Button on Taxis:
Licensing Law and Practice

Button on Taxis: Licensing Law and Practice

Fourth Edition

by

James T. H. Button
BA, Solicitor, CIoL

Bloomsbury Professional

Bloomsbury Professional

An imprint of Bloomsbury Publishing Plc

Bloomsbury Professional Ltd	Bloomsbury Publishing Plc
41–43 Boltro Road	50 Bedford Square
Haywards Heath	London
RH16 1BJ	WC1B 3DP
UK	UK

www.bloomsbury.com

BLOOMSBURY and the Diana logo are trademarks of

Bloomsbury Publishing Plc

British Library Cataloguing-in-Publication Data

A catalogue record for this book is available from the British Library.

ISBN:	HB:	978 1 78043 493 3
	ePDF:	978 1 78451 130 2
	ePub:	978 1 78451 129 6

Typeset by Phoenix Photosetting Ltd, Chatham, Kent
Printed and bound by CPI Group (UK) Ltd, Croydon, CR0 4YY

To find out more about our authors and books visit www.bloomsburyprofessional.com. Here you will find extracts, author information, details of forthcoming events and the option to sign up for our newsletters.

DEDICATION

In loving memory of Geoffrey Hamilton Button MVO, LLB,
Solicitor 1925–2016 who first read this to me

> I'm Tootles the Taxi,
> I'll give you a ride,
> Put up your hand,
> Then jump inside.
> Just watch the meter,
> You'll see the fare—
> Distance no object—
> Go anywhere!

For Daniel, Eleanor and Robert

Foreword

It is not hard to imagine what was on the minds of the great Victorian reformers who, while driving sewers through the metropolis, building the earth's first underground transportation system and laying out inspirational parks and gardens, found time to pass the London Hackney Carriages Act 1843. For just four years earlier that most influential commentator Charles Dickens had put a trenchant critique into no lesser a mouth than that of Mrs. Nickleby herself: 'Hackney coaches, my lord, are such nasty things, that it's almost better to walk at any time, for although I believe a hackney coachman can be transported for life, if he has a broken window, still they are so reckless, that they nearly all have broken windows.' Licensing followed.

Those representing constituencies beyond the bounds of the Metropolis must have tugged their collective forelocks, for four years later, Parliament deigned to revisit this less than scintillating topic, passing the Town Police Clauses Act 1847, so extending taxi licensing to the provinces.

And there, largely, the matter has rested, at least as far as Hackney Carriages are concerned. What happened in 1860, when the Lancet reported that 'It is not very agreeable to suspect that the previous occupant of the cab had small pox or typhus, scarlatina, scabies, favus or choleraic diarrhoea, or that the patient spat about or vomited amongst the straw beneath our feet?' history does not record.

Nor did Parliament respond when in 1999 Lord Justice Kennedy said in the case of *Murtagh v Bromsgrove District Council* that: 'the law needs to reflect the current state of technology and not be 23 years behind it.' Be it noted that the advanced technology he was referring to was that known as the telephone line.

Nor did it act when in 2014, the Law Commission pointed out the gaping lacunae in the system of regulation: the lack of cross-border enforcement powers; the absence of common national standards; the variable tests on matters such as disability awareness and convictions, and the lack of a clear dividing line between hackneys and private hire.

This is not a trivial topic. In England alone there are over 350,000 licensed drivers, taking passengers on nearly 600 million journeys a year costing in the region of £3 bn. The regulation of this industry is important in terms of safety of passengers and other road users, the control of rogue drivers, accessibility by disabled persons, the welfare of drivers themselves, the protection of the environment and, not least, the Treasury. The absence of a proper legislative review of taxi regulation at any point in the last 170 years therefore represents something of a monument in Parliamentary neglect.

And now, it is not the fact that the transportation is fuelled by liquid fossils rather than hay, or that the telephone line has replaced the butler as the primary mode of summoning a cab. It is that the internet has revolutionised commerce and consumer behaviour in ways unimaginable even 20 years' ago. Now we have to grapple with where a booking is accepted, when one possible answer is 'in a satellite 25 miles above earth'. Or whether a vehicle is plying for hire when a digital shadow of it appears on a hand-held telephonic device. Or whether a business 'operates' from a place occupied only by a bleeping grey box full of micro-chips. That these questions have to be answered by reference to laws printed on calf-skin to regulate the actions of horsemen in the century before last is astounding: we may as well consult Runic Law.

I suspect that after waiting for a piece of legislation to come along to sort out this imbroglio, we may find that several come along at once, maybe once Parliament is out of the legislative traffic snarl-up known as Brexit.

In the meantime, there is always Jim Button to steer us through the jam. Or rather, there is only Jim Button. Thank heaven for him. Here is the long-awaited new edition of his unrivalled textbook which subjects the field to his characteristically serious, systematic and scholarly analysis. Every case worth knowing about is covered in detail, every issue exposed. For the rest of us, for whom taxi law is just a part of what we do, it is hard to imagine how we could do without Button.

I doff my cap, wish the book and its author well, and look forward to the outworking of some of the legal debates the book highlights.

Philip Kolvin QC
Cornerstone Barristers
October 2017

Preface

This is the fourth edition of this work, and the second under the title of 'Button on Taxis: Licensing Law and Practice'. The third edition was published by Tottel, and that has now become Bloomsbury Professional. They have shown not only their faith in me as an author, but also their patience and forbearance as this volume was repeatedly delayed.

The previous three editions had appeared at roughly five yearly intervals, and that was the plan for the fourth, which would have given a publication of around 2014. However, a number of factors conspired to delay that.

In 2011 the Law Commission embarked on a review of Taxi Law as part of its 11th Programme of Law Reform[1]. That strongly suggested that new taxi law might be in the offing, and it seemed prudent to await the outcome.

That was not the only restraining factor. The Department for Transport revised the Best Practice Guidance in 2010 (a year after the publication of the third Edition) and had indicated that further revisions to the Guidance would be introduced in 2017, following consultation in January. Again, a further slight delay seemed prudent, with the hope of publishing this new edition with the most recent Guidance.

Unfortunately, due to Government inertia, any hopes of producing this new edition incorporating such developments have been dashed.

In many ways, this simply reinforces what any author of a law book will tell you: there is no right time to publish it, because the law is always changing. Notwithstanding the principle hackney carriage legislation dating back to the 19th Century[2], and private hire legislation firmly fixed in the 20th century[3]), there have been significant alterations by both statute and case law since the last edition, and we await further reform.

---

[1] See https://www.lawcom.gov.uk/project/taxi-and-private-hire-services/
[2] The London Hackney Carriage Act 1831 within Greater London and the Town Police Clauses Act 1847 outside Greater London.
[3] The Local Government (Miscellaneous Provisions) Act 1976 outside Greater London and Private Hire Vehicles (London) Act 1998 within Greater London.

In addition to the legislative and case law developments noted below, the period since the last edition has seen significant interest in hackney carriage and private hire activities.

The appalling scandals of child abuse and exploitation in Rotherham, Rochdale and Oxfordshire have involved licensed hackney carriage and private hire drivers, exposing weaknesses and failings by some local authorities. This has led in many cases to significant alterations in the way some authorities vet those who apply for licences and has alerted some sections of the public to the role played by licensees in the transportation of the most vulnerable in our society. Many local authorities have introduced compulsory Safeguarding and CSE (Child Sexual Exploitation) awareness training for licensees as a result, which is to be welcomed.

Technological advances have also given us Uber, the mobile phone app based taxi booking service. Launched in London in 2012 with a private hire operator's licence, it is primarily a private hire operator. This was not the first, or the only such system, but the widespread availability of the mobile phone app, backed by extensive and aggressive advertising across large parts of the country has led to an enormous increase in its business. Whilst arguments rage about its legality (is the booking made via the operator's computer, or via the driver) and will no doubt be answered in the fulness of time by the Senior Courts, its popularity with the public has soared. With widespread cross-border sub-contracting now possible (see below) the idea of a nationwide booking service has become a reality in many large cities and towns. Whilst it is unlikely to ever reach rural areas (the availability of significant numbers of vehicles is really an essential element of the service) it is now a dominant feature in London and elsewhere.

Opposition to Uber is plentiful and vociferous, from both hackney carriage drivers and proprietors and other private hire operators, but there is no doubt that the service has caught the public's imagination. Registered users continue to rise, and even 'dynamic pricing' (ie fares rising at periods of high demand) does not seem to deter the users. It seems clear that Uber, and/or other app based booking mechanisms are here to stay[4].

This is a brief overview of some of the many and varied changes since the last edition.

LEGISLATION

The Criminal Records Bureau was reconfigured in the 'Bonfire of the Quangos'[5] after the 2010 General Election and now Criminal Record Certificates and

---

[4]   Whilst this edition was being finalised, Transport for London refused to renew Uber's private hire operator's licence and Uber have lodged an appeal. It remains to be seen what the outcome is.

[5]   See eg https://www.instituteforgovernment.org.uk/news/latest/bonfire-quangos

other disclosures under the Police Act 1997 are provided by the Disclosure and Barring Service.

The Immigration Act 2016 introduced a requirement that all hackney carriage and private hire drivers, together with private hire operators, must demonstrate that they have the right to remain in the UK, and the right to work. From 1 December 2016 that has been a pre-requisite to the grant of a licence[6]. The provisions apply across the whole of the UK (England, Wales and Greater London being the areas covered by this work).

Under the Policing and Crime Act 2017, s 177, the Secretary of State has a power to issue Guidance to Licensing Authorities (Local Authorities and TfL) in relation to 'how their licensing functions under taxi and private hire vehicle legislation may be exercised so as to protect children, and vulnerable individuals who are 18 or over, from harm'[7].

The only other legislative change with national application is in relation to taximeters. New requirements were introduced by the Measuring Instruments Regulations 2016[8], and any new meters must comply with these.

Outside London (and not applicable within Greater London) the Deregulation Act 2015 made significant alterations to the Local Government (Miscellaneous Provisions) Act 1976. Under these provisions, hackney carriage and driver's licences are expected to be granted for a period of three years, and private hire operator's licences for a period of five years[9], although shorter periods can be specified by the local authority. This has resulted in slightly oddly worded provisions which aim to ensure that local authorities will generally grant driver's licences and private hire operator's licences that last for longer than a year.

The other relaxation introduced by the Deregulation Act 2015[10] was the ability for a private hire operator licensed outside London to sub-contract a booking to another operator licensed anywhere on mainland Britain (excluding Plymouth). Prior to the change, a private hire operator licensed in London or Scotland could subcontract to any other licensed operator, but an operator licensed in England outside London, or in Wales, could only subcontract a booking to another operator licensed within the same district. This was seen as a barrier to trade, and the difference between London and Scotland and the rest of the country was seen regarded as unfair by some operators.

This has resulted in some commercial freedom, but it has also led to a significant increase in vehicles licensed by other authorities being regularly used in areas where they are not actually licensed. This can make enforcement difficult, and

---

[6]   Immigration Act 2016, s 37 and Sch 5 which introduces additional sections to the legislation for London and elsewhere.

[7]   Policing and Crime Act 2017, s 177(1). See Appendix I.

[8]   SI 2016/1153. See Appendix I.

[9]   Deregulation Act 2015, s 11.

[10]   Deregulation Act 2015, s 12.

undermine attempts by local authorities to improve local standards of vehicles, drivers and operators.

CASE LAW

As well as alterations to the legislation, the Senior Courts have been busy with cases that either directly or indirectly impact on taxi licensing.

The need to demonstrate adoption of the Local Government (Miscellaneous Provisions) Act 1976 was reinforced in *Aylesbury Vale District Council v Call a Cab Ltd*[11] and it has also been made clear that local authorities can adopt 'bright line' policies that will say that something will never be allowed (see *R (on the application of Nicholds) v Security Industry Authority*[12] and *Habib v Central Criminal Court*[13]).

The question of how taxi licence fees are levied and what they can cover has been considered *in R (on the application of Cummings) v Council of the City & Council of Cardiff*[14] and by District (and since 2015, Local) Auditors[15].

The longstanding and vexed question of plying for hire has been examined in *Dudley Metropolitan Borough Council v Arif*[16] and *Gateshead Council v Henderson*[17], but a comprehensive definition of what is actually meant by standing or plying for hire still eludes our judges, whilst the position on insurance when a vehicle is unlawfully plying or standing for hire has been clarified in *Oldham Borough Council v Sajjad*[18]. Meanwhile *R (on the application of 007 Stratford Taxis) v Stratford on Avon District Council*[19] has confirmed that hackney carriages are constrained by the local authority's table of fares and cannot charge more, even when the journey has been arranged by a third party. Fares are usually calculated by a taximeter which is fitted to the vehicle and the decision in *Transport for London v Uber London Ltd*[20] made clear that a smart phone using an app to calculate a fare cannot be regarded as a taximeter.

Another case involving Uber has extended spoken English tests for drivers to include a written test[21] as part of the overall test of fitness and propriety. Beyond this, the courts have reinforced the important point that the only consideration in relation to taxi licensing via the 'fit and proper person' test is public safety and the livelihood of the licensee or applicant is irrelevant (*Cherwell District Council*

---

[11] [2013] EWHC 3765 (Admin), [2014] PTSR 523.
[12] [2006] EWHC 1792 (Admin), [2007] 1 WLR 2067.
[13] [2016] EWHC 2597 (Admin).
[14] [2014] EWHC 2544 (Admin).
[15] See eg, the challenge to Guildford Borough Council's taxi fees at Chapter 4, para 4.5 and http://www.guildford.gov.uk/CHttpHandler.ashx?id=6647&p=0
[16] [2011] EWHC 3880 (Admin), [2012] RTR 20.
[17] [2012] EWHC 807 (Admin), [2012] LLR 610.
[18] [2016] EWHC 3597 (Admin).
[19] [2011] EWCA Civ 160, [2012] RTR 5.
[20] [2015] EWHC 2918 (Admin), [2016] RTR 12.
[21] See *R (on the application of Uber) v Transport for London* [2017] ACD 54.

v Anwar[22]) and also that a driver's licence is not a possession for the purposes of the Human Rights Act 1998. Further consideration of the behaviour of licensees and that impact on the licence occurred in *County of Herefordshire District Council v Prosser*[23] and *Pinnington v Transport for London*[24].

Hackney carriages continue to be used for pre-booked work outside the district in which they are licensed, with no control over their booking and dispatch. The legality of this position was confirmed in *Stockton on Tees Borough Council v Fidler*[25].

English law has long regarded property rights as dominant and this approach has been continued by the Court of Appeal in *Jones v First Great Western Ltd; Jones v First Greater Western Ltd*[26] which confirmed that a landowner always retains control over access to a hackney carriage stand.

The absence of any mechanism to renew licences under the legislation led to the decision in *R (on the application of Exeter City Council) v Sandle*[27] and the longstanding practice of suspending a drivers' licence pending investigation, and then later revoking it, has been held to be unlawful in *R (on the application of Singh) v Cardiff City Council*[28], supported and explained by the High Court in *Reigate & Banstead Borough Council v Pawlowski*[29].

The power of the local authority to take action against licensed vehicles that do not comply with a local authority's requirements is the subject of an important Court of Appeal decision in *R (on the application of Wilcock) v Lancaster City Council*[30].

In addition there have been many other decisions of the Senior Courts that affect taxi licensing, and these are considered within the text.

FUTURE CHANGES

Potentially, there is the likelihood of significant developments in this area.

The Law Commission completed its investigation and reported in May 2014[31]. The Government had a year to respond. Unfortunately, at the time of writing, the Government has yet to respond to the proposals for England. In Summer 2017, a Ministerial Working Group was established to consider taxi legislation,

22   [2011] EWHC 2943 (Admin), [2012] RTR 15.
23   [2008] EWHC 257 (Admin), [2008] LLR 274.
24   [2013] EWHC 3656 (Admin), [2014] LLR 316.
25   [2010] EWHC 2430 (Admin), (2011) 175 JP 49, [2011] RTR 23.
26   [2014] EWCA Civ 301, [2015] RTR 3.
27   [2011] EWHC 1403 (Admin), [2011] LLR 480.
28   [2012] EWHC 1852 (Admin), [2013] LLR 108.
29   [2017] EWHC 1764 (Admin).
30   [2013] EWCA Civ 1607, [2014] LLR 388.
31   See https://www.lawcom.gov.uk/project/taxi-and-private-hire-services/

but it seems unlikely that there will be any developments in England until that has cogitated and reported.

Under the Wales Act 2017, taxi licensing becomes a devolved function and Welsh Government has grasped the reform nettle. Over Summer 2017 it consulted on proposals firmly based on the Law Commission's proposals, with a proposed implementation date for new taxi law in Wales of 2022[32]. It must be applauded for taking the initiative, but whether a subsequent divergence between the law of England and Wales will prove problematic remains to be seen.

Although the overall future of taxi law in England remains in doubt, the Government indicated in 2016 that it intends to continue tinkering at the edges of the existing legislation to introduce a relaxation to allow unlicensed vehicles and drivers to transport passengers from railway stations, air and sea ports to hotels or attractions[33]. If this proposal is followed through, it would appear to drive a coach and horses (and not a licensed one) through the public safety concept of hackney carriage and private hire licensing.

It is shocking that there are no national minimum standards for drivers and vehicles, with each local authority (and Transport for London) setting and then applying (or departing from) its own standards. Whilst there is an argument to say that vehicle requirements in a predominantly urban setting may differ from vehicle requirements in more rural areas, there is no justification for the situation where a person is refused a driver's licence in one district (or has that licence revoked) and can then simply obtain a licence in another, often neighbouring, district. With the relaxation in cross-border subcontracting, this can and does lead to the situation where the person who has been deemed unacceptable is actually working in that authority's area. This is a major public safety concern, which the Government has promised to address, but only through Guidance. Section 177 of the Policing and Crime Act 2017 (see above) will allow the Department for Transport to issue such Guidance[34] and it remains to be seen how effective this will be. That Guidance has yet to be published, even in draft and there is no indication at the time of writing when it is likely to be forthcoming. The Department for Transport had intended to consult on that and the revised 'Best Practice Guidance' in January 2017 but there are no indications as to when that might take place.

When these changes (and any others) are finally introduced, they will be considered on the James Button and Co., Solicitors' website[35] and readers are invited to consult that. Any comments on the book or suggestions for future editions should be sent to secretary@jamesbutton.co.uk .

---

[32]   https://consultations.gov.wales/consultations/taxi-and-private-hire-vehicle-licensing-wales
[33]   See 'Tourism Action Plan', p 11 available at https://www.gov.uk/government/publications/tourism-action-plan
[34]   See Chapter 12, para 12.61.
[35]   www.jamesbutton.co.uk

The gestation period for this new edition has been extraordinarily long and I could not have completed this new edition without the assistance, support and forbearance of a large number of people. As always, Janet, my wife and my children Robert, Eleanor and Daniel have provided unconditional support and put up with me spending inordinate amounts of time in 'taxi writing land'. I look forward to returning to a sense of normality with them.

Beyond my family, I am indebted to a large number of people who have, intentionally or not, assisted me in preparing this new edition. David Stewart, formerly Principal Legal Officer at Chichester District Council has proofread the drafts and made many helpful suggestions (not least the case summary boxes), and I have talked to and bounced ideas off, a large number of people both within and outside local government. My clients and colleagues at the Institute of Licensing have raised questions which I hope will be answered, and made suggestions which I have often incorporated. I have also received a great deal of assistance from the staff of Transport for London in relation to the London legislation, which can at times be difficult to locate. My thanks also go to Philip Kolvin QC for agreeing to write such a thought-provoking (and flattering) Foreword.

In addition to their indulgence over missed deadlines, the staff at Bloomsbury Professional have provided unflinching support and I would like to thank Leanne Barrett and Jane Bradford, together with my editor Vickie Day, for all their assistance.

Finally, as is always the case, any mistakes are mine, and mine alone (and I would be very grateful if readers would bring them to my attention – see above).

The law is stated as at 1 October 2017.

James T H Button
Rowsley
Derbyshire
October 2017

Stop Press

R (ON THE APPLICATION OF SIMMONS) v THE CROWN COURT AT GUILDFORD

As this edition was going to press, the High Court refused an application for judicial review in relation to a hackney carriage livery[1].

The history of the case of *R (on the application of Simmons) v The Crown Court at Guildford*[2] is involved and a little complex.

In December 2015, Guildford Borough Council adopted a policy that required all its licensed hackney carriages to be coloured teal by means of an all over vinyl wrap by January 2018 and any replacement vehicle would also have to be teal coloured. This wrap would have to be professionally applied, covering the entire body, bumpers etc. Before adopting this policy, the council had embarked on a lengthy and wide-ranging two-year consultation process, and the policy was adopted.

There was no challenge to that policy.

The policy was then applied. To be capable of being licensed as a hackney carriage, the vehicle would have to be the correct colour (applied by means of the vinyl wrap) and then a condition would be attached to the vehicle licence requiring the vehicle to remain that colour for the duration of the licence. This approach was permitted by the provisions of the Local Government (Miscellaneous Provisions) Act 1976, s 47 which states:

'47.— Licensing of hackney carriages.

(1) A district council may attach to the grant of a licence of a hackney carriage under the Act of 1847 such conditions as the district council may consider reasonably necessary.

---

[1]   This is a colour scheme for hackney carriages, imposed by the local authority by condition to the hackney carriage proprietor's licence. See Chapter 8, para 8.124 for more information.
[2]   CO/829/2017 Order Dated 28th September 2017 (unreported).

(2) Without prejudice to the generality of the foregoing subsection, a district council may require any hackney carriage licensed by them under the Act of 1847 to be of such design or appearance or bear such distinguishing marks as shall clearly identify it as a hackney carriage.

(3) Any person aggrieved by any conditions attached to such a licence may appeal to a magistrates' court.'

In February 2016 Mr Simmons had his vehicle liveried (at that point the council contributed towards the cost) and it was licensed by the council as a hackney carriage. He then appealed to the magistrates' court against the condition that required the vehicle to remain liveried, under the provisions of s 47(3) on the basis that he was aggrieved by the condition.

That appeal was dismissed and Mr Simmons appealed further to the Crown Court. At that hearing, it was argued by Philip Kolvin QC for the council that although there was a right of appeal aginst a condition attached to the licence under s 47(3), the underlying policy could not be challenged by way of appeal. That was accepted. The council further argued that as the condition was simply maintaining the policy, it must be reasonably necessary. To allow an appeal against a condition requiring a livery would undermine the policy and effectively be allowing a challenge to the policy.

That argument was accepted by the court, and the appeal was dismissed.

Mr Simmons then sought judicial review of the Crown Court decision, which was refused. The judge, Dove J, gave his decision in the following terms:

'I am satisfied that the Interested Party [Guildford Borough Council] is correct, and that there is settled authority to the effect that where in a licensing context an authority has adopted a policy, and it is accepted that the policy has been accurately applied in a decision upon a licence, an appeal in respect of that licence based upon the contention that the policy itself is not lawful (because, for instance, as here the policy requires the imposition of a condition which is not reasonably necessary) such an appeal would be bound to fail. An appeal brought upon such a contention is, in reality, a challenge to the legitimacy of the policy itself and not the decision which has been made faithfully applying it. Such a challenge to the policy itself would have to be brought by way of judicial review on public law grounds and promptly after the adoption of the policy. I see nothing in the language of section 47 of the Local Government (Miscellaneous Provisions) Act 1976 which would justify a different approach. The council are entitled to adopt a policy upon what they regard as being "reasonably necessary" to impose as a condition and the claimant's approach would entail that such a policy would forever be open to debate in any appeal upon a licence. In addition to being a surprising outcome, it would have the effect of sidestepping the strict timescales on bringing judicial review. The approach of the [Crown] court was therefore appropriate and there was no proper basis upon which a case could be stated.'

This decision has been described as High Court authority for a hackney carriage livery and on its own facts, in relation Guildford, it is. In the wider context, it reflects a more useful proposition, relating to the interaction between a policy and a condition.

It has been accepted here that a condition on a licence which applies or upholds a policy will be 'reasonably necessary', and it is almost impossible to challenge such a condition, because any successful challenge would effectively undermine the policy, and thereby allow a challenge to the policy.

Acknowledgment

Text and illustration from *Tootles the Taxi and Other Rhymes*

Verse by Joyce B. Clegg, illustrated by John Kenney

Copyright © Ladybird Books Ltd., 1956

Reproduced by kind permission of Ladybird Books Ltd.

Contents

Table of Statutes

References are to paragraph numbers.

Table of Statutory Instruments

References are to paragraph numbers.

Table of European Legislation

References are to paragraph numbers.

Table of Cases

References are to paragraph numbers.

C

Hackney carriage and private hire licensing

A BRIEF OVERVIEW

1.1

Every part of England and Wales has taxis. In law these are divided into hackney carriages and private hire vehicles. However, in general, the public view them collectively as 'taxis', although in London and some other areas, hackney carriages are referred to as 'cabs' and private hire vehicles are referred to as 'mini-cabs'.

1.2

There are considerable similarities between hackney carriages and private hire vehicles and their use, but there are also some significant distinctions. The differences between the two are, from a licensing perspective, important, but, from a user's standpoint, less so. One of the main similarities between the two types of vehicle (and, therefore, between those who drive them and control them) is that both transport members of the public to a specific destination upon request, in exchange for payment of a fare.

1.3

The 'public' is not a homogeneous mass, but is comprised of many individuals with different needs, abilities and, in some cases, disabilities. It is important that the service provided by hackney carriages and private hire vehicles can cope with this variety. The rationale behind a licensing regime covering this important part of the public transport of the country is the provision of a service to the public that is accessible and safe, and seen to be so. Public safety is paramount in the licensing regimes that govern these vehicles, their drivers and operators. It is the basis of decisions made as to whether or not a particular person or vehicle should be, or remain, licensed. Public safety encompasses not only the prevention of direct danger to the passenger from the driver of the vehicle or a slightly less direct danger to the passenger and other members of society from the vehicle itself or the way in which the vehicle is driven. Public safety also includes the general perception that hackney carriages and private hire vehicles provide a safe and reliable form of transport. In addition, it must not be overlooked that the hackney carriage and private hire trades employ a great many people, who also have a right to expect a fair and reasonable licensing regime to govern their activities.

1.4

The licensing of hackney carriages covers all of England and Wales, although different provisions apply in Greater London. Private hire licensing also applies across both countries, but there are three licensing regimes: the first covers all of England and Wales except the City of Plymouth; the second covers private hire in Greater London; and the third governs the use of private hire vehicles in Plymouth. According to the Department for Transport (DfT)[1], there is now only one local authority in England and Wales that has not adopted the provisions of the Local Government (Miscellaneous Provisions) Act 1976 (LG(MP)A 1976), and that is Plymouth City Council. They have no need for it because they licence private hire operations under their own local Act, the Plymouth City Council Act 1975. This means that the systems that apply when an authority that has not adopted the 1976 Act are now only of academic interest[2].

[1]   See DfT Letter to local authorities, 9 September 2002, para 25 reproduced in Appendix II.
[2]   Full details of those systems were considered in the 1st edn.

1.5

Parliament has, for the last 185 years, passed legislation covering hackney carriages, and since 1976 legislated for private hire vehicles both inside and outside London, but the actual day-to-day implementation of that legislation falls to local authorities outside Greater London and Transport for London (TfL), which exercises its functions through the London Taxi and Private Hire (LTPH) within Greater London. It is these bodies who have the complex and, at times, extremely difficult task of reconciling the needs and expectations of the public (which are often expressed through the elected politicians) with the needs and expectations of those involved in the two trades.

1.6

Local authorities are democratically elected bodies, and the Mayor of London (whose transport strategy is implemented by TfL) is also democratically elected. Accordingly, they are able to respond to the needs of their electorate and the issues which affect the area that they represent. Due to the vast range of activities which they undertake, licensing in general, and hackney carriage and private hire licensing , are seldom likely to be the priority of either an individual councillor, or that of the local electorate. However, on occasions, hackney carriage and private hire licensing can cause a great deal of concern, and absorb a lot of time and energy on the part of the administrators, enforcers and providers.

1.7

Although this is a sweeping generalisation, it appears to be the case that most of the public do not understand the distinction between hackney carriages and private hire vehicles. The public simply believe that both types are 'taxis', which will serve the purpose that they require. These purposes range from pre-booking a service to take them to a specific place through to transporting people when they are out and need to go somewhere else. In addition, hackney carriages and private hire vehicles fulfil a vital late-night role in emptying the many town and city centres of people who have gone out to be entertained for the evening and need to be taken home. When the many other uses of 'taxis' are considered (school runs and social services contracts being two of the most important), it starts to become more apparent that there is no one perfect or ideal use of a 'taxi'.

1.8

In trying to balance these conflicting needs and expectations, local authorities and TfL/LTPH are placed in an unenviable position, and may face both political and legal challenges to their decisions.

The right to challenge, however, should not simply be seen as an irritant from the administering authority's point of view. It is an important method of checking and controlling the activities of local authorities and TfL/LTPH and of protecting the interests of those involved in the trade who are directly affected by decisions such bodies make. Without such methods, the only brake on decision-making in this field would be the use of the democratic process at local government and London Mayor elections and, although the numbers of people involved in the trade across the two countries are significant, in any individual local authority it is unlikely this number would be sufficient seriously to affect the outcome of an election.

Hackney carriages

1.9

Hackney carriages are the oldest form of hire vehicle that is recognised in England and Wales. Until the Transport Act 1985 (TA 1985) reference in legislation was always made to a 'hackney carriage', but in the TA 1985 the expression 'licensed taxi' was used to mean a hackney carriage[1]. This approach has continued, and now in many circles (including Government)[2] 'taxi' means a 'hackney carriage'. Within London, the term 'London Cab' is used in both legislation and supporting documentation. This is unfortunate, as 'hackney carriage' is perfectly clear, and the use of 'taxi' for 'hackney carriage' robs us of the use of the word to describe the generic concept of a vehicle hired with a driver (ie a hackney carriage *or* a private hire vehicle). Hackney carriages have been in existence in one form or another for at least 200 years and they have been regulated in some areas for at least 185 years. The principal features of a hackney carriage are: it can carry passengers for hire and reward; it can be hailed by a prospective passenger; it can stand on a rank to await the approach of passengers; and it can be pre-booked. It must be driven by a driver who holds a hackney carriage driver's licence. The philosophy behind this licensing is that each hackney carriage is individually controlled and is available for public hire. In practice, however, in many parts of the two countries, most hackney carriage activities are more akin to private hire vehicle activities than this traditional view of the hackney carriage would suggest.

1   See TA 1985, s 13(3). See Appendix I.
2   See for example *Taxi and Private Hire Vehicle Licensing: Best Practice Guidance* issued by the DfT in October 2006, available at http://www.dft.gov.uk/pgr/regional/taxis/taxiandprivatehirevehiclelic1792. See Appendix II.

1.10

The local authority or TfL/LTPH can lay down conditions as to the type of vehicle that can be used for hackney carriage work. These can cover the size, appearance, methods of access and egress, colour, number of seats, number of doors and such specific matters as turning circle and luggage space of the vehicle. These requirements can vary widely between different councils. As TfL/LTPH is the licensing authority for the whole of Greater London, there is consistency within the Metropolis.

1.11

Outside London, the local authority has the power to limit the number of hackney carriages within its area, but only if it is satisfied that there is no significant unmet demand for hackney carriage services. A minority of local authorities do limit numbers, whilst others rely on a more laissez-faire approach, allowing market forces to determine the number of hackney carriages within the locality. Within London no limit exists on the number of hackney carriages TfL/LTPH will licence.

1.12

In relation to a hackney carriage driver, there are statutory tests that must be complied with before a person can be granted a licence. These are primarily concerned with the fitness and propriety of the individual (which, in itself, covers a wide range of areas), their right to remain and work in the UK and the length of time that they have been driving under a full driving licence. Again, there are mechanisms which allow the local authority or TfL/LTPH to impose their own tests and conditions, once again leading to wide variations in acceptable standards. A great many assess the suitability of a potential driver through such means as medical tests, driving tests, testing knowledge of the locality and, in addition, checks are made as to whether the person has any criminal convictions.

1.13

Almost all local authorities, and TfL/LTPH, prescribe the fares that the hackney carriage proprietor can charge for their services. These range from a simple charge per unit of distance travelled to complex, multi-tiered fare structures which take account of: the time of the hiring (and, in some cases, the date, eg Christmas Day); the number of people carried; the number of items of luggage carried; time spent stationary (eg at traffic lights or in traffic jams); and, in some cases, a fixed charge for cleaning the vehicle should it become soiled.

1.14

When a hackney carriage is standing for hire (either waiting on a rank or parked on a street), there are only a few reasons the driver can use to refuse to take a passenger and, once the vehicle has been hired, the hirer is then contractually bound to pay the fare. A cruising hackney carriage is not bound to respond to a hailing by a prospective passenger: the driver has discretion as to whether to accept the hiring, but again, if the hiring is accepted, the passenger is under a contractual duty to pay the fare.

1.15

It is, therefore, both in theory and generally in practice, an extremely satisfactory, reliable, safe and acceptable form of transport, with safeguards for both hirer and driver.

Private hire vehicles

1.16

Private hire vehicles are a more recent development. Adoptive legislation (excluding the then Metropolitan Area) was not available until 1976, with the Local Government (Miscellaneous Provisions) Act 1976, which was then adopted by local authorities individually over a period of 15 years or so. It has not developed in the intervening period to any great extent. The Private Hire Vehicles (London) Act 1998 introduced a broadly similar regime for Greater London, with the old Metropolitan Area being reduced in size to cover Greater London by the Greater London Authority Act 1999. At no point in any legislation are private hire vehicles referred to as 'mini-cabs', although this term is commonly used both within and outside London by the public.

1.17

A private hire vehicle cannot ply for hire or stand in a rank. It must be pre-booked with a private hire operator.

The private hire operator is the lynch-pin of the private hire vehicle licensing regime. He takes the booking for a private hire vehicle and despatches the vehicle (which must be driven by a private hire driver) to fulfil that request. A private hire vehicle cannot operate independently from a private hire operator. The legislation places considerable duties on private hire operators to ensure that the vehicles and drivers which they operate are properly licensed.

1.18

Local authorities and TfL/LTPH have various powers in relation to private hire vehicles, drivers and operators. Once again, they can consider the fitness and propriety of persons applying for a driver's or operator's licence, their right to remain and work in the UK, and in the case of drivers, how long they have held a driving licence. In relation to vehicles, they can impose conditions on the size, number of doors, passenger space, seats, luggage space, condition etc of the vehicle. They also have the power to impose conditions upon operators' and drivers' licences, in order to govern their behaviour and conduct.

1.19

Beyond the requirement for pre-booking the vehicle, the main difference between hackney carriages and private hire vehicles is in their fares. The local authority or TfL/LTPH has no power to prescribe fares for private hire vehicles. This will, therefore, be a matter for arrangement between the operator and the hirer. It has been argued that this allows for negotiation between the two parties, but, in general, the price is determined by the operator.

1.20

Neither a local authority nor TfL/LTPH has power to prescribe a maximum number of private hire vehicles within its area. Market forces, therefore, determine the number of private hire vehicles that operate within a district.

Enforcement

1.21

The local authority or TfL/LTPH not only grants licences for hackney carriages and hackney carriage drivers, private hire vehicles, drivers and operators, but it also enforces the provisions that apply to them. This means that it must ensure that licensees comply with both the legislation and any conditions that it may impose upon them. The local authority or TfL/LTPH will also take action against those who are unlicensed. Whilst the former action arguably only protects the travelling public, action against the latter protects both the public and the trade itself.

Present and future law

1.22

There have been many calls for a review of 'taxi' legislation and in 2012 the Law Commission conducted a review of Taxi and Private Hire Law and published its proposals in May 2014. The Government had a year in which to respond to that report, but at the time of writing (August 2017) no response has been forthcoming, let alone any indication that the Law Commission's proposals might be taken forward.

However, the Welsh Government has indicated that it intends to introduce new taxi law for Wales, which is a devolved function under the Wales Act 2017. This will be based largely on the Law Commission proposals with a proposed commencement date of 2022.

As it seems likely that Parliament will be tied up with the impact of Brexit for at least five years, it may well be the case that England and Wales will have different taxi legislation. This does not appear to be a satisfactory situation and it may well cause significant problems in areas each side of the England/Wales border.

1.23

That is not to say that change is not required. It is urgently needed. Whilst in general, the current legislation works and has the advantage of familiarity, that is no substitute for modern legislation. There are numerous areas where modern practice has not been reflected in developments in the law eg the use of mobile phones by drivers and/or operators; Internet and 'app' based bookings; the widespread growth of the use of pre-booked hackney carriages; to name but a few. The fact that legislation, which was designed for horse-drawn vehicles, is effectively applied to modes of transport which would have been beyond the wildest dreams of those who drafted the legislation in 1847 is a tribute to all those involved in hackney carriage and private hire licensing.

1.24

The remainder of this book will examine in detail the law and practice of the licensing of hackney carriage vehicles, hackney carriage drivers, private hire operators, private hire vehicles and private hire drivers, both outside and inside London. It will explore the interaction between these licences and other areas of transportation and will aim to demonstrate how the law is being, and can be, used to fulfil the overriding aim of public safety.

1.25

Chapter 2 covers licensing within local government and TfL/LTPH, Chapter 3 considers the appeal mechanisms, Chapter 4 looks at the fees levied for licences, whilst Chapter 5 considers the impact and working of the Rehabilitation of Offenders Act 1974 on hackney carriage and private hire licensing.

1.26

The remainder of the book has been split to cover the positions outside London, and within London, as follows:

* Chapters 6 to 14 consider the position in England and Wales outside London;
* Chapters 15 to 23 address the position within Greater London.

Finally, the Appendices contain all relevant Statutory material (Appendix I) and Extra-statutory material (Appendix II).

Licensing within local government and Transport for London

INTRODUCTION

2.1

This chapter is intended to provide a brief overview of how licensing fits within the local government framework[1]. It will also look briefly at the framework of Transport for London (TfL), of which the London Taxi and Private Hire (LTPH) is a part. Whilst TfL is part of the responsibility of the Mayor of London, it is a distinct area of local government activity. However, the elements of this chapter in relation to decision-making, policies and challenges within local authorities outside London are equally applicable to TfL/LTPH.

[1]   For a more detailed study, or to take further any of the points made here, see *Encyclopaedia of Local Government Law* (Sweet and Maxwell).

OUTSIDE LONDON – LOCAL AUTHORITIES

2.2

Local authorities have a large number of licensing and registration functions. These are generally the responsibility of district councils, metropolitan district councils, unitary authorities, London borough councils and the Common Council of the City of London in England, and county councils and county borough councils in Wales. There are some licensing and registration functions which fall to county councils in England to discharge.

2.3

Although the Town Police Clauses Act 1847 still refers to 'The Commissioners' as the body responsible for hackney carriage licencing, hackney carriage and private hire licensing is the function of a district council, unitary council or metropolitan district council in England outside the Metropolitan Area and a county or county borough council function in Wales. Although that is the case, the route the legislation has taken to reach that position is extremely complex.

Originally, the Town Police Clauses Act 1847 had to be incorporated by a special (local) Act to apply within a particular local government area. The Public Health Act 1875, s 171(4) incorporated all the 1847 Act powers in relation to hackney carriages for urban districts. The Local Government Act 1972 did not extend those powers to all areas of England and Wales (Local Government Act 1972, Sch 14, para 24(b)), but this was done by the Transport Act 1985, s 15, which extended the provisions of the Town Police Clauses Act 1847 (incorporated into the Public Health Act 1875 by the Public Health Act 1875, s 171) and Town Police Clauses Act 1889 (deemed to be incorporated in the Public Health Act 1875 by the Town Police Clauses Act 1889, s 2(2)) to all areas of England and Wales. The Greater London Authority Act 1999, s 255(2) extended the application of the Town Police Clauses Act 1847 and the Public Health Act 1875 to the districts which had, until 2000, been part of the Metropolitan Police Area.

The provisions of Part II of the Local Government (Miscellaneous Provisions) Act 1976 are adoptive[1] and the provisions of this Act will only apply where the local authority has formally adopted the provisions of Part II. The mechanism is contained in s 45[2] which states:

'45.— Application of Part II.

(1) The provisions of this Part of this Act, except this section, shall come into force in accordance with the following provisions of this section.

(2) If the Act of 1847 is in force in the area of a district council, the council may resolve that the provisions of this Part of this Act, other than this section, are to apply to the relevant area; and if the council do so resolve those provisions shall come into force in the relevant area on the day specified in that behalf in the resolution (which must not be before the expiration of the period of one month beginning with the day on which the resolution is passed).

In this subsection "the relevant area", in relation to a council, means—
(a)   if the Act of 1847 is in force throughout the area of the council, that area; and
(b)   if the Act of 1847 is in force for part only of the area of the council, that part of that area.

(3) A council shall not pass a resolution in pursuance of the foregoing subsection unless they have—
(a)   published in two consecutive weeks, in a local newspaper circulating in their area, notice of their intention to pass the resolution; and
(b)   served a copy of the notice, not later than the date on which it is first published in pursuance of the foregoing paragraph, on the council of each parish or community which would be affected by the resolution or, in the case of such a parish which has no parish council, on the chairman of the parish meeting.

(4) If after a council has passed a resolution in pursuance of subsection (2) of this section the Act of 1847 comes into force for any part of the area of the council for which it was not in force when the council passed the resolution, the council may pass a resolution in accordance with the foregoing provisions of this section in respect of that part as if that part were included in the relevant area for the purposes of subsection (2) of this section.'

Accordingly, the requirements are that there is a resolution of the authority[3] and before that resolution can be passed, the authority must have published a public notice of the proposal on two occasions in a local newspaper and copied that notice to all parish or community councils in the district (if any). The authority will need to demonstrate substantial compliance with those requirements[4].

Every authority has its own structure and procedures. This is also true where hackney carriage and private hire licensing is concerned. As a result, it is impossible to state one preferred method when there are a number of acceptable systems in operation across England and Wales.

However, there are some fundamental points which remain constant, notwithstanding the particular administrative and organisational set-up the council has adopted. These are explored in this chapter, together with specific points concerned with the licensing of hackney carriages and private hire vehicles.

[1] According to the Department for Transport (see DfT Letter to local authorities, 9 September 2002, para 25 reproduced in Appendix II), there is now only one local authority in England and Wales that has not adopted the provisions of the Local Government (Miscellaneous Provisions) Act 1976 (LG(MP)A 1976), and that is Plymouth City Council. They have no need for it because they licence private hire operations under their own local Act, the Plymouth City Council Act 1975.

[2] See para 6.3 onwards for further details.

[3] The reference in LG(MP)A, s 45 is to the 'council', but where the authority runs executive arrangements under the Local Government Act 2000, this is an executive function – see para 2.7 onwards.

[4] See *Aylesbury Vale District Council v Call a Cab Limited* [2013] EWHC 3765 (Admin), [2014] RTR 30 and Chapter 6, para 6.7.

THE LOCAL AUTHORITY ITSELF

Power to act

2.4

Local authorities are statutory creations and the basis of local authority legislation is the Local Government Act 1972 (LGA 1972). This Act has been amended considerably since it brought the, then, new authorities into existence on 1 April 1974. In terms of local authority structure, the most important subsequent legislation has been the Local Government Act 1985 (LGA 1985) (which abolished the metropolitan county councils in England and the Greater London Council), the Local Government Act 1992 (LGA 1992) (which paved the way for the creation of unitary authorities in certain parts of England (which included the abolition of the 'created' counties from the 1974 reforms – Avon, Cleveland and Humberside)), the Local Government (Wales) Act 1994 (LG(W)A 1994) (which fundamentally altered local government in Wales, replacing the former two-tier system with a Principality-wide, single-tier system of unitary authorities) and the Local Government and Public Involvement in Health Act 2007 which allowed the creation of the latest tranche of unitary authorities in England in 2009[1].

[1] Further local government reorganisation in England was halted in 2010 and the Local Government Act 2010 revoked the existing orders that had not been implemented in respect of Norwich and Exeter. Although there was a proposal by the Welsh Government for reorganisation of the 22 unitary authorities in Wales, this has now been abandoned.

2.5

Due to the statutory nature of the existence of local authorities, it is generally only possible for a local authority to undertake activities for which it is statutorily empowered. This means that for every function and action that a local authority undertakes, it must be able to show that there is either a specific statutory power for it to do so, because it is acting to discharge a specific statutory duty, or that the activity is authorised because it is incidental to another specific statutory function. That initially changed to an extent with the enactment of the Local Government Act 2000 (LGA 2000), s 2 which gives a local authority power to 'do anything which they consider is likely to achieve' the promotion of the economic, social or environmental well-being of their area (for more detail see Encyclopaedia of Local Government Law (Sweet and Maxwell)).

Over a decade later, a far wider degree of freedom was introduced by s 1 of the Localism Act 2011 which gave local authorities a general power of competence. This allows a local authority to 'do anything that individuals generally may do' but subject to limitation of existing legislative powers.

In relation to hackney carriage and private hire licensing, this point is not of enormous importance, as there are specific powers contained in the Town Police Clauses Act 1847 (TPCA 1847)[1], s 37 allied to the Transport Act 1985 (TA 1985)[2], s 15 and the Local Government (Miscellaneous Provisions) Act 1976 (LG(MP)A 1976)[3], s 45.

[1] See Appendix I.
[2] See Appendix I.
[3] See Appendix I.

Discharge of functions

2.6

The LGA 2000 requires all principal councils to adopt a constitution. In addition, it introduced the concept of Executive arrangements for local authority governance, generally replacing the earlier committee system. That was altered by the Localism Act 2011 to allow greater freedom for local authorities to determine their governance structure.

In England the council may choose one of three forms governance

(a)   Executive arrangements,
(b)   a committee system, or
(c)   prescribed arrangements[1].

If the authority decides to run Executive arrangements, those must take one of the following forms[2]:

1.   directly elected mayor and cabinet; or
2.   leader and cabinet;

In Wales, the Local Government Wales Measure 2011 allows County or County Borough Councils to operate either a Mayor and Cabinet or a Leader and Cabinet model, and the committee system is no longer available in Wales[3].

From these available models, most councils have opted for the leader and cabinet model which is the only system in Wales. In England there are a small number of directly elected mayors and some authorities retained the committee system or have reverted to it.

[1]   Local Government Act 2000, s 9B. No prescribed arrangements have been prescribed.
[2]   Local Government Act 2000, s 9C.
[3]   See Local Government (Wales) Measure 2011, Article 35.

2.7

In England (where Executive arrangements are in place) or Wales 'the council' is all the elected members of the authority, and 'the Executive' is one of the Executive arrangements outlined above, often referred to in the case of a leader and cabinet as 'the cabinet'.

The effect of the adoption of Executive arrangements is that all functions are the responsibility of the Executive, apart from those which are specified in Regulations and are allocated to the council ('Council Functions'); certain other specified functions are left for the council to choose whether to allocate to the council or the Executive.

2.8

The relevant Regulations are the Local Authorities (Functions and Responsibilities) (England) Regulations 2000, as amended, and the Local Authorities Executive Arrangements (Functions and Responsibilities) (Wales) Regulations 2007[1]. They allocate responsibility for most taxi licensing functions to the council and prohibit the Executive from exercising them. The Regulations spell out the precise functions as follows (these are identical in both sets of Regulations):

Function allocated to council	Relevant statutory provision
• Power to license hackney carriages and private hire vehicles.	As to hackney carriages: the Town Police Clauses Act 1847, as extended by the Public Health Act 1875, s 171; the Transport Act 1985, s 15; the Local Government (Miscellaneous Provisions) Act 1976, ss 47, 57, 58, 60 and 79
	As to private hire vehicles: the Local Government (Miscellaneous Provisions) Act 1976, ss 48, 57, 58, 60 and 79
• Power to license drivers of hackney carriages and private hire vehicles.	The Local Government (Miscellaneous Provisions) Act 1976, ss 51, 53, 54, 59, 61 and 79
• Power to license operators to hackney carriages and private hire vehicles.	The Local Government (Miscellaneous Provisions) Act 1976, ss 55–58, 62 and 79

¹ SI 2000/2853, as amended by numerous subsequent regulations. Although new updated Regulations were proposed in early 2015, at the time of writing (August 2017) they have yet to be made. Also SI 2007/399 (W 45).

2.9

It can be seen that in relation to hackney carriage and private hire licensing, the functions which are not the responsibility of the Executive are defined very precisely. The Regulations also state that the functions include the imposition of conditions; the determination of terms to which any licence is subject; and decisions whether and how to take enforcement action. However, it is important to recognise what is covered by the Regulations, and what is not, as those matters not expressly referred to remain the responsibility of the Executive.

Accordingly, **Council** functions are:

Hackney carriages only

- All matters covered by the TPCA 1847 as extended by the Public Health Act 1875, s 171; the Transport Act 1985, s 15 (the TPCA 1847 as extended does not apply to private hire vehicles).

Hackney carriages and private hire vehicles

- Section 47 LG(MP)A 1976 is the power to attach conditions attached to hackney carriage proprietors' licences;
- Section 48 LG(MP)A 1976 is the power to licence and attach conditions to private hire vehicle licences;
- Section 57 LG(MP)A 1976 is the power to seek information from applicants (and the offence of making a false statement);
- Section 58 LG(MP)A 1976 is the requirement to return the licence plate after expiry, suspension or revocation;
- Section 60 LG(MP)A 1976 is the power to suspend or revoke hackney carriage proprietors and private hire vehicle licences;
- Section 79 LG(MP)A 1976 allows a licence to be signed by an authorised officer of the Council, rather than having to be sealed.

Hackney carriage and private hire drivers

- Section 51 LG(MP)A 1976 is the power to licence private hire drivers;
- Section 53 LG(MP)A 1976 is the power to grant hackney carriage and private hire drivers licences for up to 3 years, charge a fee for the grant of the licence, and the power to inspect drivers' licences;
- Section 54 LG(MP)A 1976 is the power to issue, and enforcement of wearing, private hire drivers badges;
- Section 59 LG(MP)A 1976 specifies the test of suitability to be granted a hackney carriage drivers licence;
- Section 61 LG(MP)A 1976 is the power to suspend or revoke hackney carriage and private hire drivers' licences;
- Section 79 LG(MP)A 1976 allows a licence to be signed by an authorised officer of the Council, rather than having to be sealed.

Private Hire Operators and miscellaneous Hackney carriage vehicle elements

- Section 55 LG(MP)A 1976 is the power to licence private hire operators;
- Section 56 LG(MP)A 1976 are the record keeping requirements for private hire operators;
- Section 57 LG(MP)A 1976 is the power to seek information from applicants (and the offence of making a false statement);
- Section 58 LG(MP)A 1976 is the requirement to return the licence plate after expiry, suspension or revocation;
- Section 62 LG(MP)A 1976 is the power to suspend or revoke private hire operators' licences;
- Section 79 LG(MP)A 1976 allows a licence to be signed by an authorised officer of the Council, rather than having to be sealed.

It appears that all other powers and functions contained in the LG(MP)A 1976 in relation to hackney carriage and private hire licensing are **Executive** functions. These are:

- Section 45 LG(MP)A 1976 which is the process of adopting Part II of the Act;
- Section 46 LG(MP)A 1976 specifies private hire driver, vehicle and operator licence requirements and offences;
- Section 49 LG(MP)A 1976 is the requirement placed upon a hackney carriage or private hire proprietor to give notice to the Council of a transfer of an interest in the vehicle;
- Section 50 LG(MP)A 1976 is the power to require regular inspections and tests of licensed vehicles;
- Section 52 LG(MP)A 1976 is the right of appeal against refusal to grant, or conditions attached to, a private hire drivers' licence;
- Section 63 LG(MP)A 1976 is the power to create hackney carriage stands;
- Section 64 LG(MP)A 1976 creates the offence of non-hackney carriages waiting on a rank;

- Section 65 LG(MP)A 1976 is the power to fix hackney carriage fares;
- Section 66 LG(MP)A 1976 creates the offence for hackney carriage drivers of overcharging for journeys ending outside the district;
- Section 67 LG(MP)A 1976 governs the use of hackney carriages for private hire work;
- Section 68 LG(MP)A 1976 is the power of an authorised officer to inspect and suspend a hackney carriage or private hire vehicle licence;
- Section 69 LG(MP)A 1976 creates the offence for hackney carriage drivers of prolonging journeys;
- Section 70 LG(MP)A 1976 is the power to set fees for vehicle and operators licences;
- Section 71 LG(MP)A 1976 is the requirement that taximeters in private hire vehicles are tested;
- Section 72 LG(MP)A 1976 enables joint prosecution when the offences are due to the acts of a second person;
- Section 73 LG(MP)A 1976 creates the offence of obstruction of an authorised officer;
- Section 74 LG(MP)A 1976 is a saving for existing businesses on adoption of the provisions;
- Section 75 LG(MP)A 1976 contains certain exemptions to private hire licensing provisions;
- Section 76 LG(MP)A 1976 prescribes penalties on conviction;
- Section 77 LG(MP)A 1976 governs appeals;
- Section 78 LG(MP)A 1976 incorporates certain provisions of the Public Health Act 1936;
- Section 80 LG(MP)A 1976 is the interpretation section.

Clearly the fact that some of these sections are applied to the Executive rather than the Council is immaterial (eg, the offence creating provisions). However, other sections where a power is granted are important because such a power can only be exercised by the Executive. If the power is exercised by the Council, the action will be ultra vires the powers of the Council and the resulting action will be unlawful and void. The same applies in reverse if the Executive were to exercise Council functions.

The consequence of this is that there will be a split in exercise of the powers between the Executive and the Council, and these must be understood. In relation to the Executive powers, the most important appear to be the power to create stands (s 63) and the power to set fares (s 65).

In relation to fees, Schedule 1 suggests that the power to set fees for vehicles and operators licences under s 70 is an Executive function, whilst the power to set fees for drivers' licences under s 53 is a Council function. However, there is a regulation that contradicts this. Regulation 2(6) of the English Regulations[1] or regulation 3(6) of the Welsh Regulations[2] state:–

(6) The function of determining –

....

(d) whether a charge should be made for any approval, consent, licence, permit or registration the issue of which is not the responsibility of an executive of the authority; and

(e) where a charge is made for any such approval, consent, licence, permit or registration, the amount of the charge, is not to be the responsibility of an executive of the authority.

This seems to override the fact that s 70 is not listed in Schedule 1 of the Regulations and accordingly, all fee setting, under both ss 53 and 70, appears to be a Council function.

Finally, it should be noted that any decision as to how frequently vehicles must be tested under s 50 is an Executive rather than a Council function.

It seems from the above that most general day to day casework decisions about licensing matters fall to the council (and may be delegated by them to a committee or officer: see below), not to the Executive. What is perhaps less clear is, who has responsibility for adopting any general or specific policy on licensing? The adoption of such a policy is not a function expressly named in the Regulations. However, as, arguably, policy and day-to-day casework are so closely linked, it certainly makes a great deal of sense, if it is arguably not a legal requirement, for the council, not the Executive, to adopt the overall policy as well as to determine casework matters. However, for those areas which are the responsibility of the Executive, the same logic will require the Executive to make the policies. It is suggested that a joint approach is best, whereby each body drafts and adopts its own policies for its area of responsibility, but they are then noted and approved by the other part of the authority.

[1]   Local Authorities (Functions and Responsibilities) (England) Regulations 2000, SI 2000/2853, as amended.

[2]   Local Authorities Executive Arrangements (Functions and Responsibilities) (Wales) Regulations 2007, SI 2007/399 (W 45).

R (app 007 Stratford Taxis Ltd) v Stratford on Avon District Council

2.10

> Wheelchair accessibility policy for new hackney carriages. Policy adopted by the Executive rather than the Council. Was this lawful? Held: That a policy could be adopted by the Executive.

The question of where the power lay within a local authority to adopt a policy in relation to taxi licensing arose in the case of *R (app 007 Stratford Taxis Ltd) v Stratford on Avon District Council*[1] where the Court of Appeal had to determine whether the Executive or the District Council could lawfully adopt a policy relating to wheelchair accessible taxis, or whether that power was the preserve of the Council. Lady Justice Smith, President of the Queen's Bench Division, outlined the case in the following terms, explaining the problem neatly and succinctly[2].

'2. District councils comprise elected members, and a council may exercise its powers in a number of ways. These may include decisions taken by the full council. Decisions of the council may be devolved to committees, whose membership is required to represent the political composition of the full council. Since the Local Government Act 2000, decisions may also be taken by an executive, which, in the case of Stratford-on-Avon District Council, comprises a cabinet drawn from the majority party of the council. Intrinsically, questions of policy, being political in nature, are suitable for decision by such a cabinet.

3. Section 13(2) of the 2000 Act provides that any function of a local authority which is not specified in regulations under subsection (3) is to be the responsibility of an executive of the authority under executive arrangements. Section 48(4) of the 2000 Act provides that any reference to the discharge of any functions includes a reference to the doing of anything which is calculated to facilitate, or is conducive or incidental to, the discharge of those functions. Regulation 2(1) of the Local Authorities (Functions and Responsibilities (England)) Regulations 2000 provides by reference to schedule 1 that the power to license hackney carriages and private hire vehicles is not to be the responsibility of an authority's executive. On the other hand, regulation 5 of the regulations provides, with reference to schedule 4, that the adoption or approval of a plan or strategy, which might be the responsibility of an executive, shall not be the responsibility of the executive where the authority determines that the decision whether the plan or strategy should be adopted or approved should be taken by them, that is by the authority. One issue in the present appeal is whether adopting a policy that all taxis should have wheelchair access constitutes adopting a plan or strategy within regulation 5 and schedule 4, or whether it is doing something which is calculated to facilitate, or is conducive or incidental to, the discharge of the council's power to license taxis within regulation 2 and schedule 1. If it is the first, Stratford's cabinet had power to decide to adopt the wheelchair policy. If it is the second, they did not. With such nice points is 21st century appellate judicial life made interesting.'

The policy was made by the cabinet (the term used by Stratford on Avon District Council to describe their Executive) following a recommendation from the General Purposes Licensing Committee (a committee of the Council). In a complex and multi-faceted case this was the third ground of appeal[3]. The question hinged on whether the decision was 'the exercise of a function which is calculated to facilitate, or is conducive or incidental to, the discharge of the power to license hackney carriage and private hire vehicles.[4]' In which case it was a Council function (the appellants case) or alternatively, whether this decision was akin to a 'plan or strategy' in relation to licensing overall. The Court of Appeal looked at it this way[5]:

'14... . This matter turns on the construction and application of sections 13(2) and 48(4) of the 2000 Act and regulation 2(1) and schedule 1 of the 2000 regulations, to which we have already referred. In our judgment, this regulation and schedule are to be construed in the light of regulation 5(1) and schedule 4. The appellants' case is that a decision to adopt a policy that all taxis should have wheelchair access is the exercise of a function which is calculated to facilitate, or is conducive or incidental to, the discharge of the power to license hackney carriage and private hire vehicles.

15. The Recorder [at First Instance] decided that the policy did not purport to apply a condition to every licence irrespective of the individual application. The policy provided that every application would be considered against the policy. Applicants were able to ask for an exception to the policy, but must be able to demonstrate sound and compelling reasons why the committee should depart from the policy. The Recorder considered that, when the cabinet made its decision ... , it was not exercising the function of licensing hackney carriages. The appellants contend that the regulations make it clear that all powers under the 1847 Act and the power to impose conditions under the 1976 Act are for the council. Any policy is ancillary to the statutory power to license hackney carriages and is in reality part of the exercise of that power, as attaching conditions to the grant of a licence is the only way in which the policy can be enforced[6]. The respondents submit that adopting a policy (subject to exceptions in individual cases) is not exercising the power to license hackney carriages – which plainly it is not – nor is it doing something which is calculated to facilitate, or is conducive or incidental to, the exercise of the power to license hackney carriages. Mr Lock [for the local authority] draws a distinction between taking broad decisions of policy, which is the province of a political majority and appropriately exercised by a cabinet, and individual decisions about the grant or refusal of licences, which may appropriately be taken by the politically diverse council or its delegate committee. He says that this is exemplified by regulation 5 and schedule 4, by which a decision to adopt or approve a plan or strategy may be taken by a cabinet unless the council determines otherwise.

16. We have not found this ground of appeal easy to decide, since, at first blush, adopting a policy that generally all taxis should have wheelchair access may be said to be calculated to facilitate, or to be conducive or incidental to, the power to license hackney carriages. On the other hand, we accept that a policy falls within the wording "plan or strategy" used in the regulations. In our view on consideration, there is a distinction between the political decision to adopt a policy of this kind and the particular power to license hackney carriages. On this view, adopting the policy is not conducive or incidental to the power to license hackney carriages, nor is it calculated to facilitate the exercise of that power, because it does not make the exercise of the licensing power easier in individual case precisely because it is not directed to the individual exercise of the power. Logically, a plan or strategy or a policy on whether hackney carriages should have wheelchair access comes first; and that function is one that a cabinet may undertake. The function of licensing individual hackney carriages and anything that is calculated to facilitate or is conducive or incidental to the

exercise of that particular function (by the council) comes second and it is a function to be performed in the light of the plan or strategy or policy that the cabinet has determined.

17. For these reasons, in our judgment, the third ground of appeal fails. This, taken with our decision on the first ground of appeal, means that the cabinet was competent to take the policy decision that all taxis should have wheelchair access; but that their decision of 15th December 2008 was taken on consideration of significantly inadequate information.'

Accordingly, it is clear that taxi licensing policy can be the responsibility of the Executive.

1	[2011] EWCA Civ 160.
2	Paragraphs 2 and 3.
3	The other grounds were: if it was a decision for the cabinet, that body did not itself sufficiently consider and determine all the various matters that the decision-maker needed to decide and determine; it should not have been a policy, it should have been a matter for conditions attached to individual licences; there was insufficient consultation and consideration of the responses; and there was a breach of s 49A of the Disability Discrimination Act 1995. These are considered at para 2.23 onwards.
4	Para 14 above.
5	Paras 14–16 above.
6	It should be noted that this assertion is erroneous. There is no requirement for a council which licences a hackney carriage as a wheelchair accessible vehicle to attach a condition to the licence to the effect that the vehicle must remain wheelchair accessible. This is because there is no mechanism to transfer a vehicle licence from one vehicle (which is wheelchair accessible in this example) to another vehicle. See paras 8.133 onwards.

EXECUTIVE (OR CABINET) MEMBERS

2.11

The role of cabinet members who hold a licensing portfolio is sometimes unclear. In relation to the Executive functions outlined above, it may be that the authority delegate their Executive powers to the portfolio holder. In relation to the council functions, it is clear that licensing portfolio holders can be a reporting mechanism between the cabinet and the council licensing committee. They can also represent the licensing committee at the Executive, which is a useful mechanism of ensuring that the licensing functions are recognised by the Executive.

Delegation of functions

2.12

The Executive may arrange for licensing functions to be delegated. The provisions are different for England and Wales.

In England, the Leader or elected Mayor (defined in LGA 2000, s 9E(8) as the 'senior Executive member') can discharge all Executive functions, or delegate them to:

(i)   the Executive;

(ii)   another member of the Executive;

(iii)   a committee of the Executive;

(iv)   an area committee; or

(v)   an officer of the authority.

under LGA 2000, s 9E.

In Wales, the position is similar, and the Leader (under LGA 2000, s 15) or elected Mayor (under LGA 2000, s 14) can discharge all Executive functions, or delegate them to:

(i)   the Executive;

(ii)   another member of the Executive;

(iii)   a committee of the Executive; or

(iv)   an officer of the authority.

Executive Committees are rare and the Executive functions are usually either retained by the Executive as a whole, or delegated to an Executive Member. An area committee can only determine matters within its area and is therefore not relevant for taxi licensing functions.

In relation to the bulk of the licensing functions which are allocated to the council, they can be delegated by the Council to:

- a committee of the council;
- a sub-committee; or
- an officer,

under LGA 1972, s 101.

Both the Executive and Council Schemes or Schedules of Delegation are usually contained within the Councils Constitution. This will have been passed or approved by the council and is used in conjunction with the procedural rules of the council, which, again, are adopted by the council by means of resolution. These control the procedural aspects of the local authority's activities.

It is vital that the Constitution clearly and (as badly drafted provisions often are subject to challenge) accurately delegates these powers, and that the delegations are then followed. If a delegated power is exercised by a part of the authority to which the power has not been delegated (whether an Executive member, committee, sub-committee or officer under either scheme) the decision will be ultra vires the powers of the decision maker and void[1].

[1]   See eg *R (app Bridgerow Limited) v Cheshire West and Chester Borough Council v Whitefriars Resident Association* [2014] EWHC 1187 (Admin).

LICENSING COMMITTEES OF THE COUNCIL

2.13

The rules of political proportionality under the Local Government and Housing Act 1989 (LGHA 1989) will apply to the membership of a committee or sub-committee of the council.

It should be noted that a statutory licensing committee is a requirement under the Licensing Act 2003 (LA 2003). Although this is only required to determine matters governed by the LA 2003 and the Gambling Act 2005 (GA 2005) some local authorities have decided to use the same members as the licensing committee for non-LA 2003 and GA 2005 matters. If this approach is taken, it must be made clear to all concerned that this is a separately constituted committee and is not the statutory licensing committee. As it is a committee established by the authority under LGA 1972, s 101, it is not governed by any specific hearings regulations and it remains a normal council committee governed by the provisions of the LGA 1972.

2.14

There is no one particular way in which delegations are set up, although there are a number of models which are in use around the country.

Once the committee or sub-committee has been set up it is then necessary for the council itself to decide how the committee discharges the functions for which it has been created. This is usually exercised in one of two ways, either by a delegation of powers or through an investigative role. Both are an arrangement for the discharge of functions, but they are fundamentally different.

Delegation of powers means that the power or duty which lies with the council is delegated to that committee. This means that a decision of the committee is a decision of the council and no approval by any other body is required. The alternative is that the committee is asked to investigate matters and then to report its findings to the council in order to enable the council to make a decision on the basis of the information obtained by the committee.

It should be noted that Council powers can be delegated to sub-committees or to officers[1], as, indeed, can a request for investigation. In those circumstances, the effect is exactly the same as if it had been delegated to a committee.

[1]   Local Government Act 1972, s 101(1)(a).

2.15

In any proceedings, evidence should always be available in the form of a certified copy of the resolution, to show that the scheme of delegations is the current one in force[1].

[1]   Local Government Act 1972, s 234.

2.16

The council's scheme of delegations will state that a certain committee (and chief officers with a department created to support the committee) have responsibility for the licensing of hackney carriages and private hire vehicles. As stated earlier, there is no one model, and hackney carriage and private hire licensing is undertaken by a wide range of different departments. These include: regulatory departments (which often incorporate environmental health, trading standards and planning); street scene departments; environmental health departments; legal departments; Chief Executive's departments; engineer's departments; planning departments; and Town Clerk's departments. Some authorities have licensing departments, which may be autonomous or divisions of other departments, and these undertake the whole range of licensing functions applicable to that authority, whereas others tend to scatter their varying licensing functions across a number of departments. However, hackney carriage and private hire licensing do tend to stay together.

R (app Raphael) v Highbury Corner Magistrates' Court

2.17

> Power to decide whether a representation under the Licensing Act 2003 was frivolous, was delegated to Head of Service. Decision was actually made by a member of his staff. Held: It was a valid decision as a delegation covered officers acting under the control of the Head of Service.

It should be noted that it is permissible for the authority to delegate functions to a head of service or manager and then the actual decision can legitimately be taken by a more junior officer. This point was considered in *R (app Raphael) v Highbury Corner Magistrates' Court*[1]. This concerned a decision to determine that a representation in relation to a matter under the Licensing Act 2003 was frivolous or vexatious (under s 52(7)). In this case the decision was made by the licensing officer, Mr Forde, but the delegation was to the Assistant Director Environment Conservation (Public Protection). Mr Forde worked in the Assistant Director Environment Conservation (Public Protection) directorate. HHJ Mackie QC addressed the question in this way[2].

> '40. I turn next to the claim that Mr Forde did not have delegated authority to carry out delegated functions under section 52(7). That subsection, and others, spares the sub-committee from having to consider material which in the opinion of the authority is frivolous or vexatious. It is a filter to spare the members having to consider all sorts of dross. The claimant says that the delegation of that power was to the assistant director and not to Mr Forde. The submission has a superficial attraction because, of course, at least in local government, the starting point is that the person on whom a power is conferred will exercise it personally. The claimant submits that the assistant director had no power to delegate and that the papers produced do not show that that has been done.

> 41. This submission is, it seems to me, comprehensively demolished in the written skeleton argument of Mr Giffen and Mr Grant. The claim can be shortly dealt with by reference to the judgment of Turner J in *Prytherch v Conwy Borough Council*[3], with Waste Recycling Group plc as the interested party, which is case number CO/1354/2001. The learned judge said this, at paragraph 15:

>> "It was submitted that the common sense of the situation was summed up in a passage in the judgment of Shearman J, as he was, in

Cheshire CC v the Secretary of State for the Environment[4], where he said: 'The multitude of tasks which were entrusted by standing orders to the County Secretary and Solicitor is such that it is inconceivable that the council intended that all those functions should be attended to by one person or that he himself should make the relevant value judgments himself in respect of each of them.'

"I find myself in respectful submission of the obvious good sense of Shearman J's observation. It is one thing, as in Walton, for there to have been no delegation at all and for the decision taken without it to have been quashed. It is otherwise fair for there to have been formal delegation at the head of a department and for the actual decision to have been taken by a person working in that department who was informally the delegatee and answerable to that head. It then becomes a matter for the court to construe whether or not the intended scope of the delegation by the council's standing orders extended to what must be an everyday and necessary occurrence if a department is to be able to function efficiently. It plainly was."

42. It is unimaginable that the members of the committee would expect the assistant director personally to sift and distinguish the actual from the potentially frivolous and vexatious material. The informal delegation of this task by the assistant director to Mr Forde was appropriate and lawful. Indeed, if one asks oneself whether those taking the delegation decision had intended the delegation to the assistant director to be to him or her alone, their answer, to borrow a contractual law analogy, would have been, "No, of course not, we would not have expected him to deal with it personally, it should be delegated appropriately, efficiently, and economically down the line."

In relation to the scheme of delegations, it is vital to ensure that it fully covers all matters which are likely to be encountered in relation to hackney carriage and private hire licensing. Specific reference should be made to each of the pieces of legislation which cover this field[5]. The scheme of delegations may also detail which matters are the responsibility of the committee, and which are delegated to officers. It is also possible to delegate matters to an officer in consultation with the chair or deputy of the committee, which retains some member involvement, but allows for speedy decisions to be made when necessary.

[1]   [2010] EWHC 1502 (Admin).
[2]   Paras 40 to 42 above.
[3]   *R (on the application of Prytherch) v Conwy BC* [2001] EWHC Admin 869 (unreported).
[4]   [1988] JPL 30.
[5]   See Appendix I.

Overview and scrutiny of decisions

2.18

All councils must, by virtue of the LGA 2000[1], have at least one Overview and Scrutiny Committee. The function of the committee is to examine policies, services and decisions taken by or on behalf of the council and Executive and to make recommendations for improvement. In theory, the Overview and Scrutiny Committee could, therefore, call for a report from the licensing committee on a particular case and subject it to scrutiny.

Once again, there is a difference in legislation between England and Wales.

In England, a reference to the Overview and Scrutiny Committee is not possible in relation to Licensing Act 2003 matters by virtue of art 3 of The Overview and Scrutiny (Reference by Councillors) (Excluded Matters) (England) Order 2012[2]. However, there is no mention in the Order of other licensing matters (ie, not Licensing Act 2003 issues) so the position in relation to taxi licensing matters is not clear[3]. In 2001 the Government issued the following guidance:

> '[an Overview and Scrutiny Committee] should not normally scrutinise individual decisions ... particularly relating to development control, licensing, registration consents and other permissions. In particular a local authority will need to ensure such scrutiny is not an alternative to normal appeals procedures'[4].

It is suggested that this remains a sensible approach for English local authorities to take.

In relation to Wales, the position is as follows. Section 63 of the Local Government (Wales) Measure 2011 introduced s 21A into the Local Government Act 2000 covering reference of matters to scrutiny committees. Section 21A(13) introduces the concept of 'excluded matters' which are matters which cannot be referred to (and therefore considered by) overview and scrutiny committees in Welsh local authorities:

> '(13) In subsection (12) "excluded matter" means any matter which is—
>
> (a) a local crime and disorder matter within the meaning of section 19 of the Police and Justice Act 2006 (local authority scrutiny of crime and disorder matters), or
>
> (b) a matter of any description specified in an order made by the Welsh Ministers for the purposes of this section.'

At the time of writing[5] no order has been made in relation to extending the list of excluded matters under s 21A(13)(b). However, Welsh Government has issued Statutory Guidance[6] under s 21A(3) of the LGA 2000 which states:

> '6.17 It is anticipated that a Ministerial order will be made in due course to exclude certain kinds of matters from being local government matters for the purposes of section 21A.'

It can be seen that at present, in both countries, there is no bar to a local authority Member raising such an issue, which would mean that it is placed on the agenda for the Overview and Scrutiny Committee, and it would then be discussed. However, that does not mean that the Committee would have to take any action on it. It is unlikely that local authorities would scrutinise administrative decisions such as licensing decisions which have their own processes and appeals built in as they are unable to re-visit the decision once it has been made. It would, however, be possible for an Overview and Scrutiny Committee to review the overall policy on licensing and to make recommendations for improvement to the council.

1   Section 9F in relation to England, s 21 in relation to Wales.
2   SI 2012/1022.
3   Or indeed any licensing matters other than the Licensing Act, eg Gambling Act, Street trading, sex establishments etc.
4   Paragraph 3.16 of 'DETR New Council Constitutions: Local Government Act 2000 Guidance to English Local Authorities' published October 2000, amended March 2001 which forms part of the 'DETR Local Government Act 2000 New Council Constitutions – Guidance Pack'. This still appears to be extant as it has never been cancelled or replaced.
5   August 2017.
6   'Statutory Guidance from the Local Government Measure 2011' (June 2012) available at http://gov.wales/docs/dsjlg/publications/localgov/120625statguideen.pdf

DAY TO DAY DECISION MAKING AND ACTIVITY

2.19

In relation to hackney carriage and private hire vehicle licensing, the most common models employed are either a committee which undertakes all functions, or a committee which will have power to deal with all functions, but where power to grant licences in certain specified situations (usually where there are no grounds for refusal) has been delegated to officers. A few authorities have delegated the entire licensing regime to officers, with the power to both grant and refuse, but this is unusual. There were very few authorities where the entire regime was discharged by committee or sub-committee, with no officer-delegated power, but it is not clear whether this approach is still taken by any Councils.

The question as to which model is adopted is a matter for local decision, bearing in mind the need to balance the conflicting requirements of member involvement and time involved. Provided that the personnel involved understand the nature of their role and the extent of their powers, it is difficult to say whether one system is more effective or efficient than any other.

2.20

What is clear, however, is that it is essential for the committee or officer who considers a matter concerning a licence (grant, renewal, suspension or revocation) to have the delegated power to deal with that. If the findings of the officer or committee have to then be reported to another body, it is extremely difficult to ensure that every fact and furthermore every nuance is accurately and adequately reported.

R v Chester City Council, ex p Quietlynn Ltd
2.21

Sex establishment licence application. Decision delegated to a committee which set up a sub-committee to hear the application and make recommendations. Application not heard by the committee which made the

> decision, merely a report of findings. Held: This was unlawful. It was not sufficient to say that the committee could have sought information from the members of the sub- committee had they wished to.

There is a well-known passage from the judgment given by Woolf J in the case of *R v Chester City Council, ex p Quietlynn Ltd*[1] in relation to the licensing of a sex establishment. The Local Government (Miscellaneous Provisions) Act 1982, Sch 3, para 10(19) places the local authority under a statutory duty to give an applicant for a sex establishment licence an opportunity to be heard, which is not the case in hackney carriage and private hire licensing (although the rules of natural justice require this)[2]. However, the principle raised is an important one, and the following extract from *R v Chester City Council* is worth considering. Woolf J stated:

> 'Although I fully accept the importance of the use of committees and sub-committees in local government and accept that, in respect of purely administrative matters, it is quite proper for committees to act on the recommendations of other committees, it does not follow that the position is the same when the authority is performing the sort of function involved in considering applications for the grant of a licence. Such applications must be considered fairly and, in many cases it may be necessary for the determining body to have at least a summary of the representations of the applicant, whether they have been made in writing or at a hearing before another committee.'

[1]   (1983) Times, 19 October, QBD.
[2]   See paras 2.28ff below.

2.22

Notwithstanding these sentiments, the High Court decided at first instance in that case that there was no unfairness to the applicants. On appeal, the Court of Appeal did not agree and allowed one of the four appeals. However, they approved the approach outlined above by Woolf J in the High Court. Giving his judgment in the Court of Appeal, Stephen Brown LJ said[1] (at 315):

> 'It is submitted on behalf of the local authority that in this case it was not necessary that anything should be said by way of a report by the licensing panel because the decision was one which was based on locality, the characteristics of which would be known to all the members of the committee and that the five members of the licensing panel were present as members of the committee and could have given any information about the hearing and (sic) which had taken place if they had been asked. Accordingly, since the schedule provides that the hearing may be made by a sub-committee, there would be no breach of any procedural requirement such as would entitle the court to intervene in the conclusion that was reached.

It seems to me that this raises a very narrow point in this instance. I accept that the administrative functions of local authorities cover a very wide spectrum. They include the various licensing functions which fall upon local authorities. There is however an element of the judicial process in this particular function. That is made clear by paragraph 10, sub-paragraph (19) of Schedule 3 to the Act of 1982. [His Lordship read the sub-paragraph and continued:]

The principle, which is expressed in the maxim audi alterem partem, therefore is relevant and does apply, in my judgment, to this particular function.

On this occasion the uncontested facts show that no report of any kind was made to the decision-making committee. It may be that a report could have been a very short report indeed, but in my view it is a requisite of the sub-paragraph that the applicants' representations should be considered by the committee making the decision. In this case no report of any kind was made. For that reason, I take the view that there was a procedural irregularity which cannot be cured by the fact that the members of the committee could probably be expected to have known of the characteristics of the locality and could have asked, if they had wished, for details of the hearing before the panel from their members who had actually heard the applicants' representative. In my judgment this was a breach of the procedural rules which does vitiate the decision arrived at.'

[1]   *R v Chester Borough Council, ex p Quietlynn* (1984) 83 LGR 308, CA (decided jointly with *R v Havant BC, ex p Quietlynn Ltd; R v Preston BC, ex p Quietlynn Ltd; R v Swansea City Council, ex p Quietlynn Ltd; R v Trafford BC, ex p Quietlynn Ltd; R v Watford BC, ex p Quietlynn Ltd.*

R (app 007 Stratford Taxis Ltd) v Stratford on Avon District Council

2.23

> Wheelchair accessibility policy for new hackney carriages. Policy adopted by the Executive without hearing any facts, merely endorsing the Licensing Committees recommendation. Was this lawful? Held: That this was a flawed approach.

A similar point in relation to the powers of the body (or person) who heard an application to make a decision arose in the case of *R (app 007 Stratford Taxis Ltd) v Stratford on Avon District Council*[1]. The brief facts were outlined earlier[2]. The decision was made by the Executive. The first ground of challenge was that the decision was made by the Executive, but they were not provided with sufficient information to enable them to make a properly informed decision and were relying on information obtained by another body (in this case the Licensing Committee). Judgment was given by Lady Justice Smith in these terms[3]:

'9.   The appellants wished to contend before the Recorder that the cabinet, in taking the decision, did not themselves properly consider the matters relevant to the decision because they had not been provided with the material which had been provided to the committee, nor with details of the committee's recommendation... . Mr Lock [for the Council] ... accepted that the cabinet had not themselves given systematic and detailed consideration (as the committee had) to the various matters relevant to the decision. They could not be said to have done so in the short time which their consideration of this and other matters took, despite the fact that Councillor Brain, who had attended the committee meeting on 10th November 2008, was also a member of the cabinet which took the decision on 15th December 2008.

10. ...

11. Mr Lock was unable to contend that the cabinet took the decision after themselves giving sufficient material consideration to the main matters which required their consideration. Decision-making bodies in the position of the cabinet here are not required to give personal detailed attention to every strand of fact and argument capable of bearing on the decision they are making. But they are required to have drawn to their attention the main lines of relevant debate, or, as Sedley LJ put it in *R (National Association of Health Food Stores) v Secretary of State for Health* [2005] EWCA Civ 154 at paragraph 61, adopting Brennan J in *Minister of Aboriginal Affairs v Peko-Wallsend* (1986) 162 CLR 24 at paragraph 65:

> "A minister may retain his power to make a decision while relying on the department to draw his attention to the salient facts."

Here, the cabinet adopted the committee's decision upon very short consideration and without either being provided with the material that was before the committee or a résumé of the committee's consideration and reasons. If, therefore, contrary to the appellants' contention in their third ground of appeal, the cabinet was competent to take this decision, there was a significant flaw in their process.'

---

1   [2011] EWCA Civ 160.
2   See para 2.10 onwards.
3   Paragraphs 9 to 11.

2.24

From both legal and practical points of view, it is essential that the person or body who hears the application has the power to make the decision on that application. If reporting further has to be undertaken, not only will this waste both time and effort on the part of all concerned, it is likely to be a valid ground of challenge to the decision itself.

Guidance

2.25

In other areas of licensing, where recent reform of the legislation has taken place, statutory guidance is now a feature[1]. To date, no such guidance or statutory requirement for its consideration by the local authority exists in relation to hackney carriage and private hire licensing, but the Department for Transport (DfT) has issued a number of documents which must be considered by local authorities under the Wednesbury rules[2]. These include 'Taxi and Private Hire Vehicle Licensing: Best Practice Guidance'[3], 'Private Hire Vehicle Licensing – A note for guidance from the Department for Transport'[4] and 'Licensing Motorcycles as Private Hire Vehicles – A guidance note from the Department for Transport'[5]. There are also a large number of older Department of Transport Circulars which have never been cancelled. Their status seems unclear, although provided the information that they provide is not at odds with the current Guidance, they may still be considered useful.

[1]   See Licensing Act 2003, s 184 and Gambling Act 2005, s 25. In the former case the Licensing Authority must have regard to any Guidance issued by the Secretary of State by virtue of s 4(3)(b); in the latter case, the Licensing Authority must act in accordance with any Guidance issued by the Gambling Commission by virtue of s 153(1)(b).

[2]   Considered at para 2.84 onwards below.

[3]   October 2006, revised March 2010, available from http://www.dft.gov.uk/pgr/regional/taxis/taxiandprivatehirevehiclelic1792.

[4]   August 2011.

[5]   July 2012.

The decision itself

2.26

Once it has been established who or which body is empowered to make decisions relating to licensing, the actual mechanics of the decision-making process can be considered. The grant or refusal of a licence is not a criminal matter, nor is it a purely civil matter. It is an administrative matter and, accordingly, the rules which govern the operation and undertaking of that procedure are not the rules of criminal or civil evidence. This has major implications upon the way in which the decision is arrived at, and the evidence, both of type and, indeed, in some cases, quantity, that is adduced and can be considered by the decision-maker.

Administrative body

R (on the application of Hope and Glory) v Westminster Magistrates' Court and Westminster City Council

2.27

> Review of a premises licence under the Licensing Act 2003. Complaint of public nuisance. How did the court approach the appeal? Held: That licensing decisions were administrative functions at the local authority, but judicial functions at the magistrates' court.

For many years it was considered that a local authority determining licensing matters decision maker (whether a sub-committee, committee or an officer) was acting as a quasi-judicial body[1]. That view was altered in the case of *R (on the application of Hope and Glory) v Westminster Magistrates' Court & Westminster City Council*[2] where the Court of Appeal stated[3]:

> '41 As Mr Matthias [for the Council] rightly submitted, the licensing function of a licensing authority is an administrative function. By contrast, the function of the district judge is a judicial function. The licensing authority has a duty, in accordance with the rule of law, to behave fairly in the decision-making procedure, but the decision itself is not a judicial or quasi-judicial act. It is the exercise of a power delegated by the people as a whole to decide what the public interest requires. (See the judgment of Lord Hoffmann in *Alconbury*[4] at para 74.)'

It can be seen that even as an administrative body, the Court of Appeal stated that the decision maker must act fairly. How can such a body act in a fair way? It is suggested that this can be achieved by observing the rules of natural justice.

In their simplest form this means that the applicant must be treated fairly, and be seen to be treated fairly. The rules themselves are quite clear and fall neatly into two specific rules: first, that there is a right to be heard before a decision is reached; and secondly, that no person should be a judge in their own cause[5].

---

[1]   See eg *R v Liverpool Corpn, ex p Liverpool Taxi Fleet Operators' Association* [1972] 2 QB 299, CA.

[2]   [2011] EWCA Civ 31.

[3]   At para 41 per Toulson LJ.

[4]   *R (Alconbury Developments Limited) v Secretary of State for the Environment, Trade and the Regions* [2001] UKHL 23, [2003] 2 AC 295.

[5]   This was also the requirement for a quasi-judicial body, so it can be seen that there is no practical difference between the concept of the decision maker acting in a quasi-judicial capacity and acting in an administrative capacity.

A right to be heard before a decision is reached

2.28

The first rule of natural justice is *audi alterem partem*: any person who is going to be affected by the decision that is to be made has a right to be heard before the decision is reached. In relation to hackney carriage and private hire licensing, this will generally mean the applicant or licensee, depending on the situation. It will also apply where the authority is considering not renewing a licence or suspending or revoking a licence. Obviously, if the application is uncontested, ie the applicant satisfies all the criteria that the local authority has laid down, then it is unnecessary for the applicant to attend a hearing and be given a chance to speak when there are no objections against which he has to speak. However, the situation is quite different where there are prima facie grounds for refusing the licence, or when action against the licence is being considered. In those circumstances, the applicant must be given the chance to make representations. In situations where action is going to be taken urgently (eg an immediate revocation of a drivers' licence) it is also vital that the licensee is given an opportunity to make representations, although as the matter is urgent and the decision is to be taken within a short period of time, the length of time to make those representations may well be extremely short.

2.29

There is no statutory requirement that the applicant should be given the opportunity to make oral representations, but many local authorities do allow such a course of action. However, the case law supports the view that the local authority can set its own procedures and it is, therefore, open to a local authority to allow only written representations.

Selvarajan v Race Relations Board

2.30

> Allegations of racial discrimination investigated by the Race Relations Board. Held: the Board was an administrative body and under a duty to act fairly, but in the absence of external statutory rules was master of its own procedure.

This view was supported by Lord Denning MR in *Selvarajan v Race Relations Board*[1]. This case concerned an investigation into allegations of racial discrimination. These allegations were investigated by a conciliation committee of the Race Relations Board, which found discrimination but failed to achieve a settlement. The matter was then referred to the Board itself. They found no evidence of racial discrimination. The applicant for judicial review argued that the Board had failed in its duty to act fairly. He failed in that assertion. Lord Denning MR stated (at 19B):

> 'In all these cases it has been held that the investigating body is under a duty to act fairly: but that which fairness requires depends upon the nature of the investigation and the consequences which it may have on persons affected by it. The fundamental rule is that, if a person may be subjected to pains or penalties, or be exposed to prosecution or proceedings, or deprived of remedies or redress, or in some such way adversely afflicted by the investigation and report, then he should be told the case made against him and be afforded a fair opportunity of answering it. The investigating body is, however, the master of its own procedure. It need not hold a hearing. It can do everything in writing. It need not allow lawyers. It need not put every detail of the case against a man. Suffice if the broad grounds are given. It need not name its informants. It can give the substance only. Moreover, it need not do everything itself. It can employ secretaries and assistants to do all the preliminary work and leave much to them. But, in the end, the investigating body itself must come to its own decision and make its own report.'

[1]   [1976] 1 All ER 12, CA.

R v North Yorkshire County Council, ex p M (No 2)

2.31

> Local authority adoption panel. Held: The views of the guardian *ad litem* should be taken into account but the guardian *ad litem* could not dictate how the proceeding should be conducted as that decision remained with the local authority.

This approach has been supported in subsequent cases, especially in relation to oral hearings. In *R v North Yorkshire County Council, ex p M (No 2)*[1] Ewbank J, in relation to an application before an adoption panel, stated (at 80G):

> 'There is no provision for oral submissions to be made by a guardian *ad litem* in court proceedings or by any other person. Although the guardian *ad litem* may think it desirable to attend the adoption panel and put her submissions orally, this is essentially a matter for the adoption panel themselves to decide. There is no reason to suppose that the guardian *ad litem*'s views cannot be adequately expressed in the report written by her, nor adequately conveyed by the meeting she had with the principal officer and the social worker. In my view, the suggestion that the decision not to allow her to attend the adoption panel was contrary to the law is unarguable. Indeed, in my judgment, I would have thought it was good practice to come to the decision that the authority came to in this case.
>
> Although it is incumbent on a local authority when there is a court case in train to listen to the guardian *ad litem*'s views, that does not imply the guardian *ad litem* is entitled to decide how the adoption panel, or any other branch of the local authority, should conduct its affairs, nor is she entitled to insist on attending meetings.'

[1]   [1989] 2 FLR 79, QBD.

2.32

In fact, many authorities do allow persons to speak in support of or (if the situation warrants it) against an application, but these cases (and others) show that there is no right, either under statute law or common law, to require this. This can be contrasted with the position in relation to hearings concerning matters governed by the LA 2003 and GA 2005[1]. In the areas of hackney carriage and private hire licensing, it remains a matter for the discretion of the authority as to whether oral representations will be allowed. If they are, it is then a matter for the further discretion of the local authority as to whether such persons making oral representations are open to questioning.

If oral representations are allowed, consideration should be given to allowing the applicant the opportunity to be represented. This does not need to be by a legally qualified representative, but can be by someone simply acting on the applicant's behalf. However, oral representations and representatives may increase the time taken for each application, and it is for the local authority to decide on its procedures and to communicate its decision to applicants and others in advance.

1   See the Licensing Act 2003 (Hearings) Regulations 2005, SI 2005/44 as amended by the Licensing Act 2003 (Hearings) (Amendment) Regulations 2005, SI 2005/78 and the Gambling Act 2005 (Proceedings of Licensing Committees and Sub-committees) (Premises Licences and Provisional Statements) (England and Wales) Regulations 2007, SI 2007/173.

THE NEED TO KNOW ANY ALLEGATIONS OR COMPLAINTS

R v Assistant Metropolitan Police Comr, ex p Howell

2.33

> Taxi driver, licence suspended as a result of medical concerns. GP certified he was fit to drive, but a second medical opinion was obtained by the licensing authority. Driver not allowed to see the second medical report or opinion but as a consequence the licence was not renewed. Held: Decision was unlawful because the driver did not know what the concerns were and how to address them. A person must know the allegations that are made against him.

Another important consideration is the need for the person concerned to know what the allegations against him are. In *R v Assistant Metropolitan Police Comr, ex p Howell*[1], this point arose. Mr Howell had held a hackney carriage driver's licence in London for 12 years and at that time, prior to the creation of the London Mayor and TfL, the Public Carriage Office ('PCO')[2] was part of the Metropolitan Police. At the age of 50, Mr Howell had to have a medical to renew his licence, and went to his own doctor. His own doctor reported that Mr Howell had a past history of epilepsy, but that he was currently fit to drive. As a result of this, a second medical report was obtained, which concluded that Mr Howell had indeed suffered from epilepsy in the past, but that he was not affected at the present time. Notwithstanding those findings, as a consequence of this second report, the licence was not renewed. However, Mr Howell was not allowed to see the second report, nor was he told what it contained.

Ackner LJ stated (at 59H):

'The power of the assistant commissioner is to be exercised – and only to be exercised – after due consideration and determination of Mr Howell's [the applicant] fitness to drive. It is not a discretion that may be exercised arbitrarily and without accountability. The consideration must, therefore, be a fair consideration of Mr Howell's fitness to drive. The duty is, therefore to act fairly.'

The Court of Appeal held that Mr Howell had a justifiable grievance because he was not told of the contents of the report nor allowed to make representations about its contents. In addition, the decision was based on scanty and unreliable information. Ackner LJ continued (at 60H):

'In my judgment it was defective. It was defective because it did not provide Mr Howell with any indication of what were the objections which the assistant commissioner thought disentitled Mr Howell from receiving a renewal of the licence and he was thereby denied an opportunity of meeting those objections in such manner as was available. This was unfair.

I do not in any way seek to criticise the assistant commissioner for feeling anxious when he received the [second] report ... What I do criticise is his reaching his decision without communicating to Mr Howell what it was that was causing him anxiety and concern and was likely to be the operative reason for refusing to extend the licence, so as to give Mr Howell an opportunity to meet and satisfy that concern and anxiety if he could.'

This decision-making process was defective and unfair, and the matter should be reconsidered by the Assistant Commissioner. This decision was supported by both the other judges, Slade and Purchas JJ.

1   [1986] RTR 52, CA.
2   Now called London Taxi and Private Hire ('LTPH') and part of Transport for London ('TfL') which in turn is part of the responsibilities of the Mayor of London.

R v Metropolitan Police Comr, ex p Phillips

2.34

> A number of complaints were made against a taxi driver, but when the matter was considered the details of each complaint were not provided. Held: That the process was defective and the decision unlawful because the licensee must know the nature and substance of the allegations against him.

This approach was followed by the High Court in *R v Metropolitan Police Comr, ex p Phillips*[1]. A number of complaints were brought against a London hackney carriage driver ranging over a period dating from 1982 to 1985. Three matters had been taken to court and eight other complaints had been the subject of advice by the Cab Enforcement section of the Public Carriage Office, which at that time was run by the Metropolitan Police. Mr Phillips argued that when consideration was being given as to whether or not his licence should be suspended all the complainants in relation to every one of those cases should have been brought to provide evidence. On this point the judge, Mr Justice Taylor, stated (at p 3D of the transcript):

'I do not think that in the context of this inquiry it could have been realistic or appropriate for the Assistant Commissioner to muster all the complainants to come and individually stand by their original complaints and be cross-examined.'

He went on to say that in his view such an approach would be 'wholly out of proportion'.

1   (10 November 1987, unreported), QBD.

2.35

The second line of complaint was that when the matter came before the Assistant Commissioner, a Mr Sutton, the matters that were being considered were outlined by Mr Sutton. In relation to the first few matters, although he did not go into great detail, he gave an outline of each situation. This was to ensure that both he and Mr Phillips were considering the same matters. Unfortunately, he then simply went on to say:

'There is a whole list – one, two, three, four, five, six, seven, eight complaints of misbehaviour and abusive language and refusals. On each occasion you were seen and advised by B8 [a department of the PCO[1]] and all those occasions have been recorded of you being seen and advised.'

The Assistant Commissioner then went on to ask whether Mr Phillips had anything to say about all those matters, and also mentioned that there were outstanding complaints about abusive behaviour. It was this approach which was challenged as Mr Phillips did not know exactly what was being alleged.

Mr Justice Taylor took the following view[2] (at p 7E):

'On behalf of the applicant it is said that each of these complaints, if they were to be relied upon in order to found a suspension or revocation of the licence, ought to have been put with clarity to the applicant so that he could say whether he accepted them and whether he had any mitigation to raise about them or any comment at all.'

He continued (at p 9A):

'I have come to the conclusion, however, looking at the hearing as a whole, that the procedure adopted was not in accordance with the requirement that the applicant should have had an opportunity to deal with the allegations made against him. It seems to me that one is left at the end of the day, having read the transcript [of the hearing], with an uneasy suspicion that matters which had never been drawn to the applicant's attention at all may well have been taken into account.'

He concluded (at p 9G):

'It seems to me that whilst one does not wish to impose any kind of formality upon proceedings of this kind, the essentials must be observed. One of those essentials is that the matters which the Metropolitan Commissioner or his delegate have in mind to take into consideration must be spelt out to the applicant so that he can have an opportunity to deal with those specified facts. It is not sufficient in my judgment to say: "There are three or four matters which I will specify and there are eight others which I am not going to read out. Have you go anything to say about all these things?"

Where one is concerned with an applicant's livelihood I think he is entitled to know the specific matters that are relied upon against him and entitled at that time, quite apart from anything he may have said in previous years as each incident arose, to put forward what he wished to say in answer.'

As a consequence, it was decided that the procedure was defective and the decision to suspend the driver's licence was quashed.

1   See para 2.33, footnote 2.
2   *R v Metropolitan Police Comr, ex p Phillips* (10 November 1987, unreported), QBD.

R v Assistant Metropolitan Police Comr, ex p Davidson

2.36

> Taxi driver. A number of complaints were made against him but he was not shown the original letters or statements. However he was given a schedule detailing each complaint with substantial detail of each incident. Held: That this was sufficient to enable him to answer the allegations and there was no procedural impropriety.

A subsequent case of *R v Assistant Metropolitan Police Comr, ex p Davidson*[1] followed a similar line. It was alleged by Mr Davidson that as he had not seen original copies of the letters of complaint from the complainants, and also original copies of the notes made by investigating police officers, he was not aware of the substance of the allegations made against him. Mr Justice Auld considered this and stated as follows (at p 2A):

'He maintains that he was entitled to see copies of letters of complaint from the complainants themselves and also copies of notes made by the investigating police officers.

In fact what had been made available to him before the hearing and upon which he had commented in some detail in writing before the hearing was a schedule of complaints giving the date of and location where each incident complained of was said to have occurred, and, in each case, very considerable detail of the nature of the complaint.

In my judgment he was clearly entitled to know the substance of the complaints made against him, but it is not arguable that he has suffered in law or otherwise as a result of not seeing the actual letters of complaint or notes of the investigating police officers in each case. On that head, it is my view that there is no arguable case of procedural impropriety.'

1   (2 December 1992, unreported), QBD. See above at para 2.34.

R v Assistant Comr of the Metropolitan Police, ex p Foster

2.37

> Taxi driver. Action against the licence taken on the basis of complaints. Full details given to the licensee but no criminal proceedings on the basis of the complaints. Argued that these were insufficient grounds to justify action

against the licence. Held: That guilt beyond all reasonable doubt was not required as these decisions are made on the balance of probability. Licensee had full details of the allegations. No procedural impropriety and decision lawful.

Finally, mention should be made of the case of *R v Assistant Comr of the Metropolitan Police, ex p Foster*[1].

This case concerned a similar situation to that of the case of *Ex p Phillips*[2]. The suggestion was that there had been no proper steps taken to substantiate the complaints, and that they should have been dealt with by way of court proceedings before action should be taken against the licence. Mr Justice MacPherson of Cluny confirmed that the approach taken in *Ex p Phillips* was correct and in relation to Mr Foster's claim, he stated (at p 4G):

'Quite full statements (indeed in one case a long statement) were taken from the complainants. Police officers were involved in taking the complaints in more than one instance. The matters were all put fully, with chapter and verse, before the Director and before Mr Foster who was represented at the oral hearing by his solicitor.'

The matter went to the magistrates' court on appeal, and the appeal was split over two days. There was some argument as to the representation that Mr Foster had at the magistrates' court but ultimately the judge concluded (at p 9C):

'It seems to me that the Magistrate did what she was bound to do. She considered all that was put before her. I am quite certain that she listened with patience to the skilful arguments which would have been put before her by Mr Lyne, but she reached, as had the Commissioner, an overall view in an administrative sense in connection with this case.

There is no need or requirement for complaints of this kind to be proved to the point of no reasonable doubt and to clothe an investigation of this kind with the guise of a criminal proceeding. That is not what the procedure is all about. The appeal is a rehearing and a fresh look by a totally independent Magistrate at the decision which has earlier been made by the Assistant Commissioner.

I am wholly unable to see any injustice in the way in which the matter was conducted. I see no unfairness of any kind in the Magistrate's approach or in the decisions which she made as to the hearing itself. I do not accept that there was any breach of the rules of natural justice at that stage any more than there was at the earlier stage.'

He concluded (at p 10G):

'I see no procedural impropriety in this case, no unlawfulness and no unreasonableness of any kind in the approach of the Commissioner or of the Magistrate. In those circumstances, this application is dismissed.'

[1] (18 November 1994, unreported), QBD.
[2] *R v Metropolitan Police Comr, ex p Phillips* (10 November 1987, unreported), QBD.

2.38

Taken collectively these cases demonstrate two points. First, as shown in the case of *R v Assistant Metropolitan Police Comr, ex p Howell*[1] the licensee must be made aware of the allegations or complaints against him, but, secondly, provided that sufficient details are made available to the licensee to enable him to identify the complaints and the nature of the allegations, there does not have to be either presentation of witness evidence or a criminal court hearing before matters can be considered[2].

[1]   [1986] RTA 52, CA.
[2]   This is considered further in subsequent cases, including *Leeds City Council v Hussain* [2002] EWHC 1145 (Admin), [2003] RTR 199 (see para 2.111) and *Cherwell District Council v Anwar* [2011] EWHC 2943 (Admin); (see para 2.112).

No person should be a judge in their own cause

2.39

The second rule of natural justice *is nemo judex in causa sua potest*: that no person should be a judge in their own cause. This is now frequently referred to as the rule against bias, although the two concepts are not identical.

Each local authority must have its own Code of Conduct[1], covering the behaviour of members, and the approach the Council as a whole will take. In addition, the Council must maintain a register of members' interests[2].

[1]   In England this is in accordance with the Localism Act 2011, s 28 and standards are now covered by Chapter 7 (ss 26 to 37) of the Localism Act 2011. In Wales it is in accordance with Local Government Act 2000, s 51 and breaches of the Code in Wales are still considered by the Public Services Ombudsman for Wales.
[2]   Localism Act 2011, s 29 for England: Local Government Act 2000, s 81 for Wales.

2.40

There are two cases (which pre-date the Codes of Conduct)[1], where breaches of the requirement not to be a judge in your own cause were considered. They are good examples of the problems that can occur and are considered below. These are clearly useful in understanding the scope of the rule and its impact on the decision of an authority.

[1]   *Hannam v Bradford City Council* [1970] 1 WLR 937, CA and *R v Barnsley Metropolitan Borough Council, ex p Hook* [1976] 1 WLR 1052, CA.

Hannam v Bradford City Council

2.41

Dismissal of teacher by the governors of the school. Reconsideration of that decision by a local education authority committee. Three members of the appeal committee were governors, although they had not been party to the original decision. Held: This was a breach of natural justice as they were sitting as judges in their own cause.

The rule that no-one should be a judge in their own cause is well illustrated by the cases of *Hannam v Bradford City Council*[1] and *R v Barnsley Metropolitan Borough Council, ex p Hook*[2].

In *Hannam v Bradford City Council*, a teacher was dismissed by the governors of a school and, under the then current legislation and articles of government of the school, the local education authority had the power to prevent that dismissal. It was agreed that the staff sub-committee of the education authority, which considered whether or not to exercise that power, was sitting in a quasi-judicial capacity. On that sub-committee, which, on the day of the decision, consisted of ten members, were three people who were governors of the school from which the teacher had been dismissed, although they had not been present at the governors' meeting when the dismissal was approved. It was alleged that there was a risk of bias in the findings of the committee. Lord Sachs LJ said (at 942D):

'... it was abundantly clear that the staff sub-committee decision could not stand. No man can be a judge in his own cause. The governors did not, upon donning their sub-committee hats, cease to be an integral part of the body whose action was being impugned, and it made no difference that they did not personally attend the governors meeting [where the decision to dismiss was taken].'

Lord Widgery LJ added (at 946A):

'I am much impressed by the fact that when the sub-committee sat down to consider what the plaintiff would regard as an appeal, the chairman was a member of the governors against whose decision this so-called appeal was being brought. I think that if it had been disclosed at the outset that no less a person than the chairman of the sub-committee was a member of the governors in question, the immediate reaction of everyone would have been that some real likelihood of bias existed. I say that with every respect to the distinguished gentleman who chaired the sub-committee on this occasion; but when one is used to working with other people in a group or on a committee, there must be a built-in tendency to support the decision of that committee, even though one tries to fight against it, and this is so even though the chairman was not sitting on the occasion when the decision complained about was reached.'

Finally, Lord Cross LJ put forward the following suggested test for assessing whether there was any possible bias in such circumstances (at 949C):

'If a reasonable person who has no knowledge of the matter beyond knowledge of the relationship which subsists between some members of the tribunal and one of the parties would think that there might well be bias, then there is in his opinion a real likelihood of bias. Of course, someone else with inside knowledge of the characters of the members in question might say: "Although things don't look very well, in fact there is no real likelihood of bias." That, however, would be beside the point, because the question is not whether the tribunal will in fact be biased, but whether a reasonable man with no inside knowledge might well think that it might be biased.'

1   [1970] 1 WLR 937, CA.
2   [1976] 1 WLR 1052, CA; see para 2.42 below.

R v Barnsley Metropolitan Borough Council, ex p Hook

2.42

> Revocation of a market trading licence by the market manager and chairman of the markets committee. The chairman then took part in the appeal process and the markets manager was present when the members deliberated. Held: That the presence of the markets manager breached the rules of natural justice as he was a judge in his own cause.

In *R v Barnsley Metropolitan Borough Council, ex p Hook*, it was the presence of an officer, who was directly involved in the situation in question, which rendered the decision unsatisfactory. The markets manager who terminated the licence of a person to trade in the market (for urinating in an alley) then took part in the decision on the subsequent internal appeals heard by the council. Lord Scarman LJ said (at 1060D):

'In my judgment, the local authority was in breach of one rule of natural justice which is so old that it can be put in the Latin language: *nemo debet esse judex in causa propria* ... When the authority came to file its evidence, then it seems to me it did appear that Mr Fretwell, the market manager, and the chairman of the committee had participated, first, in the decision to revoke the licence; secondly, in the first appeal ... and, lastly, in the final appeal ... There can be no doubt upon the affidavit of Mr Fretwell himself that he and the chairman were parties to the original decision to revoke the licence. It seems to me an inescapable inference from the way in which Mr Fretwell has described what was then done. There can be no doubt that the two of them were both members of the first appeal committee. There can be no doubt that one of them, namely, the chairman, was a party to the final appeal, and it is clear from the evidence that, whether or not he participated in the decision, Mr Fretwell, the market manager, was present with the committee throughout the discussion, hearing, and determination of the final appeal.

... the evidence of Mr Fretwell indicates plainly his presence throughout, his participation in the first appeal, and the participation of the chairman throughout.

... In the present case the corporation was considering something very like dismissing a man from his office, very like depriving him of his property, and they were charging him with doing something wrong. It was the revocation of a licence because of misconduct that they had under consideration – not merely the man's fitness or capacity for the grant of a licence. There was, therefore, a situation here in which (using the terms broadly) Mr Hook was on trial, and on trial for his livelihood. There was a complainant, the market manager. The market manager had a professional interest in the matter since he was concerned to protect his employees, or the employees for whom he was responsible, from abuse and misconduct by stallholders in the market. Mr Fretwell was a prosecutor, a complainant; Mr Hook was a man, albeit in an administrative field, who was on trial not for his life but for his livelihood.

If ever there was a case in which it was imperative that the complainant or the prosecutor should not participate in the adjudication, I should have thought it was this one; ... most certainly the rule of *nemo debet esse judex in causa propria* should have been rigorously observed throughout the whole appellate process.'

2.43

In reality, there will be a number of occasions where local politicians, as members of the local authority, will have expressed opinions on certain subjects or even campaigned for or against matters that are now before them in the licensing committee. How does this affect their decision-making, or presence on the committee?

In 2011 the introduction of the Localism Act 2011, s 25 fundamentally altered the rules relating to bias for local authorities. Section 25 states:

25   Prior indications of view of a matter not to amount to predetermination etc.
(1) Subsection (2) applies if—
     (a) as a result of an allegation of bias or predetermination, or otherwise, there is an issue about the validity of a decision of a relevant authority, and
     (b) it is relevant to that issue whether the decision-maker, or any of the decision-makers, had or appeared to have had a closed mind (to any extent) when making the decision.
(2) A decision-maker is not to be taken to have had, or to have appeared to have had, a closed mind when making the decision just because—
     (a) the decision-maker had previously done anything that directly or indirectly indicated what view the decision-maker took, or would or might take, in relation to a matter, and
     (b) the matter was relevant to the decision.
(3) Subsection (2) applies in relation to a decision-maker only if that decision maker—
     (a) is a member (whether elected or not) of the relevant authority, or
     (b) is a co-opted member of that authority.
(4) In this section—
     "co-opted member", in relation to a relevant authority, means a person who is not a member of the authority but who—
     (a) is a member of any committee or sub-committee of the authority, or

(b)   is a member of, and represents the authority on, any joint committee or joint sub-committee of the authority,

and who is entitled to vote on any question which falls to be decided at any meeting of the committee or sub-committee;

"decision", in relation to a relevant authority, means a decision made in discharging functions of the authority, functions of the authority's executive, functions of a committee of the authority or functions of an officer of the authority (including decisions made in the discharge of any of those functions otherwise than by the person to whom the function was originally given);

"elected mayor" has the meaning given by section 9H or 39 of the Local Government Act 2000;

"member"—

(a)   in relation to the Greater London Authority, means the Mayor of London or a London Assembly member, and

(b)   in relation to a county council, district council, county borough council or London borough council, includes an elected mayor of the council;

"relevant authority" means—

(a)   a county council,

(b)   a district council,

(c)   a county borough council,

(d)   a London borough council,

(e)   the Common Council of the City of London,

(f)   the Greater London Authority,

(g)   a National Park authority,

(h)   the Broads Authority,

(i)   the Council of the Isles of Scilly,

(j)   a parish council, or

(k)   a community council.

(5)   This section applies only to decisions made after this section comes into force, but the reference in subsection (2)(a) to anything previously done includes things done before this section comes into force.

Although this is a somewhat confusing and poorly drafted section, it can be seen that it effectively allows the decision makers to express opinions before a decision, and then complicates any challenge to that subsequent decision on the basis of bias. It seems that clear predetermination will remain a ground for challenge. To date the case law on the impact of s 25 is limited, but the cases that have considered it do distinguish between what might be called 'full-blown predetermination' and simply an appearance of a closed mind.

I.M. Properties Development Limited v Lichfield District Council and others

2.44

> The principle argument concerned the vires of the Council to reconsider its local [Town and Country Planning] plan. A secondary argument relevant here concerned an apparent instruction as to which way to vote given by the Chair of the Planning Committee to the members. Held: This was covered by the Localism Act 2011, s 25 and did not amount to predetermination.

The application of s 25 was considered in some detail in *I.M. Properties Development Limited v Lichfield District Council and others*[1]. This planning case concerned a challenge to Lichfield District Council of its decision to endorse modifications to the draft Lichfield Local Plan Strategy. The principle argument was in relation to the jurisdiction of the Council to make the decision, but a subsidiary argument concerned an allegation of predetermination. The facts in relation to the predetermination point were as follows.

Four days before the matter was to be considered by full Council, Cllr Ian Pritchard, the Chair of the Planning Committee emailed the other Councillors in his political party in these terms[2]:

'Hello all,

This is to remind group members who attended the last group meeting and inform those who did not, that the group decided in government parlance to have a three line whip in place at the council meeting on Tuesday. In plain terms group members either vote in favour of the report I will be giving regarding the local plan or abstain. Also if you are approached by anyone promoting alternative sites, please make no comment. If group members are reported making negative comments it would without any doubt derail our local plan. Sorry if you find this a little heavy handed but there is an awful lot at stake. Have a kind weekend.

Kind regards,

Ian'

The argument before the court was whether that email was 'a dogmatic instruction to councillors as to how to vote'[3] which removed their individual discretion and amounted to predetermination, or was 'something said and done prior to the decision making meeting' which would engage the provisions of s 25?

The judge, Mrs Justice Patterson, recited s 25 and then said[4]:

'84 The statutory wording makes it clear that just because a decision maker has done anything directly or indirectly which indicated a view that he took or might take on a matter it was not to be taken as an appearance of a closed mind.

85 Mr Crean [for the Claimant] submits that the section is only applicable when a councillor makes a public statement. The statutory wording does not support that submission. It is broadly phrased. It refers to a decision maker having previously done "anything" in relation to a matter that was relevant to the decision. That would, in my judgment, cover the sending of the email. It was something done prior to the meeting which was relevant to the decision in that it was exhorting the recipients to vote in a particular manner. It comes within the description of doing "anything" which is the statutory wording. In my judgment the indication of the view expressed in the email would not be something that would amount to pre-determination.

86 In any event, despite Mr Crean's submissions, I do not find that the tenor of the email was so strident as to remove the discretion on the part of the recipient as to how he or she would vote. Neither the language used nor the absence of any sanction support that contention. The debate shows a far reaching discussion between members and displays no evidence of closed minds in relation to the decisions that had to be taken. A fair minded and reasonable observer in possession of all of the facts would not be able to conclude on the basis of the evidence that there was any real possibility of predetermination as a result of the email from Councillor Pritchard. This ground fails.'

This case makes it clear that the parameters of s 25 are extremely wide, but equally it demonstrates that notwithstanding s 25, predetermination remains a valid and likely ground of challenge. In addition, notwithstanding the introduction of s 25, there remains the possibility of a challenge on the natural justice principles.

1   [2014] EWHC 2440 (Admin), [2014] PTSR 1484.
2   See para 42.
3   See para 76.
4   Paragraph 84 onwards.

BIAS

Porter v Magill

2.45

Secret policy to sell council houses in marginal wards with a view to increasing the Conservative vote. This amounted to wilful misconduct. The question was whether there was bias on the part of the auditor in the light of statements made at press conferences. Held: That there was no bias as the fair-minded and informed observer would not conclude that there was.

There were a number of licensing cases where the courts took the view that members could express a view, and then put that from their minds when making a decision, which were frequently contrasted with some planning cases where the opposite view was taken.[1] Whilst these cases are important, a wider approach can and should be taken based upon the overall concept of bias[2]. The leading case is *Porter v Magill*[3]. The House of Lords reviewed a number of earlier cases relating to bias and approved (with a very minor modification) of the test laid down by the Court of Appeal in *Re Medicaments and Related Classes of Goods (No 2)*[4]. Accordingly, the test as it now stands is as follows[5]:

> 'The question is whether the fair-minded and informed observer, having considered the facts, would conclude that there was a real possibility that the tribunal was biased.'

Although this decision concerned the question of bias by a person in a judicial capacity, its application to members of local authority committees is the same.

[1]   The licensing cases were *R v Reading Borough Council, ex p Quietlynn Ltd* (1986) 85 LGR 387, QBD; *Darker Enterprises v Dacorum Borough Council* [1992] COD 465 DC and *R v Chesterfield Borough Council, ex p Darker Enterprises Ltd* [1992] COD 466, DC. The planning included *Georgiou v Enfield LBC* Admin Ct (7 April 2004, unreported) and *Bovis Homes v New Forest DC & McAlpine v S of S Environment, Transport and the Regions* (25 January 2002, unreported).

[2]   For a consideration of the law relating to bias in decision-making, please see *Encyclopaedia of Local Government Law* (Sweet and Maxwell).

[3]   [2002] 1 All ER 465, HL.

[4]   [2001] 1 WLR 700.

[5]   Per Hope LJ at para 103.

2.46

A breach of the common law test of bias may lead to a decision being quashed following a judicial review[1].

[1]   A recent example is to be found in *Kelton v Wiltshire Council* [2015] EWHC 2853 (Admin) where a councillor was a director of a housing association which had been identified by the council as its preferred partner for the affordable housing element of a new housing development. He voted for the planning permission and subsequently his association became the preferred bidder. This was held to be a clear demonstration of bias within the *Porter v Magill* test.

Policies

2.47

As with all other areas of its activity, the local authority is entitled to adopt policies in relation to hackney carriage and private hire licensing. Policies are an integral part of the decision-making process, informing and guiding the decision-makers, and providing a valuable aid to consistent decision-making. In contrast with more recent licensing regimes under LA 2003 and GA 2005 there is no statutory requirement placed upon the local authority to set hackney carriage and private hire policies. Rather, hackney carriage and private hire policies are created voluntarily by the local authority to assist with consistent decision making. They are the Council's own self-created guidelines. It must be made clear and be fully understood that a policy is not a fetter on the discretion of the local authority. Each case must continue to be judged on its own merits, but this can be done in the light of the policies that are applicable. A policy guides, but does not bind, a local authority.

R (on the application of Singh) v Cardiff City Council

2.48

> Penalty points scheme used as a means of enforcement for taxi drivers. As soon as a predetermined level was met the licence was automatically revoked. Held to be unlawful because there was no application of discretion and there was no consideration of suspension rather than revocation.

The importance of policies was neatly encapsulated by Mr Justice Singh in *R (on the application of Singh) v Cardiff City Council*[1] where he stated[2]:

> 'One of the reasons why public law recognises and indeed encourages the adoption of policies to govern the exercise of discretionary powers is not only that they assist decision makers within the relevant authority. As importantly, if not more importantly, policies signal to members of the public how discretionary powers will be exercised. In that respect they form an important function in maintaining the rule of law, because they assist individuals to be able to regulate their conduct to predict with some reasonable certainty how they will be treated by a public authority, depending on what they do.'

1   [2012] EWHC 1852 (Admin), [2013] LLR 108, Admin Ct.
2   At para 83.

Stringer v Minister of Housing and Local Government

2.49

> Planning permission. What was the effect of policy in relation to a subsequent decision? Held: Policies are quite lawful provided they are not applied unilaterally, other relevant factors are taken into account and each case is considered on its merits.

The use of policies within local government has long been recognised and judicially approved. In *Stringer v Minister of Housing and Local Government*[1] (a case concerning planning policies) Cooke J stated the following in the Divisional Court (at 1298D):

> 'It seems to me that the general effect of the many relevant authorities is that a Minister charged with the duty of making individual administrative decisions in a fair and impartial manner may nevertheless have a general policy in regard to matters which are relevant to those decisions, provided that the existence of that general policy does not preclude him from fairly judging all the issues which are relevant to each individual case as it comes up for decision.'

1   [1970] 1 WLR 1281.

British Oxygen Co Ltd v Minister of Technology

2.50

> Application for grant to develop a product. Grant refused on the basis of (so far as is relevant) the application of a policy. Held: That a policy can be applied provided each application is ultimately considered on its own merits.

This was followed by the House of Lords in *British Oxygen Co Ltd v Minister of Technology*[1]. Lord Reid took the following view (at 624G):

'It was argued on the authority of *Rex v Port of London Authority, ex p Kynoch Ltd* [1919] 1 KB 176 that the Minister is not entitled to make a rule for himself as to how he will in future exercise his discretion. In that case Kynoch owned land adjoining the Thames and wished to construct a deep water wharf. For this they had to get the permission of the authority. Permission was refused on the ground that Parliament had charged the authority with the duty of providing such facilities. It appeared that before reaching their decision the authority had fully considered the case on its merits and in relation to the public interest. So their decision was upheld.

Bankes L.J. said (at page 184):

"There are on the one hand cases where a tribunal in the honest exercise of its discretion has adopted a policy, and, without refusing to hear an applicant, intimates to him what its policy is, and that after hearing him it will in accordance with its policy decide against him, unless there is something exceptional in his case. I think counsel for the applicants would admit that, if the policy has been adopted for reasons which the tribunal may legitimately entertain, no objection could be taken to such a course. On the other hand there are cases where a tribunal has passed a rule, or come to a determination, not to hear any application of a particular character by whomsoever made. There is a wide distinction to be drawn between these two classes."

I see nothing wrong with that. But the circumstances in which discretions are exercised vary enormously and that passage cannot be applied literally in every case. The general rule is that anyone who has to exercise a statutory discretion must not "shut his ears to an application" (to adapt from Bankes L.J. at page 183). I do not think there is any great difference between a policy and a rule. There may be cases where an officer or authority ought to listen to a substantial argument reasonably presented urging a change of policy. What the authority must not do is to refuse to listen at all. But a Ministry or large authority may have had to deal already with a multitude of similar applications and then they will almost certainly have evolved a policy so precise that it could well be called a rule. There can be no objection to that, provided the authority is always willing to listen to anyone with something new to say – of course I do not mean to say that there need be an oral hearing.'

After considering the same extract from *Kynoch* Viscount Dilhorne agreed, saying (at 630H):

'Bankes L.J. clearly meant that in the latter case there is a refusal to exercise the discretion entrusted to the authority or tribunal but the distinction between a policy decision and a rule may not be easy to draw. In this case it was not challenged that it was within the power of the Board to adopt a policy not to make a grant in respect of such an item. That policy might equally well be described as a rule. It was both reasonable and right that the Board should make known to those interested the policy it was going to follow. By doing so fruitless applications involving expense and expenditure of time might be avoided. The Board says that it has not refused to consider any application. It considered the appellants.'

He concluded (at 631B)

'I must confess that I feel some doubt whether the words used by Bankes L.J. in the passage cited above are really applicable to a case of this kind. It seems somewhat pointless and a waste of time that the Board should have to consider applications which are bound as a result of its policy decision to fail. Representations could of course be made that the policy should be changed.'

1   [1971] AC 610, HL.

A-G (ex rel Tilley) v Wandsworth London Borough Council

2.51

> Intentional homelessness and the impact on the care of children. Local authority acted in accordance with the policy and the challenge was that the policy was so tightly drawn, as to fetter the discretion. Held: That the way the policy was drawn its application did fetter the discretion and was therefore unlawful.

This wide approach to policies was tightened slightly by the Court of Appeal in *A-G (ex rel Tilley) v Wandsworth London Borough Council*[1] where the Court of Appeal considered a local authority's policy in relation to homeless persons and their children. The policy had been tightly drawn and appeared to fly in the face of the requirements of the Children and Young Persons Act 1963. Templeman LJ stated thus (at 858A):

'On well recognised principles public authorities are not entitled to fetter the exercise of discretion or to fetter the manner in which they are empowered to discharge the many duties that are thrust on them. They must at all times, in every particular case, consider how to exercise their discretion and how to perform their duties.'

Templeman LJ took the view that the policy was effectively a mandatory order, notwithstanding evidence that exceptions had been made. He continued (at 858C):

'On a question of ultra vires the practice of making exceptions is irrelevant, but, for my part, even if the resolution had provided for exceptions and even if, as Mr Beloff [counsel for the defendants] urged, this was a general policy and not a mandatory order, the resolution would not get rid of the vice that a local authority, dealing with individual children, should not make a policy or order that points towards fettering its discretion in such a way that the facilities offered to the child do not depend on the particular circumstances of the child, or of the child's family, but follow some policy that it expressed to apply in general cases.'

In dismissing the local authority's appeal, he concluded (at 858G):

'In what was, if I may say so, a careful and lucid judgment, the deputy judge … correctly applied the principle that local authorities are not allowed to fetter their discretions and duties, and he reached a conclusion that I cannot fault save for this: that I am not myself persuaded that even a policy resolution hedged around with exceptions would be entirely free from attack. Dealing with children, the discretion and powers of any authority must depend entirely upon the different circumstances of each child before them for consideration.'

It can be argued that this case is, to an extent, limited to decisions involving the welfare of children, but clearly any policy can be attacked. It has also been demonstrated that where a policy has review and appeal procedures intended to emphasise that it is not binding, but merely advisory, if the evidence shows that the policy is never departed from, and it would be 'difficult to imagine precisely what extreme circumstances might serve to persuade the authority that [a departure from the policy] would be appropriate' then that policy will be susceptible to successful challenge (see *R v Warwickshire County Council, ex p Collymore*[2]).

[1]   [1981] 1 WLR 854, CA.
[2]   [1995] COD 52, QBD.

R (on the application of Westminster City Council) v Middlesex Crown Court and Chorian plc and Proud

2.52

> Application for a public entertainment licence. Refused on the basis of the council's policy relating to a 'stress area'. Held by the High Court that the authority could have a policy but it could not be applied blindly and routinely without the possibility of exception.

Within the present Millennium, in the case of *R (on the application of Westminster City Council) v Middlesex Crown Court and Chorian plc and Proud*[1], Mr Justice Scott Baker addressed the matter of policies thus:

> '19. There is no doubt that the Claimant is entitled to have a policy with regard to the grant of these licences. See for example *R v Torbay Licensing Justices, ex p White*[2] and *R v Chester Crown Court, ex p Pascoe and Jones*[3]. The policy must not, however, be applied blindly and routinely without the possibility of exception. The [Council], and also any court hearing an appeal must consider each application against the background of the policy and decide whether the circumstances of the particular case justify an exception.'

Accordingly, it is for the local authority to adopt their policies, and then have regard to them, recognising always that any person can make any application that flies in the face of the policy, and also, that they, the decision-makers, must not close their minds to such applications, but consider each and every case, fairly, on its own individual merits.

[1]   [2002] EWHC 1104 (Admin), [2002] LLR 538, Admin Ct.
[2]   [1980] 2 All ER 25.
[3]   (1987) 151 JP 752.

R (on the application of Rowe) v Revenue and Customs Commissioners

2.53

> Use of taxation schemes and consideration of the legality of notices issued under the Finance Act 2014 in accordance with HMRC policy. Held: (so far as is relevant here) that the use of policies is lawful provided they do not fetter the discretion of the decision maker.

Most recently the High Court has followed the approach taken in British Oxygen and confirms the lawful use of policy in both administrative and judicial decision-making in *R (on the application of Rowe) v Revenue and Customs Commissioners*[1]. Simler J expressed it like this[2]:

> 'Moreover as Mr Southern accepts, there can be nothing unlawful or inappropriate, in the decision-maker developing and applying a policy as to the approach to be adopted in the generality of cases, provided that the policy does not preclude the decision-maker from departing from the policy in an exceptional case: see *British Oxygen Co v Minister of Technology*[3]; and see *Assisted Reproduction and Gynaecology Centre v Human Fertilisation and Embryology Authority*[4]. This is a legitimate means of achieving consistency and certainty in decision-making.'

[1]   [2015] EWHC 2293 (Admin), [2015] BTC 27, Admin Ct.
[2]   At paragraph 101.
[3]   [1971] AC 610.
[4]   [2002] EWCA Civ 20 at para 54.

R v Nottingham City Council, ex p Howitt

2.54

> Revocation of taxi drivers licence on the basis of an agreed policy. Challenged on the grounds that this was a blanket application of a policy and amounted to a fetter on the discretion. Held: This was not a blanket approach and each case was considered on its merits, even though there was evidence to show that most cases resulted in similar decisions.

The question of the local authority fettering its discretion in relation to hackney carriage matters arose in the case of *R v Nottingham City Council, ex p Howitt*[1].

Mr Howitt held a driver's licence issued by Nottingham City Council (it is unclear from the transcript whether this was a hackney carriage driver's licence, a private hire driver's licence or whether he was the holder of both). He was convicted of plying for hire without a licence contrary to the Town Police Clauses Act 1847, s 45. He was given a 12 months' conditional discharge and ordered to pay £60 costs. At that time there was some six months before his licence expired.

The council (acting under delegated powers granted to their 'Team Leader, Taxi Licensing') decided to revoke the remainder of his licence and in addition advise that he should not apply for another licence until a period of six months had elapsed from the date of their decision.

This decision was challenged by Mr Howitt by means of judicial review on two grounds: first, that the council was applying a blanket policy of revoking the driver's licences of those convicted of plying for hire without a licence, and advising that they should not reapply for a period of at least six months; and, secondly, that the council took into account an irrelevant consideration which was the 'likelihood' that Howitt would have been driving without insurance at the time.

[1]   [1999] COD 530, QBD.

2.55

In relation to the first issue, evidence was adduced by the respondent council to the effect that there was no blanket policy applied. However, it was admitted and accepted by Mr Stevens, the Team Leader, Taxi Licensing, that in those cases the decision that he would take 'generally would mean a period of six months off the road unless there were circumstances indicating that a different decision was appropriate'. In deciding what action to take in relation to an individual's licence, the licensee would be invited for a personal interview and be given the opportunity to put their case before Mr Stevens.

There were suggestions that Mr Stevens had made remarks suggesting that a blanket policy was imposed, but in view of the conflicting evidence this was not pursued. However considerable reliance was placed upon statistics showing that between November 1994 and January 1999 there were some 96 cases of a similar nature, and of those 47 had suspensions or revocations amounting to more than six months' loss of livelihood, 24 had a period of less than six months imposed and 25 were not possible to analyse.

Although the applicant made great play of these statistics, the judge, Dyson J rejected the view that those figures showed that a blanket policy was adopted[1]. On the first point he concluded (at p 10F):

'It is not in issue that, in the absence of what Mr Stevens refers to as "appropriate mitigating factors" his policy is generally to impose a six month ban. It is clear that Mr Stevens and the Sub-committee take a strict view of the offence of plying for hire without a licence. He gives their reasons at paragraph 7 of his first affidavit. As a result, what many might regard to be a tough policy has been adopted in relation to bans. It may even be that the policy has become tougher since June 1997, although Mr Stevens does not admit this. But the only question for me in relation to the first issue is whether the decision that was made on 20th July 1998 in the case of Mr Howitt was not a true decision because it was fettered by a blanket policy of imposing bans for six months. If that was so, then the interview, which covered a number of points applicable to the particular circumstances of Mr Howitt's case, was a charade. I am not persuaded that it was. Nor am I convinced that the statistics point to the existence of a blanket policy at the material time.'

Accordingly, that first issue was rejected by the court.

[1]   *R v Nottingham City Council, ex p Howitt* [1999] COD 530, QBD.

2.56

The second ground was based on the view that Mr Stevens expressed that one of the factors that he would take into account in considering what period of suspension or revocation was the matter that 'there is a likelihood that the driver who plies for hire will be acting outside the terms of his insurance which for private hire vehicles usually excludes public hire' (at p 11F[1]). It was argued that this was an irrelevant consideration as it was a desire to punish for an offence which had not been made out. The judge dismissed this second issue thus:

'Mr Stevens has answered this ground of challenge at paragraph 5 of his second affidavit, where he says:

"I have always sought to determine the sanction that I consider appropriate, in the light of my general approach, for the offence of plying for hire. I have never sought or intended to 'punish' any one for driving without insurance nor did I do so in the case of the Applicant. It is correct to say that in my description of the reasons why in general I view the offence of plying for hire so seriously include the likelihood that a driver who plies for hire will be acting outside the terns of his insurance. My concern is the safety of the public not punishment for some separate offence. Further, I would adopt the same approach to the offence of plying for hire for the other reasons set out in paragraph 7 of my first Affidavit irrespective of the matter that I refer to in paragraph 7(c)."

In my judgment, this is a complete answer. At paragraph 7 of his first Affidavit, Mr Stevens gives five reasons why he and the Sub-committee regard the offence of plying for hire so seriously. The insurance reason is one of those. In my judgment, they are entitled to regard the likely insurance consequences of the offence as a reason for treating the offence as serious. In any event, even if it was an irrelevant consideration, it is not material to the general approach to the offence, and cannot therefore have been material to the decision of 20 July 1998.'

Accordingly, that second ground was also rejected.

1   *R v Nottingham City Council, ex p Howitt* [1999] COD 530, QBD.

2.57

The city council had challenged the proceedings on an additional ground, that there was an alternative remedy available (an appeal to the magistrates' court against revocation). The court rejected this[1].

1   For the impact of a local authority's policies on any subsequent appeal, see Chapter 3, para 3.21. (*R (on the application of Westminster City Council) v Middlesex Crown Court and Chorian plc and Proud* [2002] EWHC 1104 (Admin), [2002] LLR 538, Admin Ct. For further discussion concerning policies, see *Encyclopaedia of Local Government Law* (Sweet and Maxwell).

R (on the application of Singh) v Cardiff City Council

2.58

> Penalty points scheme used as a means of enforcement for taxi drivers. As soon as a predetermined level was met the licence was automatically revoked. Held to be unlawful because there was no application of discretion and there was no consideration of suspension rather than revocation.

The question of whether the application of a policy amounted to a fetter on the discretion of the local authority was considered in the case of *R (on the application of Singh) v Cardiff City Council*[1]. Cardiff City Council had introduced a policy of using a penalty points scheme for disciplining hackney carriage and private hire drivers[2]. Under the terms of the policy, once the specified number of points had been administered to the particular driver, there was an automatic revocation of his or her drivers' licence, with no consideration as to whether or not that was a just or reasonable action in all the circumstances. This was challenged by means of judicial review on the grounds of that it fettered the discretion of the authority. The case was heard by Mr Justice Singh, and in relation to this particular point his conclusion was that unwavering application of the policy prevented the Council from properly exercising its discretion in determining whether a driver remained a fit and proper person, and whether or not the driving licence should be suspended or revoked[3].

1   [2012] EWHC 1852 (Admin), [2013] LLR 108, Admin Ct.
2   The workings of such a scheme are considered at para 6.43.
3   Although the element in the judgment subheaded 'Fettering of discretion' (see para 92) is short, the concept of removal of discretion is fully examined in paras 68 to 91.

Nicholds v Security Industry Authority

2.59

> Challenge to an absolute prohibition in the SIA criteria which prevented an SIA licence being granted where an applicant had certain serious convictions within a specified period of time prior to the application. Held: Not a fetter on the discretion and an absolute policy was not unlawful.

It is quite clear that policies can contain absolutes, eg in certain circumstances a licence will not be granted. These are often referred to as 'bright line policies'[1]. The use of an absolute policy was considered by the High Court in *Nicholds v Security Industry Authority*[2]. The case concerned the criteria applied by the Security Industry Authority (SIA) in relation to applicants who had serious criminal convictions. The criteria adopted (under s 7 of the Private Security Industry Act 2001) automatically prevented certain applicants from being treated as fit and proper persons until a significant period of time had elapsed from the date of conviction. This was challenged on a number of grounds, the relevant one here being that it amounted to a fetter on the discretion of the authority[3]. This third ground was considered by the judge (Kenneth Parker QC (sitting as a Deputy High Court Judge)) who concluded that this was not a fetter on the discretion of the authority. He stated:

> '52 For the principle that there should generally be no fetter imposed in respect of the exercise of a statutory discretion, Mr Cragg [for the claimants] naturally relies upon the well known statement by Lord Reid in *British Oxygen Co. Ltd v Minister of Technology*[4]:
>
> > "The general rule is that anyone who has to exercise a statutory discretion must not "shut his ears to an application" ... I do not think there is any great difference between a policy and a rule. There may be cases where an officer or authority ought to listen to a substantial argument reasonably presented urging a change of policy. What the authority must not do is to refuse to listen at all. But a Ministry or large authority may have had to deal already with a multitude of similar applications and then they will almost certainly have evolved a policy so precise that it could well be called a rule. There can be no objection to that, provided the authority is always willing to listen to anyone with something new to say ...."
>
> 53 Ms Lieven, who appeared for the [Security Industry] Authority, contended that this ground was misconceived. She submitted that the authorities in which the "no fetter" principle was invoked concerned

circumstances where Parliament had conferred a broad discretion upon a public authority to take decisions conferring benefits or imposing burdens, and did not expressly empower the public authority to make rules or to establish a policy for exercising the discretion. A question has then arisen in such cases whether, and to what extent, the authority may make such rules or establish such a policy. In this case Parliament, by section 7, has expressly conferred a rule or policy making power on the Authority. The only question then is whether the authority has made rules that fall within the purpose and scope of the statutory power (the *ultra vires* test), that are rational (the Wednesbury test) and that are proportionate (if the matter has a Convention dimension). This case is on all fours with *R (Elias v Secretary of State for Defence*[5], where the executive exercised a rule making prerogative power to create an *ex gratia* scheme of compensation and was not obliged to award compensation to a person who did not satisfy the strict criteria for award of compensation.

54 In my judgment, Ms Lieven is correct in her submission.

55 The extent to which as a matter of public policy discretion should be replaced by rules is a difficult question upon which different views are strongly held: see Craig, Administrative Law, 5th edition 2003, 536–540.

56 The advantages of rules are numerous. They ensure fairness and consistency. They promote efficiency of administration. If the rules are transparent, individuals know where they stand and can plan their affairs; and they can subject the rules to searching examination and so further the public accountability of government.

57 It is not, therefore, surprising that the courts have tended to encourage, rather than discourage, public authorities from making transparent rules and developing published policies. For example, in *R (Alconbury Developments Ltd) v Secretary of State for the Environment, Transport and the Regions*[6], at [143] Lord Clyde said:

> "The formulation of policies is a perfectly proper course for the provision of guidance in the exercise of an administrative discretion. Indeed policies are an essential element in securing the coherent and consistent performance of administrative functions."

58 In *R v Southwark LBC ex p.Udu*[7] at 391 Staughton L.J. said:

> "The Council are perfectly entitled to have a policy. Fairness, after all, demands that like cases should be treated alike, and the policy will promote that objective".

59 In R v Secretary of State for the Home Department, ex p. Venables[8] at 432 Lord Woolf M.R. said:

> "The Home Secretary's discretion as to release is very wide. It is the type of discretion which calls out for the development of policy as to the way it will be exercised. This should assist in providing

consistency and certainty which are highly desirable in an area involving the administration of justice where fairness is particularly important."

60 However, in this instance Parliament has deliberately, by section 7, conferred a rule making power on the Authority. It is for the Authority to draw up what it believes are the appropriate criteria for the grant of licences for door supervisors. The criteria are challengeable only on the grounds of ultra vires, Wednesbury irrationality or lack of proportionality. I have already dealt with the challenge of invalidity; there is no challenge on Wednesbury grounds, and I shall shortly deal with proportionality.

61 It seems to me that there is also a further reason why Mr Cragg's third ground of challenge is misconceived. His argument rests upon the premise that the "no fetter" principle applies invariably wherever a discretionary power is conferred, whatever the statutory context. This argument not only infringes the prescription of the "no fetter" principle itself (as he reads it), which assumes that there is an exception to every case, but, more importantly, it is not, in my view, supported by authority or legal policy. Lord Reid was careful, in the passage cited from *British Oxygen*, to refer to "the general rule." In most instances where a discretionary power is conferred it would be wrong for the decision maker to frame a rule in absolute terms because to do so would defeat the statutory purpose. However, it seems to me that there are certain exceptional statutory contexts where a policy may lawfully exclude exceptions to the rule *because to allow exceptions would substantially undermine an important legislative aim which underpins the grant of discretionary power to the authority* [emphasis in the original judgment] . There is, for example, a well-known line of cases concerning "taxi" licensing where licensing rules, which admitted of no exceptions for any "special" circumstances, were held lawful: see, for example, *R v Manchester City Justices, ex p. McHugh*[9]; *R v Wirral MBC ex p The Wirral Licensed Taxi Owners Association*[10].

62 In my view, the statutory context must be examined with great care. In this case, for the reasons already given, the statutory context empowers the Authority to make the commission of certain serious criminal offences an absolute bar to obtaining a licence to work as a door supervisor. The rule is intra vires and rational. Not to have such a rule in respect of offences of such great gravity would tend to undermine a fundamental aim of the Act, and such a failure would be truly vulnerable to challenge on grounds both of ultra vires and Wednesbury irrationality.

63 The importance of context is demonstrated by considering certain prison cases. In *R v Secretary of State for the Home Department, ex p. Simms*[11] and in *R (Daly) v Secretary of State for the Home Department*[12], prison rules that prisoners should not receive visits from journalists acting as such and that prisoner's correspondence, including legal correspondence, should be read in the absence of the prisoner were struck down. The rules in question imposed "blanket" restrictions that did not give due regard to important

competing values. However, in a different context the court has upheld prison rules requiring category A prisoners to be strip searched after visits, a rule to which for compelling reasons no exceptions were permitted, even if the prisoner was a "model" inmate and believed that submission to such a search offended the tenets of his faith: see *R v Secretary of State, ex p Zulficar*[13]. Similarly, in the present statutory context certain offences are intrinsically so grave as to justify the imposition of an absolute bar, and no other matter is capable of counterbalancing the fact of conviction and sentence.

64 For completion, I should make one final observation in this context. It is important to bear in mind that Parliament has conferred upon the Authority the power to draw up the relevant criteria. The Authority is the industry regulator and has the experience and expertise for the task. This Court should be very cautious before seeking to "second-guess" the evaluation that the Authority has made. In my judgment, and putting aside any Convention dimension for the moment, the Court should only strike down the criteria if it could be said that there was no reasonable basis for the conclusion that certain offences were so serious as to justify the imposition of an absolute bar. For the reasons already given, I believe that the claimants in this application signally fail to show that that is the case."

1   See eg *Habib v Central Criminal Court* [2016] EWHC 2597 (Admin) at para 16.
2   *David Nicholds, Michael Hancock, Christian Thorpe v Security Industry Authority v Secretary of State for the Home Department* [2006] EWCH 1792 (Admin), [2007] 1 WLR 2067.
3   The three grounds of challenge were: (1) contravention of the Human Rights Act (considered at paragraph 2.114 below); (2) statutory interpretation as to whether the legislation allowed an absolute policy to be created under the policy-making power (it was held that it did see paras 42–50 of the judgment); and (3) did such a policy amount to a fetter on the discretion.
4   [1971] AC 610 at 625.
5   [2005] EWHC 1435.
6   [2001] UKHL 23, [2001] 2 All ER 929.
7   [1996] ELR 390.
8   [1997] UKHL 25, [1998] AC 407.
9   [1989] RTR 285, 88 LGR 180.
10   [1983] 3 CMLR 150.
11   [1999] UKHL 33, [2000] 2 AC 115.
12   [2001] UKHL 26, [2001] 2 WLR 1622.
13   Judgment of the Divisional Court, 21 July 1995.

2.60

It is interesting to note that specific reference was made to two taxi cases in this judgment[1]. Although there is no overt power contained within any hackney carriage or private hire legislation conferring a power on a local authority (or TfL) to create such rules, there is a requirement not to grant a licence unless the applicant is a fit and proper person, and accordingly, it is arguable that the position under taxi law and the Private Security Industry Act 2001 are analogous. This is certainly persuasive authority that a local authority (or TfL) can adopt an absolute policy in relation to taxi licensing.

1   *R v Manchester City Justices, ex p McHugh* [1989] RTR 285, 88 LGR 180; *R v Wirral MBC, ex p The Wirral Licensed Taxi Owners Association* [1983] 3 CMLR 150.

R (app Sayaniya v Upper Tribunal (Immigration and Asylum Chamber)

2.61

> Did mandatory rules under the Immigration Act 1971 result in a fetter on the discretion of the Home Office? Held: No, because of the statutory basis for the rules.

This approach has been followed on many occasions, most recently by the Court of Appeal in *R (app Sayaniya v Upper Tribunal (Immigration and Asylum Chamber)*[1]. This case concerned a challenge to a mandatory rule made under the Immigration Act 1971 which stated that in certain circumstances leave to enter or remain within the UK 'are to be refused'[2]. The appeal was dismissed by the Court of Appeal with judgment being given by Beatson LJ. In relation to the question of an absolute policy he stated[3]:

> '15 My starting point is that the decisions on the "non-fettering" principle relied on by Mr Malik [for the appellant] such as *Attorney General ex rel Tilly v Wandsworth LBC*[4] and *R v Secretary of State for the Home Department, ex p Venables*[5] at 469 did not concern a statute which expressly permits rules to be made, as the 1971 Act does. Neither does *British Oxygen Co Ltd v Minister of Technology*[6], which contains an earlier and classic review of the position. While, as will be seen, immigration rules are not law in the sense that a statute or a statutory instrument is, there are many decisions of the House of Lords and the Supreme Court involving the application of provisions of a mandatory nature in the Immigration Rules. They are susceptible to challenge on grounds of error of law, *Wednesbury* unreasonableness or irrationality and proportionality but in none of the cases is it suggested that their mandatory nature in itself makes them *ultra vires*. The second reason is that given by the judge when refusing permission to apply for judicial review. It is that, although paragraph 322(1A) is in mandatory terms, the Secretary of State may depart from it by making a decision more beneficial to an applicant such as to grant discretionary leave to remain "outside the rules" when the Rules provide that leave should not be given.

(i) Rules and Discretion

16 Before turning to my reasons for concluding that that this appeal should be dismissed, it is appropriate to refer to the operation of rules and discretion in our system of administrative law and the trajectory of the development of administrative law and governmental policy since the 1970s. The general difference between rules as prescriptive and mandatory and discretion as open-textured and advisory with policy statements and guidance is well recognised: see for example the statements in *R (Alvi) v Secretary of State for the Home Department*[7] at [114], [120] and see also [97]. Lord Walker in Alvi's case at [111] stated that there as a tension in public law decision-making between flexibility in the decision-making process and predictability of its outcome and that

the more there is of one, the less room there is for the other, and getting the balance right is often difficult.

17 The benefits of a system that has rules in it and thus provides some certainty and facilitates efficiency of administration are now seen more widely than they were in the middle of the twentieth century. As a result of the influence of public law and social science scholars and policy makers in this country and elsewhere, many of the developments since the 1970s have been towards a more rule-based system. Professor Kenneth Culp Davis's 1969 work, *Discretionary Justice: A Preliminary Enquiry* was particularly influential. While recognising that no legal system has ever been without significant discretionary power, which is indispensable for individualised justice, he considered that cutting back unnecessary discretionary power is important in order to provide certainty and predictability but with appropriate flexibility. In this country the influence was first seen in policy on social security. In recent years, much attention has been paid to the increasingly rule-based system of immigration control.

18 The submissions in this case need to be seen against this background. There are now many decisions of the courts on the topic. As Kenneth Parker QC (as he then was) stated in *Nicholds and others v Security Industry Authority*[8] at [57], "courts have tended to encourage, rather than discourage, public authorities from making transparent rules and developing published policies".'

1   The Queen on the application of Sandip Narpatsinh Sayaniya v Upper Tribunal (Immigration and Asylum Chamber) v Secretary of State for the Home Department [2016] EWCA Civ 85, [2016] 4 WLR 58.
2   See para 1 of the judgment.
3   Paragraphs 15–20 of the judgment.
4   [1981] 1 WLR 854.
5   [1998] AC 407.
6   [1971] AC 610.
7   [2012] UKSC 33, [2012] 1 WLR 2208.
8   [2006] EWHC (Admin), [2007] 1 WLR 2027.

2.62

This reinforces the position in relation to absolute policies, but it must always be remembered that even an absolute policy is only that, a policy. Each and every case must be considered on its own merits in the light of that policy and the policy must not be applied as a hard and fast rule, without such consideration.

All policies must be approved by the local authority (see para 2.47 above) and must be available to anybody. It therefore follows that they must be open and secret policies are unlawful. Secret policies have no place in a transparent, democratic decision-making process.

In addition, policies must be kept under review. Circumstances change, and policies must reflect the current approach of the local authority, rather than reflect dated or obsolete thinking. The statutory policies under the LA 2003 and GA 2005 must be renewed[1] regularly and it is important that taxi policies are also subjected to the same requirements.

A policy cannot be set in stone, indeed as mentioned above, it must be renewed and revised regularly to take account of altering circumstances, and it is obvious that in light of this policies must be capable of change, adaptation and updating.

[1]   The Licensing Act 2003 Statement of Policy must be renewed every five years by virtue of the Licensing Act 2003, s 5, and the Gambling Act 2005 Statement of Principles/Policy (the terms are used interchangeably in the Act) must be renewed every three years by virtue of the Gambling Act 2005, s 349.

WHAT IS THE IMPACT OF AN UPDATED POLICY ON EXISTING LICENSEES?

Wilcock v Lancaster City Council

2.63

> Hackney carriage vehicle licence. Vehicle did not comply with conditions but licence granted and renewed. Suspended when the council adopted a tougher policy on enforcement. Held: The council could change its policy and enforce more strictly.

This was acknowledged in the case of *Wilcock v Lancaster City Council*[1]. This case concerned action being taken against a hackney carriage vehicle licence which, some years after it was first licensed, was felt by City Council not comply with the vehicle conditions. Accordingly, a suspension notice was issued under s 68 of the Local Government (Miscellaneous Provisions) Act 1976, and this was challenged[2]. Although the case concerned a vehicle licence the points made by the judge (His Honour Judge Waksman QC (Sitting as a High Court Judge)) are clear indications of the powers of a local authority with regard to its policies. He stated[3]:

> "27 ... .The question then is what can properly be read into that first certificate [of compliance – issued by the Council when the vehicle has passed its mechanical and suitability test]. I can see that it can be said that under the first certificate it can be assumed that the Council's view was that the condition of the car at that time was compliant. But where does that take the claimant? I do not accept that that means clearly and unequivocally that it could never be the case during the life of that certificate, which goes on for one year, that the position on compliance could change. The Council is entitled to change its policy. It is entitled to act more strictly. That is particularly the case here, of course, because it is not suggested that it is unlawful for the council to change its approach and there is no attack on the condition itself. I do not think it can be read into the first certificate into that that the Council will never change its policy in the course or the duration of that certificate.'

If the suitability and safety of a driver or operator is substituted for the suitability and safety of the vehicle, it can be seen that this is authority for the proposition that the Council is perfectly entitled to change its policies, and also to act under those policies in a stricter way than it has done hitherto. It must be accepted that there is a significant difference between a vehicle (which can deteriorate) and a driver (who is after all human) or operator (who may be human), but the principle must remain good for all types of licence.

1   [2013] EWHC 1231 (Admin), [2013] LLR 607, Admin Ct.
2   For the implications of this judgment on vehicle suspensions, see para 8.151.
3   At paragraph 27.

LEGITIMATE EXPECTATION

R v North East Devon Health Authority, ex parte Coughlan

2.64

Another important point to consider is that of legitimate expectation. Once a licence has been granted, is there a legitimate expectation that it will continue to be granted?

There is no case directly concerning this question and taxi licences.

> Nursing home closure following a promise by the Health Authority of a 'home for life'. Did this give rise to a legitimate expectation that the nursing home provision would remain? Held: That in those circumstances the promise of a home for life did create a legitimate expectation.

The leading case on legitimate expectation generally is *R v North East Devon Health Authority, ex parte Coughlan*[1]. A legitimate expectation can arise when either a promise has been made by a public authority (as was the case in *Coughlan*) or a course of action or conduct leads to the belief that the conduct will continue. The Court of Appeal in *Coughlan* considered this at some length[2]:

'56 What is still the subject of some controversy is the court's role when a member of the public, as a result of a promise or other conduct, has a legitimate expectation that he will be treated in one way and the public body wishes to treat him or her in a different way. Here the starting point has to be to ask what in the circumstances the member of the public could legitimately expect. In the words of Lord Scarman in *In re Findlay*[3] "But what was their *legitimate* expectation?" Where there is a dispute as to this, the dispute has to be determined by the court, as happened in *In re Findlay*. This can involve a detailed examination of the precise terms of the promise or representation made, the circumstances in which the promise was made and the nature of the statutory or other discretion.

57 There are at least three possible outcomes.

(a)   The court may decide that the public authority is only required to bear in mind its previous policy or other representation, giving it the weight it thinks right, but no more, before deciding whether to change course. Here the court is confined to reviewing the decision on Wednesbury grounds (*Associated Provincial Picture Houses Ltd v Wednesbury Corpn*[4]). This has been held to be the effect of changes of

policy in cases involving the early release of prisoners: see *In re Findlay*[5];
R v Secretary of State for the Home Department, Ex p Hargreaves[6].

(b)   On the other hand the court may decide that the promise or practice
induces a legitimate expectation of, for example, being consulted
before a particular decision is taken. Here it is uncontentious that the
court itself will require *the opportunity for consultation* to be given unless
there is an overriding reason to resile from it (see *Attorney General of
Hong Kong v Ng Yuen Shiu*[7]) in which case the court will itself judge the
adequacy of the reason advanced for the change of policy, taking into
account what fairness requires.

(c)   Where the court considers that a lawful promise or practice has
induced a legitimate expectation of a *benefit which is substantive*, not
simply procedural, authority now establishes that here too the court
will in a proper case decide whether to frustrate the expectation is so
unfair that to take a new and different course will amount to an abuse
of power. Here, once the legitimacy of the expectation is established,
the court will have the task of weighing the requirements of fairness
against any overriding interest relied upon for the change of policy.

58 The court having decided which of the categories is appropriate, the
court's role in the case of the second and third categories is different from
that in the first. In the case of the first, the court is restricted to reviewing
the decision on conventional grounds. The test will be rationality and
whether the public body has given proper weight to the implications of
not fulfilling the promise. In the case of the second category the court's
task is the conventional one of determining whether the decision was
procedurally fair. In the case of the third, the court has when necessary
to determine whether there is a sufficient overriding interest to justify a
departure from what has been previously promised.'

This is the framework for deciding whether a legitimate expectation exists and
if it does, whether a subsequent decision confounds it. The Court of Appeal
concluded its lengthy examination of legitimate expectation in this way[8]:

'82 The fact that the court will only give effect to a legitimate expectation
within the statutory context in which it has arisen should avoid jeopardising
the important principle that the executive's policy-making powers should
not be trammelled by the courts: see *Hughes v Department of Health and
Social Security*[9]. Policy being (within the law) for the public authority alone,
both it and the reasons for adopting or changing it will be accepted by the
courts as part of the factual data—in other words, as not ordinarily open
to judicial review. The court's task—and this is not always understood—is
then limited to asking whether the application of the policy to an individual
who has been led to expect something different is a just exercise of power.
In many cases the authority will already have considered this and made
appropriate exceptions (as was envisaged in *British Oxygen Co Ltd v Board
of Trade*[10] and as had happened in *Ex p Hamble (Offshore) Fisheries Ltd*[11]), or
resolved to pay compensation where money alone will suffice. But where
no such accommodation is made, it is for the court to say whether the

consequent frustration of the individual's expectation is so unfair as to be a misuse of the authority's power.'

In the licensing context generally (although not taxi licensing specifically) the High Court has determined that there is no legitimate expectation that a street trading licence will continue in existence beyond the annual renewal date.[12] This decision is based largely on the ground that there are powers within the street trading legislation[13] to alter the designation of streets, revoke a licence or refuse to renew a licence.

In relation to premises licensing under the Licensing Act 2003, the Court of Appeal has also accepted that even if there was a legitimate expectation of consultation (although it was not convinced that such an expectation existed), failure to consult in breach of that expectation could not prevent the local authority from discharging its statutory duty.[14]

[1]   [2001] QB 213, CA.
[2]   At para 55 onwards.
[3]   [1985] AC 318, 338.
[4]   [1948] 1 KB 223.
[5]   [1985] AC 318 above.
[6]   [1997] 1 WLR 906.
[7]   [1983] 2 AC 629.
[8]   At para 82.
[9]   [1985] AC 766, 788, per Lord Diplock.
[10]   [1971] AC 610.
[11]   [1995] 2 All ER 714.
[12]   *R (app McMahon) v Bristol City Council* [2001] EWCA (Admin) 9, [2001] LLR 31 QBD.
[13]   Schedule 4 to the Local Government (Miscellaneous Provisions) Act 1982.
[14]   *Westminster City Council v The Albert Court Residents' Association v Corporation of the Hall of Arts and Sciences* [2011] EWCA Civ 430, [2011] LLR 240 at para 33 onwards.

HOW DOES THIS THEN APPLY TO THE QUESTION OF TAXI LICENSING?

2.64A

As all taxi licences are granted for a finite period, and there are powers to take action against that licence both during its existence and to refuse to renew at its end, there is a clear analogy with the ruling in *Bristol*[1].

In addition, in relation to both drivers (hackney carriage and private hire) and private hire operators, the local authority is prohibited from granting a licence unless it is satisfied that the applicant or an existing licensee on renewal is a fit and proper person to hold that licence[2]. The authority is therefore under a statutory duty to refuse the application unless it is so satisfied. The fundamental difference between the legislative requirements of the Licensing Act 2003 as considered in the *Albert Court* case and the taxi legislation is that the local authority has a discretion to determine fitness and propriety whereas under the Licensing Act, in the absence of relevant representations a licence must be granted and no discretion can be exercised.

The fundamental question is this: once a hackney carriage or private hire drivers' (or private hire operators') licence has been granted, in the absence of any wrongdoing or improper behaviour on the part of the licensee, is there a legitimate expectation that that licence will be renewed?

There is no specific case on this point, but in light of the decision in *Bristol*, and taking into account the Court of Appeal's comprehensive analysis in *Coughlan*, it appears that there can be no legitimate expectation that a licence will continue. It is an annual grant with discretion given to the local authority. Whilst there will certainly be an *expectation* on the part of the licensee that the licence will be renewed, that does not mean that there is, in legal terms, a *legitimate* expectation. It is difficult to see how the question posed in *Coughlan* ,'what in the circumstances the member of the public could legitimately expect[?]'[3] could be answered in any way other than 'the Council must be satisfied that the applicant is a fit and proper person in the light of the current policy'.

However, there is clearly a legitimate expectation that any application will be considered fairly and properly in the light of any new, updated or revised policy. This accords with the first possibility outlined in *Coughlan*[4] (see above).

1   *R (app McMahon) v Bristol City Council* [2001] EWCA (Admin) 9, [2001] LLR 31, QBD.
2   Local Government (Miscellaneous Provisions) Act 1976 above: s 51 in respect of private hire drivers; s 59 in respect of hackney carriage drivers; s 55 in respect of private hire operators.
3   [2001] QB 213 CA at para 56.
4   [2001] QB 213 CA at para 57.

Procedure

THE HEARING

2.65

To enable the applicant to be given a fair hearing, it is necessary for him to know what the rules are by which his application will be considered; if the council has approved any policies or general conditions which apply, then these should be brought to the attention of the applicant before his application is made. They should be available, in full and in time, to enable the applicant to fully appreciate their implications and to formulate his arguments against them, if need be.

HEARSAY EVIDENCE

2.66

In relation to the hearing itself, it is important to recognise that, it is an administrative process, and the hearing is an administrative one. It is not a criminal hearing, nor is it a civil hearing, and accordingly neither the criminal or civil rules governing admissibility of evidence apply.

Kavanagh v Chief Constable of Devon and Cornwall

2.67

Application for a shotgun licence. Hearsay evidence considered by the decision maker. Held: That in decsions such as this hearsay could be legitimately taken into account.

The case of *Kavanagh v Chief Constable of Devon and Cornwall*[1] is useful in respect of this question. It concerned an appeal against a refusal by the Chief Constable to grant a shotgun certificate to the appellant and to register the appellant as a firearms dealer under the provisions of the Firearms Act 1968. Such licences and registrations could only be granted if the Chief Constable was 'satisfied' of certain matters. The Chief Constable considered hearsay material in discharging his duty. The question to be determined by the Court of Appeal was whether the Crown Court could consider hearsay evidence in determining a subsequent appeal against refusal to grant such registrations and certificates. Lord Denning stated (at 698G):

> '... I think [the Crown Court] should act on the same lines as any administrative body which is charged with an enquiry. They may receive any material which is logically probative even though it is not evidence in a court of law. Hearsay can be permitted where it can be fairly regarded as reliable. No doubt they must act fairly. They should give the party concerned an opportunity of correcting or contradicting what is put against him. But it does not mean that he has to be given a chance to cross examine. It is enough if they hear what he has to say ... In an appeal under the Firearms Act 1968, it seems to me essential that the Crown Court should have before it all the material which was before the chief officer of police ... If he refuses [the application] and the applicant appeals to the Crown Court, then the Crown Court must see whether or not the chief officer was right in refusing. For that purpose the Crown Court ought to know the material that was before him and what were the reasons which operated on his mind. It can also consider any other material which may be placed before it. In the end it must come to its own decision whether a firearm certificate should be granted or refused, or whether a person should be registered as a firearms dealer.'

[1]   [1974] 2 All ER 697, CA.

Westminster City Council v Zestfair Ltd

2.68

> Refusal to grant a night-café licence. Hearsay evidence ruled inadmissible by the magistrates' court; challenged by way of case stated. Held: Hearsay was admissible both before the local authority and the magistrates' court on appeal.

In the case of *Westminster City Council v Zestfair Ltd*[1], the reasoning in *Kavanagh*[2] was followed. The *Zestfair* case concerned a refusal to grant a night café licence under the Greater London Council (General Powers) Act 1968. At the subsequent appeal to the magistrates' court, the stipendiary magistrate had ruled that hearsay evidence was not admissible and, as a consequence, granted a licence. The council appealed by way of case stated and the High Court granted the appeal.

Pill J stated (at 291):

'It is common ground that the court should rehear the application on the merits and not simply decide whether the council were wrong in law. At the hearing of the complainants' complaint before the magistrates' court oral evidence was given by four witnesses for the council and one witness for the complainants. The council then sought to put in evidence all of the matters that had been placed before the licensing sub-committee.

The practical question, as appears from counsel's submissions, was whether an officer or officers of the council could give evidence to the court of complaints made to them as to nuisance alleged to have been caused by reason of the conduct of the premises. It is common ground that the licensing sub-committee, provided they act fairly, are entitled to have regard to material which would not ordinarily be admissible in a civil proceeding in a court of law.'

He went on to conclude (at 294):

'The two tribunals should approach the issue in section 49(2) [of the Greater London Council (General Powers) Act 1968] on the same evidential basis and the parties should have the opportunity to call evidence on the same basis.'

Accordingly, it is quite clear that hearsay evidence can be admitted, but caution must be exercised with regard to the weight that is attached to any such evidence.

1   (1990) 88 LGR 288, DC.
2   *Kavanagh v Chief Constable of Devon and Cornwall* [1974] 2 All ER 697, CA; see para 2.67 above.

McCool v Rushcliffe Borough Council

2.69

> Taxi driver assaulted female passenger, but acquitted at the criminal trial. Local authority and magistrates' court considered hearsay evidence of the assault. Held: That hearsay evidence was admissible.

This view has been supported in the case of *McCool v Rushcliffe Borough Council*[1]. In this case, a private hire driver was prosecuted for committing an indecent assault on a passenger. At the first trial, the jury failed to reach a verdict. At the retrial, the complainant did not appear because she could not face the trauma of giving evidence again. As a result, McCool was acquitted. Rushcliffe Borough Council refused to renew his licence, as they did not feel he was a fit and proper person. That decision was upheld by the magistrates' court on appeal. Mr McCool appealed by way of case stated. On the question of the admissibility of hearsay evidence, Bingham LCJ said (at 893F):

'It is common ground that in reaching their decision the justices were entitled to rely on hearsay evidence. That is in my judgment clear from section 51(1)(a) of the Act [Local Government (Miscellaneous Provisions)

Act 1976] and also from *Kavanagh v Chief Constable of Devon and Cornwall*[2],
... It is also in my judgment plain from the judgment of Pill J in *Westminster
City Council v Zestfair*[3]. I conclude that, in reaching their respective
decisions, the Borough Council and the justices were entitled to rely on
evidential material which might reasonably and possible influence the
making of a responsible judgment in good faith on the question in issue.
Some evidence such as gossip, speculation and unsubstantiated innuendo
would rightly be disregarded. Other evidence, even if hearsay, might by its
source, nature and inherent probability carry a greater degree of credibility.
All would depend on the particular facts and circumstances.'

[1]   [1998] 3 All ER 889, QBD.
[2]   [1974] 2 All ER 697, CA; see para 2.67 above.
[3]   [1990] 88 LGR 288, DC; see para 2.68 above.

Leeds City Council v Hussain

2.70

> Taxi driver charged with an offence of violent disorder. Council suspended
> licence before court proceedings and using hearsay evidence. Held: Hearsay
> was admissible.

Subsequently this question was raised again in the case of *Leeds City Council v
Hussain*[1]. The council decided to suspend Mr Hussain's private hire driver and
vehicle licences. The reason for these suspensions was that he had been charged
with an offence of violent disorder, which involved a number of private hire
drivers and their vehicles.

The council took into account a report by a police officer into the events
which led to Hussain being charged, but did not hear live evidence from him.
On appeal against the decision of the council, the magistrates' court found in
the council's favour, but on further appeal to the Crown Court, the decision was
overturned. The question of the admissibility of hearsay was one of the questions
raised by the Crown Court.

In the Administrative Court, Silber J gave his views as follows:

'The hearsay evidence issue

18. The Crown Court in issue (v) raised the question of whether it
is necessary in a case of the holder of a private hire vehicle and driver's
licences who has been charged with serious criminal conduct committed
in the course of his employment to hear witnesses to the offence for which
he has been charged before a decision can properly be made as to whether
there is any "reasonable cause" to suspend the licence. This raises the issue
as to whether hearsay evidence is admissible.

19. In *Westminster City Council v Zestfair* [1989] 88 LGR 288, the Divisional
Court had to deal with the issue of whether hearsay evidence was admissible
in magistrates' courts' hearings of an appeal relating to an application to

grant a licence to a night cafe. Pill J, giving the only reasoned judgment with which Neill LJ agreed, adopted a statement of Cusack J in *Kavanagh v Chief Constable of Devon and Cornwall* [1974] QB 624 (which was quoted at page 629 where it was expressly adopted in that case by Roskill LJ in the Court of Appeal) to the effect that if some of the matters before the court "are hearsay and are not supported by the evidence of witnesses in the Crown Court ... it will be for that [court] to consider carefully what weight is to be attached to the evidence which is put before it in that fashion".

20. It is noteworthy that section 51(1)(a) of the Act provides that:

"... a district council shall, on the receipt of an application from any person for the grant to that person of a licence to drive private hire vehicles, grant to that person a driver's licence: Provided that a district council shall not grant a licence – (a) unless they are satisfied that the applicant is a fit and proper person to hold a driver's licence ..."

21. Subsection (1A), inserted by amendment, reads:

"For the purpose of satisfying themselves as to whether an applicant is a fit and proper person to hold a driver's licence, a council may send to the chief officer of police for that police area in which the council is situated – (a) a copy of that person's application, and (b) a request for the chief officer's observations; and the chief officer to respond to that request."

22. More recently in *McCool v Rushcliffe Borough Council²* Lord Bingham said at page 893G:

"It is common ground that in reaching their decision the justices were entitled to rely on hearsay evidence. That is in my judgment clear from s 51(1)(a) and also from *Kavanagh v Chief Constable of Devon and Cornwall* ... It is also in my judgment plain from the judgment of Pill J in *Westminster City Council v Zestfair* ... I conclude that, in reaching their respective decisions, the borough council and the justices were entitled to rely on any evidential material which might reasonably and properly influence the making of a responsible judgment in good faith on the question in issue. Some evidence such as gossip, speculation and unsubstantiated innuendo would be rightly disregarded. Other evidence, even if hearsay, might by its source, nature and inherent probability carry a greater degree of credibility. All would depend on the particular facts and circumstances."

23. Thus, hearsay is admissible when considering the suspension of licences for "any reasonable cause".'

It is quite clear from this line of cases that hearsay evidence is admissible before the local authority and on any subsequent appeal before either the magistrates' court or Crown Court.

1   [2002] EWHC 1145 (Admin), [2003] RTR 13.
2   [1998] 3 All ER 889 – see para 2.69 above.

Committee procedure

2.71

When considering an application most local authorities have standard procedures which they follow, covering such matters as: is there to be an oral hearing? If so, can the applicant be accompanied and by whom? Can the applicant bring witnesses? Can witnesses be cross-examined? Can the applicant ask questions of officers or other witnesses? Are there any time-limits placed on the presentation that an applicant, objector or witnesses can make? And so on.

2.72

Assuming that this is a decision being made by a committee or sub-committee, there will be a considerable number of people in the room, who will be not only the members of the committee, but also officers who are there to advise the committee. It must be made clear to all concerned and then made demonstrably clear by their actions that the officers do not take part in the decision-making, they merely advise the members as to their powers. This should be emphasised by the fact that officers withdraw for the decision. The only exception to this could be the lawyer advising the committee, who can remain, not to influence the committee or take any part in the decision, but merely to advise them on points of law and procedure that may arise.

In some authorities, the procedure is for all officers to withdraw and the committee calls the legal adviser back, if they need legal advice. In others, the lawyer remains, but then withdraws after any such points have been raised.

If the lawyer has advised the committee in private, it is good practice for them to either repeat the advice in the presence of all the parties, or to explain the substance and nature of the advice that has been provided[1].

In all cases, the decision must be made solely by members, unless the power is delegated to an officer. In this case, the officer must place himself in the same position as the members.

1   See Practice Direction (Criminal: Consolidated) made 8 July 2002, amended 29 July 2004 and *Clark v Kelly* [2004] 1 AC 681, PC. Although neither is binding on the local authority (the Practice Direction applying to the Criminal Courts and *Clark v Kelly* being only persuasive) this approach reduces any doubt in the minds of the parties as to what has been said.

2.73

Another important matter to consider is whether such hearings are in public or in private. If the matter is being decided by an officer, then there is no problem, because that can quite properly and legitimately be decided in private, but if the matter takes the form of a committee meeting, then the provisions of the Local Government Act 1972, Pt VA apply with regard to access to both information and the meeting.

2.74

The Local Government Act 1972, s 100A states that 'a meeting of a principal council shall be open to the public except to the extent that they are excluded ...'[1] and that includes meetings of Committees and Sub-committees.

It is possible for a meeting to be held in the absence of the press and public if a resolution to exclude them and move into private session is passed in accordance with s 100A(4) on the basis that the meeting will be considering exempt information, as defined in s 100I. Such a resolution must be based on one of the descriptions of exempt information contained in Schedule 12A to the LGA 1972 and once that resolution has been passed, the subsequent session is usually referred to as Part 2 or Part B and the reports for those items are exempt reports, as they do not have to be published in the usual way for public inspection.

This approach is usually taken by Licensing Committees and sub-committees when considering matters concerning existing and potential hackney carriage and private hire drivers, operators and (occasionally) proprietors. This is because they will be appearing before the committee as there is some element of their application that means that they do not fall within the Council's policy (in which case the matter could usually be determined by officers under delegated powers) and therefore fall to be determined by the Committee.

The usual justification for excluding the press and public is one of the paragraphs of Schedule 12A which describe exempt information. These include 'information relating to any individual' (paragraph 1 for England) or 'information relating to a particular individual' (paragraph 12 for Wales) and 'information which is likely to reveal the identity of an individual' (paragraph 2 for England and paragraph 13 for Wales).

Once the resolution has been passed, no reporting of the matter can take place and the usual detailed minutes need not be produced, although there must be a written summary of the proceedings which provides a reasonably fair and coherent record without disclosing the exempt information (see s 100C).

It can therefore be seen that if the Council decide to treat an application, or consideration of an existing licence, as exempt information, then none of that exempt information can be revealed. This would include any information that would identify the person if either paragraphs 1, 2, 12 or 13 were used as the basis of the exempt information. In these circumstances it would appear that the written summary would only be able to refer to 'an applicant' or 'an existing licensee', or possibly, if slightly more information is felt to be warranted, 'a male/female applicant' or 'an existing male/female licensee'. Even using initials would be sufficient to identify the person, especially in the closed community of licensees.

It does remain open to the Council not to treat such applications as being exempt information and therefore to hear all such matters in public, as the process contained in s 100(4) is discretionary. This approach is taken by a small number of authorities and in those cases full details of the applicant or licensee can be made public, although not any further information covered by the Data Protection Act such as criminal convictions, medical concerns etc. If those matters are to be discussed, it would still be necessary for the resolution to be passed and the Committee/Sub-committee to exclude the press and public, unless the applicant/licensee consented to such information being disclosed.

¹ This provision is the same in both England and Wales.

2.75

An alternative approach involves the use of the Local Government Act 1972, Sch 12A, para 5 (England) or 16 (Wales) which state:

'Information in respect of which a claim to legal professional privilege could be maintained in legal proceedings.'

This requires the acceptance that, in relation to any licence application, legal professional privilege applies to the information, which will probably be the case.

2.76

It seems that local authorities are rarely, if ever, challenged on the matter of conducting hackney carriage and private hire licensing matters in private, but it is an area where the authority should be satisfied as to its powers to exclude the press and public. It must not merely take it for granted that such considerations will automatically be heard in private.

It is not clear, however, what sanction, if any, can be applied to the local authority if it can be shown that it exceeded its powers by excluding the press and public wrongly. Any decision made when the press and public have been wrongly excluded does not appear to be either void or voidable, and the only avenue for challenge would seem to be an allegation of maladministration to the Ombudsman.

THE COMMITTEE MEETING

2.77

Turning to the procedure that is adopted at the committee meeting, again, this is a matter for each local authority to decide upon. However, some basic points are important and must be considered. Under the Licensing Act 2003 and Gambling Act 2005, procedures for the statutory Licensing Committee have been specified by Regulations¹. These are not mandatory for other committees, and as they prescribe procedures that are complex and in some cases rather unwieldy they are probably not particularly useful as a guide.

First, the procedure should be agreed in advance and it makes sense to have one standard procedure, which is always used. This has the advantage of allowing the applicant and the applicant's representative to be given it in advance, so that they know what to expect. There is also certainty for officers and members of the authority, as they will always be following the same procedure. Finally, it should have been approved by the local authority lawyers to ensure that it is an acceptable procedure.

1   See the Licensing Act 2003 (Hearings) Regulations 2005, SI 2005/44 as amended by the Licensing Act 2003 (Hearings) (Amendment) Regulations 2005, SI 2005/78 and the Gambling Act 2005 (Proceedings of Licensing Committees and Sub-committees) (Premises Licences and Provisional Statements) (England and Wales) Regulations 2007, SI 2007/173.

2.78

The applicant should be called and asked to confirm his name and address. It may be helpful to identify the members of the committee (although it is not necessary to do so by name, this is merely to differentiate them from officers) and the officers who are advising the committee. If the applicant has representatives, they should also introduce themselves.

2.79

The matter under consideration should be outlined. In some authorities, this is done by the chair of the committee. In others, either the clerk to the committee, the lawyer advising the committee or the licensing officer outlines the matter in question.

2.80

If the hearing concerns the granting of a licence to a driver (either hackney carriage or private hire) or a private hire operator, the grounds for objecting to the application should be made clear. This is most likely to concern previous convictions, which may prevent the applicant being considered a 'fit and proper person, but can also include medical matters, or failure to meet a required standard in council approved tests'[1].

It will not be necessary to read out the previous convictions or other concerns (if this is an open meeting, that approach should be treated with caution), as it is sufficient to have them printed and distributed. The applicant should be asked whether he agrees with the list of previous convictions and, if the answer is in the negative, the matter should be adjourned to clarify the position.[2] Assuming, however, that the applicant does agree that the list is accurate, the spokesperson for the council should explain why these convictions would lead to the refusal of the application, referring to any policy guidelines that the council may have adopted. The applicant should then be given a chance to explain the circumstances surrounding the convictions in question and any other relevant information. Following this, officers and councillors may ask questions to clarify the situation and establish to their satisfaction whether or not this person is a fit and proper person[3] to be granted a licence. Thereafter, the applicant should be asked whether or not there is anything else he wishes to add and then all interested parties should withdraw (applicant and applicant's representative, officers of the local authority and, if they are present, any members of the public).

1   See Chapter 5 in relation to 'spent' convictions.
2   See in particular the 'Revised Code of Practice for Disclosure and Barring Service Registered Persons' published by the Home Office November 2015 available at https://www.gov.uk/government/

uploads/system/uploads/attachment_data/file/474742/Code_of_Practice_for_Disclosure_and_
Barring_Service_Nov_15.pdf

3   For an explanation of the concept of 'fit and proper' please see Chapter 10, para 10.21 onwards.

THE DECISION

2.81

The members will then make their decision. It should be noted that only members who have heard the entire application are able to consider the decision. This prevents a member taking part if they arrived late for the item in question or left for part of the matter, returning before the decision was made. It is arguable that this would include any physical inspection of e.g. a vehicle, meaning that a member of the committee who did not take part in such an inspection could not take part in the decision.

2.82

Most authorities invite the applicant back in to the meeting to inform them verbally whether or not they have been successful, but some will only impart that information later in writing. Even if the decision is given verbally, it must be confirmed in writing as soon as possible.

2.83

Whilst the usual and most common method of challenge to a decision of the licensing committee is by way of one of the statutory appeals that lie to the magistrates' court (or, in one particular circumstance, direct to the Crown Court), there is also the wider application of judicial control of the decision-making process itself. This is by means of the judicial review procedure which allows the High Court to consider the approach to the decision which the local authority has made.

Reasonableness

2.84

Assuming that the decision-making body had the power to make the decision, that is to say, the delegated powers were in place and 'Procedure Rules'[1] were followed, a judicial review will concern itself with the reasonableness, or otherwise, of the decision that was reached, whether the rules of natural justice were followed and any breach of the Human Rights Act 1998.

The usual test of reasonableness is the 'Clapham omnibus' test. This asks what a normal person (who has no particular knowledge, training or skill in the area concerned) would do in the situation in question.

1   These are the replacement for what were formally called 'Standing Orders'. They are the mechanism used by the council for decision making and are now usually contained in the Council's Constitution.

Associated Provincial Picture Houses Ltd v Wednesbury Corpn

2.85

> Application for a cinema licence granted subject to a condition that no child under 15 could be admitted to a Sunday performance. The question was whether this was a reasonable restriction imposed by means of a condition. Held: The court could not intervene and override the decision unless the decision itself was so unreasonable that no reasonable body would have made that decision, having taken into account all relevant factors and not having taken into account any irrelevant ones.

In relation to local government decision-making (and, indeed, other public body decision-making), the test of reasonableness is not the 'Clapham omnibus' test, but the rather more refined test originating in the case of *Associated Provincial Picture Houses Ltd v Wednesbury Corpn*[1]. Lord Green MR laid down the following principles (at 228–230):

'When discretion ... is granted the law recognises certain principles upon which that discretion must be exercised ... What then are those principles?

... The exercise of such a discretion must be a real exercise of the discretion. If, in the statute conferring the discretion, there is to be found expressly or by implication matters which the authority exercising the discretion ought to have regard to, then in exercising the discretion it must have regard to those matters. Conversely, if the nature of the subject-matter and the general interpretation of the Act make it clear that certain matters would not be germane to the matter in question, the authority must disregard those irrelevant collateral matters ...

It is true the discretion must be exercised reasonably. Now what does that mean? Lawyers familiar with the phraseology commonly used in relation to exercise of statutory discretions often use the word "unreasonable" in a rather comprehensive sense. It has frequently been used and is frequently used as a general description of the things that must not be done. For instance, a person entrusted with a discretion must, so to speak, direct himself properly in law. He must call his own attention to the matters which he is bound to consider. He must exclude from his consideration matters which are irrelevant to what he has to consider. If he does not obey those rules, he may truly be said, and often is said, to be acting "unreasonably". Similarly, there may be something so absurd that no sensible person could ever dream that it lay within the powers of the authority ...

... It is true to say that, if a decision on a competent matter is so unreasonable that no reasonable authority could ever have come to it, then the courts can interfere. That, I think, is quite right; but to prove a case of that kind would require something overwhelming ...'

[1]   [1948] 1 KB 223, CA.

Council of Civil Service Unions v Minister for the Civil Service

2.86

> Decision taken without consultation or prior notice to ban trade union membership at GCHQ on the grounds of national security. Challenged by way of judicial review. Held by the House of Lords that the decision was susceptible to judicial review, and would be unfair due to the lack of consultation, but the requirements of national security outweighed those factors.

This test has itself been re-addressed frequently in the last 60 years. In *Council of Civil Service Unions v Minister for the Civil Service*[1], Lord Diplock used the expression 'irrationality'. He said (at 410F):

> 'By "irrationality" I mean what can by now be succinctly referred to as "*Wednesbury* unreasonableness". It applies to a decision which is so outrageous in its defiance of logic or of accepted moral standards that no sensible person who applied his mind to the question to be decided could have arrived at it.'

This term is now widely accepted as being interchangeable with '*Wednesbury* unreasonableness'. It is imperative that a decision is not unreasonable in '*Wednesbury*' terms if it is to remain unchallenged.

[1]   [1985] AC 374, HL.

2.87

It must be both recognised and appreciated that the judicial review process is available when it is the reasonableness of the decision-making process, or a question over the exercise of powers or duties or application of the law, which is open to challenge, rather than the decision itself. If the decision leads to a statutory ground of appeal, then those should be exhausted before any judicial review is considered, unless exceptional circumstances exist[1].

[1]   See eg *R v Blackpool Borough Council, ex p Red Cab Taxis Ltd* [1994] RTR 402, QBD. See Chapter 3, para 3.49.

Reasons

2.88

There is no doubt whatsoever that reasons should be given for the decision. Although there is no statutory requirement to give reasons for any decision in relation to any matter connected with hackney carriage or private hire licensing, the decision of the Court of Appeal in *R (on the application of Hope and Glory Public House Ltd) v Westminster City Magistrates' Court*[1] makes it clear that in relation to all licensing decisions, the giving of reasons and the detail of those reasons are essential to enable the authority to defend its position on appeal.

This can be contrasted with sex establishment licensing, where the applicant can request a written statement of the reasons for refusal to renew a sex establishment licence[2] and decisions under the LA 2003 and GA 2005 where the legislation requires reasons to be given[3].

The earlier general cases are really now of academic interest[4], and the judgment in *Hope & Glory* addresses the point clearly and succinctly. However, one earlier case bears inspection because it relates to private hire licences.

[1]   [2011] EWCA Civ 31, [2011] 3 All ER 579.
[2]   See Local Government (Miscellaneous Provisions) Act 1982, Sch 3, para 10(20).
[3]   See LA 2003, s 23 and GA 2005, ss 164, 165.
[4]   See eg *R v Civil Service Appeal Board, ex p Cunningham* [1991] IRLR 297, CA; *R v Secretary of State for the Home Department, ex p Doody* [1994] 1 AC 531, HL; *Stefan v General Medical Council* (1999) 143 Sol Jo LB 112, PC.

R v Burton-upon-Trent Justices, ex p Hussain

2.89

> Refusal to renew a taxi drivers licence. Appeal to the magistrates' court was dismissed and an appeal by way of case stated was considered by the High Court. Held: The failure to give reasons for the decision amounted to a denial of natural justice.

In *R v Burton-upon-Trent Justices, ex p Hussain*[1] judicial review was sought of the failure by the magistrates to give reasons for their decision, on an appeal against a refusal to grant a private hire driver's licence and operator's licence by the local authority.

In relation to drivers' licences, the provisions of the Local Government (Miscellaneous Provisions) Act 1976, s 61(1) and (2) apply and, in relation to the private hire operator's licence, s 62(1) and (2) of the Act apply. In both those sections sub-s (2) states:

> 'Where a district council suspend, revoke or refuse to renew any licence under this section they shall give to the driver (61(2)(*a*) [or] operator 62(2)) notice of the grounds of which the licence has been suspended or revoked or on which they have refused to renew such licence ...'

Those grounds are in each case contained in sub-s (1) of the relevant section.

[1]   (1996) 9 Admin LR 233.

2.90

In the *Burton-upon-Trent* case[1], it was argued that it was insufficient to simply state that the reason for the refusal to renew the licence in question was one of the grounds contained in either the Local Government (Miscellaneous Provisions) Act 1976, s 61(1)(a) or (b) or s 62(1)(a)–(d).

Potts J stated (at 236H):

'Mr Storey [for the applicant] submits that the expression "notice of the grounds" has the effect of requiring the licensing authority to give reasons for reaching its decision.'

He went on (at 237A):

'The licensing authority in the present case … simply informs the applicant that his driver's licence was revoked under s 62(1)(b) and his operator's licence revoked under s 62(1)(a), (b), (c) and (d), but failed to specify what the applicant had done or failed to do in order to justify revocation.

In my judgment, there is force in this submission. The decision letter did not sufficiently inform the applicant of the ground or grounds on which the licensing authority had concluded that revocation was appropriate.

This failure could not be decisive of this application since the decision under review is that of the justices. But, as I have sought to indicate, the justices made no findings of fact and gave no reasons for their decision. In my judgment, they ought to have done both. Had they made findings of fact, the court may well not have been faced with the problem identified above in relation to the first ground of application, namely, conflicting accounts on affidavit as to what occurred in court.

Furthermore, the applicant would have been informed of the basis upon which the court reached its decision. In my judgment, the applicant was entitled to be so informed.

In any event, I am satisfied that the justices ought to have had in mind the provisions of ss 61 and 62 of the 1976 Act, as they were concerned (as Mr Hibbert pointed out in his affidavit) with a rehearing of the original panel meeting.

Therefore the justices ought to have related their findings of fact to the provisions of s 62(1)(b) (reasonable cause) and of s 62(1) and identified the reasons and ground in respect of which revocation of the applicant's licence was thought appropriate. For example, under s 61(1)(b), the applicant was entitled to know what the "reasonable cause" was. The failure to make findings of fact and to give reasons relating to s 61(1)(b) and s 62(1) of the Act, in my judgment, amounted to a denial of natural justice[2].'

¹   *R v Burton-upon-Trent Justices, ex p Hussain* (1996) 9 Admin LR 233.
²   See *R v Harrow Crown Court, ex p Dave* [1994] 1 WLR 98, 158 JP 250.

2.91

This case is interesting in that the legislation requires notice of the grounds for the refusal (or revocation or suspension) to be given and specifically states what grounds are available for such action to be taken. It would appear that the court, in this case, has extended the requirement from simply stating which ground has been relied upon to actually requiring the magistrates' court and, by logical extension, the local authority to give reasons for such action over and above the statutory requirement.

R (app Hope and Glory Public House Ltd) v Westminster City Magistrates' Court

2.92

> Review of a premises licence under the provisions of the Licensing Act 2003. On appeal the magistrates court district judge outlined the procedure, which was largely upheld by the Court of Appeal. Held that reasons should be given and the fuller and more detailed those reasons, the more likely it was that was the appeal court would uphold the local authority's decision.

R (app Hope and Glory Public House Ltd) v Westminster City Magistrates' Court[1] concerned a review of a premises licence which had been granted in respect of a public house under the Licensing Act 2003. Following complaints of noise nuisance[2], Westminster City Council imposed conditions on the licence. These conditions were appealed to the magistrates' court, and the High Court case resulted from a judicial review of the magistrates' decision.[3] In relation to reasons, Toulson LJ (giving the judgment of the court) stated[4]:

> 'The statutory duty of the licensing authority to give reasons for its decision serves a number of purposes. It informs the public, who can make their views known to their elected representatives if they do not like the licensing sub-committee's approach. It enables a party aggrieved by the decision to know why it has lost and to consider the prospects of a successful appeal. If an appeal is brought, it enables the magistrates' court to know the reasons which led to the decision. The fuller and clearer the reasons, the more force they are likely to carry.'

Whilst there is no statutory duty in relation to taxi licensing decisions, the principle remains the same.

[1]   [2011] EWCA Civ 31, [2011] 3 All ER 579 CA.
[2]   The case concerns the concept of public nuisance, the appeals process itself (see para 3.17).
[3]   *R (on the application of Hope & Glory Public House Ltd) v City of Westminster Magistrates' Court* [2009] EWHC 1996 (Admin), [2010] ACD 12, Admin Ct.
[4]   At para 43.

R (on the application of Merlot 73 Ltd) v City of Westminster Magistrates' Court

2.93

> Review of a premises licence under the Licensing Act 2003 and some reasons given but not full reasons. Appeal against the decision dismissed by magistrates' court on appeal. Judicial review of the decision. Held: Where reasons were given they were taken into account; equally where no reasons were given the court could draw its own conclusions.

This case has been followed in *R (on the application of Merlot 73 Ltd) v City of Westminster Magistrates' Court*[1], again, a Licensing Act case. Here the Licensing Authority attached conditions following a review of a premises licence. It gave reasons for one of those conditions, but not for others. The challenge (on this point) was that the magistrates' court had attached the wrong weight to those conditions where no reasons were given. Blair J in his judgment addressed that point in these terms[2]:

'(2) Weight of reasons

31. The claimant says, and the district judge pointed out in his judgment, that the conditions relating to the service of drinks in glass containers, and the limit on playing recorded music to 0300, were imposed without any discussion and without any reasons given. (This was not the case as regards the condition as to no admittance after midnight.) In those circumstances, the claimant contends that the judge accorded weight to the decision of the Committee which it did not merit.

32. This issue was dealt with authoritatively in the Hope and Glory case. At [47] Toulson LJ (giving the judgment of the court with Laws LJ and Sir Nicholas Wall P) refers to earlier authority to the effect that the magistrate should pay " … great attention to the decision of the elected local authority and should only reverse it if he was satisfied that it was wrong". However, as the court also pointed out, the weight which magistrates should ultimately attach to the reasons given by the authority " … must be a matter for their judgment in all the circumstances, taking into account the fullness and clarity of the reasons, the nature of the issues and the evidence given on the appeal". As the court put it, the fuller and clearer the reasons, the more force they are likely to carry ([43]).

33. The district judge cited the relevant passages from the H.pe and Glory case in paragraph 15 of his judgment, and it is plain that he applied them throughout. Where the authority gave reasons (as it did in relation to the last entry condition), he took those reasons into account. Where no reasons were given, he equally took their absence into account. His approach in this regard cannot in my view be criticised.'

[1]   [2013] EWHC 3416 (Admin).
[2]   At paras 31 to 33.

2.94

It can be seen that in relation to hackney carriage and private hire licensing in light of the decision in *R v Burton-upon-Trent Justices, ex p Hussain*[1] and particularly *Hope and Glory Public House Ltd) v Westminster City Magistrates' Court*[2], it is vital to give reasons to enable the local authority to be in a position to defend any subsequent appeal. In addition, providing detailed reasons will help unsuccessful applicants either to re-apply, in the light of the reasons that led to initial failure or to accept defeat and not waste time and money on appeals that are unlikely to succeed.

1   (1996) 9 Admin LR 233; see para 2.89 above.
2   [2011] EWCA Civ 31, [2011] 3 All ER 579, CA.

2.95

This in turn leads to the difficulty of actually formulating the reasons for refusing to grant the licence, although LA 2003 experiences have undoubtedly assisted in making this be recognised as part and parcel of the decision-making process. It is essential that the reasons cited are the actual reasons which led to the refusal and not some spurious afterthought designed to justify an, otherwise, insupportable decision. Likewise, the reasons must be the reasons that the committee (or other decision-making body) actually formulate, rather than reasons created by officers to support the decision.

2.96

Making decisions on a licensing committee is an onerous duty; the livelihoods of the applicants are at stake and this has to be balanced by risk to the safety of both the travelling public and the public at large. Members of such committees should not approach the task lightly (very few do) and they must appreciate the gravity of the situation in which they find themselves.

The local authority can set policies, but must be careful not to fetter its discretion. It is important that the policies are both worded initially and then subsequently approached in such a way as to enable deviation from them to be undertaken in appropriate circumstances, when justice demands.

It is this application of discretion which is a fundamental part of the local authority licensing process; it allows for a human element in what would, otherwise, simply be a box-ticking, rubber-stamping exercise. However, like all things, it must be exercised judiciously and should not be used simply as a method of ignoring or avoiding policies which have previously been approved.

2.97

It will be appreciated that the licensing committees' deliberations are important from a number of perspectives. Whilst it is impossible to guarantee that any decision will be completely watertight legally, it is important from the local authority's point of view that the correct considerations are applied to any decision – appeals and judicial reviews are costly and should be avoided, if at all possible.

From the applicant's perspective, it is equally important that the hearing is conducted correctly and fairly, and the decision is communicated in such a way as to explain to the applicant where there are grounds for improvement in their approach or why they will find it extremely difficult to obtain a licence from that authority for the foreseeable future.

Having said that, it is equally important that those involved in this decision-making are not overawed by such considerations and are prepared to undertake the function that is imposed upon them.

Consequences of mistakes made by the local authority

2.98

If the local authority makes a mistake, its decision is capable of challenge, either by judicial review or appeal[1]. If the challenge is upheld, the effects of the decision will be reversed in some way. However, one important question in relation to the local authority's decision-making process is if there is any right to compensation should the council make some mistake, either in the interpretation of the law or in its procedures.

[1]   See Chapter 3.

R v Knowsley Metropolitan Borough Council, ex p Maguire

2.99

> Application for hackney carriage licence. Authority altered its approach during the application process. Applicant claimed damages for maladministration. Held: Claim was dismissed as without negligence by the authority, there was no right to damages resulting from a local authority exercising its statutory powers.

This was the question that was considered in the case of *R v Knowsley Metropolitan Borough Council, ex p Maguire*[1]. The claim arose out of an application for hackney carriage proprietors' licences, after the passing of the TA 1985, s 16 (which removed the absolute discretion that the local authority had to limit the number of hackney carriage proprietors' licences that it would grant)[2]. A procedure was adopted by Knowsley Metropolitan Borough Council whereby licences would be granted to all who applied and met specified criteria, until such time as the results of surveys to assess demand were known. Letters were sent to applicants explaining this and detailing the criteria. One element of the criteria was that a suitable vehicle (in this case, a purpose-built hackney carriage – an FX4) should be presented.

Following the ruling in *R v Reading Borough Council, ex p Egan*[3] Knowsley Metropolitan Borough Council revised its decision, as it appeared that their policy was unlawful. As a consequence, the local authority refused to grant the applicants their licences, notwithstanding the fact that they had purchased vehicles. Although that decision was quashed and the applicants received the licences they had applied for, they maintained that they had suffered damage as a result of the local authority's illegal action. They claimed compensation under a number of heads: first, that the local authority was in breach of its statutory duty; secondly, that the local authority had been negligent; thirdly, that the local authority was in breach of contract; and, finally, on the grounds that the local authority should be estopped (that is to say prevented) from effectively changing its mind.

Schiemann J dismissed the claim under each head.

1   (1992) 90 LGR 653.
2   See Appendix I.
3   (1987) [1990] RTR 399n; see Chapter 8, para 8.178. This judgment ruled that allocating a small number of new hackney carriage proprietors licences, then assessing the impact on supply and demand for hackney carriages before issuing any more was unlawful. It was subsequently disapproved in the later case of *Ghafoor v Wakefield Metropolitan District Council* [1990] RTR 389, QBD. See Chapter 8, para 8.191.

2.100

In relation to breach of statutory duty, he stated[1] (at 660):

'In the present case, there is no indication at all in the legislative provisions that they were passed for the benefit of would-be cab drivers rather than the public at large. A refusal of a licence gives rise to a right of appeal to the crown court. The imposition of a condition alleged to be unlawful gives rise to a right of appeal to the magistrates' court. I am not persuaded that Parliament intended anyone to have a private right of action in respect of any failure by a licensing authority to exercise its powers lawfully. In consequence the claim fails under this head.'

In relation to negligence, he stated (at 661):

'I am entitled to form my own view as to whether or no[t] what the local authority did amounted to negligence and I do not think it did.

"As is well-known, anybody, even a judge, can be capable of misconstruing a statute; and such misconstruction, when it occurs, can be severely criticised without attracting the epithet 'negligent'. Obviously, this simple fact points rather to the extreme unlikelihood of a breach of duty being established in these cases[2]."

Mr Braithwaite [for the council] submits that the local authority found themselves overwhelmed with applications at a time when they had not done a demand survey, that the local authority were in principle entitled to balance supply and demand for cabs and were not negligent during the interim period in which they were establishing the demand position in adopting a policy of excluding those who had had the benefit of one licensed cab and had chosen to sell it. I think there is force in this submission and that he is entitled to make it, notwithstanding the judgment of Otton J.

Since I do not find the local authority negligent I do not need to consider the difficult question of law of whether the local authority were under a duty of care owed to the applicants not to be negligent in their construction of the statute. As appears from Takaro (above), the answer is not self-evident.'

1   *R v Knowsley Metropolitan Borough Council, ex p Maguire* (1992) 90 LGR 653.
2   See *Rowling v Takaro Properties Ltd* [1988] AC 473 at 502, PC.

2.101

On the argument that the local authority were in breach of contract Schiemann J found that they were not and that the correspondence that had been entered into did not amount to a contract[1]. He stated (at 663):

'He [Mr Braithwaite] submits that we are not here in the field of contract at all but rather in the field of local government administration. Local authorities are always adumbrating policy documents but those are not to be construed as offers to the world at large and that the same applies to letters setting out policy.

In my judgment this submission is well founded. There is no reason to suppose that neither the local authority nor the applicants ever thought in terms of contract. That is not conclusive and I accept that there are cases where courts will after considering the relevant documentation and actions find that the parties have entered into a contract notwithstanding the fact that they may never have applied their minds consciously to doing so. A good example is *Carlill v Carbolic Smoke Ball Co*. But it will be remembered that in that case the defendants offered their reward in order to persuade people to buy their product.

"If the vendor of an article ... with a view to increase its sale or use, thinks fit publicly to promise to all who buy or use it that, to those who shall not find it as surely efficacious as it is represented by him to be he will pay a substantial sum of money, he must not be surprised if occasionally he is held to his promise[2]."

In the present case to construe the letter of 18 May as a contractual offer seems to me to be to lose touch with reality and to insert the law of contract into an inapposite situation.'

1   *R v Knowsley Metropolitan Borough Council, ex p Maguire* (1992) 90 LGR 653.
2   *Carlill v Carbolic Smoke Ball Co* [1892] 2 QB 484 at 489, per Hawkins J.

2.102

The last claim was that of estoppel which was dealt with in the following way[1] (at 664):

'Finally, Mr Davies [for the applicants] sought to mount a submission on the basis of estoppel of convention. In substance this was a submission that, although in truth the local authority were not contractually liable to the applicants, the local authority had acted as though there was such a contract and the local authority are now estopped from contending the contrary. It is true that the local authority – rightly in my view – perceived those who had acted on the indication given in the letter of 18 May as having a strong claim to a licence, but there is no indication before me that the local authority ever represented that they ever thought of such a claim as a *contractual* claim as opposed to a claim based on a desire to administer well and fairly.'

1   *R v Knowsley Metropolitan Borough Council, ex p Maguire* (1992) 90 LGR 653.

2.103

Although the court found against the claimants on all heads, the decision is extremely important as an indication of the way in which the law may develop[1]. The conclusion drawn by the judge[2] was (at 664):

'It follows that the applicants' claims fail. They fail because we do not have in our law a general right to damages for maladministration.'

And (at 665):

'The arguments ingeniously advanced by Mr Davies are an attempt to remedy what from the point of view of his clients are shortcomings of our administrative law by extending the concepts of negligence, contract and estoppel. While I have considerable sympathy with his clients I do not think that I am at liberty to extend the law in the way he suggests. The applications fail.'

[1]   Reference was made to the findings of two investigations, the Law Commission in 1969 and the Committee of the Justice – All Souls Review of the Administrative Law of the United Kingdom – *Administrative Justice; some necessary reforms* (1988).
[2]   *R v Knowsley Metropolitan Borough Council, ex p Maguire* (1992) 90 LGR 653.

2.104

Since the *Knowsley* case[1] there have been some developments in this field, although as yet they still fall short of providing the right to damages for those affected by administrative decisions.

The House of Lords in the case of *Phelps v Hillingdon London Borough Council*[2] ruled that a local education authority could be vicariously liable for the acts of its employees if an employee was negligent in circumstances where a duty of care was owed to an individual. Although this case is clearly not limited to its facts (dyslexic children who alleged that lack of appropriate education for pupils with special educational needs had affected their academic performance and general life), the House of Lords warned that courts should be slow to find such negligence as to do so might interfere with the performance of the authorities' duties.

To date no case has occurred using this argument in the field of local authority licensing and the question must be asked as to when or if a duty of care would arise in a licensing situation.

[1]   *R v Knowsley Metropolitan Borough Council, ex p Maguire* (1992) 90 LGR 653.
[2]   [2001] 2 AC 619, HL.

2.105

Although this is clearly both an important and interesting area, it has not progressed in the last quarter of a Century. Clearly there remains a potential claim and one which may lead to more litigation before the questions are finally settled. Although it may be seen as an area where the law might develop, the absence of progress suggests otherwise and at the moment local authorities may feel that they are protected from the financial consequences of any mistakes that they may make in statutory interpretation or application of the general law.

Human Rights Act 1998

2.106

The Human Rights Act 1998 (HRA 1998) has now been in force for over 17 years, and has had a fundamental impact on the way in which local authorities approach their decision-making in a number of areas[1].

[1]   For more information on Human Rights see Lester, Pannick and Herberg, *Human Rights Law and Practice* (3rd edn, LexisNexis).

2.107

In relation to hackney carriage and private hire licensing under the Human Rights Act 1998, there are three principal articles of the ECHR which may be relevant: Art 6, Art 8 and Art 1 of Protocol 1.

ARTICLE 6 – THE RIGHT TO A FAIR TRIAL

2.108

Article 6 states:

> '1. In the determination of his civil rights and obligations or of any criminal charge against him, everyone is entitled to a fair and public hearing within a reasonable time by an independent and impartial tribunal established by law. Judgment shall be pronounced publicly but the press and public may be excluded from all or part of the trial in the interest of morals, public order or national security in a democratic society, where the interests of juveniles or the protection of the private life of the parties so require, or to the extent strictly necessary in the opinion of the court in special circumstances where publicity would prejudice the interests of justice.'

The right to engage in commercial or business activities is a civil right (eg *Kaplan v United Kingdom*[1], *Pudas v Sweden*[2], *Gasper v Sweden*[3]) and, accordingly, when the local authority considers the application for a licence, or whether the licensee can continue trading on the same terms and subject to the same conditions or indeed can continue trading at all will be a consideration of his civil rights. Article 6 therefore comes into play[4].

[1]   Application 7598/76 (1980) 4 EHRR 64.
[2]   (1987) 10 EHRR 380, ECtHR.
[3]   (1998) 26 EHRR CD 30.
[4]   In relation to criminal prosecutions and Art 6, see Chapter 6, para 6.10 onwards, Enforcement.

2.109

It is clear that a local authority committee, sub-committee or officer making a decision on the question as to whether or not to grant a licence cannot fulfil the requirement for a hearing before 'an independent and impartial tribunal'. However, the fact that there is, in relation to every licence relating to hackney carriage and private hire matters, a statutory right of appeal to an independent tribunal (either a magistrates' court or Crown Court), means that the requirements of Art 6 of the ECHR in respect of independence and impartiality are not compromised and it is unlikely that a successful challenge could be launched against the local authority determining the question (see *Albert and Le Comptre v Belgium*[1]).

Where there is no right of appeal, the availability of judicial review (however unlikely this may be in practical terms) is sufficient to ensure that the matter can be determined by an independent and impartial tribunal[2].

[1]   (1982) 5 EHRR 533.
[2]   This was decided by the European Court of Human Rights in Bryan v United Kingdom (1995) 21 EHRR 342, and domestically by the House of Lords in *R (on the application of Holding & Barnes plc) v Secretary of State for the Environment, Transport and the Regions* [2001] 2 WLR 1389.

ARTICLE 8 – THE RIGHT TO RESPECT FOR PRIVATE AND FAMILY LIFE

2.110

Article 8 relates to the private life of a person, and protects interference with that unless it can be justified. The article states:

'1. Everyone has the right to respect for his private and family life, his home and his correspondence.

2. There shall be no interference by a public authority with the exercise of this right except such as is in accordance with the law and is necessary in a democratic society in the interests of national security, public safety or the economic well-being of the country, for the prevention of disorder or crime, for the protection of health or morals, or for the protection of the rights and freedoms of others.'

Under English case law, the position seems clear that this does not impact on the grant or retention of a licence. The purpose or legitimate aim behind the licensing regime is public safety and accordingly a licence can be refused or removed without consideration of the impact on a person's family (except in exceptional circumstances).

Leeds City Council v Hussain

2.111

Taxi driver charged with an offence of violent disorder. Council suspended licence before court proceedings and using hearsay evidence. Was the impact on his livelihood of a suspension a relevant factor? Held: No because the overriding aim of the legislation was public safety.

This was the decision of the High Court in *Leeds City Council v Hussain*[1]; which was followed by the decision in *Cherwell DC v Anwar*[2].

In *Leeds City Council v Hussain*[3] the case arose following the suspension of a drivers' licence following his arrest and being charged with an offence of violent disorder. He appealed against that decision and the magistrates' court upheld that appeal. The Council then appealed by way of case stated to the High Court. There were a number of questions posed[4] and in particular, question (d) which asked:

> '(d) Whether, in the case of a holder of private hire vehicle and driver's licences who has been charged with a serious criminal offence committed in the course of his employment, the impact of the suspension of those licences upon his livelihood and the absence of any compensation if he is ultimately acquitted of the criminal charge are circumstances which can properly be taken into account when deciding whether there is 'any … reasonable cause' to suspend his licences.'

Mr Justice Silber gave the answer in these terms[5]:

> '24. The Crown Court asks in question (d) whether the impact of a suspension of licences upon the likelihood of a driver, in the absence of any compensation if he is ultimately acquitted of the criminal offence, is a circumstance which can properly be taken into account in deciding whether there is "any reasonable cause" to suspend his licence.
>
> 25. There is indeed no authority on this point, but as Lord Bingham explained in the passage in McCool that I have already quoted, the purpose of the power of suspension is to protect users of licensed vehicles and those who are driven by them and members of the public. Its purpose, therefore, is to prevent licences being given to or used by those who are not suitable people taking into account their driving record, their driving experience, their sobriety, mental and physical fitness, honesty, and that they are people who would not take advantage of their employment to abuse or assault passengers. In other words, the council, when considering whether to suspend a licence or revoke it, is focusing on the impact of the licence holder's vehicle and character on members of the public and in particular, but not exclusively, on the potential users of those vehicles.
>
> 26. This does not require any consideration of the personal circumstances which are irrelevant, except perhaps in very rare cases to explain or excuse some conduct of the driver.'

Unfortunately, the judge gave no indication as to what such "very rare cases" might be, but it is suggested that as the overriding purpose is to protect public safety, it would need to be a matter that could not jeopardise public safety in any way.

[1]   [2003] RTR 13.
[2]   [2012] RTR 15.
[3]   [2003] RTR 13.

4   See paragraph 8 of the judgment: '(a) Whether, in the case of a holder of private hire vehicle and driver's licences who has been charged with a serious criminal offences committed in the course of his employment, it is necessary for there to be a finding of guilty in relation to that criminal charge before a decision can properly be made as to whether there is 'any ... reasonable cause' to suspend his licences; (b) Whether, in the case of a holder of private hire vehicle and driver's licences who has been charged with a serious criminal offence committed in the course of his employment, it is necessary to hear live witness evidence from witnesses to the offence with which he has been charged before a decision can properly be made as to whether there is 'any ... reasonable cause' to suspend his licences; (c) Whether, in the case of a holder of private hire vehicle and driver's licences who has been charged with a serious criminal offence committed in the course of his employment, it is necessary to reach the conclusion that there is at least a reasonable chance of him being convicted of this offence before his licences can properly be suspended;' – see para 2.70 for further information on the first three questions.

5   See paragraphs 24–26.

Cherwell DC v Anwar

2.112

> Taxi driver convicted of assaulting his wife. Local authority refused renewal of his licence. Appeal to the magistrates' court successful because the court took into account the impact on his family. Local authority appealed by way of case stated. Held: The impact on a licensee's family was not a relevant consideration.

In *Cherwell DC v Anwar*[1] the case concerned another appeal by way of case stated from the magistrates' court, which had allowed an appeal against a refusal to renew the driver's hackney carriage and private hire drivers' licences. The initial decision of the local authority was based on a conviction of the driver for assault by beating.

The relevant question raised in the case stated was[2]:

'(a)   Whether in determining this appeal and in the light of the decision in *Leeds City Council –v- Hussain*, we were right to consider and take account of the need for Mr Anwar to provide for his family and the personal circumstances of his wife and children.'

After quoting the passages from *Leeds*, cited above, in their entirety, the judge (His Honour Judge Bidder QC, sitting as a Deputy High Court Judge) stated[3]:

'25. Silber J. in consequence, answered the 4th question posed in that case in the negative. It has been ingeniously argued by counsel for the Respondent, that it is possible that the future impact of the removal of a licence on a licence holder's family would serve as a deterrent to him and thus might be relevant to the primary issue of the safety of the public. If, however, the magistrates had followed that subtle line of argument, one would have expected them to have included that in their reasons and to link it with their conclusion that the applicant was not a danger to the public. They did not and I therefore conclude that they regarded the hardship to his wife and children as a completely separate factor to the issue of the safety of the public and, from their reference to it in (h) clearly regarded it as an important reason for differing from the council's decision. That is simply not in line with the Hussain case.

26. Thus I answer the first question posed for my decision in the negative.'

The European Court of Human Rights has made it clear that there is no right to employment or work protected by the convention but there have been occasional cases where the ECHR has intervened in relation to employment issues and Article 8. In *Sidabras v Lithuania*[4] the Court held that a long term prohibition on work for the state was an infringement of Article 8, although whether this would apply to a licensing issue is less clear.

A refusal to grant a drivers' licence by one council does not automatically mean that other councils will take the same view. In every case the local authority must consider each case on its merits and therefore has a discretion as to whether or not to grant the licence. Accordingly, it seems unlikely that any such refusal to grant, or any action taken against a licence (suspension, revocation or refusal to renew) would infringe Article 8.

[1]   [2012] RTR 15.
[2]   See para 23 of the judgment.
[3]   At paras 25 and 26.
[4]   (2006) 42 EHRR 6.

ARTICLE I PROTOCOL I – THE PROTECTION OF PROPERTY

2.113

The third area of concern in relation to licensing is Article 1 of Protocol 1 of the ECHR. This states:

'Every natural or legal person is entitled to the peaceful enjoyment of his possessions. No one shall be deprived of his possessions except in the public interest and subject to the conditions provided for by law and by the general principles of international law.

The preceding provisions shall not, however, in any way impair the right of a State to enforce such laws as it deems necessary to control the use of property in accordance with the general interest or to secure the payment of taxes or other contributions or penalties.'

As a licence permits a person to undertake his civil right to carry on in business, it is often stated that it has been held by the European Court of Human Rights that any such licence constitutes a possession (see *Tre Traktörer Aktiebolag v Sweden*[1]). However, as can be seen from later cases, the question is much more involved.

There are two types of licences relating to hackney carriages and private hire vehicles that local authorities grant; vehicle licences (both hackney carriage and private hire) that can be transferred to another party (often at a premium); and hackney carriage and private hire drivers' licences, and private hire operators' licences which are personal and therefore have no transfer value.

It does appear that there is a distinction between these two types of licence in relation to the Human Rights Act 1998.

Unfortunately, there is no single English authority on the point, with a variety of cases arriving at different conclusions. The matter is then compounded by the varying approaches taken by the ECHR (and on occasions The European Commission on Human Rights which prior to 1998 produced reasoned opinions which would then be confirmed by the Committee of Ministers).

1   (1989) 13 EHRR 309, ECtHR.

R (app Nicholds) v Security Industry Authority

2.114

> Application for SIA registration refused due to criminal convictions. Argued that this infringed Article 8 as previous registration as a doorman under local schemes had been replaced by the new national regime. Held: That at that time (and the court acknowledged the law was developing) a personal licence was a possession.

In R (app Nicholds) v Security Industry Authority[1] the case concerned registration with the Security Industry Authority as a registered door supervisor. The High Court reviewed the law up to then and Kenneth Parker QC (sitting as a Deputy High Court Judge) concluded reluctantly (at paragraph 83) that a personal licence which had no separate value and was not marketable, was a possession for the purposes of Article 1 Protocol 1.

This was based on the authorities of Tre Traktörer Aktiebolag v Sweden[2] (a decision of the ECHR), the High Court cases of R (Quark Fishing Ltd) v Secretary of State for Foreign & Commonwealth Affair[3], R (app Malik) v Waltham Forest Primary Care Trust[4], and the Court of Appeal in Crompton v Department of Transport North Western Area[5].

The three English cases all relied upon the decision in Tre Traktörer Aktiebolag that a licence was a possession. It is worth noting that in Nicolds the judge was dubious as to whether Tre Traktörer Aktiebolag really did come to that conclusion (see paragraph 79).

Since then, the case law has developed. Malik was considered by the Court of Appeal in 2007[6] and was referred to in the High Court in Cherwell DC v Anwar[7].

Malik concerned a removal from the medical performers list. This removal prevented Dr Malik from practising as a GP for the NHS. It was found by the High Court that the removal was unlawful (due to procedural irregularities) and the High Court further held that it amounted to an interference with possessions contrary to Article 1 Protocol 1. The question for the Court of Appeal in Malik was whether the right to practice as a GP did amount to a possession. The Court of Appeal found that it did not as it was a personal right and any goodwill in the practice could not be sold by virtue of a statutory bar contained within the NHS legislation.

1   [2007] 1 WLR 2067.
2   (1989) 13 EHRR 309.
3   [2003] EWHC 1743 (Admin).

4   [2006] EWHC 487 (Admin).
5   [2003] EWCA Civ 64.
6   *R (app Malik) v Waltham Forest Primary Care Trust* [2007] 1 WLR 2092.
7   [2012] RTR 15.

Cherwell DC v Anwar

2.115

> Taxi driver convicted of assaulting his wife. Local authority refused renewal
> of his licence. Appeal to the magistrates' court successful because court
> took into account the impact on his family. Local authority appealed by way
> of case stated. Secondary question as to whether a drivers' licence was a
> possession. Held: A drivers' licence was not a possession for the purposes of
> Article 1 Protocol 1.

In *Cherwell* (which concerned non-renewal of a hackney carriage and private
hire combined drivers licence) there was agreement between the parties that
a hackney carriage and private hire drivers' licence was not a possession for
the purposes of Article 1 Protocol 1. Although this was an agreed position, the
judge (His Honour Judge Bidder QC sitting as a Deputy High Court Judge)
had considered the point before agreement was made and concluded that
the decision in *Crompton v Department of Transport North Western Area*[1] was
distinguishable.

He preferred the conclusion of the Court of Appeal in *Malik* which regarded
the decision on the point in *Crompton* as having been made *per incurium*. He said
(at paragraphs 14 to 16):

> '14 At this stage of my judgement I should deal, briefly, with the issue
> of whether this licence constitutes a "possession" within the meaning of
> that term in Article 1 of the First Protocol of the European Convention
> of Human Rights. Counsel before me were agreed that it did not. I agree
> with their concession. While the contention that the licences in this case
> were "possessions" might appear to be supported by the Court of Appeal
> decision in *Crompton –v-Department of Transport North-Western Area*[2],
> that the licence in that case was a "possession" was assumed by the court
> without argument.
>
> 15 Before Counsel's agreement I had concluded that the later decision
> of the Court of Appeal in *Waltham Forest NHS Primary Care Trust and
> Secretary of State for Health –v-Malik*[3] does appear to be indistinguishable
> from this case. Here, as in *Malik*, there is no evidence that the refusal to
> renew the licence would affect any "goodwill" of Mr Anwar's business,
> nor that it would diminish any of the other assets of the business. The
> licence itself is not marketable, nor does it bear any premium. It is not
> bought at a market value. Crompton is cited in *Malik* and the court in
> *Malik* appears to have regarded it as a decision made per incuriam. That
> is, I consider I am bound by *Malik*, and indeed that decision appears to me

to be completely consistent with a not always easily interpretable line of European authorities.

16 I therefore conclude that the licences in this case do not comprise "possessions" within the meaning of article 1.'

1   [2003] EWCA Civ 64.
2   [2003] EWCA Civ 64.
3   [2007] EWCA Civ 265.

Malik v UK

2.116

> Removal of a GP from the NHS practitioners' list. Did this amount to a possession? Held: It was a personal registration which could not attract goodwill, was not transferable and therefore was not a possession for the purposes of Article 1 Protocol 1.

In 2012 *Malik* was considered by the ECHR[1] which upheld the decision of the Court of Appeal. In arriving at its decision the court considered the case law to date (at paragraphs 88 to 93) and concluded as follows (at paragraph 96):

'96. In view of its review of the case-law, the Court does not consider that the applicant's inclusion in the Performers List in England constituted a "possession" for the purposes of Article 1 of Protocol No. 1. In order for that Article to apply, it must be established that there was an underlying professional practice of a certain worth that had, in many respects, the nature of a private right and thus constituted an asset and therefore a "possession" within the meaning of the first sentence of Article 1 (see paragraph 89 above).'

It is clear that a large part of the reasoning for this conclusion was that the professional practice that *Malik* built up was not capable of being sold with any premium for goodwill. Accordingly, the inclusion on the list of practitioners was akin to a personal licence.

On the basis of the decision in *Malik* by the ECHR it would appear that a driver's or operator's licence is not a possession, as it cannot be sold and cannot generate goodwill.

This might appear to contrast with the decision in *Gudmundson v Iceland*[2] which actually concerned a taxi driver's licence. However firstly, *Gudmundson* is a decision of the European Commission on Human Rights, rather than the EHCR, although such judgments are still important. Secondly and perhaps more importantly, *Gudmundson* is a decision which does not necessarily seem to apply to the law relating to taxi drivers in England and Wales. In *Gudmundson* the court said this:

'As regards the question as to whether a licence to conduct certain economic activities could give the licence-holder a right which is protected under

Article 1 of Protocol No. 1 , the Commission considers that the answer will depend inter alia on the question whether the licence can be considered to create for the licence-holder a reasonable and legitimate expectation as to the lasting nature of the licence and as to the possibility to continue to draw benefits from the exercise of the licensed activity. Furthermore, the Commission notes that a licence is frequently granted on certain conditions and that the licence may be withdrawn if such conditions are no longer fulfilled. In other cases, the law itself specifies certain situations in which the licence may be withdrawn.

It follows, in the Commission's opinion, that a licence-holder cannot be considered to have a reasonable and legitimate expectation to continue his activities, if the conditions attached to the licence are no longer fulfilled or if the licence is withdrawn in accordance with the provisions of the law which were in force when the licence was issued (cf. No. 10426/83, Dec. 5.12.84, D.R. 40 p. 234).'

It can be seen that as a taxi driver's licence can be withdrawn in accordance with the provisions of the law (eg suspended, revoked or refused to be renewed on one of the grounds contained in s 61 of the Local Government (Miscellaneous Provisions) Act 1976) the decision in *Gudmundson* does not seem to apply to a driver's licence in England and Wales.

This then reveals a stark contrast with a licence which can be transferred and which can generate goodwill. Vehicle licences fall into this category and do appear to be possessions following the reasoning in the case law above.

It can therefore be seen that if a local authority is considering action against a drivers' licence, there is no need to consider the impact of Article 1 Protocol 1.

However, from the above analysis, in relation to a goodwill generating, transferable licence such as a vehicle licence, Article 1 Protocol 1 will come into play and the authority will then have to be able to demonstrate that its decision did not unjustifiably infringe the human rights of the licensee.

[1]   *Malik v UK* [2012] Med LR 270.
[2]   (1996) 21 EHRR CD 89.

R (On the Application of Begum (By Her Litigation Friend, Rahman)) v Headteacher, Governors of Denbigh High School

2.117

> School uniform in relation to Muslim observance. Did refusal to allow pupils to wear a jilbab interfere with her right to manifest her religion under Article 9? Held: That it did not, and the question was whether a person's human rights had been violated rather than the process that had been followed.

It is important to be clear on decision-making where there is an infringement of human rights. The decision of the House of Lords in *R (On the Application of*

Begum (By Her Litigation Friend, Rahman)) v Headteacher, Governors of Denbigh High School[1] made it clear that the question is whether a person's rights have been infringed, rather than the process by which the decision was made. Lord Bingham put it like this[2]:

'29. I am persuaded that the Court of Appeal's approach to this procedural question was mistaken, for three main reasons. First, the purpose of the Human Rights Act 1998 was not to enlarge the rights or remedies of those in the United Kingdom whose Convention rights have been violated but to enable those rights and remedies to be asserted and enforced by the domestic courts of this country and not only by recourse to Strasbourg. This is clearly established by authorities such as *Aston Cantlow and Wilmcote with Billesley Parochial Church Council v Wallbank*[3]; *R (Greenfield) v Secretary of State for the Home Department*[4]; and *R (Quark Fishing Ltd) v Secretary of State for Foreign and Commonwealth Affairs*[5]. But the focus at Strasbourg is not and has never been on whether a challenged decision or action is the product of a defective decision-making process, but on whether, in the case under consideration, the applicant's Convention rights have been violated. In considering the exercise of discretion by a national authority the court may consider whether the applicant had a fair opportunity to put his case, and to challenge an adverse decision, the aspect addressed by the court in the passage from its judgment in Chapman quoted above. But the House has been referred to no case in which the Strasbourg Court has found a violation of Convention right on the strength of failure by a national authority to follow the sort of reasoning process laid down by the Court of Appeal. This pragmatic approach is fully reflected in the 1998 Act. The unlawfulness proscribed by section 6(1) is acting in a way which is incompatible with a Convention right, not relying on a defective process of reasoning, and action may be brought under section 7(1) only by a person who is a victim of an unlawful act.

30. Secondly, it is clear that the court's approach to an issue of proportionality under the Convention must go beyond that traditionally adopted to judicial review in a domestic setting. The inadequacy of that approach was exposed in *Smith and Grady v United Kingdom*[6], and the new approach required under the 1998 Act was described by Lord Steyn in *R (Daly) v Secretary of State for the Home Department*[7], in terms which have never to my knowledge been questioned. There is no shift to a merits review, but the intensity of review is greater than was previously appropriate, and greater even than the heightened scrutiny test adopted by the Court of Appeal in *R v Ministry of Defence, Ex p Smith*[8]. The domestic court must now make a value judgment, an evaluation, by reference to the circumstances prevailing at the relevant time (*Wilson v First County Trust Ltd (No 2)*[9]. Proportionality must be judged objectively, by the court (*Williamson*, above, para 51). As Davies observed in his article cited above, "The retreat to procedure is of course a way of avoiding difficult questions". But it is in my view clear that the court must confront these questions, however difficult. The school's action cannot properly be condemned as disproportionate, with an

acknowledgement that on reconsideration the same action could very well be maintained and properly so.

31. Thirdly, and as argued by Poole in his article cited above[10], I consider that the Court of Appeal's approach would introduce "a new formalism" and be "a recipe for judicialisation on an unprecedented scale". The Court of Appeal's decision-making prescription would be admirable guidance to a lower court or legal tribunal, but cannot be required of a head teacher and governors, even with a solicitor to help them. If, in such a case, it appears that such a body has conscientiously paid attention to all human rights considerations, no doubt a challenger's task will be the harder. But what matters in any case is the practical outcome, not the quality of the decision-making process that led to it.'

As can be seen, this is a fundamentally different approach from that undertaken on a judicial review of a local authority decision, and will depend on the facts of the case much more than the methodology.

1   [2006] 2 WLR 719.
2   At para 29 onwards.
3   [2003] UKHL 37, [2004] 1 AC 546, paras 6–7, 44.
4   [2005] UKHL 14, [2005] 1 WLR 673, paras 18–19.
5   [2005] UKHL 57, [2005] 3 WLR 837, paras 25, 33, 34, 88 and 92.
6   (1999) 29 EHRR 493, para 138.
7   [2001] UKHL 26, [2001] 2 AC 532, paras 25–28.
8   [1996] QB 517, 554.
9   [2003] UKHL 40, [2004] 1 AC 816, paras 62–67.
10   'Of headscarves and heresies: The *Denbigh High School* case and public authority decision making under the Human Rights Act' [2005] PL 685 at 691–695.

Belfast City Council v Miss Behavin' Ltd

2.118

> Application for a sex establishment licence. Refused and an appeal considered the right to freedom of expression under Article 10. Held: The question of breach of human rights was for the court to decide, on the basis of the restriction. The process by which the decision was arrived at was immaterial.

From a licensing perspective, this approach was followed and endorsed by the House of Lords in *Belfast City Council v Miss Behavin' Ltd*[1]. In particular, Baroness Hale explained he position as follows[2]:

'31 The ... straightforward, question is who decides whether or not a claimant's Convention rights have been infringed. The answer is that it is the court before which the issue is raised. The role of the court in human rights adjudication is quite different from the role of the court in an ordinary judicial review of administrative action. In human rights adjudication, the court is concerned with whether the human rights of the claimant have in fact been infringed, not with whether the administrative decision-maker properly took them into account. If it were otherwise, every policy decision taken before the 1998 Act came into force but which engaged a Convention right would be open to challenge, no matter how obviously compliant with the right in question it was. That cannot be right, and this House so decided in *R (SB) v Governors of Denbigh High School*, in relation to the decisions of a public authority.'

1   [2007] UKHL 19, [2007] 1 WLR 1420.
2   At paragraph 31.

2.119

These decisions do not mean that the Human Rights Act 1998 can be ignored or disregarded. Local authorities must be fully aware of the Act and its impact upon their decision-making.

WITHIN LONDON —TRANSPORT FOR LONDON

2.120

Hackney carriage and private hire licensing within London is the responsibility of Transport for London (TfL) which is a body corporate created by s 154 of the Greater London Authority Act 1999 and which is accountable to the Mayor of London and responsible for delivering the Mayor's Transport Strategy. It has a separate Board, which is chaired by the Mayor of London and comprises 15 other members. As a result of the creation of TfL, previous references in London hackney carriage legislation to the Metropolitan Police were amended to refer to TfL[1]. TfL is also 'the licensing authority' for the purposes of private hire licensing and enforcement under the provisions of the Private Hire Vehicles (London) Act 1998[2].

1   By virtue of Greater London Authority Act 1999, Sch 20.
2   See Appendix I.

2.121

The ultimate power in relation to both hackney carriage and private hire licensing within London lies with the Board of Transport for London. Powers are given directly to TfL under the London Hackney Carriages Acts of 1843, 1850, 1853[1], the Metropolitan Public Carriage Act 1869[2], the London Cab and Stage Carriage Act 1907[3], the London Cab Act 1968[4] and the Private Hire Vehicles (London) Act 1998[5]. The board of TfL has powers to make regulations and is the ultimate decision-making body for hackney carriage and private hire licensing within London.

TfL discharges its day-to-day hackney carriage and private hire functions via London Taxi and Private Hire ('LTPH') formerly known as the Public Carriage Office.

Although member involvement is limited to board decisions, and all other LTPH activities are effectively officer decisions, all the points made in relation to decision-making within local government above are equally applicable to TfL/ LTPH.

1   See Appendix I.
2   See Appendix I.
3   See Appendix I.
4   See Appendix I.
5   See Appendix I.

Power to act

2.122

TfL/LTPH is a statutory creation, and, as with local authorities, can therefore only undertake activities for which it is statutorily empowered.

In relation to hackney carriage and private hire licensing, this point is not of enormous importance, as there are specific powers contained in the Greater London Authority Act 1999.

The decision itself

2.123

The grant or refusal of a licence by TfL/LTPH is governed by the same rules as apply to decisions made by local authorities outside London. It is not a criminal matter, nor is it a purely civil matter. It is an administrative matter and, accordingly, the rules which govern the operation and undertaking of that procedure are not the rules of criminal or civil evidence. Although it is an administrative, rather than quasi-judicial body, it must still act fairly and the best approach to fair decision making is to observe and have regard to the rules of natural justice. This is true whether it is a decision of the TfL board, or a LTPH officer.

Policies

2.124

As with local authorities, TfL/LTPH is entitled to adopt policies in relation to hackney carriage and private hire licensing. As with local authorities, they must be correctly approved and made available.

Procedure

The Hearing

2.125

Although hearings will be before an officer, rather than a committee (as is often the case outside London), the same rules in relation to the fairness of the hearing apply, although there will be no requirement for the matter to be heard in public.

Reasonableness

2.126

As a public body, TfL/LTPH are required to act reasonably in accordance with *Wednesbury* principles in the same way as local authorities.

Reasons

2.127

TfL/LTPH are under the same common law duty to provide reasons for their decision-making as local authorities.

Human Rights Act 1998

2.128

TfL/LTPH is a public body, and therefore bound by the requirements of the Human Rights Act 1998 (HRA 1998). The impact of the Human Rights Act on TfL/LTPH is therefore the same as the impact of the Human Rights Act on local authorities.

Chapter 3

Appeals

3.1

Decisions made by local authorities and Transport for London (TfL)[1], are open to challenge. That can be by way of a statutory right of appeal or by judicial review.

Licensing appeals in general and hackney carriage and private hire licensing appeals in particular, are unusual as they are not governed by either the Civil Procedure Rules[2] or the Criminal Procedure Rules[3]. There are still governed by the Magistrates' Courts Rules 1981[4] and the Crown Court Rules 1982[5].

[1] Within Greater London, hackney carriage and private hire licensing is the responsibility of the Mayor of London, exercised via Transport for London (TfL). The department of TfL that deals with hackney carriage and private hire licensing is called 'London Taxi and Private Hire' and was formerly called the Public Carriage Office (PCO).

[2] SI 1998/3132.

[3] SI 2012/1726.

[4] SI 1981/552.

[5] SI 1982/1109. Although both the Magistrates' Courts Rules 1981, SI 1981/552 and the Crown Court Rules 1982, SI 1982/1109 were ostensibly repealed by the Criminal Procedure Rules 2005, SI 2005/384 as amended, now the Criminal Procedure Rules 2015, SI 2015/1490 (CPR), the CPR clearly state that they only apply to criminal cases in criminal courts (see ss 69(1) and 68 of the Courts Act 2003 and CPR r 2.1), and therefore hackney carriage and private hire appeals to both the magistrates' court and the Crown Court are still governed by the Magistrates' Courts Rules 1981 and the Crown Court Rules 1982. This appears to have been confirmed by the addition of explicit case management powers for both magistrates courts and Crown Courts in relation to civil proceedings from 5 April 2010 – see The Magistrates' Courts (Amendment) Rules 2009, SI 2009/3362 and the Crown Court (Amendment) Rules 2009, SI 2009/3361.

In *Stockton-on-Tees Borough Council v Latif* [2009] EWHC 228 (Admin), [2009] LLR 374 it was stated to be common ground that the CPR (Civil Procedure Rules) applied (see para 8). This was not explored by the High Court but in the light of the above, appears to have been a mistaken assumption.

OUTSIDE LONDON

Statutory rights of appeal

3.2

Although there are two different approaches to statutory appeals, depending upon whether the Local Government (Miscellaneous Provisions) Act 1976

(LG(MP)A 1976) has been adopted or not, for the reasons explained in Chapter 1[1], only the procedure applicable in 'controlled districts' where LG(MP)A 1976 has been adopted is considered here.

When LG(MP)A 1976 has been adopted, there are statutory rights of appeal to the magistrates' court against almost all the decisions of the local authority. With two exceptions, these are available, both against a refusal to grant or renew a licence and a decision to suspend or revoke a licence that is in existence, as well as a right to appeal against any conditions which may have been imposed on any such licence by the local authority.

[1] See Chapter 1, para 1.4.

3.3

The exceptions are: first, an appeal against a refusal to grant a hackney carriage proprietor's licence, which lies directly to the Crown Court; and secondly, a decision to suspend a vehicle licence (applicable to both hackney carriages and private hire vehicles) under the LG(MP)A 1976, s 68 against which there is no right of appeal.

3.4

The following rights of appeal are to be found in LG(MP)A 1976:

- Appeal against conditions imposed on a hackney carriage proprietor's licence (LG(MP)A 1976, s 47).
- Appeal against refusal to grant a private hire vehicle licence, or conditions imposed on such a licence (LG(MP)A 1976, s 48).
- Appeal against refusal to grant a private hire driver's licence, or conditions imposed on such a licence (LG(MP)A 1976, s 52).
- Appeal against refusal to grant a private hire operators' licence, or conditions imposed on such a licence (LG(MP)A 1976, s 55).
- Appeal against refusal to grant a hackney carriage driver's licence (LG(MP)A 1976, s 59).
- Appeal against suspension, revocation or refusal to renew a hackney carriage or private hire vehicle licence (LG(MP)A 1976, s 60).
- Appeal against suspension, revocation or refusal to renew a hackney carriage or private hire driver's licence (LG(MP)A 1976, s 61).
- Appeal against suspension, revocation or refusal to renew a private hire operators' licence (LG(MP)A 1976, s 62).

3.5

LG(MP)A 1976, s 77 states:

'**Appeals**

77–(1) Sections 300 to 302 of the Act of 1936, which relate to appeals, shall have effect as if this Part of this Act were part of that Act.

(2) If any requirement, refusal or other decision of a district council against which a right of appeal is conferred by this Act—

(a) involves the execution of any work or the taking of any action; or

(b) makes it unlawful for any person to carry on a business which he was lawfully carrying on up to the time of the requirement, refusal or decision;

then, until the time for appealing has expired, or, when an appeal is lodged, until the appeal is disposed of or withdrawn or fails for want of prosecution—

(i) no proceedings shall be taken in respect of any failure to execute the work, or take the action; and

(ii) that person may carry on that business.

(3) Subsection (2) of this section does not apply in relation to a decision under subsection (1) of section 61 of this Act which has immediate effect in accordance with subsection (2B) of that section'

The reference to 'the Act of 1936' is to the Public Health Act 1936. The provisions of the Public Health Act 1936, ss 300–302[1] are a well-known, workable method of seeking an appeal against a decision of a local authority. By virtue of s 301 of the Act there is then a further appeal, as of right, to the Crown Court from the decision of the magistrates' court.

[1]   See Appendix I.

3.6

In general, the effect of LG(MP)A 1976, s 77(2) is to stay any action pending the determination of an appeal. There is an exception in relation to a hackney carriage or private hire driver's licence when the local authority has decided that the licence should be suspended or revoked with immediate effect in the interests of public safety. Unless that applies (and this is considered further in para 3.7 below), this means that, if the appeal is against a refusal to renew a licence or a decision to suspend or revoke a licence, the licence is deemed to remain in force, pending the determination of the appeal. Any action against the licence in the form of a suspension or revocation does not in fact take place immediately, but is delayed until the time period for appealing against the decision has expired. That period is 21 days from the date on which 'notice of the councils requirement, refusal or other decision was served upon the person desiring to appeal' (Public Health Act 1936, s 300(2) applied by LG(MP)A 1976, s 77(1)).

This means that there is at least three weeks before the action against the licence takes effect, and, of course, if an appeal is lodged, the delay can be of some considerable length[1].

[1]   See para 3.38 in relation to extensions of the time limit.

3.7

Section 52 of the Road Safety Act 2006 inserted sub-ss (2A) and (2B) into LG(MP)A 1976, s 61 under which it is possible for a local authority to suspend or revoke a drivers' licence with immediate effect if the local authority determine that such action is 'necessary in the interests of public safety'[1]. The appeal period remains the same at 21 days; the only difference is the fact that the driver cannot use the licence unless and until the appeal is decided in his favour.

[1] For further details on the grounds for suspension or revocation of a driver's licence, see Chapter 6, paras 6.34 onwards and 6.42 onwards. This leads to the question of what is meant by the phrase 'necessary in the interests of public safety'. The local authority can only take action where it considers that the driver is not a fit and proper person as a result of one of the factors referred to in LG(MP)A 1976, s 61(1).

3.8

As noted above, it is possible to appeal to the Crown Court against the decision of the magistrates' court under the Public Health Act 1936, s 301. No time-limit for launching this appeal is specified within s 301, but the time-limit is 21 days from the date of the decision in the magistrates' court by virtue of the Crown Court Rules 1982, r 7(3)[1]. Again, the usual effect of such an appeal is that any action is stayed until the expiry of that time, and if a Crown Court appeal is launched, there is a further extension of that stay until the determination by that Court.

[1] SI 1982/1109.

3.9

Where a suspension or revocation was declared by the local authority to have had immediate effect, the position would appear to be that the suspension or revocation remains in effect until the Crown Court appeal is determined or abandoned. If the appeal to the magistrates' court by the driver was unsuccessful, an appeal by the driver would then extend the suspension or revocation until the Crown Court decision. It would also seem to apply where the appeal was successful before the magistrates, but the local authority exercised its right to appeal under the decision in *Cook v Southend Borough Council*[1]. In that situation, the effect of the magistrates' decision would not take effect for 21 days and provided the local authority appealed within that time, the ban on the use of the licence would remain in place until the Crown Court determination. Although s 302 of the Public Health Act 1936 states that:

'Where upon an appeal under this Act a court varies or reverses any decision of a council, it shall be the duty of the council to give effect to the order of the court and, in particular, to grant or issue any necessary consent, certificate or other document, and to make any necessary entry in any register.'

It is submitted that s 302 must only apply where all appeals under the Act have been exhausted, otherwise the position would be that an immediate revocation that had been upheld by the magistrates' court could be overcome by lodging a further appeal to the Crown Court, allowing the driver to use the licence pending the final appeal, which must be seen as frustrating the aim behind the power of immediate action against a drivers' licence. This view is reinforced by the fact that where the appeal to the magistrates' court was unsuccessful, there has been no variation or reversal of the Council's decision and s 302 does not apply.

¹   *Cook v Southend Borough Council* [1990] 2 QB 1, CA; see para 3.29 below.

3.10

In matters concerning the use of a hackney carriage or private hire vehicle or a private hire operators licence, the staying effect of any appeal can lead to concern from the local authority where the decision has a direct bearing upon public safety, eg where a vehicle is unsafe or an operator has been accused of or convicted of a serious crime.

In relation to a vehicle, if the vehicle is unfit, an authorised officer of the local authority, or a police constable can suspend the licence with immediate effect under LG(MP)A 1976, s 68¹.

Unfortunately there is no mechanism which allows immediate action to be taken against a private hire operator's licence, even in the case of an operator who has been accused or convicted of a serious crime, and when the local authority feels that he should no longer be in a position of responsibility, holding, as he does, details of persons' movements (eg periods when residences are empty because the occupiers are on holiday).

¹   See Chapter 8, para 8.150.

Expiry of licence during the appeal

3.11

The situation can occur where the licence expires during the appeal process. The impact of this now varies, depending on whether the licence (in the case of a driver) was suspended or revoked with immediate effect, or not.

In the first situation where the licence was revoked or suspended with immediate effect, the driver cannot drive. However, he should apply to renew his licence in the normal way, before its expiry date to preserve his rights if his appeal is ultimately successful. If he does not do this, although the licence would be re-instated following a successful appeal, it would immediately expire as the expiry date would have passed. Renewal would only be possible if an application had been made before the licence expired, as it is usually the case that something that has expired cannot be renewed¹. A new application could be detrimental to a driver as they may have to undertake tests or checks which would not be required for a renewing driver.

In relation to the second situation where the action against the licence does not have immediate effect, clearly, the licence still has effect, and can be used pending the appeal, as outlined above, but what happens after the determination of the appeal?

If an application to renew the licence has not been received by the local authority before the expiry of the licence on its original expiry date, the licence cannot exist after a successful appeal. Although the effect of a successful appeal is to overturn the decision of the local authority, there is no power given to the court to extend the life of the original licence. Accordingly, in such a situation, the licensee has no current licence.

¹   However see *Exeter v Sandle* [2011] EWHC 1403 (Admin), [2011] LLR 480, para 8.244 for an example of where the courts have allowed renewal after expiry.

3.12

In either situation, to preserve his rights in the event of a successful appeal, it is therefore essential for the licensee to apply to renew his licence in the usual way, before it expires¹. The local authority will have to consider this, and could grant it without prejudice and subject to the outcome of the appeal. If the appeal is unsuccessful, the licence will not then be issued, but if the appeal is successful, the licence can be issued in the normal way from the date of expiry of the original licence. Alternatively, the local authority could refuse to renew the licence. This could then be appealed in the normal way and listed to be dealt by the magistrates' court at the same time as the appeal against suspension or revocation.

¹   See paras 8.242 onwards; 10.156 onwards; 12.85 onwards; 13.126 onwards and 14.22 onwards.

3.13

The staying effect of an appeal is only effective where there is a licence already in existence. If the application was for a new licence, then as there is no licence already in force, the mechanism does not work and the licence will not be deemed to come into existence until the court overturns the decision of the local authority or, if it is an appeal to the Crown Court from the decision at the magistrates' court, the decision of the Crown Court.

3.14

Where LG(MP)A 1976 has been adopted, the only licence which carries a right of appeal directly to the Crown Court on refusal is a hackney carriage proprietor's (vehicle) licence. The reasons for this are as follows.

Originally, the Town Police Clauses Act 1847 had to be incorporated by a special (local) Act. Then the Public Health Act 1875, s 171(4) incorporated all the 1847 Act powers in relation to hackney carriages for urban districts. The Local Government Act 1972 did not extend those powers to all areas of England and Wales (Local Government Act 1972, Sch 14, para 24(b)), but this was done by the Transport Act 1985, s 15, which extended the provisions of the Town Police Clauses Act 1847 (incorporated into the Public Health Act 1875 by the Public Health Act 1875, s 171) and Town Police Clauses Act 1889 (deemed to be incorporated in the Public Health Act 1875 by the Town Police Clauses Act 1889, s 2(2)) to all areas of England and Wales. The Greater London Authority Act 1999, s 255(2) extended the application of the Town Police Clauses Act 1847 and the Public Health Act 1875 to the districts which had, until 2000, been part of the Metropolitan Police Area.

3.15

For some inexplicable reason, LG(MP)A 1976 did not grant a specific right of appeal to the magistrates' court against a refusal to grant a hackney carriage proprietor's licence. Accordingly, the appeal lies under the pre-1976 regime. It is covered by the Public Health Acts Amendment Act 1907, s 7 which, by virtue of s 2(1), is construed as one with the Public Health Act 1875. Section 7 states:

'**Appeals to Crown Court, etc**

7–(1) Except where this Act otherwise expressly provides any person aggrieved—
(a) By any order, judgment, determination, or requirement of a local authority under this Act;
(b) By the withholding of any order, certificate, licence, consent or approval, which may be made, granted, or given by a local authority under this Act;
(c) By any conviction or order of a court of summary jurisdiction under any provision of this Act;
     may appeal to the Crown Court.'

The time period for lodging an appeal to the Crown Court is 21 days from the decision of the local authority[1].

[1]   See rr 6(1) and 7(3) of the Crown Court Rules 1982, SI 1982/1109.

All appeals

3.16

Such hearings are neither criminal nor civil. The court is sitting in a judicial capacity hearing an appeal against an administrative decision.

R (on the application of Hope and Glory) v City of Westminster Magistrates' Court

3.17

> Appeal against conditions imposed following review of a premises licence under Licensing Act 2003. Decision of magistrates' court challenged by judicial review. Was the process used by the Stipendiary Magistrate correct? Leave refused but granted on appeal. Judgment given by the Court of Appeal.

This was stated clearly in the decision of the Court of Appeal in *R (on the application of Hope and Glory) v City of Westminster Magistrates' Court*[1] where Touslon LJ stated (at para 41):

'As Mr Matthias rightly submitted, the licensing function of a licensing authority is an administrative function. By contrast, the function of the district judge is a judicial function. The licensing authority has a duty, in accordance with the rule of law, to behave fairly in the decision-making procedure, but the decision itself is not a judicial or quasi-judicial act. It is the exercise of a power delegated by the people as a whole to decide what the public interest requires.'

1   [2011] 3 All ER 579.

3.18

The Court of Appeal has restated the principles applying to licensing appeals in the *Hope and Glory*[1] case, reinforcing the position established by *Stepney Borough Council v Joffe*[2] and *Sagnata Investments Ltd v Norwich Corpn*[3].

It is quite clear that such hearings are hearings *de novo* (which is to say, that they are a completely fresh hearing). The court places itself in the position of the body whose decision is being appealed against, whether that is the local authority or the magistrates' court. The appeal court has to substitute its decision for the decision of the local authority and must satisfy itself on the same principles as the local authority must have satisfied itself to start with.

What then is the practical effect of this? As the Court of Appeal observed in *Hope and Glory*[4]:

'the appeal is a rehearing at which the affected parties are all entitled to call evidence, and that the court must make its decision on the full material before it.'

If there are any new developments or if any new information is obtained between the date of the local authority hearing decision and the date of the appeal being determined, that can be adduced before the appeal court. This, of course, works both ways and is open for the appellant and the respondent to produce any new material which may be relevant to their appeal. This proposition is supported by the case of *Rushmoor Borough Council v Richards*[5].

However, the local authority has come to a position and it has been given the power to adjudicate on such applications and other matters. What then is the impact of its decision on a subsequent appeal? Is the court hearing the appeal entitled to disregard the decision being appealed, or must it take it into account? If it is to be taken into account, how much weight must it be given?

1   *R (on the application of Hope and Glory) v City of Westminster Magistrates' Court* [2011] 3 All ER 579.
2   [1949] 1 KB 599, DC; see para 3.19 below.
3   [1971] 2 QB 614, CA; see para 3.20 below.
4   *R (on the application of Hope and Glory) v City of Westminster Magistrates' Court* [2011] 3 All ER 579.per Toulson LJ at para 28.
5   (1996) 160 LGR 460 QBD; see para 3.22.

Stepney Borough Council v Joffe

3.19

Revocation of street traders licences. Appeal is a hearing *de novo*, but the court must consider the local authorities decision and not overturn it lightly.

In the *Stepney* case[1], this matter was considered. The case concerned a decision by the council to revoke street trading licences which had been granted to three traders, under the provisions of the London County Council (General Powers) Act 1947. The argument had been put forward that the magistrate on an appeal was not entitled to substitute his decision for that of the local authority. That view was not accepted by the Divisional Court. Lord Goddard CJ stated (at 602):

'It is said that, on an appeal … the magistrate is not entitled to substitute his opinion for the opinion of the borough council; that all he can decide is whether there was evidence upon which the council could come to that conclusion. I find myself quite unable to accept that argument. If that argument be right, the right of appeal … would be purely illusory. Such an appeal would … really be only an appeal on the question of law whether there was any evidence upon which the borough council could have formed an opinion. If their decision were a mere matter of opinion and that opinion were to be conclusive, I do not know that the borough council would be obliged to have any evidence. They could simply say "In our opinion this person is unsuitable to hold a licence". It is true that they must give a sufficient reason, but they could give any reason they liked and say: "That is sufficient in our opinion". I do not know how a court could then say on appeal that that was not a sufficient reason. If the reason need only be one which is sufficient in the opinion of the borough council, it is difficult to see how any court of appeal could set aside their decision. It seems to me that [London County Council (General Powers) Act 1947, s 25(1)] gives an unrestricted right of appeal, and if there is an unrestricted right of appeal it is for the court of appeal to substitute its opinion for the opinion of the borough council.'

In relation to the question of the relevance of the previous decision by the local authority, Lord Goddard CJ said (at 602):

'That does not mean to say that the court of appeal, in this case the metropolitan magistrate, ought not pay great attention to the fact that the duly constituted and elected local authority have come to an opinion on the matter, and it ought not lightly to reverse their opinion. It is constantly said (although I am not sure that it is always sufficiently remembered) that the function of a court of appeal is to exercise its powers when it is satisfied that the judgment below was wrong, not merely because it is not satisfied that the judgment was right.'

[1]   *Stepney Borough Council v Joffe* [1949] 1 KB 599, DC.

Sagnata Investments Ltd v Norwich Corpn

3.20

Refusal of gaming machine permit. Appeal is a hearing *de novo* but the court must give considerable weight to the decision of the local authority.

In the *Sagnata* case[1] the Court of Appeal upheld both elements of the *Stepney*[2] judgment: that such an appeal is a hearing *de novo*, a completely fresh hearing; and that the court should take account of and give considerable, but not overwhelming, weight to the fact that the local authority came to the decision that it did. Edmund Davies LJ cited with approval the judgment of Lord Goddard CJ in the *Stepney* case (at 149G and 150G).

It is therefore clear that an appeal is a rehearing. What then can the court take into account?

[1]   *Sagnata Investments Ltd v Norwich Corpn* [1971] 2 QB 614, CA.
[2]   *Stepney Borough Council v Joffe* [1949] 1 KB 599, DC.

R (on the application of Westminster City Council) v Middlesex Crown Court and Chorian plc and Proud

3.21

> Refusal to grant public entertainment licence. Position of the court on appeal. Court stands in the shoes of the local authority and must consider local authority policy.

It is clear that the relevant policies of the local authority must be taken into account, and indeed in general, followed by the court hearing any appeal. In the case of *R (on the application of Westminster City Council) v Middlesex Crown Court and Chorian plc and Proud*[1] the question was raised as to whether the court hearing an appeal was bound by the policy of the local authority. Mr Justice Scott Baker stated:

> '21. How should a Crown Court (or a Magistrates' Court) approach an appeal where the council has a policy? In my judgment it must accept the policy and apply it as if it was standing in the shoes of the council considering the application. Neither the Magistrates' Court nor the Crown Court is the right place to challenge the policy. The remedy, if it is alleged that a policy has been unlawfully established, is an application to the Administrative Court for judicial review. In formulating a policy the council will no doubt first consult the various interested parties and then take into account all the various relevant considerations.'

In coming to this conclusion he referred to the decisions in the cases of *R v Sheffield Crown Court, ex p Consterdine*[2] and *R v Chester Crown Court, ex p Pascoe and Jones*[3].

It is also clear from the cases of *Kavanagh v Chief Constable of Devon and Cornwall*[4], *Westminster City Council v Zestfair*[5], *McCool v Rushcliffe Borough Council*[6] and *Leeds City Council v Hussain*[7] that hearsay evidence is admissible on appeal, just as it is before the local authority[8].

If a party wishes to rely on hearsay evidence in the magistrates' court, it appears that he must comply with the requirements of the Magistrates' Courts (Hearsay Evidence in Civil Proceedings) Rules 1999[9]. There is some doubt over this, however, as the appeal itself is arguably not 'civil proceedings' as it is not covered by the Civil Procedure Rules, but compliance with the requirements would be sensible and will remove any doubt as to admissibility.

1   (29 May 2002, unreported), Admin Ct.
2   (1998) 34 Licensing Review 19.
3   (1987) 151 JP 752.
4   [1974] 2 All ER 697; see Chapter 2, para 2.67.
5   (1989) 88 LGR 288, DC; see Chapter 2, para 2.68.
6   [1998] 3 All ER 889, QBD; see Chapter 2, para 2.69.
7   See Chapter 2, para 2.70.
8   [2002] EWHC 1145 (Admin), [2003] RTR 199.
9   SI 1999/681. These require notice of hearsay to be given by the party wishing to rely on it to all other parties and file copy with the court not less than 21 days before the date of the hearing (rule 3). It is possible to seek a witness summons in relation to proposed hearsay evidence under rule 4.

Rushmoor Borough Council v Richards

3.22

Appeal against refusal to vary public entertainment licence. New evidence of events occurring between the date of the council decision and the appeal can be adduced at the appeal.

In *Rushmoor Borough Council v Richards*[1] the question arose as to whether the court on an appeal in a licensing matter (in that case, an appeal concerning a public entertainment licence granted under the Local Government (Miscellaneous Provisions) Act 1982) could consider evidence of events that had occurred after the decision that was the subject of the appeal. The magistrate's court on appeal had refused to admit or consider such evidence and allowed the appeal.

Tuckey J reviewed the cases of *Sagnata Investments Ltd v Norwich Corpn*[2], *Kavanagh v Chief Constable of Devon and Cornwall*[3] and *Westminster City Council v Zestfair Ltd*[4].

Each of those cases concerned a different type of licence, under different legislation, but all agreed on the approach to be taken. Tuckey J concluded:

'These cases support the view that I form from looking at the legislation, that appeals under this legislation are by way of rehearing *de novo* and that Magistrates are not restricted to hearing evidence about events before the authority's decision under appeal. They are able and, indeed, must consider all the relevant evidence that is put before them whether it relates to events before or after the decision under appeal.

It follows that I do not think the Magistrates made the correct ruling in this case. Turning to the question for which the opinion of the court is requested, which reads as follows:

"When considering an appeal against a Local Authority's decision pursuant to the Local Government (Miscellaneous Provisions) Act

1982, were the Justices correct in disregarding evidence placed before them which related to matters arising between the date when the Council made its decision which was the subject of an appeal and the date of appeal hearing before the Magistrates?"

The answer must be "no". They were not correct.'

It is therefore clear that, provided the material is relevant, evidence of matters that have arisen since the council's decision, but before the appeal, can be adduced. The same would therefore apply to any new developments between the decision of the magistrates' court and any subsequent appeal to the Crown Court.

1   (1996) 160 LGR 460, QBD.
2   [1971] 2 QB 614, CA.
3   [1974] QB 624, CA.
4   (1990) 88 LGR 288.

R (on the application of Hope and Glory) v Westminster Magistrates Court [1]

3.23

> Appeal against conditions imposed following review of a premises licence under Licensing Act 2003. Decision of magistrates' court challenged by judicial review. Was the process used by the Stipendiary Magistrate correct? Leave refused but granted on appeal. Judgment given by the Court of Appeal.

This case concerned an appeal against the imposition of conditions imposed on a premises licence following a review under the Licensing Act 2003. The licensee appealed against the conditions to the magistrates' court which conducted a hearing. That decision was challenged by way of judicial review to the High Court, where the principal argument concerned the approach taken to the appeal by the District Judge in the magistrates' court. The High Court found that his approach was correct, and a further appeal was brought to the Court of Appeal.

In the light of both *Joffe*[2] and *Sagnata*[3], the district judge stated that the approach he would take to the appeal was as follows[4]:

'I will therefore

(1) Note the decision of the licensing sub-committee.

(2) Not lightly reverse their decision.

(3) Only reverse the decision if I am satisfied it is wrong.

(4) I will hear evidence.

(5) The correct approach is to consider the promotion of the Licensing Objectives. To look at the Licensing Act 2003, the Guidance made under section 182 LA03, Westminster's Statement of Licensing Policy and any legal authorities.

(6) I am not concerned with the way in which the Licensing Sub-Committee approached their decision or the process by which it was made. The correct appeal against such issues lies by way of Judicial Review.'

The Court of Appeal was asked to consider whether this was the correct approach and in particular the impact of the decision of the local authority on the appeal court. The Court of Appeal concluded that the district judge had been correct on the first five points, but had misdirected himself on the final point. They concluded[5]:

> 'It is right in all cases that the magistrates' court should pay careful attention to the reasons given by the licensing authority for arriving at the decision under appeal, bearing in mind that Parliament has chosen to place responsibility for making such decisions on local authorities. The weight which the magistrates should ultimately attach to those reasons must be a matter for their judgment in all the circumstances, taking into account the fullness and clarity of the reasons, the nature of the issues and the evidence given on the appeal.'

They fully upheld the approach of the judge in the High Court in finding that the approach taken by the District Judge was correct in relation to steps 1–5, and in coming to that conclusion, they dismissed the argument that there was a distinction between decisions based upon policy and those which were not. They were not convinced by the 6th point, and felt that the magistrates' court could consider the way in which the licensing authority had made their decision, however it is suggested that that is limited to Licensing Act appeals[6].

---

[1]   *R (on the application of Hope and Glory) v City of Westminster Magistrates' Court* [2011] EWCA Civ 31, [2011] 3 All ER 579.

[2]   *Stepney Borough Council v Joffe* [1949] 1 KB 599, DC.

[3]   *Sagnata Investments Ltd v Norwich Corpn* [1971] 2 QB 614, CA.

[4]   *R (on the application of Hope and Glory) v City of Westminster Magistrates' Court* [2011] EWCA Civ 31, [2011] 3 All ER 579, per Toulson LJ at para 7.

[5]   See para 45.

[6]   See paras 51 and 52. Because s 181(2) of the Licensing Act allows the magistrates' court to 'remit the case to the licensing authority to dispose of it in accordance with the direction of the cour' the Court of Appeal took the view that the way in which the licensing authority dealt with the matter was relevant to the appeal. As no such specific statutory powers exist for hackney carriage and private hire appeals, it is suggested that this 6th point remains the correct approach for such appeals.

3.24

As noted above, the appeal is not governed by either set of judicial rules[1], but is subject to the Magistrates' Courts Rules 1981[2] and rule 14 lays down the procedure that is to be followed on the hearing of a complaint.

> '14.— Order of evidence and speeches: complaint
> (1) On the hearing of a complaint, except where the court determines under section 53(3) of the Act of 1980 to make the order with the consent of the defendant without hearing evidence, the complainant shall call his evidence, and before doing so may address the court.

(2) At the conclusion of the evidence for the complainant the defendant may address the court, whether or not he afterwards calls evidence.

(3) At the conclusion of the evidence, if any, for the defence, the complainant may call evidence to rebut that evidence.

(4) At the conclusion of the evidence for the defence and the evidence, if any, in rebuttal, the defendant may address the court if he has not already done so.

(5) Either party may, with the leave of the court, address the court a second time, but where the court grants leave to one party it shall not refuse leave to the other.

(6) Where the defendant obtains leave to address the court for a second time his second address shall be made before the second address, if any, of the complainant.'

In other words, the running order laid down by Rule 14 is as follows:

(1) Complainant/Appellant opening speech;

(2) Complainant/Appellant calls evidence by means of witnesses and/or hearsay;

(3) Defendant/Respondent challenges evidence (cross examination of witnesses);

(4) Defendant/Respondent addresses court (irrespective of whether he is to produce evidence) but if does so, cannot address court again at the end – see (8) below;

(5) Defendant/Respondent calls evidence by means of witnesses and/or hearsay;

(6) Complainant/Appellant challenges evidence (cross examination of witnesses);

(7) Complainant/Appellant may call evidence to rebut Defendant/Respondent's case;

(8) Defendant/Respondent addresses court (closing speech) only if not done so at end of Complainant/Appellant case – see (4) above;

(9) With the leave of the court, either party can address the court again, but if one does, the other must be able to as well;

(10) If second addresses, Complainant/Appellant always has the last word.

Notwithstanding these Rules, many local authorities and magistrates' courts have evolved their own procedure.

The most striking part of these informal procedures is that it is often agreed that the respondent local authority should present their case first and the appellant should then respond to that. The thinking behind this is to enable the court to understand what the appellant is appealing against, rather than having the somewhat awkward and potentially confusing situation of the appellant explaining his reasons for appeal, followed by the respondent explaining why the appeal should not be granted. If this approach is not agreed, then the appellant will present his case first. In those circumstances, it is very helpful for the court if the respondent local authority outlines the law and background to the court by way of opening before the appellant puts his case.

If this approach is undertaken, it is important that the respondent local authority should reserve their right to address the court before the appellant's summing up.owever, it should be noted that the Court of Appeal in *Hope and Glory* questioned this informal approach and stated[3]:

'It is normal for an appellant to have to show that the order challenged was wrong. The only unusual feature about this type of appeal is that all parties have carte blanche to call evidence. It does not, however, follow that the respondent to the appeal should bear the responsibility of showing that the order should be upheld and so should be required to present its case first.'

It reinforces that view later in the judgment by adding[4]:

'48 It is normal for an appellant to have the responsibility of persuading the court that it should reverse the order under appeal, and the Magistrates Courts Rules envisage that this is so in the case of statutory appeals to magistrates' courts from decisions of local authorities. We see no indication that Parliament intended to create an exception in the case of appeals under the Licensing Act.

49 We are also impressed by Mr Matthias's point that in a case such as this, where the licensing sub-committee has exercised what amounts to a statutory discretion to attach conditions to the licence, it makes good sense that the licensee should have to persuade the magistrates' court that the sub-committee should not have exercised its discretion in the way that it did rather than that the magistrates' court should be required to exercise the discretion afresh on the hearing of the appeal.'

It appears therefore that rule 14 of the Magistrates Courts Rules 1981 will apply unless there is an agreement by the court with the consent of both parties to depart from that prescribed procedure.

[1]   Civil Procedure Rules 1998, SI 1998/3132 and Criminal Procedure Rules 2012, SI 2012/1726.
[2]   SI 1981/552.
[3]   *R (on the application of Hope and Glory) v City of Westminster Magistrates' Court* [2011] 3 All ER 579 per Toulson LJ at para 35.
[4]   *R (on the application of Hope and Glory) v City of Westminster Magistrates' Court* [2011] 3 All ER 579 per Toulson LJ at paras 48 and 48.

3.25

It is open to the appeal court to substitute its decision for the decision which is being appealed against. This can include modifying or varying the decision which is being appealed against. The court also has the discretion to award costs.

Costs

Bradford Metropolitan Borough Council v Booth

3.26

Appeal against refusal to renew private hire operators' licence. Appeal successful. Should costs follow the cause and be awarded against the council? No, provided the local authority had acted properly.

Clearly the magistrates' court has the power to award costs. This power is found in the Magistrates' Courts Act 1980, s 64. The question which often arises is whether or not they should. The risk of costs being awarded against a party is a powerful deterrent to litigation. It can also be a deterrent to effective decision-making and enforcement. This point was raised in the case of *Bradford Metropolitan Borough Council v Booth*[1]. This case concerned an appeal against a decision to refuse to renew Mr Booth's private hire operator's licence. The appeal to the magistrates' court was successful and Mr Booth applied for costs against the council. There was considerable argument in the magistrates' court as to whether costs should be awarded, with Mr Booth's representative arguing that costs should follow the cause, and the council arguing that reliance can be placed on *R v Merthyr Tydfil Crown Court, ex p Chief Constable of Dyfed Powys*[2] and that costs should only be awarded if the local authority had acted unreasonably or in bad faith.

In the Queen's Bench Division judgment was given by Lord Bingham LCJ. He quoted from the judgment of Lightman J in *R v Merthyr Tydfil Crown Court, ex p Chief Constable of Dyfed Powys*[3], who in turn quoted from Roch J in the earlier case of *R v Totnes Licensing Justices, ex p Chief Constable of Devon and Cornwall*. Roch J stated (quoted by Bingham LCJ at para 11 of the judgment in *Bradford Metropolitan Borough Council v Booth*):

'In my judgment it was wrong for the justices to treat this matter as civil proceedings between two private litigants and to ignore the factor urged upon them by the solicitor appearing for the police authority, namely, that the police have a function which they are required to perform. They are required to supervise the proper conduct of the licensed premises and to object in those cases where there are good grounds for objecting to the renewal of the licence. That that is the police's function is clearly demonstrated by the provisions in the Licensing Act which give the police power to enter licensed premises whether at the invitation of the licensee or not.

In addition, in my view, the police authority must also bring to the attention of the licensing justices matters of which the police know and which can fairly and properly be said to amount to misconduct by the licensee or those for whom he is responsible ...'

This was quoted with approval by Lightman J, who added (quoted by Bingham LCJ at para 13 of the judgment in *Bradford Metropolitan Borough Council v Booth*):

'In my view, the position is quite clear: the same principle applies before the Crown Court as before the licensing justices. The language of the relevant rules is for all practical purposes identical. This is reinforced by the consideration that the proceedings before the Crown Court take place by way of rehearing. In the same way as the justices need the assistance of the police in respect of the provision of any information which may assist them in deciding whether or not the Applicant is a fit person to hold a licence, the Crown Court requires that assistance. It seems to me that no order can properly be made against the police simply on the basis that costs follow the event. The Crown Court can only make such an order if it can be shown that the police's position has been totally unreasonable or prompted by some improper motive.'

The Lord Chief Justice concluded the *Bradford* case as follows:

'22. It seems to me that the justices in this case misdirected themselves, first, in relying on a principle that costs should follow the event, that misdirection being compounded by their view that the reference in section 64 to the order being just and reasonable applied to quantum only. On the other hand, in my judgment the submissions made by Mr Blair-Gould on behalf of the local authority go too far the other way since to give effect to the principle for which he contends would deprive the justices of any discretion to view the case in the round which is in my judgment what section 64 intends.

23. I would accordingly hold that the proper approach to questions of this kind can for convenience be summarised is three propositions:

24. Section 64(1) confers a discretion upon a magistrates' court to make such order as to costs as it thinks just and reasonable. That provision applies both to the quantum of the costs (if any) to be paid, but also as to the party (if any) which should pay them.

25. What the court will think just and reasonable will depend on all the relevant facts and circumstances of the case before the court. The court may think it just and reasonable that costs should follow the event, but need not think so in all cases covered by the subsection.

26. Where a complainant has successfully challenged before justices an administrative decision made by a police or regulatory authority acting honestly, reasonably, properly and on grounds that reasonably appeared to be sound, in exercise of its public duty, the court should consider, in addition to any other relevant fact or circumstances, both (i) the financial prejudice to the particular complainant in the particular circumstances if an order for costs is not made in his favour; and (ii) the need to encourage public authorities to make and stand by honest, reasonable and apparently sound administrative decisions made in the public interest without fear of exposure to undue financial prejudice if the decision is successfully challenged.'

1   [2000] COD 338, QBD.
2   [1998] 46 LS Gaz R 35.
3   (1990) 156 JP 587, Times, 28 May.

Powell v City and County of Swansea

3.27

Appeal against refusal to grant hackney carriage vehicle licences. Council had failed to process the applications correctly. Appeal successful. Costs awarded distinguishing *Bradford v Booth* because council acted unreasonably.

It can be seen that *Bradford Metropolitan Borough Council v Booth*[1] is an extremely important case which recognises that for local authorities to adequately be able to discharge their functions the threat of costs must only apply in extraordinary circumstances[2]. However it must also be realised that this is not an automatic bar to costs being awarded against the local authority. In *Powell v City and County of Swansea*[3] there was a failure on the part of the Council to correctly process applications for the renewal and transfer of four hackney carriage vehicle licences. As a consequence the applications were refused. This was overturned by the magistrates on appeal, and the magistrates refused to award costs against the council on the basis of the decision in *Bradford Metropolitan Borough Council v Booth*. The successful licensee appealed this part of the judgment. The case was heard by Mr Justice Pitchford. He concluded:

'9. While the justices found that the primary duty to make completed applications to the respondent [the council] in due time rested upon the appellant [Mr Powell], their reason for allowing the appeal was that he had complied. He had served the applications upon the respondent within due time, namely before the end of the expiration of the current licence. While the justices found that the respondent acted in accordance with its policies, the respondent had conceded during the hearing that the policy was wrongly applied to these applications, since these applications should have been treated as applications for renewal, to which the policy did not apply. Given these findings, it seems to me that the reasons given by the justices did not in fact support the justices' decision to decline an award of costs, since on their finding there was nothing more that the appellant either should have done or could have done in the absence of instruction received from the respondent. They could not, in other words, support the view that the respondent acted reasonably in refusing the applications upon procedural grounds.

10. In accordance with the guidance provided by Lord Bingham [in *Bradford Metropolitan Borough Council v Booth* 3 at para 26], it was necessary first for the justices to consider whether the regulatory authority acted "honestly, reasonably, properly and on grounds that reasonably appeared to be sound". There can be no doubt that the respondent acted honestly in the exercise of its public duty. The issue before the justices was whether in the light of the court's findings the decision of the regulatory authority could be said to have been reached reasonably and properly and on grounds that reasonably appeared to be sound at the time. The submission made to the justices on the appellant's behalf was the respondent had not acted reasonably. Considerations of financial prejudice did not arise. It is my judgment that the justices erred in concluding that the decision was made on grounds that reasonably appeared to be sound. In view of their findings this was plainly a case for an award of costs, since the respondent had purported to apply to the applications a policy which it could not apply.

11. I would answer the stated question ["In view of the findings of fact in this case, did the Magistrates err in law (or were the magistrates wrong

in law) in refusing the Appellant his costs in whole or in part?" at para 8] "yes". I would find that this was plainly a case for an award of costs in favour of the appellant and ... I would remit the case to the justices for further consideration of the sum to be awarded.'

Accordingly, unless the local authority acted not only honestly, but also reasonably and properly, costs may be awarded against them.

1   [2000] COD 338, QBD.
2   For applications of the principle in *Bradford v Booth* see eg, *R (app Cambridge City Council) v Alex Nestling Limited* [2006] EWHC 1374 (Admin) [2006] LLR 397.
3   (30 July 2003, unreported), Admin Ct.

R (app Perinpanathan) v Westminster Magistrates' Court and another

3.28

> Seizure of cash under Proceeds of Crime Act 2002. Successful appeal. Costs not awarded against police. *Bradford v Booth* followed and approved by Court of Appeal.

The question of whether the decision in *Bradford v Booth*[1] was correct was considered by the Court of Appeal in *R (app Perinpanathan) v Westminster Magistrates' Court and another*[2]. The case concerned a successful defence of proceedings brought by the police for the confiscation of cash which had been seized by the police under the provisions of the Proceeds of Crime Act 2002. At the magistrates' court where the decision was made, the court refused to award costs against the successful defendant on the basis of the ruling in *Bradford v Booth*[3] and because the 'application was reasonably made [by the Police].' The decision to refuse costs was judicially reviewed and dismissed by the High Court. It was appealed to the Court of Appeal, where the principal judgment was given by Stanley Burnton LJ. His views were supported by Neuberger MR and Maurice Kay LJ.

Stanley Burnton LJ reviewed a number of authorities and concluded[4]:

'The effect of the authorities

40. I derive the following propositions from the authorities to which I have referred:

1.   As a result of the decision of the Court of Appeal in *Baxendale-Walker*[5], the principle in the *City of Bradford* case is binding on this Court. Quite apart from authority, however, for the reasons given by Lord Bingham LCJ I would respectfully endorse its application in licensing proceedings in the magistrates' court and the Crown Court.

2.   For the same reasons, the principle is applicable to disciplinary proceedings before tribunals at first instance brought by public authorities acting in the public interest: *Baxendale-Walker.*

3.   Whether the principle should be applied in other contexts will depend on the substantive legislative framework and the applicable procedural provisions.
4.   The principle does not apply in proceedings to which the CPR apply.
5.   Where the principle applies, and the party opposing the order sought by the public authority has been successful, in relation to costs the starting point and default position is that no order should be made.
6.   A successful private party to proceedings to which the principle applies may nonetheless be awarded all or part of his costs if the conduct of the public authority in question justifies it.
7.   Other facts relevant to the exercise of the discretion conferred by the applicable procedural rules may also justify an order for costs. It would not be sensible to try exhaustively to define such matters, and I do not propose to do so.

41. Lord Bingham LCJ stated that financial prejudice to the private party may justify an order for costs in his favour. I think it clear that the financial prejudice necessarily involved in litigation would not normally justify an order. If that were not so, an order would be made in every case in which the successful private party incurred legal costs. Lord Bingham LCJ had in mind a case in which the successful private party would suffer substantial hardship if no order for costs was made in his favour. I respectfully agree with what Toulson J (with whom Richards LJ agreed) said in *R (Cambridge City Council) v Alex Nestling Ltd*[6]:

> 12. As to the financial loss suffered by the successful appellant, a successful appellant who has to bear his own costs will necessarily be out of pocket, and that is the reason in ordinary civil litigation for the principle that costs follow the event. But that principle does not apply in this type of case. When Lord Bingham referred to the need to consider the financial prejudice to a particular complainant in the particular circumstances, he was not in implying that an award for costs should routinely follow in favour of a successful appellant; quite to the contrary.

42. I would also comment that there may have been a tendency to focus more on Lord Bingham LCJ's answer to the straightforward issue defined in paragraph 1 of his judgment than to the more nuanced propositions set out under paragraph 23. Ultimately, the duty of the magistrates' court is to make such order as to costs as is just and reasonable, subject to the constraint imposed by section 64."

It is therefore clear that the principle in *Bradford v Booth*[7] was not only correct but was also correctly applied.

1   [2000] COD 338, QBD above.
2   [2010] EWCA Civ 40, [2010] 1 WLR 1508.
3   [2000] COD 338, QBD above.
4   [2010] EWCA Civ 40, [2010] 1 WLR 1508 at paragraph 40.
5   *Baxendale-Walker v the Law Society* [2007] EWCA Civ 233, [2008] 1 WLR 426.

6   R (app Cambridge City Council) v Alex Nestling Limited [2006] EWHC 1374 (Admin), [2006] LLR 397.

7   [2000] COD 338, QBD above.

Meaning of 'person aggrieved'

Cook v Southend Borough Council

3.29

> Revocation of hackney carriage drivers licence. Appeal to magistrates' court successful. Decided by Court of Appeal that Council could appeal that decision to the Crown Court as they were a 'person aggrieved'.

The wording of most of the appeal provisions is that an appeal is available to any 'person aggrieved'. This is usually taken as meaning a person who is not granted a licence or is granted a licence subject to conditions which they find unacceptable. Since the case of *Cook v Southend Borough Council*[1] it has become clear that a local authority can be a 'person aggrieved' for the purposes of such appeals.

In this case, the Court of Appeal considered whether it was possible for a local authority to be a 'person aggrieved' after a decision by a magistrates' court, following an appeal against the local authority's decision in relation to hackney carriage and private hire licensing.

In a comprehensive judgment, Woolf LJ stated as follows (at 7B):

'In these circumstances it is, I hope, useful if I set out certain general propositions which I would expect to apply where the expression "a person aggrieved" is used in relation to a right of appeal in the absence of a clear contrary intention in a particular statutory context. (1) A body corporate including a local authority is just as capable of being a person aggrieved as an individual. (2) Any person who has a decision decided against him (particularly in adversarial proceedings) will be a person aggrieved for the purposes of appealing against that decision unless the decision amounts to an acquittal of a purely criminal offence. In the latter case the statutory context will be all important. (3) The fact that the decision against which the person wishes to appeal reverses a decision which was originally taken by that person and does not otherwise adversely affect that person does not prevent that person being aggrieved. On the contrary it indicates that he is a person aggrieved who is entitled to exercise the right of appeal in order to have the original decision restored.

Turning to the circumstances giving rise to this appeal, in the absence of authority I would have no hesitation in coming to the conclusion that irrespective of whether or not the justices had made an order for costs, the council had a right of appeal under section 301.'

1   [1990] 2 QB 1, CA.

3.30

There had been a number of earlier cases which his Lordship considered at length, most of which made a distinction between the position of a council which had had costs awarded against it by the magistrates' court and those where no such costs were awarded against a council. This had led to the anomalous situation whereby a council was actually in a better position if it had had costs awarded against it, because it had a right of appeal, as opposed to a council where no costs had been awarded against it and had no right of appeal. His Lordship took the view that this was absurd and that the question of costs was irrelevant. The grievance felt by the local authority was in losing the appeal, rather than in having costs awarded against it, and he concluded[1] (at 18H):

> 'I would therefore dismiss this appeal on the basis that the council was a person aggrieved by the decision of the Southend justices quite apart from the order for costs which was made against the council. However, even if this is not the position, the effect of the order for costs is to make this case indistinguishable from the decision of the House of Lords in *Jennings v Kelly* [1940] AC 206.
>
> It follows in my view this appeal must be dismissed.'

[1] *Cook v Southend Borough Council* [1990] 2 QB 1, CA.

3.31

This has wide-ranging implications, as it allows the local authority to appeal when it feels that the decision of the magistrates, on overturning the local authority's decision, was wrongly made and enables it to then appeal to the Crown Court. This ability has been used on a number of occasions since 1990, with varying success.

Swansea City and County Council v Davies

3.32

> Condition requiring notice to be displayed on private hire vehicles. Appeal brought against that condition by a hackney carriage proprietor. Was he a 'person aggrieved' notwithstanding the condition had not been attached to his licence? Held: That he was, as close relationship between both types of vehicle.

It is also possible for others to fall within the definition of 'person aggrieved', beyond the unsuccessful applicant or existing licensee and the council. In the case of *Swansea City and County Council v Davies*[1], it was held that a hackney carriage proprietor could be a person aggrieved and therefore appeal against a condition which had been attached to a private hire proprietor's licence. The facts were as follows.

The council of the City and County of Swansea adopted a policy and accordingly, imposed a condition on private hire vehicle licences, that private hire vehicles would: 'be required to display signs identifying the name and telephone number of the company under which the vehicle operated together with a statement "pre-booked fares only". The signs would be 37cm × 10cm, illuminated and displayed in the top right hand corner of the front windscreen and on the rear windscreen not illuminated and displayed in the top left hand corner. The word "Taxi" should not be included on the signs.'

This condition was imposed under LG(MP)A 1976, s 48(2). The proposal caused considerable controversy with the hackney carriage licensed proprietors, who felt that it would lead to confusion between the two types of vehicle. Mr Davies was a hackney carriage proprietor and he appealed against the condition imposed on the private hire vehicle licences, arguing that he was 'Any person aggrieved by ... any conditions specified in such a [private hire vehicle] licence' and as a result 'may appeal to a magistrates' court' within the meaning of s 48(7).

The council contended that he did not have locus standi to bring an appeal, but the magistrates found in Davies' favour on the preliminary question as to whether or not he was in fact a person aggrieved. The council appealed by way of case stated to the Queens Bench Division before Munby J. The arguments centred on whether a 'person aggrieved' was limited to a private hire vehicle licence holder or whether it could have a wider meaning.

Munby J addressed the issue thus:

'19. Although a number of authorities have been referred to in the course of argument, neither Mr Thomas [for the Council] nor Mr Maddox [for Mr Davies], as I indicated, suggest that any particular case is more than illustrative of past approaches. Mr Thomas has very helpfully drawn to my attention a passage in Halsbury's Laws in England, Volume 1(1), paragraph 56. That passage reads as follows:

"The meaning of a 'person aggrieved' may vary according to the context, but a person will not be held to be aggrieved by a decision if that decision is not materially adverse to him or if the tribunal to which he seeks to appeal has no jurisdiction to find in his favour. Nor, in general, is it enough for a person to show that he is dissatisfied with the order made or that his interests are likely to be prejudiced by the outcome. He is normally required to establish that he has been denied of deprived of something to which he is legally entitled, or that the decision has imposed a legal burden on him, or that (as in the case of a licensing decision against which a right of appeal is provided by statute) the adverse impact of the decision on his interests is so direct that he must be regarded as falling within the statutory category of persons aggrieved by it. In some contexts, however, the expression has been interpreted more broadly to include persons objecting to a licensing application that has been granted, and other persons who have a substantial grievance in respect of an order, proposal or decision prejudicially affecting their interests but not encroaching directly upon them."

20. Both Mr Thomas and Mr Maddox, as I understand their respective submissions, accept that as being a fair, accurate and useful summary of the relevant principles.

21. Ultimately, it seems to me, this appeal turns on the meaning and the interpretation to be given to the words in this particular statute having regard to the particular statutory context. At the end the day, it seems to me, there are three considerations which point to the conclusion at which I have arrived, namely that the Justices were correct in their determination that the respondent was a "person aggrieved". The first is Mr Maddox's submission that if the draftsman had intended to limit the persons entitled to exercise the right under section 48(7) as Mr Thomas would have it, he could and would have achieved that objective by more narrowly drawn language. Secondly, and reinforcing that argument, it does seem to me that in this case the draftsman has in the other sections of the Act which were brought to my attention been able to use appropriately confined language on those occasions when he intended to achieve such a result. That is indicative of an intention in section 48(7) to have, if anything, a wider rather than a narrower class of person who is to be entitled to exercise a right to appeal.

22. That is not to say that the class is limitless. Nothing which I say today is to be taken as indicating that the class of "persons aggrieved" under section 48(7) extends any further than the class of persons who are represented, as it were, by the respondent. I am certainly not indicating that the class of "persons aggrieved" would extend, for example, to the public generally or to any other section of the community.

23. That leads me to the third matter. Having regard to the statutory context, it seems to me that it is appropriate in construing section 48(7) to have regard to the statutory principle in proviso (a)(ii) to section 48(1) of the Act, that licences for private hire vehicles are not to be granted by a district council if the vehicle in question is such that either in design or appearance it may lead any person to believe that the vehicle is a Hackney Carriage. It seems to me that that is indicative of a context under which the statutory mechanism in section 48 is seeking to draw a clear distinction between two different categories of vehicles, that is to say, on the one hand Private Hire Vehicles and, on the other hand Hackney Carriages. That seems to me something to which one should have regard in forming a view as to the width of section 48(7) and it does seem to me that that is supportive of [sic 24] Mr Maddox's submission that the respondent, as the holder of a Hackney Carriage licence is, as I find him to be, a "person aggrieved" within the meaning of section 48(7).

25. I return to the question which the justices have raised for the opinion of the High Court:

"Can the respondent in this case, a hackney carriage vehicle licence holder be a 'person aggrieved' by a condition imposed on a private hire vehicle licence for the purposes of an appeal on section 48(7) of the Local Government (Miscellaneous Provisions) Act 1976."

26. I answer that question in the affirmative.'

Notwithstanding the limiting of this judgment in para 22, this is clearly a very important decision, which can enable a wider range of people to challenge certain decisions of local authorities by using the easier, quicker and cheaper route of an appeal to the magistrates' court, when without this case, they would have had to seek redress in the Administrative Court via judicial review proceedings.

[1]   [2001] RTR 54, QBD.

Peddubriwny v Cambridge City Council

3.33

> Enquiry made to local authority about a private hire driver's licence, but no application made or licence granted. No right of appeal against a condition on such a licence arose as no licence held.

A slightly different point was raised in the case of *Peddubriwny v Cambridge City Council*[1]. Mr Peddubriwny held a hackney carriage driver's licence issued by Cambridge City Council. He inquired about obtaining a private hire driver's licence, and was told that police checks would have to be undertaken before the licence could be issued initially and then would need to be repeated every three years.

He never applied for a private hire driver's licence, but appealed to the magistrates' court on the basis that he was a person aggrieved by a condition attached to a private hire driver's licence, namely the requirement to undergo a police check every three years. He based his appeal on LG(MP)A 1976, s 52 which states:

'Any person aggrieved by—
(1)   the refusal of the district council to grant a driver's licence under section 51 of this Act; or
(2)   any conditions attached to the grant of a driver's licence;
       may appeal to a magistrates' court.'

The magistrates dismissed his appeal as he was not a person aggrieved, and so did the Crown Court on a subsequent appeal from the decision of the magistrates. He appealed to the High Court by way of case stated.

[1]   [2001] EWHC 200 (Admin), [2001] RTR 461.

3.34

The case of *Swansea City and County Council v Davies*[1], was cited, but dismissed. The court held that it was quite clear that unless a person had either been refused a private hire driver's licence, or had such a licence grated subject to conditions, no appeal under LG(MP)A 1976, s 52 was possible. Mr Justice Silber stated:

'19. If I had been in any doubt about the need for an actual application, I would have reached an identical conclusion by analysing section 52, the triggering event for which is a refusal or the imposition of conditions attached to the grant of licences and those triggering events can only follow an actual application being made. A potential applicant for a licence does not, in my view, have the standing to bring an appeal under section 52.

20. Indeed, to find otherwise would entail rewriting section 52(2) so that it would cover not as at present any conditions attached to the grant of a driver's licence but with emphasis added "any conditions that might be attached to the grant of a driver's licence." I do not believe there is any justification whatsoever for rewriting section 52(2) in this way or at all. The legislature has made the position quite clear and the stark fact is that a person has to have made an application before he can have the right to bring an appeal under section 52(2).'

It was contended by Peddubriwny that the effect of that was to require any person who might in the future, if granted a private hire driver's licence, be aggrieved by the conditions that would be attached to the licence, to seek judicial review of the policy that would lead to those conditions, thereby placing him in a less advantageous position than a licensee. He contended this created an anomaly. Again, this was dismissed by Silber J:

'25. It is also argued on behalf of the appellant that the approach of the crown court would mean that he would be placed in an anomalous position as he would have to resort to judicial review proceedings. I do not understand what is anomalous about it. The legislature has made a clear decision to who should have the right of appeal in the Magistrates' Court and my task is to follow their intention and not to query it. Even if I thought, which is not the case, that it was anomalous, it must not be forgotten that the remedy of judicial review is a valuable and important remedy available to the parties.'

His conclusion was as follows:

'26. As I have had the benefit of full arguments on the conditions that have to be satisfied before an appeal can be brought under section 52, I believe that I should state that I believe that Mr Miller, on behalf of the respondents [Cambridge City Council], was right when he submitted that a party can only bring an application under section 52 if:

(a) he has made an application for a licence;

(b) such application has been received by the council;

(c) the application was either refused or granted with conditions attached and

(d) the Applicant is aggrieved by (c) namely the refusal of the application or the conditions attached to the grant of it.

27. On the facts of this case, the appellant fails on each of the grounds (a), (b), (c) and (d). I must now return to the question which was posed for this Court which was:

> "Whether we were correct in holding that in the circumstances, the Appellant, not having in July 1999 applied for a licence to drive private hire vehicles and not having been refused such a licence nor had a licence issued with conditions, was not a person aggrieved within the meaning of section 52 of the Act and in consequences [sic] could not bring a complaint under that action against the Respondent."

28. For the reasons which I have given, and notwithstanding the careful and able arguments of Miss Garner [for Mr Peddubriwny], the answer to that question raised must be in the affirmative. The appeal is therefore dismissed.'

[1] [2001] RTR 54, QBD; see para 3.32 above.

Time limits for Appeals

3.35

The time-scales involved in an appeal to the magistrates' court are contained within the Public Health Act 1936, s 300. This requires any appeal to be brought within 21 days 'from the date on which notice of the council's requirement, refusal or other decision was served upon the person desiring to appeal'. Such an appeal is by way of complaint.

3.36

Most local authorities communicate their decision to the applicant in writing and the 21 days to make an appeal takes effect from the date on which that letter is deemed to have been received by the unsuccessful applicant. By virtue of the Interpretation Act 1978, s 7, service is deemed to be effected 'at the time at which the letter would be delivered in the ordinary course of post'. As a consequence of a Practice Direction[1], for a letter sent first class, it will be the second working day after posting, and the fourth working day after posting if sent second class, subject to any proof to the contrary. This is notwithstanding the fact that the applicant may well have been told of the decision in person at the determination of the hearing. This simply gives the applicant slightly longer to get his appeal lodged and it would appear difficult to argue successfully that such verbal notice is the date from which time runs.

[1] [1985] 1 All ER 889.

3.37

The Public Health Act 1936, s 300(3) states:

> 'in any case where such an appeal lies, the document notifying to the person concerned the decision of the council in the matter shall state the right of

appeal to a court of summary jurisdiction and the time within which such an appeal may be brought.'

It is therefore vital that the letter or notice informing the applicant of the decision contains details of his right of appeal and the time-scales involved.

Extension of Appeal Period

3.38

Is the 21-day appeal period from the decision of the council for a magistrates' appeal and from the decision of the magistrates for a Crown Court appeal an absolute limit, or can it be extended at the discretion of the court? This was the question that arose in *Stockton-on-Tees Borough Council v Latif*[1].

[1]   [2009] EWHC 228 (Admin), [2009] LLR 374.

Stockton-on-Tees Borough Council v Latif

3.39

> Appeal against a decision to revoke his hackney carriage and private hire vehicle licences. Beyond 21 day limit. Held: Appeal period cannot be extended.

In the case of *Stockton-on-Tees Borough Council v Latif*[1] the appellant lodged his appeal against a decision to revoke his hackney carriage and private hire vehicle licences[2], but the appeal was lodged outside the 21-day period. The magistrates refused to hear the appeal. Latif appealed to the Crown Court which 'for reasons that are not apparent to [the Judge] the Crown Court assumed that the Magistrates' Court decision was based on a refusal to extend time on the basis of discretion rather than lack of jurisdiction'[3] allowed the appeal and remitted the case to the magistrates' court for a rehearing on the merits.

Stockton-on-Tees BC challenged that decision by way of case stated and three questions were posed for the High Court:

'(i)   Whether the court was wrong in law to allow an extension of the time for appealing from the licensing committee to the Magistrates' Court when the Public Heath Act 1936 and the Local Government (Miscellaneous Provisions) Act 1976 do not provide for any statutory extension of the 21 day appeal period.

(ii)   Whether the court was wrong in law to apply the Civil Procedure Rules, r 3,1(2)(a) and r 52 in extending the statutory time for the appeal.

(iii) Whether the Magistrates' Court, and/or the Crown Court on appeal from the Magistrates' Court have power to extend the 21 day time for appealing under s 300 of the Public Health Act 1936.'[4]

The conclusions reached were as follows[5]:

'[20] The terms of the s 300 of the Public Health Act 1936 are, in my view clear. A fixed period of 21 days is given to bring an appeal. Parliament did not provide for an extension of time which it clearly could have done if that had been the intention. In addition Parliament made it mandatory that the document notifying the person of the decision should state the right of appeal and the time within which such an appeal might be brought. That, it seems to me, is a pointer to the importance of compliance with the time limit and would militate against any implied right of extending the time.

[21] Similarly applying a purposive approach there does not seem to me to be any good reason not to apply the clear meaning of the words. I have mentioned the requirement to tell the Applicant of the time limit. But the failure to comply is not all that draconian. It is open to the former licence holder to apply for a new licence which is likely to be granted or rejected on similar grounds as before and an appeal can if necessary follow. It does not therefore seem to me there is any compelling reason to reach the conclusion that Parliament could not have intended a strict time limit as the words suggest.

[22] It does not seem to me that the rules of court can assist here. CPR 3.1(2)(a) refers to "any rule, practice direction or court order" none of which apply here and I respectfully adopt the views of Latham LJ in *Barcys* set out above.

[23] It follows that in my opinion the Crown Court was wrong to extend the time limit in this case since there was no jurisdiction to do so. I should point out that the court did not have the benefit of the Extradition cases which were placed before me.

[24] The answer to the questions posed in para 3 above is therefore:

(i) Yes.
(ii) Yes.
(iii) No.'

Accordingly it is clear that there is no ability on the part of a court (either magistrates or Crown), or indeed a local authority, to allow any extension to the 21-day time limit for appeals.

[1] [2009] EWHC 228 (Admin), [2009] LLR 374.
[2] The transcript refers to 'a combined Hackney Carriage and Private Hire Vehicle licence', but it is suggested that this must in fact have been a combined Hackney Carriage and Private Hire *drivers'* licence.
[3] Per Mr Christopher Symons QC (sitting as a deputy judge of the High Court) at para 8.
[4] [2009] EWHC 228 (Admin), [2009] LLR 374 at para 3.
[5] [2009] EWHC 228 (Admin), [2009] LLR 374 at para 20 onwards.

3.40

A further right of appeal lies to the Crown Court by virtue of the Public Health Act 1936, s 301. In this situation, the Crown Court sits as an appeal court against the decision of the magistrates' court below. The method of commencing such an appeal is laid down in the Crown Court Rules 1982, Pt III[1].

The procedure in the Crown Court is much the same as the procedure in the magistrates' court. The Crown Court sits with a judge and two magistrates from jurisdictions other than that which heard the appeal to the magistrates' court[2]. In the case of an appeal against a refusal to grant a hackney carriage proprietor's licence, or in areas where LG(MP)A 1976 has not been adopted, magistrates should be from a jurisdiction other than that which covers the authority against whom the decision is being made.

[1]   SI 1982/1109. Within this chapter, reference is still made to the Magistrates' Courts Rules 1981, SI 1981/552 and the Crown Court Rules 1982, SI 1982/1109. Although both of these were ostensibly repealed by the Criminal Procedure Rules 2005, SI 2005/384 as amended (CPR), the CPR clearly state that they only apply to criminal cases in criminal courts (see ss 69(1) and 68 of the Courts Act 2003 and CPR r 2.1), and therefore it appears to be the case that hackney carriage and private hire appeals to both the magistrates' court and the Crown Court are still governed by the Magistrates' Courts Rules 1981 and the Crown Court Rules 1982.
[2]   Senior Courts Act 1981, s 74.

3.41

Once again, the Crown Court has a discretion to award costs under the Crown Court Rules 1982, r 12[1] and can substitute its decision for that of the magistrates' court or local authority. Evidential and procedural matters remain as for the magistrates' court. As the situation in respect of costs in the Crown Court is the same as the magistrates' court it would appear that the ruling in *Bradford Metropolitan Borough Council v Booth*[2] applies equally. If hearsay evidence is to be admitted in an appeal to the Crown Court, the requirements of the Civil Evidence Act 1995 must be complied with.

[1]   SI 1982/1109. See footnote to para 3.40 above.
[2]   [2000] COD 338; see para 3.26 above.

Further appeals

3.42

The magistrates' court and Crown Court are the only venues for statutory rights of appeal, but it is possible to appeal further, on a point of law, against the decision of either the magistrates' court or Crown Court, by way of 'case stated'.

3.43

In the case of an appeal from the Crown Court, this is an appeal to the High Court under the provisions of the Senior Courts Act 1981, s 28 and is available on the grounds that the 'order, judgment or other decision' was 'wrong in law, or is in excess of the jurisdiction'.

3.44

If the appeal is from the magistrates' court, the provisions of the Magistrates' Courts Act 1980, s 111 apply to any 'conviction order, determination or other proceeding of the Court' on the grounds that it was 'wrong in law, or is in excess of the jurisdiction'.

3.45

The procedure for both applications is contained in the Civil Procedure Rules, Part 52 rule 52.19.

R v Reading Crown Court, ex p Reading Borough Council

3.46

> Refusal to renew a private hire driver's licence because of his previous convictions. Successful appeal at Crown Court. Local Authority sought to appeal by way of case stated. Refusal by Crown Court to state case. Judicial review of that decision failed.

In *R v Reading Crown Court, ex p Reading Borough Council*[1], the Crown Court judge refused to state a case at the request of the local authority. The local authority had refused to renew a private hire driver's licence because of his previous convictions. In 1993, the first check was made of his criminal record by the local authority and the full extent of his record was revealed – this included an assault, when acting as a taxi driver (which would appear to be an early example of road rage), an offence of driving without due care and attention and a conviction for theft as a result of shop-lifting. There were numerous other convictions which had taken place over previous years. The applicant appealed to the magistrates' court, which dismissed his appeal. He then appealed to the Crown Court, which upheld his appeal. The local authority sought a judicial review of the judge's decision not to state a case. This was dismissed. The High Court decided that there were no grounds on which a case could be stated and, even though the decision to allow the appeal may have been surprising, it was not so extraordinary that no reasonable judge could have reached it. Collins J concluded:

> 'It may be that this was an unexpected decision. But the test is not whether I would have reached the same decision or whether another court would have reached the same decision. The test is whether this decision is such that no reasonable body could have reached it. In my judgment, it cannot be so described. It seems to me that it was a decision to which the learned judge and his colleagues were entitled to come on the material before them. In those circumstances, there were no grounds upon which a case could properly be stated. Even if the case should have been stated, the inevitable result would have been that the appeal would be dismissed. Accordingly, it seems to me that both these applications must be refused.'

This case provides a salutary lesson that, occasionally, decisions seem wrong, but that this has to be accepted by the losing party. Sometimes, there is nothing that can be done about an appeal result.

[1]   [1996] COD 90.

Judicial review

3.47

There are occasions when it is the decision-making process of the local authority which is open to challenge and, when that is the case, the method of challenge is by way of judicial review of the local authority's decision.

R v Halton Borough Council, ex p Poynton

3.48

> No application actually made to the council for a licence. No decision to refuse or grant taken. No locus for judicial review as no decision made.

Before that can be done, however, the local authority has to have taken a decision. This was demonstrated in the case of *R v Halton Borough Council, ex p Poynton*[1]. Halton Borough Council had a policy of only granting private hire drivers' licences to people who would work as full-time private hire drivers. Mr Poynton completed an application form and stated he was already in full-time employment and intended to drive a private hire vehicle on a part-time basis. He was told by the local authority that it would not be able to accept his application. The local authority subsequently accepted that it was wrong to refuse to accept his application and that it would consider his case on its merits. Correspondence took place between the local authority and the solicitors acting for Mr Poynton; however, no application was actually received by the local authority. An application for leave to seek judicial review was therefore made. This was unsuccessful, for the reasons given by Otton J:

> 'In my judgment in the absence of any decision on the application made by this applicant this court does not have jurisdiction or power to order mandamus against the council to act or refrain from acting in a situation where the appropriate committee has had no opportunity to consider the matter at all. It is manifest from the correspondence that the council has been ready and willing to consider the application and to determine it on its merits.
>
>   It is thus open to the applicant to argue that the policy is ultra vires or that he falls outside it or that the only power the council has to limit his activities is to attach to the grant of a licence such conditions as they consider reasonably necessary under subsection (2) of section 51 [LG(MP)A 1976, s 51(2)].
>
>   I am satisfied that it would be wrong for this court to attempt to deal with this application in vacuo and in the absence of any decision one way or the other. In reality, I consider that this application is an attempt to obtain from judicial review a writ of certiorari to bring up and quash a policy as it exists and which has been in existence for three years. This in my judgment is an inappropriate use of judicial review powers and procedures.

In arriving at this conclusion I also bear in mind that there is an alternative remedy open to the applicant in the event of an adverse finding by the council. He would be free to go to the magistrates and he may … succeed either before the justices or before the Crown Court. I see nothing oppressive or unjust in requiring Mr Poynton to pursue this remedy.

This application is therefore refused.'

1 (1989) 1 Admin LR 83.

R v Blackpool Borough Council, ex p Red Cab Taxis Ltd

3.49

> Conditions attached to private hire licences. Judicial review sought rather than appealing to magistrates' court. Held: Usually any statutory appeal should be exhausted before judicial review pursued.

However, judicial review is not generally appropriate when there is a statutory right of appeal against a decision or action of the local authority[1]. This view was upheld by Judge J in *R v Blackpool Borough Council, ex p Red Cab Taxis Ltd*[2], where judicial review was sought relating to the imposition of conditions on private hire vehicle licences. As there was a statutory right of appeal to the magistrates' court and subsequently to the Crown Court, that route had to be used in preference to judicial review. Judge J said (at 410E):

'In exercising my discretion I have attempted to balance the very many differing factors, some of which stand together and weigh down on one side, and some of which of course are diametrically opposed. Having reflected on the matter, my conclusion is that, notwithstanding that the decision-making process was flawed, the main issue in the case, the condition, in the overall interests of everyone – the council, the applicants, the drivers of taxis and the people living locally – should have been, and still could be best considered and decided by the justices in Blackpool in accordance with their statutory procedures. Such proceedings would have been more rapid and cheaper and ultimately of greater practical value to all those involved, including the applicants themselves.'

1 For occasions when it may be see *R v Lincoln City Council, ex p King and Cook* and *R v Luton Borough Council, ex p Mirza* (2 February 1995, unreported), CA.
2 [1994] RTR 402, QBD.

R (app Wilford) v Financial Services Authority

3.50

> Statutory appeals should be used in preference to judicial review, except in exceptional circumstances.

This approach has been reinforced by subsequent decisions. In *R (app Wilford) v Financial Services Authority*[1] Moore-Bick LJ stated[2]:

> 'The starting point, as emphasised by cases such as *Preston*[3], *Calveley*[4], *Ferrero*[5], *Falmouth*[6] and *Davies*[7], is that only in exceptional cases will the court entertain a claim for judicial review if there is an alternative remedy available to the applicant. The alternative remedy will almost invariably have been provided by statute and where Parliament has provided a remedy it is important to identify the intended scope of the relevant statutory provision. For example, in the context of legislation to protect public health the court is very likely to infer that Parliament intended the statutory procedure to apply, even in cases where it is alleged that the decision was arrived at in a way that would otherwise enable it to be challenged on public law grounds, because it enables the real question in dispute to be decided. That will be particularly so if the procedure allows a full reconsideration on the merits of a decision which has direct implications for public health and safety. A remedy by way of judicial review, although relatively quick to obtain, simply returns the parties to their original positions. It does not enable the court to determine the merits of the underlying dispute. In a few cases strong reasons of policy may dictate a different approach: see *R v Hereford Magistrates' Court, ex parte Rowlands*[8]; but such cases are themselves exceptional and do not in my view detract from the general principle. Ultimately, of course, the court retains a discretion to entertain a claim for judicial review, but whether it will do so in any given case depends on the nature of the dispute and the particular circumstances in which it arises.'

1   [2013] EWCA Civ 677 (unreported).
2   [2013] EWCA Civ 677 (unreported) at paragraph 36.
3   *Re Preston* [1985] AC 835.
4   *R v Chief Constable of Merseyside Police, ex p Calveley* [1986] QB 424.
5   *R v Birmingham City Council, ex p Ferrero Ltd* [1993] 1 All ER 830.
6   *R v Falmouth and Truro Port Health Authority ex p South West Water* [2001] QB 445.
7   *R (Davies) v Financial Services Authority* [2003] EWCA Civ 1128, [2004] 1 WLR 185.
8   [1998] QB 110.

R (on the Application of Great Yarmouth Port Company Ltd) v Marine Management Organisation

3.51

> Guidance on what might constitute 'exceptional circumstances' which would allow judicial review to be sought in preference to exercising a statutory right of appeal.

The question of what might constitute 'exceptional circumstances' was addressed by Hickinbottom J in R *(on the Application of Great Yarmouth Port Company Ltd) v Marine Management Organisation*[1].

It was addressed in this fashion:

'52 "Exceptional circumstances" is, of course, a term that defies precise definition; but the higher courts have given guidance. Their Lordships said in both *Preston*[2] and *Harley Development Inc*[3] that, whilst shutting no doors, usually such circumstances would involve something tantamount to an abuse of process by the relevant decision-maker. I find the older cases to which Mr Drabble referred me — such as *R v Paddington Valuation Officer ex parte Peachey Property Corporation*[4] especially at page 400; and *R v Hallstrom ex parte W*[5] at page 852 — to be of less help, because they do not grapple with the important constitutional issues and, over the last few decades, the position of tribunals within the justice system has fundamentally changed and, with that change, the respect accorded to them by the higher courts has risen. Nevertheless, in *Peachey Property Corporation*[6] Lord Denning still set a high bar. He said (at page 400) that prerogative remedies would only be available where the alternative statutory course was "nowhere near so convenient, beneficial and effectual." With the evolution of tribunals over the intervening years, in my respectful view the bar is much higher yet.

53 These authorities, and more, were recently considered by the Court of Appeal in *Willford*[7]. Moore-Bick LJ, giving the judgment of the court, stressed that where Parliament has set up a sophisticated appeal scheme, there is very likely to be an inference that Parliament intended that scheme to apply to the exclusion of judicial review "even in cases where it is alleged that the decision was arrived at in a way that would otherwise enable it to be challenged on public law grounds", including, of course, where the challenge is based upon the proposition that the decision-maker had acted outside his statutory powers. He said that the court would not ordinarily allow a claimant to proceed by way of judicial review, save in exceptional circumstances, "usually because it is satisfied that the alternative remedy is for some reason clearly unsatisfactory."

54 The court [of Appeal] (in particular, at [20], [26] and [30]) identified some of the factors that may be relevant in the exercise of deciding whether the alternative remedy is clearly unsatisfactory, such as the suitability of the statutory appeal in the context of the particular case; the relevant circumstances, including the comparative speed, expense and finality of alternative processes; the need and scope of fact-finding; the desirability of an authoritative ruling on any point of law arising, including, in words of Glidewell LJ in *ex parte W*[8] (at page 852G-H), "whether the alternative statutory remedy will resolve the question at issue fully and directly"; and, finally, although with the caveat "perhaps", the apparent strength of the applicant's substantive challenge. Like others before it, the court emphasised the very rarity of circumstances in which a statutory appeal would be found to be clearly unsatisfactory. I would add that the circumstances will be rare indeed where the alternative remedy falls to the reformed tribunal system which is intended and designed to be comprehensive and sufficient to deal with all issues of fact and law in virtually all circumstances.'

Although it is arguable that the mechanism of appeal in the taxi cases (the magistrates' court, followed by the Crown Court) may not be regarded as a 'reformed tribunal system', there is no doubt that it is a simple, straightforward, reasonably quick and reasonably cheap method of challenging a decision of the local authority. It therefore seems that the likelihood of leave for seeking judicial review being obtained where there is a statutory right of appeal is low[9].

1   [2013] EWHC 3052 (Admin), [2014] LLR 361.
2   R v Inland Revenue ex p Preston [1985] AC 835.
3   Harley Development Inc v Commissioner of Inland Revenue [1996] 1 WLR 727.
4   [1966] 1 QB 380.
5   [1986] QB 824.
6   [1966] 1 QB 380.
7   R (app Wilford) v Financial Services Authority [2013] EWCA Civ 677 (unreported).
8   R v Hallstrom, ex p W [1986] QB 824.
9   This supports the older case of R v Lincoln City Council, ex p King and Cook and R v Luton Borough Council, ex p Mirza (2 February 1995, unreported), CA. The cases concerned wheelchair-accessible hackney carriages, and are considered in detail in Chapter 8, para 8.116.

3.52

There may be some exceptional situations where there is an overlap with some elements of a decision, which could be subject to judicial review, concerning perhaps the vires or power of a policy, as well as other elements, which could be appealed to the magistrates' court. In those situations, judicial review could be launched as well. The conventional wisdom has been that, the magistrates could not reasonably consider the question of vires, but that has been questioned by *R (app Wilford) v Financial Services Authority*[1] and also by *R (on the application of Hope and Glory) v City of Westminster Magistrates' Court*[2]. It remains to be seen what direction the senior courts take in the future on this complex issue.

1   [2013] EWCA Civ 677 (unreported) above.
2   [2011] EWCA Civ 31, [2011] 3 All ER 579, per Toulson LJ at para 7.

R v Leeds City Council, ex p Hendry

3.53

> Judicial review allowed in preference to a right of appeal because incorrect interpretation of policy used to refuse the grant of a private hire licence.

A case where judicial review was granted notwithstanding the existence of a right of appeal was *R v Leeds City Council, ex p Hendry*[1]. In this case, a private hire vehicle licence was refused by the council because, it was alleged, a policy had been adopted whereby any vehicle which was presented for a new licence (and, in this case, the vehicle had previously been licensed as a private hire vehicle, but the licence had lapsed prior to the application, so it was a new application, rather than a renewal) should not be granted one unless (para 441B):

> 'the vehicle was first registered on or after April 1st 1987 and was fitted with inertia reel seat belts of the three point type to all rear seats.'

The applicant sought a judicial review of his refusal, as he felt that the statement was not an accurate statement of the policy which had been adopted by Leeds City Council. On investigation, that proved to be true and the policy in fact was that (para 441G):

> 'The council shall not grant a hackney carriage or private hire vehicle licence, unless the vehicle was manufactured on or after April 1st 1987, or already fitted with only inertia reel seat belts of the three point belt type to all outboard rear seats.'

Latham J considered whether the judicial review was the appropriate means of seeking relief, when an appeal was available by virtue of LG(MP)A 1976, s 48(7), and whether such appeal procedures should be exhausted before judicial review is contemplated. He stated (at para 443C):

> 'In general terms that principle is correct and has been repeatedly affirmed, in particular recently in the case of *R v Birmingham City Council, ex p Ferrero Ltd* [1993] 1 All ER 530. The Court of Appeal once again said that where there is an alternative remedy, and especially where Parliament has provided a statutory appeal procedure, it is only exceptionally that judicial review should be granted. However, the question which has to be asked in every case such as this is not simply whether or not there is an alternative statutory appeal procedure but whether in the context of that procedure the real issue to be determined can sensibly be determined by that means. If it can, then clearly the statutory procedure should prevail and should be the route adopted by any person aggrieved. If on the other hand the statutory appeal procedure is not apt to deal with the question that is raised in the given case, then there is nothing to prevent an applicant from seeking relief by way of judicial review.
>
> In the present case, although Mr Straker on behalf of the council made a valiant attempt to say that the real issue was whether or not a vehicle was (if I can put it this way) safe for the purposes of hiring on the roads, it seems to me that this is not essentially the question in this case. The question in this case is very simply whether or not the officer purporting to refuse the application made by Mr Hendry, the applicant, was acting in accordance with the policy of the council or not. If he was not and therefore acting outside the authority that he had, it does not seem to me that the magistrates' court is the appropriate forum in which to ventilate that in order to come to any conclusion about it.
>
> In the circumstances I decline to say that it was inappropriate for judicial review proceedings to have been bought in this case. I say and repeat "in this case". It may be that there would be circumstances where there is an overlap between the issues of vires and the issue which can be resolved by the magistrates such as to make it sensible to say that it is the magistrates' court which should in fact deal with the matter. That does not apply here.'

---

[1]   (1994) 6 Admin LR 439, QBD. A similar conclusion, that judicial review was appropriate, notwithstanding the availability of an appeal to the magistrates' court was reached in *R v Nottingham City Council, ex p Howitt* [1999] COD 530, QBD. See Chapter 2, para 2.54.

3.54

As the time-limits for launching a judicial review are tight[1], it is important to decide at an early stage what the grounds for any judicial challenge are to be. It is then important to decide on the forum for such challenge and, if necessary, to pursue it.

1   Civil Procedure Rules, rule 54.5 '(1) The claim form must be filed—
     (a) promptly; and
     (b) in any event not later than 3 months after the grounds to make the claim first arose.'

3.55

Accordingly, it is important for potential litigants to stage a challenge to the local authority in the correct manner. Obviously, appeals to magistrates' courts are much more straightforward, faster and, perhaps above all, cheaper than embarking upon a judicial review. It is difficult to see why, if an appeal procedure is available, judicial review would seem to be a preferable approach.

3.56

Judicial review is in fact a two-stage process[1]. The first stage is to seek leave to apply for a judicial review and, only if this is successful, is the second stage, the judicial review itself, undertaken.

1   For further information on Judicial Review see Mark de Blacam, *Judicial Review* (Bloomsbury Professional).

R v Darlington Borough Council, ex p Association of Darlington Taxi Owners and Darlington Owner Drivers' Association

3.57

> Application for judicial review brought by unincorporated association against a decision to remove limit on hackney carriage numbers. Dismissed as the body had no legal capacity to bring proceedings.

Judicial review is governed by the Civil Procedure Rules 1998, Pt 54. In the context of judicial review, it is important to be aware of the ability of the parties to bring proceedings. It is important that any judicial review is brought by a person, or incorporated association (ie a limited company). Some older cases were brought by Taxi Associations[1]. This was clearly demonstrated as not being possible in *R v Darlington Borough Council, ex p Association of Darlington Taxi Owners and Darlington Owner Drivers' Association*[2]. This case concerned an application for judicial review of the decision of Darlington Borough Council to remove the limit on the number of hackney carriages which would be licensed and also to end a concessionary fare scheme for wheelchair-accessible vehicles.

However, the case did not consider the merits of that point and instead addressed a far more important and useful question: whether an unincorporated association (that is, a group of individuals, rather than one individual or a limited company) is able to issue legal proceedings against a local authority in order to challenge a decision of that local authority.

It was decided by Auld J that an unincorporated association was not able to bring proceedings in such a case, as it lacked the legal capacity to do so. As a result, the application for judicial review was dismissed and the merits of the case were not considered.

[1] See eg *R v Liverpool Corpn, ex p Liverpool Taxi Fleet Operators' Association* [1972] 2 QB 299.
[2] [1994] COD 424.

R v Darlington Borough Council, ex p Association of Darlington Taxi Owners and Darlington Owner Drivers' Association (No 2)

3.58

> Where judicial review was refused because applicant had no legal standing, costs could still be awarded against such a body.

This led, however, to a second case, *R v Darlington Borough Council, ex p Association of Darlington Taxi Owners and Darlington Owner Drivers' Association (No 2)*[1]. This was an application brought by the local authority, seeking the costs of the original hearing from the unincorporated associations (the Association of Darlington Taxi Owners and the Darlington Owner Drivers' Association). This was challenged by the two Associations on the grounds that, as they had no standing to bring proceedings, they therefore had no liability in costs. However, this view was rejected again by Auld J, who held that, notwithstanding the fact that the proceedings were struck out, proceedings had been issued and, therefore, liability and costs accrued. In fact, the costs order was made against all the members of the two Associations at the time of the application for leave to apply for judicial review and that order was enforceable jointly and severally.

[1] [1995] COD 128.

3.59

These cases make it clear that only an individual or a limited company can bring proceedings in hackney carriage and private hire licensing matters and that, if an unincorporated association brings proceedings, not only will they fail, but they will also incur a liability for costs.

The Ombudsman

3.60

In addition, in certain circumstances there is the possibility of a challenge to a local authority via the Ombudsman. In England, The Ombudsman (correctly termed the Commissioner for Local Administration) was created and is controlled by, the

Local Government Act 1974, Pt III[1]. In Wales the Public Services Ombudsman for Wales was created under the Public Services Ombudsman (Wales) Act 2005.

[1]   For further information see *Encyclopaedia of Local Government Law* (Sweet and Maxwell).

3.61

In both countries, the Ombudsman can investigate complaints made by members of the public that they have suffered injustice due to maladministration on the part of a local authority. 'Maladministration' is not defined in either of the pieces of legislation. However, reference is often made to the 'Crossman catalogue' which includes 'bias, neglect, inattention, delay, incompetence, ineptitude, perversity, turpitude, arbitrariness and so on'.

3.62

In relation to hackney carriage and private hire licensing matters, the role of the Ombudsman in both England and Wales is severely limited by virtue of s 26(6) of the Local Government Act 1974, and s 9 of the Public Services Ombudsman (Wales) Act 2005 both of which prevent any investigation into a matter where there is a right of appeal to 'a tribunal constituted under an enactment' which would include both a magistrates' court and the Crown Court.

3.63

Obviously, in most situations in relation to hackney carriage or private hire matters, there is a right of appeal if it is the applicant who is affected by the decision of the local authority. The role of the Ombudsman is probably more relevant in relation to a complaint by a member of the public concerning the method or manner in which a local authority has exercised its powers with regard to hackney carriage and private hire licensing.

3.64

In addition it should be recognised that the findings of the Ombudsman are not binding on the local authority, although certain actions, including advertising the findings of the Ombudsman, are required. If the Ombudsman recommends that a financial award should be made, there is no power to enforce that if the Local Authority decide not to follow the recommendation.

It is a matter for individual local authorities as to how they react to an Ombudsman's investigation. Some authorities take the view that an investigation is merely an exercise in time-wasting and clearly have no intention in complying with any findings that the Ombudsman may make, whilst other authorities, at the other extreme, react with such speed to any suggestion that the Ombudsman might be involved, so as to almost make a mockery of any suggestion of corporate independence.

It will be realised that neither approach is correct and the rational view of the Ombudsman is that it provides a cost-effective alternative method of addressing peoples' grievances which might result from the actions of local authorities.

WITHIN GREATER LONDON

Hackney carriages

3.65

In respect of the vehicle and drivers' licences (issued under the Metropolitan Public Carriage Act 1869, ss 6 and 8 respectively) a right of appeal against refusal to grant or suspension or revocation of the licence lies to the magistrates' court by virtue of the Transport Act 1985, s 17.

'17–(1) In this section—

"licence" means a licence under section 6 of the Metropolitan Public Carriage Act 1869 (taxi licences) or under section 8 of that Act (taxi driver licences); and

"licensing authority" means the person empowered to grant a licence.

(2) Where the licensing authority has refused to grant, or has suspended or revoked, a licence the applicant for, or (as the case may be) holder of, the licence may, before the expiry of the designated period—

(a) require the authority to reconsider his decision; or

(b) appeal to a magistrates court.

(3) Any call for a reconsideration under subsection (2) above must be made to the licensing authority in writing.

(4) On any reconsideration under this section the person calling for the decision to be reconsidered shall be entitled to be heard either in person or by his representative.

(5) If the person calling for a decision to be reconsidered under this section is dissatisfied with the decision of the licensing authority on reconsideration, he may, before the expiry of the designated period, appeal to the a magistrates court.

(6) On any appeal to it under this section, the court may make such order as it thinks fit; and any order which it makes shall be binding on the licensing authority.

(7) Where a person holds a licence which is in force when he applies for a new licence in substitution for it, the existing licence shall continue in force until the application for the new licence, or any appeal under this section in relation to that application, is disposed of, but without prejudice to the exercise in the meantime of any power of the licensing authority to revoke the existing licence.

(8) For the purposes of subsection (7) above, where the licensing authority refuses to grant the new licence the application shall not be treated as disposed of—

(a) where no call for a reconsideration of the authority's decision is made under subsection (2) above, until the expiry of the designated period;

(b) where such a reconsideration is called for, until the expiry of the designated period which begins by reference to the decision of the authority on reconsideration.

(9) Where the licensing authority suspends or revokes a licence, or confirms a decision to do so, he may, if the holder of the licence so requests, direct that his decision shall not have effect until the expiry of the designated period.

(10) In this section
    "designated period" means such period as may be specified for the purpose by London cab order;
    "London cab order" means an order made by Transport for London.

(11) Any power to make a London cab order under this section includes power to vary or revoke a previous such order.'

3.66

It is interesting to note that the applicant or licence holder can seek a reconsideration of the decision before embarking upon appeal to the magistrates' court. This clearly has considerable advantages from the appellant's perspective in terms of cost and although it is referred to in the Transport Act 1985, s 17(2) as being an alternative, requesting a reconsideration does not prevent a subsequent appeal against that reconsidered decision.

3.67

Any appeal must be lodged within 28 days of the date of the notice of the licensing authority: London Taxis (Licensing Appeals) Regulations 1986, reg 2[1].

¹   SI 1986/1188. See Appendix I.

3.68

In contrast to the situation outside London, there is no further right of appeal to the Crown Court against decisions of the magistrates. This means that the only method of challenging the decision of the magistrates is to the High Court by way of case stated. This clearly applies to both applicants and licensees, and to the licensing authority.

Private hire licences

3.69

In relation to private hire licences, rights of appeal are contained within the Private Hire Vehicles (London) Act 1998. Section 3(7) relates to operators' licences:

'(7) An applicant for a London PHV operator's licence may appeal to a magistrates' court against—

(a) a decision not to grant such a licence;

(b) a decision not to specify an address proposed in the application as an operating centre; or

(c) any condition (other than a prescribed condition) to which the licence is subject.'

Section 7(7) relates to vehicle licences:

'(7) An applicant for a London PHV licence may appeal to a magistrates' court against a decision not to grant such a licence or against any condition (other than a prescribed condition) to which the licence is subject.'

Section 13(6) relates to drivers' licences:

'(6) An applicant may appeal to a magistrates' court against a decision not to grant a London PHV driver's licence or against any condition to which such a licence is subject.'

3.70

These sections relate to applicants. Once a licence is in existence, the powers contained in the Private Hire Vehicles (London) Act 1998, s 16 in relation to suspension or revocation come into play, and a right of appeal against a decision under s 16 is contained in s 17(4).

'16–(1) The licensing authority may suspend or revoke a licence under this Act for any reasonable cause including (without prejudice to the generality of this subsection) any ground mentioned below.

(2) A London PHV operator's licence may be suspended or revoked where—

(a) the licensing authority is no longer satisfied that the licence holder is fit to hold such a licence; or

(b) the licence holder has failed to comply with any condition of the licence or any other obligation imposed on him by or under this Act.

(3) A London PHV licence may be suspended or revoked where—

(a) the licensing authority is no longer satisfied that the vehicle to which it relates is fit for use as a private hire vehicle; or

(b) the owner has failed to comply with any condition of the licence or any other obligation imposed on him by or under this Act.

(4) A London PHV driver's licence may be suspended or revoked where—

(a) the licence holder has, since the grant of the licence, been convicted of an offence involving dishonesty, indecency or violence;

(b) the licensing authority is for any other reason no longer satisfied that the licence holder is fit to hold such a licence; or

(c) the licence holder has failed to comply with any condition of the licence or any other obligation imposed on him by or under this Act.'

3.71

The Private Hire Vehicles (London) Act 1998, s 26 stays the effect of any suspension or revocation at the very least until the time for launching the appeal (21 days see s 25(4)) unless s 17(2) has been invoked. This states:

'(2) If the licensing authority is of the opinion that the interests of public safety require the suspension or revocation of a licence to have immediate effect, and the authority includes a statement of that opinion and the reasons for it in the notice of suspension or revocation, the suspension or revocation takes effect when the notice is served on the licence holder or vehicle owner (as the case may be).'

3.72

There is no right of appeal against the decision of the licensing authority to use the provisions of the Private Hire Vehicles (London) Act 1998, s 17(2) to suspend or revoke a licence with immediate effect and, accordingly, the only method of challenging that element of the decision (but not the decision to suspend or revoke the licence) would appear to be either judicial review or a complaint to the ombudsman.

3.73

In contrast to the situation pertaining to hackney carriage licences within London, s 25(6) allows a further appeal to the Crown Court against the decision of the magistrates' court.

3.74

Finally it is interesting to note that the Private Hire Vehicles (London) Act 1998, ss 3(7), 7(7) and 13(6) give right of appeal to applicants rather than persons aggrieved which will prevent a hackney carriage vehicle proprietor challenging a condition imposed on a private hire vehicle licence[1]).

In all other respects, the same considerations will apply to the appeal process within London as apply outside.

[1]   See in relation to *Swansea City and County Council v Davies* [2001] RTR 54, QBD, para 3.32 above.

Judicial review

3.75

The position relating to judicial review is no different from that outside London.

The Ombudsman

3.76

Finally, the Ombudsman's remit extends to both the Greater London Authority and Transport for London: Local Government Act 1974, s 25(1)(aaa) and (cc) respectively.

Chapter 4

Fees for licences

LICENCE FEE LEVYING GENERALLY (OUTSIDE AND WITHIN LONDON)

4.1

There is considerable case law developing around licence fee setting by local authorities. Although many of the cases do not directly relate to hackney carriage and private hire licence fees, the principles that they establish are vital. It is therefore necessary to examine these principles before moving on to consider the specific fee levying powers outside and within London in detail.

The Provision of Services Directive[1] was incorporated into English Law by the Provision of Services Regulations 2009[2] with effect from 28 December 2009. The aim of the Directive is to allow pan-European trade and any licences that are required must be available across the European Union. This requires mechanisms for electronic remote application. The Directive also requires that licence fees are proportionate to the costs involved, are not set at a level to discourage applications, and cannot be used to generate revenue. In addition, enforcement costs cannot be assimilated with the licence fee. These regulations apply to and affect most licence fees, but they do not apply to hackney carriage or private hire licensing by virtue of paragraph 21 of the Directive[3]. As a consequence they do not have a direct impact on taxi licensing, but they do affect some of the more recent case law.

[1] Directive 2006/123/EC of the European Parliament and of The Council of 12 December 2006 on services in the internal market.
[2] SI 2009/2999.
[3] Directive 2006/123/EC.

R v Manchester City Council, ex p King

4.2

Variable fees set by local authority for street trading licences dependent on location. Significant increase on fees levied under previous statutory regime. Held: Licensing fees are not a revenue raising measure and must relate to the cost of the licensing regime. A surplus is not unlawful provided it is carried forward and accounted for in subsequent years.

The provisions of LG(MP)A 1976 do not give the authority discretion to charge whatever it likes for the grant of a licence. The cost of a licence has to be related to the cost of the licensing scheme itself. That is apparent from the wording used, as will be seen below, but the question of the level of fee is also governed by the decision in the case of *R v Manchester City Council, ex p King*[1]. Although this was a case concerning the street trading provisions of the Local Government (Miscellaneous Provisions) Act 1982 (LG(MP)A 1982), the judgment has relevance to all local authority licensing fees and was approved by the recent decisions in *Hemming*[2].

[1]   (1991) 89 LGR 696, DC.
[2]   *R (app Hemming and Ors) v Westminster City Council* [2012] EWHC 1260 (Admin) upheld in Court of Appeal [2013] EWCA 591 and Supreme Court [2015] UKSC 25.

4.3

In the *King* case[1], Manchester City Council argued that the wording of LG(MP)A 1982 allowed them to set fees for street trading licences that reflected the commercial nature of the sites on which traders traded and that they did not have to be related to the cost of the street trading licensing and registration scheme. The High Court disagreed. Roch J stated (at 709):

'... it would be surprising if Parliament had intended to include a general revenue-raising provision in a schedule which deals solely with street trading. The purpose of that part of the Act is to establish a general scheme for street trading which local authorities may adopt if they so desire ...

The fees charged, in my judgment, must be related to the street trading scheme operated by the district council and the costs of operating that scheme. The district council may charge such fees as they reasonably consider will cover the total cost of operating the street trading scheme or such lesser part of the cost of operating the street trading scheme as they consider reasonable. One consequence of the wording used is that, if the fees levied in the event exceed the cost of operating the scheme, the original decision will remain valid provided it can be said that the district council reasonably considered such fees would be required to meet the total cost of operating the scheme.'

The effect of this decision is vital in relation to local authority licence fee setting. A local authority cannot use licence fees to raise revenue. Any surplus must be carried forward at the year end and be applied to the same account in following years. Likewise, under the ruling in *R v Westminster City Council, ex p Hutton*[2] the authority can raise fees in subsequent years to recoup any shortfall from licence fee revenue.

[1]   *R v Manchester City Council, ex p King* (1991) 89 LGR 696, DC.
[2]   (1985) 83 LGR 461.

R (app Hemming and Ors) v Westminster City Council

4.4

> Sex establishment licence fees set to recover the costs of enforcement against
> unlicensed traders. Challenged after the introduction of the European Union
> Services Directive. Held: The licence fee cannot recover enforcement costs
> but a separate 'retention fee' could be levied to cover the shortfall.

The decision in *King* was upheld by the High Court, Court of Appeal and the
Supreme Court in the long running series of cases concerning sex establishment
licence fees[1]. The specific question being considered was whether Westminster
City Council could recover the costs of enforcement against unlicensed traders
by means of the licence fee paid by those who held sex establishment licences. In
addressing this question, the High Court reviewed the law on licence fees and
summarised the position like this:[2]

> '24... .It is not disputed that [the Council's] determination of the fee will
> have to be informed by the need to ensure that it does not make a profit
> out of the fee which it charges. That is no more than the law dictates. The
> power of a local authority to charge a reasonable fee for the grant, for
> example, of a street trading licence was said in *R v Manchester City Council
> ex p. King*[3] to preclude the raising of revenue for purposes other than street
> trading. As Roch J (as he then was) said at pp. 709–710:
>
>> "The fees charged ... must be related to the street trading scheme
>> operated by the district council and the costs of operating that scheme.
>> The district council may charge such fees as they reasonably consider
>> will cover the total cost of operating the street trading scheme or
>> such lesser part of the cost of operating the street trading scheme as
>> they consider reasonable. One consequence of the wording used is
>> that, if the fees levied in the event exceed the cost of operating the
>> scheme, the original position will remain valid provided that it can be
>> said that the district council reasonably considered such fees would
>> be required to meet the total cost of operating the scheme."
>
> 25. There are two important issues of principle which affect how the
> Council may determine the licence fee ... First, is the Council obliged
> to adjust what would otherwise have been an appropriate fee ... to reflect
> any previous surplus or deficit? Secondly, can the costs of enforcing the
> licensing system be reflected in the licence fee? It is necessary to deal with
> each of these issues in turn.
>
> 26. Carrying forward surpluses or deficits. The first of these issues arose
> in *R v Westminster City Council ex p. Hutton*, which was one of a number
> of cases tried together and reported collectively as *R v Birmingham City
> Council ex p. Quietlynn Ltd and ors*[4]. *Hutton* related to the licence fee for a sex
> establishment in Westminster. The administrative costs on which the fee

was based in the year in question included a sum representing the supposed shortfall in fee income against administrative costs in the previous year. The question was whether the fee was lawful. Forbes J held that it was. At pp. 518–519, he said:

> "I accept entirely that to carry forward a deficit from one year to another may result in anomalies when considering the effect of that process on applicants for grants or renewal of what are annual licences. The persons who, in the year in which the deficit is brought in, seek the grant or renewal of licences may well not be the same people who sought the grant or renewal in the previous year. Those in the previous year may have been fortunate to be undercharged. There is no certainty that, by bringing the deficit into the next year's accounts and therefore recouping from the next year's applicants, the authority will be exacting the money from those who morally ought to pay. But to my mind such a comparison is itself irrelevant in the context of local authority finance. The statutory accounts of local authorities are structured on the basis that shortfalls in one year must be carried into the next year's accounts. The identity of the ratepayers who contribute to the General Rate Fund is changing all the time. If an authority, as a matter of policy, which is itself not challenged on the ground of immateriality, decides that the cost of a service from year to year shall not fall on the ratepayers, that decision would benefit ratepayers of different identities and may disadvantage or advantage from year to year different persons who benefit from the service. I accept [Westminster's counsel's] contention that when a charge is based on an annual budget, which must be concerned with situations which themselves will not be verifiable until after the end of the year in question, the only sensible way to fix the level of the charge is to take one year with another."

It does not necessarily follow that just because a local authority acts lawfully in carrying forward a deficit from one year to the next, it acts unlawfully when it declines to carry forward a surplus. But if the justification for carrying forward a deficit from one year to the next is because it is not known in the current year what the expenditure on administering and enforcing the system will be, that reasoning should apply to a surplus just as much. If a local authority were to be treated as acting lawfully if it failed to carry forward a surplus from one year to the next, the making of profits would become legitimized.

27. It follows that the Council has to determine the annual licence fee for sex establishments by adjusting what would otherwise have been the appropriate fee to reflect any previous deficit or surplus. That is an uncontroversial requirement bearing in mind that that has been the Council's policy for many years … However, it does not have to adjust the licence fee every year to reflect any previous deficit or surplus, so long as it "all comes out in the wash" eventually. And the adjustment does not have

to be precise: a rough and ready calculation which is broadly correct will do.'

¹   *R (app Hemming and Ors) v Westminster City Council* [2012] EWHC 1260 (Admin) upheld in Court of Appeal [2013] EWCA 591 and Supreme Court [2015] UKSC 25.
²   *R (app Hemming and Ors) v Westminster City Council* [2012] EWHC 1260 (Admin) per Keith J at para 24 onwards.
³   (1991) 89 LGR 696.
⁴   (1985) 83 LGR 461.

4.5

It can be seen that each year does not have to be calculated precisely, but any surplus ***must*** be carried forwards, and deficits *can* be carried forwards. This will not be in the following year, but in the year after that, due to the mechanisms of accounting and local authority financial years. A licence fee will be set ahead of the start of the municipal year in April, and then levied from April until the following March. Before the end of that year (if required) a new fee will be set for the second year but in setting that fee, it will not be possible to take into account a surplus or deficit from the first year as those results will not be known until well after the end of that first year and into the period of levying the second year's fee. The only practical method of taking those surpluses or deficits into account is to take those from the first year into account when setting the third year's fees. Likewise, any surplus or deficit on the second year is carried forward to the fourth year and the process continues. This 'leapfrogging' approach is the only practical way to set lawful licence fees.

It is also vital that each fee levying power is accounted for and calculated separately. In relation to taxis there are two fee levying mechanisms: LG(MP)A 1976, s 53 in relation to drivers' licences and LG(MP)A 1976, s 70 in relation to vehicle operators' licences. Each of these is a separate budget and a separate account[1].

¹   This point was considered by the District Auditor in relation to the fees levied by Guildford Borough Council. He found that there was no split in relation to costs and expenditure between the two fee levying provisions. For the full determination see: http://www.guildford.gov.uk/CHttpHandler.ashx?id=6647&p=0

There is a suggestion contained in an Order made by the High Court following a judicial review that in fact there should be five separate accounts: Hackney carriage driver; private hire driver; Hackney carriage vehicle; private hire vehicle; private hire operator. However, as this does not form part of the judgment it does not appear to be a binding precedent. See *R (on the application of Cummings) v Council of the City and Council of Cardiff* [2014] EWHC 2544 (Admin) at para 4.9.

4.6

Returning to *Hemming*, the key question was whether the costs of enforcement could be recovered by the licence fee. Under the provisions of Sch 3, para 19 to the Local Government (Miscellaneous Provisions) Act 1982 a local authority can charge a 'reasonable fee' for the grant or renewal of a sex establishment licence. As sex establishments are covered by the provisions of the European Union Services Directive[1] a licence fee (termed a 'charge' in the Directive and the Regulations) cannot cover more than the costs of the 'procedures and formalities' associated with the authorisation scheme[2] and in particular cannot either raise funds, *or* be used as a deterrent to apply for such a licence[3].

Westminster City Council levied fees which covered not only the costs of issuing the licence, but which also covered the costs of enforcement against unlicensed traders[4].

Both the High Court and Court of Appeal found in favour of the traders and determined that the Services Directive prohibited the Council from recovering the costs of enforcement. A distinction was made between 'enforcement' which was the costs of enforcing the legislation against unlicensed operators, and 'compliance' which covered the costs of ensuring that the licensed traders were complying with the requirements of their licence and the legislation. The Court of Appeal put it like this[5]:

'101. (v) The distinction between enforcement against licensed operators and unlicensed operators: I have referred (see [para 33]) to the distinction the judge drew between the costs of enforcement against unlicensed operators and the costs of compliance monitoring and enforcement against licensed operators. The Council maintains that there is no such distinction in the language of either the Directive or the Regulations. It also contends that the distinction between the two types of enforcement drawn by the judge (first judgment, [35]) and in the terms of the declaration granted (see [4] above) is not reflected by the construction he adopted in paragraph [44] of his first judgment, which appears to suggest that the Council is precluded from recovering the costs of any enforcement activity through the licence fee.

102. It is clear that the judge intended to distinguish between the costs of monitoring compliance and enforcement in respect of licensed operators, and the costs of enforcement against unlicensed operators. It was only the latter which he held fell outside Article 13(2) and Regulation 18(4). Unsurprisingly, since neither the Directive nor the Regulations refer to the costs of enforcement at all, the distinction between these two types of enforcement does not reflect their express terms. But for the reasons in the next paragraph, I agree with the judge that the cost of compliance monitoring and enforcement against an applicant who is given a licence can fall within the costs of the "authorisation procedures".

103. It is clear and undisputed that costs incurred in investigating the suitability of an applicant for a licence can be reflected in the fee. In the case of an application to renew a licence, I consider that the costs of monitoring the applicant's continued suitability can include the costs of monitoring compliance with the terms of their licences in the past. Once the Council knows what those costs are in broad terms, as it does by reference to what has happened in the past, it is, in my judgment, entitled to include them in the calculation for the next year's licence. There may be a formulaic element to this calculation. But the example of *European Commission v Spain*[6] (as to which see [81] – [85]) is a strong indication that using a

formula that proceeds on the basis of the cost of the actual authorisation process is justified.

104. For these reasons, I reject the contention that it is not lawful to draw a distinction between the two types of enforcement. The distinction, incidentally, is similar to the distinction that applies (see [94]) in respect of enforcement in the case of barristers and those who impersonate barristers.'

1   Introduced into English Law from 28 December 2009 by the Provision of Services Regulations 2009, SI 2009/2999.
2   Provision of Services Regulations 2009, SI 2009/2999, reg 18(4).
3   Taxi licences (both hackney carriage and private hire) are not covered by the EU Services Directive, and as a result the *Hemming* judgments are not directly applicable. However, the principles are relevant to taxi licence fee setting.
4   This had been challenged in 1984 and was found by the High Court to be lawful in *R v Westminster City Council, ex p Hutton* (1985) 83 LGR 516. The position changed after the introduction of the Provision of Services Regulations 2009, SI 2009/2999 in December 2009.
5   *R (app Hemming and Ors) v Westminster City Council* Court of Appeal [2013] EWCA 591 per Beatson LJ at paras 101 onwards.
6   *Re Shopping Centres Licensing: European Commission v Spain* Case C-400/08 [2011] 2 CMLR 50.

4.7

The Supreme Court went further and generally overturned the decision of the Court of Appeal. In giving the unanimous judgment of the Court, Lord Mance agreed that the licence fee could not cover the enforcement costs (as opposed to compliance costs) but then went on[1]:

'17. It follows from paras 15 and 16 above that article 13(2) (and so regulation 18) is concerned – and concerned only – with charges made in respect of authorisation procedures and their cost, and that nothing in article 13(2) precludes a licensing authority from charging a fee for the possession or retention of a licence, and making this licence conditional upon payment of such fee. Any such fee would however have to comply with the requirements, including that of proportionality, identified in section 2 of Chapter III and section 1 of Chapter IV. But there is no reason why it should not be set at a level enabling the authority to recover from licensed operators the full cost of running and enforcing the licensing scheme, including the costs of enforcement and proceedings against those operating sex establishments without licences.'

This raises a number of issues. In relation to a power to levy a 'reasonable fee' (which is the wording used for both street trading and sex establishment licences under the LG(MP)A 1982[2]), the Supreme Court is suggesting that such a power extends beyond the licence fee and an additional charge can be levied. But what power does a local authority have to levy arbitrary powers without specific lawful authority? Section 93 of the Local Government Act 2003 allows a payment to be charged for discretionary services, but clearly enforcement is not a discretionary service, although it is the exercise of a discretion by the local authority rather than the discharge of a statutory duty. Section 1 of the Localism Act 2011, allows the local authority to do 'anything that individuals generally may do', but a normal person cannot levy a charge for enforcement. It remains unclear where the power identified by the Supreme Court lies and as a consequence, it is suggested that this judgment be treated with some caution in relation to its wider application.

1   R (app Hemming and Ors) v Westminster City Council [2015] UKSC 25.
2   Local Government (Miscellaneous Provisions) Act 1982, Sch 4, para 9 in relation to street trading licences and consents, and Sch 3, para 19 in relation to sex establishment licence fees.

4.8

As the wording in LG(MP)A 1976 is more specific than that in LG(MP)A 1982 (for street trading) this may not seem particularly relevant, but it both cases are important in relation to the concept of a licensing regime. The licence fees in relation to hackney carriage and private hire licensing must be related to the costs of the regime as specified in LG(MP)A 1976.

R (on the application of Cummings) v Council of the City and Council of Cardiff

4.9

> Judicial review based on failure to carry forward surpluses from year to year and incorporating the costs of taxi marshals within the licence fees. Held: Surpluses must be carried forwards and taxi marshal costs are not recoverable.

R (on the application of Cummings) v Council of the City and Council of Cardiff [1] concerned a challenge to the fees set by and levied by Cardiff City Council over a period of five years from 2009 to 2013. In essence the challenge was that the council had failed to take into account surpluses from previous years when setting subsequent years' fees, and had unlawfully included within the fee structure the costs of 'taxi marshals' used to regulate the taxi ranks and queues of people waiting for taxis within the city. The reported judgment does not address many of the issues, because the position had been conceded and agreed by the time of the decision, which is unfortunate. The council conceded the points, and agreed to re-determine the fees for the years 2009–2013, carrying forward surpluses and deficits, removing the costs of taxi marshals and removing any cross subsidy between the various categories of licence. The judgment concerned an application to amend the original application for judicial review to seek restitution back to 1978 rather than 2009. This application was refused on the basis that the claimants could bring their own separate action for restitution.

As a consequence, the judgment does not detail the legal requirements, apart from a brief reference to *Hemming*[2]. The detail, such as it is, is contained in the Order that was made following the concessions by the council[3] which states[4]:

'4. It be declared that:

4.1 A local authority when determining hackney carriage and private hire licence fees under section 53 and 70 of the Local Government

(Miscellaneous Provisions) Act 1976 must take into account any surplus or deficit generated from fees levied in previous years in respect of meeting the reasonable costs of administering the licence fees as provided by section 53 and 70.

4.2 A local authority must keep separate accounts for and ensure when determining hackney carriage and private hire licence fees under sections 53 and 70 of the Local Government (Miscellaneous Provisions) Act 1976 that any surplus or deficit accrued under each of the Hackney carriage and private hire licensing regimes, and between each licence within those regimes, are only accounted for and taken into account within the regime under which they have accrued and a surplus from one licensing regime shall not be used to subsidise a deficit in another.'

It can be seen that this statement goes further than previous court decisions or interpretations of the law by auditors in two ways: firstly it suggests that deficits have to be taken into account in future years and; secondly there should be a separate account for the five different taxi licence fees.

Previous decisions have made it clear that there is a discretion over carrying forward deficits and this element of the Order does not accord with the decisions in *Hutton*[5] or *Hemming*[6].

In relation to the suggestion that should be five separate accounts, again this does not appear to accord with the legislative requirements. There are two distinct fee levying provisions (ss 53 and 70). Section 53(1) does not specify that there too should be two accounts for drivers. Section 70(1) specifically states that the fees and charges should be sufficient 'in the aggregate' to cover the matters specified in s 70(1)(a) to (c).

This leads to an important question over the status of a High Court Order. It is clear that it is only the *ratio decidendi*[7] of a Senior Court decision which is a binding precedent. The remainder of the judgment will only be persuasive. A High Court Order does not form part of the judgment and is therefore not binding and at best can only be regarded as persuasive[8].

It therefore appears that *Cummings* is binding authority for very little, and creates no new law. The persuasive nature of the judgment reinforces what is already known, and the Order simply demonstrates an agreed procedure for one authority.

1   [2014] EWHC 2544 (Admin).
2   At paragraph 13.
3   Available at http://www.stjohnschambers.co.uk/dashboard/wp-content/uploads/Cummings-Others-v-Cardiff-11.pdf
4   At paragraph 4 of the Order.
5   *R v Westminster City Council, ex p Hutton* (1985) 83 LGR 516.
6   *R (app Hemming and Ors) v Westminster City Council* [2012] EWHC 1260 (Admin) upheld in Court of Appeal [2013] EWCA 591 and Supreme Court [2015] UKSC 25.
7   *Ratio decidendi* – 'The enunciation of the reason or principle upon which a question before a court has been decided is alone binding as a precedent' *Halsbury's Laws of England* Volume 11 (2015), para 25.
8   This area is explained very clearly in *Halsbury's Laws of England* Volume 11 (2015), para 25. In particular footnote 2 states:

'A subsequent court is not bound by a proposition of law which has been assumed by the previous court and not decided by it: *R (on the application of Kadhim) v Brent London Borough Council Housing Benefit Review Board* [2001] QB 955, [2000] All ER (D) 2408, CA'.

OUTSIDE LONDON

4.10

Each of the licences outlined in Chapter 1 – hackney carriage drivers' and hackney carriage proprietors' (vehicle) licences, private hire operators' licences, private hire drivers and private hire vehicle licences – attracts a fee payable to the local authority.

4.11

Under the Local Government (Miscellaneous Provisions) Act 1976 (LG(MP)A 1976)[1], the provisions controlling the levying of these fees are:

- LG(MP)A 1976, s 53(2), in respect of drivers' licences for both hackney carriages or private hire vehicles; and
- LG(MP)A 1976, s 70 for hackney carriage proprietors' licences, private hire vehicle licences and private hire operators' licences[2]

and these will be considered in turn.

[1]   As the Local Government (Miscellaneous Provisions) Act 1976 (LG(MP)A 1976) has apparently been adopted by all local authorities in England and Wales except Plymouth City Council, consideration will not be given in this chapter to the situation with regard to fees that applies where LG(MP)A 1976 has not been adopted. Details of this can be found in the first edition of this work.

[2]   The European Union Provision of Services Directive (Directive 2006/123/EC of the European Parliament and of The Council of 12 December 2006 on services in the internal market) were incorporated into English Law by the Provision of Services Regulations 2009, SI 2009/2999 with effect from 28 December 2009. By virtue of paragraph 21 of Directive 2006/123/EC of the European Parliament and of the Council they do not apply to hackney carriage or private hire licensing, and as a consequence are not of direct application.

Drivers' licence fees

4.12

LG(MP)A 1976, s 53(2) states:

'53–(2) Notwithstanding the provisions of the Act of 1847 [Town Police Clauses Act 1847], a district council may demand and recover for the grant to any person of a licence to drive a hackney carriage, or a private hire vehicle, as the case may be, such a fee as they consider reasonable with a view to recovering the costs of issue and administration and may remit the whole or part of the fee in respect of a private hire vehicle in any case in which they think it appropriate to do so.'[1]

It is clear that the fees for drivers' licences for both hackney carriages or private hire vehicles, when covered by these provisions, have to be both reasonable and imposed 'with a view to recovering the costs of issue and administration'. This will cover the costs of assessing the suitability of the applicant. It will also include the costs of the issue of the badge and other associated administrative tasks.

Pre-application requirements or tests such as Disclosure and Barring Service (DBS) checks, medical tests, driving and knowledge tests should be charged as separate items and not included in the licence fee. This is because the licence fee can only be levied 'for the grant to any person of a licence'. If the application is refused and no licence is granted, no fee is payable.

However, it seems that no provision can be made for the costs of enforcement undertaken by the authority against either licensed or unlicensed drivers. There is no case directly on the point and to permit such costs to be recovered, it would be necessary to show that enforcement was covered by the term 'administration'. In the Court of Appeal in *Hemming*[2] the Court was prepared to accept that the overall costs of 'authorisation procedures' could also include the costs of enforcement against existing licensed operators. This has become known as 'compliance' and must be contrasted with 'enforcement' which is action against unlicensed traders[3]. Does this equate to 'Administration'? Although this may appear an attractive argument for local authorities, it is by no means certain for a number of reasons: *Hemming* concerns different legislation – the Local Government (Miscellaneous Provisions) Act 1982 – and was primarily concerned with the application of the European Union Services Directive as applied by the Provision of Services Regulations 2009, SI 2009/2999. In that case the relevant legislation was Article 13 of the Directive which states:

> 'Authorisation procedures and formalities shall not be dissuasive and shall not unduly complicate or delay the provision of the service. They shall be easily accessible and any charges which the applicants may incur from their application shall be reasonable and proportionate to the cost of the authorisation procedures in question and shall not exceed the cost of the procedures.'

The arguments against the application of the *Hemming* approach to taxi licensing are that the legislation is different, and the fee levying provisions for taxi licensing in the LG(MP)A 1976[4] are much more prescriptive than those contained in LG(MP)A 1982[5] for fees for sex establishment licences. In addition, taxi licensing is not subject to the provisions of the European Union Services Directive. It is therefore difficult to sustain the argument that the reference in *Hemming* to 'authorisation procedures' means the same as 'the costs of issue and administration' (s 53) or 'administrative or other costs' (s 70).

In conclusion, it does not seem possible for a local authority to recover general compliance or enforcement costs for hackney carriage or private hire driver licensing via the licence fees[6].

---

[1]　It has never been clear why s 53(2) states that a district council 'may remit the whole or part of the fee in respect of a private hire vehicle in any case in which they think it appropriate to do so' when this section does not relate to private hire vehicles. If this were regarded as a misprint and reference should have been to private hire drivers, it seems anomalous that the legislature would

allow refunds for private hire drivers but not for hackney carriage drivers when the criteria for both in relation to grant and action against the licence are identical. As a consequence, it is suggested that this element of s 53(2) is meaningless.

2   *R (app Hemming and Ors) v Westminster City Council* [2013] EWCA 591, CA.
3   See paragraphs 101–104 of the Court of Appeal judgment.
4   LG(MP)A 1976, ss 53 and 70.
5   Local Government (Miscellaneous Provisions) Act 1982, Sch 3 para 19.
6   The position is slightly different in relation to vehicle proprietors – see para 4.17 below.

Vehicle and operators' licences

4.13

In relation to the fees for both hackney carriage and private hire vehicle licences and private hire operators' licences, LG(MP)A 1976, s 70 states:

'Fees for vehicle and operators' licences

70–(1) Subject to the provisions of subsection (2) of this section, a district council may charge such fees for the grant of vehicle and operators' licences as may be resolved by them from time to time and as may be sufficient in the aggregate to cover in whole or in part—

(a) the reasonable cost of the carrying out by or on behalf of the district council of inspections of hackney carriages and private hire vehicles for the purpose of determining whether any such licence should be granted or renewed;

(b) the reasonable cost of providing hackney carriage stands; and

(c) any reasonable administrative or other costs in connection with the foregoing and with the control and supervision of hackney carriages and private hire vehicles.

(2) The fees chargeable under this section shall not exceed—

(a) for the grant of a vehicle licence in respect of a hackney carriage, twenty-five pounds;

(b) for the grant of a vehicle licence in respect of a private hire vehicle, twenty-five pounds; and

(c) for the grant of an operator's licence, twenty-five pounds per annum;
     or, in any such case, such other sums as a district council may, subject to the following provisions of this section, from time to time determine.

(3)(a) If a district council determine that the maximum fees specified in subsection (2) of this section should be varied they shall publish in at least one local newspaper circulating in the district a notice setting out the variation proposed, drawing attention to the provisions of paragraph (b) of this subsection and specifying the period, which shall not be less than twenty-eight days from the date of the first publication of the notice, within which and the manner in which objections to the variation can be made.

(b) A copy of the notice referred to in paragraph (a) of this subsection shall for the period of twenty-eight days from the date of the first publication thereof be deposited at the offices of the council which published the notice and shall at all reasonable hours be open to public inspection without payment.

(4) If no objection to a variation is duly made within the period specified in the notice referred to in subsection (3) of this section, or if all objections so made are withdrawn, the variation shall come into operation on the date of the expiration of the period specified in the notice or the date of withdrawal of the objection or, if more than one, of the last objection, whichever date is the later.

(5) If objection is duly made as aforesaid and is not withdrawn, the district council shall set a further date, not later than two months after the first specified date, on which the variation shall come into force with or without modification as decided by the district council after consideration of the objections.

(6) A district council may remit the whole or part of any fee chargeable in pursuance of this section for the grant of a licence under section 48 or 55 of this Act in any case in which they think it appropriate to do so.'

Kelly v Liverpool City Council

4.14

> Challenge by way of judicial review against the practice of levying a fee to test a vehicle when the vehicle failed the test and as a consequence no licence was granted. Held: Fees for vehicle tests could be levied even when a licence was not granted.

What can be recovered via the licence fee under LG(MP)A 1976, s 70? Does this only allow a single payment when the licence is granted, or can an overall licence fee include mid-term charges and fees when no licence is granted because a vehicle fails its test?

The case of *Kelly v Liverpool City Council*[1] raised the question of whether a district council could charge for the inspections of vehicles which were submitted for acceptance as either hackney carriages or private hire vehicles, but refused a licence. Liverpool City Council lost at first instance in the Divisional Court, and appealed to the Court of Appeal. The argument centred around the wording in s 70(1) 'a district council may charge such fees for the grant ...' The point raised was that if the vehicle failed the test, there was no grant of a licence and therefore no power to charge a fee. Judgment was given by Schiemann LJ. Having outlined the background to the licensing regime, he stated (at para 4):

> '4. The 1976 Act [LG(MP)A 1976] in terms, and the 1847 Act [Town Police Clauses Act 1847] arguably by implication, obliges councils to inspect the vehicle which it is sought to licence. The inspection process costs money. Parliament has authorised authorities to charge fees so that they may reimburse themselves this cost.'

He continued (at para 7):

'7. The Judge decided that Councils could only charge those to whom they granted licences. The authority contend that they are empowered to charge all those whose vehicles they inspect whether or not a licence is eventually granted. The authority point out that a consequence of the judge's decision is that the cost of inspecting vehicles which should not have been submitted for testing falls upon those who ensure that their vehicles are up to scratch before they submit them for testing.'

[1]   [2003] EWCA Civ 197, [2003] 2 All ER 772.

4.15

The judgment considered a number of different factors. First, the question was 'is it lawful to charge those to whom no licence is granted?' which was considered as follows[1] (at para 9ff):

'9. The judge considered that it was not lawful to charge those who had not been granted licences. His reasoning was simple and understandable. He rightly said that the section provided for the charging of fees "for the grant of ... vehicle licences". He was of the view that it followed that if no licence was granted no fees could be charged.

10. Mr Fraser [for Liverpool City Council] submitted that the provision that the council may charge "for the grant" of licences merely meant that any fees charged must arise out of functions properly associated with the function of granting a licence and that inspection for the purposes of ascertaining whether to grant a licence was fundamental to this function.

11. He submitted that the phrase was ambiguous. It could be limited in the way that the judge had held but it was also capable of bearing the interpretation which he submitted was the correct one.

12. We agree. The phrase is ambiguous and can bear either meaning. ...

15. At first it seems odd that an unsuccessful applicant for a licence should need to bear a proportion of the costs of providing hackney carriage stands of which he will not have any need if he is refused a licence. However, there are a number of answers to this point. The first is that it only runs in relation to hackney carriages and not in relation to private hire vehicles and yet the answer to the question must be the same for both. The second is that it is not an unavoidable consequence of the wording of the section that all applicants must bear the cost of providing hackney carriage stands. It seems to us possible to charge applicants for a licence the costs of inspecting their vehicle and administrative costs involved in determining whether the licences should be granted or renewed without charging them the costs of providing hackney carriage stands. Apart from anything else subsection (6) gives the utmost flexibility ...

17. We have been persuaded that the judge was wrong in the view which he apparently held that it was wrong to charge fees to those applicants whose vehicles did not pass the test and were thus not granted a licence first time. His conclusion involves the proposition that either the Council or those who present first class vehicles for licensing must pay for the inspection costs of those who repeatedly present substandard vehicles. We cannot believe that this was intended by parliament.'

The second question addressed was 'is it lawful to charge the costs of inspection separately from other costs?' This arose because Liverpool City Council, in common with many other councils had a policy of charging £30 for the first test, then an additional £25 for each and every subsequent test if the initial test was failed.

This was answered simply (at para 19):

'We see nothing wrong in what we are told is the widespread practice of authorities, namely, to charge for each inspection at the time that it is carried out.'

The third question raised was 'what impact do the maximum fee provisions contained in s 70(2) have on inspection charges?'. The court decided (at para 20):

'20. The broad policy of the charging section is clear. The fees charged for the grant of licences are not to be used as a revenue raising measure. On the other hand authorities are entitled to charge sums sufficient to cover the costs of doing the things set out in subsection [70](1). ...

25. Subsection [70](2) itself sets out a maximum in respect of each of the three types of licence there set out. However it expressly provides that "in any such case" (e.g. in the case of a vehicle licence in respect of a hackney carriage) the fees chargeable shall not exceed "such other sums as the district council may determine". The words "in any such case" indicate that, for the purposes of construing the rest of the subsection, one must proceed case by case.

26. The plural "sums" is in our judgment significant. We accept that the plural could have been inserted merely to justify a second increase after a first increase. However it was not necessary to use the plural for that purpose. Even had the singular been used the Council would have been able to substitute a new maximum as they "from time to time determine". See also in this context section 12 of the Interpretation Act 1978.

27. In our judgment the plural entitles a district council to specify a maximum sum in respect of the first vehicle inspection, a maximum sum in respect of a second vehicle inspection and a maximum sum in respect of administrative costs and so on, without specifying an overall maximum figure.

28. What is clearly important is that any proposed increase is advertised and considered in the way envisaged in subsections [70](3)–(5).'

In conclusion, the court stated (at para 29):

> '29. The Council had a regime which specified that £30 should be paid prior to and in respect of the first test and £25 prior to and in respect of each subsequent test. Once the vehicle had passed the test a further sum of £120 had to be paid for the licence. We see nothing legally objectionable in such a scheme which we understand is similar to that adopted by many other councils.
>
> 30. We therefore allow the appeal …'

[1] *Kelly v Liverpool City Council* [2003] EWCA Civ 197, [2003] 2 All ER 772; see para 4.14 above.

4.16

It is clear from this decision that different fees can be levied for hackney carriages, private hire vehicles and private hire operators licences, and that those fees can be levied in stages if there are specific reasons for doing so, as in the *Liverpool* case[1]. The inspection fee, repeat test fee and then the licence cost, covering the costs of administration, enforcement and so on.

[1] *Kelly v Liverpool City Council* [2003] EWCA Civ 197, [2003] 2 All ER 772; see para 4.14 above.

4.17

It seems that the following costs can be recovered via the fee under LG(MP)A 1976, s 70. The initial inspection of the vehicle, the cost of providing taxi ranks (referred to in the legislation as hackney carriage stands), and then by virtue of para (c) everything else that is connected with the administration and enforcement of the entire hackney carriage vehicle and private hire vehicle operation. This will include vehicle inspections, administration of vehicle records, random checks, hackney carriage demand surveys etc. The *Liverpool* decision[1] also means that the fees can be differentiated to enable the costs of hackney carriage stand provision to only be recovered from the hackney carriages that use them. This seems to be completely proper, as it would be inequitable to charge private hire vehicle proprietors and private hire operators for the cost of something that they are prohibited from using.

[1] *Kelly v Liverpool City Council* [2003] EWCA Civ 197, [2003] 2 All ER 772; see para 4.14 above.

4.18

The wording of LG(MP)A 1976, s 70(1)(c) clearly envisages the inclusion of the costs of enforcement, and subsequent legal proceedings, as being part of the costs relating to the vehicles themselves. The way in which the section is worded must be considered carefully because it is not immediately clear whether this relates to any hackney carriage or private hire vehicle or only hackney carriages and private hire vehicles licensed by that particular authority. The costs that can be recovered are those 'in connection with … the control and supervision of hackney carriages and private hire vehicles.'

The definitions of hackney carriage and private hire vehicle contained in s 80 of LG(MP)A 1976[1] suggest that it will apply to any vehicle acting as a hackney carriage or private hire vehicle because in both cases the definition relates to the use of the vehicle, rather than the existence of a licence. This would mean that enforcement action against the proprietors of vehicles being used to unlawfully ply for hire could be recovered via these fees[2]. It would not appear to extend to recovering the costs of prosecution against the drivers of such vehicles.

[1]   '"Hackney carriage" has the same meaning as in the Act of 1847;' which states: '38 What vehicles to be deemed hackney carriages Every wheeled carriage, whatever may be its form or construction, used in standing or plying for hire in any street within the prescribed distance, and every carriage standing upon any street within the prescribed distance, having thereon any numbered plate required by this or the special Act to be fixed upon a hackney carriage, or having thereon any plate resembling or intended to resemble any such plate as aforesaid, shall be deemed to be a hackney carriage within the meaning of this Act; and in all proceedings at law or otherwise the term "hackney carriage" shall be sufficient to describe any such carriage:'
    '"Private hire vehicle" means a motor vehicle constructed or adapted to seat fewer than nine passengers, other than a hackney carriage or public service vehicle [or a London cab] [or tramcar], which is provided for hire with the services of a driver for the purpose of carrying passengers;'.
[2]   The offence of unlawfully plying for hire contained in Town Police Clauses Act 1847, s 45 applies to both the driver and any 'proprietor or part proprietor of any carriage, …[who] permits the same to be used as a hackney carriage plying for hire within the prescribed distance without having obtained a licence … for such carriage'.

4.19

It seems clear that the costs of enforcement, in relation to operators' licences, cannot be included in the fee, as the wording of LG(MP)A 1976, s 70(1)(c) appears to limit the use of that section to the vehicles themselves. Although private hire operators' licences are referred to in s 70(1), nowhere else within the section is there any reference to operators' licences, apart from the standard fee of £25 per year contained in s 70(2)(c).

4.20

The overall effect of the provisions contained within LG(MP)A 1976, in respect of fees for licences, would appear to be, therefore, that, in relation to drivers, the costs of issue and administration can be recovered; in relation to vehicles, the costs of inspection, ranks, control and supervision (including enforcement), and the administration connected with it, can be recovered; and, in relation to operators' licences, it appears that only the costs of administration are recoverable.

4.21

In order to be able to justify a fee levied under either LG(MP)A 1976, ss 53 or 70, it will be necessary to be able to differentiate between the two provisions[1]. This will mean that there must be at least two identifiable accounts relating to the fees levied under each section, and if different fees are levied under each section in respect of the different licences covered by the provision, there must be a separate account breakdown for each[2].

1   This was considered above; see para 4.11.
2   This point was considered by the District Auditor in relation to the fees levied by Guildford Borough Council. Three complaints were made: that the council had not properly advertised that it was going to charge fees of more than £25; that the council did not keep proper records of costs and fees for each type of licence; and finally that fees were in excess of costs. The district auditor found that the correct advertisements had not been placed and accordingly the fees charged for that particular year were unlawful. He also found that there were insufficient records of expenditure and costs and most importantly that there was no split in relation to costs and expenditure between the two fee levying provisions. He did not find that there was overcharging in respect of those costs. For the full determination see: http://www.guildford.gov. uk/CHttpHandler.ashx?id=6647&p=0

Notice provisions

4.22

Under LG(MP)A 1976, s 53(2)[1] the fee for hackney carriage and private hire driving licences simply has to be related to the recoverable costs and there are no statutory requirements for advertisements, notices, consultation or representations. In addition, there is no restriction on the number of times that the local authority can increase the fees. However, their actions must be reasonable, in accordance with the *Wednesbury* principles.

The provisions of s 53(2) can be contrasted with the requirements under LG(MP)A 1976, s 70[2] in relation to:

•   hackney carriage proprietors' licences;
•   private hire vehicle licences; and
•   private hire operators' licences.

1   See Appendix I.
2   See Appendix I.

4.23

The district council can charge more than the fees laid down in LG(MP)A 1976, s 70(2). If the fees are to be greater, then the following procedure must be followed:

1.   A notice must be published in a local newspaper, stating the proposed fees which exceed those laid down in s 70(2).
2.   This must specify a date, not less than 28 days from the date on which the notice is first published. That date has two functions:
     (a)   it is the date by which any objections must be lodged; and
     (b)   it is the date on which the revised fees will come into effect if either –
          (i)   no objections are received; or
          (ii)   any objections received have been withdrawn before that specified date.
3.   It must also state where objections should be addressed and how they can be made. Obviously, it is desirable for such objections to be lodged in writing, as opposed to any other method (although an objection by a fax or email should be acceptable).

4.   A copy of the notice must be available at the council offices for inspection, free of charge, 'at all reasonable hours' (s 70(3)(b)).
5.   Once the objection period (usually 28 days) has expired, if there have been no objections received or those received have subsequently been withdrawn, then the new fees take effect, either at the end of the objection period, or when the last objection is withdrawn (s 70(4)).
6.   However, if objections are made and are not withdrawn, then the council must consider the objections.
7.   In the light of those objections (although it must consider them, it does not have to vary the proposal as a result of them) the council then sets a second date, which cannot be more than two months after the first date specified, when the new fees come into force (see the flowchart below). It appears that if an alteration is required after consideration, the fees could be increased as well as decreased.

A failure to comply with all these requirements would render the fees invalid, and this is reinforced by the remarks of Schiemann LJ in *Kelly v Liverpool City Council*[1] where, in relation to fees levied under s 70 he stated:

'28. What is clearly important is that any proposed increase is advertised and considered in the way envisaged in subsections [70](3)–(5).'

This is clearly correct as evidenced by the approach of the District Auditor in the Guildford case[2].

[1]   [2003] EWCA Civ 197, [2003] 2 All ER 772.
[2]   See para 4.5 above and http://www.guildford.gov.uk/CHttpHandler.ashx?

4.24

Although LG(MP)A 1976, s 53 contains no requirement for consultation, a local authority would be ill-advised not to embark upon some element of consultation with those persons who would be affected by an increase in fees (eg, the drivers of both hackney carriages and private hire vehicles).

Although it is not a statutory requirement, it would seem sensible for local authorities to follow the same procedure as contained in LG(MP)A 1976, s 70 for increases in fees under s 53, so as to provide the consultation which is required and to demonstrate that they are approaching the matter in a reasonable fashion.

Fees in general

4.25

It is important to appreciate that a statutory power to levy a fee does not give a local authority an absolutely free hand in relation to the scale of the fee that is levied. The impact of any increase upon the livelihood of those affected has to be taken into account, as does the scale of the increase itself. Consultation must take place with interested parties, whether this is a statutory requirement or not, and results of that consultation must be considered by the local authority before the decision is finally made. It is important that any such consultation is undertaken

FLOW CHART FOR FEES SET UNDER SECTION 70 OF THE LOCAL GOVERNMENT (MISCELLANEOUS PROVISIONS) ACT 1976

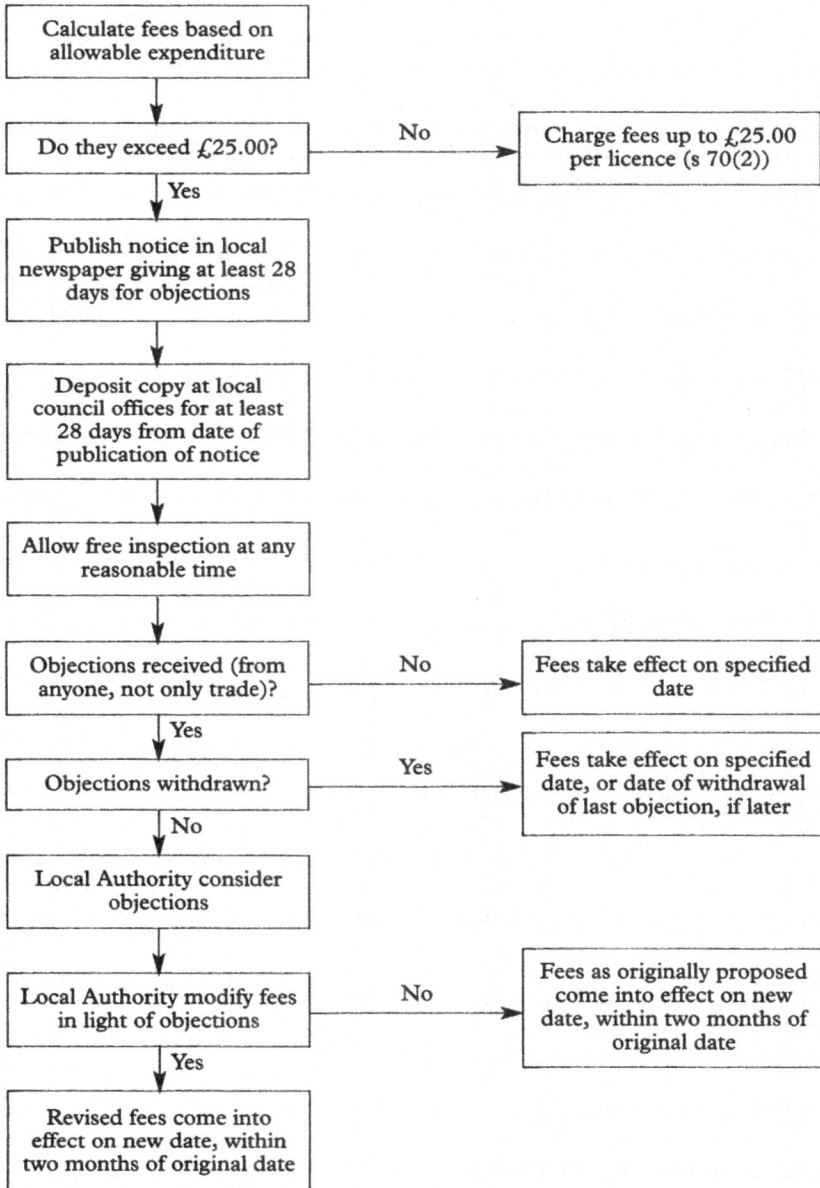

Calculate fees based on allowable expenditure

↓

Do they exceed £25.00? — No → Charge fees up to £25.00 per licence (s 70(2))

↓ Yes

Publish notice in local newspaper giving at least 28 days for objections

↓

Deposit copy at local council offices for at least 28 days from date of publication of notice

↓

Allow free inspection at any reasonable time

↓

Objections received (from anyone, not only trade)? — No → Fees take effect on specified date

↓ Yes

Objections withdrawn? — Yes → Fees take effect on specified date, or date of withdrawal of last objection, if later

↓ No

Local Authority consider objections

↓

Local Authority modify fees in light of objections — No → Fees as originally proposed come into effect on new date, within two months of original date

↓ Yes

Revised fees come into effect on new date, within two months of original date fairly and that the results are then considered properly by the local authority. Any suggestion that the consultation process is a sham would be grounds for an application for leave to seek a judicial review of the final decision.

4.26

It must also be borne in mind that when Parliament has given a local authority power to raise money to pay for an activity, then that power should not be rejected lightly. The control of hackney carriage and private hire vehicles, and associated drivers and operators, is a time-consuming and costly exercise and it is quite legitimate for a local authority to recover as much of their costs as they are able to in relation to this. Those involved in the hackney carriage and private hire trades are in a business and it would be difficult to justify an approach whereby a local authority subsidises private enterprise by refusing to recover as much of the costs associated with its statutory duties as it is able to do so. Such a subsidy would be at the expense of the other services the council could provide to its council tax payers, if full cost recovery was undertaken.

This is obviously a matter of politics and, as ever, it will be for the elected members to make the final decision. However, the overriding aim must be to protect the public and, within the statutory mechanisms, to provide an efficient and effective service for all concerned: those involved in the trade, the council itself and those who elect the council and pay for its activities: the council tax payers.

WITHIN LONDON

Hackney carriage vehicles

4.27

Fees are payable to Transport for London (TfL) for licences for both hackney carriage vehicle and hackney carriage driver's licences.

The power to levy a fee for a hackney carriage vehicle licence is contained in the Metropolitan Public Carriage Act 1869, s 6(5) (MPCA 1869). This power is multi-layered, as a fee can be levied on application, for any examinations or tests that may be required and then, when the licence is finally granted.

4.28

MPCA 1869, s 6(5) states:

'(5) A fee of such amount (if any) as Transport for London may determine shall be paid to Transport for London—
(a) by any applicant for a licence under this section, on making the application for the licence;
(b) by any applicant for the taking or re-taking of any test or examination, or any part of a test or examination, with respect to any matter of fitness, on making the application for the taking or re-taking of the test, examination or part; and

(c) by any person granted a licence under this section, on the grant of the licence.'

4.29

This power is extended by MPCA 1869, s 6(7) and (8) which states:

'(7) Different amounts may be determined under subsection (5) of this section for different purposes or different cases.

(8) Transport for London may remit or refund the whole or part of a fee under subsection (5) of this section.'

4.30

This can be contrasted with the powers contained in LG(MP)A 1976, s 70 in respect of hackney carriage proprietor's licences outside London, where there are specified matters that can be taken into account in deciding the fee. MPCA 1869, s 6 gives TfL an absolute discretion in setting the fee, and whether to vary the fee in different cases, and also whether to refund all or part of it. The overriding principle that licence fees cannot be used as a revenue raising tool, and the associated requirements of carrying forward surpluses etc will apply to TfL in the same way as they would apply to a local authority[1].

1   See above para 4.2 onwards.

4.31

The only method of challenge would appear to be judicial review. The possible grounds would seem to be either *Wednesbury* reasonableness or exceeding lawful authority. Whilst the absence of any limiting factors to take into account in determining the fee might suggest that TfL have a completely free rein in relation to fee setting, the general case law makes it clear that they are limited in their scope.

Hackney carriage drivers

4.32

Identical provisions exist in respect of hackney carriage driver's licences. They are contained in MPCA 1869, s 8(8), (10) and (11). As the wording is identical, the same comments apply as outlined above at paras 4.28–4.31.

Private hire

4.33

The Private Hire Vehicles (London) Act 1998, s 20 provides for fees to be levied on application for a London private hire operator's, vehicle or driver's licence. The fees themselves are prescribed by the licensing authority by means of regulations.

London operators

4.34

By virtue of the Private Hire Vehicles (London) (Operators' Licences) Regulations 2000, reg 4[1] (as amended) a fee is payable on application for a grant of an operator's licence. For a variation a fee is also payable. Once the licence is granted, a further fee of is payable. This latter fee covers a period of five years.

[1]   The original Private Hire Vehicles (London) (Operators' Licences) Regulations 2000, SI 2000/3146 is a Statutory Instrument. Subsequent amendments have been made by TfL under the powers contained in powers contained in s 32 of the Private Hire Vehicles (London) Act 1998. These can be found at https://tfl.gov.uk/corporate/publications-and-reports/taxi-and-private-hire?intcmp=3162#on-this-page-3 and see Appendix I.

4.35

There are no criteria laid down as to how these fees are calculated. Unlike the situation outside London, any fee can be set by Transport for London, but the general rules for fee setting will still apply[1]. Whilst the initial Regulations were made by the Secretary of State for Transport, amendments (including fee alterations) are made by TfL and would therefore be susceptible to judicial review[2].

[1]   See above para 4.2 onwards and see Appendix I.
[2]   See eg, The Private Hire Vehicles (London) (Operators' Licences) (Amendment) Regulations 2006 available at http://content.tfl.gov.uk/phv-london-operators-licences-amendment-regulations-2006.pdf

London drivers and vehicles

4.36

For drivers, the fees are set by the Private Hire Vehicles (London PHV Driver's Licences) Regulations 2003 (as amended)[1]. Again, no obvious routes of challenge exist to the level of the fee that may be set. Again, because these are made by TfL, any alterations to the fees by means of these Regulations would be susceptible to judicial review.

[1]   Although referred to as 'Regulations', these are not Statutory Instruments, but are made by TfL under powers contained in s 32 of the Private Hire Vehicles (London) Act 1998. The original Private Hire Vehicles (London PHV Driver's Licences) Regulations 2003 are available at http://content.tfl.gov.uk/private-hire-drivers-regulations-2003.pdf and the Private Hire Vehicles (London PHV Drivers Licences) (Amendment) Regulations 2004 are available at http://content.tfl.gov.uk/phv-london-phv-drivers-licences-amendment-regulations-2004.pdf and see Appendix I.

Chapter 5

Rehabilitation of Offenders Act 1974

INTRODUCTION

5.1

The existence (or otherwise) of previous criminal convictions can have a major impact upon the suitability of an applicant for a hackney carriage or private hire licence. This chapter examines the workings and impact of the Rehabilitation of Offenders Act 1974 (ROA 1974), as amended by the Legal Aid, Sentencing and Punishment of Offenders Act 2012 and its application to hackney carriage and private hire licensing outside and within London, together with the use of the Disclosure and Barring Service (DBS).

ROA 1974 introduced a mechanism whereby a person could 'lose' their criminal record in certain circumstances. This was designed to remove what were regarded by many as unfair consequences for people who had, perhaps, only committed one crime, possibly in their youth, which affected the rest of their lives in an unfair and disproportionate way. For example, they might not be able to obtain employment or, at best, be discriminated against by prospective employers and, likewise, obtaining insurance or consumer credit and so on might be difficult in some cases. It was felt that such persons should not be treated in the same fashion as 'hardened' criminals with lengthy criminal records. The result of this was the Rehabilitation of Offenders Act 1974.

THE WORKINGS OF THE REHABILITATION OF OFFENDERS ACT 1974

5.2

The consequence of ROA 1974 is that 'rehabilitation' occurs in certain situations. Convictions can become spent after a certain period of time and, once spent, for many purposes, a person is quite entitled not to disclose that they were ever convicted of such an offence. Although it is often felt that this applies to 'less serious' offences, this is incorrect, as both the possibility of rehabilitation and the length of time before rehabilitation occurs depends upon the sentence imposed, not the offence committed, as stated in ROA 1974, s 1:

> **'Rehabilitated persons and spent convictions**
>
> (1)   Subject to subsections (2), (5) and (6) below, where an individual has been convicted, whether before or after the commencement of this Act, of any offence or offences, and the following conditions are satisfied, that is to say—
>
> (a)   he did not have imposed on him in respect of that conviction a sentence which is excluded from rehabilitation under this Act; and
>
> (b)   he has not had imposed on him in respect of a subsequent conviction during the rehabilitation period applicable to the first-mentioned conviction in accordance with section 6 below a sentence which is excluded from rehabilitation under this Act;
>
> then, after the end of the rehabilitation period so applicable (including, where appropriate, any extension under section 6(4) below of the period originally applicable to the first-mentioned conviction) or, where that rehabilitation period ended before the commencement of this Act, after the commencement of this Act, that individual shall for the purposes of this Act be treated as a rehabilitated person in respect of the first-mentioned conviction and that conviction shall for those purposes be treated as spent.'

There are certain sentences which, when imposed, mean that a conviction can never become spent, as defined in ROA 1974, s 5(1), but, other than those, the theory is that any other conviction can in due course become spent for the purposes of the Act.

5.3

The period that has to elapse before a conviction becomes spent depends on the sentence imposed, rather than the crime committed, and these are contained in the table in s 5(2).

In March 2014[1] there was a significant reduction in the rehabilitation periods[2]. The revised rehabilitation periods took effect on 10 March 2014 and apply to all convictions, both before and after that date, and the rehabilitation period runs from the date of conviction in accordance with s 5(2)(a).

---

[1]   The reduction in rehabilitation periods was contained within s 139 of the Legal Aid, Sentencing and Punishment of Offenders Act 2012 which amended s 5 of the ROA 1974.

[2]   For example, prior to March 2014 the rehabilitation period for an adult sentenced to a fine was five years. It is now one year.

PROTECTED CONVICTIONS AND CAUTIONS

5.4

In 2013 the Court of Appeal ruled that revealing cautions for minor matters on an Enhanced CRB (now a DBS) disclosure was incompatible with Article 8 of the European Convention on Human Rights and Fundamental Freedoms incorporated into the Human Rights Act 1998 (HRA 1998)[1] and accordingly made a Declaration of Incompatibility under HRA 1998, s 4[2]. Although the Court of Appeal stated that the judgment would not take effect until the matter had been considered by the Supreme Court, the Government acted and introduced amendments to the Rehabilitation of Offenders (Exceptions) Order 1975[3]. The Rehabilitation of Offenders Act 1974 (Exceptions) Order 1975 (Amendment) (England and Wales) Order 2013[4] introduced two new concepts: a 'protected caution' and a 'protected conviction', neither of which will generally be released in any DBS certificate.

Both of these concepts are defined in Article 2A of the Rehabilitation of Offenders Act 1974 (Exceptions) Order 1975[5].

'(1) ...a caution is a protected caution if it was given to a person for an offence other than a listed offence and—

(a) where the person was under 18 years at the time the caution was given, two years or more have passed since the date on which the caution was given; or

(b) where the person was 18 years or over at the time the caution was given, six years or more have passed since the date on which the caution was given.'

'(2) ... a person's conviction is a protected conviction if the conditions in paragraph (3) are satisfied and—

(a) where the person was under 18 years at the time of the conviction, five years and six months or more have passed since the date of the conviction; or

(b) where the person was 18 years or over at the time of the conviction, 11 years or more have passed since the date of the conviction.'

The conditions contained in paragraph (3) in relation to a protected conviction are:

- the conviction cannot have been for a 'listed offence';
- the sentence did not involve custody or service detention; and
- the person has no other criminal convictions.

The listed offences are defined in paragraph (5) and are all reasonably serious:

'(a) an offence under section 67(1A) of the Medicines Act 1968;

(b) an offence under any of sections 126 to 129 of the Mental Health Act 1983;

(c) an offence specified in the Schedule to the Disqualification from Caring for Children (England) Regulations 2002;

(d) an offence specified in Schedule 15 to the Criminal Justice Act 2003;

(e) an offence under section 44 of, or under paragraph 4 of Schedule 1 or paragraph 4 of Schedule 4 to, the Mental Capacity Act 2005;

(f) an offence under section 7, 9 or 19 of the Safeguarding Vulnerable Groups Act 2006;

(g) an offence specified in section 17(3)(a), (b) or (c) of the Health and Social Care Act 2008, apart from an offence under section 76 of that Act;

(h) an offence specified in the Schedule to the Safeguarding Vulnerable Groups Act 2006 (Prescribed Criteria and Miscellaneous Provisions) Regulations 2009;

(i) an offence specified in Schedule 2 or 3 of the Childcare (Disqualification) Regulations 2009;

(j) an offence superseded (whether directly or indirectly) by any offence falling within paragraphs (a) to (i);

(k) an offence of—

(i) attempting or conspiring to commit any offence falling within paragraphs (a) to (j), or

(ii) inciting or aiding, abetting, counselling or procuring the commission of any such offence,

or an offence under Part 2 of the Serious Crime Act 2007 (encouraging or assisting crime) committed in relation to any such offence;

(l) an offence under the law of Scotland or Northern Ireland, or any country or territory outside the United Kingdom, which corresponds to any offence under the law of England and Wales falling within paragraphs (a) to (k);

(m) an offence under section 42 of the Armed Forces Act 2006 in relation to which the corresponding offence under the law of England and Wales (within the meaning of that section) is an offence falling within paragraphs (a) to (k); or

(n) an offence under section 70 of the Army Act 1955, section 70 of the Air Force Act 1955 or section 42 of the Naval Discipline Act 1957 of which the corresponding civil offence (within the meaning of that Act) is an offence falling within paragraphs (a) to (k).'

As a consequence, for most purposes including taxi licensing, a DBS certificate (whether standard or enhanced) will not reveal the existence of either a protected caution or a protected conviction (see Article 3(2) of the 1975 Order).

However, there are exceptions contained in Article 3ZA (which does not exclude protected cautions and convictions) so a Standard or Enhanced DBS Certificate will reveal protected cautions or convictions in relation to questions asked about the suitability of a person to work in certain fields as defined in Article 3ZA, none of which concern any hackney carriage or private hire licences.

As a protected conviction or caution must be for a minor matter which was committed a significant time ago, it is highly unlikely that any of these would have had an impact on the grant or continued retention of any hackney carriage or private hire licences, and accordingly the impact on taxi licensing of this alteration is negligible. However, it is important to recognise that even an enhanced DBS certificate will not reveal all convictions and cautions[6].

---

[1] For consideration of human rights in general and its impact on licensing, please see Chapter 2, para 2.106.

[2] See *R (app T) v Chief Constable of Greater Manchester and others* [2013] EWCA Civ 25, [2013] 1 WLR 2515. This decision was overturned by the Supreme Court in June 2014 (see [2014] UKSC 35, [2015] AC 49) so it is clear that the government rather jumped the gun. However, at the time of writing (August 2017) the matter is still being considered by the courts

with the latest decision being that of the Court of Appeal in *R (app P) v Secretary of State for the Home Department* [2017] EWCA Civ 321, [2017] 2 Cr App R 12.

3   SI 1975/1023.

4   SI 2013/1198.

5   SI 1975/1023.

6   The Disclosure and Barring Service has published a list of convictions which will always be disclosed. It is available at https://www.gov.uk/government/publications/dbs-list-of-offences-that-will-never-be-filtered-from-a-criminal-record-check

Cautions

5.5

A simple caution (often still referred to by the earlier terms of formal or police cautions) can be administered by the police and other enforcement agencies, although only the police can issue conditional cautions. The process is covered by the Ministry of Justice Guidance '*Simple Cautions for Adult Offenders*'[1]. In relation to the effect of a caution, the Guidance states:

'A) Significance of the admission of guilt

66. A simple caution is an admission of guilt to committing an offence and forms part of an offender's criminal record.

B) Criminal record: retention and disclosure of the simple caution

67. The simple caution forms part of an offender's criminal record and a record will be retained by the police for future use. It may also be referred to in future legal proceedings.

68. A simple caution may be revealed as part of a criminal record check. Separate guidance governs the disclosure of criminal record information.

69. All information relating to simple cautions (as well as convictions) for a recordable offence is retained on the Police National Computer ("PNC"). ACPO guidelines set out how long this information will be retained for. The information is kept for police operational reasons and in the interest of prevention and detection of crime.

70. Legislation which came into effect in December 2008 brought simple cautions within the ambit of the Rehabilitation of Offenders Act 1974 ("ROA"). This means that simple cautions become spent immediately they are administered10. This means that an individual does not need to disclose a simple caution when asked unless they are seeking work in an occupation that is listed in the Exceptions Order to the ROA such as working with children and vulnerable adults or for other excepted purposes such as seeking to obtain certain licences. Cautions will also be disclosed under Disclosure and Barring Service ("DBS") standard and enhanced checks. Further information can be obtained from the DBS11.'

Section 8A and Sch 2 to the ROA 1974 address the question of cautions and rehabilitation. The effect of s 8A and Sch 2 is that a simple caution is spent at the time the caution is given, whilst conditional cautions remain live for three months from the date on which the caution was given.

Table of Rehabilitation Periods – ROA 1974, s 5(2)

Sentence	End of rehabilitation period for adult offenders	End of rehabilitation period for offenders under 18 at date of conviction
A custodial sentence of more than 30 months and up to, or consisting of, 48 months	The end of the period of 7 years beginning with the day on which the sentence (including any licence period) is completed	The end of the period of 42 months beginning with the day on which the sentence (including any licence period) is completed
A custodial sentence of more than 6 months and up to, or consisting of, 30 months	The end of the period of 48 months beginning with the day on which the sentence (including any licence period) is completed	The end of the period of 24 months beginning with the day on which the sentence (including any licence period) is completed
A custodial sentence of 6 months or less	The end of the period of 24 months beginning with the day on which the sentence (including any licence period) is completed	The end of the period of 18 months beginning with the day on which the sentence (including any licence period) is completed
Removal from Her Majesty's service	The end of the period of 12 months beginning with the date of the conviction in respect of which the sentence is imposed	The end of the period of 6 months beginning with the date of the conviction in respect of which the sentence is imposed
A sentence of service detention	The end of the period of 12 months beginning with the day on which the sentence is completed	The end of the period of 6 months beginning with the day on which the sentence is completed
A fine	The end of the period of 12 months beginning with the date of the conviction in respect of which the sentence is imposed	The end of the period of 6 months beginning with the date of the conviction in respect of which the sentence is imposed

Sentence	End of rehabilitation period for adult offenders	End of rehabilitation period for offenders under 18 at date of conviction
A compensation order	The date on which the payment is made in full	The date on which the payment is made in full
A community or youth rehabilitation order	The end of the period of 12 months beginning with the day provided for by or under the order as the last day on which the order is to have effect	The end of the period of 6 months beginning with the day provided for by or under the order as the last day on which the order is to have effect
A relevant order	The day provided for by or under the order as the last day on which the order is to have effect	The day provided for by or under the order as the last day on which the order is to have effect

¹   With effect from April 2015. Available at https://www.gov.uk/government/uploads/system/uploads/attachment_data/file/416068/cautions-guidance-2015.pdf

The effects of re-offending

5.6

If a person commits another offence during the rehabilitation period for the first offence, then the rehabilitation period for the earlier offence is extended until the rehabilitation period for the subsequent offence has expired. ROA 1974, s 6(4) states:

'6–(4) Subject to subsection (5) below, where during the rehabilitation period applicable to a conviction—
(a)   the person convicted is convicted of a further offence; and
(b)   no sentence excluded from rehabilitation under this Act is imposed on him in respect of the later conviction;
if the rehabilitation period applicable in accordance with this section to either of the convictions would end earlier than the period so applicable in relation to the other, the rehabilitation period which would (apart from this subsection) end the earlier shall be extended so as to end at the same time as the other rehabilitation period.'

This does not apply to disqualifications, disabilities, prohibitions or other penalties which are not covered by the Table in s 5(2)¹. Whilst this clearly has important implications in relation to some subsequent offences the effect of s 6 is that some recidivists are never rehabilitated due to persistent re-offending, and their convictions will never be spent. The number of people so affected has reduced significantly as a result of the reductions in rehabilitation periods from March 2014.

¹   See ROA 1974, s 6(5).

The effects of rehabilitation

5.7

Once a person has been rehabilitated, the provisions contained in ROA 1974, s 4(1) come into effect:

'4.— Effect of rehabilitation.

(1) Subject to sections 7 and 8 below, a person who has become a rehabilitated person for the purposes of this Act in respect of a conviction shall be treated for all purposes in law as a person who has not committed or been charged with or prosecuted for or convicted of or sentenced for the offence or offences which were the subject of that conviction; and, notwithstanding the provisions of any other enactment or rule of law to the contrary, but subject as aforesaid—

(a)   no evidence shall be admissible in any proceedings before a judicial authority exercising its jurisdiction or functions in England and Wales to prove that any such person has committed or been charged with or prosecuted for or convicted of or sentenced for any offence which was the subject of a spent conviction; and

(b)   a person shall not, in any such proceedings, be asked, and, if asked, shall not be required to answer, any question relating to his past which cannot be answered without acknowledging or referring to a spent conviction or spent convictions or any circumstances ancillary thereto.'

On the face of it, this would prevent a local authority, in the discharge of its hackney carriage and private hire licensing functions, from enquiring about any spent convictions.

ROA 1974, s 4(2) prevents any questions about spent convictions being asked other than by a judicial authority.

5.8

The Rehabilitation of Offenders Act 1974 (Exceptions) Order 1975¹, as amended, was made under ROA 1974, s 4(4). Article 3 excludes the provisions of s 4(2) from applying in relation to questions asked by a person in the course of their duties or employment who is ascertaining the suitability of an individual in relation to certain occupations. These occupations are listed in the Rehabilitation of Offenders Act 1974 (Exceptions) Order 1975, Schedules 1 and 2. Since March 2002 hackney carriage and private hire drivers, both outside and within London, have been listed (referred to in the Order as 'taxi drivers') as 'regulated occupations' in Rehabilitation of Offenders Act 1974 (Exceptions) Order 1975,

Sch 2 para 4. The effect of this in relation to hackney carriage and private hire drivers is to render ROA 1974 inapplicable. For all practical purposes, it is as if ROA 1974 had never been passed for taxi drivers.

¹   SI 1975/1023. See Appendix I.

5.9

Hackney carriage proprietors and private hire operators and proprietors are not listed in the Rehabilitation of Offenders Act 1974 (Exceptions) Order 1975¹.

In relation to unlisted occupations it was recognised that there was a danger to the public in certain situations where a person with undesirable convictions could seek the grant of a licence, and as a consequence the provisions of ROA 1974, s 7(3) were enacted.

¹   SI 1975/1023.

Using 'spent' convictions

5.10

ROA 1974, s 7(3) states:

'(3) If at any stage in any proceedings before a judicial authority in England and Wales (not being proceedings to which, by virtue of any of paragraphs (a) to (e) of subsection (2) above or of any order for the time being in force under subsection (4) below, section 4(1) above has no application, or proceedings to which section 8 below applies) the authority is satisfied, in the light of any considerations which appear to it to be relevant (including any evidence which has been or may thereafter be put before it), that justice cannot be done in the case except by admitting or requiring evidence relating to a person's spent convictions or to circumstances ancillary thereto, that authority may admit or, as the case may be, require the evidence in question notwithstanding the provisions of subsection (1) of section 4 above, and may determine any issue to which the evidence relates in disregard, so far as necessary, of those provisions.'

5.11

The question is whether a hearing by a local authority licensing committee constitutes 'proceedings before a judicial authority'. This is defined in ROA 1974, s 4(6):

'4–(6) For the purposes of this section and section 7 below "proceedings before a judicial authority" includes, in addition to proceedings before any of the ordinary courts of law, proceedings before any tribunal, body or person having power—

(a)   by virtue of any enactment, law, custom or practice;

(b)   under the rules governing any association, institution, profession, occupation or employment; or

(c)   under any provision of an agreement providing for arbitration with
respect to questions arising thereunder;

to determine any question affecting the rights, privileges, obligations or
liabilities of any person, or to receive evidence affecting the determination
of any such question.'

Adamson v Waveney District Council

5.12

Application for hackney carriage drivers licence refused. Spent convictions
placed before the local authority (and the magistrates on appeal). Was it
possible to take spent convictions into account prior to the alterations to
the Rehabilitation of Offenders Act in 2002 to exclude the provisions of the
Act from applying to taxi drivers? Held: The local authority was a judicial
authority for the purposes of the Act and relevant spent convictions could be
taken into account.

The case of *Adamson v Waveney District Council*[1] makes it clear that a local
authority determining a licensing application, or taking action against a licence
is a judicial authority for these purposes. The judgment in this case was delivered
by Sedley J.

On the specific question as to whether s 7(3) applied to a decision to grant a
hackney carriage driver's licence, Sedley J said (at 900F):

'It is common ground in this case that the initial consideration by the local
authority of an application under section 59 of the Act of 1976 [Local
Government (Miscellaneous Provisions) Act 1976] for a hackney carriage
driver's licence is a proceeding before a judicial authority within this
provision.'

It is difficult to see any argument that would prevent this principle being applied
to all the hackney carriage and private hire licences, not just hackney carriage
drivers. As such, it is an extremely useful statement[2].

[1]   [1997] 2 All ER 898.
[2]   This applies to any licensing regime where the primary legislation does not prevent the use of
spent convictions (eg, Licensing Act 2003, s 114 specifically prohibits consideration of spent
convictions in relation to a personal licence application). The impact of *Adamson v Waveney
District Council* was acknowledged by the Home Office when it altered its '*Scrap Metal Dealers
Act 2013 Determining suitability to hold a scrap metal dealer's licence*' Guidance in May 2014.

5.13

At the time of the case, ss 51(1A) (in relation to private hire drivers) and 59(1A)
(in relation to hackney carriage drivers) of the Local Government (Miscellaneous
Provisions) Act 1976 (LG(MP)A 1976) allowed for the observations of the chief
officer of police to be sought by the local authority. This was at that time usually

done by means of a print-out of the person's record from the Police National Computer. These provisions have subsequently been repealed, but that does not affect the principles in this judgment[1].

The judgment of Sedley J continued[2] (at 900G):

'It appears to follow that by virtue of section 4(2) [of ROA 1974] the chief constable may treat the question put to him by the local authority as relating to spent as well as to unspent convictions ... It poses an immediate problem if the recipient local authority is to receive the whole of a previous offender's record, spent and unspent, relevant or irrelevant.'

He then attempted judicial assistance with the problem that he has identified:

'It may be that what I have to say shortly will help to resolve the problem that this, on the face of it, poses.'

[1]   See para 5.16 below.
[2]   *Adamson v Waveney District Council* [1997] 2 All ER 898.

5.14

The judgment is well reasoned. However, the judge required local authorities to seek and obtain a high level of co-operation from chief constables. His suggestion was that the Chief Constable, in framing his response to the request for his observations, should[1] (at 904C):

'... give careful consideration to what spent convictions, if any, are capable of relating to the issue which the local authority will have to decide, and to ensure that his disclosure (which is, after all, in the form of observations, according to the statutory language) is limited to what is capable of being relevant.'

[1]   *Adamson v Waveney District Council* [1997] 2 All ER 898.

5.15

This would (in the judge's view) allow the following procedure (which he suggested for appeals from the local authority) to apply to decisions of the local authority itself. His suggested procedure was as follows[1] (at 904A):

'... it seems to me that the following stages have to be gone through in any application such as that with which the justices were here concerned. First, with the help of the advocates before them, they have to identify what the issue is to which any spent convictions must relate if they are to be admitted. The issue here was the fitness of the applicant to hold the material licence. Secondly, those responsible for presenting material to the court must give their own objective, professional consideration to the question whether any or all of the spent convictions on the record are capable of having a real relevance to the issue which has been identified. When the matter is before justices, it will be the advocate for the local authority who must consider that. When the matter is before the local authority, it will be the chief constable who must consider it.'

Once that had been accomplished, the following should occur (at 904E):

'Next, the "judicial authority", as the Act calls it, has to consider whether it should admit the convictions in the light of the issue before it. Inevitably there will be procedural differences between what can happen before a local authority committee and what will happen before justices. These may, however, be able to be brought satisfactorily into line in the following way. Before justices I have no doubt that the right course is for the local authority advocate to indicate what is the class of offence, the age of the offence and perhaps, in broad terms, the apparent seriousness (gauged by penalty) of the offence shown by the record before him. That is the best that can be done, without pre-empting the very decision that the justices have to take, to enable the justices to decide (having heard anything the applicant wishes to say to the contrary) whether to admit any spent convictions. They may decide that some but not others in the list ought to be put before them.'

1　*Adamson v Waveney District Council* [1997] 2 All ER 898.

5.16

To assist the local authority at what might be termed 'first instance', Sedley J added[1] (at 904G):

'Translating this back to the stage where the matter is before the local authority, it may very well be that the chief constable should correspondingly be invited to provide a covering letter giving the same broad indications, but no more, so that the committee can decide whether it needs to go into some or all of those offences, the existence of which has been indicated to them. That indication will of course, as I have said, already have been pruned of those which are clearly not relevant and should not be considered under any circumstances.'

1　*Adamson v Waveney District Council* [1997] 2 All ER 898.

5.17

Assuming that there were some relevant convictions (whether spent or not), the next stage would be[1] (at 904H):

'Once some or all of the spent convictions are admitted in evidence, either before the local authority committee or before justices, the applicant is then entitled naturally to be heard, not by way of suggesting that the convictions were incorrectly arrived at but in order to persuade the judicial authority that they are either, in truth, irrelevant or such, by reason of their age, circumstances or lack of seriousness, that they should not jeopardise his application. All of that is simple natural justice.'

And then, finally (at 904J):

'The judicial authority must then come to its own dispassionate conclusion, having in mind not only the interests of the applicant as a person with spent convictions but also the interests of the public in whose interests these exceptional powers are being exercised.'

1   *Adamson v Waveney District Council* [1997] 2 All ER 898.

County of Herefordshire District Council v Prosser

5.18

> Application for a hackney carriage and private hire drivers licence (dual licence). Refused because of previous convictions. Decision overturned on appeal to the magistrates' court on the basis that the convictions were minor, irrelevant and spent. Appeal by way of case stated to the High Court. Held that the particular convictions were not minor, all convictions were relevant and no convictions were spent for taxi drivers.

In *County of Herefordshire District Council v Prosser*[1] an application was made to the district council for a combined hackney carriage and private hire drivers licence[2]. The application was refused due to Prosser's previous convictions 'which consisted of 14 appearances in court for offences including assaults, Public Order Act offences, criminal damage, driving offences and dishonesty offences'[3]. Prosser appealed to the magistrates' court who granted the appeal. They took the view that the sentences were spent under ROA 1974[4]. The council appealed by way of case stated and the particular point on the question of whether the offences were spent was considered by the judge[5]:

> '9 Mr Savill [for the Council] submits that [the magistrates] ... second error was in concluding that it would be "unreasonable to regard [the respondent's] spent convictions as still relevant." The Justices were wrong in law in that, first, by operation of the Rehabilitation of Offenders Act 1974 (Exceptions) (Amendment) Order 2002, hackney carriage drivers and private hire drivers are regulated occupations for the purposes of the Rehabilitation of Offender's Act 1974 Schedule 1 Part III and as such are exempt from the provisions of the Act. There is therefore no such thing as a "spent" conviction in relation to these occupations. As such, to dismiss them as irrelevant was an error of law.'

His conclusion on this point was clear[6]:

> 'Further, the Justices erred in finding that the offences were spent. I am satisfied that by operation of the 2002 Order, the convictions against the respondent were not spent. Such convictions, in the present circumstances, do not become spent. The *Adamson*[7] case that was referred to is not relevant in the light of the 2002 Order.'

This judgment is a clear reinforcement of the effect of the amendment to the Rehabilitation of Offenders Act 1974 (Exceptions) Order 1975[8], and that there are no spent convictions for taxi drivers (although it must be recognised that neither a protected caution or conviction will be revealed on an enhanced DBS certificate[9]).

The question that it raises is what the judge meant by saying that the judgment in *Adamson v Waveney District Council* was irrelevant? It appears clear that he is referring to the ability to take what were then spent convictions (in 1997 at the date of the *Adamson* judgment) into account in relation to determining the fitness and propriety of a taxi driver. That clearly altered in 2002.

It is important however to recognise that hackney carriage and private hire vehicle proprietors and private hire operators are not exempted occupations under the Rehabilitation of Offenders Act 1974 (Exceptions) Order 1975[10] and accordingly the ruling in *Adamson* remains not only relevant but vital in allowing local authorities to take spent convictions into account for those applicants and licensees.

What is less clear is whether the Prosser case alters the rationale in *Adamson* that notwithstanding the ability to consider all convictions, only 'relevant' convictions should be placed before the decision maker. This is not addressed in the later judgment, and indeed it is clear that all the convictions recorded against Prosser were indeed relevant for his proposed role as a taxi driver[11].

No legislative changes or judgements since *Adamson* have directly altered the approach taken in that case that:

> 'those responsible for presenting material to the court [or local authority committee or officer] must give their own objective, professional consideration to the question whether any or all of the spent convictions on the record are capable of having a real relevance to the issue which has been identified.'[12]

It is clear that if the word 'spent' is removed from the above, it must still be the correct approach, and as a consequence it is suggested that the *Adamson* approach is the correct one and only relevant convictions should be presented to the decision-maker.

[1]   [2008] LLR 274, QBD.

[2]   As the criteria for granting drivers licences for hackney carriages and private hire vehicles outside London are identical, and the power to take action against these licences are also the same, a number of local authorities grant 'dual' or 'combined' licences which act as both a hackney carriage driver's licence and a private hire driver's licence. For more detail see Chapters 9 and 14.

[3]   Per Michael Supperstone QC (Sitting as a Deputy High Court Judge) at paragraph 4.

[4]   Full consideration of the impact of those offences and the question of fitness and propriety is contained in Chapter 10, para 10.21 onwards.

[5]   Above at para 9.

[6]   Above at para 12.

[7]   *Adamson v Waveney District Council* [1997] 2 All ER 898 above.

[8]   it should be noted that the Rehabilitation of Offenders Act 1974 (Exceptions) (Amendment) Order 2002, SI 2002/441 is not a stand-alone provision as it might appear from this particular judgment, but rather it amended the Rehabilitation of Offenders Act 1974 (Exceptions) Order 1975, SI 1975/1023.

[9]   See para 5.4 above.

[10]   SI 1975/1023.

11   See Chapter 10, para 10.23 onwards. for an analysis of these offences and their impact on an application for a hackney carriage and private hire driver's licence.
12   *Adamson v Waveney District Council* [1997] 2 All ER 898 per Sedley J at 904A.

The Disclosure and Barring Service

5.19

The difficulty with this was that a great deal of reliance was placed on the Chief Constable.

Since March 2002 the mechanism for obtaining information about previous convictions has changed. The Police Act 1997, Pt V (PA 1997) is implemented by the Disclosure and Barring Service (DBS), which is an executive non-departmental public body, sponsored by the Home Office[1]. The DBS provides three types of disclosure: basic, standard and enhanced. These relate to the certificates defined in PA 1997, Pt V.

1   The disclosure system was previously run by the Criminal Records Bureau, and the 'CRB Certificate' is still the common method of referring to the (now) DBS Certificate.

5.20

'Basic disclosure' is the equivalent of a criminal conviction certificate (PA 1997, s 112) and is available to any individual[1]. The disclosure is sent to the applicant, and it lists all current convictions within the meaning of ROA 1974. An employer or a local authority could ask an individual to provide an up-to-date basic disclosure certificate, and no registration with the DBS is necessary. Of course, an individual may refuse to obtain, or provide, a basic disclosure certificate, but that may adversely affect their chances of employment or of obtaining a licence.

1   Basic Disclosures are only available from Disclosure Scotland, but can be obtained by any UK resident.

5.21

'Standard disclosure' is the equivalent of a criminal record certificate (PA 1997, s 113A). This is only available to bodies or organisations that have registered with the DBS in respect of employment and positions which are excluded from the effects of ROA 1974 by the Rehabilitation of Offenders Act 1974 (Exceptions) Order 1975[1], as amended.

Standard disclosures vary depending on whether the subject has only one conviction, or more convictions.

Where the subject has only one conviction, the certificate will only contain details of any current convictions (ie unspent convictions), any convictions which resulted in a custodial sentence (spent or unspent), any convictions for an offence specified in PA 1997, s 113(6D), any current caution for a s 113(6D) offence, or a current caution for any other offence.

Where a subject has more than once conviction, the certificate will contain details of all convictions, current cautions for a s 113(6D) offence, or current cautions for any other offence.

In all cases, the standard DBS Certificate is sent to the subject, who then has to provide it to the relevant body or organisation.

1   SI 1975/1023.

5.22

There are two types of enhanced disclosure: an enhanced disclosure and an enhanced disclosure with checks of the barred lists.

An enhanced disclosure certificate is the equivalent of an enhanced criminal record certificate (PA 1997, s 113B).

As with a standard disclosure, this is only available in respect of employment and positions which are excluded from the effects of ROA 1974 by the Rehabilitation of Offenders Act 1974 (Exceptions) Order 1975[1], as amended, but in addition, it must also be in respect of a purpose or occupation which is covered by the Police Act 1997 (Criminal Records) Regulations (as amended)[2] Enhanced disclosures contain details of all current convictions, as well as spent convictions and cautions, reprimands or final warnings, plus details of other information held by the police . As with standard disclosures, the application must be countersigned by an authorised person on behalf of a body or organisation that has registered with the DBS[3]. Again, the applicant is sent the DBS certificate, and then he has to show that to the local authority or TfL.

An enhanced disclosure with checks of the barred lists is the equivalent of an enhanced criminal record certificate (PA 1997, s 113B) plus the information accessed under ss 113BA and 113BB. This is available for purposes and occupations that are prescribed under regulations made under s 125.

1   SI 1975/1023.
2   SI 2002/233, reg 5(a)(zf) covers 'considering the applicant's suitability to obtain or hold a taxi driver licence'.
3   A physical signature is not required if the application is made on-line in accordance with the DBS requirements: s 113(2A).

5.23

As a taxi driver is a regulated occupation by virtue of the Rehabilitation of Offenders Act 1974 (Exceptions) Order 1975, Sch 1, Part III[1] an enhanced disclosure is required in relation to applicants for new drivers' licences, or renewals of existing licences. The section of the application form (Section X) which asks what the 'position applied for' is should be completed with 'other workforce' to ensure that there is a check of the adult and child barred lists, as well as common law disclosure. This is in accordance with the DBS Guidelines[2].

1   SI 1975/1023.
2   'How employers or organisations can request DBS checks for potential employees' section x61 (available at https://www.gov.uk/guidance/dbs-check-requests-guidance-for-employers#avoiding-common-mistakes-on-the-dbs-application-form). This make it clear that applications that do not involve working with adults or children must use the description 'other workforce'. This accords with the The Safeguarding Vulnerable Groups Act 2006 (Miscellaneous Provisions) Regulations 2012, SI 2012/2112. Regulations 24 and 25 define regulated activity in relation to vulnerable adults, but these regulations are specifically excluded for hackney carriage and private hire drivers by reg 26. It is generally argued that a hackney carriage or private hire drivers does not

'work' with adults or children in the way specifically covered by the Safeguarding Vulnerable Groups Act 2006.

CHALLENGING A DBS CERTIFICATE

5.24

It is possible to challenge the information contained in a DBS Certificate if it is incorrect and that challenge can be brought by either an applicant or an employer (or local authority). These provisions are contained in PA 1997, s117

PA1997, s 118 allows a person to challenge the information included in the certificate which is covered by s 113BA (relating to children) on the grounds that it was either not relevant for the post applied for, or should not have been included.

In relation to incorrect information, an application must be made in writing to the DBS, which must then consider if the information is correct or not. Where the dispute concerns the additional information, the appeal lies to the Independent Monitor. This post was created by PA 1997, s 119B.

PRACTICAL EFFECT OF CRIMINAL CONVICTIONS ON APPLICANTS AND LICENCE HOLDERS

5.25

As only taxi drivers are mentioned in the Rehabilitation of Offenders Act 1974 (Exceptions) Order 1975[1], enhanced disclosures are not available for hackney carriage proprietors or private hire operators and proprietors. Information concerning any previous convictions for applicants for these licences should be obtained by means of a recent basic disclosure obtained by the applicant and a statutory declaration (see para 5.47 onwards).

[1]   SI 1975/1023.

5.26

Once disclosure has been obtained, then it will be necessary for the local authority or TfL/TPH to decide on the relevance or otherwise of any spent convictions to the particular application.

Criminality itself, on a single occasion, is not necessarily a bar to the grant of a licence, whether that is a driver's, operator's or proprietor's licence. Consideration must be given to the nature of the offence the relevance of that offence to the particular licence, the gravity of the offence and the age of the offence. In addition, an isolated offence will carry less weight than numerous offences, whether those are similar or disparate.

5.27

The purpose of hackney carriage and private hire licensing is to protect the public. As a consequence, there are many licences that it would be inappropriate to grant to those with a criminal conviction.

5.28

Notwithstanding this, the term 'criminal' tends to be a sliding one and it is important that the nature of a person's convictions, and possible threat that they may pose to the public bearing in mind the activity that their licence may allow, is very carefully considered.

5.29

As a result, the implications of ROA 1974, in relation to spent and unspent convictions, are important.

In relation to the relevance of a criminal conviction to the holder of a licence relating to hackney carriage or private hire matters, it is worth considering the following. It is suggested that criminal offences fall into one of 14 categories:

1. Offences of dishonesty.
2. Offences of violence (including sexual violence and other forms of abuse).
3. Motoring offences.
4. Offences involving substance abuse (both alcohol and drugs).
5. Offences of damage (criminal damage, arson, vandalism etc).
6. Offences that are contraventions of licensing laws or conditions.
7. Offences involving obscene materials.
8. Offences involving consensual but under-age sex.
9. Local authority offences, eg health and safety, food safety, trading standards, breach of planning and statutory nuisance notices etc.
10. Offences of discrimination.
11. Offences relating to the Administration of Justice (eg not surrendering to bail).
12. Animal Cruelty, dangerous dogs etc.
13. Kerb-crawling or other sexual offences including living off immoral earnings etc.
14. Treason.

It is suggested that there are no other categories and that all criminal offences fall into one of the above. When the licensed roles relating to hackney carriages and private hire vehicles are considered, it can be seen that some or all of these categories of offence and subsequent criminal conviction are relevant for those purposes.

5.30

The public needs to be protected and it is only too easy to foresee the temptations that could be put in the way of an habitually dishonest licence holder involved in the hackney carriage or private hire trade.

This ranges from a driver simply over-charging or providing the wrong change through to drivers and operators taking advantage of the knowledge that a person is away from their property for a period. There have been incidents reported around the country where people used a hackney carriage or private hire vehicle to take them to an airport for a holiday and who have returned to find their house burgled. In one incident, a spate of such crimes was directly linked to the drivers working for a particular private hire operator. In addition, the use of vehicles as conveyances for stolen or smuggled goods, or other forms of contraband is a legitimate concern. The use of hackney carriages and private hire vehicles to move people around for criminal purposes, such as prostitutes, or children to facilitate abuse should also not be overlooked.

5.31

Likewise, a driver with violent tendencies, whether it is aggression towards men or women or sexual aggression, may not be a suitable person to drive the public around, bearing in mind that, on occasions, the public can be difficult and uncooperative and, on other occasions, the driver will be dealing with people who are travelling on their own and may be extremely vulnerable for whatever reason.

5.32

Motoring offences are equally important in relation to someone who intends to earn their living driving the public. They will arguably carry less weight in relation to merely providing vehicles in which the public will be conveyed via a private hire operators licence, but could well be important in relation to a vehicle proprietor if the convictions relate to the condition of a vehicle, or insurance offences.

5.33

Offences involving substance abuse may indicate an inability to control the use of such substances, with a potentially highly detrimental effect upon passengers. Any tendency towards drinking and driving or towards abuse of controlled drugs, which may impair a driver's ability, should be viewed with extreme caution. Similarly, any supply of illegal substances may well have a bearing on the suitability of a proprietor to hold a vehicle licence, due to the potential for the use of a vehicle for movement of such items.

5.34

Criminal damage, and other forms of property injury will be relevant, either because the conviction indicates a pre-meditated desire to cause damage and loss, or because it indicates a failure to control emotions sufficiently in extreme circumstances.

5.35

Any contravention of licensing laws or conditions, irrespective of whether or not these are related to hackney carriage or private hire licensing, are important as they suggest a disregard of the importance of those requirements.

5.36

Any convictions in relation to obscene materials should be viewed with concern, although it is accepted that such convictions do not necessarily indicate violent tendencies. Again, the use of licensed vehicles to transport such material should also be considered.

5.37

Convictions obtained against people for having consensual sex with others under the age of consent, whether heterosexual or homosexual, are also a cause for concern. Although these do not involve violence, they do indicate a disregard for the law, and hackney carriages and private hire vehicles carry great numbers of under-age persons, who could be vulnerable to such advances. It has become apparent that hackney carriages and private hire vehicles are also used for the transporting children for sexual purposes.

5.38

Local authority offences, although not necessarily directly relevant to taxi licensing, should not be discounted lightly by decision-makers.

5.39

Offences of discrimination are a concern to all within our society, representing as they do a totally unacceptable treatment of certain sections of society. They should be taken extremely seriously and would therefore be seen to have considerable impact upon a current or potential licensee.

5.40

Failure to comply with bail requirements, or other non-compliance with justice requirements demonstrate a flagrant disregard for legal rules and requirements and must be considered seriously.

5.41

Any offences involving misuse or mistreatment of animals indicates a character lacking in either compassion or empathy, both of which are important for taxi drivers.

5.42

Kerb crawling and other sexual offences will always be matters of serious concern due to the dominating position of the offender in relation to the victim.

5.43

Convictions for treason are extremely rare and therefore unlikely to feature in a taxi licensing situation[1].

1   Convictions for treason are extremely rare, with only a handful of cases resulting in conviction since the beginning of the 20th century. The last person to be executed for treason was William Joyce (known as Lord Haw-Haw) in 1946, but there was a conviction in 1981 under the Treason Act 1842 (Marcus Serjeant was sentenced to five years' imprisonment after firing blanks at the Queen during Trooping the Colour).

5.44

Relevance does not only emanate from the nature of the crime that was committed, but is also dependent on the quantity of crimes that are committed. A single minor offence of eg, dishonesty committed when an individual was a minor 20 or 30 years previously will be relevant but will carry very little weight. Conversely a series of convictions for matters which in isolation would not be relevant to the activity covered by the licence would become relevant because of quantity and the evidence that the individual has difficulty complying with legislative requirements.

As noted above, criminality itself on an isolated occasion is not an automatic bar to holding a hackney carriage or private hire licence, but it is vital that it is fully understood that the purpose of licensing is to ensure the protection of the public, rather than a mechanism to enable persons to work. As the Department for Transport's *'Taxi and Private Hire Licensing Best Practice Guidance'* makes clear[1], public protection is the overriding consideration, although it is fully acknowledged that from an applicant's perspective, a licence is either the passport or barrier to employment.

Decisions as to whether or not to grant a licence (or take action against an existing licence) must be based upon safety considerations and as the courts have made clear, questions of livelihood or impact on an individual's family are not relevant[2].

1   Paragraph 8 states: 'The aim of local authority licensing of the taxi and PHV trades is to protect the public.' The Guidance was first published in 2006 and revised in March 2010. It is available at https://www.gov.uk/government/publications/taxi-and-private-hire-vehicle-licensing-best-practice-guidance
2   See in particular *Leeds City Council v Hussain* [2003] RTR 13 and *Cherwell DC v Anwar* [2012] RTR 15.

Government guidelines

5.45

All local authorities and TfL/LTPH should have adopted policies in relation to criminal convictions. In 1992, local authorities were given powers to seek the views of the police in relation to an applicant for a hackney carriage or private hire driver's licence. Accompanying these powers, a joint Department of Transport and Home Office circular[1] was issued to local authorities which included (at Annex D) some suggested guidelines for dealing with criminal convictions. An updated version was produced by Local Government Regulation (formerly LACORS) in September 2010[2]. Criminal records are now available via the DBS[3].

1   DoT circular 2/92, HO circular 13/92. See Appendix II.
2   Available at http://www.ihsti.com/lacors/ContentDetails.aspx?id=24387
3   See para 5.19 onwards above.

5.46

Many local authorities adopted the guidelines contained in the 1992 circular[1] wholesale, whilst others have used them as the basis for their own modified policy. A policy on previous convictions in relation to each type of licence is vital. It makes it easier for applicants, who will then know what considerations will be taken into account in relation to their application. It should also promote consistency of decision-making on the part of the local authority or TfL/LTPH. All applicants should be given a copy of the policy guidelines adopted by the local authority or TfL/LTPH when they are given their application form and other information. Provided such a policy is used as a policy and not as hard and fast rules, this is quite acceptable, notwithstanding the repeal of the provisions which the circular referred to. However, as with any policy, this must be kept under review and up to date[2].

1   DoT circular 2/92, HO circular 13/92. See Appendix II. Other models have been produced by LGR Regulation (part of LACORS) and the Local Government Association. At the time of writing (August 2017) the Institute of Licensing is working on a new approach – see www. instituteoflicensing.org
2   Due to the passage of time, any local authority which based their previous convictions policy on the 1992 Circular and has not updated it, is likely to find it wanting.

Statutory declarations

5.47

Notwithstanding the requirement for a local authority to seek enhanced disclosure from the DBS in respect of taxi drivers, a statutory declaration can still prove useful. It is even more important in relation to operators and proprietors when the basic disclosure will only reveal current live convictions. Many authorities still require a statutory declaration to be completed in relation to all applications. This has the advantage of revealing (assuming that it is completed correctly) any convictions that do not appear on the Police National Computer, together with matters that are not convictions, such as Fixed Penalty Notices, ASBOS and injunctions and cautions (although these should be recorded on the PNC).

In addition, the application form should make it clear that the questions are being asked under the powers contained in LGMPA 1976, s 57, and that any false declaration is an offence by virtue of s 57(3) outside London. Within London the equivalent provisions are the London Hackney Carriages Act 1843, s 14 for hackney carriage drivers licences, Order 15 of the London Cab Order 1934 in respect of hackney carriage proprietors licences, and the Private Hire Vehicles (London) Act 1998, s 28 for private hire operators, drivers and vehicle licences.

5.48

Motoring offences do not automatically appear on the Police National Computer (and therefore on DBS Disclosures[1]) and to check for these, a search of the Driver and Vehicle Licensing Agency (DVLA) records can be made. Although this can be useful, it should be recognised that, if a driver has received a period of disqualification, for whatever reason, upon reinstatement of the licence, the DVLA records are cleared. As a result, there are occasions when such a search could be useful, but it should not be seen as either an automatic requirement or foolproof.

[1]   See para 5.19 onwards.

5.49

There are, in fact, a number of such convictions, where a body other than the Crown Prosecution Service or the police (prior to 1 January 1986) brought the prosecution. These include prosecutions by the DSS, in relation to benefit fraud; by local authorities, in relation to housing benefit fraud, hackney carriage and private hire matters, other licensing matters, trading standards offences (which include matters relating to motor cars, such as safety), environmental and planning offences and, possibly, matters such as harassment of tenants; by HMRC, in relation to tax matters, VAT offences and smuggling matters; and by the RSPCA in respect of animal cruelty offences.

IMPORTANCE OF STATUTORY DECLARATION'S TRUTHFULNESS

5.50

It can be seen that the offences which may not appear on a DBS disclosure can be extremely serious, which any local authority would wish to know about. These should be revealed on a statutory declaration or application form. Although there is no method of checking the accuracy of these disclosures, most authorities retain applications from previous years and many have a policy of checking the offences revealed on each year's statutory declaration and/or application form against those of previous years. In addition, they can be checked against either the enhanced or basic disclosure that has been obtained or provided. This is not in conflict with the Data Protection Act 1998, because the fifth principle of data protection (Data Protection Act 1998, Sch, 1, para 5) states:

> 'Personal data processed for any purpose or purposes shall not be kept for longer than is necessary for that purpose or those purposes'

which would appear to allow application forms and other documents relating to a licence to be kept for as long as the licensee continues to hold any type of licence.

If there is a discrepancy, the applicant can be asked to explain it. This may be a simple oversight or mistake, or a more serious matter of intentionally not revealing criminal convictions. In cases involving intentional non-disclosure of offences, there are two possible courses of action.

In the case of a false statutory declaration, the file can be passed to the police, with a view to an investigation and subsequent prosecution by the Crown Prosecution Service for perjury being instigated under the Perjury Act 1911, s 5.

Alternatively, it is possible for the local authority to prosecute the person under LG(MP)A 1976, s 57(3), provided the local authority have asked about previous convictions on the application form. A statutory declaration would appear to satisfy this requirement.

Section 57(3) states:

'57–(3) If any person knowingly or recklessly makes a false statement or omits any material particular in giving information under this section, he shall be guilty of an offence.'

5.51

It is important that local authorities do all they can to ensure that the applicant has submitted their correct and full names on any licence application: omitting a middle name or adding a middle name can, on occasions, produce a disclosure which relates to a different person. Disclosures should be checked against current DVLA driving licences to ensure that the names given are the same.

5.52

If the disclosure reveals offences which do not correspond with offences revealed on the applicant's statutory declaration, it is good practice for the local authority to interview the person to establish why other offences have been revealed. It may be that there is a mistake on the records held by the police or that they may have omitted to reveal all of their offences on the statutory declaration. Either way, it is important that the position is clarified, so that the local authority knows exactly what offences do comprise the person's record.

HE'S PAID HIS PRICE; HE'S DONE HIS TIME

5.53

An argument often put forward against the use of previous convictions is that, once a person has served their sentence, their 'debt to society' has been paid and it is wrong to keep bringing a matter up and punishing them again for the same offence, eg, by revoking a licence or refusing to grant or renew, thereby depriving them of their livelihood. However, the local authority is not punishing them, it is protecting the public from a person who has demonstrated a propensity towards wrongdoing. Accordingly, it is both correct and essential that convictions, both current and spent, are considered.

Chapter 6

Enforcement outside London

INTRODUCTION

6.1

Any legal requirements are meaningless and pointless unless they are enforced. If there is no sanction applied for breach of the law, the law is worthless. This is true of hackney carriage and private hire licensing, just as much as it is true of any other area of law.

Enforcement of hackney carriage and private hire matters outside Greater London falls to local authorities. From April 2014 local authorities must have regard to the requirements of the Regulators' Code[1]. This is a Statutory Code of Practice made under the Legislative and Regulatory Reform Act 2006.

Local Authorities should also have regard to their own enforcement and prosecutions policy (if any). This is important following the decision in *R v Adaway*[2]. This case shows that if a local authority either fails to have regard to its own enforcement policy, or departs from it without good reason, an application for a stay in criminal proceedings can be made. The decision has been distinguished in subsequent cases[3]. The current position is that an application for a prosecution to be stayed as it amounts to an abuse of process will only be likely to succeed if the decision to prosecute is *Wednesbury* unreasonable, taking into account any enforcement policy the authority may have.

[1] Available at https://www.gov.uk/government/uploads/system/uploads/attachment_data/file/300126/14-705-regulators-code.pdf
[2] [2004] EWCA Crim 2831, [2005] LLR 142.
[3] See *R (on the application of Mondelly) v Commissioner of Police for the Metropolis* (2007) 171 JP 121, [2006] EWHC 2370 (Admin) and *London Borough of Wandsworth v Rashid* [2009] EWHC 1844, (Admin) [2009] LLR 788.

CRIMINAL ENFORCEMENT

6.2

The duties to implement hackney carriage legislation are applied to local authorities by virtue of the Town Police Clauses Act 1847 (TPCA 1847), the Public Health Act 1875, the Local Government Act 1972 and the Transport Act 1985.

The TPCA 1847 was originally intended to be incorporated into local Acts, but it now stands as a complete Act in its own right, in relation to hackney carriages. It was incorporated (together with the Town Police Clauses Act 1889) into the Public Health Act 1875 by the Public Health Act 1875, s 171 and then applied to the whole of England and Wales by the Transport Act 1985, s 15. If any local authority which had local legislation incorporating the provisions of TPCA 1847 but which excluded the hackney carriage provisions within TPCA 1847, those exclusions were also repealed by the Transport Act 1985, s 15.

6.3

In relation to the Local Government (Miscellaneous Provisions) Act 1976 (LG(MP)A 1976), which applies to both hackney carriages and private hire vehicles, this is enforced by the local authority, but only after LG(MP)A 1976, Pt II has been adopted by the local authority under the provisions of LG(MP)A 1976, s 45. There is one exception to the requirement to adopt the Act and that is where the area of the council, or part of area of the council was, prior to 2000, within the Metropolitan Police area. Until the reduction of the Metropolitan Police area, hackney carriage licensing fell to the Public Carriage Office, and it was not possible to adopt LG(MP)A 1976. However, the Greater London Authority Act 1999, s 255(4) applies LG(MP)A 1976, Pt II to the whole or part of any district outside Greater London which was formally in the Metropolitan Police area without the need for any adoption.

Criminal enforcement is the responsibility of the local authority in whose area the offence was committed, rather than the authority that granted the licences (if any). These may be the same, but the vehicle may have travelled over a local authority border.

6.4

If enforcement involves prosecution for offences, it is essential that the local authority can demonstrate they can fulfil two prerequisites:

1.   In all cases, they must be able to show that they have authority to bring proceedings. This will be a decision by the council or the committee, sub-committee or officer who has the delegated power to make the decision to prosecute in the particular case.
2.   If the prosecution is for an offence committed under LG(MP)A 1976, it must be demonstrated that the Act has been adopted. Again, this will be by means of a certified copy of a resolution adopting the Act, plus copies of the statutory notices published in a local newspaper and evidence that notice was given to any parish councils within the council's area[1]. If, since the adoption of the Act, reorganisation of local government has taken place within the area, it will also be necessary to demonstrate how and why an adoption by an authority, which has since been reorganised, still has application to the new authority bringing the proceedings.

These points are often overlooked, but are fundamental and essential to the question of a prosecution.

¹   See para 6.3 onwards for full details on the adoption process and requirements for the Local
     Government (Miscellaneous Provisions) Act 1976.

Dee and Clwyd River Authority v Parry

6.5

> Prosecution for water pollution. No minute of the resolution to commence
> proceedings was produced. Case dismissed by the magistrates' court. Water
> Authority appealed by way of case stated. Appeal dismissed as the High
> Court agreed that the water authority was analogous to a local authority
> and could only commence legal proceedings following a resolution to do so,
> which had to be evidenced by the minutes themselves or a certified copy of
> the minutes.

The first point was considered in the case of *Dee and Clwyd River Authority v
Parry*[1] where the Divisional Court upheld the view of the magistrates' court that
a minute recording the decision to institute a prosecution (or a certified copy of
such a minute) was essential to demonstrate that the prosecuting authority had
taken such a decision[2].

¹   (1967) 65 LGR 488, DC.
²   The power for a local authority to commence legal proceedings is now contained in the Local
     Government Act 1972, s 222.

Kingston-upon-Hull City Council v Wilson

6.6

> Prosecution for using, driving and operating a private hire vehicle without
> the required licences. Defence raised the question of whether the Local
> Government (Miscellaneous Provisions) Act 1976 had been adopted and
> that adoption demonstrated by the prosecution. Held: That the prosecution
> had not shown adoption was in place and therefore the prosecution could
> not succeed.

The second point was considered in the case of *Kingston-upon-Hull City Council
v Wilson*[1]. Although this was a case primarily concerned with other points, the
question of failing to demonstrate adoption would have been fatal in other
circumstances. Buxton J stated the following:

> 'A question, however, arises as to how the matter should be resolved.
> Towards the end of his argument Mr Neish drew our attention to the
> fact that it was nowhere below proved, on behalf of the local authority,
> that a resolution has, in fact, been passed under section 45 of the Act
> [LG(MP)A 1976], applying that Act to the district of the City of Hull.
> Therefore, the fact at the basis of all this law that this is a controlled district
> was never proved. Mr Sampson [for the local authority], who has dealt
> with this matter very fairly on behalf of the prosecutor, accepted that it was

incumbent upon the local authority to prove (no doubt as a formal matter, but it was not done) that the Act applied to the Hull district and therefore the necessary precondition of all these offences, that Mr Wilson [the defendant in the original prosecution] was acting in a controlled district, had not been made out.

I see no answer to this objection. It may be regarded as a technical, and even unattractive, point but it is properly taken. That means that there would be no point in remitting this case to the Magistrates because even if it were remitted there would be a fatal gap in the evidence that was before them on the first occasion, which could not now be filled; as I put to Mr Sampson in argument, and he properly accepted, if Mr Wilson has been represented below, and that representative has properly waited until the end of the prosecution case and then submitted there was no case to answer because of this defect in the prosecution evidence, it would have been extremely difficult for the prosecutor to argue that he should be allowed to reopen his case.

For that reason, therefore, I would not remit this case to the Magistrates.'

1   (1995) Times, 25 July; see further Chapter 13, para 13.72.

Aylesbury Vale District Council v Call a Cab Limited

6.7

> Prosecution for acting as a private hire operator without a licence. Defence raised the question of adoption during the hearing. Prosecution adjourned and evidence of non-compliance with the adoption process adduced. Defendant acquitted as evidence did not show correct adoption. Appeal by way of case stated. Local Authority demonstrated substantial compliance with adoption process and therefore held that the Local Government (Miscellaneous Provisions) Act 1976 had been correctly adopted.

The question of adoption of the 1976 Act was considered in *Aylesbury Vale District Council v Call a Cab Limited*[1]. Call a Cab Ltd was prosecuted for operating without a private hire operator's licence. At the hearing the question of adoption of the 1976 Act was raised at a late stage. As a result, the hearing was adjourned by the court for a month to enable the local authority to provide evidence of the resolution. When the hearing resumed, evidence of non-compliance with the requirements of the adoption process under s 45 was adduced. In particular, this concerned the failure by the local authority to notify the Parish Councils in accordance with s 45(3)(b). It was alleged that an analysis of a random sample of 12 out of a total of 112 Parish Council records showed no evidence that the required notice had been given by the district council. There was also a question over the validity of the resolution and whether it complied with the requirements of s 45(2). As a consequence of the concerns over the validity of the adoption of the legislation, the defendant was acquitted.

The council appeal by way of case stated and the first question was:

'1. Whether there was sufficient evidence on which the court could reasonably conclude that the requirements of section 45(3)(b) of the Local Government Miscellaneous Provisions Act 1976 had not been satisfied?'

The principal judgment was given by Ouseley J who addressed the question in the following way[2]:

'It is agreed that the question which has to be asked is whether the conclusion which the District Judge reached was irrational. That is, was it irrational for him to conclude that the defendant had succeeded on the balance of probabilities of showing that 12 Parish Councils had not been notified? If the District Judge was entitled to reach that conclusion, then the answer to question 1 is yes. The framing of the question reflects the fact that the defendant bore the burden of proof on the civil standard. True it is that there is a presumption of regularity upon which the Council could rely before him. But in my judgment that presumption is merged into the question of whether the defendant has succeeded in showing, on the balance of probabilities, that there was no notice given to the 12 parishes.'

On this first question, he concluded[3]:

'17. I start from this premise. The District Judge was entitled, upon analysis of the minutes of the Parish Council which he had received, to infer that their record-keeping minuting, including minuting of correspondence was sufficiently detailed and thorough that the receipt of a notice would have been minuted. That was an inference which it was open to him to draw having examined in considerable detail the contents of the minutes. It was therefore open to him to conclude that something was missing from those minutes and that was because the notice had not been served as required.

18. Faced with that, he then was entitled to ask what it was that the Council had produced beyond a presumption that it would have done what it had intended to set out to do. There was no specific evidence from the Council, not evidence even in the form of a report to the full Council stating that the notices had been sent out to the Parish Councils or a minute to that effect or a recital to the resolution. It is said that nothing can be inferred from that silence and, even if further records had been produced, Parish Councils might have differed in the way in which they recorded the receipt of such notification. That is as may be but it does not show that the conclusion of the District Judge on the evidence he had in relation to what happened to each of those 12 Councils was irrational. There was no evidence that 12 Parish Councils were rural or that Parish Councils in a rural area were disinclined to record notices received of a particular nature.

19. In substance, the factors which Mr Findlay [for the Appellant Council] contends were ignored, were not in reality ignored, they were arguments which the District Judge considered, but which he rejected. It is my conclusion therefore that the question should be answered in favour of the defendant: yes.

20. I understand the concern which the Local Authority at this distance in time has about any such conclusion, particularly as after the passage of such time it would regard the presumption of legality as a solid basis upon which to resist such a defence. I accept that the concern is such that legislative changes are considered. I would emphasize the limited nature of the decision here. It does not prevent the Council in a subsequent case producing better evidence of what underlay the resolution, supported perhaps by a contemporaneous report showing or asserting contemporaneous compliance with section 45(3), a state of affairs which would have been of considerable assistance. It does not stop them researching whether other Parish Council records show that notice was given, which would support its contention that there was no great weight to be attached to non-minuting by other Councils, because a random process of sending out notices might be regarded as less probable than a random recording process. Indeed, it can go through the adoption process again. But none of those possibilities is a reason for holding that the District Judge's conclusion in this respect was an irrational one, one which he was not entitled to come to.'

It is therefore clear that the question of adoption can be legitimately raised[4] by the defence and it is for the council to demonstrate that it has properly adopted the provisions of Part II of the 1976 Act. The court then went on to consider what was required to demonstrate adoption.

The question was whether there had to be complete compliance with the entirety of the requirements contained in s 45, or whether some deviation was allowable[5]:

'The argument which this revolves around is whether and to what extent a failure to comply with the giving of notice under section 45(3)(b) necessarily, and without any other matters being brought into play, invalidates the resolution so that it is of no effect.'

The court's conclusion was this:

'22. We have been taken through a substantial number of authorities to provide assistance as to what the effect of the non-compliance found by the District Judge would be. I do not consider it necessary to go through the detail of those submissions. What the cases all show is that the question of whether non-compliance has the effect of invalidating an administrative act is a matter that depends in the first place on the construction of the statute, read as a whole in order to determine the imputed intention of Parliament as to what the consequences of non-compliance with a procedural requirement should be. Here Mr Kolvin [for the respondent defendant] prays in aid the negative language of section 45(3)(b): the resolution is not to be passed without compliance with those provisions. Criminal liability can ensue, although part 2 of the 1976 Act goes considerably wider than merely to create a criminal offence in respect of a business activity, up to that moment, still lawful.

23. The notification requirements are an important part of making the public aware of the imminent passing of a resolution. There is no provision whereby an individual is entitled to be notified just because that individual is affected, and there is no means whereby an individual can appeal against the administrative act when first it begins to bite upon him. He drew analogies with the decision of Forbes J in *R v Birmingham City Council ex p. Quietlynn Ltd*[6]. He emphasized that, this being a criminal prosecution, a defendant should not be in peril of conviction upon an act which would be invalidated by the Administrative Court. Indeed, the decision in *Boddington v British Transport Police*[7] suggested that the powers which the Administrative Court might have to exercise its discretion against quashing an administrative act, or refusing relief on the grounds that it had not been sought timeously, would not apply so as to bar reliance upon invalidity by a defendant to a criminal charge.

24. Mr Findlay submitted that whatever the particular language of section 45 in terms of prohibition, the statutory provisions read as a whole showed that the notice requirement was no more than a notification requirement. It did not incept a process of consultation, nor was it there obviously to give rise to a right of objection. There was no obligation on a Parish Council to do anything with the notice when received apart perhaps, with the benefit of hindsight, to note that the post had arrived. There was no requirement that the notice be sent to the operators of private hire vehicles businesses who might, in 1989, have been affected.

25. Plainly there was no prejudice suffered by these defendants from any failings since even had they been in business in 1989 they would not have received notice and as they were not in business then they could not have received notice, nor was there any obligation to provide notice of the resolution to businesses coming to existence after the passing of the resolution. The notice to the public at large should be regarded as effectively provided by the notice to the press advertisement which requirement was complied with. The fact as is true that these failures were not failures in relation to timing but, as found by the District Judge, failures in relation to giving notice at all did not prevent the failure to meet the requirement being one which did not necessarily give rise to invalidity.

26. In my judgment, although the language of section 45(3) clearly makes it a requirement, mandatory if you will at this stage, that notice be given to each Parish Council, reading the statute as a whole and recognising the complete lack of prejudice to the defendants from non-compliance with the statutory requirements beyond the fact that non-compliance might give them an argument whereas validity would deprive them of it, the factors I have discussed here show that, if there is substantial compliance with the statutory provision, the act is not invalid.'[8]

Substantial compliance is therefore sufficient. But what does this mean? In *Aylesbury*, the argument was accepted that evidence of notification to some Parish Councils was sufficient[9], and therefore it was reasonable to assume that notification to all Parish Councils had been made, notwithstanding the facts that in some cases the Parish Council had not recorded that it had ever received the notice.

Clearly each case would be determined on its own facts, but it is suggested that absence of any evidence of notification, or of the required notices in the press, might result in a different decision. It is also clear that if there is no evidence of the resolution to adopt, or that resolution is flawed, such deficiencies might well be viewed as amounting to less than substantial compliance.

1   [2013] EWHC 3765 (Admin), [2014] RTR 30.
2   At para 14.
3   Paragraph 17 onwards.
4   At an early stage of the proceedings. This was made clear by Treacy LJ at para 33 where he said:

>   'I would only add to the remarks of my Lord that I was concerned on reading these papers to see that the issue of the validity of the by-law (sic) [not a by-law, but adoption of the Act] had not been raised at the case management hearing, nor had it been raised in the defence statement. Good practice, and the observations on a number of occasions by this court, dictate that an issue of this nature should be raised well in advance of the hearing so that all parties are in a position to present relevant evidence to the tribunal at the time when the case is listed for hearing. In this instance an adjournment of over a month was necessary and a further day of court time was taken up. In reality, the raising of the issue at such a late stage can properly be described and has been described as tantamount to an ambush. I repeat that it is not good practice and it should not happen in the future.'

5   Per Ouseley J at para 21.
6   [1985] 83 LGR 461.
7   [1999] 2 AC 143.
8   In the official transcript ([2013] EWHC 3765 (Admin)), and the reports in Licensing Law Reports ([2014] LLR 261) and the Road Traffic Reports ([2014] RTR 30) some vital words are missing from paragraph 26. The only appear in the Public and Third Sector Law Reports ([2014] PTSR 523) where for some reason, the particular paragraph is both complete and numbered 25!
9   Although not stated in the report, the inference is that it was unlikely that a random selection of Parish Councils to receive the notification was made.

Nottingham City Council v Rashid and Taj

6.8

> Unlicensed private hire operator, continuing to operate and drive unlicensed vehicles. The argument was presented that the City Council had not adopted the Local Government (Miscellaneous Provisions) Act 1976 correctly because at the time of adoption the 1847 Act was not in force throughout the district. Held: That the adoption was valid and an injunction was granted to prevent further breaches of the criminal law.

Another point that has arisen is whether the LG(MP)A 1976 can be adopted and apply in places where the TPCA 1847 did not apply before local government re-organisation in 1974. This was considered in the case of *Nottingham City Council v Rashid and Taj*[1]. The defendants maintained that they did not require any licences to run a private hire business (operators', vehicle or drivers' licences) as the LG(MP)A 1976 did not apply in Nottingham. This was considered by

Frances Kirkham J in connection with an application for an injunction sought by Nottingham City Council to restrain the defendants from repeated breaches of the LG(MP)A 1976. She dismissed the defendants' contentions, stating:

'23. Mr Rashid and Mr Taj contend that the claimant has no legal right to succeed in this application because it does not have a lawful licensing regime. Their case is that the claimant has failed to adopt Part 2 of the 1976 Act. It follows, they say, that the claimant has no power to license any private hire vehicles. They contend that their convictions were unlawful. This is the position on which Mr Rashid has taken, with respect to every set of proceedings involving questions of licensing. They refer to Public Health Act 1875, Town Police Clauses Act 1847 and Transport Act 1985.

24. Mr Zaman has taken me through the legislative history relevant to this issue. Part 2 of the 1976 Act deals with the licensing of hackney and private hire vehicles. It is an "adoptive" Act i.e. it must be adopted by the claimant. Section 45(2) of the 1976 Act provides:

"If the Act of 1847 is in force in the area of the district council, the council may resolve that the provisions of this part of the Act, other than this section, are to apply to the relevant area …"

25. The reference to the Act of 1847 is a reference to the Town Police Clauses Act 1847. Section 1 of that Act provides:

"This Act shall only extend to such towns or districts in England or Ireland as shall be comprised in any Act of Parliament hereafter to be passed which shall declare that this Act shall be incorporated therewith …"

26. Section 5 of the Public Health Act 1875 defined districts as urban sanitary districts and rural sanitary districts. Accordingly, by the provisions of the 1875 Act, the 1847 Act was to apply to all urban districts. Nottingham was such a district.

27. Section 171 of the 1875 Act provides:

"The provisions of the Town Police Clauses Act 1847 with respect to the following matters, namely

…

(4) with respect to hackney carriages

shall for the purposes of regulating such matters in urban districts be incorporated with this Act …"

In other words, the provisions of the 1874 Act with respect to hackney carriages were incorporated into the 1875 Act.

28. Section 56 of the Nottingham Corporation Act 1882 made reference to the 1847 Act:

"The terms 'hackney carriage' or 'carriages' whenever used in Sections 37, 39 to 52 … 58 and 60 to 68 … of the Town Police

Clauses Act 1847 as incorporated with the Public Health Act 1875 shall be deemed to include ..."

Section 118 of the Nottingham Corporation Act 1923 also makes reference to the 1874 Act:

"The provisions of the Town Police Clauses Act 1847 and the byelaws of the Corporation for the time being in force with respect to hackney carriages shall be as fully applicable in all respects to hackney carriages standing or plying for hire ..."

In addition, Section 52 of the Nottingham Corporation Act 1925, which dealt with byelaws as to hackney carriages, referred to the provisions of the Town Police Clauses Act 1847:

"The power to make byelaws conferred upon the Corporation by Section 68 of the Town Police Clauses Act 1847 shall be extended ..."

29. Those references reinforce the claimant's case, which I accept, that the relevant provisions of the 1847 Act apply to it.

30. The boundaries of Nottingham City have been extended by the provisions of the Nottingham Corporation Act 1932 and the Nottingham City and County Boundaries Act 1951. It follows that the private hire vehicle business which the defendants run in Alfreton Road is within the claimant's boundary.

31. The major local government reorganisation pursuant to the Local Government Act 1972 abolished urban districts and vested the powers of those districts in district councils. With effect from 1 April 1974, Nottingham City became the district council for the district of Nottingham. By Section 180 of the 1972 Act, the powers under the Public Health Acts 1875 to 1925 were vested in the district councils.

32. The defendants rely on paragraphs 2325 of Schedule 14 of the 1972 Act, which deal with the Public Health Acts 1875 to 1925. Paragraph 23 provides that the Public Health Acts 1875 to 1925 are extended throughout England & Wales, whether or not they so extended before 1 April 1974. Paragraph 23 provides that paragraph 23 shall not apply to various enactments and including Section 171(4) of the Public Health Act 1875, and that those enactments shall, subject to paragraph 25, apply to those, and only those, to which they applied immediately before 1 April 1974. Paragraph 25 permitted the local authority to resolve that any of the enactments referred to in paragraph 171(4) of the 1875 Act had to have been passed before 1 April 1975; sub-paragraph 4 of paragraph 25 required the Secretary of State to approve any such resolution.

33. On 27 June 1978 the claimant council resolved that the provisions of Part 2 were to be brought into effect in the city of Nottingham with effect from 4 September 1978.

34. The defendants rely on Section 15 of the Transport Act 1985. This provides:

> "(1) Where immediately before the commencement of this section, the provisions of the Town Police Clauses Act 1847 with respect to hackney carriages ... (as incorporated in ... the Public Health Act 1875) were not in force throughout the whole of the area of a district council in England & Wales, these provisions shall:
> (a) if not then in force in any part of the council's area, apply throughout that area: and
> (b) if in force in part only of its area, apply also in the remainder of that area."

There is, in my judgment no merit in the defendants' arguments in relation to this provision. The effect of that provision is that the hackney carriage provisions of the 1874 Act applied where they had not previously applied.'

This confirms that the adoption of the 1976 Act can apply to any district within England and Wales, and the only questions will be whether or not the authority has firstly adopted the Act and secondly, can then demonstrate that.

[1]   (24 February 2006, unreported), QBD (injunction application).

GENERAL POINTS

6.9

As with any criminal investigation and subsequent prosecution, the general rules applicable to such investigations must be followed. These include compliance with the requirements of eg, the Police and Criminal Evidence Act 1984 (PACE), the Criminal Procedure and Investigations Act 1996, the Regulation of Investigatory Powers Act 2000 etc.

6.10

In addition, Art 6 of the European Convention on Human Rights and Fundamental Freedoms (ECHR), as incorporated in the Human Rights Act 1998, enshrines the right to a fair trial. A full discussion on criminal prosecutions and human rights is beyond the scope of this book, but one particular point in relation to hackney carriage and private hire enforcement is usefully worth mentioning.

6.11

Many authorities use entrapment actions to enforce the Town Police Clauses Act 1847, s 45 (TPCA 1847). Section 45 states:

'Penalty for plying for hire without a licence

If the proprietor or part proprietor of any carriage, or any person so concerned as aforesaid, permits the same to be used as a hackney carriage plying for hire within the prescribed distance without having obtained a licence as aforesaid for such carriage, or during the time that such licence is suspended as hereinafter provided, or if any person be found driving, standing, or plying for hire with any carriage within the prescribed distance for which such licence as aforesaid has not been previously obtained, or without having the number of such carriage corresponding with the number of the licence openly displayed on such carriage, every such person so offending shall for every such offence be liable to a penalty not exceeding level 4 on the standard scale.'

6.12

It can be seen that it is an offence under TPCA 1847, s 45 to ply for hire in any vehicle that is not a hackney carriage, or by using a hackney carriage that is not licensed within the district in which it is plying for hire[1].

[1]   See Chapter 8, para 8.7 onwards for consideration of what constitutes plying for hire.

Nottingham City Council v Amin

6.13

> A hackney carriage was hailed by undercover police officers in a district for which it was not licensed. The driver responded to that hailing and picked up the passengers. On a prosecution for unlawful plying for hire a successful defence was raised of entrapment which breached the right to a fair trial under Art 6 of the European Convention on Human Rights and that the evidence should be excluded under s 78 of the Police and Criminal Evidence Act 1984. That argument was successful and the defendant was acquitted. The council appealed by way of case stated and it was held that provided a simple opportunity to commit a crime was presented, without any encouragement, that did not amount to a breach of the requirements for fairness.

6.14

The method frequently employed by local authorities to establish whether there is an illegal plying for hire is to use an undercover officer (or other undercover person, such as a police officer) to attempt to hire the vehicle. If that is successful, then an offence has been committed. This approach was used in Nottingham and led to a challenge under Art 6 of the ECHR as to the fairness of this method of obtaining the evidence in the case of *Nottingham City Council v Amin*[1].

[1]   [2000] 2 All ER 946, QBD.

6.15

The argument raised before the stipendiary magistrate was that the evidence obtained by the undercover officers should be excluded under PACE, s 78 as the use of entrapment had been ruled unacceptable by the European Court of Human Rights in relation to the fair trial protected by Art 6 of the ECHR.

6.16

In this case it was a hackney carriage from another, adjoining district which was successfully flagged down by undercover officers. The situation was summarised by Bingham LCJ giving the judgment of the court[1] (at 2D):

'The respondent was the driver of a licensed taxi from an area adjoining, but not including, the area of the Nottingham City Council. That licensed vehicle was G312 BUY, the subject of the information. On 22 October 1998 the respondent was driving this car in Lower Parliament Street, Nottingham, in the area of the Nottingham City Council in which the vehicle was not licensed. The vehicle was fitted with a roof light which was capable of being lit, but which was not lit up at the time of the relevant encounter.

Two special constables in plain clothes flagged the car down and the respondent stopped. The two constables asked the respondent to take them to a specified destination. He agreed and carried them to that destination in the car. On reaching the destination they paid him the fare for the journey, which he accepted. Also at the destination the respondent spoke to two enforcement officers of the Nottingham City Council.

On the stipendiary magistrate's findings there was no evidence to show that the respondent had offended on any earlier occasion or on this particular evening until this event. The stipendiary magistrate described the special constables as "agents provocateurs", but in my judgment that is to treat as a primary fact a judgmental issue at the heart of the case.

The respondent gave evidence at the trial and said that he had been under a mistake when he picked up the passengers, but the stipendiary magistrate rejected that evidence. He found that there was no conversation in which the respondent had asked the officers for identification and that he had not in the course of that conversation suggested that he was in the city to collect a pre-arranged fare. The magistrate found that the respondent's spoken English was not good, but that his understanding was better, and that there had been no misunderstanding when he had accepted the passengers. The magistrate rejected the evidence of the respondent when it conflicted with that of the constables.

Thus, in a nutshell, the respondent was driving in the middle of Nottingham a car which was licensed as a taxi, but not for that area. Two pedestrians hailed him. He stopped, picked them up and carried them for a fare to their destination. The stipendiary magistrate was in the event left with no explanation why the respondent was in the middle of Nottingham in the car, where he was coming from or where he was going, and there was no explanation which the magistrate accepted as to why the respondent had picked up the passengers when he was not licensed to do so. There was, however, no evidence of any pressure exerted by the constables or any persuasion of the respondent, and he was not wheedled into doing what he did.

In para 6 of the case stated the magistrate said:

"I was of opinion that: (a) based on my findings of fact, there could be no question of the Respondent being in any misunderstanding as to the circumstances in which he accepted the two fares as passengers. As his evidence was not believed, there was no basis of fact upon which he could be acquitted."'

It was accepted, following the decision of the House of Lords in *R v Sang*[2] that there was no defence of entrapment in English law. A number of other cases were referred to by the judge who summarised the position in English law as follows (at 6A):

'It seems to me that the court has adopted a fairly consistent line. On the one hand, it has been recognised as deeply offensive to ordinary notions of fairness if a defendant were to be convicted and punished for committing a crime which he only committed because he had been incited, instigated, persuaded, pressurised or wheedled into committing it by a law enforcement officer. On the other hand, it has been recognised that law enforcement agencies have a general duty to the public to enforce the law and it has been regarded as unobjectionable if a law enforcement officer gives a defendant an opportunity to break the law, of which the defendant freely takes advantage, in circumstances where it appears that the defendant would have behaved in the same way if the opportunity had been offered by anyone else.'

[1]   *Nottingham City Council v Amin* [2000] 2 All ER 946, QBD.
[2]   [1980] AC 402.

6.17

However, the question to be answered was whether this approach was inconsistent with the rulings of the European Court of Human Rights, which would lead to the evidence being excluded as being prejudicial to a fair trial under art 6 of the ECHR. Three cases were considered by the Lord Chief Justice: *Schenk v Switzerland*[1], *Lüdi v Switzerland*[2] and (at some length) *Teixeira de Castro v Portugal*[3].

[1]   (1988) 13 EHRR 242, ECtHR.
[2]   (1992) 15 EHRR 173, ECtHR.
[3]   (1998) 28 EHRR 101, ECtHR.

6.18

The facts in *Teixeira de Castro v Portugal*[1] as outlined by Bingham LCJ[2] were as follows (at 9D):

'It is plain that the public security police initially approached a suspected drug dealer named VS in order to obtain hashish from him. He having, despite a number of approaches, failed to put them in touch with a hashish supplier, they approached him again to see if he could put them in touch with a supplier of heroin. At this stage he mentioned the name of the applicant, as a result of which an approach was made to the applicant which led to a deal on the strength of which the applicant was prosecuted, convicted and sentenced.'

There was a distinction in Portuguese law between an undercover agent and an agent provocateur, and significant other differences between this case and an investigation and prosecution undertaken in England. Bingham LCJ made the role of the court clear when he stated (at 12A):

'The court's [the European Court of Human Rights] task under the convention was not to give a ruling as to whether statements of witnesses were properly admitted as evidence, but rather to ascertain whether the proceedings as a whole, including the way in which evidence was taken, were fair.'

The conclusion of the European Court of Human Rights in *Teixeira de Castro v Portugal* was (at 116):

'39. In the light of all these considerations, the court concludes that the two police officers' actions went beyond those of undercover agents because they instigated the offence and there is nothing to suggest that without their intervention it would have been committed. That intervention and its use in the impugned criminal proceedings meant that, right from the outset, the applicant was definitively deprived of a fair trial. Consequently, there has been a violation of art 6(1).'

The conclusion of Bingham LCJ was (at 13C):

'It is in my judgment apparent that there are various matters to which the court [the European Court of Human Rights] attached significance ... which would not be readily applicable in English proceedings: for example (and obviously) no anti- drug-trafficking operation would be ordered or supervised by a judge. Similarly, if there were evidence pointing to the propensity of a given defendant to commit an offence of a certain kind, that would not be adduced in evidence before the trial court. Nor in the ordinary course would there be evidence of whatever report or suspicion had given rise to the presence of the two police officers who were in Nottingham on the occasion in question.

None the less, Mr Beloff [for the respondent, Amin] is entitled to, and does, attach significance to the precise language which the court uses in para 38 of the judgment. He submits that the two police constables in Nottingham did not confine themselves to investigating the respondent's criminal activity and did not do so in an "essentially passive manner". Accordingly he submits that they are to be regarded, in the light of that authority, as having instigated the offence or incited it and so as having acted as agents provocateurs so as to render the proceedings as a whole unfair, there being no other significant evidence against the respondent.

While I for my part am willing to accept that, on a precise and literal reading of the court's language, Mr Beloff is entitled to make that submission, I am wholly unwilling to accept the far-reaching proposition which he bases on it. It seems to me that that conclusion has to be understood in the context of the whole argument before the court on that occasion and on the special facts of that case.

It is true that in the present case the criminal activity alleged was much more minor. It is also true that the facts are much simpler and that they simply cannot lend themselves to the construction that this respondent was in any way prevailed upon or overborne or persuaded or pressured or instigated or incited to commit the offence. The question for the stipendiary magistrate was whether, on the facts which he found, the admission of this evidence had such an adverse effect on the fairness of the proceedings that he should exclude it, or whether (to put the test in a different way) the effect of admitting it was to deny the respondent a fair trial.

In my opinion the only possible answer to both questions was No. If an affirmative answer had been possible then the question became one for the judgment of the stipendiary magistrate and for his exercise of discretion. In my judgment, however, an affirmative answer was not possible and it follows that the stipendiary erred in law in ruling as he did [that the evidence should be excluded].'

1   (1998) 28 EHRR 101, ECtHR.
2   *Nottingham City Council v Amin* [2000] 2 All ER 946, QBD.

6.19

The effects of this case are that enforcement by way of entrapment is permissible, provided that the undercover officers do not incite, encourage, persuade or coerce the suspect to commit the offence.

6.20

This view has been upheld by the House of Lords in *R v Loosley*[1] where it was accepted that the courts had the power to stay proceedings as an abuse of the process if the entrapment involved coercion or persuasion, and evidence obtained in those ways could be excluded under PACE, s 78. However, the House of Lords also upheld the approach that provided the entrapment operation merely presented the defendant with the opportunity to commit a crime, the evidence should not be excluded under s 78 and there was no infringement of the defendant's rights under Art 6 of the ECHR.

The requirements of the Regulation of Investigatory Powers Act 2000 (RIPA) must also be considered. In general covert surveillance by local authorities is restricted and in some cases prohibited.

1   [2001] UKHL 53, [2001] 4 All ER 897. This ruling has been consistently followed, most recently in *R v Palmer (Tre)* [2014] EWCA Crim 1681, [2015] Crim LR 153.

ENFORCEMENT UNDER THE TOWN POLICE CLAUSES ACT 1847

6.21

Under the hackney carriage provisions of TPCA 1847, there is no specific reference to a particular officer empowered to enforce the provisions of the Act. This means that the power to enforce lies with the local authority itself, rather than a specific statutorily designated officer, and it will be for the local authority to delegate its powers of enforcement to whichever department and officers it sees fit.

6.22

There are a number of offences contained within the provisions of TPCA 1847 which fall to the local authority to enforce, although the police could take action, if they wished, as they are no longer prevented from doing so. Until the passing of LG(MP)A 1976, s 27, the police were prevented from prosecuting by the Public Health Act 1875, s 253, unless specifically authorised to do so by the relevant section.

6.23

Table 6.2 gives a brief outline of the offences under TPCA 1847. These are all summary offences as a consequence of the Public Health Act 1875, s 251. This was repealed for all purposes, except for the prosecution of offences under TPCA 1847, by the Public Health Act 1936, s 346 and Sch 3, Pt I.

6.24

Fine 'levels' refer to the concept of the standard scale of fines, which were introduced by the Criminal Justice Act 1982, ss 37, 38 and 46. These replaced fixed fines specified in a huge number of legislative provisions. The amount equating to each level can be increased, allowing fine levels to maintain a sensible level when inflation is taken into account. Currently the fine levels are show in the tables below[1].

Table 6.1

Standard Scale Fine Levels

Level	Maximum Fine
1	£200.00
2	£500.00
3	£1,000.00
4	£2,500.00
5	Unlimited

Table 6.2

Enforcement table – Town Police Clauses Act 1847

Section	Offence	Maximum Penalty
40	Giving false information on application for HC proprietor's licence	Level 1
44	Failure to notify change of address of HC proprietor	Level 1
45	Plying for hire without a HC proprietor's licence	Level 4
47	Driving a HC without a HC driver's licence	Level 3
47	Lending or parting with a HC driver's licence	Level 3
47	HC proprietor employing unlicensed driver	Level 3
48	Failure by HC proprietor to hold HC driver's licence	Level 1
48	Failure by HC proprietor to produce HC driver's licence	Level 1
52	Failure to display HC plate	Level 1
53	Refusal to take a fare	Level 2
54	Charging more than the agreed fare	Level 1
55	Obtaining more than the legal fare	Level 3 and 1 month imprisonment until the excess is refunded
56	Travelling less than the lawful distance for an agreed fare	Level 1
57	Failing to wait after a deposit to wait has been paid	Level 1
58	Charging more than the legal fare	Level 3
59	Carrying other person than the hirer without consent	Level 1
60	Driving a HC without proprietor's consent	Level 1
60	Person allowing another to drive a HC without proprietor's consent	Level 1
61	Drunken driving of HC	Level 1
61	Wanton or furious driving or wilful misconduct leading to injury or danger	Level 1

Section	Offence	Maximum Penalty
62	Driver leaving hackney carriage unattended	Level 1
64	HC driver obstructing other HCs	Level 1

The penalty for breach of byelaws made under s 68 of this Act or s 6 of the Town Police Clauses Act 1889 is a fine not exceeding level 2 by virtue of s 183 of the Public Health Act 1875.

[1]   Level 5 was £5000 until 12 March 2015 when it became an unlimited amount. The Government had proposed increasing the levels for 1 to 4 but at the time of writing (August 2017) those increases have yet to be implemented.

ENFORCEMENT UNDER THE LOCAL GOVERNMENT (MISCELLANEOUS PROVISIONS) ACT 1976

6.25

Under LG(MP)A 1976, there are a number of offences relating to both hackney carriages and private hire vehicles. Again, enforcement falls to the local authority, but the Act introduces the concept of an authorised officer. This is defined in LG(MP)A 1976, s 80 as:

'"authorised officer" means any officer of a district council authorised in writing by the council for the purposes of this Part of this Act;'

There is also a specific offence of obstruction of authorised officers contained in LG(MP)A 1976, s 73:

'73–(1) Any person who—

(a)   wilfully obstructs an authorised officer or constable acting in pursuance of this Part of this Act or the Act of 1847; or

(b)   without reasonable excuse fails to comply with any requirement properly made to him by such officer or constable under this Part of this Act; or

(c)   without reasonable cause fails to give such an officer or constable so acting any other assistance or information which he may reasonably require of such person for the purpose of the performance of his functions under this Part of this Act or the Act of 1847;

shall be guilty of an offence.

(2) If any person, in giving any such information as is mentioned in the preceding subsection, makes any statement which he knows to be false, he shall be guilty of an offence.'

6.26

It can be seen that an authorised officer is a person appointed by the district council to act on their behalf, in relation to enforcement activities under

LG(MP)A 1976 and TPCA 1847. It will be necessary for such an officer to demonstrate his authorisation, if required and that authorisation must be in writing to satisfy the requirements of LG(MP)A 1976, s 80.

Table 6.3 outlines the hackney carriage offences under LG(MP)A 1976 and Table 6.4 and Table 6.5 outline the private hire offences. Again, these are all summary offences by virtue of either LG(MP)A 1976, s 76:

'Penalties

76 Any person who commits an offence against any of the provisions of this Part of this Act in respect of which no penalty is expressly provided shall be liable on summary conviction to a fine not exceeding level 3 on the standard scale.'

or the relevant section which defines the offence.

Table 6.3

Enforcement table – hackney carriage provisions – Local Government (Miscellaneous Provisions) Act 1976

Section	Offence	Maximum Penalty
49	Failure to notify transfer of HC proprietor's licence	Level 3 (by virtue of s 76)
50(1)	Failure to present HC for inspection as required	Level 3 (by virtue of s 76)
50(2)	Failure to inform LA where HC is stored if requested	Level 3 (by virtue of s 76)
50(3)	Failure to report an accident to LA	Level 3 (by virtue of s 76)
50(4)	Failure to produce HC proprietor's licence and insurance certificate	Level 3 (by virtue of s 76)
53(3)	Failure to produce HC driver's licence	Level 3 (by virtue of s 76)
53A(9)	Failure to return driver's licence and badge after ceasing to be in force for immigration reasons	Level 3 and daily penalty of £10 for each day of non-compliance after conviction
57	Making false statement or withholding information to obtain HC driver's licence	Level 3 (by virtue of s 76)
58(2)	Failure to return plate after notice given after expiry, revocation or suspension of HC proprietor's licence	Level 3 plus daily fine of £10

Section	Offence	Maximum Penalty
61(2)	Failure to surrender driver's licence after suspension, revocation or refusal to renew	Level 3 (by virtue of s 76)
64	Permitting any vehicle other than HC to wait on a HC stand	Level 3 (by virtue of s 76)
66	Charging more than the meter fare for a journey ending outside the district, without prior agreement	Level 3 (by virtue of s 76)
67	Charging more than the meter fare when HC used as private hire vehicle	Level 3 (by virtue of s 76)
69	Unnecessarily prolonging a journey	Level 3 (by virtue of s 76)
71	Interfering with a taximeter	Level 3 (by virtue of s 76)
73(1)(a)	Obstruction of authorised officer or constable	Level 3 (by virtue of s 76)
73(1)(b)	Failure to comply with requirement of authorised officer or constable	Level 3 (by virtue of s 76)
73(1)(c)	Failure to give information or assistance to authorised officer or constable	Level 3 (by virtue of s 76)

Table 6.4

Enforcement table – private hire provisions – Local Government (Miscellaneous Provisions) Act 1976

Section	Offence	Maximum Penalty
46(1)(a)	Using an unlicensed PH vehicle	Level 3 (by virtue of s 76)
46(1)(b)	Driving a PH vehicle without a PH driver's licence	Level 3 (by virtue of s 76)
46(1)(c)	Proprietor of a PH vehicle using an unlicensed driver	Level 3 (by virtue of s 76)
46(1)(d)	Operating a PH vehicle without a PH operator's licence	Level 3 (by virtue of s 76)
46(1)(e)	Operating a vehicle as a PH vehicle when the vehicle is not licensed as a PH vehicle	Level 3 (by virtue of s 76)
46(1)(e)	Operating a PH vehicle when the driver is not licensed as a PH driver	Level 3 (by virtue of s 76)

Section	Offence	Maximum Penalty
48(6)	Failure to display PH vehicle plate	Level 3 (by virtue of s 76)
49	Failure to notify transfer of PH vehicle licence	Level 3 (by virtue of s 76)
50(1)	Failure to present PH vehicle for inspection as required	Level 3 (by virtue of s 76)
50(2)	Failure to inform LA where PH vehicle is stored if requested	Level 3 (by virtue of s 76)
50(3)	Failure to report an accident to LA	Level 3 (by virtue of s 76)
50(4)	Failure to produce PH vehicle licence and insurance certificate	Level 3 (by virtue of s 76)
53(3)	Failure to produce PH driver's licence	Level 3 (by virtue of s 76)
53A(9)	Failure to return drivers' licence and badge after ceasing to be in force for immigration reasons	Level 3 and daily penalty of £10 for each day of non-compliance after conviction
54(2)	Failure to wear PH driver's badge	Level 3 (by virtue of s 76)
55ZA(8)	Failure to return operators licence after ceasing to be in force for immigration reasons	Level 3 and daily penalty of £10 for each day of non-compliance after conviction
55B	Subcontracting PH Operator knowing that the subcontractor will use and unlicensed vehicle or driver	Level 3 (by virtue of s 76)
56(2)	Failure by PH operator to keep records of bookings	Level 3 (by virtue of s 76)
56(3)	Failure by PH operator to keep records of PH vehicles operated by him	Level 3 (by virtue of s 76)
56(4)	Failure to produce PH operator's licence on request	Level 3 (by virtue of s 76)
57	Making false statement or withholding information to obtain PH driver's or operator's licence	Level 3 (by virtue of s 76)
58(2)	Failure to return plate after notice given after expiry, revocation or suspension of PH vehicle licence	Level 3 plus daily fine of £10

Section	Offence	Maximum Penalty
61(2)	Failure to surrender drivers licence after suspension, revocation or refusal to renew	Level 3 (by virtue of s 76)
67	Charging more than the meter fare when HC used as private hire vehicle	Level 3 (by virtue of s 76)
69	Unnecessarily prolonging a journey	Level 3 (by virtue of s 76)
71	Interfering with a taximeter	Level 3 (by virtue of s 76)
73(1)(a)	Obstruction of authorised officer or constable	Level 3 (by virtue of s 76)
73(1)(b)	Failure to comply with requirement of authorised officer or constable	Level 3 (by virtue of s 76)
73(1)(c)	Failure to give information or assistance to authorised officer or constable	Level 3 (by virtue of s 76)

Table 6.5

Enforcement table – private hire provisions – Transport Act 1980

Section	Offence	Maximum Penalty
Section 64(2)(a)	Driving a PH vehicle with a roof sign which contravenes section 64(1)	Level 3
Section 64(2)(b)	Causing or permitting a PH vehicle to be driven with a roof sign which contravenes section 64(1)	Level 3

PROSECUTING UNDER BYELAWS

6.27

A district council has a power to make bylaws for the control and supervision of hackney carriages under s 68 of the Town Police Clauses Act 1847 for a variety of purposes:

'For regulating the conduct of the proprietors and drivers of hackney carriages plying within the prescribed distance in their several employments, and determining whether such drivers shall wear any and what badges, and for regulating the hours within which they may exercise their calling: For regulating the manner in which the number of each carriage, corresponding with the number of its licence, shall be displayed: For regulating the number of persons to be carried by such hackney carriages, and in what manner such number is to be shown on such carriage, and what number of horses or other animals is to draw the same, and the placing of check strings to the carriages, and the holding of the same by the driver, and how such hackney carriages are to be furnished or provided: For fixing the stands of such hackney carriages, and the distance to which they may be compelled to take passengers, not exceeding the prescribed distance: For fixing the rates or fares, as well for time as distance, to be paid for such hackney carriages within the prescribed distance, and for securing the due publication of such fares: For securing the safe custody and re-delivery of any property accidentally left in hackney carriages, and fixing the charges to be made in respect thereof.'

Many authorities do have such bylaws and the current model is contained in the DFT Circular 'Guidance notes and model byelaws'[1]. Some of these were made by authorities which have been reorganised by local government reorganisations from 1974 on.

All pre-1974 local authorities were abolished on 31 March 1974 and new authorities came into existence on 1 April 1974. Many local authorities use hackney carriage byelaws, which were made before 31 March 1974, by local authorities whose area is now part of the 'new' authority.

Section 238 of the Local Government Act 1972 ('the 1972 Act') lays down the procedure which is required to prove the existence of byelaws, although this is aimed at byelaws made by a post-1 April 1974 authority. Article 9 of the Local Authorities etc (Miscellaneous Provisions) Order 1974, made under s 254 of the 1972 Act covers the point.

If the byelaws were made by a county council pre-1 April 1974 in respect of matters which after 1 April 1974 would be district council matters, then the provisions of art 9(3) apply. In respect of byelaws relating to matters which were district council pre-1 April 1974 and were district council matters post-1 April 1974, art 9(4) applies:

'The production of a printed copy of any byelaw to which paragraph (3) does not apply made by any authority described in column (1) of Part I or II of Schedule 4 to the Local Authorities (England) (Property etc.) Order 1973 or the Local Authorities (Wales) (Property etc.) Order 1973 upon which is endorsed a certificate purporting to be signed by the proper officer of the authority specified in respect of such authority in column (2) stating:-

(a) that the byelaw was made by the first mentioned authority;
(b) the matters set out in (b), (c) and (d) of section 238 of the Act [the 1972 Act]

shall be prima facie evidence of the facts stated in the certificate, and without proof of the handwriting or official position of any person purporting to sign the certificate'

The columns referred to in the 1973 Orders list the old authorities and the successor authorities.

Accordingly, the method of evidencing the byelaws is similar for both pre- and post-1 April 1974 byelaws, and it appears that pre-1974 byelaws are just as valid for successor authorities as any byelaws which were actually made by the post-1 April 1974 authority.

> [1]   There is no number for this Guidance, and it does not appear to be available on the DfT Website, but as far as can be established it has not been cancelled or replaced. It is in Appendix II.

6.28

The case of *Boddington v British Transport Police*[1] should be noted in relation to prosecution for breach of byelaws. In this case, the House of Lords decided that it was possible for a defendant, being prosecuted for breach of byelaws, to raise the validity of the byelaws, particularly whether they were intra vires (within the powers) the byelaw-making power.

Breach of any requirement of a hackney carriage byelaw is an offence by virtue of Byelaw 18 of the Model Byelaws and on summary conviction is punishable by a fine not exceeding level 2 on the standard scale[2]. The penalty is imposed by s 183 of the Public Health Act 1875[3]. It is possible for a local authority to depart from the model byelaws, but in most cases they are identical to the model byelaws.

Enforcement Table – Hackney Carriage Byelaws (based on the 2005 Department for Transport Model) 1115

Model Byelaw No	Offence	Penalty
2	Concealing the vehicle number whilst the HC is standing or plying for hire	Level 2 by virtue of PHA 1875, s 183
2	Standing or plying for hire with a defaced or illegible plate	Level 2 by virtue of PHA 1875, s 183
3	Failure to provide sufficient means by which any person in the carriage may communicate with the driver	Level 2 by virtue of PHA 1875, s 183
3	Failure to cause the vehicle roof or covering to be kept water-tight	Level 2 by virtue of PHA 1875, s 183
3	Failure to provide any necessary windows and a means of opening and closing not less than one window on each side	Level 2 by virtue of PHA 1875, s 183
3	Failure to cause the seats to be properly cushioned or covered	Level 2 by virtue of PHA 1875, s 183
3	Failure to cause the floor to be provided with a proper carpet, mat or other suitable covering	Level 2 by virtue of PHA 1875, s 183
3	Failure to cause the fittings and furniture generally to be kept in a clean condition, well maintained and in every way fit for public service	Level 2 by virtue of PHA 1875, s 183

Model Byelaw No	Offence	Penalty
3	Failure to provide means for securing luggage	Level 2 by virtue of PHA 1875, s 183
3	Failure to provide an efficient fire extinguisher in a readily available location	Level 2 by virtue of s 183 PHA 1875
3	Failure to provide at least two passenger doors and a separate door for the driver	Level 2 by virtue of PHA 1875, s 183
4(e)	Failure to position the taximeter so that it is plainly visible to passengers and suitably illuminated	Level 2 by virtue of PHA 1875, s 183
5(a)	Turning the meter on when standing or plying for hire	Level 2 by virtue of PHA 1875, s 183
5(b)	Starting the meter before the beginning of a journey charged by distance and time	Level 2 by virtue of PHA 1875, s 183
5(c)	Failure to illuminate the meter properly between sunrise and sunset, or at the request of a passenger	Level 2 by virtue of PHA 1875, s 183
6	Tampering with the fittings or seals on a taxi-meter	Level 2 by virtue of PHA 1875, s 183
7(a)	Failure to proceed to a hackney carriage stand when plying for hire	Level 2 by virtue of PHA 1875, s 183
7(b)	Failure to proceed to another hackney carriage stand when plying for hire if the first stand is full	Level 2 by virtue of PHA 1875, s 183
7(c)	Failure to wait behind the last hackney carriage on a stand that is not full	Level 2 by virtue of PHA 1875, s 183
7(d)	Failure to move up when the carriage in front moves up	Level 2 by virtue of PHA 1875, s 183
8	Using another person to importune a person to hire the carriage	Level 2 by virtue of PHA 1875, s 183
9	Failure to behave in a civil and orderly manner	Level 2 by virtue of PHA 1875, s 183
9	Failure to take all reasonable precautions to ensure safety of passengers during the journey and on entering and leaving the vehicle	Level 2 by virtue of PHA 1875, s 183
10	Failure to arrive on time for a pre-booked journey	Level 2 by virtue of PHA 1875, s 183

Model Byelaw No	Offence	Penalty
11	Carrying more passengers than the vehicle licence permits	Level 2 by virtue of PHA 1875, s 183
12	Failure to wear the drivers' badge in a position and manner that is plainly visible	Level 2 by virtue of PHA 1875, s 183
13	Failure to convey a reasonable amount of luggage	Level 2 by virtue of PHA 1875, s 183
13	Failure to afford reasonable assistance in loading and unloading luggage	Level 2 by virtue of PHA 1875, s 183
13	Failure to afford reasonable assistance in removing luggage to or from the entrance of any building, station or place at which the driver may take up or set down such person	Level 2 by virtue of PHA 1875, s 183
14(ii)	Demanding more than the metered fare	Level 2 by virtue of PHA 1875, s 183
15(i)	Failure to display the table of fares	Level 2 by virtue of PHA 1875, s 183
15(ii)	Wilfully or negligently concealing or rendering illegible the table of fares	Level 2 by virtue of PHA 1875, s 183
16	Failure to carefully search the vehicle for lost property after each hiring	Level 2 by virtue PHA 1875, s 183
17	Failure to deliver any lost property to the local authority (or police)[4] within 48 hours of finding it	

1   [1999] 2 AC 143, HL.

2   The power to make byelaws is contained within TPCA 1847, s 68 which applies to local authorities by virtue of the Public Health Act 1875, the Local Government Act 1972 and the Transport Act 1985. The TPCA 1847 was originally intended to be incorporated into local Acts, but it now stands as a complete Act in its own right, in relation to hackney carriages. It was incorporated (together with the Town Police Clauses Act 1889) into the Public Health Act 1875 by the Public Health Act 1875, s 171 and then applied to the whole of England and Wales by the Transport Act 1985, s 15. If any local authority which had local legislation incorporating the provisions of TPCA 1847 but which excluded the hackney carriage provisions within TPCA 1847, those exclusions were also repealed by the Transport Act 1985, s 15.

3   Section 183 of the Public Health Act 1875 imposes the penalty for breach of bylaws which is currently level 2 on the standard scale. The section was originally enacted with a maximum penalty of £5 for breach of the bylaws. This was amended by s 31(2) of the Criminal Law Act 1977 to a maximum of £50, which was then replaced by reference to level 2 on the standard scale by s 40 of the Criminal Justice Act 1982.

4   This will depend on the wording of the byelaws in any individual authority.

CAUTIONS

6.29

A number of authorities use simple cautions[1] as a method of dealing with less serious cases[2]. Briefly, a simple caution is not a conviction, but they can be cited before a court on a subsequent conviction, but should be kept separate from any list of previous convictions. Two preconditions are required before a simple caution can be offered:

- there has to be sufficient evidence to have led to a prosecution; and
- the offender must admit his guilt.

In addition, the offender must agree to accept a simple caution. Under the Rehabilitation of Offenders Act 1974 a caution is deemed to be spent as soon as it is administered[3].

[1]   Simple cautions refer to what were previously called formal cautions to differentiate them from Conditional Cautions introduced by Part 3 of the Criminal Justice Act 2003.

[2]   Guidance on the use of formal cautions is contained in Home Office publication '*Simple Cautions for Adult Offenders*' available at https://www.gov.uk/government/uploads/system/uploads/attachment_data/file/416068/cautions-guidance-2015.pdf

[3]   Rehabilitation of Offenders Act 1974, s 8A and Sch 2.

6.30

If criminal sanctions are not sufficient to prevent a person offending, it is possible for a local authority to obtain an injunction to enforce the criminal law by restraining the person. This was the ruling in *Stoke-on-Trent City Council v B & Q (Retail) Ltd*[1]. This has been used by at least one authority to prevent a licensed driver from driving an unlicensed hackney carriage.

[1]   [1984] AC 754, HL.

DEFENCES

6.31

Apart from technical defences (e.g. failure to demonstrate adoption of LG(MP)A 1976), there are some points worth mentioning here in relation to prosecution for non-compliance with certain provisions.

In relation to any offence under LG(MP)A 1976, s 46, it is necessary to show 'knowledge' on the part of the defendant. Quite why this is the case is unclear, as most other offences in relation to hackney carriage and private hire licensing are strict liability offences. However, that is the situation.

Reading Borough Council v Ahmad

6.32

> Driver borrowed a friend's car, not knowing it was a licensed private hire vehicle. As he did not have knowledge of that fact, or that he was in a controlled district, no offence was committed.

The case of *Reading Borough Council v Ahmad*[1] reinforces this point. In this case, a prosecution was brought for driving a private hire vehicle without holding a private hire driver's licence. The High Court held that the offence contained in LG(MP)A 1976, s 46(1)(b) and (2) requires knowledge on the part of the person driving without a driver's licence, that he was in a controlled district (that is, a district which has adopted the provisions of LG(MP)A 1976), was driving a licensed private hire vehicle and did not hold a private hire vehicle driver's licence. It is immaterial whether or not money changed hands at the time of the offence or, indeed, whether any passengers had been carried at the time. The ruling in *Benson v Boyce*[2] makes it clear that a private hire vehicle is always a private hire vehicle.

[1]   (1998) 163 JP 451, QBD.
[2]   [1997] RTR 226; see para 13.72 onwards.

Latif v Middlesbrough Borough Council

6.33

> Owner of a private hire vehicle allowed another to drive it. The driver did not hold a driver's licence, but the vehicle owner had given him the money to obtain a licence, and although he had not done so, the owner had not turned a blind eye to the situation. Held: That he did not have knowledge that driver was unlicensed.

Another case relating to 'knowledge' is that of *Latif v Middlesbrough Borough Council*[1], where a private hire operator was prosecuted under LG(MP)A 1976, s 46(1)(e) for operating a vehicle when the driver did not hold a private hire driver's licence. His conviction was quashed, as he had provided the driver with the money to obtain a licence and had not 'turned a blind eye' to the situation.

[1]   [1997] COD 486; see Chapter 12, para 12.78.

Eden District Council v Braid

6.34

> Prebooked hackney carriage and 11 people got into the vehicle, which was licensed for six. Driver refused to drive until some got out but he was threatened. In fear for damage to the vehicle of harm to himself, he carried

> them. Prosecuted for carrying more than the licence permitted and pleaded duress. Held on appeal, this was a permissible defence.

A very different defence was used successfully in the case of *Eden District Council v Braid*[1]. In this case, a defence of duress was pleaded against a charge of carrying more passengers than the byelaw allowed. The situation arose at the Appleby Horse Fair, when a booking was made for a customer. When the customer emerged from the premises, he got into the front seat of the hackney carriage and, a few moments later, four more adults, one teenager and four children also emerged from the premises and got into the hackney carriage. The carriage was licensed to carry six people, including the driver, but was now carrying 11. The driver refused to drive until some of them got out, but they refused to leave the vehicle and said that the driver would have to remove them physically if he wanted them out. The driver was aware that they were smelling of drink and he feared physical harm to himself and damage to his vehicle. Accordingly, he drove them to where they wanted to go. This had been observed by an enforcement officer from the local authority, although when he approached the driver and passengers at the end of the journey, there was a great potential for violence and the enforcement officer retreated. The magistrates found that a plea of duress had been established and acquitted the driver. The local authority appealed, by way of case stated, on the grounds: first, that duress was not available for an offence of strict liability and, secondly, whether it was open to the magistrates to find that the defence had been made out on the facts.

In relation to the first question, Bingham LCJ giving judgment said:

> 'In challenging the justices' decision on behalf of the local authority Mr Dutchman-Smith first submits in his skeleton argument that a defence of duress is not available where the alleged offence is one of strict liability. That is a proposition which he has not sought to pursue in argument and for which no authority is cited. It appears to me to run counter to the clear understanding of the defence of duress as described, for example, in Smith and Hogan "Criminal Law" (8th edition) 238 and 240; Blackstone's Criminal Practice 1998 at paras. A3.20 and A3.23; and Archbold at s 17–119. It would also seem to me to be wrong in principle. Even in an offence of strict liability there must be an intention to do the act which the law proscribes. If the only reason why the defendant does the act which the law proscribes is because he is subjected to a threat of serious personal injury which he reasonably thinks will be carried out in circumstances where a reasonable person of ordinary firmness with the same apprehension might act in the same way, I can for my part see no reason why the defence of duress should not be available.'

On the second point his judgment was as follows:

> 'The appellant's more substantial ground is an argument that there was no evidence upon which a reasonable bench could have concluded that on the facts the defence of duress was tenable. In making that submission Mr

Dutchman-Smith relies in particular on the acceptance by the respondent that he could have got out of the vehicle, gone into the club and rung the police, and could have dialled 999 and could have left the car. Those are, of course, matters which the justices had fully in mind. It was, however, very much a matter for them as to what the respondent could or should reasonably have done in the circumstances. Our attention has been drawn to *R v Hudson and Taylor* [1971] 2 QB 202, [1971] 2 All ER 244 in which a judgment prepared by Widgery LJ was read by Parker LCJ. At page 207G the court said:

> "In the opinion of this court it is always open to the Crown to prove that the accused failed to avail himself of some opportunity which was reasonably open to him to render the threat ineffective, and that upon this being established the threat in question can no longer be relied upon by the defence. In deciding whether such an opportunity was reasonably open to the accused the jury should have regard to his age and circumstances, and to any risks to him which may be involved in the course of action relied upon."

The justices plainly had this matter in mind and they made findings that no other viable options were available to the respondent at the time; and that he had every reason to believe that he would be set upon and suffer serious physical injury as a result of the gypsies' threat if he did not do as they asked. Plainly the justices were not of the opinion that the respondent could, without fear of being attacked, have simply left the vehicle with the passengers in it and gone into the club.

Reliance is also placed by the appellant on the statement by the respondent that he feared damage being caused to his car. That, counsel submits, does not support a plea of duress. It is, however, to be noted that the respondent quite plainly feared injury to himself as well as damage to his vehicle, and a threat of injury to himself certainly does support a plea of duress, even if a threat of damage to the vehicle does not.

In my judgment, whether or not I would myself have reached the same decision as the justices, this is not an appeal which should be allowed. The justices were correctly advised in law and there is no hint in the case that they misapplied the law in any way. They made findings of fact which were in my judgment open to them. These findings may to some extent be regarded as surprising, but one should be very slow to think that the Divisional Court sitting in London is better placed than Appleby Justices to understand the factual situation prevailing in Kirkby Stephen during the Appleby Horse Fair. It is true that this is a defence which can very rarely succeed and its bounds should not be widened. It is not, however, irrelevant in my judgment that the byelaw in question here was one made for the safety of persons to be carried in this taxi; that the very persons to be carried were those who were coercing the respondent to act as he did; and that the offence which he committed was one for which the maximum penalty was £50. It would not of course be the wish of this court in any way to encourage breaches of any law or byelaw, but it is perhaps right to point out that the criminal act which the respondent performed, even in the absence of duress, was one ranking relatively low in any scale of criminal heinousness. In my judgment the justices reached a sustainable conclusion. I would dismiss this appeal.'

¹   [1999] RTR 329.

NON-CRIMINAL ENFORCEMENT

6.35

Enforcement of the hackney carriage and private hire provisions can also be effected by means of action taken against the licence held by the person who has transgressed. That transgression may be evidenced by a criminal conviction, but it need not be¹. In addition, an injunction can be obtained under the Local Government Act 1972, s 222 to reinforce the criminal law in appropriate cases where someone flagrantly flouts the licensing regime².

¹   For example, the cases of *R v Maidstone Crown Court, ex p Olson* [1992] COD 496 (see Chapter 10, para 10.139); *R v Assistant Metropolitan Police Comr, ex p Foster* (18 November 1994, unreported) (see Chapter 2, para 2.37); *McCool v Rushcliffe Borough Council* [1998] 3 All ER 889, QBD (see Chapter 10, para 10.142); and *Leeds City Council v Hussain* [2002] EWHC 1145 (Admin), [2003] RTR 199 (see Chapter 10, para 10.146) clearly demonstrate that action can be taken against a licence where no criminal conviction was ultimately obtained.

²   See *Stoke-on-Trent City Council v B & Q (Retail) Ltd* [1984] AC 754, HL.

6.36

Under TPCA 1847, s 50, the council can revoke a hackney carriage proprietor's or hackney carriage driver's licence if the licence holder has been convicted of two offences under TPCA 1847.

6.37

Under LG(MP)A 1976, suspension or revocation of hackney carriage or private hire vehicle licences (proprietors, in the case of hackney carriages) is possible under LG(MP)A 1976, s 60:

'Suspension and revocation of vehicle licences

60–(1) Notwithstanding anything in the Act of 1847 [TPCA 1847] or in this Part of this Act, a district council may suspend or revoke, or (on application therefor under section 40 of the Act of 1847 or section 48 of this Act, as the case may be) refuse to renew a vehicle licence on any of the following grounds—

(a)   that the hackney carriage or private hire vehicle is unfit for use as a hackney carriage or private hire vehicle;

(b)   any offence under, or non-compliance with, the provisions of the Act of 1847 or of this Part of this Act by the operator or driver; or

(c)   any other reasonable cause.

(2) Where a district council suspend, revoke or refuse to renew any licence under this section they shall give to the proprietor of the vehicle notice of the grounds on which the licence has been suspended or revoked or on which they have refused to renew the licence within fourteen days of such suspension, revocation or refusal.

(3) Any proprietor aggrieved by a decision of a district council under this section may appeal to a magistrates' court.'

6.38

Similar sanctions are available against drivers' licences (for both hackney carriages and private hire vehicles) under the provisions of LG(MP)A 1976, s 61:

'Suspension and revocation of drivers' licences

61–(1) Notwithstanding anything in the Act of 1847 [TPCA 1847] or in this Part of this Act, a district council may suspend or revoke or (on application therefor under section 46 of the Act of 1847 or section 51 of this Act, as the case may be) refuse to renew the licence of a driver of a hackney carriage or a private hire vehicle on any of the following grounds—
(a) that he has since the grant of the licence—
   (i) been convicted of an offence involving dishonesty, indecency or violence; or
   (ii) been convicted of an offence under or has failed to comply with the provisions of the Act of 1847 or of this Part of this Act; or
(b) any other reasonable cause.

(2)(a) Where a district council suspend, revoke or refuse to renew any licence under this section they shall give to the driver notice of the grounds on which the licence has been suspended or revoked or on which they have refused to renew such licence within fourteen days of such suspension, revocation or refusal and the driver shall on demand return to the district council the driver's badge issued to him in accordance with section 54 of this Act.
(b) If any person without reasonable excuse contravenes the provisions of this section he shall be guilty of an offence and liable on summary conviction to a fine not exceeding level 1 on the standard scale.

(2A) Subject to subsection (2B) of this section, a suspension or revocation of the licence of a driver under this section takes effect at the end of the period of 21 days beginning with the day on which notice is given to the driver under subsection (2)(a) of this section.

(2B) If it appears that the interests of public safety require the suspension or revocation of the licence to have immediate effect, and the notice given to the driver under subsection (2)(a) of this section includes a statement that that is so and an explanation why, the suspension or revocation takes effect when the notice is given to the driver.

(3) Any driver aggrieved by a decision of a district council under subsection (1) of this section may appeal to a magistrates' court.'

6.39

Finally, in relation to private hire operators' licences only, LG(MP)A 1976, s 62 allows suspension and revocation:

'Suspension and revocation of operators' licences

62–(1) Notwithstanding anything in this Part of this Act a district council may suspend or revoke, or (on application therefor under section 55 of this Act) refuse to renew an operator's licence on any of the following grounds—

(a) any offence under, or non-compliance with, the provisions of this Part of this Act;

(b) any conduct on the part of the operator which appears to the district council to render him unfit to hold an operator's licence;

(c) any material change since the licence was granted in any of the circumstances of the operator on the basis of which the licence was granted; or

(d) any other reasonable cause.[1]

(2) Where a district council suspend, revoke or refuse to renew any licence under this section they shall give to the operator notice of the grounds on which the licence has been suspended or revoked or on which they have refused to renew such licence within fourteen days of such suspension, revocation or refusal.

(3) Any operator aggrieved by a decision of a district council under this section may appeal to a magistrates' court.'

[1]   For the use of 'any other reasonable cause' see Chapter 8, para 8.137 onwards.

6.40

In each case, the effect of a suspension or revocation is not immediate, with one important exception for drivers' licences which is considered below[1]. A decision to revoke or suspend a licence does not take effect for 21 days, and if an appeal is lodged within that time, that period is extended until the appeal is determined or abandoned. This lack of immediacy is a result of the combined effect of LG(MP)A 1976, s 77 and PHA 1936, s 300. Section 77 states:

'77 Appeals

(1) Sections 300 to 302 of the Act of 1936, which relate to appeals, shall have effect as if this Part of this Act were part of that Act.

(2) If any requirement, refusal or other decision of a district council against which a right of appeal is conferred by this Act—

(a) involves the execution of any work or the taking of any action; or

(b) makes it unlawful for any person to carry on a business which he was lawfully carrying on up to the time of the requirement, refusal or decision;

then, until the time for appealing has expired, or, when an appeal is lodged, until the appeal is disposed of or withdrawn or fails for want of prosecution—

(i) no proceedings shall be taken in respect of any failure to execute the work, or take the action; and

(ii) that person may carry on that business.

(3) Subsection (2) of this section does not apply in relation to a decision under subsection (1) of section 61 of this Act which has immediate effect in accordance with subsection (2B) of that section.'

[1] See para 6.42 below.

6.41

As can be seen, the combined effect of PHA 1936, s 300 (and LG(MP)A 1976, s 61(2A) in respect of drivers' licences[1]) and LG(MP)A 1976, s 77 is to allow the licence to be used for 21 days from the decision to suspend or revoke and, if an appeal is launched, can be further used until the appeal is determined or abandoned.

That extends to both the magistrates' and Crown Court appeals.

The one significant exception to that usual rule is in relation to a driver's licence (either hackney carriage or private hire) where immediate suspension is possible under s 61(2B). The effect of this is that a local authority can suspend or revoke a driver's licence with immediate effect. There is still a right of appeal, but the licence cannot be used during the time until that appeal is heard.

[1] Section 61(2A) effectively restates the Public Health Act 1936 (PHA 1936), s 300(2) making it clear that the appeal period is 21 days from the date on which the notice of the decision was given to the person concerned.

SUSPENSION OR REVOCATION OF DRIVERS LICENCES

6.42

As detailed above[1] powers are contained within section 61 of the 1976 Act to suspend or revoke a drivers licence, and that action can be taken with immediate effect if that is necessary in the interests of public safety using the powers contained in s 61(2B). It is important that the power to take immediate action against a driver's licence is available immediately. To enable such decisions to be taken quickly, the power should be delegated to an officer in consultation with the Chair or Deputy of the Licensing (or appropriate) committee. This will continue member involvement, whilst allowing for speed of decision making.

[1] See para 6.40.

R (app Singh) v Cardiff City Council

6.43

> Use of penalty points as a control measure for drivers' licences, resulting in automatic revocation when a fixed number of points had been reached. Held: That penalty points per se were a lawful control measure but automatic revocation was not. Also, whilst suspension could be used as a punishment, if a licence was suspended, it could then not be revoked.

An important question over the use of suspension followed by revocation was raised in the case of *R (app Singh) v Cardiff City Council*[1]. This case was principally concerned with the question of whether or not a 'penalty points scheme' for drivers licences was lawful[2]. However two further matters were considered by the judge in the judgment: was it possible to suspend a drivers licence and then subsequently revoke it; and could the power of suspension be used as a punishment?

For many years the power of suspension of a driver's licence had been used by local authorities as a way of taking intermediate action (often with immediate effect) following serious allegations or complaints made against the licensee (eg, violence, sexual assaults, dishonesty etc) to protect the public while an investigation takes place[3]. The effect of an immediate suspension was to prevent the driver from using the licence to drive a licensed hackney carriage or private hire vehicle and thereby offer an immediate degree of protection to the public. During the period of suspension, the local authority would investigate the allegations or complaints and then determine whether the licence should be revoked in the light of its findings. If the complaint was not substantiated, or the allegations were shown to be false, the suspension would then be lifted and the driver would be free to continue work.

This approach was ruled unlawful by Mr Justice Singh in *R (app Singh) v Cardiff City Council*[4] who made it clear that suspension of a driver's licence is a final decision on the question of a person's fitness and propriety and suspension cannot be used as an interim measure pending further investigation into a drivers conduct and ultimate fitness and propriety. He stated[5]:

> '103. In my judgment, the way in which the concept of suspension is used by Parliament is section 61 of the 1976 Act is not, as it were, to create a power of interim suspension, it is rather after a considered determination in other words a final decision on whether a ground for either revocation, or suspension of a licence is made out, for there to be either revocation or, as a lesser sanction, a sanction of suspension.
>
> 104. By way of analogy, one can envisage for example in a professional context a solicitor or a barrister can be disciplined on grounds of his conduct. The relevant disciplinary body may conclude that even if the misconduct has been established, that the appropriate sanction should be something less than complete revocation of the practising certificate for

the relevant lawyer. It may be, for example, a suspension for a period of 1 year, will constitute sufficient sanction in the interests of the public.

105. It is in that sense, in my judgment, that Parliament uses the concept of suspension in section 61 of the 1976 Act. It does not use, as it were, to create an interim power, before a reasoned determination has been made, that the grounds in subsection (1A) or (1B) have been made out. It is not, as it were, a protective or holding power. It is a power of final suspension, as an alternative to a power of final revocation.'

This judgment prevents local authorities from suspending a driver's licence pending further investigation if there is a possibility that the licence should ultimately be revoked. In the light of this, what options are available to a local authority to protect the public in the light of serious complaints or allegations?

It would appear that the only approach that can be taken is to decide upon the sanction on the basis of the allegation and suspend or revoke this driver's licence (which could be with immediate effect in the interests of public safety under s 61(2B)). The delegations to allow such decisions to be taken quickly need to be clearly set out. It must be considered carefully whether a period of suspension will be sufficient to protect the public. If it will not be, then the decision must be taken to revoke the licence.

In addition, it is essential that the driver has a chance to answer the allegations and put forward his case. This can be a short period of time, communicated by telephone, text, e-mail, fax or in person, but failure to factor this into the process would lead to a successful challenge on the basis that he did not have an opportunity to be heard by the decision maker[6].

If the driver then appeals, any new evidence resulting from the investigation can be adduced at the magistrates' court to justify the decision, as an appeal is a rehearing[7].

[1]   [2012] EWHC 1852 (Admin), [2013] LLR 108.
[2]   This is considered at para 6.47 below.
[3]   It is clear that action can be taken against a licence where no criminal conviction has occurred. This includes situations where a police investigation is continuing and the licensee has been bailed, but not charged: see *Leeds City Council v Hussain* [2002] EWHC 1145 (Admin), [2003] RTR 13; where there has been an acquittal see *McCool v Rushcliffe Borough Council* [1998] 3 All ER 889, QBD and *R v Maidstone Crown Court, ex p Olson* [1992] COD 496, 136 Sol Jo LB 174.
[4]   [2012] EWHC 1852 (Admin), [2013] LLR 108.
[5]   At paras 103 to 105.
[6]   One of the rules of natural justice. For details see Chapter 2, para 2.27 onwards.
[7]   See Chapter 3.

6.44

It is also important to have a mechanism to enable the driver to be relicensed (or the suspension lifted) if the investigation does not reveal sufficient evidence to justify the earlier decision. Clearly, a suspension can simply be lifted which would lead to the driver being able to resume using the licence.

In relation to a revocation, the licence cannot be re-instated and will need to be re-issued. It would seem reasonable in these circumstances for the local authority to accept any pre-grant enquiries (eg, medical tests, knowledge, DBS checks etc) that existed in relation to the previous licence, up to the point at which they would have required renewing had the licence not been revoked. Again, the delegation to enable this decision to be taken quickly is important, as in both these cases there is no justification in preventing the driver from working.

It has been suggested that the judge, Singh J, did not intend this consequence. At paragraph 102 of the judgment he stated:

'Returning to the language of section 61, I remind myself that this was not a case in which any attempt was made to activate the suspension of the licence to have immediate effect pursuant to the interest of public safety basis in subsection (2B). The notice sent to Mr Morrissey did not purport to invoke that provision or to make the suspension immediately effective.'

Unfortunately it is difficult to see how this comment alters the impact of his judgment. The powers contained in s 61(1) are:

'(1) Notwithstanding anything in the Act of 1847 or in this Part of this Act, a district council may suspend or revoke or (on application therefor under section 46 of the Act of 1847 or section 51 of this Act, as the case may be) refuse to renew the licence of a driver of a hackney carriage or a private hire vehicle on any of the following grounds—
(a)   that he has since the grant of the licence—
    (i)   been convicted of an offence involving dishonesty, indecency or violence; or
    (ii)   been convicted of an offence under or has failed to comply with the provisions of the Act of 1847 or of this Part of this Act; or
(b)   any other reasonable cause.'

Section 61(2B) does not alter this power, it simply allows a decision to suspend or revoke to take place with immediate effect (in contrast to s 61 (2A) where there is no effect for 21 days):

'(2B) If it appears that the interests of public safety require the suspension or revocation of the licence to have immediate effect, and the notice given to the driver under subsection (2)(a) of this section includes a statement that that is so and an explanation why, the suspension or revocation takes effect when the notice is given to the driver.'

Accordingly, it would appear that any decision under s 61 must be to *either* suspend *or* revoke the licence, and once that decision has been made by the authority, no further action in relation to that licence can be taken, irrespective of whether it was an immediate suspension under s 61(2B) or a 'normal' suspension under s 61(1)[1].

There is nothing else in the judgment in *Singh* which provides any argument for distinction between the two mechanisms and it seems that the Judge's statement in paragraph 102 does not alter the effects of the judgment overall[2].

[1]   The same argument would also apply to action against an operator's licence under s 62 of the 1976 Act. However, as there is no power to take any immediate action against an operator's licence and the powers of both suspension and revocation do not take effect for 21 days and are

stayed if an appeal is lodged, it is difficult to see why any authority would consider suspending an operator's licence as a prelude to possible revocation of the same.

2   It may well be the case that this was not the intention of the draughtsman or Parliament when the legislation was first promoted, or subsequently amended to allow for immediate suspension or revocation, but unfortunately in the light of this judgment that does appear to be the situation.

Reigate and Banstead Borough Council v Pawlowski

6.45

> Is it correct that a local authority cannot suspend a drivers' licence as an interim measure, pending subsequent revocation? Held: That is correct and suspension cannot be used as an interim measure.

The decision that a licence cannot be suspended as an interim measure and then subsequently revoked has been reconsidered and upheld in *Reigate and Banstead Borough Council v Pawlowski*[1]. Pawlowski was a licensed private hire driver who was arrested and charged with drink-driving on 2 August 2015. The council was informed on 4 August, and revoked his driver's licence with immediate effect on 5 August. On 28 October 2015, Pawlowski was acquitted following a trial. He had appealed against the revocation of his driver's licence and that was heard on 2 February 2016. The magistrates allowed the appeal, having concluded that Pawlowski was a fit and proper person to hold a private hire driver's licence. They took the view that revocation was not an appropriate sanction, but that suspension would have been, thereby flying in the face of the judgment in *Singh*[2]. They also awarded costs against the council on the basis of the hardship suffered by *Pawlowski*[3]. The council appealed by way of case stated to the High Court.

Judgment was given by HH Judge Keyser QC sitting as a judge of the High Court and the material part of the judgment is to be found at paragraphs 21 to 26 where he stated:

> '21 However, in the light of the views expressed by the Justices and the concerns expressed by the Council, and in the hope of providing a small measure of assistance for the future, I offer some very limited observations of a general nature.
>
> 22 The decision in *R (Singh) v Cardiff City Council*[4] caused a degree of consternation among local authorities. A fairly widespread practice appears to have developed, whereby a licensing authority that learned of a criminal charge or summons or other allegation of wrongdoing against a licence-holder would impose a suspension of the licence pending either determination of the criminal proceedings or investigation of the allegation and would then, in the light of the outcome, take such further action as might appear to be merited, perhaps involving revocation of the licence if the charge or allegation were proved. The decision in *R (Singh) v Cardiff City Council*[5] shows that suspension of a licence pursuant to section 61(1) can only be achieved by a substantive decision on the basis that one of the grounds in that subsection is made out. Suspension cannot be imposed as a

holding exercise, pending consideration whether a ground is made out. In that sense, suspension is a final decision.

23 In his skeleton argument, Mr Douglas-Jones on behalf of Mr Pawlowski submitted that, despite the prohibition on interim suspensions in *R (Singh) v Cardiff City Council*[6], it would be open to a local authority, in a suitable case, to make a substantive decision to suspend on learning that a licence-holder had been charged and to make a further substantive decision to revoke on learning that he had been convicted on the charge: the fact of the charge would amount to a "reasonable cause" under section 61(1)(b), and the fact of conviction would amount to new circumstances entitling the local authority to exercise afresh its judgment and discretion under section 61. Although it would be inappropriate for me to attempt to say anything definitive about that suggestion, in circumstances where my observations are not made with reference to specific facts and are unnecessary for my decision, I am of the view that the suggested approach is not helpful as a general guide to local authorities' conduct.

24 *R (Singh) v Cardiff City Council*[7] establishes that it is unlawful for a local authority to use suspension as a holding operation pending further investigation. So a council cannot lawfully suspend by reason of a criminal charge on a "wait and see" basis. It follows that it cannot use the cloak of a substantive decision to suspend to achieve the same holding operation. If it suspends the licence, it must do so by way of a substantive decision on the fitness of the driver to hold the licence, after giving the driver a proper opportunity to state his case, not merely as a means by which to maintain a position pending the final outcome of the criminal proceedings. Once it is seen that suspension is not a holding operation but a substantive decision, it becomes apparent (in my view) that suspension will rarely be the appropriate course where a driver is charged with a matter for which, if convicted, he would be subject to revocation of his licence. If such a charge merits action, and if the action is not by way of an interim measure pending determination of the facts at criminal trial, revocation will generally be the appropriate course. To suspend a licence because an allegation is made and then revoke it because the allegation is proved is, as it seems to me, contrary to the decision in *R (Singh) v Cardiff City Council*[8], even if the former decision is dressed up as a substantive rather than a merely provisional or holding decision.

25 This is not to say that, once a decision has been taken to suspend upon notification of a charge or allegation of wrongdoing, no subsequent decision to revoke can ever be taken. Although the submission accepted by Singh J in *R (Singh) v Cardiff City Council* referred to the council being *functus officio*, a licensing authority will never be *functus officio* with respect to section 61 in the sense that it no longer has duties to discharge and powers to exercise. The point rather is that any decision to suspend, though in one sense final, can only be made on the basis of the information available at the time the decision was made. When faced with a decision

under section 61, the council must fully consider the available information, afford the licence-holder the opportunity to state his case, and exercise the judgment and discretion identified by Singh J. Thus, as Mr Douglas-Jones submitted orally when acting in the role of an amicus curiae , it is possible to envisage a case where, although the information provided to a local authority concerning a criminal charge leads it to consider that suspension is a sufficient sanction, facts thereafter emerging in the course of the criminal trial put a different complexion on the matter and require revocation. It does not seem to me that the initial suspension would necessarily rule out a subsequent revocation in such circumstances, having regard in particular to the fact that the council's powers are conferred for purposes of public protection. Such a case, however, is very different from the case considered in *R (Singh) v Cardiff City Council*[9], where suspension is simply in the nature of a holding measure pending a substantive decision as to what if any sanction is appropriate.'

26 The effect of this is that, although the decision in each case will be one for the judgment and discretion of the council, where a licence-holder is charged with an offence the commission of which would be considered to render him unfit to hold a licence, the council is likely to consider it appropriate to revoke the licence at that stage. For reasons already stated, to suspend the licence merely because of the charge and revoke it merely because of the ensuing conviction would in my view conflict with the decision in *R (Singh) v Cardiff City Council*[10] as to the scope of the power under section 61. Any decision to revoke will be subject to a statutory right of appeal. Further, if it should later transpire, for example by reason of acquittal at trial, that the former licence-holder is indeed a fit and proper person to hold a licence, provision can be made for expeditious re-licensing.'

This is an important judgment which reinforces the view expressed in *Singh*[11] that suspension cannot be used as an interim measure. The judge considered all the arguments put forward against the decision in *Singh*, and found them wanting. He also emphasised the point made above that if the grounds for revocation are subsequently found to be unsubstantiated, a mechanism must be available to allow the licence to be reinstated as quickly as possible.

[1]   [2017] EWHC 1764 (Admin), (13 July 2017, unreported).
[2]   *R (app Singh) v Cardiff City Council* [2012] EWHC 1852 (Admin), [2013] LLR 108; see para 6.43 above.
[3]   In relation to costs on a successful appeal, *Bradford MBC v Booth* [2000] All ER (D) 635 and *R (app Perinpanathan) v Westminster Magistrates' Court and Another* [2010] EWCA Civ 40, [2010] WLR 1508. For full details see Chapter 3, para 3.26 onwards.
[4]   [2012] EWHC 1852 (Admin), [2013] LLR 108.
[5]   As above.
[6]   As above.
[7]   As above.
[8]   As above.
[9]   As above.
[10] As above.
[11] *R (app Singh) v Cardiff City Council* [2012] EWHC 1852, (Admin), [2013] LLR 108; see para 6.43 above.

6.46

In relation to costs on a successful appeal, *Bradford MBC v Booth and R (app Perinpanathan) v Westminster Magistrates' Court and Another*[1] will continue to apply, and provided the authority did not act negligently, capriciously or incompetently in arriving at its decision it should not be penalised in costs even if the subsequent decision of the magistrates is to uphold the appeal. As the law now prevents suspension for the purposes of investigation it is difficult to see how an authority that had acted in this way could be said to have acted improperly.

The question of the use of immediate revocation of drivers' licences is an important one. Clearly it is a significant step, although the impact on the livelihood of the driver is not a relevant factor[2], and should not be taken lightly by a local authority. However, the overriding purpose of hackney carriage and private hire licensing is public safety[3], and where there is a risk to public safety, action should be taken as soon as possible to minimise that risk. In its *'Taxi and Private Hire Vehicle Licensing: Best Practice Guidance'*[4], the DfT make the following statement:

> '88. Section 52 of the Road Safety Act 2006 amended the Local Government (Miscellaneous Provisions) Act 1976 such that local authorities can now suspend or revoke a taxi or PHV driver's licence with immediate effect on safety grounds. It should be stressed that this power can only be used where safety is the principal reason for suspending or revoking and where the risk justifies such an approach. It is expected that in the majority of cases drivers will continue to work pending appeal and that this power will be used in one-off cases. But the key point is that the law says that the power must be used in cases which can be justified in terms of safety. The Department is not proposing to issue any specific guidance on this issue, preferring to leave it to the discretion of licensing authorities as to when the power should be used.'

This suggests that there may be reasons apart from public safety where a local authority might be considering suspending or revoking a licence. Apart from suspending a licence as a punishment for repeated non-compliance over minor matters[5], it is difficult to see how this might occur. The driver must be fit and proper at application, and must therefore remain fit and proper for the duration of that licence. If they are not, then they must present a risk to public safety. As such, it is suggested that the DfT Guidance is unfortunate and the reality must be that in the majority of cases (with very few exceptions), where a licence is revoked, it must be with immediate effect to protect public safety.

---

[1]   [2000] All ER (D) 635 and [2010] EWCA Civ 40, [2010] WLR 1508. For full details see Chapter 3, para 3.26 onwards.

[2]   See *Leeds City Council v Hussain* [2003] RTR 13 and *Cherwell DC v Anwar* [2012] RTR 15 Chapter 2, paras 2.111 and 2.112.

[3]   This is made clear in paragraph 8 of the Department for Transport's *Taxi and Private Hire Vehicle Licensing: Best Practice Guidance* (October 2006, revised March 2010) available at http://www.dft. gov.uk/pgr/regional/taxis/taxiandprivatehirevehiclelic1792

[4]   DfT, *'Taxi and Private Hire Vehicle Licensing: Best Practice Guidance'* (October 2006, revised March 2010), available from http://www.dft.gov.uk/pgr/regional/taxis/taxiandprivatehirevehiclelic1792.

[5]   See para 6.49.

PENALTY POINTS SCHEMES

6.47

The powers available to a local authority to deal with transgression or wrongdoing on the part of a licensee are to suspend, revoke or refuse to renew the licence. For minor misdemeanours those are draconian steps, and some more graduated response is required. Many authorities use a system of warnings, followed by written warnings, but these can be unclear as to their effect, and uncertain as to their duration.

Those uncertainties can be overcome to a large extent by the use of a penalty points scheme. These are enforcement tools utilised by a number of local authorities. In concept it is not dissimilar from driving licence points resulting from convictions or fixed penalty notices on a DVLA driving licence.

The authority sets a maximum number of points that can be accrued on a licence[1]. It determines how long any points should remain on the licence, and what the period is after which the licence is wiped clean. It then sets a tariff of points for various misdemeanours. In some cases, these are fixed and in other cases there can be a sliding scale. Points can be awarded by officers or committees and sub-committees. Some schemes carry a right of appeal to a committee or sub-committee against an award of points by officers, with powers given to the committee to quash the award, reduce the number of points, increase the number of points or take action against the licence[2].

When the maximum number of points is reached, it triggers an opportunity for the authority to consider whether action should be taken against the licence. That could be a suspension as a punishment[3], revocation or refusal to renew. It is vital that there is no automatic action taken once the maximum number of points is reached.

[1]   This can be any of the taxi licences: hackney carriage driver; private hire driver; private hire operator; hackney carriage proprietor/vehicle; private hire proprietor/vehicle.
[2]   Suspend or revoke.
[3]   See para 6.49.

6.48

It was a points scheme which formed the basis of the challenge in *R (app Singh) v Cardiff City Council*[1]. Cardiff City Council had introduced a penalty points scheme some years earlier, in around 1988. There were some slight modifications later (the exact history of the approval of the policy is unclear) and in the words of the judge, Mr Justice Singh[2]:

'it is common ground before me that the document which is before the court does set out the policy as it was in force at the time of the two individual decisions which are in issue in the present case. The document is headed "Penalty point system" and states:

"The Licensing Committee agreed to introduce a Penalty Point system to be utilised in the event of misconduct by licensed Hackney Carriage/Private Hire Drivers. As a consequence the Licensing

Committee defined guidelines for the administration of the system and resolved that.

(i) the categories of offences, together with the range of penalty points listed below be adopted as guidelines, and each matter be considered on its merits and depend on the circumstances surrounding each case."

There then followed headed (a) to (g) a number of types of incident, for example assault, harassment, deception etc with a points range set out for each type of incident. The policy continued at paragraph 2:

"the accumulation of 10 or more points in any period of 3 years will normally result in the automatic revocation of the licence."'

The judge noted that there had been a modification to the policy[3]:

'the policy was amended after the particular decisions under challenge in this case in December 2011, paragraph 2 of the policy now states:

"The accumulation of 10 or more points in any period of 3 years will normally result in the revocation of the licence."'

The challenges to the policy were twofold.

Firstly, that the penalty points scheme itself was ultra vires the powers of the authority and unlawful[4]. It was suggested by the claimants that the council had created a separate disciplinary scheme to run parallel with the powers contained in s 61 of the 1976 Act[5]. This argument was rejected by the judge in the following terms[6]:

'64. In my judgment that argument is not well-founded. I accept the arguments in this regard on behalf of the defendant. In my judgment, what the defendant sought to do and has done is to adopt a policy to govern the exercise of its undoubted discretion under section 61 of the 1976 Act. A public authority is perfectly entitled to adopt policies which will regulate the exercise of a given discretionary power. In my judgment there is nothing wrong in principle with a licensing authority, such as the present, taking the view that the public interest justifies adopting a policy which would not lead to the suspension or revocation of a driver's licence, for example, for a single incident.

65. In my view, there is nothing wrong in principle with the defendant authority such as the present, adopting the policy, which seeks, both in fairness to the driver potentially affected and also to protect the public interest, to have, as it were, a staged process by which the cumulative effect of incidents of misconduct may well lead ultimately to the conclusion that in the judgment of the local authority, a person is not a proper person to continue to enjoy the relevant licence.'

The second argument was that once the driver accumulated 10 penalty points, the revocation of his licence would be 'automatic', and that did not allow a proper exercise of discretion as required by s 61[7]. On this point, the judge examined what s 61 actually required[8]:

'69. Before addressing that submission in more detail, I would note that in my view section 61 does not confer only a discretion. In my view, it includes an element what may be called the exercise of a judgment in particular in subsection (1)(b) which requires there to be any other reasonable cause. It was common ground before me, in substance, for present purposes, that means whether a person continues to be a fit and proper person to hold a driver's licence.

70. As I have said, that is not a pure exercise of discretion, it is rather an exercise which calls for judgment to be performed on whether the statutory question has been answered in favour of or against the relevant driver.

71. That is a threshold question before which the exercise of discretion does not exist. Even once the threshold question has been answered against a driver, there still exists in the local authority a discretion. Section 61 provides that in those circumstances a Council may, not that it must, suspend or revoke a licence. So at that stage of the process discretion does come into it. That discretion of course must be exercised lawfully according to well-known principles of public law.'

He then moved on to consider how Cardiff City Council approached that process.

'74. There are three ways at least in which the point can be formulated and was on behalf of the claimant. These three submissions in essence summarise the fundamental defects in law, as I see them to be in the policy of the Council as adopted and applied. The first is that the policy calls for the automatic revocation of a licence if 10 points have been accumulated in a 3-year period. That, on its face, leaves no room for judgment or discretion.

75. I will return in a moment to the evidence as to how matters were actually carried out in practice.

76. The second fundamental defect is that this means that there is no consideration required, or it would appear perhaps even permitted by the policy of the underlying facts which lay behind the earlier imposition of points which a driver may have. That may, as the case of Mr Singh illustrates, be some years before the decision of the Committee which eventually decides to revoke a licence.

77. Fundamentally, as was put by the claimants and I accept, this leads to the wrong question being asked. Not the statutory question of whether there is any reasonable cause, in other words whether in all the circumstances of the case a driver is a fit and proper person to continue to enjoy licence, rather the question at worst could be reduced to a mathematical one of whether, for example, six points plus four points equals 10 points.

78. The third fundamental defect, in my judgment, again accepting the claimant's submissions in this regard is that the policy does not recognise that the outcome even of concluding that a person is not a fit and proper

person is not necessarily revocation, it may be under section 61 the sanction of suspension.

79. I turn briefly in this regard to the new policy as reformulated in December 2011. That, in my judgment, may have the effect of mitigating to some extent the inflexibility of the earlier formulation of the policy. However what it does not do, in my judgment, is address all of the fundamental defects which I have identified. For example it still does not direct the local authority to ask itself the right question in law under section 61 and the Committee may well still be distracted, in my view, by the wrong question, for example a mathematical question. Further and in any event the reformulated policy still does not recognise that the appropriate sanction, even when a reasonable cause has been established, would be that of suspension and not revocation.'

It can therefore be seen that a penalty points scheme is lawful, provided the sanction is not automatically applied and the decision maker undertakes the correct process when determining what sanction, if any, should apply. The accumulation of penalty points over a short period of time can indicate a propensity for a driver to have little regard for conditions of licence, or standards of behaviour expected by the council, and that can directly impact upon the continuing requirement to remain a fit and proper person. The process is to ask and then determine in the light of the evidence, whether the driver is a fit and proper person and if not, then what is the appropriate sanction.

1   [2012] EWHC 1852 (Admin), [2013] LLR 108.
2   At para 15.
3   At para 16.
4   Detailed at para 62.
5   Local Government (Miscellaneous Provisions) Act 1976, s 61 contains the power allowing a local authority to take action against a drivers' licence.
6   At paras 64 and 65.
7   Detailed at para 68.
8   See para 69 onwards.

SUSPENSION AS A PUNISHMENT

6.49

What can be done about drivers (and private hire operators) who repeatedly fail to comply with licensing and legislative requirements? Obviously, if the matter is serious and public safety is directly affected, the licence can be revoked[1], but what can be done if the matter is more minor, but repeated? The use of a penalty points scheme[2] or a system of warnings is useful, but what happens if the licensee still does not comply? Can suspension of a licence be used in these circumstances as a punishment?

The use of suspension as a punishment is considered in *R (app Singh) v Cardiff City Council*[3]. It had previously been thought that short suspensions, as a punishment for transgressions which did not ultimately render the driver no longer fit and proper to hold the licence were difficult to justify, due to the underlying question of fitness and propriety and how that could be lost and then regained in a short period of time. This was addressed quite simply by Singh J in Singh where he stated[4]:

> '103. In my judgment, the way in which the concept of suspension is used by Parliament is section 61 of the 1976 Act is not, as it were, to create a power of interim suspension, it is rather after a considered determination in other words a final decision on whether a ground for either revocation, or suspension of a licence is made out, for there to be either revocation or, as a lesser sanction, a sanction of suspension.

> 104. By way of analogy, one can envisage for example in a professional context a solicitor or a barrister can be disciplined on grounds of his conduct. The relevant disciplinary body may conclude that even if the misconduct has been established, that the appropriate sanction should be something less than complete revocation of the practising certificate for the relevant lawyer. It may be, for example, a suspension for a period of 1 year, will constitute sufficient sanction in the interests of the public.

> 105. It is in that sense, in my judgment, that Parliament uses the concept of suspension in section 61 of the 1976 Act. It does not use, as it were, to create an interim power, before a reasoned determination has been made, that the grounds in subsection (1A) or (1B) have been made out. It is not, as it were, a protective or holding power. It is a power of final suspension, as an alternative to a power of final revocation.'

It can be seen that this is the same passage as quoted above in relation to interim suspensions and has already been considered. That is true, but it reinforces the idea, particularly in paragraph 104, that suspension is a final decision, and not the precursor to other action. Accordingly, it is clear that suspension can therefore be simply used as a punishment. Although this case concerned drivers' licences and the powers available to a local authority under s 61 of the 1976 Act, there seems to be no reason why the same approach cannot be used in relation to private hire operators when taking action under s 62 of the same Act.

[1] See para 6.42 onwards.
[2] See para 6.47 above.
[3] [2012] EWHC 1852 (Admin), [2013] LLR 108.
[4] As above at para 103 onwards.

CONCLUSIONS

6.50

It was stated at the commencement of this chapter that it is only through enforcement that any laws have any meaningful effect and this is true of hackney carriage and private hire legislation just as much as it is of other areas. Vigorous enforcement of hackney carriage and private hire provisions is essential if the ultimate aim of the licensing regime, to protect the travelling public, is to be achieved. There is no doubt that enforcement is expensive in terms of both the staff and legal costs involved, but, unless it is undertaken, the licensing of hackney carriages and private hire vehicles becomes a merely administrative exercise. That is of benefit to no one, except unscrupulous persons who do not comply with the requirements.

6.51

Licensees who pay licence fees are entitled to expect an enforcement regime which aims not only to protect the public, but also to protect them from those who do not comply with the requirements, notwithstanding the fact that enforcement costs cannot be generally recovered via the licence fees[1]. Local authorities without effective enforcement policies and procedures are not only letting down their population and anyone who visits their area, but also letting down the vast majority of people involved in the hackney carriage and private hire trades who abide by the rules and work hard to provide a good, safe and reliable service to the public.

[1]   See Chapter 4, para 4.12 onwards.

Chapter 7

Hackney carriages outside London: an introduction

LEGISLATION

The Town Police Clauses Act 1847

7.1

Hackney carriages are an extremely old form of public transport and have been subject to statutory control for over three centuries[1]. Outside London they are governed primarily by the provisions of the Town Police Clauses Act 1847 (TPCA 1847).

'Clauses Acts' were popular in the last century and were intended as a set of acceptable sections which could be adopted and incorporated into local Acts of Parliament promoted by local authorities.

[1]   The first legislation for control of hackney carriages in London was 'An Ordinance for the Regulation of Hackney-Coachmen in London and the places adjacent' and was approved by Parliament in 1654 during the Commonwealth interregnum of Oliver Cromwell. It is available at http://www.british-history.ac.uk/no-series/acts-ordinances-interregnum/pp922-924

7.2

TPCA 1847 no longer needs such specific incorporation within local legislation as it stands as a complete Act in its own right, in relation to hackney carriages. It was incorporated (together with the Town Police Clauses Act 1889) into the Public Health Act 1875 by the Public Health Act 1875, s 171 and then applied to the whole of England and Wales by the Transport Act 1985, s 15. If any local authority had local legislation incorporating the provisions of TPCA 1847 but which excluded the hackney carriage provisions within TPCA 1847, those exclusions were also repealed by the Transport Act 1985, s 15.

The net effect of this is that TPCA 1847 applies throughout England and Wales (outside Greater London) and provides the bedrock of the legislation relating to hackney carriages.

7.3

TPCA 1847 has been modified and amended over the last 150 years and it appears that, in the absence of new 'taxi' legislation, it will continue to be amended as new ideas emerge and new problems need to be solved[1].

[1]　In 2014 the Law Commission reported on its investigation into *'Taxi and Private Hire Services'* which is available at http://lawcommission.justice.gov.uk/areas/taxi-and-private-hire-services. htm. At the time of writing (August 2017) no further developments have taken place in relation to England, but the Welsh Government is consulting on the introduction of new legislation in Wales with likely implementation in 2022.

7.4

A hackney carriage is a vehicle licensed by the district council in the area in which it undertakes its business, is driven by a person who holds a hackney carriage driver's licence granted by the same local authority and which falls within the definition contained in TPCA 1847, s 38. To fall within this definition, the vehicle must seat fewer than nine passengers, but other than that, it can be of any type or description. In 1847, the internal combustion engine was in its infancy as a power plant and, accordingly, it is not a requirement that a hackney carriage is powered by an internal combustion engine. The licensing regime can apply to horse-drawn vehicles and to human-propelled vehicles just as effectively.

7.5

A hackney carriage can ply for hire and also wait at a hackney carriage stand (generally referred to as a taxi rank). It is also possible for hackney carriages to be pre-booked and act in a way similar to private hire vehicles.

7.6

Once a hackney carriage has been approached on a stand, the driver must take the person to the destination requested, provided it is within the 'prescribed distance' (which is defined as the area of the district council in question[1])[2].

[1]　See Chapter 8, para 8.1.
[2]　See TPCA 1847, s 53; see Appendix I.

7.7

In exchange for carrying that passenger or passengers, the driver is entitled to charge a fare, which may be regulated by the local authority. If it is regulated, then the driver cannot charge more than the fare for a journey within the district, but can charge less; if the local authority does not set the fares, then the fare must be reasonable.

7.8

The district council can make byelaws to control the conduct of both the proprietors and the drivers.

7.9

The vehicles themselves must be inspected by the local authority, which must be satisfied that they are mechanically sound and comply with any particular conditions before the proprietor's licence can be granted. Records of licences granted must be kept by the local authority.

TPCA 1847 contains considerably more provisions than those mentioned here, but they will be considered in detail in the subsequent chapters which relate to hackney carriage vehicles and hackney carriage drivers.

The Town Police Clauses Act 1889

7.10

The Town Police Clauses Act 1889 allows proprietors' and drivers' licences to be granted for less than a year (Town Police Clauses Act 1889, s 5) and extends the range of topics which can be covered by byelaws made by the local authority (Town Police Clauses Act 1889, s 6).

The Local Government (Miscellaneous Provisions) Act 1976

7.11

The Local Government (Miscellaneous Provisions) Act 1976 (LG(MP)A 1976) has considerable impact on hackney carriages, notwithstanding its overriding aim being to regulate private hire vehicles. This includes:

- power to attach conditions to hackney carriage proprietors' licences;
- transfer of hackney carriages;
- testing of hackney carriage vehicles;
- various provisions relating to drivers' licences, badges etc;
- powers for suspension and revocation of drivers and vehicle licences
- charging of fees for licences; and
- has considerable impact on the provision of hackney carriage stands.

In addition, LG(MP)A 1976, s 65 provides an alternative method of fixing fares to that contained within the byelaws procedure and also includes provisions whereby obstruction of authorised officers is an offence (LG(MP)A 1976, s 73).

7.12

LG(MP)A 1976 is adoptive and it is for local authorities to adopt its provisions if they wish. Such adoption is wholesale: that is to say, the district council must adopt the whole of LG(MP)A 1976, Pt II and cannot pick specific sections that it wishes to adopt.

7.13

The process of adoption is contained in LG(MP)A 1976, s 45, and the process is straightforward.

7.14

Other primary legislation also affecting hackney carriages includes the Transport Act 1981, the Transport Act 1985 and the Equality Act 2010.

The Transport Act 1985

7.15

After 1976, the next significant impact on hackney carriage licensing was the Transport Act 1985. This introduced the idea of hackney carriages being hired to more than one person at a time, with each person paying separate fares. The hire of the carriage could be either immediately or by booking in advance, and could also be used to provide local services under a restricted public service vehicle operator's licence. As already seen, it extended the impact of TPCA 1847 to the whole of England and Wales.

7.16

Possibly the most important alteration resulting from the introduction of the Transport Act 1985 was the abolition of the unfettered ability of the district council to set a maximum number of licences which it would grant for hackney carriage proprietors or vehicles[1].

[1]   This area is looked at in further detail in Chapter 8, para 8.166 onwards.

The Equality Act 2010

7.17

The Equality Act 2010 replaced the Disability Discrimination Act 1995. It contains significant measures relating to hackney carriages, although as yet only a few have been implemented. The provisions in force to date are: a requirement in most cases for a driver to carry assistance dogs in hackney carriages where a passenger makes use of such help; and a power to allow a local authority to maintain a list of wheelchair accessible vehicles When such a list is maintained, in most cases a driver must provide mobility assistance to wheelchair bound passengers.

Byelaws

7.18

Finally, consideration must be given to byelaws. These can be made under either TPCA 1847, s 68 or the Town Police Clauses Act 1889, s 6. They require the approval of the Secretary of State for Transport, but the Department for Transport is unlikely to approve byelaws which depart from the model byelaws which they provide unless the local authority can provide good reasons for the departure[1].

The model byelaws, are reproduced at Appendix II. They were originally issued as an annex to Department of Transport circular 8/86, but have since been revised[2]. The procedure for making byelaws is contained in the Local Government Act 1972, s 236[3].

[1]   '26. For the purposes of consistency, we would expect draft byelaws to be based on the model. That is not to say that we would automatically dismiss any deviation from the wording of the model; it is fully realised that licensing authorities often want to tailor their licensing policies to their own circumstances. However, when a deviation is proposed, we do need to be satisfied that there is a genuine reason for it and that it is not simply change for the sake of change': Department for Transport letter to local authorities dated 9 September 2003. See Appendix II.

[2]   The revisions take account of the fact that all local authorities in England and Wales have adopted the LG(MP)A 1976 (except the City of Plymouth which has its own local legislation).

[3]   See *Encyclopaedia of Local Government Law* (Sweet and Maxwell).

Chapter 8

Hackney carriage vehicles outside London: definition and demand

WHAT IS A HACKNEY CARRIAGE?

8.1

Section 37 of the Town Police Clauses Act 1847 gives a power to the 'Commissioners' to licence hackney carriages. It states:

> 'The commissioners may from time to time licence to ply for hire within the prescribed distance, or if no distance is prescribed, within five miles from the General Post Office of the city, town, or place to which the special Act refers, (which in that case shall be deemed the prescribed distance,) hackney coaches or carriages of any kind or description adapted to the carriage of persons'.

The 'Commissioners' are now construed as being a reference to the district, borough, metropolitan borough, unitary or Welsh county or county borough council[1].

The reference to the prescribed distance is now a reference to the area of the district council (or unitary, metropolitan district, Welsh county or county borough council), unless the council has hackney carriage zones, in which case it will be the area of the zone in question. This is as a result of the Public Health Act 1875, s 171, which incorporated the provisions of TPCA 1847 and the Town Police Clauses Act 1889 for all urban districts. The Local Government Act 1894 and the Local Government Act 1933 extended hackney carriage licensing to all urban districts, boroughs and county boroughs, and this continued under LGA 1972. Paragraph 2 of Sch 14 to the LGA 1972 makes it clear that any reference to an urban or rural authority is now a reference to a local authority within the meaning of the 1972 Act, and the powers contained in TPCA 1847, s 37 are now granted to the local authority and all references to the commissioners are now construed as references to the local authority. The Transport Act 1985 extended hackney carriage licensing to all districts in England and Wales. As a consequence, the reference to the radius of five miles from the GPO is now merely of historic interest.

The definition of a hackney carriage is contained in the Town Police Clauses Act 1847, s 38 (TPCA 1847):

'What vehicles to be deemed hackney carriages

38 Every wheeled carriage, whatever may be its form or construction, used in standing or plying for hire in any street within the prescribed distance, and every carriage standing upon any street within the prescribed distance, having thereon any numbered plate required by this or the special Act to be fixed upon a hackney carriage, or having thereon any plate resembling or intended to resemble any such plate as aforesaid, shall be deemed to be a hackney carriage within the meaning of this Act; and in all proceedings at law or otherwise the term "hackney carriage" shall be sufficient to describe any such carriage: Provided always, that no stage coach used for the purpose of standing or plying for passengers to be carried for hire at separate fares, and duly licensed for that purpose, and having thereon the proper numbered plates required by law to be placed on such stage coaches, shall be deemed to be a hackney carriage within the meaning of this Act.'

It is interesting to note that, in all subsequent Acts, the above definition is used for a hackney carriage[2] and, even where the legislation has started to use the word 'taxi', it is made clear that a 'taxi' means a hackney carriage, eg:

- the Transport Act 1980, s 64(3);
- the Transport Act 1985, s 13(3); and
- the Equality Act 2010, s 173(1).

The approach to the concept of a hackney carriage is in itself quite clever. It is the use of the vehicle that makes it a hackney carriage, as opposed to the appearance, construction or existence of a licence. The question then moves on to whether or not a vehicle that is being used in such a way is correctly licensed. If it is, then that use is lawful. If not, then an offence under s 45 of the TPCA 1847 is committed[3].

[1]   See paragraph 2.3 above.
[2]   See the Local Government (Miscellaneous Provisions) Act 1976, s 80.
[3]   See Appendix I.

8.2

The plate is issued by the Local Authority and must be affixed to the vehicle (see TPCA 1847, ss 51 and 52 and byelaw 2 of the model byelaws). TPCA 1847, s 51 specifies the size of the letters that must be used for the phrase on the plate 'To carry … persons'. This phrase must be must be painted 'in legible letters, so as to be clearly distinguishable from the colour of the ground whereon the same are painted, one inch in length, and of a proportionate breadth' on the plate, which itself must be 'placed on some conspicuous place on the outside of such carriage'. Local authorities use a wide variety of different styles of plates for hackney carriages, and it would seem that many of them do not comply with this requirement. This statutory requirement can be contrasted with the position relating to private hire vehicles, where the design of the plate is wholly at the discretion of the local authority[1].

[1]   See Chapter 13, para 13.31.

8.3

The maximum number of passengers that can be carried in a vehicle for it to be capable of being licensed as a hackney carriage is eight. Any vehicle which carries more than eight is classified as a public service vehicle (PSV) under the Public Passenger Vehicles Act 1981, s 1(1).

STATUS OF A HACKNEY CARRIAGE

Hawkins v Edwards

8.4

> Licensed hackney carriage not displaying plate. Argued that the plate did not have to be displayed when it was not being used as a hackney carriage. Held: Once a vehicle has been licensed as a hackney carriage, it retains that status for the duration of the licence, irrespective of whether it is being used for hackney carriage purposes at any given time.

In the case of *Hawkins v Edwards*[1], the question of whether a licensed hackney carriage was always a hackney carriage was considered. Mr Hawkins held a hackney carriage proprietor's licence and was prosecuted for failing to display the plate correctly. He argued that, at the time, the vehicle was not acting as a hackney carriage, was therefore not a hackney carriage and, therefore, he did not need to display the plate. The matter was considered in the High Court and Alverstone LCJ gave the judgment of the court (supported by Lawrance J). He stated (at 172):

> 'The point raised in this case is one of some nicety, and requires consideration. I confess I was at first struck with the hardship which, it was said, might arise through holding that a person could not employ his carriage, if it was licensed as a hackney carriage, in any other way than as a hackney carriage. But upon consideration I think the grievance is one which we need not take into account. The general purview of the by-law is to protect the public: the object is to provide for a proper supervision of carriages which are licensed to stand or ply for hire as hackney carriages. I think that if a man elects to have the privilege of keeping a carriage which is licensed, he elects to devote that carriage to the services indicated in the by-law. The words of the by-law, "while such carriage may stand, ply, or be driven for hire", in my view, are merely meant to indicate a period during which the hackney carriage is a thing which must have its number shewn, and we ought not to accede to the argument of the appellant's counsel that

the by-law only applies whilst the carriage is actually standing, plying, or being driven for hire. I think the right view is that the carriage is licensed for a period, and if used during that period in standing or plying for hire the number must be shewn for the whole period. The language of s 38 of the Town Police Clauses Act 1847, means, I think, that every wheeled carriage which is in fact from time to time used in standing or plying for hire is to be deemed to be a hackney carriage for the whole period during which it is so from time to time used, and the language of the section does not limit the period to the time during which the carriage is in fact used for standing or plying for hire in a street.'

[1]   [1901] 2 KB 169.

Yates v Gates

8.5

> An unlicensed driver drove a hackney carriage, and was acquitted of driving without a licence contrary to TPCA 1847, s 46 because the vehicle was not standing or plying for hire. The prosecutor appealed by way of case stated and it was held that a hackney carriage cannot change its character from moment to moment and once licensed it is always a hackney carriage.

The question of the status of a hackney carriage was reconsidered by the High Court in the case of Yates v Gates[1]. In fact, this was a second question in relation to the case, the primary point concerning the necessity to obtain positive consent from a passenger hiring a hackney carriage to the carrying of another person[2].

[1]   [1970] 1 All ER 754, QBD.
[2]   See Chapter 10, para 10.115.

8.6

However, the question as to whether a hackney carriage was always a hackney carriage and therefore whether anyone driving a vehicle which was licensed as a hackney carriage needed a hackney carriage driver's licence, irrespective of whether or not the vehicle was working at the time, was raised. Parker LCJ gave the judgment of the court[1] and he stated (at 756B):

'The second information charged the respondent that on the same day he drove a hackney carriage which was duly licensed to ply for hire not having obtained a licence to act as such driver. The justices took the view that since on the occasion in question the sign "For Hire" was not illuminated, and in the circumstances that the respondent was not driving the vehicle for hire, therefore did not require a licence, and dismissed the information. In regard to that, s 46 of the Act [TPCA 1847] in question provides:

"No person shall act as driver of any hackney carriage licensed in pursuance of this or the special Act to ply for hire ... without first obtaining a licence from the commissioners..."

Section 47 provides the penalty: "If any person acts as such driver as aforesaid without having obtained such licence ..." he shall be guilty of an offence.

Pausing there, it is undoubtedly true that the respondent did not have the necessary licence, and that the vehicle in question was itself licensed to ply for hire. The justices, however, took the view that unless the vehicle was plying for hire it would not be a hackney carriage the driver of which would require a licence. That of course envisages that a vehicle licensed as a hackney carriage as defined in s 38 of the 1847 Act must change its character from moment to moment; when it is not plying for hire it is not a hackney carriage, and when it is plying for hire it is a hackney carriage.

In my judgment s 46 is perfectly plain. No person shall drive any vehicle which is licensed as a hackney carriage, whatever it may be doing at that particular moment unless he himself has a licence as required by s 46. Support for this view may be found in *Hawkins v Edwards*[2], where the argument which apparently found favour with the justices in this case was not acceded to in the Divisional Court.

In my view this case should go back to the justices with a direction to convict ...'

[1]   *Yates v Gates* [1970] 1 All ER 754, QBD.
[2]   [1901] 2 KB 169; see para 8.4 above.

PLYING AND STANDING FOR HIRE

8.7

The question of what is meant by plying or standing for hire is fundamental to both hackney carriage and private hire activities. Only hackney carriages can ply or stand for hire; private hire vehicles cannot. As a result, this question has been a major source of contention over a long time. The right to ply or stand for hire is jealously guarded by hackney carriage proprietors as this is, to a large extent, the most important distinction between the two types of vehicle. It is an offence for any vehicle other than a hackney carriage, licensed within the district in which it is found (or zone if the district has hackney carriage zones) to stand or ply for hire by virtue of TPCA 1847, s 45 which states:

'Penalty for plying for hire without a licence

45 If the proprietor or part proprietor of any carriage, or any person so concerned as aforesaid, permits the same to be used as a hackney carriage plying for hire within the prescribed distance without having obtained a licence as aforesaid for such carriage, or during the time that such licence is suspended as hereinafter provided, or if any person be found driving, standing, or plying for hire with any carriage within the prescribed distance for which such licence as aforesaid has not been previously obtained, or without having the number of such carriage corresponding with the number of the licence openly displayed on such carriage, every such person

so offending shall for every such offence be liable to a penalty not exceeding level 4 on the standard scale.'

And 'street' is defined in TPCA 1847, s 3 as:

'The word "street" shall extend to and include any road, square, court, alley, and thoroughfare, or public passage, within the limits of the special Act:'

As a result, this area of law has been the subject of considerable litigation over the last century or so and a large body of case law has built up. Unfortunately, that is not perhaps as helpful as it might at first appear. Parker LCJ observed in *Cogley v Sherwood*[1] (at 323):

'The court has been referred to a number of cases from 1869 down to the present day dealing with hackney carriages and stage carriages. Those decisions are not easy to reconcile, and ... I have been unable to extract from them a comprehensive and authoritative definition of "plying for hire".'

and in over half a century since that case, no complete definition has emerged.

[1] [1959] 2 QB 311; see para 8.10 below.

8.8

One of the difficulties which has led to this is the age of the legislation. As has been stated elsewhere, TPCA 1847 was passed at a time when the internal combustion engine was in its infancy and the present road transport, traffic, communications and social climate could not even have been imagined. As a result, the legislation addresses itself to horse-drawn vehicles from another era and the case law has struggled to apply that to an ever-changing reality. This evolution has been compounded by the existence of lawfully licensed private hire vehicles since 1976.

It is important to recognise that the concepts of 'plying' and 'standing' are separate and distinct and it is unfortunate that the terms tend to be conflated into one indivisible concept[1]. 'Standing' refers to a stationary vehicle, either at a hackney carriage stand or lawfully parked elsewhere, whist 'plying' refers to a cruising vehicle. When the legislation is analysed, it can be seen that some elements concern plying, others concern standing, and some parts cover both activities.

The breakdown is as follows:

- Section 37 of the 1847 Act allows the district council to licence Hackney carriages to 'ply for hire'.
- Section 38 introduces the concept of vehicles 'standing or plying for hire', which is necessary as a vehicle undertaking either activity is deemed to be a hackney carriage.
- The undertaking of standing as well as plying for hire is again present in s 45 (in relation to the penalty for doing either without a licence).
- Sections 53 and 64 – 'standing for hire' with no reference to 'plying'.

- Byelaws 2, 5 and 8 – clear distinctions.
- Byelaw 7 – only 'plying'.

¹   See eg, *Milton Keynes Borough Council v Barry* (3 July 1984, unreported), DC.

Case law

Sales v Lake

8.9

> Pre-booked seats on a charabanc outing, and passengers picked up at an arranged point. Held: To be plying for hire.

In *Sales v Lake*¹ the proposition that the vehicle and driver must be exhibited to the prospective customer was established. Lake sold tickets for a charabanc excursion to Brighton and arranged a time and location when the passengers, who had all purchased a ticket, were to be picked up. The driver of the charabanc did so and was prosecuted and convicted for unlawfully plying for hire. An appeal was launched by way of case stated and the conviction was upheld by a majority decision. The majority judgments handed down by Avory J (with a simple agreement by McCardie J) are difficult to reconcile, and appear to support the dissenting judgment. However, the important principle is outlined by Trevethin LCJ in his (minority) judgment where he summarised the concept of plying for hire:

> 'In my judgment a carriage cannot accurately be said to ply for hire unless two conditions are satisfied.
> (1.) There must be a soliciting or waiting to secure passengers by the driver or other person in control without any previous contract with them, and
> (2.) the owner or person in control who is engaged in or authorizes (sic) the soliciting or waiting must be in possession of a carriage for which he is soliciting or waiting to obtain passengers.'

This established the proposition that the vehicle must be exhibited and there must be a driver present with that vehicle for there to be either a plying or standing for hire.

¹   [1922] 1 KB 553.

Cogley v Sherwood

8.10

> Chauffeur driven vehicles available at London airport. The vehicles were not visible to passengers but were allocated once a booking had been made. Held: Not to be standing or plying for hire.

In *Cogley v Sherwood*[1], the court considered and reviewed a number of the older cases. This case concerned an operation at London Airport. There was a desk that was staffed at the airport, where cars could be booked or hired for immediate transport. The vehicles that were supplied were not hackney carriages and also, crucially, were not visible at the time the booking or hiring was made. They were prosecuted for unlawful plying for hire, contrary to the Metropolitan Public Carriage Act 1869, s 7. The drafting differs from that of TPCA 1847, but the question which was central to this case was whether by this mechanism the vehicles were plying for hire. This determination is applicable both within and outside London. Parker LCJ, in a lengthy judgment, considered a large number of previous cases. He stated (at 323):

> 'The court has been referred to a number of cases from 1869 down to the present day dealing with hackney carriages and stage carriages. Those decisions are not easy to reconcile, and like the justices, with whom I have great sympathy, I have been unable to extract from them a comprehensive and authoritative definition of "plying for hire." One reason, of course, is that these cases all come before the court on case stated, and the question whether a particular vehicle is plying for hire, being largely one of degree and therefore of fact, has to be approached by considering whether there was evidence to support the justices' finding.'

[1]   [1959] 2 QB 311.

8.11

Parker LCJ considered that the cases of *Allen v Tunbridge*[1], *Armstrong v Ogle*[2], *Case v Storey*[3] and *Clarke v Stanford*[4] all indicated that the vehicle in question must be exhibited in order for there to be a plying for hire. He continued[5] (at 325):

> 'In the ordinary way, therefore, I should, apart from authority, have felt that it was of the essence of plying for hire that the vehicle in question should be on view, that the owner or driver should expressly or impliedly invite the public to use it, and that the member of the public should be able to use that vehicle if he wanted to. Looked at in that way, it would matter not that the driver said: "Before you hire my vehicle, you must take a ticket at the office," aliter [otherwise], if he said: "You cannot have my vehicle but if you go to the office you will be able to get a vehicle, not necessarily mine.'

He took the view that the decisions in *Gilbert v McKay*[6] and *Cavill v Amos*[7] did not apply because, in those cases, there was an exhibition of vehicle, and in the present case (*Cogley v Sherwood*) that was absent. He considered the case of *Griffin v Grey Coaches Ltd*[8] as distinguishable on its facts, as it concerned stage carriages. His conclusion was that, in this circumstance, there was no plying for hire as there was no exhibition of the vehicles themselves.

[1]   (1871) LR 6 CP 481.
[2]   [1926] 2 KB 438.
[3]   (1869) LR 4 Exch 319.
[4]   (1871) LR 6 QB 357.

5　　*Cogley v Sherwood* [1959] 2 QB 311.
6　　[1946] 1 All ER 458.
7　　(1899) 16 TLR 156.
8　　(1928) 45 TLR 109.

8.12

That judgment was supported by Donavan J[1], who stated (at 328):

'The expression "ply for hire" is not defined in the statute, and I would respectfully concur in the justices' finding that no comprehensive definition is to be found in the decided cases. But the term does connote in my view some exhibition of the vehicle to potential hirers as a vehicle which may be hired. One can perhaps best explain the reason by taking an example. It is a fairly common sight today to see in smaller towns and villages a notice in the window of a private house "Car for Hire". If the car in question is locked up in the owner's garage adjacent to the house, it could not in my view reasonably be said that at that moment the car was "plying for hire". If a customer wishes to hire it, he comes and makes his terms with the owner. On the return journey the owner might exhibit a sign on its windscreen, as some of them do, "Taxi" and then clearly he would be plying for hire. Similarly, if he left the car outside his house, the same notice on the car would involve, I think, that the car was then plying for hire, and the notice in the window might also then have the same effect.'

He took the view that both *Gilbert v McKay*[2] and *Griffin v Grey Coaches Ltd*[3] were distinguishable: *Gilbert* on its facts; and *Griffin* because it was a stage carriage. He concluded that the vehicles which were the subject of the bookings in this situation, were not plying for hire.

1　　*Cogley v Sherwood* [1959] 2 QB 311.
2　　[1946] 1 All ER 458.
3　　(1928) 45 TLR 109.

8.13

The final judgment was given by Salmon J[1] who agreed with the views expressed by the two previous judges (at 330):

'I also agree, although not without some doubt, that, for the reasons stated by my Lord, this appeal should be allowed. Such doubt as I feel springs not from the words of the statute, which appear to me to be reasonably plain, but from the multifarious decisions upon it. If the matter were *res integra*, I should have thought that it was obvious that the words "plying for hire" have a meaning different from and narrower than "letting for hire" or "carrying on a private hire business". But for authority, I should have thought that a vehicle plies for hire if the person in control of the vehicle exhibits the vehicle and makes a present open offer to the public, an offer which can be accepted, for example, by the member of the public stepping into the vehicle.

But from time to time in the past people owning vehicles which were plying for hire have exercised their ingenuity for circumventing the provisions of the Act of 1869 [Metropolitan Public Carriage Act 1869], and on a large number of occasions this court has had to consider those attempts. During the course of the years, observations have been made which deal with the particular circumstances of a case, and these have been adopted and expanded in other cases; and so we have come to a position where, on the authorities, it is possible, ... to make a powerful argument, ... for holding that this Act means something quite different from what any ordinary man would think that it meant on reading it.

Indeed, this court, to my mind, is driven to the very brink of saying that whenever a private hire firm has a fleet of motor-cars in its garage and advertises for customers, those motor-cars are plying for hire. That seems to me to be quite wrong. It was never within the contemplation of the legislature that the job-master (who was the counterpart in 1869 of the car hire service of 1959), should be within the Act, as was pointed out by Montague Smith J, in *Allen v Tunbridge*[1] as long ago as 1871. I do not feel that we are constrained by authority to cross the brink. Although authority precludes a finding that the making of a present open offer is a necessary part of "plying for hire", I do not feel compelled by any authority to find that a vehicle plies for hire unless it is exhibited. In this case the vehicles were not, as my Lords have pointed out, exhibited, and for that reason I agree that this appeal should be allowed.'

[1]   (1871) LR 6 CP 481.

8.14

As *Cogley v Sherwood*[1] provides a comprehensive assessment of the cases which had been decided prior to that date, there seems little point in considering them at length. From 1959 (the date of *Cogley v Sherwood*), it has been quite clear that for there to be a plying for hire, there has to be an exhibition of the vehicle in question and this applies both within and outside London. That view has been clearly supported by *Rose v Welbeck Motors Ltd*[2], *Newman v Vincent*[3] and *Vant v Cripps*[4].

[1]   [1959] 2 QB 311.
[2]   [1962] 1 WLR 1010; see para 8.16 below.
[3]   [1962] 1 WLR 1017; see para 8.17 below.
[4]   (1963) 62 LGR 88; see para 8.18 below.

Alker v Woodward

8.15

Identifiable minicab (with a telephone number displayed) parked for 15 minutes. Held: To be standing for hire.

This was followed by *Alker v Woodward*[1]. An unlicensed minicab equipped with a radio was parked for 15 minutes on a road where there was a licensed hackney carriage stand. It was identified by a card in the windscreen reading 'radio taxis' and a telephone number. When questioned, the driver said that he was waiting for a call. The High Court concluded that:

> 'it was of the essence of plying for hire that the vehicle should be on view, that the driver or owner should expressly or impliedly invite members of the public to use it, and that the member of the public could use it if he wanted to. Here the car was on view and the notice invited its use for hiring. There was therefore a prima facie case [of unlawful plying for hire] ... '[2].

[1] [1962] Crim LR 313, QBD. There does not appear to be a full transcript of the judgment and the only report is in the Criminal Law Review.
[2] Quotation taken from the Criminal Law Review which is itself a summary of the judgment.

Rose v Welbeck Motors Ltd

8.16

> Marked minicab parked on a bus turn-around. It moved up when the bus came, but was in the vicinity for at least 50 minutes. Held: To be plying for hire.

Rose v Welbeck Motors Ltd[1] is a London case which concerned a prosecution for plying for hire under the Metropolitan Public Carriage Act 1869. As noted above, the wording of that Act is slightly different from the wording in TPCA 1847. In *Rose*, a mini-cab was parked on a bus standby, an area where buses turn round. When a bus came along, the mini-cab moved some ten yards further along the road. In total, it was there for 50 minutes. The question was whether the driver of the mini-cab was plying for hire. Parker LCJ gave the principal judgment of the court. He considered the case of *Cogley v Sherwood*[2] and then stated (at 1014):

> 'That the vehicle in the present case was on exhibition in the sense that it was on view to the public is undoubted. The real question, as it seems to me, is whether a prima facie case was made out that the vehicle in question was impliedly inviting the public to use it. Whether in any case such a prima facie case is made out must, of course, depend upon the exact circumstances, and I certainly do not intend anything I say in this judgment to apply to any facts other than those here. What are the facts here? One starts with the fact that this vehicle was of a distinctive appearance, regarding its colour, its inscriptions, its equipment in the form of radio communication, and its type. Secondly – and this is equally important – it was standing with the driver at the steering wheel for some fifty minutes in a public place on public view and at a place where buses turned round: in other words, at a place where many members of the public would be getting off the buses and where many members of the public would forgather to board

the buses. Moreover, when requested to leave, the driver drove away only to return immediately almost to the same place.'

He concluded (at 1015):

'In my judgment, there is no real difference between the expression, "taxi" and "cab" and, in the particular circumstances of this case, it seems to me that any tribunal would be bound to hold that this vehicle was exhibiting itself as a vehicle for hire. Therefore, this case ought to be remitted to the justices with the direction that there was a case to answer and that they should continue the hearing of the case. I deliberately refrain from saying what, in my judgment, might amount to a defence.'

[1]   [1962] 1 WLR 1010.
[2]   [1959] 2 QB 311; see para 8.10 above.

Newman v Vincent

8.17

> Marked minicab parked for 20 minutes, during which time it was approached by at least 2 people asking if it was available for hire. Held: To be plying for hire.

On the same day, the same court gave a similar ruling in another London case, *Newman v Vincent*[1]. The facts were very similar to those in *Rose v Welbeck Motors Ltd*[2], except that the vehicle was only parked for some 20 minutes. However, it did have a notice attached to the passenger-side sun visor, which read 'Mini-cab Booking'. The matter of the notice on the sun visor seemed extremely important in the mind of Parker LCJ, who gave judgment (at 1019):

'It is quite true that in some respects this is a weaker case than the case of *Rose v Welbeck Motors Ltd*, in which we have just given judgment, because the period of time in the present case was 20 minutes and, although the vehicle was on a public street, it was not at a bus turn-round, and may well have given the appearance of waiting outside a private house. On the other hand, it has the exceptional feature of the sun vizor (sic) but, more important to my mind, the evidence that its appearance and conduct was such that two members of the public came up and asked if it was for hire. For my part I find it quite impossible in those circumstances to say that there was not a prima facie case of the vehicle's plying for hire in the sense of being on view to the public and inviting the public to use it.'

It seems that the apparent emphasis placed on the words on the sun visor are unfortunate, and the most important element of this judgment is the appearance of the vehicle and its location leading prospective passengers to approach it to enquire whether it was for hire.

[1]   [1962] 1 WLR 1017.
[2]   [1962] 1 WLR 1010.

Vant v Cripps

8.18

> Unattended car with a sign reading 'Barry's Taxis, Moortown' and a telephone number parked outside a house, which had a sign on it saying 'taxi' and the same telephone number. Held: This was unlawfully plying for hire.

Vant v Cripps[1], a decision outside London, concerned a private hire vehicle (although it was not licensed as this case dates from 1963, some period before the introduction of the Local Government (Miscellaneous Provisions) Act 1976) which was parked outside a house on one occasion, and was parked on the driveway of the same house on another. On the rear of the vehicle was a sign, measuring eight inches by six inches, which read 'Barry's Taxis, Moortown' and gave a telephone number. On the house itself was an electric light with a rectangular globe which had the word 'Taxi' on it and the same telephone number. On both occasions the vehicle was unattended (ie, there was no driver in the vehicle). The proprietor and the usual driver were prosecuted for unlawfully plying for hire and both he and the proprietor were prosecuted for not having the relevant insurance.

[1]   (1963) 62 LGR 88.

8.19

Parker LCJ gave the judgment of the court[1] and stated (at 92):

> 'Their real trouble here is that albeit they are running, or said to be running, a genuine private hire business, they kept this vehicle outside their house with a great sign on it at the back, "Barry's Taxis", and a telephone number. On top of that, at the corner of the house was an electric light fitting with a rectangular globe on which appeared the word "Taxi" and the telephone number.
>
> Accordingly, anyone walking up the street and seeing the car outside the house and the sign at the corner of the house would say "Here is a car waiting to be hired" – not a private car but what is known as a taxi, a cab.'

He continued, explaining that a police officer had interviewed both defendants (at 92):

> '… it appeared that while he [the police officer] was there, in the kitchen of the house, somebody came along who had seen the car outside and the two signs, the one on the car, and the one on the house, and came in and attempted to hire the car, and was refused. The relevance of that is that it appeared at any rate to one member of the public that the car was outside plying for hire.
>
> The magistrate found – and this must be almost entirely a question of fact – that this vehicle with this sign and standing under the electric sign on the house could do no other than cause a member of the public to assume

that the vehicle was available in the business for hire without a previous contract being made, and, as I have said, he found the defendants guilty on these charges.'

He concluded (at 93):

'In my judgment, the defendant, Barry Vant, was properly convicted here. On the facts it is perfectly clear that this vehicle was plying for hire. I say that bearing in mind the cases which have been decided under section 7 of the Act of 1867[2] and in particular *Rose v Welbeck Motors Ltd* [1962] 1 WLR 1010, 60 LGR 423. That is the position with regard to the vehicle. So far as Barry Vant is concerned, he was clearly the person in charge of the vehicle in the sense that he was in the house; he was the person who would drive the vehicle if it was used; and he knew that the vehicle was outside with this sign on it and standing under the sign that was on the house, and, accordingly plying for hire. In those circumstances, it seems to me quite impossible to contend that he himself was not plying for hire in the sense of being in charge of a vehicle which was itself plying for hire.'

Ashworth J agreed and quoted from *Cogley v Sherwood*[3]. He stated (at 93):

'In my view this passage precisely fits the present case. Donovan J said (at 328–9):

"The expression 'plying for hire' is not defined in the statute, and I would respectfully concur in the justices' finding that no comprehensive definition is to be found in the decided cases. But the term does connote in my view some exhibition of the vehicle to potential hirers as a vehicle which may be hired. One can perhaps best explain the reason by taking an example. It is a fairly common sight today to see in smaller towns and villages a notice in the window of a private house 'Car for Hire'. If the car in question is locked up in the owner's garage adjacent to the house, it could not in my view reasonably be said that at that moment the car was 'plying for hire'. If a customer wishes to hire it, he comes and makes his terms with the owner. On the return journey the owner might exhibit a sign on its windscreen, as some of them do, 'Taxi' and then clearly he would be plying for hire. Similarly, if he left the car outside his house, the same notice on the car would involve, I think, that the car was then plying for hire, and the notice in the window might also then have the same effect."

If one substitutes for the notice in the window the lettering on the electric light globe, that passage precisely fits this case.'

This is a surprising decision, principally because the vehicle was unattended and since the decision in *Sales v Lake*[4] the principle has been that there must be an exhibition of the vehicle and the driver must also be present. It therefore demonstrated a significant tightening of the concept of plying or standing for hire.

1   (1963) 62 LGR 88.
2   Parker LCJ is referring here to the Metropolitan Public Carriage Act 1869. On this and one other occasion (at page 92) the transcript refers to 'the Act of 1867' as opposed to the correct reference of the Act of 1869.
3   [1959] 2 QB 311; see para 8.10 above.
4   [1922] 1 KB 553

8.20

Those cases all predate the regulation of private hire vehicles under the Local Government (Miscellaneous Provisions) Act 1976. Once this was enacted and available for adoption by local authorities[1], a greater difficulty arose because there were other licensed vehicles: private hire vehicles, which could provide a transport service to the public, but which could quite clearly not ply or stand for hire. When this is considered, it makes sense for the original test to have been developed in the light of modern circumstances. Unless every private hire vehicle could be hidden in a garage when not carrying out a hiring, it would appear possible to argue that it was plying or standing for hire.

1   See Chapter 2, para 2.3 for adoption processes and Chapter 6, para 6.7 for its impact.

Eldridge v British Airport Authority: the expression 'standing'

8.21

> Hackney carriage driver loaded passengers at Heathrow at a place which was not a stand. Proescuted for 'standing for hire'. Held: 'Standing' meant waiting or parking and did not mean 'stationary'.

Eldridge v British Airport Authority[1] concerned Heathrow airport. Under the London legislation[2], any hackney carriage found standing was deemed to be plying for hire. Eldridge loaded passengers at a point on the highway which was not a stand. That was an action which was contrary to the airport bylaws in force at the time. He argued that the bylaws were repugnant to the parent act. It was held that they were not repugnant because the expression of 'standing in any street' was a restricted concept. As the London legislation is different from TPCA 1847, the case itself is not of enormous importance, but it contains a useful statement by Donaldson J (at 396E):

> 'In my judgment "standing" in the context of that section means something akin to waiting or parking. It does not mean being stationary. Were it otherwise, the licensed driver in an ordinary taxi cab who was stopped at traffic lights would be at the mercy of everyone who wished to hire a cab. A similar problem would confront a driver who stopped momentarily whilst seeking a petrol pump on his way home. This would be an intolerable situation for taxi-cab drivers.'

This shows a very sensible and practical approach to the question of 'standing'.

1   [1970] 2 QB 387.

²   London Hackney Carriage Act 1831, s 35: '35. Every hackney carriage which shall be found standing in any street or place, shall, unless actually hired, be deemed to be plying for hire, although such hackney carriage shall not be on any standing or place usually appropriated for the purpose of hackney carriages standing or plying for hire; and the driver of every such hackney carriage which shall not be actually hired shall be obliged and compellable to go with any person desirous of hiring such hackney carriage; and upon the hearing of any complaint against the driver of any such hackney carriage for any such refusal such driver shall be obliged to adduce evidence of having been and of being actually hired at the time of such refusal, and in case such driver shall fail to produce sufficient evidence of having been and of being so hired as aforesaid he shall forfeit level 1 on the standard scale.[in 1970 the fine was 40 shillings]'.

Milton Keynes Borough Council v Barry

8.22

> Private hire vehicle parked close to hackney carriage stand. Approached by passengers. Driver refused the hire until he had radioed the request to his operator. Held: That he was plying for hire because of the location of the vehicle close to a location where hackney carriages would usually be found.

In 1984 the High Court considered the case of *Milton Keynes Borough Council v Barry*[1]. This was an appeal by way of case stated against an acquittal on a charge of unlawful plying for hire brought by Milton Keynes Borough Council, and therefore engaged legislation applicable outside London. The facts were that Mr Barry was a licensed private hire driver, driving a licensed private hire vehicle. That vehicle had the words 'Quick Cars' displayed somewhere on the front doors. He dropped a fare off at Bletchley bus station, which was within the district of Milton Keynes Borough Council and then parked his car close to a hackney carriage stand near to the bus station. It was not actually parked in the stand itself, but was, from the facts of the case, close to it. He then used his radio to inform the operator that he was free and was awaiting further instructions.

About two minutes later two people approached the car and asked to be taken to a specific destination. The driver declined, saying that the vehicle had to be pre-booked. However, he then called the operator on his radio and told him of this request. He was then told by his operator that he had been booked for these people and could undertake the journey.

1   (3 July 1984, unreported), DC.

8.23

The matter was investigated by Milton Keynes Borough Council. Their vehicle licensing officer interviewed the operator and the driver and it was clear that there were no records in place recording the booking. Evidence was heard by the magistrates from both the vehicle licensing officer and a hackney carriage driver who 'happened to be near the respondent at the relevant time in his cab and gave evidence to the justices about they way in which he said the respondent had behaved'. The driver, Mr Barry and his operator also gave evidence to the effect that they had simply failed to make a record of the facts as stated. The magistrates accepted the arguments presented by the driver and operator, and rejected the arguments presented by the hackney carriage driver and the Council's vehicle licensing officer.

This is one of many cases where the High Court fails to recognise the important distinction between 'plying' and 'standing' for hire. In this case the vehicle was stationary, but all the references in the judgment are to 'plying for hire'. Whilst it probably would not have altered the decision, it is a good example of the conflation of and confusion between, the two terms.

8.24

The first judgment was given by Lord Justice Watkins[1]. He referred to *Cogley v Sherwood*[2] and then said (at 4D):

'We have been referred also to Clarke v Stanford (1871) QB 357, Foinett v Clark (1877) 41 JP 359 and to Rose v Welbeck Motors Limited and another (1962) 1 WLR 10. It is abundantly clear from those cases that the question of what is meant by plying for hire has occupied the courts for some time for well over a century. Decisions go back to the days when broughams and landaus were used. What is meant by plying for hire is, for taxi drivers who are licensed to operate to take part in a taxi service, of great importance. ...

There is a great temptation, no doubt, to those who do not have a licence and who are employed by private car hire firms, to take as passengers people who have not previously arranged or agreed with the owner of the car to be carried; in other words, to behave as though they were licensed and accordingly to pick up passengers when and where the opportunity arises upon the streets.'

He continued (at 5E):

'The question is therefore: Can it be said that no reasonable bench of justices could draw the inference that these justices obviously did? That inference obviously was that the respondent was in a position adjacent to the hackney carriage rank for a wholly innocent purpose and was entitled to be there for that purpose without it being found that he was plying for hire – the innocent purpose being that he was awaiting instructions from his employers as to where he should proceed from the place where he had dropped off passengers whom he had been carrying.

In coming to my conclusion, I ignore altogether, of course, the evidence which the justices rejected: that is to say the evidence of the taxi driver which was clearly hostile to the respondent. Nevertheless I fail to understand how any reasonable bench of justices could have avoided inferring from the circumstances as found that the respondent, in remaining where he was, adjacent to the hackney carriage rank, was there in the hope and expectation that he would be able, within a relatively short period of time, to attract custom to himself and avail himself of it as and when presented. It was not known nor could it have been known by anyone just how long he would have to wait for further instructions from his employer. It may have been two or three minutes. It may have been a quarter of an hour or a good deal longer than that. Presumably, therefore, the respondent would have remained where he was for whatever period of time elapsed between his arrival at the bus station and further instruction coming from his employers.

It cannot have been without his contemplation, in my judgment, that during that time, he being in the position he was and bearing all the hallmarks upon his cab of a person who is employed for the purposes of carrying passengers, that he would be approached or was likely to be approached by people who wished to avail themselves of the services of a taxi. Taking all those considerations in account and looking squarely at them, I do not comprehend how any reasonable bench of justices could have avoided coming to the conclusion that this respondent was plying for hire. In coming to the conclusion which they did they it seems to me failed to see what was staring them in the face, namely, a less than innocent sojourn by this respondent in his position adjacent to the hackney carriage rank.'

[1]   *Milton Keynes Borough Council v Barry* (3 July 1984, unreported), DC.
[2]   [1959] 2 QB 311; see para 8.10 above.

8.25

This view was supported by Mr. Justice McCullough[1]:

'On the facts found a strong prima facie case was raised that Mr Barry was parked where he was with the intention that members of the public would see his vehicle and, in particular, its sign saying "Quick Cars", and would approach him in the belief that his vehicle was available for immediate hire. Within one or two minutes that is exactly what happened. A couple approached him and after a brief radio call to his controller a contract of hire was entered into. By the time the couple approached him the driver had already told the controller that he had completed his previous engagement. Nevertheless he remained, waiting for his next engagement. How long would he have stayed had the couple not approached so soon? The inference is that he would have remained until, as would be likely early on a Saturday evening, someone passing through the bus station wanted to hire his taxi. I see nothing in the evidence to rebut the strong presumption that he was intending to exhibit his vehicle to potential hirers as a vehicle which might there and then be hired. In my judgment, therefore, conviction was inevitable.'

However, he went on to say (at 7G):

'Plying for hire is largely a matter of fact and degree. Each case depends upon its own facts ... I can visualise cases in which it might be held that the contract made in such circumstances led on its own to a finding that the vehicle was plying for hire in the period of the conversations. I visualise other circumstances in which such a conclusion could not properly be drawn.'

1   *Milton Keynes Borough Council v Barry* (3 July 1984, unreported), DC.

8.26

Whilst it may It appear that the decisive factor in this case was the proximity of the private hire vehicle to the hackney carriage stand, the court is following a long line of similar High Court decisions.

The difficulty with this approach is that at no point is the question addressed as to what private hire vehicles should do whilst waiting for the next booking. They clearly cannot be expected to drive continually for fear of being accused of plying for hire whenever they stop; neither can they be expected to return to some covered building where they cannot be seen[1].

1   There are a few local authorities that have had a condition on private hire licences that require the driver to return to the operator's base after each hiring, before starting the next hiring. Such a condition, it is submitted, is manifestly absurd, and would result in may hundreds of thousands of miles of unnecessary car journeys for no useful or reasonable purpose.

8.27

Milton Keynes[1] is yet another authority for the situation where a private hire vehicle is and giving every indication, on the facts of the particular case, that it is awaiting custom and therefore plying for hire. It does not, however, answer the question posed above, namely: can a private hire vehicle park lawfully awaiting the next booking being radioed through by the operator?

None of the cases lay down any periods of time which the courts would consider it reasonable for a private hire vehicle to wait for a booking to be radioed through. Guidance as to time does exist in other areas eg, the law relating to pedlars[2], and a similar indication would provide significant assistance in this area.

1   *Milton Keynes Borough Council v Barry* (3 July 1984, unreported), DC.
2   See eg, *Croydon LBC v Burdon* [2002] EWHC 1961 (Admin), [2003] EHLR 1.

8.28

What is less clear is whether *Milton Keynes*[1] is authority for the proposition that a private hire driver cannot contact an operator on behalf of a prospective customer. The court does not say that this is in itself unlawful land neither does the later case of *Chorley Borough Council v Thomas*[2]. Clearly, in such circumstances the driver would be acting as agent for the customer in the same way as a hotel would act as an agent when arranging a private hire vehicle for a guest. There is nothing in the Local Government (Miscellaneous Provisions) Act 1976, any reported case or the general law of agency to prevent a driver acting as a passenger's agent in these circumstances.

Assuming that the ruling in *Milton Keynes* is limited to confirming the earlier decisions that parking where prospective passengers would expect to find a hackney carriage and exhibiting the vehicle and driver is plying for hire, it is suggested that if the private hire vehicle was not waiting unlawfully (eg, on private land which is not a street for the purposes of the 1847 Act[3]), the actions of the driver in contacting his operator to inquire whether a vehicle can be booked (which may or may not happen to be that particular vehicle) on behalf of prospective customers is not in itself unlawful.

The question of parking arose again in the case of *Ogwr Borough Council v Baker*[4].

[1]   *Milton Keynes Borough Council v Barry* (3 July 1984, unreported), DC.
[2]   [2001] EWHC Admin 570, [2001] LLR 62, QBD. See para 8.37 below.
[3]   See *Young v Scampion* (1988) 87 LGR 240, QBD and *Eastbourne Borough Council v Stirling* [2001] RTR 7 below.
[4]   [1989] COD 489; see para 8.29 below.

Ogwr Borough Council v Baker

8.29

> Private hire vehicle parked by a line of hackney carriages near to a hot dog stand. Approached by two passengers who had booked a vehicle with the same firm. The driver radioed through to check the booking and was told not to take them, but then told he could because the name of one passenger was the same as the booking. Held: To be plying for hire.

In relation to 'plying', the approach in *Cogley v Sherwood*[1], *Rose v Welbeck Motors Ltd*[2], *Newman v Vincent*[3] and *Vant v Cripps*[4] was followed in the case of *Ogwr Borough Council v Baker*[5].

In this case, a police officer observed a private hire vehicle which was parked near to some hackney carriages outside a night-club in Bridgend. The private hire vehicle was also parked near to a hot dog van. A couple were observed to approach the private hire vehicle and inquire whether that vehicle had been sent to fulfil their booking. The driver ascertained from the operator that they had booked a private hire vehicle with the same firm. However, he had not been sent to the location by the firm to fulfil that or any other booking. However, they got into the car, and when approached by the police officer the driver admitted that this was not a pre-arranged booking. He was acquitted of plying for hire contrary to TPCA 1847, s 45, but the local authority appealed by way of case stated.

Again, the references are to 'plying for hire' notwithstanding that at all material times the vehicle was stationary.

[1]   [1959] 2 QB 311; see para 8.10 above.
[2]   [1962] 1 WLR 1010; see para 8.16 above.
[3]   [1962] 1 WLR 1017; see para 8.17 above.
[4]   (1963) 62 LGR 88; see para 8.18 above.
[5]   [1989] COD 489.

8.30

On its facts therefore, this would appear to be a straightforward case of unlawful plying for hire. However, the case goes a little further than that. It was established in the magistrates' court that the driver often parked where he had that night, and that sometimes he bought a hot dog, although he had not done so on this occasion.

8.31

In the magistrates' court, no authorities were cited. Neither were any authorities cited in the High Court[1]. Considering the wealth of cases concerning this area, that seems somewhat surprising. The case was heard by Bingham LJ and Leggatt J, who gave the first judgment. After outlining the facts and the magistrates' decision, he stated (at 3C):

'This is the latest in a line of cases stretching back over a century in which the court has been asked by local authorities to stiffen the resolve of magistrates in convicting unlicensed cab drivers of plying for hire.'

Later he outlined the approach of the court on that occasion to this question (at 3F):

'The question which it is acknowledged that the justices had to ask themselves is whether by parking the vehicle where he did the respondent was in the circumstances impliedly soliciting custom, that is, exhibiting the vehicle to the public as one which might be hired. To this question, however formulated, it seems to me there could only be one answer.

The justices in the case stated gave reasons in support of their decision: First they said: "Although the defendant's private hire vehicle was on view to the public there was no evidence that the vehicle carried any visible invitation to the public to use it, for example, a 'For Hire' sign." But it did bear, as they found, on its windscreen the name of the taxi service, "Allways," which is no doubt known locally to people who have occasion to hire vehicles, and as such it was recognisable as a private hire vehicle. Next the justices said: "Nor was there any evidence that the defendant by any means whatever invited the public to use his vehicle: rather the reverse was true." They added: "The defendant was chosen by passengers, who had already booked with his firm, as the defendant immediately tried to confirm by radio." But the respondent's presence in the vehicle with the name of the taxi service on the windscreen near a line of hackney carriages outside a night-club at 1.30 in the morning could not but constitute an invitation. It is true that the passengers may have booked with the respondent's firm, but the respondent was not there for the purpose of fulfilling that booking.

The justices then say: "As to the place where the defendant's vehicle was found, it appeared to us that (although he might put himself under suspicion by being near a place where hackneys were plying for hire) there was a reasonable and valid excuse, if any were needed to exculpate him on that ground, for his being near the hot-dog stand whose facilities he sometimes used."

The respondent was admittedly near the hackneys and therefore in a place to which people wishing to hire cars would be likely to come but to speak of the hot-dog stand as providing a reasonable and valid excuse for his presence seems to me absurd. There is no suggestion that the respondent used the hot-dog stand on the relevant occasion. Indeed, as I have already commented, he gave no explanation at all for being where he was.

The question is not whether he may have stopped where he did in case he felt like eating a hot dog at some stage but whether in so doing he was exhibiting his car to the public as being available for hire. He probably was and indeed he must have known that he was and done so intentionally.

The justices say finally: "We could not reasonably draw inferences from the evidence which would have constrained us to the view that we were sure of the defendant's guilt." This court will not likely[2] interfere with findings of fact by justices but since there is no dispute that the justices were properly directed or properly directed themselves, the conclusion is irresistible that their finding was one which no reasonable bench could in the circumstances have made.'

This view was supported by Bingham LJ, who added (at 6C):

'My initial impression on reading this case was, I confess, that it was a very clear case of plying for hire by an unlicensed vehicle. I have, accordingly, scrutinised the justices decision with great care to make sure that there is not some factor which may have justified them in reaching the decision they did. I can find none.'

1   *Ogwr Borough Council v Baker* [1989] COD 489.
2   As reported, but should it read 'lightly'?

8.32

Albeit in the absence of cited authorities, but undoubtedly following the line of precedent, this judgment seems to take no account of the fact that there are licensed private hire vehicles which must be able to stop and wait for a booking to be relayed to them by their operator and is therefore similar approach to *Milton Keynes Borough Council v Barry*[1].

1   (3 July 1984, unreported), DC; see para 8.22 above.

Nottingham City Council v Woodings
8.33

> Private hire vehicle was parked on the public highway to allow the driver to use the public toilets. Driver then sat in his vehicle and was approached by prospective passengers, who asked if he was free. Held: That merely parking the vehicle was not an offence, but accepting a fare without a booking having been made via the private hire operator was illegal.

A decade later, however, in *Nottingham City Council v Woodings*[1], a case outside London, the approach differed significantly, although again referred exclusively to 'plying for hire'. The case concerned a private hire car licensed by Nottingham

City Council parked in Nottingham city centre. The driver, who was only licensed as a hackney carriage driver[2], was sitting in the car. The driver got out of the car and went to some nearby public toilets. When he returned to the car, he was approached by two plain-clothes police officers. The defendant was asked 'Are you free?', to which he replied 'Yes'. He was then asked if he could take the two men to a destination and, when asked how much it was going to be, the driver replied 'Depends on where you are going'. The two plain-clothes officers then got in to the car and revealed their identity. Woodings was prosecuted for unlawfully plying for hire, contrary to TPCA 1847, s 45. He was convicted by the magistrates' court, but appealed successfully to the Crown Court. The local authority appealed to the Divisional Court by way of case stated. The specific question raised was:

> 'does the driver of a marked minicab whose vehicle is not a licensed hackney carriage ply for hire, within the meaning of the Town Police Clauses Act 1847, if he, without more, is approached by a member of the public and then enters into and/or concludes negotiations for the hire of the vehicle?'

[1]   [1994] RTR 72.
[2]   The fact that a private hire vehicle can only be driven by a private hire driver, and any other person drives it an offence is committed (see s 46(1)(b) of the 1976 Act) was not considered in the judgment.

8.34

Judgment was given by Rose LJ[1]. He referred to a number of cases, including *Cavill v Amos*[2], *Sales v Lake*[3], *Cogley v Sherwood*[4], *Rose v Welbeck Motors Ltd*[5], and *Vant v Cripps*[6], and then stated (at 78A):

> 'In the light of those authorities, Mr Lewis [for the City Council] submits that a person plies for hire within section 45 of the Act of 1847 if, with his vehicle, he is available for hire by a member of the public. In the present case, the defendant had in a public street a car recognisable as a minicab available for hire, and when he, the defendant, sitting in the driving seat, was asked if he was free, he indicated that he was and that he was prepared, for reward, to take the prospective passengers.
>
>   Mr Lewis's alternative submission is that the defendant in the present case was soliciting custom expressly or impliedly, by having a car identifiable, as I have indicated, available in the street and if, on the authorities, it is necessary for a car to be exhibited, then this car was exhibited.'

Having clearly considered the consistent approach contained within those authorities, he then came to the following conclusion (at 78D):

> 'In my judgment, when the defendant parked the marked car in the street, for the purpose of going to the toilet, he was not plying for hire, and when he came out of the toilet, he was not plying for hire. But when, having sat in the driver's seat, he told the prospective passengers that he was free to carry them, at that stage he was, bearing in mind where the car was and what the car looked like, plying for hire.

It may be that, in approaching this matter, the Crown Court to some extent confused the question of whether the car was standing in the street with the question of whether the defendant was plying for hire with the carriage. No doubt, as I have said, when he parked the marked vehicle so that it was merely standing in the street, he was not committing an offence. But it seems to me that plying for hire sufficient to constitute the offence took place when, sitting in the car, he answered the question in the way which I have indicated.'

He then added, although this does not appear relevant at this point (at 78G):

'For my part, I accept Mr Lewis's submission [for the local authority] that it is not a necessary ingredient of this offence under section 45, as distinct from an offence under section 7 of the Metropolitan Public Carriage Act 1869, for the car to be exhibited. Clearly, if a car is exhibited as a taxi and the driver is sitting in it, those are highly material circumstances when one comes to consider the question of whether he is plying for hire with a carriage. But it does not seem to me that it is a necessary ingredient in this offence that the vehicle should be exhibited in the way which was a necessary requirement in *Cogley v Sherwood* and *Rose v Welbeck Motors Ltd*. The vehicle must, of course, be with the accused driver because that is what section 45 requires. No doubt, that will normally mean it is somewhere very near, but whether or not the vehicle is itself plying for hire within *Cogley v Sherwood* and *Rose v Welbeck Motors Ltd* is not, in my view, determinative of whether or not the driver is plying for hire with a carriage.'

---

1   *Nottingham City Council v Woodings* [1994] RTR 72. The second judge, Waller J simply stated 'I entirely agree.'
2   (1900) 16 TLR 156.
3   [1922] 1 KB 553.
4   [1959] 2 QB 311; see para 8.10 above.
5   [1962] 1 WLR 1010; see para 8.16 above.
6   (1963) 62 LGR 88; see para 8.17 above.

8.35

Neither *Milton Keynes Borough Council v Barry*[1] nor *Ogwr Borough Council v Baker*[2] were mentioned in *Nottingham*[3] and, indeed, *Nottingham* appears to be in conflict with those two earlier decisions, as well as the cases that were considered.

No indication is given as to why this judgment was such a departure from the previous decisions. The judge did not give any reasons for distinguishing the previous decisions but has arrived at a significantly different conclusion.

There are obvious reasons why a different conclusion was reached, although they are not mentioned in the judgment. These are the practical difficulties of a private hire vehicle and driver whilst awaiting the next booking. How long can they wait at a specific location for another booking? Can they wait within an area where they know pre-booked journeys are likely to commence? Where can they go if these options are not open to them?

The principles in *Nottingham* were summarised with judicial approval in the later case of *Dudley Metropolitan Borough Council v Arif*[4] in the following way:

'I accept Mr De Mello's [Counsel for Dudley MBC, the appellants] formulation of the principles stated in *Nottingham City Council v Woodings*:

"(a) A carriage cannot accurately be said to ply for hire unless two conditions are satisfied.

   (1) There must be a soliciting or waiting to secure passengers by the driver or other person in control without any previous contract with them, and

   (2) The owner or person in control who is engaged or authorises the soliciting or waiting must be in possession of a carriage for which he is soliciting or waiting to obtain passengers: Sales v Lake[5];

(b) A vehicle plies for hire if the person in control of the vehicle exhibits the vehicle and makes a present open offer to the public, an offer which can be accepted, for example, by a member of the public stepping into the vehicle: Cogley v Sherwood"[6].'

[1]   (3 July 1984, unreported), DC; see para 8.22 above.
[2]   [1989] COD 489; see para 8.29 above.
[3]   *Nottingham City Council v Woodings* [1994] RTR 72.
[4]   [2011] EWHC 3880 (Admin), [2012] RTR 20 per Beatson J at para 23.
[5]   [1922] 1 KB 553.
[6]   [1959] 2 QB 311 at 331.

8.36

With subsequent judicial approval, the ruling in *Nottingham*[1] appears to be a reasonable, accurate, up-to-date and sensible interpretation of the law. Unfortunately, the position is by no means clear, and as as subsequent cases show, the law surrounding plying for hire is still subject to uncertainty[2].

[1]   *Nottingham City Council v Woodings* [1994] RTR 72.
[2]   See below at para 8.49 onwards.

Chorley Borough Council v Thomas

8.37

> Private hire vehicle parked outside a pub. Passengers got in with no pre-booking and driver radioed the booking through to the operator before the journey commenced. Held: To be unlawful plying for hire.

Once again, *Chorley Borough Council v Thomas*[1] (a case outside London) followed the pre-*Nottingham* approach. The facts were as follows: a licensed private hire vehicle, driven by a licensed driver was parked outside a pub, *The Ridgeway*. The driver was approached by a prospective passenger and the passenger asked the driver whether he was free. The driver responded that he was and the passenger got into the vehicle. The driver asked him his name, and where he was going to. On being told the destination (another pub called *The White Bear*) the driver said that the fare would be £1.40. The driver then contacted the operator via his radio to book the journey. The vehicle did not move until that booking had been made. On arrival at the destination, the fare was paid, plus a 50p tip.

A prosecution for unlawful plying for hire contrary to TPCA 1847, s 45 followed, where the District Judge found the following facts (at para 3) and accepted an application of no case to answer.

'(a) There was no evidence for how long the vehicle had been stationary.
(b) A booking was made to the base station almost immediately after Mr Liptrot entered the vehicle.
(c) The booking was in fact supported by documentation.
(d) The journey commenced after the booking was made.
(e) In those circumstances there was no evidence that the respondent had been plying for hire.'

The prosecution was dismissed and the council appealed to the High Court by way of case stated. The question posed for the High Court was as follows:

'whether the driver of a marked mini-cab whose vehicle was not a licensed hackney carriage was plying for hire within the Town Police Clauses Act 1847 if, he, without more, was asked by a member of the public if his vehicle was free and, having indicated that his vehicle was available and received details of the prospective journey and disclosed the price for it, placed a booking with his taxi operating base before the journey started'

The judge Maurice Kay J considered a number of earlier judgments including *Cogley v Sherwood*[2], *Sales v Lake and Others*[3], *Rose v Welbeck Motors Ltd and Another*[4], *Ogwr Borough Council v Baker*[5] and *Nottingham City Council v Woodings*[6].

The judge made it clear that he found himself in some difficulty over the fact that this case had ended as a result of a submission of no case to answer, and that the point he had to decide was whether, at that point, a prima facie case had been made that the offence had been committed. This was a rather different position to be in from an appeal after a decision, where both prosecution and defence arguments would have been heard and deliberated upon. His conclusion was as follows (at para 17):

'I, of course, accept that each of these cases is little more than a decision on its own facts, and I also indicate the reluctance that one has to part company with an experienced district judge sitting in his jurisdiction. However, in my judgment, the reasons given by the learned district judge for finding no case to answer in the present case indicate that he was influenced by matters not relevant to the issue of "plying for hire" in the circumstances of this case. I accept Mr Carter's [for the appellant Local Authority] primary submission that, in the circumstances of this case, there was a prima facie case to answer upon the evidence contained in paras (a)–(d) inclusive of the district judge's findings of fact. What took place immediately after that, whether it is characterised as a booking via the base station or as a confirmation of a booking that had already taken place at the scene, is, in my judgment, neither here nor there when considering whether a prima facie case had been made out on the evidence in this case. Relying on the approach exhibited in all the authorities to which I have referred, I feel compelled to the conclusion that in this case the prosecution had established a prima facie case and that any decision to the contrary was legally unsound.'

What conclusions can be drawn from this case? In the High Court the judge decided that the facts – parking the vehicle outside the pub, and then saying that he was free – amounted to a prima facie case of plying for hire. That is not to say that a defence that a booking was indeed in existence before the hiring commenced would not have been successful. As the judge said, cases such as these are dependent upon their own facts. Some weight was attached to the fact that there was no evidence as to how long the vehicle had been stationary before the approach by the passenger was made. This was contrasted with the situation in *Rose v Welbeck Motors Ltd and Another*[7] where the vehicle had been observed stationary for some 50 minutes, and returned to almost the same place when told to move on.

[1]   [2001] EWHC Admin 570, [2001] LLR 62, QBD.
[2]   [1959] 2 QB 311; see para 8.10 above.
[3]   [1922] 1 KB 553.
[4]   [1962] 1 WLR 1010; see para 8.16 above.
[5]   [1989] COD 489; see para 8.29 above.
[6]   [1994] RTR 72; see para 8.33 above.
[7]   [1962] 1 WLR 1010; see para 8.16 above.

Dudley Metropolitan Borough Council v Arif

8.38

> Private hire vehicle booked for a pick up at a specified time and location to take a person to an identified destination. The driver was approached at that place by a person of the same gender as the booked person soon after the specified time and asked if the driver could take her to the specified place. The driver does so without asking for her identity. The person carried was not the person who was booked. Was this plying for hire? Held: This was a mistake of fact and therefore not plying for hire.

In *Dudley Metropolitan Borough Council v Arif*[1] the facts were as follows. A private hire vehicle was booked at a specified time to take 'Jenny' from the Showcase Cinema in Dudley to Kingswinford (a suburb of Dudley). The driver arrived at the pick-up and was parked outside the cinema and was approached by a woman soon after the booked pick up time and she asked if the driver could take her to the specified place. The driver did so without asking for her identity and it transpired that the person carried was not the person who had made the booking. The magistrates' court acquitted the driver on a prosecution of unlawful plying for hire contrary to TPCA 1845, s 45. The council challenged that decision by way of case stated to the High Court.

The case was heard by Beatson J and having considered the facts, he concluded in the following fashion[2]:

'24 It is suggested Mr Mills [Counsel for the appellant Council] that if the plying for hire cannot occur in the instant of agreeing or negotiating a journey with people who are "in fact not a pre-booked fare" it would mean that private hire companies could easily cover such instances by private hire drivers simply "calling in a non-booked fare and it being entered in the journey logs". That would be an undoubted mischief, but I reject the submission that this is so in the present case because it goes behind the magistrates' findings of fact … ..

25 I have referred to Mr Mills' argument that a mistake of fact as to whether a person is a driver's fare is irrelevant and cannot afford the driver a defence. This argument does not sit altogether comfortably with the statements of Lord Parker CJ in *Cogley v Sherwood*[3] and of Maurice Kay J in the *Chorley*[4] case that the question whether a particular vehicle is plying for hire is largely one of degree and therefore of fact. The issue is whether the driver has committed the actus reus of section 45. The actus reus is "driving, standing or plying for hire with any carriage within the prescribed distance". What the driver thought he was doing is relevant to whether he was "plying for hire". Moreover, logically on Mr Mills' submissions, the position would have been the same even if the driver had asked the two women who approached him whether they had booked and they said they had. He even considered, when asked, that this might be so if the driver had asked for their names. In the language used in his skeleton arguments, those people would still be "people who are in fact not a pre-booked fare" and on his argument those questions by the driver and the answers given to him are relevant only to sentence. But the question is surely whether, on the evidence before them, it was open to the magistrates in this case to find that the driver was not plying for hire. I have concluded that it was.

26 I turn to ground 2. Mr Mills submitted that the magistrates' conclusion that it would have been unreasonable to expect the driver to have made further inquiry of the fares given that their request matched the booking he was required to collect only five minutes earlier ignored what he described in paragraph 40 of his skeleton argument as a "credibility stretching coincidence". This was that Mr Arif happened to be at the cinema 15 minutes before he was "apparently" radioed at 12.20 with a booking for a Jenny from the Showcase cinema to Kingswinford and that there just happened to be a booking which matched the journey which the officers asked for a few minutes later.

27 Again, this comes close to going behind the facts found by the magistrates. The submission is that, since the purpose of the Section 45 offence is to protect members of the public, it was insufficient in law for the driver to rely on assumptions. He was expected to take necessary steps to satisfy himself that he had the correct fare. I also reject this submission. The magistrates, having heard evidence which I have set out earlier in

this judgment, concluded that the respondent was not plying for hire. They were entitled to consider all the facts irrespective of the fact that the offence was one of strict liability. They were also entitled to take into account the driver's purpose for being outside the Showcase cinema. They stated this was not to solicit or wait for passengers without any previous contract. They were also entitled to take account of the evidence of the booking records at ABC Taxis that there was a pre-booked fare for a woman wishing to travel to Kingswinford, and the other matters to which I have referred.

28 For those reasons this appeal must be dismissed.'

This is a useful decision which provides a sensible approach to the question of pre-booking. Whilst it would be ideal if every booking for a private hire vehicle made with a private hire operator included comprehensive details (e.g. full name and address of the hirer, full details of the pick-up location to a 5 yard margin of error, likewise for the drop of location, the identity of the vehicle and driver and the fare agreed) this is often not the case. To penalise a driver who in good faith collected a female passenger who had booked a vehicle from that firm, for that location because it was not the actual passenger would seem to be harsh.

1   [2011] EWHC 3880 (Admin), [2012] RTR 20.
2   Above at para 24 onwards.
3   [1959] 2 QB 311.
4   *Chorley BC v Thomas* [2001] EWHC (Admin) 570.

Gateshead Council v Henderson

8.39

> Private hire vehicle dropping passenger off. An enforcement officer got into the vehicle and invited his colleague to join him, having asked if the driver would take them to an hotel. Acquitted of unlawful plying for hire at the magistrates' court and the council appealed by way of case stated. Held: On the facts it was not an unreasonable conclusion for the magistrates to reach, and the appeal was dismissed.

The case of *Gateshead Council v Henderson*[1] relies principally on the decisions in both *Ogwr BC v Baker*[2] and *Nottingham City Council v Woodings*[3], but reaches a different conclusion. Two enforcement officers saw a licensed private hire vehicle parked on the highway, where a passenger was completing their hiring by paying the driver. There was some dispute as to the facts, but the magistrates found the following[4]:

'Having heard all the evidence we made the following findings of fact in relation to the contentious issues. We found that Mrs Hunter [the passenger who was completing her transaction] had not alighted from the vehicle prior to Mr Lines [the first enforcement officer] knocking on the window and making his repeated requests. Furthermore Mrs Hunter was still in the rear of the vehicle completing her transaction when Mr Lines physically entered the vehicle and made a request to be taken to the Hilton Hotel. In our view we could not be sure that the respondent had either expressly or by inference, invited or encouraged a member of the public to use his vehicle. Therefore we dismissed the allegation of plying for hire ...'

The arguments concerned the question of whether this was a reasonable decision for the magistrates to make. In the case stated, the magistrates stated that they had been referred to both the *Ogwr* and *Nottingham* decisions, and in the light of those had concluded[5]:

'In relation to the interpretation of the word "plying" we have drawn a distinction between a driver agreeing to complete an unsolicited request, as in the instant case, and a driver who solicits the trade directly or indirectly by parking up or lingering for longer than is necessary in the expectation or hope of further custom. This was clearly not the situation in this case, where the driver was still in the process of concluding a legitimate fare when engaged by the council officers.'

Two submissions were made by Ms Smith, Counsel for the council[6]:

'First at para 53 of her skeleton argument she submits that:

"The bench failed to take into consideration the factors relating to the alleged offence and paid too much regard to matters that were irrelevant."

Secondly ... she submitted that the bench erred in their construction of the words 'plying for hire' in s 45 of the Town and Police Clauses Act 1847 because the driver of a private hire car commits an offence if he agrees to carry a passenger who has not pre–booked the vehicle.'

Those submissions were both rejected by the judge, Supperstone J in these terms[7]:

'16 As for the first submission, Ms Smith relies on the cases of *Ogwr Borough Council v Baker*[8] and *Nottingham City Council v Woodings*[9]. The case of *Ogwr* concerned a line of hackney carriages and private hire vehicles parked outside a nightclub. The hackney carriages were plying for hire by persons emerging from the nightclub. Also in the street was a hotdog van. It was parked about 10 yards away from the nightclub and the respondent's private hire vehicle was parked near to the hotdog van. A couple emerged from the nightclub, walked past some hackney carriages and went up to the respondent's vehicle. It bore on its windscreen a sticker saying "Always", which the justices found was the name of the firm that employed the respondent. It made available private hire vehicles. The couple approached the driver and asked him whether he was for them and he then communicated with his controller for the purpose of ascertaining whether the couple had indeed booked a private hire vehicle from his firm. It was established they had although the respondent had not been sent there by his firm for the purpose of fulfilling that booking. The justices found that the respondent sometimes parked in the position where he was when accosted by the couple for the purpose of using, as they put it, the facilities of the hotdog van, but as the police constable observed the respondent did not get out of his vehicle for that purpose on this occasion. The officer approached the vehicle and asked the respondent the names and addresses of his passengers. He did not know either and confirmed that this was not a pre–arranged pick up.

17 Leggatt J identified the question which the judges had to ask themselves as being:

"Whether by parking the vehicle where he did the respondent was in the circumstances impliedly soliciting custom – that is, exhibiting the vehicle to the public as one which might be hired."

18 In his judgment the respondent's presence in the vehicle with the name of the taxi service on the windscreen near a line of hackney carriages outside a nightclub at 1.30 am in the morning could not but constitute an invitation. As Bingham LJ observed, this was a very clear case of plying for hire by an unlicensed vehicle. The facts of the present case can in my view be distinguished from those in *Ogwr* in two material respects. First, the vehicle was stationary but not parked, the transaction with Mrs Hunter still being in progress when the vehicle was first sighted by the enforcement officers and approached by Mr Lines; secondly, the respondent's vehicle was not near a taxi rank.

19 In *Woodings* the defendant was sitting in the driver's seat of a private hire vehicle, recognisable as a minicab by signs on the side of the car. The car was parked and there was no passenger in the vehicle. Rose LJ said at 75DE:

"In my judgment, when the defendant parked the marked car in the street, for the purpose of going into the toilet, he was not plying for hire, and when he came out of the toilet, he was not plying for hire. But when, having sat in the driver's seat, he told the prospective passengers that he was free to carry them, at that stage he was, bearing in mind where the car was and what the car looked like, plying for hire."

20 Again, as the justices noted at para 22 of the statement of case, the facts of the present case can be distinguished from those in the *Woodings* case. The respondent had not parked his vehicle and Mrs Hunter, his passenger, was still in the vehicle completing her transaction when Mr Lines approached and made his request.

21 In my judgment the decision of the justices in the present case was one to which a reasonable bench, applying their minds to proper considerations and giving themselves proper directions, could come on the findings of fact that they made. Accordingly, I reject Ms Smith's first submission.

22 Ms Smith's second submission, which Mr Holland for the respondent describes as a bold submission, I also reject. In my view it plainly runs

counter to the analysis of Leggatt J, with whom Bingham LJ agreed in *Ogwr*, and of Rose LJ with which Waller J agreed in *Woodings*. Mr Holland submits that there is no comprehensive and authoritative definition of plying for hire. It is a question of fact and agree in each case. In *Cogley v Sherwood; Car Hire Group (Skyport) Ltd v Same; Howe v Kavanaugh; Car Hire Group (Skyport) Ltd v Same [1959] 2 QB 311* Lord Parker CJ said at 325–326:

> "In the ordinary way, therefore, I should, apart from authority, have felt that it was of the essence of plying for hire that the vehicle in question should be on view, that the owner or driver should expressly or impliedly invite the public to use it, and that the member of the public should be able to use that vehicle if he wanted to."

23 Ms Smith noted that that case was determined under a different statute, namely the Metropolitan Public Carriage Act 1869. However, Rose LJ in *Woodings* cited it with approval. In my view both *Cogley* and *Sales v Lake and Others* [1922] 1 KB 553, a case also involving the 1869 Act to which Mr Holland referred, support the approach adopted in *Woodings* and in *Ogwr*. Accordingly this appeal is dismissed.'

This is rather an unusual case and it is suggested that it is largely confined to its own facts. Had the enforcement officers waited until the existing passenger had left the vehicle and then taken the approach they took, the answer might well have been different. It certainly does not appear to be authority for private hire vehicles and drivers to take fares without a prior booking being made.

The following two cases *Young v Scampion*[10] and *Eastbourne Borough Council v Stirling*[11] are considered out of chronological order because they involve the additional element that the vehicles were situated on private land. This is clearly a complicating factor as a vehicle must be located on a 'street' within the definition in TPCA 1847, s 3 to be standing or plying for hire.

[1]   [2012] EWHC 807 (Admin), [2012] LLR 610.
[2]   [1989] COD 489, QBD.
[3]   [1994] RTR 72, QBD.
[4]   At para 9.
[5]   At para 10.
[6]   At paras 14 and 15.
[7]   At paras 16 to 23.
[8]   [1989] COD 489.
[9]   [1994] RTR 72.
[10]   (1988) 87 LGR 240, QBD; see para 8.40 above.
[11]   [2001] RTR 7; see para 8.46 above.

Young v Scampion

8.40

> Vehicles which were not hackney carriages licensed by Solihull MBC were located on a private hackney carriage rank at Birmingham Airport, which was within the district of Solihull, and were available for immediate hire.

> Was this a 'street' for the purposes of the Town Police Clauses Act 1847?
> Held: Using a multi-faceted test, that on its facts, this location was not a
> 'street' and therefore no offence had been committed.

The decision in *Young v Scampion*[1] also concerns the immediate hiring of vehicles,
but on private land as opposed to a street. It is of considerable importance
in relation to the use of both hackney carriages and private hire vehicles. It
concerned a prosecution brought by Solihull Metropolitan Borough Council,
relating to the use of hackney carriages at Birmingham International Airport,
which lies within the metropolitan district of Solihull. There was a private road,
known as Airport Way, at the airport where there was a hackney carriage stand.
That road was not a public highway, although it was a continuation of the public
highway. At the demarcation point of the public highway and private road there
was, in fact, a barrier, although this was apparently only ever closed on Christmas
Day. To all intents and purposes, traffic could pass and re-pass over the private
road, despite a sign that indicated that parking was not allowed, apart from in
specified authorised areas. The defendants in the case were hackney carriage
drivers licensed by Birmingham City Council, driving hackney carriage vehicles
licensed by Birmingham City Council. They stood on the rank at Birmingham
Airport on Airport Way and, when they got to the front, they took passengers
to destinations within Solihull. They were convicted of standing, plying for hire
and driving a hackney carriage at Airport Way and also of driving in the street in
Solihull when they had no licence to ply for hire in Solihull. They appealed by
way of case stated. The matter was heard by Mann LJ and Auld J.

[1]　(1988) 87 LGR 240, QBD.

8.41

There were a number of questions raised by the magistrates in their stated case.
First:

> 'whether the words "any carriage" in the second limb of section 45
> [TPCA 1847, s 45] means "any hackney carriage".'

Auld J found that they did and stated[1] (at 251):

> 'In my view no offence is committed under either limb of section 45 unless
> the vehicle is a hackney carriage within the meaning of the Act.'

[1]　*Young v Scampion* (1988) 87 LGR 240, QBD.

8.42

The second question was:

> 'Whether the justices were entitled to find, as they did, that the defendants'
> vehicles were hackney carriages, and thus subject to the control in section
> 45 [TPCA 1847, s 45], because they were designed and/or normally used
> as hackney carriages, or whether they should have been constrained by

section 38 only so to find if the vehicles were "used in standing or plying for hire in any street" within the Solihull area.'

This turned upon:

'the status of … a [hackney carriage] vehicle outside its own licensing area where it was not licensed and not required to carry … a [hackney carriage] plate, and where there is no evidence that it had stood or plied for hire in any street over which the public had a legal right of standing or passage. As counsel for the defendants in this case put it, a Birmingham licensed taxi does not lose its character as a Birmingham taxi when it enters Solihull, but it does not thereby become, in addition, a Solihull taxi' (at 253, per Auld J[1]).

He continued:

'In considering this question it is important to remember that in every case the use of a vehicle in question is that in the area of the local authority seeking to enforce their licensing control. Before that authority can mount a prosecution under section 45 they must be in a position to prove that the taxi in question is a hackney carriage in their own area. The need for such local control arises out of the local *use* [Auld J's emphasis] of a vehicle, in the words of section 38, "whatever may be its form or construction" as a hackney carriage or, in today's language, as a taxi.

A vehicle's design or normal use in some other local authority area must be irrelevant to a local authority's control if the vehicle does not stand or ply for hire within their area, but only passes through it with fares taken up in some other area. If that were not the case, no taxi driver could pick up a fare in one area and convey him to any other area unless he was licensed there; and if on a long journey and passing through several local areas of control, he would require a licence for each area through which he passes. The absurdity of such interpretation is reflected in a comparatively recent provision introduced in the Local Government (Miscellaneous Provisions) Act 1976, which consolidated a number of provisions found in a number of local Acts concerning the control of hackney carriages and private hire vehicles, and provided for their adoption by local authorities in whose areas the Act of 1847 was already in force. Section 75(1)(a), referring to *its* [Auld J's emphasis] provisions in the Act of 1976, not those of the Act of 1847, set out the following saying:

"Nothing in this Part of this Act shall – (a) apply to a vehicle used for bringing passengers or goods within a controlled district in pursuance of a contract for the hire of the vehicle made outside the district if the vehicle is not made available for hire within the district."

In my view, it would be absurd for there to be a saving for vehicles coming into a controlled area applicable to supplemental provisions gathered together in the Act of 1976 if the basic provisions in the Act of 1847 applied to vehicles across local authority boundaries whether or not they stand or ply for hire outside the area for which they are licensed.'

He continued (at 254):

> 'The horse-drawn carriage has given way to the taxi cab, which itself has evolved over recent years, ranging in design from the London black cab to ordinary saloon cars distinguishable as taxis only by their licence plates. It follows that the only constant and sensible definition of a hackney carriage within the meaning of the Act of 1847 is by reference to its use, not its design.
>
> In my view, the legislature, in section 38, has defined and territorially limited that use to standing or plying for hire in any street in the area of the borough seeking to enforce their control.'

1   *Young v Scampion* (1988) 87 LGR 240, QBD.

8.43

The third question concerned the meaning of 'street' in TPCA 1847, s 38 and whether that meant only a street to which the public have a legal right of access, or any street irrespective of the right of access[1]. Auld J took the view that the definition in TPCA 1847, s 3 only referred to public streets[2]. He stated (at 255):

> 'If I had been looking at this question without the benefit of authority, I would have had little difficulty in concluding that what Parliament intended to refer to here was a public street in the sense of a street where a carriage was entitled as of right to ply for hire (subject to the licensing provisions of the Act of 1847) and where the public were entitled as of right to go. I say that, not only because of the clear purpose of the legislation to which I have referred, but also because of the definition of the word "street" in section 3, the interpretation section, of the Act of 1847. As I have already noted, it provides that the word "shall extend to and include any road, square, court, alley and thoroughfare, or *public passage* within" the borough [emphasis added]. In my view, the qualification of word "passage" with the word "public" was clearly not intended to distinguish between it and other listed locations. It cannot have been intended that plying for hire on public or private streets and roads etc qualified for control, whereas plying for hire in private passages did not. The introduction of the qualifying word "public" for the word "passage" is, in my view, a clear indication that the public nature of the place, obvious in the other locations listed, but not so obvious in the case of a passage, should be underlined.
>
> My view is supported by authority. *Curtis v Embery* (1872) LR 7 Exch 369 and *Jones v Short* (1900) 69 LJQB 473.'

He concluded on this point by saying (at 258):

> 'The restriction of the control of the Act of 1847 to vehicles standing or plying for hire on public property has been recognised by Parliament in that in 1925 it specifically extended that control to railway premises: see section 76 of the Public Health Act 1925.'

1   'Street' is defined in TPCA 1847, s 3: 'The word "street" shall extend to and include any road, square, court, alley, and thoroughfare, or public passage, within the limits of the special Act:'

2   *Young v Scampion* (1988) 87 LGR 240, QBD.

8.44

This then led on to the fourth question. Was Airport Way a street? Auld J concluded that it was not a street[1]. He found that the earlier cases of *Birmingham and Midland Motor Omnibus Co v Thompson*[2] and *White v Cubitt*[3] were distinguishable, as, in those cases, vehicles were parked, albeit on private land, but in order to draw custom from the general public in the adjoining street. He followed the rulings in *Curtis v Embery*[4] and *Jones v Short*[5], which had concerned carriages parked on railway property. He stated (at 260):

'In *Curtis v Embery* and *Jones v Short*, the railway cases, the carriages were parked on railway land to draw custom from those members of the public using the railway, that is people on the railway company's private property. Both the carriages and the behaviour of the railway travellers using them were, when on that land, subject to the control of the railway company.

Here, the defendants were parked on the airport authority's private property in order to draw custom from those using the airport. They were not soliciting custom from those using the public streets of Solihull, and, whilst there, were physically separated from such general custom more completely than were the vehicles in the railway cases or those relied upon by Solihull Council. Whilst there, they and their potential customers were subject to the control of the airport authority as expressed in its byelaws and as exercisable by it as owner of the land. The various matters relied upon by the justices in the case stated going to the lack of any physical restriction or sign of change at the boundary between the public highway and the start of Airport Way are no more relevant than the lack of physical divide between the road and hackney carriage stand in the railway cases. The principle applied in those cases, with which, as I have said, I agree, is that land is not a "street" for the purpose of section 38 unless the public, including taxi drivers in their taxis, have a legal right of access to it. The fact that the public, including taxi drivers, in fact resort to a particular location in large numbers, as they do to modern railway stations, airports and hotel entrances, and the like, cannot of itself make such a location a street for this purpose.'

Accordingly, it was concluded that a hackney carriage did not have to be licensed by the borough in which it was standing either at a rank or on other land, if it was on a private road to which the public did not have a legal right of access and was there for the purposes of people who were not generally passing on public streets.

1   *Young v Scampion* (1988) 87 LGR 240, QBD.

2   [1918] 2 KB 105.

3   [1930] 1 KB 443.

4   (1872) LR 7 Exch 369.

5   (1900) 69 LJQB 473.

8.45

The final question was, once having picked up a passenger, could a hackney carriage drive on roads within the area of a council with which it was not licensed? In relation to that question Auld J stated[1] (at 261):

'... the mere driving by the defendants of their taxis through the streets of Solihull could not make them so. The functional definition in section 38 refers only to standing or plying for hire. They are in no different position from a licensed Birmingham taxi, or a taxi licensed in any other local authority area, conveying a passenger taken up within their own area into the Solihull area.

In short, a vehicle licensed in one area does not need a licence from any other authority into whose area it is driven or in which it solicits or accepts passengers from private land.'

Although considerable emphasis was placed on the fact that Airport Way at Birmingham Airport was not only a private road, but was in the control of Birmingham Airport and was subject to byelaws made by the airport authority, it would appear from this ruling that hackney carriages from another district could park on private land provided they have the permission of the land owner to do so and if it could be argued that they are not plying or standing for hire for the benefit of persons moving along a public highway but for persons who are on private land. An obvious example of this would be a rank created at a large shopping centre for the purposes of persons using the shopping centre, which due to its geographical location would be unlikely to attract pedestrians from other public roads. It remains to be seen whether this would be possible in practice[2].

[1]   *Young v Scampion* (1988) 87 LGR 240, QBD.
[2]   As a result of the decision in *Young v Scampion*, hackney carriage and private hire vehicles from outside the district are regularly used to undertake immediate hirings at many airports throughout England and Wales.

Eastbourne Borough Council v Stirling

8.46

> Private hire vehicles which were not hackney carriages licensed by Eastbourne BC located on private land at Eastbourne Railway station. Bookings made directly with the drivers and therefore the vehicles were available for immediate hire. Was this a 'street' for the purposes of the Town Police Clauses Act 1847? Held: This location was a 'street' and therefore the offence of unlawfully standing for hire had been committed.

In *Eastbourne Borough Council v Stirling*[1], the argument accepted by the court in *Young v Scampion*[2] was used by both sides. It was an appeal by way of case stated by the prosecutor against a decision of a stipendiary magistrate who acquitted two drivers of private hire vehicles of charges of unlawfully plying for hire on the west forecourt of Eastbourne railway station. They argued that as the forecourt was private land, the fact that the vehicles they were driving were private hire vehicles, not hackney carriages, did not mean that they had committed an offence contrary to TPCA 1847, s 37. The defence argued that for there to be a plying for hire the vehicle must be parked or standing on a street to which the public had access as of right. As there was no right of access to the station forecourt, no offence was committed. The prosecution (later the appellants) argued that there was plying for hire if the effect of parking the vehicles was to attract custom from those using the public highway.

The facts were as follows: the local railway company had reached an agreement with a local hackney carriage and private hire company to allow two hackney carriages and one private hire vehicle to use the west forecourt of Eastbourne railway station. The agreement, which had been approved by the Council, required that the private hire driver must remain outside the private hire vehicle. In theory, each private hire journey would be pre-booked with the operator.

On two occasions enforcement action was undertaken. In the words of the judge, Pill LJ the situation was as follows:

> '[3] On each occasion, Mr Douglas Lindsay, an environmental health officer, approached a [private hire] vehicle in that position. On 28 May, he asked Mr Stirling if he had a fare and Mr Stirling replied that he did not and where did Mr Lindsay want to go. On 29 May he asked Mr Morley if he had a booking and when, Mr Morley gave a negative answer, told Mr Morley that he was plying for hire. Having referred to the authorities, the learned magistrate concluded that:

>> "the prosecution had not shown that the west forecourt at Eastbourne railway station is a 'street' for the purposes of this prosecution and therefore the application of no case to answer must succeed."

> It is not disputed that the west forecourt is owned by Railtrack and is therefore private property.'

---

1   [2001] RTR 7.
2   *Young v Scampion* (1988) 87 LGR 240, QBD; see para 8.40 above.

8.47

The court decided that there was a plying for hire in this case[1]. The argument was that whilst *Young v Scampion*[2] was not incorrect, the distance from the public highway was vital. In *Young v Scampion*, the hackney carriages were 'well away' (per Pill LJ at para 17) from the public highway and as a result it was extremely unlikely that anyone using the public highway would be attracted to use the hackney carriages. In *Eastbourne Borough Council v Stirling* the distance was considerably less. The court concluded that, as the parked vehicles were exhibited to persons using the public highway, were in very close proximity to the public highway and on the facts, were available for immediate hire without pre-booking, they were standing or plying for hire on a street. Pill LJ stated (at para 5):

'the taxi rank is very close to the public highway. Indeed one end of the taxi rank is extremely close to, if not on, the boundary between the forecourt and the public highway.'

Pill LJ summed the case up as follows:

'[18] I would apply the White [*White v Cubitt* [1930] 1 KB 443] principle in this case. The taxi rank is situated immediately adjacent to a public street in what is plainly a busy part of Eastbourne where many commercial premises are situated and pedestrian traffic will be high. A vehicle on the rank is plainly likely to attract custom from members of the public using the adjoining street in a busy part of the town. The respondents were plying for hire in a street within the meaning of s.38 [TPCA 1847, s 38].

[19] As a matter of language, I have no difficulty in construing the expression "plying for hire in any street" as covering a situation in which the vehicle is in a prominent position just off the street and the public are in numbers on the street. The same point arose in the context of the Street Offences Act 1959 in Smith v Hughes [1960] 2 All ER 859, [1960] 1 WLR 830 where this Court considered whether a prostitute who solicits men in a street from the balcony of a house or from behind closed or open ground floor or first floor windows of a house adjoining the street commits the offence of soliciting "in a street or public place" contrary to s.1(1) of that Act. Lord Parker stated, at p 861B:

"Observe that it does not say there specifically that the person who is doing the soliciting must be in the street. Equally it does not say that it is enough if the person who receives the solicitation or to whom it is addressed is in the street. For my part, I approach the matter by considering what is the mischief aimed at by this Act. Everybody knows that this was an Act intended to clean up the streets, to enable people to walk along the streets without being molested or solicited by common prostitutes. Viewed in that way, it can matter little whether the prostitute is soliciting while in the street or is standing in a doorway or on a balcony, or at a window, or whether the window is shut or open or half open; in each case her solicitation is projected to and addressed to somebody walking in the street. For my part, I am content to base my decision on that ground and that ground alone. I think that the magistrate came to a correct conclusion in each case, and that these appeals should be dismissed."

[20] That the services offered in that case were different from those in the present case needs no underlining but the reasoning of Lord Parker applies in the present context. The driver is plying for hire in the street if his vehicle is positioned in circumstances such that the offer of services is "projected to and addressed to" members of the public in the street.'

¹   *Eastbourne Borough Council v Stirling* [2001] RTR 7.
²   *Young v Scampion* (1988) 87 LGR 240, QBD; see para 8.40 above.

8.48

The decision in *Eastbourne v Stirling* follows the line of decisions before *Nottingham*[1] in relation to the presence of the vehicle and the driver, but does not address the question of pre-booking.

If the vehicles had been pre-booked, would there have been an offence? If there had been an office of some description which prospective passengers were required to visit in order to book the vehicle and any passenger who directly approached the vehicle without first having made a booking at the office had been turned away, or directed to the office by the driver, would the vehicles still have been plying for hire? From the conclusions drawn above, it seems that such an approach would be lawful.

Likewise, there is no mention of the length of time the vehicles had been waiting before accepting a booking. Does that make a difference? Again, following the conclusions above, the answer would be no.

Finally, had there been a close boarded two metre high fence between the public highway and the place the vehicles were parked, would that have made a difference? It is suggested that this would have made a difference as the vehicles would not be exhibited to those using the highway. This follows the decision in both *Young v Scampion*[2] and a number of the older cases including *Cogley v Sherwood*[3].

[1]   *Nottingham City Council v Woodings* [1994] RTR 72 QBD; see para 8.33 above.
[2]   (1988) 87 LGR 240, QBD; see para 8.40 above.
[3]   [1959] 2 QBD 311; see para 8.10 above.

Conclusions

8.49

What conclusions can be drawn about 'plying for hire' from these cases?

There is a consistent line of High Court decisions and one significant case which has taken a similar approach but reached a slightly different conclusion. The case which appears to depart from the reasoning first established in *Sales v Lake*[1] is *Nottingham City Council v Woodings*[2]. That decision did take account of a number previous of decisions and certainly seems to represent a practical and to an extent, pragmatic view.

However, the conclusion in *Nottingham* appears at odds with the conclusions arrived at in all the previous cases. The subsequent cases of *Chorley BC v Thomas*[3], *Dudley Metropolitan Borough Council v Arif*[4] and *Gateshead Council v Henderson*[5] all refer to the *Nottingham* decision but arrive at conclusions which are clearly based on all the cases apart from *Nottingham*.

It is clear that the simple question of where the vehicle is parked is too crude an indicator as to whether or not it is plying for hire, and it is surely the case that the courts must acknowledge the existence of licensed private hire vehicles and the requirements that they have to wait for the next booking being communicated by the operator. The *Nottingham* decision certainly does that, but stands alone, both in relation to the earlier cases, and subsequent decisions. As a consequence, it should perhaps be viewed with caution. It is suggested that these cases show that there is a difference between a private hire vehicle parking in a car park, or down a side street awaiting a booking being radioed through and a similar vehicle located outside a pub, nightclub or supermarket, knowing it may be approached by prospective passengers who have not pre-booked a journey.

¹   [1922] 1 KB 553.
²   *Nottingham City Council v Woodings* [1994] RTR 72.
³   [2001] EWHC Admin S70, [2001] LLR 62 QBD; see para 8.37 above.
⁴   [2011] EWHC 3880 (Admin), [2012] RTR 20.
⁵   [2012] EWHC 807 (Admin), [2012] LLR 610.

8.50

How should *Young v Scampion*¹ and *Eastbourne Borough Council v Stirling*² be viewed? They follow the vast majority of the decisions. *Young* is authority for the question of whether a specific location is a 'street' for the purposes of the 1847 Act as there was no doubt the vehicles were standing for hire. Although *Eastbourne* appears to consider similar issues, they are not the determining factor that they were in *Young*, and other elements came into play.

¹   (1988) 87 LGR 240, QBD; see para 8.40 above.
²   [2001] RTR 7; see para 8.46 above.

8.51

Wherever a vehicle is located on private land, whether it is standing or plying for hire now seems to be a matter of distance from the public highway as much as whether there is an exhibition of the vehicle. This is unsatisfactory as there is no clear indication of the distance that may be required – somewhere between a yard or two in *Eastbourne Borough Council v Stirling*¹ and half a mile in *Young v Scampion*². Other factors may also come into play. In the case of an out-of-town shopping centre, the likelihood of a member of the public using the proximate public highway must be seen as relevant. If the public highway is a motorway from which pedestrians are banned, or a busy dual carriageway with no pavements or footpaths, then the distance may be less than the situation where the public highway is further away but heavily used by potential passengers for hackney carriage or private hire vehicles.

¹   [2001] RTR 7; see para 8.46 above.
²   (1988) 87 LGR 240, QBD; see para 8.40 above.

8.52

The court in *Chorley*¹ agreed with the decision in *Nottingham*² that whether or not a vehicle is plying for hire is a matter of fact in each case. Beyond that the decisions seem to diverge. What is the current position in regard to plying for hire?

The judgment in *Chorley*, although taking into account the decision in *Nottingham*, appears at first glance to be at odds with it. The question of the length of time that the vehicle was stationary was not addressed, and did not seem important. The case hinged on the immediate acceptance of the request to be carried by the prospective passenger. In *Chorley*, there was not an immediate acceptance of the request, but an entry into a procedure whereby there was a booking in existence before the hiring was commenced. However, further analysis reveals that the time is a red herring, and that the cases are in fact in accord.

This is due to the vital question concerning a possible defence of a booking being made before the hiring commenced. If the prima facie offence is made out by parking the vehicle outside the pub, and the driver then saying that he was free (which the court in *Chorley* clearly felt was the case), is it possible to prevent an offence by subsequent actions on the part of the driver by making a booking? In other words, is it possible to make an unlawful act lawful by subsequent (rather than prior) action?

The answer to this should be no. As the offence in s 45[3] is a strict liability offence, without any requirement for knowledge or intention, the illegal act itself should be sufficient to constitute the crime, but *Dudley*[4] and *Gateshead*[5] show that again, the matter will ultimately be dependant on the particular facts of the case.

[1]   [2001] EWHC Admin S70, [2001] LLR 62 QBD; see para 8.37 above.
[2]   [1994] RTR 72, QBD; see para 8.33 above.
[3]   See Appendix I.
[4]   [2011] EWHC 3880 (Admin), [2012] RTR 20.
[5]   [2012] EWHC 807 (Admin), [2012] LLR 610.

8.53

It is necessary to examine the legislation governing private hire bookings at this point. The 1847 Act was passed before private hire vehicles were envisaged, but now they exist and must of necessity operate in conjunction with hackney carriages.

The requirement that private hire vehicles must be pre-booked is contained in s 56(2) of the Local Government (Miscellaneous Provisions) Act 1976:

'(2) Every person to whom a licence in force under section 55 of this Act has been granted by a district council shall keep a record in such form as the council may, by condition attached to the grant of the licence, prescribe and shall enter therein, before the commencement of each journey, such particulars of every booking of a private hire vehicle invited or accepted by him, whether by accepting the same from the hirer or by undertaking it at the request of another operator, as the district council may by condition prescribe and shall produce such record on request to any authorised officer of the council or to any constable for inspection.'

The crucial element is contained in the words 'shall keep a record … and shall enter therein, before the commencement of each journey, such particulars of every booking of a private hire vehicle invited or accepted by him' and on initial examination, provided that such a booking has been correctly made and logged, that must be sufficient to prevent an allegation of plying for hire.

It is immediately obvious why this is such an important question. Can private hire vehicles park on or off road, in locations where such parking by any type of vehicle is lawful, awaiting a radio message from their operator? Will it matter how long they are so parked, or the place in which they are parked (whether near to places where prospective passengers may be found or not)? From the above cases, it seems this may be the case, and location is a consideration in the overall facts of a particular case.

Alternatively a private hire vehicle will be prevented from stopping anywhere near potential passengers unless they already have a booking. They will therefore either have to drive around until they receive their next booking, or park somewhere well away from any prospective passengers.

Although the latter appears to be an absurd situation in an environment where fuel consumption, pollution and emissions are of major concern, the enormous numbers of vehicles congregating in areas where entertainments are centred is causing problems in many towns and cities, especially late at night. When the fact that many of these vehicles and drivers are not licensed by the particular local authority in whose area they are located ('remote working') is also considered, it must be recognised that this is a problem in many parts of the country. At present, the case law does not decide definitively when a vehicle and driver are standing for hire, although a line of reasoning can be discerned through the cases.

All the cases have decided that immediate hire via the driver is illegal (including using the driver as an agent to contact the operator on the passenger's behalf) and whilst there is legitimate judicial concern over vehicles waiting, no case has specifically decided that a private hire vehicle cannot park lawfully to await the next booking via the operator.

The conclusion drawn from judicial decisions of equal standing would therefore seem to be as follows:

1. Only hackney carriages can ply or stand for hire. The test of plying or standing for hire, following all the case law is that the vehicle is exhibited and available for immediate hire without a pre-booking being made.
2. Plying is where a vehicle is moving and responds to a hailing by a prospective passenger; standing is when the vehicle is stationary at a rank or other location.
3. Nothing in the legislation or case law prevents a private hire vehicle parking lawfully to await a booking made via the operator, provided that the vehicle is not standing for hire (see 1 and 2 above).
4. The test of whether or not the vehicle is available for hire (ie standing for hire) is based on the intentions of the driver, as evidenced by his actions if approached by a prospective passenger, once any current passenger has left the vehicle.
5. A defence is available if a passenger of a similar appearance and/or description to the one booked is carried.

8.54

The effects of this conclusion are therefore as follows:

(a) Private hire vehicles do not have to 'hide' and a private hire vehicle can park lawfully anywhere that a private vehicle can so park to await the next booking received from the operator provided that does not amount to standing for hire (this obviously excludes hackney carriage ranks and may exclude areas of public attractions).

(b) A prospective passenger can make a booking with the operator by telephone, having read the telephone number from the details displayed on the private hire vehicle, and can then be directed, by the operator, to the vehicle which has been lawfully parked and exhibited, because the driver had no involvement in the booking process (and advertising a private hire service is lawful – see *Windsor & Maidenhead RBC v Khan*)[1].

(c) A prospective passenger can use a computer programme, the internet or an 'app' to book a private hire vehicle.

(d) If the driver is approached by the prospective passenger and asked if he is free, provided he replies that a booking must be made, he can direct the passenger to the operator by providing his firm's telephone number or app and the passenger then follows procedures (b) or (c) above.

(e) If however, the driver takes an active part in facilitating the booking via the operator, for example by making the booking via his radio, as in *Milton Keynes* or *Chorley*, or by providing a mobile telephone directly connected to the operator, that evidences the fact that his purpose in parking the vehicle was to be available for immediate hire and the offence will have been made out.

(f) It is clear that the booking does not have to be made by the passenger personally, as a third party can act as an intermediary or agent (eg a receptionist at a hotel, a work colleague, a pub landlord etc), but as noted at (d) above, the driver cannot fulfil the role of agent.

As can be seen, this is an area of the law that is complex, confusing and (notwithstanding the conclusions drawn above) uncertain and almost six decades after Lord Parker LCJ observed in *Cogley v Sherwood*[2]:

> 'The court has been referred to a number of cases from 1869 down to the present day dealing with hackney carriages and stage carriages. Those decisions are not easy to reconcile, and … I have been unable to extract from them a comprehensive and authoritative definition of "plying for hire".'

the precise meaning of plying and standing for hire still awaits judicial discovery.

It remains an area which is ripe for conflicting arguments and it is hoped that at some future date, the Senior Courts finally and conclusively determine what is meant by 'standing or plying for hire'.

---

[1] This is reinforced by conditions attached to private hire vehicles by some councils requiring signs to be displayed saying '*Advanced Bookings Only*' or '*Pre-booked Only*' which can be distilled into the concept of 'No phone call, No ride'.

[2] [1959] 2 QB 311 at 323.

8.55

Table 8.1   Plying and standing for hire

Case	Summary	Conclusion
Sales v Lake [1922] 1 KB 553 Para 8.9	Tickets sold for a charabanc excursion to Brighton and pre-arranged a time and location when passengers were to be picked up. The driver of the charabanc did so and was convicted of unlawfully plying for hire. On appeal the conviction was upheld. Prosecution for unlawful plying for hire contrary to Metropolitan Public Carriage Act 1869, s 7 (see Appendix I) (slightly differently drafted from TPCA 1847, s 47 (see Appendix I)).	Established that there cannot be a plying for hire unless two conditions are satisfied: (1) There must be a soliciting or waiting to secure passengers by the driver or other person in control without any previous contract with them and (2) the owner or person in control who is engaged in or authorises the soliciting or waiting must be in possession of a carriage for which he is soliciting or waiting to obtain passengers.
Cogley v Sherwood [1959] 2 QB 311 Para 8.10	London airport desk staffed for booking or hiring immediate transport. Vehicles not hackney carriages not visible. Prosecution for unlawful plying for hire contrary to Metropolitan Public Carriage Act 1869, s 7 (see Appendix I) (slightly differently drafted from TPCA 1847, s 47 (see Appendix I)). Were the vehicles by this mechanism plying for hire?	Court considered a number of older authorities. *Allen v Tunbridge* (1871) LR 6 CP 481 *Armstrong v Ogle* [1926] 2 KB 438 *Case v Storey* (1869) LR 4 Exc 319 *Clarke v Stamford* (1871) LR 6 QB 357 All of which determine that vehicle must be exhibited. Court indicated that vehicle should be on view. There should be an express or implied invitation to the public. A member of the public should if they want to be able to use the vehicle. Court distinguished *Gilbert v Mckay* [1946] 1 All ER at 458 and *Cavilll v Amos* (1899) 16 TLR 156 as there was exhibition. *Griffin v Grey Coaches Limited* (1928) 45 TLR 104 was further

Case	Summary	Conclusion
		distinguished as the latter concerned stage carriage.
		Although the court could not find a comprehensive previous legal definition, they found that as there was no exhibition there was no plying for hire.
Rose v Welbeck Motors Limited [1962] 1 WLR 1010 Para 8.16	Prosecution under Metropolitan Carriage Act 1869, s 7 (see Appendix I). Mini cab parked on bus stand where buses turned. When bus came vehicle moved some 10 yards, parked there 50 minutes in all. Was the vehicle plying for hire?	*Cogley v Sherwood* considered. Judgment was on the facts of this matter only. Vehicle was of distinctive appearance, colour, and inscription and as to its radio equipment. The driver was at the wheel and was 50 minutes in a public place and on public view and at a bus turn around where the public would be. The driver kept moving and returning. It was held there was no distinction between a 'taxi' and a 'cab', and any tribunal would be bound to hold there was the exhibiting of a vehicle for hire.
Newman v Vincent [1962] 1 WLR 1017 Para 8.17	Similar facts to Rose above, but vehicle only parked for 20 minutes. Did have *notice* on passenger sun visor, 'MINI-CAB BOOKING'.	Notice was very material and important in the eyes of the court. It recognised that the vehicle might have appeared simply to be outside a private house however it attracted two members of the public who asked if it was for hire. Court found it therefore impossible to say that there was no prima facie case of plying for hire as vehicle on view and inviting the public to use it.

Case	Summary	Conclusion
Vant v Cripps (1963) 62 LGR 88 Para 8.18	Private hire vehicle not licensed as pre LGMPA 1976. Vehicle parked outside house and on driveway of same house on another occasion. Sign in rear 8" × 6" 'Barry's Taxis Mooretown' with a telephone number. Light on house with word 'Taxi' on it. Prosecution for plying for hire (driver) and with no insurance (driver and operator).	Court considered a proper conviction by the magistrates. *Rose v Welbeck Motors* considered. Although an apparent private hire business, anyone passing would see a car and sign and would discern a car waiting to be hired. Not a private car but a taxi. Although plying for hire not statutorily defined court found that clearly the accused was in charge of the vehicle and he would drive it. He was aware that it stood outside with a sign on it and it stood under an illuminated sign. On the evidence one member of the public was attracted to try to hire the vehicle. Perfectly clear vehicle was plying for hire.
Eldridge v British Airport Authority [1970] 2 QB 381 Para 8.21	'Meaning of standing in any street' (London Hackney Carriage Act 1831, s 35 (see Appendix I)). NOTE: The London Legislation is different from the TCPA 1847.	'Standing' means something akin to waiting or parking. Does not mean stationary. Otherwise waiting at traffic lights for example would be 'standing' and unworkable.
Milton Keynes Borough Council v Barry (3 July 1984, unreported), DC Para 8.22	Appeal by way of case stated against an acquittal for unlawful plying for hire brought by Milton Keynes. Private hire driver and private hire vehicle. 'Quick Cars' displayed on front door of car. Dropped off fare parked close to hackney carriage stand near bus station. Advised by radio to base he was free. Approached by two people. Driver advised he had to be pre-booked. Called base who advised he was booked to take them as passengers. On later investigation no records of such procedure found.	Court considered *Cogley v Sherwood*. Court referred to *Clarke v Stamford* [1871] QB 357; *Foinett v Clarke* (1877) 41 JP 359 and *Rose v Welbeck Motors* [1962] 1 WLR 10. Court felt there was temptation for those who were not appropriately licensed employed by private hire firms to take passengers not pre-booked. Court could not see how any reasonable bench would have avoided inferring that driver remaining where he was adjacent to hackney carriage rank was there in hope and expectation of attracting custom. The position he adopted bore all

Case	Summary	Conclusion
		the hallmarks of someone employed for the purpose of carrying passengers and he was likely to be approached accordingly. No reasonable bench could have drawn any other conclusion. It was a less than innocent sojourn at the rank.

AUTHOR'S NOTE: Although the deciding factor appears to be the proximity to the Hackney Carriage stand, it s mere presence there does not appear unlawful, as there is nothing in the 1976 Act or case law, to prevent a vehicle parking adjacent to a hackney carriage stand.

Case	Summary	Conclusion
Ogwr Borough Council v Baker [1989[COD 489 Para 8.29	Police officer observed private hire vehicle near hackney carriages outside night club near hot dog van. Windscreen exhibited the name 'Allways' recognising it as a private hire vehicle. Couple approached who had booked with *firm* but subject vehicle had *not* been sent. When confronted thereafter by Police Officer driver admitted not pre-booked. Acquitted of plying for hire contrary to TCPA 1847, s 45 (see Appendix I) but local authority appealed by way of case stated.	Court strictly followed *Cogley v Sherwood*, *Rose v Welbeck Motors Limited*, *Newman v Vincent* and *Vant v Cripps* despite no authorities being cited in the High Court or the court below. Court had to ask whether in parking where he did there was an implied soliciting of customer ie exhibiting to the public for hire. The court felt examining the justices' decision that irrespective of there being no 'for hire' sign only the firm name 'Allways' on the windscreen the fact that the driver with the vehicle with the name of the service on the windscreen near a line of hackney carriages outside a night club at 1.30 in the morning could only constitute an invitation. The court further considered that on the facts the assertion that the respondent made intermittent use of the hot dog stand was of no evidential value as he gave no explanation for being where he was at the time of the offence. The court ruled that the finding was one which no reasonable bench in the circumstances could have made.

Case	Summary	Conclusion

AUTHOR'S NOTE: The judgment is surprising for as previously noted it takes no account of private hire vehicles ability to be able to stop and wait for a booking to be relayed by their operator.

Case	Summary	Conclusion
Nottingham City Council v Woodings [1994] RTR 72 Para 8.33	What is meant by 'plying for hire'? The case concerns a private hire vehicle licensed by Nottingham City Council parked in its city centre. The licensed private hire driver went to some public toilets; when he returned to the vehicle he was approached by two plain clothed police officers. He was asked if he was free. He confirmed. He was then asked if he could take them to a destination and when questioned on the fare he replied 'depends on where you are going'. The police entered the car and identified themselves. He was prosecuted for unlawfully plying for hire contrary to the TPCA 1847, s 45 (see Appendix I). He was convicted, appealing successfully to the Crown Court. The Authority appealed to the Divisional Court by way of case stated. The issue was whether the driver of a marked mini cab which was *not* a licensed hackney carriage plies for hire within the meaning of the 1847 Act if without more he is approached by the public and concludes negotiations for hire.	The court referred to a number of cases including *Cavill v Amos* (1900) 16 TLR 156, *Sales v Lake* [1922] 1 KB 553, *Cogley v Sherwood*, *Rose v Welbeck Motors* and *Vant v Cripps* above. The court found that when a marked car was parked in the street and the driver went to the toilet there was no plying. When he came out and sat in the car he was not doing so, however when he advised prospective passengers he was free, bearing in mind the position of the vehicle and what it looked like, there was plying for hire. The court ruled that the vehicle must be with the accused driver, meaning somewhere near.

AUTHOR'S NOTE: *Milton Keynes Borough Council v Barry* and *Ogwr Borough Council v Baker* were not referred to in *Nottingham* and it appears to be in conflict with the earlier decisions. See para 8.34 for comments on *Nottingham* as the better decision, and to para 8.47 for overall conclusions.

Case	Summary	Conclusion
Young v Scampion (1988) 87 LGR 240 Para 8.40	This matter concerned a prosecution brought by Solihull MBC relating to the use of Hackney Carriages at Birmingham International Airport within its district. A private road known as Airport Way had a hackney carriage stand. That road was not a public highway but a continuation of it. There was a barrier although this was only closed once a year. Traffic could pass and repass. The defendants were hackney drivers licensed by Birmingham City Council driving vehicles licensed by them. They stood on the Airport Way rank and took passengers to destinations in Solihull. They were convicted of standing plying for hire and driving a hackney at Airport Way and also of driving in the streets in Solihull when they had no licence to ply for hire in Solihull. The defendants appealed by way of case stated.	Court found that for an offence the vehicle had to be a hackney carriage within the meaning of the 1847 Act by reference to its use not its design. Court also addressed at length the meaning of a street in TCPA 1837, s 39 and whether public access was a necessary test. The court ruled following *Birmingham and Midland Motor Omnibus v Thompson* [1981] 2 KB 105 and *White v Cubitt* [1931] KB 443 that these earlier cases were distinguishable as vehicles were parked, albeit on private land but to draw custom from the public in an adjoining street. The court followed *Curtis v Embury* (1872) LR 7 Exc 369 and *Jones v Short* (1900) 69 LJ QB 473 concerning carriages parked on railway property. Here the defendants were parked on the Airport's private property to draw custom from the Airport. They were not soliciting custom from the public streets of Solihull. There was a general physical separation from the highway. Court also found that even though large numbers of people resorted to airports and railway stations etc it did not make such locations a street. Accordingly the court ruled that a hackney carriage did not have to be licensed by the Borough in which it was standing at a rank if that rank was on a private road for the purposes of people who were not generally passing on public streets. It was further held that having picked up a passenger a hackney carriage could drive on roads within the area of the council with which it was *not* licensed.

Case	Summary	Conclusion
		That followed the purpose of the statutory control allowing a taxi licensed in one local authority area to convey a passenger through another without a need for a separate licence.
Chorley Borough Council v Thomas [2001] EWHC Admin 570 QBD [2001] LLR 62 Para 8.37	Case outside London. Licensed private hire vehicle with licensed driver. Parked outside public house. Driver approached by prospective passenger asked if free. Driver said yes. Passenger entered car. Driver asked passenger name and destination. Told another public house. Driver said fare would be £1.40. Driver contacted operator by radio to book journey. No movement until booking made. Fare paid at destination plus 50p tip. Prosecution for unlawful plying for hire contrary to TCPA 1847, s 45 (see Appendix I). Application for no case accepted at first instance on the basis: • No evidence how long vehicle stationary • Booking made to base station almost immediately passenger enters vehicle • Booking supported by documentation • Journey commenced after booking made • Therefore no evidence of plying for hire. Chorley appealed to High Court by way of case stated.	*Cogley v Sherwood* *Sales v Lake* *Rose v Welbeck Motors* *Ogwr Borough Council v Baker* *Nottingham City Council v Woodings* considered. Judge had no prosecution or defence arguments for consideration from the lower court as submission of no case led to case dismissal. Judge found on facts set out in the summary of reasons ante that there was a prima facie case to answer. The judge did not rule on the 'booking' procedure as he did not consider it relevant in relation to the determination of a prima facie case being made out.

AUTHOR'S NOTE: Parking outside public house indicating he was free and then making a booking via the operator provided a prima facie case for prosecution. However, there is nothing to say that a booking in existence prior to hiring would not provide a defence. See para 8.37.

Case	Summary	Conclusion
Eastbourne v Stirling [2001] RTR 7 Para 8.46	Decision as to whether private hire vehicle was plying or standing for hire when parked on the station forecourt. Local railway company in Eastbourne reached an agreement with local private hire company to allow its vehicles to use west forecourt of station. Each hiring would be pre-booked with the operator who had a shed on-site for bookings. Arrangements supplanted and replaced earlier hackney rank at station. On two separate occasions Environmental Health Officer approached drivers. On the first, the driver said he did not have a fare and asked where the officer wanted to go. On the second after he asked the driver if he had a booking and was told no the Officer told the driver he was plying for hire. At first instance the magistrate concluded the prosecution had not shown that the forecourt of the station was a street for the purpose of the prosecution and there was no case to answer. The matter was appealed to the High Court by the Council by way of cases stated following the acquittal of the drivers.	The defence argued that for these to be a plying for hire a vehicle must be parked or standing on a street to which the public has access of right – as there was no access, no offence committed. The appellant said that there was plying for hire as the effect of parking the vehicle was to attract custom from the public highway. The court decided there *was* plying for hire. *Young v Scampion* was not incorrect but distance from the highway vital. In *Young v Scampion* hackney carriages were well away from the public highway, it being very unlikely anyone would be attracted to use them. In Eastbourne the distance was considerably less. *White v Cubit* [1930] 1 KB 443 applied. Judge found that the vehicle on the rank would be plainly likely to attract custom from members of the public using the adjoining street in a busy part of the town, respondents were therefore plying for hire in the street within the meaning of TCPA 1847, s 38 (see Appendix I).
Dudley Metropolitan Borough Council v Arif [2012] RTR 20 Para 8.38	The driver of a private hire vehicle was booked to pick up a female passenger from a cinema and was given only the first name of the passenger and the locality of the destination. He arrived early and was approached by a woman who asked to go to the same locality. He did not ask her name but assumed she was his booked	Held: Dismissing the appeal that this was a case of a mistake of fact and must be accepted by the court on those terms. For the High Court to dig deeper risked going behind the facts found by the magistrates' court. The defence of mistake was not unreasonable.

Case	Summary	Conclusion
	passenger. She was not. He was prosecuted for unlawful plying for hire, but acquitted by the magistrates' court. The council appealed by way of case stated.	
Gateshead Council v Henderson [2012] LLR 610, Admin Ct Para 8.39	Private hire vehicle dropping off passenger. Approached by a new passenger without a booking who got into the vehclie. Aquitted at the magistrates' court of unlawfully plying for hire. Prosecutor appealed by way of case stated.	Held: Dismissing the appeal that there was no deliberate exhibition of the vehicle, and therefore no offence had been committed.

Plying for Hire – Author's Summary Conclusion

1. Only hackney carriages can ply or stand for hire. The test of plying or standing for hire, following both the decisions in *Nottingham* and *Chorley* is that the vehicle is exhibited and available for hire.

2. Nothing in the legislation or case law prevents a private hire vehicle parking lawfully to await a booking made via the operator, provided that the vehicle is not standing or plying for hire (see 1 above).

3. The length of time that a private hire vehicle is lawfully parked is irrelevant.

4. The test of whether or not the vehicle is available for hire (ie plying for hire) is based on the intentions of the driver, as evidenced by his actions if approached by a prospective passenger.

8.56

For consideration of what constitutes a 'booking' for the purposes of private hire bookings, see Chapter 12, para 12.2 onwards.

TOUTING FOR HIRE

8.57

The Criminal Justice and Public Order Act 1994, s 167 makes it an offence 'in a public place, to solicit persons to hire vehicles to carry them as passengers'. The problem that this section was intended to address was where people were approached at railway and bus stations, airports etc by people asking them if they wanted a 'taxi'. In many cases the intention was to divert a person, especially tourists and foreigners who may not be familiar with the concept of a hackney carriage, away from a regulated, licensed vehicle, and into an unlicensed, unregulated and unlawful vehicle. This would allow excessive fares to be charged, at the very least and robberies and assaults in more extreme cases.

8.58

There is no definition of the word 'solicit' in the Criminal Justice and Public Order Act 1994. In the case of *Weisz v Monahan*[1] the question was considered as to whether a card displayed on a notice board in a street which offered the services of a prostitute amounted to 'soliciting' for the purpose of the Street Offences Act 1959, s 1(1) which made it an offence for a common prostitute to loiter or solicit in a street or public place for the purpose of prostitution. Lord Parker CJ stated (at 665):

> 'She was clearly not loitering. The only question is: was she soliciting? For my part, I am quite satisfied that soliciting in that connection involves the physical presence of the prostitute and conduct on her part amounting to an importuning of prospective customers. An advertisement is more in the nature of a notice, and though in one sense it may be said to be soliciting custom, certainly something much more than that is needed in the commission of the offence of soliciting by a prostitute.'

[1]   [1962] 1 All ER 664.

8.59

This was immediately followed by the case of *Burge v Director of Public Prosecutions*[1] where Lord Parker CJ stated that in order to commit an offence which required a person to 'solicit', 'it must involve the physical presence of the alleged offender' (at 667).

[1]   [1962] 1 All ER 666.

8.60

Both these cases considered the question of using an advertisement to solicit custom. The courts have taken a consistent approach in a situation where a person is present. In *Behrendt v Burridge*[1] the question arose as to whether a woman sitting in a window was soliciting. Boreham J took the view that she was (at 288):

> 'This young woman, sitting on a stool scantily clad, in a window bathed in red light and in an area where prostitutes were sought, might just as well have had at her feet an advertisement saying: "I am a prostitute. I am ready and willing to give the services of a prostitute and my premises are now available for that purpose." It is clear, in my judgment, that she was soliciting in the sense of tempting or alluring prospective customers to come in for the purpose of prostitution and projecting her solicitation to passers by.'

[1]   [1976] 3 All ER 285.

8.61

It appears from these judgments that there must be a physical presence for there to be a solicitation. How then does this apply to the Criminal Justice and Public Order Act 1994, s 167? Section 167(2) states:

'(2) Subsection (1) above does not imply that the soliciting must refer to any particular vehicle nor is the mere display of a sign on a vehicle that the vehicle is for hire soliciting within that subsection.'

Which suggests that a mere indication that a vehicle is a private hire vehicle is not an offence under s 167. This view is supported by Department of Transport circular 4/94 which states: '"Soliciting" is normally a proactive process' and continues:

'Subsection (2) provides that a taxi driver merely sitting in a taxi with a "For Hire" or "Taxi" sign displayed will not be committing an offence; nor will the driver of a taxi or private hire vehicle with a sign indicating that it can be hired by telephone.'

It can be seen that this view appears to accord with the decision in *Nottingham City Council v Woodings*[1].

[1]   [1994] RTR 72; see para 8.33 above.

Oddy v Bug Bugs Ltd

8.62

> Pedicab (an unlicensed, pedal powered rickshaw) available for immediate hire in London. Private prosecution brought alleging the vehicle was illegally plying for hire. Acquitted at the magistrate's court. Prosecution appealed by way of case stated. Held: Dismissing the appeal that something more than the mere presence of a vehicle and driver was required for the offence.

In *Oddy v Bug Bugs Ltd*[1] it was decided that whether or not soliciting had taken place would always depend on the particular circumstances of the case but that something more than mere progress down the street was required. 'Plying for hire' and 'soliciting' were not coterminous. In the latter case some form of invitation to a client was needed.

[1]   [2003] EWHC 2865 (Admin), [2004] LLR 124, Admin Ct. This case concerned trishaws in London and is considered at Chapter 18, para 18.25.

8.63

Until the decision in *Oddy v Bugbugs* Ltd[1] there was no reported decision on the section and a number of local authorities had used it successfully to prosecute the drivers of private hire vehicles which had been parked where potential passengers were likely to congregate, eg outside nightclubs. To achieve this, it had to be accepted that the mere presence of a private hire vehicle, waiting for a booking to be called through to the driver, would amount to touting. In the light of *Oddy v Bugbugs*, it is suggested that approach is incorrect. Private hire vehicles can park wherever any other vehicle can lawfully park and as they are lawfully licensed vehicles, it seems perverse if, when they do park, they are committing an offence. The offence should only be committed when the mischief aimed at is present, and there has been an approach made to a prospective hirer.

¹ [2003] EWHC 2865 (Admin), [2004] LLR 124, Admin Ct.

Hulin v Cook

8.64

A slightly different point was raised in *Hulin v Cook*¹. This case concerned the question of whether the provisions of TPCA 1847, in relation to plying for hire, extended to hackney carriage stands provided by the then British Railways Board on railway property outside railway stations. Byelaw 22(2) of the British Railways Board Byelaws required a hackney carriage proprietor to apply for permission from the British Railways Board before the hackney carriage could be used on a British Rail stand, this being in addition to the requirement to hold a licence under TPCA 1847, s 38. In this case no such permission had been obtained and the prosecution was brought against both the proprietor and the driver of the hackney carriage in question. They contended that the Public Health Act 1925, s 76 meant that, because the general provisions of the hackney carriage licensing regime were extended to stands at railway stations, they did not need the permission of the British Railways Board. That view was accepted by the magistrate, who acquitted the driver and proprietor. The prosecution appealed by way of case stated. Widgery LCJ gave the judgment of the court. He noted that s 76 of the 1925 Act had been passed because cases prior to that supported the view that a licence was not required if the person was plying for hire on private property. He concluded (at 349L):

'It is contended however that under section 76 some new right to ply for hire was thereby conferred, but, in my judgment, that is not so. The position after the passing of the Act of 1925 was that the licensing system under the Act of 1847 was extended to a new area. It was extended to the area of the railways and to railway premises, and anyone wishing to ply for hire on railway premises thereafter required a licence under the Act of 1847, despite the fact that the property was private property, but nothing in the way of a further right was thereby conferred.

Once the Act of 1925 was passed, the position in Cardiff, and for all I know in other places as well, was simply this. The typical taxi driver who wished to serve customers in the area, whether they came from airport, railway stations, bus stations or elsewhere, would need the ordinary 1847 Act licence in order to carry on his trade in Cardiff at all. In addition to that, if he wanted to serve passengers in Cardiff Central Station he would have to make his peace with the Railways Board in as much as he would require their consent under their byelaws before he could ply for hire within the confines of the railway property. That, in my understanding of the position, is how the law now stands, and it follows from that that the magistrate was in error when he considered, as he evidently did from the form of his case, that the effect of section 76 was to give a new right which had not previously existed in that it licensed taxi drivers to ply for hire in Cardiff.'

[1]   [1977] RTR 345.

Kahn v Evans

8.65

> When does a hailing of a hackney carriage translate into a hiring? A passenger hailed a hackney carriage whilst standing on railway premises although the vehicle was on the street when it responded. The question was whether the driver was plying for reward on railway property? He argued that as he had already been hailed there was a contract existence and therefore he was not guilty of the offence. Held: That until the destination had been agreed, there was no contract in existence.

A different question, although it initially concerned a railway station stand, was answered in *Kahn v Evans*[1]. The question was when did a contract between driver and passenger come into existence? *Kahn v Evans* concerned a prosecution of a licensed hackney carriage driver for plying for reward on railway premises without authority to do so, contrary to the British Railways Board Byelaws 1965, byelaw 22(2). His defence was that, as he had been hailed before he was on railway premises, when he actually entered the railway premises he was already under contract to the persons who had hailed him to take them anywhere they wished to go and, consequently, he was not plying. That defence failed before the magistrates and Mr Kahn appealed by way of case stated to the High Court. Judgment was given by Robert Goff LJ, who stated (at 37C):

> 'Three questions are posed for our consideration by the justices. They ask whether they were correct in law in holding that:
>> "(1) the process of plying for reward continues until a contract was made between the driver of a hackney carriage and a prospective passenger to convey that passenger for reward;
>> (2) no such contract could be made merely by the prospective passengers hailing the driver of the hackney carriage and his responding to the hail by driving from the public road on to railway premises; and
>> (3) such a contract did not come into existence until the driver of the hackney carriage has spoken to the prospective passenger and agreed to convey him or her."

For the defendant [the driver], Mr Irvine addressed no argument to us on the first question. He therefore accepted that the first question should be answered in the affirmative.

I turn then to the second and third questions. On these questions, Mr Irvine made the following submissions. He submitted that when the defendant was driving his taxi along the public road with his "For Hire" sign displayed, his conduct amounted to an invitation to treat. Next he submitted that the action of the two women in hailing the defendant amounted to an offer to hire him. Then, when the defendant decided to accept that offer and changed course, turning towards the two women, his conduct in so doing amounted to an acceptance of that offer, whereupon a contract came into existence. It follows that on those submissions the contract was made before the defendant's hackney carriage entered upon the railway premises. So, says Mr Irvine, no offence was committed on the facts of the present case.

I am perfectly content to view the action of a cab driver such as the defendant in driving along a road with the "For Hire" sign exhibited on his cab as constituting an invitation to treat in the sense of an invitation to enter into negotiations for a contract, which does not bind anybody and is simply a preliminary to a contract possibly coming into existence.

I then come to Mr Irvine's second submission, which was that when the two women hailed the cab they were making an offer to hire the cab, by which he must have meant an offer which if accepted would result in a binding contract. The difficulty with this proposition as I see it is that the terms of any such offer are not known; and in particular it is not known to what destination the person hailing the cab wishes to be taken, or what fare would be charged for conveying him to that destination.

An example was put to Mr Irvine in the course of argument. Let it be supposed that somebody standing at Brighton station sees a cab coming along the road with its "For Hire" sign displayed. He hails it, intending to ask to be taken to John O'Groats. If Mr Irvine's submission is right, as soon as that cab driver seeing the passenger on the side of the road turns his cab towards that person with the intention of accepting him as a fare a binding contract comes into existence. It must follow, if this submission is right, that that passenger is bound to go in that cab to John O'Groats and that the cab driver is bound to take him there. It also follows that the only way in which the fare could be ascertained for that journey would be on the basis that a reasonable fare would be charged and paid. It only needs an example such as that to reveal the difficulties which Mr Irvine faces in putting his argument.

Another example put to Mr Irvine in the course of argument was this. Let it be supposed that a prospective passenger standing on the side of the road wants to be taken home. He sees a cab coming along displaying a "For Hire" sign. He hails it and it turns towards him but gets stuck for a moment in the traffic. Thereupon another cab driver passing by sees him standing at the side of the road and drives up to him, and he gets into that second cab. On Mr Irvine's example the passenger would at that point of time be guilty of a breach of contract vis-à-vis the first driver and it is possible that the second driver would be guilty of the wrong of inducing a breach of contract between the passenger and the first driver. Again the example, in my judgment, reveals the problems underlying Mr Irvine's argument.

In my judgment, as a matter of sheer common sense, when a prospective passenger sees a cab coming along the public highway showing a "For Hire" sign and hails it, all he is doing is indicating to the cab driver a wish or intention to hire his cab. He is doing no more than indicating a desire to negotiate with the cab driver for the purpose of making a contract of carriage. The material terms have not been agreed at that point in time. When the cab driver drives up in answer to that hail, his action is still part and parcel of the process of negotiation which may lead to a binding contract. When the driver comes to the side of the road and lowers his window and the passenger says, "Will you please take me to –" whatever the address may be and the driver says "Yes", there may be at that point in time a contract, but certainly not before that point of time. If the destination is within the area to be served it may be that the cab driver is bound to accept the passenger. If it is outside a certain area it may be that he is at liberty to refuse to take the passenger, but a bargain can be struck as to the fare to be paid for carrying the passenger to that place. But of course none of the facts giving rise to problems of that kind are made known by the simple act of the person standing on the pavement and hailing the cab, or by the cab driver answering the hail.

All of this demonstrates, in my judgment, that at that point of time the parties are still in the stage of what is called invitation to treat or negotiation, but that no offer capable of being accepted and so creating a binding contract has yet been made.

For those reasons I am unable to accept Mr Irvine's submissions.

It is right that I should record that Mr Irvine referred us to section 53 of the Town Police Clauses Act 1847, but I do not think it is necessary to go into that section which in my judgment has no bearing upon the question in this case.

Addressing myself to the second and third questions posed by the justices, I for my part would answer both those questions in the affirmative.'

Whilst this judgment obviously applies to the question of when a hiring is made on railway premises, the concept of contract in relation to hackney carriage hiring is a an important and useful point.

¹   [1985] RTR 33.

HACKNEY CARRIAGE ZONES

8.66

Most local authorities license hackney carriages to ply throughout the area of their district. However, there are some districts where there are zones for hackney carriages. This means that the district is subdivided and hackney carriages are licensed in that zone, rather than within the whole district. The existence of zones is a consequence of history, as explained below. If no zones exist within a district, they cannot be created by the local authority.

8.67

The existence of hackney carriage zones stems from local government reorganisation in 1974 under the terms of the Local Government Act 1972 (LGA 1972)[1].

[1]   For a concise overview of the history of zoning, see the explanatory notes issued by the Department of the Environment, Transport and the Regions (in May 1997 in relation to England, and February 1998 in relation to Wales), reproduced in Appendix II.

Local government reorganisation

8.68

Briefly, hackney carriages are licensed by local authorities under the provisions of the Town Police Clauses Acts of 1847 and 1889. Although TPCA 1847 originally had to be incorporated within a local Act, it was applied to all urban sanitary districts by the Public Health Act 1875, s 171. These became either urban districts or boroughs under the Local Government Act 1894. By virtue of the Local Government Act 1933, hackney carriage licensing was an urban district council, borough council and county borough council function, although there were a few rural district councils which also undertook hackney carriage licensing until the application of LGA 1972 on 1 April 1974.

LOCAL GOVERNMENT ACT 1972

8.69

LGA 1972 created two tiers of local government within England and Wales, and amalgamated many of the former smaller areas of local government that had been responsible for hackney carriage licensing. Under LGA 1972, urban district councils, rural district councils, borough councils and county borough councils were abolished and replaced with district councils and metropolitan district councils. The areas of the new districts were sometimes the area of a previous authority, but, in many cases, were amalgamations of a number of previous authorities and parts of other previous authorities.

8.70

LGA 1972, s 180 and LGA 1972, Sch 14, Pt II had the effect of applying the Public Health Act 1875, s 171(4) (which applied hackney carriage licensing to urban districts and specified that the prescribed distance was within the area of any urban district) to the areas which it had applied to immediately before the establishment of the new authorities on 1 April 1974. This meant that hackney carriage licensing could only take place in those parts of the country where it had taken place prior to 31 March 1974.

8.71

A consequence of this was that there were districts (both metropolitan and non-metropolitan) in England and Wales where hackney carriage licensing did not

apply throughout the area of the entire district, but only where it had applied
before 1 April 1974.

8.72

It was possible for the new district council to pass a resolution under LGA 1972,
Sch 14, Pt II, para 25. By that resolution, the council could abolish hackney
carriage licensing within their district by stating that the Public Health Act 1875,
s 171(4) should not apply throughout the district. However, such a resolution
had to be passed before 1 April 1975 (within one year of the creation of the new
authority).

8.73

Alternatively, the new authority could pass a resolution, under LGA 1972,
Sch 14, Pt II, para 25(3), applying the provisions of hackney carriage licensing to
its entire district. That would have the effect of extending the licensing regime
from the areas where it had applied before reorganisation to the entire post-
reorganisation district, as one area with no zones.

8.74

A third possibility was that the new local authority did nothing and continued
to have zones, and also the possibility of areas where there was no licensing of
hackney carriages in the district.

8.75

As a result, a number of authorities have, in fact, had hackney carriage zones
since 1974 and, as there was no mandatory requirement to extend hackney
carriage licensing under LGA 1972, there were also a number of areas where
there was no licensing of hackney carriages.

TRANSPORT ACT 1985

8.76

That situation changed with the introduction of the Transport Act 1985, s 15.

'Extension of taxi licensing in England and Wales

15–(1) Where, immediately before the commencement of this section, the
provisions of the Town Police Clauses Act 1847 with respect to hackney
carriages and of the Town Police Clauses Act 1889 (as incorporated in
each case in the Public Health Act 1875) were not in force throughout the
whole of the area of a district council in England and Wales whose area
lies outside the area to which the Metropolitan Public Carriage Act 1869
applies, those provisions (as so incorporated) shall—
(a) if not then in force in any part of the council's area, apply throughout
that area; and

(b) if in force in part only of its area, apply also in the remainder of that area.

(2) Where part only of a district council's area lies outside the area to which the Act of 1869 applies, that part shall, for the purposes of subsection (1) above, be treated as being the area of the council.

(3) So much of any local Act as enables a district council to bring to an end the application of the provisions mentioned in subsection (1) above to the whole or any part of their area shall cease to have effect.'

It can be seen that s 15(1)(a) provides that if there had been no hackney carriage licensing in any part of the council's area, then the provisions of the Town Police Clauses Acts of 1847 and 1889 would apply throughout its area; and, if the hackney carriage licensing provisions of those two Acts only applied in part of the local authority area, then they would also apply in the remainder of the local authority's area.

8.77

The Department of Transport[1] took the view that the effect of the Transport Act 1985, s 15, in areas where hackney zoning existed, was not to abolish zones, but rather to create an extra zone in the part of the local authority's district where hackney carriage licensing had not applied up until the introduction of s 15.

[1]   Circular 8/86; see Appendix II.

8.78

Again, at any time after 1985, a local authority could pass an extension resolution under LGA 1972, Sch 14, Pt II, para 25 to abolish zones within its district and to have one area for hackney carriage licensing which would cover the entire area of the district.

8.79

It seems that, if hackney carriage zones did exist, then byelaws could only be passed by the post-1974 district council in relation to those zones within its district where hackney carriage licensing applied. If the new authority inherited byelaws from a previous constituent authority, then those byelaws would only be enforceable in the zone to which they now applied.

8.80

If an authority had zones, then each zone was effectively a district and any licence which was granted would only be effective within the zone. In addition, any question over numbers would relate to the zone and each zone could have its own limit on hackney carriages (provided that there was no significant demand for hackney carriage services which remained unmet within the zone).

8.81

That, then, was the situation after the introduction of the Transport Act 1985.

THE 1990s REORGANISATION

8.82

The situation was then further complicated by the new local government reorganisation which took place in the 1990s. For the first time, England and Wales were treated differently and, although the rationale behind the reorganisations in both countries was the same, the consequences were slightly different[1].

> [1] See the Department of the Environment, Transport and the Regions guidance notes: Appendix II.

8.83

The effects of the 1990s reorganisation are, in many ways, much the same as the effects of the reorganisation of 1974. If a new authority comprises parts of two or more post-1974 districts, then each of those constituent parts will constitute a zone for the purposes of hackney carriage licensing. Licences which cover an old district (a new zone within a new authority) will be valid only within the area of the old district. This will be so irrespective of new authority boundaries, so, if an old district has been bisected and split between two new authorities, a hackney carriage licence for the old district will be effective in the area of the old authority (which now lies in two new local authority areas), but will be ineffective in any areas of either of the new authorities which lie outside the area of the former council. The same will apply to byelaws inherited by new authorities from constituent authorities: they will remain enforceable within the area of the previous district, possibly by two or more new authorities, depending upon the geography of the situation.

THE 2000s REORGANISATION

8.84

The final reorganisations of local government (for the present time) took place in 2009 when the counties of Northumberland, County Durham, Shropshire, Wiltshire, Bedfordshire, Cheshire and Cornwall became unitary with either one or more authorities replacing the county council and district councils. In these areas zones were created and authorities have taken different approaches, with some de-zoning and others retaining their pre-reorganisation hackney carriage boundaries.

The DfT considers hackney carriage zones in its 'Best Practice Guide'[1] where it states (at paras 60 to 62):

'TAXI ZONES

89. The areas of some local licensing authorities are divided into two or more zones for taxi licensing purposes. Drivers may be licensed to ply for hire in one zone only. Zones may exist for historical reasons, perhaps because of local authority boundary changes.

90. The Department recommends the abolition of zones. That is chiefly for the benefit of the travelling public. Zoning tends to diminish the supply of taxis and the scope for customer choice – for example, if fifty taxis were licensed overall by a local authority, but with only twenty five of them entitled to ply for hire in each of two zones. It can be confusing and frustrating for people wishing to hire a taxi to find that a vehicle licensed by the relevant local authority is nonetheless unable to pick them up (unless pre-booked) because they are in the wrong part of the local authority area. Abolition of zones can also reduce costs for the local authority, for example through simpler administration and enforcement. It can also promote fuel efficiency, because taxis can pick up a passenger anywhere in the local authority area, rather than having to return empty to their licensed zone after dropping a passenger in another zone.

91. It should be noted that the Government has now made a Legislative Reform Order which removed the need for the Secretary of State to approve amalgamation resolutions made by local licensing authorities The Legislative Reform (Local Authority Consent Requirements)(England and Wales) Order 2008 came into force in October 2008. Although these resolutions no longer require the approval of the Secretary of State, the statutory procedure for making them – in paragraph 25 of schedule 14 to the Local Government Act 1972- remains the same.'

[1]   DfT, '*Taxi and Private Hire Vehicle Licensing: Best Practice Guidance*' (October 2006, revised March 2010) available at http://www.dft.gov.uk/pgr/regional/taxis/taxiandprivatehirevehiclelic1792.

Passing an extension resolution

8.85

The only way to overcome this is for the new authority to pass an extension resolution under LGA 1972, Sch 14, Pt II, para 25, abolishing zones and applying hackney carriage licensing throughout the area of the new authority. This route is also open to any local authority which has zones as a result of the 1974 reorganisation, and wishes to remove these so as to have a single hackney carriage licensing regime throughout the area of the district. Paragraph 25(1) of Sch 14 requires that notice of the proposed resolution be given in accordance with para 25(5) but the original requirement for the approval of the Secretary of State or Welsh Ministers has been removed.

8.86

As the Secretary of State or Welsh Ministers are no longer required to approve the resolution, passing an extension resolution is now be a reasonably straightforward administrative matter.

8.87

Unless, and until, such a resolution is passed in any authority which has zones, irrespective of whether these are post-1974 authorities or authorities that have been created as a result of the latest reorganisation in both England and Wales, zones will continue to apply. The effect of this is that the authority is unable to treat its area as one hackney carriage licensing district and must continue to treat each zone separately.

8.88

Although there is nothing to prevent the local authority granting what are, in effect, multiple licences to a hackney carriage to enable it to ply for hire in all the zones within its district, the local authority cannot pass district-wide byelaws or impose a district-wide fare structure. This does not mean that different byelaws or fares need to apply in different zones, although they could do so if that was the desire of the authority, but it does mean that each zone will require its own byelaws and fare structure, and any fare increases must be treated on a zone basis. This means that although the same fares can apply, they will have to be implemented by means of two or more fare increases.

8.89

In relation to fees for hackney carriage proprietor's licences and drivers' licences, again, these can only be levied on a zoned basis.

8.90

It can be seen that zones can and do exist, but the only action that a local authority can take is to remove all zones or accept the situation as it is. There is no power available to a local authority to either merge some zones to create a smaller number or, alternatively, to create new zones, thereby further subdividing its district.

A HACKNEY CARRIAGE CAN PLY THROUGHOUT THE DISTRICT

8.91

Once a hackney carriage proprietor's licence has been granted to a vehicle, that vehicle can ply or stand for hire throughout the area of the district (or the appropriate zone if the authority has zones)[1]. It is not possible for a local authority to limit the area of the district. Some years ago, one local authority (Reigate and Banstead Borough Council) did issue some hackney carriage proprietor's licences with conditions attached preventing the use of certain ranks within the district, although that condition was later removed. TPCA 1847, s 37 states:

> 'The commissioners may from time to time licence to ply for hire within the prescribed distance, or if no distance is prescribed, within five miles from the General Post Office of the city, town, or place to which the special Act refers, (which in that case shall be deemed the prescribed distance,) such number of hackney coaches or carriages of any kind or description adapted to the carriage of persons as they think fit.'

The reference to the prescribed distance is now a reference to the area of the district council (or unitary, metropolitan district, Welsh county or county borough council), unless the council has hackney carriage zones, in which case it will be the area of the zone in question[2].

1   See para 8.66 onwards.
2   See para 8.1 above for an explanation of this.

R (on the application of Maud) v Castle Point Borough Council

8.92

> Proposal to delimit hackney carriage numbers. It was argued that any new licences should have a condition attached to them preventing use at a particularly popular hackney carriage rank. Held: A local authority cannot restrict where a hackney carriage can work within a district.

As a consequence, it is clear that a hackney carriage can ply throughout the area of the district (or zone) and any reduction in that area is not permitted. This view was upheld by the Court of Appeal in the case of *R (on the application of Maud) v Castle Point Borough Council*[1]. Castle Point Borough Council commissioned an independent survey, which reported that there was unmet demand, both patent and latent (the question of demand in this judgment is considered at para 8.203 below) for hackney carriages. As a consequence of this, the council decided to increase the number of hackney carriages that they would licence. The challenge was brought by an existing hackney carriage proprietor and (as is relevant here) he argued that the council should have attached a condition to the new licences preventing them from using the most popular ranks within the district. He took the view that such a condition could be attached to the new licences by use of the LG(MP)A 1976, s 47(1). The council refused to do this, feeling it had no power to attach such a condition and the aggrieved hackney carriage licensee sought judicial review (not limited to this argument). On this point he lost in the Administrative Court, and subsequently on appeal to the Court of Appeal. In the Administrative Court[2], Mr Justice Wilson rejected the argument thus:

> '21. The parameters of section 47(1) have not been the subject of widespread judicial consideration. The source of guidance most helpful to me is the decision in *R v Wirral MBC, ex parte The Wirral Licensed Taxi Owners Association* [1983] 3 CMLR 150, in which Glidewell J upheld the validity of a condition which specified the type of vehicle covered by a licence. The judge
> (a) noted at 159 that words of the section were very wide but that it had been agreed on all sides that there were some limits upon the discretion thereby conferred;
> (b) cited at 160 *Pyx Granite Co Ltd v Ministry of Housing and Local Government* [1958] 1 QB 554, in which it was held that the exercise of an analogous power given to planning authorities should fairly and reasonably relate to the permitted development and not be in furtherance of an ulterior object, however desirable; and

(c)   suggested at 161 that the Council's functions under the taxi licensing legislation were to achieve:

"... the safety, convenience and comfort of passengers in hackney carriages, the safety of other road users and to ensure that there is some way in which those who wish to use either hackney carriages or private hire vehicles can readily distinguish the one type of vehicle from another."

22. I have significant doubt whether a condition can lawfully be imposed under section 47(1) which precludes a taxi from operating within part of the district. The legal foundation of the licence is section 37 of the Act of 1847 which refers to a licence to ply for hire "within the prescribed distance". By section 171(4) of the Public Health Act 1875, that expression means "within any urban district". Prior to 1 April 1975 a local authority had power to resolve to disapply that meaning: see paragraphs 24, 25(1) and 25(2)(a) of schedule 14 to the Local Government Act 1972. But there was no such resolution in this case. In other words, there was in the past a facility for zones to be set up which would limit the geographical area of a taxi licence. Although I accept that the law sometimes permits a result to be achieved by more than one route, I consider that it would surprising if zoning could still be achieved by the attachment of a condition. In particular I consider, on balance, that such would run counter to the founding statute which provides for the grant of a licence "to ply for hire within the [borough]". Would not the suggested condition limiting the licence to ply for hire to within a specified part of the borough derogate from the width of the licence in statutory contemplation?

23. As I canvassed with Mr Wolfe [for the claimant, Mr Maud], there might have been a further argument that, even had it been lawful to attach the suggested condition to all extra licences, it would have been irrational for the defendants to do so. What would be the justification for making all newly licensed vehicles second-class, unable to ply for hire at the most profitable rank? Should not market forces be allowed to operate outside Benfleet station, as elsewhere? And if, as to which the defendants have clearly harboured concern, taxis waiting outside the station may create congestion, productive of danger for pedestrians and difficulty for private motorists, that problem might rationally be addressed by specifying the size of the rank, presently such as to cover 12 taxis, and actively obliging taxis unable to stand within the rank to proceed to another rank.

24. But Mr Muir [for the local authority] has not clearly argued any such hypothetical irrationality. And Mr Wolfe has convincingly demonstrated that the defendants would have wished at least to consider making the grant of licences conditional in that respect if they had not been advised that such course was closed to them. I propose to leave that point open and it remains for me only to decide the bare point relating to the parameters of section 47(1).

25. Both admirable counsel will not mind my confessing to a sensation of unease that, relevant to my decision this afternoon, there may be more law, present and past, relating to the geographical ambit of taxi licences, which has not been brought to my attention. But, by a narrow margin, the doubt, considerations and question articulated in paragraph 22 above lead me to conclude that there is no power under section 47(1) of the Act of 1976 to limit by condition the area of the licensed vehicle's operation within the borough.'

The Court of Appeal dismissed the subsequent appeal on this point in the following term (Keene LJ giving the judgment of the court):

'15. The judge below had taken the view that section 37 of the 1847 Act, by its language, only permitted the licence to be granted for a taxi to ply for hire across the whole of an authority's area. That was based on the words in that section, as amended by the 1875 Act, "a licence to ply for hire within any urban district". It is submitted by Mr Wolfe [for the appellant, Mr Maud] that those words do not have the meaning adopted by the judge but merely denote the area of the licensing authority's jurisdiction. In other words, they define the geographical extent of that jurisdiction. They do not, contends Mr Wolfe, require the licence to be granted for the whole of the district in question. Therefore, one should simply apply the conventional administrative law principles. Here, the purpose of the condition would have been within the legislative object of the powers under Section 47 of the 1976 Act, and emphasis is placed on the broad wording, as it is described, of that empowering section which deals with conditions.

16. For my part, I prefer the judge's construction of Section 37, particularly bearing in mind the history of the phrase now under consideration. In its original form the words read that the commissioners might "from time to time license to ply for hire *within the prescribed distance*"; I emphasise the last four words. An alternative to the prescribed distance was then given. It seems to me that those words "within the prescribed distance" did not relate – or certainly did not relate solely – to the jurisdictional area of the commissioners. They denoted where the hackney carriages, as they truly were at that time, could ply for hire. Those words were later replaced by the words "within any urban district", as Mr Wolfe emphasises. But I cannot accept that that alteration was intended to render the phrase solely a jurisdictional one rather than one dealing with the area where the vehicle could ply for hire.

17. There is to my mind an even stronger point against Mr Wolfe's contention. If he were right, it would enable an authority to create by its licensing system two classes of taxis: one unrestricted as to where a taxi could ply for hire and the other restricted. The latter would patently be a second class type of taxi which could not operate from all the stands or perhaps all the streets in the borough or district. That seems to me to be contrary to the whole legislative approach adopted more recently by Parliament in this area of activity, the approach being to allow, as far as

possible, open competition in the trade. As Lord Justice Woolf said in *R v Great Yarmouth Borough Council ex p Sawyer* [1989] RTR 297 at 298, the policy of the Transport Act 1985 is –

"… to remove restraints and allow market forces to take their course in a way which did not exist before Section 16 of the Transport Act 1985 came into effect."

In the same case Lord Justice Bingham (at page 303) referred to the Act of 1985 substituting "a free market policy" so long as the authority was not satisfied that there was no unmet demand. To bring into being a two-tier structure of licensed taxis within a district would fly in the face of that legislative approach.

18. In my view a condition preventing a taxi from plying for hire from a particular taxi stand or stands, or in a particular street or streets, would fall outside the scope of the powers granted by Parliament.

19. Despite Mr Wolfe's attractive submissions, I conclude that the authority was right to adopt the advice it had been given by counsel on this particular point.'

---

1   [2003] RTR 7.
2   *R (on the application of Maud) v Castle Point Borough Council* [2002] EWHC 273 (Admin), [2002] LLR 374, Admin Ct.

HACKNEY CARRIAGE PROPRIETOR'S LICENCE

The granting of the licence

8.93

A hackney carriage needs a licence granted by the district council under TPCA 1847, s 37. Such a licence is referred to in the legislation as a hackney carriage proprietor's licence, but is often referred to in day-to-day usage as a hackney carriage vehicle licence.

'**Commissioners may licence hackney carriages**

37. The commissioners may from time to time licence to ply for hire within the prescribed distance, or if no distance is prescribed, within five miles from the General Post Office of the city, town, or place to which the special Act refers (which in that case shall be deemed the prescribed distance), hackney coaches or carriages of any kind or description adapted to the carriage of persons.'[1]

---

1   The reference to the prescribed distance is now a reference to the area of the district council (or unitary, metropolitan district, Welsh county or county borough council), unless the council has hackney carriage zones, in which case it will be the area of the zone in question. This is as a result of the Public Health Act 1875, s 171, which incorporated the provisions of TPCA 1847 and the Town Police Clauses Act 1889 for all urban districts. The Local Government Act 1894 and the Local Government Act 1933 extended hackney carriage licensing to all urban districts, boroughs and county boroughs, and this continued under LGA 1972. LGA 1972, Sch 14, para 2

makes it clear that any reference to an urban or rural authority is now a reference to a local authority within the meaning of the 1972 Act, and the powers contained in TPCA 1847, s 37 are now granted to the local authority, and all references to the commissioners are now construed as references to the local authority. The Transport Act 1985 extended hackney carriage licensing to all districts in England and Wales.

8.94

The local authority can limit the numbers of hackney carriage proprietor's licences that it is prepared to grant, but only if it is 'satisfied that there is no significant demand for the services of hackney carriages (within the area to which the licence would apply) which is unmet'[1].

[1]   This is considered in more detail at paras 8.165–8.234 below.

8.95

TPCA 1847, s 40, in addition to laying down the requirement to apply for a licence, also places a requirement upon the proprietor or proprietors to sign 'a requisition' for a licence, now commonly referred to as an application form. This details the information that should be contained within that requisition, including the full name and address of the applicant, together with anyone else who is involved in the keeping, employ or letting for hire of the hackney carriage in question. In the case of there being more than one proprietor, eg a partnership, each person with an interest in the vehicle has to complete a requisition.

8.96

In 1847 there was no reference in the law to any person who had lent any money for the purchase of a vehicle, but by 1976 hire-purchase or other credit agreements to fund a new hackney carriage were commonplace. The question has been raised as to whether the finance company is a part-proprietor and can be named on the licence? From the finance company's perspective, this is seen as a way of protecting their interest, akin to a mortgage over a property. However, others express concern that this is a method by which finance companies can acquire hackney carriages without either applying for a licence or, in areas where there is a limit on the number of licences that will be granted, without paying a premium to existing licensees.

8.97

'Proprietor' is not defined in TPCA 1847, but the wording of TPCA 1847, s 40 suggests that the proprietor is one, or one of a number of persons in partnership, who is actually involved in the day-to-day activity of the use of the vehicle as a hackney carriage. Section 40 specifies that the requisition, must state:

'... the name and surname and place of abode of the person applying for such licence, and of every proprietor or part proprietor of such carriage, or person concerned, either solely or in partnership with any other person, in the keeping, employing, or letting to hire of such carriage; ...'

This is reinforced by the Local Government (Miscellaneous Provisions) Act 1976 ('LG(MP)A 1976'), s 80, which defines 'proprietor' as follows:

> '"proprietor" includes a part-proprietor and, in relation to a vehicle which is the subject of a hiring agreement or hire-purchase agreement, means the person in possession of the vehicle under that agreement;'

which suggests that a finance company, however the purchase of the vehicle is being funded by them, hire-purchase, lease purchase, personal loan or whatever, is not a proprietor. Accordingly, a finance company should not be mentioned on the requisition, nor should they be recorded on the vehicle licence.

Suitability of the Applicant/Proprietor

8.98

At this point it is worth considering what a hackney carriage actually does. Clearly they transport people from where they are, to where they want to be, in a convenient, safe and comfortable manner, but the impact of a licensed hackney carriage goes beyond that.

Hackney carriages are seen everywhere across the United Kingdom, at all times of the day and night, in any location. As a result the presence of a hackney carriage does not elicit any interest or curiosity. This can be contrasted with the unexpected presence of a van in the small hours of the morning.

As a consequence of this, hackney carriages provide the ideal transportation system for any form of contraband, whether that is drugs, guns, illicit alcohol or tobacco, male or female prostitutes, or children who may be at risk of, or are being, abused.

In relation to hackney carriages[1] there is no test of fitness and propriety for the proprietor. This can be contrasted with the position in relation to both hackney carriage and private hire drivers and private hire operators[2]. However TPCA 1847, s 37 gives the local authority complete discretion over granting the licence, and the only situation where that changes is where there is significant unmet demand for hackney carriage services within the district (or zone)[3].

This discretion is usually exercised in respect of the vehicle, both its size and specification and also its mechanical suitability, but it is equally applicable in respect of the suitability of the proprietor.

The local authority would not want to grant a hackney carriage licence (or a fleet of hackney carriage licences) to a drug dealer, gun-runner, person controlling prostitutes, or child abuser and accordingly local authorities must make suitable and appropriate enquiries about the character of such applicants.

Unlike hackney carriage and private hire drivers, the Rehabilitation of Offenders Act 1974 (Exceptions) (Amendment) Order 2002 does not cover hackney carriage proprietors who are therefore not excluded from the workings of the Rehabilitation of Offenders Act 1974 ('ROA 1974'). This means that convictions become 'spent' in relation to a hackney carriage proprietor. However, the ruling of the High Court in *Adamson v Waveney District Council*[4] means that local authorities can take spent convictions into account when determining the suitability of an applicant to hold a hackney carriage proprietors licence.

In addition, the fact that the role of the hackney carriage proprietor is not an exempt occupation for ROA 1974 means that it is not possible to obtain an Enhanced DBS check. However, the applicant (or licensee on renewal) can be asked to obtain a Basic Disclosure from Disclosure Scotland. This can be combined with a statutory declaration as part of the application process requiring the applicant to list all previous convictions, together with other relevant material information in a similar fashion to hackney carriage and private hire drivers[5].

Although this is by no means a perfect system, it does give local authorities a reasonable basis for making an informed decision as to the safety and suitability of an applicant or existing hackney carriage proprietor.

As with hackney carriage and private hire drivers, it is not only permissible but eminently sensible to have a clear and transparent policy in relation to previous convictions and other matters for hackney carriage proprietors.

To enable consistent and informed decisions to be made, it is useful to have a working test of safety and suitability for hackney carriage proprietors licence. A possible test would be:

'Would I be comfortable allowing this person to have control of a licensed vehicle that can travel anywhere, at any time of the day or night without arousing suspicion and be satisfied that he/she would not allow it to be used for criminal or other unacceptable purposes and be confident that he/she would maintain it to an acceptable standard throughout the period of the licence?'

It can be seen that this also encompasses a requirement on the applicant to maintain the vehicle to an acceptable standard, and this will be considered below at para 8.144.

It is also useful to note that s 57(1) of LG(MP)A 1976 allows the local authority to:

'require any applicant for a licence under the Act of 1847 or under this Part of this Act to submit to them such information as they may reasonably consider necessary to enable them to determine whether the licence should be granted and whether conditions should be attached to any such licence.'

Section 57(2)(c) allows the local authority to enquire about the character of directors and company secretaries where an application for a private hire operator's licence is made by a limited company. Although s 57(2)(c) is stated to only apply to applications for a private hire operator's licence, as that is clearly stated to be without prejudice to subsection (1), therefore the local authority can make any enquiries that it feels are necessary and can clearly investigate and consider the fitness and propriety of limited companies, their secretaries and directors and any convictions recorded against the company whilst an applicant was a secretary or director.

---

[1] Exactly the same considerations apply to private hire vehicles – See Chapter 13, para 13.6.

[2] See Chapter 10, para 10.21 onwards for consideration of fitness and propriety for hackney carriage and private hire drivers and private hire operators.

3   See para 8.167 onwards below.
4   [1997] 2 All ER 898, QBD – see Chapter 5, para 5.11.
5   See Chapter 10, para 10.21 onwards.

Key Cabs Ltd T/A Taxifast v Plymouth City Council

8.99

> Does an application for hackney carriage proprietor's licence have to relate to a specific vehicle, or can it be an application in principle for a particular type of vehicle? Held: It must relate to a specific vehicle.

The case of *Key Cabs Ltd T/A Taxifast v Plymouth City Council*[1] considered the question of an application for a hackney carriage proprietor's licence, specifically whether the application had to relate to a vehicle owned by the applicant, or whether it could be an application in principle and then a suitable vehicle would be acquired if the application was successful. The applicant had intended to apply for 30 hackney carriage proprietor's licences (Plymouth being an authority that had a limit on the number of hackney carriage proprietor's licences it would issue) and after a long and involved period[2] appealed against the perceived refusal by Plymouth to grant the licences. The 'applications' were made by means of a letter and at the appeal heard before the Crown Court, the council raised the point that TPCA 1847, s 40 required the application to be made in respect of an identified vehicle owned by the applicant. This was considered and the rulings in both *R v Weymouth Borough Council ex parte Teletax (Weymouth) Ltd*[3] and *R (Kelly) v Liverpool Crown Court and another*[4], but there was no conclusive earlier decision.

Mitting J then gave his judgment in the following terms[5]:

'23. Accordingly, the question is open for decision by me without there being binding authority directly in point either way. However, for the reasons which I have indicated in the wording of the statute and in the observations of Lord Goddard CJ in *ex parte Teletax*, there can only be one answer to the underlying question. This regulatory regime requires, at a minimum, that the vehicle or vehicles in respect of which a requisition is made must be identified – and in the ordinary case in existence – when the requisition is made. Otherwise it is difficult to see how the requirements of section 40 could be complied with, or indeed how the person making the requisition could avoid committing the low-level criminal offence specified in the section. It is simply not possible to identify a proprietor of a vehicle in the absence of an identified vehicle. In the ordinary case that will require a vehicle to be in existence, even though not necessarily in the ownership of the person making the requisition. It is theoretically possible to envisage such a person applying in respect of vehicles which have not yet been manufactured, but in respect of which the manufacturer is able to offer advance identification, by chassis number or some other such means, of a vehicle which will be built. But that situation is unlikely to arise often.

24. That ruling has, of course, for the operators of taxis unfortunate economic consequences. It means, as the appellant contends, that a proprietor of a taxi business may incur very substantial expenditure on equipping himself with a fleet (or putting himself in a position to acquire such a fleet) in circumstances in which he does not know one way or other whether or not licences will be granted. That is an unsatisfactory aspect of this regulatory regime, but it is for Parliament and not the courts to address it.'

Accordingly, any application for a hackney carriage proprietor's licence must identify the specific vehicle which is the subject of the application.

Most local authorities have standard forms for this application, or requisition, for a hackney carriage proprietor's licence.

1   [2007] EWHC 2837 (Admin), [2008] LLR 68, Admin Ct.
2   Considered at paras 2 to 8 per Mitting J.
3   [1947] KB 583.
4   [2006] EWCA Civ 11.
5   Key Cabs Ltd T/A Taxifast v Plymouth City Council [2007] EWHC 2837 (Admin) (8 November 2007) at paras 23 and 24.

Cannock Chase District Council v Alldritt

8.100

> Does a certificate of insurance for hackney carriage use have to accompany an application for a hackney carriage proprietors licence? Held: No, the licence can be granted on the principle that it will not be issued until a certificate of insurance is provided.

One of the standard requirements in a hackney carriage proprietor's licence application (and, indeed, in a private hire vehicle application) is a requirement that the application must be accompanied by a registration document for the vehicle and a valid insurance certificate for the vehicle. In the case of *Cannock Chase District Council v Alldritt*[1] (a case which primarily concerns the granting of hackney carriage proprietor's licences), a second question arose. It was considered in the judgment of Mann LJ as follows (at 4B):

'A second point raised by the Crown Court, and which arose out of a consideration of the applications made by Mr. Alldritt [the applicant for a number of hackney carriage proprietor's licences] was this:

"Was the Crown Court correct in holding as unlawful the condition imposed by the District Council, that an applicant for a hackney carriage licence must present, with his application, a certificate of insurance in respect of the vehicle it is sought to licence that is valid at the time of making the application?"

The district council has, as might be expected, a form of application for licence in respect of Hackney carriage vehicles, and it seeks information.

Under the rubric "insurance" there are questions as to the name of the company, as to whether all third party and passenger risks are covered, as to the period of the policy and as to its date. Overleaf there is the admonition, "This application must be accompanied by the following: (i) Registration Document for the Vehicle (ii) Valid Insurance Certificate, (iii) Fee".

The Crown Court seems to have proceeded upon the basis that an application would be treated as invalid by the district council unless accompanied by a valid insurance certificate. Mr. Stephens on behalf of the council disclaims, as I understand him, that position. He draws attention to section 57(1) of the Local Government (Miscellaneous Provisions) Act 1976 which provides:

> "A district council may require any applicant for a licence under the Act of 1847 or under this Part of this Act to submit to them such information as they may reasonably consider necessary to enable them to determine whether the licence should be granted and whether conditions should be attached to any such licence."

Mr. Stephens submits that the insurance requests are requests which are reasonable within the meaning of that power. I agree with that submission without hesitation. I also agree that where there is a certificate of insurance it would be reasonable to require its production for inspection. However, I could not agree that an application should not be considered unless it is accompanied by a certificate of insurance. That requirement is not one which in my view is authorised by section 57, or for that matter any other provision in relation to the licensing of vehicles, and accordingly a refusal to entertain on that ground would in any judgement be unlawful.

As I understand it, the district council does not dissent from that and is content that its request for information might be answered "not yet arranged" or "to be arranged". Such an answer might well be one for a person who has not previously had a licence for his vehicle and who does not wish to incur expenditure on insuring it as a Hackney before he gets a plate for it. I think the difficulty would be removed if the form made it clear that there was a qualification [This application must be accompanied by the following: ... (ii) Valid Insurance Certificate] "... if any".

Thus, if the question posed by the Crown-Court which I have read is read in the sense in which I think it is intended to be read the answer is that it is unlawful to refuse to consider an application unless a certificate of insurance is in force. However, a request for information is in my view perfectly appropriate.'

It therefore seems that an application can be made on the basis that if it is successful, a policy of insurance will be provided, rather than it being a condition precedent to the consideration of the application. This certainly seems reasonable, although a local authority would be well advised not to part with the licence, once it has been granted, until they confirm the existence of the insurance policy. This principle would appear to be capable of being extended to the matter of the vehicle registration document as well. An applicant may be reluctant to invest in a vehicle until he is certain that he will be granted a licence. A similar approach would appear reasonable.

[1]   (28 January 1993, unreported), DC.

Challoner v Evans

8.101

> Can a licensed hackney carriage be sold whilst the licence plate is retained by the vendors? Held: No. The vehicle and licence plate (and therefore licence) are indivisible.

The case of *Challoner v Evans*[1] makes it clear that the plate belongs to the local authority and cannot be disposed of separately from the vehicle. In this case, the defendant sold the vehicle, but attempted to retain the plate and 'rent' the plate to the purchaser of the vehicle. When he applied for renewal of the licence, he committed an offence under TPCA 1847, s 40, as he declared that he was the proprietor of the hackney carriage when he had, in fact, sold the vehicle. In that case, Croom-Johnson LJ concluded:

> 'In my view, on the facts as the Justices found them, Mr Evans [who applied for the renewal] was not concerned in the employment for hire of any Hackney carriage by Mr Holledge [the owner of the vehicle]. It was Mr Holledge who was employing the Vauxhall Cavalier for hire. The same position would have continued had the licence been granted in accordance with the application which was made on the 29th November 1984. It is quite clear on the facts found by the justices that it was Mr Holledge and nobody else who was the proprietor of the Hackney carriage. In those circumstances, in filling in his own name as the sole proprietor of the vehicle Mr Evans did commit the offence with which he was charged.'

[1]   (1986) Times, 22 November.

Procedure

8.102

There are specific points which need to be contained within the licence itself as issued by the local authority and those are laid down in TPCA 1847, s 41[1]. They include:

- the name and address of everyone who is either a proprietor or who has an interest in the vehicle; and
- the number of the licence which corresponds to the number on the plate attached to the hackney carriage.

In addition, local authorities are given a wide discretion, by s 41, to include any other information that they think may be relevant. This will often include the make and model of the vehicle that has been licensed together with the registration number, the seating capacity of the hackney carriage, together with any conditions that are attached to the licence under LG(MP)A 1976, s 47[2].

1   See Appendix I.
2   See para 8.106 below.

8.103

The local authority must register the licence, after it has been completed and that registration must be recorded in 'a book to be provided by the Clerk of the Commissioners' for that purpose. It is certainly implied that the Register will contain all the details that are required to be included in the licence, and that would be a sensible approach, as otherwise the Register could easily be both meaningless and useless. TPCA 1847, s 42[1] goes on to state that there should be 'columns or places for entries to made of every offence committed by any proprietor or driver or person attending such carriage'. It is quite sensible that this information be recorded and that it should be recorded by the local authority. What is less clear is whether compliance with the law is achieved if the information is recorded in any form other than in a book. Most local authorities use computer programs for recording this information, and the use of 'a book' is now extremely antiquated[2].

1   See Appendix I.
2   Any authorities that do not use computers will use card indexes or some other filing mechanism.

8.104

Whatever method is used, to comply fully with the requirements of TPCA 1847, s 42, it must be open to inspection by anyone, not just someone either involved in the trade or from the local authority itself, at any reasonable time and without payment. 'Reasonable time' is usually taken to mean during the normal office hours of the local authority concerned.

8.105

The question of recording of criminal offences raises some important points. Does this mean all criminal convictions, or is it limited to those offences related to hackney carriage use? The wording in the Act is not limited, and therefore appears to mean all criminal offences, irrespective of subject matter. If this is the case, does the Rehabilitation of Offenders Act 1974 apply? As a hackney carriage proprietor is not a listed occupation in the Rehabilitation of Offenders (Exemptions) Order 1975, it appears that it does. What then is the practical impact of this requirement?

Applicants for hackney carriage proprietor's licences should already have revealed their criminal convictions as part of their application process[1]. They should then be made aware of this requirement and it should be made clear that live convictions will be placed on the public register and then be accessible to the general public on request. As this information will then be revealed with the consent of the applicant, this will overcome any concerns relating to the Data Protection Act.

There is a further problem in relation to offences that are not disclosed by the applicant, but which are then revealed on a DBS check. The local authority cannot publish these without the consent of the applicant as to do so would be a breach of the Police Act 1997, s 124. Accordingly, it appears that it also needs to be made clear on the application form that the applicant consents to the publication of any convictions that they have not revealed but which come to light as a result of the DBS check.

Finally, the local authority must ensure that once a conviction is spent under the Rehabilitation of Offenders Act 1974, it is removed from the public register.

It is not clear how many, if any, local authorities take this approach.

1   See para 8.98 above.

Conditions

8.106

The LG(MP)A 1976, s 47 gives the local authority discretionary powers in relation to hackney carriage proprietor's licences:

'Licensing of hackney carriages

47–(1) A district council may attach to the grant of a licence of a hackney carriage under the Act of 1847 such conditions as the district council may consider reasonably necessary.

(2) Without prejudice to the generality of the foregoing subsection, a district council may require any hackney carriage licensed by them under the Act of 1847 [TPCA 1847] to be of such design or appearance or bear such distinguishing marks as shall clearly identify it as a hackney carriage.

(3) Any person aggrieved by any conditions attached to such a licence may appeal to a magistrates' court.'

8.107

The power to attach conditions is extremely wide. There is a wide range of conditions imposed by local authorities, eg the appearance of the vehicle, including size, colour and age. Any conditions that may be attached will be dependent upon the policies of the local authority. Conditions should only be attached to reflect the policy of the local authority and it is important that the policies have been correctly made and approved[1]. If a policy is not backed up by conditions attached to the licence, it will be unenforceable. Conversely, conditions attached without the preceding policy may be ultra vires, depending upon which part of the council (full council, licensing committee or officer) imposed the condition. If the authority has yet to grant a licence subject to any condition, it needs to express itself as adopting a policy that such conditions will be attached to hackney carriage proprietor's licences in the future.

A right of appeal exists against any condition attached to a hackney carriage proprietor's licence (see LG(MP)A 1976, s 47(3) and para 8.126 below).

There are a number of common conditions attached to hackney carriage proprietor's licences by local authorities under LG(MP)A 1976, s 47(1), which generally do not attract controversy. These include:

- at least 400mm width per person across the back seat[2];
- carrying of first aid kits[3];
- cleanliness and tidiness of the vehicle;
- carrying of a fire extinguisher[4];
- advertising to be displayed on or in the vehicle only with the approval of the local authority.

Policies and conditions are frequently challenged. A policy can only be challenged by means of judicial review in the High Court. Where a condition is attached to a licence, it can be challenged by appeal to the magistrates' (using the right of appeal contained in LG(MP)A 1976, s 47(3)) and subsequent appeals to the High Court by way of case stated or judicial review

The following paragraphs examine some of those appeals that have been considered by the High Court or Court of Appeal (although there are some references to Crown Court decisions where there is no High Court decision on the point).

[1]   For consideration of the policy making process, please see Chapter 2, para 2.47 onwards.
[2]   There is no national standard for the minimum seat size for a passenger seat in a hackney carriage. The 400mm width is derived from para 9 of Sch 6 to the Road Vehicles (Construction and Use) Regulations 1986, SI 1986/1078 in relation to minibuses. Notwithstanding the lack of statutory requirement, it is a measurement in common use.
[3]   This is a requirement for self employed drivers under the Health and Safety (First-Aid) Regulations 1981, SI 1981/917 made under the Health & Safety at Work Etc. Act 1974.
[4]   This is required under byelaw 3(h) of the model byelaws. See Appendix II.

AGE AND TYPE OF VEHICLE

R v Hyndburn Borough Council, ex p Rauf and Kasim

8.108

> Can a council introduce an age policy for vehicles which does not contain an 'exceptional condition' clause? Held: Yes, because a Council can always depart from a policy.

In the case of *R v Hyndburn Borough Council, ex p Rauf and Kasim*[1], the High Court held that it was possible, under LG(MP)A 1976, s 47(1)[2], to impose the condition on the grant of a licence that no licence would be granted to a vehicle that was over a specified age. Hyndburn Borough Council had introduced the following policy to improve the reliability, safety and overall standards of the vehicles licensed by the council:

'(1)   That private hire and hackney carriage vehicles must be no more than 3 years old when first registered [ie licensed as a private hire and hackney carriage vehicle];

(2) That the maximum age of a private hire and hackney carriage vehicle must be no more than 7 years;

(3) That the maximum age of an FX4 [purpose-designed and built hackney carriage] must be no more than 11 years.'

This was challenged on the grounds that it was unlawful, going beyond the powers contained in either LG(MP)A 1976, s 47(1), in relation to hackney carriages, or LG(MP)A 1976, s 48(2), in relation to private hire vehicles; that it fettered the discretion of the authority; and was *Wednesbury* unreasonable. Dismissing the application, Kennedy J stated (at 16C):

'In the present case ... this local authority did give such consideration as was appropriate to this application. It indicated in the letter which it wrote in reply to it that the application was refused in line with the policy and that did not indicate that it was shutting its ears to any application, either considered individually or an application which amounted to an application to change the policy as a whole.

In those circumstances, it seems to me, the stance adopted by the local authority in relation to the application was a lawful one and therefore on the substantive ground ... the application fails.'

[1]   (12 February 1992, unreported), QBD.

[2]   See Appendix I.

8.109

It is worth noting that the reason for the distinction made between the 'ordinary' vehicles and FX4s was because London-style cabs had a separate chassis and were designed for the hackney carriage trade, whereas saloon vehicles were of a unitary or chassis-less construction and were not purpose-designed. This remains true for Metrocabs (the original is no longer in production, but still popular as second hand vehicles, but a new Metrocab is about to be launched) and the London Taxis International ('LTI') vehicles (FX4 and TX1, TX11 and TXIV). Recent years have seen a further blurring of the traditional distinctions by the introduction of MPVs (eg Volkswagen Sharan) and the Eurotaxi. In addition, Transport for London has approved the Mercedes Benz Vito Taxi which is of unitary construction.

8.110

Some authorities had imposed age policies, but allowed an 'exemption clause' to prevent an allegation that, by imposing such a policy, they were fettering their discretion[1]. These policies were usually worded to allow vehicles to be licensed by the local authority if they were older than allowed by the age policy, but only if they were 'exceptionally well-maintained' or in 'exceptional condition'. Such wording led to appeals against refusals because of different interpretation of 'exceptional' etc. As there was no 'exemption clause' in the policy of Hyndburn Borough Council, the judgment in the case supports the view that exemption clauses are not necessary, provided the policy is just that, a policy, not an immutable rule[2].

The DfT '*Best Practice Guide*' addresses age of vehicles and is dubious about the use of age policies[3]:

'Age Limits. It is perfectly possible for an older vehicle to be in good condition. So the setting of an age limit beyond which a local authority will not license vehicles may be arbitrary and inappropriate. But a greater frequency of testing may be appropriate for older vehicles – for example, twice-yearly tests for vehicles more than five years old.'

Whilst it is accepted that older vehicles can be used successfully as hackney carriages, this seems to rather miss the point. The purpose of any age limit is to try and ensure that the licensed vehicles are as safe, reliable and comfortable as possible. Any age policy would not in itself be arbitary, because it must be a policy and the local authority must then consider any application that falls outside the age policy on its own individual merits.

[1] Chapter 2, para 2.47 onwards.
[2] *R v Hyndburn Borough Council, ex p Rauf and Kasim* (12 February 1992, unreported), QBD.
[3] DfT, '*Taxi and Private Hire Vehicle Licensing: Best Practice Guidance*' (October 2006, revised March 2010 at para 22), available at http://www.dft.gov.uk/pgr/regional/taxis/taxiandprivatehirevehiclelic1792. See also Appendix II.

8.111

LG(MP)A 1976, s 47(2)[1] allows the local authority to impose conditions specifically in relation to the design or appearance of the hackney carriages which they license and this has been the subject of a number of court cases.

[1] See Appendix I.

R v Wirral Metropolitan Borough Council, ex p the Wirral Licensed Hackney Carriage Owners Association

8.112

> Can a local authority have a policy that only particular types of vehicle will be licensed as hackney carriages? Held: Yes, provided the policy is based upon a specification, rather than a make and model.

Notwithstanding subsequent cases, possibly the most important is the case of *R v Wirral Metropolitan Borough Council, ex p the Wirral Licensed Hackney Carriage Owners Association*[1] as it forms the basis of the later decisions. Wirral Metropolitan Borough Council resolved that from a certain date, all hackney carriages licensed by the council would have to be of a purpose-built type. Originally, the resolution specifically stated 'FX4', but it was suggested, and accepted, that this might conflict with art 30 of the Treaty of Rome. The resolution was amended to become a specification, rather than a specific make or model of vehicle. One of the reasons for this policy was that it was important for the public to be able to distinguish between hackney carriages and private hire vehicles. Another reason concerned the general suitability of that type of vehicle for hackney carriage work. The Wirral Licensed Taxi Drivers Association challenged the decision. In dismissing the application, Glidewell J said (at 161, para 39):

> 'What are the Council's functions under this legislation in relation to the licensing of taxi cabs? As I see it they are to achieve, so far as they can, the safety, convenience and comfort of passengers in hackney carriages, the safety of other road users and to ensure that there is some way in which those who wish to use either hackney carriages or private hire vehicles can readily distinguish the one type of vehicle from another. That the last is a proper object is to my mind made clear by section 47(2) of the 1976 Act [LG(MP)A 1976, s 47(2)]. I conclude, on the material before me, that the Council's primary purpose was indeed … to introduce a requirement which served to distinguish hackney carriage vehicles from private hire vehicles. But I cannot find that it was the sole purpose, nor can I find that in arriving at its decision, the Council did not take into account other factors. Putting it the other way round, I am satisfied on the material before me that the Council did take into account other factors: safety and convenience. It was not only entitled to do so, but was obliged to do so and it did so. What I think in effect the Council has done, through its relevant committee and the assistance of various reports it has had, is, it has said:
>
> > "We want to ensure that hackney carriages are readily distinguishable from private hire vehicles. We are told that it could be done simply by ensuring that hackney carriages are all of one colour, or bearing distinguishing signs, or we could require that they are all of a particular description. If we adopt the latter requirement it will have the added advantage that we shall be ensuring that the vehicle does have the advantages of robustness, added safety, added convenience of passengers, and that is our view. Thus we take those matters into account in deciding that that is the best way of distinguishing."
>
> I know I am interpreting what the Council has said. This is in effect what is to be read into the reports [placed before it]. I cannot say that in arriving at its decision the Council either took some irrelevant consideration into account, or came to a conclusion to which no reasonable authority could ever have come.'

[1]   [1983] CMLR 150.

WHEELCHAIR-ACCESSIBLE

R v Manchester City Council, ex p Reid and McHugh

8.113

Is a policy that all new hackney carriage licences can only be granted to wheelchair accessible vehicles, and all existing vehicles must be wheelchair accessible within 3 years lawful? Held: Yes it is.

Some authorities went further (and the trend continues) and have required not only an all-London-style cab fleet, but that the fleet itself should be comprised of all wheelchair-accessible vehicles. This was pioneered in the late 1980s by Manchester City Council and was challenged in the case of *R v Manchester City Council, ex p Reid and McHugh*[1]. In the mid-1980s, Manchester City Council was concerned about the provision of transport services for disabled people who used wheelchairs and, when they decided to increase the size of the hackney carriage fleet in Manchester by 100 vehicles, they imposed a condition upon those licences requiring the successful applicants to provide vehicles which were not only based on a London-style cab, but also either already converted for wheelchair access or to be converted within a specified period of time at their own expense. This condition was challenged as being unreasonable. Simon Brown J heard the application for judicial review. He considered the judgment in *R v Wirral Metropolitan Borough Council*[2] and stated (at 185):

'The decision [in the *Wirral* case] is, of course, authority for saying that a council is obliged to have regard to safety and convenience, but not for the converse proposition that the safety, convenience and comfort of passengers are the *only* considerations (apart from section 47(2) of the Act of 1976 question of identification) open to an authority determining what conditions to impose. As it seems to me conditions imposed for the other considerations could well be legitimate, for instance those controlling the display of advertisements, such, indeed, as formed part of the city council's own standard conditions. Even, however, were this not so, I have no difficulty whatever in regarding a facility for transporting the wheelchair-bound disabled as directly relating to the "safe, comfortable and convenient functioning of the taxi" and thus squarely within Mr Frizgerald's [who appeared for the applicants] own formulation. Nor am I in the least attracted to the submission that the wheelchair-bound disabled (or rather that proportion of them who are particularly advantaged by being enabled to remain in their chairs) are too small a minority of the population to be properly regarded as an integral part of the general public. On the contrary, I prefer Mr Hugill's approach that the general public must be taken to comprise many physical minority groups, including for instance the obese, the unusually tall, young children and the disabled.

Ultimately, it must always be a question of fact and degree whether the minority is so small or the advantage to them is so slight or the cost of complying with the provision is so great that the imposition of such a condition cannot be justified.

Mr Fitzgerald further stresses the phrase "reasonably necessary" within the condition-making power. He contends that even putting the city council's case at its highest it was their conclusion only that the proposed facility was an ideal rather than a necessity, their evidence being couched in the explicit language of desirability, not need. This submission also I reject. It seems to me that desirability shades into necessity: what is clearly desirable in the interests of the safety and comfort can by the same token properly be regarded as reasonably necessary.

Nor do I accept Mr Fitzgerald's argument that the conversion condition can be impugned as not reasonably relating to the purpose of the condition-making power, but imposed rather for an ulterior object, that of solving the wider and more general problem of the disabled within Manchester's public transportation system. The contention here is that the council were exercising the power of compulsion over new taxi drivers to make good deficiencies elsewhere in the transport system. But I can see no objection to the council having regard to the existence or lack of alternative facilities for the disabled when deciding how to exercise this condition-making power.'

[1]   (1989) 88 LGR 180.
[2]   [1983] CMLR 150; see para 8.112 above.

8.114

In fact subsequent developments prior to this hearing took the policy of Manchester City Council even further. They had by then imposed a condition requiring all existing licensed hackney carriages within the City to be converted to carry wheelchairs, or failing that, the replacement of the vehicles with purpose-built, wheelchair-accessible vehicles. The cost for this was to be recovered through an increase in fares and as a consequence, by the beginning of 1992, Manchester had the first English fleet of hackney carriages which were all accessible for wheelchair-using travellers.

8.115

Similar policies have now been adopted by a number of local authorities throughout England and Wales.

R v Lincoln City Council, ex p King and Cook, R v Luton Borough Council, ex p Mirza

8.116

> Can a local authority refuse to grant vehicles licences (either new or on renewal) to vehicles which do not comply with a purpose built vehicle policy? Held: Yes it can.

This has been followed in the joined Court of Appeal cases of *R v Lincoln City Council, ex p King and Cook, R v Luton Borough Council, ex p Mirza*[1]. Both were appeals against unsuccessful applications for judicial review.

[1]   (2 February 1995, unreported), CA.

8.117

Both Lincoln City Council and Luton Borough Council had adopted policies that all hackney carriages licensed within their districts had to be wheelchair accessible. The challenge to Lincoln City Council was against a refusal to grant hackney carriage licences to non-wheelchair accessible vehicles owned by

Mr King and by Mr Cook. The challenge Luton Borough Council faced was slightly different. Mr Mirza had an accident in his hackney carriage and could not afford to repair it, so asked Luton Borough Council if they would allow him to run a saloon vehicle as a hackney carriage in the intervening period. This was considered by the local authority and rejected.

8.118

An application for judicial review by King and Cook was rejected as there was another remedy available, namely an appeal against the refusal to grant the licences using the powers contained in LG(MP)A 1976, s 60(3)[1]. The same point was made in relation to the application by Mirza, which was also rejected.

[1]   See Appendix I.

8.119

Two other grounds were argued on behalf of Mirza. They were:
1.   that the policy conflicted with art 30 of the Treaty of Rome, and
2.   that the decision was *Wednesbury* unreasonable.

8.120

In *Mirza*'s case[1] the Divisional Court judgment concentrated on the question of alleged incompatibility between the policy and art 30 of the Treaty of Rome. The decision in *R v Metropolitan Borough Council of Wirral, ex p The Wirral Licensed Taxi Owners Association*[2] was approved, as were some obiter remarks in the unreported case of *R v Doncaster Metropolitan Borough Council, ex p Kelly*[3], where Harrison J approved the *Wirral* approach. Although the European cases of *Keck*[4] and *Boermans*[5] were referred to, these did not detract from the principle in the *Wirral* case. Brooke J stated:

> 'I accept Mr Calver's [for the Council] submissions that the wide policy provided by the Council in this case does not offend against art 30 of the Treaty of Rome. The provisions apply, so far as Mr Mirza is concerned, if he wishes to acquire a vehicle which would qualify for a licence under the Council's policy, to all relevant traders operating within the national territory as well as to the traders abroad within the other Member States. They affect in the same manner, in law and in fact, the marketing of the products in each country.
> Although Mr Crystal valiantly sought to argue that the judgments of the English Courts, particularly, the judgment of Glidewell J, went on a misunderstanding of the principles of European Law, I am completely satisfied that the present jurisprudence of the court makes it quite clear that a provision, such as that laid down by the Luton Borough Council, does not offend art 30. Accordingly, I regard the art 30 point, as did Glidewell J eleven years ago and Harrison J on a provisional basis last July, as unarguable.'

Finally, he rejected the argument that the decision of the local authority was unreasonable in *Wednesbury* terms by saying:

> 'At all events, I have seen a great mass of evidence which shows that this was a policy which the Council, in the exercise of the discretion given to it by statute, could reasonably and lawfully enter into.'

1   *R v Luton Borough Council, ex p Mirza (Riaz Ahmed)* [1995] COD 231, QBD.
2   [1983] CMLR 150; see para 8.112 above.
3   (20 October 1994, unreported).
4   *Keck and Mithouard* Case C-267 268/91 [1993] ECRI-6097, [1995] 1 CMLR 101, ECJ.
5   *Re criminal proceedings against Tankstation't Heukske VOF and JBE Boermans* Case C-401/92 402/92 [1994] ECRI-2199, [1995] 3 CMLR 501, ECJ.

8.121

The appeal to the Court of Appeal was on the basis that the decisions in both King and Cook's[1] cases and Mirza's[2] case were wrong. An additional ground was argued before the Court of Appeal, that Lincoln City Council could not refuse to renew the licences for King and Cook's vehicles, solely because they were not wheelchair-accessible vehicles, by use of LG(MP)A 1976, s 60[3].

1   *R v Lincoln City Council, ex p King and Cook* (20 July 1994, unreported), QBD.
2   *R v Luton Borough Council, ex p Mirza (Riaz Ahmed)* [1995] COD 231, QBD.
3   See Appendix I.

8.122

The court addressed the arguments separately, taking the art 30 of the Treaty of Rome point first. The other aspects of this judgment[1] will be considered at para 8.140 below.

Swinton Thomas LJ took into account the cases considered by Brooke J in the Divisional Court, and concluded (at 6G):

> 'It is said that the policy adopted creates a preference for goods of local manufacture. It is said that the only vehicles which have been specifically manufactured as a taxi and will fulfil the conditions laid down by the policy, are in reality London black cabs. However, with respect to that submission, it does not seem to me to be correct. It is clear from the policy documents themselves that the Councils will license other vehicles, some of them manufactured in other ECC [sic] countries, which are capable of accommodating a person in a wheelchair and will also license vehicles which have been adapted for that purpose.'

He continued (at 7F):

> 'It is true, of course, that the policies adopted by the Councils will result in the vehicles being more expensive for taxi proprietors to buy. That does not, in my judgment, in any way offend Article 30 in itself.

In *R v Metropolitan Borough of Wirral ex parte The Wirral Licensed Taxi Owners Association* [1983] CMLR 150, Glidewell J (as he then was) considered a very similar argument to the one put forward by Mr Langstaff in relation to hackney carriages. There were some factual differences between that case and these cases, but those differences are, in my view, immaterial.

It was suggested that the policy of the Wirral Council offended Article 30. Glidewell J formed the view that that argument was wholly unarguable. Mr Langstaff, in effect, submits that the learned judge was wrong to come to that conclusion.

In *R v Doncaster Metropolitan Borough Council, ex parte Paul Michael Kelly* [20 October 1994, unreported] Harrison J, when considering this point said:

> "Whilst it is not necessary to decide the point, my provisional view is that there is no substance in the argument, because the terms of the policy do not refer to any specific vehicle manufactured in this country, but rather to black London-style purpose-built Hackney Carriage with wheelchair facilities. That does not restrict, in any way, the place where such a vehicle is manufactured. It is open to any manufacturer in a Member State to manufacturer such a vehicle and for it to be imported into this Country. Whether they would do so or not is unknown."

Harrison J decided that application on the basis that the Applicant had a suitable alternative remedy.

In *R v Birmingham City Council, ex parte Wesson* [1992] 3 CMLR 377, a case which appears in the judgment of Brooke J, and a case which did concern quite different facts, Rose J (as he then was) said:

> "The mere fact that the measure may lead to a reduction in the imports to the United Kingdom is not … sufficient to lead to the assumption that Article 30 applies to the measure. … Measures which apply without distinction to imported and domestically produced goods and not intended to regulate trade in goods, and which do not prevent the import or sale of goods even if they effect the outlets through which the goods are distributed, are not caught by Article 30."

The conditions laid down by the two Councils before they will grant licences apply equally to all producers and manufacturers throughout the Community.

In my judgment, contrary Mr Langstaff's [for the appellants, Cook, King and Mirza] submissions, these policies are not discriminatory policies and do not place other manufacturers outside the United Kingdom at a disadvantage. They are simply designed for the assistance of the disabled. Any manufacturer throughout the European Community can comply with those requirements. I agree with the finding of Brooke J that the submission that Article 30 renders these decisions and the policies of the Councils illegal is unarguable.'

Leggatt LJ agreed in the following terms (at 13F):

'On 24 November 1993 the European Court in the joined cases of Keck and Mithourd C-267, C-268/91 reappraised its approach to the interpretation of the Rules of the EEC Treaty relating to competition and freedom of movement within the Community. At paragraph 16 of the judgment of the Court, it was said:

> "… contrary to what has previously been decided, the application to products from other Member States of national provisions restricting or prohibiting certain selling arrangements is not such as to hinder directly or indirectly, actually or potentially, trade between Member States within the meaning of the Dassonville judgment (Case 8/74 [1974] ECR 837), provided that those provisions apply to all affected traders operating within the national territory and provided that they affect in the same manner, in law and in fact, the marketing of domestic products and of those from other Member States."

The policies of the two Councils with which this Court is concerned are not intended to regulate, and do not regulate, trade in goods within the Community. The policies apply to all traders in the United Kingdom; they affect the marketing of domestic products in the same way as those from other Member States; there is no restriction on importation; and manufacturers in the United Kingdom and in other EEC countries have to fulfil the same conditions in order to produce a vehicle which fulfils the Council's requirements.

In my judgment, in neither of the present cases is there any quantitative restriction on imports capable of constituting a breach of Article 30 of the Treaty.'

Finally the court considered the question of whether such policies were unreasonable in *Wednesbury* terms[2]. This argument was dismissed by Swinton Thomas LJ in this way (at 11D):

'Mr Langstaff [for the Appellants, Cook, King and Mirza] submits that the refusal of the Lincoln City Council to grant licences to Mr Cook and Mr King was Wednesbury unreasonable. It is said that it was perverse of the Council to adopt a policy that all taxis should have wheelchair access. It is stressed that these applications were applications for renewal as opposed to new applications. It is said in particular that there was no evidence to support a need for this condition to be included in the licences and indeed, by reference to the bundle, that there was evidence to the contrary effect.

This policy is one which has been adopted – and this is common ground – by a number of Councils, and has been considered previously by the Courts. In these cases there are certainly matters on the facts and on the merits of the applications which might be considered by Magistrates, or by the Crown Court if the appeal is pursued. However, in my judgment it is quite impossible to argue that no local Council, applying its mind properly to the problem, could have reached the decision reached by the Lincoln City Council, either in adopting the policy or in refusing the applications made by Mr King and Mr Cook. Insofar as the reasons for the decisions are concerned, the reasons given were plain and clear, namely that the vehicles failed to comply with condition (3).'

That view accorded with the approach taken by Leggatt LJ who agreed in the following, concise fashion (at 15B):

'I do not regard it as arguable that, in formulating their policy as they have, either Council acted perversely or without due consultation.'

This judgment reinforces the decision in the *Wirral* and *Manchester* cases[3], and removes any doubt that may have lingered that an 'all purpose built' hackney carriage policy is lawful.

The adoption by local authorities of such a policy of only granting hackney carriage proprietor's licences to London-style cabs has become increasingly popular in urban areas and is often referred to as a 'mandatory order'. This has no legal meaning, but is generally accepted to refer to a situation where an all-London-style cab policy is in force.

[1] *R v Lincoln City Council, ex p King and Cook and R v Luton Borough Council, ex p Mirza* (2 February 1995, unreported), CA.

[2] For the other arguments concerning art 30 of the Treaty of Rome, refusal to renew a proprietor's licence and the availability of alternative remedies, see para 8.116 onwards above.

[3] *R v Metropolitan Borough Council of Wirral, ex p The Wirral Licensed Taxi Owners Association* [1983] CMLR 150; see para 8.112 above and *R v Manchester City Council, ex p Reid and McHugh* (1989) 88 LGR 180, see para 8.113 above.

8.123

As was outlined in the *Wirral* case[1], such policies must be worded extremely carefully to avoid any charge of anti-competitive behaviour under European law. The Court of Appeal reinforced this by approving the policies of both Lincoln City Council and Luton Borough Council and reinforcing the fact that such policies did not infringe art 30 of the Treaty of Rome. Policies that refer to specific makes of vehicle are unlikely to succeed should such a challenge be mounted. The most successful way of wording the policy is by measurement of internal and external features, door openings, turning circle etc. The specification adopted by the Public Carriage Office (PCO) in London appears to satisfy the most stringent criteria available, but does not allow Eurotaxis[2] to be used as hackney carriages. Accordingly, if a local authority wished to allow MPVs and Eurotaxis to be licensed, some variation to the PCO specification would be required.

Such a policy must also be viewed in the light of the *Taxi and Private Hire Vehicle Licensing: Best Practice Guidance* re-issued by the DfT in March 2010[3]. Although not statutory guidance to which local authorities are duty bound to have regard to, it must be recognised as being a relevant consideration in *Wednesbury*[4] terms which must be taken into account when considering matters it covers. One such area is the kind of vehicle that the local authority will licence as a hackney carriage.

'VEHICLES

Specification Of Vehicle Types That May Be Licensed

26. The legislation gives local authorities a wide range of discretion over the types of vehicle that they can license as taxis or PHVs. Some authorities specify conditions that in practice can only be met by purpose-built vehicles but the majority license a range of vehicles.

27. Normally, the best practice is for local licensing authorities to adopt the principle of specifying as many different types of vehicle as possible. Indeed, local authorities might usefully set down a range of general criteria, leaving it open to the taxi and PHV trades to put forward vehicles of their own choice which can be shown to meet those criteria. In that way there can be flexibility for new vehicle types to be readily taken into account.

28. It is suggested that local licensing authorities should give very careful consideration to a policy which automatically rules out particular types of vehicle or prescribes only one type or a small number of types of vehicle. For example, the Department believes authorities should be particularly cautious about specifying only purpose-built taxis, with the strict constraint on supply that that implies. But of course the purpose-built vehicles are amongst those which a local authority could be expected to license. Similarly, it may be too restrictive to automatically rule out considering Multi-Purpose Vehicles, or to license them for fewer passengers than their seating capacity (provided of course that the capacity of the vehicle is not more than eight passengers).'

The impact of such a policy on hackney carriage proprietors must also be considered. Wheelchair accessible vehicles are more expensive that saloons and the benefit to the wheelchair-bound disabled must be balanced against a possible overall reduction in the number of hackney carriages.

However, the suitability of wheelchair accessible vehicles for disabled people who are not wheelchair bound is open to question[5]. This is considered in the DfT *Taxi and Private Hire Vehicle Licensing: Best Practice Guidance* in the following terms[6]:

'ACCESSIBILITY

13. The Minister of State for Transport has now announced the way forward on accessibility for taxis and PHVs. His statement can be viewed on the Department's website at: http://www.dft.gov.uk/press/speechesstatements/statements/accesstotaxis. The Department will be taking forward demonstration schemes in three local authority areas to research the needs of people with disabilities in order to produce guidance about the most appropriate provision. In the meantime, the Department recognises that some local licensing authorities will want to make progress on enhancing accessible taxi provision and the guidance outlined below constitutes the Department's advice on how this might be achieved in advance of the comprehensive and dedicated guidance which will arise from the demonstration schemes.

14. Different accessibility considerations apply between taxis and PHVs. Taxis can be hired on the spot, in the street or at a rank, by the customer

dealing directly with a driver. PHVs can only be booked through an operator. It is important that a disabled person should be able to hire a taxi on the spot with the minimum delay or inconvenience, and having accessible taxis available helps to make that possible. For PHVs, it may be more appropriate for a local authority to license any type of saloon car, noting that some PHV operators offer accessible vehicles in their fleet. The Department has produced a leaflet on the ergonomic requirements for accessible taxis that is available from: http://www.dft.gov.uk/transportforyou/access/taxis/pubs/research'

It remains to be seen what view will be taken in the future by the courts in relation to proposals by local authorities for all purpose built/wheelchair accessible hackney carriages[7].

1   *R v Metropolitan Borough Council of Wirral, ex p The Wirral Licensed Taxi Owners Association* [1983] CMLR 150; see para 8.112 above.

2   See especially *R (on the application of Lunt) v Liverpool City Council* [2009] EWHC 2356 (Admin), [2010] RTR 5, [2010] 1 CMLR 14 at Chapter 9, para 9.53.

3   DfT, *'Taxi and Private Hire Vehicle Licensing: Best Practice Guidance'* (October 2006, revised March 2010), available from http://www.dft.gov.uk/pgr/regional/taxis/taxiandprivatehirevehiclelic1792 See Appendix I.

4   *Associated Provincial Picture Houses Ltd v Wednesbury Corpn* [1948] 1 KB 223, CA; see Chapter 2, para 2.70 onwards for further details.

5   See Chapter 9, para 9.48 onwards.

6   DfT, *'Taxi and Private Hire Vehicle Licensing: Best Practice Guidance'* (October 2006, revised March 2010), available from http://www.dft.gov.uk/pgr/regional/taxis/taxiandprivatehirevehiclelic1792 See Appendix I.

7   The provisions of the Equality Act 2010 in relation to wheelchair accessible hackney carriages are considered in Chapter 9 at para 9.54 onwards.

LIVERY OR COLOUR SCHEMES

8.124

In addition to the actual mechanical specification of the vehicle, conditions can be attached in relation to its visual appearance and a number of authorities have liveries for their hackney carriages. In some cases, this is the traditional black, especially in the case of purpose-built vehicles, but other authorities are rather more imaginative and have contrasting bonnet and boot lids or doors. Once again, the justification for this is to assist the travelling public in identifying a hackney carriage. Other conditions of a similar type include the requirement for illuminated roof signs, possibly with or without specified wording, badges affixed to the vehicles in prominent places (on the doors, wings, bonnets and boot lids, on the roof or wherever the council may think fit) and the presence of specified wording on the vehicles' sides.

8.125

Some authorities allow advertising on the vehicles, either by means of advertisements being allowed on specified areas of the vehicle (often with maximum sizes for the adverts) or by means of 'sponsored' vehicles, whereby the vehicle is decorated[1] all over in a particular livery advertising a certain product or company. This is popular in large cities on purpose-built vehicles, but seems less common on either saloon-type vehicles or in rural areas. Of those authorities that do allow such sponsored vehicles, a number have within the conditions requirements that the design must be submitted to the council for prior approval and some stipulate that any sponsorship that endorses alcohol products will not be accepted. It is not entirely clear the extent of the powers a local authority has to limit the type of advertisement which it will allow through sponsored vehicles, other than preventing advertisements which in themselves would be unlawful. Any form of filtering or censorship of otherwise lawful advertisements might render the condition itself unreasonable.

[1] This is usually by means of vinyl covering, rather than paint. It does change the appearance of the vehicle, and it seems that the DVLA V5 registration document (the 'log-book') should be amended to reflect a change in colour.

Appeal against any conditions imposed

8.126

A right of appeal is conferred by LG(MP)A 1976, s 47(3)[1], which provides that 'any person aggrieved by any conditions attached to such a [hackney carriage proprietor's] licence may appeal to a magistrates' court'[2]. It should be noted that it is only when the condition has been attached to such a licence that an appeal can be brought, and that a proposal made by the council that a condition will be imposed or the adoption of a policy to that effect is not sufficient to trigger the appeal mechanism.

Any such appeal must be brought within 21 days from the date on which the requirement was imposed. This will be when the licence is first granted, or renewed. Accordingly, every year there is an opportunity to challenge any conditions, although if the condition was accepted in previous years, it may be difficult to justify what amounts to an extremely delayed appeal against a requirement that has been accepted in the past.

[1] See Appendix I.
[2] For the mechanics of this, see Chapter 3, para 3.4 onwards on appeals.

8.127

It is worth making the point here that as there is a statutory appeal mechanism, in general, that mechanism should be exhausted before the question of judicial review arises[1]. However, in the situation outlined above, where the condition has yet to be applied to any licence but the proposal has been approved or the policy has been adopted by the council in respect of future licences, it seems that there would then be a possibility of seeking a judicial review of that decision. Although this is possible, in practical terms, especially in relation to cost, it would probably be more effective for the aggrieved parties (which will undoubtedly be more than one member of the trade) to wait until the condition is actually applied to a licence and then back an appeal by that licence holder against the provision rather than seek a judicial review[2].

¹   See eg *R v Blackpool Borough Council, ex p Red Cab Taxis Ltd* [1994] RTR 402, QBD; Chapter 3,
     para 3.49.
²   See Chapter 3, para 3.47 for more details of judicial review.

THE LICENCE ITSELF

Procedure

8.128

Although TPCA 1847, s 43¹ makes it a requirement that the licence should
be sealed by the district council and should not last for more than a year,
LG(MP)A 1976, s 79² means that it is acceptable for the licence simply to be
signed by an authorised officer rather than sealed.

¹   See Appendix I.
²   See Appendix I.

8.129

LG(MP)A 1976, however, makes no alteration to the prohibition on granting
hackney carriage proprietor's licences for more than a year. The Town Police
Clauses Act 1889, s 5¹ allows for licences to be granted for a shorter period, and
a number of district councils use this provision to take the licence up to a general
renewal date that the council specifies. Some authorities have hackney carriage
proprietor's licences which all expire on the same date, with the inevitable spike
in administration that will create. Others take the view that the licence will run
for a year from whenever the licence is granted and, accordingly, their renewals
are staggered throughout the year. This evens out the administrative process.

¹   See Appendix I.

8.130

TPCA 1847, s 44¹ requires a proprietor to inform the council within seven
days of a change of address and imposes a penalty for failing to comply with
this requirement of a fine not exceeding level 1 on summary conviction. It also
requires the council 'by their clerk' to endorse the change on the licence and
sign it. Again, many authorities issue a substitute licence in these circumstances
and, whilst this may not be absolutely legally correct, it will certainly make for
greater clarity in situations where proprietors move more than once within the
year. It does not take a great deal of imagination to realise how complex a licence
could become if the proprietor moved two or three times throughout the life of
the licence.

¹   See Appendix I.

8.131

If the proprietor transfers his interest to another person he must, under
LG(MP)A 1976, s 49¹, inform the council of this change within 14 days of the

transfer. This must be notified in writing and he must specify the name and address of the person to whom his interest has been transferred. Once such a notice has been received by the district council, then, under TPCA 1847, s 42[2], the council must register it. Provided that such notice is given to the council within the 14-day period, the council cannot refuse to register it.

[1]   See Appendix I.
[2]   See Appendix I.

R v Weymouth Borough Council, ex p Teletax (Weymouth) Ltd
8.132

> Can a local authority refuse to register a transfer of a vehicle licence from one proprietor to another? Held: No, any such transfer must be acknowledged and accepted by the local authority.

This was confirmed in the case of *R v Weymouth Borough Council, ex p Teletax (Weymouth) Ltd*[1], which addressed the question of whether a local authority had to record a transfer of a hackney carriage proprietor's licence on the sale of such a licence from one licensee to another. This point is not specifically addressed in the legislation. In this case, Teletax Ltd bought five hackney carriages from existing proprietors who had current licences and applied to Weymouth Borough Council for those licenses to be transferred to them. The council was reluctant to do this, apparently because it felt that by purchasing the licences, Teletax had acquired proprietor's licences ahead of people who had been in a waiting list for some time.

Goddard LCJ stated (at 590):

> 'What then is the effect of these sections [of TPCA 1847]? In my opinion, they clearly show that the licence is granted to the carriage, and that the licence remains in force for a year from the time when it is granted, or until the next annual licensing meeting of the commissioners, if they appoint a date before the annual granting of these licences. What then is to happen if during that a year a change of proprietorship takes place? There is the vehicle; it has a licence attached to it. There is nothing in this Act which says that the vehicle may not be sold, or may only be sold with the consent of the council. There is no provision here to say that if a person has obtained a licence for a cab and disposes of it, or dies, that he or his personal representatives must surrender the licence. What is necessary is that the register should be kept in order and kept up to date. Therefore, it seems to me that, by necessary implication, a person who buys a cab which has been licensed is under a duty to go to the local authority and say: "I am now the proprietor of this cab which you licensed for a year; please therefore enter me in the register as the proprietor, and substitute my name on the licence granted in respect of the cab, in the place of the name of the earlier proprietor."'

His Lordship took the view that there was no power for the local authority not to register the transfer of these licences. Atkinson J concurred with Lord Goddard and added (at 593):

> 'There is one consideration, however, which I think assists the applicants here, and that is the position of the proprietor who has sold his hackney carriage. He must be entitled to have his name removed from the register, and to have his name removed from the licence which has been granted. If he gave notice to the commissioners, similar to the notice required by section 44, I should have thought that if they refused to remove his name from the register, he could come here for mandamus[2] to make them do so. This seems to indicate that the council must be bound to take notice of changes of ownership and to keep their register accurate in accordance with the true position. If the old proprietor has a right to his name removed, I should have thought it was equally clear that the new proprietor has a right to have his name inserted in the place of that of the old proprietor.'

However, the council may then refuse to renew the licence for the new proprietor under LG(MP)A 1976, s 60(1)[3]. This would be necessary where the new proprietor was not a safe and suitable person, or who had a poor record of vehicle maintenance[4].

[1]   [1947] KB 583.
[2]   Now a mandatory order under the Civil Procedure Rules 1998.
[3]   See Appendix I.
[4]   See para 8.98 above.

Transfer of vehicles

8.133

Within the lifetime of a licence, it may be necessary or desirable to replace the original vehicle with another, eg because it is newer or because of accident, damage or breakdown. Strangely, there is no mention within the legislation of transferring the licence to a substitute vehicle. How then can this be achieved?

8.134

In the absence of a statutory mechanism, a practical approach is required. It is necessary for the proprietor to surrender his licence in respect of the original vehicle, and the local authority then issues a new licence in respect of the replacement vehicle.

8.135

That process poses no problems where there is an unlimited number of hackney carriages, but if there is a limit in place, it is essential that this process is undertaken in the clear recognition that the original licensee will be granted the new licence. To achieve this it is vital that this process is not regarded as the issue of a surrendered licence, but rather, the only mechanism whereby a replacement vehicle can be licensed.

8.136

As this is the only mechanism whereby a different vehicle can be used as a hackney carriage under an existing proprietor's licence, the same approach must be taken in respect of vehicles which have been damaged as a result of an accident, or which need to be taken off the road for a lengthy period for maintenance. No matter how long the replacement vehicle is to be used for, a 'transfer' as outlined above must be undertaken for the replacement vehicle, and again when the original vehicle is returned to service.

8.137

It is interesting to note that in neither TPCA 1847 nor LG(MP)A 1976 are there any qualification requirements for hackney carriage proprietors on first application, although as there is a discretion to grant the licence (TPCA 1847, s 47), clearly the local authority could refuse if they felt that the applicant was not a suitable person. On renewal, LG(MP)A 1976, s 60(1)(b) and (c)[1] may have an effect if the council take the view that the proprietor has either committed an offence under either TPCA 1847 or LG(MP)A 1976, in the case of s 60(1)(b), or 'any other reasonable cause', in relation to s 60(1)(c). That wording does not have to be construed ejusdem generis with the wording contained in s 60(1)(a) or (b). That means that 'any other reasonable cause' does not have to be linked in any way with an offence committed under hackney carriage legislation and the council can take any other matter into account that is reasonable in the circumstances.

[1]   See Appendix I.

Norwich City Council v Thurtle and Watcham

8.138

> Do the words 'any other reasonable cause' relate to the committing of an offence under either the 1847 or 1976 Acts? Held: No, they are not related and can refer to any matter.

This was the decision in the case of *Norwich City Council v Thurtle and Watcham*[1]. Mr Watcham had held eight private hire vehicle licences and was convicted for dishonestly handling goods. The goods were car seats which had been stolen and which he used as seats in one of his private hire cars. On conviction, Norwich City Council revoked his vehicle licences under the powers contained in LG(MP)A 1976, s 60(1)(c). Mr Thurtle, who held a private hire driver's licence, was convicted of being concerned with another in stealing a motor car. Again, on conviction Norwich City Council revoked his driver's licence under s 1(1)(b). Both appealed to the magistrates' court, who ruled that 'any other reasonable cause' had to be construed ejusdem generis with the grounds contained in either s 60(1)(a) and (b), in the case of a vehicle licence, or LG(MP)A 1976, s 6(1)(a), in the case of a driver's licence. As a consequence, the magistrates upheld the appeals. Norwich City Council appealed by way of the case stated and the matter was considered by Comyn J. He dealt with the actual question very briefly (at 2C):

'In my judgment the justices were not correct to construe the words in question as applicable only to matters *ejusdem generis* with those immediately before set out.'

The judge then spent some considerable time expanding on this statement and giving his reasons (at 2E):

'In my judgment the words "any other reasonable cause" are at large and cover anything and everything which might be regarded as a reasonable reason for depriving a person of his vehicle licence. It is impossible to define in any general terms what circumstances might arise. Endless possibilities suggest themselves. The all-important word is "reasonable".'

He continued (at 2G):

'I would only add at this stage that criminal convictions of any kind – in particular criminal convictions relating to motor vehicles, or motor vehicle parts or accessories – could, in my judgment, amount to "any other reasonable cause". Equally I wish to make it quite plain that, in my judgment, they do not automatically do so. Every case has got to be considered in its own context as to whether there is or is not a reasonable cause.

Furthermore, it would not be a reasonable cause in my judgment that revocations had been made of drivers' licences under section 61 or operators' licensed under section 62. This matter of reasonable cause must be decided in every case on its own facts and in a common sense, down-to-earth way. It would not be right to seek to fetter a court in how it approaches the matter.'

This comment related to the argument which was advanced that, as a person's private hire driver's licence was being revoked, there was no point in not revoking his vehicle licences. This argument seems difficult to follow, as it would be possible for a vehicle proprietor to allow other licensed drivers to drive his cars. It found no favour with the judge, who said 'I do not agree. These are all separate matters'. He then concluded as follows (at 4C):

'The Case Stated goes on to say that the justices were asked to construe the section, and in particular sub-section (1)(*c*). They say that it was argued on the respondent's behalf that handling stolen goods could not be a ground for revoking his vehicle licence. I have already indicated that I do not agree with that. It could be a ground. Whether it should have been a ground is another matter and is a matter for the justices now to decide.

The Case Stated goes on to say that the appellant (the council) argued that the Public Health Committee had an unfettered discretion within the normal meaning of the words. I agree with that statement and that contention, but only to this extent. They had the discretion within the wide meaning, as I find it, of those words; not a discretion so unfettered as to make them feel that they were compelled by reason of the conviction to suspend or revoke the licence.'

[1]   (21 May 1981, unreported), DC.

8.139

Accordingly, 'any other reasonable cause' could relate to any other ground on which the council felt the new proprietor was unsuitable. The most obvious grounds would be that he has a criminal record, possibly unrelated to taxis, which would cause the council concern if he was to be involved in the hackney carriage trade or that there was some other reason which makes him unsuitable. It is not necessary for the council to consider whether or not the new proprietor is a fit and proper person, but that is probably as good a test as any.

R v Lincoln City Council, ex p King and Cook and R v Luton Borough Council, ex p Mirza

8.140

> Could a local authority refuse to renew a vehicle licence under 'any other reasonable cause' for a vehicle that did not comply with a WAV policy? Held: Yes it could.

In the joined Court of Appeal cases of *R v Lincoln City Council, ex p King and Cook and R v Luton Borough Council, ex p Mirza*[1] the question arose again, but in a slightly different set of circumstances. Lincoln City Council had adopted a policy that all hackney carriages should be wheelchair accessible. Two existing licensees applied for renewal of their proprietor's licences for non-wheelchair accessible vehicles. Their applications were refused.

[1]   (2 February 1995, unreported), CA.

8.141

The Court of Appeal considered whether or not Lincoln City Council could refuse to renew the licences for King and Cook's vehicles, solely because they were not wheelchair-accessible vehicles, by use of LG(MP)A 1976, s 60. Swinton Thomas LJ viewed this argument as follows[1] (at 10C):

> 'Lincoln Council purported to refuse these applications under s 60(1)(c) namely "any other reasonable cause". Clearly the vehicles did not come within (a) or (b); the refusal could only be covered by (c). It is submitted that first applications for a licence are distinct from renewals. That is correct. They are dealt with separately in the relevant Acts. Accordingly,

it is submitted by Mr Langstaff [for the Appellants, King & Cook] that an application for a renewal should be treated differently from an application for a fresh licence. Mr Langstaff submits that the section envisages an event or events which have occurred in the year prior to the application for renewal.

I do not myself accept that contention, but even if it be correct then, in my judgment, a change of policy on behalf of the Council could be such an event. It is then submitted that, under (c) "any other reasonable cause" must be construed ejusdem generis with (a) and (b) and the fact that the taxis did not have wheelchair accessibility was not a proper ground for refusing a renewal.

I do not for my part agree that the words "any other reasonable cause" must be construed ejusdem generis with the matters contained in (a) and (b). The phrase "any other reasonable cause" is extremely wide. It would, in my judgment, be an affront to the words used to construe those words ejusdem generis with the limited matters contained in (a) and (b). The failure of the vehicle to comply with a prerequisite lawfully laid down by the Council must, in my judgment, fall within the phrase "any other reasonable cause".'

Again, Leggatt LJ agreed (at 14F):

'I do not consider that it is seriously capable of argument that the words "or any other reasonable cause" in s 60 of the Local Government (Miscellaneous Provisions) Act 1976 should, supposedly by application of the ejusdem generis rule, be temporarily confined so as to apply only to a cause arising within the currency of the annual licence, the renewal of which is under consideration. Without qualification, the words of the section mean what they say.'

1   (2 February 1995, unreported), CA.

8.142

It is therefore clear that the words 'any other reasonable cause' can be applied to anything. It is arguable that where there is a numbers policy in force a council could refuse a transfer to a new proprietor because there is a waiting list of people for hackney carriage proprietor's licences. However, this would not be reasonable, as it would effectively amount to a ban on transfer of a hackney carriage vehicle licence, which is not prohibited by the legislation. Indeed, the legislation in LG(MP)A 1976, s 49[1] would appear to specifically envisage such transfers taking place naturally.

1   See Appendix I.

Inspection of vehicles

8.143

It is vital that hackney carriages are safe at all times and proprietors are responsible for the continued maintenance of the vehicle. Local authorities need to be satisfied that the hackney carriages operating within their area are safe to do so, both before the vehicle is licensed and during the currency of the licence. Cars (including private hire vehicles) need an MOT certificate after they have been registered for three years by virtue of the Road Traffic Act 1988, s 45(1) ('RTA 1988'). They must be tested in accordance with s 47(2). Hackney carriages (referred to as a taxi in s 47(3)) require an MOT after one year[1]. That can be an MOT issued by any testing station. A person appointed by a local authority can be a vehicle inspector provided they are approved by the Secretary of State for Transport under s 45(3) and then undertake MOT tests.

In addition to generally testing vehicles, it is also possible for local authorities to test hackney carriages (and private hire vehicles) and issue a 'Certificate of Compliance' instead of an MOT Certificate[2]. The mechanism for this is as follows. RTA 1988, s 44 allows the Secretary of State to specify types of vehicles which can be used on public highways without a test certificate issued under s 45 being in force. Regulation 6 of the Motor Vehicles (Tests) Regulations 1981 ('the 1981 Regulations') allows an exemption from an MOT certificate provided the local authority is authorised to provide such a certificate by the Secretary of State.

Regulation 6(1) states:

'(1) Pursuant to section 44(4) the Secretary of State hereby prescribes the following vehicles as those to which section 44 does not apply:—

...

(xviii) subject to the provisions of paragraph (4), a hackney carriage or a cab in respect of which there is in force a licence under—
  (a) section 6 of the Metropolitan Public Carriage Act 1869, or
  (b) the Town Police Clauses Act 1847, the Burgh Police (Scotland) Act 1892 or any similar local statutory provision,
  to ply for hire;
(xix) subject to the provisions of paragraph (4), a private hire car in respect of which there is in force a licence granted by a local authority or Transport for London, or, in Scotland, by a local authority or a police authority.'

but the non-application of RTA 1988, s 44 only applies when the provisions of reg 6(4) are met:

'(4) The exemptions specified in paragraph (1)(xviii) and (xix) do not obtain unless the authority which issued the licence ("the licensing authority") holds a certificate issued by the Secretary of State evidencing that he is satisfied that the issue of the licence is subject to the vehicle first passing an annual test relating to the prescribed statutory requirements; and, as from 1st January 1983,
  (a) in the case of a vehicle of a kind mentioned in paragraph (1)(xviii) first used more than one year before the licence there mentioned was issued, or
  (b) in the case of a vehicle of a kind mentioned in paragraph (1)(xix) first used more than three years before the licence there mentioned was issued

the licensing authority also issued to the licensee a certificate recording that on the date on which the certificate was issued that authority was, as a result of a test, satisfied that the prescribed statutory requirements were satisfied.'

'Private hire car' is defined in reg 5:

> '"private hire car" means a motor vehicle which is not a vehicle licensed to ply for hire under the provisions of the Metropolitan Public Carriage Act 1869, Town Police Clauses Act 1847, the Burgh Police (Scotland) Act 1892 or any similar local statutory provision with respect to hackney carriages but which is kept for the purpose of being let out for hire with a driver for the carrying of passengers in such circumstances that it does not require to be licensed to ply for hire under the said provisions'

These provisions enable local authorities to not only test vehicles to MOT standards, but also to incorporate within that test other additional requirements to satisfy themselves as to the suitability and safety of the vehicle for use as a hackney carriage (or private hire vehicle). They are widely used by local authorities and in those cases, the MOT and suitability test are combined.

Not all authorities use this approach, and there are local authorities who require the proprietor to obtain an MOT certificate and then the authority conducts a separate inspection of the vehicle for licensing purposes.

¹   Road Traffic Act 1988, s 47(3)(b). The definition of 'taxi' is by reference to Transport Act 1980, s 64(3) (s 64 prohibits the use of certain words on roof signs of vehicles other than hackney carriages) and is:
    'In this section "taxi" means a vehicle licensed under section 37 of the Town Police Clauses Act 1847, section 6 of the Metropolitan Carriage Act 1869, [section 10 of the Civic Government (Scotland) Act 1982] ² or any similar local enactment.'
²   This is not an MOT Certificate and will not be recorded on the DVLA database, so vehicle proprietors should ensure that an MOT Test Certificate is also issued.

8.144

LG(MP)A 1976, s 50(1)¹ allows the local authority to request the proprietor to present the vehicle for test at whatever place the council specifies. It is interesting to note that the place of test must be 'within the area of the council' and, if the council use test facilities which are actually outside their council area, then a hackney carriage proprietor could legitimately refuse to attend at that location for a test during the duration of the licence.

¹   See Appendix I.

8.145

If the hackney carriage is not being used (and this would appear to indicate that it is off the road for some considerable period rather than simply not working at that precise time), then the council can by notice ask the proprietor where it is. The proprietor must tell them its location and allow them to inspect and test. Again, it appears that the legislation specifically envisages that the vehicle will be tested wherever it is currently stored, which may well be in conditions which would not allow for a complete test. Obviously, if the vehicle is not insured, taxed, tested or roadworthy it would not be possible to require it to be moved to the council's test site, but if those considerations do not apply, then, to enable a test to be undertaken, it would need to be moved to the council's test site, although the legislation does not specifically allow this. It will probably be necessary to move the vehicle to an approved testing site to ensure that the provisions of the Health and Safety at Work etc Act 1974 are maintained in respect of the testers themselves.

8.146

LG(MP)A 1976, s 50(2) also applies in relation to vehicles which are the subject of an application for a hackney carriage proprietor's licence, but for which no licence has been in force previously and again, it is likely that they would need to be transported to the council's test site to enable a comprehensive and acceptable test to be undertaken.

8.147

Testing of vehicles is obviously important if the hackney carriage has been involved in any kind of accident. LG(MP)A 1976, s 50(3) requires the proprietor to inform the district council 'as soon as reasonably practicable' and, in any case, within 72 hours of any accident causing 'damage materially affecting the safety, performance or appearance of the hackney carriage ... or the comfort or convenience of persons carried therein'. Once such a notice has been received the local authority will undoubtedly wish to inspect the vehicle and can use the provisions of s 50(1) to require the vehicle to be presented for testing, if it is still running, or if it is off the road, the provisions of s 50(2) can be used to require an inspection.

8.148

LG(MP)A 1976, s 50(4) allows an authorised officer of the council to inspect both the licence and the insurance policy in force for the vehicle.

8.149

LG(MP)A 1976, s 50(1) limits the number of times that an inspection can be made of a hackney carriage to three in any one year and most authorities use this for their regular inspections. Some inspect bi-annually, but very few appear to make full use of the provision for three inspections per year.

The DfT 'Best Practice Guidance'[1] suggests the following in relation to vehicle inspections:

'Vehicle Testing

32. There is considerable variation between local licensing authorities on vehicle testing, including the related question of age limits. The following can be regarded as best practice:

Frequency Of Tests. The legal requirement is that all taxis should be subject to an MOT test or its equivalent once a year. For PHVs the requirement is for an annual test after the vehicle is three years old. An annual test for licensed vehicles of whatever age (that is, including vehicles that are less than three years old) seems appropriate in most cases, unless local conditions suggest that more frequent tests are necessary. However, more frequent tests may be appropriate for older vehicles (see 'age limits' below). Local licensing authorities may wish to note that a review carried out by the National Society for Cleaner Air in 2005 found that taxis were more likely than other vehicles to fail an emissions test. This finding, perhaps suggests that emissions testing should be carried out on ad hoc basis and more frequently than the full vehicle test.

Criteria For Tests. Similarly, for mechanical matters it seems appropriate to apply the same criteria as those for the MOT test to taxis and PHVs*. The MOT test on vehicles first used after 31 March 1987 includes checking of all seat belts. However, taxis and PHVs provide a service to the public, so it is also appropriate to set criteria for the internal condition of the vehicle, though these should not be unreasonably onerous.

   *A manual outlining the method of testing and reasons for failure of all MOT tested items can be obtained from the Stationary Office see http:www.tsoshop.co.uk/bookstore.asp?FO=1159966&Action=Book&From=SearchResults&ProductID=0115525726

Age Limits. It is perfectly possible for an older vehicle to be in good condition. So the setting of an age limit beyond which a local authority will not license vehicles may be arbitrary and inappropriate. But a greater frequency of testing may be appropriate for older vehicles – for example, twice-yearly tests for vehicles more than five years old.

Number Of Testing Stations. There is sometimes criticism that local authorities provide only one testing centre for their area (which may be geographically extensive). So it is good practice for local authorities to consider having more than one testing station. There could be an advantage in contracting out the testing work, and to different garages. In that way the licensing authority can benefit from competition in costs. (The Vehicle Operators and Standards Agency – VOSA – may be able to assist where there are local difficulties in provision of testing stations.)

33. The Technical Officer Group of the Public Authority Transport Network has produced Best Practice Guidance which focuses on national inspection standards for taxis and PHVs. Local licensing authorities might find it helpful to refer to the testing standards set out in this guidance in carrying out their licensing responsibilities. The PATN can be accessed via the Freight Transport Association.'

It is clear that the DfT view testing in a different light from some local authorities. The suggestion that an annual test is sufficient for a vehicle which may travel up to 80,000 miles per year (equivalent to eight years' average private car use) is regarded as surprising by many involved in licensing hackney carriages and private hire vehicles, and indeed by some operators. The DfT suggestion for bi-annual tests after five years (by which time it is entirely possible that the vehicle may have travelled 150,000 miles, and conceivably approaching 400,000 miles) seems to undervalue the importance of vehicle testing in relation to passenger carrying vehicles such as hackney carriages and private hire vehicles.

¹   DfT, '*Taxi and Private Hire Vehicle Licensing: Best Practice Guidance*' (October 2006, reissued March 2010) available at http://www.dft.gov.uk/pgr/regional/taxis/taxiandprivatehirevehiclelic1792. See Appendix II.

8.150

With regard to irregular or 'spot' inspections, the local authority can make use of LG(MP)A 1976, s 68, which allows inspection of a hackney carriage or private hire vehicle by an authorised officer of the council or a police constable:

'Fitness of hackney carriages and private hire vehicles

68 Any authorised officer of the council in question or any constable shall have power at all reasonable times to inspect and test, for the purpose of ascertaining its fitness, any hackney carriage or private hire vehicle licensed by a district council, or any taximeter affixed to such a vehicle, and if he is not satisfied as to the fitness of the hackney carriage or private hire vehicle or as to the accuracy of its taximeter he may by notice in writing require the proprietor of the hackney carriage or private hire vehicle to make it or its taximeter available for further inspection and testing at such reasonable time and place as may be specified in the notice and suspend the vehicle licence until such time as such authorised officer or constable is so satisfied:

Provided that, if the authorised officer or constable is not so satisfied before the expiration of a period of two months, the said licence shall, by virtue of this section, be deemed to have been revoked and subsections (2) and (3) of section 60 of this Act shall apply with any necessary modifications.'

This allows the authorised officer to inspect and test the vehicle. If it does not satisfy the council's requirements then a notice can be issued requiring the vehicle to be submitted for a re-test and the licence can be suspended until such time as the vehicle satisfactorily passes any subsequent test. This is an extremely useful provision and is essential for keeping the hackney carriage vehicles operating within the area of the council in a satisfactory and safe condition.

It is interesting to note that, if the vehicle is not presented in a fit condition within two months of the date of the original suspension notice being issued under LG(MP)A 1976, s 68, then the licence itself is deemed to be revoked. If the licence is deemed to be revoked after the expiry of the two-month period, then there is a right of appeal against that revocation by virtue of LG(MP)A 1976, s 60(2) and (3). However, there is no right of appeal against the suspension of the vehicle pending the improvements required in the notice. Although s 60 allows the council to suspend or revoke the proprietor's licence on the grounds that 'that the hackney carriage … is unfit for use as a hackney carriage' (s 60(1)(a)), if the suspension has been imposed under s 68 after an inspection then such right of appeal does not to exist.

8.151

At first sight, this seems anomalous, as both sections refer to the fitness of the hackney carriage as being the reason for action being taken. Whilst it may seem unjust that a local authority can avoid having its decision being challenged by means of appeal if it uses the LG(MP)A 1976, s 68 procedure as opposed to the LG(MP)A 1976, s 60 procedure, it is clearly unsatisfactory to allow a vehicle assessed to be unfit to continue being used for both the 21 day appeal, and if an appeal is lodged, until the appeal is determined. As a result s 68 is the only practical method of taking action against unroadworthy vehicles.

This position was confirmed by the High Court and Court of Appeal in *R (on the application of Wilcock) v Lancaster City Council*[1].

[1]   [2013] LLR 607 Admin Ct and [2014] LLR 388, CA.

R (on the application of Wilcock) v Lancaster City Council

8.152

> Does 'fitness' of the vehicle in LG(MP)A 1976, s 68 relate only to mechanical fitness, or can it apply to all the requirements of the local authority? Held: It can apply to any non-compliance with the local authorities conditions, as well as mechanical fitness.

The limits of the powers contained in s 68 were considered in *R (on the application of Wilcock) v Lancaster City Council*[1]. Mrs Wilcock purchased a Fiat Scudo vehicle in 2008 and it was adorned by the vendor with signage stating 'Taxi'. That was in breach of the council's conditions for hackney carriage vehicle licenses, but despite that, the licence was granted following the issue of a certificate of compliance. The certificates and licence were renewed until 2012. In 2012 the council received complaints about the signage, and instructed Mrs Wilcock to remove them. She refused and in November a suspension notice was issued under s 68. Mrs Wilcock sought judicial review. After proceedings had been commenced, becuase the certificate of compliance and the vehicle licence expired in December, Mrs Wilcock applied to renew the licence. Notwithstanding the judicial review proceedings, the licence was renewed, with the condition prohibiting the signs. In addition to the judicial review, Mrs Wilcock also appealed to the magistrates' court against the condition limiting signage. In the words of the judge in the High Court, His Honour Judge Waksman QC[2] the position before the High Court was thus:

> 'What all of that means is that the suspension issue in fact has been and gone. The issues before me are now entirely academic as far as Mrs Wilcock

is concerned, because in due course the whole question of the imposition of that condition will be debated in full before the magistrates. But in deference to the arguments made, which may still have some significance as far as costs are concerned, and because I am told that one point concerning section 68 is of wider interest, I shall deal with all the grounds that have been advanced before me. They are three:

(1)   Was the suspension notice itself in breach of the claimant's substantive legitimate expectation?

(2)   Was it *ultra vires*, because section 68, properly construed, did not permit a suspension notice to be issued in these sort of circumstances? And/or

(3)   Did the defendant act disproportionately in the circumstances of this case in a human rights sense in seeking to serve a suspension notice on the facts here when it did?

I deal with each of those matters in turn.'

In relation to legitimate expectation, there was some dispute as to whether the vehicle was originally purchased before the first certificate of compliance was issued, or the other way round[3], but the judge concluded[4]:

'27 … .I can see that it can be said that under the first certificate it can be assumed that the Council's view was that the condition of the car at that time was compliant. But where does that take the claimant? I do not accept that that means clearly and unequivocally that it could never be the case during the life of that certificate, which goes on for one year, that the position on compliance could change. The Council is entitled to change its policy. It is entitled to act more strictly. That is particularly the case here, of course, because it is not suggested that it is unlawful for the council to change its approach and there is no attack on the condition itself. I do not think it can be read into the first certificate into that that the Council will never change its policy in the course or the duration of that certificate.

28. Defects of course can arise during the course of a certificate. Whether it would be unconscionable to change midway, as it were, seems to me to depend on the facts of the particular case…. . However, the matter does not end there because it is not possible to find breach of legitimate expectation unless one is also to find that there is overall unfairness or unconscionability in the light of that. Here, in my judgment, there is clearly none.

…

31. Given, therefore, (a) the timing of this and the earlier notification; (b) the ease with which the matter could be rectified *pro tem*; and (c) the fact that within a month all of this could then be the subject of a proper appeal, I am afraid that I find it quite impossible to see how there is any breach of legitimate substantive expectation here. Ground 1 therefore fails'.

This seems to be a sensible approach and is particularly important as it confirms that a local authority can not only alter its policies, it can also alter its approach to enforcement and in both cases that can legitimately be applied to an existing licensee.

From a vehicle perspective, the second question concerning the limits (if any) of s 68 is the most important element of the judgment. The judge analysed the situation and took the following approach[5]:

'32. I now turn to ground 2, which concerns the interpretation of section 68. I have already pointed out that it is accepted that the word "fitness" under section 60 includes matters such as breach of licence conditions[6]. I have also pointed out that until a suspension turns into a revocation there is no statutory right of appeal against a suspension notice, though of course it can always be susceptible to being challenged by way of judicial review.

33. What then is the interpretation of section 68 claimed for by Mr Rothschild [for Mrs Wilcock]? There have been various formulations put forward, but the essence is that where the word "fitness" appears in the second line of section 68 it should be read as "roadworthiness", or "suitable mechanical condition", or, if he is wrong about that, something a rather wider, but which in any event would not catch breach of a licence condition, or perhaps not a breach of this licence condition. If that is right, then of course the first point to make is that it is a construction which is radically narrower than the construction of a similar word which appears in section 60, a few sections earlier in this statute. *Prima facie*, that would be odd, in my view.'

The judge dismissed the argument that the legislative history of the LG(MP)A 1976 limited the powers within s 68[7]. The second point that the signage issue was trivial also received short shrift:

'40. Therefore, to the extent that it affects the issue of interpretation, I reject the notion that this case is a typical example of a piece of trivia that should not fall within section 68 at all, but should only be left to section 60[8].

41. Why then should it be that section 68 more generally should confine itself more generally to questions of roadworthiness? As it seems to me, the virtue of section 68 is that it provides a swift and summary process, both for the Council and for the operator to deal with and hopefully get rid of problems which arise in the currency of the licence concerning the vehicle which are capable of being disposed of quickly. This would have the virtue of not involving either party in expensive legal proceedings. In that sense it is a different creature from section 60 and has clearly been regarded as such by the legislators for a very considerable period of time.

42. Indeed it actually seems to me that section 68 is technically apposite to less serious matters because those are the kind of matters which ought to be capable of being dealt with very swiftly and without the need for the incentive of a deterrent of a suspension notice. This itself is confined only to a relatively short period, though of course I accept that a period of two months is significant for someone who plies their trade and earns their living in that way, and I do not underestimate that at all.

43. It follows from that that I do not accept that the fact that this matter could have been dealt with under section 60 means that it has to have been dealt with under section 60 or that it is a reason why the word "fitness" should be read down as a matter of interpretation.

...

44. Mr Rothschild pointed out that the word "test" has been inserted into section 68. It was not in all of its statutory predecessors. He says that "test" would indicate something to do with mechanical features of the vehicle. That is obviously right, where that is the sort of problem that has occurred. I have little doubt that the reason why "test" was not there originally is because technology has probably moved on and there is a need and a point in having something a little more intrusive than a mere inspection to see whether the car is fit or not. But none of that entails the conclusion that fitness can only be concerned with matters of roadworthiness. In a case like this, of course, testing would not be required, but inspection certainly would.

45. For these brief reasons I am quite unable to see, as a matter of common-law, as it were, that section 68 should be read down. Nor do I see that it should be read down simply because there is no right of appeal in respect of the suspension period. As I have indicated, it is a limited period. It is susceptible of judicial review in any case, and the circumstances where a challenge would be made would, I would have thought in the normal course of things, be rare. But the fact that there is no substantive right of appeal from that suspension notice does not, in my judgment, help Mr Rothschild here.'

The judge also concluded that the hackney carriage proprietors licence was not a possession for the purposes of Article 1 Protocol 1 of the European Convention on Human Rights and Fundamental Freedoms[9], and his final analysis of s 68 was as follows[10]:

'57. On that footing, therefore, I have reached the clear view that the word "fitness" in section 68 means precisely the same as it means in section 60. I have already indicated that, in my judgment, the fact that in some cases the process could be issued under section 60 as opposed to section 68 does not mean that the narrower interpretation has to be given under section 68. There is some issue about the extent to which the Council in fact uses section 60 for cases such as this. It appears that there is delegated power, in fact, at least so far as suspensions is concerned, to go under section 60 and section 68, so that an authorised officer could suspend against either, and I am content to proceed on that basis. I also accept what Mr Holland [for the Council] says, which is that there are a number of cases of suspension which come under section 60, though not always, and there are clearly a large number of notices which come under section 68, but I do not think that that makes any difference here. Ground 2 therefore fails.'

Finally, the judge made it clear that the use of a s 68 suspension notice was not a disproportionate interference with the licence by the Council[11]:

'59. For the factual reasons already given, it is manifestly not disproportionate to serve a suspension notice here when (a) the matter could easily be cured; (b) it is of limited duration; (c) it can be challenged on the merits later on; and (d) there was prior notice not later than the defect notice.

60. I accept that section 60 and 68 are different creatures, as already indicated, and I see no reason why the Council is bound to go under section 60 when there is a short and convenient summary process available under section 68. Nor do I regard the issue of the suspension notice as disproportionate because there is no full right of appeal.'

Mrs Wilcock was not satisfied with that outcome, and made 2 attempts to have the matter considered by the Court of Appeal. The first (paper) application was refused, and then the matter was considered on an oral application by Maurice Kay LJ[12] who introduced the judgment in the following terms[13]:

'Mrs Wilcock is a Lancaster taxi driver. This momentous dispute relates to what the Council consider to be a breach of conditions attached to her licence.'

and he then determined the application[14]:

'4. In the court below Judge Waxman QC described the effect of section 68 in this way at paragraph 8:

"Under section 68 a licence for a vehicle can be suspended for no longer than two months and if the relevant matter is rectified before the end of that two-month period the suspension will end then. The suspension is not capable of extension. If not rectified and the two months have expired, it turns into a revocation which will then trigger a right of appeal as in under section 60."

The grievance nurtured by Mrs Wilcock is that whereas there is an initial right of appeal following a suspension, revocation or refusal under section 60, there is no such right of appeal following a notice under section 68 although there is a right to apply for permission to seek judicial review.

5. A number of grounds of challenge were ventilated before Judge Waxman but today there is only one ground of appeal pursued by Ms Dring on behalf of Mrs Wilcock. It is the simple one of statutory interpretation. The submission is that in the circumstances which arose in this case, which did not deal with mechanical defects or road worthiness, the Council's only power was to proceed under section 60, thereby triggering a right of appeal rather than under section 68.

6. In order to sustain such an argument, Ms Dring has to submit that "unfitness for use as a Hackney carriage" in section 60 is addressing something different from "fitness of the Hackney carriage" under section

68. Judge Waxman rejected that submission. In paragraph 33 of his judgment he said:

"What then is the interpretation of section 68 claim for (on behalf of Mrs Wilcock) there have been various formulations put forward but the essence is that where the word "fitness" appears in the second line of section 68 it should be read as "road worthiness" or, "suitable mechanical condition" or, if he is wrong about that, something rather wider but which in any event would not catch breach of a licence condition or perhaps not a breach of this licence condition. If that is right then, of course, the first point to make is that it is a construction which is radically narrower than the construction of a similar word which appears in section 60, a few sections earlier in the statute. Prima facie that would be odd in my view."

In the following paragraphs he gave reasons why he was not going to perpetuate that oddity. When Lord Justice Davis refused permission to appeal he said:

"The judge's interpretation of and approach to section 60 and section 68 seems to me plainly right."

7. I have come to the same conclusion. It would be quite remarkable if the statute had been using "fitness" and "unfitness" by reference to a different hinterland in section 60 and section 68. In truth, section 60 and section 68 are simply two different powers which a council can use when the pre-conditions exist. Sometimes they will exist under both cases and it is a matter for judgment on behalf of the council as to which power they use. They are different in substance because section 68 is time limited to a maximum of two months but in fact, for obvious commercial and other reasons, will generally produce the desired results in a shorter time than that.

8. Section 60, as I have indicated, would involve in the present circumstances suspension and triggering of a right of appeal with interim relief pending appeal, which might go on for a considerable time and incur considerable expense.

9. I do not propose to say any more. I am satisfied that the judge was correct and I agree with Lord Justice Davis about this particular ground of appeal. I sense that it is being advanced as a kind of test case. We are now a considerable time down the road from when this dispute first arose. There have been parallel proceedings in the Magistrates' Court which apparently came to an end after Judge Waxman's decision, but I do not consider it necessary or appropriate to grant permission to get a decision from this court on a point on which the decision of the High Court seems to me to be correct and seems to have clarified whatever dispute exists in Lancaster or elsewhere about the Act. Accordingly I shall refuse permission.'

This is clear authority for the proposition that s 68 can be used wherever and whenever a vehicle is not only mechanically unfit, but where there is non-compliance with any of the conditions attached to that vehicle licence.

1   [2013] LLR 607, Admin Ct.
2   At para 23.
3   See paras 24–26.
4   At para 27 onwards.
5   Paragraphs 32–46.
6   Section 60(1) states:

> **'60 Suspension and revocation of vehicle licences**
>
> (1) Notwithstanding anything in the Act of 1847 or in this Part of this Act, a district council may suspend or revoke, or (on application therefor under section 40 of the Act of 1847 or section 48 of this Act, as the case may be) refuse to renew a vehicle licence on any of the following grounds—
>
> (a) that the hackney carriage or private hire vehicle is unfit for use as a hackney carriage or private hire vehicle;
>
> (b) any offence under, or non-compliance with, the provisions of the Act of 1847 or of this Part of this Act by the operator or driver; or
>
> (c) any other reasonable cause.'

7   See para 34.
8   See para 40 onwards.
9   This does not actually appear to be correct, as it is a transferable licence – see Chapter 2, para 2.109 onwards.
10 At para 57.
11 See paras 59 and 60.
12 [2014] LLR 388, CA.
13 At para 2.
14 Paragraphs 4–9.

8.153

There has been some debate as to when such tests can be undertaken and which vehicles can or should be selected for testing. A number of local authorities have embarked upon high profile pro-active testing regimes. These often involve the police, VOSA, the Benefits Agency and the Border Force and take place at times of heavy use of hackney carriages and private hire vehicles. Vehicles are identified by licensing officers, stopped by the police and then directed to a testing station, where, if appropriate, suspensions under LG(MP)A 1976, s 68 and VOSA stop notices can be issued. If the vehicle is carrying passengers when stopped, depending on the nature of the infringement, the driver is allowed to continue to his destination and then proceed to the testing station.

This has raised questions as to whether such enforcement activity can be undertaken, both at all and especially at times of peak demand. For example, if a suspension notice under s 68 is issued on a Friday night, in most cases the testing station will not be available to test the vehicle after repairs have been made with a view to the lifting of the notice until Monday morning, thereby preventing the use of the vehicle for the remainder of the weekend. This is seen as unreasonable by those affected, whose vehicles fail the inspections.

The answer to both these questions appears to be yes. Section 68 is not limited to a total number of inspections in any specified period and it seems reasonable that vehicles are inspected when they are working or available to work, as that is when the public (who are the parties most at risk from unroadworthy vehicles) are being carried.

8.154

As was explained at paras 8.4–8.6 above, a hackney carriage is always a hackney carriage[1] and as a consequence must always be driven by a person who holds a current hackney carriage driver's licence issued by the same authority that licensed the vehicle. The only exception to this is when the vehicle is being tested. This is provided by the Transport Act 1985, s 139(2) and Sch 7, para 3, which states:

> 'Section 46 of the Town Police Clauses Act 1847 (drivers not to act without first obtaining a licence) shall not apply to a person driving a hackney carriage licensed under that Act for the purpose of or in connection with—
>
> (a) any test of the mechanical condition or fitness of the hackney carriage or its equipment carried out for the purposes of [section 45 of the Road Traffic Act 1988] (tests of satisfactory condition of vehicles other than goods vehicles) or for the purposes of any requirements with respect to such condition or fitness imposed by or under any other enactment; or
>
> (b) any test of that person's competence to drive a hackney carriage carried out for the purposes of any application made by him for a licence to drive a hackney carriage.'

It is clear that a hackney carriage can be driven by somebody other than a hackney carriage driver for the purpose of the test. It appears to extend to driving to and from a pre-booked hackney carriage test, as that appears to be the only explanation for the inclusion of the words 'in connection with' in para 3.

[1]   See *Hawkins v Edwards* [1901] 2 KB 169 at para 8.4 above.

WHERE SHOULD THE APPLICATION BE MADE?

8.155

An application for a hackney carriage proprietor's licence should be made to the authority in whose area the applicant intends to use the vehicle to stand or ply for hire. However, because a hackney carriage can undertake pre-booked work anywhere in England or Wales, in recent years applications have been made in authorities where the standards or fees may be lower and then the vehicles undertake pre-booked work in locations that are remote from the authority in which they are licensed. This was the situation which was considered by the High Court in *R (App Newcastle City Council) v Berwick-upon-Tweed Borough Council*[1].

[1]   [2008] EWHC 2369 (Admin), [2009] RTR 34, Admin Ct.

R (App Newcastle City Council) v Berwick-upon-Tweed Borough Council

8.156

> Can a local authority grant hackney carriage proprietors' licences without consideration of the use that those vehicles will be put to? Held: That the local authority must consider the remote use of a hackney carriage for pre-booked work.

The case of *R (App Newcastle City Council) v Berwick-upon-Tweed Borough Council*[1] arose following concerns by Newcastle City Council ('Newcastle') that a significant number of its former private hire vehicles had relinquished their Newcastle private hire vehicle licences and had become licensed as hackney carriages by Berwick-upon-Tweed Borough Council ('Berwick') and were then continuing to work for private hire purposes within Newcastle.

The decision in *Brentwood Borough Council v Gladen*[2] made it clear that a person who accepted advanced or pre-bookings for a hackney carriage did not require a private hire operator's licence, and that judgment itself does not limit such a person to using only hackney carriages licensed within the district in which the booking agent is situated.

This was the 'freedom' being exploited by the operators in Newcastle. The attractions of Berwick as a licensing authority included lower licence fees, the absence of a knowledge test for drivers, no age limit for vehicles and a no prohibition on the licensing of vehicles which had dark tinted glass in passenger compartment windows.

Berwick did not impose any numerical limit on its hackney carriage fleet (unlike Newcastle which had a numerical limitation) and Berwick took the view that provided the vehicle was suitable for use as a hackney carriage and the proprietor a fit and proper person, it was not entitled to inquire what use would be made of the vehicle.

This view was in part based on the common understanding (accepted and agreed by both Newcastle and Berwick) that a licensed hackney carriage can not only ply or stand for hire within the district in which it is licensed, but can also undertake pre-booked work anywhere else in England or Wales. That inherent right existed before the introduction of the Town Police Clauses Act 1847 and no subsequent legislation (including the Local Government (Miscellaneous Provisions) Act 1976) had altered that.

Newcastle's counter-argument was that the purpose and object of the 1847 Act was to enable a local authority to licence hackney carriages to ply for hire within its district and the licensing authority must both inquire as to proposed use and then refuse to grant if the proposed use was other than plying for hire within the district.

This matter was of concern to both parties. The number of hackney carriages licensed by Berwick increased from 46 in April 2006 to 672 by August 2008 and the majority of those additional licences were granted to proprietors who were resident outside the district and the additional hackney carriages were seldom if ever used to ply (or stand) for hire in Berwick. Newcastle felt that this removed their ability to control vehicles which were predominantly used in their area and Berwick considered that they were required to grant such licences as they were unable to inquire as to use because of the inherent and established rights connected to a hackney carriage proprietors' licence.

[1]   [2008] EWHC 2369 (Admin), [2009] RTR 34, Admin Ct.
[2]   [2004] EWHC 2500 (Admin), [2005] RTR 12; see Chapter 13, para 13.98 onwards.

8.157

Newcastle therefore sought judicial review and asked for three remedies:

1.   An order quashing the decision of the Defendant [Berwick] ... of its refusal to cease granting licences under s 37 of the Town Police Clauses Act 1847 to proprietors of vehicles who do not intend that the vehicles will be used to ply for hire within the area of the Defendant.
2.   A Mandatory Order compelling the Defendant to exercise its power pursuant to section 57 of the Local Government (Miscellaneous Provisions) Act 1976 to require any proprietor of a vehicle applying for the grant of a licence under s 37 of the Town Police Clauses Act 1847 who is resident in the area of the Claimant [Newcastle] to submit such information as will enable the Defendant to ascertain if the proprietor intends that the vehicle will (if so licensed) be used to ply for hire within the area of the Defendant.
3.   A declaration that the Defendant may not lawfully grant a licence under s 37 of the Town Police Clauses Act 1847 to any proprietor in respect of a vehicle which it is not satisfied will (if so licensed) be used to ply for hire within the area of the Defendant.

8.158

The case was complicated by the involvement of two interested parties. The first was a George Richardson, acting for and on behalf of the Berwick Borough Taxi Association and the second was Ian Shanks and others, who collectively ran a private hire firm licensed by North Tyneside Council (an adjoining authority to Newcastle) called Blue Line Taxis.

Richardson's argument was that a licensed Newcastle operator could not take bookings for, or dispatch, any vehicle other than a licensed Newcastle private hire vehicle, driven by a licensed Newcastle private hire driver. If this was successful, it would prevent a licensed Newcastle private hire operator taking bookings for and then dispatching, a Berwick hackney carriage to fulfill the booking.

Shanks's argument was supportive of the approach taken by Berwick and was based upon his experiences as a Berwick hackney carriage proprietor.

The case was heard by Mr Christopher Symons QC, sitting as a deputy High Court judge.

The argument put forward by Newcastle was that by granting licences to proprietors who they knew would not use their vehicles to ply for hire within the district in Berwick-upon-Tweed, inherently demonstrated that Berwick was acting unlawfully because it was not acting within the policy and objects of the Act as detailed in *Padfield v Minister of Agriculture, Fisheries and Food*[1].

Berwick's defence was that the only grounds to refuse an application for a hackney carriage proprietor's licence made by a suitable applicant providing a suitable vehicle, was on the grounds of limitation of numbers as provided by s 16 of the Transport Act 1985. Thereafter any duly licenced person could use a Berwick hackney carriage to discharge the inherent right of a hackney carriage proprietor to undertake pre-booked hirings anywhere in England or Wales. Accordingly it would be irrational (and therefore unlawful) to refuse to grant a licence simply because it could or would be used lawfully for pre-booked purposes in Newcastle upon Tyne.

Richardson supported his argument that a Newcastle licensed private hire operator could only dispatch a Newcastle licensed private hire vehicle by reference to the decision in *Kingston upon Hull City Council v Wilson*[2]. Richardson further argued that this judgment made it a criminal offence for both a licensed private hire proprietor to dispatch a licensed hackney carriage and for a licensed hackney carriage driver to drive such a pre-booked hackney carriage.

Shanks's argument supported Berwick's position by indicating that, in addition to hackney carriage and private hire activities, there was a third category of hire of vehicles with drivers, outside the scope of both hackney carriage and private hire vehicle licensing. These exist under the ruling in *Young v Scampion*[3], whereby completely unlicensed vehicles and drivers can stand for hire at ranks which are on private land which is remote from the public highway and does not form part of a 'street' as defined in s 3 of the 1847 Act. This included situations such as that found at Newcastle Airport, where such vehicles could work, but the contractual rules imposed by the owners of the rank (the airport company) required any such vehicles to have a hackney carriage proprietor's licence, albeit not one necessarily issued by Newcastle within whose boundary the airport lies.

[1]   [1968] AC 997 at 1030.
[2]   CO 1249-95; 29 June 1995.
[3]   (1988) 87 LGR 240, QBD.

8.159

In a lengthy judgment, the judge identified the purpose of the Town Police Clauses Act 1847:

> '22. In my judgment the major purpose behind the 1847 Act, and indeed the 1976 Act, is the safety of the public by which I include both the travelling public as passengers and other road users. Thus the scheme of the legislation is directed towards having safe vehicles, fit and proper drivers and appropriate conditions of hire. To ensure this safety a form of enforcement is provided for with a system of penalties for non-compliance.'

He went on to address the concerns that arose from the concept of vehicles working remotely from the licensed area:

> '23. If hackney carriages are working remote from their licensing authority a number of, at the least potentially, undesirable consequences follow.

The licensing authority will not easily keep their licensed fleet under observation. It will be carrying out its enforcement powers from a distance. The licensing authority where the hackney carriage has chosen to operate will have no enforcement powers over the vehicle although it is being used in its area. Further, unlike its own licensed vehicles, the hackney carriage from remote areas will not be subject to the same conditions and byelaws as the local vehicles. It is no surprise that the legislation provides for testing and testing centres to be within the licensing authority's area.'

and then reinforced the concept of local licensing in control in the following way:

'29. Section 37 of the 1847 Act gives the authority concerned a discretion as to whether to grant a licence or not. Hence the use of the word "may". The exercise of that discretion falls to be considered against the background of the legislation and in my judgment should be used "to promote the policy and objects of the Act" [*footnote in judgment: Padfield v. Minister of Agriculture, Fisheries and Food* [1968] AC 997 at 1030]. The licence permits the vehicle to ply for hire in the prescribed area. The authority, if it wishes, can restrict the number of licences it issues based on demand within the area [*footnote in judgment*: Section 16 of the 1985 Transport Act]. The local authority can issue it its own conditions and make its own byelaws. It can make provision for its own inspections of the hackney carriages. Thus the licensing regime is local in character. In addition it can be seen that most of the provisions have public safety much in mind. The local imposition of conditions and byelaws, local testing and enforcement, together with the other statutory provisions I have referred to all seem to me to point clearly to the conclusion that it was the intention behind the licensing system that it should operate in such a way that the authority licensing hackney carriages is the authority for the area in which those vehicles are generally used. Further the 1847 Act provides for licences to be granted for hackney carriages to ply for hire within the prescribed distance (i.e. within the area of the licensing authority).

30. Having regard to the policy and objects of the Act in my judgment Berwick in exercising its discretion under section 37 of the 1847 Act should take into account where the hackney carriage will be used.'

8.160

He dismissed the argument that it was not for the licensing authority to consider the lawful use of the vehicle for private hire purposes in the following way:

'31. It seems to me that the question to be asked is not whether a hackney carriage proprietor once a licence is granted would be acting lawfully but rather whether in exercising their discretion a licensing authority can use its discretion to ensure that it maintains control over those vehicles it has licensed.'

and went on to say[1]:

'In my judgment a local authority, properly directing itself, is entitled, and indeed obliged, to have regard to whether the applicant intends to use the licence to operate a hackney carriage in that authority's area and also to have regard to whether in fact the applicant intends to use that hackney carriage predominantly, or entirely, remotely from the authority's area. This should result in each local authority licensing those hackney carriages that will be operating in their own area and should reduce the number of hackney carriages which operate remotely from the area where they are licensed.'

The judge reinforced in the importance of local control in the following way:

'34. I am anxious not to direct how Berwick, or any other local authority, should exercise their discretion which must be a matter for their own judgment taking into account the need to have available safe and suitable hackney carriages and having proper regard to the safety of the public. However it would seem to me to be difficult for any local authority to justify exercising their discretion by granting a hackney carriage licence to an applicant when the authority knows that the applicant has no intention of using that licence to ply for hire in its area. This is particularly so when the local authority also knows that the intention is to use the hackney carriage in an area remote from that authority's area. I say that because it seems to me it is very difficult to exercise proper control over hackney carriages which are never, or rarely, used in the prescribed area. It is also undesirable for authorities to be faced with a proliferation of hackney carriages licensed outside the area in which they are being used and therefore not subject to the same conditions and byelaws as apply to those vehicles licensed in the area.'

The judge went on to say that the intention as to use could, but did not have to be, gleaned from questions asked by the local authority that received the application for the hackney carriage proprietors licence using the powers provided in LG(MP)A 1976, s 57[2].

[1]   Also at paragraph 31 of the judgment.
[2]   See paragraph 35 of the judgment.

8.161

Newcastle's third claim for remedy was a declaration that it was not lawful to grant a hackney carriage proprietor's licence to a vehicle which would be used remotely for private hire purposes. This was rejected by the judge where he stated:

'38. It must be a matter for Berwick to exercise its own discretion in this matter taking into account the terms of this judgment. While I cannot at the moment conceive of it being rational to grant a licence to those who intend to operate their hackney carriages remotely from Berwick-on-Tweed I am not prepared to say that it is bound to be unlawful. I certainly do not think it is essential that Berwick use section 57 of the 1976 Act.'

As a consequence, it is submitted that a local authority can grant a licence to a hackney carriage for remote use, but must exercise its discretion carefully in doing so. In exercising such a discretion it would have to ensure the decision was not unreasonable in *Wednesbury*[1] terms. This is reinforced by paragraph 39 of the judgment where the judge addressed this issue in the following way:

'39. It is clear that there has been a good deal of communication between the various local authorities and no doubt that will continue. Sensible cooperation between for example Berwick, Newcastle and the immediately adjacent councils may well assist in ensuring that licences are sought where they are intended to be used. There will be proprietors who wish to use their vehicles in a number of different authorities' areas[2] and in that case no doubt there will be flexibility in the exercising of the discretion. Matters such as where the proprietor is based and where most of the business comes from will be material matters to consider.'

In relation to the claim brought by Newcastle against Berwick the judge concluded as follows:

'40. In conclusion in my judgment Berwick has a discretion under section 37 of the 1847 Act to refuse to issue licences to those who have no intention of exercising their right to ply for hire in Berwick and/or to those who intend to use the vehicle predominantly in an area remote from Berwick.'

[1]   *Associated Provincial Picture Houses Ltd v Wednesbury Corpn* [1948] 1 KB 223, CA.
[2]   *Footnote in judgment*: Although they will only be able to ply for hire in the area where the licence is granted.

8.162

Considerable time in both the hearing and the judgment was taken up by the arguments brought by Richardson (that only Newcastle licensed private hire vehicles can be dispatched by a Newcastle licensed private hire operator), which argument was resisted by both Claimant (Newcastle) and Defendant (Berwick). After lengthy consideration the judge concluded that argument in the following way:

'56. The Court is therefore in the position that both the Claimant and the Defendant (supported by Blue Line Taxis, the Second Interested party) are agreed that Newcastle has no power to prosecute those private hire operators licensed under section 55 of the 1976 Act who use hackney carriages to fulfil pre-booked hirings provided the hackney carriage and the driver are properly licensed. The authority of this Court in *Gladen*[1] in my judgment supports that view. On the opposite side appears to me to be the decision in *Wilson*[2] and the decision of the District Judge in *Whalley*[3] which will shortly be coming to this Court. I am told by Mr. Richardson, through, Mr. Maddox that this matter is of national significance.

57. While, as may be apparent from my remarks in paragraph 45 above, I have considerable sympathy with the argument persuasively put by Mr. Maddox, I am not prepared to do other than follow *Gladen* which is a

decision of this Court which I am certainly not prepared to say is obviously wrong. Mr. Maddox sought to persuade me that since that case involved section 46(1)(d) the submission now advanced on behalf of Mr. Richardson was not fully argued. However it is clear from the judgment in that case that the Court considered section 46(1)(d) and (e) and expressed its conclusions and I do not think it is possible to distinguish it.

58. So it follows that I am not prepared to hold that Newcastle can prosecute those using hackney carriages to fulfil pre-booked hirings in Newcastle Upon Tyne albeit that their hackney carriage licence is obtained from a local authority remote from Newcastle.'

That dealt with the argument brought by Richardson and the overall conclusions of the court in relation to the claim by Newcastle were:

(i) 'In the proper exercise of its statutory discretion under section 37 of the Town Police Clauses Act 1847 a licensing authority is obliged to have regard (a) to whether the applicant intends that the hackney carriage if licensed will be used to ply for hire within the area of that authority, and (b) whether the applicant intends that the hackney carriage will be used (either entirely or predominantly) for private hire remotely from the area of that authority.'

(ii) 'A licensing authority may in the proper exercise of its discretion under the said section 37 refuse to grant a licence in respect of a hackney carriage that is not intended to be used to ply for hire within its area and/or is intended to be used (either entirely or predominantly) for private hire remotely from the area of that authority.'

(iii) 'In determining whether to grant a licence under the said section 37 a licensing authority may require an applicant to submit information pursuant to section 57 Local Government (Miscellaneous Provisions) Act 1976 in order to ascertain the intended usage of the vehicle.'

1   *Brentwood Borough Council v Gladen* [2004] EWHC 2500 (Admin), [2005] RTR 12.
2   *Kingston upon Hull City Council v Wilson* CO 1249-95; 29 June 1995.
3   A decision of District Judge Andrew Shaw sitting in Wrexham Magistrates' Court in the case of *Wrexham County Borough Council v Debbie Whalley and Jonathan Higgins* (2008, unreported). At the time of the hearing, it was suggested to the High Court that this case was being appealed by way of case stated and would be considered by the High Court in due course. For reasons reportedly connected to funds, the High Court challenge never took place.

What then is the practical impact of this decision?

8.163

Clearly local authorities following the decision will have to establish the intended use of a hackney carriage. This can be, but does not have to be, by means of seeking information under the power contained in LG(MP)A 1976, s 57, although if s 57 is not used, in many cases it is difficult to see how the local authority will ascertain that intention – the judge took the view that local knowledge on the part of the local authority's licensing staff might suffice[1], however this may be hearsay or anecdotal and not wholly reliable.

The judge also observed, quite rightly, that any false statements made on an application for a licence are an offence and further that failure to act honestly on a drivers' part will go to the issue of fitness and propriety.

Once that intended use has been established, the local authority will then have to decide how to exercise their discretion as to whether or not to grant a hackney carriage proprietor's licence under TPCA 1847, s 37. Such exercise must not be *Wednesbury*[2] unreasonable. The judgment says that if the entire or predominant intended use of the hackney carriage is pre-booked hirings remote from the area of the local authority, then the local authority can exercise its discretion and refuse the grant of the licence. However, in exercising that discretion the local authority must also consider 'proprietors who wish to use their vehicles in a number of different authorities' areas[3]'.

This places local authorities in a difficult position in the proper exercise of a discretion requiring them to balance the right to be granted a hackney carriage proprietor's licence against the discretion to refuse if the declared entire or predominant use is for remote pre-booked hirings.

The decision further impinges on circumstances where an applicant may require a hackney carriage proprietor's licence to enable him to undertake lawful immediate hirings at locations which do not constitute a 'street' for the purposes of the TPCA 1847, such as Newcastle Airport, under the ruling in *Young v Scampion*[4]. It would clearly be extremely difficult to refuse an application for a licence where the applicant intended that use on the basis of this ruling.

Finally, consideration must also be given to the applicant who declares quite openly that he does not intend to use his vehicle to ply or stand for hire within the district of the local authority that grants the hackney carriage licence, but the purpose of his application is to avail himself of the inherent right to use his vehicle for pre-booked purposes elsewhere. Such inherent right to use is clearly lawful (and this judgment does not in any way impinge on the lawful use), and is envisaged by the judge to a degree in his comments at paragraph 39 of the judgment[5], but it is difficult to see how the granting local authority can approach this.

There is no doubt that the intention of the judge was to address what he described as the 'undesirable ...proliferation of hackney carriages licensed outside the area in which they are being used'[6], whilst recognising, albeit tacitly, the inherent right of a hackney carriage proprietor to undertake pre-booked hirings anywhere in England or Wales. Unfortunately his conclusions have led local authorities into difficult situations in relation to the exercise of their discretion in trying to balance the potential lawful and unlawful grant with the consequent and inevitable risks of challenge by those who are adversely affected by the decisions resulting from that exercise.

As a consequence of the *Berwick-upon-Tweed*[7] judgment, a number of local authorities have introduced so called 'intended use policies'. These aim to ensure that a hackney carriage is used predominantly within the district in which it is licensed and local authorities will refuse to either grant or renew a licence where that requirement cannot be, or has not been satisfied.

1   See paragraph 38 of the judgment.
2   *Associated Provincial Picture Houses Ltd v Wednesbury Corpn* [1948] 1 KB 223, CA.
3   See paragraph 39 of the judgment.
4   (1988) 87 LGR 240, QBD.
5   'There will be proprietors who wish to use their vehicles in a number of different authorities'
     areas and in that case no doubt there will be flexibility in the exercising of the discretion.'
6   See paragraph 34 of the judgment.
7   [2008] EWHC 2369 (Admin), (5 November 2008, unreported).

APPLICANTS FOR PROPRIETOR'S LICENCES

8.164

On an application for a proprietor's licence, the district council is not provided with any specific requirements that have to be met by the applicant. However, as the power to issue a licence is discretionary, not mandatory, the authority can refuse to issue a licence if the vehicle or applicant are not suitable. The only situation in which a licence specifically cannot be refused (assuming that the applicant and vehicle are acceptable) is if there is a significant demand which remains unmet.

'No significant demand which is unmet'

8.165

Until the introduction of the Transport Act 1985, local authorities had an unrestricted discretion to limit the number of hackney carriages which they would licence. The Transport Act 1985, s 16 removed that discretion by amending the wording of TPCA 1847, s 37[1]. Section 16 stated:

'Taxi licensing: control of numbers

16 The provisions of the Town Police Clauses Act 1847 with respect to hackney carriages, as incorporated in any enactment (whenever passed), shall have effect—

(a)   as if in section 37, the words "such number of" and "as they think fit" were omitted; and

(b)   as if they provided that the grant of a licence may be refused, for the purpose of limiting the number of hackney carriages in respect of which licences are granted, if, but only if, the person authorised to grant licences is satisfied that there is no significant demand for the services of hackney carriages (within the area to which the licence would apply) which is unmet.'

Accordingly, s 37 reads as follows:

'The commissioners may from time to time licence to ply for hire within the prescribed distance, or if no distance is prescribed, within five miles from the General Post Office of the city, town, or place to which the special Act refers, (which in that case shall be deemed the prescribed distance,)

... 'hackney coaches or carriages of any kind or description adapted to the carriage of persons ... [and] the grant of a licence may be refused, for the purpose of limiting the number of hackney carriages in respect of which licences are granted, if, but only if, the person authorised to grant licences is satisfied that there is no significant demand for the services of hackney carriages (within the area to which the licence would apply) which is unmet.'

The effect of this provision was described by Wilson J in *R (on the application of Maud) v Castle Point Borough Council*[2]:

'6. The legal position has thus become as follows:
(a) before a local authority can refuse an application for a vehicle licence in order to limit the number of licensed taxis, they must be satisfied that there is no significant demand for the services of taxis, within the area to which the licence would apply, which is unmet;
(b) if the local authority are thus satisfied, a discretion, as opposed to an obligation, arises to refuse the grant of a licence; but
(c) if the local authority are not so satisfied, they cannot refuse to grant a licence for the purpose of limiting the number of licensed taxis and are thus obliged to grant it.'

This assessment was approved by the Court of Appeal[3].

[1] See Appendix I.
[2] (18 February 2002, unreported), Admin Ct; see para 8.204 onwards below.
[3] *R (on the application of Maud) v Castle Point Borough Council* [2002] EWCA Civ 1526, [2003] LGR 47, at para 5.

8.166

As stated above, the consequence of the introduction of the Transport Act 1985, s 16 is that there are two types of local authority: those which do limit the number of hackney carriages and those which do not.

Deregulation of hackney carriages or delimitation of numbers?

8.167

The removal of the numerical limit is often (and misleadingly) referred to as 'deregulation of hackney carriages'. This is an unfortunate and emotive turn of phrase which suggests that if the number is not set, there is no regulation whatsoever of hackney carriages. This is not the case, as all quality controls remain on both the vehicle and the driver, and it is only the quantity control which is removed. A better expression is 'delimitation of numbers' which more accurately reflects the action that is taken.

8.168

The rationale behind the introduction of the Transport Act 1985, s 16 was that local authorities would no longer be able to control the numbers of hackney carriages. However, it has not worked out like that in many parts of the country and some 25% of local authorities still limit the number of hackney carriages that they will licence.

8.169

The litigation in this area has been considerable. This is understandable, as many persons' livelihoods are at stake. In areas where a limit on hackney carriage numbers is maintained, hackney carriage proprietor's licences have a value. As with any market, these values fluctuate according to demand and that demand varies between local authority areas and also in response to other factors. Some years ago, reports indicated that market value for hackney carriage proprietor's licences ranged from around £2,000 to upwards of £50,000, with the current highest value being £80,000[1]. However, with the increase in private hire numbers these values appear to have fallen. Obviously, if someone has invested considerable sums in such a licence, they will be loath to see that value wiped out by a decision by the local authority to delimit numbers. On the other hand, many local authorities take the view that limiting hackney carriage numbers is an unacceptable form of protectionism, which does not provide the travelling public with the best service.

[1]   Oxford City Council as at April 2008 – source www.taxidriver.co.uk – building on information contained in the Office of Fair Trading report *The regulation of licensed taxi and PHV services in the UK* (OFT676 available at www.oft.gov.uk/news/publications/leaflet+ordering.htm), the results of its investigation into UK Taxi Services, at para 4.43. No more recent information appears to be available.

8.170

As with any dispute, there are strong arguments on both sides. An unregulated 'free-for-all' in the provision of hackney carriage services would not be acceptable. However, as mentioned above, if number restrictions are removed, all quality control provisions remain in place and the market will find the level for the number of hackney carriages which an area can sustain.

8.171

It is often argued that delimitation will lead to congestion and unacceptably high numbers of hackney carriages plying and ranking within the local authority area. Such vast increases appear to be rare among those authorities which have delimited numbers, especially bearing in mind the capital outlay which is required to invest in a suitable vehicle on the part of a potential proprietor. When this is offset against the uncertainty of the rewards which a hackney carriage proprietor's licence is likely to return, it is understandable why the threatened exponential rise in hackney carriage numbers in many areas has not been experienced. In addition, in areas where delimitation has taken place, some private hire vehicle licensees surrender their licences and apply for hackney carriage licences instead (obviously subject to provision of a suitable vehicle), again reducing the potential for a huge increase in hackney carriage numbers.

8.172

The arguments in relation to overcrowding and congestion are also difficult to translate into reality. Even if a local authority experienced an increase in hackney carriage numbers of some two to three hundred vehicles, in terms of the actual traffic flow in most town centres, that would represent a very small percentage increase.

8.173

It is undoubtedly true that an increase in hackney carriage numbers can lead to additional pressure on hackney carriage stands, but there appear to be only a handful of local authorities in England and Wales which are able to provide stands for all their hackney carriages. This is notwithstanding the requirement contained in byelaw 7 of the model byelaws, which requires the driver of a hackney carriage, when plying for hire and not actually hired, to:

'(a) proceed with reasonable speed to one of the stands appointed by the Council;

(b) if a stand, at the time of his arrival, is occupied by the full number of carriages authorised to occupy it, proceed to another stand.'

Realistically, it must always be expected that some vehicles will be unable to rank at any given time and they will be either plying for hire, undertaking hire or simply not working at that particular time.

8.174

Provided that the local authority maintains quality control, delimitation should not be a problem for hackney carriage services. A number of local authorities have combined delimitation with the introduction of vehicle specifications (including wheelchair accessibility), age policies and liveries with a view to using the change as a method of increasing the quality of the hackney carriage fleet, as well as using the increase in outlay required for a person to enter the trade as a method of tempering significant rapid increases in hackney carriage numbers, which may lead to the congestion difficulties and unacceptable losses for existing trade members.

Guidance for local authorities

8.175

In 1985, the Department of Transport issued a circular[1] giving guidance on the then new restriction on the power of local authorities to limit the number of hackney carriages that they would licence. Paragraphs 26–28 stated:

'*Grant of taxi licences*

26. Section 16 [Transport Act 1985] will also be brought into effect on 6 January [1986]. This section qualifies the power which district councils now have under the Town Police Clauses Act 1847 to refuse to grant taxi licences in support of a policy of limiting the number of taxis in their area. Under the section a district council may refuse an application for a licence in order to limit the number of taxis if, but only if, they are satisfied that there is no significant unmet demand for taxi services within the area to which the licence would apply. An applicant whose licence is refused by a district council has a right of appeal to the Crown Court. The section does not require district councils to limit the number of taxi licences they issue for this reason; it forbids them to restrict numbers for any other reason. The powers of district councils to refuse licences or put conditions on them, relating to the fitness of the applicant or his vehicle are undiminished. In view of the fact that these vehicles may now be authorised to carry passengers at separate fares, district councils may wish to review the conditions of fitness laid down for these vehicles and the enforcement of maintenance standards. The attention of district councils is drawn to the provisions of paragraph 1 of Schedule 7, which establishes that taxis may be licensed with up to eight passenger seats.

Advice on the grant of taxi licences

27. District councils may wish to review their policy on the control of hackney carriage numbers in the light of the section [Transport Act 1985, s 16]. Limitation of taxi numbers can have many undesirable effects – an insufficiency of taxis, either generally or at particular times or in particular places; insufficient competition between the providers of taxi services, to the detriment of their customers; and prices for the transfer of taxi licences from one person to another which imply an artificial restriction of supply. Under the section a district council may refuse a licence to restrict numbers only if satisfied that there is not significant unmet demand for taxis in the relevant area. If there is an appeal, it will be for the council to convince the court that they had reasonable grounds for being so satisfied. It will not, in general, be sufficient for a district council to rely on the assertion of existing taxi licence holders that the demand is already catered for. They have evidence only of the demand which they satisfy and it will be for the council themselves to seek for and examine the evidence of unmet demand. There may be those who have given up trying to use taxis because of the inadequacy of the service and there may be latent demand in parts of a district that have not been adequately served – where those who wish to use taxis may not have demonstrated their demand since there had been no opportunity of having it satisfied. Moreover, if the applicant for a new taxi licence proposed to use it to provide a new service – for instance under section 12 – and had reasonable grounds to believe that there would be a demand for his service if he provided it, a council which wished to refuse a licence would have to satisfy themselves that the demand would not be forthcoming. Overcrowding at taxi ranks is not of itself evidence that there is no unmet demand. It may be that the provision of ranks has hitherto been too limited and the council should look actively for sites for further ranks.

This circular was modified by Department of Transport circular 4/87[2] following some early delimitation cases[3]. The conclusion of the Circular was[4]:

'8. It follows from these judgments that:

a. A council may adopt a policy of de-restricting the number of taxi licences that it issues, without considering the question of demand;

b. It is not open to a Council which is unsure of the presence or absence of significant unmet demand to refuse to grant any application for a taxi licence for the purpose of limiting the number of taxi licences; and

c. A Council which believes that there is significant unmet demand and is able to quantify the extent of that demand must grant at least such number of taxi licences as it considers necessary to ensure that no significant unmet demand remains.

9. It is, of course, open to a Council which is satisfied that there in no significant unmet demand to refuse to grant additional taxi licences.

10. The advice contained in Paragraph 28 of Circular 3/85 is now withdrawn[5].'

Collectively these circulars are now over 30 years' old and although they have never been formally cancelled, they have been superseded by the Department for Transport *Best Practice Guidance*[6]. They remain important however, as they informed many of the important judgments that related to limitation or delimitation of hackney carriage numbers.

[1] DoT circular 3/85, reproduced in Appendix II.
[2] See Appendix II.
[3] *R v Great Yarmouth Borough Council, ex p Sawyer* (1987) [1989] RTR 297n, CA; see para 8.180 below; *R v Reading Borough Council, ex p Egan* (1987) [1990] RTR 399n; see para 8.179 below.
[4] DoT circular 3/85, paras 8–10.
[5] Paragraph 28 stated:
       "**28.** There are a number of district councils which already exercise no control on the number of taxis in their areas without causing problems of over supply. However, the Department [of Transport] accepts that in some areas the total abandonment of quantity control could lead to an initial over-supply of taxis before market forces could bring about an equilibrium between supply and demand. In order to avoid possible disruption, a district council faced with a large number of new applicants, could, in the Department's view, reasonably grant a proportion of the applications, deferring consideration of the remainder until the effects of granting the first tranche could be assessed.'"
[6] DfT, '*Taxi and Private Hire Vehicle Licensing: Best Practice Guidance*' (October 2006, revised March 2010) available at http://www.dft.gov.uk/pgr/regional/taxis/taxiandprivatehirevehiclelic1792. See Appendix II.

8.176

The current guidance from the DfT is contained in the *Best Practice Guide*[1] in the following terms:

'QUANTITY RESTRICTIONS OF TAXI LICENCES OUTSIDE LONDON

45. The present legal provision on quantity restrictions for taxis outside London is set out in section 16 of the Transport Act 1985. This provides

that the grant of a taxi licence may be refused, for the purpose of limiting the number of licensed taxis 'if, but only if, the [local licensing authority] is satisfied that there is no significant demand for the services of hackney carriages (within the area to which the licence would apply) which is unmet'.

46. Local licensing authorities will be aware that, in the event of a challenge to a decision to refuse a licence, the local authority concerned would have to establish that it had, reasonably, been satisfied that there was no significant unmet demand.

47. Most local licensing authorities do not impose quantity restrictions; the Department regards that as best practice. Where restrictions are imposed, the Department would urge that the matter should be regularly reconsidered. The Department further urges that the issue to be addressed first in each reconsideration is whether the restrictions should continue at all. It is suggested that the matter should be approached in terms of the interests of the travelling public – that is to say, the people who use taxi services. What benefits or disadvantages arise for them as a result of the continuation of controls; and what benefits or disadvantages would result for the public if the controls were removed? Is there evidence that removal of the controls would result in a deterioration in the amount or quality of taxi service provision?

48. In most cases where quantity restrictions are imposed, vehicle licence plates command a premium, often of tens of thousands of pounds. This indicates that there are people who want to enter the taxi market and provide a service to the public, but who are being prevented from doing so by the quantity restrictions. This seems very hard to justify.

49. If a local authority does nonetheless take the view that a quantity restriction can be justified in principle, there remains the question of the level at which it should be set, bearing in mind the need to demonstrate that there is no significant unmet demand. This issue is usually addressed by means of a survey; it will be necessary for the local licensing authority to carry out a survey sufficiently frequently to be able to respond to any challenge to the satisfaction of a court. An interval of three years is commonly regarded as the maximum reasonable period between surveys.

50. As to the conduct of the survey, the Department's letter of 16 June 2004 set out a range of considerations. But key points are:

> **the length of time that would-be customers have to wait at ranks.** However, this alone is an inadequate indicator of demand; also taken into account should be...

> **waiting times for street hailings and for telephone bookings.** But waiting times at ranks or elsewhere do not in themselves satisfactorily resolve the question of unmet demand. It is also desirable to address...

latent demand, for example people who have responded to long waiting times by not even trying to travel by taxi. This can be assessed by surveys of people who do not use taxis, perhaps using stated preference survey techniques.

peaked demand. It is sometimes argued that delays associated only with peaks in demand (such as morning and evening rush hours, or pub closing times) are not 'significant' for the purpose of the Transport Act 1985. The Department does not share that view. Since the peaks in demand are by definition the most popular times for consumers to use taxis, it can be strongly argued that unmet demand at these times should not be ignored. Local authorities might wish to consider when the peaks occur and who is being disadvantaged through restrictions on provision of taxi services.

consultation. As well as statistical surveys, assessment of quantity restrictions should include consultation with all those concerned, including user groups (which should include groups representing people with disabilities, and people such as students or women), the police, hoteliers, operators of pubs and clubs and visitor attractions, and providers of other transport modes (such as train operators, who want taxis available to take passengers to and from stations);

publication. All the evidence gathered in a survey should be published, together with an explanation of what conclusions have been drawn from it and why. If quantity restrictions are to be continued, their benefits to consumers and the reason for the particular level at which the number is set should be set out.

financing of surveys. It is not good practice for surveys to be paid for by the local taxi trade (except through general revenues from licence fees). To do so can call in question the impartiality and objectivity of the survey process.

51. Quite apart from the requirement of the 1985 Act, the Department's letter of 16 June 2004 asked all local licensing authorities that operate quantity restrictions to review their policy and justify it publicly by 31 March 2005 and at least every three years thereafter. The Department also expects the justification for any policy of quantity restrictions to be included in the Local Transport Plan process. A recommended list of questions for local authorities to address when considering quantity controls was attached to the Department's letter. (The questions are listed in Annex A to this Guidance.)'

In April 2017 the Competition and Markets Authority ('CMA') issued guidance to Local Authorities in relation to limitation of hackney carriage numbers[2]. This makes it clear that in the opinion of the CMA, restriction of hackney carriage numbers harms consumer choice. They stated:

'Quantity restrictions are not necessary to ensure the safety of passengers, or to ensure that fares are reasonable. However, they can harm passengers by reducing availability, increasing waiting times, and reducing the scope for downward competitive pressure on fares.

The CMA takes the view that concerns around congestion, air pollution and enforcement costs can generally be addressed through measures less harmful to passengers' interests than quantity restrictions.'

1   DfT, '*Taxi and Private Hire Vehicle Licensing: Best Practice Guidance*' (October 2006, revised March 2010) available at http://www.dft.gov.uk/pgr/regional/taxis/taxiandprivatehirevehiclelic1792. See Appendix II.

2   *Regulation of taxis and private hire vehicles: understanding the impact on competition* – Competition and Markets Authority, April 2017 available at https://www.gov.uk/government/uploads/system/uploads/attachment_data/file/624539/taxi_phv_la_guidance.pdf; see Appendix II.

Increasing numbers of hackney carriages and surveys: case law

8.177

It is not surprising that there has been significant litigation on this area. Although some of the cases appear to conflict, it is possible to discern a line of reasoning. The cases are considered in chronological order.

Tudor v Ellesmere Port and Neston Borough Council

8.178

> Application for two new hackney carriage vehicle licences, which was refused. At the Crown Court an assertion was made in closing arguments by the Council which the appellant was not given any opportunity to rebut. Held: That this was a breach of the rules of natural justice, and those rules apply to the decision making process and any appeal.

The first reported High Court decision was that in *Tudor v Ellesmere Port and Neston Borough Council*[1]. This case is authority for the view that the rules of natural justice must be followed in an appeal against refusal to grant a hackney carriage proprietor's licence. An assertion that the applicant was not a fit and proper person was introduced during the final speech made on behalf of the council and the appellant had no opportunity to rebut the allegations. In relation to unmet demand, it was decided that, although an application for two licences had been made and turned down by the council, by the time the appeal was heard by the Crown Court, the provisions of the Transport Act 1985 were in force and in the absence of any evidence as to the demand, the council conceded that it could no longer refuse to grant the licences merely by reason of numbers.

1   (1987) Times, 8 May.

R v Reading Borough Council, ex p Egan

8.179

> Could a council grant a batch of new hackney carriage licences and then wait and see if there was no unmet demand? Held: In the absence of evidence to show that there was no unmet demand, irrespective of a recent grant of licences, an application for additional licences must be granted.

The next case to be considered was *R v Reading Borough Council, ex p Egan*[1]. The facts are that, on the introduction of the Transport Act 1985, s 16, Reading Borough Council followed the advice given in the Department of Transport circular 3/85. Until the introduction of the Transport Act 1985 the council had licensed 50 hackney carriages. It was then proposed to grant an additional 30 licences, then 'wait and see' and assess the impact of those additional licences on the demand for hackney carriages, in accordance with the circular. This was challenged by means of judicial review. Judgment was handed down by Nolan J. His decision was as follows (at 404A):

> 'The question before me, however, is a different one, namely, whether a council which is unsure of the presence or absence of unmet demand, but which fears that immediate and total de-restriction may cause over-provision, is entitled to issue a limited number of further licences as a temporary measure, and as a means of obtaining the evidence by which the presence or absence of unmet demand can finally be established.
>
> I wish that I could answer this question in the affirmative. The dangers of over-provision were clearly accepted by the law prior to 1985, as is shown by the judgment of Lord Goddard CJ in *Rex v Weymouth Borough Council, ex p Teletax (Weymouth) Ltd* [1947] KB 583 and are recognised in paragraph 28 of the circular as still existing. If there is an unnecessarily large number of taxis, there may be great and unnecessarily difficulties in supervising and controlling them. The fact that a policy of total de-restriction has worked without problems in other areas does not mean it will work without problems in Reading. But in my judgment the language of section 16 is too clear to allow these considerations to prevail. By its own admission the council was not satisfied on 28th January 1986 and for that matter is not satisfied now as to the absence of unmet demand. It is surprising, but clear, that the Act of 1985 made no provision for any interim period during which licensing authorities might have an opportunity to establish, by market research or otherwise, the presence or absence of unmet demand. It follows that from the time section 16 came into force on 6th January 1986 the council and any other council which is unable to feel satisfied that there is no significant unmet demand had been obliged to grant applications for licences in respect of suitably qualified vehicles without limit of number. Paragraph 28 of the circular appears to me to incorporate an erroneous view of the law.'

[1]   (1987) [1990] RTR 399n (the case dates from 1987, but was not reported until 1990).

R v Great Yarmouth Borough Council, ex p Sawyer

8.180

> The council decided to remove the limit on hackney carriage numbers
> without any independent survey. Held: That was lawful, and the only possible
> challenge was that the decision was unreasonable on *Wednesbury* grounds.

The next case, *R v Great Yarmouth Borough Council, ex p Sawyer*[1], is important in
relation to the making of the decision of whether or not to delimit the number
of hackney carriages. When the Transport Act 1985, s 16 was first proposed in
the Transport Bill, Great Yarmouth Borough Council considered its position in
relation to hackney carriage licensing. Until then the number had been limited,
but, prior to the introduction of the Act, consideration of the position took place.
At that time the council reconsidered. The Transportation Sub-Committee took
the view that the number should be maintained as there was no significant unmet
demand, but also asked the trade to look into methods of providing evidence to
support that view. The sub-committee did not have delegated powers but was
reporting to the full committee and at the full committee the decision was made
to delimit the number of hackney carriages operating within the borough. That
decision was approved by full council. Judicial review was sought of that decision
on the basis that it was, first, unreasonable in *Wednesbury* terms and, secondly,
that irrelevant matters had been taken into account. The irrelevant matters were
alleged to be a consideration by Great Yarmouth Borough Council as to what
actions were being taken in respect of the new legislative requirements by other
authorities in Norfolk.

[1]   (1987) [1989] RTR 297n, CA.

8.181

In relation to the argument of irrationality, Woolf LJ stated[1] (at 301L):

> '... looking at the position, as this court does, on appeal from Hodgson
> J and as did the judge [in the Crown Court], on the basis of the material
> which was available to the committee when it came to its decision, the
> position is clear. There is not the beginning of a case to show that the
> decision of the transportation committee was irrational.'

Woolf LJ carried on and stated that the appeal was bound to fail (at 302K):

> 'In coming to that conclusion, I would emphasise two matters. First of
> all, the role of the judge was an extremely limited role, having regard to
> the provisions of the Act to which I have made reference. The judge, in
> coming to his conclusion, was not purporting to express any view as to
> the merit of the decision of the authority. The authority was given the
> responsibility, under the licensing legislation, as amended, of coming to
> a decision with regard to whether or not they were prepared to maintain
> their previous policy. They came to that decision, and the courts can only

intervene if it is shown that the authority has gone about its task in a way which was unlawful.

The other matter which I would mention is that clearly, on the material put before this court, the individual taxi drivers may suffer material hardship as a result of the change of policy. With regard to their problems, the court has in mind the evidence, but because of the role of the courts to which I have already made reference, there is no basis for intervening on the grounds of the individual hardship of individual drivers.'

Bingham LJ considered the matter and came to the same conclusion. He stated (at 303G):

'In the council reaching that decision, a number of matters entered into the council's thinking. The members plainly knew of the council's own previous policy. They also clearly knew of the policy of the Act. They appreciated the difficulty of proving the lack of unmet demand, despite the strong representations of the local taxi proprietors. They appreciated the cost of defending proceedings unsuccessfully. Inquiries showed that most authorities in the area were adopting a policy of de-restriction. Accordingly, the council decided that it would adopt a policy of de-restriction.

I see nothing irrational or unlawful in that process of consideration. A council does not need a reason under the Act to adopt a policy of de-restriction. Therefore, a decision to de-restrict is very hard to challenge on the grounds of irrationality, although no doubt, that could be done if the decision was made for obviously unsustainable reasons.'

Finally, Dillon LJ gave a concurring judgment which led to a unanimous decision of the Court of Appeal. In a short judgment he stated (at 304B):

'On the facts, I see no indication that the council took into account matters that they should not have taken into account. In particular, I think they were entitled to be told what action other district councils in Norfolk would be taking in relation to the Act. Beyond that I see no basis on the facts for any conclusion that the council acted unreasonably in forming the view, as deposed to by Mr Emslie, that they could not be satisfied that there was no unmet demand for hackney carriages in the area, and in consequently deciding to de-restrict the number of hackney carriages operating in the borough. They could not decide to restrict the number unless they were satisfied that there was no significant unmet demand. They were not bound to make further inquires or have surveys conducted in order to see more clearly whether there was or was not unmet demand.'

[1]   *R v Great Yarmouth Borough Council, ex p Sawyer* (1987) [1989] RTR 297n, CA.

8.182

This case is authority for the proposition that a local authority can at any time decide to delimit the number of hackney carriages for which it will grant licences, subject only to the proviso that that decision must not, of itself, be *Wednesbury* unreasonable. Provided that the council has taken into consideration the relevant matters and, conversely, has not considered anything irrelevant, it can decide to take that course of action.

8.183

As to what would be relevant matters will be a matter of fact in every case, but obvious ones would include:

- The financial impact on existing licence holders who may have invested in their licence.
- The potential reduced custom for existing licence holders.
- Congestion on hackney carriage stands.
- Congestion on the roads generally.
- Benefits to the travelling public of additional vehicles.
- The opportunity for others to become involved in the trade as a means of securing a livelihood.
- The costs of commissioning a survey.
- The costs of allocating a small number of additional licences.
- The costs of defending appeals against refusals to grant licences, either with or without a survey.

Stevenage Borough Council v Younas

8.184

> There was evidence of a period of unmet demand at night in the vicinity of a particular nightclub. Was this sufficient to prevent the council refusing an application for a new hackney carriage licence? Held: That it was not, it was evidence of unmet demand, but not evidence of the significance of that unmet demand.

The case of *Stevenage Borough Council v Younas*[1] is a High Court decision, which follows the view given by the Court of Appeal in the *Great Yarmouth* case[2], eg that the broad approach could be adopted. Stevenage Borough Council commissioned a survey and the Crown Court gave the following case for an appeal against a refusal to grant a licence to Mr Younas (at 406L):

'We were satisfied that it had been demonstrated that there was no significant demand for the services of hackney carriages within the area of the Stevenage Borough Council which was unmet subject to one proviso. This proviso is as follows. We heard certain evidence relating to the demand for the services of hackney carriages near a particular night-club in Stevenage after midnight. This evidence was to some extent conflicting and we did not find it necessary to resolve such conflicts in the evidence as there were although we were not prepared to reject the appellant's on this point.

We concluded, however, that bearing in mind the evidence relating to the demand for the services of hackney carriages after midnight, the council could not be satisfied that there was no significant demand for the services of hackney carriages within the area of Stevenage Borough Council which was unmet.

The question for the opinion of the court was stated as follows:

"... whether on the evidence before the court" – that is, before the Crown Court –

"It was correct in law to hold that the council could not be satisfied that there was no significant demand for the services of hackney carriages within the area of the council which was unmet".'

Pill J concluded (at 408G) that the findings of the Crown Court did not:

'in my judgment prevent the council from being satisfied in the terms of the section. A broader approach is legitimate on the wording of the section. The Crown Court were wrong in law in reaching the conclusion which they did ... I accept that the burden upon the council is a heavy one. The Crown Court found however that, subject to one point, that burden had been satisfied.'

This case supports the view that, even if a survey finds that there is some unmet demand at some place in the district at a particular time, this itself is not sufficient to demonstrate significant unmet demand, if the rest of the time demand is satisfied. It is a test of the degree of significance of the unmet demand, rather than simply the existence of it.

[1]   (1988) [1990] RTR 405n, QBD.
[2]   *R v Great Yarmouth Borough Council, ex p Sawyer* (1987) [1989] RTR 297n, CA; see para 8.180 above.

R v Halton Borough Council, ex p Gunson

8.185

> Having decided to delimit hackney carriage numbers, following lobbying by the hackney carriage trade, the authority re-imposed a limit without any evidence of demand. Held: To be unlawful.

R v Halton Borough Council, ex p Gunson[1] concerned a decision by Halton Borough Council to re-impose a numerical limit on the number of hackney carriage proprietor's licences which it would grant. Before the introduction of the Transport Act 1985 there were 60 hackney carriage vehicles and 261 private hire vehicles. On 1 April 1986 the authority delimited the number of hackney carriage vehicle licences it would issue and, by December 1986, there were 158 hackney carriages and only 66 private hire vehicles. Representations were received by the council from the trade to the effect that there were too many hackney carriages. As a result, the authority set up a 'taxi working party'. This inquired into all aspects of hackney carriage and private hire provision and reported that, although there were a lot of hackney carriages, there was a sparse service in some parts of the borough and recommended that no limit should be imposed. It warned that if a limit was imposed, the present inadequate service would deteriorate even further. This was to be reported to a meeting of the taxi committee (the panel which considered the granting of hackney carriage vehicle licences and setting a number limit) and, two days before that meeting, a circular was published by the taxi driver association to all the members of the committee. It was argued that as a consequence of that circular, the committee departed from the recommendation in the taxi working party's report and imposed a limit which was the number of hackney carriage licences in existence on that date. Challenge was made by way of judicial review to the imposition of the numerical limit on the grounds that it was unreasonable and, on a second ground, that an assurance had been given by a councillor that no limit would be imposed.

1   (29 July 1988, unreported).

8.186

In allowing the application, Otton J stated[1]:

'In approaching this case and in arriving at my conclusions. I start with the effect of section 16 of the 1985 Act [Transport Act 1985]. It is clear that the effect of the amendment to sub-paragraph (*b*) is to transform the permissive "may" from the earlier Act into a partial mandatory "must". Unless the authority is "satisfied there is no significant demand which is unmet it is obliged to issue a licence to an otherwise suitable applicant". It also has the effect that an authority can adopt a policy of no numerical restriction of licences. By the use of the double negative and the emphatic phrase "if but only if", the construction becomes clear in the way that I have adumbrated. It may be that the Committee did in fact carry out the necessary exercise under section 16 of the Town Police Clauses Act 1847. Unfortunately, there is no evidence, or insufficient evidence, that they did. There is no adequate minute of the meeting. There is no adequate record of what occurred at the meeting. This is surprising in view of the fact that it was of such importance and one would have expected a proper record to be kept by the officials to the borough council, including its Chief Executive, or affidavits to be sworn covering these proceedings. The affidavit of Mr Redican [a member of the Committee who proposed the introduction of the numerical limit] only speaks for himself and the affidavit falls short of showing that even he had section 16 clearly and accurately in his mind in proposing the motion that he did. There is no affidavit from the Chairman of the Committee. There is no affidavit from the Chief Executive. The affidavit from Miss Kenny does not take the matter further in this regard. There is no evidence that they even considered the Working Party report, apart from the record that I have read, leading up to the resolution and recommendation. If they did carry out an extensive debate on the implication of the Working Party report, they did not record any evidence of "no significant unmet demand". Indeed, the record of the Working Party suggested and recommended to the contrary. There is no evidence that the Committee correctly considered or complied with their statutory duty under section 16. It is true that the 8th July document from the taxi drivers was before them but there is no suggestion that this document was tested or evaluated. In any event, it did not directly address the question of unmet demand but only the hardship to existing taxi drivers which is not the same thing.

In the surprising absence of any evidence as to how the decision was arrived at, I am left with an overwhelming sense of unease that they were too readily persuaded to bring down the shutter at the behest of the taxi drivers lobby and in particular as a result of its circular letter of the 8th July two days before the meeting. Consequently, I am not prepared to draw the inference that they did reach their conclusion correctly or reach a lawful conclusion. In my judgment the burden of proof on this aspect is upon the council and in spite of Miss Hamilton's [for the council] tenacious argument I have come to the conclusion that the burden has not been discharged. Consequently, I have no option but to rule that the decision is unlawful.'

On the second ground he found that the statement which had been made by the Chairman of the Working Party, that there would be no change in policy without prior notice was not binding. He stated:

'... this statement ... is distinguishable from the statements made in *R v Liverpool Corpn, ex p Liverpool Taxi Fleet Operators Association* [1972] 2 QB 299. The statement which came from the Chairman of the Working Party was not binding and was not meant to be binding either upon the Committee or upon the Council.'

¹   *R v Halton Borough Council, ex p Gunson* (29 July 1988, unreported).

8.187

This case is, effectively, the antithesis of the *Great Yarmouth* decision¹ where it was held that the authority could decide to deregulate unless that decision was in itself *Wednesbury* unreasonable. In the present case of *R v Halton Borough Council, ex p Gunson*², it was decided that as the decision to re-limit was not based on any evidence at all, it was in itself irrational and, therefore, unlawful.

¹   *R v Great Yarmouth Borough Council, ex p Sawyer* (1987) [1989] RTR 297n, CA; see para 8.180 above.
²   *R v Halton Borough Council, ex p Gunson* (29 July 1988, unreported).

R v Brighton Borough Council, ex p Bunch

8.188

Following a survey conducted by an independent body which showed times of sparse supply of hackney carriages, the council resolved not to issue any more hackney carriage licences. This was challenged as not taking into account latent demand. Held: The council could only take account of demand for services only hackney carriages could provide, ie immediate hiring and not other transport needs that could be satisfied by private hire vehicles or buses. The judgment also provided judicial approval of independent surveys.

The next case, dating from 1989, is *R v Brighton Borough Council, ex p Bunch*[1]. Brighton Borough Council commissioned a survey in June 1986 which found that there was no significant unmet demand for hackney carriage services within the borough. As a result, they resolved not to issue any new hackney carriage licences, but decided to have a second survey in the following year. This was undertaken and the conclusions were reported to the licensing sub-committee of the council in November 1987. This showed that, generally, there was no change in the position from the previous year (that is, there was no significant unmet demand) but that there were times of poor service. The report to the sub-committee stated:

> 'Poor service is not caused by a shortage of licensed taxis but is due to the reluctance of existing drivers to work anti social hours ... The council have undoubtedly licensed sufficient taxis for all reasonable needs and there would be no problems in meeting demand if better operating practices were adopted.'

The council accepted this view and resolved that no new hackney carriage licences would be granted. This was challenged on a number of grounds by way of judicial review and the matter was considered by Kennedy J in the Divisional Court. The first ground was that the minutes of the meeting did not accurately reflect the decision. That was rejected.

The second ground was that the council had failed to take into account properly the results of the surveys which showed that there were periods of unmet demand. In relation to this Kennedy J outlined the arguments and stated (at p 6):

> '1. That demand may not be visible. It may be latent because a person who knows that it will be difficult to get a taxi may well make some other arrangements, so that he will not be there to be counted if, for example, a count is made of the numbers in a taxi queue, and

> 2. That "the services of hackney carriages" should be interpreted as meaning all services which a hackney carriage can give, and not just those such as standing for hire in a taxi rank, and responding to the customer who hails a taxi in the street which are services which only a hackney carriage can provide.

> Mr Norman [For the applicants, Bunch and others] submits that Mr Corner's [the surveyor from Sussex University] surveys make no attempt to measure latent demand, and concentrate far too much on the services which only a hackney carriage can provide.

> For the respondents, Mr McCarthy submits that the approach adopted by Mr Corner was correct not only because it is necessary, as we said

in *Sawyer v Gt Yarmouth Borough Council* (unreported), to adopt a broad approach but also because when Parliament enacted the proviso which appears in section 16 of the Transport Act 1985 it contemplated the licensing authority being satisfied of the present non-existence of any significant unmet demand. The statutory use of the present tense must render it unnecessary to consider latent demand and anyway the authority could only be satisfied by evidence of such demand as is measurable, which is only patent demand. I accept that submission.

As to the services of hackney carriages, Mr McCarthy submits that in the context of section 16 of the Transport Act 1985 those words must mean the services which only a hackney carriage can provide, an interpretation which commended itself to the Portsmouth Crown Court on 24th October 1988 in the case of *Portsmouth City Council v Brown* (unreported). Here again it seems to me that Mr McCarthy is right because section 37 of the Town Police Clauses Act 1847 is concerned with licensing hackney carriages to ply for hire, and it would be surprising if a licensing authority were bound to licence hackney carriages because it could not be satisfied that there was no significant unmet demand for services which could be performed equally well by other types of vehicle (such as a private hire vehicle or a bus).'

Although it was accepted that the surveys had shown that there were periods of unmet demand, the argument that the council had failed to take the surveys correctly into account was unsuccessful.

The third ground was that the council had taken into account an irrelevant factor when it brought into question the working practices of the existing hackney carriage drivers. Kennedy J stated (at – again, as indicated on the transcript)):

'On the evidence before it the sub-committee was entitled to conclude that there was no significant unmet demand even if one member of the majority [party on the committee] did think that there was an unmet demand (albeit insignificant) which may be relieved by certain changes in traffic management and work practices. And, in any event, as I have already indicated I am not satisfied in relation to Councillor Hawkes that the recollection of Mr Bunch is correct.'

and as a consequence that ground of challenge failed.

The final ground was that the conclusions reached by the Council that there was no significant unmet demand was unreasonable or irrational. This called into question the validity of the surveys and failed.

The overall conclusion was that the approach of the Court of Appeal in the *Great Yarmouth* case[2] was correct and that a broad approach could be taken by looking at the area of the borough council as a whole. As a result, short periods of poor service did not automatically mean that there was unmet demand.

[1]   [1989] COD 558.

[2]   *R v Great Yarmouth Borough Council, ex p Sawyer* (1987) [1989] RTR 297n, CA; see para 8.180 above.

8.189

It is interesting to note that it was recognised by the court that the approach taken by the surveyors was correct. Kennedy J stated (at 7–8):

> 'Here many of the detailed complaints relate to matters I have already considered, but complaint is also made of the respondents' failure to obtain evidence of demand for hackney carriage services from consumers.
>
> That in my judgment is answered by Mr Corner in his 1987 survey where he says at page 47 why he did not attempt to consult the public. His report continues: "People do not maintain accurate records of such mundane matters as taxi use. There is abundant evidence that people are extremely poor at estimating waiting times. Careful observation of ranks is of much greater value than selective and probably inaccurate recollections of actual or potential taxi users about their experiences and attitudes."
>
> In more general terms complaint is made that the respondents failed to inquire into the level of unmet demand, but that I cannot accept. It is abundantly clear to me that a competent person was instructed to carry out an independent survey, that he did so with skill and care, and that the respondents then took proper steps to circulate and to receive comments upon the survey which had been produced. No more could reasonably be required of them.'

It can be seen that this is judicial approval of an independent survey.

8.190

The application for judicial review was dismissed and Kennedy J stated that the challenge should not have been made by way of judicial review, but rather should have been by way of an appeal to the Crown Court against the refusal to grant the licence applied for. This case once again supports the view that the broad approach can be taken, when considering the question of the significance of any unmet demand for hackney carriage services.

Ghafoor v Wakefield Metropolitan District Council

8.191

> The council decided to issue a batch of licences and then assess the impact. This was challenged by unsuccessful applicants. Held: (departing from the Reading approach) that this was lawful, and that a broad approach to demand could be taken.

The approach in *R v Reading Borough Council, ex p Egan*[1] was not followed in the case of *Ghafoor v Wakefield Metropolitan District Council*[2]. Until the introduction of the Transport Act 1985, s 16, Wakefield Metropolitan District Council had maintained a limit on the number of hackney carriages it would licence. The council commissioned a survey which stated that there was an unmet demand for hackney carriage services. As a consequence, the council decided to issue five licences. The unsatisfied applicants, who had not received a licence, appealed to the Crown Court, which dismissed the appeal. A further appeal was made to the High Court. Four specific questions were raised:

'1.   What was the correct approach for the Crown Court to adopt in determining appeals from the local authority? Should the Crown Court seek to determine how a reasonable council would have acted if it had heard the evidence heard by the Crown Court or should it exercise its own judgment?

2.   Did the Crown Court apply the law correctly in this case, in particular:

(*a*)   did the Crown Court apply the correct burden of proof?

(*b*)   did the Crown Court apply the correct standard of proof?

(*c*)   was the Crown Court right in adopting a broad approach to the question of demand?

3.   Was the Crown Court right in concluding that there was no significant unmet demand for taxi services in Wakefield?

4.   In the light of the Crown Court's determination in September 1987 that the council had failed to establish that there was a significant unmet demand for hackney carriages in Wakefield and in the light of the Crown Court's present findings on the question of delay [at hackney carriage ranks], would the applicants have a sense of grievance that could result in their having a genuine and reasonable feeling that justice had not been seen to be done?'

[1]   (1987) [1990] RTR 399n; see para 8.179 above.
[2]   [1990] RTR 389, QBD.

8.192

Webster J considered para 28 of DoT circular 3/85. Although that approach had been ruled unlawful by Nolan J in *R v Reading Borough Council ex p Egan*[1], Webster J disagreed with that interpretation and stated[2] (at 394J):

'With great respect to the judge, I cannot agree either with that view or his decision that section 16 obliged local authorities which were unable to feel satisfied that there was no significant unmet demand to issue new hackney carriage licences without limit of number. In my view the effect of section 16 is, as I have said, merely to deprive the licensing authority of the discretion, which it would otherwise have, to refuse a particular application by a fit and proper person for the purpose of limiting the number of taxis except when it is satisfied that there is no significant unmet demand within the area; but there is nothing, in my view, to prevent an authority from advising itself in one way or another about the number of taxis which would have to be licensed in order to meet all significant demand and, having granted licences up to that number, from refusing the next application or applications after that number had been reached unless, by that time, the circumstances have changed so that the authority could no longer be satisfied that there was, given the total number of licences then issued, no significant unmet demand.'

He continued (at 395E):

> 'I therefore conclude that the council in the present case were acting perfectly properly in assessing the number of licences needed to satisfy the significant unmet demand and, having done so, in issuing only that number of licences provided that, when any further application was made, they satisfied themselves afresh as to the absence of significant unmet demand before deciding to refuse that application.'

In relation to the specific questions, Webster J decided that the Crown Court did apply the correct burden of proof and were correct in their approach, that it is upon the local authority to show that there is no unmet demand. In relation to standard of proof, it is that which is applicable in civil proceedings (ie the balance of probabilities). Finally, he accepted the Court of Appeal's view that a broad approach in relation to demand could be taken, rather than a narrow approach on the basis that there was a specific delay at a specific rank at a specific time.

[1]   (1987) [1990] RTR 399n; see para 8.179 above.
[2]   *Ghafoor v Wakefield Metropolitan District Council* [1990] RTR 389, QBD.

R v Middlesbrough Council, ex p I J H Cameron (Holdings) Ltd

8.193

> The council deferred making a decision on an application for new hackney carriage licences until a survey had been commissioned and the results received, whereupon six months later they determined there was no unmet demand and refused the application. Held: A deferment for a short period of time did not amount to a refusal (but see *Wirral* below).

The approach taken in *Wakefield*[1], rather than the *Reading*[2] approach, was followed in *R v Middlesbrough Council, ex p I J H Cameron (Holdings) Ltd*[3]. The question in this case was whether a deferral of a decision as to whether or not to grant a hackney carriage proprietor's licence amounted to a refusal. In this case, an application was made for 25 hackney carriage proprietor's licences in January 1989. No response was received from the local authority, so, in March of the same year, the solicitors for the applicant wrote to the council asking for a decision. In April, the council committee deferred the issue of additional licences until a survey had been undertaken to ascertain whether or not there was significant unmet demand. The results of that survey were received by the council in June and in July 1989, the applicant was notified that his applications had been refused. The applicant asserted that the delay amounted to a refusal and that if the council could not satisfy itself as to the extent of any unmet demand, following the ruling in *R v Reading Borough Council, ex p Egan*[4], they must grant the licences applied for. The High Court (in front of Popplewell J) held that a deferral for a comparatively short period of time, in order to conduct a survey as to unmet demand, did not amount to a refusal and, therefore, it did not follow the decision of Nolan J in the *Reading* case.

1   *Ghafoor v Wakefield Metropolitan District Council* [1990] RTR 389 QBD; see para 8.191 above.
2   *R v Reading Borough Council, ex p Egan* (1987) [1990] RTR 399n; see para 8.179 above.
3   [1992] COD 247.
4   (1987) [1990] RTR 399; see para 8.179 above.

Cannock Chase District Council v Alldritt

8.194

> Application for hackney carriage licences in a district where there was overall no unmet demand, but short supply in one particular town where the applicant intended to use the new vehicles. Refused by the council but on a challenge to the Crown Court decision to refuse the licences by way of case stated. Held: That the area could be a small part of the district, and not the whole of the district.

Cannock Chase District Council v Alldritt[1] concerned an application for six hackney carriage proprietor's licences. Cannock Chase District Council had a policy of limiting numbers, which was supported by a survey. Mr Alldritt applied for six hackney carriage licences with a view to operating in the town of Rugeley. The district of Cannock Chase comprises significant areas of rural countryside and three quite distinct towns: Cannock, Hednesford and Rugeley. The assertion made by Mr Alldritt was that there was unmet demand in Rugeley and that was where he proposed to use the vehicles, if successful in his application. The view of the council, based on their survey, was that, although there was greater demand in Rugeley than elsewhere in the district, taking the district as a whole, there was no significant unmet demand. They refused the applications. Mr Alldritt appealed to the Crown Court and the Crown Court upheld his appeal. The district council appealed by way of case stated and the High Court dismissed their appeal. The High Court does not appear to have been referred to any other cases. In the Crown Court, the view was quite clearly taken that the expression 'the area' could include a part of the area of the district council and did not have to relate to the entire area. The matter was considered by the High Court, and Mann LJ gave the following judgment (at 3A):

> 'The council is concerned at certain of the language employed by the Crown Court in its decision. In particular it is concerned that the Crown Court is indicating to the council that the phrase "the area" in section 16 means in effect any part of the area. I can understand that concern. However, although I understand the concern, it seems to me to be a point of no materiality in the instant proceedings. These proceedings were not review proceedings. Were they such, this court would have had to consider whether the council had properly directed itself, and if it had whether its conclusion was perverse. However, that did not arise because the appeal to the Crown Court involves a hearing de novo. It is the Crown Court which then becomes vested with the power of refusing by reference to the consideration in section 16 of the Act of 1985. I emphasise "power" because as a matter of statutory language there is no obligation to refuse upon that

ground. It is quite plain that in this case the Crown Court considering the matter de novo decided not to exercise the power conferred by section 16. The observations about the council's entitlement to do so I, for my part, would regard as by the way. The court was not concerned with the council's entitlement. It was exercising the powers of licensing de novo. The Crown Court was perfectly entitled to proceed in the way in which it did. There is here no question on the construction of the Act of 1847, as enlarged by section 16 of the Act of 1985.'

1   (28 January 1993, unreported), DC.

8.195

This judgment[1] seems at odds with the decision in *R v Brighton Borough Council, ex p Bunch*[2]. Whether the same result would have been obtained had the court had the benefit of reference to such cases as *Brighton* and *R v Great Yarmouth Borough Council, ex p Sawyer*[3] is a matter of some conjecture. However, the geography of the area appears to have been an overriding consideration in the minds of both the Crown Court and the High Court. It appears that this case should not be taken as indicating that the rulings in *Bunch* and *Sawyer* are wrong, but rather that the courts will on occasion tailor their judgments to the reality of the situation.

1   *Cannock Chase District Council v Alldritt* (28 January 1993, unreported), DC.
2   [1989] COD 558; see para 8.188 above.
3   (1987) [1989] RTR 297n, CA; see para 8.180 above.

R v Leeds City Council, ex p Mellor

8.196

> The council deferred an application pending a survey, and then allocated additional licences by means of a points system. Challenged as unlawful on both approaches. Held: That a deferment was not a refusal, and allocation by a points system was not unlawful provided there was a mechanism for consideration of the circumstances of individual applicants.

The approach that a deferral did not amount to a refusal was followed in *R v Leeds City Council, ex p Mellor*[1]. This case concerned two points. First, there was an assertion that an application for a hackney carriage vehicle licence was effectively refused when the decision was deferred to obtain more information as to unmet demand. Having considered the cases of *R v Reading Borough Council, ex p Egan*[2], *Ghafoor v Wakefield Metropolitan District Council*[3] and *R v Middlesbrough Borough Council, ex p IJH Cameron (Holdings) Ltd*[4]. Hutchison J concluded (at p 7):

> 'My conclusions as to the effect of those authorities is as follows. Like Popplewell J[5], I am persuaded that I should not follow the decision of Nolan J[6] that an authority which is not satisfied that there is no unmet demand must accede to all and any applications before them and may

not defer. I prefer the views of Webster J[7] and in reliance on Popplewell J's decisions and that of Webster J, I would summarise the position as I conceive it to be as follows. First, it is undoubtedly the case that where on an application for a new licence is made and the authority cannot be satisfied that there is no unmet demand, it has no discretion to refuse, for the purpose of limiting numbers, to grant the licence. Secondly, however, there is nothing to prevent an authority from taking steps to inform itself, or further to inform itself, on the question whether there is unmet demand and if necessary to enable it to do so, it may defer consideration of an application or applications. Thirdly, while there may be circumstances in which deferment would amount to refusal in which the case the further question as to whether the purpose of that refusal was the limiting of numbers would have to be addressed, a bona fide deferment will not be construed ordinarily as amounting to a refusal. In this context, there is plainly an obligation on the authority, given the purpose of the 1985 Act and the amendments effected by it, to keep themselves reasonably well informed as to such matters, but plainly information may need updating from time to time because of changed circumstances or, as here, because of the fact that the application introduces a new factor into the equation, the impact of which has not previously been, and requires to be, considered.'

The second point concerned the method of allocation of new licences. Leeds City Council had used, for many years, a 'points system' to allocate the (very few) new hackney carriage vehicle licences which it had hitherto issued. In 1990 a decision was taken to issue 20 new licences for wheelchair accessible vehicles. They amended their existing points system to allocate the new licences. It was argued that by using such a system, proper consideration was not be given to merits of individual applications even though the system had some flexibility built in, as special consideration to individual applications could be given outside the points system and, as a consequence, the council was fettering its discretion. Hutchison J addressed this point as follows (at p 8):

'The second argument is advanced in this way. It is submitted by Mr MacDonald [for the Applicant, Mr Mellor] that in imposing the points system, the applicant was adopting a blanket policy by which no true consideration could be given to the merits of individual applications, in particular the application of Mr Mellor. It is suggested that it was illegitimate so to fetter their discretion. Mr MacDonald referred me to authority on this subject, though I think it is unnecessary to cite it for this reason. He conceded that in the last resort, the question whether it was legitimate for the authority to adopt the criteria which it did in this case, depended on the Wednesbury (see *Associated Provincial Picture Houses v Wednesbury Corporation* [1948] 1 KB 223, [1947] 2 All ER 680) test, that essentially the question was: Could any reasonable authority, addressing itself to the legislative framework and other material considerations, conclude that it was appropriate to apply with modifications the longstanding points system to the allocation of these 20 licences designed for disabled persons. In particular, could it reach that conclusion, apropos a point systems which had been introduced before the 1985 Act in the light of the liberalising policy introduced by that Act?

Mr MacDonald makes the point that the criteria restrict the ambit of those entitled effectively to apply for new licences to a small part of the driving population. He points out that given that the last new licences before this date were issued in 1979, the overwhelming impression is that the local authority were committed to a policy of severely limiting the number of licences which is inconsistent with the general tenor of the 1985 Act and that, in fact, what they were doing by the re-adoption with modifications of these criteria was to perpetuate a situation where the grant of the licence depended on its being, as he put it in what he conceded was an inelegant phrase, Buggins's turn. He submitted that that was out of tune with the approach introduced by the 1985 Act.

Addressing that, ... I unhesitatingly conclude that it cannot be said that it was impermissible for the local authority to adopt these criteria. Opinions might differ as to whether they were the best way of going about it but that is not the test. Opinions certainly could not differ as to whether some form of limitation was appropriate and I need not refer to the authorities which Mr Allen [for the City Council] mentioned on the issue of whether individual consideration in every case was necessary or whether some form of policy was appropriate. It goes without saying that in this context, it is not impermissible to introduce a policy. The question is whether the policy in fact introduced was self-evidently one which no reasonable authority could have adopted. In my judgment, it cannot realistically be argued that it was and I dismiss for that reason this ground of attack.'

The final relevant consideration[8] was whether the council had treated Mr Mellor fairly by baldly applying the policy, without applying any special considerations Hutchison J addressed this point as follows (at page 9 of the judgment):

'However, Mr MacDonald's next ground of challenge, which I have already indicated I accept, is that in the event no proper consideration was given to Mr Mellor's application and, in particular, to the question whether the exempting powers contained in the [points] criteria should be exercised in his case. It is pointed out that there were undoubtedly considerations which should have led the local authority, at any rate, to address the question. He had been the originator of the idea [to increase hackney carriage numbers to accommodate wheelchair accessible vehicles]. He had had an application on the table for approaching two years. He was, it is accepted, in every other way qualified for the grant of such licences and on those general grounds a powerful case could be made for saying that Mr Mellor was somebody who deserved the exercise of the special power to override the strict points system. I say in parenthesis that no separate attack is mounted on *Wednesbury* (see *Associated Provincial Picture Houses v Wednesbury Corporation* [1948] 1 KB 223, [1947] 2 All ER 680) grounds under this head, ie, on the grounds that no reasonable authority could have failed to exercise the exempting powers. The attack is confined to the contention that the evidence establishes that they did not ever address their minds to the question whether that exempting power should be exercised. It is that contention that I have found to be established.

. ... There is no evidence at all that either the Council officers — and it would, I think, have been inappropriate for them to address this point — or the Committee themselves ever adverted to, or considered in any way, the powers that they had power to override the points system. On the contrary, there is inferentially some evidence to suggest that they never did. First of all, there is the fact that the officers ... were charged with the task of, as it were, calculating the points on the basis of the information provided in the 140 odd applications. They did so and their report was received by the Council on the very day (19th December) on which the decisions were made. Arrangements had been made on that day for the 20 successful applicants to attend, for perfectly legitimate reasons, meetings. This was to do with the imposition of the conditions which particularly applied to the grant of these 20 licences for use by disabled people. It therefore seems to me to be almost inescapably clear that it was assumed on that date, and before the Committee ever considered the matter, that subject to their being agreeable to the conditions in question, the 20 successful points applicants, if I may so describe them, were the 20 to whom licences were going to be granted.

Against that background, and in the absence of a scrap of evidence to suggest that the question of special treatment of any applicant and, in particular, Mr Mellor was considered, it seems to me to be established that the approach was on the points basis only and that the power to treat any applicant in a particular manner was never considered and certainly the possibility of exercising it was never taken into account. The officers, it is conceded, carried out a mechanical exercise. I am satisfied on the evidence that I have seen that it is clear that the members of the Committee did the same. Mr Mellor was, in my judgment, entitled to have considered the question whether special consideration should be given to him because of the special position in which he was. He never received that consideration and in that respect I consider that the procedure was flawed and he is entitled to the relief which he seeks.'

1   [1993] COD 352.
2   [1990] RTR 399n; see para 8.179 above.
3   [1990] RTR 389, QBD; see para 8.191 above.
4   [1992] COD 247; see para 8.193 above.
5   *R v Middlesborough Borough Council, ex p IJH Cameron (Holdings) Ltd* [1992] COD 247; see para 8.193 above.
6   *R v Reading Borough Council, ex p Egan* [1990] RTR 399n; see para 8.179 above.
7   *Ghafoor v Wakefield Metropolitan District Council* [1990] RTR 389, QBD; see para 8.191 above.
8   There was a final argument over the correctness of the application for judicial review over an appeal to the Crown Court following a refusal to grant a hackney carriage licence. It was decided that in this case, this was an acceptable approach.

8.197

This judgment is extremely useful, as many authorities which limit the numbers of hackney carriages they will licence, conduct surveys to ascertain whether there is any significant unmet demand. If the survey finds that there is unmet demand, a recommendation is usually made as to how many extra vehicle licences should be granted to satisfy that demand. The local authority then has the difficulty of trying to determine which applicants should be granted licences. Many authorities have drawn up points systems based upon a number of criteria to determine the allocation. The *Leeds* case[1] is extremely important and it supports the view that such a process is acceptable, provided the mechanism is not, in itself, *Wednesbury* unreasonable. However, it is clear from the judgment that such a system must have the flexibility to take account of an individual applicants special circumstances.

[1]   *R v Leeds City Council, ex p Mellor* [1993] COD 352; see para 8.196 above.

Kelly and Smith v Wirral Metropolitan Borough Council

8.198

> An application was made for two hackney carriage licences, which were granted on appeal to the Crown Court, who ordered their issue. That was challenged as others had been on the waiting list for longer. Held by the Court of Appeal, that it was for the authority to determine who should receive licences when there was unmet demand and they should not be simply awarded to a successful litigant. In addition, deferment of a decision did amount to a refusal and trigger a right of appeal.

The Court of Appeal case of *Kelly and Smith v Wirral Metropolitan Borough Council*[1] considered a number of points. These included the mechanism of allocation to be employed when it is found that there is significant unmet demand, whether that finding is by the council or the Crown Court, and the question of deferred decisions.

The case concerned two applications to Wirral Metropolitan Borough Council for hackney carriage proprietor's licences. Wirral Metropolitan Borough Council had a policy of limiting the number of hackney carriages that it would license at the time. Mr Kelly applied for ten hackney carriage proprietor's licences which were refused on the ground that there was no significant unmet demand. He appealed to the Crown Court which upheld his appeal and ordered the council to issue the ten licences to Mr Kelly. The council appealed against that to the High Court, which upheld the appeal by deciding that the Crown Court should not have ordered the issuing of the licences to Mr Kelly but should have remitted the matter back to the council for consideration in the light of the Crown Court's conclusion on demand. Mr Kelly appealed against that decision to the Court of Appeal. The argument against the granting of the ten licences centred on the fact that there were other people on the waiting list who had applied for licences a great deal earlier than Mr Kelly and they would be prejudiced if he was granted ten licences and they received none.

[1]   (1996) 160 JP Rep 1047, CA.

8.199

Auld LJ noted the approach of Webster J in *Ghafoor v Wakefield Metropolitan District Council*[1]. He went on to say[2]:

'In my judgment, it is a necessary part of the licensing function that the licensing authority, whether a local authority or the Crown Court on appeal from it, or a combination of the two of them, apply in relation to each applicant a system which is fair to all current applicants. That can only be done in any particular application where a local authority maintains that there is no significant unmet demand, by a determination of its extent and how it is to be matched with all the current competing applications, including that of the particular applicant. Picking up Laws J's words in relation to Mr Kelly that I have already cited, "it follows, as night the day, that a further process of inquiry had to take place before a ... decision could be made whether to grant the licences" to him. In my judgment also, there is nothing in Section 16 of the 1985 Act [Transport Act 1985], in its requirement that a licensing authority must grant a licence if it is not satisfied that there is no significant unmet demand, to prevent the authority, whether council or court, from examining in the context of an individual application the general state of unmet demand by reference to all outstanding applications. A court, like a local authority may be faced with a number of applications/appeals; in such a circumstance, the court cannot sensibly or properly consider each application in isolation.'

He concluded:

'Accordingly, I am of the view that Laws J correctly remitted Mr Kelly's applications to the Council for its consideration in the light of the Crown Court's unchallenged conclusion on demand.'

[1]   [1990] RTR 389, QBD; see para 8.191 above.
[2]   *Kelly and Smith v Wirral Metropolitan Borough Council* (1996) 160 JP Rep 1047, CA.

8.200

Mr Smith's appeal was similar, but concerned a particularly important point, which was whether a right of appeal arose when a local authority failed to grant a hackney carriage proprietor's licence within a reasonable period of time. No specific decision had been made to refuse, but there was delay. This delay could occur because the council wished to commission a survey, or simply through failure on the part of council to reach a decision. The argument raised by Mr Smith was that such a delay amounted a 'withholding' of a licence and, accordingly, gave rise to a right of appeal under the Public Health Act (Amendment) Act 1907, s 7. Again, Auld LJ gave the judgment of the court[1] and stated:

'In my judgment, the words and intention of section 7 are plain. In the context of licensing, section 7(1)(*b*) provides a right of appeal where a local authority has made a determination whether to grant or refuse a licence, and section 7(1)(*b*) provides the same right where a local authority, by its failure to make a determination, withholds a licence. Here, the Council withheld a licence from Mr Smith by not deciding on his application. As Laws J mentioned, this interpretation may pose difficulties in determining the date of withholding for the purpose of fixing the start of the three weeks' appeal period, for example, where the local authority has no established cycle of licensing meetings. But the Crown Court will need to consider the particular circumstances of each case, bearing in mind always that withholding is a form of continuing inaction and that it may not be appropriate to adopt an overly rigorous attitude to the time limit for appealing in such a case. That is not an issue that could cause any difficulty for Mr Smith. Shortly after his third and last application for a licence in January 1993, his solicitors wrote to the Council seeking a decision within 28 days, and he lodged his appeal within a day or two of the end of that period.'

[1] *Kelly and Smith v Wirral Metropolitan Borough Council* (1996) 160 JP Rep 1047, CA.

8.201

It can be seen, therefore, that simply succeeding on appeal at the Crown Court by demonstrating that there is unmet demand for hackney carriage services which is significant is not, in itself, sufficient to guarantee the appellant a hackney carriage proprietor's licence, as the council will then have to consider the fact that there is unmet demand and decide upon its criteria for granting licences. This point was addressed by Staughton LJ in the *Kelly* case[1]:

'I agree that these appeals should be dismissed for the reasons given by Auld LJ. The only point that has made me pause is the thought that Mr Kelly and Mr Smith, having borne the heat and burden of litigation while others have done nothing, may end up with no licences and see others profit by their efforts. It may be that Mr Smith is in no danger in that respect, as he has been an applicant since 1986. But is there a risk that Mr Kelly will receive nothing? I would hope that the Council can take into account, amongst other relevant circumstances, the fact that he has shown himself so keen to have a licence that he has even engaged in litigation for that purpose, while others have not. But it is for the Council, in the first instance, to decide whether any and if so what weight should be given to that factor.

If it were only a question of assessing the number of new licences required to meet demand, I would have thought that the question could have been remitted to the Crown Court. Unless they merely acted on the absence of evidence that there was no unmet demand, they must have had evidence of unmet demand. That evidence could well have established the extent of the shortfall. But as the claims of other subsisting applicants also fall to be considered, I agree that the application should be remitted to the Wirral Council for reconsideration.'

[1] *Kelly and Smith v Wirral Metropolitan Borough Council* (1996) 160 JP Rep 1047, CA.

Regina v Council of the City and District of St Albans

8.202

> Decision to delimit following a short (two week consultation). Challenged as
> a disproportionate decision, inadequate consultation and absence of survey.
> Held: Not disproportionate as the goal was more WAV hackney carriages,
> the trade had responded to the consultation so no prejudice, and a survey not
> required to de-limit.

Regina v Council of the City and District of St Albans[1] concerned a decision taken
by St Albans District Council to delimit the number of hackney carriage licences
it would grant. Historically it is interesting because until 1995, there had never
been a limit on numbers applied, but one was introduced and by 1999 it was felt
by the council that this was too restrictive and there was a desire to increase the
number of wheelchair accessible vehicles.

A preliminary decision was taken to grant hackney carriage proprietor's licences
for an additional five vehicles which would have to be wheelchair accessible, to
commission an unmet demand survey and to refuse a request for a fare increase
for the period over the Millennium New Year. Following protestation by the
trade and a threatened 'strike' by taxi drivers over the forthcoming Millennium
New Year, a subsequent decision was taken to remove the limit.

There was a period of consultation of just over two weeks, which resulted
in 'a petition, a number of letters of protest against the proposal explaining the
serious consequences of this decision upon the existing licences and a full and
detailed letter from their solicitor dealing with the various arguments on the
issue'[2]. Although this period may seem short, no complaint was made at the time
by any respondent and although the point was raised at the subsequent hearing,
the absence of protest over the time scale at the time was telling.

Following the representations, the decision was confirmed that the limit
should be removed with immediate effect.

The applicants sought both judicial review and an injunction against the issue
of further licences, and were successful in both. The injunction was granted until
the trial. At the full hearing, three arguments were put forward by the applicants:
the Standing Orders of the Council; Proportionality and The Timing of the
Consultation Process.

In relation to the question of the council's standing orders Lightman J did not
find any irregularity[3].

With regard to proportionality he stated as follows (at para 16):

'16 The second complaint relates to whether the decision was proportionate.
Where the goal sought to be achieved can be achieved at less cost to
third parties than that which is proposed to be adopted, the doctrine
of proportionality generally requires the goal to be achieved in the way
which occasions the lesser cost to third parties. The critical question when
applying that principle in this case is to decide what was the goal that was
sought to be achieved here. If the goal was limited to increasing the number

of wheelchair-accessible taxis, then it may have been disproportionate to abolish all restrictions. If the goal was to punish the association of licensees for their threat of strike action, then it would be open to objection on any basis. This would not be the case if the goal was to remove vulnerability to such a threat in the future. But I am satisfied that the goal behind the council resolution was to restore the situation which had prevailed prior to 1995 and to establish an open market. The Council's decision embraced three further considerations which were the consequences of establishing on open market, namely (1) there would be no risk in the future of further threats of strike action; (2) there would be, or there would be likely to be, more wheelchair-accessible taxis; and (3) there would be a saving of the costs of triennial surveys as to the demand for taxis in the future. But the overall decision and the overall goal aimed to be achieved was indeed one of abolishing all restrictions on numbers immediately, and if that was the goal then the question of proportionality does not arise. The Council was entitled to adopt this as its goal and, having adopted this course as its goal, no question arises of considering whether the consequences on the existing licensees render the decision of itself, on grounds of proportionality, invalid. Of course the effect on the existing licensees was a relevant question for the Council to take into account and this brings me on to the third challenge.'

The final and arguably most significant challenge was the question of the length of time allowed for consultation. Generally speaking a period of two weeks would be viewed as being extremely short and this was the argument put forward by the applicants. Unfortunately, as they had not raised the issue of a lack of time during the consultation process itself, the judge took the view that as they had managed to respond within the time limit set by the council and had not sought any increase in that length of time they had not been prejudiced in any way. He drew particular attention to the conclusion of the letter sent by the solicitors for the applicants during the consultation process which stated:

'We have not commented on the affect of de-regulation [sic] on the livelihood of hackney carriage drivers by your council as we think the petition already presented to the council speaks for itself in this regard.

Please will you include a copy of the letter of the Officer's report to the meeting of the full Council on 14 July.'[4]

and the judge concluded (at para 21):

'21 In my view, as a matter of fact, a sufficient time was given for making representations, but, if I had any doubts, this letter [from the applicants' solicitors] was a clear representation by the applicants that there was indeed sufficient time and that the Council should proceed as it did. It therefore seems to me that any suggestion that the Council failed sufficiently to take into account representations or failed to give sufficient time to the applicants to make representations and put material before them, whether regarding the effect of the decision on the livelihood of the existing licence holders or otherwise, appears to me to lack any substance.'

The question as to whether or not the survey was required before a delimitation decision was made had been raised in the course of arguments, together with the suggestion that a financial impact survey should also have been conducted. The judge dismissed both these arguments in the following terms[5]:

'22 It has been further suggested that the Council could or should have gone further. The applicants first suggested that the Council should have obtained a full survey on the issue as to unsatisfied demand for hackney carriages in the area. But of course if the policy decision was being adopted to abolish all restrictions on numbers, there was no relevance in any such survey, and there was absolutely no need for the Council to proceed in that way. It is to be noted that there was no suggestion in the solicitor's letter that it should do so.

23 Secondly, it has been suggested that the Council should have conducted a survey or obtained expert advice regarding the financial impact on the existing licensees. As a matter of principle there was no obligation to do so. There was ample material available to the Council for this purpose. In any event their solicitor himself said there was sufficient material before the Council for making its determination. I do not see how there can be any question of any lack of sufficient material before the Council or there was any failure of duty on the part of the Council to obtain any further material.'

The judge also made reference to and acknowledged, the commercial hardship which would be borne by those who had invested in a hackney carriage proprietor's licence at a premium, but emphasised that this was a commercial decision and that hardship alone could not in any way affect the validity of the council's decision. He explained it thus[6]:

'25 The other matter I should refer to is the matter of obvious hardship which this decision of the Council may occasion to existing licensees and, in particular, those who have mortgaged their assets and their future to pay for licences. I regret to say that the purchase of such licences at premiums was at all times a risky investment. There was never any assurance given by the Council (if any assurances could lawfully be given) that the value of the licences would not be diluted by the opportunities given to further individuals to obtain licences by an increase in licences available and granted. The only protection to which existing licensees were entitled was the opportunity to make representations to the Council before any decision was made to change the basis on which licences were granted and that full opportunity has, as I have held, been given in this case.

26 The sad fact is that some of the existing licensees may have proceeded with their purchases on the basis that the monopoly which determined the value of their licences would continue for the foreseeable future. I regret to say that they had no legitimate expectation to this effect and the value of the licences they purchased was at all times at risk of dilution if the Council took such action as it has done.'

This case shows that if consultation takes place and those affected respond without alerting the council to the fact that they are prejudiced through lack of time, a subsequent argument relating to a short consultation period is unlikely to find favour. Whilst there was clearly a suspicion in the minds of the applicants that this decision was predicated by the threat of a strike at what would undoubtedly be an extremely busy time for hackney carriage services, on its own particular facts there were sufficient other reasons to justify the decision was taken. It also shows that the courts are cognisant of the commercial realities facing hackney carriage proprietors, and the necessity to balance that against the lawful decision making of the council.

1   [2001] LLR 38, QBD.
2   [2001] LLR 38 QBD, per Lightman J at para 5.
3   [2001] LLR 38 QBD, per Lightman J at paras 10–14.
4   [2001] LLR 38, QBD, per Lightman J at para 19.
5   [2001] LLR 38, QBD, per Lightman J at paras 22 and 23.
6   [2001] LLR 38, QBD, per Lightman J at paras 25 and 26.

R (on the Application of Nemeth) v West Berkshire District Council

8.203

> Additional licences issued in 1997 following a survey. In 2000 council changed policy to one of managed growth leading to delimitation within four years. Challenged as legitimate expectation that limit would remain and impact on the commercial viability of existing licensees. Held: No legitimate expectation that the policy would continue and council had considered commercial impact.

In the case of *R (on the Application of Nemeth) v West Berkshire District Council*[1] the argument was raised that the council was required to maintain its existing policy in relation to any additional proprietor's licences to be granted.

West Berkshire District Council limited the number of hackney carriage licences that it would issue. An additional five licences were issued in 1997, the grant of which were subject to a stringent points system which effectively required the provision of a wheelchair accessible vehicle. Nemeth was one of the successful applicants in 1997 and was aggrieved when, in 2000, the council changed its policy to one of managed growth (in this case a delimitation over a three and a half year period) with all vehicles to be wheelchair accessible by the end of that time.

The questions were whether there was a legitimate expectation that the policy dating from 1997 would continue indefinitely and secondly whether the council failed to take into account the impact of the changes of that policy on the claimant and the other four licensees who were issued licences in 1997.

The matter came before Hunt J in December 2000 and he addressed the two points as follows:

In relation to the legitimate expectation point he said (at paras 6–10):

'6. Was there a legitimate expectation that the 1997 policy would remain in force for any particular length of time or beyond the next review? Was there an alleged conduct of the council such as to lead to such legitimate expectation? I find there was not. It was clear from the 1997 report that the defendants could review the policy at any time. It was clear from a later meeting with the hackneyhackney Owners' Association in January 1998 that the defendants were not saying a change such as that now agreed could not happen. Plainly, the council said its committee could not bind the future policy, nor did they seek to say they could.

7. I find that there had been no promise made or assurance given to the claimant, and certainly none in the nature of an agreement or contract such as operated in the case of *R v North and East Devon Health Authority, ex parte Coughlan* [2000] 2 WLR 622, in which case there were statements, conduct and a letter in unqualified terms.

8. This claimant made a sensible commercial decision in 1997 and has operated in the light of that. Having had the option, he bought a new vehicle, not a secondhand one, and has no doubt benefited to date from that. The defendants are now changing the status quo, as they must in law, to meet the unmet demand which has now been ascertained. They were entitled to do what they have done. The claimant's complaint is, I find, in reality about deregulation and numbers. The defendants illustrate this by the fact that, when their first stance in June was deregulation and all new licences to be disabled access vehicles, it was opposed by the claimant.

9. It is plain that in this case there was consultation between June and 3rd July. It is plain that the committee were aware of the previous policy and the taxi drivers' position and they considered it. A number of options were open to the committee, and in choosing option 5, but expanding slowly, the committee have continued the objective of having as many as possible suitably adapted vehicles but phasing them in. In short, the requirement to consider the policy and consult properly, including taking into account the taxi drivers' position before changing the policy, has been met.

10. I find that the expectation is not established nor has the council's conduct amounted to an abuse of power.'

Turning to the question of the impact on the claimant, the matter was dealt with in a very similar fashion to the decision in *Regina v Council of the City and District of St Albans*[2]. Earlier in the judgment (at paragraph 8) the judge recognised the commercial decisions that had been made by the claimant. He concluded (paragraphs 11–14):

'11. I turn to the alleged failure to take into consideration in particular the impact of the changes in policy on the claimant and the other four in a similar position who took up the 1997 licences.

12. It is plain that there were two discussions between June and the 3rd July meetings, and the minutes of the 3rd July meeting recognised the

difficulties of increased numbers for the trade. In addition, the individual councillors had received a letter from the claimant personally, it is correct to say that it was before the June meeting, setting out his case, including in particular the large investment made by those who had taken the previous five plates.

13. It is also correct that the specific complaint he now makes was not spelt out on 3rd July, although I find as a fact that the members would be aware of it through his letter in June. However, he was present on 3rd July at the meeting and did not ask to speak to put the case as now presented, although he could have asked to do so if he wished. In addition, the members of the town association were represented and they declined an invitation to speak.

14. I find that it is not now open to the claimant to say that the point was not before the committee when he could easily have emphasised it if he felt that they were unaware of it. In addition, as I have already found, they were individually aware of it in any event and cannot have failed to take it into account.'

This case clearly reinforces the fact that a council is free to alter its policy at any time, provided it consults those who are likely to be affected and reinforces the point that provided the commercial impact on existing licensees is considered, delimitation decisions can be taken.

¹   8 December 2000 Admin Ct 2000 WL 33122488.
²   [2001] LLR 38, QBD; see para 8.202 above.

R (on the application of Maud) v Castle Point Borough Council

8.204

> In assessing unmet demand, could so called 'latent demand' (the use of private hire vehicles taking immediate hirings) be considered? Held: Yes, as this amounted to hackney carriage work.

The question of delimitation came before the courts again in the case of *R (on the application of Maud) v Castle Point Borough Council*[1]. Castle Point is a district which covers both Benfleet and Canvey Island in Essex. These are distinct areas but, in the absence of hackney carriage zones, fall within the same licensed district. The council had a limit of 37 on the number of hackney carriage licences that it would grant. A survey was conducted by independent consultants Halcrow Fox which considered the question of demand for hackney carriages within the district. It concluded that there was unmet demand. The survey went further than that and concluded that there was what Halcrow Fox referred to as latent unmet demand as well as patent unmet demand. They arrived at this conclusion because in Castle Point some 90% of the hackney carriage work originated from a rank outside Benfleet Railway Station. There was very little hackney carriage activity elsewhere but there was considerable private hire activity. They observed around 150 private hire vehicles leaving other ranks and other places within the district with passengers, which had not been pre-booked. They described this in the following way:

'The analysis of the rank observations revealed that a large proportion of the activity at the ranks away from Benfleet Station was carried out by the private hire trade. This amounted to 150 rank hirings with a further 250 empty departures per week. These hirings are in effect pseudo hackney carriage activity and as such should in law be undertaken by an appropriately licensed vehicle.'

[1]   [2002] EWHC 273 (Admin), [2002] LLR 374.

8.205

The report concluded that the issue of five additional hackney carriage licences would satisfy demand but concluded that delimitation would be preferable as it would:

'legitimise the activities of what were currently the private hire vehicles, many of which would be likely to be the subject of applications to be taxis [hackney carriages], and would provide the best chance of achieving a genuine service for the whole borough.'

8.206

After consultation with the trade, the Council decided to delimit. This was challenged by Mr Maud who was a hackney carriage driver.

8.207

The matter was considered by Wilson J[1], who summarised the legal position as follows (at para 6):

'(a) before a local authority can refuse an application for a vehicle licence in order to limit the number of licensed taxis, they must be satisfied that there is no significant demand for the services of taxis, within the area to which the licence would apply, which is unmet;
(b) if the local authority are thus satisfied, a discretion, as opposed to an obligation, arises to refuse the grant of a licence; but
(c) if the local authority are not so satisfied, they cannot refuse to grant a licence for the purpose of limiting the number of licensed taxis and are thus obliged to grant it.'

[1]   R (on the application of Maud) v Castle Point Borough Council [2002] EWHC 273 (Admin), [2002] LLR 374.

8.208

Castle Point relied strongly upon the ruling in R v Great Yarmouth Borough Council, ex p Sawyer[1]. The council's argument was summarised by Wilson J[2] as follows (at para 12):

'He submits that in the circumstances the presence or absence of significant unmet demand is irrelevant. He says that, before they refused to grant a licence in order to maintain a limit upon the total number in issue, the defendants would have to have been satisfied of its absence; but that what the defendants resolved to do was, subject to their other criteria, to grant all such licences without reference to a limit; and that they were entitled to do so without being satisfied of its presence.'

1   [1989] RTR 297; see para 8.180 above.
2   *R (on the application of Maud) v Castle Point Borough* [2002] EWHC 273 (Admin), [2002] LLR 374.

8.209

This did not find automatic favour with the judge, who stated[1] (at para 13):

'On the facts of the present case I find myself unable to despatch the application by reference to Mr Muir's very general point. Central to the examination of the issue by these defendants was the determination of the presence or absence of significant unmet demand. Such a determination was the first main heading of their remit to Halcrow Fox. It was highly relevant in law. If the defendants were satisfied of its absence, a discretion would arise and require to be exercised. If they were not so satisfied, the defendants were in the realms of obligation rather than of discretion. In my view it must theoretically be open to the claimant to allege that the defendants' conclusion that it was present (or, more particularly, their failure to conclude that it was absent) was reached invalidly, with the result that they failed to appreciate that they had a discretion which was required to be exercised.'

1   *R (on the application of Maud) v Castle Point Borough Council* [2002] EWHC 273 (Admin), [2002] LLR 374.

8.210

The judge then considered the possible arguments against the decision to delimit being a valid decision and the first point concerned the question of latent unmet demand. He was not impressed by the distinction between patent and latent unmet demand and stated[1] (at para 15):

'I find the significance, and indeed the actual parameters, of the suggested distinction somewhat elusive. If, as I assume, latent means "not apparent on the surface" and patent means "apparent on the surface", why should the defendants have to ignore unmet demand in the former category? The reference to demand in section 16 of the Act of 1985 is unqualified. If a man is observed to be waiting for a taxi for 20 minutes, such is an instance of patent unmet demand. If another man, when interviewed, explains that he did not wait for a taxi because bitter experience led him to expect that he would have to wait for 20 minutes and so instead he persuaded his wife to meet him by car, I take such to be an instance of latent unmet demand. But each is an instance of precisely the same problem and, I apprehend, of equal significance to the decision-maker. When they observed a mass of people boarding private hire vehicles at informal ranks and embarking on journeys which the drivers undertook unlawfully, Halcrow Fox described their observations as latent unmet demand for taxis. To me, that unmet demand seems, at least arguably, to have been patent.'

[1]   *R (on the application of Maud) v Castle Point Borough Council* [2002] EWHC 273 (Admin), [2002] LLR 374.

8.211

It can be seen that the judge did not accept the distinction between latent and patent unmet demand, because on the basis of the facts in this case he took the view that all the unmet demand was in fact patent. He declined to follow the ruling in *R v Brighton Borough Council, ex p Bunch*[1], where the court had ruled that latent unmet demand could not be taken into account. His conclusion was 'that it was valid for the defendants to have regard to latent unmet demand'[2] (at para 16).

[1]   [1989] COD 558; see para 8.188 above.
[2]   *R (on the application of Maud) v Castle Point Borough Council* [2002] EWHC 273 (Admin), [2002] LLR 374.

8.212

The second argument again derived from the ruling in *R v Brighton Borough Council, ex p Bunch*[1] where the court stated that only demand for hackney carriage services could be taken into account and not the demand for private hire services. The claimant argued that by taking into account the 150 private hire departures with passengers per week observed by the consultants the Council had taken into account an irrelevant factor. This was dismissed by Wilson J because he took the view[2] (at para 18) that:

'the stark statistic of 150 private hire vehicles leaving the informal ranks with passengers each week… clearly represents significant demand for taxi services, unmet by the taxis.'

[1]   [1989] COD 558; see para 8.188 above.
[2]   *R (on the application of Maud) v Castle Point Borough Council* [2002] EWHC 273 (Admin), [2002] LLR 374.

8.213

There was further argument concerning the possibility of imposing a condition restricting any new hackney carriage vehicles from working from the most popular rank but this was also dismissed[1]. Accordingly, his conclusion was that the decision by the Council to delimit was a valid decision and was not *Wednesbury* unreasonable as it was not founded upon irrelevant considerations.

[1]   See para 8.92 above.

8.214

Maud appealed to the Court of Appeal[1]. The majority of the judgment concerned the question of restricting the use of the licence[2].

[1]   R (on the application of Maud) v Castle Point Borough Council [2002] EWCA Civ 1526, [2003] RTR 7.
[2]   See para 8.92 above.

8.215

The Court of Appeal addressed the question of the validity of the decision and the consideration of irrelevant matters, judgment being given by Keene LJ with the agreement of Kennedy and Buxton LJJ. In relation to the question of latent demand reference was once again made to the decision in *R v Brighton Borough Council, ex p Bunch*[1]. In that case the court decided that only patent unmet demand could be taken into account (at p 10):

'The statutory use of the present tense must render it unnecessary to consider latent demand and anyway the authority could only be satisfied by evidence of such demand as is measurable, which is only patent demand. I accept that submission.'

[1]   [1989] COD 558.

8.216

That was relied upon by Maud as authority that only patent unmet demand could be taken into account by the council. In *Maud*[1] the court took the following view (at para 22):

'It appears to me that this submission misinterprets what was being said in Bunch, probably because of the use of the phrase "latent demand". In Bunch there was no evidence, so far as one can discern, from the surveys of any significant unmet demand – patent or latent. It was simply being argued that the committee should have assumed that a number of people were making alternative arrangements and the consultant should have gone out to try to ascertain this, and all of this was then described as latent demand.

In contrast, in the present case one at least of the two components of the so-called "latent demand" consisted of private hire vehicles being used illegally as taxis, in that they were being engaged by passengers at ranks where they were waiting. This was especially true at ranks on Canvey Island. To my mind it is a misnomer to call that latent demand, as Halcrow Fox did. It is a clearly manifested demand for a taxi service, and it is a current demand. None of the arguments about the use of the present tense in the statutory provisions in any way prevents that evidence from being taken into account by the authority.

I would also emphasise that there may be more than one method of assessing the current demand for taxis. The appropriate methods are not necessarily confined to counting passenger queues or calculating the delays to passengers. If there is convincing evidence of suppressed demand that may be relevant. For example, if it can be established by interview that there are a number of people in the district who wanted a taxi on certain occasions but could not find one and in the end, as a second best, resorted to choosing a less satisfactory alternative solution, that to my mind would be relevant evidence of current demand. The local authority would have to be satisfied that the demand was, first, and foremost, for a taxi, so that inconvenience was being caused to the public through the shortage of taxis. It is in the end all a question of evidence.

I cannot see that the respondent went wrong in law in having regard to what Halcrow Fox termed "latent demand", although the phrase was perhaps, in the light of the case law, an unfortunate one. In my judgment this particular ground has no validity.'

1   *R (on the application of Maud) v Castle Point Borough Council* [2002] EWCA Civ 1526, [2003] RTR 7.

8.217

The final argument, that the survey had taken into account private hire services rather than hackney carriage services was dismissed because it was the consultants who identified the 150 trips in question as work of a hackney carriage type[1] (at para 26):

'It is said that there is no evidence that in those instances those vehicles were plying for hire. They may have been pre-booked and so were acting lawfully as private hire vehicles.

Yet it was the consultants, Halcrow Fox, whose survey identified those 150 trips by observation and who themselves concluded that those trips were being done illegally. They described them in paragraph 28 of the executive summary as "rank hirings", by which I take them to mean that the vehicles were being hired at the rank in question. That was a conclusion to which those consultants were entitled to come, given the expert observations they were carrying out. It does not seem to me that the respondent can be faulted for having based its decision on the conclusions of an independent firm of reputable consulting engineers and for having accepted that evidence contained in their report.'

1   *R (on the application of Maud) v Castle Point Borough Council* [2002] EWCA Civ 1526, [2003] RTR 7.

8.218

The Court of Appeal concluded that the High Court decision was correct and that no irrelevant considerations had been taken into account by the council in arriving at its decision.

R (on the application of Royden) v Metropolitan Borough of Wirral

8.219

> Decision to de-limit subject to all new hackney carriage being WAV. Challenged on four grounds: failure to consult; failure to take account of relevant information; unlawful interference with property rights under HRA 1998; failure to provide insufficient reasons. Held: Sufficient consultation, relevant information considered, no interference with property rights and sufficient reasons given.

The question of delimitation arose again in the case of *R (on the application of Royden) v Metropolitan Borough of Wirral*[1]. A significant element of the argument in this case concerned the question of the implications of the Human Rights Act 1998 in relation to a delimitation decision[2]. The facts which led to this case were as follows.

[1]   [2003] BLGR 290, Admin Ct.
[2]   The challenge related to the impact of Article 1, Protocol 1 on the reduction in value of a hackney carriage proprietor's licence following a decision to de-limit hackney carriage numbers. Since that decision the case law has developed and the current position is detailed in Chapter 2, para 2.113 onwards.

8.220

Wirral Metropolitan Borough Council limited the number of hackney carriage licences that it would grant until the early 1990s. There was then considerable litigation until 1997, when the limit was increased by 15 to 101. This limit was challenged by unsuccessful applicants and unmet demand was established. Following the ruling in *Kelly and Smith v Wirral Metropolitan Borough Council*[1], the matter was remitted to the council to decide on the grant of further licences. The council then commissioned a report from Maunsell Transport Planning, who concluded that overall there was no significant unmet demand. However, it went further to say that the market for hackney carriages within the borough had become distorted over time, leading to a larger than usual quantity of private hire vehicles. The hackney carriage vehicles tended to be limited to certain parts of the borough (which was a large geographic area with distinct town centres within it) and it concluded:

> 'Evaluation of the current observed structure of both hackney carriage and private hire industries suggests the need for policy revision and issue of further plates to ensure the provision of the type of service required by customers in the Wirral. Improved training for drivers and standards for both hackney and private hire vehicles are needed.
>
> To ensure the hackney trade has the opportunity to develop steadily and firmly in rising to its full potential, the consultant recommends the issue of a further 25 plates. The effect of these must be monitored to allow further tranches to be released if this is proven necessary for market development.'

As a consequence of that, the decision was taken by the Council to issue 25 licences. For these there were 58 applicants and, as a consequence, in 1999 the number of licences issued increased to 126.

1   (1996) 160 JP Rep 1047, CA; see para 8.198 above.

8.221

By late 2001 the matter had come to consideration again by the council following regular discussions about the possibility of delimitation at the Consultative Committee which had been established by the council with the trade (both hackney carriage and private hire).

8.222

In late 2001 the council indicated that it was going to review its policy on hackney carriage numbers and in February 2002 issued a questionnaire to all hackney carriage and private hire drivers, proprietors and operators in the district as well as other interested parties. There were also public notices seeking representations.

8.223

After some argument about the contents of the questionnaire with the applicant, the results were assessed and a report was presented to the licensing committee. The decision was taken to remove the limit subject to every new vehicle being wheelchair accessible and less than three years' old at the date of first registration as a hackney carriage. The decision was challenged by way of judicial review. There were four grounds for that challenge.

8.224

The first ground was that there had been a failure to consult. The court stated[1] (at para 54):

> 'As regards the obligation to consult said to arise out of the circumstances of the case and past practice, a licensing authority is under no statutory duty of prior consultation when exercising its powers under section 37 of the Town Police Clauses Act 1847, as amended. However, in this case the defendant has conceded that there was an obligation of prior consultation, and did in fact embark upon a consultation exercise. In those circumstances it is unnecessary for me to consider the precise legal basis of any obligation to consult there may be. As the Court of Appeal said in *Coughlan*[2] cited above, at paragraph 108:

>> "whether or not consultation of interested parties and the public is a legal requirement, if it is embarked upon it must be carried out properly."

> I must therefore determine whether the consultation which in fact took place was proper and sufficient in the circumstances of this case, as far

as the claimant and his colleagues were concerned. In *Coughlan's* case the Court of Appeal said, also (at para 108):

"To be proper, consultation must be undertaken at a time when proposals are still at a formative stage; it must include sufficient reasons for particular proposals to allow those consulted to give intelligent consideration and an intelligent response; adequate time must be given for this purpose; and the product of consultation must be conscientiously taken into account when the ultimate decision is taken: *R v Brent London Borough Council, ex p Gunning* (1985) 84 LGR 168." '

The conclusion of the court in this case was that there had been consultation, that consultation had been conducted correctly and that there had been no legitimate expectation of further consultation.

¹   *R (on the application of Royden) v Metropolitan Borough of Wirral* [2003] BLGR 290, Admin Ct.
²   *R v North and East Devon Health Authority, ex p Coughlan* [2000] 3 All ER 850.

8.225

Grounds 2, 3 and 4 were failure to take account of necessarily relevant information, interference with property and violation of art 1 of the First Protocol to the European Convention on Human Rights and insufficient reasons. These were considered together and the human rights element failed[1]. In relation to the question of delimitation alone, the judge, Sir Christopher Bellamy QC, took the view that the decision in *R v Great Yarmouth Borough Council, ex p Sawyer*[2] was correct and stated[3] (at para 99):

'99. ... it seems to me established that, subject to any relevant human rights considerations, as a matter of law the defendant was entitled, under the Act of 1847 [TPCA 1847], to 'de-restrict' the number of hackney carriage vehicle licences in issue, and that no prior survey of demand was required by that section before any such decision was taken. Conscious though the court is of the potential impact of the decision on individual taxi drivers, Lord Woolf's comments in the *Great Yarmouth* case show that the court is bound by the law and cannot intervene on grounds of hardship.'

¹   See para 118 onwards of the judgment.
²   (1987) 86 LGR 617. See para 8.180 above.
³   *R (on the application of Royden) v Metropolitan Borough of Wirral* [2003] BLGR 290, Admin Ct.

8.226

The question then was raised as to whether the Council had taken into account the relevant factors and had not taken into account any irrelevant factors. The judge reviewed the matter in the following way[1] (at para 100):

'100. The Report to the Licensing Committee and the minute of the meeting of 18 March 2002 show that the Licensing Authority took into account a large number of facts and matters before reaching their decision. After setting out the legal position under the Act of 1847 [TPCA 1847] and the guidance issued by the Department of Transport, the Report to the Licensing Committee draws attention to: (i) the value of the existing licences, and the fact that "Existing licensees have invested in a licence at some stage in the past and put some reliance on their ability to sell it to secure their financial future"; (ii) the possible reduction in earnings of existing licence holders; (iii) possible additional pressure on hackney carriage stands; (iv) the availability of service to disabled passengers; (v) the benefit to the public of more vehicles being available; (vi) the enforcement of vehicle standards; (vii) the limitation on opportunities to enter the trade; (viii) illegal plying for hire; and (ix) the situation in other licensing authorities (see paragraphs 32 to 37 above).

101. The Report to the Licensing Committee then goes on to identify the three options facing the defendant. The Report points out that if a restriction on licences were maintained, there would have to be a survey, the defendant would need to defend any appeals, and the cost of both of those matters would have to be recouped by increasing licence fees. If the limit were removed, a number of issues would have to be considered, including the provision of hackney ranks. As regards the option of the controlled release of additional plates, the Report recalls that the Maunsell Report had found a severely distorted market. If an additional but restricted number of licences were to be issued, the defendant would have to decide on the number. A survey would be necessary since the defendant would have to justify to the court that there was unmet demand and how it had decided on the number of additional licences to be issued (see paragraph 37 above).

102. After referring to the results of the consultation (see paragraph 38 above) Ms Miller expressed the view in the Report that "doing nothing is not an option". She said notably:

> "The limit on numbers could be removed without controls. However I would suggest that the limit on numbers of hackney carriage vehicles is removed with controls such as an age limit. This would let market forces find an equilibrium

The situation would be kept under review and it would always be open to the Council to re-impose a numerical limit on the number of hackney carriage vehicle licences if the evidence indicated that this was appropriate.'

[1]   *R (on the application of Royden) v Metropolitan Borough of Wirral* [2003] BLGR 290, Admin Ct.

8.227

In addition, it was clear that the committee also took into account the views of those who had addressed the committee, which included members of the trade. The judge concluded[1] (at para 105):

> '105. Taking all the foregoing into account, it seems to me that it would be impossible to hold that the decision of 18 March 2002 is unlawful, applying the conventional grounds of judicial review. The decision is not in my

view irrational or unreasonable in the sense of *Associated Picture Houses v Wednesbury Corporation* [1948] 1 KB 223. Relevant factors, including the impact of the decision on existing licence holders have been taken into account, and no irrelevant factors have been considered. The decision is not perverse, nor procedurally unfair, nor erroneous in point of law.

106. The position is, therefore, that applying the normal principles of English law, the contested decision has been regularly adopted according to law.'

[1]   *R (on the application of Royden) v Metropolitan Borough of Wirral* [2003] BLGR 290, Admin Ct.

8.228

The human rights argument also failed[1] and accordingly the challenge to the decision of Wirral Metropolitan Borough Council was unsuccessful.

[1]   See paras 118 onwards of the judgment.

R (on the application of Johnson) v Reading Borough Council

8.229

> A survey found unmet demand and recommended the grant of eight licences to remove that. Council decided to issue 30. Challenged on the basis that it could only issue eight on the basis of the survey. Held: Whilst it would struggle to justify issuing less than that recommended by the survey, there was no prohibition on issuing more.

In *R (on the application of Johnson) v Reading Borough Council*[1] the question of the impact of an unmet demand survey arose.

Reading BC limited the number of hackney carriages that it would licence to 138 and commissioned an unmet demand survey. That found unmet demand and recommended that the granting of eight new licences would remove the unmet demand (and take the overall fleet number to 146, an increase of 6%). In addition they recommended some alterations to existing ranks and the creation of two new ranks.

Four possible courses of action were detailed in the committee report prepared by Mr Mortlock, Team Leader Licensing and Enforcement Officer[2]:

'Option 1

The first option is to have regard to the results of the survey and to issue the minimum number of hackney carriage vehicle licences as detailed in the survey ... A minimum number of plates must be issued.

Option 2

The second option would be to move towards a position where the number of hackney carriages was determined by market forces rather than by local authority control. In law, persons who currently own hackney carriages have a legitimate expectation that the prevailing status quo will not change overnight. It would not be reasonable to lift the limit on the number of hackney carriages without some warning. Therefore if a move towards market forces determining the number of hackney carriages is the favoured option, this would need to be phased in over a period of time. Three to five years would be the minimum period of time that would be necessary to move towards such a position. A number of hackney carriage vehicle licences would need to be issued this year and again in the following years prior to de-limiting occurring in the final year.

From an officer perspective, it is felt that an appropriate number of hackney carriage vehicle licences to issue, in order to move towards de-limiting, would be 30 per year...

... Central government is considering removing the local authority powers to restrict hackney carriage licence numbers in their area.

Option 3

Members may, if thought appropriate, issue in excess of 8 new licences without moving towards de-limiting.

Option 4

Members may choose to disregard the result of the survey ... However [this] is likely to lead to an appeal where an applicant for a hackney carriage vehicle licence is refused ...'

In the end, after considerable debate, the council decided to issue 30 new licences, but not move towards delimitation. In other words, this was a finite increase, rather than managed growth.

The decision was as follows[3]:

'In reaching the decision the Committee had taken into account:

The unmet demand identified by the survey.

The representations of the [claimants]

The likelihood that the government would remove the right of local authorities to determine the number of hackney carriage licences in its area against the legitimate expectation of the [claimants] under the status quo.

The representations of other persons for more than 8 licences, e.g. Chair of Reading Transport Limited.

The knowledge that there was unmet demand throughout the town and not just in popular pick-up points such as Reading station due to the high instances of private hire vehicles plying for hire around the town.

It was therefore agreed that 30 would not be an unreasonable increase, bearing in mind that this was the Head of Environment Consumer Services' recommendation if the Committee wished to adopt option 2 as set out in the report. The Committee was also mindful that it would need to review the situation at the end of the first twelve months after the increase to assess the impact.'

This decision was challenged by way of judicial review, and the applicant argued six points[4]:

'The Claimants' submissions

45. Mr Patel on behalf of the claimants submits that the council's decision was based upon a wrong interpretation of the TPI report. The council assumed that the recommendation of 8 new licences applied only to unmet demand at the railway station: that if only 8 new licences were issued there would still exist unmet demand elsewhere in Reading. He makes the following points.

46. First, TPI were commissioned to determine whether there was significant unmet demand for the whole of Reading. There was no geographical restriction.

47. Second, TPI did not limit itself to empirical data obtained during rank observations but also considered anecdotal evidence in coming to its conclusion and recommendations. The pedestrian survey indicated that delay at ranks was only a minor deterrent to hackney carriage use.

48. Third, the council was irrational in concluding that if 8 new licences were issued there would remain unmet demand. Such a conclusion was not supported by any evidence. Insofar as it relied upon the members' own observations it was based upon improper and irrelevant considerations. Insofar as it relied upon the observations in the survey of informal rank activity by private vehicles, it was wrong and/or a misinterpretation of the report. The TPI report concluded that the presence of private hire vehicles was a consequence of existing hackney carriage vehicles being reluctant to operate in those areas.

49. Fourth, the choice of 30 new hackney carriage licences was irrational. It was based upon Mr Mortlock's option 2. That figure was put forward by him as appropriate in the context of de-restriction. Moreover, he never sought to justify it.

50. Fifth, even if the TPI report could be read as being limited to the railway station there was no, or no proper basis for concluding that 22 new licences would be required. By far the greatest demand was and would be at the railway station.

51. Sixth, monitoring the number of licences in twelve months' time would not help. By then the damage would be done. The council would not be empowered to cancel a licence at that time."

These were countered by the Council in the following terms[5]:

'The Defendants' submissions

52. Mr Harrison on behalf of the defendants makes a number of points.

53. First, he submits that the council had an unfettered discretion to issue any number of taxi licences it wished. The only statutory restriction was

as to the circumstances in which it could choose to limit the number of licences issued. I do not take that to be in issue.

54. Second, he submits that there was on the evidence sufficient opportunity to the claimants to put their case to the relevant committee. This application could only succeed if the decision to issue the additional 22 licences to the 8 suggested by TPI was irrational in the Wednesbury sense. Although there is some criticism by the claimants of the consultation process, essentially there is no dispute about that proposition.

55. Third, he emphasised the deference which should be accorded a decision taken by democratically elected councillors following a meeting. As it was put in the Great Yarmouth case (see above) the court should not consider such decisions with over-refinement.

56. Fourth, the purpose of the survey was limited. It was to tell the councillors the minimum number of licences needed if the Council was to act lawfully in refusing any application for a licence. 8 new licences would achieve that object.

57. Fifth, as to the survey itself, he submits that while it did contain information relating to the Borough as a whole, the analysis which led to the key conclusions was that at the railway station. There was nothing irrational in the Councillors considering the report's conclusions in the way they did. There was nothing too in the report dealing with the peak Saturday night hours.

58. Sixth, Mr. Harrison refers to the letter from the Transport and General Union of 23 May 2003. That shows, he submitted, that option 3 was a live option.

59. Seventh, Mr. Harrison took me through the record of the meeting at which the decision was made. He submits that it is plain this matter was carefully and rationally considered by the councillors. The comments I have quoted above were rational. There was evidence of a premium on plates. The private hire association was asking for 30 to 40 licences. The possible options were before them. Their legitimate concerns were expressed. A suggestion of 16 new licences was rejected as not enough. As to the choice of 30 new licences, that reflected their view that such a number would be an improvement to the town and was consistent with the legitimate expectations of the claimants. It was rational in deciding upon 30 to take into account what had been said to the councillors by their professional and expert adviser. Moreover, although they knew (as the Union letter makes plain) there was the possibility of more than 8 new plates being put forward by the Committee, no alternative number was put forward by the claimants.'

Goldring J then delivered his conclusions[6]:

'60. It seems to me Mr. Harrison is right.

61. First, although I am conscious that *Regina v Great Yarmouth Borough Council* (see above) on its facts concerned the Council's policy decision to de-restrict, some of the observations within it seem to me appropriate in the present case. Real deference should be paid to the decision of decision takers who are democratically elected and who take their decision following at least adequate consultation (as in my view this undoubtedly was) with interested parties. That decision should not be judged in an over refined and over legalistic way.

62. Second, the widest possible discretion is given to the Council. It can de-restrict entirely (subject only to the legitimate expectations of those affected, not something raised in argument before me). Any decision taken to increase the number of licences should be looked at bearing in mind the width of the discretion it has.

63. Third, it seems to me the essential purpose of the survey was to ensure that the Council did not act unlawfully by refusing applications for plates because there was unmet demand. The fact that it suggested that unmet demand could be met as required by Section 37 of the Town Clauses Act, as amended, by 8 new licences did not in any way fetter the Council's discretion in deciding to grant more than eight.

64. Fourth, I agree with Mr. Harrison; although the Report was said to cover the whole Borough, someone deciding the number of additional licences was entitled to come to the view there was concentration on the area of the railway station, particularly as far as the analysis was concerned.

65. Fifth, there was before the councillors a great deal of local information. The police expressed views. So did the local private hire organisation. There was some evidence of plates being at a premium. I see nothing objectionable in local councillors, plainly familiar with Reading, using their local knowledge of how the taxi system operates in practice. Indeed, they would be failing in their duty as councillors if they ignored their local knowledge.

66. Further, the Committee knew the government was contemplating the possibility of requiring total de-restriction.

67. As to the views the councillors expressed, they seem to me to deal with the relevant factors in a sensible and rational way. Different councillors expressed different views which, Report or no Report, they were entitled to hold.

68. Sixth, it is clear from the documents that it was known to the claimants that the Council was contemplating a greater number of additional licences than eight. It was mentioned in the meeting of 14 May 2003. The Trade Union knew. Mr. Mortlock put it forward as an option. It was known too that. Mr. Mortlock, albeit in the context of de-restriction, had suggested that 30 additional licences would not be unlawful. In spite of that, the claimants did not put forward an alternative additional number of licences

other than eight. They restricted themselves to referring to the need to maintain balance.

69. Seventh, when deciding upon 30 extra licences the Committee in part relied upon the expert advice of Mr. Mortlock to the effect that that would be lawful (albeit in the context of de-restriction). No-one suggested to the contrary. The Committee was entitled to rely on that advice.

70. Eighth, having regard to what Mr. Mortlock said and the factors identified in paragraphs 63-7 above, and bearing in mind the extent of the discretion vested in the Council, it seems to me the Committee was entitled to take the decision it did for the reasons expressed in the Minutes. It was not in my view a decision which could be described as irrational.

71. In short, I have concluded that this application for judicial review must fail.'

This case demonstrates that a survey is evidence for refusing applications for additional licences, because it is the only acceptable method of demonstrating that there is no significant unmet demand for hackney carriage services. However, a survey is immaterial where a council wishes to increase hackney carriage numbers, unless the argument is advanced that even with the increase in vehicles, there remains unmet demand. As here, the decision was to issue more licences than the survey recommended; the survey could not be used to support opposition to such a decision. This reinforces the ruling in *Castle Point v Maud*[7].

It is also a useful judicial view on what can legitimately be taken into account in arriving at a decision to issue additional hackney carriage licences, and recognises the importance of local knowledge in such a decision making process.

[1] [2004] EWHC 765 (Admin), [2004] All ER (D) 90 (Apr).

[2] *R (on the application of Johnson) v Reading Borough Council* [2004] EWHC 765 (Admin), [2004] All ER (D) 90 (Apr) at para 27.

[3] *R (on the application of Johnson) v Reading Borough Council* [2004] EWHC 765 (Admin), [2004] All ER (D) 90 (Apr) at para 43.

[4] *R (on the application of Johnson) v Reading Borough Council* [2004] EWHC 765 (Admin), [2004] All ER (D) 90 (Apr), per Goldring J at paras 45-51.

[5] *R (on the application of Johnson) v Reading Borough Council* [2004] EWHC 765 (Admin), [2004] All ER (D) 90 (Apr), per Goldring J at paras 53-59.

[6] *R (on the application of Johnson) v Reading Borough Council* [2004] EWHC 765 (Admin), [2004] All ER (D) 90 (Apr), per Goldring J at paras 60-71.

[7] *R (on the application of Maud) v Castle Point Borough Council* [2002] EWHC 273 (Admin), [2002] LLR 374, Admin Ct at para 6; see para 8.204 above.

Cummings v Cardiff County Council

8.230

A decision to grant six new licences was challenged and the council then resolved to de-limit. Challenged that a flawed initial decision impugned the later decision. Held: That was not the case; the later decision stood on its own and confirmed that a decision to delimit was only susceptible to challenge on *Wednesbury* grounds.

The case of *Cummings v Cardiff County Council*[1] is one of the few de-limitation cases that has reached the Court of Appeal[2] and again concerns the process used by the council in reaching a decision to remove the limit on hackney carriage licences.

Cardiff had a limit on its hackney carriage numbers, and Mr Cummings owned or controlled a large proportion of those that the Council had licensed (58 out of 480, or some 12%). Occasionally additional licences were issued, and a decision was taken in January 2003 to issue six more. The history of the issue of licences within Cardiff is detailed with some particularity at paragraphs 16 to 21.

In early 2003 the council, which had commissioned a survey from the Halcrow Group Ltd, decided to issue six new licences, based upon the conclusions of the survey which concluded that there was unmet demand, which would be met by the issue of these additional licences.

This decision then led to the question of the method of allocation of those additional licences. The Halcrow report addressed this[3] thus:

'If the Council pursues the option of issuing six additional licences there are three options the Council could pursue;
- Issue licences according to the Council's waiting list, for example, i.e. the driver has been on the waiting list for the longest is issued a licence first, for example, Selby District Council; or
- If no waiting list is available all potential drivers could be interviewed and graded according to a set of pre-determined criteria, both Manchester and Leeds City Councils use such a system; or
- Use a lottery system, for example, Southampton City Council.'

The council decided on the lottery option at its meeting in January 2003. Mr Cummings sought both judicial review of the decision, and an injunction preventing both the use of a lottery or the grant of any additional licences.

His argument was based on three grounds which can be summarised as:

1. overlooking or being misled over the existence of a waiting list;
2. irrationality of the use of a lottery; and
3. failure to consider each application on its own merits[4].

As a result of this challenge, the council reconsidered its position, and in April deferred the lottery and decided to pursue delimitation of numbers. This was the subject of consultation with the hackney carriage trade, and a report was submitted to a meeting in October 2003. At that meeting, the decision was taken to remove the limit on the number of hackney carriage licences that would be granted and the committee based its findings on the following:

'Having considered all the evidence, the Committee then discussed the implications of such a proposal [to delimit] in Cardiff. The Committee found that:
- From the Halcrow survey and report, and their own experience of Cardiff on a Friday and Saturday night, that there was an unmet demand for hackney carriage services in the city;

- The market for hackney carriage services will find its own sustainable level and number of vehicles;
- The local authority could maintain quality control over the services through introducing conditions as part of the vehicle licensing process;
- Recognise that the initial outlay of a new car could be prohibitive for some potential owners, and therefore a three year vehicle age limit would be introduced as part of the conditions of licence.'

Mr Cummings then issued a further challenge to the second decision by way of judicial review and the applications were considered together.

At the hearing the argument was put forward by the claimant that the decision in January was flawed, and as consequence, that impugned the integrity of the later decision to delimit in October.

Moses J considered the whole matter carefully. There was considerable argument as to whether the report in January was misleading over the existence and status of the waiting list, and whether the choice of a lottery as a means of allocation was lawful. He found that report had been misleading, but that the choice of a lottery was lawful. As the January decision had been superseded by the October decision, and the latter decision was not prejudiced by the earlier decision, it was not necessary to rule on the consequences of the misleading report[5].

'26 However, I reject the second and third grounds of challenge to the Committee's decision to select applicants by lottery. There is no basis for saying that it was irrational to use a lottery merely because earlier applications had been deferred. It is plain from an analysis of the history that on each occasion a decision was reached to issue fresh licences, a fresh decision was made as to the method of allocation. Mr Cummings does not suggest that he had any legitimate expectation that the same system would be adopted on each occasion a decision was made to issue fresh licences. On the contrary, the history shows that there was no basis for such an expectation. Nor was it, in my view, irrational to reject a method of allocation, which included consideration of the merits of any particular application. The Committee was entitled to take the view that any system which laid down a criterion of merit was difficult, cumbersome and expensive, for reasons identified by the Chairman, Mr Pinnell.

27 There remains the issue as to the effect of the misleading report. It seems to me wrong to reach any conclusion as to the effect of that report on the decision of 14th January 2003 when that decision has itself been rescinded. The importance of the decision to use a lottery is only of any relevance if it has an impact on the decision to delimit the issue of licences. The effect of the misleading report is only of relevance if it has an impact upon the decision under challenge in the second Judicial Review proceedings, the decision dated 7th October 2003. I should, therefore, before considering the impact of the misleading report, turn to the events leading to the decision of 7th October 2003 and to that decision itself.'

In relation to the second decision, once again there was considerable argument. A lot of this was based on the attempt to link the two decisions, which, had it been successful, would have led to the problems with the first decision affecting the second decision. However, the judge found no link between the two. Accordingly, the second decision was then considered in isolation on its own merits. He concluded[6]:

'37 It was a matter for the Committee to decide what arguments were relevant to the issue of whether there should be de-restriction or not. It was not and it cannot be suggested that any of the considerations they did take into account were irrelevant. The Committee was entitled to take the view that the issue before it, in October, was whether the advantages of de-restriction outweighed the disadvantages. It was under no obligation to take into account the issue of a fair method of allocation, should it continue to issue a limited number of licences. In the light of the essential question, whether to de-restrict or not to de-restrict, the issue as to a fair method of allocation, should the Committee continue to issue a limited number of licences, simply did not arise.

38 I accept that had it not been for the earlier decision in January and the challenge mounted by the claimant it is unlikely that the Committee would have ever turned to consider the question of de-restriction. But the fact that the earlier decision and the challenge triggered consideration of the issue does not mean to say that any defect in the process, by which the first decision was reached, tainted the second decision. The trigger for the decision to de-restrict played no part in the actual consideration as to whether to de-restrict. It could hardly be said that the decision was taken in order to deprive the claimant of licences to which he would otherwise have be entitled. After all, his challenge in January was made for the purpose of securing an entitlement to consideration of the grant of licences ahead of others. A decision in October resulted in him having any licences he wanted. The damage to him, which was advanced in his letter and, accordingly, considered by the Committee was in the damage to the market in transfer of licences. The Committee was entitled to reject the claimant's arguments in relation to damage to the market in transfer of licences and it was not argued before me to the contrary.

39 For those reasons I reject the submission that any defects in the process by which the January decision was reached affected the second decision so as to make it unlawful. The Committee properly considered the merits of de-restriction, taking into account the consultation with the trade and the arguments against it.'

Mr Cummings then appealed this decision to the Court of Appeal, where similar arguments were rehearsed. Once again the applicant (now appellant) Mr Cummings attempted to join the two decisions, and once again, this approach failed.

Scott-Baker J put it this way[7]:

'27. A decision whether or not to de-limit is entirely separate and independent of a decision upon how to allocate licences within the context of limitation. On the face of it, therefore, in the absence of bad faith or bias on the part of the authority it is difficult to see how the later decision can be tainted by any deficiencies in the earlier decision. No bad faith or bias is alleged in the present case, ... Let me say at once that there is no evidence that any official or counsellor (sic) behaved other than honestly and fairly. In so far as anything was misrepresented at either of the meetings it seems to me that it was entirely innocent.'

He noted that the report considered by the councillors at the second meeting in October addressed the issues of de-limitation, with factors both in favour and against being identified. He considered the three points argued and he concluded[8]:

'36. In my judgment, and bearing in mind the respondent's position, the answer to the appellant's three complaints seem to me to be as follows. As to the first point, that a decision had already been made on 14 January not to delimit the number of hackney carriage licences, first of all that is a decision that could be revisited by the Council at any time; and secondly, on examination of what was considered on 14 January 2003 there was, in my judgment, no considered decision on that issue on the merits. The matter was put before the Council members by the officials really on the basis that there would be no change from the practise that had obtained for many years in the past that there would be a limit on the number of licences which would be controlled in so far as the granting of further licences was concerned by unmet demand.

37. As to the second point, that the counsellors (sic) were kept in the dark about advice from Halcrow not to delimit, in my judgment Halcrow's advice on examination was nothing like as strong as Mr Bromley-Martin [for the appellant] suggests. Indeed it was, I would say, more accurately described as equivocal. In any event there was reference to Halcrow in the decision of the Committee in October, and perhaps of much greater significance all the arguments for and against delimitation were carefully rehearsed in the official's report to the Council.

38. As to the third and final point that the waiting list was inaccurately described, in my judgment that contention is made out. It was not, as Moses J found, an accurate assessment of the true position, but it was, in my view, completely irrelevant to the decision that the Council had to take on 7 October.

39. Standing back for a moment from the particular facts of this case and moving to the general from the particular, it seems to me that the decision of 7 October falls to be examined on classic *Wednesbury* grounds. I can see nothing that the Council took into account that they should not have taken into account; nothing that they left out of account that they should have considered. Far from concluding that the decision was irrational, in

my judgment it was an entirely rational one and one which they were fully entitled to reach.'

That view was supported by both the other judges, Buxton LJ and Phillips MR.

Whilst this is a complex case, it is ultimately another Court of Appeal authority that delimitation can take place at any time, subject only to a challenge on *Wednesbury* principles. In this, it follows directly from the decision in *R v Great Yarmouth Borough Council, ex p Sawyer*[9] some 18 years before.

It is unfortunate that, considering the length of the arguments surrounding the possibility of the allocation of extra plates by means of a lottery, neither court in this case declared unequivocally whether such a method of allocation was lawful, as it is a method used by a number of authorities that continue to limit hackney carriage numbers when allocating new licences.

[1]   [2004] EWHC 2295 Admin Ct, [2005] LLR 27, [2005] EWCA Civ 1061, [2005] LLR 687.
[2]   The others being *R v Great Yarmouth Borough Council, ex p Sawyer* (1987) [1989] RTR 297n, CA; see para 8.180 above. *Kelly and Smith v Wirral Metropolitan Borough Council* (1996) 160 JP Rep 1047, CA; see para 8.198 above; and *R (on the application of Maud) v Castle Point Borough Council* [2003] RTR 7, CA; see para 8.204 above.
[3]   Paragraph 17.3.1 of the report, quoted at para 10 of the Admin Ct judgment.
[4]   See para 11 of the Admin Ct judgment.
[5]   Per Moses J at paras 26 and 27 of the Admin Ct judgment.
[6]   Per Moses J at paras 37–39 of the Admin Ct judgment.
[7]   At para 27 of the Court of Appeal judgment.
[8]   At paras 36–39 of the Court of Appeal judgment.
[9]   (1987) [1989] RTR 297n, CA; see para 8.180 above.

Sardar v Watford Borough Council

8.231

> Had sufficient consultation been undertaken at the correct stage? Held: No, and therefore the decision was quashed.

Sardar v Watford Borough Council[1] concerned the process of consultation before a delimitation decision was taken. It is a case which is entirely dependent on its own facts and does not advance the legal position beyond reinforcing the law relating to consultation and the practicalities of consulting in relation to a delimitation decision.

The decision hinged on the question of whether or not the decision to delimit had in fact been taken before the consultation exercise was conducted. If it had, the council would have fettered its discretion and the decision would be unlawful. If not, the decision could stand.

Watford Borough Council had been operating a 'managed growth' policy in regard to hackney carriage numbers from 2003. Following the Office of Fair Trading report in 2003[2], a change to taxi arrangements at Watford Junction railway station, and a large number of appeals against refusals to grant hackney carriage proprietor's licences being lodged with the Crown Court, the council reconsidered its policy. A consultation exercise was undertaken between March and mid-summer, and steps were put in place to arrange an unmet demand survey.

A report was prepared for the next licensing committee meeting on 5 September 2005 when the matter would be discussed, which contained alternative recommendations[3]:

'(a) That no further hackney carriage vehicle licences be granted pending the result of an unmet demand survey/or

(b) that the existing policy of "managed growth" be maintained notwithstanding the Council's decision to undertake a survey into unmet demand.'

Following a meeting of the majority political group two days before this meeting, an 'amendment' was produced which stated[4]:

'As it is the intention of the council to delimit the number of hackney carriage vehicle licences that are available, the recommendations contained in this report are to be deleted and replaced by:

11 Recommendation [substituted]:

That officers prepare a detailed report for the meeting of this committee to agree the manner under which delimitation will take effect. This will include the provision of options for the committee to consider in relation to vehicle specifications and standards, vehicle livery, and changes to pre-licensing requirements for first time holders of Watford Borough Council driver's licences.

That any applicants for hackney carriage vehicle licences between now and the next meeting be informed of the Council's intentions and asked to withdraw their application. Should they not withdraw then the Council will defer any determination until after the next meeting,

That those persons currently with appeals against the Council's refusal to grant a hackney carriage vehicle licence be informed of the Council's intentions.'

This substituted recommendation resulted in the following decision[5]:

'1. That officers prepare a detailed report for the next meeting of this committee to agree the manner under which delimitation will take effect. This will include the provision of options for the committee to consider in relation to vehicle specification and standards, vehicle livery and changes to pre-licensing requirements for first time holders of Watford Borough Council driver's licenses ...'

This in turn led to a consultation exercise and a further meeting in October where the recommendation was[6]:

'1. Under the Transport Act 1985 the Council has the power to limit the number of hackney carriage vehicle licences that it issues within the borough subject to satisfying itself that having set the limit there is no unmet demand. The Council has exercised this power to restrict the number of licences that have been issued and, save for a small increase in 1995, has adopted a policy of managed growth since March 2003. The Council now wishes to remove the limit on the number of licences it issues.

13 Recommendations

1. That the council no longer exercises its discretion under section 16 of the Transport Act 1985 to limit policy outlined in policy LC23 of 10 March 2003 and limits on the number of hackney carriage vehicle licences that it issues and that the current policy outlined in minute LC23 of 10 March 2003 be ended with immediate effect ...'

The recommendation was adopted, and that decision was challenged by way of judicial review.

The case hinged on the following, point, identified and encapsulated by Wilkie J[7]:

'17 It is not in dispute that there could be no change of policy without consultation. Equally it is not in dispute that there was no consultation prior to 5 September 2005 on delimitation.

18 It, therefore, follows that if, and to the extent that, there was a decision on 5 September 2005 to delimit the number of hackney carriage licences to be issued then that decision was taken unlawfully.'

And the arguments were expanded by the judge at paras 29 and 30:

'29 In my judgment, having had regard to the totality of the evidence, the Council on 5 September took a decision in principle to de-limit. Further, in my judgment, the policy of delimitation, by virtue of that decision, ceased to be a policy which was at the formative stage. The description "a formative stage" may be apt to describe a number of different situations. A Council may only have reached the stage of identifying a number of options when it decides to consult. On the other hand it may have gone beyond that and have identified a preferred option upon which it may wish to consult. In other circumstances it may have formed a provisional view as to the course to be adopted or may "be minded" to take a particular course subject to the outcome of consultations. In each of these cases what the Council is doing is consulting in advance of the decision being consulted about being made. It is, no doubt, right that, if the Council has a preferred option, or has formed a provisional view, those being consulted should be informed of this so as better to focus their responses. The fact that a Council may have come to a provisional view or have a preferred option does not prevent a consultation exercise being conducted in good faith at a stage when the policy is still formative in the sense that no final decision has yet been made. In my judgment, however, it is a difference in kind for it to have made a decision in principle to adopt a policy and, thereafter, to be concerned only with the timing of its implementation and other matters of detail. Whilst a consultation on the timing and manner of implementation may be a proper one on these issues it cannot, in my judgment, be said that such a consultation, insofar as it touches upon the question of principle, is conducted at a point at which policy on that issue is at a formative stage.

30 The question arises in this case, however, what is the position where, as here, there has, after the decision in principle has been taken, been a full blown consultation in the course of which views were invited, and were expressed, on the issue of de-limitation, where the report to the committee, on 20 October, set out in full the outcome of that consultation, including the question of principle, where the report to the committee presented a series of possible decisions including deciding not to de-limit, where the report to the committee set out in full the various arguments for and against de-limitation, and where it is apparent that the debate in the committee dealt fully with the question of de-limitation and debate was not foreclosed on the footing that a decision in principle had already been taken?'

It was accepted that the law governing consultation was as laid down by the Court of Appeal in *R v North and East Devon HA ex parte Coughlan*⁸ and was as follows (at para 108):

'It is common ground that, whether or not consultation of interested parties and the public is a legal requirement, if it is embarked upon it must be carried out properly. To be proper, consultation must be undertaken at a time when proposals are still at a formative stage; it must include sufficient reasons for particular proposals to allow those consulted to give intelligent consideration and intelligent response; adequate time must be given for this purpose; and the product of consultation must be conscientiously taken into account when the ultimate decision is taken.'

Was this the case here? The judge found not. Having found that

'... in my judgment, of these four conditions, the second and third have manifestly been satisfied. I am also satisfied that the product of the consultation was conscientiously taken into account when the decision was made on the 20 October. In so deciding I bear in mind the approach to bias, in a different context, referred to by the defendant and described in the decision in *Georgiou*. The problem, however, is with satisfying the first principle and whether the conscientious consideration of the consultation was applied, in effect, to the question whether to reverse a decision which had already been made rather than taking a decision untrammelled by any prior decision.'

He found that the decision had in effect been taken in September and as a result the consultation was not effective, and as a consequence, the claim would succeed.

As stated earlier, this case is very largely concerned with its own facts, but it is a useful reminder of the need for consultation to be undertaken correctly, in accordance with the principles laid down in *R v North and East Devon HA ex parte Coughlan*⁹.

¹   [2006] EWHC 1590 (Admin), [2007] LLR 54, Admin Ct.

2   *The regulation of licensed taxi and PHV services in the UK* (OFT676 available at www.oft.gov.uk/
    news/publications/leaflet+ordering.htm), the results of its investigation into UK Taxi Services.
3   *Sardar v Watford Borough Council* [2006] EWHC 1590 (Admin), [2007] LLR 54, Admin Ct at
    para 9.
4   *Sardar v Watford Borough Council* [2006] EWHC 1590 (Admin), [2007] LLR 54, Admin Ct at
    para 11.
5   *Sardar v Watford Borough Council* [2006] EWHC 1590 (Admin), [2007] LLR 54, Admin Ct at
    para 12.
6   *Sardar v Watford Borough Council* [2006] EWHC 1590 (Admin), [2007] LLR 54, Admin Ct at
    para 13.
7   *Sardar v Watford Borough Council* [2006] EWHC 1590 (Admin), [2007] LLR 54, Admin Ct at
    paras 17 and 18.
8   [2001] QB 213.
9   [2001] QB 213.

Saltax v Salford

8.232

> Following lengthy consultation, a decision was taken to delimit hackney
> carriage numbers. Challenged by judicial review. Held: This was a
> satisfactory consultation, no survey was required before delimitation, and
> sufficient reasons had been given.

Another case which is largely concerned with its own particular facts is *Saltax Ltd
v Salford City Council*[1]. This was an application for judicial review of the decision
by Salford City Council to remove the limit on hackney carriage numbers. Before
this decision was made, the council had undertaken a wide ranging consultation,
including questionnaires to members of the public in each ward of the city, the
business community, wheelchair users and local councillors, hackney carriage
proprietors and drivers, and private hire operators, proprietors and drivers. This
process also included producing a draft hackney carriage and private hire policy,
as up until that point, Salford had not had one comprehensive policy covering
these functions. That was also the subject of consultation. The consultation
process was lengthy and involved[2], culminating in a decion to adopt the new
policy and delimit the hackney carriage numbers.

An application for judicial review was made and was considered by Mr Justice
Kenneth Parker. His opening remarks on the grounds of challenge set the scene
for the remainder of his judgment[3]:

> '49 I should say at the outset that the claimants have on this application
> adopted a scattergun approach. Mr Hercock's skeleton argument runs to
> 40 pages of dense type, purporting to chronicle a myriad of very detailed
> criticisms of the decision-making process. Many of these criticisms were
> not pursued at the hearing. Many could not possibly ground a challenge to
> the legality of the decision. I am concentrating therefore on what I see as
> potential grounds that could be advanced in a claim for judicial review of
> this decision, taking account of the nature of the decision, the background
> to the decision and the circumstances in which it was taken.'

The potential grounds were distilled by the judge to be as follows:

1. Was a survey required before a decision to delimit could be made?
2. Were the views of residents correctly assessed?
3. The results of the questionnaires were not properly reported to the Councillors by Mr Pinnington, the officer responsible for licensing.
4. The consultation with the trade was flawed generally and in particular by the absence of any focus group meetings.
5. No reasons were given for the decision, and
6. The decision could not be taken by a single portfolio holder.

Each of these arguments was rejected in turn.

1. He followed the ruling in *R v Great Yarmouth Borough Council, ex p Sawyer*[4] and agreed with subsequent cases that no survey was required before a decision to remove a limit could be made[5]. Such an argument was in the judge' view "fundamentally misconceived"[6].

2. Whilst the return rate for the public questionnaire was poor, it was clear that public opinion had been canvassed:

    "It could not therefore be said that the general public interest case was not substantially supported at grass roots level"[7].

3. The judge said that Mr Pinnington

    "was always scrupulous to show the basis of his calculation so that the reader would know precisely how the percentage was calculated and could thus form his or her own assessment of the value of the assessment"[8].

4. In relation to the consultation the judge addressed his comments as follows[9]:

    "the evidence in this case clearly shows that the Council engaged fully with the trade. It sent a questionnaire, invited and received written representations and held two meetings. The Council could have been left in no doubt as to the extent of opposition among operators of licensed taxis to the removal of quantity restrictions and to the nature of that opposition. At each stage Mr Pennington scrupulously set out in his reports both the nature and extent of opposition, that was then plain for all to see.

    The principal criticism of the process was that the Council failed to hold focus group meetings with the trade. Given the nature of the opposition to removal of quantity restrictions, it is wholly unclear to me what additional value such focus groups would have contributed to the decision making process in this particular case, but in any event there was plainly no duty on the Council to consult through such fora."[10]

    And he concluded this point by saying[11]:

"There is no suggestion that during the decision-making process the Council closed its mind to any relevant evidence gathered from experience elsewhere that could usefully have informed its final decision in relation to Salford."

5.   The reasons given were sufficient[12]:

"Looking at the decision-making process as a whole, including the extensive consultation with the trade and its final outcome, I have no doubts at all that those affected by the decision perfectly well knew and understood the basis upon which the decision had been taken."

6.   Finally, the Scheme of Delegations clearly gave the Lead Cabinet Member the power to make such a decision, and the fact that it was a pooicy decision did not alter that delegation.

"I see no reason in policy terms why a matter of the nature in question should not be delegated to an individual lead member"[13].

This case shows that if the consultation process is thorough, and at a formative stage, it is very hard to overturn a considered decision to delimit hackney carriage numbers.

[1]   [2009] EWHC 3798 (Admin), (18 December 2009, unreported).
[2]   See paragraphs 13 to 48 of the judgment.
[3]   At paragraph 49.
[4]   (1987) [1989] RTR 297n, CA; see para 8.180 above.
[5]   *R (on the application of Royden) v The Wirral Metropolitan Borough Council* [2002] All ER (D) 256, distinguishing *R (on the application of Maud) v Castlepoint Borough Council* [2002] EWHC 273 (Admin).
[6]   Per Kenneth Parker J at paragraph 50.
[7]   Per Kenneth Parker J at paragraph 57.
[8]   Per Kenneth Parker J at paragraph 60.
[9]   Per Kenneth Parker J at paragraphs 62.
[10]   Per Kenneth Parker J at paragraphs 62 and 63.
[11]   Per Kenneth Parker J at paragraph 65.
[12]   Per Kenneth Parker J at paragraph 68.
[13]   Per Kenneth Parker J at paragraph 71.

Conclusion to be drawn

8.233

What then is the net result of these cases?

- Full and genuine consultation must take place before the decision to delimit is taken (*Watford*[1] and *Salford*[2]).
- The laws of natural justice apply to the process (*Ellesmere Port and Neston*[3]).
- If the authority cannot demonstrate there is no unmet demand, the licences must be granted (*Ellesmere Port and Neston, Wirral (Kelly and Smith)*[4]).
- It is possible to delimit at any time, subject only to the requirement that such a decision must not be *Wednesbury* unreasonable (*Great Yarmouth*[5], *Wirral*

(*Royden*)[6], *St Albans, West Berkshire, Castle Point*[7], *Cardiff*[8] *and Salford*[9]), or indeed re-limit subject to the same requirements (*Halton*[10]).

- Consideration must be given to the commercial impact of a delimitation decision, but provided that is done, commercial impact alone is not a ground for challenge (*St Albans*[11] and *West Berkshire*[12]).
- In assessing unmet demand, a broad approach should be taken and small areas or times of short supply may not indicate a need for more licences (*Great Yarmouth, Stevenage*[13], *Brighton*[14], but consider *Cannock Chase*[15]).
- Private hire use and latent unmet demand cannot be considered (*Brighton*), but patent demand for hackney carriage services can be considered (*Castle Point*[16]).
- The conclusions of a survey cannot prevent more licences being granted than the survey recommends, provided the decision is not unreasonable in *Wednesbury* terms (*Reading*[17]).
- If a limit is in place and additional licences are to be granted to meet any unmet demand, they can be allocated in batches, allowing the impact of each tranche to be assessed (*Wakefield*[18], not following *Reading*[19]).
- Additional licences can be allocated by means of a 'points system' provided it is not unreasonable and individual circumstances are also considered (*Leeds*[20]).
- A deferment in making a decision amounts to a refusal (*Wirral* (*Kelly and Smith*), not following *Middlesbrough*[21] and *Leeds*).
- If licences are to be granted following an appeal, it is for the local authority to allocate them, according to its criteria, not the court, according to the success of the appeal (*Wirral* (*Kelly and Smith*)).

[1]   *Sardar v Watford Borough Council* (30 June 2006, unreported), Admin Ct; see para 8.231 above.
[2]   *Saltax Ltd v Salford City Council* [2009] EWHC 3798 (Admin), (18 December 2009, unreported), see para 8.323 above.
[3]   *Tudor v Ellesmere Port and Neston Borough Council* (1987) Times, 8 May; see para 8.178 above.
[4]   *Kelly and Smith v Wirral Metropolitan Borough Council* (1996) 160 JP Rep 1047, CA; see para 8.198 above.
[5]   *R v Great Yarmouth Borough Council, ex p Sawyer* (1987) [1989] RTR 297n, CA; see para 8.180 above.
[6]   *R (on the application of Royden) v Metropolitan Borough of Wirral* [2003] BLGR 290, Admin Ct; see para 8.219 above.
[7]   *R v Halton Borough Council, ex p Gunson* (29 July 1988, unreported); see para 8.185 above.
[8]   *Cummings v Cardiff County Council* [2005] EWCA Civ 1061; see para 8.230 above.
[9]   *Saltax Ltd v Salford City Council* [2009] EWHC 3798 (Admin), (18 December 2009, unreported), see para 8.232.
[10]   *R (on the application of Maud) v Castle Point Borough Council* [2003] RTR 7, CA; see para 8.204 above.
[11]   *R v Council of the City and District of St Albans* [2001] LLR 38, QBD ; see para 8.202 above.
[12]   *R (on the Application of Nemeth) v West Berkshire District Council* 2000 WL 33122488 (8 December 2000) Admin Ct; see para 8.203 above.
[13]   *Stevenage Borough Council v Younas* (1988) [1990] RTR 405n, QBD; see para 8.184 above.
[14]   *R v Brighton Borough Council, ex p Bunch* [1989] COD 558; see para 8.188 above.
[15]   *Cannock Chase District Council v Alldritt* (28 January 1993, unreported); see para 8.194 above.
[16]   *R (on the application of Maud) v Castle Point Borough Council* [2002] EWCA Civ 1526, [2003] RTR 7, CA; see para 8.204 above.
[17]   *R (on the application of Johnson) v Reading Borough Council* [2004] EWHC 765 (Admin), [2004] All ER (D) 90 (Apr); see para 8.229 above.

18   *Ghafoor v Wakefield Metropolitan District Council* [1990] RTR 389, QBD; see para 8.191 above.
19   *R v Reading Borough Council, ex p Egan* (1987) [1990] RTR 399n; see para 8.179 above.
20   *R v Leeds City Council, ex p Mellor* [1993] COD 352; see para 8.196 above.
21   *R v Middlesbrough Council, ex p I J H Cameron (Holdings) Ltd* [1992] COD 247; see para 8.193 above.

8.234

Table 8.2   Increasing Numbers of Hackney Carriages and Surveys – Case Law Summary

Case	Summary	Conclusion
Tudor-v-Ellesmere Port and Neston Borough Council (1987) The Times, 8 May Para 8.178 High Court decision of the Queens Bench Division.	First reported decision in the High Court, on increasing numbers. Authority for the view that rules of natural justice are to be followed in an appeal regarding refusal to grant hackney carriage proprietor's licence. Assertion applicant not fit and proper introduced late in Counsel's final speech. No opportunity therefore to rebut. Application made for two licences and refused, however Transport Act 1985 in force by Crown Court appeal hearing.	In absence of evidence as to demand, council conceded it could no longer refuse grant merely by reason of numbers.
R v Reading Borough Council, ex p Egan (1987) [1990] RTR 399A (not reported until 1990) Para 8.179 High Court decision, QBD.	On introduction of Transport Act 1985, s 16, Reading took advice from the DOT circular 3/85. Previously had only licensed 50 hackney carriages. Proposed to grant 30 additional licences then 'wait and see' and assess additional demand for hackney carriages based on such grant. Challenged by way of judicial review.	Nolan J dealt with the question as to whether the fear of total derestriction might cause over provision and whether the council was entitled to issue limited number of further licences as a means of obtaining the evidence to establish presence or absence of unmet demand. He stated that the dangers of over provision were accepted in law prior to 1985: *R v Weymouth Borough Council, ex p Teletax (Weymouth) Limited* [1947] KB 583.

Case	Summary	Conclusion
		May be difficult to supervise and control a large number of taxis. The Act makes no provision for an interim period to establish by market research or otherwise presence or absence of unmet demand. Follows that from s 16 coming into force on 6 January 1986 a council which is unable to feel satisfied that there is no significant unmet demand is obliged to grant applications for suitably qualified vehicles without limit of numbers. He further stated that paragraph 28 of the circular appeared to incorporate an erroneous view of the law.
R v Great Yarmouth Borough Council, ex p Sawyer (1987) [1989] RTR 297 N, CA Para 8.180 Court of Appeal decision	When s 16 first proposed in the Transport Bill, council considered its position. Numbers had been limited. Council reconsidered. Sub-committee took the view that the number should be maintained, no significant unmet demand. Asked trade to provide evidence to support the view. Ultimately however decision made by full council to delimit. Judicial review sought of decision that unreasonable in *Wednesbury* terms and irrelevant matters taken into account, namely the action being taken by other authorities in Norfolk.	Judgments were given by Woolf LJ, Bingham LJ and Dillon LJ. In summary the Lord Justices decided that a local authority can at any time decide to delimit the number of hackney carriage licences which it will grant provided its decision is not *Wednesbury* unreasonable. Their Lordships said there was no basis for intervening on the basis that individual drivers would suffer hardship by the increase in the number of taxis. Council was entitled to be told and to consider what action other District Councils in Norfolk were taking. Not bound to make further enquiries or to have surveys conducted.

AUTHOR'S NOTE: As to what will be relevant matters is a factual issue in each case but see para 8:171 for the author's suggestions as to those which are predominant.

Case	Summary	Conclusion
Stevenage Borough Council v Younas (1988) [1990] RTR 405 N QBD Para 8.184 High Court decision, QBD	High Court decision of the Queens Bench Division following the *Great Yarmouth* case above regarding the adoption of a broad approach, to delimitation, matter went to Crown Court by way of appeal against refusal to grant Mr Younas a licence, thence to the Divisional Court.	Crown Court indicated it was satisfied that it was demonstrated there was no significant demand at the services of hackney carriage within Stevenage Borough Council area which was unmet. Subject only to one proviso, concerning demand for the services of hackneys near a particular night club after midnight. Crown Court found that that requirement did *not* allow the council to be satisfied that there was no significant demand. Pill LJ in the High Court concluded that the findings the Crown Court were wrong and did not prevent the Council from being satisfied in the terms of section. A broad approach was legitimate.

AUTHOR'S NOTE: This case supports the view that even if a survey finds there is unmet demand at some place at a particular time that is *not* sufficient to demonstrate significant unmet demand if the rest of the time demand is satisfied. The test is one of significance rather than existence.

R v Halton Borough Council, ex p Gunson (29 July 1988, unreported) Para 8.185 High Court decision, QBD	Halton reimposed numerical limits on hackney carriage proprietor's licences. Before the Transport Act 1985 there were 60 hackney carriage and 261 private hire. On 1 April 1986 they delimited the number of hackney vehicle licences and by December 1986 there were 158 hackney carriages and 66 private hire. The trade made representations to the council that there were too many hackney carriages.	Otten J stated that effect of Transport Act 1985, s 16, transfers permitted 'may' to 'partially mandatory must' different from prior legislation. Unless authority satisfied no significant demand which is unmet obliged to issue a licence to suitable applicant. Policy of no numerical restriction can be adopted. Court indicated there was insufficient evidence of the committee proceedings and records and adequate statements. Insufficient evidence of the implications of the working party report.

Case	Summary	Conclusion
	Authority set up taxi working party, made full enquiries. Despite 'sparse service' in some parts of the borough, recommended no limit should be imposed. Warned if limit imposed, inadequate service would deteriorate further. Two days before the taxi committee meeting (to whom working party would report), circular published by Taxi Drivers' Association to all committee members. Argued that as result committee departed from recommendation in working party's report, imposing a limit. Challenged by judicial review imposition of a limit unreasonable and that an assurance had been given by a councillor that no limit would be imposed.	No evidence committee considered or complied with their statutory duty under s 16; taxi drivers circular only dealt with hardship. Court could only conclude in the absence of evidence as to how any decision was arrived at that committee were persuaded to act at the behest of the drivers, decision therefore unlawful. Statement of the chairman not binding on the authority being distinguishable from the statements in *R v Liverpool Corporation, ex p Liverpool Taxi Fleet Operators Association* [1972] 2 QB 299.

AUTHOR'S NOTE: The opposite of the *Great Yarmouth* decision in that as decision to delimit was not evidence based, it was irrational and unlawful on *Wednesbury* grounds.

R v Brighton Borough Council, ex p Bunch [1989] COD 558 Para 8.188 High Court decision, QBD	Survey commissioned June 1986: no significant unmet demand thereafter no new hackney carriage licences issued. Decided second survey in following year showed no change in position, report suggested shortage of taxis due to reluctance of drivers to work unsocial hours. View accepted no new licence issued. Challenged by way of judicial review.	Kennedy J, in the Divisional Court, indicated that demand may be latent, services of hackney carriages should be interpreted as meaning all services, latent demand should not be considered and only measurable demand should be taken into account. Argument that council had failed to take surveys directly into account or to inquire as to the level of unmet demand was unsuccessful, nor was council's conclusion unreasonable or irrational.

AUTHOR'S NOTE: Broad approach should be taken. Short periods of poor service did not signify unmet demand. Case demonstrates judicial approval of an independent survey.

Case	Summary	Conclusion
Ghaffor v Wakefield Metropolitan District Council [1990] RTR 389, QBD Para 8.191 High Court decision, QBD	This does not follow the approaching *R v Reading Borough Council, ex p Egan.* Until the introduction of the Transport Act 1985 Wakefield had maintained a limit on the number of hackney carriages licensed. Council commissioned survey; stated there was unmet demand. Council issued five licences. Dissatisfied applicant who did not receive a licence appealed to Crown Court. Appeal dismissed. Appeal made to High Court. Four specific matters raised: (1) What was the correct approach for the Crown Court to take: in determining appeals should it stand in the shoes of the council or make its own judgment? (2) Did the Crown Court apply law correctly in relation to burden and standard of proof and a broad approach? (3) Was the Crown Court right in concluding that there was no significant unmet demand for taxi services in Wakefield? (4) In the light of the Crown Court's determination that the council had failed to establish that there was significant unmet demand for hackney carriages and the Crown Court's finding that there was a delay at ranks, would applicants have a sense of grievance that justice had not been done?	Mr Justice Webster considered paragraph 28 of the DOT circular 3/85. Although that approach had been ruled unlawful by Nolan J in *Reading Borough Council, ex p Egan,* Webster J disagreed with that interpretation. He found that the effect of s 16 was to deprive the local authority of a discretion to refuse the application except when it is satisfied there is no significant unmet demand. Nothing in his view prevented the authority from advising itself in one way or another about the number of taxis which would have to be licenced in order to meet all significant demand. The council in the present case were acting perfectly properly in assessing the number of licences and issuing only that number provided they satisfied themselves afresh as to further unmet demand before refusing further applications. Webster J decided that the Crown Court approach on burden of proof, standard of proof were correct and a broad approach in relation to demand should be taken.

Case	Summary	Conclusion
R v Middlesbrough Council, ex p IJH Cameron (Holdings) Limited [1992] COD 247 Para 8.193 High Court decision, QBD	*Reading* decision followed here. Question of whether deferral of a decision as to whether or not to grant hackney carriage proprietor's licence amounted to refusal. Application for 25 licences January 1989. April 1989 council committee deferred licence issue until survey undertaken. Survey received and in July 1989 applicant notified application refused. Applicants asserted delay amounted to refusal and following Reading Borough Council authority must grant.	In the High Court, Popplewell J held that a deferral for a short period of time to conduct a survey did not amount to refusal. Did not therefore follow the decision of Nolan J in the *Reading* case.
Cannock Chase District Council v Alldritt (28 January 1993, unreported), DC Para 8.194 High Court decision, QBD	Application for six hackney carriage proprietor's licences. Cannock had a policy of limitation supported by survey. Distinction made as to demand in three significant geographical areas of the local authority district. Appellants contended there was unmet demand in one area. Appeal to Crown Court. Crown Court upheld appeal. District Council appealed by way of case stated; High Court dismissed the application. Its appears High Court was not referred to any other cases.	Judgment of Mann LJ. Appeal to Crown Court is a hearing de novo. Crown Court vested with the power of grant or refusal. As such the court not concerned with council's entitlement. Court decided not to exercise the power conferred by s 16, the Crown Court perfectly entitled to proceed in the way it did.

AUTHOR'S NOTE: Judgment seems at odds with *Brighton Borough Council, ex p Bunch* and whether the same result would have obtained had the court had reference to *Great Yarmouth Borough Council, ex p Sawyer* is a matter for conjecture. Geography appears to be the overriding consideration both in Crown and High Court. It appears the court tailors judgment to the reality of the situation, but is effectively introducing some form of HC zoning, for grant, if not use.

Case	Summary	Conclusion
R v Leeds City Council, ex p Mellor [1993] COD 352 Para 8.196 High Court decision, QBD	Approach that deferral did not amount to refusal followed in this case. First assertion that an application was refused when the decision was deferred for more information. Second consideration was the points allocation of new licences used by Leeds.	Court considered *R v Reading Borough Council, ex p Egan*, *Ghaffor v Wakefield Metropolitan District Council* and *R v Middlesbrough Borough Council, ex p IJH Cameron Holdings Ltd*. Hutchinson J concluded that the effect of the authorities was that he should not follow the decision of Nolan J in the *Reading* case, that an authority which is not satisfied that there is no unmet demand must accede to all applications and may not defer. It is the case that when application is made and the authority cannot be satisfied that there is no unmet demand, it has no discretion to refuse for the purpose of limiting numbers. However authority is entitled to take steps to inform itself as to unmet demand and may defer for that consideration. Obligation on the authority to keep themselves reasonably well informed as to such matters information may need updating from time to time. Court analysed at length the points system for the allocation of licences, deciding that a point system is satisfactory if *Wednesbury* reasonable and there is a facility for special consideration of individual applicant's circumstances.

AUTHOR'S NOTE: Many authorities limiting numbers do so by survey. A recommendation is then made as to how many extra vehicle licences should be granted. The determinant as to who should be granted licences can be decided on a points system based on a number of criteria. The *Leeds* case supports the view such approach is acceptable, provided it is flexible.

Case	Summary	Conclusion
Kelly and Smith v Wirral Metropolitan Borough Council (1996) 160 JP REP 1047, CA Para 8.198 Court of Appeal decision	Court of Appeal decision concerning number of issues. Mechanism of allocation when there is significant unmet demand and deferred decisions. Wirral MBC had applications for hackney carriage proprietor's licences. Had a policy of limiting the number of hackneys. Mr Kelly applied for 10 hackney carriage proprietor's' licences. Refused on the ground there was no significant unmet demand. Appeal to Crown Court. Appeal upheld. Licences all to be issued. Council appealed to High Court which ruled that the decision as to whom to issue the licences to (but not the question of how many to issue) should be remitted to the council, overruling part of the Crown Court decision. Mr Kelly appealed to the Court of Appeal. Argument centred on others on the waiting list who had applied for licences earlier than Mr Kelly. Mr Smith appealed similarly. Concerned whether a right of appeal arose when local authority failed to grant a hackney carriage proprietor's licence within reasonable time. No specific decision to refuse, but there was delay. Appellant argued delay amounted to withholding.	On the matter of allocation of the licences, Auld LJ noted judgment of Webster J in *Ghaffor v Wakefield Metropolitan District Council*. Court ruled that the local authority or Crown Court should apply a system fair to all applicants. Nothing in s 16 of the 1985 Act requiring that a licensing authority must grant a licence if not satisfied there is no significant demand to prevent the authority from examining in the context of an individual application the general state of unmet demand by reference to all outstanding applications. On a successful appeal it was correct that the Crown Court remit the decision as to whom the licences should be issued to back to the council and that those ahead of the successful appellant on the waiting list might then benefit over the appellant. On the matter of when the decision to refuse a hackney carriage proprietor's licence application was made triggering an appeal to the Crown Court, Lord Justice Auld gave the judgment of the court. Courts needed to consider the particular circumstances for each case as withholding is a continuing form of inaction but it may not be appropriate to adopt an overly rigorous attitude to time limits. However, inaction or delay amounts to a refusal, triggering a right of appeal.

Case	Summary	Conclusion

AUTHOR'S NOTE: Success at appeal demonstrating unmet demand; no guarantee of hackney carriage proprietor's licence as council will have to decide upon criteria for granting licences.

Case	Summary	Conclusion
R v Council of the City and District of St Albans [2001] LLR 38 QBD	Decision by St Albans to delimit the number of hackney carriage licences.	No irregularity found in Council's Standing Orders by Lightman J.
Para 8.202 High Court decision of the Queens Bench Division	Preliminary decision to grant an additional five licences, commission unmet demand survey and refuse request for fare increase.	With regard to proportionality, the court found goal was to establish an open market. This had the consequence of removing vulnerability to a threat in the future of strike action.
	Following trade protest, decision taken to remove limit.	Likelihood of more wheelchair accessible taxis and a saving of costs of triannual surveys for taxi demands in the future.
	Consultation over a period of two weeks, no complaints received as to shortness of time.	Question of proportionality did not arise if the goal was one of abolishing all restrictions on numbers immediately.
	After representations agreed limit should be removed with immediate effect.	
	Applicants sought judicial review and an injunction which was granted.	Council are entitled to adopt this as their goal.
	Arguments concerned Council's Standing Orders, proportionality in the timing of the consultation process.	In respect of consultation, two weeks viewed as extremely short. Judge heard that as they had managed to respond within the time limits set by the council and had not sought any increase in that length of time, there was no prejudice.
		Judge dismissed arguments on the issue of whether or not a survey was required before a delimitation decision was made and that in every case a financial impact survey should have been commissioned.
		Court found that there was no obligation to assess financial impact.
		Judge also made reference to commercial hardship borne by those who had invested the hackney carriage

Case	Summary	Conclusion
		proprietor's licence at a premium.
		Court felt that investment in licences by drivers was a risk investment and no promises that the licences would not be diluted.

AUTHOR'S NOTE: If consultation takes place without consultees alerting the Council to the lack of time, short duration arguments not likely to succeed. Courts understand the commercial realities facing drivers.

Case	Summary	Conclusion
R (on the application of Nemeth) v West Berkshire District Council (8 December 2000) Admin Ct 2000 WL 33122488 Para 8.203 High Court decision of the Admin Ct, QBD	Argument raised that council was required to maintain its existing policy in relation to additional proprietor's licences. West Berkshire DC limited number of hackney carriage licences it would issue. Additional five licences issued 1997 subject to stringent points system, Nemeth successful applicant. Mr Nemeth aggrieved when, in 2000, council changed policy to manage growth. Question was whether there was a legitimate expectation that the policy dating from 1997 would continue indefinitely and whether council failed to take account of impact on the appellant and four other licencees.	Hunt J in December 2000 did not find any conduct on behalf of the council leading to legitimate expectation, no promises or assurances given. Court found that there was sufficient consultation including the taxi drivers' position, therefore expectation not established nor was council's conduct in abuse of power. Meeting with council recognised the difficulties of increased numbers for the trade and investments taken in buying plates. But more or less the council is free to alter its policy at any time provided it consults those likely to be affected. Provided the commercial impact on existing licensees is considered delimitation decisions can be taken.
R (on the application of Maud) v Castlepoint Borough Council [2002] EWHC 273 (Admin), [2002] LLR 374, Admin Ct Para 8.204 High Court decision of the Admin Ct – QBD, appealed to the Court of Appeal [2002] EWCA Civ 1526, [2003] RTR 7.	Castlepoint is a district covering Benfleet and Canvey Island in Essex both, in the absence of hackney carriage zones, falling within the same licence district. Council had limit of 37 hackney carriage licences; independent consultants prepared demand report, concluded unmet demand.	Matter considered by Wilson J. Castlepoint relied strongly on the ruling in *R v Great Yarmouth Borough Council ex p Sawyer*. Analysis of the exercise of discretion or obligation in relation to met/unmet demand. Court not impressed by distinction between patent and latent unmet demand.

Case	Summary	Conclusion
	Report referred also to latent unmet demand as well as patent in view of station rank generating high percentage of work. Five additional licences would satisfy demand. Council delimited after consultation. Challenged by Mr Maud, a hackney carriage driver.	Court took the view that all unmet demand was patent. The court did not follow ruling in *R v Brighton Borough Council, ex p Bunch*, where only HC services could be taken into account. Further arguments considered possibility of imposing condition that new licensed vehicles could not work from the most popular rank. Dismissed. Matter appealed to the Court of Appeal. Matter considered by Keene, Kennedy and Buxton LJJ. In relation to latent and patent demand. Reference made to *R v Brighton Borough Council ex p Bunch*. Appeal Court view was that all methods should be used for assessment of demand – latent demand unfortunate phrase. The fact that survey had taken into account private hire rather than hackney was dismissed. Court of Appeal concluded High Court decision correct. No irrelevant considerations taken into account in decision.
R (on the application of Roydon) v Metropolitan Borough of Wirral [2003] BLGR 290 Admin Ct Para 8.219 High Court decision of the Admin Ct, QBD	Delimitation with significant argument in relation to Human Rights Act 1988 relating to the decision. Wirral limited the number of hackney carriage licences until the 1990s. Considerable litigation until 1997 when limit increased by 15 to 101. Limit challenged by unsuccessful applicants.	Matter remitted to council to grant further licences. Court held there had been consultation conducted correctly. Court took the view that *Great Yarmouth ex p Sawyer* correct. Council were entitled to derestrict subject to human rights considerations. No prior survey was necessary.

Case	Summary	Conclusion
	Unmet demand established. Council commissioned report.	Consideration then given by the court to *Wednesbury* reasonableness. Court held it was impossible to hold decision unlawful applying conventional grounds of judicial review. Was not *Wednesbury* unreasonable, nor perverse procedurally unfair nor erroneous in any in point of law.
	Decision was taken by council to issue 25 licences. There were 58 applicants and in 1999 number of licences increased to 126.	
	February 2002 questionnaire issued to operators.	
	Some argument about contents of questionnaire with applicant but results assessed and report prepared for committee.	Also held that the value in the licence was not protected by Article 1 Protocol 1 of the European Convention and the Human Rights Act 1998.
	Decision taken to remove limit for wheelchair accessible vehicles less than three years old.	
	Challenged by way of judicial review on basis of failure to consult and failure to take account of relevant information, interference with property and violation or Article 1 of the First Protocol and insufficient reasons.	
R (on the application of Johnson) v Reading Borough Council [2004] EWHC 765 Admin; [2004] All ER(D) 90 (Apr, Admin Ct) Para 8.229 High Court decision of the Admin Ct, QBD	Council limited the number of hackney carriages it would licence to 138, commissioned unmet demand survey.	Goldring J delivered his decision. Cited *R v Great Yarmouth Borough Council*. Deference should be paid to decision of democratically elected decision takers who follow an at least adequate consultation.
	Recommended granting of eight new licences, would remove unmet demand. Increase of 6%.	
	Recommended alterations to ranks and new ranks.	Should not be judged in an over refined and over legalistic way.
	Committee report detailed various courses of action.	Council has wide discretion.
	After debate council decided to issue 30 new licences but not move towards delimitation.	Purpose of survey was to ensure council did not act unlawfully.
	Finite increase, not managed growth.	Was an entitlement to look at a concentrated area. No objection to councillors using local knowledge.

Case	Summary	Conclusion
	Decision challenged by way of judicial review. Seven points argued:	Committee knew government was contemplating total derestriction.
	(1) wrong interpretation of report;	Councillors' views dealt with in a sensible and rational way.
	(2) lack of geographical restriction;	Conflict over the actual numbers of applicable licences.
	(3) anecdotal evidence considered;	
	(4) irrational conclusion in relation to grant of licences meeting unmet demand;	Committee were entitled to rely on the expert advice of the licencing and enforcement officer.
	(5) irrational choice of 30 new hackney licences;	Decision therefore could not be described as irrational and the judicial review must fail.
	(6) no proper basis for concluding demand in relation to the railway station; and	
	(7) monitoring licences would be of no assistance.	
	Council could not retract licences. Council made detailed submissions in response to these points of challenge.	

AUTHOR'S NOTE: Case demonstrates the survey is evidence for refusing applications for additional licences, but it is not evidence for and cannot prevent the council deciding to grant extra licences. Surveys therefore meaningless in relation to situation where the council wishes to increase numbers. This reinforces the ruling in both *Great Yarmouth* and *Castlepoint*.

Cummings v Cardiff County Council [2004] EWHC 2295, [2005] LLR 27, Admin Ct, [2005] EWCA Civ 1061, [2005] LLR 687 CA	A delimitation case that reached the Court of Appeal concerning the process used by council to reach decision to remove the limit on hackney carriages.	Moses J in the Divisional Court considered the matter fully.
Para 8.230	Cardiff had limits on hackney numbers.	Generally report found misleading, but choice of lottery lawful.
High Court decision of the Admin Ct, QBD appealed to the Court of Appeal.	Mr Cummings owned and controlled a large proportion of them at 58 out of 480.	Matter for committee to decide what arguments were relevant to the issue and whether to derestrict or not. Whether advantage of derestriction outweighed disadvantage. Rejection of the submission that defects in the process by which the first decision was made affected the second decision to make it unlawful.
	Decision based on survey to issue six more on the basis that the council concluded that there was unmet demand which would be met by that issue. Decision	

Case	Summary	Conclusion
	led to the question of the method of allocation. Council decided on the option of a lottery and Mr Cummings sought judicial review of the decision and an injunction based on being overlooked or misled over the existence of the waiting list, irrationality of use of the lottery and failing to consider each application on its own merits. Council as a result reconsidered its position, decided to pursue delimitation of numbers. Consultation took place with hackney carriage trade. Committee considering report found that there was an unmet demand, market for hackney services would find its own level, quality control could be maintained by the authority, new cars would be financially prohibitive, therefore three year vehicle age limit would be introduced. Mr Cummings then appealed the decision to the Court of Appeal where similar arguments took place.	Mr Cummings then appealed to the Court of Appeal where several arguments were raised. Scott Baker J decided that decision whether or not to delimit entirely separate and independent of decision on how to allocate licences within limitation context. Facts in the case appear complex but Court of Appeal authority that delimitation can take place any time subject to a challenge on *Wednesbury* principles. This follows *Great Yarmouth Borough Council, ex p Sawyer* in 1987.

AUTHOR'S NOTE: Despite legal arguments of allocation of plates by lottery no unequivocal declaration made by the court as to the legality of such a method of allocation.

Case	Summary	Conclusion
Sardar and Watford Borough Council (30 June 2006, unreported), Admin Ct	Concerned process of consultation before delimitation decision taken.	Wilkie J identified the issues.
Para 8.231	Matter dependent on its own facts.	Not in dispute, there could be no change of policy without consultation.
High Court decision of the Admin Ct, QBD	Reinforces law relating to consultation and its practicalities in the delimitation decision.	Equally not in dispute no consultation prior to 5 September 2005.
	Watford had been operating managed growth policy in regard to hackneys from 2003 following an OFT report there was a change to taxi arrangements at Watford Junction Railway Station.	There was a decision to delimit then that decision was necessarily taken unlawfully.
	A large number of appeals against refusals to grant lodged with Crown Court.	The law governing consultation was laid down by the Court of Appeal in *R v North and East Devon Health Authority, ex p Coglan* considered that court set out the basis for proper consultation. The court found that the decision had been taken at a point prior to the consultation being effective; as a consequence the claim would not succeed.
	Council had reconsidered policy.	
	Consultation exercise took place.	
	Committee recommendation was that no further hackney carriage licences to be granted pending survey or existing policy of managed growth be maintained.	As council took a decision on 5 September to delimit, policy to delimit therefore ceased to be in the formative stage.
	Majority of political group changed the recommendation to agree a manner under which delimitation would take effect.	The conduct for such consultation was not satisfied in full. He found that the decision had in effect been taken in September. Consultation was not effective and the claim would therefore succeed.
	Further report prepared, consultation exercise and ultimately a recommendation was adopted to delimit and this was challenged by way of judicial review.	

AUTHOR'S NOTE: This case is largely on its own facts. It is a useful reminder for correct consultation to be taken in accordance with *R v North and East Devon Health Authority, ex p Coglan*.

Case	Summary	Conclusion
Saltax Ltd v Salford City Council [2009] EWHC 3798 (Admin); 18 December 2009 QBD (Admin Ct) Para 8.232	Decision to de-limit made by the lead Cabinet Member following lengthy and detailed consultation, challenged by way of judicial review on six grounds: 1. Was a survey required before a decision to delimit could be made? 2. Were the views of residents correctly assessed? 3. The results of the questionnaires were not properly reported to the Councillors by Mr Pinnington, the officer responsible for licensing. 4. The consultation with the trade was flawed generally and in particular by the absence of any focus group meetings. 5. No reasons were given for the decision. 6. The decision could not be taken by a single portfolio holder.	Every argument was rejected by the judge and the decision was upheld.

AUTHOR'S NOTE: This case is largely on its own facts, but it usefully restates that no survey is required to delimit. As regards the decision taken by the lead cabinet member, it should be compared with *R (app 007 Stratford Taxis Ltd) v Stratford on Avon District Council* [2011] EWCA Civ 160 see Chapter 2, para 2.23.

Waiting lists

8.235

Those authorities that do maintain a limit on the number of hackney carriages that they will licence often make use of waiting lists. This is seen as a mechanism whereby those who wish to have a hackney carriage licence can express their interest to be considered if and when any further licences become available. There is a question over the status of these waiting lists and clearly (following the ruling in *Kelly and Smith v Wirral Metropolitan Borough Council*[1]), the presence on a waiting list may well influence the final allocation of licences if an increase in number is decided upon by the Council[2].

[1]   (1996) 160 JP Rep 1047, CA; see para 8.198 above.

²   There are some authorities who run an extraordinary system whereby they have a waiting list
to be placed on the waiting list, as the first waiting list is full! In these circumstances, it is not
clear what criteria are used to determine how many names should reasonably or practically be
contained on the principal waiting list.

8.236

The question that arises, however, is whether being placed on a waiting list
amounts to a refusal. This would appear to depend to an extent on the facts of
the particular case.

8.237

If an individual makes an informal inquiry about the possibility of obtaining
a hackney carriage proprietor's licence and is informed that there is a limited
number, that the allocation is currently taken up and that the council will inform
the individual if and when any further licences are available, then that is simply
a method of maintaining a list of interested parties if and when further licences
are issued.

8.238

One significant problem with waiting lists from the perspective of the council
is keeping them up to date. With changes of name, changes of circumstance,
people moving away from the area and death, waiting lists can rapidly become
inaccurate. Indeed, to maintain the effectiveness and validity of a waiting list it
is probably necessary for the local authority to contact the people on that list
at regular intervals to ascertain whether or not they wish to remain on the list[1].

¹   It is occasionally claimed that a person's place on a waiting list can be passed on death by will
or intestacy. Although beyond the scope of this book, this seems unlikely as a place on a waiting
list does not appear to be a 'chose in action' which is capable of assignment to a third party. Any
authority that is creating a new waiting list should consider making it clear on the face of the
waiting list that a place on the waiting list is personal, and cannot be transferred, assigned or
bequeathed. See *Theobald on Wills* (18th edn, Sweet and Maxwell, 2016).

R v Tower Hamlets London Borough Council, ex p Kayne-Levenson

8.239

> Where a council has a limit on hackney carriage numbers, if an applicant is
> placed on a waiting list, does that amount to a refusal? In a case concerning
> street trading Held: Yes it does and thereby triggers a right of appeal.

However, if an application is made for a hackney carriage proprietor's licence
and the council respond to that by placing the applicant on a waiting list due
to the fact that there is a limited number and no licences are available at that
particular time, then it would seem that would amount to a refusal to grant a
licence and would trigger the right of appeal contained in the Public Health
Acts Amendment Act 1907, s 7[1]. This approach is supported by the judgment of

Lord Denning in *R v Tower Hamlets London Borough Council, ex p Kayne-Levenson*[2], where he stated:

> 'In this state of affairs, the borough council have taken this course: they have a number of applicants for one pitch: they grant the licence to one, and put the others on the "waiting list." They write to each of the unsuccessful applicants and tell him that his name will be placed on the "waiting list." This "waiting list" is a list of applicants for a pitch in that street. Names are added in order of date. Then when any pitch in that street becomes vacant, it is offered to the names in that list. If the first one does not want it, it is offered to the next, and so forth. If any applicant refuses it twice, he goes down to the bottom of the list. The waiting list for some streets is so long that a person may have to wait for years before he will be offered a pitch in it.
>
> It appears that, in practice, when the borough council put a name on a waiting list, they do not treat it as a refusal, and accordingly they do not give him formal notification, or tell him that he can appeal.
>
> I see no objection to the council keeping a waiting list or operating it as they do. It is a convenient piece of administration. But I think they should alter their form of notification. To put an application on the waiting list is tantamount to a refusal. They should treat it as such and tell him so. It is a refusal on the ground that there is no space available: see section 21 (3) (b) [of the London County Council (General Powers) Act 1947]. They should notify him that it is a refusal and tell him of his right to appeal. This is of little use to him. But they can soften the blow by telling him that his name will be put on the waiting list.'

Accordingly, councils who accept applications for hackney carriage proprietor's licences and then deal with the application by adding a person's name to a waiting list are in fact refusing the application, and should communicate that fact to the applicant, thereby enabling him to appeal if he wishes.

1   See Chapter 3, paras 3.3 and 3.15.
2   [1975] QB 431, CA. This case concerned street trading licences under the London County Council (General Powers) Act 1947.

Surveys

8.240

Finally, it is necessary to mention surveys. They are the only acceptable method of demonstrating whether demand for hackney carriage services is met or, if it is not, the extent of the shortfall. However, they are of limited use where the authority is considering increasing numbers or delimiting altogether. They are not required before delimiting[1]. If an authority wishes to increase numbers, provided the increase is equal to or more than the number suggested by the survey to meet any unmet demand, again the survey becomes immaterial[2].

In *R v Brighton Borough Council, ex p Bunch*[3], an independent survey carried out by a competent person attracted judicial approval. Surveys conducted by the council's officers are likely to be seen as partial and therefore, unlikely to be capable of being relied on in any appeal against a refusal to grant a hackney carriage proprietor's licence. However, even independent surveys can cause problems as was highlighted in the *Key Cabs Ltd v Plymouth City Council* case[4].

[1]   See *R v Great Yarmouth Borough Council, ex p Sawyer* (1987) [1989] RTR 297n, CA (see para 8.180 above) and *R (on the application of Maud) v Castle Point Borough Council* [2002] EWHC 273 (Admin), [2002] LLR 374, Admin Ct and *R (on the application of Maud) v Castle Point Borough Council* [2002] EWCA Civ 1526, [2003] RTR 7, CA (see para 8.204 above).

[2]   *R (on the application of Johnson) v Reading Borough Council* [2004] EWHC 765 (Admin), [2004] All ER (D) 90 (Apr), Admin Ct (see para 8.229 above).

[3]   [1989] COD 558: see in particular the remarks of Kennedy J at 7–8, reproduced at para 8.188 above.

[4]   *Key Cabs Ltd v Plymouth City Council* Plymouth Crown Court (7 March 2006, unreported). This was an appeal against a refusal to grant a hackney carriage proprietor's licence. Plymouth had commissioned a demand survey from TPI, who in turn subcontracted some of the data collecting to another company. This sub-contractor produced results which were inaccurate and had apparently been created falsely and threw the whole TPI survey results into doubt.

8.241

Independent surveys are expensive to commission, but essential if the local authority is successfully going to defend a refusal to grant additional licences. The costs of such a survey can be recovered from the hackney carriage trade via an increase in licence fees. In areas where LG(MP)A 1976 has been adopted, LG(MP)A 1976, s 70(1)(c) allows the recovery of:

> 'any reasonable administrative or other costs in connection with the foregoing and with the control and supervision of hackney carriages and private hire vehicles.'

This approach is supported by the DfT in its Best Practice Guidance[1] where it states (at para 34):

> '**financing of surveys**. It is not good practice for surveys to be paid for by the local taxi trade (except through general revenues from licence fees). To do so can call in question the impartiality and objectivity of the survey process.'

This is an approach which can prove unpopular with the hackney carriage trade, as it will increase their fees, but as the maintenance of a limit on numbers is arguably in the interests of the existing licence holders, such complaints seem ill-founded.

[1]   DfT, *'Taxi and Private Hire Vehicle Licensing: Best Practice Guidance'* (October 2006, revised March 2010) available at http://www.dft.gov.uk/pgr/regional/taxis/taxiandprivatehirevehiclelic1792

Application for renewal

8.242

It is only on renewal that the provisions of LG(MP)A 1976, s 60(1) expressly come into play. On an application for a renewal, these provisions are extremely useful. They allow the council to refuse an application on the grounds either that the vehicle itself is unsuitable or that the applicant himself is unsuitable for some reason. This will often involve a consideration of the applicant's criminal record. It is possible, using the powers contained in LG(MP)A 1976, s 57[1] to require applicants to obtain a basic DBS disclosure which will reveal current live convictions[2]. This must be obtained by the applicant, as it cannot be obtained by the local authority and the local authority will need to decide how recent it must be. In addition it is advisable to require the applicant to complete a statutory declaration listing his previous convictions. This statutory declaration, should make it clear that, following the *Waveney* case[3], spent convictions can be considered and that, therefore, all convictions, (whether spent or otherwise) should be included in the list. The council can then consider any convictions revealed on either the DBS search or the statutory declaration in accordance with its policy, as it would do in relation to a driver's licence.

[1]   See Appendix I.
[2]   Basic Disclosures are only available from the Disclosure and Barring Service in Scotland, but can be obtained by residents in England and Wales – see https://www.mygov.scot/disclosure-types/?via=http://www.disclosurescotland.co.uk/basic.htm.
[3]   *Adamson v Waveney District Council* [1997] 2 All ER 898; see Chapter 5, para 5.11 onwards.

8.243

Many authorities do require applicants for all licences, in relation to hackney carriage and private hire activities, to complete a statutory declaration in these terms and then take the precaution of keeping them in the applicant's file from year to year. On a number of occasions, comparison between a current application and a former one may reveal that some offences have been omitted. As the information is contained in a statutory declaration, such lack of information is prima facie perjury and a number of authorities have passed such information to the police who in turn have successfully prosecuted for perjury. Such conviction is then, of course, an additional conviction which must be revealed in future applications.

One of the strange omissions within the legislation is the absence of any renewal mechanism for hackney carriage proprietors licences[1]. In the absence of any statutory process, local authorities need to determine the approach that they will take, and this should be clearly stated within their policies.

In relation to a vehicle licence, as the vehicle will need to have a test before the licence can be renewed, it is very unlikely that any authority will permit the use of a vehicle after the expiry of the licence.

[1]   The same applies to all these licences. There is clearly an expectation that licences can be renewed, because the local authority has the power to refuse to renew any licence, but the renewal mechanism itself is absent. See LG(MP)A 1976: s 60(1) in respect of renewal of vehicle licences; s 61(1) in respect of renewal of drivers' licences; s 62(1) in respect of renewal of operators' licences. This can be contrasted with most other licensing regimes where once a licence is in existence, provided the application for renewal is made before the current licence expires, the current licence is deemed to continue on the same terms and conditions until the renewal determination. See eg, Local Government (Miscellaneous Provisions) Act 1982, Sch 3, para 11 in respect of sex establishment licences and Scrap Metal Dealers Act 2013, Sch 1, para 1.

R (on the application of Exeter City Council) v Sandle

8.244

> Could a hackney carriage proprietors' licence be renewed after it had expired? Held: Yes it could provided the application was made within a short time of expiry and there was a good reason for the delay in applying.

The question of whether it was possible for a local authority to renew a hackney carriage proprietors' licence that had expired was considered in *R (on the application of Exeter City Council) v Sandle*[1]. Mr Sandle was a hackney carriage proprietor who applied to renew his hackney carriage proprietors' licence the day after it had expired. That was refused and, because at that time Exeter had a limit on hackney carriage nmbers, the vehicle licence was allocated and granted to the person at the top of the waiting list. Sandle appealed the refusal to the Crown Court[2] which allowed the appeal and decided that the licence could have been renewed and in any event, a new licence should have been granted. Exeter granted the new licence but challenged the decision by way of case stated to establish whether a licence could be renewed once it had expired.

Judgment was given by Collins J who summed up the point at contention thus[3]:

> '2. The court decided that notwithstanding that the licence had expired when the application for its renewal was made, it was capable within the meaning of the legslation of being renewed and it ought to have been renewed. However, in addition the court had decided that a fresh licence should have been in the circumstances granted. The appellant council does not challenge that decision. Accordingly, this appeal in so far as Mr Sandle is concerned is academic because he has the licence which he wished for. But it is of some importance to the Appellant Council because I am told that it, and indeed a considerable number of licensing authorities, have taken the view that the terms of section 43 of the Town Police Clauses Act 1847 prevent a renewal because they limit the licence granted to a period of 12 months.
>
> 3. The statutory provision in question, section 43, reads as follows. Under the heading "Licence to be enforced for one year only":

> > "Every licence so to be granted shall be under the common seal of the commissioners, if incorporated, or, if not incorporated, shall be signed by two or more of the commissioners..."

> Perhaps that in itself is not particularly material now:

> > "... and shall not include more than one carriage so licensed, and shall be in force for one year only from the day of the date of such licence, or until the next general licensing meeting, in case any general licensing day be appointed by the commissioners."

In reality nowadays, as I understand it, the local authorities will normally act on the basis of the licence being valid for one year only within the terms of section 43.'

Exeter had a condition attached to the licence that an application for renewal had to be made not more than 14 days' before the expiry of the licence.

In relation to the first question stated in the case:

'(1) Is a Hackney Carriage Licence capable of renewal in the sense envisaged by section 60 Local Government (Miscellaneous Provisions) Act 1976[4] before the expiration of the one year period prescribed by section 43 Town Police Clauses Act 1847?'

Collins J answered yes, for the following reasons:

'7. It seems to me that the word "renew" can quite properly mean "grant afresh". That is to say, to permit the licence that has been granted to be treated as a new licence. That is a perfectly normal use of the English language and one which is clearly recognised by section 60 of the 1976 Act. Thus, an individual licence can only last for 12 months. That licence can be renewed and therefore is treated as a new licence which again will last for a period of 12 months and so on, if application is made. If it is a question of renewal then renewal will normally only be able to be made upon the same terms, that is to say it is a mechanical exercise unless there are reasons why such renewal should not be permitted.

8. In the case of Exeter, and I suspect in the case of other authorities, there is a condition attached to a licence that an application for renewal must be made before the licence comes to an end – that is to say before the 12-month period expires. In fact, the condition imposed by Exeter requires that such an application be made not more than 14 days before the 12-month period comes to an end, but can be made at any time up to the expiry of that 12-month period. That means inevitably that if the application is left until the last day of the validity of the licence it is unlikely to be processed until the following day at the earliest and if weekends intervene it will be longer than the following day. Thus, any renewal will have to take place after the licence has expired. I am told that there is what I am bound to say seems to be a little bit of a fudge applied in those circumstances because, albeit it is granted in those circumstances, it is treated as a fresh licence – that is to say as if it were not a renewal but a grant of a fresh licence which means that the conditions that normally have to apply in order to enable a new licence to be obtained are not imposed in such a case. It seems to me that that is a wholly unnecessary provision. There is nothing that prevents a licence which has expired from being renewed. As a matter of English, if for example one forgot to renew a driving licence the normal expression to be used when one remembered is "I forgot to renew, I must renew now" and no one, as it seems to me, could suggest that that was a misuse of the English language. As it seems to me that is entirely consistent with the approach indicated by the Act of 1976.

9. Although in the case of Exeter no doubt a renewal can be dealt with speedily, it may be that in other cases it will take a few days for the matter to be considered or there may be questions as to whether a renewal is permissible in an individual case because there may be concerns that there possibly has been a breach of conditions or there are grounds for refusing to renew and thus it could take a few days to sort that out. It would be somewhat absurd if in taking those few days so that the licence had expired it then became impossible to renew it within the meaning of the legislation. Accordingly, I take the view that not only is it permissible to renew when the licence still exists, but also it is possible to renew a licence, that is to say effectively to grant what amounts to a new licence, after the original has expired and that is no breach of section 43.

In relation to the question of the grant in those circumstances when there was a limit on licences, and in the case of a delay in renewing, the licence had been allocated to someone else, Collins J placed great weight on the renewal condition attached to the licence.

'11. It seems to me the answer to that problem lies in the condition. The applicant will know that he must make his application before the licence expires and if he does not do so he will find that his application is likely to be rejected. Indeed, unless he has a very good reason for the failure that will almost certainly be the case. I am told that there are problems in deciding how long a period should be left before a decision is made to grant a fresh licence to take the place of the one in respect of which no application for renewal has been made. The simple answer to that surely is that certainly a couple of days, perhaps three days, who knows, but a very short period is one which is appropriate just in case there is a good reason for the delay. In fact in this case the application was made a day late and the Crown Court decided that there was indeed a very good explanation – I think the individual who was deputed to make the application had a sick child at the material time and accordingly had been distracted but had realised quickly and tried to make his application but the weekend had come upon him and thus the application was only a day late and, perhaps slightly unsurprisingly, the Crown Court took the view that in those circumstances it was not reasonable for the council to have refused to entertain the application for a renewal. But I must make it clear that if it is apparent from the conditions that the application has to be made within the period the licence is in force, it will take very strong case and very exceptional circumstances for an applicant who fails to make his application for renewal in time to be able to justify a claim that the council ought in the circumstances to have granted his licence. Such exceptional circumstances can exist and as I say it would be sensible for a council to give two or three days at least before taking the step of deciding to grant it to someone else. After all, I suppose such an application can for example be made by post and if there are postal difficulties that would be a good reason no doubt to defer any action to make sure that there had not been a delay in the post. One can imagine other circumstances which might make it obvious that it would be prudent to give a little extra time in all circumstances. It is obviously impossible to spell those out, but as I say suffice it to say that if the condition is not met it will be proper for the council to take the view that they will only allow renewal in exceptional circumstances.'

Not only does this deal with the question of the re-allocation of the licence, it also gives an indication as to the period of time after expiry during which an application for renewal might be successful. The judge mentioned "two or three days at least" and it would seem that perhaps a period of 5 working days would be reasonable in many cases, but each case will depend on its own particular facts.. This was reinforced by the judge's answer to the second question posed:

'(2) Is a Hackney Carriage Licence capable of renewal, in the same way, after the expiration of that one year period? Answer: "Yes". If so, how long after does it cease to be so capable? Answer: "There is no particular period, but as I have indicated it would only be in exceptional circumstances that a delay of more than a few days would be permissible."'

It is therefore clear that the imposition of a condition relating to renewal of the licence is vital.

1   [2011] EWHC 1403 (Admin), [2011] LLR 480.
2   It appears from the High Court judgment that this was an appeal directly to the Crown Court against a refusal to grant a new hackney carriage proprietors licence in accordance with Public Health Acts Amendment Act 1907, s 7, rather than an appeal to the Crown Court from a decision of the magistrates' court in relation to the refusal to renew the licence, which would lie under LG(MP)A 1976, s 60(3).
3   At paragraphs 2 and 3.
4   Section 60(1) states:
    '60 Suspension and revocation of vehicle licences
    (1) Notwithstanding anything in the Act of 1847 or in this Part of this Act, a district council may suspend or revoke, or (on application therefor under section 40 of the Act of 1847 or section 48 of this Act, as the case may be) refuse to renew a vehicle licence on any of the following grounds—
    (a) that the hackney carriage or private hire vehicle is unfit for use as a hackney carriage or private hire vehicle;
    (b) any offence under, or non-compliance with, the provisions of the Act of 1847 or of this Part of this Act by the operator or driver; or
    (c) any other reasonable cause.'

Chapter 9

Hackney carriages outside London: the use of hackney carriages

INTRODUCTION

9.1

This chapter will address the practical aspects of hackney carriages, including consideration of the use of seat belts, taximeters and fares; disabled people; stands; non-motorised hackney carriages; hiring hackney carriages at separate fares; and the use of bus lanes.

SEAT BELTS AND MOBILE TELEPHONES

9.2

The general rule is that seat belts must be worn by adults travelling in a motor vehicle, if they are fitted to that vehicle (Motor Vehicles (Wearing of Seatbelts) Regulations 1993, reg 5[1] made under the Road Traffic Act 1988, s 14 (RTA 1988)). However, drivers of hackney carriages (referred to in the Regulations as 'licensed taxi') and drivers of private hire vehicles have a limited exemption from this requirement. The Motor Vehicles (Wearing of Seatbelts) Regulations 1993, reg 6 provides that the requirements of reg 5 do not apply to:

'(g) the driver of:
(i) a licensed taxi while it is being used for seeking hire, or answering a call for hire, or carrying a passenger for hire, or
(ii) a private hire vehicle while it is being used to carry a passenger for hire.'

[1]   SI 1993/176.

9.3

Other than that, the only other relevant exception is if the person holds a medical certificate as defined in the Motor Vehicles (Wearing of Seatbelts) Regulations 1993, Sch 1[1].

[1]   SI 1993/176.

9.4

It can therefore be seen that there is not a blanket exemption for drivers of hackney carriages and private hire drivers from the general requirement to wear a seat belt and that it does not apply when the vehicle is not working but is being driven for private use. In such situations, it should be remembered, both hackney carriages and private hire vehicles remain as licensed vehicles and must only be driven by persons who hold the appropriate hackney carriage or private hire drivers' licence[1].

[1]   *Hawkins v Edwards* [1901] 2 KB 169; *Benson v Boyce* [1197] RTR 226.

9.5

Clearly, the requirement to wear a seat belt also applies to passengers in hackney carriages and private hire vehicles. If an adult passenger (any person over the age of 14 years – see RTA 1988, ss 14 and 15) fails to wear a seatbelt, the passenger commits a criminal offence, not the driver of the vehicle (RTA 1988, s 14(3)). This would also be the case if the passenger is in a wheelchair and refuses to be properly secured in a vehicle which is capable of carrying wheelchair-bound passengers[1].

[1]   In those circumstances it would seem advisable for the driver not to carry the passenger, as the safety of the passenger, the driver and other road users could be severely compromised by an unrestrained wheelchair rolling around in a vehicle. That would seem to be a 'reasonable excuse' for not taking the passenger and a defence to a charge brought under the Town and Police Causes Act 1847, s 53; see para 9.49 onwards in relation to carrying disabled people in hackney carriages, and Chapter 10, para 10.93 in relation to the duty to take a fare.

9.6

The situation is slightly different in respect of children under the age of 14. In vehicles other than hackney carriages (and private hire vehicles), the driver of the vehicle commits an offence if the requirements[1] are not complied with. Generally these require a child under 135cm in height (approximately 12–13 years of age) to use a child restraint (a child seat or harness of an appropriate size for the height of the child). However, in respect of hackney carriages (and private hire vehicles) reg 10(1)(b) and (c) of the Motor Vehicles (Wearing of Seatbelts) Regulations 1993[2] alters that requirement and allows unrestrained children under three years' old, and children over three years' old to use an adult seat belt in hackney carriages (and private hire vehicles) if no appropriate seat belts are available. These provisions state:

'(1) The prohibitions in section 15(3) and (3A) of the Act do not apply in relation to—

...

(b)   a small child aged under 3 years who is riding in a licensed taxi or licensed hire car, if no appropriate seat belt is available for him in the front or rear of the vehicle;

(c)   a small child aged 3 years or more who is riding in a licensed taxi, a licensed hire car or a small bus and wearing an adult belt if an appropriate seat belt is not available for him in the front or rear of the vehicle;

…'[3]

It can therefore be seen that children can be carried lawfully in hackney carriages (and private hire vehicles) without the correctly sized child restraints. It will remain the parents' or carers' decision as to whether the obvious risks associated with such a course of action are acceptable.

These requirements are summarised in Table 9.1 below.

Table 9.1

Wearing of Seatbelts and Use of Child Seats as at June 2016[4]

Person	Front seat	Rear seat	Who is responsible?
Driver	Seat belt MUST be worn if fitted.		Driver
Children under three years' old	Correct child restraint MUST be used.	Correct child restraint MUST be used If one is not available in a licensed taxi or private hire vehicle, the child may travel unrestrained.	Driver
Child Aged 3–11 and under 135cms in height (about 4.5 Feet)	Correct child restraint MUST be used	Correct child restraint must be used if seat belts are fitted. If a child seat is not available, a child may travel using just the seat belt in these situations : – In a licensed taxi or private hire vehicle – For a short distance if the journey is unexpected and necessary – There isn't room to fit a third child seat	Driver
Child Aged 12 or 13 years or younger child 135 cms or more In height	Adult seat belt must be worn if fitted	Adult seat belt must be worn if fitted	Driver
Passengers aged 14 years and over	Must be worn if fitted	Must be worn if fitted	Passenger

1   The requirements are contained in RTA 1988, s 15, the Motor Vehicles (Wearing of Seatbelts) Regulations 1993, SI 1993/176, Pt III, Motor Vehicles (Wearing of Seat Belts by Children in Front Seats) Regulations 1993, SI 1993/31 and the Motor Vehicles (Wearing of Seat Belts) (Amendment) Regulations 2006, SI 2006/1892.

2   SI 1993/176 as amended by reg 16 of The Motor Vehicles (Wearing of Seat Belts) (Amendment) Regulations 2006, SI 2006/1892.

3   Regulation 2 of the Motor Vehicles (Wearing of Seatbelts) Regulations 1993, SI 1993/176 defines the terms 'licensed taxi' and 'licensed hire car' by reference to s 13(3) of the Transport Act 1985, which in turn defines 'licensed taxi' as:

'(a) in England and Wales, a vehicle licensed under—
   (i)   section 37 of the Town Police Clauses Act 1847; or
   (ii)   section 6 of the Metropolitan Public Carriage Act 1869;
or under any similar enactment;'

and 'licensed hire car' as:

'a vehicle which is licensed under section 48 of the Local Government (Miscellaneous Provisions) Act 1976 or section 7 of the Private Hire Vehicles (London) Act 1998;'.

4   Available   at   http://www.rospa.com/road-safety/advice/vehicles/in-car-safety-and-crash worthiness/seat-belts-law/

MOBILE TELEPHONES

9.7

As a result of considerable concern over the dangers of drivers using hand-held mobile telephones, legislation was introduced with effect from 1 December 2003 to limit their use[1]. These provisions however do not apply to the use of two-way radios, as fitted to many hackney carriages. Accordingly, the use of these devices, even while driving, remains lawful. However, in respect of a mobile telephone, hackney carriage (and private hire) drivers are bound by the same restrictions as others driving motor vehicles.

1   Regulation 110 of the Road Vehicles (Construction and Use) Regulations 1986, SI 1986/1078 inserted by The Road Vehicles (Construction and Use) (Amendment) (No 4) Regulations 2003, SI 2003/2695.

SMOKING

9.8

All hackney carriages (and private hire vehicles) are smoke-free vehicles and it is an offence for any driver or passenger to smoke within the vehicle.

The Health Act 2006 introduced a ban on smoking in enclosed public places, and s 5 of the Act allows the devolved administrations to make regulations concerning smoking in vehicles.

'Smoking' is defined as:

'(a) *"smoking"* refers to smoking tobacco or anything which contains tobacco, or smoking any other substance, and

(b) smoking includes being in possession of lit tobacco or of anything lit which contains tobacco, or being in possession of any other lit substance in a form in which it could be smoked.'

The English and Welsh regulations vary slightly, but both prohibit smoking in hackney carriages (or private hire vehicles). Because both types of vehicle retain their characteristics at all times (ie, a hackney carriage is always a hackney carriage irrespective of what use it is being put to at any given time, likewise a private hire vehicle[1]) no smoking can take place in any licensed vehicle.

In England, the regulations[2] apply to an enclosed vehicle or enclosed part of a vehicle:

'(1) Subject to the following paragraphs of this regulation, an enclosed vehicle and any enclosed part of a vehicle is smoke-free if it is used—
(a)   by members of the public or a section of the public (whether or not for reward or hire); or
(b)   in the course of paid or voluntary work by more than one person (even if those persons use the vehicle at different times, or only intermittently).
…

(2) A vehicle or part of a vehicle is enclosed for the purposes of paragraphs (1) and (1A) where it is enclosed wholly or partly by a roof and by any door or window that may be opened.'

In Wales, the regulations[3] also apply to enclosed vehicles or enclosed parts of vehicles, but the wording is slightly different:

'(1) Subject to the following paragraphs of this regulation, a vehicle shall be smoke-free if it is used—
(a)   for the transport of members of the public or a section of the public (whether or not for reward or hire); or
(b)   for work purposes by more than one person (even if the persons who use it for such purposes do so at different times, or only intermittently).

(2) This regulation applies to vehicles and parts of vehicles which are enclosed.

(3) A vehicle or part of a vehicle is enclosed for the purposes of paragraph (2) where it has doors or windows which may be opened but it is not enclosed unless it is wholly or partly covered by a roof.'

In both countries, 'no smoking' signs must be displayed on the vehicle[4] and it is then an offence to smoke in a smoke-free vehicle[5] or to permit smoking in a smoke-free vehicle[6].

Fixed penalty notices can be issued in respect of failing to display no smoking signs, or smoking in a smoke-free place. They are not available in relation to permitting or allowing smoking the smoke-free place which can only be enforced by means of a summary prosecution.

It is clear therefore that there should be no smoking at any time in any hackney carriage (or private hire vehicle). This applies not only when the vehicle is carrying passengers, but also when it is awaiting the next hiring and when it is being used for social domestic and pleasure purposes.

The Health Act 2006 only applies to smoking tobacco or other substances which are lit and accordingly does not apply to the use of electronic cigarettes (often referred to as 'vaping'). A number of authorities have introduced conditions on their vehicle licences prohibiting the use of electronic cigarettes within the vehicle.

1   See *Hawkins v Edwards* [1901] 2 KB 169; Chapter 8, para 8.4 and *Yates v Gates* [1970] 1 All ER 754, QBD; Chapter 8, para 8.5 in relation to hackney carriages; *Benson v Boyce* [1997] RTR 226; Chapter 13, para 13.72 in relation to private hire vehicles.
2   Smoke-free (Exemptions and Vehicles) Regulations 2007, SI 2007/765, reg 11.
3   Smoke-free Premises etc (Wales) Regulations 2007, SI 2007/787, reg 4.
4   Health Act 2006, s 6 (for England); Smoke-free Premises etc. (Wales) Regulations 2007. SI 2007/787, reg 6 (for Wales).
5   Health Act 2006, s 7 for both England and Wales.
6   Health Act 2006, s 8 for both England and Wales.

TAXIMETERS

9.9

Almost all hackney carriages have a taximeter fitted, but this is not a statutory requirement. There is nothing in either the Town Police Clauses Act 1847 (TPCA 1847) or the Local Government (Miscellaneous Provisions) Act 1976 (LG(MP)A 1976) which requires hackney carriages to have meters, but most local authorities do make it a requirement, either by means of byelaws made under TPCA 1847, s 68[1] or as a condition attached to the hackney carriage proprietor's licence under LG(MP)A 1976, s 47(1)[2]. In each case, those provisions, whether byelaws or conditions, will require the meter to be calibrated and sealed. LG(MP)A 1976, s 68 allows inspection of the meter and subsequent suspension of the proprietor's licence if the accuracy of the taximeter is unsatisfactory.

1   See Appendix I.
2   See Appendix I.

9.10

Most local authorities have a number of different types of meter which are acceptable to them and hackney carriage proprietors can use any from the approved list. The EU Measuring Instruments Directive (MID) (2004/22/EC – OJ No. L135, 30.4.04) was carried into national regulations in the Measuring Instruments (Taximeters) Regulations 2006[1]. Notwithstanding the repeal of that Directive and its replacement by the EU Measuring Instruments Directive (MID) (2014/32/EU – OJ No. L96, 29.03.14)[2] these remain in force and govern the overall approval of taximeters. They are not of direct concern to local authorities, who will only approve taximeters which have already been shown to comply with the Regulations.

1   SI 2006/2304.
2   In April 2016, the revised Measuring Instruments Directive came into effect. Any new meters which are placed on the market after that date will have to comply with the new requirements, but any existing meters will not need to be replaced. See paragraph (4) of the preamble to the directive which states:

    '(4) This Directive covers measuring instruments which are new to the Union market when they are placed on the market; that is to say they are either new measuring instruments made by a manufacturer established in the Union or measuring instruments, whether new or second-hand, imported from a third country.'

This is further reinforced by the Technical Briefing Note published by the National Measurement and Regulation Office on 28 October 2015 (see https://www.gov.uk/government/uploads/system/uploads/attachment_data/file/471912/Technical_Briefing_Note_-_Introduction_of_new_weighing_and_measuring_instruments_European_Directives_on_20_Apr_ver_2.pdf) which states:

> 'All instruments placed on the market after 20th April 2016 will have to comply with the requirements in the new Directives and Regulations'.

It is clear that a new meter is not required. That is made clear by Article 50 of the Directive which states that all existing measuring instruments covered by, and compliant with the previous Directive (2004/22/EC) can still be available on the market and/or put into use provided they were placed on the market before 20 April 2016.

THE POWER OF THE LOCAL AUTHORITY TO SET FARES

9.11

Local authorities have a power to set fares for hackney carriages and many, but not all, do. This can be done in one of three ways:

1.   under a special (local) Act of Parliament;
2.   under byelaws made under TPCA 1847, s 68; or
3.   under LG(MP)A 1976, s 65.

9.12

The first and second methods are now obsolete, which means that fares must be set using the powers and mechanism contained in LG(MP)A 1976, s 65.

'Fixing of fares for hackney carriages

65–(1) A district council may fix the rates or fares within the district as well for time as distance, and all other charges in connection with the hire of a vehicle or with the arrangements for the hire of a vehicle, to be paid in respect of the hire of hackney carriages by means of a table (hereafter in this section referred to as a "table of fares") made or varied in accordance with the provisions of this section.

(2) (a) When a district council make or vary a table of fares they shall publish in at least one local newspaper circulating in the district a notice setting out the table of fares or the variation thereof and specifying the period, which shall not be less than fourteen days from the date of the first publication of the notice, within which and the manner in which objections to the table of fares or variation can be made.

(b) A copy of the notice referred to in paragraph (a) of this subsection shall for the period of fourteen days from the date of the first publication thereof be deposited at the offices of the council which published the notice, and shall at all reasonable hours be open to public inspection without payment.

(3) If no objection to a table of fares or variation is duly made within the period specified in the notice referred to in subsection (2) of this section, or if all objections so made are withdrawn, the table of fares or variations shall

come into operation on the date of the expiration of the period specified in the notice or the date of withdrawal of the objection or, if more than one, of the last objection, whichever date is the later.

(4) If objection is duly made as aforesaid and is not withdrawn, the district council shall set a further date, not later than two months after the first specified date, on which the table of fares shall come into force with or without modifications as decided by them after consideration of the objections.

(5) A table of fares made or varied under this section shall have effect for the purposes of the Act of 1847 as if it were included in hackney carriage byelaws made thereunder.

(6) On the coming into operation of a table of fares made by a council under this section for the district, any hackney carriage byelaws fixing the rates and fares or any table of fares previously made under this section for the district, as the case may be, shall cease to have effect.

(7) Section 236(8) (except the words "when confirmed") and section 238 of the Local Government Act 1972 (except paragraphs (c) and (d) of that section) shall extend and apply to a table of fares made or varied under this section by a district council in England as they apply to byelaws made by a district council in England .

(7A) Section 8(5) and section 19 of the Local Government Byelaws (Wales) Act 2012 shall extend and apply to a table of fares made or varied under this section by a council for a county or county borough in Wales as they apply to byelaws made by a council for a county or county borough in Wales.'

9.13

At first sight, this seems a cumbersome procedure, but is in fact not particularly difficult. However it must be remembered that this is an executive function, and not a Council function[1].

1. A notice must be published in a local newspaper, stating the proposed fares or variation of the fares.
2. This must specify a date, not less than 14 days from the date on which the notice is first published. That date has two functions:
    (a) it is the date by which any objections must be lodged; and
    (b) it is the date on which the revised fares will come into effect if either –
        (i) no objections are received; or
        (ii) any objections received have been withdrawn before that specified date.
3. It must also state where objections should be addressed and how they can be made. Obviously, it is desirable for such objections to be lodged in writing, as opposed to any other method (although an objection by a fax or email should be acceptable).
4. A copy of the notice must be available at the council offices for inspection, free of charge, 'at all reasonable hours' (LG(MP)A 1976, s 65(1)(b)).

FLOW CHART FOR SETTING HACKNEY CARRIAGE FARES

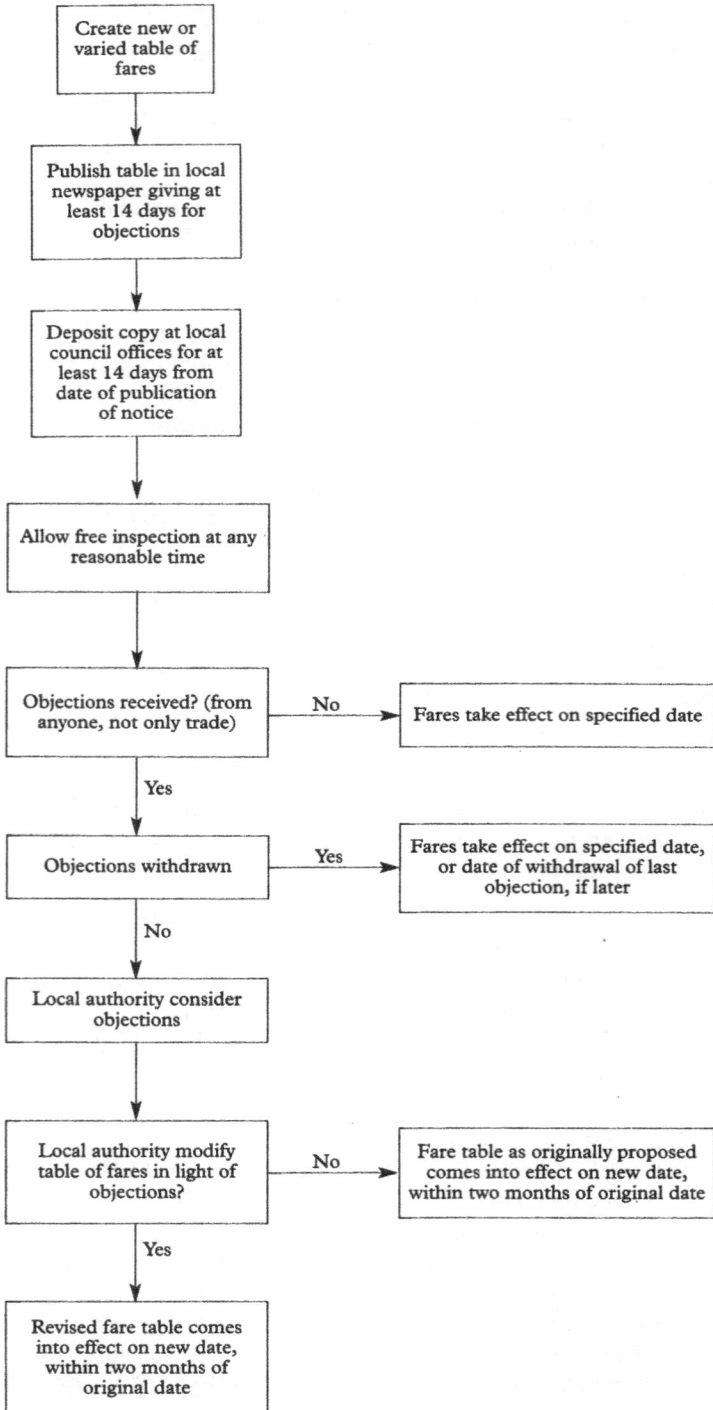

```
┌─────────────────┐
│  Create new or  │
│ varied table of │
│      fares      │
└─────────────────┘
         │
         ▼
┌─────────────────┐
│Publish table in local│
│newspaper giving at│
│least 14 days for│
│   objections    │
└─────────────────┘
         │
         ▼
┌─────────────────┐
│Deposit copy at local│
│council offices for at│
│least 14 days from│
│date of publication│
│    of notice    │
└─────────────────┘
         │
         ▼
┌─────────────────┐
│Allow free inspection at any│
│   reasonable time   │
└─────────────────┘
         │
         ▼
┌─────────────────┐         ┌─────────────────────────┐
│Objections received? (from│  No  │Fares take effect on specified date│
│anyone, not only trade)│ ───► └─────────────────────────┘
└─────────────────┘
         │ Yes
         ▼
┌─────────────────┐         ┌─────────────────────────┐
│Objections withdrawn│  Yes │Fares take effect on specified date,│
│                 │ ───►  │or date of withdrawal of last│
└─────────────────┘         │    objection, if later    │
         │ No              └─────────────────────────┘
         ▼
┌─────────────────┐
│Local authority consider│
│   objections    │
└─────────────────┘
         │
         ▼
┌─────────────────┐         ┌─────────────────────────┐
│Local authority modify│  No  │Fare table as originally proposed│
│table of fares in light of│ ───► │comes into effect on new date,│
│   objections?   │         │within two months of original date│
└─────────────────┘         └─────────────────────────┘
         │ Yes
         ▼
┌─────────────────┐
│Revised fare table comes│
│into effect on new date,│
│within two months of│
│  original date  │
└─────────────────┘
```

5. Once the objection period (usually 14 days) has expired, if there have been no objections received or those received have subsequently been withdrawn, then the new fares take effect, either at the end of the objection period or when the last objection is withdrawn (LG(MP)A 1976, s 65(3)).

6. However, if objections are made and are not withdrawn, then the council must consider the objections.

7. In the light of those objections (although it must consider them, it does not have to vary the proposed fare as a result of them) the council then sets a second date, which cannot be more than two months after the first date specified, when the new fares come into force.

[1] See Chapter 2, para 2.7 onwards.

9.14

The provisions of LG(MP)A 1976, s 65(5)[1] are worth noting, in that if the district council has byelaws, the table of fares made under the provisions of LG(MP)A 1976, s 65 is deemed to be the table of fares in the byelaws, and will supersede any earlier fares set by previous byelaws.

[1] See Appendix I.

9.15

It is important to further note that miles, yards, feet and inches must be used when setting hackney carriage fares, although it is permissible for the metric equivalents to be shown as well. That is as a result of reg 5(2) of the Units of Measurement Regulations 1995[1], which excludes the application of metric units from road traffic signs, distance and speed measurement where miles, yards, feet and inches remain the lawful unit of measurement. As a taximeter measures by distance and time, it would appear to fall within the exception contained in reg 5(2) and therefore taximeters and the corresponding fare cards should be calibrated in imperial units, rather than metric.

[1] SI 1995/1804.

Parsons v South Kesteven District Council

9.16

Appeal lodged against the table of fares as a 'condition' attached to a hackney carriage proprietor's licence. Held by the Crown Court that the table of fares was connected to the condition to have a meter fitted to the vehicle and therefore could be challenged by way of appeal.

It is interesting to note that there is no right of appeal against the fares once set. It would therefore appear that the only remedy is judicial review. However, a Crown Court decision seems to indicate otherwise. In the case of *Parsons v South Kesteven District Council*[1] the following argument was put. The requirement to fit a taximeter was a condition attached to a hackney carriage proprietor's licence under LG(MP)A 1976, s 47[2] and there was a right of appeal against such a condition by virtue of s 47(3). As the table of fares would be meaningless without the condition to have a meter, by extension there must also be a right of appeal against the table of fares themselves. This argument was accepted by the Crown Court, which decided that there was a right of appeal. The judge (Richard Pollard J) stated:

> 'We [himself and the magistrates sitting with him] believe that it is sophistry to say that we can look at the requirement of a taximeter but that we cannot look at the Table of Fares. We reject the contention that the Table can only be looked at by way of judicial review. We cannot make any sense of the appellate jurisdiction given to the magistrates and to this court without looking at the Table and its inevitable effect, particularly as the table has effect, for the purposes of the 1847 Act as if it were included in hackney carriage byelaws (s 65(5) of the 1976 Act). Taximeters are meaningless without a table of fares. The real effect of the Respondents condition that there be a taximeter was that the council were imposing a condition as to fares that could be charged.'

[1] (1996, unreported).
[2] See Appendix I.

9.17

Unfortunately, the matter has never been considered by the High Court, and the Crown Court decision is only persuasive.

9.18

The argument was clearly effective before the Crown Court, but whether it is correct is another matter. LG(MP)A 1976, s 47 allows the council to attach conditions to a hackney carriage licence and s 47(3) allows 'any person aggrieved by any conditions attached to such a licence' to appeal to the magistrates' court. There is no reference in s 47 to the provisions of LG(MP)A 1976, s 65 (which is the power to set the fares for hackney carriages), neither is there any reference in s 65 to an appeal being launched using the powers contained in s 47(3). It is true that there is no right of appeal contained within s 65. However, it would seem that the wording in s 47(3) limits the appeals quite clearly to conditions that are attached under s 47. Although, clearly, the requirement to have a taximeter is going to be such a condition, it may well be stretching the point too far to then argue that the fares are also a condition, when they are quite clearly not a condition attached to the licence.

BOOKING FEE

9.19

Although the case of *House v Reynolds*[1] apparently outlaws the charging of a booking fee, it is possible to incorporate such a fee within the table of fares. This is as a result of the wording of LG(MP)A 1976, s 65(1):

'65–(1) A district council may fix the rates or fares within the district as well for time as distance, and all other charges in connection with the hire of a vehicle or with the arrangements for the hire of a vehicle, to be paid in respect of the hire of hackney carriages …'

¹   [1977] 1 WLR 88, QBD; see Chapter 10, para 10.106.

9.20

A booking fee would fall within the words 'and all other charges in connection with the hire of a vehicle or with the arrangements for the hire of a vehicle' and is therefore lawful provided it has been approved by the local authority. *House v Reynolds*[1] is still authority for the fact that an unauthorised booking fee is unlawful.

¹   [1977] 1 WLR 88, QBD.

9.21

It is worth noting that if any post-1974 local Act of Parliament incorporated the provisions of TPCA 1847 and that local Act set fares for hackney carriages, then it would appear that the local authority is unable to use the provisions of LG(MP)A 1976, s 65 to vary those fares and must seek repeal of that section of the local Act before any fares set under s 65 would take effect. This is because, although s 65(5) specifically states that any fares made by byelaws are overridden, it does not apply to special Acts of Parliament. It is not clear whether any local authorities have such local legislation.

9.22

Once the fares have been made, by whatever method, they then apply to hackney carriages which are licensed to ply for hire within the district.

9.23

It is possible for a local authority to abandon regulation of fares once they have been applied by either method, byelaws or LG(MP)A 1976, s 65. If the fares were set by byelaws, it is possible to revoke or amend the byelaws that refer to the setting of fares by virtue of the Interpretation Act 1978, s 14. If the fares have been set using s 65, it appears to be possible by using the same mechanism, because s 65 makes it clear that a table of fares is akin to a byelaw. However, in this case it would seem to be prudent to follow the fare-setting procedure to publicise the proposed removal of the table of fares.

The use of the meter

9.24

If a vehicle is fitted with a meter and the local authority has hackney carriage byelaws, the meter must be used for all journeys charged by time and distance. This is the requirement contained in model byelaw 5(b):

'5. The driver of a hackney carriage provided with a taximeter shall:

(a)   ...

(b)   before beginning a journey for which a fare is charged for distance and time, bring the machinery of the taximeter into action by moving the said key, flag or other device so that the word "HIRED" is legible on the face of the taximeter and keep the machinery of the taximeter in action until the termination of the hiring'.

Therefore, the meter must be used for all journeys within the district unless a fixed fare has been agreed in advance of the hiring. In those cases, the driver must ensure that the fare will not exceed the maximum that could be charged for that hiring and it is therefore clearly good practice to activate the meter. This protects the driver from any allegation of overcharging, whilst allowing the passenger to see what a 'bargain' they have successfully negotiated.

The meter must not be brought into action until 'before the beginning of the journey'. It is important to consider the position with disabled and wheelchair bound passengers. The 'journey' does not commence until the passenger is securely seated, or the wheelchair has been correctly loaded and secured, the ramps have been properly stowed and the journey commences. If the meter is commenced before the loading commences, and continues until the unloading has finished, there is direct discrimination because the disabled passenger is being treated less favourably than an able-bodied passenger , contrary to s 13 of the Equality Act 2010[1].

[1]   Section 13(1) states:

'(1) A person (A) discriminates against another (B) if, because of a protected characteristic, A treats B less favourably than A treats or would treat others.'

and disability is a protected characteristic by virtue of s 6.

The fare shown on the meter

OFFENCE TO CHARGE MORE THAN THE FARE SHOWN

9.25

Within the district, it is an offence under TPCA 1847, s 58[1] to charge more than the fare shown on the meter[2], plus any legitimate extras and this is punishable by a fine not exceeding level 3 on the standard scale. This also applies to fares made under LG(MP)A 1976, s 65[3], notwithstanding the fact that s 58 refers to either byelaws or special Acts. This is because s 65(5) makes it clear that fares made under provisions of s 65 take effect as if they were contained in byelaws.

[1]   See Appendix I.

[2]   Section 58 states: 'Every proprietor or driver of any such hackney carriage who is convicted of taking as a fare a greater sum than is authorized by any byelaw made under this or the special Act shall be liable to a penalty not exceeding level 3 on the standard scale ... '. The reference 'a fare set by byelaws' is now construed to be a reference to fares set by the local authority under LG(MP)A 1976, s 65 and as the meter cannot be set to a greater rate than those fares, it is an offence to charge more than the metered fare.

[3]   See Appendix I.

Stratford-on-Avon District Council v Dyde

9.26

> Pre-booked hackney carriage for a journey within the district at an agreed price which was significantly higher than the metered fare would have been. Held that an offence was committed under s 67, notwithstanding that the agreement was between the passenger and a taxi company, not the driver.

The case of *Stratford-on-Avon District Council v Dyde*[1] arose from a test purchase undertaken by officers from Stratford-on-Avon District Council. They contacted a local taxi company and booked a journey wholly within the district. A fare of £32 was agreed. When the hackney carriage arrived at the pick-up point, the driver did not turn his meter on. The journey was undertaken and the passengers charged the £32. It was clear from measuring the distance that the fare should have been around £20.10. Dyde was prosecuted for charging more than the metered fare contrary to s 67(1) of the 1976 Act and failing to activate the meter contrary to byelaw 5(b). The case was dismissed by the magistrates on the basis that it amounted to entrapment and the evidence of the undercover officers was excluded under s 78 of the Police and Criminal Evidence Act 1984.

The council appealed by way of case stated. The High Court held that the evidence could be admitted[2]. It further found that[3]:

'As a licensed hackney carriage driver, the Respondent [Dyde] would have been well aware of two matters in particular:
(1) that although it was permissible for a taxi to undertake journeys for a fixed price ("a fixed job", as it was put on the Respondent's behalf), it was a criminal offence to do so at a fixed price that was in excess of the metered fare (see s 67(1));
(2) that a metered fare from Walton Hotel, Wellesbourne to Gaydon would not be nearly as much as £32. The Respondent might not have known that the metered fare would be precisely £20.10, as alleged in the information, but, given the considerable discrepancy between the two figures, he would have been in no doubt that a fare of £32 was significantly in excess of the metered fare and was therefore unlawful.

[25] The magistrates do not appear to have considered the implications of s 67 of the 1976 Act in this respect. Looking at their conclusions in paras 18 and 19 of the case stated, the fact that the Respondent was not a party to the original discussion about the fare, and that he confirmed with the officers that the fare had been negotiated by them with 007 Taxis, and the fact that he was not asked to switch on his taxi meter, are all beside the point if the Respondent knew, as he should have done, as a licensed hackney carriage driver, that any fixed fare agreed by a third party had to be equal to or not greater than the metered fare, and that the metered fare would not be as much as £32.'

This case shows that a hackney carriage driver cannot charge more than the metered fare (or the fare on the table of fares if no meter is fitted, eg, on a horse drawn hackney carriage) for a journey wholly within the district. If they do so, they commit an offence under TPCA 1847, s 58. It is no defence to say that they were not a party to any agreement. This raises the question of how should a driver avoid such a crime? Although the model byelaws do not require a driver to activate the meter when a fixed price has been agreed, doing so protects the driver from overcharging. It will also reassure the passenger that they are in fact paying less than, or equal to the metered fare.

This places a hackney carriage at a disadvantage when compared to a private hire vehicle for certain contractual journeys. Many education authorities contract with hackney carriage and private hire drivers and proprietors to transport children, often at a significant cost. Whilst a private hire driver/proprietor can agree any fare, a hackney carriage driver is limited to the metered fare if the journey is wholly within the district.

[1] [2009] EWHC 3011 (Admin), [2010] RTR 13.
[2] See paras 12–18 of the judgment.
[3] See para 24 onwards.

AGREEMENTS AS TO FARES

9.27

TPCA 1847, s 54[1] allows agreement to be made in advance of the hiring of a hackney carriage that a sum less than that shown at the end of the hiring will be paid and once such an agreement has been made it is an offence for the proprietor or driver to demand more than was agreed in advance. This situation only covers specific occasions when the agreement is clearly made in advance and does not cover the situation where, at the end of the hiring, the hirer either disputes the fare or does not have sufficient means of payment to cover the fare. In those cases, the fare itself is due under the contract entered into between the hirer and the driver or proprietor.

[1] See Appendix I.

ACCEPTING LESS THAN THE FARE SHOWN

9.28

There seems to be no doubt that the driver is entitled to both demand and accept less than the fare shown on the meter. This is a matter of contract and a party to a contract is able to agree to a mutual variation of the terms at any point. As has been seen, the only legislative controls concern not charging or demanding more than the fare shown on the meter. The Office of Fair Trading has confirmed this in its report *The regulation of licensed taxi and PHV services in the UK*, the results of its Investigation into UK Taxi Services[1].

[1] OFT676, available at www.oft.gov.uk/news/publications/leaflet+ordering.htm.

R v Liverpool City Council, ex p Curzon Ltd

9.29

> Liverpool City Council introduced a two-rate table of fares, with an increased
> rate to be charged between midnight and 5am. Curzon Ltd, who operated
> a fleet of hackney carriages, wanted to charge a single day rate at all times.
> Held: That the meter could be set to a lower rate than that authorised by the
> council under the table of fares.

The point has been accepted in the case of *R v Liverpool City Council, ex p Curzon
Ltd*[1]. This case considered two questions:

1. whether it was lawful for a hackney carriage driver to charge less than the
    fare shown on the meter; and
2. whether the meter had to be calibrated to show the fares that the City
    Council had set or whether, if the proprietor of the hackney carriage was
    prepared to offer a universal discount on those fares, it could be calibrated
    to reflect the lower fare.

In this particular case, Liverpool City Council had introduced a two-tier rate of
fares, the difference being between a daytime rate and a night-time rate. Curzon
Ltd (who ran a fleet of hackney carriages) wished to continue to run simply at
the daytime rate and not charge passengers the extra for hirings which took place
when the night-time rate was in force. The City Council suspended the licences
of the vehicles that were not equipped with the new meter under LG(MP)A
1976, s 68[2] and Curzon Ltd challenged the lawfulness of that suspension by way
of judicial review. The case was heard before McCullough J, who reviewed both
the legislation and Liverpool City Council's byelaws.

[1]   (1983, unreported).
[2]   See Appendix I.

9.30

In answer to the first question (whether the driver had to charge the fare that was
shown on the meter), McCullough J stated[1]:

> '... I am persuaded that the statutes do not empower a district council to
> impose on drivers, whether by making bylaws or fixing a table of fares, a
> fare structure to which they must adhere. Such doubt as there is should
> be resolved in favour of the less restrictive construction. It is my view that
> the statutes prevent a driver from charging more than the fare prescribed,
> but not less, they do not empower a district council to prevent him from
> charging less.
>
> The great majority of drivers will, no doubt, want to charge the
> full prescribed fare. But if others do not, they may, at least before the
> commencement of the hiring, agree to take less. Whether a district
> council may prevent a driver, at the end of or during the period of hire,

from waiving part (or, indeed, the whole) of the charge which the law entitles him to demand is perhaps less clear, in that no section in either Act expressly contemplates such waiver. Mr. Braithwaite [for the City Council] said that, other than that such a driver would commit no criminal offence, he reserved the question.

I see nothing in the Acts which gives power to the council to prevent such waiver. There must have been, during the 146 years since 1847, many thousands of occasions when passengers have discovered that the fare exceeds the amount of money they are carrying and drivers have let them off the difference. Waiver in similar circumstances is commonplace in many areas of life. In my judgment, short of contractual restriction, there is nothing to prevent a driver from doing this if he wants.'

In relation to the second question of the calibration of the meter, he considered at length the meaning of the word 'accuracy' in LG(MP)A 1976, s 68. He stated:

'Mr Braithwaite's submission that an accurate meter is one which displays the fare prescribed in the table of fares assumed that the council was empowered to require a driver to charge according to the current table of fares, which is a proposition I have rejected. He concedes that if, as I have held, a driver is entitled to charge what he likes up to the prescribed maximum, his meter is accurate if it is set according to his own scale of charges. This effectively concludes the second question against the council.

I can see why he [Mr Braithwaite] made the concession. It fits well with clause 5 c of the bylaws. What the passenger wants to know is what he has to pay. The driver is only entitled to charge what is displayed on his meter ... If the driver is only going to charge, say, half the rate allowed in the table of fares, then half that rate is what the passenger will expect to see on the meter. Similarly, as with the drivers of Curzon Ltd's cabs, if they are only going to charge day rates at night, then what the meter should show is the fare according to the day rate. The concession makes it unnecessary for me to consider whether, even although a driver proposes to charge less than the fare allowed by the table of fares, his meter should nevertheless display the fare according to the table of fares, leaving it to him to tell the passenger that he will take less.'

It was held, therefore, that a one-tier meter which only charged the daytime rate was not unlawful for lacking accuracy, despite the fact that the City Council wished to impose two-tier charging for its hackney carriages.

---

[1] *R v Liverpool City Council, ex p Curzon Ltd* (1983, unreported).

CONDITIONS TO PREVENT THE DRIVER ACCEPTING LESS THAN THE FARE SHOWN

9.31

R v Liverpool City Council, ex p Curzon Ltd[1] appears to settle the matter. However, there is a view that it is possible to prevent a hackney carriage driver accepting less than the fare shown on the meter by means of a condition applied to the hackney carriage proprietor's licence. The question which would apply in this case is whether the condition was 'reasonably necessary', and this is debatable. The argument in favour of such a condition is to prevent squabbles on hackney carriage stands when the second or third cab in line is known to offer discounts on the meter fare and the first two do not. However, apart from the possible threat to public order that such a situation may present, it is difficult to see how such a condition is required to protect the public, as it must be beneficial to the public to be able to take advantage of reduced fares, if the drivers and proprietors are prepared to offer them.

[1]   (1983, unreported); see para 9.29 above.

No MEANS TO PAY THE FARE

9.32

What is the situation when the hirer does not have the means to pay the fare at the end of the journey, commonly referred to as 'bilking'? TPCA 1847, s 66[1] states that in the case of refusal to pay the fare, the fare itself, together with any costs, can be recovered before 'one justice'. This would utilise the provisions of the Magistrates' Court Act 1980, s 58 for recovery of a civil debt. It is not clear, in practice, how often this is undertaken, but, if it is, such action would be by way of complaint. This action was taken and was the subject of a High Court decision in *R v Kingston-upon-Thames Justices, ex p Martin*[2]. The case turned on the question of whether an adjournment should have been allowed and that is not relevant here. What is of interest is the fact that a hackney carriage driver sought to recover the sum of £34.60 in this fashion. The passenger refused to pay the amount shown on the meter, as he said that an agreement in advance had been for a fare of £15.00. In the absence of the defendant, the matter was proved and the driver recovered the sum owing.

[1]   See Appendix I.
[2]   [1994] Imm AR 172.

THE APPROACH TAKEN BY THE DRIVER

9.33

In practice, the approach employed by hackney carriage drivers, when faced with the situation of passengers who cannot pay the fare, is to return them to the point at which they were picked up. Although this incurs additional costs for the driver, it ensures that the passenger has not actually benefited from their breach of contract. It is, of course, open to passengers to negotiate with the driver to accept a lesser fare or possibly to accept property as security for the fare to be paid in due course. As with any contractual dealings, such agreements must not be arrived at by the use of threats, force or violence, as the parties must be able to bargain freely.

9.34

Another practice is for the driver to take the passenger to the nearest police station. Since the introduction in January 2007 of s 11 of the Fraud Act 2006 this is a criminal matter and the police should take such deliveries of passengers and reports by drivers seriously. It is suggested that this might be more effective than returning them to their pick-up point.

9.35

Although it is possible to understand the provocation which might lead a taxi driver to use intimidatory methods to recover the fare, such action is, of course, completely unacceptable. In some areas, especially on late-night hirings, some drivers ask for either a deposit to be made against the fare before the hiring commences, or full fixed payment in advance (which must not exceed the metered fare). Provided that the balance is returned where the final fare does not exceed the deposit, then this is an acceptable and indeed, reasonable method of operation. Whilst the protection of the travelling public is the paramount aim of the licensing regime, it must always borne in mind that those involved in the trade are trying to earn a living and must be allowed to take all reasonable steps to achieve this.

AGREEMENTS TO PAY MORE THAN THE FARE SHOWN

9.36

TPCA 1847, s 55 outlaws any agreement to pay more than the fare shown on the meter, irrespective of what may have been agreed beforehand. If any overpayment of this nature is made, it can be recovered through the magistrates' courts as a civil debt[1]. In addition, the driver who demanded the excess can not only be prosecuted and fined, but also, if the excess demanded has not been repaid, he can be imprisoned for up to one month, unless the excess is repaid during that time. This seems to be an extraordinary provision and one can only think that such agreements were a major problem in the middle of the 19th century. The fine is level 3 on the standard scale and no other legislative provision governing hackney carriages or private hire vehicles carries a risk of imprisonment for breach. No records of any imprisonment for such a transgression have been found and it is difficult to say what view modern magistrates would take of such a situation.

[1]   See para 9.32 above.

TIPPING

9.37

This does not, however, prohibit the tipping of a hackney carriage driver at the end of the hiring. This is one area of service where a tip is often given and provided no agreement to tip was made in advance (in which case it would be outlawed by TPCA 1847, s 55)[1], the hirer is at liberty to tip whatever amount they may wish. As this is a gratuity and there is no contractual provision covering it, the driver should not expect this and although he may feel aggrieved if a tip is not forthcoming, no action can be taken against the passenger.

[1]   See Appendix I.

POTENTIAL HIRER WITH INSUFFICIENT FUNDS

9.38

The situation where the potential hirer does not have sufficient funds to take him the distance which he wishes to travel according to the fares set can be overcome in one of two ways: either by the driver discounting the fare at the end of the hiring or, alternatively, by an agreement to take the hirer a specified distance in exchange for a specified sum. This is governed by TPCA 1847, s 56[1], which allows passengers (up to the maximum number that the hackney carriage is permitted to carry) to be carried a specified distance in return for a specified sum of money. In this latter case, the distance agreed to be carried must not be less than that which the agreed sum of money would have entitled the passengers to be carried under the table of fares. If it is a shorter distance, then the driver has committed an offence under TCPA 1847, s 56.

[1]   See Appendix I.

'WAITING TIME'

9.39

If the hire is to include a period during which the driver must wait, eg, whilst a visit is made by the hirer to a cash-point before being taken to the final destination, then TPCA 1847, s 57[1] allows a deposit to be made by the hirer to the driver to cover not only his fare, but also any anticipated waiting time. Once that deposit has been made it is an offence for the driver to refuse to wait.

[1]   See Appendix I.

9.40

Most local authorities build 'waiting time' into their fare structure, but if they have not done so, TPCA 1847, s 57 provides a statutory fee of 7p per half hour of waiting time. It is not known whether there are any authorities who expect their drivers to wait for such rates of payment.

OTHER FARE PROVISIONS

9.41

There are two provisions in LG(MP)A 1976 in relation to fares other than the setting of them and these are to be found in LG(MP)A 1976, s 66[1] and LG(MP)A 1976, s 69[2].

[1]   See Appendix I.
[2]   See Appendix I.

FARE GREATER THAN THAT SHOWN ON METER

9.42

LG(MP)A 1976, s 66 prohibits any demand of a fare greater than that shown on the meter for hirings which end outside the area of the district council in which the hackney carriage is licensed, unless an agreement to pay more than the metered fare has been made in advance of the hiring commencing. In practice, when the hirer states the destination to the driver, the driver will probably realise if the destination is outside the district and should explain to the hirer that this will be for an agreed fare, as opposed to metered fare, but if this is not the case, the driver is bound to charge not more than the fare shown on the meter. If this provision is not complied with an offence is committed under s 66(2).

PROLONGATION OF JOURNEY

9.43

The other provision contained in LG(MP)A 1976, in s 69, concerns the prolongation of journeys, either by distance or time where it was not reasonably necessary. This covers the situation where a taxi driver literally and metaphorically takes a passenger 'for a ride', exploiting the fact that the passenger does not know the area, solely to increase the fare. It must be recognised that this has to be unreasonable prolongation and therefore, legitimate deviation from the shortest route to avoid congestion, roadworks or other similar situations is not unlawful. Equally, if the passenger specifically requests to go via a certain point, then that is a request made by the hirer, to which the driver should acquiesce.

9.44

Enforcement of LG(MP)A 1976, s 69 can be extremely difficult in situations where hirers feel that they have been taken further than was necessary, but do not know the area and are not only unsure as to where they should have been taken, but are also in most cases unsure where they actually were taken. In addition, a great many hirers do not appreciate the significance of waiting times in most fare structures and that hirings at busy periods of time in congested cities can cost considerably more than a similar hiring at quiet, off-peak times.

TRAILERS AND ROOF RACKS

9.45

Can a trailer or a roof rack be used on a hackney carriage? There is no reference in the legislation or DfT Guidance[1], and no senior court case on either point, so it is left to each local authority to consider. It appears that there are some authorities which permit the use of either or both without any formality and a number which seem to actively prohibit their use.

Obviously, there are occasions when the driver and passenger might find the use of a trailer or a roof rack beneficial (journeys to and from airports and seaports being obvious examples).

---

[1]   DfT, '*Taxi and Private Hire Vehicle Licensing: Best Practice Guidance*' (October 2006, revised March 2010) available from http://www.dft.gov.uk/pgr/regional/taxis/taxiandprivatehirevehiclelic1792.

Trailers

9.46

Apart from concerns over the roadworthiness of the trailer, there seem to be no obvious reasons to prohibit their use, apart from possible concerns over the obscuring of the vehicle plate from behind the trailer itself. This raises an interesting point, because the trailer does not obscure the plate from all angles, and it will still be visible. However, it will certainly be difficult to see if not impossible when viewed from behind at some distance, for example by a following vehicle. If this is seen as a prohibiting factor, it could be partially overcome by the issue of a 'trailer plate'.

A local authority cannot licence a trailer, but there is no prohibition on an authority testing it, and it could then issue a 'trailer plate'. If this was clearly and obviously different from the vehicle plate, but carried the same number, it would demonstrate that the trailer had been approved and could only be used with the specified vehicle. This cannot be achieved under taxi legislation, because the trailer is not a hackney carriage and therefore the authority must use other powers.

In England, the authority could use the general power of competence contained in the Localism Act 2011, s 1[1] as the power to inspect the vehicle, and issue the 'trailer plate' and the power to charge for discretionary services under s 93 of the Local Government Act 2003[2] as the power to charge for those activities. In Wales the position is slightly different as the Localism Act provisions do not apply. The 2003 Act applies in Wales, but in relation to the power to test and issue a plate, the alternative is to use the Local Government Act 1972, s 111[3] which allows a local authority to undertake activities which are incidental to its functions.

The authority might then want to attach a condition to the vehicle licence to the effect that the vehicle can use a trailer, but only one that has been approved and carries a trailer plate bearing the same number as the vehicle licence.

The driver would remain responsible for the use of the trailer, in terms of maximum weights, brakes, tyres etc, just as he is responsible for the vehicle itself. The driver must also have a DVLA licence that allows him to use a trailer. People who have passed their car driving test since the end of 1996 do not have an automatic right to tow a trailer, and need to pass an additional test. It would also be necessary to ensure that a waterproof cover is used to protect the luggage if the trailer is not waterproof.

[1]   Section 1 of the Localism Act 2011 states:

'**1 Local authority's general power of competence**
(1) A local authority has power to do anything that individuals generally may do.
(2) Subsection (1) applies to things that an individual may do even though they are in nature, extent or otherwise—
　　(a)   unlike anything the authority may do apart from subsection (1), or
　　(b)   unlike anything that other public bodies may do.
...'

[2]   Section 93(1) of the Local Government Act 2003 allows a local authority in England or Wales to:

' ... charge a person for providing a service to him if—
(a) the authority is authorised, but not required, by an enactment to provide the service to him, and
(b) he has agreed to its provision.
...'

[3] Section 111(1) of the Local Government Act 1972 states:

    '111.— Subsidiary powers of local authorities.

    (1) Without prejudice to any powers exercisable apart from this section but subject to the provisions of this Act and any other enactment passed before or after this Act, a local authority shall have power to do any thing (whether or not involving the expenditure, borrowing or lending of money or the acquisition or disposal of any property or rights) which is calculated to facilitate, or is conducive or incidental to, the discharge of any of their functions.'

Roof racks

9.47

A roof rack or roof box might well either obscure or interfere with a roof-sign which the vehicle conditions require to be fitted and illuminated. This in itself is not a reason to prohibit the use of roof racks, as it can be overcome. Where a roof rack will be used, the authority could issue an additional light or roof sign. One could then be fitted at the front of the roof rack, and the other at the rear.

As with a trailer, the driver will be responsible for ensuring that the roof rack is properly and securely fixed to the vehicle and then luggage carried on it is also properly secured. It would also be necessary to ensure that a waterproof cover is used to protect the luggage if an open roof rack is used.

DISABLED PEOPLE AND HACKNEY CARRIAGES

'London-style' vehicles and other vehicles

9.48

Hackney carriages provide a valuable transport service for a great many disabled people, offering, as they do, a door-to-door service, in reasonable comfort, with personal service on a one-to-one basis from the driver. This has long been recognised both within local authorities and the trade itself.

Disabled persons with mobility problems

9.49

Vehicles for use as hackney carriages which have been specially adapted or designed to carry passengers who wish to remain in a wheelchair for the journey have been available for a number of years. Originally these were usually 'London-style' vehicles, which since the late 1980s have been built to accommodate one wheelchair in the passenger compartment, but in recent years, a number of other vehicles have become available. These are sometimes referred to as 'alternative taxis' ('AT'), and are based upon vans or Multi-Purpose Vehicles ('MPV'). In general, all vehicles that are capable of carrying wheelchair-bound passengers are referred to as "Wheelchair Accessible Vehicles ('WAV'). In the case of the purpose-built hackney carriages, access is gained via ramps from the near-side of the vehicle and the passenger travels in their wheelchair facing backwards and secured by means of special seat-belts, and the ramps are carried in the boot when not being used. In most of the ATs, access is via the rear of the vehicle, either via ramps or mechanical lifts. The direction of travel of the wheelchair bound passenger varies, depending on the vehicle in question.

Both approaches provide a good method of transport for wheelchair-using disabled persons. The ATs are considerably cheaper than the purpose built hackney carriages, but some local authorities will not licence ATs[1].

[1]   Many local authorities use the TfL/LTPH Conditions of Fitness as the basis for their vehicle specifications for purpose built hackney carriages and these will not allow ATs, due to the requirement for a very tight turning circle and a one piece rear window. The TfL/LTPH Conditions of Fitness can be viewed at http://www.tfl.gov.uk/businessandpartners/taxisandprivatehire/1386.aspx.

9.50

In addition, for non-purpose-built vehicles (ie ordinary saloon cars in areas where there are no 'mandatory orders'), swivel seats are available from a number of manufacturers. These replace the front passenger seat and actually swing either round, or round and out, to make it easier for people to get in. For the non-wheelchair user, these can be extremely satisfactory, but, as always, this is dependent upon the nature of the disability the person has.

9.51

It is important to recognise that not all disabled people use wheelchairs all the time. As disabilities take many forms, such vehicles are not always ideal for persons who are not wheelchair-dependent all the time.

9.52

It was the availability of the London-style cabs, which were actually purpose-built to carry wheelchairs, which led Manchester City Council, in the mid-1980s, to consider the service of transport for disabled people, as outlined earlier[1]. Arguments have raged over the worth of such an approach: primarily over the question of how much use is actually made of these vehicles by people using wheelchairs and whether that use is justified in relation to the costs involved. As all new purpose-built vehicles are built to carry wheelchairs and as the number of older vehicles that would need converting to be able to be granted a licence in such circumstances reduces, this argument carries less weight. In addition, reports from disabled individuals and groups have emphasised the reassurance that people who use wheelchairs feel in any town or city where all the hackney carriages are wheelchair-accessible. They know that they are always able to get home by making their way to a hackney carriage stand and will be able to get the first hackney carriage in the rank rather than having either to wait on the off-chance that an accessible vehicle appears or to phone and make booking arrangements.

[1]   See Chapter 8, para 8.113.

R (on the application of Lunt) v Liverpool City Council

9.53

> Liverpool City Council refused to licence an E7 EuroTaxi as a hackney carriage because it required all hackney carriages to meet the TfL Conditions of Fitness, which meant the E7 was unacceptable. This was challenged by way of judicial review as conflicting with the Disability Discrimination Act 1995, that the decision was based on a material mistake as to fact and was contrary to the free movement of goods across the European Union. Held: The decision would be quashed as all the grounds of challenge were successful.

The question of the suitability of some wheelchair accessible vehicles ('WAV') to carry certain types of wheelchair bound passengers was considered in *R (on the application of Lunt) v Liverpool City Council*[1]. Liverpool City Council, in common with around 20 other local authorities and TfL, relied on the TfL Public Carriage Office[2] 'Conditions of Fitness' ('CoF') to determine whether a vehicle was suitable to be licensed as a hackney carriage.

Since the early 1990s, those conditions had mandated the use of a WAV, but only one that complied with the overall CoF including turning circle, side loading for wheelchairs etc. In practice this limited the acceptable vehicle to the purpose built 'London Taxi' models[3].

In 2007 an application was made by the manufacturer of the E7 taxi to have it approved for use as a hackney carriage within Liverpool[4]. That application was supported by Mrs Lunt, who was disabled and confined to a wheelchair. The nature of her disability meant that she required a larger, semi-reclining wheelchair, which would not fit safely within the existing CoF approved vehicles.

There was involved negotiation between Allied Taxis and the City Council and although it is clear from the judgment that the precise details were sometimes in question[5], the final conclusion of the Licensing Committee was to refuse approval of the E7 for use as a hackney carriage by a vote of four votes to two. The reasons, summarised in the judgment[6] stated that although the Council was:

> 'conscious of the need to give due regard to the Disability Discrimination Act, but three features caused it concern about the E7: firstly, the sliding doors and safety issues arising therefrom (the Council, it should be noted, had looked at the E7 itself); secondly, the size of an intermediate step; and thirdly, the turning circle needed in Liverpool where some ranks in the City Centre would need a three-point turn without the tight London-style turning circle.'

The claim raised four issues[7]:

> '1.   The decision amounted to unjustified discrimination contrary to section 21D and E of the Disability Discrimination Act 1995 (DDA), as amended with effect from 4 December 2006.

2. It failed to have due regard to its duty under section 49(1) of the DDA, introduced in June 2006, of the need to eliminate discrimination and promote equality of opportunity.
3. It exercised its public law discretion as to whether to license the E7 on the basis of a material and undisputed error of fact. Its judgment was thus based on a decisive error. There were also other grounds of unfairness argued.
4. In reaching the decision that it did, the City Council breached Article 28 of the European Union Treaty in that it imposed a product requirement (or similar requirement) that had equivalent effect to a quantative restriction on imports of material from an EU state without justification.

32. Although those four submissions raised some disputed issues of law to be addressed by this court in due course, the challenges at common law under the DDA and under community law all eventually shared a common factual foundation, and it is submitted that, in each case, the decisions were undermined by the error of fact made by the Council that at least includes the following:
1. The defendant through its officer, Mr Edwards, and consequently the chair, failed to understand that not all its licensed hackney carriage fleet was accessible to all wheelchair users, irrespective of their particular conditions and the size and characteristics of their wheelchairs.
2. The defendant misunderstood and therefore mis-stated the impact of the maintenance of the present practice as merely restricting the choice and the convenience of wheelchair users as opposed to the ability of some users, including Mrs Lunt, to use the present licensed taxis in Liverpool at all in the safe position. It could therefore reach no lawful judgment on the merits of the application and the extent to which it constituted discrimination, and the comparative safety benefits when considering the matter more generally.
3. Insofar as in its response to the DDA point and the Community law claims the Council sought to base a justification of its decision on safety considerations, the material upon which it relied was inadequate, and it failed to obtain relevant evidence from a competent source to advise it on the question.'

The judge accepted that the decision was susceptible to judicial review and the challenge was successful on all four grounds.

In relation to the errors of fact, judgment was as follows[8]:

'44. A lawful exercise of discretion could not have been performed unless the Committee properly understood the problem, its degree and extent. The margin of discretion as to fact and policy that the common law affords to decision-makers under the test in the Wednesbury Corporation case only applies to decision-makers who have acted fairly and directed themselves accurately on the relevant considerations to be weighed in making a matter of judgment or exercise of discretion. However, whether the failures came about as a result of the deficiencies in Mr Edwards' report, or a failure by the Committee to take into consideration and understand the factual position emerging from the documentary submissions and annexes in the second claimant's written submissions, the result is the same.

45. The Committee clearly based its decision on the erroneous belief that:
1. all its existing fleet of 1400 London-style taxis were accessible to wheelchair users generally, and that must mean to all wheelchair users;
2. problems as to the safe position and strapping of wheelchairs were the result of driver error rather than the result of constrictions of space;
3. it was dealing merely with a wish by wheelchair users to greater choice rather than something that restricted their ability to access the benefits provided by the licensing regime at all.

46. Since this error was critical to its decision in respect of its DDA duties, the balance of competing considerations if EC law was engaged and generally, it must be quashed and the matter remitted for reconsideration unless Ms Patterson [for the Respondent City Council] could satisfy me that it could make no difference to the outcome. I conclude that she cannot so satisfy me.'

In relation to the points concerning the Disability Discrimination Act 1995[9], the court found as follows. Sections 21D and 21E of the DDA 1995, imposed duties on local authorities as public bodies to consider the impact of their decisions on disabled people[10]. The court accepted a six-step approach to this duty in the following way[11]:

'1. Did the Council have a practice policy or procedure?
2. Did that practice policy or procedure make it impossible or unreasonably difficult for disabled persons to receive any benefit that is, or may be, conferred by the Council?
3. If so, is it under a duty to take such steps as is reasonable in all the circumstances of the case for it to change that practice policy and procedure so it no longer has that effect?
4. Has the Council failed to comply with its duty to take such steps?
5. If so, is the effect of that failure such as to make it unreasonably difficult for Mrs Lunt to access such benefit?
6. If so, can the Council show that its failure to comply is justified in that either-
   (a) it reasonably holds an opinion that the non-compliance is necessary in order not to endanger the health or safety of any other person; or
   (b) its failure is justified as a proportionate means of achieving another legitimate aim?'

The conclusion was that the council had failed in its duty under s 21. Blake J concluded this point by saying[12]:

'60. I accordingly conclude that it is misdirection for the Council to consider that because some wheelchair users can access the London taxi in dignity and safety that there is accessibility to wheelchair users as a class, and that any problem that Mrs Lunt has must be regarded as entirely individual to her. I accept that there must be a class of persons rather than mere problems encountered by a single individual, but the written and oral evidence presented to the Committee and its officers upon its true construction, as in the witness statements on behalf of the claimants in this case, showed serious difficulties for a class of wheelchair users that was wider in extent than Mrs Lunt personally, and that of that class there are some, like Mrs Lunt, who could not access the safe and secure position at all. As already indicated, that evidence has increased with the post-decision material now available for consideration.'

It also failed in in its duties under s 49 of the DDA[13]. This was summed up in the following way[14]:

'62. Both sides accept that this is a mandatory relevant consideration to be considered, even apart from section 21 duties. Clearly a proper analysis of the section 21 duties on reconsideration may well reveal unjustified discriminatory treatment that requires addressing. The Council's retention of the turning circle requirement in its policy is one that makes it more difficult for a class of wheelchair users to access public hire taxis.

.... .

64. The duty is to have regard rather than merely to achieve the improvement of the equality considerations at stake, but it is to have *due* regard, which must mean proper regard and full weight to the issue must be given.'

Finally, the question of Article 28 of the Treaty of Europe was considered[15]. Did the refusal to approve the E7 amount to an a quantitative restriction? The judge concluded that it did[16]:

'74. In my judgment, the policy provides a substantial restriction on the use of the vehicle in Liverpool, as the E7 is designed specifically as a public hire taxi, but it cannot be sold for such a purpose in Liverpool because the policy being impugned prevents its use as such.'

The matter was remitted to Liverpool City Council for reconsideration. They now licence a range of vehicles as hackney carriages, all of which are WAV and either purpose built or approved conversions.

[1]   [2009] EWHC 2356 (Admin), [2010] RTR 5, Admin Ct.
[2]   Now London Taxi and Private Hire.
[3]   At the time of the issue, these comprised FX4, TX1-4, and Metrocabs. They now include the Mercedes Vito.
[4]   'The E7 is a vehicle developed in consultation with [Allied Taxis] and Peugeot based in France. It is manufactured by [Allied Taxis] in the United Kingdom using a chassis base imported from France that is used in the Peugeot Expert Tepee range of vehicle. The Expert Tepee is a commercial passenger carrying vehicle that is also used as a taxi in many European cities. The E7 is a purpose-built design for publicly hired taxis in the United Kingdom.' Per Blake J at para 2 above.
[5]   See paras 7–28 of the judgment.

⁶   At para 29.

⁷   Per Blake J at paras 31 and 32.

⁸   Per Blake J at para 45 onwards.

⁹   The Disability Discrimination Act 1995 was repealed and replaced by the Equality Act 2010 in October 2010.

¹⁰   This duty has been replaced by a broader and more generic duty under the Equality Act 2010, s 29.

¹¹   Per Blake J at para 53.

¹²   Per Blake J at para 60.

¹³   Section 49 (now repealed) stated:

> 'Every public authority shall in carrying out its functions have due regard to –
> (a) the need to eliminate discrimination that is unlawful under this Act;
> (b) the need to eliminate harassment of disabled persons that is related to their disabilities;
> (c) the need to promote equality of opportunity between disabled persons and other persons;
> (d) the need to take steps to take account of disabled persons' disabilities, even where that involves treating disabled persons more favourably than other persons;
> (e) the need to promote positive attitudes towards disabled persons; and
> (f) the need to encourage participation by disabled persons in public life.'

¹⁴   Per Blake J at para 62 onwards.

¹⁵   Article 28 states 'Quantitative restrictions on imports and all measures having equivalent effect shall be prohibited between Member States.'

¹⁶   Per Blake J at para 74.

The Equality Act 2010 ss 160–173

9.54

The aim of making more, if not all, hackney carriages WAV was taken a stage further (at least in theory) by the passing of the Disability Discrimination Act 1995 (DDA 1995) as amended, which was repealed and replaced by the Equality Act 2010 ('EA 2010').

EA 2010, Pt 12 (ss 161–173)[1] applies to hackney carriages, and in some cases, private hire vehicles. This legislation refers to hackney carriages as 'taxis', the definition in EA 2010, s 173(1) making it clear that 'taxi' means a hackney carriage, but it does exclude hackney carriages drawn by horses or other animals. References within the EA 2010 are to the 'licensing authority' which means either a local authority or Transport for London.

EA 2010 contains a number of provisions relation to hackney carriages and disabled people and some of those also extend to private hire vehicles[2]. Although at the time of writing, a few have been brought into effect and these are considered below, the remaining provisions, including the making of accessibility regulations and the granting of additional hackney carriage licences for WAV remain enacted but unimplemented[3].

¹   See Appendix I.

²   The relevant sections are contained in Appendix I.

³   The Department for Transport issued guidance for licensing authorities, drivers and operators in October 2010 when the Equality Act provisions replaced the disability discrimination act requirements. It is available at https://www.gov.uk/government/uploads/system/uploads/attachment_data/file/3543/equality-act-taxis-annexa.pdf and https://www.gov.uk/government/uploads/system/uploads/attachment_data/file/3544/equality-act-taxis-annexb.pdf

9.55

During the 15-year lifetime of the DDA 1995, the Government made various announcements about the introduction of the WAV provisions, but ultimately, little happened. The current position is referred to in the revised DfT *Best Practice Guide* which states the following (at para 13–14)[1]:

'**Accessibility**

13. The Minister of State for Transport has now announced the way forward on accessibility for taxis and PHVs. His statement can be viewed on the Department's website at: http://www.dft.gov.uk/press/speechesstatements/statements/accesstotaxis. The Department will be taking forward demonstration schemes in three local authority areas to research the needs of people with disabilities in order to produce guidance about the most appropriate provision. In the meantime, the Department recognises that some local licensing authorities will want to make progress on enhancing accessible taxi provision and the guidance outlined below constitutes the Department's advice on how this might be achieved in advance of the comprehensive and dedicated guidance which will arise from the demonstration schemes.

14. Different accessibility considerations apply between taxis and PHVs. Taxis can be hired on the spot, in the street or at a rank, by the customer dealing directly with a driver. PHVs can only be booked through an operator. It is important that a disabled person should be able to hire a taxi on the spot with the minimum delay or inconvenience, and having accessible taxis available helps to make that possible. For PHVs, it may be more appropriate for a local authority to license any type of saloon car, noting that some PHV operators offer accessible vehicles in their fleet. The Department has produced a leaflet on the ergonomic requirements for accessible taxis that is available from: http://www.dft.gov.uk/transportforyou/access/taxis/pubs/research'

Since 2010 there has been no further movement in relation to the provision of vehicles, but there are requirements for assistance dogs to be carried and drivers must provide assistance to wheelchair bound passengers. Over two decades since the passing of legislation which was designed to make hackney carriages wheelchair accessible, there has been no improvement on this provision as a result of national legislation and this remains a significant failure to make transport available nationally for wheelchair-bound members of the population.

The provisions that are in force will be considered, followed by a summary of the remainder of the provisions.

[1]   *Taxi and Private Hire Vehicle Licensing: Best Practice Guidance* issued by the DfT in March 2010, available at https://www.gov.uk/government/uploads/system/uploads/attachment_data/file/212554/taxi-private-hire-licensing-guide.pdf .

Provisions in effect

A DRIVER MUST CARRY ASSISTANCE DOGS

9.56

Equality Act 2010, s 168 places a duty on the driver of a hackney carriage (referred to as a 'taxi') to carry an assistance dog[1]:

'168 Assistance dogs in taxis

(1) This section imposes duties on the driver of a taxi which has been hired—
    (a) by or for a disabled person who is accompanied by an assistance dog, or
    (b) by another person who wishes to be accompanied by a disabled person with an assistance dog.
(2) The driver must—
    (a) carry the disabled person's dog and allow it to remain with that person;
    (b) not make any additional charge for doing so.
(3) The driver of a taxi commits an offence by failing to comply with a duty imposed by this section.
(4) A person guilty of an offence under this section is liable on summary conviction to a fine not exceeding level 3 on the standard scale.'

'Assistance dog' is defined in s 173(1) as meaning:

'"assistance dog" means—
(a) a dog which has been trained to guide a blind person;
(b) a dog which has been trained to assist a deaf person;
(c) a dog which has been trained by a prescribed charity to assist a disabled person who has a disability that consists of epilepsy or otherwise affects the person's mobility, manual dexterity, physical co-ordination or ability to lift, carry or otherwise move everyday objects;
(d) a dog of a prescribed category which has been trained to assist a disabled person who has a disability (other than one falling within paragraph (c)) of a prescribed kind[2];'

Additional Assistance dogs are prescribed by reg 3 of the Disability Discrimination Act 1995 (Taxis) (Carrying of Guide Dogs etc.) (England and Wales) Regulations 2000, SI 2000/2990 as amended and include:

'3. Prescribed charities

Each of the following is a prescribed charity for the purposes of paragraph (c) of the definition of "assistance dog" in section 173(1) of the 2010 Act (so far as that definition applies for the purposes of section 168 of that Act)—
(a) "Dogs for the Disabled" registered with the Charity Commission under registration number 1092960;
(b) "Support Dogs" registered with the Charity Commission under registration number 1017237; and

(c) "Canine Partners for Independence" registered with the Charity Commission under registration number 803680.'.

A driver is exempted from this requirement if he holds an exemption certificate issued by the local authority on medical grounds under the provisions of EA 2010, s 169:

'169 Assistance dogs in taxis: exemption certificates

(1) A licensing authority must issue a person with a certificate exempting the person from the duties imposed by section 168 (an "exemption certificate") if satisfied that it is appropriate to do so on medical grounds.

(2) In deciding whether to issue an exemption certificate the authority must have regard, in particular, to the physical characteristics of the taxi which the person drives or those of any kind of taxi in relation to which the person requires the certificate.

(3) An exemption certificate is valid—
   (a)   in respect of a specified taxi or a specified kind of taxi;
   (b)   for such period as is specified in the certificate.

(4) The driver of a taxi is exempt from the duties imposed by section 168 if—
   (a)   an exemption certificate issued to the driver is in force with respect to the taxi, and
   (b)   the prescribed notice of the exemption is exhibited on the taxi in the prescribed manner.
   The power to make regulations under paragraph (b) is exercisable by the Secretary of State.

(5) In this section *"licensing authority"* means—
   (a)   in relation to the area to which the Metropolitan Public Carriage Act 1869 applies, Transport for London;
   (b)   in relation to any other area in England and Wales, the authority responsible for licensing taxis in that area.'

Clearly such a certificate can only be issued on medical grounds, which tend to relate either to allergies to dogs, or phobia of dogs. However, the local authority (or TfL in the case of a London driver) must also have regard to the vehicle the driver will be driving. Where there is an all WAV policy in place, this might be a straightforward consideration, but it will be more complex where there is a mixed vehicle fleet. As a hackney carriage driver can theoretically drive any hackney carriage licensed by the same authority and there is no mandatory linking of a driver and a particular vehicle, it will be for the local authority (or TfL) to determine how the characteristics of different vehicles will affect individuals.

If such an exemption certificate is granted, it must be in the form specified in the Disability Discrimination Act 1995 (Taxis) (Carrying of Guide Dogs etc) (England and Wales) Regulations 2000 (as amended), reg 2 and Sch 1 (in England) or Sch 2 (in Wales)[3]. Once such a certificate has been granted, it must be displayed in accordance with reg 2(2):

'2–(2) The prescribed manner of exhibiting a notice of exemption for the purposes of section 169(4)(b) of the 2010 Act shall be by either—

(a) affixing it in a prominent position on the dashboard of the taxi, facing upwards; or

(b) affixing it to the windscreen of the taxi, facing outwards.'

There is a right of appeal against a refusal by the licensing authority to issue an exemption certificate. This is contained in EA 2010, s 172 which states:

'(1) A person who is aggrieved by the refusal of a licensing authority in England and Wales to issue an exemption certificate under section 166, 169 or 171 may appeal to a magistrates' court before the end of the period of 28 days beginning with the date of the refusal.'

If the appeal is successful, the magistrates can order the licensing authority to issue the certificate (see s 172(3)).

Breach of the duty placed upon a hackney carriage to carry an assistance dog in the passenger compartment contrary to EA 2010, s 168 is a criminal offence under s 168(3). As the Equality Act is silent as to which body can prosecute such an offence, it is a general criminal offence and can therefore be investigated by the police and prosecuted by the Crown Prosecution Service. However it can also be investigated by, or prosecuted by the local authority under the powers contained in s 222 of the Local Government Act 1972[4]. As the local authority is the enforcing authority for all other taxi legislation, it would seem to be both reasonable and expedient for the local authority to prosecute cases such as this.

[1]   Similar provisions apply to private hire vehicles under EA 2010, s 170.
[2]   The Disability Discrimination Act 1995 (Taxis) (Carrying of Guide Dogs etc.) (England and Wales) Regulations 2000, SI 2000/2990 as amended are now deemed to have been made under the Equality Act, and were amended by the Equality Act 2010 (Commencement No. 4, Savings, Consequential, Transitional, Transitory and Incidental Provisions and Revocation) Order 2010, SI 2010/2317.
[3]   SI 2000/2990.
[4]   Section 222 states:

   '(1)Where a local authority consider it expedient for the promotion or protection of the interests of the inhabitants of their area—
     (a) they may prosecute or defend or appear in any legal proceedings and, in the case of civil proceedings, may institute them in their own name, and
     (b) they may, in their own name, make representations in the interests of the inhabitants at any public inquiry held by or on behalf of any Minister or public body under any enactment.
   (2) In this section "local authority" includes the Common Council and the London Fire and Emergency Planning Authority.'

9.57

In relation to assistance dogs, again, there have been a number of reported problems where carriage of the dog has been refused on the grounds that it may make a mess of the vehicle, either by deposit of dog hairs or worse. In addition to a breach of EA 2010, s 168, this is also a breach of the conditions of many local authorities.

In April 2017, EA 2010, ss 165 and 167 came into force, together with the full provisions of s 166 and regulations relating to the exemption notices[1]. These allow a licensing authority (a local authority or TfL in London) to create a list of 'designated vehicles' which are capable of carrying passengers in wheelchairs and then require drivers of those vehicles to provide mobility assistance. These vehicles can be either hackney carriages or private hire vehicles. Section 166 is an exemption provision. Guidance was issued in February 2017 to assist licensing authorities and driver's with the introduction of these provisions[2].

[1]   Equality Act 2010 (Taxis and Private Hire Vehicles) (Passengers in Wheelchairs – Notices of Exemption) Regulations 2017, SI 2017/342.
[2]   *Access For Wheelchair Users To Taxis And Private Hire Vehicles – Statutory Guidance'*
       Department for Transport February 2017 available at https://www.gov.uk/government/publications/access-for-wheelchair-users-to-taxis-and-private-hire-vehicles

9.58

The starting point for these provisions lies with s 167:

'167 Lists of wheelchair-accessible vehicles

(1)   For the purposes of section 165, a licensing authority may maintain a list of vehicles falling within subsection (2).
(2)   A vehicle falls within this subsection if—
       (a)   it is either a taxi or a private hire vehicle, and
       (b)   it conforms to such accessibility requirements as the licensing authority thinks fit.
(3)   A licensing authority may, if it thinks fit, decide that a vehicle may be included on a list maintained under this section only if it is being used, or is to be used, by the holder of a special licence under that licence.
(4)   In subsection (3) *"special licence"* has the meaning given by section 12 of the Transport Act 1985 (use of taxis or hire cars in providing local services).
(5)   "Accessibility requirements" are requirements for securing that it is possible for disabled persons in wheelchairs—
       (a)   to get into and out of vehicles in safety, and
       (b)   to travel in vehicles in safety and reasonable comfort,
       either staying in their wheelchairs or not (depending on which they prefer).
(6)   The Secretary of State may issue guidance to licensing authorities as to—
       (a)   the accessibility requirements which they should apply for the purposes of this section;
       (b)   any other aspect of their functions under or by virtue of this section.
(7)   A licensing authority which maintains a list under subsection (1) must have regard to any guidance issued under subsection (6).'

9.59

It can be seen that this is a power rather than a duty, but the guidance issued by the Department for Transport encourages licensing authorities to create and maintain a list of vehicles which are capable of carrying passengers in wheelchairs[1]:

> '1.11 Section 167 of the Act permits, but does not require, LAs to maintain a designated list of wheelchair accessible taxis and PHVs.
>
> 1.12 Whilst LAs are under no specific legal obligation to maintain a list under section 167, the Government recommends strongly that they do so. Without such a list the requirements of section 165 of the Act do not apply, and drivers may continue to refuse the carriage of wheelchair users, fail to provide them with assistance, or to charge them extra.'

[1] Paras 1.11 and 1.12 of *Access For Wheelchair Users To Taxis And Private Hire Vehicles – Statutory Guidance*, Department for Transport February 2017 available at https://www.gov.uk/government/publications/access-for-wheelchair-users-to-taxis-and-private-hire-vehicles

9.60

Although a mechanism exists which would allow a local authority to specify ('list') a vehicle as only being suitable for carrying wheelchair-bound passengers when it is being used and the local bus service ('a special licence' in accordance with sub-s (3) and (4)) it is difficult to see why that would be the case. As the overriding consideration must be the safety of the passengers, it would appear to be immaterial whether the vehicle is being used for regular hackney carriage services or a local bus service.

In relation to the listing of vehicles, the guidance states:

> '1.14 The Act states that a vehicle can be included on a licensing authority's list of designated vehicles if it conforms to such accessibility requirements as the licensing authority thinks fit. However, it also goes on to explain that vehicles placed on the designated list should be able to carry passengers in their wheelchairs should they prefer.
>
> 1.15 This means that to be placed on a licensing authority's list a vehicle must be capable of carrying some – but not necessarily all – types of occupied wheelchairs. The Government therefore recommends that a vehicle should only be included in the authority's list if it would be possible for the user of a "reference wheelchair"[1] to enter, leave and travel in the passenger compartment in safety and reasonable comfort whilst seated in their wheelchair.
>
> 1.16 Taking this approach allows the provisions of section 165 of the Act apply to a wider range of vehicles and more drivers than if LAs only included on the list vehicles capable of taking a larger type of wheelchair.
>
> 1.17 The Government recognises that this approach will mean that some types of wheelchair, particularly some powered wheelchairs, may be unable to access some of the vehicles included in the LA's list. The

Act recognises this possibility, and section 165(9) provides a defence for the driver if it would not have been possible for the wheelchair to be carried safely in the vehicle. Paragraph 3.10 of this guidance below aims to ensure that users of larger wheelchairs have sufficient information about the vehicles that will be available to them to make informed choices about their journeys.'

If the licensing authority decide to create a list of wheelchair accessible vehicles, they must then publish this[2]. Interestingly, the guidance goes on to suggest that licensing authorities should create a supplemental list (not a statutory list) of other vehicles that whilst not capable of carrying a passenger seated in the wheelchair, can carry a passenger seated in a normal seat and a wheelchair in the boot[3].

1   As defined in Sch 1 of the Public Service Vehicles Accessibility Regulations 2000, SI 2000/1970.
2   See paragraphs 1.18 to 1.20 of *Access for Wheelchair Users to Taxis and Private Hire Vehicles – Statutory Guidance*, Department for Transport February 2017 available at https://www.gov.uk/government/publications/access-for-wheelchair-users-to-taxis-and-private-hire-vehicles
3   Above at paras 1.21 and 1.22.

9.61

There is a right of appeal contained in s 172(4). This gives 'A person who is aggrieved by the decision of a licensing authority to include a vehicle on a list maintained under section 167' a right to appeal. It is interesting to note that this right lies with 'a person' rather than the proprietor of a vehicle which has been listed. It remains to be seen whether it will be possible for people who are not proprietors to appeal against the listing. The guidance also provides information on appeals[1].

1   Above at para 1.23.

9.62

Once a vehicle has been listed under s 167, it is then referred to as either a 'designated taxi' or a 'designated private hire vehicle' and the driver of any such vehicle who is not in possession of an exemption certificate issued under s 166 is then under a statutory duty to carry wheelchair-bound passengers and to provide 'mobility assistance'.

The duty applies when the vehicle has been hired:

'165 (1) This section imposes duties on the driver of a designated taxi which has been hired—
   (a) by or for a disabled person who is in a wheelchair, or
   (b) by another person who wishes to be accompanied by a disabled person who is in a wheelchair.
(2)   This section also imposes duties on the driver of a designated private hire vehicle, if a person within paragraph (a) or (b) of subsection (1) has indicated to the driver that the person wishes to travel in the vehicle.'

9.63

The duties imposed on the driver are detailed in EA 2010, s 165(4) and (5). Subsection (4) contains the general duties and subsection (5) details what is meant by 'mobility assistance'.

The general duties are[1]:

'(a) to carry the passenger while in the wheelchair;
(b) not to make any additional charge for doing so;
(c) if the passenger chooses to sit in a passenger seat, to carry the wheelchair;
(d) to take such steps as are necessary to ensure that the passenger is carried in safety and reasonable comfort;
(e) to give the passenger such mobility assistance as is reasonably required.'

And mobility assistance:

'is assistance—
(a) to enable the passenger to get into or out of the vehicle;
(b) if the passenger wishes to remain in the wheelchair, to enable the passenger to get into and out of the vehicle while in the wheelchair;
(c) to load the passenger's luggage into or out of the vehicle;
(d) if the passenger does not wish to remain in the wheelchair, to load the wheelchair into or out of the vehicle.'

Neither of those duties require a driver to carry a passenger in circumstances where it would be lawful for him to refuse the hiring, eg for a journey from a hackney carriage stand which will terminate outside the district (or hackney carriage zone)[2]. In addition, unless the vehicle is of a description prescribed by the Secretary of State, the driver cannot be compelled to carry more than one wheelchair or wheelchair-bound passenger[3].

Failure to provide mobility assistance or to carry the passenger or discharge any of the other duties contained in s 165 (4) is a criminal offence by virtue of sub-s (8), but there is a defence if the driver can show that it would not have been possible for the wheelchair to be carried safely in the vehicle (sub-s (9)(b)).

[1]   EA 2010, s 165(4).
[2]   EA 2010, s 165(6)(b).
[3]   EA 2010, s 165(6)(a).

9.64

A licensed hackney carriage or private hire driver can apply for a certificate of exemption from the duties imposed under s 165. This process is governed by s 166 and application is made to the licensing authority. Neither the legislation nor the guidance provide any assistance to the licensing authority on how it is to determine such applications. The legislation simply states:

'166 Passengers in wheelchairs: exemption certificates

(1) A licensing authority must issue a person with a certificate exempting the person from the duties imposed by section 165 (an "exemption certificate") if satisfied that it is appropriate to do so—

    (a)   on medical grounds, or

    (b)   on the ground that the person's physical condition makes it impossible or unreasonably difficult for the person to comply with those duties.

(2)   An exemption certificate is valid for such period as is specified in the certificate.

(3)   The driver of a designated taxi is exempt from the duties imposed by section 165 if—

    (a)   an exemption certificate issued to the driver is in force, and

    (b)   the prescribed notice of the exemption is exhibited on the taxi in the prescribed manner.

(4)   The driver of a designated private hire vehicle is exempt from the duties imposed by section 165 if—

    (a) an exemption certificate issued to the driver is in force, and

    (b) the prescribed notice of the exemption is exhibited on the vehicle in the prescribed manner.

(5)   For the purposes of this section, a taxi or private hire vehicle is "designated" if it appears on a list maintained under section 167.

(6)   In this section and section 167 *"licensing authority"*, in relation to any area, means the authority responsible for licensing taxis or, as the case may be, private hire vehicles in that area.'

The guidance states that local authorities should take an objective view of such applications and ideally have independent medical assessment[1]. There is no prescribed form of Exemption Certificate but there is a prescribed form of Exemption Notice. This is contained in the Equality Act 2010 (Taxis and Private Hire Vehicles) (Passengers in Wheelchairs – Notices of Exemption) Regulations 2017[2]. This notice must then be displayed within the nearside windscreen of the vehicle when it is being driven by the holder of the exemption certificate[3].

Section 172(1) provides a right of appeal to the magistrates' court against a refusal to grant an exemption certificate. The guidance also provides information on appeals and suggests that licensing authorities may wish to establish their own internal appeals procedure before the matter gets to the magistrates' court[4]. It is difficult to see how this can work, because once the decision of the licensing authority has been made, as a matter of law the right of appeal lies to the magistrates' court and he is arguable that the licensing authority no longer has any jurisdiction to consider the matter.

[1]   See paras 1.31–1.34 of *Access For Wheelchair Users To Taxis And Private Hire Vehicles – Statutory Guidance*, Department for Transport, February 2017 available at https://www.gov.uk/government/publications/access-for-wheelchair-users-to-taxis-and-private-hire-vehicles

[2]   SI 2017/342.

[3]   The prescribed forms of notice are contained in Schedule 1 (for England) and Schedule 2 (for Wales) of the Equality Act 2010 (Taxis and Private Hire Vehicles) (Passengers in Wheelchairs – Notices of Exemption) Regulations 2017, SI 2017/342. Regulation 2(2) specifies that the notice must measure 10 cm × 10 cm, and whilst the prescribed notice for England is square, it is unfortunate that the prescribed notice for Wales is rectangular.

[4]   See paragraphs 1.41 and 1.42 of *Access For Wheelchair Users To Taxis And Private Hire Vehicles – Statutory Guidance*, Department for Transport, February 2017 available at https://www.gov.uk/government/publications/access-for-wheelchair-users-to-taxis-and-private-hire-vehicles

9.65

As noted above, there are a number of further provisions contained within the Equality Act relating to hackney carriages and private hire vehicles, but in relation to these, there are apparently no current plans to bring them into effect.

Section 160 gives power to the Secretary of State for transport to make 'taxi accessibility regulations'. These would be wide-ranging regulations relating to the specification of hackney carriages to enable them to carry wheelchair-bound passengers. Section 160(3) also provides for the regulations to impose duties on the drivers of such vehicles to comply with provisions relating to access ramps and the way in which the wheelchair is secured.

Section 161 will require a local authority which limits the overall number of hackney carriages that it will license to grant a licence for a wheelchair accessible vehicle, irrespective of the overall number of vehicles already licensed, unless the proportion of WAV to non-WAV is greater than that prescribed by the Secretary of State. There is currently no indication as to what that proportion might be.

Section 162 will allow a local authority to require wheelchair accessible vehicles to be made available where there is any contract with a single company (hackney carriage or private hire) at any port, airport, railway station or bus station (referred to as a 'transport facility').

Section 163 will require all new hackney carriages to be WAV unless it is a renewal of a licence for a vehicle which was not a WAV. This requirement can be removed under s 164 if the local authority applies to the Secretary of State for an exemption on the basis that it would be inappropriate for that requirement to apply and if it did the results would be an unacceptable reduction in the number of hackney carriages within the area.

9.66

It is, therefore, widely accepted that hackney carriages provide an extremely useful and usable form of transport for disabled persons. However, until the remaining provisions of EA 2010 come into force for every district council, the provision of a genuinely useful service across the whole of England and Wales for persons with varying types of disability will not occur, and disabled people will be discriminated against by their location, local geography and local and national politics.

HACKNEY CARRIAGE STANDS

9.67

One of the distinguishing features of hackney carriages is that they can 'rank up'. Hackney carriages can wait at approved ranks, referred to as 'stands' in the legislation, and await the arrival of a hirer.

Once a hackney carriage stand has been created and where there are hackney carriage bylaws in force, the driver of a hackney carriage is required to proceed to a hackney carriage stand when it is not actually hired. Model byelaw number 7 states:

> '7. The driver of a hackney carriage shall, when plying for hire in any street and not actually hired:
> (a) proceed with reasonable speed to one of the stands appointed by the Council;
> (b) if a stand, at the time of his arrival, is occupied by the full number of carriages authorised to occupy it, proceed to another stand;'

The effect of this requirement was considered by the Court of Appeal in *Jones v First Greater Western Ltd*[1] where Floyd LJ took the following view[2]:

> '31 Thus I was not persuaded that Byelaw 3 [which is the equivalent of model bylaw number 7] of the taxi byelaws was of any assistance. Quite apart from the point that the byelaws cannot legitimately be used as an aid to construction of primary legislation, the byelaws do not impose an obligation to proceed to the nearest stand. If the byelaw had meant to create such an obligation, it would have said so. Instead the byelaw requires the taxi to proceed "with reasonable speed to one of the stands". Even if the byelaw bore the meaning contended for, it carries no implication that a space will be available for the taxi when it arrives at any given stand. If that is so, it is difficult to see how a driver could be in breach of this byelaw if access were prevented to a stand (e.g. one on private land) by other means.'

[1]   Initially heard in the High Court as *Patricia Jones, Mourad Tighilt (Suing on behalf of themselves and all other members of the Bristol Branch of the National Taxi Association) v First Greater (sic) Western Limited* [2013] EWHC 1485 (Ch), [2014] LLR 16, ChD and then in the Court of Appeal as *Jones v First Greater Western Ltd* [2014] EWCA Civ 301, [2015] RTR 3, CA. This case is considered in detail at para 9.87.

[2]   At para 31.

Creation of a stand

9.68

Originally, hackney carriage stands were created by a local authority by means of byelaws made under TPCA 1847, s 68. Where the LG(MP)A 1976 is in force, the byelaws route is no longer available, and any stands made under byelaws are now deemed to have been made under s 63[1].

It is also possible for a highway authority to prohibit parking or waiting on a street by means of Traffic Regulation Orders under the provisions of the Road Traffic Regulation Act 1984, ss 32–37, but this is outside hackney carriage licensing control[2].

[1]   LG(MP)A 1976, s 63(4).
[2]   See para 9.83 below.

9.69

Therefore the only method of creating hackney carriage stands is contained in LG(MP)A 1976, s 63. This allows district councils to 'appoint stands for hackney carriages' either on public highways or private land and the stands can be for either continual or part-time use.

PRIVATE STANDS

R v Great Western Trains Ltd, ex p Frederick

9.70

> Exclusive use granted to one hackney carriage company to use a railway station rank (located on railway owned land). Challenged by the other hackney drivers who were excluded from the rank. Held: This was not part of the statutory duty of the railway company and was not susceptible to judicial review.

If the land in question does not form part of the highway, then the consent of the owner of the land is required. 'Private' stands were considered in *R v Great Western Trains Ltd, ex p Frederick*[1]. This case concerned an application for leave to apply for judicial review of a decision of Great Western Trains Ltd to grant sole and exclusive rights to one company to ply for hire from the hackney carriage stand at Newport Central Station. The decision was challenged by hackney carriage drivers who were excluded from using the station rank by virtue of the new agreement.

[1]   [1998] COD 239.

9.71

Five points were considered by Popplewell J[1]. First, had there been sufficient consultation with the trade (represented by the applicants) by Great Western Trains Ltd to enable the trade to put forward arguments as to why the proposed arrangements should not have gone ahead? As a letter had been sent to each of the existing hackney carriage drivers, who had permission to use the station rank, explaining the situation and as it was made clear that their permissions to use the station stand were going to expire on a set date, Popplewell J found that there was sufficient consultation, even taking into account the ruling in *R v Liverpool Corpn, ex p Liverpool Taxi Fleet Operators' Association*[2].

[1]   *R v Great Western Trains Ltd, ex p Frederick* [1998] COD 239.
[2]   [1972] 2 QB 299, CA.

9.72

The second point was, if there had not been consultation, was the application for leave for judicial review out of time? – to which the judge found that it was.

9.73

The third question raised an argument that the agreement between Great Western Trains Ltd and the taxi company was contrary to TPCA 1847, s 64 because it required the taxi company to supply Great Western Trains Ltd with, amongst other things, the names of responsible persons such as supervisors who would be responsible for policing the hackney carriage stand. Under the agreement there was an obligation on the proprietor to police the area of the stand. Popplewell J dismissed this argument, but gave some useful indications of what is meant by s 64[1]:

> 'As I understand the argument, by giving exclusive use of the stand to Dragon Taxis, there is said to be a breach of section 64, because it will hinder or obstruct the driver of the applicant's vehicles contrary to that section. If, as I indicated in the course of argument, all that was required was for the proprietor, either himself or through the respondents, to take out an injunction against the applicants, that is also said to be something which would hinder the drivers like the applicants.
>
> It seems to me that section 64, to put it in a very simple way, is there to prevent a punch-up between rival licence holders. The whole language of "obstruct", "hinder", "wrongfully", "in a forcible manner" and so on is not dealing with the situation in this case, when one lot of drivers have been given the right and the others have not. It is to deal with the situation on the ground when rival drivers may take the matter into their hands. I am wholly unpersuaded that section 64 has any bearing on the facts of the instant case.'

[1]   *R v Great Western Trains Ltd, ex p Frederick* [1998] COD 239.

9.74

The fourth question was whether an agreement, in relation to the use of a hackney carriage stand which was sited on private land, was susceptible to judicial review. Popplewell J concluded that the provision of a hackney carriage stand was not part of the statutory function of the railway company under the provisions of the Railways Act 1993 and that the provision of a hackney carriage stand was ancillary to its statutory function and, accordingly, not susceptible to judicial review, although, in relation to their statutory matters, he stated[1]:

> '... in my judgment, the Great Western Train Company are susceptible to judicial review, that susceptibility exists only in relation to those of the decisions which in some way are either statutorily underpinned or involve some other sufficient public law element.'

[1]   *R v Great Western Trains Ltd, ex p Frederick* [1998] COD 239.

9.75

Finally, in relation to the fifth point, he concluded that the application itself was out of time.

9.76

This case is useful to the extent that it demonstrates (albeit that it is only an application for leave and not a full judicial review of the situation) that a railway company can enter into an exclusive arrangement with one hackney carriage 'company' to use a hackney carriage stand at a railway station. In the case of a railway company, that decision itself is not subject to judicial review and any policing of the arrangements that are imposed upon the hackney carriage company are not in breach of TPCA 1847, s 64. By extension, it would appear that such an arrangement could apply to an airport or, indeed, at any other large undertaking where there is private land upon which a hackney carriage stand could be created, eg out-of-town shopping centres or sports centres, entertainment complexes etc.

PUBLIC HIGHWAY STANDS

9.77

If the stand is to be on a public highway, the consent of the highway authority is required. In areas with county councils, the highway authority is the county council, but, in unitary and metropolitan areas, it is the same council discharging both highway and hackney carriage licensing functions. Whether this actually makes it any easier in practice to obtain the consent of the highway authority seems to be open to question, but, in theory, it should ease the process considerably.

9.78

Under LG(MP)A 1976, s 63(1)[1], the district council can determine the number of hackney carriages that can use the stand and it also has a power to vary that number.

[1]   See Appendix I.

9.79

Before a new stand is created (or removed) or the maximum number of vehicles which can use the stand is varied, notice must be given to the Chief Officer of Police. A public notice must also be provided in one local newspaper. Any objections which are received within 28 days of the first publication of the public notice must be taken into account, together with the comments of the Chief Officer of Police, before such a stand is appointed or the number is varied. There are limitations on the siting of hackney carriage stands and these are contained within LG(MP)A 1976, s 63(3). They are effectively to prevent obstructions or impediments caused by hackney carriage stands in relation to premises or any buses or other public service vehicles (PSVs) that may be using the road or any depots or bus stations nearby.

9.80

It should be noted that once a hackney carriage stand has been created, it is possible to alter it, or remove it by using the same mechanism that was used to create it. These powers are contained in LG(MP)A 1976, s 63(5). It is important that ranks which are no longer used are removed, and new ones created which are located as conveniently as possible.

FLOW CHART FOR GRANTING HACKNEY CARRIAGE STANDS

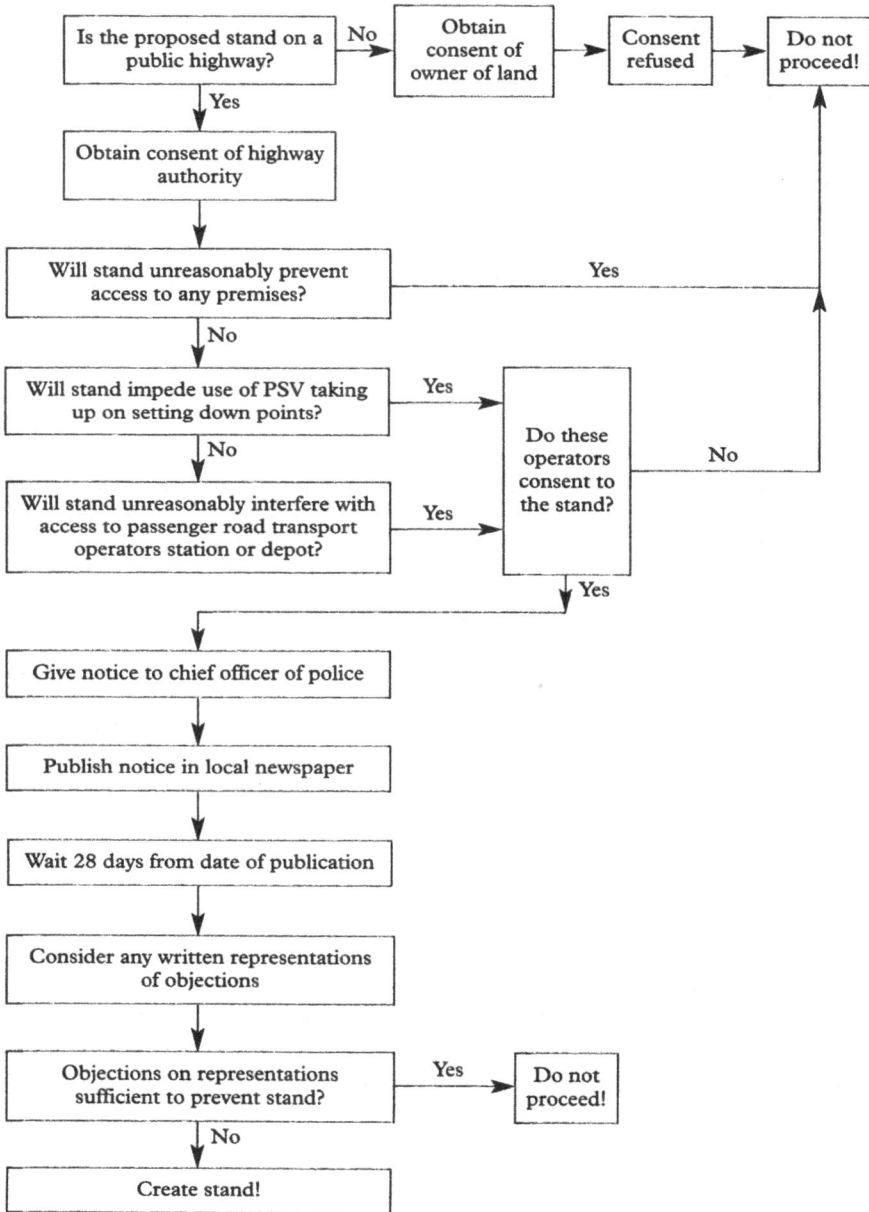

9.81

Hackney carriage stands are an important feature of both the trade and urban life and their existence and use should be subject to frequent evaluation. Towns and cities are dynamic places and the need for stands varies as time goes by. What may have been a busy area as recently as three or four years ago (let alone 10 or 20 years ago), leading to the provision of viable, well-used stands, may have altered significantly as a result of development. There are a great many stands around the country which have fallen into disuse but which still exist under the legislation. Equally, there are many areas of the country where hackney carriage stands would be extremely useful and heavily used, but where no provision has been made in recent years. This leads to the problem of hackney carriage drivers creating unofficial ranks in areas of high demand. The difficulties that these can give rise to are those of congestion, obstruction of access to premises and bus stops, parking offences and the fact that the stand itself is not protected solely for the use of hackney carriages.

9.82

Hackney carriage stands on the public highway must be marked out and signed in accordance with the Traffic Signs Regulations and General Directions 2016[1], Sch 7, Part 4, Item 5 . In particular, the road markings must be coloured yellow and white markings cannot be used. If a stand was marked in white, it would still be a stand, but the council could not enforce the provisions preventing any other vehicle from parking or waiting on it[2].

[1]   SI 2016/362.
[2]   This was the decision of the Chief Adjudicator of the National Parking Adjudication Service, appointed under the Road Traffic Act 1991, s 73, in Case No MD 284 *Darius v Maidstone Borough Council* (2002). This case concerned the earlier Traffic Signs Regulations and General Directions 1994, SI 1994/1519, the relevant provisions of which are identical to the current 2002 Regulations, SI 2002/3113.

THE USE OF TRAFFIC REGULATION ORDERS

9.83

A number of local authorities create what are referred to as hackney carriage ranks by means of Traffic Regulation Orders ('TRO'). It is important to recognise that this process imposes waiting or parking restrictions on the location, which can be applied in such a way as to only permit hackney carriages to use the facility, but they are not hackney carriage stands within the meaning of the TPCA 1847, the LG(MP)A 1976, hackney carriage byelaws or any other legislative provisions referring to hackney carriage stands.

The powers to make a TRO are contained within Pt 1 of the Road Traffic Regulation Act 1984 and give powers to the traffic authority to make a TRO in respect of a road (s 1)[1].

The powers contained in s 1 are extremely wide and can be used to apply a parking restriction to any vehicle which is not a hackney carriage, thereby creating a reserved space for hackney carriages to park, but it does not constitute a hackney carriage rank within the meaning of either bylaws or the LG(MP)A 1976.

Once a TRO is in force, unlawful parking can be enforced by means of fixed penalty notices, but no offences under either LG(MP)A 1976, s 64 or hackney carriage byelaws can be committed.

[1]   'Road' is defined in section 142 in the following terms:

      '"*road*"—

      (a) in England and Wales, means any length of highway or of any other road to which the public has access, and includes bridges over which a road passes,'

Railway Station Ranks

9.84

Originally, because hackney carriage stands at railway stations were located on private land owned by the railway company, there was uncertainty as to whether the control provisions contained within the byelaws applied to them. This was addressed by s 76 of the Public Health Act 1925 which stated that the provisions of the 1847 Act will apply to 'any railway station or railway premises ... as if such railway station or railway premises were a stand for hackney carriages or a street'.

Section 63 of the 1976 Act makes it clear that a rank can be created by the local authority (or deemed to have been created that way because it was created by byelaws) on private land with the consent of the landowner. This was confirmed by the Court of Appeal in *Jones v First Greater Western Ltd* where Floyd LJ stated (at para 9), '[Section 63 of the] 1976 Act extended the power of local authorities to appoint taxi stands, with the consent of the owner of the land, on any land not forming part of the highway.'[1] Accordingly, the provisions in s 64 restricting the use of that stand to hackney carriages will apply, and the first element of PHA 1925, s 76 is therefore redundant.

However, the second element, which deems all railway premises to be a street for the purposes of the 1847 Act is very important. Neither 'railway station' or 'railway premises' are defined and will therefore carry their everyday meaning and as this is not limited to hackney carriage stands, this will apply to all railway premises.

It is vital to ensure that s 76 has been correctly applied in the local authority's area. The mechanism is contained in Sch 14, para 25 to the Local Government Act 1972[2].

[1]   *Jones v First Greater Western Ltd* [2014] EWCA Civ 301, [2015] RTR 3, CA at para 9. This case is considered in detail at para 9.87 below.

[2]   If s 76 of the Public Health Act 1925 was in force in all or part of the area of a district created under the Local Government Act 1974, the new local authority could give notice that it will apply throughout the new authority's area, or not apply throughout the area. If the notice was to disapply the provisions of s76, that resolution had to be passed before 1 April 1975. A resolution applying s 76 to the whole area can be made at any time. Unless such a resolution has been passed, it appears that s 76 only applies to the parts of the district where it applied before local government re-organisation in 1974.

The use of the stand

9.85

Once the stand has been created under LG(MP)A 1976, s 63, whether directly or deemed to be created under s 63 by virtue of appearing in former byelaws, then LG(MP)A 1976, s 64[1] protects that stand during the hours of use for the benefit of hackney carriages.

[1]   See Appendix I.

9.86

LG(MP)A 1976, s 64(1) makes it an offence for any person to 'cause or permit any vehicle other than a hackney carriage to wait on any stand for hackney carriages' and this is a comprehensive ban on all other vehicles. The only defence which is available is under s 64(5), in relation to a PSV, and that is only on the grounds of avoiding obstruction to traffic to enable passengers to be dropped off or 'other compelling reason[s]'. It is not actually clear what reason would be so compelling to afford a defence under this section, but it would seem reasonable that any action taken to avoid an accident or to protect life or health would be a good defence. Conversely, it is less likely to succeed if the justification is that the bus stop ahead was full.

In addition, the model byelaws (byelaw no 7(c) and (d))[1] regulate the use of the stand by hackney carriages.

'7. The driver of a hackney carriage shall, when plying for hire in any street and not actually hired:

...

(c) on arriving at a stand not already occupied by the full number of carriages authorised to occupy it, station the carriage immediately behind the carriage or carriages on the stand and so as to face in the same direction; and

(d) from time to time, when any other carriage immediately in front is driven off or moved forward cause his carriage to be moved forward so as to fill the place previously occupied by the carriage driven off or moved forward.'

It can be seen that these require the vehicles to stand in line and move up as required. Although it is part of our culture[2], there is no legal requirement that a passenger must take the first hackney carriage in the line of vehicles at a stand, although that is certainly the convention. The hirer is free to choose any vehicle that they might prefer. However, in many cases the drivers will refuse to take a fare unless they are the first vehicle. Whether this is lawful will depend on whether refusing to take fare because they are not the first vehicle is a 'reasonable excuse' under TPCA 1847, s 53[3]. On most occasions, the drivers further back on the rank will refuse to take a passenger, and direct them to the first hackney carriage. However, that will not be the case if the later vehicles are charging lower fares.

1   See Appendix II.
2   See for example, the 'cab-rank' rule referred to by barristers which requires them to take any
     case (equivalent to a fare) that is offered to them.
3   See Chapter 10, para 10.93.

Jones v First Great Western Ltd

9.87

> A railway company can control access to a rank, notwithstanding that fact
> that the rank is a statutory one created under byelaws or s 63 of the Local
> Government (Miscellaneous Provisions) Act 1976.

The case of *Jones v First Greater Western Ltd*[1] confirms that when a hackney
carriage stand is located on private land, access to that stand by hackney carriages
can be controlled by the landowner, notwithstanding the requirement contained
in the byelaws that a hackney carriage that is not hired should proceed to a stand,
and if it is not full, position itself behind the last hackney carriage on the stand[2].

Bristol City Council had created a hackney carriage stand at Bristol Temple
Meads railway station, with the consent of the landowner at the time, British
Rail[3] in 1974 although no charge was made to use it. First Great Western who
took over the station in 2006 introduced a charge from 2011. Hackney carriage
proprietors would have to pay £375 per year to use the stand and those who did
not pay would not be able to use it.

This was a challenged by Jones and others on behalf of the Bristol Hackney
Carriage Association. In the High Court, the judgment was in favour of the
landowners, First Greater Western. In a lengthy judgment, His Honour Judge
McCahill QC (Sitting as a High Court Judge) dismissed all the arguments
presented by the taxi trade. He concluded:

'Under what right or power was the permit scheme introduced or
permission revoked?

275 In my judgment, it was introduced by FGW as landowner. This is
the major thrust of what FGW argued to BCC and to the claimants,
albeit backed up by the byelaws. Independently of the private rights as
landowner, I am satisfied that the byelaws too, given my construction of
them, also conferred power on FGW to restrict taxis soliciting custom
without proper authorisation.

Is the permit scheme invalid?

279 In my judgment, no. Even if the byelaws did not permit its introduction,
and even if FGW had wrongly invoked byelaw powers, its position as
private landowner, with power to control those who came on to its land,
justified and rendered lawful the permit scheme. No possible prejudice was
suffered by the claimants thereby, and the outcome would not have been
different in any respect. The permit scheme would have been introduced,
as FGW was resolved to introduce it from late 2010 onwards.'

Leave to appeal to the Court of Appeal was given and in the Court of Appeal, judgment was also given for the railway company. The principle judgment was given by Floyd LJ who commenced his conclusions in the following way[4]:

'27 It is beyond dispute that Parliament has, in the successive Acts, consistently left to the private landowner the power to withhold consent to the fixing of a taxi stand on its private land. The issue at the heart of this appeal is what consequences follow for the landowner when he does give consent and the stand is fixed. In particular, is it necessary or legitimate to imply into the statute a consent on behalf of the landowner, so long as the stand is so fixed, to permit unrestricted access to the stand by licensed taxis?'

He continued:

'34 In my judgment the reasons advanced against the implication of an unrestricted consent to access are far more compelling. Firstly, the landowner would lose, if the appellants are right, important aspects of its ability to control the use of its land. This is not a conclusion to which the court will readily come unless there are good reasons to do so.

35 Secondly, it is not difficult to find in the statutory scheme a purpose for the requirement of the owner's consent. The requirement is, as Mr Small submits, not only necessary in order to avoid the imposition on the landowner of a taxi stand at all, but also to give the landowner control over the precise placing of the stand, and other aspects of its operation. The landowner, by withholding his consent, can impose conditions on its consent which the authority can either accept or lose the opportunity of placing the stand on that land at all. One clear purpose of the requirement, in my judgment, is therefore to ensure the preservation of the owner's rights of control of its land so far as consistent with the appointment of the stand.

36 Thirdly, and following on from the second reason, I see no reason why the landowner should not give its consent on the express basis that it reserves the right to charge (or, as might have been the case with British Rail in 1974, continue to charge) a fee for entry. If it is open, as I believe it is, to the landowner to protect itself in this way, then it is difficult to see why the requirement for consent to the fixing of a stand should necessarily imply unrestricted access to the stand.

37 Fourthly I reject Mr Fletcher's attempted dichotomy between public and private stands. Once it is appreciated that the ability to withhold consent allows the landowner to control the terms on which the stand is fixed on his land, there is nothing inherently contradictory in a stand which is on private land where entry is subject to a charge.

38 Fifthly, it is not at all clear to me how, on the appellants' case, the landowner regains control of its land once it has given its consent. The appellants' case involves the proposition that consent to the appointment

of a taxi stand on private land implies a necessary consent on the part of a landowner to allow unrestricted access to the stand until the stand ceases to be designated by byelaw. As Mr Fletcher recognises, causing the stand to cease to be an appointed stand is something over which the landowner has no direct control. He described it as a political process. The amendment to the byelaw would require the consent of the local authority and approval of the Minister. The effect would be that the land would, on the appellants' argument, be burdened with an obligation which it would be impossible for the landowner to remove at will, and which would reduce the value of the land in the event of a change of use, insolvency of the owner or proposed sale. That consideration, it seems to me, makes it all the more unlikely that it was Parliament's intention to create this right.

39 Finally, it is of course possible to postulate extreme examples where, if the respondent is right and it retains a right to restrict access, the purpose of the appointment of a stand would be defeated. One example might be imposing such an exorbitant fee for the permit that no taxi driver would be prepared to pay. Another might be barring all access for no reason. However, these examples are more theoretical than real. In reality the landowner who has consented to the appointment of a stand on its land is not likely to wish to prevent taxis from using it altogether, at least for as long as he wants a stand on his land at all. I consider it much more likely that Parliament intended to leave landowners with the ability to control access, than to burden the landowner with an obligation to grant an unrestricted right of access which it might prove difficult or impossible to remove.

40 I accept Mr Small's submission that the landowner's consent to the appointment of the stand carries with it no more than that which the statutory context requires, namely that there is a taxi stand on the land subject to the regulation of the authority. This does not go far enough for the appellants' purposes. There is no reason why the landowner should not restrict access or charge a fee. It follows that I consider that the judge reached the right conclusion on this issue.

41 I would add that I have been able to reach this conclusion without the reliance which the judge understandably placed on Hulin v Cook. It is not completely clear that the appellant's argument in this case, based on the alleged consequences of consent to the appointment of the stand, was raised in Hulin v Cook. In the event, the conclusion I have reached is consistent with the conclusion reached by the Divisional Court in that case.'

It is therefore clear that notwithstanding the fact that the local authority has created a hackney carriage stand on private land, because firstly the consent of the landowner is required and secondly because the landowner's rights are paramount, the landowner has both the right and the power to prevent access to that stand. It is up to the landowner to decide how that access will be granted and provided there is no infringement of the Equality Act 2010, the landowner can employ any mechanism they wish. The most common being payment of a fee.

1   Initially heard in the High Court as *Patricia Jones, Mourad Tighilt (Suing on behalf of themselves and all other members of the Bristol Branch of the National Taxi Association) v First Greater (sic) Western Limited* [2013] EWHC 1485 (Ch), [2014] LLR 16, ChD and then in the Court of Appeal as *Jones v First Greater Western Ltd* [2014] EWCA Civ 301, [2015] RTR 3, CA.
2   Model byelaw no 7.
3   For a detailed history of the situation, see the High Court judgment. This is also informative reading for anyone with an interest in the history of hackney carriage legislation, local government reorganisation, or rail nationalisation and privatisation.
4   At para 27.

Rodgers v Taylor

9.88

> Hackney carriage parked (as opposed to waiting) on a hackney carriage stand. There were parking restrictions on the street with an exception for hackney carriages on a stand. Held: The vehicle could only wait for the next hiring – it could not be parked on the hackney carriage stand.

It is also possible to have a hackney carriage stand on a street where there are parking restrictions. This was the situation in *Rodgers v Taylor*[1] which confirms that if there is a parking restriction on a street and there is also a hackney carriage stand on that street, hackney carriages can only wait on the stand whilst they are plying for hire or waiting for a fare. They cannot simply use it as a parking place. In this case, the defendant was a licensed hackney carriage driver who parked his hackney carriage on a hackney carriage stand on a street in which there was a waiting restriction. As the judge put it succinctly[2]:

> 'There is no dispute but that Eastgate Street in Gloucester was a restricted street [i.e. there was a parking restriction in place] in which there was at the material time a hackney carriage stand. The Crown Court found, as the justices had found, that the vehicle referred to in the information was a licensed hackney carriage. It was at all material times waiting at a licensed hackney carriage stand on Eastgate Street, Gloucester, during a period for which the stand was authorised to operate. They also found that the vehicle was left locked and unattended by the appellant for a period of approximately an hour and that during that time he had been about some business of his own.
>
> The defendant contended before the Crown Court that he was entitled to leave his licensed hackney carriage at the authorised hackney carriage stand, and the reason he did that, and the time for which he did it, was immaterial. The Crown Court took the view that that contention was not correct, and that the prosecutor was right in contending that the regulations impliedly restricted licensed hackney carriages to wait at authorised hackney carriage stands only when they were plying for hire or waiting for a fare. The defendant at that time was not plying for hire or waiting for a fare. He had, to put it in the vernacular, parked up in the stand and gone about his own business.'

He was prosecuted under the Road Traffic Regulation Act 1984, s 5(1) and the City of Gloucester (Eastgate Street) (Waiting Regulation) Order 1982, art 5(1) (c). There was an exception within the traffic order whereby a vehicle could wait for 'so long as may be necessary' for a number of specified reasons, which included 'if the vehicle is a licensed hackney carriage, to wait at an authorised hackney carriage stand, during the period of time for which the stand is authorised to operate'. There was no time-limit on the operation of the stand and it was argued that that exception allowed the defendant to use the stand as a parking place.

McNeill J gave the judgment of the court and concluded (at 766):

'I take the view that the only sensible construction of those words is "so long as may be necessary to enable it to wait as a licensed hackney carriage for the purposes of the licensed hackney carriage stand", that is to say, for the period during which the licensed driver is entitled to operate as such with his licensed carriage.'

It is therefore an offence for the driver of a hackney carriage to park the vehicle on a hackney carriage stand.

Accordingly, enforcement of the use of a stand only by hackney carriages is possible in two ways. If there is a hackney carriage stand created under s 63 (or by byelaws), then other vehicles are prohibited from waiting on the stand by virtue of s 64. The actual use of the stand by hackney carriages will be regulated by the byelaws (model byelaw no 7).

However, it is also possible to have a parking restriction, expressed to exclude hackney carriages waiting at a stand. In that case, as long as the hackney carriage is using the stand correctly (ie, waiting for the next fare, and moving up when required to do so), they would not be breaching the parking restriction, but if a hackney carriage was parked on the stand, or any other vehicle was, that would be a breach of the restriction.

1   [1987] 85 LGR 762.
2   Per McNeil J.

Bradford Metropolitan Borough Council v Obaid

9.89

> Private hire driver dropped passengers off by stopping on a hackney carriage stand. Held: This was an offence because even a nominal period of being stationary amounted to 'waiting'.

In *Bradford Metropolitan Borough Council v Obaid*[1] a private hire driver dropped his passengers off at a hackney carriage stand. He was prosecuted under LG(MP)A 1976, s 64. He was acquitted by the magistrates and Bradford Metropolitan Borough Council appealed by way of case stated to the High Court. The question raised was:

'… whether stopping a motor vehicle on a taxi rank (being a stand for hackney carriages during a period of which the stand has been appointed, or is deemed to have been appointed by a District Council under the provisions of s.63 of the Local Government (Miscellaneous Provisions) Act 1976 in order to set down passengers amounts to causing or permitting it to wait there contrary to s.64(1) of the Local Government (Miscellaneous Provisions) Act 1976.'

1   [2001] EWHC Admin 536, [2001] LLR 4, QBD.

9.90

It was argued by the council that as there was a statutory defence in LG(MP)A 1976, s 64(4) allowing PSVs to wait on a stand in cases of obstruction of traffic flow, no other vehicle could wait on a stand for any reason.

9.91

Judgment was given by Latham LJ[1], with the agreement of Forbes J (at para 10):

'10. On behalf of the appellant Council, Mr Blair-Gould submitted that the existence of the special statutory defence in section 64(4) of the 1976 Act [LG(MP)A 1976, s 64(4)] suggests that Parliament recognised that, were it not for that special defence, such conduct on the part of the public service vehicle might otherwise amount to an offence under section 64(1) and (3). He submitted that stopping in order to set down passengers amounts to causing a vehicle to wait. He argued that the only reason the word "wait" is used rather than "stop" is to allow for momentary stops. "Wait", he submitted, does not mean wait for something but means to remain. Mr BlairGould suggested that this appears to be borne out by the decision in *Rodgers v Taylor* [1987] RTR 86, where the court held that a taxi could not wait at a taxi stand except in order to operate the vehicle as a taxi. In that particular case the court approved a concession by the prosecutor that there was an implied limitation of the word "wait" in such circumstances where, for example, a car had been brought to a standstill for a short period of time by a traffic jam. Mr BlairGould submitted that the purpose of the prohibition in the legislation is to allow taxis to have unrestricted access to a taxi rank and to prevent any risk of unauthorised vehicles plying for hire or being mistaken for taxis. Therefore, he argued, the time taken to set down passengers and to receive payment from them cannot be treated as *de minimis* or too short to be considered. It is central to the purpose of a taxi rank that it should be reserved for taxis and not used by private hire vehicles.

11. In my judgment, Mr BlairGould's submissions are correct and are supported by the existence of the special statutory defence in section 64(4) of the 1976 Act. The word "wait" is a word which is frequently used in English and should be given its natural and ordinary meaning, that meaning being the one which is appropriate to the context in which the

word is used. I put it that way because, like many commonly used words, "wait" is capable of a number of meanings, or shades of meaning, and its particular meaning in any given case will be that which is appropriate to its context.

12. In my view, in the context in which it is used in the present case, "to wait" means to remain in the same place for a period of time which is other than purely nominal. In my judgment, on the facts as found by the justices, although it was very short in duration, the period of time during which the respondent's motor car remained within the hackney stand in question whilst the respondent dropped off his passengers, cannot properly be regarded as purely nominal. The existence of the statutory defence under section 64(4) clearly supports that conclusion. I am of the firm opinion that the justices should have come to the conclusion that, on the facts of this case, the respondent did cause his motor car to wait on the hackney stand in question.

13. Accordingly, I would give the answer "yes" to the question posed by the justices. I would, therefore, allow this appeal, quash the order of the justices and remit the matter to the Magistrates' Court for reconsideration by a differently constituted Bench of magistrates.'

1   *Bradford Metropolitan Borough Council v Obaid* [2001] EWHC Admin 536, [2001] LLR 4, QBD.

9.92

This reinforces the view that, apart from the very limited defence given to PSVs in LG(MP)A 1976, s 64(4), hackney carriage stands are for the exclusive use of hackney carriages to wait for the next hiring.

9.93

LG(MP)A 1976, s 63 and LG(MP)A 1976, s 64 provide a useful and workable framework for the provision of hackney carriage stands. Stands are vital if the hackney carriage trade is to be able to perform its functions and fully realise its potential of providing transport for individuals. It is especially important that ranks are provided at locations that are suitable for disabled persons and at other locations which are convenient for use by persons for whom other forms of transport are less accessible, such as parents with prams or pushchairs and those who are infirm, as opposed to disabled.

9.94

To enable these provisions to work effectively, vigilance is required on the part of local authorities in taking action against those who park on hackney carriage stands illegally and also in assessing whether the stands are in the right place, whether new ones should be created or whether obsolete ones should be removed.

Picking up passengers

McKenzie v DPP

9.95

> Hackney carriage stopped at the side of the road on a stretch with double white (no overtaking) lines in the middle to pick passengers up. Was this an offence as parking in such situations would be? Held: Not an offence and a hackney carriage can stop in such a location to pick up and drop passengers off.

Consideration has been given to hackney carriages parking on hackney carriage stands[1], but the case of *McKenzie v DPP*[2] concerned a hackney carriage picking up a fare where double white lines (no overtaking) were painted in the middle of the road. It was decided that the driver of a hackney carriage did not commit an offence if he stopped to pick up or drop off passengers at a point where double white lines were painted down the centre of the road. It is usually an offence for a vehicle to park on such a stretch of road as a result of the Traffic Signs Regulations and General Directions 2016, reg 2; Sch 9, Pt 7, para 9 6[3]. There are some exceptions contained in Sch 9, Pt 7, para 9, reg 26 and the High Court decided that the use of a hackney carriage when somebody is boarding or alighting fell within the exception now contained in Sch 9, Pt 7, para 9(3), reg 26(3) and 26(4) (which was contained in reg 27(3)(a)(i) of the Traffic Signs Regulations and General Directions 1994[4] at the time of this case) 'to enable a person to board or alight from the vehicle … the vehicle cannot be used for such a purpose without stopping on the length of road'.

[1]   *Rodgers v Taylor* (1986) 85 LGR 762; see para 9.88 above.
[2]   [1997] RTR 175.
[3]   SI 2016/362 and SI 2002/3113.
[4]   SI 1994/1519.

TAXI HAILING POINTS

9.96

In the mid-1990s one local authority (Kirklees Metropolitan Borough Council) introduced what it referred to as 'taxi hailing points'. These were intended to provide an alternative to a stand, either where there was insufficient space for a stand or the location would not prove sufficiently popular with the public or the trade to justify the creation of a stand.

9.97

A hailing point is just that. It is a specific point where the public know that they will be able to hail a hackney carriage. Although the public can hail a hackney carriage anywhere and no particular provision is required, the theory behind hailing points is that the drivers will know where they are and will ensure that they pass them on a regular basis.

9.98

The pilot scheme of Kirklees Metropolitan Borough Council was a success and more hailing points have been created. As there is no provision for the hackney carriage to wait, as there is on a stand, no lengthy procedures are required before a hailing point is created, as all that is required is the erection of a suitable sign, and also making the public and hackney carriage drivers aware of the locations of the hailing points.

9.99

It should be noted that a hailing point is not an 'authorised place' for the purposes of hiring a taxi at separate fares under the provisions of the Transport Act 1985, ss 10–13[1]; it is simply somewhere to hail a hackney carriage for use at a single fare.

[1]   See para 9.120 onwards, below.

BYELAWS

9.100

Byelaws have already been referred to and can be made under TPCA 1847, s 68[1] and the Town Police Clauses Act 1889, s 6[2] to regulate a large variety of matters relating to hackney carriage operation, both of the vehicles and the drivers, together with such matters as stands.

[1]   See Appendix I.
[2]   See Appendix I.

9.101

The entire scope of the powers are to be found in the specific sections, but the main matters of concern today include:

- conduct of proprietors and drivers (TPCA 1847, s 68);
- wearing of badges by drivers (TPCA 1847, s 68);
- display of the licence number (TPCA 1847, s 68);
- number of seats in the vehicle (TPCA 1847, s 68);
- safe keeping and return of lost property (TPCA 1847, s 68); and
- notice of fares to be levied (Town Police Clauses Act 1889, s 6).

9.102

Model byelaws have been produced by the Department for Transport. Although there are no apparent plans update the model byelaws, in its Guidance Note of July 2005 to licensing authorities, it reminds them of their byelaw-making powers, and states:

'(ii) Model byelaws

11. The Department has produced a set of model byelaws as a basis for local licensing authorities. This is attached at Annex **A.** The model byelaws cover the range of standard controls which most local authorities would want to impose and we would expect local authorities to base their byelaws on the model.

(iii) Deviations from the model

12. Where a local authority wishes to introduce a byelaw which deviates from the model, we shall expect local authorities to take a rigorous approach in drafting to ensure that the tests of legal validity are met. These are set out in *Kruse* v *Johnson* [1898] 2 QB 911 as comprising **4** elements essential to validity:

- byelaws must be within the powers of the local authority which makes them;
- byelaws must not be repugnant to the general law;
- byelaws must be certain and positive in their terms; and
- byelaws must be reasonable.

13. If a local authority identifies a policy objective which it wishes to reflect in byelaws, the onus will be on the local authority to draft a suitable byelaw to put to the Department for provisional approval.

14. The onus will also be on the local authority to satisfy itself as to the validity of any proposed byelaw which it submits to the Department for approval. We would expect local authorities to have sought their own legal advice and to provide an explanation as to why they consider that any proposed byelaw is valid. We would stress that confirmation by the Secretary of State does not endow the byelaws with legal validity – only the courts can determine whether a byelaw is valid. To this extent, it is crucial that any draft byelaws are seen and approved by the Council's legal advisers. Any request for provisional approval of byelaws which deviate from the model should be accompanied by an explanation of the policy objective, a justification of their validity and confirmation that the byelaws have been approved by legal advisers.'

9.103

The penalty for breach of byelaws made under s 68 of this Act or s 6 of the Town Police Clauses Act 1889 is a fine not exceeding level 2 on summary conviction by virtue of s 183[1], of the Public Health Act 1875. Such offences are summary only.

[1]   See Chapter 6, para 6.27.

9.104

Byelaws can be revoked, amended or re-enacted by virtue of the Interpretation Act 1978, s 14.

NON-MOTORISED HACKNEY CARRIAGES

Same statutory provisions as motorised vehicles

9.105

It must be borne in mind that not all vehicles that carry the public are motorised. Many seaside resorts and other towns visited by a large number of tourists have horse-drawn carriages[1] which are licensed as hackney carriages. If they are hackney carriages, then all the statutory provisions applicable to motorised vehicles apply to them. There are no exceptions contained within the legislation for vehicles which are not motorised (other than in relation to EA 2010[2]). Clearly, the local authority will need to have policies in relation to the type of vehicle that it will license covering accommodation, safety features etc in the same way that those policies exist for motorised hackney carriages. Any horse-drawn hackney carriage licences must have conditions attached which reflect those polices. Accordingly, it will be necessary for a driver of a horse-drawn hackney carriage to hold a hackney carriage driver's licence and the prerequisite to that is that he holds a DVLA licence.

[1]   The DfT issued a 'Code of Practice for Horse Drawn Vehicles' in April 2011, available at https://www.gov.uk/government/uploads/system/uploads/attachment_data/file/291347/code-of-practice-for-horse-drawn-vehicles.pdf

[2]   See para 9.54 above.

WHETHER A VEHICLE IS A HACKNEY CARRIAGE

R v Cambridge City Council, ex p Lane

9.106

> Application to licence a trishaw/pedicab. Council took the view it was a hackney carriage and therefore driver must hold a hackney carriage drivers licence, as opposed to an omnibus. Held: That a trishaw was a hackney carriage.

In recent years another type of vehicle has also made its presence felt – the pedal-powered rickshaw often referred to as either a 'trishaw' or 'pedicab'. This was defined in the case of *R v Cambridge City Council, ex p Lane*[1] by Sir Richard Scott V-C (at 157) as:

> 'A trishaw is a cross between a rickshaw and a tricycle. Like a tricycle it has three wheels, a single front wheel and two rear wheels. Over the rear wheels a compartment in which passengers may sit is suspended. The vehicle is an adaptation of a rickshaw, replacing the individual running on the ground and pulling the vehicle with an individual using the cycle technique to provide the power for propelling the vehicle.'

The question arose in this case as to whether a trishaw was a hackney carriage or a stage coach. This distinction was important because if it was a hackney carriage, Cambridge City Council could impose conditions on both vehicle and driver licences[2]. This matter was heard by the Court of Appeal in July 1998 and in a lengthy judgment, Sir Richard Scott V-C considered the legislation in detail. This included full consideration of the distinction between a hackney carriage and a stage coach. His determination was follows (at 167):

> 'I have come to the conclusion that Mr Lane's trishaws are within the definition of a hackney carriage in section 38 [LG(MP)A 1976, s 38] and are not excluded by the proviso. They are, therefore, licensable under section 37 and, if that is right, sections 47 and 59 of the 1976 Act apply to them.'

This view was supported by Peter Gibson J and Schiemann LJ, who were also sitting.

[1]   [1999] EHLR 156, CA.
[2]   At the time that Cambridge City Council was involved in this case, there was an argument that a local authority could attach conditions to a hackney carriage driver's licence. This was rejected in the case of *Wathan v Neath Port Talbot County Borough Council* ([2002] EWHC 1634 (Admin), [2002] LLR 749, Admin Ct – see Chapter 10, para 10.74 onwards.

9.107

It is clear, therefore, that both horse-drawn and person-drawn vehicles are hackney carriages. This does, however, give rise to some difficulties. If a local authority has a numerical limit on the number of hackney carriage proprietors' licences that it will grant, that must include any horse or person-drawn vehicles. There is no provision within the legislation for there to be a test for the demand for motorised hackney carriages as opposed to non-motorised hackney carriages. They are all treated the same and accordingly, any non-motorised hackney carriages must be included in any surveys to assess demand and, likewise, licences granted to non-motorised hackney carriages must be included in the total number of licences that the authority will grant.

9.108

Also, the horse and person powered hackney carriages will also be bound by the fare table set by the local authority, and, as above, there is no mechanism for different fares to be set for, or charged by, hackney carriages that are non-motorised.

9.109

Another problem is the requirement that a hackney carriage driver cannot refuse to take a fare within the district (or zone if they exist within the district) unless he has a reasonable excuse[1]. If the horse is tired, or the person peddling the trishaw likewise, that might not be seen as a reasonable excuse. The same would apply to a journey which would encounter a large number of hills. As a consequence, the existence and popularity of horse-drawn hackney carriages and trishaws are largely limited by the geography of a district.

[1]   TPCA 1847, s 53. See Chapter 10, para 10.93.

9.110

The most significant problem will arise when the provisions of EA 2010 are finally introduced in relation to wheelchair accessible vehicles. This is because EA 2010, s 173(1) states:

> '"taxi"—
> (a) means a vehicle which is licensed under section 37 of the Town Police Clauses Act 1847 or section 6 of the Metropolitan Public Carriage Act 1869, and
> (b) … applies to Scotland,
> but does not include a vehicle drawn by a horse or other animal;'

Although this will overcome any difficulty in relation to horse-drawn vehicles, trishaws do not appear to be exempt from EA 2010 and it is difficult to see how a trishaw can be made accessible for wheelchairs.

HORSE DRAWN OMNIBUSES

9.111

It is possible for a horse drawn vehicle (but not a person powered vehicle) to be licensed by the local authority as an omnibus under the provisions of the TPCA 1899, and byelaws made under s 6 of the 1889 Act. Although repealed for motorised public service vehicles by the provisions of the Road Traffic Act 1930, these provisions remain in force for non-motorised vehicles. This allows the omnibus to follow a fixed route and charge the passengers separate fares. This may be a more suitable method of licensing both horse drawn vehicles and pedicabs in tourist areas.

HIRING HACKNEY CARRIAGES AT SEPARATE FARES

9.112

The Transport Act 1985 introduced the concept of hackney carriages being used as part of a local transport service. With the deregulation of buses, which the Transport Act 1985 also introduced, an opportunity was seen for hackney carriages to be used effectively as small buses to enable groups of people to be transported at separate fares by hackney carriage, rather than by a PSV[1].

[1] These provisions are contained in the Transport Act 1985, ss 10–13. See Appendix I.

A scheme must be created by the local authority

9.113

Before hackney carriages can be used in this way, a scheme has to be created by the local authority. Local authorities have a discretion as to whether or not to do this, but are placed under a duty to do it if a request is made in writing by least

10% of the current (at the time that the request is made) holders of hackney carriage proprietors' licences[1].

[1]   Transport Act 1985, s 10(4).

9.114

The scheme must specify where hackney carriages can be hired, referred to as 'authorised places' and must also 'specify the requirements to be met for purposes of the scheme in relation to the hiring of taxis at separate fares'. It is less than clear what this means, but it would appear to include the frequency of hackney carriages visiting authorised places and other matters of that nature.

9.115

Under the Transport Act 1985, s 10(6), the local authority is given a discretion in relation to the scheme to include provisions relating to fares, any kind of indication on the vehicle that it is available for the hiring at separate fares, the type of arrangements that are in place for such use and any conditions that they may wish to apply. Once a scheme is in place, it can be varied by the local authority if they wish to modify it in any way[1].

[1]   Transport Act 1985, s 10(7).

9.116

Finally, the Secretary of State is also given a power to impose schemes by order should he think fit.

9.117

It is not clear how many schemes have been created since the introduction of this legislation. However, such a scheme has been used annually by Rushmoor Borough Council in Hampshire since 2004 to service the Farnborough Air Show which has been extremely effective.

Advance bookings

9.118

The Transport Act 1985, s 11 allows advance booking of both hackney carriages and private hire vehicles at separate fares, provided that all the passengers book the journey in advance and each of them agree to the fact that other people would be present paying their own fare. No scheme is required to enable this to take place and the arrangement can be made at any time. Again, no data appears to exist as to how often this provision is used, but there are probably occasions when it might prove useful.

9.119

When a hackney carriage is being used under the terms of the Transport Act 1985, ss 10 or 11, it is still subject to the same controls as it would be if it was used conventionally as a hackney carriage. Enforcement of the scheme will lie with the local authority.

A restricted PSV operator's licence

9.120

The final possibility introduced by the Transport Act 1985 is contained in the Transport Act 1985, s 12, which enables the hackney carriage proprietor to apply to the Traffic Commissioners for a restricted PSV operator's licence. This would enable him then to use his hackney carriage to provide 'a local service with one or more stopping places within the area of the authority which granted the taxi licence of the vehicle in question'. Section 12 is subject to the provisions contained in the Local Services (Operation by Taxis) Regulations 1986[1]. Again, it is not clear how many restricted PSV operators' licences have been granted to hackney carriage proprietors since the availability of this power[2].

[1]   SI 1986/587. See Appendix I.
[2]   See Department of Transport circular 7/86 explaining these provisions at Appendix II. Note should also be taken of the provisions of the Transport Act 2000, s 265, which allows a PSV operator to run small PSVs to undertake private hire work in certain circumstances. This is considered at Chapter 12, para 12.45ff.

9.121

The Transport Act 1985 was seen as a great liberalising piece of legislation which would open up transport services to competition. In relation to hackney carriages, its success has been limited. A large number of local authorities still impose quantity restrictions on hackney carriages, thereby automatically reducing competition in that area of the local transport field and the idea of hackney carriages becoming an integral part of a deregulated local bus service does not appear to have fulfilled the expectations of the Government of the time. This may change if the power to limit the numbers of hackney carriage licences is removed[1]), but that will remain to be seen.

[1]   See Chapter 8, para 8.164.

9.122

The DfT *Best Practice Guide*[1] makes reference to all these above provisions:

'FLEXIBLE TRANSPORT SERVICES

92. It is possible for taxis and PHVs to provide flexible transport services in a number of different ways. Such services can play a valuable role in meeting a range of transport needs, especially in rural areas – though potentially in many other places as well. In recent years there has been a

significant increase in the provision of flexible services, due partly to the availability of Rural Bus Subsidy Grant and Rural Bus Challenge Support from the Department.

93. The Department encourages local licensing authorities, as a matter of best practice, to play their part in promoting flexible services, so as to increase the availability of transport to the travelling public. This can be done partly by drawing the possibilities to the attention of taxi and PHV trade. It also should be borne in mind that vehicles with a higher seating capacity than the vehicles typically licensed as taxis (for example those with 6, 7 or 8 passenger seats) may be used for flexible services and should be considered for licensing in this context.

94. The main legal provisions under which flexible services can be operated are:

Shared taxis and PHVs – advance bookings (section 11, Transport Act 1985): licensed taxis and PHVs can provide a service at separate fares for up to eight passengers sharing the vehicle. The operator takes the initiative to match up passengers who book in advance and agree to share the vehicle at separate fares (lower than for a single hiring). An example could be passengers being picked up at home to go to a shopping centre, or returning from the shops to their homes. The operator benefits through increased passenger loadings and total revenues.

Shared taxis – immediate hirings (section 10, Transport Act 1985): such a scheme is at the initiative of the local licensing authority, which can set up schemes whereby licensed taxis (not PHVs) can be hired at separate fares by up to eight people from ranks or other places that have been designated by the authority. (The authority is required to set up such a scheme if holders of 10% or more of the taxi licences in the area ask for one.) The passengers pay only part of the metered fare, for example in going home after a trip to the local town, and without pre-booking, but the driver receives more than the metered fare.

Taxibuses (section 12, Transport Act 1985): owners of licensed taxis can apply to the Traffic Commissioner for a 'restricted public service vehicle (PSV) operator licence'. The taxi owner can then use the vehicle to run a bus service for up to eight passengers. The route must be registered with the Traffic Commissioner and must have at least one stopping place in the area of the local authority that licensed the taxi, though it can go beyond it. The bus service will be eligible for Bus Service Operators Grant (subject to certain conditions) and taxibuses can be used for local authority subsidised bus services. The travelling public have another transport opportunity opened for them, and taxi owners have another business opportunity. The Local Transport Act 2008 contains a provision which allows the owners of PHVs to acquire a special PSV operator licence and register a route with the traffic commissioner. A dedicated leaflet has been sent to licensing authorities to distribute to PHV owners in their area alerting them to this new provision.

95. The Department is very keen to encourage the use of these types of services. More details can be found in the Department's publication 'Flexible Transport Services' which can be accessed at: http://www.dft.gov. uk/pgr/regional/buses/bol/flexibletransportservices'

---

¹   DfT, *'Taxi and Private Hire Vehicle Licensing: Best Practice Guidance'* (October 2006, revised March 2010), paras 92–95 available from http://www.dft.gov.uk/pgr/regional/taxis/taxiandprivatehirevehiclelic1792. See Appendix II.

BUS LANES AND DOUBLE WHITE LINES

9.123

In a number of parts of the country, hackney carriages are allowed to use bus lanes under the provisions of the Road Traffic Regulation Act 1984. Those who support this, take the view that hackney carriages are an integral part of public transport and therefore should be entitled to use bus lanes in the same way as buses.

R v Oxfordshire County Council, ex p Measor

9.124

> Decision by Highway Authority to prohibit hackney carriages from using bus lanes because not 'public transport' Held: Not an unreasonable decision.

The case of *R v Oxfordshire County Council, ex p Measor*[1] concerned a decision by Oxfordshire County Council to prohibit the use of bus lanes in certain parts of Oxford City by hackney carriages. This was challenged by means of judicial review by the Secretary of the City of Oxford Licensed Taxi Cab Association. The challenge was based on the grounds that: first, the County Council was wrongly advised in law in that it was not possible to devise a sign which allowed the use by bus lanes of hackney carriages; secondly, that the decision to ban hackney carriages from the bus lanes was taken without any proper inquiry in to the effect that would be caused if hackney carriages were allowed to use the bus lanes; thirdly, that there should have been a public inquiry; and finally, that the decision was contrary to the County Council's transport policy, which was to give priority to public transport. The matter was considered by Popplewell J, who dismissed the application. He took the view that the incorrect advice concerning the sign was 'a comparatively small part of the decision-making process' and he decided 'in my judgment, it played little or no part in the decision of the councillors'.

In relation to the second point concerning the absence of proper inquiry he stated:

'The question arises, were the County Council entitled, through their members and all these various committees, to use their own observations and common sense to decide whether the presence of taxis in a bus lane was likely to be of advantage in the flow of traffic for the public generally? They concluded that the buses were more likely to travel more speedily and without interference if there were not taxis in the bus lane. It is very difficult to fault that conclusion. It is, to me, self-evident, the more traffic there is in the bus lanes, the less speedily buses will move. They were entitled to form the view which they had formed from their own observations that this was the risk. I do not put it any higher than that. There was a risk that if taxis went down the bus lane then private hire vehicles would follow. Again, it is self-evident, irrespective of taxis going in the bus lanes, that private citizens do use bus lanes. But anything that discourages private citizens from using the bus lane is to be encouraged. The whole purpose of this exercise was to ensure that the general public had the use of public service vehicles to the best advantage of the public.

Accordingly, I am not persuaded that it was unreasonable for these bodies to form their own view, either from their own experience, or applying their own sense, and to come to a conclusion that the exclusion of taxis from bus lanes was likely to be conducive to the proper movement of public service vehicles in these particular roads.'

He concluded that the County Council was quite within its rights to decide not to hold a public inquiry.

Finally, in relation to the argument that the County Council had departed from their policy to give priority to public transport, he stated the following:

'Finally it is submitted that the respondent's policy was to give priority to public transport and public transport means, and it is accepted, taxis. The failure to allow taxis is therefore in breach of that policy. I take the view that the County Council were perfectly entitled, in relation to giving priority to public transport, to make a distinction between various forms of public transport. They were not bound under the policy to give priority to taxis in addition to giving priority to buses. Giving priority to public transport is a general phrase which they have followed, namely, by providing bus lanes for public service vehicles.'

1   (4 July 1997, unreported), [1997] CLY 4303.

9.125

This case demonstrated that it will ultimately be a matter for the local authority (being the highway authority) to decide whether or not to allow hackney carriages to use bus lanes. There will always be variation across the country as different local authorities will have different views. The same would apply to the use of bus lanes by private hire vehicles. Indeed, it is difficult to see the strength of an argument that would prohibit private hire vehicles from using bus lanes whilst allowing hackney carriages to do so, but that is the stance that is currently taken by many local authorities.

Chapter 10

Hackney carriage drivers outside London

INTRODUCTION

10.1

The role of the hackney carriage driver is important in a number of ways.

Firstly, only a licensed hackney carriage driver can drive a hackney carriage[1], as the cases of *Hawkins v Edwards*[2] and *Yates v Gates*[3] show[4].

Secondly, the responsibilities placed on and the power and control available to, a hackney carriage driver are significant. A hackney carriage driver is responsible not only for their passengers, but also for the control of the vehicle and all other road users. Also, a hackney carriage driver has almost complete control over the passengers, especially in the case of a lone passenger.

This chapter examines how such a licence is obtained and to whom it can be granted.

---

[1] In relation to private hire vehicles, many local authorities issue 'restricted' driver's licences for the spouses and other relatives of private hire vehicle proprietors to enable them to drive the private hire vehicle when it is not working. This is achieved by means of conditions attached to the driver's licence. See Chapter 14, para 14.24 onwards for more details. As conditions cannot be attached to a hackney carriage driver's licence (see *Wathan v Neath Port Talbot CBC* (12 July 2001, unreported), Admin Ct; para 10.74 onwards below), such an approach is not possible for hackney carriages, and accordingly, any one driving a hackney carriage must pass the same tests, and meet the same criteria.

[2] [1901] 2 KB 169; Chapter 8, para 8.4.

[3] [1970] 1 All ER 754; Chapter 8, para 8.5.

[4] See Chapter 8, paras 8.4–8.6.

GRANTING THE LICENCE

10.2

The requirement to hold a hackney carriage driver's licence is contained in the Town Police Clauses Act 1847, s 46 (TPCA 1847).

'Drivers not to act without first obtaining a licence

46 No person shall act as driver of any hackney carriage licensed in pursuance of this or the special Act to ply for hire within the prescribed distance without first obtaining a licence from the commissioners, which licence shall be registered by the clerk to the commissioners, and such fee as the commissioners may determine shall be paid for the same; and every such licence shall be in force until the same is revoked except during the time that the same may be suspended as after mentioned.'

It can be seen that this requires the district council to register the drivers' licences, which it issues, and allows the district council to charge 'such fee as [it] may determine shall be paid'. It is also clear from the wording that the driver's licence must have been issued by the same authority that licensed the hackney carriage[1].

[1]   See *Darlington Borough Council v Thain* [1995] COD 360 QBD; see para 10.6 below.

10.3

Further provisions relating to the actual grant of a driver's licence are contained in the Local Government (Miscellaneous Provisions) Act 1976 (LG(MP)A 1976), especially LG(MP)A 1976, s 53(1)(b)[1], which was amended in 2015 to introduce a presumption that driver's licences should be granted for a three-year duration. The wording of the revised subsection is somewhat peculiar:

'(b) Notwithstanding the provisions of the Public Health Act 1875 and the Town Police Clauses Act 1889 , but subject to section 53A, every licence granted by a district council under the provisions of the Act of 1847 to any person to drive a hackney carriage shall remain in force for three years from the date of such licence or for such lesser period, specified in the licence, as the district council think appropriate in the circumstances of the case.'

This is therefore not a mandatory three-year driver's licence, but rather an indication that drivers licences should last three years. There is no further guidance as to what a district council might think to be appropriate circumstances and therefore this will remain a matter for the local authority's discretion.

[1]   See Appendix I.

10.4

The DfT Best Practice Guide[1] has not been reissued since the introduction of the amendment and currently states suggests that local authorities should usually grant three year licences:

'Duration Of Licences

55. It is obviously important for safety reasons that drivers should be licensed. But it is not necessarily good practice to require licences to be renewed annually. That can impose an undue burden on drivers and

licensing authorities alike. Three years is the legal maximum period and is in general the best approach. One argument against 3-year licences has been that a criminal offence may be committed, and not notified, during the duration of the licence. But this can of course also be the case during the duration of a shorter licence. In relation to this, authorities will wish to note that the Home Office in April 2006 issued revised guidance for police forces on the Notifiable Occupations Scheme. Paragraphs 62–65 below provide further information about this scheme.

56. However, an annual licence may be preferred by some drivers. That may be because they have plans to move to a different job or a different area, or because they cannot easily pay the fee for a three-year licence, if it is larger than the fee for an annual one. So it can be good practice to offer drivers the choice of an annual licence or a three year licence.'[2]

It does seem clear that an authority cannot insist on granting a three-year licence and if for some reason an applicant wants a one-year licence, the authority should oblige. That request and the subsequent one-year licence would appear to be 'appropriate in the circumstances of the case' as the exercise of the local authority's discretion.

[1]   DfT, *'Taxi and Private Hire Vehicle Licensing: Best Practice Guidance'* (October 2006, updated March 2010), available at http://www.dft.gov.uk/pgr/regional/taxis/taxiandprivatehirevehiclelic1792.

[2]   That extract is obsolete, but as it is the most recent published information by the Department of Transport in relation to drivers' licences it is worth noting. It is also important to recognise that the Home Office Notifiable Occupations Scheme was cancelled in March 2015.

10.5

TPCA 1847, s 47[1] makes it an offence for anyone to drive a hackney carriage unless they hold a current hackney carriage driver's licence. This section also makes it clear that even if a driver's licence is held but has been suspended, then in fact the person does not hold a licence and would commit an offence under s 47.

[1]   See Appendix I.

Darlington Borough Council v Thain

10.6

A hackney carriage proprietor had been refused a renewal of his hackney carriage drivers licence. He drove his licensed hackney carriage for the purposes of collecting his daughter from a party. Held: That he was not a licensed driver, and as a hackney carriage was always a hackney carriage the offence under section 47 had been committed.

A hackney carriage proprietor will breach TPCA 1847, s 47 by allowing an unlicensed hackney carriage driver to drive the vehicle. In the case of *Darlington Borough Council v Thain*[1], the view that a hackney carriage could only be driven by a person who held a hackney carriage driver's licence was restated. The argument that a hackney carriage could be driven by anyone when it was not working as a hackney carriage was rejected. Judgment was given by Tuckey J who stated:

'*Yates v Gates* [1972] QB 27, [1970] 1 All ER 754 is a decision of this court. In his judgment the Lord Chief Justice, Lord Parker, at P31.H says:

> "The justices took the view that since on the occasion in question the sign "for hire" was not illuminated, and in the circumstances that the defendant was not driving the vehicle for hire, therefore he did not require a license,"

He then says that the Justices in that case dismissed the information on that basis. After referring to s 46 he said:

> "Pausing there, it is undoubtedly true that the defendant did not have the necessary licence, and that the vehicle in question was itself licensed to ply for hire. The justices, however, took the view that unless the vehicle was plying for hire it would not be a hackney carriage, the driver of which would require a licence. That, of course, envisages that a vehicle licensed as a hackney carriage as defined in section 38 of the Town Police Clauses Act, 1847, must change its character from moment to moment; when it is not plying for hire it is not a hackney carriage, and when it is plying for hire it is a hackney carriage."

He then says, and these are the important words:

> "In my judgment section 46 is perfectly plain. No person shall drive any vehicle which is licensed as a hackney carriage, whatever it may be doing at the particular moment, unless he himself has a licence as required by section 46."

The Court allowed the prosecutors appeal.

With that very clear statement of principle it is not surprising, in my judgment, that the Justices were (when they reconsidered the case) decided that they had got it wrong. In my judgment they had. This offence is committed whenever a licensed taxi is driven by someone who is not licensed to do so, irrespective of his intention at the material time.

The question which the Justices posed for our consideration is whether in law a person who is not the holder of a Hackney carriage driver's licence may drive his own motor vehicle for a private purpose, if that motor vehicle is licensed as a Hackney carriage, and on the face of it bears the appearance of a Hackney carriage. I would answer that question, "no".'

---

[1]   [1995] COD 360.

10.7

In addition, the lending or parting with a hackney carriage driver's licence is also an offence. The only occasion in which a hackney carriage driver's licence can be parted with is to comply with TPCA 1847, s 48[1], which requires the proprietor of a hackney carriage to retain the licences of those he employs as drivers.

[1]   See Appendix I.

10.8

A fee can be charged for the grant of a hackney carriage driver's licence[1].

[1]   See Chapter 4, para 4.12 onwards.

Criteria for the grant of a licence

10.9

It is now necessary to consider what criteria must be met before a person can be granted a hackney carriage driver's licence.

10.10

TPCA 1847 is silent as to any qualification that the driver must hold or any criteria that must be met before a hackney carriage driver's licence can be granted. Such requirements are however, contained in LG(MP)A 1976, s 59(1) and are also subject to the overriding aim of hackney carriage and private hire licensing as stated in the DfT's '*Taxi and Private Hire Vehicle Licensing: Best Practice Guidance*'[1]:

'The aim of local authority licensing of the taxi and PHV trades is to protect the public.'

The LG(MP)A 1976 states:

'Qualifications for drivers of hackney carriages

59(1) Notwithstanding anything in the Act of 1847, a district council shall not grant a licence to drive a hackney carriage—
(a)   unless they are satisfied
    (i)   that the applicant is a fit and proper person to hold a driver's licence; and
    (ii)   that the applicant is not disqualified by reason of the applicant's immigration status from driving a hackney carriage; or
(b)   to any person who has not for at least twelve months been authorised to drive a motor car, or is not at the date of the application for a driver's licence so authorised.'

[1]   October 2006, revised March 2010, available from http://www.dft.gov.uk/pgr/regional/taxis/taxiandprivatehirevehiclelic1792.

10.11

There are three requirements contained within LG(MP)A 1976, s 59 that must be satisfied by a potential hackney carriage driver.

1.   That the 'applicant is a fit and proper person to hold a [hackney carriage] driver's licence'.

2.   That the 'applicant is not disqualified by reason of the applicant's immigration status from driving a hackney carriage'.

3.   That the person must have 'been authorised to drive a motor car' for at least 12 months before the date of application, not the date of grant.

In reality, the third requirement may lead to a situation where a full driving licence has been held for considerably longer than 12 months by the time the grant of the licence is made, due to delays in the administrative process.

These requirements be considered in reverse order.

Authorised to drive a motor car

Crawley Borough Council v Crabb

10.12

> Licensed private hire driver was disqualified from driving for six months. At the end of that period he applied for a new private hire driver's licence which was refused on the basis that he had not held a full licence for 12 months at the date of application. Held: That a period of 12 months after the disqualification was not required.

The case of *Crawley Borough Council v Crabb*[1] deals with the situation where a person has been disqualified from driving. This can be as a result of too many points being added to a licence as a result of road traffic offences[2] (commonly referred to as 'totting'[3]) or for any other reason, eg, with drink-driving the mandatory minimum one-year ban[4]. In *Crabb*, a private hire driver had held a DVLA licence since 1974. On 16 August 1993, he was disqualified from driving for six months. That disqualification ended on 24 February 1994 and on 2 March 1994, he applied to Crawley Borough Council for a private hire driver's licence. The council refused the application on the grounds that he had not held a licence for a 12-month period prior to the date of application. Mr Crabb appealed and the magistrates granted him a licence. The council appealed, by way of case stated and judgment was given by Carnwath J. He stated (at 206D):

> 'As a matter of ordinary language, it seems to me that a person who has held a licence for 12 months in the past, and does in fact hold a licence at the date of application, is entitled to qualify, notwithstanding that there is no continuity between the two periods.
>
> If that interpretation leads to unworkability, or to an absurdity, then no doubt one would seek to adjust the reading accordingly. However, I do not think that can be said here. One could understand a policy that a period of 12 months following a disqualification should be required, but equally one can see, if someone has served his disqualification period and is considered to be a fit and proper person to hold a licence (under section 51(1)(*a*) [LG(MP)A 1976, s 51(1)(a)]) then he should be entitled to claim a new licence and should not be further penalised. I cannot say that

the interpretation taken by the justices is so absurd or unjust as to justify changing or reinterpreting the words.

It is also necessary to bear in mind that the section is not specifically concerned with the consequences of the disqualification. It is concerned with the general position in relation to the grant of licences. It would not be right to interpret it by reference to some supposed purpose which is related to problems arising from disqualification.'

This confirms that following a disqualification, a further period of one year does not have to elapse after the applicant has been allowed to drive again, before he can seek a hackney carriage driver's licence. Provided that at least one year has elapsed since he passed his driving test and was originally authorised to drive, then the statutory test is satisfied.

1   [1996] RTR 201, QBD.
2   Road Traffic Offenders Act 1988, ss 28, 29, 35 and Sch 2, amended by the Road Traffic Act 1991.
3   Short for 'totting up' ie adding together the number of penalty points accumulated on the licence.
4   Road Traffic Act 1988, s 4 and the Road Traffic Offenders Act 1988, ss 34, 97 and Sch 2.

10.13

However, at least one local authority has a policy of not granting a hackney carriage driver's licence until at least two years have elapsed following the return of the licence after any period of disqualification. This is one of its tests of fitness and propriety and, as such, is considered below.

The situation is different if following a conviction, the person's DVLA licence is revoked and the DVLA driving test has to be taken again[1]. The person would therefore need to hold their new driver's licence for at least 12 months before applying for a hackney carriage or private hire driver's licence.

1   This can occur when a 'new driver' (that is a driver within two years of passing their driving test) accumulates six penalty points. Revocation is automatic under the provisions of the Road Traffic (New Drivers) Act 1995 and a new licence cannot be issued unless and until the person passes a full driving test.

10.14

With regard to the second requirement, 'authorised to drive a motor car' is defined in LG(MP)A 1976, s 59(1A) This states:

'59–(1A) For the purposes of subsection (1) of this section a person is authorised to drive a motor car if—
(a)   he holds a licence granted under Part III of the Road Traffic Act 1988 (not being a provisional licence) authorising him to drive a motor car, or
(b)   he is authorised by virtue of section 99A(1) or section 109(1) of that Act to drive in Great Britain a motor car.'

10.15

The Road Traffic Act 1998, s 99A(1) allows a person who holds a 'Community licence' to drive vehicles in Great Britain which he would be allowed to drive in his own country. A Community licence is defined in the Road Traffic Act 1988, s 108 as a driving licence issued by a state that is a party to the Agreement on the European Economic Area ('EEA') (other than the UK) signed at Oporto on 2 May 1992, as amended by the Brussels Protocol dated 17 March 1993. The countries to which this applies are:

EU countries: Austria, Belgium, Bulgaria, Croatia, Republic of Cyprus, Czech Republic, Denmark, Estonia, Finland, France, Germany, Greece, Hungary, Ireland, Italy, Latvia, Lithuania, Luxembourg, Malta, Netherlands, Poland, Portugal, Romania, Slovakia, Slovenia, Spain, Sweden.

Non-EU countries: Iceland, Liechtenstein and Norway.

10.16

The Road Traffic Act 1988, s 109(1) allows a person who holds a Northern Ireland driving licence to drive vehicles in Great Britain which he is licensed to drive in Northern Ireland and the Deregulation (Taxis and Private Hire Vehicles) Order 1998[1] allows a Northern Ireland driving licence to be sufficient for the purposes of obtaining a hackney carriage licence in England and Wales.

[1]   SI 1998/1946.

10.17

It is also possible to drive under the Road Traffic Act 1988, Pt III with certain foreign driving licences if the licence is an 'exchangeable licence' as defined the Road Traffic Act 1988, s 108. Countries whose licences fall within this definition include: Gibraltar (Road Traffic Act 1988, s 108), Andorra, Australia, Barbados, British Virgin Islands, Republic of Cyprus, The Falkland Islands, The Faroe Islands, Guernsey, Hong Kong, Isle of Man, Japan, Jersey, Malta, Monaco, New Zealand, Republic of Korea, Singapore, Switzerland, Zimbabwe by virtue of the Driving Licences (Exchangeable Licences) Order 1999[1] as amended.

A person who is lawfully resident in the UK can drive on an exchangeable driving licence for up to 12 months[2]. After that period they must apply to exchange that driving licence for a UK one and provided that application is made within[3] five years of the date of becoming resident, a UK licence will be granted in exchange[4].

[1]   SI 1999/1641.
[2]   See reg 80 of the Motor Vehicles (Driving Licences) Regulations 1999, SI 1999/2864.
[3]   See Road Traffic Act 1988, ss 97 and 97A.
[4]   See reg 10 of the Motor Vehicles (Driving Licences) Regulations 1999, SI 1999/2864.

10.18

Provided one of these full driving licences has been held for at least one year at the date of application, the driver satisfies the criteria contained in LG(MP)A 1976, s 59(1)(b), even if he has not been driving in the UK during that time.

10.19

Although many local authorities prefer the driving licence to reflect the address in the UK where the applicant resides, there is no requirement for the holder of an

EEA driving licence to exchange it for a UK driving licence[1]. However, because the holder of an exchangeable driving licence can only use it for 12 months from the date of becoming resident, after 12 months it must be exchanged for a UK licence which will then reflect the UK address of the licensee.

[1]   Road Traffic Act 1988, s 99A.

The applicant must not be 'disqualified by reason of the applicant's immigration status from driving a hackney carriage'

10.20

The Immigration Act 2016 ('IA 2016') amended the LG(MP)A 1976 to add an additional criterion to the requirements to be satisfied before a hackney carriage drivers licence can be granted. An applicant for a new hackney carriage drivers' licence, or the renewal of a driver's licence granted before the introduction of this amendment[1], must not be disqualified from holding a hackney carriage driver's licence by reason of his immigration status. Only persons with a right to both remain in the UK and also work in the UK can be granted a hackney carriage driver's licence and if either of those requirements are lost, any such licence that has been issued will lapse.

Sections 79A and 79B have been inserted into LG(MP)A 1976 which detail those who are disqualified from holding any hackney carriage drivers' (or private hire drivers or operators licence) by reason of immigration status, and explain the meanings of immigration offences and immigration penalties:

'79A Persons disqualified by reason of immigration status

(1) For the purposes of this Part of this Act a person is disqualified by reason of the person's immigration status from carrying on a licensable activity if the person is subject to immigration control and—
(a)   the person has not been granted leave to enter or remain in the United Kingdom; or
(b)   the person's leave to enter or remain in the United Kingdom—
   (i)   is invalid;
   (ii) has ceased to have effect (whether by reason of curtailment, revocation, cancellation, passage of time or otherwise); or
   (iii) is subject to a condition preventing the person from carrying on the licensable activity.

(2) Where a person is on immigration bail within the meaning of Part 1 of Schedule 10 to the Immigration Act 2016—
(a)   the person is to be treated for the purposes of this Part of this Act as if the person had been granted leave to enter the United Kingdom; but
(b)   any condition as to the person's work in the United Kingdom to which the person's immigration bail is subject is to be treated for those purposes as a condition of leave.

(3) For the purposes of this section a person is subject to immigration control if under the Immigration Act 1971 the person requires leave to enter or remain in the United Kingdom.

(4) For the purposes of this section a person carries on a licensable activity if the person—
(a) drives a private hire vehicle;
(b) operates a private hire vehicle; or
(c) drives a hackney carriage.'

Section 79B defines what is meant by 'Immigration offence' and 'immigration penalty':

'79B Immigration offences and immigration penalties
(1) In this Part of this Act "immigration offence" means—
(a) an offence under any of the Immigration Acts;
(b) an offence under section 1 of the Criminal Attempts Act 1981 of attempting to commit an offence within paragraph (a); or
(c) an offence under section 1 of the Criminal Law Act 1977 of conspiracy to commit an offence within paragraph (a).
(2) In this Part of this Act "immigration penalty" means a penalty under—
(a) section 15 of the Immigration, Asylum and Nationality Act 2006 ("the 2006 Act"); or
(b) section 23 of the Immigration Act 2014 ("the 2014 Act").
(3) For the purposes of this Part of this Act a person to whom a penalty notice under section 15 of the 2006 Act has been given is not to be treated as having been required to pay an immigration penalty if—
(a) the person is excused payment by virtue of section 15(3) of that Act; or
(b) the penalty is cancelled by virtue of section 16 or 17 of that Act.
(4) For the purposes of this Part of this Act a person to whom a penalty notice under section 15 of the 2006 Act has been given is not to be treated as having been required to pay an immigration penalty until such time as—
(a) the period for giving a notice of objection under section 16 of that Act has expired and the Secretary of State has considered any notice given within that period; and
(b) if a notice of objection was given within that period, the period for appealing under section 17 of that Act has expired and any appeal brought within that period has been finally determined, abandoned or withdrawn.
(5) For the purposes of this Part of this Act a person to whom a penalty notice under section 23 of the 2014 Act has been given is not to be treated as having been required to pay an immigration penalty if—
(a) the person is excused payment by virtue of section 24 of that Act; or
(b) the penalty is cancelled by virtue of section 29 or 30 of that Act.
(6) For the purposes of this Part of this Act a person to whom a penalty notice under section 23 of the 2014 Act has been given is not to be

treated as having been required to pay an immigration penalty until such time as—

(a) the period for giving a notice of objection under section 29 of that Act has expired and the Secretary of State has considered any notice given within that period; and

(b) if a notice of objection was given within that period, the period for appealing under section 30 of that Act has expired and any appeal brought within that period has been finally determined, abandoned or withdrawn.'

In addition, by virtue of s 51(1ZA) the local authority must have regard to the Guidance issued by the Secretary of State:

'(1ZA) In determining for the purposes of subsection (1) whether an applicant is disqualified by reason of the applicant's immigration status from driving a private hire vehicle, a district council must have regard to any guidance issued by the Secretary of State.'

The Guidance was issued on 1 December 2016[2] and details the three steps that a local authority must take to ensure that an applicant satisfies the test[3]. In brief the steps are:

1. Original documents from specified lists (Annex A) must be provided by the applicant;
2. The documents must be verified and examined in the presence of the applicant; and
3. A copy of all the documents must be made and retained.

These checks must be made in respect of every applicant from December 2016, but need only be undertaken on renewals where the applicant has a 'time-limited immigration permission to be in the UK and work'[4].

Where a driver only has a limited time to remain in the UK, s 53A prevents a local authority from granting a drivers' licence beyond the period of permission to remain, and it can be for a shorter period. If the applicant has an extended leave to remain, the local authority cannot grant a licence for more than six months, but again it can be for a shorter period.

'53A Drivers' licences for persons subject to immigration control

(1) Subsection (2) applies if—

(a) a licence within section 53(1)(a) or (b) is to be granted to a person who has been granted leave to enter or remain in the United Kingdom for a limited period ("the leave period");

(b) the person's leave has not been extended by virtue of section 3C of the Immigration Act 1971 (continuation of leave pending variation decision); and

(c) apart from subsection (2), the period for which the licence would have been in force would have ended after the end of the leave period.

(2) The district council which grants the licence must specify a period in the licence as the period for which it remains in force; and that period must end at or before the end of the leave period.'

If a licensed driver loses the right to remain in the UK during the currency of a licence, the licence ceases to have effect[5]. This is covered by s 53A(6) and no action needs to be taken by the local authority (eg, revocation) because simply, the licence ceases to be of effect. In those circumstances, the licence and badge must be returned to the local authority within seven days of the expiry of the licence[6].

In any case where the licence has either ended or ceases to have effect, failure to surrender it within seven days is an offence under s 53A(9). The maximum penalty on summary conviction is a fine not exceeding Level 3 on the standard scale, and there is also provision for a continuing daily penalty of £10 for each day after conviction. Those fine levels can be altered by the Secretary of State under s 53A(10).

[1]   These provisions came into effect on 1 December 2016.
[2]   '*Guidance for Licensing Authorities to Prevent Illegal Working in the Taxi and Private Hire Sector in England and Wales*' available at https://www.gov.uk/government/uploads/system/uploads/attachment_data/file/574059/Guidance-for-licensing-authorities-to-prevent-illegal-working-in-the-taxi-and-private-hire-sector-in-England-and-Wales.pdf See Appendix II.
[3]   Above at page 10 onwards.
[4]   Above at page 12.
[5]   Although the licence will lapse, there is no mechanism contained within the legislation for the Border Force to notify a local authority when a right to work or remain ceases.
[6]   See s 53A(7).

The applicant must be a 'fit and proper person'

10.21

It is the requirement that no licence should be granted to someone unless they are a fit and proper person[1] that contains the biggest area of difficulty and causes committees or officers the most concern.

What is meant by the term 'fit and proper person' and how is a local authority to determine whether an applicant is indeed fit and proper to hold a hackney carriage drivers' licence?

'Fit and proper person' is a phrase that occurs in legislation but has never been defined with any degree of particularity. It does have a certain archaic ring to it, and in the second decade of the 21st Century, a satisfactory alternative expression is 'safe and suitable person'. That appears to neither add nor detract from the original, but does bring it more up to date, in a phrase that is more readily understood and acted upon by all parties concerned in the consideration of an applicant or existing licensee.

It is vital that the role of a hackney carriage driver is properly understood by local authorities and unless it is, there is a considerable risk that unsuitable people will be granted licences, leading to both direct potential danger to passengers and other road users and a loss of confidence in the whole hackney carriage and private hire licensing regime[2].

A hackney carriage driver has significant power and with such power comes significant responsibility. When a passenger gets into a hackney carriage, following a hailing, a hiring from a rank or a pre-booking, they are placing themselves in the hands of the driver. The passenger and all other road users rely on the assumption that the driver is a good driver, with sufficient driving experience to safely negotiate the perils of the public highway. The passenger (or passengers) also rely on the expectation that they will not be harmed in any way during that journey. That harm could arise from a road traffic accident (which should be covered by the first assumption) but could also result from the actions of the driver towards the passenger. The driver's behaviour should be above reproach at all times and should never cause the passenger to have any concerns about their safety or welfare.

The driver has the ability to take a passenger to a remote or secluded place for nefarious purposes and there is little a passenger can do to prevent such a journey taking place. It is equally possible for a driver to rob a passenger, overcharge a passenger, or abuse a passenger either physically or verbally.

Passengers come from every section of society, and encompass persons of all colours, creeds, abilities and disabilities. A great many passengers are vulnerable persons, due to age, infirmity or disability, intoxication or drug use, as well as emotional issues. Drivers must ensure that the welfare of the passenger is their overriding aim and act accordingly.

Within this context, drivers should also take sensible steps to protect themselves from accusations of questionable behaviour. This includes caution about making contact with passengers on social media, particularly if the passengers are children or vulnerable adults.

It is also important to recognise that a hackney carriage driver must be and must remain, a safe and suitable person at all times, not simply when they are driving a hackney carriage. The character of a person does not alter simply because they are wearing a badge and driving a licensed vehicle.

People who are prone to violence do not become meek and mild; the dishonest person does not become honest; the poor driver does not become better; the person with alcohol or drug problems does not become clean and sober; and the sexual predator does not lose their tendencies simply because they are driving a hackney carriage. Councils must look at the whole of a person's character before determining their safety and suitability to hold or retain a hackney carriage drivers' licence.

In light of all the above considerations, it may seem surprising that there is no judicially approved test of fitness and propriety.

In the absence of such a test, a number of local tests have developed. These tend to be based on a test similar to the following:

> 'Would you (as a member of the licensing committee or other person charged with the ability to grant a hackney carriage driver's licence) allow your son or daughter, spouse or partner, mother or father, grandson or granddaughter or any other person for whom you care, to get into a vehicle with this person alone?'

If the answer to this question (or a similar test) is an unqualified 'Yes', then the test is probably satisfied. If there are any doubts in the minds of those who make the decision, then further consideration should be given as to whether this person is a fit and proper person to hold a hackney carriage driver's licence[3].

[1]   LG(MP)A 1976, s 59(1)(a). See Appendix I.
[2]   It is reasonable to refer to both hackney carriage and private hire drivers here, because the criteria for grant of a licence are identical.
[3]   It is important to recognise that the role of the local authority is not to interview the applicant for a job, neither does the local authority have the ability to offer any kind of job to the applicant. The local authority must limit its consideration to the fitness and propriety of the individual – see para 10.23 onwards below.

10.22

Bingham LCJ made the following observation in the case of *McCool v Rushcliffe Borough Council*[1], a case concerning the refusal to grant a private hire driver's licence:

> 'One must, as it seems to me, approach this case bearing in mind the objectives of this licensing regime which is plainly intended, among other things, to ensure so far as possible that those licensed to drive private hire vehicles are suitable persons to do so, namely that they are safe drivers with good driving records and adequate experience, sober, mentally and physically fit, honest, and not persons who would take advantage of their employment to abuse or assault passengers.'

This was then effectively restated by Mr Justice Silber in the case of *Leeds City Council v Hussain*[2]. In the context of a suspension of a driver's licence 'for any other reasonable cause' he said (at [25]):

> '... the purpose of the power of suspension is to protect users of licensed vehicles and those who are driven by them and members of the public. Its purpose, therefore, is to prevent licences being given to or used by those who are not suitable people taking into account their driving record, their driving experience, their sobriety, mental and physical fitness, honesty, and that they are people who would not take advantage of their employment to abuse or assault passengers.'

These passages clearly support the above test for fitness and propriety.

[1]   [1998] 3 All ER 889.
[2]   [2002] EWHC 1145 (Admin), [2003] RTR 199; see para 10.67 below.

Matters to take into account when determining fitness and propriety

CONSIDERATION OF PREVIOUS CONVICTIONS

10.23

Since March 2002, hackney carriage (and private hire) drivers have been included within the Rehabilitation of Offenders Act 1974 (Exceptions) Order 1975[1]. The consequence of this is that all convictions, irrespective of age, sentence imposed or offence committed, remain live for an applicant for a hackney carriage driver's licence. This means that they can all be taken into account, although following the approach taken in the *Waveney* case[2], it seems reasonable that the local authority should only take convictions into account which are relevant to an application for a licence[3].

1   SI 1975/1023.
2   *Adamson v Waveney District Council* [1997] 2 All ER 898; see Chapter 5, para 5.12 onwards.
3   The question of previous criminal convictions and the effect of the Rehabilitation of Offenders Act 1974 were considered in Chapter 5. Local authorities must require the applicant to obtain an enhanced disclosure from the Disclosure and Baring Service (DBS).

10.24

The DfT Best Practice Guide states[1]:

'Criminal Record Checks

58. A criminal record check is an important safety measure particularly for those working closely with children and the vulnerable. Taxi and PHV drivers can be subject to a Standard Disclosure (and for those working in "Regulated Activity" to an Enhanced Disclosure) through the Criminal Records Bureau. Both levels of Disclosure include details of spent and unspent convictions, cautions reprimands and final warnings. An Enhanced Disclosure may also include any other information held in police records that is considered relevant by the police, for example, details of minor offences, non-conviction information on the Police National Computer such as Fixed Penalty Notices and, in some cases, allegations. An Enhanced Disclosure is for those working in Regulated Activity (footnote: "Regulated Activity" is defined in The Safeguarding Vulnerable Groups Act 2006 (Miscellaneous Provisions) Regulations 2009) .and the Government has produced guidance in relation to this and the new "Vetting and Barring Scheme" which is available at www.isagov.org.uk/default.aspx?page=402. [The Department will issue further advice as the new SVG scheme develops.]

59. In considering an individual's criminal record, local licensing authorities will want to consider each case on its merits, but they should take a particularly cautious view of any offences involving violence, and especially sexual attack. In order to achieve consistency, and thus avoid the risk of successful legal challenge, local authorities will doubtless want to have a clear policy for the consideration of criminal records, for example the number of years they will require to have elapsed since the commission of particular kinds of offences before they will grant a licence.

60. Local licensing authorities will also want to have a policy on background checks for applicants from elsewhere in the EU and other overseas countries. One approach is to require a certificate of good conduct authenticated by the relevant embassy. The Criminal Records Bureau website (www.crb.gov.uk) gives information about obtaining certificates of good conduct, or similar documents, from a number of countries.

61. It would seem best practice for Criminal Records Bureau disclosures to be sought when a licence is first applied for and then every three years,

even if a licence is renewed annually, provided drivers are obliged to report all new convictions and cautions to the licensing authority.'

Unfortunately this is obsolete in a number of ways[2], but the overall message is still sound. The next step is to obtain details of those convictions.

[1]   DfT, *'Taxi and Private Hire Vehicle Licensing: Best Practice Guidance'* (October 2006, revised March 2010), paras 58–61 available from http://www.dft.gov.uk/pgr/regional/taxis/taxiandprivate hirevehiclelic1792. See Appendix II.

[2]   1. All hackney carriage and private hire applicants must produce an enhanced DBS Certificate.
      2. The Criminal Records Bureau is now the Disclosure and Barring Service.
      3. The Safeguarding Vulnerable Groups Act and the Vetting and Barring Scheme have not been applied to hackney carriage and private hire drivers.
      4. The Guidance suggests that drivers should be required to repot new convictions and cautions to the local authority, but this may be problematic as conditions cannot be attached to a hackney carriage drivers' licence.

10.25

The guidance in the Department of Transport and Home Office circular 2/92[1] is still relevant, albeit dated and superseded by the DfT *Best Practice Guide*[2] in relation to the consideration of criminal convictions, but the parts of it relating to the police checks under LG(MP)A 1976, s 51(1A) and LG(MP)A 1976, s 59(1A) are now obsolete.

[1]   See Appendix II.

[2]   DfT, *'Taxi and Private Hire Vehicle Licensing: Best Practice Guidance'* (October 2006, revised March 2010), paras 42–44, available at http://www.dft.gov.uk/pgr/regional/taxis/ taxiandprivatehirevehiclelic1792. See Appendix II.

10.26

The local authority will require the applicant to obtain an Enhanced Disclosure from the Disclosure and Barring Service[1] and in addition as a matter of prudence, many local authorities require applicants to complete a statutory declaration listing all convictions, both spent and unspent as well as other matters that might be relevant such as cautions, fixed penalty notices, ASBOs, Civil Injunctions, County Court Judgments and so on.

[1]   See Chapter 5, para 5.19 onwards.

10.27

The consideration of criminal convictions in relation to the holding of a licence is by no means an exact science. In 1992, the Department of Transport and Home Office Circular 2/92 contained (at Annex D) guidelines relating to the relevance of convictions. LACORS (Local Authorities Coordinators of Regulatory Services – later renamed as LG Regulation) issued updated guidelines in 2010[1]. A number of local authorities still base their policies on one or the other of these documents, but a significant number of have altered their policies and substantially tightened the criteria. However it has been created, it is vital that it has a policy in respect of previous convictions for hackney carriage (and also private hire) drivers and that policy is regularly reviewed. This will lead to greater consistency in decision-making, and also provide guidance to applicants on the approach that the council is likely to take in respect of any previous convictions they may have[2].

1   'Taxi and PHV Licensing Criminal Convictions' Policy' available at http://www.ihsti.com/ lacors/ContentDetails.aspx?id=24387 . In January 2017 the LGA consulted on a new draft policy.
2   See Chapter 5, para 5.38.

R v Crewe and Nantwich Borough Council, ex p Barker

10.28

> Revocation of PH Drivers' licence, following an application which did not reveal guilty pleas on dishonesty offences as he had yet to be sentenced. On a Judicial Review it was argued that the licence could not be revoked as the offences had not been committed since the grant. Held: The Council could consider the convictions and take action against the licence.

The case of *R v Crewe and Nantwich Borough Council, ex p Barker*[1] concerned a decision by Crewe and Nantwich Borough Council to revoke a private hire driver's licence which had been granted to Mr Barker[2]. There had been some history of complaints and concerns about Mr Barker and he had been warned in the past about his behaviour in relation to his licence. He applied for renewal of his licence on 2 September 1994 and on the application form he referred to a conviction for 'handling'. He did not reveal that he had pleaded guilty to a number of offences but was awaiting sentence. In giving judgment, MacPherson J stated:

> 'That was totally inaccurate. The offences were fourfold offences which took place on various dates in 1993 to which I have already referred. He was arrested in July 1994, I was told today. He may have appeared before the court in August 1994, on the way to his eventual conviction and sentence, but to say that he was convicted of an offence and to indicate "August 1994 – handling in Crewe" was not correct. What took place was that on 7 September 1994 he did appear in the magistrates' court and pleaded guilty to four serious offences. The Memorandum of Conviction … records convictions on 5 October 1994 and thus includes the sentence to which I have referred, namely 80 hours of community service, and reveals that he was convicted, on his own plea at summary trial, of using an MOT certificate which he believed to be false with the intention of inducing the Sun Alliance Insurance Company to accept it as genuine. He also admitted dishonestly receiving a stolen MOT certificate. There were two further offences which were parallel, but separate, one of using an MOT certificate with the intention of inducing the Highways Motor Policies of Lloyds to accept it as genuine and another of receiving stolen goods, namely, that MOT certificate.'

There was a meeting between an officer of the local authority and Mr Barker, during which time Mr Barker informed the local authority that the conviction was still pending and the case needed to go back to court. The local authority conducted the police check, but that did not reveal any offences because sentence was not passed until about a week after the search was conducted. The judge stated:

'The long and the short of it is, however, that it is palpable, in my judgment, and certainly probable, that on 15 September this man, Mr Barker, did not inform the Council that he had pleaded guilty to four serious offences.'

He continued:

'Why he did not do that and indicated that the matter was still pending is, perhaps, obvious. If he had disclosed the full situation then and there he would never have been granted a licence. It seems to me to be absurd to think that somebody who has been convicted of offences in relation to MOT certificate, and handling of stolen goods, and inducing insurance companies to think that the certificate is genuine, would or could or should ever be granted a driver's licence to drive a taxi or a hire car. That man is palpably dishonest. I cannot believe that it can be tolerated that people who have been dishonest in connection with motor vehicle documentation of that kind would be granted a licence. However, that is, to some extent, irrelevant. My views on that matter are strong and I express them.'

1   [1996] CLY 3969.
2   Although the case concerned a private hire driver, it is relevant in the case of a hackney carriage driver as the criteria for issue, suspension, revocation or refusal to renew are identical.

10.29

The question was then raised as to whether these were offences which had been committed since the grant of the licence, in which case the local authority could take action under LG(MP)A 1976, s 61(1)(a)[1], or whether they were offences that had been committed prior to the grant of the licence, in which case the local authority would have to take action under s 61(1)(b). Reference was made by MacPherson J to the case of *R v Recorder of Manchester*[2] [sic] as to whether a conviction is a conviction on the entering of a guilty plea or only on sentencing. The judge concluded[3]:

'It seems to me, in the circumstances of this case, that the dual nature of the conviction referred to in the authority, to which both counsel have referred in their skeletons, means that in this case and for the purposes of a licence and proceedings of this kind the conviction was not complete until sentence.'

However, that argument seems to be unresolved in this case because the local authority revoked the licence under s 61(1)(b) – any other reasonable cause – the judge concluded:

'Looking at the whole picture, as they were entitled to do, in my judgment, they were able, under 61(1)(b), with the information which they then had in full, including the evidence from Mr Lee [from the council] and Mr

Barker as to what happened on 15 September, to say that this man's licence should be revoked. That is what they did. It seems to me unlikely that any other body, looking at the same information, would have reached any different decision.'

1   See Appendix I.
2   This appears to be a reference to *S (an infant) v Manchester City Recorder* [1969] 3 All ER 1230, although this is not made at all clear in the judgment.
3   *R v Crewe and Nantwich Borough Council, ex p Barker* [1996] CLY 3969.

10.30

There was an argument raised that the decision to revoke was *Wednesbury* unreasonable, but that was not pursued with any great vigour. MacPherson J concluded[1] by saying:

'I conclude simply by saying this. If, in strictly legal terms, there had been something in Mr Wood's argument about s 61(1)(*b*) and if, therefore, there had been some legal flaw in the consideration of this case I would undoubtedly not have exercised my discretion to grant relief in the circumstances of this case. I have to look at the whole picture. Here is a man with previous history, with serious convictions in MOT certificates and insurance fraud, and giving misleading history. Here was a man who did not give full information to the person to whom he applied for the renewal of his licence. It seems to me that he has absolutely no merit whatsoever and he would not be entitled to the relief which is or may have been granted at the discretion of this court. On all hands, therefore, or on all sides, or in all directions, this application fails and it is dismissed.'

This case is useful as it gives a graphic illustration of judicial displeasure in relation to a person with serious convictions seeking a private hire driver's licence.

1   *R v Crewe and Nantwich Borough Council, ex p Barker* [1996] CLY 3969.

Nottingham City Council v Farooq (Mohammed)

10.31

> Refusal to renew a driver's licence because driver had failed to reveal convictions for dishonesty. Discovered on a police check and council felt not a fit and proper person. On appeal the magistrates allowed the appeal. The council appealed by way of case stated. Held: A local authority or a court on appeal must accept convictions and not seek to go behind them or reconsider them.

R v Crewe and Nantwich Borough Council, ex p Barker[1] was followed in terms of judicial displeasure, rather than on any particular principles, by the case of *Nottingham City Council v Farooq (Mohammed)*[2]. This case concerned a licensed private hire driver who did not inform Nottingham City Council of his conviction for theft and obtaining property by deception[3]. That was in breach of the conditions applied to his licence. Subsequently, he applied to renew his licence and he failed to mention the convictions. As a consequence of a police check, the convictions came to light and the local authority decided not to renew his licence on the grounds that he was not a fit and proper person, as evidenced by the fact that he had not informed the authority of his convictions at the time and had then subsequently failed to declare them on his application form. He appealed and the magistrates granted him a licence as he maintained that he had not committed the offences, but he had accepted responsibility for them to assist a friend. He also claimed that he had overlooked the need to report the matter to the local authority as he had completed the form in haste. In the magistrates' court his licence was granted because the magistrates accepted his arguments and despite the advice of their clerk, went behind the convictions, concluding that he was a person who had behaved foolishly, rather than a person who at any stage had been deliberately deceitful. Nottingham City Council appealed by way of case stated and the matter was heard by Tucker J.

1   [1996] CLY 3969.
2   [1998] CLY 4865.
3   Again, this case concerned a private hire driver, but it is relevant in the case of a hackney carriage driver as the criteria for issue, suspension, revocation or refusal to renew are identical.

10.32

The first question which had been raised by the justices in the case was:

'Were we, the Justices, acting as a civil appeal court, entitled to review the merits of the respondent's convictions for theft and deception?'

Tucker J stated[1]:

'To that my answer is unhesitatingly "No". The reason for that is that the convictions were recorded on a plea of guilty, and if they had been contested would have had to be proved so as to make the Justices sure of their truth. In other words, the Justices would have had to be satisfied beyond reasonable doubt of the respondent's guilt, whereas in a civil case a very different standard of proof applies, that is to say the balance of probabilities.

In my opinion it is not open to Justices on a civil appeal such as this to review convictions, and I am glad to see that my opinion coincides with that of the Justices' clerk.'

Tucker J then referred to the case of *Adamson v Waveney District Council*[2] and *Hunter v Chief Constable of the West Midlands Police*[3]. He continued:

'So, although I have already indicated my answer to the question, my complete answer to the first question is this: that Justices acting as a Civil Appeal Court are not entitled to review the merits of the respondent's convictions for theft and deception.'

1   *Nottingham City Council v Farooq (Mohammed)* [1998] CLY 4865.
2   [1997] 2 All ER 898; see para 5.12 onwards.
3   [1982] AC 529.

10.33

The second question concerned the possibility of an adjournment to enable the council to deal with the assertion that the appellant was not guilty of the matters for which he was convicted. Tucker J dismissed that as irrelevant because the magistrates could not go behind the conviction.

10.34

Three further questions which were contained in the case stated are extremely important and the views of Tucker J are useful in relation to establishing fitness and propriety of an applicant for a licence. As a consequence, the remainder of his judgment[1] is reproduced below:

'Then I come to the third question which is:

"In concluding that the incorrect completion of the forms for renewal of the respondent's licence, by omitting reference to the convictions, was through foolishness and ignorance rather than deliberate deception, was the court entitled to hold that the respondent was nonetheless a fit and proper person within the meaning of section 61 of the Local Government (Miscellaneous Provisions) Act 1976 to hold a licence?"

My answer to that question is in these terms. The Magistrates' Court is not precluded from finding that they are not satisfied that a person is not a fit and proper person within s 61 of the 1976 Act to hold a licence merely because he has not been guilty of deliberate deception. Failing to comply with the requirements of the 1976 Act due to extreme foolishness rather than deliberate deception is not a basis for holding that they are satisfied that the person is a fit and proper person to hold a driver's licence.

The Justices' fourth question is:

"Where a local authority had decided that a person was not a fit and proper person within the meaning of section 61 of the Local Government (Miscellaneous Provisions) Act 1976 because he made a false statement for the purposes of obtaining a combined hackney carriage driver's licence and private hire vehicle driver's licence and where the Justices are satisfied as a fact that the statement was false, should the Justices, in considering an appeal against the decision, have regard to whether the statement was made knowingly or recklessly in determining whether the person was a fit and proper person?"

Pausing there. It is, of course, material to consider the terms of the appropriate section of the 1976 Act, which is section 57, subsection (1) of which provides:

"A district council may require any applicant for a licence ... to submit to them such information as they may reasonably consider necessary to enable them to determine whether the licence should be granted ..."

Subsection (3) of that section provided:

"If any person knowingly or recklessly makes a false statement or omits any material particular in giving information under this section, he shall be guilty of an offence."

So my answer to the fourth question is this. The magistrates ought to consider whether an applicant making a false statement to obtain a licence did so knowingly or recklessly in considering whether he is a fit and proper person to hold a licence.

The fifth and final question which the Justices ask is:

"Was the decision one which no reasonable court could reach in the light of the case law in *Stepney Borough Council v Joffe* [1949] 1KB 599, DC[2] and the guidance contained in DOT Circular 2/92, Annex D, 13/97[3]?"

I have already referred to the decision in the Case mentioned by the Justices. As to the circular, that contains guidelines relating to the relevance of convictions. The general policy is set out, including the fact that the overriding consideration should be the protection of the public.

So far as offences of dishonesty are concerned, they are referred to under para 3(*g*) of the document in these terms:

"Hackney carriage and PHV drivers are expected to be persons of trust. The widespread practice of delivering unaccompanied property is indicative of the trust that business people place in drivers. Moreover, it is comparatively easy for a dishonest driver to defraud the public by demanding more than the legal fare etc. Overseas visitors can be confused by the change in currency and become 'fair game' for an unscrupulous driver. For these reasons a serious view should be taken of any conviction involving dishonesty. In general, a period of three to five years free of convictions should be required before entering an application."

Therefore, in answer to the question which the Justices posed, I am obliged to say that the decision was not one that the Magistrates' Court could reasonably come to on the material before it.'

1   *Nottingham City Council v Farooq (Mohammed)* [1998] CLY 4865.
2   See Chapter 3, para 3.19.
3   See Appendix II.

10.35

It is thus clear from the case that a conviction which has not been appealed is a conviction, irrespective of the motives or circumstances which led to a plea of guilty being entered.

Secretary of State for Transport, Local Government and the Regions v Snowdon

10.36

> PCV (bus) driver convicted of two counts of indecent assault on a 15 year old during a coach trip when he was the driver. His appeal to the magistrates' court against the finding of the Traffic commissioner was successful. This was appealed by the Secretary of State (ie, the Traffic Commissioner) by way of case stated. Held: The magistrates could take into account his livelihood, and entry on the Sexual Offenders Register was not an automatic bar to holding a PCV drivers licence.

The case of *Secretary of State for Transport, Local Government and the Regions v Snowdon*[1] concerned a man who had been licensed to drive passenger carrying vehicles (under a passenger carrying vehicle or PCV driver's licence). He was convicted during the currency of the licence of two offences of indecent assault on a female, for which he was sentenced to 100 hours community service on each count, to be served concurrently and his name was to be entered on the Sex Offenders Register for a period of five years under the provisions of the Sex Offenders Act 1997. As a consequence of the discovery of that offence, which concerned a 15-year-old girl who was travelling as a passenger on the coach driven by Mr Snowdon during the course of a school excursion to Spain, the Traffic Commissioner (who licences such drivers) concluded that Mr Snowdon did not meet the criteria to continue to hold a licence. The determination of that question is given to the Traffic Commissioner by virtue of the Road Traffic Act 1988, ss 112 and 113. The requirement placed upon the Traffic Commissioner is that he 'shall determine whether the applicant for a licence is or is not, having regard to his conduct, a fit person to hold a licence to drive ... passenger carrying vehicles'.

[1]   [2003] RTR 15.

10.37

Mr Snowdon appealed to the magistrates, who upheld his appeal, taking into account the fact that he needed the licence for his livelihood, that his employers had agreed both to continue to employ him as a driver and had presented references to the magistrates who heard the appeal, and also that he had expressed his regret for the offences.

10.38

The Secretary of State for Transport, Local Government and The Regions appealed against that finding by way of case stated. The arguments were that:

1.   His holding of a licence and the employment that flowed from that was not a relevant consideration when determining his fitness to hold such a licence.

2. Registration on the Sex Offenders Register was incompatible with holding a PCV drivers licence.

10.39

Both these arguments were rejected by Mr Nigel Pleming QC (sitting as a deputy High Court judge). He took the view that if the effect of the Sex Offenders Act 1997 had been intended to prevent such offenders from holding a PCV licence, that would have been made clear in the Act. He also took the view that the matters that the magistrates took into account, namely his employment, references and the fact that his employer had continued to employ him, were not irrelevant matters and as a consequence the magistrates were correct to have regard to them.

10.40

In relation to the first point Mr Pleming stated[1]:

'34. Whether or not the Magistrates were right to regard the current employment status of Mr Snowdon as being a relevant and compelling consideration. As already noted, the Secretary of State's contention is that "employment status is an irrelevant consideration" when considering that (sic) Section 112 and 121 of the Act. I accept and proceed upon that basis that "conduct" referred to in Section 112 suggests what has been done, how a person has behaved etc. However, the person's conduct must also be considered in context and in the round. Here, Mr Snowdon's convictions do, of course, raise questions that must be given the most careful consideration. But it does not follow that references from an employer, for example, are irrelevant, or that explanations as to the detail of a person's life –both private and commercial, after the incident and/or the conviction – should not also be taken into account. Any other approach, in my opinion, would be too arid and would not allow an applicant's personal circumstances to be considered. Here, it is indeed unfortunate that Mr Snowdon's case was not referred to the Secretary of State on conviction. However, as a matter of fact it was not and, it would in my opinion be wrong to deny Mr Snowdon the opportunity of relying on evidence from his employer who had stood by him both during and after his conviction and, apparently, with full knowledge that Mr Snowdon's name is now on the Sex Offenders Register.

35. The Magistrates had to form their own judgment and, as with the Secretary of State or the Traffic Commissioners, they were only obliged to "have regard to his conduct" before moving on to decide whether or not Mr Snowdon was a fit and proper person to hold the licence applied for. Ms Rahman's [for the Secretary of State] submission to me was, in effect, that having regard to this person's conduct, (the commission of two sex offences on a young girl when she was a passenger on his bus) was so serious that no reasonable decision-maker – here the Magistrates – could have concluded that he was "a fit person to hold the licence applied for". I accept, of course, that the Magistrates could have reached the same conclusion as the Traffic

Commissioner but I do not accept that it was the only conclusion they could have reached. If it was Parliament's intention that conviction of a sex offence and/or presence on the Sex Offender's Register *automatically* disqualifies a bus driver from holding a PCV licence, then it could have said so. There has been ample opportunity in the statutory provisions referred to in the earlier parts of this judgment for Parliament to have adopted that course. But so long as Magistrates are allowed to form their own judgment and reach their own conclusions as to whether or not, "having regard to his conduct", the person before them is a fit person to hold the licence applied for, then the court should be loathe to interfere with the decision eventually made.'

[1]   *Secretary of State for Transport, Local Government and the Regions v Snowdon* [2003] RTR 15.

10.41

In relation to the second point, the judge stated[1]:

'36. Whether the Magistrates were right to regard registration on the Sex Offenders Register as not being incompatible with holding a passenger carrying vehicle driver's licence. The Secretary of State questions whether the Magistrates were right to regard registration of the Sex Offenders Register as not being incompatible with holding a passenger carrying vehicle driver's licence. The Secretary of State argues that presence on the Sex Offenders Register automatically equates to unfitness to hold any PCV licence. During the course of her submissions Ms Rahman put it in a slightly different way, but substantially to the same effect. She argued that the circumstances of the offence involving a fifteen year old female passenger on a bus, coupled with registration on the Sex Offenders Register is such as to have led the Magistrates to only one conclusion, that Mr Snowdon should not be licensed to drive such a vehicle. I accept that the existence of such a conviction, or convictions, is a very powerful indicator that such a person is not a fit person to hold the licence applied for. Certainly, applying the extended meaning of 'conduct' as set out in section 121(1)(b) [Public Passenger Vehicles Act 1981] the decision-maker is allowed to take account of, indeed obliged to take account of, any conduct which is "in any other respect relevant to his holding a passenger carrying vehicle driver's licence". Clearly there are strong arguments for concluding that Mr Snowdon should not have been allowed to continue his former occupation as a bus driver. Another bench of Magistrates may, reasonably and rationally, have reached the decision that Mr Snowdon's appeal should have been dismissed. However, as already noted, if the intention of Parliament was that the presence of a person's name on the Sex Offenders Register automatically deprived that person of the right, or ability, to drive a passenger carrying vehicle, Parliament could, and should, have said so. Parliament did not so provide. In my judgment, the question of fitness, and the impact on the question of fitness of registration on the Sex Offender's Register is essentially a matter – when on appeal – for the Magistrates. Referring to Ms Rahman's additional note, set out in part above, I do not accept her proposition "that the presence of an applicant for a licence on the Sex Offenders' Register is determinative of the issue of risk". Under the licensing legislation the assessment process calls for a move sophisticated, and wide-ranging approach than that statement suggests.'

1   *Secretary of State for Transport, Local Government and the Regions v Snowdon* [2003] RTR 15.

10.42

This case makes it clear that in relation to a PCV licence an entry on the Sex Offenders Register is not an automatic barrier to the grant of a driver's licence. It should be noted that the wording of the Public Passenger Vehicles Act 1981 is slightly different from LG(MP)A 1976: for the PCV licence the person has to be a 'fit person', whereas for a hackney carriage licence a person has to be a 'fit and proper person'. Accordingly, it cannot be regarded as a direct authority on the point in relation to hackney carriage drivers. It must be contrasted with the decisions in *Leeds City Council v Hussain*[1] and *Cherwell DC v Anwar*[2] where it was expressly stated that the impact of losing or not obtaining a driver's licence on the livelihood and family of the individual was not a relevant consideration in determining whether the person was 'fit and proper' to hold a driver's licence.

1   [2003] RTR 13.
2   [2012] RTR 15.

10.43

Ultimately this case is stating that each decision has to be judged on its merits, and that the magistrates are quite capable of making that decision on an appeal from the Traffic Commissioners, or in relation to hackney carriages from the local authority. An entry on the Sex Offenders Register is not an automatic bar to holding such a licence, but it is clearly a relevant consideration that should be taken into account. Equally, it is useful to note that the court was not impressed with the argument that references, employment status and loss of livelihood were irrelevant factors. Whilst this case is not authority for a proposition that in a certain set of circumstances a driver should not be granted a licence, neither is it authority that in a certain set of circumstances a driver must be granted a licence. It is merely a reminder that magistrates, the superior courts and local authorities can properly come to different conclusions on a similar set of facts.

Pinnington v TfL

10.44

Hackney carriage driver convicted of possession of cannabis who also failed to renew his licence and drove for five months unlicensed and uninsured. Licence application to renew was refused and that was upheld on appeal. On a challenge to the High Court. Held: That there was insufficient evidence to determine that he was not a fit person to hold a hackney carriage driver's licence within London.

Pinnington v Transport for London[1] is a case where the facts, if not unique, are certainly unusual. Pinnington was a hackney carriage driver in London. He failed to inform TfL of a change of address, because his renewal reminder was sent to the wrong address. He then failed to renew his driver's licence and also had a conviction for possession of cannabis. His application for a new driver's licence was refused. That decision was upheld by the magistrates and he challenged that by way of case stated to the High Court.

As already mentioned, the facts were unusual. Pinnington had become a hackney carriage driver in 2006, following his father into the trade. There were no complaints and he had a good driving record. His father became ill and had grown cannabis at home for personal use only, to relieve the symptoms, and before he died, asked Pinnington to dispose of the plants after his death as he did not want any trouble for his relatives. This was what Pinnington was attempting to do on 29 March 2009, but he was stopped by the police, who found the drugs, and he was arrested. He did not inform TfL of his arrest (there was no requirement to do so) and he was not charged until 1 June 2010.

By the time he was charged, he was no longer working as a taxi driver. His licence had expired on 27 December 2009 but he did not realise, and continued working until May 2010 when the fact he had been driving without a licence for five months came to light at a routine check. At that point he handed in his (expired) licence.

He pleaded guilty and was convicted of possession of cannabis on 5 July 2010, when the magistrates refused a prosecution request to consider an adjournment to establish whether a caution should be offered. He was sentenced to a community order of six months with a requirement for 80 hours of unpaid work.

He then applied for a new hackney carriage driver's licence on 1 February 2011 and disclosed his conviction. 'It took TFL a long time to deal with the application'[2] and on 25 August 2011 the application was refused. The London legislation allows an applicant to seek a review of the decision by TfL[3], followed by an appeal to the magistrates' court. Pinnington requested such a review. After a meeting with a TfL officer, Mr Kennedy, the recommendation was made that the licence be granted. The Deputy Director who made the final decision did not follow the recommendation and refused the application, but the reasons for the refusal were sparse:

'All he [stated was] that "taking all the circumstances into account that Mr Pinnington raised at the hearing, I support the original decision not to re-issue the licence therefore disagree with the recommendation from the personal hearing."[4]'

Pinnington appealed to the magistrates' court, but the appeal was dismissed. The magistrates took the view that they could not go behind the conviction[5], they had to follow the TfL policy, driving without a licence and insurance meant he was not a fit person, the conviction for possession of cannabis meant he was not a fit person, but little weight was to be placed on the failure to notify the change of address. Pinnington then appealed by way of case stated to the High Court.

[1]   [2013] EWHC 3656 (Admin), [2014] LLR 316, Admin Ct.
[2]   Per Mrs Justice Andrews DBE at paragraph 7.
[3]   See the Transport Act 1985, s 17.

4   Per Mrs Justice Andrews DBE at paragraph 9.
5   This is correct , see *Nottingham City Council v Farooq (Mohammed)* [1998] CLY 4865; see para 10.31 above.

10.45

The case was heard by Mrs Justice Andrews DBE who took the view in relation to his drugs conviction, that had he appealed, the conviction would have been set aside under the ruling in *R v Murphy*[1]. In addition, he was not working as a taxi driver at the time of his conviction, as he had handed his lapsed licence back.

Turning to the decision of TfL and the subsequent appeal to the magistrates' court, the judge agreed that it was correct that the magistrates could not go behind the drugs conviction, but stated[2]:

'19 The Justices were quite right to say that they could not go behind the conviction. This was an answer to an argument that was raised before them to the effect that Mr Pinnington's solicitors might have advised him wrongly that the case of Murphy deprived him of a defence. But the fact of the conviction should have been the starting point of their consideration not the end of it.'

The judge had already considered the policy and its impact[3]:

'16 The Justices were also obliged to have regard to any relevant policy of the licensing authority. In this case, the policy relating to drugs offences appears in the staff manual (version 8):

"i. 3.3.17   Drugs

ii. A serious view is taken of any drug related offence. The nature and quantity of the drugs, whether for personal use or supply are issues which should be considered. An application from an applicant who has an isolated conviction for an offence related to the possession of drugs within the last 3–5 years may be considered, but consideration must be given to the nature and quantity of the drugs, as well as the sentence imposed by the court."

17 Thus, as a matter of policy, an application by someone who has an isolated conviction for the possession of drugs would not normally be entertained until at least three years had elapsed since the conviction. However there remains a discretion to entertain such an application notwithstanding that three years have not elapsed. Although policy considerations are of importance, the policy has to be applied in a manner that is consistent with the proper approach to the underlying issue, namely, is the applicant a fit and proper person to hold a taxi licence notwithstanding that he has a conviction for the possession of drugs?'

She continued[4]:

'At the [appeal] hearing TFL had originally argued that policy could only be departed from in "exceptional circumstances". That put the bar too high and was accepted as doing so later in the hearing. What the Justices were saying, therefore, albeit somewhat inelegantly, was that the fact that both parties now agreed that it was unnecessary to show "exceptional circumstances" made no difference to their decision. However, this statement reveals nothing about the basis on which that decision was reached. That is set out in points 3, 4 and possibly 5. I shall deal with these in reverse order.'

In relation to the failure to notify the change of address, she said[5]:

'It would plainly not be a point which in and of itself could lead the Justices to conclude that he was not a fit and proper person to hold a license. It has nothing to do with his driving skills or the safety of passengers, though it may be of small significance in assessing whether he has the right attitude towards matters of regulation.'

The two key elements were the conviction and the driving whist unlicensed.

'22 One then turns to the conviction. This is where it seems to me the Justices clearly fell into error.... it [is] obvious that they felt that the mere existence of the conviction and the sentence, in and of themselves, were enough to justify a conclusion that Mr Pinnington was not a fit and proper person to hold a licence. That means that the Justices did not take into account any of the extenuating circumstances, including the facts giving rise to the commission of the offence; the fact that the possession was not for supply or even for personal use, but in order to destroy the plants; the fact that the sentence was plainly unduly harsh; and the fact that Mr Pinnington was honest enough to admit his guilt... . this is ...at odds with ...the approach that the policy itself requires to be taken for cases where an application is made after three years. The policy makes it clear that the nature and quantity of the drugs, whether for personal use or supply, are issues which should be considered. There is no indication that these matters were addressed, and if they were, I would expect something to have been said about them in the reasons. Instead, the Justices expressed themselves in a way that suggests that they felt the conviction and sentence were enough in and of themselves to justify the conclusion that he was not fit to hold a licence. In so doing they plainly erred in law and reached a decision that they were not entitled to reach.'

Finally, there was the question of the unlicensed driving[6]:

'25 It is interesting that TFL placed little reliance on Mr Pinnington's failure to renew his licence at the earlier stages of this matter. The focus was always on the conviction. At most it was prayed in aid as a supporting reason to conclude that he was not a fit and proper person. Like Mr Kennedy, I regard this as a serious matter for which there has been no proper excuse. Mr Pinnington was always responsible for ensuring that he was licensed. It is not a satisfactory explanation that he relied upon his father to help him with matters of administration and paperwork. There is also the serious problem that failure to renew a licence may be a breach of the terms and conditions of a driver's motor insurance policy, and indeed

Mr Pinnington admitted in cross-examination that in consequence of the non-renewal he was driving the cab without insurance for five months. Mr Paul [for Mr Pinnington] sought to play down that admission on the basis that there was no evidence of the terms of the insurance policy but I am not impressed by that submission. Nor am I impressed by the submission that driving without insurance cover has no real effect on the safety of his passengers. If there had been an accident, and insurance cover was denied, any passenger who was injured would be left with recourse to the MIB or Mr Pinnington himself.

26 On the other hand, renewal of a licence is an administrative matter which is not predicated upon a fresh assessment of safety or qualifications. There is nothing in the relevant legislation or regulations providing for summary revocation of a licence on these grounds. In fact the policy of TFL, which was not before the Justices, indicates that a person who works after his licence has expired may be allowed a new licence with a written warning if it is an isolated occurrence. However different considerations may apply to someone who has been working unlicensed for more than three months or who does so after a warning.

27 Mr Ustych [for TfL] submitted that in this case Mr Pinnington had been working without a licence for five months and that alone justified the conclusion that he was not a fit and proper person. He pointed to the fact that driving without a licence leads to a financial penalty, a fine up to level three, under the Order. He submitted that the reason why the failure to renew is said to have happened, namely, the failure by Mr Pinnington to advise TFL of his change of address, aggravated the offence. Initially, I found those submissions persuasive, but having considered this case in the round I have concluded that the Justices could not fairly and properly have reached the view that Mr Pinnington was not a fit and proper person on the basis of the non-renewal alone. It was a first time offence. Mr Pinnington was wholly misguided to have left these matters to his father but his father was not a stranger to the job, he was an experienced cabbie. His father's illness, death and the depression that this caused Mr Pinnington to suffer also had some bearing on his ability to cope with such matters. Like Mr Kennedy, I also bear in mind the fact that he was not driving his cab for some 18 months, partly in consequence of the delay by TFL in dealing with his application for a fresh licence'

The conclusion was that the decision of the magistrates should be quashed and TfL should issue Pinnington with a hackney carriage drivers' licence.

---

[1] *R v Murphy* [2002] EWCA Crim 1587. There is a defence to possession of drugs under s 5(4)(a) of the the the Misuse of Drugs Act 1971 which provides that a possessor had a defence where 'as soon as possible after taking possession of [the drug] he took all such steps as were reasonably open to him to destroy the drug'. *R v Murphy* considered this defence and determined that in a case where a son discovered cannabis belonging to his father in the glove box of his car, burying the cannabis was not sufficient to amount to a defence as relying on the forces of nature to destroy the drug was not enough. However, the Court of Appeal viewed this as an offence of the utmost technicality and substituted an absolute discharge for the two years' conditional discharge the Crown Court had imposed.

² Per Mrs Justice Andrews DBE at paragraph 19.
³ Per Mrs Justice Andrews DBE at paragraphs 16 and 17.
⁴ Above at para 20.
⁵ Above at para 21.
⁶ Above at paras 29 onwards.

10.46

Although this case is very much limited to its own unusual facts, there are some useful points. A conviction *per se* is not a reason to refuse to renew a licence (or refuse to grant) and the circumstances of that conviction must be considered, whilst being careful not to go behind it.

Failure to notify a change of address alone cannot mean that a person is not fit and proper, but driving without a licence is a serious issue[1]. Mr Pinnington was successful, but another person in similar circumstances might not be so fortunate.

[1]   It is interesting to note TfL's policy on driving when a licence has expired. This would usually lead to a written warning but would not prevent a new licence being granted. Some local authorities would regard this as a very lenient approach, whilst others would take a more serious view of such a mistake.

County of Herefordshire District Council v Prosser

10.47

> Application for a hackney carriage and private hire driver's licence (dual licence). Refused because of previous convictions. Decision overturned on appeal to the magistrates' court on the basis that the convictions were minor, irrelevant and spent. Appeal by way of case stated to the High Court. Held: That the particular convictions were not minor, all convictions were relevant and no convictions were spent for taxi drivers.

In *County of Herefordshire District Council v Prosser*[1] an application was made to the district council for a combined hackney carriage and private hire driver's licence[2]. The application was refused due to Prosser's previous convictions:

'which consisted of 14 appearances in court for offences including assaults, Public Order Act offences, criminal damage, driving offences and dishonesty offences'[3].

Prosser appealed to the magistrates' court who granted the appeal. They took the view that the sentences were spent under ROA 1974 and:

'although numerous and relating to assault and matters affecting public safety, his actions tended towards being at the less serious end of the spectrum and indeed several dated back to the early '90s. Given the nature and limited seriousness of the offences he had committed and his attempts to improve his behaviour since his last offence, it would be unreasonable to regard his spent convictions as still relevant'[4], and refusing to grant the licence:

> 'purely on the grounds that his offences involved assault etc did not seem reasonable'.

The council appealed by way of case stated and the salient issues were identified by the judge[5]:

> '9 Mr Savill [for the Council] submits that there were four errors of law on the part of the Hereford Justices: first, in a case concerning an applicant who had been sentenced variously to imprisonment, a community service order of 150 hours and a probation order of the then maximum duration, the Justices' conclusion that the respondent's "actions tended towards being at the less serious end of the spectrum" was wrong in law. This was so on two grounds; first, as being a conclusion which no reasonable bench of justices, properly directing themselves, could reach; and second, as appearing to offend the principle laid down in Nottingham City Council v Farooq (Mohammed) (Times, 28 October 1998) that a civil appeal court is not entitled to review the merit of a criminal conviction. The second error was in concluding that it would be "unreasonable to regard [the respondent's] spent convictions as still relevant." The Justices were wrong in law in that, first, by operation of the Rehabilitation of Offenders Act 1974 (Exceptions) (Amendment) Order 2002, hackney carriage drivers and private hire drivers are regulated occupations for the purposes of the Rehabilitation of Offender's Act 1974 Schedule 1 Part III and as such are exempt from the provisions of the Act. There is therefore no such thing as a "spent" conviction in relation to these occupations. As such, to dismiss them as irrelevant was an error of law. In any event the Justices were wrong in law to disregard previous convictions as irrelevant, given the overriding principle of protection of public safety, previous convictions of the types found in this case must always be relevant. The proper question is whether other factors have outweighed the relevant convictions. The Justices therefore applied the wrong test. Further the conclusion was one which no reasonable Bench of Justices, properly directing themselves, could reach. Third, having regard to the exemption from the provisions of the 1974 Act for hackney carriage/private hire drivers, the Justices erred in law in concluding that the respondent "had earned the right to expect [the Justices] to rely upon the accepted position that convictions normally become spent after five or seven years", when there was at law no such "accepted position", and accordingly no entitlement to such an expectation. Fourth, in view of the totality of the respondent's previous convictions and the overriding consideration of public safety, the conclusion that the respondent was a fit person to be granted a hackney carriage/private hire driver's licence was wrong in law as being a conclusion which no reasonable bench of justices, properly directing themselves, could reach.'

When viewed together, these cases demonstrate that, quite correctly, each case must be decided on its own merits, and different tribunals (whether that is the local authority, a magistrates' court, Crown Court or the High Court) can come to different conclusions. Provided the overriding aim of public safety and protection is not lost, this is a reflection of the flexibility in the mechanism of determining suitability to hold a driver's licence.

¹   [2008] LLR 274, QBD.
²   As the criteria for granting drivers' licences for hackney carriages and private hire vehicles outside London are identical, and the power to take action against these licences are also same, a number of local authorities grant 'dual' or 'combined' licences which act as both a hackney carriage drivers licence and a private hire drivers licence. For more detail see Chapters 9 and 14.
³   Per Michael Supperstone QC (Sitting as a Deputy High Court Judge) at paragraph 4.
⁴   Above at para 7.
⁵   Above at para 9.

OTHER INFORMATION AS IS CONSIDERED NECESSARY

10.48

However, criminal convictions are not the only criteria and authorities will require further information before they will consider an application. LG(MP)A 1976, s 57(1) allows a district council to require an applicant:

'to submit to the local authority such information as they may reasonably consider necessary to enable them to determine whether the licence should be granted or whether conditions should be attached to any such licence.'

10.49

LG(MP)A 1976, s 57(2)¹ specifically allows a local authority to require a medical certificate certifying that the applicant is physically fit to be the driver of a hackney carriage. It also allows examination of the driver by a doctor² to assess his physical fitness. Guidance concerning medical fitness of drivers in general and taxi drivers in particular is available³. Some caution, however, must be exercised before guidelines are adopted in their entirety. For example, a reference in the guidelines to a medical report accompanying each application for a licence, which in many authorities could mean annual medicals where licences are only granted for one year, may not be felt to be appropriate for hackney carriage (or private hire) drivers. The DfT Best Practice Guide states⁴,

'Medical fitness

67. It is clearly good practice for medical checks to be made on each driver before the initial grant of a licence and thereafter for each renewal. There is general recognition that it is appropriate for taxi/PHV drivers to have more stringent medical standards than those applicable to normal car drivers because:

they carry members of the general public who have expectations of a safe journey;

they are on the road for longer hours than most car drivers; and

they may have to assist disabled passengers and handle luggage.

68. It is common for licensing authorities to apply the "Group 2" medical standards – applied by DVLA to the licensing of lorry and bus drivers – to taxi and PHV drivers. This seems best practice. The Group 2 standards preclude the licensing of drivers with insulin treated diabetes. However, exceptional arrangements do exist for drivers with insulin treated diabetes, who can meet a series of medical criteria, to obtain a licence to drive category C1 vehicles (ie 3500–7500 kgs lorries); the position is summarised at Annex C to the Guidance. It is suggested that the best practice is to apply the C1 standards to taxi and PHV drivers with insulin treated diabetes.'

1   See Appendix I.
2   LG(MP)A 1976 uses the term Registered Medical Practitioner.
3   The Guidance for all drivers is 'Assessing Fitness to Drive – A Guide for Medical Professionals' (which replaced the previous 'At a Glance Guide to the Current Medical Standards of Fitness to Drive') and is published by DVLA available from https://www.gov.uk/government/publications/assessing-fitness-to-drive-a-guide-for-medical-professionals.

Advice on best practice for local authorities issuing taxi licences is given by the booklet, 'Fitness to drive: a guide for health professionals', published in 2006 by The Royal Society of Medicine (RSM) on behalf of the Department for Transport (ISBN reference 9781853156519).

This states (at page 64): 'For taxi drivers, the House of Commons Select Committee report, *Taxi and Private Hire Vehicles*, recommended in 1995 that taxi licence applicants should pass a medical examination. The Medical Commission for Accident Prevention recommended in 1995 that Group 2 medical standards should be used because of the need to ensure that fare-paying passengers were not put at unnecessary risk. Its recommendation has been endorsed by various expert bodies subsequently. It is, however, contested at times, especially in relation to the risk of seizures and to diabetes that appears to be reliably managed on insulin.'

4   DfT, '*Taxi and Private Hire Vehicle Licensing: Best Practice Guidance*' (October 2006, revised March 2010), available from http://www.dft.gov.uk/pgr/regional/taxis/taxiandprivatehirevehiclelic1792.

DRIVING TESTS

10.50

A number of authorities require applicants for hackney carriage drivers' licences to undertake driving tests (over and above the DVLA driving test). The DfT *Best Practice Guide* addresses this as follows[1],

'Driving Proficiency

70. Many local authorities rely on the standard car driving licence as evidence of driving proficiency. Others require some further driving test to be taken. Local authorities will want to consider carefully whether this produces benefits which are commensurate with the costs involved for would-be drivers, the costs being in terms of both money and broader obstacles to entry to the trade. However, they will note that the Driving Standards Agency provides a driving assessment specifically designed for taxis.'

As noted by the DfT above, the Driving Standards Agency did provide a test for hackney carriage drivers[2], but this was abandoned at the end of 2016. A number of local authorities have arrangements with other providers of similar courses and assessments. During the currency of the DSA test, the question of whether this should be a requirement for all hackney carriage drivers, or only new applicants was raised.

¹   DfT, '*Taxi and Private Hire Vehicle Licensing: Best Practice Guidance*' (October 2006, revised March 2010), available from http://www.dft.gov.uk/pgr/regional/taxis/taxiandprivatehirevehiclelic1792.
²   See http://www.dsa.gov.uk/Taxis.asp.

Darlington BC v Kaye

10.51

> Council introduced a requirement that all existing drivers, as well as new applicants had to pass the DSA drivers test. An existing driver refused and his licence was not renewed. Granted on appeal and the council challenged the decision by way of case stated. Held: This was not an unlawful condition on the licence, but was a legitimate element in determining the fitness and propriety of a driver.

This was the basis of the case of *Darlington BC v Kaye*¹. Mr Kaye had been a hackney carriage driver licensed by Darlington BC for over 25 years. The council introduced a requirement that all hackney carriage drivers should pass the DSA Driving Test before a licence would be renewed, as well as initially granted. Mr Kaye refused to take the test, and his application to renew his licence was refused. He appealed to the magistrates' court and was successful. Darlington BC appealed to the High Court by way of case stated.

¹   [2005] RTR 14, Admin Ct.

10.52

At the magistrates' court, the argument had been accepted that the requirement to pass the DSA test was a condition attached to the hackney carriage driver's licence, which was not possible following the ruling in *Wathan v Neath Port Talbot CBC*¹.

¹   [2002] EWHC 1634; see para 10.74 onwards.

10.53

The case was heard by Wilkie J. He set out the background, stating¹:

'2. The respondent has worked as a hackney carriage driver in Darlington since 1970. He has held a full driving licence for 35 years. He has never been the subject of a complaint from a passenger. In that 35 years of driving he has received one three point penalty on his licence arising from a speeding conviction dated 9 March 2002.'

And he then detailed the decision that had led to the alteration in policy by the Council²:

'4. On a date in September 2002, the precise date being unclear, the appellant passed the following resolution:
a)   That the council's current policy be amended to introduce the Driving Standards Agency taxi test as a pre requirement of any grant

of hackney carriage and private hire driver licences for those drivers who have driven hackney carriages or private hire vehicles for less than six months together with experienced drivers who have allowed a licence to lapse, the proposed start date for this group of drivers being 4 November 2002.

b) The council's current policy be amended to introduce the Driving Standards Agency taxi test as a requirement for the renewal of all hackney carriage and private hire licences for those drivers whose medical and/or police check are due, the proposed start date for this group of drivers being 1st April 2003.

c) That drivers be asked to pass the Driving Standard Agency test on one occasion only.

d) That the use of the Driver Improvement Scheme be approved as a disciplinary tool that may be used by the licensing committee as an alternative to suspension for drivers with nine or more penalty points or a history of poor driving, the proposed start date being the November 2002 licensing committee and that the Director of Development and Environment make the necessary arrangements to establish a referral system for taxi drivers to the Durham, or alternatively the Cleveland, national driver improvement scheme as outlined in paragraph 30 of the submitted report.

The reasons annexed to the minute recording these decisions read as follows:

a) To raise the standard of driving skills for the benefit of all road users.

b) To provide reassurance to the public and the fare paying passengers that all drivers have achieved the necessary minimum professional standard of driving skill.'

The council argued that the requirement to pass the DSA test was permissible, as it fell within the powers available to the local authority to seek information from applicants under LGMPA 1976, s 57(1) and (2). The respondent argued that it was an unlawful condition attached to the licence.

1   [2005] RTR 14 at para 2.
2   At para 4.

10.54

The magistrates formulated two questions for the High Court to address and Wilkie J quoted them in reverse order[1]:

'11. ... I set them out in reverse order to that in which they appear in the case stated as it appears to be more logical to do so. They were as follows:

a) Was the requirement to pass the DSA driving test a request for information as envisaged by section 57 Local Government (Miscellaneous Provisions) Act 1976 or did it amount to a condition to the grant of a license which must be fulfilled before the Borough Council would consider whether or not to grant a hackney carriage driver's license?

b)   Was the information as to whether an applicant or a hackney carriage driver's license had passed the DSA driving test reasonably required and necessary to establish whether the respondent was a fit and proper person to hold a license under section 59 Local Government (Miscellaneous Provisions) Act 1976?'

After considering the legislation, and the decision in *Wathan v Neath Port Talbot CBC*[2] he concluded[3]:

'23. In my judgment the District Council, in deciding whether it is satisfied that an applicant is a fit and proper person, is entitled to have regard to the applicant's standard of driving. It is not to be artificially limited to considering evidence about that standard which happens to have arisen because of criminal convictions. Nor is it precluded from having any regard to an applicant's standard of driving merely because he has held a driver's license for 12 months. It is a matter for the District Council to set the standard of what will amount to a fit and proper person by reference to, amongst other things, the applicant's standard of driving provided in so doing they taken into account all relevant matters and leave out of account irrelevant matters and come to a decision to which a reasonable licensing body could come. Furthermore it is entitled to have a policy which it applies in the generality of cases provided it is prepared to be " willing to listen to anyone with something new to say" (see Lord Reid in *British Oxygen Company v Board of Trade* (1971) AC 610, *625D*).

24. It follows, in my judgment, that the appellant was entitled, after due consideration and proper consultation, which plainly took place, to adopt a policy that it would not regard a person as a fit and proper person to have a license who had not first passed the specific DSA taxi driver test. It further follows that, given that policy, it was entitled to consider that it was reasonably necessary for it, in order to form a view whether a person was a fit and proper person to have a license, to require information from an applicant whether he or she had passed that test.

25. Thus, addressing the questions posed by the magistrates in their case stated, in my judgment the requirement to pass the DSA driving test was not a condition attached to the grant of a license which must be fulfilled before the Borough Council would consider whether or not to grant a hackney carriage driver's license. Rather, it was a policy which the District Council applied when considering whether an applicant was a fit and proper person to whom to grant or renew a license. Given that policy, the District Council was reasonably entitled to consider it necessary that it should receive information whether the applicant had or had not passed the DSA driving test. Accordingly, the requirement that the applicant should so inform the District Council was a requirement for information within section 57 of the 1976 Act.

26. It therefore follows that, in my judgment, the magistrates misdirected themselves in concluding that the requirement for that information was outwith the terms of the statute.'

1   At para 11.
2   [2002] EWHC 1634; see para 10.74 onwards.
3   [2005] RTR 14, at paras 23–26.

10.55

This case is important for two reasons. Firstly, it confirms that the DSA Taxi Test (or any similar requirement as the DSA test no longer exists) is a reasonable pre-requisite for a hackney carriage (or indeed private hire) driver. Secondly, it addresses the important point concerning conditions on a hackney carriage licence. Whilst there is little doubt that *Wathan v Neath Port Talbot*[1] is correct (and this case does not challenge that) in preventing conditions being attached to a hackney carriage driver's licence, the decision in *Darlington v Kaye*[2] makes it clear that pre-requisites, whether they are the DSA test, medicals, knowledge tests or whatever, are not conditions attached to the licence and accordingly, they are acceptable provided the council is acting reasonably within its powers under LGMPA 1976, s 57 in requesting that information or qualification.

1   [2002] EWHC 1634; see para 10.74 onwards.
2   [2005] RTR 14.

KNOWLEDGE AND OTHER TESTS

10.56

Some local authorities test the applicant's knowledge of the locality and others also test the ability to speak English.

10.57

The knowledge tests take a number of forms. They generally require applicants to answer a number of questions about the best routes to take between specified places. This can include variations to take account of the time of day and rush hour traffic. Such tests are considered desirable by the DfT in its *Best Practice Guide*[1]:

> **'Topographical Knowledge**
>
> 75. Taxi drivers need a good working knowledge of the area for which they are licensed, because taxis can be hired immediately, directly with the driver, at ranks or on the street. So most licensing authorities require would-be taxi-drivers to pass a test of local topographical knowledge as a pre-requisite to the first grant of a licence (though the stringency of the test should reflect the complexity or otherwise of the local geography, in accordance with the principle of ensuring that barriers to entry are not unnecessarily high).'

With the widespread availability of satellite navigation devices ('SatNav'), either as a built in feature on the vehicle, or as a separate device, whether it is a dedicated SatNav, or contained within a mobile telephone, some question the continuing need to test local geographic knowledge. As yet this has not been considered by the Senior Courts, and until that time, it is arguable that to be a fit and proper person to hold a hackney carriage drivers licence, a certain minimum standard of geographic and local knowledge of the district is a reasonable requirement.

¹ DfT, '*Taxi and Private Hire Vehicle Licensing: Best Practice Guidance*' (October 2006, revised March 2010), para 49, available at http://www.dft.gov.uk/pgr/regional/taxis/taxiandprivatehire vehiclelic1792. See Appendix II.

10.58

The test of the applicant's ability to speak English is considered especially important in areas with airports or seaports, but is becoming increasingly common across the whole of England and Wales. A question that arises frequently is the legality of a spoken English test. Provided it is a requirement for all applicants or drivers it is not a breach of the Equality Act 2010¹. Any breach would only occur where the requirement was not applied universally, but there was some kind of selection before the test was required. That would amount to unlawful discrimination. However, if the local authority is satisfied that there is a genuine requirement that all hackney carriage drivers can communicate in English to a minimum standard, then such a test will be lawful if universally applied.

¹ Under the Equality Act 2010, s 9, race is a protected characteristic, and includes colour, nationality, ethnic and national origins. For further information please see *Discrimination Law* (Bloomsbury Professional).

10.59

Is such a requirement necessary? As the role of a hackney carriage driver is to provide transport to the public by means of a hackney carriage, and as English is the de facto official language of England¹ and one of the two languages given equal status in Wales² and is the first language of the majority of residents of both countries, it seems a reasonable requirement. By extension, in theory it would be possible to apply a similar requirement in Wales for both Welsh and English, although it seems that no local authority in Wales has taken such a step.

¹ There is no defined official language in England or Wales, or indeed the United Kingdom as a whole, although until 2012 the Government appeared to believe otherwise and stated that 'English is the official language of the United Kingdom and is spoken by around 400 million people around the world.' – see http://www.direct.gov.uk/en/Governmentcitizensandrights/LivingintheUK/DG_10012519 . This page has now been archived on the Government website and no obvious replacement exists. English is the de facto official language across the whole UK, and in Wales, Welsh is a de jure official language, whilst English remains de facto official.

² See the Welsh Language Act 1967, the Welsh Language Act 1993, the Welsh Language (Wales) Measure 2011 and the National Assembly for Wales (Official Languages) Act 2012. These combine to place Welsh and English on an equal basis.

R (on the application of Uber) v Transport for London

10.60

> Was it reasonable for the licensing authority (in this case Transport for London) to require applicants for private hire drivers' licences to pass a spoken and written test in English? Held: Yes it was.

The question of a written and spoken English test was considered in *R (on the application of Uber) v Transport for London*[1]. TfL introduced a requirement that all private hire drivers had to be able to communicate in English to Level B1 of the Common European Framework of Reference for languages (B1 CEFR), which required speaking, listening to, reading, and writing English at an appropriate level.

This was challenged by Uber as being disproportionate, although they did not contest the need for drivers to be able to speak and verbally communicate in English. Uber argued that the English language requirements were contrary to EU law, discriminatory on grounds of nationality or national or ethnic origins and disproportionate[2].

Judgment was given by Mitting J. Firstly he considered the potential grounds of challenge[3]:

'14. It is common ground that a measure which has had and will have such an impact on so many people must be strictly justified. European Union law is engaged in two ways: because the English language requirement affects the right of EEA nationals to "take up and pursue activities as selfemployed persons" under Article 49 of the Treaty on the Functioning of the European Union; and, because they discriminate indirectly against nonUK nationals whose first language is not English, Article 2 of Council Directive 2000/431/EC of 29th June 2000 is engaged.

It provides:

"1) For the purposes of this Directive, the principle of equal treatment shall mean that there shall be no direct or indirect discrimination based on racial or ethnic origin

(b) Indirect discrimination shall be taken to occur where an apparently neutral provision, criterion or practice would put persons of a racial or ethnic origin at a particular disadvantage compared with other persons, unless that provision, criterion or practice is objectively justified by a legitimate aim and the means of achieving that aim are appropriate and necessary."

Article 3 deals with the scope of measure:

"(1) Within the limits of the powers conferred upon the Community, the Directive shall apply to all persons as regards both the public and private sectors including public bodies in relation to:

(a) conditions for access to employment, to selfemployment and to occupation, including selection criteria and recruitment conditions whatever the branch of activity and at all levels of the professional hierarchy, including promotion."

15. Effect is given to this Directive by section 19 of the Equality Act 2010, which provides:

"(1) A person (A) discriminates against another (B) if (A) applies to (B) a provision, criterion or practice which is discriminatory in relation to a relevant protected characteristic of (B's).

2) For the purpose of subsection (1) a provision, criterion or practice is discriminatory in relation to a relevant protected characteristic of (B's), if:

(a) (A) applies, or would apply it to persons with whom (B) does not share the characteristic.

(b) It puts or would put persons with whom (B) shares the characteristic at a particular disadvantage, when compared with persons with whom B does not share it.

(c) It puts or would put (B) at a disadvantage.

(d) (A) cannot show it to be a proportionate means of achieving a legitimate aim."

The relevant protected characteristics include race, which, by virtue of section 9(1) includes nationality and ethnic or national origins.

16. Application of these principles requires TfL as a public authority to establish that the measure is proportionate in the EU law sense. It was helpfully and comprehensively explained in the joint judgments of Lord Reed and Lord Toulson on *R (ota Lumsden and others) v Legal Services Board* [2016] AC 697:

"33 Proportionality as a general principle of EU law involves a consideration of two questions: first, whether the measure in question is suitable or appropriate to achieve the objective pursued; and secondly, whether the measure is necessary to achieve that objective, or whether it could be attained by a less onerous method.".

In two circumstances, proportionality is applied "more strictly": when measures interfere with fundamental freedoms guaranteed by the treaties, and when they derogate from them in purported compliance with EU law, see paragraphs 37 and 38. The approach to evidence deployed in support of the measure was explained in paragraph 56:

"The justification for the restriction tends to be examined in detail, although much may depend upon the nature of the justification, and the extent to which it requires evidence to support it. For example, justifications based on moral or political considerations may not be capable of being established by evidence. The same may be true of justifications based on intuitive common sense. An economic or social justification, on the other hand, may well be expected to be supported by evidence."'

The judge explained that any measure which restricted freedoms must be proportionate and would be unlawful if the required level of protection could be achieved by less restrictive means[4]. The need for the requirement was explained as follows[5]:

'The public interests in question are the safety and welfare and convenience of the passengers. The level of protection of those interests which TfL has determined is necessary to protect them is that private hire vehicle drivers must have a sufficient command of spoken English to be able to understand their requirements, including those arising unexpectedly, for example, in a medical emergency; to discuss a route or fare with them, and to explain safety requirements to them; and of written English, to understand regulatory communications to them, and traffic and other information supplied to them by TfL.'

The judge determined that the protection required by the requirement was acceptable within the margin of appreciation, and then considered whether there were less onerous means of achieving it. The test required applicants to write a short essay on a topic which was unrelated to private hire activity. This was only 100 to 130 words and he concluded[6]:

'In my judgment, TfL have demonstrated that they were and are entitled to require drivers to demonstrate that level of competence in written as well as spoken English. There is now and for the foreseeable future no practicable alternative means of achieving the protection of the legitimate public interests which TfL have identified to the level properly set by them. In reaching that conclusion, I have not found the Central Government requirement for "public facing" officials to have a sufficient command of spoken English only to deal with a comparable set of circumstances. For the reasons explained, drivers must do more than converse with passengers and understand spoken English.'

This judgment demonstrates clearly that a requirement to speak and write in English to a basic level is a reasonable requirement for private hire drivers, and by extension, hackney carriage drivers[7].

[1] [2017] ACD 54, Admin Ct.
[2] There were two other challenges brought by Uber against TfL, relating to insurance and the need for a private hire operator to provide a permanently staffed telephone service. These were dismissed by the High Court and will be considered in Chapter 12, para 12.103 onwards relating to private hire operators and Chapter 22, para 22.31 in relation to private hire vehicles.
[3] At para 14.
[4] See paras 17 and 18.
[5] See para 19.
[6] At para 27.
[7] At the time of writing (August 2017), both parties have indicated that they are seeking leave to appeal to the Court of Appeal.

AGE LIMITS

10.61

A number of local authorities have age limits beyond which drivers are either required to submit to more frequent medical testing, or in some cases, will not be considered for a licence at all. The DfT Best Practice Guide states[1]:

'**Age Limits**

69. It does not seem necessary to set a maximum age limit for drivers provided that regular medical checks are made. Nor do minimum age

limits, beyond the statutory periods for holding a full driver licence, seem appropriate. Applicants should be assessed on their merits.'

In relation to Age Policies, it is necessary to consider whether a policy which treats older drivers in a different way from their younger colleagues is lawful[2].

[1]   DfT, *'Taxi and Private Hire Vehicle Licensing: Best Practice Guidance'* (October 2006, revised March 2010), para 46, available at http://www.dft.gov.uk/pgr/regional/taxis/taxiandprivatehirevehiclelic1792. See Appendix II.

[2]   For example, a number of authorities require triennial or quinquennial medical checks for hackney carriage and private hire drivers until they reach their 65th birthday, and then annual medicals thereafter.

10.62

Age discrimination is governed by the Equality Act 2010 ('the 2010 Act'). Under the 2010 Act, age is a protected characteristic under s 4 and is defined in s 5 in the following terms:

'**5 Age**

(1) In relation to the protected characteristic of age—

(a)   a reference to a person who has a particular protected characteristic is a reference to a person of a particular age group;

(b)   a reference to persons who share a protected characteristic is a reference to persons of the same age group.

(2) A reference to an age group is a reference to a group of persons defined by reference to age, whether by reference to a particular age or to a range of ages.'

Generally, direct discrimination is unlawful, but there is an exception in relation to age. Section 13 subsections (1) and (2) state:

'**13 Direct discrimination**

(1) A person (A) discriminates against another (B) if, because of a protected characteristic, A treats B less favourably than A treats or would treat others.

(2) If the protected characteristic is age, A does not discriminate against B if A can show A's treatment of B to be a proportionate means of achieving a legitimate aim.'

A local authority does not employ a hackney carriage or private hire driver, but does provide them with the means to obtain work by granting a licence. If there are additional tests imposed by a local authority based on the age of the applicant or licensee, those will not be unlawful provided they are a proportionate means of achieving a legitimate aim.

It will therefore be necessary firstly to identify the legitimate aim. In this case it is the safety of the public[1] and it will then be necessary to show that the age of the driver can affect that. Provided that evidence is available, it would seem that policies which require more frequent medical and driving tests as people become older would be lawful. It is unlikely that a stated age beyond which a licence will not be granted would be lawful.

10.63

In relation to proportionality, it would appear to be necessary to show that, for example, drivers over 65 are more likely to have medical conditions which would render them less safe to drive hackney carriages or private hire vehicles than those under 65 and that those medical conditions could reasonably and realistically be expected to be detected by annual medicals as opposed to triennial or quinquennial medicals.

10.64

To be able to demonstrate this, some credible research would be required that has been conducted in relation to the safety of older drivers. Assuming that research both exists and confirms that those over 65 are more susceptible to accident inducing illnesses than those under 65, then a local authority should be able to justify its policy. However in the absence of that evidence, such a policy is prima facie unlawful.

10.65

Other factors that can be considered when assessing the fitness and propriety of an applicant include the applicant's demeanour, appearance and behaviour before either officers or members. Again, the local authority should have a clear policy on what factors may be taken into account in determining fitness and propriety. The DfT in its *Best Practice Guide* makes reference to 'Other Training' and says[1]:

> **'Other training**
>
> 72. Whilst the Department has no plans to make training courses or qualifications mandatory, there may well be advantage in encouraging drivers to obtain one of the nationally-recognised vocational qualifications for the taxi and PHV trades. These will cover customer care, including how best to meet the needs of people with disabilities. More information about these qualifications can be obtained from GoSkills, the Sector Skills Council for Passenger Transport. GoSkills is working on a project funded by the Department to raise standards in the industry and GoSkills whilst not a direct training provider, can guide and support licensing authorities through its regional network of Regional Managers.
>
> 73. Some licensing authorities have already established training initiatives and others are being developed; it is seen as important to do this in consultation with the local taxi and PHV trades. Training can cover customer care, including how best to meet the needs of people with disabilities and other sections of the community, and also topics such as

the relevant legislation, road safety, the use of maps and GPS, the handling of emergencies, and how to defuse difficult situations and manage conflict. Training may also be considered for applicants to enable them to reach an appropriate standard of comprehension, literacy and numeracy. Authorities may wish to note that nationally recognised qualifications and training programmes sometimes have advantages over purely local arrangements (for example, in that the qualification will be more widely recognised).

Contact details are:

GoSkills, Concorde House, Trinity Park, Solihull, Birmingham, B37 7UQ.
Tel: 0121-635-5520
Fax: 0121-635-5521
Website: www.goskills.org
e-mail: info@goskills.org

74. It is also relevant to consider driver training in the context of the 2012 Olympic and Paralympic Games which will take place at a number of venues across the country. One of the key aims of the Games is to "change the experience disabled people have when using public transport during the Games and to leave a legacy of more accessible transport". The Games provide a unique opportunity for taxi/PHV drivers to demonstrate their disability awareness training, and to ensure all passengers experience the highest quality of service.'

¹   DfT, '*Taxi and Private Hire Vehicle Licensing: Best Practice Guidance*', (October 2006, revised March 2010), paras 72–74, available at http://www.dft.gov.uk/pgr/regional/taxis/taxiandprivate hirevehiclelic1792. See Appendix II.

IMPACT ON LIVELIHOOD AND FAMILY

10.66

On two occasions the High Court has given judgment on the question of whether the impact on the persons livelihood and family of either not being granted, or losing a hackney carriage or private hire drivers licence were matters that could be taken into account. The first was *Leeds City Council v Hussain*¹, which was then followed by *Anwar v Cherwell DC*².

In both cases, it was made abundantly clear that the only consideration was the fitness and propriety of the person, considered against the overall aim of the licensing regime of protecting public safety.

¹   [2002] EWHC 1145 (Admin), [2003] RTR 199; see para 10.67 below.
²   [2011] EWHC 2943 (Admin), [2012] RTR 15. See para 10.72 below.

Leeds City Council v Hussain

10.67

Private hire driver was arrested but not charged and the council suspended his licence. His appeal to magistrates' court failed, but the subsequent appeal to the Crown Court was successful, because he had not been charged, the evidence of the matter was hearsay and the suspension affected his livelihood. The council challenged that to the High Court. Held: No requirement for a conviction or even a charge to take action against a licence; hearsay evidence was admissible; the impact on the drivers' livelihood was irrelevant.

In *Leeds City Council v Hussain*[1] Hussain was a private hire driver[2] and Leeds City Council suspended his licence because he had been charged with an offence of violent disorder arising out of an incident which involved a number of private hire drivers and their vehicles. He appealed to the magistrates' court, which dismissed the appeal, upholding the decision of the City Council. He further appealed to the Crown Court and was successful. Leeds City Council appealed against that decision by way of case stated. One ground of the findings of the Crown Court was that no live evidence had been called[3]. Another was the question of whether action could be taken before a criminal conviction had been secured[4], the third was whether there had to be a reasonable chance of conviction before any action could be taken[5] and the final one concerned the impact of a suspension on the drivers' livelihood, which is considered here.

[1]   [2002] EWHC 1145 (Admin), [2003] RTR 199.
[2]   The powers to take action against a private hire driver's licence are identical to those for hackney carriage drivers, both being contained in LG(MP)A 1976, s 61, so this case is relevant to hackney carriage drivers as well as private hire.
[3]   This matter is considered in Chapter 2, para 2.66.
[4]   This is considered at para 10.146 below.
[5]   This is considered at para 10.146 below.

10.68

The pertinent question raised by the Crown Court was:

'(a) …[the need for a conviction question];
(b) … [The live evidence question][1];
(c) …[the likelihood of a conviction question]
(d) Whether, in the case of a holder of private hire vehicle and driver's licences who has been charged with a serious criminal offence committed in the course of his employment, the impact of the suspension of those licences upon his livelihood and the absence of any compensation if he is ultimately acquitted of the criminal charge are circumstances which can properly be taken into account when deciding whether there is "any … reasonable cause" to suspend his licences.'

[1]   See Chapter 2, para 2.66.

10.69

The judge, Mr Justice Silber, broke these into three broad headings:

1.   the need for conviction issue[1];
2.   the hearsay evidence issue[2]; and
3.   the licence holder's personal circumstances issue.

1   Considered at para 10.146 onwards below.
2   Considered in Chapter 2, para 2.66.

10.70

The licence holder's personal circumstances were considered and the judge acknowledged that there was no authority on the point. He then stated as follows[1] (at para 25):

> '25. There is indeed no authority on this point, but as Lord Bingham explained in the passage in *McCool*[2] that I have already quoted
>
> > [at page 891F, quoted at para 13 of the judgment: "One must, as it seems to me, approach this question bearing in mind the objectives of this licensing regime which is plainly intended, among other things, to ensure so far as possible that those licensed to drive private hire vehicles are suitable persons to do so, namely that they are safe drivers with good driving records and adequate experience, sober, mentally and physically fit, honest, and not persons who would take advantage of their employment to abuse or assault passengers."]
>
> , the purpose of the power of suspension is to protect users of licensed vehicles and those who are driven by them and members of the public. Its purpose, therefore, is to prevent licences being given to or used by those who are not suitable people taking into account their driving record, their driving experience, their sobriety, mental and physical fitness, honesty, and that they are people who would not take advantage of their employment to abuse or assault passengers. In other words, the council, when considering whether to suspend a licence or revoke it, is focusing on the impact of the licence holder's vehicle and character on members of the public and in particular, but not exclusively, on the potential users of those vehicles.
>
> 26. This does not require any consideration of the personal circumstances which are irrelevant, except perhaps in very rare cases to explain or excuse some conduct of the driver.'

1   *Leeds City Council v Hussain* [2002] EWHC 1145 (Admin), [2003] RTR 199.
2   *McCool v Rushcliffe Borough Council* [1998] 3 All ER 889, QBD; see para 10.142 below.

10.71

As this is a High Court decision, it is in itself authority for the proposition that the council (or court on appeal) should not take into account the livelihood of the applicant or licensee when considering their fitness and propriety to drive a hackney carriage.

Anwar v Cherwell DC

10.72

> Hackney carriage driver convicted of assault. Local authority refused renewal of licence, but the appeal to the magistrates' court was successful.

> The magistrates took into account the hardship he and his family would suffer if the licence was removed. The local authority appealed to the High Court. Held: The impact on his and his family's livelihood was not a matter that could be considered.

This principle was followed in *Anwar v Cherwell DC*[1]. Anwar had been a licensed driver (Cherwell DC issued dual or combined hackney carriage and private hire drivers' licences) since 2003, and applied to renew his licence in June 2009. At that point he revealed that he had been convicted in March 2009 on a guilty plea, of assault by beating contrary to s 39 of the Criminal Justice Act 1988 and had been sentenced to a community order with a 15 month supervision requirement and ordered to pay £300 in costs. Cherwell refused his renewal application on the basis that he was not a fit and proper person, having regard to their policy, which at that time stated:

> 'Convictions and driving licence endorsements
>
> A person with a current conviction for a serious crime need not be permanently barred from obtaining a licence but will be expected to remain free of conviction for at least three years, according to the circumstances, before an application is entertained. Some discretion will be applied if the offence is isolated and there are mitigating circumstances. However, the overriding consideration will be the protection of the public.
>
> Violence
>
> As hackney carriage and PHV drivers maintain close contact with the public, a firm line will be taken with applicants who have convictions involving violence. At least three years free of such convictions would normally need to be shown before an application is entertained.'

Anwar appealed to the magistrates' court and the appeal was successful. Cherwell DC appealed that decision by way of case stated. The case was heard by His Honour Judge Bidder QC (Sitting as a Deputy High Court Judge). The key issue before the magistrates was whether Anwar was a fit and proper person, and the questions in the case stated were:

> '(a) Whether in determining this appeal and in the light of the decision in *Leeds City Council –v- Hussain*, we were right to consider and take account of the need for Mr Anwar to provide for his family and the personal circumstances of his wife and children.
>
> (b) Having found that the council were entitled to come to the decision that they did, had acted in good faith and had taken into account all relevant matters, was our decision one which no reasonable court could have reached.'

The judge outlined the facts as follows[2]:

> '18. It is the case that the respondent did not disclose his conviction to the local authority immediately, although it was a condition he should do so, but rather he disclosed that at the time of his renewal application.

19. The court noted that this was a case of domestic violence. The assault had followed an argument with his wife about their children and there was evidence that the couple had reconciled with no further difficulties. The magistrates did not consider that the respondent posed any risk to the public in the light of the conviction and they also took into account the council's policy, the respondent's previous good character, the fact that there had been no complaint in relation to his standard of driving, the fact that there was no evidence he posed a risk to the public and the needs of his wife and children.

20. They correctly directed themselves at the council's policy gave some discretion, even where a driver was convicted of an offence of violence. However, looking at the policy and page 20 of the appellant's bundle it does appear that that discretion is specifically related to mitigating circumstances in relation to the offence.

21. Paragraph (h) of the case stated reads as follows:

"We accept that the council acted in good faith at all times and were entitled to reach the decision that they did. However, we are of the opinion that they exercised their discretion incorrectly and that we are entitled to take into account the needs of his family."

22. It seems to me, looking at the judgement overall, that it is obvious that the magistrates considered that the needs of the respondent's family were an important factor in persuading them to overturn the council's decision.'

The judge considered the decision in *Leeds City Council v Hussain*[3] and accepted the decision of Silber J in that case that personal circumstances were not a matter that could be taken into account. An interesting argument had been put before the court by counsel for Anwar and the judge concluded the case thus[4]:

'25. It has been ingeniously argued by counsel for the Respondent, that it is possible that the future impact of the removal of a licence on a licence holder's family would serve as a deterrent to him and thus might be relevant to the primary issue of the safety of the public. If, however, the magistrates had followed that subtle line of argument, one would have expected them to have included that in their reasons and to link it with their conclusion that the applicant was not a danger to the public. They did not and I therefore conclude that they regarded the hardship to his wife and children as a completely separate factor to the issue of the safety of the public and, from their reference to it in (h) clearly regarded it as an important reason for differing from the council's decision. That is simply not in line with the *Hussain* case.

26. Thus I answer the first question posed for my decision in the negative.

27. Although it has been argued that that does not necessarily mean that I must answer the second question in the affirmative, it is really quite impossible for me to conclude that the magistrates did not place any significant weight on the hardship point. Indeed, looking at the decision fairly and as a whole, they plainly regarded the hardship to the wife and children as important enough to differ from the council. They took into

account an irrelevant reason, which no reasonable court would have done. I cannot speculate on what their decision would have been absent the taking into account of the hardship issue – had they not taken that into account it is difficult to see that they could, while having proper regard to the council's decision, have made the generous decision they did. In any event, I should not speculate and I am driven to the conclusion that I should answer the second question in the affirmative.'

It is therefore quite clear that in determining whether a person is, or remains, a fit and proper person, the only considerations that can be taken into account are those relating to public safety. Livelihood and family considerations are not relevant. In arriving at that conclusion, which is based on clear and conclusive high court authorities[5], the point made by Silber J in *Leeds City Council v Hussain* at paragraph 26 of needs to be considered. He said[6]:

'26. This does not require any consideration of the personal circumstances which are irrelevant, except perhaps in very rare cases to explain or excuse some conduct of the driver.'

It is difficult to think of any situation where the personal circumstances of an applicant or driver are sufficiently important to overcome the conclusion that they are not a safe and suitable person to undertake the role and responsibilities of a hackney carriage driver.

[1]   [2011] EWHC 2943 (Admin), [2012] RTR 15.
[2]   At paragraphs 18 to 22.
[3]   [2002] EWHC 1145 (Admin), [2003] RTR 199.
[4]   Above at paras 25 to 27.
[5]   *Leeds City Council v Hussain* [2002] EWHC 1145 (Admin), [2003] RTR 199; see para 10.67 above and *Anwar v Cherwell DC* [2011] EWHC 2943 (Admin), [2012] RTR 15; see para 10.72 above.
[6]   [2002] EWHC 1145 (Admin), [2003] RTR 199; see para 10.67 above.

10.73

If the decision is taken that the licence should not be granted, then LG(MP)A 1976, s 59(2) gives the applicant a right of appeal[1] to a magistrates' court against such refusal if they are 'aggrieved' by that refusal.

'(2) Any applicant aggrieved by the refusal of a district council to grant a driver's licence on the ground that he is not a fit and proper person to hold such licence may appeal to a magistrates' court.'

[1]   The requirements in relation to appeals are fully considered in Chapter 3.

Conditions, byelaws and Codes of Conduct

Wathan v Neath Port Talbot County Borough Council

10.74

Local authority imposed conditions on a hackney carriage drivers' licence. These were not complied with and the licence was suspended by the council.

> On appeal it was argued that there was no power to attach conditions to a hackney carriage drivers' licence, and the appeal was dismissed. The driver challenged to the High Court. Held: There was no power to attach conditions to a hackney carriage driver's licence.

It is clear that a local authority cannot attach conditions to a hackney carriage driver's licence[1]. This was the decision in the case of *Wathan v Neath Port Talbot County Borough Council*[2]. Prior to this case, a great many local authorities imposed conditions on hackney carriage driver's licences. Although there was no express power to attach conditions, it was argued that LG(MP)A 1976, s 57(1) permitted it.

[1]   However the DfT has an alternative view; see para 10.80 below.
[2]   [2002] EWHC 1634 (Admin), [2002] LLR 749, Admin Ct.

10.75

LG(MP)A 1976, s 57(1) states:

> 'A district council may require any applicant for a licence under the Act of 1847 or under this Part of this Act to submit to them such information as they may reasonably consider necessary to enable them to determine whether the licence should be granted and whether conditions should be attached to any such licence.'

This indicates that conditions can be attached to any licence granted under TPCA 1847, and that therefore conditions could be attached to a hackney carriage driver's licence. The argument found support in LG(MP)A 1976, s 52(3) which allows a person aggrieved by any conditions attached to the grant of a driver's licence to appeal to a magistrates' court. Unfortunately, s 52(2) is silent as to whether this right of appeal is in relation to a private hire or hackney carriage driver's licence.

10.76

Neath Port Talbot County Borough Council attached conditions to the hackney carriage drivers' licences that it issued. One of those conditions required the licensee to notify the council of certain convictions recorded during the currency of the licence, within a specified time. Mr Wathan held such a licence, had convictions recorded against him, and did not inform the Council. They suspended his licence. He appealed against that decision to the magistrates' court. At that hearing, the argument was raised that the council had no power to attach conditions to a hackney carriage driver's licence. The magistrates rejected that view, and dismissed the appeal. Mr Wathan appealed by way of case stated to the High Court.

10.77

The case was heard by Sir Edwin Jowitt[1]. He summed up the situation and delivered his judgment succinctly:

'4. What has been said and what has been urged upon me today by Mr Thomas, for the defendant [council], is that section 57(1) [LG(MP)A 1976, s 57(1)] not only provides the power to require information to be given, it also provides the power to issue licences both for hackney carriages and for private hire vehicles and to impose conditions upon their grant. I am bound to say that is not the natural way one would read that subsection. But his difficulty is made the greater when one bears in mind the earlier sections to which it is sufficient for me to refer without going through them in any detail.

5. The Act distinguishes between the operator of a vehicle, the driver of the vehicle and the vehicle itself. Section 55 of the 1976 Act empowers the District Council to issue a licence to the operator of a private hire vehicle and to impose conditions upon that licence. Section 51 makes similar provision in the case of a driver of a private hire vehicle, and section 48 contains the power to grant licences in respect of the private hire vehicle itself and to impose conditions in respect of it.

6. So, if Mr Thomas is right, one has in section 57 the creation of a power to grant licences and also to impose conditions upon the grant of those licences, whereas, in the preceding sections, that has already been dealt with by the sections to which I have referred. This, in my judgment, reinforces my reading of section 57: that it simply provides additional power to the District Council when it comes to decide whether to grant a licence and, where, it is empowered to impose conditions, whether to impose conditions. That is why section 57 comes in the place in this part of the Act which it does, after the sections which deal with the issue of licences and attaching conditions to them.

7. Mr Thomas realistically accepts that one has to give the same meaning to section 57 whether one is seeking to apply it to a hackney carriage or to a private hire car. That really should be sufficient to dispose of this argument. The magistrates were wrong when they considered that section 57 gave the powers that it does, and the submission to them that it did that was also wrong.'

[1]   *Wathan v Neath Port Talbot County Borough Council* [2002] EWHC 1634 (Admin), [2002] LLR 749, Admin Ct.

10.78

The judge went on to consider the LG(MP)A 1976, s 52(2) argument outlined above (the right of appeal), and found it wanting. He concluded[1]:

'20. But, I repeat, although anomalies sometime occur in statutes, that does not allow the court to ignore the plain wording of the section and substitute some variation which seeks to remove the anomaly. Where there is an ambiguity that may be possible, but there is no ambiguity here. I turn then to the question which magistrates posed in their case. In paragraph 7 of the case stated, the questions are these:

"(i) Whether the Magistrates were correct in law in finding that S57(1) Local Government (Miscellaneous Provisions) Act 1976 empowers the Respondent to attach Conditions to the Appellant's Hackney Carriage Driver Licence thereby purporting to regulate the conduct of the Appellant in his role as a Hackney Carriage Driver especially in the circumstances where no information was obtained by the Respondent to justify the Condition prior to the Licence having been issued."

21. I ignore for the moment the words which follow "especially in the circumstances" and answer the question no, and merely add that that answer is not affected by those words which I have just ignored.

22. The second question:

"(ii) Whether the Magistrates were correct in law in finding that Condition 27 of the Respondent's Conditions of Licence is enforceable as against the Appellant in this case."

23. Again, the answer to that is no. There are no powers under section 57 to make conditions which attach to the licence of a driver of a hackney carriage and the District Council has not issued any byelaws, which is what has given rise to the difficulty in this case.

24. The third and final question:

"(iii) Whether the conduct of a Hackney Carriage Driver (if to be regulated) should in law be regulated by way of Byelaws approved by the Secretary of State for Transport in accordance with S68 Town Police Clauses Act 1847."

25. I have not been addressed upon the particular method by which byelaws under section 68 [TPCA 1847, s 68] have to be promulgated and brought into effect by the District Council, but I merely say that any regulation of a hackney carriage driver has to be covered by such byelaws, and however it is that they have to be brought into force. The result is that this appeal is allowed.'

Accordingly, in the absence of a power to attach conditions to hackney carriage drivers' licences, local authorities must rely on byelaws to regulate the conduct of their hackney carriage drivers.

[1]   *Wathan v Neath Port Talbot County Borough Council* [2002] EWHC 1634 (Admin), [2002] LLR 749, Admin Ct.

10.79

This ruling has caused difficulties for many local authorities, as the model byelaws are nowhere near as comprehensive as the conditions some local authorities had attempted to impose on hackney carriage driver's licences.

This is especially true in relation to the requirement which formed the basis of the *Neath Port Talbot* case[1], namely the requirement to inform the local authority if, during the currency of a licence, any convictions were recorded against the licensee.

1   *Wathan v Neath Port Talbot County Borough Council* [2002] EWHC 1634 (Admin), [2002] LLR 749, Admin Ct.

10.80

The DfT put forward an argument that, notwithstanding the decision in *Neath Port Talbot*, conditions could be attached to a hackney carriage proprietor's licence. This was detailed in their note to local authorities dated July 2005. It stated:

'3. It appears to have been accepted amongst local licensing authorities that the judgment in the case of *Wathan* v *Neath and Port Talbot CBC* [2002 EWHC 1634] established a principle that there was no power available in law to attach conditions to a hackney carriage driver's licence.

4. The Department's view is that the decision in *Wathan* is being misinterpreted; and that the power to grant a licence to a hackney carriage driver under s.46 of the Town Police Clauses Act 1847 implies a power to attach conditions to that licence.

5. *Hewison v Skegness Urban District Council [1963 1 QB 584]* (sic) held that whether or not an authority could impose conditions to a licence depended on what the statutory power to grant the licence said or implied. In deciding whether conditions can be imposed on a hackney carriage driver's licence, certain considerations must be taken into account, including (i) whether or not the statutory regime contains preconditions for the grant of a licence – an absence of statutory criteria makes it easier to imply a power to impose conditions; and (ii) enforcement. There is a mechanism to enforce any breach of a condition under section 50 of the 1847 Act and section 61 of the 1976 Act.

6. These considerations have informed our view that the power to grant a licence to a hackney carriage driver under section 46 of the 1847 Act implies a power to attach conditions to that licence.

7. By contrast, in the case of *Wathan* v *Neath and Port Talbot CBC*, the court was asked if section 57 of the Local Government (Miscellaneous Provisions) Act 1976 empowers authorities to attach conditions to a hackney carriage driver's licence. The court held that it did not, because section 57 concerns licence applications and whether conditions should be attached to a licence. We accept the conclusion of the court in relation to the question put to it; section 57 does not, as the judgment makes clear, confer a power to impose conditions. However this was, in our view, because section.57 impliedly assumes that there was already such a power, presumably deriving from section 46 of the 1847 Act.

8. We recognise that there are arguments against this view, and it will be a matter for each licensing authority, in conjunction with its own legal

advisers, to determine whether it is proper to attach conditions to a licence. Ultimately, of course, whether section 46 provides such a power will be a matter for the courts to decide.

9. While, in the Department's opinion, there is no need – at least on legal grounds – for licensing authorities to abandon their conditions of licence and re-enact the relevant obligations or prohibitions in byelaws, some local licensing authorities might decide that hackney carriage byelaws suit their purposes better than conditions of licence (eg the varying approaches to penalties for offences or consequences for breaches might be a relevant consideration).'

Is this a valid argument? There is no doubt that the decision in the *Skegness UDC* case[1] makes it clear that the ability of a local authority to impose conditions is dependant upon the legislation in question. The matter then hinges on whether the provisions of the TPCA 1847 allow such conditions to be imposed.

[1]   *Hewison v Skegness Urban District Council* [1963] 1 QB 584.

10.81

Section 46 states:

'Drivers not to act without first obtaining a licence

46 No person shall act as driver of any hackney carriage licensed in pursuance of this or the special Act to ply for hire within the prescribed distance without first obtaining a licence from the commissioners, which licence shall be registered by the clerk to the commissioners, [and such fee as the commissioners may determine shall be paid] for the same; and every such licence shall be in force until the same is revoked except during the time that the same may be suspended as after mentioned.'

and it can be seen this contains no indication of a condition imposing power. The DfT also state that s 50[1] of TPC 1847 gives a power to enforce any conditions that might be imposed. Unfortunately s 50 does not give such a power; rather it enables action to be taken by the local authority against the licence for non-compliance with the provisions of the legislation or byelaws.

Indeed, within the 1847 Act itself there is no concept of any type of condition being imposed on any licence. This, allied to the fact that the LG(MP)A 1976 specifically provides for conditions to be attached to hackney carriage proprietor's licences under s 47(1) reinforces the view that there is no inherent power to attach conditions to a hackney carriage driver's licence contained within the 1847 Act. The DfT suggest that the absence of a specific power in the 1976 Act demonstrates that there must be a power in the 1847 Act; it is suggested that the absence of a specific power in the 1976 Act is more correctly viewed as a legislative oversight.

It is not clear whether any authorities have accepted the DfT view and imposed conditions on hackney carriage driver's licences using the 1847 Act.

[1]   See Appendix I.

10.82

The problem of reporting convictions to the local authority can be addressed by either the issue of 'dual licences' or by means of a Code of Conduct for Drivers.

A dual or combined licence is where the local authority grants a driver's licence which allows the licensee to drive both hackney carriages and private hire vehicles[1]. Clearly, conditions can be attached to a private hire driver's licence (LG(MP)A 1976, s 51(2))[2]. Whilst these are unenforceable against the hackney carriage element of a dual licence, in relation to information about convictions, the overall benefit is significant.

[1]   See Chapter 14, para 14.2 onwards.
[2]   See Appendix I.

10.83

If that condition is attached to a dual licence, the driver must report a conviction to prevent action being taken against his private hire driver's licence for non-compliance with a condition.

10.84

Arguably, in that situation, the authority would then have to 'split' the licences, to revoke or suspend his private hire licence as appropriate, for non-compliance with a condition but allow him to continue driving a hackney carriage, as there is no requirement to inform the authority of such a conviction in relation to the hackney carriage element of the licence.

10.85

However, the authority may also wish to consider taking action in addition against his hackney carriage driver's licence as a result of the conviction itself. It does not appear to matter that the information was obtained in connection with another licence, as it is all connected with his suitability to continue driving a hackney carriage (and, as the case may be, a private hire vehicle).

10.86

Byelaws can be made under the powers contained in TPCA 1847, s 68 and Town Police Clauses Act 1889, s 6, both of which contain provisions for such byelaws to regulate the behaviour of hackney carriage drivers. Many local authorities use byelaws which were made by former local authorities prior to local government re-organisation in 1974 (and possibly again in the mid 1990s) and which were abolished but whose area is now part of the 'new' authority. This is possible by virtue of the Local Authorities etc (Miscellaneous Provisions) Order 1974, art 9[1] and the Local Government Act 1972, s 238. Model byelaws were published by Department of Transport circular 3/85[2] and the mechanism for making byelaws is contained in the Local Government Act 1972, s 235.

[1]   SI 1974/482.

²   See Chapter 6, para 6.27 and Chapter 9, para 9.100 onwards and Appendix II. They have
    been re-issued on occasions to reflect the fact that it is believed that all authorities (apart from
    Plymouth City Council) have adopted the LG(MP)A 1976.

10.87

The model byelaws are very weak in relation to control of hackney carriage
drivers and updated byelaws are still required as a matter of urgency. The DfT
does not appear to intend to issue revised model byelaws and has not made any
announcements relating to byelaws since 2005 when they issued a Guidance
Note[1]. In that the DfT considered the bylaw making powers and also explained
the possibility for deviations from the model byelaws (which were annexed to the
Guidance Note).

'**Considerations when making hackney carriage byelaws**

(i) Extent of vires

10. Having considered the matter carefully, we take the view that the
byelaw-making power in the 1847 Act should be considered in the context
of local authorities' wider responsibilities in relation to hackney carriage
licensing ie. that the purpose of the power is to enable local licensing
authorities to regulate hackney carriage drivers and proprietors in such
a way as to ensure that they are fit and proper persons and in order to
ensure the safety of the travelling public. In reaching this conclusion, it
is relevant to note that the 1847 Act refers to the conduct of both drivers
and proprietors "plying ... in their several employments', suggesting
that plying is not restricted just to drivers seeking hirings, but is a way of
defining the running of a taxi business.

Moreover, section 68 also refers to regulating things such as the maintenance
of the carriage. We therefore take the view that section 68 allows byelaws to
cover all areas associated with the business of running hackney carriages in
which the licensing authority has a genuine and legitimate interest.

(ii) Model byelaws

11. The Department has produced a set of model byelaws as a basis for
local licensing authorities. This is attached at Annex A. The model byelaws
cover the range of standard controls which most local authorities would
want to impose and we would expect local authorities to base their byelaws
on the model.

(iii) Deviations from the model

12. Where a local authority wishes to introduce a byelaw which deviates
from the model, we shall expect local authorities to take a rigorous approach
in drafting to ensure that the tests of legal validity are met. These are set
out in *Kruse* v *Johnson* [1898] 2 QB 911 as comprising **4** elements essential
to validity:
*   byelaws must be within the powers of the local authority which
    makes them;
*   byelaws must not be repugnant to the general law;

- byelaws must be certain and positive in their terms; and
- byelaws must be reasonable.

13. If a local authority identifies *a* policy objective which it wishes to reflect in byelaws, the onus will be on the local authority to draft a suitable byelaw to put to the Department for provisional approval.

14. The onus will also be on the local authority to satisfy itself as to the validity of any proposed byelaw which it submits to the Department for approval. We would expect local authorities to have sought their own legal advice and to provide an explanation as to why they consider that any proposed byelaw is valid. We would stress that confirmation by the Secretary of State does not endow the byelaws with legal validity – only the courts can determine whether a byelaw is valid. To this extent, it is crucial that any draft byelaws are seen and approved by the Council's legal advisers. Any request for provisional approval of byelaws which deviate from the model should be accompanied by an explanation of the policy objective, a justification of their validity and confirmation that the byelaws have been approved by legal advisers.'

Whilst it could be argued that this was an acceptance (or possibly even encouragement) by the DfT that local authorities may wish to develop their own byelaws as a method of control for both Hackney carriage drivers and vehicles, as far as can be established, no byelaws that depart from the model byelaws have been approved by the DfT in the last decade.

[1]   Department for Transport *Hackney Carriage Byelaws – Guidance Notes and Model Byelaws* July 2005, paras 10–14. See Appendix II.

CODES OF CONDUCT

10.88

An alternative approach to the control of drivers is a Code of Conduct. This can apply to both hackney carriage and private hire drivers and can cover all aspects of their behaviour. It is not in itself a condition attached to the licence and therefore does not fall foul of the ruling in *Wathan v Neath Port Talbot County Borough Council*[1].

However, the local authority can state that this is the standard of behaviour and conduct expected of a licensed driver and if the driver falls short, the council will then consider whether they remain a fit and proper person to hold the licence.

[1]   [2002] EWHC 1634 (Admin), [2002] LLR 749, Admin Ct.

A LICENSED HACKNEY CARRIAGE DRIVER

Driver's hours

10.89

There are no direct controls over the hours that a hackney carriage driver can work[1]. However, the Working Time Regulations 1998 as amended apply to hackney carriage drivers. Regulation 24A requires such employed drivers to have adequate rest periods[2].

[1] This can be contrasted with HGV and PSV drivers whose driving hours are regulated. There have been suggestions that hackney carriage drivers' hours should be limited, but there are no current proposals. The matter was raised in 2015 by a Councillor Adrian Lawrence, Cabinet Member for Housing and Community at the Borough Council of King's Lynn & West Norfolk who raised it with his MP, Elizabeth Truss. This led to a response from the then Secretary of State for Transport, Patrick McLoughlin (in an undated letter received on 28th October 2015).

> 'Cllr Lawrence makes an important point about safety, a priority and concern that I share. It is vitally important that licensed drivers are fit to drive safely and that members of the public can use taxis and private hire vehicles in the knowledge that they are a safe form of transport.
>
> Self-employed taxi and private hire vehicle drivers can choose the hours they work and there are no rules to limit the number of hours they can work in a day or a week. The issue of licensed drivers' hours has been reviewed in the past; however it was concluded that there was no real case for amending the licensing regime to provide for the regulation of drivers' hours. Responses received at the time from road safety and regulatory organisations and from local and police authorities suggested that the hours worked by taxi drivers were not considered to give rise to a safety problem. Taxis and private hire vehicles typically cover relatively short distances which are generally interspersed with rest breaks, so the total time spent driving is considerably less than the time spent on call. Enforcement is also a relevant consideration; restricting the hours of taxi and private hire vehicle drivers or imposing requirements for rest in a trade consisting predominantly of self-employed individuals would prove both difficult and costly to enforce, with or without a tachograph in the vehicle.
>
> That said, local licensing authorities have a key role to play in maintaining safety. Where concerns about the operation of taxis and private hire vehicles are brought to their attention they could — and should — take immediate action if there is any evidence of unsafe activity.'

[2] 'Adequate rest' is defined in reg 24A(3): '"*adequate rest*" means that a worker has regular rest periods, the duration of which are expressed in units of time and which are sufficiently long and continuous to ensure that, as a result of fatigue or other irregular working patterns, he does not cause injury to himself, to fellow workers or to others and that he does not damage his health, either in the short term or in the longer term.'

10.90

This only applies to drivers who are employed and working under a contract of employment and does not apply to self-employed drivers. It is therefore of limited application in relation to the hackney carriage trade, where the vast majority of drivers are self-employed.

10.91

In relation to those who are employed, the employed can opt out of the application of the Regulations by agreeing in writing that they should not apply in accordance with reg 4(1) (this must voluntary and the driver cannot be forced to opt out by the employer).

Provisions affecting drivers under the Town Police Clauses Act 1847

10.92

There are a number of provisions applying to hackney carriage drivers which exist with a view to protecting the public.

PROVISIONS AFFECTING DRIVERS UNDER THE DUTY TO TAKE A FARE

10.93

Under TPCA 1847, s 53 the hackney carriage driver waiting on a hackney stand, or on the street is under a duty to take a fare[1]. It states:

> **'Penalty on driver for refusing to drive**
>
> 53   A driver of a hackney carriage standing at any of the stands for hackney carriages appointed by the commissioners, or in any street, who refuses or neglects, without reasonable excuse, to drive such carriage to any place within the prescribed distance, or the distance to be appointed by any byelaw of the commissioners, not exceeding the prescribed distance, to which he is directed to drive by the person hiring or wishing to hire such carriage, shall for every such offence be liable to a penalty not exceeding level 2 on the standard scale.'

[1]   As regards 'cruising' hackney carriages, see *Hunt v Morgan* at para 10.99 below and Chapter 19, para 19.40.

10.94

There are a number of matters to be considered in relation to TPCA 1847, s 53. First, it should be noted that this is not a blanket requirement, as the driver can refuse if he has a 'reasonable excuse'.

10.95

There is no reported High Court decision relating to the question of what is a 'reasonable excuse'. In the absence of such a decision, it will be a subjective matter for the magistrates to consider whether the refusal was reasonable in the particular circumstances of the case before them. In certain areas of some large cities in England and Wales, hackney carriage drivers refuse to take fares after a certain time of night, due to their concerns about being assaulted either by the passengers themselves or by persons in the area to which they have been asked to travel. It would appear to be difficult to argue against this, as the safety of the driver and, indeed, in certain circumstances, his passengers would appear to be a reasonable excuse for not taking the fare. This has serious implications for people who live in areas that are viewed in this light by the hackney carriage drivers, but a prosecution would appear unlikely to succeed.

10.96

Beyond that, other 'reasonable excuses' would include the behaviour of the prospective passenger. It would seem to be reasonable for a driver to refuse to take a passenger who was abusive, racist, sexist, foul mouthed, extremely drunk etc. This could also extend to those who refused to stop smoking or eating, or had been sick over themselves or soiled themselves in other ways, or where there were legitimate concerns that the passenger might damage the vehicle.

10.97

The second point concerns the area within which a hackney carriage driver must take a fare. TPCA 1847, s 53 refers to the 'prescribed distance, or the distance to be appointed by the byelaw ... not exceeding the prescribed distance'. The prescribed distance is now the area of the district council (or unitary, metropolitan district, Welsh county or county borough council), unless the council has hackney carriage zones, in which case it will be the area of the zone in question[1].

[1]   This is as a result of the provisions of the Public Health Act 1875, s 171, which incorporated the provisions of TPCA 1847 and the Town Police Clauses Act 1889 for all urban districts. The Local Government Acts 1894 and 1933 extended hackney carriage licensing to all urban districts, boroughs and county boroughs and this continued under the Local Government Act 1972. The Transport Act 1985 extended hackney carriage licensing to all districts in England and Wales.

10.98

Some local authorities may have byelaws which reduce the prescribed distance from the area of the local authority and there are some local Acts which extend it, eg the Greater Manchester Act 1981, which in relation to the ten metropolitan districts within Greater Manchester extends the prescribed distance to any hiring commencing within the district and extending up to four miles from the district boundary, provided it is within the county of Greater Manchester.

HAILING A CAB

10.99

Does a 'cruising' hackney carriage have to respond to a prospective passenger hailing the cab? In other words, is a refusal to stop and pick a fare on the street (as opposed to a passenger approaching a hackney carriage on the rank or stand, or stationary on the street) an offence? From the wording of TPCA 1847 s 53[1] the answer appears to be clear, that only a refusal to take a fare from the rank or a street (within the meaning of the definition contained in TPCA 1847, s 3[2]) constitutes an offence. This has never been the subject of a superior court decision outside London, but the London case of *Hunt v Morgan*[3] suggests strongly such a refusal to respond to a hailing is not an offence.

[1]   See Appendix I.
[2]   'Street' is defined in TPCA 1847, s 3: 'The word "street" shall extend to and include any road, square, court, alley, and thoroughfare, or public passage, within the limits of the special Act:'
[3]   [1948] 2 All ER 1065 QBD – fully considered in Chapter 19, para 19.40.

10.100

As is often the case, the legislation applicable in London is similar, but not identical to the outside London legislation. Whilst TPCA 1847, s 53 requires a driver to take a fare when 'standing at any of the stands for hackney carriages appointed by the commissioners, or in any street' unless there is a reasonable excuse, the requirement in London is wider. Section 7 of the London Hackney Carriage Act 1853 requires a driver 'which shall ply for hire at any place within the limits of this Act' to take a fare (unless there is a reasonable excuse). In *Hunt v Morgan*[1] the question arose as to 'whether a cruising taxicab driver is bound to accept anyone who hails him. It is obviously one of general importance, not only to cab drivers, but also to the members of the public, and it seems never to have been the subject of a decision. There is, no doubt, a widely held belief that a cabman, whether on the rank or not, is bound to accept a fare unless he has a reasonable excuse for refusing'.[2] The answer in London was that there is no requirement to take such a fare, which, although clearly viewed a surprising by the court, was the position under the legislation.

[1]   As above.
[2]   [1948] 2 All ER 1065 QBD, per Goddard LCJ at 1066.

10.101

When the differences between the two regulatory regimes are considered, it seems that, in the absence of any other statutory requirements, which are not to be found in any of the nationally applicable legislation[1], it is clear that a hackney carriage which is travelling, albeit one which is not hired at the time, is under no legal requirement to respond to a hailing by a prospective passenger. This allows the driver to be selective about those he decides to pick up.

[1]   Town Police Clauses Act 1847 or Local Government (Miscellaneous Provisions) Act 1976.

AGREEMENTS AS TO FARES

10.102

An agreement can be made in advance of the hire that a certain fare will be paid, which must be less than the fare which would be shown on the meter. TPCA 1847, s 54[1] prohibits any increase in that agreed fare being made either during or at the conclusion of the hiring and if a driver attempted to charge more than the agreed fare, this would be an offence under that section. This does not, of course, prohibit charging less than the fare that is shown on the meter at the end of the journey if no agreement was made in advance[2].

[1]   See Appendix I.
[2]   See Chapter 9, para 9.27 onwards.

AGREEMENT TO PAY MORE THAN THE LEGAL FARE

10.103

TPCA 1847, s 55 makes it an offence for a driver to demand more than the fare shown on the meter[1]. In such circumstances it is possible for the local authority to prosecute the driver and on conviction a fine not exceeding level 3 on the standard scale can be imposed.

'Agreement to pay more than the legal fare

55 No agreement whatever made with the driver, or with any person having or pretending to have the care of any such hackney carriage, for the payment of more than the fare allowed by any byelaw[2] made under this or the special Act, shall be binding on the person making the same; and any such person may, notwithstanding such agreement, refuse, on discharging such hackney carriage, to pay any sum beyond the fare allowed as aforesaid; and if any person actually pay to the driver of any such hackney carriage, whether in pursuance of any such agreement or otherwise, any sum exceeding the fare to which such driver was entitled, the person paying the same shall be entitled, on complaint made against such driver before any justice of the peace, to recover back the sum paid beyond the proper fare, and moreover such driver shall be liable to a penalty for such exaction not exceeding level 3 on the standard scale; and in default of the repayment by such driver of such excess of fare, or of payment of the said penalty, such justice shall forthwith commit such driver to prison, there to remain for any time not exceeding one month, unless the said excess of fare and the said penalty be sooner paid.'

[1] See Chapter 9, para 9.36.
[2] LG(MP)A 1976, s 65(5) states that if the district council has byelaws, the table of fares made under the provisions of LG(MP)A 1976, s 65 is deemed to be the table of fares in the byelaws, and will supersede any earlier fares set by previous byelaws.

10.104

TPCA 1847, s 56[1] allows an agreement to be struck with the driver (or proprietor) of a hackney carriage that for a specified sum of money the passengers will be carried a fixed distance. This is subject to the proviso that the actual charge does not work out as being greater than that which would be allowed by the meter[2].

[1] See Appendix I.
[2] See Chapter 9, para 9.38.

PENALTY ON PROPRIETORS ETC CONVICTED OF OVERCHARGING

10.105

TPCA 1847, s 58 prohibits a driver charging more than is displayed on the meter. This can be contrasted with TPCA 1847, s 55, which actually makes unlawful an agreement to pay more than the amount which would be displayed on the meter at the end of the journey.

'Penalty on proprietors, etc convicted of overcharging

58 Every proprietor or driver of any such hackney carriage who is convicted of taking as a fare a greater sum than is authorised by any byelaw made under this or the special Act shall be liable to a penalty not exceeding

level 3 on the standard scale, and such penalty may be recovered before
one justice; and in the conviction of such proprietor or driver an order
may be included for payment of the sum so overcharged, over and above
the penalty and costs; and such overcharge shall be returned to the party
aggrieved.'

House v Reynolds

10.106

> Booking fee for a hackney carriage added to the fare by the driver. Held:
> This was an offence as it was charging more than the fare allowed by the
> table of fares.

This distinction is usefully illustrated by the case of *House v Reynolds*[1]. In this case,
convictions had been secured against a number of hackney carriage drivers and
hackney carriage proprietors for contravention of both TPCA 1847, s 55 and
TPCA 1847, s 58. A group of proprietors had arranged a centralised telephone
booking service and prospective passengers who used this service were told
that to book a hackney carriage by this method would incur a booking fee of
10p. That sum was collected at the end of the journey at the same time as the
recorded fare was obtained from the passenger.

[1]   [1977] 1 WLR 88, QBD.

10.107

The first question was whether such a fee was contrary to the provisions of
TPCA 1847, s 55. Eveleigh J gave the leading judgment of the court[1]. He quoted
s 55 and then said (at 92C):

> 'In my view that section is striking at the payment by the passenger of
> something apart from, or over and above, the fare itself. It is aimed at
> a collateral agreement to the agreement to hire. Of course there has to
> be a connection between such agreement and the contract of hire. The
> words "No agreement whatever" are clearly to be read in the context of
> a hiring agreement but relate to something collateral thereto. In my view
> the booking agreement with which we are concerned in this case was an
> agreement collateral to the hiring agreement, but it did provide for the
> payment of such a sum more than the fare that was allowed. Consequently,
> there has been a breach of section 55.'

[1]   *House v Reynolds* [1977] 1 WLR 88, QBD.

10.108

Slynn J agreed (as did Widgery LCJ). Slynn J stated[1] (at 92H):

> 'Section 55 [TPCA 1847, s 55], … is wide enough to cover a collateral
> agreement to pay money and covers the taking by a driver of a sum of over

and above what is in the strict sense a fare. The agreement to pay a booking fee and the taking of a booking fee by the driver in the present case in my judgment fell within that section.'

[1] *House v Reynolds* [1977] 1 WLR 88, QBD.

10.109

It is interesting to note that it was argued that no offence had been committed by the 'driver, or with any person having or pretending to have the care of any such hackney carriage' because the arrangement to pay the 10p was made with the umbrella booking organisation. Eveleigh J defeated that argument with the following[1] (at 92F):

'I should refer to one final argument addressed to the court by Mr Farquharson [for the defendants], who said that section 55 [TPCA 1847, s 55] related to an agreement made with the driver or any person having or pretending to have the care of the hackney carriage, and he said that in the present case the agreement could not be said to have been made with the defendants, be it with the owner or be it with the driver, because the agreement was made with the organisation Streamline Taxis.

In my view that argument does not prevail. The telephonist was in my opinion acting as an agent on behalf of the defendants, be it the driver or be it the owner, or, to put it another way, the agreement was being made with the owner and the driver through the telephonist.'

[1] *House v Reynolds* [1977] 1 WLR 88, QBD.

10.110

It is quite clear, therefore, that this case outlaws a booking fee being levied for a telephone booking of a hackney carriage, unless that booking fee is incorporated into the Table of Fares (Chapter 9, para 9.19).

10.111

In relation to TPCA 1847, s 58, Eveleigh J considered the matter (and it should be recognised that convictions had been obtained in *House* under both TPCA 1847, ss 55 and 58) and his judgment was as follows[1] (at 92E):

'I turn now to section 58. It is important to emphasise the words in that section "taking as a fare". These are clearly to be contrasted with the words in section 55 which referred to the payment of "any sum exceeding the fare". Consequently, it seems to me that section 58 is dealing with the fare itself, with a sum of money paid and received as the fare. As I have already come to the conclusion that the 10p in this case was not paid as the fare but was something collateral thereto, it would follow that there is no offence under section 58.'

[1] *House v Reynolds* [1977] 1 WLR 88, QBD.

10.112

It would seem that the offence under TPCA 1847, s 58 is committed at the end of the journey when the demand is made for more than the fare that is shown on the meter (plus any allowable extras). This may affect in which magistrates' court the information should be laid, as it may be that the end of the hiring was in a different Local Justice Area from that which covers the area of the local authority that licensed the hackney carriage and driver.

Ely v Godfrey

10.113

> Driver overcharged a fare at the end of the journey which was outside the local authority's area. The local authority that licensed the vehicle and driver prosecuted. This was appealed. Held: That the court had no jurisdiction because the offence was committed in another local authority area.

This point was considered in the case of *Ely v Godfrey*[1], which concerned a prosecution under the Salford Improvement Act 1862, s 309. A hackney carriage driver had charged considerably more than the fare which was allowed by the byelaws for a journey which commenced within the borough of Salford but ended some 8.5 miles beyond the borough boundary. The correct fare, as indicated by the byelaws, would have been 13 shillings but, in fact, the driver charged 25 shillings. Section 309 was extremely similar in wording to TPCA 1847, s 55 and the driver was prosecuted in Salford Magistrates' Court. He appealed against conviction. One of the grounds for appeal was that the stipendiary magistrate sitting in Salford had no jurisdiction to try the case, as the alleged offence had taken place in another borough, some 8.5 miles away from the Salford boundary. Salter J stated (at 84):

> 'I am of the opinion that this conviction cannot stand, on the ground that the learned magistrate who dealt with this matter had no jurisdiction to deal with it.
>
> In my opinion the offence of which this man was convicted was committed wholly on the arrival of the cab at Mile End Lane [in Stockport], at which time and place, as found in the case, the driver asked and received the sum of 25 shillings. If that was excess of the amount to which he was lawfully entitled, he committed the offence then and there; and that was a distance of seven or eight miles from the boundary of the jurisdiction of the stipendiary magistrate who dealt with this matter.'

[1] (1922) 86 JP 82.

How many people can be carried in a hackney carriage?

10.114

It is for the local authority to decide how many passengers the hackney carriage can be licensed to carry, which is then detailed on the licence in accordance with TPCA 1847, s 41 ('in every such licence shall be specified … such other particulars as the commissioners think fit')[1]. The number of passengers is then shown on the plate[2].

TPCA 1847, s 52 makes it an offence for the driver to refuse to carry any number of persons up to that maximum when required to do so by the hirer, but TPCA 1847 and LG(MP)A 1976 are both silent as to the maximum number of passengers that can be carried.

That restriction is contained in byelaws and can be found in byelaw 11 of the model bylaws, which states:

'11. A proprietor or driver of a hackney carriage shall not convey or permit to be conveyed in such carriage any greater number of persons than the number of persons specified on the plate affixed to the outside of the carriage.'

Neither the byelaws, TPCA 1847 or LG(MP)A 1976 address the question of children. The London Cab Order 1934, art 33[3] restricts the number of passengers to the maximum that the carriage is licensed to carry, but states:

'in computing such number, an infant in arms shall not count as a person and two children under 10 years of age shall count as one person.'

There are some local authorities which have used this approach, either by means of conditions attached to the hackney carriage proprietor's licence, or informally when assessing whether an offence has been committed, but it is suggested that such an approach must be considered very carefully, bearing in mind the dangers involved in children not having proper restraints, or sharing an adult seatbelt[4].

[1]   See Chapter 8, para 8.102.
[2]   See para 8.2.
[3]   SI 1934/1346; see Appendix I.
[4]   The idea or practice of two children sharing one adult seatbelt is now so obsolete and dangerous that it is not even mentioned (even as being unacceptable and dangerous) in official Government advice.

CARRYING PERSONS OTHER THAN THE HIRER

Yates v Gates

10.115

> Driver carried a woman and child as well as the hirer and his companion. Was this contrary to s 59? Held: It was, as no express consent had been given by the hirer.

TPCA 1847, s 59 prohibits a driver (or proprietor) of a hackney carriage from carrying persons other than the hirer, unless the hirer has given his express consent. This was the principal point considered in *Yates v Gates*[1]. The situation was that two people (who were actually employees of the local authority) approached a hackney carriage. The driver was not present, but was in a nearby house. When he emerged from the house he was accompanied by a woman and a child. The two officers asked to hire the vehicle to take them to a destination. The driver stated that he would take the two officers first, then take the women and the child to their destination and all five people got into the vehicle. The question which arose was whether the express consent which was required under s 59 could be obtained by acquiescence. Parker LCJ gave the judgment of the court (at 755J):

> 'The question ... left to the court is: "Can consent be expressed by actions without words; if so, were Mr Smith's actions capable in law of amounting to express consent?" In my judgment express consent in this provision, whatever it may mean elsewhere, means positive consent, not an acquiescence in the form of an implied consent. It envisages that a driver of a taxi cab should ask the hirer whether he objects to somebody else being carried. Of course if he says "I have no objection", there is the express consent. It may be also, in answer to the first question raised by the justices, that the action might amount to consent, in that he might nod his head in answer to the question, but mere acquiescence, as I have said, would not in my judgment amount to express consent within the Act.'

1   [1970] 1 All ER 754, QBD.

Those who are prohibited from driving a hackney carriage

10.116

A person is prohibited from driving a hackney carriage without the consent of the proprietor under TPCA 1847, s 60[1]. Additionally, a hackney carriage driver who does have the consent of the proprietor to drive, but who allows another person who does not have such consent to drive, also commits an offence. In addition, any driver of a hackney carriage must hold a hackney carriage driver's licence[2].

1   See Appendix I.
2   See *Hawkins v Edwards* [1901] 2 KB 169 and *Yates v Gates* [1970] 1 All ER 754, QBD. See Chapter 8, para 8.4 onwards and Chapter 10, para 10.1.

10.117

In reality, although criminal offences exist, the resulting action is more likely to be taken by the proprietor himself under contract, rather than to rely on the local authority to take action under TPCA 1847, s 60.

The effect of other legislation on the Town Police Clauses Act 1847

10.118

TPCA 1847, s 61[1] has effectively been rendered obsolete by the provisions of the Road Traffic Act 1988. In 1847, there were no provisions concerning drunken driving or 'wanton and furious driving', but there are now and it is most unlikely that the local authority would take action under s 61 in such circumstances. The police would undoubtedly be involved and would wish to take action under the Road Traffic Act 1988 for either dangerous driving, contrary to the Road Traffic Act 1988, s 2 or careless and inconsiderate driving, contrary to the Road Traffic Act 1988, s 3.

[1] See Appendix I.

Morris v Preston Crown Court and Blackpool BC

10.119

> Prosecution of a horse drawn hackney carriage driver for exposing persons to the risk of injury by the manner of his driving. Argued that the byelaw in question only applied to the horse, not the carriage. Held: The offence related to the carriage.

Notwithstanding the above, a prosecution for furious driving was brought by Blackpool Borough Council against the driver of a horse drawn hackney carriage in *Morris v Preston Crown Court and Blackpool BC*[1]. That was dropped but the driver was convicted of breaching Byelaw 20 of the Blackpool BC byelaws[2]. The driver, Mr Morris was observed driving a horse-drawn hackney carriage carrying himself and four passengers speeding through a red light and over white lines into the oncoming traffic, before returning to the correct side of the road. He was convicted by the magistrates, and his appeal to the Crown Court was dismissed. Morris sought judicial review of the interpretation of Byelaw 20, arguing that it did not apply to the way in which the carriage was driven, only the treatment of the horse.

Byelaw 20 states:

> '(i) The proprietor or driver of a hackney carriage shall not whilst standing, plying or driving for hire, drive or allow to be driven, or harness or allow to be harnessed to the carriage any animal in such condition as to expose any person conveyed or being in such a carriage, or any person traversing any street, to risk of injury.'

It was held that it did apply to the way in which the carriage was driven. Judgment was given by Hickenbottom J[3]

> '20 It seems to me that the determinative question for this application is this: what is the object of "drive or allow to be driven" in byelaw 20? Is it a hackney carriage, as referred to previously in the provision, as in essence contended for by the council: or is it the animal (ie the horse) referred to later in the provision? So far as "driving" is concerned, does the byelaw mean: "The proprietor or driver of a hackney carriage shall not … drive [the carriage], or allow [the carriage] to be driven … as to expose a person [in the defined categories] to risk of injury?". Or does it mean: "The proprietor or driver of a hackney carriage shall not … drive [the horse] or allow [the horse] to be driven as to expose a person [in the defined categories] to risk of injury?".

21 In my judgment, on its true construction, it is unambiguously the former. In the context of horse-drawn hackney carriages, "driving" ordinarily, naturally and plainly means driving the carriage, not simply the horse. But, in any event, byelaw 20 does not refer simply to a horse, but to a horse "in such condition as to expose any [relevant] person ... to risk of injury". On the construction propounded by the claimant [Morris, the driver], the risk that must arise for the byelaw to apply has to arise from the condition of the horse. As I have indicated, it is common ground that the byelaw prohibits a driver from harnessing a horse in such condition as to expose a relevant person to the risk of injury. In my view, the claimant's construction consequently renders the words "drive or allowed to be driven" otiose, because for a horse to be driven it must be harnessed.'

He concluded[4]:

'28 For those reasons, I accept the substance of para 4.4 of the council's detailed grounds of response to this application, which says succinctly:
(i) "Put simply, bylaw 20 requires that:
(1) a driver shall not drive so as to expose persons to risk of injury; and
(2) that the driver shall not harness an animal to the carriage in such condition that would expose such persons to risk of injury."

29 The reference to "allow to be driven" and "allow to be harnessed" is relevant to the way in which a proprietor may commit those two modes of offending.'

This case is clearly limited to authorities where a similar byelaw is in force, and does not alter the assertion that TPCA 1847, s 61 is obsolete.

---

[1] [2012] EWHC 2134 (Admin), [2013] LLR 423, Admin Ct.
[2] This is a byelaw that is only usually found where the authority licences horse drawn hackney carriages.
[3] Above at para 20 onwards.
[4] Above at para 28.

10.120

Likewise, TPCA 1847, s 63[1] is obsolete. This allows anyone who is hurt or has damage caused to themselves or their property by the driver of a hackney carriage to seek compensation through the magistrates' court. However, as this compensation cannot exceed £5, any claim for compensation would appear to be best directed against the driver under the general civil law.

---

[1] See Appendix I.

10.121

TPCA 1847, s 62[1] still has some relevance. It is an offence for the driver of a hackney carriage to 'leave it in any street or in any place of public resort or entertainment, whether it be hired or not, without someone proper to take care of it' and is punishable to a penalty on conviction not exceeding level 1 on the standard scale. In addition, a police constable can remove the hackney carriage to a place of safe custody. The section, in fact, refers to removing the hackney carriage and any horses harnessed to it to a livery stable, but in the age of motorised hackney carriages that is unlikely to be a common occurrence, unless the area has horse-drawn hackney carriages, which do exist in some seaside and tourist towns.

[1]   See Appendix I.

10.122

It is interesting to note that, on the face of it, TPCA 1847, s 62 would apply to any hackney carriage which is parked on a street or at any other public place, irrespective of whether it is locked or not. This would appear to suggest, if interpreted literally, that a hackney carriage can only be parked on private land to which the public has no access (although it is less than clear whether that access should be as of right or of fact). This seems most unreasonable in today's situation regarding motorised hackney carriages, and it would seem unlikely that any prosecution in relation to a hackney carriage that was properly parked would succeed. However, in *Attridge v Attwood*[1] a hackney carriage driver parked his vehicle with the handbrake on and the engine switched off. He was prosecuted under s 62. He asserted that the section only applied to horse-drawn vehicles, but that was rejected. The High Court held that it would be a matter of fact and degree as to whether a driver had taken sufficient precautions to satisfy the requirements of s 62. The case of *Rodgers v Taylor*[2] should also be noted.

[1]   [1964] Crim LR 45.
[2]   (1986) 85 LGR 762. See Chapter 9, para 9.88 in relation to a hackney carriage parking on a stand.

10.123

If one driver attempts to prevent another hackney carriage from being hired in preference to his, he commits an offence under TPCA 1847, s 64[1], as does someone who obstructs other hackney carriages. In relation to obstruction of other hackney carriages, this is more appropriately dealt with under other legislation, eg the Highways Act 1980, s 137 (wilfully obstructing the passage of a highway) or the Road Vehicles (Construction and Use) Regulations 1986, reg 103[2] (causing or permitting a motor vehicle or trailer to stand on a road so as to cause unnecessary obstruction of the road). However, there may be situations where the drivers are in dispute as to whom should take the particular fare. In those circumstances s 64 may still be relevant[3].

[1]   See Appendix I.
[2]   SI 1986/1078.
[3]   This point was considered in *R v Great Western Trains Ltd, ex p Frederick* [1998] COD 239. See Chapter 9, para 9.70 onwards.

10.124

If a prosecution is brought against a driver for an offence under any provision of TPCA 1847 and the driver is acquitted, TPCA 1847, s 65[1] allows him to claim 'such compensation for his loss of time in attending the said Justice touching or concerning such complaint or information as to the said Justice seems reasonable'. It is interesting to note that such compensation is to be paid irrespective of whether or not the driver is legally represented and it enables a person who is acquitted to claim compensation for his loss of time, and not just for costs involved in instructing a solicitor. It is unclear how often this section is used when a local authority either fails to secure a conviction or withdraws a summons before trial, although it has been used in recent years when a prosecution has not been successful[2].

1   See Appendix I.
2   An award of £100 for loss of earnings was made by Swansea magistrates' court following a prosecution by the City & County of Swansea which was unsuccessful in March 2008.

Provisions affecting drivers under the Local Government (Miscellaneous Provisions) Act 1976

REQUIREMENT TO PRODUCE HACKNEY CARRIAGE DRIVER'S LICENCE

10.125

LG(MP)A 1976, s 53(3)[1] requires a hackney carriage driver to produce his driver's licence to either an authorised officer of the council or a police constable, if so requested. It must be produced forthwith or within a five-day period[2] to either the council offices or the police station. 'Forthwith' has been defined as 'as soon as possible in all the circumstances, the nature of the act being done to be taken into account' in *Sameen v Abeyewickrema*[3]. It is unlikely that a hackney carriage driver would be able to produce his driver's licence immediately as, by virtue of TPCA 1847, s 48, the licence has to be retained by the proprietor of the hackney carriage. Unless the driver is also the proprietor, he is unlikely to have the licence with him, but it should not take him too long to be able to produce it, having obtained it from the proprietor for that purpose.

1   See Appendix I.
2   LG(MP)A 1976, s 53(3)(a) and (b).
3   [1963] AC 597, PC.

Duties under the Equality Act 2010

A DRIVER MUST CARRY ASSISTANCE DOGS

10.126

The Equality Act 2010, s 168 places a duty on the driver of a hackney carriage (referred to as a 'taxi') to carry an assistance dog[1]:

> **'168 Assistance dogs in taxis**
> (1) This section imposes duties on the driver of a taxi which has been hired—
>   (a) by or for a disabled person who is accompanied by an assistance dog, or

(b) by another person who wishes to be accompanied by a disabled person with an assistance dog.

(2) The driver must—

(a) carry the disabled person's dog and allow it to remain with that person;

(b) not make any additional charge for doing so.

(3) The driver of a taxi commits an offence by failing to comply with a duty imposed by this section.

(4) A person guilty of an offence under this section is liable on summary conviction to a fine not exceeding level 3 on the standard scale.'

'Assistance dog' is defined in s 173(1) as meaning:

' "assistance dog" means—

(a) a dog which has been trained to guide a blind person;

(b) a dog which has been trained to assist a deaf person;

(c) a dog which has been trained by a prescribed charity to assist a disabled person who has a disability that consists of epilepsy or otherwise affects the person's mobility, manual dexterity, physical co-ordination or ability to lift, carry or otherwise move everyday objects;

(d) a dog of a prescribed category which has been trained to assist a disabled person who has a disability (other than one falling within paragraph (c)) of a prescribed kind[2];'

---

[1] Similar provisions apply to private hire vehicles under EA 2010, s 170.

[2] The Disability Discrimination Act 1995 (Taxis) (Carrying of Guide Dogs etc.) (England and Wales) Regulations 2000, SI 2000/2990 as amended are now deemed to have been made under the Equality Act, and were amended by the Equality Act 2010 (Commencement No. 4, Savings, Consequential, Transitional, Transitory and Incidental Provisions and Revocation) Order 2010, SI 2010/2317.

10.127

Additional Assistance dogs are prescribed by reg 3 of The Disability Discrimination Act 1995 (Taxis) (Carrying of Guide Dogs etc.) (England and Wales) Regulations 2000, SI 2000/2990 as amended and include:

' "3. Prescribed charities

Each of the following is a prescribed charity for the purposes of paragraph (c) of the definition of "assistance dog" in section 173(1) of the 2010 Act (so far as that definition applies for the purposes of section 168 of that Act)—

(a) "Dogs for the Disabled" registered with the Charity Commission under registration number 1092960;

(b) "Support Dogs" registered with the Charity Commission under registration number 1017237; and

(c) "Canine Partners for Independence" registered with the Charity Commission under registration number 803680.'

10.128

A driver is exempted from this requirement if he holds an exemption certificate issued by the local authority on medical grounds under the provisions of EA 2010, s 169:

'**169 Assistance dogs in taxis: exemption certificates**

(1)   A licensing authority must issue a person with a certificate exempting the person from the duties imposed by section 168 (an "exemption certificate") if satisfied that it is appropriate to do so on medical grounds.

(2)   In deciding whether to issue an exemption certificate the authority must have regard, in particular, to the physical characteristics of the taxi which the person drives or those of any kind of taxi in relation to which the person requires the certificate.

(3)   An exemption certificate is valid—
(a)   in respect of a specified taxi or a specified kind of taxi;
(b)   for such period as is specified in the certificate.

(4)   The driver of a taxi is exempt from the duties imposed by section 168 if—
(a)   an exemption certificate issued to the driver is in force with respect to the taxi, and
(b)   the prescribed notice of the exemption is exhibited on the taxi in the prescribed manner.
The power to make regulations under paragraph (b) is exercisable by the Secretary of State.

(5)   In this section "licensing authority" means—
(a)   in relation to the area to which the Metropolitan Public Carriage Act 1869 applies, Transport for London;
(b)   in relation to any other area in England and Wales, the authority responsible for licensing taxis in that area.'

Clearly such a certificate can only be issued on medical grounds, which tend to relate either to allergies to dogs, or phobia of dogs. However, the local authority (or TfL in the case of a London driver) must also have regard to the vehicle the driver will be driving. Where there is an all WAV policy in place, this might be a straightforward consideration, but it will be more complex where there is a mixed vehicle fleet. As a hackney carriage driver can theoretically drive any hackney carriage licensed by the same authority and there is no mandatory linking of a driver and a particular vehicle, it will be for the local authority (or TfL) to determine how the characteristics of different vehicles will affect individuals.

If such an exemption certificate is granted, it must be in the form specified in the Disability Discrimination Act 1995 (Taxis) (Carrying of Guide Dogs etc) (England and Wales) Regulations 2000 (as amended), reg 2 and Sch 1 (in England) or Sch 2 (in Wales)[1]. Once such a certificate has been granted, it must be displayed in accordance with reg 2(2):

'**2–(2)** The prescribed manner of exhibiting a notice of exemption for the purposes of section 169(4)(b) of the 2010 Act shall be by either—

(a) affixing it in a prominent position on the dashboard of the taxi, facing upwards; or

(b) affixing it to the windscreen of the taxi, facing outwards.'

There is a right of appeal against a refusal by the licensing authority to issue an exemption certificate. This is contained in s 172(1) which states:

'(1) A person who is aggrieved by the refusal of a licensing authority in England and Wales to issue an exemption certificate under section 166, 169 or 171 may appeal to a magistrates' court before the end of the period of 28 days beginning with the date of the refusal.'

If the appeal is successful, the magistrates can order the licensing authority to issue the certificate (see s 172(3)).

[1]   Deemed to be made under the Equality Act 2010.

10.129

Breach of the duty placed upon a hackney carriage to carry an assistance dog in the passenger compartment contrary to EA 2010, s 168 is a criminal offence under s 168(3). As the Equality Act is silent as to which body can prosecute such an offence, it is a general criminal offence and can therefore be investigated by the police and prosecuted by the Crown Prosecution Service. However it can also be investigated by, or prosecuted by the local authority under the powers contained in s 222 of the Local Government Act 1972[1]. As the local authority is the enforcing authority for all other taxi legislation, it would seem to be both reasonable and expedient for the local authority to prosecute cases such as this.

[1]   Section 222 states:

'(1) Where a local authority consider it expedient for the promotion or protection of the interests of the inhabitants of their area—

(a) they may prosecute or defend or appear in any legal proceedings and, in the case of civil proceedings, may institute them in their own name, and

(b) they may, in their own name, make representations in the interests of the inhabitants at any public inquiry held by or on behalf of any Minister or public body under any enactment.

(2) In this section "local authority" includes the Common Council and the London Fire and Emergency Planning Authority.'

10.130

In relation to assistance dogs, again, there have been a number of reported problems where carriage of the dog has been refused on the grounds that it may make a mess of the vehicle, either by deposit of dog hairs or worse. In addition to a breach of EA 2010, s 168, this is also a breach of the conditions of many local authorities.

PROVISION OF MOBILITY ASSISTANCE

10.131

Sections 165 and 167 of EA 2010 came into force in April 2017. These allow a licensing authority (a local authority or TfL in London) to create a list of 'designated vehicles' which are capable of carrying passengers in wheelchairs, and then require drivers of those vehicles to provide mobility assistance. These vehicles can be either hackney carriages or private hire vehicles. Section 166 is an exemption provision.

10.132

The starting point for these provisions lies with s 167:

'**167 Lists of wheelchair-accessible vehicles**
(1) For the purposes of section 165, a licensing authority may maintain a list of vehicles falling within subsection (2).
(2) A vehicle falls within this subsection if—
  (a) it is either a taxi or a private hire vehicle, and
  (b) it conforms to such accessibility requirements as the licensing authority thinks fit.
(3) A licensing authority may, if it thinks fit, decide that a vehicle may be included on a list maintained under this section only if it is being used, or is to be used, by the holder of a special licence under that licence.
(4) In subsection (3) "special licence" has the meaning given by section 12 of the Transport Act 1985 (use of taxis or hire cars in providing local services).
(5) "Accessibility requirements" are requirements for securing that it is possible for disabled persons in wheelchairs—
  (a) to get into and out of vehicles in safety, and
  (b) to travel in vehicles in safety and reasonable comfort,
  either staying in their wheelchairs or not (depending on which they prefer).
(6) The Secretary of State may issue guidance to licensing authorities as to—
  (a) the accessibility requirements which they should apply for the purposes of this section;
  (b) any other aspect of their functions under or by virtue of this section.
(7) A licensing authority which maintains a list under subsection (1) must have regard to any guidance issued under subsection (6).'

Once a vehicle has been listed under s 167, it is then referred to as either a 'designated taxi' or a designated private hire vehicle and the driver of any such vehicle who is not in possession of an exemption certificate issued under s 166 is then under a statutory duty to carry wheelchair-bound passengers and to provide 'mobility assistance' by virtue of s165.

The duty applies when the vehicle has been hired:

'165(1) This section imposes duties on the driver of a designated taxi which has been hired—
(a) by or for a disabled person who is in a wheelchair, or
(b) by another person who wishes to be accompanied by a disabled person who is in a wheelchair.

(2) This section also imposes duties on the driver of a designated private hire vehicle, if a person within paragraph (a) or (b) of subsection (1) has indicated to the driver that the person wishes to travel in the vehicle.'

The duties imposed on the driver are detailed in sub-ss (4) and (5). Subsection (4) contains the general duties and sub-s (5) details what is meant by 'mobility assistance'.

The general duties are[1]:

'(a) to carry the passenger while in the wheelchair;
(b) not to make any additional charge for doing so;
(c) if the passenger chooses to sit in a passenger seat, to carry the wheelchair;
(d) to take such steps as are necessary to ensure that the passenger is carried in safety and reasonable comfort;
(e) to give the passenger such mobility assistance as is reasonably required.'

And mobility assistance:

'is assistance—
(a) to enable the passenger to get into or out of the vehicle;
(b) if the passenger wishes to remain in the wheelchair, to enable the passenger to get into and out of the vehicle while in the wheelchair;
(c) to load the passenger's luggage into or out of the vehicle;
(d) if the passenger does not wish to remain in the wheelchair, to load the wheelchair into or out of the vehicle.'

Neither of those duties require a driver to carry a passenger in circumstances where it would be lawful for him to refuse the hiring, eg for a journey from a hackney carriage stand which will terminate outside the district (or hackney carriage zone)[2]. In addition, unless the vehicle is of a description prescribed by the Secretary of State, the driver cannot be compelled to carry more than one wheelchair or wheelchair-bound passenger[3].

Failure to provide mobility assistance or to carry the passenger or discharge any of the other duties contained in s 165(4) is a criminal offence by virtue of sub-s (8), but there is a defence if the driver can show that it would not have been possible for the wheelchair to be carried safely in the vehicle (sub-s (9)(b)).

[1]   EA 2010, s 165(4).
[2]   EA 2010, s 165(6)(b).
[3]   EA 2010, s 165(6)(a).

Suspension and revocation of hackney carriage drivers' licences

10.133

LG(MP)A 1976, s 61 gives the local authority powers to suspend, revoke or (on an application for renewal) refuse to renew a hackney carriage driver's licence. The grounds are contained in s 61(1)(a) and (b) and are wide-ranging[1].

The procedure contained in TPCA 1847, s 50 is obsolete when LG(MP)A 1976 has been adopted.

10.134

LG(MP)A 1976, s 61 states:

'Suspension and revocation of drivers' licences

61–(1) Notwithstanding anything in the Act of 1847 [TPCA 1847] or in this Part of this Act, a district council may suspend or revoke or (on application therefor under section 46 of the Act of 1847 or section 51 of this Act, as the case may be) refuse to renew the licence of a driver of a hackney carriage or a private hire vehicle on any of the following grounds—
(a) that he has since the grant of the licence—
   (i) been convicted of an offence involving dishonesty, indecency or violence; or
   (ii) been convicted of an offence under or has failed to comply with the provisions of the Act of 1847 or of this Part of this Act; or
(b) any other reasonable cause.

(2)(a) Where a district council suspend, revoke or refuse to renew any licence under this section they shall give to the driver notice of the grounds on which the licence has been suspended or revoked or on which they have refused to renew such licence within fourteen days of such suspension, revocation or refusal and the driver shall on demand return to the district council the driver's badge issued to him in accordance with section 54 of this Act.
(b) If any person without reasonable excuse contravenes the provisions of this section he shall be guilty of an offence and liable on summary conviction to a fine not exceeding level 1 on the standard scale.

(2A) Subject to subsection (2B) of this section, a suspension or revocation of the licence of a driver under this section takes effect at the end of the period of 21 days beginning with the day on which notice is given to the driver under subsection (2)(a) of this section.

(2B) If it appears that the interests of public safety require the suspension or revocation of the licence to have immediate effect, and the notice given to the driver under subsection (2)(a) of this section includes a statement that that is so and an explanation why, the suspension or revocation takes effect when the notice is given to the driver.

(3) Any driver aggrieved by a decision of a district council under subsection (1) of this section may appeal to magistrates' court.'

10.135

It should be noted, however, that for action to be taken under s 61(1)(a), the offence has to have been committed since the grant of the licence. No consideration can be given under s 61(1)(a) to any offence which took place before the grant of the licence, but there is no time limitation on what can be considered under s 61(1)(b) as 'any other reasonable cause'. Accordingly, in any situation where a licensing committee decides to tighten their criteria in relation to criminal offences[1], action could be taken under s 61(1)(b) to revoke or refuse to renew a licence if the offence was committed before the licence was originally granted[2].

Local authorities should receive information from the police when the police have relevant intelligence relating to a taxi driver, whether that is a conviction, arrest, caution or other intelligence. This can be provided by the police using Common Law Police Disclosure[3].

[1] See Chapter 2, para 2.59 in respect of the application of a revised, tighter policy.

[2] For consideration of immediate action against driver's licences, see Chapter 6, para 6.42 onwards.

[3] The guidance '*Common Law Police Disclosure – Guidance for employers and regulatory bodies*' states:

'Common Law Police Disclosure (CLPD) ensures that where there is a public protection risk, the police will pass information to the employer or regulatory body to allow them to act swiftly to put in measures to mitigate any danger.'

This is available at https://www.gov.uk/government/uploads/system/uploads/attachment_data/file/452650/CLPD_Guidance_0_4.pdf

10.136

LG(MP)A 1976, s 61(1)(a) includes offences of dishonesty, indecency or violence or offences under TPCA 1847 or LG(MP)A 1976. Section 61(1)(b) allows such action to be taken for 'any other reasonable cause'[1]. This includes any action falling short of a criminal conviction and could include a situation that led to a failed prosecution.

[1] This can be for any matter: see *Norwich City Council v Watcham and Thurtle* (21 May 1981, unreported). See Chapter 8, para 8.138.

10.137

This can occur where the local authority or the Crown Prosecution Service has brought a prosecution and the driver has been acquitted. It is still open to the local authority to consider the driver's position in relation to his driver's licence notwithstanding the acquittal. Depending on the circumstances, such action may constitute a reasonable cause for not renewing, suspending or revoking a driver's licence. On a subsequent appeal[1] the matter would be considered on the basis of the civil standard of proof (the balance of probabilities) as opposed to the criminal standard of proof (beyond all reasonable doubt).

[1] Under LG(MP)A 1976, s 61(3).

10.138

It is a fundamental rule of English law that a person cannot be tried twice for the same crime[1]. However, considering a person's previous convictions as evidence of his fitness and propriety to drive a hackney carriage does not amount to trying him twice. The rule that prevents double jeopardy is only applicable to criminal prosecutions and the consideration of a person's suitability to drive a hackney carriage is not a criminal matter. Such action is not unlawful as it does not amount to double jeopardy and no plea of autrefois acquit or autrefois convict can be made. Those pleas can only be made before a criminal court if it is alleged that a person is being tried for the same matter twice and that he has already been acquitted of the charge (autrefois acquit) or convicted of the charge (autrefois convict). Provided the consideration of non-convictions is taken in the interests of protecting the public, the local authority would appear to be able to take such action. It remains to be seen whether it would be successful on a subsequent appeal, ie whether the court felt that the action taken was reasonable in the circumstances, but the line of action is open to it.

[1]   Although this has changed in relation to serious crimes as defined in Sch 5, Pt 1 of the Criminal Justice Act 2003 by virtue of Pt 10 of the same Act.

R v Maidstone Crown Court, ex p Olson

10.139

> Conviction in Crown Court quashed on appeal, and evidence of that acquittal excluded by the magistrates on appeal from a refusal to grant a drivers' licence. Held: By the High Court that such evidence was admissible before the council or on appeal.

This view is supported by a series of cases, the first of which is *R v Maidstone Crown Court, ex p Olson*[1]. In this case, Mr Olson was a hackney carriage driver and had been so for nine years. In June 1988, he was convicted of indecently assaulting a 15-year-old girl on her evidence that he had committed the assault in a country lane when she did not have enough money to pay her fare home. Upon conviction, Ashford Borough Council, who had granted him the hackney carriage licence, revoked it. However, in January 1989 the conviction was quashed on appeal on the grounds of misdirection of the jury. By virtue of the Criminal Appeal Act 1968, that counted as an acquittal. Accordingly, Mr Olson had never been convicted of the offence. He applied for another hackney carriage driver's licence, but the local authority was not satisfied that he was a fit and proper person and refused to grant the licence. Mr Olson appealed to the magistrates' court and the magistrate refused to allow the local authority to call the girl, who had been the complainant in the criminal case, to give evidence. As a consequence of this, there was effectively no evidence against Mr Olson and the magistrates allowed his appeal. Ashford Borough Council appealed to the Crown Court and argued that the magistrates had been wrong to exclude the complainant's evidence. As a preliminary point, the Crown Court judge was asked to rule on the admissibility or otherwise of the complainant's evidence. He ruled it admissible. The case was then adjourned so that Mr Olson could seek a judicial review of that decision.

[1]   [1992] COD 496.

10.140

The questions posed for the High Court were:

1. The jurisdiction of the High Court to consider the point.
2. The merits of the argument as to whether or not the evidence was admissible.
3. Where the burden of proof lay.
4. What the standard of proof was.
5. Whether there were grounds for estoppel or arguing an abuse of process.

10.141

The case was heard by Watkins LJ and May J[1]. They decided (at 498) they did not have any jurisdiction to consider the matter. Notwithstanding that, on the application of both parties they were prepared to consider the merits:

> '*Burden of proof:* It was for the applicant to establish that he was a fit and proper person. It was accepted that he would discharge that burden if the local authority were not permitted to call the complainant to give evidence. It followed that the evidential burden shifted to the local authority. It should not, however, be overlooked that what they were seeking to do was to rebut the applicant's case that he was a fit and proper person. They were not seeking to prosecute him a second time.
>
> *Standard of proof:* It was necessary to the applicant's argument that the standard of proof in relation to the facts which the local authority sought to prove was the criminal standard. But these were not criminal proceedings. They were proceedings relating to the grant of a taxi licence. It was for the applicant to establish on the balance of probabilities that he was a fit and proper person. In seeking to rebut the applicant's contention that he was such a person, the local authority needed only to satisfy the civil standard of proof, even if the substance of what they sought to prove amounted to a criminal offence. Parliament did not intend that local authorities had to refuse licenses under this head only if they were *sure* that an applicant alleged to have committed a relevant offence had indeed committed it. The balance of public interest to see that those who drove taxis were fit and proper persons to do so did not argue for a criminal standard of proof here. The local authority had to establish what they sought to prove to a civil standard of proof commensurate with the occasion and the proportionate to the subject matter.
>
> *Estoppel and abuse:* There was no estoppel or abuse. The local authority were entitled to go behind the applicant's acquittal for the different purpose of seeking to rebut his contention that he was a fit and proper person to hold a taxi driver's licence. To that end, they were entitled to call the complainant to give evidence.'

[1] *R v Maidstone Crown Court, ex p Olson* [1992] COD 496, QBD.

McCool v Rushcliffe Borough Council

10.142

> Taxi driver prosecuted for indecent assault on a passenger. Jury failed to
> reach a verdict and a retrial was ordered. Victim did not give evidence at
> retail due to the trauma of doing so at the first trial. Defendant acquitted for
> lack of evidence. Could the evidence be used in considering his suitability to
> hold a drivers' licence? Held: Yes it could.

This approach was followed in *McCool v Rushcliffe Borough Council*[1], where the
High Court not only agreed with the decision in *Olson*[2] and allowed hearsay
evidence of an indecent assault which had not resulted in a conviction[3] but, in
addition, confirmed that the standard of proof in licensing matters was a civil
one (the balance of probabilities) rather than the higher criminal test (beyond all
reasonable doubt).

1   [1998] 3 All ER 889, QBD.
2   *R v Maidstone Crown Court, ex p Olson* [1992] COD 496; see para 10.139 above.
3   *Westminster City Council v Zestfair Ltd* (1989) 88 LGR 258 and *Kavanagh v Chief Constable of
     Devon and Cornwall* [1974] QB 624; see Chapter 2, para 2.66 onwards.

10.143

The facts that led to the case were detailed in the judgment[1]:

'On the hearing of the complaint on 19 June the magistrates made the
following findings set out in paragraph 3 of the case stated:

"(a) Mr John McCool, the applicant, had been a taxi driver for a
number of years. He had been charged and tried for an allegation
of indecent assault on a 42-year-old lone female passenger. This
was initially a charge of abduction but this was withdrawn by the
Crown Prosecution Service. (b) At the applicant's first trial at the
Nottingham Crown Court on 5 March 1996 the jury failed to reach
a verdict and at the retrial the passenger did not attend court and
the applicant was therefore acquitted. Her reason for not attending
court was that she was not prepared to go through the trauma of
giving evidence again. This was also the reason as to why she did
not attend court in relation to the hearing on 19 June 1997. (c) That
the incident happened on 22 September 1995 when the applicant
took a fare from the Black Orchid Nightclub at Nottingham. The
lone female passenger asked to be taken home. (d) He turned down
an unlit country road and stopped the taxi. The applicant then put
his arm through the gap between the seats and began clawing at her
legs. The female passenger was absolutely terrified and jumped out
and ran around the back of the cab. The applicant got out of the cab
and caught her and then wedged her up against the car, put his hand
up her skirt and pulled at her underwear. The applicant then said he

would take her home and started apologising and then he dropped her off near a pub."'

McCool's application to Rushcliffe Borough Council for a private hire driver's licence was refused on the basis of these facts, the conclusion being that he was not a fit and proper person to be granted a licence.

¹   [1998] 3 All ER 889, QBD.

10.144

McCool appealed to the magistrates' court, but was unsuccessful. The justices' reasons were also detailed in the judgment as follows:

'We found that the applicant had thereby committed an indecent assault. (e) The applicant lied in his police interview since he denied ever being at the scene of the incident. He admitted that this was a lie. (f) At the second police interview he denied being at the scene again but it was only after he was shown video evidence that he admitted being involved in the incident. (g) The applicant admitted lying to the Crown Court as to why he touched the female passenger's leg. (h) We rejected the applicant's explanation for these lies as untruthful and found him to be an unreliable witness. (i) The applicant was not a fit and proper person to hold a private hire licence.'

10.145

McCool appealed to the High Court by way of case stated. Judgment was given by Bingham LCJ(at 896A):

'It is in my judgment very important to bear in mind the basis upon which that case [*R v Maidstone Crown Court, ex p Olson*] was proceeding before this court, namely that the applicant was entitled to be regarded as a fit and proper person unless evidence of indecent assault could be adduced against him. It is also in my judgment very important to bear in mind the regulatory framework to which I have already made reference.

I return to section 51(1) [LG(MP)A 1976, s 51(1)], from which it is plain that a district council has a mandatory obligation to grant a licence to an applicant for a licence to drive private hire vehicles, but that it is prohibited from granting a licence unless it is satisfied that the applicant is a fit and proper person to hold a driver's licence. It is no doubt right to regard an applicant as fit and proper if adequate evidence of good character and record is adduced and there is no reason to question or doubt it. But the local authority, or on complaint to them the justices, are not permitted to grant the licence unless they are satisfied that the applicant is fit and proper. They may fail to be satisfied because adequate information of character and record is not forthcoming, as would be the case if an applicant failed to respond adequately to a request under section 57(1); or they might fail to be satisfied for any other good reason. It is in my view impossible to be prescriptive as to what might amount to a good reason. What will be (or may be) a good reason will vary from case to case and vary according to the context in which those words appear. The decision maker may take account of hearsay (as already indicated), provided it is hearsay which is not unreasonably thought to be worthy of credence, and such evidence need not be evidence which will withstand scrutiny according to the formal rules of a court of law. It is not a good reason if a local authority or justices rely on prejudice or assertions shown to be ill-founded or gossip or rumour or any other matter which a reasonable and fair-minded decision maker acting in good faith and with proper regard to the interests both of the public and the applicant would not think it right to rely on. But it is appropriate for the local authority or justices to regard as a good reason anything which a reasonable and fair-minded decision maker, acting in good faith and with proper regard to the interests both of the public and the applicant, could properly think it right to rely on. In my judgment the justices in this case did not exceed the bounds of appropriate evidence in reaching their decision.

I said earlier that the questions posed by the justices in my view called for reformulation. I would propose to reformulate the questions as follows:

"(1) Were we entitled to have regard to hearsay evidence of the indecent assault alleged against Mr McCool without direct evidence of it?"

To that question I would answer "Yes".

"(2) Did we apply a correct standard proof to the question for our determination?"

Again I would answer "Yes", save that the justices may well have applied a more rigorous standard than was called for in the circumstances.

"(3) Were we entitled on the findings made, if properly made, not to be satisfied that Mr McCool was a fit and proper person to be granted a private vehicle licence?"

To that question I would answer "Yes".'

Leeds City Council v Hussain

10.146

> Private hire driver charged with violent disorder. Council suspended his licence. Appeal at magistrates' court dismissed, but successful at Crown Court. Council appealed. Held: No conviction or prosecution was required, and the facts could be taken into account when considering his suitability to hold a drivers' licence.

A similar approach was seen in *Leeds City Council v Hussain*[1]. Hussain was a private hire driver[2] and Leeds City Council suspended his licence because he had been charged with an offence of violent disorder arising out of an incident which involved a number of private hire drivers and their vehicles. He appealed to the magistrates' court, which dismissed the appeal, upholding the decision of the City Council. He further appealed to the Crown Court and was successful. Leeds City Council appealed against that decision by way of case stated. One ground of the findings of the Crown Court was that no live evidence had been called[3].

1   *Leeds City Council v Hussain* [2002] EWHC 1145 (Admin), [2003] RTR 199. This case has already been considered in relation to the impact on a person's livelihood of losing a licence (see para 10.67 above) but the remaining issues of hearsay and the ability of the local authority to take action against a licence in the absence of a criminal conviction are considered here.

2   The powers to take action against a private hire driver's licence are identical to those for hackney carriage drivers, both being contained in LG(MP)A 1976, s 61, so this case is relevant to hackney carriage drivers as well as private hire.

3   This matter is considered in Chapter 2, para 2.66.

10.147

The remaining questions raised by the Crown Court were:

'(a)   Whether, in the case of a holder of private hire vehicle and driver's licences who has been charged with a serious criminal offences committed in the course of his employment, it is necessary for there to be a finding of guilty in relation to that criminal charge before a decision can properly be made as to whether there is "any … reasonable cause" to suspend his licences;

(b)   … [The live evidence question][1];

(c)   Whether, in the case of a holder of private hire vehicle and driver's licences who has been charged with a serious criminal offence committed in the course of his employment, it is necessary to reach the conclusion that there is at least a reasonable chance of him being convicted of this offence before his licences can properly be suspended;

(d)   … [The personal circumstances of the driver question][2].

1   See Chapter 2, para 2.66.
2   See para 10.67 above.

10.148

The judge, Mr Justice Silber, broke these into three broad headings:

1.   the need for conviction issue;
2.   the hearsay evidence issue[1];
3.   the licence holder's personal circumstances issue[2].

He concluded, having taken into account the rulings in *McCool v Rushcliffe Borough Council*[3] and *R v Maidstone Crown Court, ex p Olson*[4] that the words in LG(MP)A 1976, s 61(1)(b) – 'any other reasonable cause' allowed action to be taken in circumstances where the driver had not been convicted. He stated[5] (at para 14 of the judgment):

'I do not think as a matter of principle that before a licence can properly be suspended there is any need for a conclusion to be reached by the Magistrate that in the wording of question (c) and the issues raised in the case stated there is at least a reasonable chance [of the respondent] being convicted of [a serious] offence.'

He also added (at para 17 of the judgment) that a vehicle licence could be suspended for the same reason under LG(MP)A 1976, s 60 even the though the driver of that vehicle had not been convicted.

1   Considered in Chapter 2, para 2.66.
2   Considered at para 10.146 above.
3   [1998] 3 All ER 889, QBD.
4   [1992] COD 496.
5   *Leeds City Council v Hussain* [2002] EWHC 1145 (Admin), [2003] RTR 199.

10.149

This case clearly supports the line of reasoning in *Maidstone*[1] and *McCool*[2], and is a robust judgment on its facts.

1   *R v Maidstone Crown Court, ex p Olson* [1992] COD 496; see para 10.139 above.
2   *McCool v Rushcliffe Borough Council* [1998] 3 All ER 889, QBD; see para 10.142 above.

R v Chester Crown Court (on the application of Wrexham County Borough Council)

10.150

> Does the Crown Court on an appeal from the magistrates' court have to attach the same weight to any evidence as the magistrates' court, or the council did? Held: No, it was a matter for the Crown Court to determine what weight to attach to any particular piece of evidence.

The decision in *R v Chester Crown Court (app Wrexham CBC)*[1] followed the same principles as the previous cases[2], but arrived at a different conclusion, based upon its own particular facts.

Mr Jones was a licensed private hire driver and when he had originally applied for his licence in 2001, he revealed that he had convictions for offences committed as a young man. At the time of his initial application these were spent[3]. Later that year, he was involved in an incident which is detailed in the judgment as follows[4]:

'2. On 23rd September 2001 a complaint was made to North Wales Police that a gang of youths, including Mr Jones, had gathered around a house occupied by two men and that there had then ensued an affray in which the two men were assaulted and in which damage was caused to the house.

4. Mr Jones, ... was arrested and interviewed. ... he admitted being present outside the premises and becoming involved in an assault upon one of the men, although he denied using or possessing any weapon. ... he was charged with burglary and affray but that the case was discontinued

on advice from the Crown Prosecution Service. No evidence was offered against Mr Jones and accordingly he was discharged.'

These facts came to light in 2003 as a result of a CRB Disclosure[5], and led to the council officers wanting to question Jones about the matter. He was provided with a series of questions in advance and on the advice of his representative, he refused to answer them. The material questions were as follows (although Mitting J makes the point that they were statements, rather than questions):

'The council's copy of the disclosure was received in February 2003 and it contained information, which did not result in a prosecution, that related to an incident on the 23rd September 2002 [this should read 2001]. (The information was read out)

The information contained in the "relevant information" of the CRB form is such that had it been known at the time you renewed your private hire driver's licence would have been sufficient for the facts to have been submitted to the council's Environmental Licensing Committee for their consideration.

Section 61 of the Local Government (Miscellaneous Provisions) Act provides that the council may suspend, revoke or refuse to renew the driver of a private hire driver's licence on certain grounds under subsection (b) it states any other reasonable cause.'

The council revoked his driver's licence. The decision was described in the following manner by Mitting J[6]:

'7. The committee based its decision to revoke his licence on three factors: first, the previous convictions originally disclosed by Mr Jones, which had been spent and had not led to any difficulties in the grant of his licence in the first place; secondly, the refusal to answer the questions or to respond to the statements I have indicated; and, thirdly, the information contained in the police document about the incident on 23rd September 2001. They decided that, taken together, those factors meant that there was reasonable cause to revoke Mr Jones' licence, essentially on the basis that he was not a fit and proper person to have a licence.'

Jones appealed to the magistrates' court, arguing that the note was incorrect, as he did not admit affray, although he admitted his presence at the scene. His appeal was dismissed, and he appealed to the Crown Court. The Crown Court allowed the appeal and the council asked the court to state a case. It refused and the council challenged that decision by way of judicial review.

[1]   [2004] EWHC 1591 (Admin), [2004] LLR 802.
[2]   *R v Maidstone Crown Court, ex p Olson* [1992] COD 496; see para 10.139 above; *McCool v Rushcliffe Borough Council* [1998] 3 All ER 889, QBD; see para 10.142 above and *Leeds City Council v Hussain* [2002] EWCA 1145 (Admin), [2003] RTR 199; see para 10.146 above.
[3]   As this was prior to 2002 when taxi drivers (both hackney carriage and private hire) were exempted from the provisions of the Rehabilitation of Offenders Act 1974.
[4]   *R v Chester Crown Court (app Wrexham CBC)* [2004] EWHC 1591 (Admin), [2004] LLR 802 per Mitting J at paras 2 and 4.
[5]   Although the judgment is silent as to why the information came to light in 2003, it is suggested that it would have been on renewal of his licence.
[6]   Outlined by Mitting J at para 7.

10.151

Mr Justice Mitting considered the judicial review on the same basis as an appeal by way of case stated.

10.152

The council conceded that the first two factors (the previous conviction which had not prevented grant in the past and his refusal to answer questions) were not sufficient, either alone or combined, to amount to 'any other reasonable cause' to revoke the licence. This left the final factor; the incident which did not lead to criminal proceedings. In relation to this the judge found[1]:

'12. The issue before the Crown Court and before me turns upon the third proposition. Mr Abberton puts it in this way, as he put it before the Crown Court: the information given by the police was admissible hearsay, it called for an answer and, in the absence of an answer, the court could and should have concluded that Mr Jones was not a fit and proper person to have a private hire driver's licence so there was reasonable cause to revoke it. The previous convictions and the failure to answer questions were prayed in aid in support of that basic proposition, but unless the basic proposition stands then, as I understand his submissions, Mr Abberton accepts that the decision of the Crown Court is not open to successful challenge.

13. What the Crown Court said about that was this, in paragraph 24:

"We are well aware of where the allegation emanates from, well aware that hearsay has its place in any hearing and it is proper to take into account, but what we can't ignore in this instance is that the allegation is there, there is an allegation made but this court knows that it led to proceedings being discontinued."

14. In that passage the court correctly accepted that hearsay evidence was admissible, and their reasoning in that respect is not challenged. Its conclusion is set out in paragraph 25 and was:

"When the court knows that for a fact, it seems to this court to be entirely inappropriate on the facts of this case for the court then to really start to make any adverse inference against him as a result of that course of action being taken and it is not safe, this court concludes, to come to any decision as to the reliability or credibility of what is being said in that document when considered action has been taken and proceedings, whatever be the reason, proceedings have simply been discontinued. Unless one starts embarking on a considered view of the evidence, effectively trying this matter, that is about the only way in which it perhaps could ever be resolved, but that is not the position this court is put in. It knows an allegation is made, it knows an allegation was denied, because the defendant didn't plead guilty to these matters and it knows that the prosecuting authorities decided to take no steps.

26. In these circumstances, no reasonable cause existed as far as this court is concerned under the provisions of the relevant Act for this licence in those circumstances to be suspended or revoked ..."

15. That is a passage that Mr Abberton criticises. He says, as I have indicated, that having accepted that the police report was admissible hearsay, it was duty bound to require Mr Jones to give evidence or, at the very least, to afford him the opportunity of giving evidence, and I infer that if he declined to take it to draw an inference adverse to him, not under statutory provisions but at common law in relation to civil proceedings, which these were.

16. The law is authoritatively stated by the Divisional Court in *McCool v Rushcliffe Borough Council*, a court presided over by the then Lord Chief Justice, Lord Bingham, on Wednesday, 1st July 1998, in upholding the decision of the justices to revoke a licence in the case of a man who had been accused of an indecent assault on a passenger, who had been prosecuted for it before the Crown Court, whose trial had resulted in the disagreement of the jury in the first instance and in the offering of no evidence in the second instance, when the complainant declined to give evidence for a second time. Thus, superficially, the facts bore some resemblance to those in this case: there was a charge, there was no conviction, the driver in each case fell therefore to have his case considered on the basis that there had been no conviction. But an examination of the facts in *McCool* reveals highly significant differences. First, the driver in that case admitted that he had lied to the police in pretending in interview that no incident of any kind had occurred, admitted that he had lied on oath in the Crown Court and had advanced a case that, although he had touched his passenger indecently, he had done so with her consent or encouragement. There was, in addition, available to the justices a newspaper report of the complainant's account given in the Crown Court which was accepted by the driver as an accurate record of what she said. The justices concluded, having heard him give evidence, that he was, on the balance of probabilities, guilty of the offence of indecent assault with which he had been charged. Having so concluded, then the justices, as the Divisional Court held, were plainly entitled to conclude that he was not a fit and proper person to hold a private hire licence.

17. The Divisional Court held that the justices were entitled to take into account the hearsay that they had and noted that their decision was not based only on hearsay, but also on the additional factors, principally the driver's admitted lies to which I have referred. For those reasons, the decision of the magistrates was upheld.

18. A moment's thought reveals that there are factual differences between that case and this, because in this case the driver disputed not only that he was guilty of the offence for which he had been arrested and charged, but also that he had made admissions recorded in the police note. The Crown Court, like the committee and the justices, did not have any transcript of

the interview so as to judge whether or not his denial of those admissions was well-founded or not. But not only were there those differences of fact, but there is a fundamental difference in the legal position. In *McCool* the Divisional Court was asked to consider whether or not the justices were entitled to take into account the evidence that they did to reach the conclusion that they did. The court held that they were. In this case the Council submit that the Crown Court should have taken into account the police report and, in consequence, required Mr Jones to give evidence or offered him the opportunity of doing so.

19. That is not a proposition which can be founded on the reasoning in *McCool*. Whether or not a court gives weight to material before it is a matter for the court, in particular, if the material is, as here, partially disputed hearsay. Whether or not a court takes into account in a way adverse to a driver an accusation made but not proceeded with is pre-eminently a matter for the court. It is simply impossible to say that this court's decision that this withdrawn charge did not call for any further answer from Mr Jones was wrong. It is impossible to say that this court''s decision that the withdrawn charge did not give rise to the conclusion that there was reasonable cause for revoking the licence was irrational or wrong in law. It was pre-eminently a matter for the court to weigh up and to decide. Its decision simply is not open to criticism on the principles that this court applies, and for that reason this application must be dismissed.'

This case clearly accepts that the reasoning in *McCool*[2] was correct, but then asserts that the weight to be attached to any such evidence is a matter for the court (or the local authority) hearing the matter, and it is quite possible for different courts to come to different conclusions on the same facts.

[1]   At paras 12–19.
[2]   *McCool v Rushcliffe Borough Council* [1998] 3 All ER 889, QBD; see para 10.142 above.

10.153

Likewise, where a person is accused of a criminal offence, action can be taken before the hearing of the prosecution, provided that there is sufficient evidence to support the view that the action taken against the licence is on the basis of 'any other reasonable cause'. Local authorities must tread carefully in this area, for if there is insufficient evidence, the action may be unreasonable. It is necessary for local authorities to balance their duties to the public against their duties to the drivers that they licence and such decisions can be difficult.

Suspension of a hackney carriage driver's licence

10.154

One further area concerns the suspension of a hackney carriage driver's licence. Refusal to renew or revocation is reasonably straightforward. Provided that the grounds laid down in LG(MP)A 1976, s 61(1)(a) or (b) have been met, then the local authority can come to the conclusion that the person is no longer a fit and proper person to drive a hackney carriage. However, the use of a suspension presents more complex considerations.

Can a local authority suspend a hackney carriage driver's licence as a punishment? This was an element of the matter considered in *R (app Singh) v Cardiff City Council*[1] and the judge, Singh J concluded that such a power was contained in the wording of s 61. He stated[2]:

'103. In my judgment, the way in which the concept of suspension is used by Parliament is section 61 of the 1976 Act is not, as it were, to create a power of interim suspension, it is rather after a considered determination in other words a final decision on whether a ground for either revocation, or suspension of a licence is made out, for there to be either revocation or, as a lesser sanction, a sanction of suspension.

104. By way of analogy, one can envisage for example in a professional context a solicitor or a barrister can be disciplined on grounds of his conduct. The relevant disciplinary body may conclude that even if the misconduct has been established, that the appropriate sanction should be something less than complete revocation of the practising certificate for the relevant lawyer. It may be, for example, a suspension for a period of 1 year, will constitute sufficient sanction in the interests of the public.

105. It is in that sense, in my judgment, that Parliament uses the concept of suspension in section 61 of the 1976 Act. It does not use, as it were, to create an interim power, before a reasoned determination has been made, that the grounds in subsection (1A) or (1B) have been made out. It is not, as it were, a protective or holding power. It is a power of final suspension, as an alternative to a power of final revocation.'

This is clear authority for the use of suspension as a punishment. Any such suspension should be for a definite period of time, to enable the driver to decide whether to appeal the decision. It is also unlikely that a suspension for a punishment would be justified if it was to take immediate effect[3]. A suspension could be stated to be until a particular requirement was met, provided the driver has the responsibility for meeting any such requirement. Examples include: a requirement to pass a driving course, or to attend an anger management course. It could also be used in situations where the driver has medical problems, and the suspension would be until a satisfactory medical report was produced.

[1]   [2012] EWHC 1852 (Admin), [2013] LLR 108.
[2]   At para 103 onwards.
[3]   See Chapter 6, para 6.42 onwards for consideration of the powers of immediate action against a drivers' licence.

10.155

Finally, as a means of transparent and proportionate enforcement, a number of local authorities have introduced 'points systems' for hackney carriage drivers[1].

[1]   Such schemes are considered in detail in Chapter 6, para 6.47 onwards.

Renewal of a hackney carriage driver's licence

10.156

One of the strange omissions within the legislation is the absence of any renewal mechanism for hackney carriage drivers' licences.[1] In the absence of any statutory process, local authorities need to determine the approach that they will take and this should be clearly stated within their policies.

There are four possible approaches that the local authority can take.

1. No over-run – if renewal of the licence was not applied for and granted before expiry of the existing or current licence, it cannot be used, and the driver cannot drive a hackney carriage until the renewal application has been determined.
2. Issue of short term 'without prejudice' licence – from the expiry of the old licence until the determination of the renewal, provided the application was made before the expiry of the existing or current licence.
3. Informal acceptance of old licence 'continuing' (ie, remaining valid) until the determination of the renewal, provided the application was made before the expiry of the existing or current licence.
4. 'Turn a blind eye' to use of expired licences.

It is clear that neither 3 nor 4 are acceptable. In neither case is there a valid licence in existence to allow the person to drive a hackney carriage and accordingly the driver would commit an offence under TPCA 1847, s 46.

This leaves options 1 and 2, both of which are lawful and are widely used by local authorities.

Option 1 has the advantage of certainty and clarity and places the onus firmly on the licensee to ensure that renewal is made in a timely fashion, allowing sufficient time for all required checks and tests to be made (including the DBS check which can take a considerable period). However, it is viewed by some authorities as being overly harsh, especially if unforeseen delays occur which are beyond the control of the applicant.

Option 2 addresses that and again, provided the application has been properly made before the current licence expires, a short term licence can be issued to enable the driver to continue to work pending the determination of the renewal application. It must be made completely clear that such a licence is issued 'without prejudice' to any subsequent decision that the authority may make when the renewal application is considered in the light of all the information that becomes available. This is to prevent any suggestion being made that the authority had deemed the applicant fit and proper at the time that the short-term licence was issued. This approach allows drivers to continue working when either there are delays in obtaining the required information or the application has been left late.

The authority must also consider what action to take when application to renew a driver's licence is made after the expiry of the current licence. This was considered in the context of a hackney carriage vehicle licence in *R (on the application of Exeter City Council) v Sandle*[2].

In that case, the judge concluded that it was possible to renew a hackney carriage proprietor's licence that had expired, but such an application should only be successful where there were extremely good reasons for the application not being made before expiry and the delay in applying after expiry was only a matter of a few days.

Whilst this case only concerned a hackney carriage proprietors licence, it clearly impacts upon drivers' licences, because the judge was firmly of the view that an expired licence could be renewed and as the wording of LG(MP)A 1976, s 60 (in relation to renewal of vehicle licences) is identical to s 61 (in relation to renewal of drivers' licences), the principle must also apply to drivers' licences.

[1] The same applies to all these licences. There is clearly an expectation that licences can be renewed, because the local authority has the power to refuse to renew any licence, but the renewal mechanism itself is absent. See LG(MP)A 1976: s 60(1) in respect of renewal of vehicle licences; s 61(1) in respect of renewal of drivers' licences; s 62(1) in respect of renewal of operators' licences.

This can be contrasted with most other licensing regimes where once a licence is in existence, provided the application for renewal is made before the current licence expires, the current licence is deemed to continue on the same terms and conditions until the renewal determination. See eg Sch 3, para 11 of the Local Government (Miscellaneous Provisions) Act 1982 in respect of sex establishment licences and Sch 1, para 1 of the Scrap Metal Dealers Act 2013.

[2] [2011] EWHC 1403 (Admin). This is considered in Chapter 8, para 8.243 onwards.

Chapter 11

Private hire vehicles outside London: an introduction

11.1

Private hire vehicles represent a second category or type of vehicle that provide services to the public by way of private independent transportation.

11.2

The rise in the numbers of 'mini-cabs' during the 1960s and early 1970s led to the passing and introduction of the Local Government (Miscellaneous Provisions) Act 1976 (LG(MP)A 1976), which introduced a regulatory framework for the control of private hire vehicles outside Greater London.

11.3

These provisions are adoptive, but there is only one local authority in England and Wales that has not adopted them: Plymouth City Council, which controls private hire vehicles by a local Act[1].

[1]   According to the DfT in their letter dated 9 September 2002 to Local Authorities concerning 'Taxi and Private Hire Vehicle Licensing Issues' at para 25. The legislation within Plymouth is contained within the Plymouth City Council Act 1975.

11.4

A private hire vehicle differs from a hackney carriage in a number of fundamental ways:

1.   The vehicle itself cannot resemble a hackney carriage. This is to enable it to be readily identified by the public as a private hire vehicle.
2.   A private hire vehicle cannot ply for hire (that is, cruise the streets of the district until hailed by a prospective passenger[1]).
3.   A private hire vehicle cannot stand for hire (that is, use a hackney carriage stand or park and undertake an immediate hiring with a passenger unless a booking has been made via a private hire operator[2]).
4.   A private hire vehicle must be driven by a person who holds a private hire driver's licence issued by the same local authority that licences the vehicle (in this aspect the situation is similar to the rules governing hackney carriages).

5.   However, the similarity ends at this point because a private hire operator must control each and every private hire vehicle. The operator is the person who takes the bookings from the customer and arranges for the vehicle to go to wherever the customer requests. This is the only way in which private hire vehicles are able to collect their customers.

¹   See Chapter 8, para 8.7 onwards.
²   See Chapter 8, para 8.7 onwards.

11.5

It can therefore be seen that there are three players involved in the private hire function: the private hire driver; the private hire operator; and the private hire vehicle. This can be contrasted with the situation that applies to hackney carriages, where all that is required is a licensed vehicle and licensed driver.

11.6

There are further variations between the two licensing regimes:

1.   No limit can be placed upon the number of private hire vehicles that a local authority will license.
2.   The local authority has no power to prescribe fares for private hire vehicles.
3.   The local authority does not have any power to prescribe the type of vehicle, other than the requirement that the vehicle is satisfactory for its purpose, although the council can lay down minimum specifications for private hire vehicles and the vehicle cannot resemble a hackney carriage.

11.7

There are no private hire zones. The area for private hire operation is the total area of the local authority that has adopted LG(MP)A 1976.

11.8

Although the private hire regime is slightly different from the hackney carriage regime, the overriding aims of providing the public with a safe and convenient method of transport remain the same and the differences in approach in no way undermine that fundamental consideration.

11.9

Almost all the legislative requirements concerning private hire vehicles are contained in LG(MP)A 1976, but there are some provisions relevant to private hire vehicles and drivers in other Acts, including Transport Act 1980, Transport Act 1985, Equality Act 2010, Immigration Act 2016 and the Policing and Crime Act 2017.

11.10

One other area of considerable difference between the two regimes is that of byelaws. The use of byelaws, in relation to hackney carriages, is well established and governed by the provisions of the Town Police Clauses Act 1847 and the Town Police Clauses Act 1899. In relation to private hire vehicles, there is no overt power to make byelaws to regulate their conduct. It seems that such byelaws could be made by a local authority using the powers contained in the Local Government Act 1972, s 235. This enables the local authority to make byelaws 'for the good rule and government' of its area. It is suggested that private hire byelaws could be made under this provision, if it could be demonstrated that the effect of such byelaws could be to improve the life of the citizens of the area. As yet, no authority has taken this route and it remains to be seen whether a council would feel that the benefits of doing so would be worthwhile, considering the time and costs involved. It also remains to be seen what a local authority would attempt to regulate by such byelaws.

Chapter 12

Private hire operators outside London

INTRODUCTION

The term 'operate'

12.1

A private hire vehicle can only be despatched to a customer by a private hire operator. That is, a person who holds an operator's licence under the Local Government (Miscellaneous Provisions) Act 1976, s 55 (LG(MP)A 1976). This licence allows him to operate private hire vehicles. 'Operate' is defined in LG(MP)A 1976, s 80 as follows:

> '"operate" means in the course of business to make provision for the invitation or acceptance of bookings for a private hire vehicle; ...'

And

> '"private hire vehicle" means a motor vehicle constructed or adapted to seat , other than a hackney carriage or public service vehicle, which is provided for hire with the services of a driver for the purpose of carrying passengers;'.

St Albans District Council v Taylor

12.2

> Unlicensed vehicle and unlicensed driver provided at no charge by a licensed private hire operator. Did this constitute 'operating'? Held: Yes, because there was a provision for the invitation of bookings, and the legislation specifies 'hire' without any requirement for 'reward'.

It was decided in the case of *St Albans District Council v Taylor*[1] that there did not have to be any payment for there to be a hiring and, therefore, if the operator supplied vehicles at no charge, he was still operating. Taylor was a private hire operator and was prosecuted for knowingly using an unlicensed private hire vehicle and an unlicensed private hire driver. Short of both vehicles and drivers to fulfil a booking, Taylor asked his wife to drive his customers to the destinations that they had asked to be taken to. He told her not to make any charge for the journey, nor to accept a tip. He was acquitted by the magistrates, who took the view that there was no hiring, as no money had changed hands. On appeal by way of case stated, the matter was heard by Russell LJ and Hodgson J. Russell LJ gave the leading judgment and concluded that there was no doubt that Mr Taylor was acting 'in the course of business and therefore operating under the terms of section 80 [LG(MP)A 1976, s 80]'. However, as the vehicles used were not licensed as private hire vehicles, he continued:

> 'Much more difficult, however, is whether it is right to find, contrary to the findings of the justices, that the defendant was "operating" his wife's vehicles as private hire vehicles. I have come to the conclusion that he was because, in telling his wife to drive her own vehicle, he was making provision for the acceptance of the bookings that had been made by his customers within the meaning of "operate" to be found in section 80. There was no cancellation of those bookings; on the contrary the defendant was fulfilling them. He was not engaging upon a purely domestic arrangement such as would arise if Mrs Taylor was being asked to give a lift to friends of the defendant. The customers remained customers of the defendant despite what they were told by Mrs Taylor. whilst the wording of section 80 might have been more happily phrased I do not think that to say Mr Taylor was making "provision for the ... acceptance of bookings" unduly strains the language when applied to the unusual circumstances of this case. This construction of the section certainly achieves the purpose of the legislation to which I have earlier referred.
>
> There remains for consideration the words "private hire vehicle". Was the vehicle used by Mrs Taylor operated as a private hire vehicle? Private hire vehicle is also defined in section 80. It reads so far as material:

> > "... 'private hire vehicle' means a motor vehicle ... which is provided for hire with the services of a driver for the purpose of carrying passengers."

> By paragraph 7 of the case the justices found

> > "that there had been no hiring in respect of the informations relating to 7 and 13 July 1989 and that the vehicles were not operated as private hire vehicles ..."

> For my part I have to disagree with this finding. It is true that no payment in respect of the journeys was sought or paid. However, I am quite unable to accept that the journeys were undertaken without any consideration on a purely domestic or social, as opposed to a commercial, basis. Mr Taylor arranged for the carriage of his customers in order to fulfil what he regarded as his contractual obligation. Without that contractual obligation he would not have carried his customers on the journeys that they had booked with Mr Taylor's private hire vehicle business. No doubt in doing as he did Mr

Taylor was protecting the good will of that business rather than let down his customers or transfer their custom to a competitor.

To constitute a hiring it is not necessary, in my judgment, that in all the circumstances there should be the payment of money. If the hirer can fairly be said to derive commercial benefit from the transaction then a hiring may take place, and in my view it did take place in the unusual circumstances of this case.

Accordingly, for the reasons I have endeavoured to outline, I have come to the conclusion that the justices fell into error by dismissing these informations.'

This view was supported by Hodgson J.

¹ [1991] Crim LR 852.

12.3

This is an important case as it makes very clear that money does not need to change hands for there to be a hiring in the course of business and also that if the vehicle is used as a private hire vehicle, even if it is not a licensed private hire vehicle, it falls within the definition.

R (on the application of Arun District Council) v Spooner

12.4

> Was a vehicle that was used as a pet ambulance, which occasionally carried the owners as well, a private hire vehicle and was the person who arranged the journeys an operator? Held: This was not a private hire vehicle despite the fact that it occasionally carried passengers and as a consequence, no operators licence was required.

*R (on the application of Arun District Council) v Spooner*¹ considered whether a pet ambulance fell within the definition of 'operating'. The facts were outlined by Thomas LJ²:

'2. I think it is right to begin by summarising, in a sentence or two, the activity for which this local authority decided to prosecute the respondent, in this case Mr Spooner, at the time a man of 70 and now 72 years of age. He provided what was essentially a charitable service, though it is right to accept he might have got some small incidental benefit for himself. However, he gave of his own time and took no money, apart from money required to defray the costs of his activities, by providing a service to, what the magistrates found were, elderly people within the area of this district council in taking their pets to the vet.

3. For that, in circumstances in which we shall set out in detail, he was prosecuted for not having a licence. The magistrates dismissed that, as we have said. The matter was brought to this court at no doubt considerable

further expense to the ratepayers of the Arun District Council. Yet we were told that the decision made to appeal to this court, despite the acquittal before the magistrates, was as a matter of policy. I shall return further to that issue at the conclusion of this judgment.

This was originally a service whereby elderly people were taken to the vets with their pets in the pet ambulance, which was a converted estate car. Following discussions with Arun District Council, that service was discontinued, but was reinstated some six months later but in a slightly different way. The new service was simply a pet only carriage service, and in 95% of journeys the animal was carried alone. However, in five per cent of the cases, where the vet requires the owner's attendance or in an emergency, the owner was taken in the vehicle, but no further charge was made. The service was an appointment only service; bookings were made and the fee normally charged was £6. No fee, as I have said, was charged for those occasions where in an emergency, or the vet required it, the owner accompanied the vehicle.'[3]

---

[1] [2007] EWHC 307 (Admin), [2007] All ER (D) 73 (Jan).
[2] As above at paras 2 and 3.
[3] Per Thomas LJ at para 5.

12.5

Thomas LJ continued:

'6. Although some of the advertising material suggested that longer journeys might be made, for which some further charge was to be levied, those were in fact not undertaken and £6 was charged for taking each animal to the clinic and bringing it back again. The service was always non-profit making, though it was not registered as a charity or a trust. The respondent and his wife gave up their time on a voluntary basis. No one was paid wages and the money that was charged was to cover the costs of the vehicle and other incidental expenses. The majority of the takings were retained for expenses, normally 75 to 80 per cent and the remainder normally, 20 to 25 per cent, was paid to a charity. The vehicle was classed by the DVLA as an ambulance and nil rated. The magistrates found that the respondent had fully comprehensive insurance for the vehicle.'

The council discovered the existence of the revised service and interviewed Mr Spooner under caution. They mistakenly believed that the service had not altered and prosecuted Spooner for three offences:

- using a vehicle as a private hire vehicle without a licence contrary to s 46(1)(a);
- being an unlicensed driver of a private hire vehicle contrary to s 46(1)(b); and
- operating the vehicle without an operator's licence contrary to s 46(1)(d).

The magistrates found that no offence was committed because the vehicle did not fall within the definition of a private hire vehicle.

12.6

In relation to the definition of a private hire vehicle, Thomas LJ stated that[1]:

'11. On that definition, on the facts of this case, four subissues arose. First, was the vehicle constructed to carry fewer than nine passengers? It is common ground that it was. The second sub-issue that arose: was the vehicle provided with the services of the driver? Again it is common ground that it was. The third subissue which arose is whether the vehicle was provided for hire. Again it was accepted that it was, in the light of the findings made. It is therefore unnecessary for me to refer to the judgment of Lord Justice Russell in *St Albans District Council v Taylor* [1991] RTR 400 where he discusses, at page 404, the issues relating to what amounts to a hiring.

12. The fourth and final subissue that arose is whether the hire was for the purpose of carrying passengers. It is on that sole issue that the dispute arose before this court. There is little by way of authority to help. It is useful to refer briefly to the judgment of Mance J, as he then was, in *Benson v Boyce* [1997] RTR 226, where, in considering the relevant provisions, he considered that what mattered in determining whether a vehicle was a private hire vehicle was that one looked at its characteristic use, rather than its use on a specific occasion.

13. Taking that guidance, I asked myself the question whether on the primary findings of fact made by the magistrates, which I have set out, they were entitled to find whether the purpose of the hire was for the purpose of carrying passengers or some other purpose. In the submissions before us it was not suggested by the local authority that a finding made by the Justices that the purpose was not the carriage of passengers, but the carriage of pets, was perverse. However, it was contended by the local authority that if passengers were carried on one single occasion, even though the underlying purpose of a hire might have been the carriage of animals or goods, because one person was carried on one occasion, the purpose of that hiring became purpose of carrying passengers.

14. It seems to me that if the relevant statutory provision had read, 'which is provided for hire with the service of a driver during which passengers are carried' there could be no doubt that that contention was correct. But that is not what the legislation provides. The legislation requires the trier of fact to ask the question: what was the purpose of the hire? That, it seems to me, is purely a factual question to be determined on the evidence. On the facts, as set out by the Justices, it seems to me clear that they were entitled to find that the purpose was not the carriage of passengers, but the carriage of pets.

15. It seems to me that the basic underlying finding that supported that conclusion was the fact that no additional charge was made for the carriage of a passenger, that a passenger was only carried in an emergency or where the vet required the attendance of the owner, and that the charge that was

made was for the pet and in the overwhelming number of cases where pets were carried, the pet alone was carried. In those circumstances it seems to me that the magistrates were entitled to come to the conclusion that they did, and which I have set out, and as there is no suggestion that their finding was perverse, the local authority's appeal on that issue must fail.

16. As it was essential for the local authority to establish, in respect of each of the informations laid, that the vehicle was a private hire vehicle, it follows, in my judgment, that the magistrates were right to come to the conclusion that they did, and dismiss the information.'

The court then considered a second question which was whether this activity amounted to 'operating' within the meaning of the 1976 Act. The magistrate had taken the view that no personal profit had accrued to Mr Spooner, he was not operating a business and therefore not 'operating' within the meaning of the Act. In relation to this, Thomas LJ made the following finding[2]:

'17. ... As I have set out, it was the view of the Justices that because no personal profit accrued to the respondent he was not conducting a business. Therefore he was not, within the definition of the word "operating" in section 80 of the Act, carrying out an activity in the course of a business. It seems to me, and this has essentially been accepted by Mr Lamb, that their reasoning was fallacious.

18. On the facts, the respondent was plainly carrying on a business. He was operating a booking system and had a specially adapted vehicle. A charge was made. The charge made resulted in a profit being made in the ordinary sense of the word in that the expenses of the business were far less by a matter of 20 or 25 per cent than the costs of the operation. The fact that the Respondent then donated that excess of 20 to 25 per cent to charity cannot possibly mean the activity is not a business. If a profit, as is the case here, was made from this activity, the use of that profit is entirely irrelevant; the activity must have constituted a business. That, however, makes no difference to the overall conclusion, to which I have come, as it is clear, as I have already stated, that the appeal must fail because of the first issues in relation to the definition of a private hire vehicle.'

This is an important decision, as it reinforces the view expressed in *Benson v Boyce*[3] that is necessary to look at the characteristic use of the vehicle, rather than a single specific occasion. Generally this vehicle did not carry passengers, and even when passengers were carried no extra charge was made. It is also important from the point of view of the question of operating a business, that the fact that no personal benefits accrued to Mr Spooner, did not prevent his activity from amounting to a business[4].

1   Per Thomas LJ at paras 11–16.
2   Per Thomas LJ at paras 17 and 18.
3   [1997] RTR 226; see para 13.72.
4   It is also worth noting that the High Court was critical of the local authority for having firstly brought the prosecution, and then secondly pursued on appeal. This was outlined by Thomas LJ at paras 21 and 22 of the judgment in the following terms:

'21. It follows, therefore, that the magistrates were correct in my judgment in dismissing the information. It seems to me a matter of regret (but I say no more) that in the circumstances which I outlined at the beginning of this judgment, the local authority decided, after they had discovered the change in the way in which the service provided by the respondent had been conducted, to pursue the matter before the court.

22. It is a matter of even greater regret that significant sums of ratepayers' money have been expended in an appeal to this court in the circumstances of a case where what the respondent was doing was a charitable service intended to help elderly people in this local authority's area taking their pets to the vet. It is difficult to think of a case where a prosecutor should not have thought much more clearly about whether really this was a case where an appeal should have been pursued to this court.'

When an application for full costs to reimburse the legal aid fund which had funded Mr Spooner was resisted by Counsel for the local authority, both Thomas LJ and Mrs Justice Dobbs made their views extremely clear, describing the matter as 'a disgraceful appeal' (at para 25) and 'a case that should never have been brought in the first place and to pursue it against a 72-year-old man to this court was a disgrace' (at para 32).

All three licences must be issued by the same authority

12.7

A private hire operator can only operate a private hire vehicle which has been licensed by the same authority as that which granted his operator's licence. In addition, it must be driven by a private hire driver licensed by the same authority. This was made clear in the cases of *Dittah v Birmingham City Council, Choudhry v Birmingham City Council*[1], *Murtagh v Bromsgrove District Council*[2] and *Shanks v North Tyneside Borough Council*[3], all of which are considered below. This triad of licences is sometimes referred to as the 'happy family of private hire licensing'.

[1]   [1993] RTR 356.
[2]   (1999) Independent, 20 November, QBD.
[3]   [2001] EWHC 533 (Admin).

Dittah v Birmingham City Council, Choudhry v Birmingham City Council

12.8

> Can a private hire operator only operate vehicles and drivers licensed by the same authority that licences the operator? Held: Yes, all three licences must have been issued by the same local authority.

The cases of *Dittah v Birmingham City Council, Choudhry v Birmingham City Council*[1] concerned private hire operators licensed by Birmingham City Council who were operating private hire vehicles licensed by Solihull Metropolitan Borough Council and driven by drivers also licensed by Solihull. Messrs Dittah and Choudhry (the operators) were prosecuted for knowingly operating a private hire vehicle which did not have a private hire driver's or vehicle licence, contrary to LG(MP)A 1976, s 46(1)(e)(i) and (ii). The argument was that they were licensed, albeit not by Birmingham City Council and, accordingly, no offence had been committed. The counter-argument on behalf of the prosecution was that to satisfy s 46, the operator, vehicle and driver all had to be licensed by the same authority. The case was heard by Kennedy LJ and Clarke J, with Kennedy LJ giving the judgment. He referred to (at 363):

'... a letter dated 25th June 1992 from the Department of Transport to the district secretary of the Bromsgrove District Council, paragraph 3 of which reads:

"In our view applying section 80(2) to sections 46(1)(*d*) and (*e*) has the effect that an operator requires a licence from the area in which he intends to operate and may operate only in that area vehicles and drivers licensed by the same district. This has the practical effect that an operator licensed in area A may only use vehicles and drivers licensed in area A but these vehicles and drivers will by virtue of section 75(2) exemption be able to go anywhere in the course of hiring."'

He continued (at 363):

'That in my judgment is an accurate statement of the law, whatever may have been said elsewhere in the past.'

As a consequence of that he concluded (at 363):

'Accordingly, in my judgment the answer to the question posed in each case must be that, as postulated, section 46(1)(*e*) of the Act of 1976 must be read subject to the provisions of section 80(2) of that Act, so as to require private hire operators licensed under section 55 of the Act to make use only of vehicles and drivers licensed by the council of the district by which the operators are licensed when operating in that controlled district. The alternative construction cannot be supported, and these appeals must be dismissed.'

[1]   [1993] RTR 356. These were separate cases raising similar points and the appeals were heard together and reported together.

12.9

This case has been followed by *Murtagh (t/a Rubery Rednal Cars) v Bromsgrove District Council*[1] and *Shanks v North Tyneside Borough Council*[2]. In both these cases the ruling in *Dittah and Choudrey*[3] that all three licences must be issued by the same local authority was followed with approval.

[1]   [2001] LLR 514, QBD.
[2]   [2001] EWHC 533 (Admin).
[3]   *Dittah v Birmingham City Council, Choudhry v Birmingham City Council* [1993] RTR 356; see para 12.8 above.

Murtagh (t/a Rubery Rednal Cars) v Bromsgrove District Council

12.10

> A Freephone line was installed in a supermarket in Birmingham, linking directly to an operator's base in Bromsgrove (a neighbouring borough). A booking was fulfilled using a Birmingham City Council licensed vehicle and driver, dispatched by a Bromsgrove District Council operator. Was this lawful? Held: No, as all three licences had to be issued by the same local authority.

In *Murtagh v Bromsgrove District Council*[1] Ms Murtagh and her partner were licensed as operators by Bromsgrove District Council. They also had a private hire operator's licence issued by Birmingham City Council, which was a neighbouring district. They had freephone telephone lines in supermarkets situated in Birmingham. These connected to their office in Bromsgrove. On three occasions they discharged bookings received at their Bromsgrove office with a car and driver, both of which were licensed by Birmingham City Council, rather than Bromsgrove. This put them in conflict with the ruling in *Dittah v Birmingham City Council, Choudhry v Birmingham City Council*[2] and they were prosecuted by Bromsgrove District Council. The magistrates convicted them and they appealed against that decision. The arguments were as follows (as outlined by Mr Justice Jowitt):

> 'It was contended by the appellants [Murtagh and partner] before the magistrates that by reason of the dedicated telephone lines in Birmingham they had made provision for the invitation there of bookings for a private hire vehicle, and so were operating within the Birmingham controlled district, and could respond to bookings by providing a private hire vehicle licensed by and driven by a driver licensed by the Birmingham City Council.
>
> The respondent's contention was that there was no provision in Birmingham for the invitation of bookings and that bookings were accepted in the Bromsgrove controlled district so that the vehicle and its driver had both to be licensed by Bromsgrove. Moreover, it was contended, even if the appellants operated also within the Birmingham controlled district by virtue of the dedicated telephone lines, that did not affect the statutory requirement arising from the fact of operating in Bromsgrove.
>
> The magistrates accepted the respondent's contentions. They concluded that the appellants were operating in the Bromsgrove controlled district and were not operating in the Birmingham controlled district. They concluded that the use of the vehicle on the three occasions did require a vehicle and driver licensed by Bromsgrove, and that accordingly all five offences were made out.'

1   [2001] LLR 514 , QBD.
2   [1993] RTR 356; see para 12.8 above.

12.11

The question that had to be addressed by the High Court was:

'... whether, since undoubtedly the appellants were operating in Bromsgrove (because that is where they accepted bookings), it is to be said that not only had the operators to have their licences, but the vehicles and their drivers also had to have their licences issued by Bromsgrove.'

12.12

Mr Justice Jowitt, giving the first judgment[1], found that *Dittah v Birmingham City Council, Choudhry v Birmingham City Council*[2] applied and he concluded:

'It follows in my judgment that, although the appellants held operators' licences issued both by Birmingham as well as by Bromsgrove, they were not entitled to operate private hire vehicles which were not licensed by and driven by drivers licensed by Bromsgrove.'

[1]   *Murtagh (t/a Rubery Rednal Cars) v Bromsgrove District Council* [2001] LLR 514, QBD.
[2]   [1993] RTR 356; see para 12.8 above.

12.13

It can be seen that this case not only follows, but also approves of the ruling in *Dittah v Birmingham City Council, Choudhry v Birmingham City Council*[1].

[1]   [1993] RTR 356; see para 12.8.

Shanks v North Tyneside Borough Council

12.14

Could an operator licensed by North Tyneside Borough Council dispatch a vehicle and driver licensed by Newcastle City Council? Held: No, as all three licences had to be issued by the same local authority.

In *Shanks v North Tyneside Borough Council*[1], the question that was raised was whether *Dittah v Birmingham City Council, Choudhry v Birmingham City Council*[2] had been correctly decided. Considerable arguments were adduced to the court to persuade them to depart from the decision in *Dittah*, but Lord Justice Latham, giving the judgment of the court, stated (at para 22):

'Not only do I consider that it has not been shown [in the arguments in *Shanks*] that the decision of Dittah was per incuriam and therefore a case which we can revisit, but I have come to the firm conclusion that it was correctly decided.'

[1]   [2001] EWHC 533 (Admin).
[2]   [1993] RTR 356; see para 12.8 above.

12.15

It is therefore clear that an operator, licensed in that case in North Tyneside could only dispatch vehicles licensed by North Tyneside and which were driven by North Tyneside licensed drivers.

12.16

Both these cases show that *Dittah*[1] was clearly correctly decided.

[1]   *Dittah v Birmingham City Council, Choudhry v Birmingham City Council* [1993] RTR 356; see para 12.8 above.

12.17

Further questions that arise concerning private hire operators are:

- whether a private hire operator can take a booking for a journey which commences outside the area in which he is licensed;
- whether a private hire operator can take a booking for a journey which terminates outside the area in which he is licensed;
- whether a private hire operator can take a booking for a journey which goes outside the area in which he is licensed on the course of its journey; and
- whether a private hire operator can take a booking for a journey that never comes within the area in which he is licensed.

12.18

LG(MP)A 1976, s 75(1)(a) is of some assistance in this regard:

'75–(1) Nothing in this Part of this Act shall—
(a)   apply to a vehicle used for bringing passengers or goods within a controlled district in pursuance of a contract for the hire of the vehicle made outside the district if the vehicle is not made available for hire within the district; …'

12.19

Controlled district is defined in LG(MP)A 1976, s 80(1):

'"controlled district" means any area for which this Part of this Act is in force by virtue of a resolution passed by a district council under section 45 of this Act; …'

12.20

LG(MP)A 1976, s 75(2) also assists in relation to these points:

'75–(2) Paragraphs (*a*), (*b*) and (*c*) of section 46(1) of this Act shall not apply to the use or driving of a vehicle or to the employment of a driver of a vehicle while the vehicle is used as a private hire vehicle in a controlled district if a licence issued under section 48 of this Act by the council whose area consists of or includes another controlled district is then in force for the vehicle and a driver's licence issued by such a council is then in force for the driver of the vehicle.'

12.21

It is clear that, provided the three licences required in relation to a private hire vehicle (operator, vehicle and driver) have all been issued by the same authority, that is to say they 'match', then the private hire vehicle can undertake journeys anywhere in England and Wales. That is irrespective of the local authority area where the journey commences, areas through which the journey passes and, ultimately, the area where the journey ends. In addition, advertisements for a private hire service can be placed anywhere and are not limited to the geographical area of the local authority which licenses the operator of the private hire service. These are the conclusions which can be drawn from the cases of *Adur District Council v Fry*[1] and *Windsor and Maidenhead Royal Borough Council v Khan*[2].

[1]   [1997] RTR 257 considered at para 12.94 below.
[2]   [1994] RTR 87 considered at para 12.95 below.

THE PREMISES AND FLEET OF AN OPERATOR

12.22

The practical effect of the requirement to hold an operator's licence is that a private hire operator will have to have premises from which he controls a fleet of vehicles. There is no maximum limit to the size of this fleet, although the minimum would be one, as even a single private hire vehicle must be controlled by an operator to comply with the legislative requirements.

12.23

These premises, which are usually referred to as the private hire operator's 'base', will usually be equipped with telephone lines (although an increasing number of private hire bookings are made over the internet) and may also be able to deal with personal callers. The customer visits the operator's base, telephones or uses the internet or an app and asks for a private hire vehicle to collect them from a certain point at a certain time. The operator will normally establish not only the collection point, but also the destination and will then arrange for a vehicle from his fleet to satisfy the booking. This is usually achieved by means of radio, with transmission from the base to one or more of the vehicles, but could involve the use of mobile telephones or the internet to a smartphone.

12.24

The operator will usually charge the driver or owner of the vehicle a fee for being part of that particular operator's fleet. Those fees can be a flat rate per week, a percentage of fares taken, a combination of the two or any other arrangement that the parties agree to.

12.25

The operations of private hire operators range from small concerns operating one or two vehicles up to sizeable undertakings in urban areas where an individual operator controls many hundreds of private hire vehicles. Notwithstanding the size of the fleet, the basic provisions remain the same and are considered in detail below.

12.26

The starting point is LG(MP)A 1976, s 46(1)(d), which states:

'46–(1) Except as authorised by this Part of this Act— ...
(d)   no person shall in a controlled district operate any vehicle as a private hire vehicle without having a current licence under section 55 of this Act; ...'

12.27

Contravention of this requirement is an offence by virtue of LG(MP)A 1976, s 46(2), for which the maximum penalty is a fine not exceeding level 3 on the standard scale[1].

Although not overtly stated within the legislation, it is clearly the case that the operator not only takes the booking and dispatches the vehicle and driver, but also remains responsible for both vehicle and driver for the duration of that hiring.

It is important that the operator, driver and vehicle proprietor (if different from the driver) are all clear about the contractual arrangements that exist between them. Whilst the legislation is clear that the contract for the hire of the vehicle and driver is between the hirer and the operator[2], it is silent as to the arrangements between the three licensees.

An operator will wish to ensure that those driving for him are satisfactory (in addition to holding a private hire drivers' licence) and will attend to bookings punctually and provide a professional service to customers. The operator will also need to ensure that vehicles are not only licensed, but also kept clean and tidy and in a good state of mechanical repair. All these matters should be covered by the contracts between the parties.

[1]   LG(MP)A 1976, s 76.
[2]   LG(MP)A 1976, s 56(1). See para 12.57 below.

APPLICATION FOR AN OPERATOR'S LICENCE

12.28

As outlined above[1], a private hire vehicle must be controlled by a private hire operator who holds a licence under LG(MP)A 1976, s 55. To comply with the legislation, a prospective operator must make an application to the district council under LG(MP)A 1976, s 55(1). This states:

'55–(1) Subject to the provisions of this Part of this Act, a district council shall, on receipt of an application from any person for the grant to that person of a licence to operate private hire vehicles grant to that person an operator's licence:

Provided that a district council shall not grant a licence unless they are satisfied
(a)   that the applicant is a fit and proper person to hold an operator's licence; and
(b)   if the applicant is an individual, that the applicant is not disqualified by reason of the applicant's immigration status from operating a private hire vehicle.

(1A) In determining for the purposes of subsection (1) whether an applicant is disqualified by reason of the applicant's immigration status from operating a private hire vehicle, a district council must have regard to any guidance issued by the Secretary of State.[2]

(2) [Subject to section 55ZA, every licence granted under this section shall remain in force for five years or for such lesser period, specified in the licence, as the district council think appropriate in the circumstances of the case.'

[1]   See para 12.1 above.
[2]   See para 12.33 below for details on immigration status.

12.29

Once an application has been received, the council is then under a duty to grant an operator's licence to that person subject to determining that they are 'a fit and proper person to hold an operator's licence' and, in the case of an individual or partnership, the person (or persons) has the right to remain and work in the UK. These are the only grounds on which an application can be refused[1].

[1]   These considerations are similar to those which apply to other licences and which have been considered in Chapter 5. See also Chapter 10, para 10.21 onwards.

Power to require applicants to submit information

12.30

Under LG(MP)A 1976, s 57, the local authority is given wide-ranging powers to seek information about a prospective private hire operator. Section 57(1) is a general power in relation to any licence, but s 57(2)(b) and (c) specifically relates to private hire operators.

'Power to require applicants to submit information

57–(1) A district council may require any applicant for a licence under the Act of 1847 [Town Police Clauses Act 1847] or under this Part of this Act to submit to them such information as they may reasonably consider necessary to enable them to determine whether the licence should be granted and whether conditions should be attached to any such licence.

(2) Without prejudice to the generality of the foregoing subsection—

…

(b) a district council may require an applicant for an operator's licence to submit to them such information as to—
   (i)   the name and address of the applicant;
   (ii) the addresses or address whether within the area of the council or not from which he intends to carry on business in connection with private hire vehicles licensed under this Part of this Act;
   (iii) any trade or business activities he has carried on before making the application;
   (iv) any previous application he has made for an operator's licence;
   (v)   the revocation or suspension of any operator's licence previously held by him;
   (vi) any convictions recorded against the applicant;
   as they may reasonably consider necessary to enable them to determine whether to grant such licence;
(c) in addition to the information specified in paragraph (b) of this subsection, a district council may require an applicant for an operator's licence to submit to them—
   (i)   if the applicant is or has been a director or secretary of a company, information as to any convictions recorded against that company at any relevant time; any trade or business activities carried on by that company; any previous application made by that company for an operator's licence; and any revocation or suspension of an operator's licence previously held by that company;
   (ii) if the applicant is a company, information as to any convictions recorded against a director or secretary of that company; any trade or business activities carried on by any such director or secretary; any previous application made by any such director or secretary for an operator's licence; and any revocation or suspension of an operator's licence previously held by such director or secretary;
   (iii) if the applicant proposes to operate the vehicle in partnership with any other person, information as to any convictions recorded against that person; any trade or business activities carried on by that person; any previous application made by that person for an operator's licence; and any revocation or suspension of an operator's licence previously held by him.'

12.31

It is important to recognise that the local authority can ask for any information that is reasonably required to enable them to determine an application and the questions contained in LG(MP)A 1976, s 57(2)(b) and (c) are not exclusive.

12.32

LG(MP)A 1976, s 57(3) is a wide-ranging offence provision:

'57–(3) If any person knowingly or recklessly makes a false statement or omits any material particular in giving information under this section, he shall be guilty of an offence.'

The two requirements that must be satisfied before an operator's licence can be granted, that the applicant must be a fit and proper person and must not be prohibited from holding an operator's licence by reason of their immigration status will be considered in reverse order.

The applicant must not be 'disqualified by reason of the applicant's immigration status from operating a private hire vehicle'

12.33

The Immigration Act 2016 ('IA 2016') amended the LG(MP)A 1976 to add an additional criterion to the requirements to be satisfied before a private hire operators licence can be granted. An individual applicant[1] for a new private hire operator's licence, or the renewal of an operator's licence granted before the introduction of this amendment[2], must not be disqualified from holding a private hire operator's licence by reason of their immigration status. Only persons with a right to both remain in the UK and also work in the UK can be granted a private hire operator's licence and if either of those requirements are lost, any such licence that has been issued will lapse.

Sections 79A and 79B have been inserted into LG(MP)A 1976 which detail those who are disqualified from holding any private hire operator's licence (or hackney carriage driver's or private hire driver's licence) by reason of immigration status, and explain the meanings of immigration offences and immigration penalties.

'79A Persons disqualified by reason of immigration status

(1) For the purposes of this Part of this Act a person is disqualified by reason of the person's immigration status from carrying on a licensable activity if the person is subject to immigration control and—

(a)   the person has not been granted leave to enter or remain in the United Kingdom; or

(b)   the person's leave to enter or remain in the United Kingdom—

    (i)   is invalid;

    (ii)   has ceased to have effect (whether by reason of curtailment, revocation, cancellation, passage of time or otherwise); or

    (iii)   is subject to a condition preventing the person from carrying on the licensable activity.

(2) Where a person is on immigration bail within the meaning of Part 1 of Schedule 10 to the Immigration Act 2016—

(a)   the person is to be treated for the purposes of this Part of this Act as if the person had been granted leave to enter the United Kingdom; but

(b)   any condition as to the person's work in the United Kingdom to which the person's immigration bail is subject is to be treated for those purposes as a condition of leave.

(3) For the purposes of this section a person is subject to immigration control if under the Immigration Act 1971 the person requires leave to enter or remain in the United Kingdom.

(4) For the purposes of this section a person carries on a licensable activity if the person—

(a)   drives a private hire vehicle;

(b)   operates a private hire vehicle; or

(c)   drives a hackney carriage.'

Section 79B defines what is meant by 'Immigration offence' and 'immigration penalty'.

'79B Immigration offences and immigration penalties

(1) In this Part of this Act "immigration offence" means—

(a)   an offence under any of the Immigration Acts;

(b)   an offence under section 1 of the Criminal Attempts Act 1981 of attempting to commit an offence within paragraph (a); or

(c)   an offence under section 1 of the Criminal Law Act 1977 of conspiracy to commit an offence within paragraph (a).

(2) In this Part of this Act *"immigration penalty"* means a penalty under—

(a)   section 15 of the Immigration, Asylum and Nationality Act 2006 ("the 2006 Act"); or

(b)   section 23 of the Immigration Act 2014 ("the 2014 Act").

(3) For the purposes of this Part of this Act a person to whom a penalty notice under section 15 of the 2006 Act has been given is not to be treated as having been required to pay an immigration penalty if—

(a)   the person is excused payment by virtue of section 15(3) of that Act; or

(b)   the penalty is cancelled by virtue of section 16 or 17 of that Act.

(4) For the purposes of this Part of this Act a person to whom a penalty notice under section 15 of the 2006 Act has been given is not to be treated as having been required to pay an immigration penalty until such time as—

(a)   the period for giving a notice of objection under section 16 of that Act has expired and the Secretary of State has considered any notice given within that period; and

(b)   if a notice of objection was given within that period, the period for appealing under section 17 of that Act has expired and any appeal brought within that period has been finally determined, abandoned or withdrawn.

(5) For the purposes of this Part of this Act a person to whom a penalty notice under section 23 of the 2014 Act has been given is not to be treated as having been required to pay an immigration penalty if—

(a)   the person is excused payment by virtue of section 24 of that Act; or

(b)   the penalty is cancelled by virtue of section 29 or 30 of that Act.

(6) For the purposes of this Part of this Act a person to whom a penalty notice under section 23 of the 2014 Act has been given is not to be treated as having been required to pay an immigration penalty until such time as—

(a)   the period for giving a notice of objection under section 29 of that Act has expired and the Secretary of State has considered any notice given within that period; and

(b)   if a notice of objection was given within that period, the period for appealing under section 30 of that Act has expired and any appeal brought within that period has been finally determined, abandoned or withdrawn.'

In addition, by virtue of s 55(1A) the local authority must have regard to the Guidance issued by the Secretary of State:

'(1A) In determining for the purposes of subsection (1) whether an applicant is disqualified by reason of the applicant's immigration status from operating a private hire vehicle, a district council must have regard to any guidance issued by the Secretary of State.'

The Guidance was issued on 1 December 2016[3] and details the three steps that a local authority must take to ensure that an applicant satisfies the test[4]. In brief the steps are:

1.   Original documents from specified lists (Annex A) must be provided by the applicant;

2.   The documents must be verified and examined in the presence of the applicant; and

3.   A copy of all the documents must be made and retained.

These checks must be made in respect of every applicant from December 2016, but need only be undertaken on renewals where the applicant has a 'time-limited immigration permission to be in the UK and work'[5].

Where an operator only has a limited time to remain in the UK, s 55ZA prevents a local authority from granting an operator's licence beyond the period of permission to remain and it can be for a shorter period. If the applicant has an extended leave to remain, the local authority cannot grant a licence for more than six months, but again it can be for a shorter period.

'55ZA Operators' licences for persons subject to immigration control

(1) Subsection (2) applies if—

(a)   a licence under section 55 is to be granted to a person who has been granted leave to enter or remain in the United Kingdom for a limited period ("the leave period");

(b) the person's leave has not been extended by virtue of section 3C of the Immigration Act 1971 (continuation of leave pending variation decision); and

(c) apart from subsection (2), the period for which the licence would have been in force would have ended after the end of the leave period.

(2) The district council which grants the licence must specify a period in the licence as the period for which it remains in force; and that period must end at or before the end of the leave period.'

If a licensed operator loses the right to remain in the UK during the currency of a licence, the licence ceases to have effect[6]. This is covered by s 55ZA(5) and no action needs to be taken by the local authority (eg, revocation) because simply, the licence ceases to be of effect. In those circumstances, the licence must be returned to the local authority within seven days of the expiry of the licence[7].

In any case where the licence has ceased to have effect, failure to surrender it within seven days is an offence under s 55ZA(8). This is not a 'grace' period: the seven days is apparently simply for administrative convenience. The maximum penalty on summary conviction is a fine not exceeding level 3 on the standard scale and there is also provision for a continuing daily penalty of £10 for each day after conviction. Those fine levels can be altered by the Secretary of State under s 55ZA(9).

[1]   Although the legislation is silent, it is suggested that these requirements will apply to all members of a partnership as well an individual applicant.
[2]   These provisions came into effect on 1 December 2016.
[3]   'Guidance for Licensing Authorities to Prevent Illegal Working in the Taxi and Private Hire Sector in England and Wales' available at https://www.gov.uk/government/uploads/system/uploads/attachment_data/file/574059/Guidance-for-licensing-authorities-to-prevent-illegal-working-in-the-taxi-and-private-hire-sector-in-England-and-Wales.pdf. See Appendix II.
[4]   As above at page 10 onwards.
[5]   As above at page 12.
[6]   Although the licence will lapse, there is no mechanism contained within the legislation for the Border Force to notify a local authority when a right to work or remain ceases.
[7]   See s 55ZA(6).

The applicant must be a 'fit and proper person'

12.34

The second requirement is that the applicant must be a 'fit and proper person'. As with drivers[1] a 'safe and suitable person' is a satisfactory alternative expression.

[1]   See Chapter 10, para 10.21 onwards.

12.35

As with drivers, it is useful to have a test of fitness and propriety, or safety and suitability for a private hire operator and to inform such a test, it is necessary to understand the role of a private hire operator.

When a booking is made for a private hire vehicle, the person booking that vehicle will provide significant amount of generally personal information to that operator. This can include the times that they leave and return to their home, where they are travelling, the frequency of those visits, whether they are going on holiday for a period of time and so on. It is essential that the recipients of that information, the operator, ensures that the information is not used for criminal or other unacceptable purposes. For example, it would be very easy to use the knowledge that a family was on holiday for a fortnight to burgle their house, or use the knowledge of regular and illicit rendezvous with third parties to blackmail an individual.

Once again, there is no judicially approved test of fitness and propriety for private hire operators, so it is reasonable to use a variation on the approach used for drivers and a test similar to the following would seem appropriate:

'Would I be comfortable providing sensitive information such as holiday or business plans, movements of my family or other personal information to this person and feel safe in the knowledge that such information will not be used or passed on for criminal or unacceptable purposes?'

If the answer to this question (or a similar test) is an unqualified 'Yes', then the test is probably satisfied. If there are any doubts in the minds of those who make the decision, then further consideration should be given as to whether this person is a fit and proper person to hold private hire operators licence[1].

[1]   It is important to recognise that the role of the local authority is not to interview the applicant for a job, neither does the local authority have the ability to offer any kind of job to the applicant. The local authority must limit its consideration to the fitness and propriety of the individual.

Matters to take into account when determining fitness and propriety

CONSIDERATION OF PREVIOUS CONVICTIONS

12.36

It is not possible to obtain an enhanced Disclosure and Barring Service check for private hire operators. They do not appear within the Rehabilitation of Offenders Act 1974 (Exceptions) Order 1975[1], as amended. Notwithstanding that, a basic disclosure can be obtained[2], allied to a statutory declaration[3]. This view is supported by the DfT *Best Practice Guide* which states[4]:

'Criminal Record Checks

78. PHV operators (as opposed to PHV drivers) are not exceptions t the Rehabilitation of Offenders Act 1974, so Standard or Enhanced disclosures cannot be required as a condition of grant of an operator's licence. But a Basic Disclosure, which will provide details of unspent convictions only, could be seen as appropriate, after such a system has been introduced by the Criminal Records Bureau[5]. No firm date for introduction has yet been set; however, a feasibility study has been completed; the Criminal Records Bureau is undertaking further work in this regard. Overseas

applicants may be required to provide a certificate of good conduct from the relevant embassy if they have not been long in this country. Local licensing authorities may want to require a reference, covering for example the applicant's financial record, as well as the checks outlined above.'

Although operators are unlikely to have direct contact with an individual passenger and certainly do not have the same degree of control over a passenger as a driver does, it is important that they are a person of integrity. They receive and then hold personal information as outlined above and the public must have confidence in their honesty.

Local authorities should have a policy in relation to the impact of previous convictions on an applicant for a private hire operator's licence and this may be similar in concept, although not content, to the drivers and proprietors equivalents[6].

The impact of certain offences will differ from drivers (eg, a motoring conviction) but the overall approach will be similar[7].

[1] SI 1975/1023.

[2] Only available from Disclosure Scotland See http://www.disclosurescotland.co.uk/basic.htm.

[3] See Chapter 5, para 5.46.

[4] DfT, 'Taxi and Private Hire Vehicle Licensing: Best Practice Guidance' (October 2006, revised March 2010), para 52, available at http://www.dft.gov.uk/pgr/regional/taxis/taxiandprivatehirevehiclelic1792. See Appendix II.

[5] This should now be read as a reference to the Disclosure and Barring Service. Basic disclosures are still not available in England or Wales and a Basis DBS Certificate is only available from Disclosure Scotland.

[6] It should be noted that all the current published previous convictions policies (DfT and LGR – see Chapter 10, para 10.27) consider drivers and are silent in relation to operators.

[7] Accordingly, all the considerations detailed in respect of drivers in Chapter 10, para 10.21 onwards, will apply to operators.

OTHER INFORMATION AS IS CONSIDERED NECESSARY

12.37

Local authorities can require an applicant for an operator's licence to satisfy any pre-application requirements they feel are necessary. Although not driving, some knowledge of the area might be a sensible requirement, or an assessment of their knowledge of the requirements of operating private hire vehicles. It is not clear how many local authorities do impose any similar requirements.

IMPACT ON LIVELIHOOD AND FAMILY

12.38

As with drivers, in considering an application, the local authority can only consider the safety of the public[1] and the impact of not being granted a licence (or action being taken against a licence – suspension, revocation or refusal to renew) on the livelihood or the family of the applicant is not a factor that can or should be considered[2], whatever hardship may be caused.

It is then important to ensure that those individuals who work for that operator (where the operator is not a sole operator, driver and proprietor) are also subjected to a similar test. These are the people who actually take the bookings and dispatch the vehicles. A condition should be placed on a private hire operator's licence requiring the operator to ensure that all staff are also fit and proper people on the same test, and if it becomes apparent that the operator is not applying similar criteria, then that inevitably will call into question the continuing fitness and propriety of the operator.

1   See DfT, '*Taxi and Private Hire Vehicle Licensing: Best Practice Guidance*' (October 2006, revised March 2010), para 8, available from http://www.dft.gov.uk/pgr/regional/taxis/taxiandprivatehirevehiclelic1792

2   See *Leeds City Council v Hussain* [2002] EWHC 1145 (Admin), [2003] RTR 199; see Chapter 10, para 10.67 onwards; and *Anwar v Cherwell DC* [2011] EWHC 2943 (Admin), [2012] RTR 15; see Chapter 10, para 10.72.

12.39

LG(MP)A 1976, s 55(4) allows an applicant aggrieved by either a failure to grant an operator's licence or by the conditions attached to that licence to appeal to the magistrates' court.

LICENCE DURATION

12.40

The licence itself can be granted for any period of up to five years[1] and in October 2015 the legislation was amended to provide a presumption that an operator's licence would last for five years, but the re-worded legislation (LG(MP)A 1976, s 55(2)) is slightly peculiar.

'(2) Subject to section 55ZA, every licence granted under this section shall remain in force for five years or for such lesser period, specified in the licence, as the district council think appropriate in the circumstances of the case.'

This is therefore not a mandatory five-year driver's licence, but rather an indication that operators' licences should last five years. There is no further guidance as to what a district council might think to be appropriate circumstances and therefore this will remain a matter for the local authority's discretion.

The DfT Best Practice Guide[2] has not been reissued since the introduction of the amendment and currently suggests that local authorities should usually grant five year licences:

'Licence Duration

81. A requirement for annual licence renewal does not seem necessary or appropriate for PHV operators, whose involvement with the public is less direct than a driver (who will be alone with passengers). Indeed, a licence period of five years may well be appropriate in the average case. Although the authority may wish to offer operators the option of a licence for a shorter period if requested.'

It is not clear what 'the average case' means, but it would seem to mean the usual case.

1   LG(MP)A 1976, s 55(2).
2   DfT, 'Taxi and Private Hire Vehicle Licensing: Best Practice Guidance' (October 2006, revised March 2010), available at http://www.dft.gov.uk/pgr/regional/taxis/taxiandprivatehirevehiclelic1792.

12.41

It is important that local authorities are aware of any criminal convictions or other matters imposed on a private hire operator during the period of the licence. This is addressed by most local authorities who impose a condition on an operator's licence under LG(MP)A 1976, s 55(3) requiring the holder of such a licence to inform the authority, within a specified period (either seven or 14 days), of any conviction for any offence recorded against them or other matters (eg, cautions, fixed penalty notices etc) during the currency of the licence.

Conditions applied to private hire operators' licences

12.42

LG(MP)A 1976, s 55(3) allows the local authority to impose any conditions that it 'considers reasonably necessary' on a private hire operator's licence. The conditions that are imposed under this power vary widely from local authority to local authority, but they can include:

- ensure any vehicle hired attends punctually;
- if any rooms are provided for the public, for waiting or making bookings, they must be clean, adequately heated and ventilated and lit;
- no booking should be accepted unless the hirer knows the basis of the hire charge;
- not to permit people who are drunk to remain on the premises; and
- no maintenance of vehicles at the base.

ADDRESS FROM WHICH THE OPERATOR MAY OPERATE

Kingston upon Hull City Council v Wilson

12.43

Does a private hire operators licence relate to any premises within the district, or only to premises specified in the licence? Held: Only to the specific premises.

In addition, the local authority will specify the address or addresses from which the operator may operate. It is important that these are correct and that, if the operator moves, he not only informs the local authority, but also ensures that a revised licence is issued. This point was made clear in the case of *Kingston upon Hull City Council v Wilson*[1]. This was an appeal by way of case stated against a decision by Kingston upon Hull City Magistrates to acquit Mr Wilson of three charges. Two involved the use of a private hire vehicle[2], but the remaining charge was operating a vehicle as a private hire vehicle in a controlled district without holding an operator's licence, contrary to LG(MP)A 1976, s 46(1)(d). Mr Wilson did, in fact, hold a private hire operator's licence, but for a different address from that which was apparently being used by him to operate the vehicle. It was argued that Mr Wilson had an operator's licence (which he did), but the operator's licence had a condition imposed on it that it was to operate vehicles from Francis Street in Hull and not Jipdane, another road in the city and therefore he had operated without a licence. Buxton J stated (at p 18E):

> 'Mr Neish also argues that, nonetheless, Mr Wilson did have an operator's licence. Of course, he had a licence to operate private hire vehicles from Francis Street, in the city of Hull, as the Magistrates found. I do not accept, however, that that is an answer to this charge. First of all, it is clear that the condition imposed by the local authority was to operate vehicles from Francis Street and not from 4 Jipdane. I do not accept that operating a vehicle in breach of a condition of the licence is sufficient defence to a charge under section 46(*d*). Further, and this may be the same point, the section says:
>
> > "no person shall in a controlled district operate any vehicle as a private hire vehicle without having a current licence under section 55 of this Act;"
>
> That must, in common sense, mean without having a licence that currently applies to that operation, and clearly, on the findings of the Magistrates, Mr Wilson's Francis Street licence did not. Therefore the charge under section 46(1)(*b*) was made out.'

[1]   (1995) Times, 25 July.
[2]   See Chapter 13, para 13.72, footnote 3.

PARKING AT THE OPERATOR'S BASE

12.44

A number of authorities require a minimum number of parking places to be available at the premises used by the operator at their base. However, other authorities actually impose a condition that no private hire vehicles can park at the operator's base. The reasons for this difference seem to be based upon the concept of 'ranking'.

12.45

The local authorities that require operators to have parking places justify it on the grounds of easing congestion. In many (but by no means all) cases, private hire drivers do tend to return to their base between jobs and they park their cars nearby. If it is a sizeable operation, this can lead to serious congestion on adjoining roads, to the detriment of local residents and general passenger traffic. Accordingly, it is felt by some local authorities that it is best that there are some car-parking spaces which are available only for the private hire vehicles operated by that particular operator, as a way of easing this problem. This has the added advantage that if a person wishes to take the services of a private hire vehicle by entering and making the booking at the premises, then there is the possibility that a vehicle will be immediately available.

RANKING

12.46

One argument that is used against a provision of car parking is that, where two or more private hire vehicles have stopped together (as they would be outside their premises in a designated car park), this constitutes an unlawful rank. This is seen by some as an offence, as only hackney carriages can rank, and even then only at designated hackney carriage stands. This argument is not supported by authorities on plying or standing for hire[1] and is not in itself sufficient to warrant the policy of no parking places at a private hire operator's premises. Even though a private hire vehicle has stopped, possibly in company with other private hire vehicles, this does not make it an unlawful rank. As a private hire vehicle cannot be booked from a rank (lawful or otherwise), it is difficult to see how the presence of such a vehicle stationary on the street, or any other area to which the public has access, such as a car park, can constitute a rank. It is simply a stationary private hire vehicle. This view is reinforced when it is considered that where an approach has been made to the driver of a stationary vehicle, assuming that he is sitting in it, by a prospective customer with a view to using the services of the vehicle, the driver would be duty-bound to refer the prospective customer to the operator to make the booking.

[1]   See Chapter 8, para 8.7 onwards.

12.47

Whilst it is accepted that unlawful plying for hire does take place, this is a matter which can and should be controlled by enforcement action, rather than by conditions against car parking spaces.

12.48

A better argument against the requirement to provide car-parking spaces concerns the nature of the premises in question. A great many private hire operators use small offices as their base and, when this is taken into account, together with the overall number of off-road car parking spaces available in many towns and cities, it is felt that it would not be reasonable to require an operator to be able to provide car parking spaces.

PARKING WITHIN A SPECIFIED DISTANCE OF THE BASE

12.49

Some authorities have attempted to impose a condition which prohibits more than a specified number (usually very few, ie two or three) of private hire vehicles operated by that particular operator from parking within a specified distance of their base. Whilst the philosophy behind such a condition is understandable (to prevent congestion), it is difficult to see how such a condition can be enforced and, indeed, whether it is reasonable. Any vehicle which is insured, taxed and has (if necessary) a current MOT certificate can be parked at any legitimate parking place on the public highway at any time, subject only to parking restrictions. It is difficult to see how a local authority can erode those rights by a condition applied to the licence granted to a private hire operator.

PRIVATE HIRE VEHICLE MUST RETURN TO BASE

12.50

This can be contrasted with a condition, which is applied by at least one local authority, that, after each booking has been completed, the private hire vehicle must return to its operator's base before it can be despatched by the operator on another hiring. It is difficult to see what the justification is behind this condition. It would appear to be a recipe for considerable congestion in the vicinity of the private operator's base, a waste of time and fuel and a method of greatly increasing both environmental pollution and wear and tear on the vehicles involved. If the district in question is sizeable (and a great many districts are large geographic areas, both in England and Wales) and the operator is based near to a boundary with another district, the situation could arise that a vehicle is being despatched on a hiring across the district, returning across the district to the base, then being sent back from whence it came to pick up the next fare which was very close to the destination of the original fare. Such a condition would be manifestly absurd[1].

[1]   In 2007 Liverpool City Council was proposing that such a requirement should be imposed nationally by legislation. This proposal did not find any favour with central Government.

PLANNING PERMISSION

12.51

An important question is whether planning permission should be in place before an application for an operator's licence is considered or such licences granted, or whether planning permission can be sought subsequently.

12.52

Some local authorities take the view that planning permission is a condition precedent to the grant of an operator's licence. In those cases, no application for an operator's licence will be considered until permission for the use of the premises in question has been granted by the relevant local authority. The justification for this approach appears to be that once a private hire operator's licence has been granted, the licence holder may take the view that they can commence trading without the need for planning permission.

12.53

The counter view is that licensing and planning, notwithstanding the fact that both are considered by the same local authority, are separate and distinct matters.

Provided it is made clear to the licence holder that the grant of an operator's licence does not allow the use of the premises as a private hire operator's base in the absence of planning permission, the difficulty should not arise.

12.54

This is not a point that has ever been challenged by the courts and it is a matter for local authorities to consider. It is suggested, however, that the latter approach is the better. It is also worth adding that the standard wording of planning consents is that the permission granted thereby does not constitute any authorisation required under other legislation, which reinforces the view that planning permission is not to be regarded as a condition precedent for the grant of an operator's licence[1].

---

[1] This accords with the provisions and practice under the Licensing Act 2003 in relation to premises licences, and seems to be commonly understood. It is also worth noting that s 210 of the Gambling Act 2005 makes it clear that the grant of a premises licence for gambling purposes is not dependent on the existence of either planning permission or building regulation consent.

BOOKINGS

12.55

It is the operator with whom the public has direct initial contact, in order to obtain the services of a private hire vehicle. LG(MP)A 1976, s 56 lays down the fundamental requirements that cover a provision of a private hire vehicle by an operator.

Booked in advance

12.56

Any hiring of a private hire vehicle must be arranged in advanced ('booked') via a private hire operator. Whilst this is undoubtedly the case, this fundamental requirement is reasonably well concealed within the legislation. It can be found in s 56(2) which states:

'(2) Every person to whom a licence in force under section 55 of this Act has been granted by a district council shall keep a record in such form as the council may, by condition attached to the grant of the licence, prescribe and shall enter therein, before the commencement of each journey, such particulars of every booking of a private hire vehicle invited or accepted by him, whether by accepting the same from the hirer or by undertaking it at the request of another operator, as the district council may by condition prescribe and shall produce such record on request to any authorised officer of the council or to any constable for inspection.'

A section 55 licence is an operator's licence and as can be seen, the operator must record the details of each and every booking 'before the commencement of each journey'.

CONTRACT IS DEEMED TO BE MADE WITH THE OPERATOR

12.57

LG(MP)A 1976, s 56(1) makes it clear that the contract which covers the journey made in the vehicle is between the person booking the vehicle and the operator, even if the car is provided by an independent third party, who has himself a contract with the operator. Section 56(1) states:

'56–(1) For the purposes of this Part of this Act every contract for the hire of a private hire vehicle licensed under this Part of this Act shall be deemed to be made with the operator who accepted the booking for that vehicle whether or not he himself provided the vehicle.'

12.58

This has obvious implications in the event of any dispute over the service that is provided. It provides an easy method for the customer to take action against the operator, who is likely to be well known through advertisements and generally in the locality, whereas it may be difficult for a customer to identify which particular driver or vehicle he used on the occasion in question.

12.59

If action is taken by an aggrieved customer against the operator under LG(MP)A 1976, s 56, it will then be open to the operator to seek redress from the driver. This will be on the basis that the driver failed to deliver the expected level of service under the contract which existed between the operator and driver-and-car combination, by which the use of the operator's services are obtained.

For the benefit of all parties, operators should ensure that all contracts for the provision of drivers and vehicles with them are in writing, and service levels are clearly specified[1].

[1]   This is not a legal requirement but the words attributed to Sam Goldwyn are instructive: 'A verbal contract isn't worth the paper it's written on.'

SUBCONTRACTING

12.60

In October 2015 two new sections were introduced to the LG(MP)A 1976 by the Deregulation Act 2015. Sections 55A and 55B allow a private hire operator to sub-contract a booking to another private hire operator, irrespective of where either is licensed within the UK mainland, with the exception of Plymouth[1].

This change brought to an end the former prohibition on a sub-contract other than between operators licensed by the same authority[2].

The legislation is unwieldy and arguably unnecessarily complex, but the principles are relatively straightforward.

Section 55A states:

'55A Sub-contracting by operators

(1) A person licensed under section 55 who has in a controlled district accepted a booking for a private hire vehicle may arrange for another person to provide a vehicle to carry out the booking if—

    (a) the other person is licensed under section 55 in respect of the same controlled district and the sub-contracted booking is accepted in that district;

    (b) the other person is licensed under section 55 in respect of another controlled district and the sub-contracted booking is accepted in that district;

    (c) the other person is a London PHV operator and the subcontracted booking is accepted at an operating centre in London; or

    (d) the other person accepts the sub-contracted booking in Scotland.

(2) It is immaterial for the purposes of subsection (1) whether or not subcontracting is permitted by the contract between the person licensed under section 55 who accepted the booking and the person who made the booking.

(3) Where a person licensed under section 55 in respect of a controlled district is also licensed under that section in respect of another controlled district, subsection (1) (so far as relating to paragraph (b) of that subsection) and section 55B(1) and (2) apply as if each licence were held by a separate person.

(4) Where a person licensed under section 55 in respect of a controlled district is also a London PHV operator, subsection (1) (so far as relating to paragraph (c) of that subsection) and section 55B(1) and (2) apply as if the person holding the licence under section 55 and the London PHV operator were separate persons.

(5) Where a person licensed under section 55 in respect of a controlled district also makes provision in the course of a business for the invitation or acceptance of bookings for a private hire car or taxi in Scotland, subsection (1) (so far as relating to paragraph (d) of that subsection) and section 55B(1) and (2) apply as if the person holding the licence under section 55 and the person making the provision in Scotland were separate persons. In this subsection, "private hire car" and "taxi" have the same meaning as in sections 10 to 22 of the Civic Government (Scotland) Act 1982.

(6) In this section, "London PHV operator" and "operating centre" have the same meaning as in the Private Hire Vehicles (London) Act 1998.'

[1] Private hire licensing in Plymouth is governed by the Plymouth City Council Act 1975, rather than LG(MP)A 1976, and the amendments do not apply to the Plymouth legislation.

[2] This was made clear in *Shanks v North Tyneside Borough Council* [2001] EWHC Admin 533, [2001] All ER (D) 344 (Jun), QBD.

12.61

As a consequence of this section, a private hire operator licensed under the 1976 Act can subcontract a booking to a licensed private hire operator in another district, in London or in Scotland[1]. This power overrides any contractual restriction on the subcontracting in the original contract between the hirer and the first private hire operator[2] and in addition, the consent of the hirer is not required.

The initial private hire operator commits an offence if he knows that the second private hire operator is going to use an unlicensed vehicle or driver to fulfil the subcontracted booking[3].

This relaxation is causing significant problems. Local authorities which have high standards for private hire vehicles (eg, mandatory CCTV, age and emission policies etc) are having their attempts to maintain and raise private hire standards undermined by vehicles and drivers from other authorities being used to provide subcontracted vehicles.

Provided the second private hire operator dispatches a vehicle and driver licensed by the same authority as that operator, the hirer has no control over the origin of the vehicle and driver that undertakes the journey.

This has led to widespread concern[4] and the introduction of the Policing and Crime Act 2017, s 177. This will allow the Department for Transport to publish Guidance, to which local authorities must have regard, 'as to how their licensing functions under taxi and private hire vehicle legislation may be exercised so as to protect children, and vulnerable individuals who are 18 or over, from harm'[5].

It remains to be seen how effective Guidance will be at rectifying a situation which has been permitted by legislation.

[1]   Section 55A(1).
[2]   Section 55A(2).
[3]   Section 55B(3).
[4]   See eg, the Report of the Communities and Local Government Committee of Parliament into 'Government interventions: the use of Commissioners in Rotherham Metropolitan Borough Council and the London Borough of Tower Hamlets' which stated at para 16:

> 'We believe that local authorities must be able to apply particular measures in relation to taxi licensing in their areas, such as requiring taxis to have CCTV installed, without those measures being undermined by taxis coming in from other areas. *We recommend that, in order to ensure that lessons are learned from experiences in Rotherham, DCLG works with the Home Office and the Department for Transport on the preparation of statutory guidance under the Policing and Crime Bill in relation to taxi licensing. That guidance should be brought forward without delay. Once the guidance has been introduced, the Government should monitor the extent to which it ensures consistently high standards in taxi licensing across the country, and also enables local authorities to put in place and enforce specific measures which are appropriate for their local circumstances. If guidance is not able to achieve this, the Government should consider legislation.*'

[5]   At the time of writing (August 2017), no draft guidance has been produced, but a DfT briefing at the Local Government Association in November 2016 (available at http://www.local.gov.uk/sites/default/files/documents/taxi-and-phv-policy-paul--573.pdf) stated that any such guidance would address the following matters:

> 'practical measures that local authorities can consider adopting to better safeguard children and vulnerable individuals, including:
> * Emphasising that passenger safety should be at the forefront of licensing policies and the consideration of committees;
> * Tests that can be used to ensure that licensed drivers are 'fit and proper' to work with children and vulnerable adults;
> * Making best use of local intelligence, including use of DBS checks;

- Immigration checks [NB: a legal requirement in their own right] and Certificates of Good Character;
- Safeguarding and CSE awareness training;
- Enforcement.'

Bookings by and for disabled people accompanied by assistance dogs

12.62

Section 170 of the Equality Act 2010 (EA 2010) makes it an offence for a private hire operator to fail or refuse to take a booking for a private hire vehicle:

'(a) if the booking is requested by or on behalf of a disabled person or a person who wishes to be accompanied by a disabled person, and

(b) the reason for the failure or refusal is that the disabled person will be accompanied by an assistance dog.'

It is also an offence by virtue of EA 2010, s 170(2), for the operator to make any additional charge as a result of the need to carry an assistance dog.

'Assistance dog' is defined in s 173(1) as meaning:

'"assistance dog" means—

(a) a dog which has been trained to guide a blind person;

(b) a dog which has been trained to assist a deaf person;

(c) a dog which has been trained by a prescribed charity to assist a disabled person who has a disability that consists of epilepsy or otherwise affects the person's mobility, manual dexterity, physical co-ordination or ability to lift, carry or otherwise move everyday objects;

(d) a dog of a prescribed category which has been trained to assist a disabled person who has a disability (other than one falling within paragraph (c)) of a prescribed kind[1];'

Additional Assistance dogs are prescribed by reg 3 of The Disability Discrimination Act 1995 (Taxis) (Carrying of Guide Dogs etc.) (England and Wales) Regulations 2000[2] (as amended) and include:

'3. Prescribed charities

Each of the following is a prescribed charity for the purposes of paragraph (c) of the definition of "assistance dog" in section 173(1) of the 2010 Act (so far as that definition applies for the purposes of section 168 of that Act)—

(a) "Dogs for the Disabled" registered with the Charity Commission under registration number 1092960;

(b) "Support Dogs" registered with the Charity Commission under registration number 1017237; and

(c) "Canine Partners for Independence" registered with the Charity Commission under registration number 803680.'

These provisions and the accompanying provisions affecting private hire drivers[3] are vitally important as they should prevent discrimination against those people who need to use assistance dogs, and also place private hire vehicles in the same position as hackney carriages[4].

1   The Disability Discrimination Act 1995 (Taxis) (Carrying of Guide Dogs etc.) (England and Wales) Regulations 2000, SI 2000/2990 as amended are now deemed to have been made under the Equality Act, and were amended by the Equality Act 2010 (Commencement No. 4, Savings, Consequential, Transitional, Transitory and Incidental Provisions and Revocation) Order 2010, SI 2010/2317.
2   SI 2000/2990.
3   See Chapter 13, para 13.82 onwards.
4   See Chapter 9, paras 9.54 onwards.

Records kept by operators

12.63

LG(MP)A 1976, s 56(2) and (3) places a duty on a private hire operator to keep various records. However, it is left up to the council to decide what records are required both in relation to the journeys that are booked (s 56(2)) and the vehicles used (s 56(3)).

JOURNEYS BOOKED

12.64

LG(MP)A 1976, s 56(2) states:

> '56–(2) Every person to whom a licence in force under section 55 of this Act has been granted by a district council shall keep a record in such form as the council may, by condition attached to the grant of the licence, prescribe and shall enter therein, before the commencement of each journey, such particulars of every booking of a private hire vehicle invited or accepted by him, whether by accepting the same from the hirer or by undertaking it at the request of another operator, as the district council may by condition prescribe and shall produce such record on request to any authorised officer of the council or to any constable for inspection.'

12.65

It can be seen that this is a wide-ranging power that allows the local authority to impose a great many requirements as to record-keeping. This is implemented in different ways by various councils, but almost all insist on a bare minimum of records, including:

- the name of the hirer;
- the location of the pick-up point;
- the location of the destination;
- the time the private hire vehicle is required; and
- the time that the booking was made;
- the identity of the vehicle and driver allocated to fulfil the booking.

Other details that some local authorities require include:

- whether the booking was made by telephone or in person;
- the fare quoted for the journey;
- other remarks, including details of whether the booking is a sub-contract from another operator or is to be sub-contracted by this operator; and
- the method of recording the booking[1].

[1]   Traditionally, this was by means of pen and paper, but with the advent of electronic systems, there may only be a voice recording, or a printout from a computer. Local authorities must ensure their conditions are compatible with modern technology.

12.66

The DfT Best Practice Guide suggests the following records should be kept[1]:

'79. It is good practice to require operators to keep records of each booking, including the name of the passenger, the destination, the name of the driver, the number of the vehicle and any fare quoted at the time of booking. This information will enable the passenger to be traced if this becomes necessary and should improve driver security and facilitate enforcement. It is suggested that 6 months is generally appropriate as the length of time that records should be kept.'

This list of suggested information seems to miss out the most fundamental point – the time of the booking. Without that information, it will be impossible to use the records to prove that there was a booking in existence before the hiring commenced, which will be essential to prove that the vehicle was not plying or standing for hire.

[1]   DfT, '*Taxi and Private Hire Vehicle Licensing: Best Practice Guidance*' (October 2006, revised March 2010), para 79, available from http://www.dft.gov.uk/pgr/regional/taxis/taxiandprivatehirevehiclelic1792. See Appendix II.

12.67

These conditions:

1. enable the operator to identify a particular booking;
2. enable the operator to despatch a car at the right time to the right place;
3. enable the local authority to ensure that a booking was made for a particular journey; and
4. provide a comprehensive record of bookings taken by the private hire operator.

12.68

From an enforcement perspective, it is the confirmation that a booking has been made before the journey was undertaken that is important.

It is an offence for a private hire vehicle to ply for hire[1]; that is, to respond to anything other than a pre-booking and this can frequently be evidenced by the fact that the operator has no record of the trip which was taking place when the vehicle was apprehended by enforcement officers.

¹ TPCA 1847, s 45 and see Chapter 8, para 8.7 onwards.

Multiple operators' licences

12.69

There is no prohibition on one person or company holding more than one operator's licence. If these are within the same district and therefore issued by the same authority, the records must be kept separate, although the cars and drivers may be interchanged, subject to any local requirements imposed by the local authority to notify which vehicle and driver is working for which operator at any particular time.

12.70

If the operators' licences have been granted by different authorities, then whilst it is quite possible to pass a booking from an operator licensed in one district to another operator licensed in a different district (sub-contracting in accordance with ss 55A and 55B of LG(MP)A 1976) each operator must maintain their own records of those sub-contracts and ultimate vehicle bookings.

Vehicles used

12.71

The second category of records that is required to be kept is outlined in LG(MP)A 1976, s 56(3):

'56–(3) Every person to whom a licence in force under section 55 of this Act has been granted by a district council shall keep such records as the council may, by condition attached to the grant of the licence, prescribe of the particulars of any private hire vehicle operated by him and shall produce the same on request to any authorised officer of the council or to any constable for inspection.'

12.72

Again, the onus is placed upon the council to state, by way of condition attached to the licence, precisely what records are required in relation to vehicle. The more usual ones include some method of identifying the vehicle that was used (registration number, plate number) and the driver who was driving at the time. In some cases, the records are maintained in a simple hand-written form in a notebook, but many larger operators have computerised records and methods of tracking the vehicles that are providing private hire services to that particular operator, enabling the operator to despatch the most conveniently situated vehicle. In some systems, the computer actually selects the nearest vehicle and communicates the booking to the driver of that vehicle.

Inspection of records

12.73

By virtue of LG(MP)A 1976, s 56(4) any authorised officer of the council or a police constable can, on request, inspect the records maintained, by virtue of LG(MP)A 1976, s 56(2) and (3).

12.74

The local authority, through its officers, undertakes private hire enforcement. The powers in LG(MP)A 1976 are given to authorised officers, who are defined in LG(MP)A 1976, s 80(1) as 'any officer of a district council authorised in writing by the council for the purposes of this Part of this Act'.

12.75

This is the framework within which a private hire operator must work. The conditions imposed by local authorities are not especially onerous and most operators find it easy to comply with the requirements. If it appears to an operator that any condition imposed is too onerous and, as a consequence, is unreasonable, there is a power of appeal contained in LG(MP)A 1976, s 55(4). This applies to an applicant who is aggrieved by 'any conditions attached to the grant of such a licence'. As is usual in the 1976 Act, the right of appeal lies to the magistrates' court and is by way of complaint[1].

[1]   See Chapter 3, para 3.4.

Operator must hold licences for vehicle and driver

12.76

One condition that is often imposed upon private hire operators, under LG(MP)A 1976, s 56(3), is the requirement that the operator holds both the private hire vehicle licence of any vehicle that he is operating and the private hire driver's licence of any driver who is driving any such vehicle. This is a useful provision for both the local authority and the operator himself. From the local authority's perspective, it should enable it to satisfy itself reasonably easily and quickly that the operator is indeed using licensed vehicles and drivers. From the operator's point of view, provided that he complies with the conditions and does indeed hold these licences, it should provide him with a complete defence to any charge under LG(MP)A 1976, s 46(1)(e).

'46–(1) Except as authorised by this Part of this Act— ...
(e)   no person licensed under the said section 55 shall in a controlled district operate any vehicle as a private hire vehicle—
   (i)   if for the vehicle a current licence under the said section 48 is not in force; or
   (ii)   if the driver does not have a current licence under the said section 51.

(2) If any person knowingly contravenes the provisions of this section, he shall be guilty of an offence.'

Knowingly to contravene

12.77

The use of the word 'knowingly' in LG(MP)A 1976, s 46(2) requires the prosecution to prove knowledge or intent and it is strange that this is not a strict liability offence, which is the case with a great many other licensing offences enforced by local authorities.

Latif v Middlesbrough Borough Council

12.78

> Operator gave a driver the money to renew his drivers' licence, but the driver failed to do so. No further enquiries were made by the operator. Was this sufficient to amount to a defence that he 'knowingly' used an unlicensed driver? Held: Yes it was.

The case of *Latif v Middlesbrough Borough Council*[1] relates to this 'knowledge'. A private hire operator was prosecuted under LG(MP)A 1976, s 46 for two offences concerning the employment of an unlicensed private hire driver, in relation to his vehicle licence and also in relation to his operator's licence. He was convicted at the magistrates' court and his appeal to the Crown Court was dismissed. He then appealed to the High Court by way of case stated.

[1]   [1997] COD 486.

12.79

Latif employed a Mr Din as a driver and, at the time the alleged offence was committed, Din did not have a private hire driver's licence. At some time prior to that, Latif had given Din the money to renew his private hire driver's licence, but Din had not done so. The question raised was whether Latif 'knowingly' used an unlicensed private hire driver. It was argued that Latif had done sufficient to overcome any suggestion that he had knowingly used an unlicensed driver, by providing Din with the money to renew his licence. The counter-argument was that Latif should have done more to ensure that his driver was licensed.

12.80

Newman J stated[1]:

> 'On the facts found the court concluded that being put on notice that Mr Din's licence was to expire on some date prior to 16 April and failing to make enquiries to ascertain the true position meant that the defendant

had acted knowingly. In my judgment, there is no warrant for the word "knowingly" being construed so broadly as to encompass the facts as found. The facts went no further than establishing that the defendant was on notice that a situation might prevail on a particular day when it is alleged the offence was committed. Further, having given money to Mr Din to obtain a licence the defendant had good reason to believe he would have obtained one. Upon the facts as found and giving the word "knowingly" its normal meaning, which, in my judgment, in this statute it should have, the charges had not been made out.'

[1]   *Latif v Middlesbrough Borough Council* [1997] COD 486.

12.81

Newman J reviewed a number of cases concerning knowledge which supported this view. He came to the conclusion that, as the defendant had not deliberately shut his eyes as to whether Din had a licence or not, he could not be deemed to have been reckless as to whether or not he held a private hire driver's licence. Accordingly, on the facts, the appeal was allowed.

12.82

Knowledge is always extremely difficult to prove in any event, but it does not seem that this case makes it any more difficult. It is, to a large extent, confined to its own particular facts and if a condition is applied to both private hire vehicle licences and private hire operators' licences, requiring the proprietor or operator to hold a driving licence of anyone they employ, it would then be more difficult to demonstrate a lack of knowledge. In addition, even if the local authority is unsuccessful in securing a conviction under LG(MP)A 1976, s 46(1)(e), breach of a condition imposed under LG(MP)A 1976, s 56 is itself an offence by virtue of s 56(5). Accordingly, a prosecution under that section may prove successful. Informations should be laid for both offences and, in fact, two convictions may be obtained.

12.83

It can be seen that it is vital for private hire operators to comply with the requirements of the local authority, in relation to conditions, and also to comply with the legislative requirements that are placed upon them.

12.84

It is also important that the local authority carefully considers what conditions should be imposed on private hire operators and that those conditions are subsequently fully enforced. If there is any failure of compliance on the part of the operator, in addition to criminal sanctions, action can be taken by the local authority on renewal of the licence or, in serious situations, the licence can itself be suspended or revoked.

SUSPENSION, REVOCATION OR REFUSAL TO RENEW AN OPERATOR'S LICENCE

12.85

The provisions contained in LG(MP)A 1976, s 62 give the council significant powers to suspend or revoke an operator's licence or to refuse an application for renewal. Section 62 states:

'**Suspension and revocation of operators' licences**

62–(1) Notwithstanding anything in this Part of this Act a district council may suspend or revoke, or (on application therefor under section 55 of this Act) refuse to renew an operator's licence on any of the following grounds—

(a) any offence under, or non-compliance with, the provisions of this Part of this Act;

(b) any conduct on the part of the operator which appears to the district council to render him unfit to hold an operator's licence;

(c) any material change since the licence was granted in any of the circumstances of the operator on the basis of which the licence was granted;

(ca) that the operator has since the grant of the licence been convicted of an immigration offence or required to pay an immigration penalty; or

(d) any other reasonable cause.

(1A) Subsection (1)(ca) does not apply if—

(a) in a case where the operator has been convicted of an immigration offence, the conviction is a spent conviction within the meaning of the Rehabilitation of Offenders Act 1974, or

(b) in a case where the operator has been required to pay an immigration penalty—

(i) more than three years have elapsed since the date on which the penalty was imposed, and

(ii) the amount of the penalty has been paid in full.

(2) Where a district council suspend, revoke or refuse to renew any licence under this section they shall give to the operator notice of the grounds on which the licence has been suspended or revoked or on which they have refused to renew such licence within fourteen days of such suspension, revocation or refusal.

(3) Any operator aggrieved by a decision of a district council under this section may appeal to a magistrates' court.'

12.86

It can be seen that an offence (that is, a conviction) for any matter under LG(MP)A 1976 is a ground for such action to be taken. LG(MP)A 1976, s 62(1)(a) goes considerably further than that because non-compliance with any provision of LG(MP)A 1976 is also a ground. Whilst such action would need to be reasonable, it does not have to be evidenced by a criminal conviction[1] and this gives the local authority considerable power, should it wish to exercise it.

[1] See *R v Maidstone Crown Court, ex p Olson* [1992] COD 496 (Chapter 10, para 10.139); *McCool v Rushcliffe Borough Council* [1998] 3 All ER 889, QBD (Chapter 10, para 10.142); and *Leeds City Council v Hussain* [20020] EWHC 1145 (Admin), [2003] RTR 199 (Chapter 10, para 10.146), *R (on the application of Wrexham CBC) v Chester Crown Court* (2004) (25 June 2004 unreported), Admin Ct (Chapter 10, para 10.150).

12.87

LG(MP)A 1976, s 62(1)(b) goes further still, by allowing the local authority to suspend, revoke or refuse to renew an operator's licence for 'any conduct on the part of the operator which appears to the district council to render him unfit to hold an operator's licence'. Again, no criminal conviction is necessary to support this and the test of whether such action is justified will be one of *Wednesbury* reasonableness.

12.88

LG(MP)A 1976, s 62(1)(c) is a general power which enables the local authority to consider any changes that have taken place to the operator or other related matters since the licence was first granted and whether they are grounds for suspension, revocation or refusal to renew the operator's licence.

12.89

LG(MP)A 1976, s 62(1)(d) enables the local authority to take this action for 'any other reasonable cause'. The decision in *Norwich City Council v Watcham and Thurtle*[1] was that 'any other reasonable cause' does not have to be construed *ejusdem generis* with the grounds set out in sub-s (1)(a)–(c). This means that the 'any other reasonable cause' does not have to be similar to the matters listed in the other subsections.

[1] (21 May 1981, unreported); see Chapter 8, para 8.138.

12.90

As is common with other suspensions or revocations under the LG(MP)A 1976 the effect of the decision by the council is not effective until 21 days have passed and if, during that period, an appeal to the magistrates' court is lodged, the effect is stayed pending the determination or abandonment of the appeal. A further appeal to the Crown Court extends that effect once again.

It is important to note that there is no power to take immediate action against a private hire operator's licence. Accordingly, even in the most serious circumstances, the licence will remain in force for the appeal period of 21 days and if an appeal is lodged during that time, the licence can be used until the appeal is determined or abandoned.

12.91

Thus, it can be seen that the powers of a local authority to take action, in respect of an operator's licence, are extremely wide. Such actions should not be undertaken lightly by the local authority, but, if the circumstances require such action, they are useful powers.

12.92

There is a right of appeal given under LG(MP)A 1976, s 62(3) to an operator who is aggrieved by such an action. Section 62(2) requires the local authority to provide written notice of the grounds on which the action has been taken. In addition, it must provide reasons[1].

[1] See Chapter 3 regarding appeals in general, and Chapter 2, para 2.84 onwards in relation to reasons.

PRIVATE HIRE OPERATORS: PROBLEM AREAS

12.93

There are a number of areas of activity in relation to private hire vehicles that have caused difficulties in the past.

Private hire vehicle can undertake journeys anywhere in England and Wales

Adur District Council v Fry

12.94

Can a private hire vehicle undertake a pre-booked journey that is wholly outside the district in which it is licensed? Held: Yes it can. There are no restrictions on where a private hire vehicle can pick up a pre-booked passenger, transport them or drop them off.

In *Adur District Council v Fry*[1], the situation concerned a booking for a journey by a private hire vehicle which commenced, ended and throughout its length was within the district of Adur District Council. It was, however, undertaken by a private hire vehicle licensed by Hove Borough Council, driven by a driver who held a private hire driver's licence issued by Hove Borough Council and the booking was made with an operator based outside the area of Adur District Council, who also held an operator's licence issued by Hove Borough Council. It can be seen, therefore, that all three licences matched and the only question was whether it was lawful to undertake a journey in the area of another district council. The High Court decided that it was, judgment being given by Kay J. He concluded that no offence was committed in those circumstances due to the limited meaning of 'operate' contained in LG(MP)A 1976, s 80(1). In coming to that conclusion, he relied upon the judgments in *Dittah v Birmingham City Council, Choudhry v Birmingham City Council*[2], *Britain v ABC Cabs (Camberley) Ltd*[3] and *Windsor and Maidenhead Royal Borough Council v Khan*[4]. As a result the meaning of operate meant 'in the course of business to make provision for the invitation or acceptance of booking for a private hire vehicle' and could not be construed more widely. His conclusion was this (at 263A):

'The question posed in the case stated is:

"Whether it was correct to say that the word 'operate' in section 46(1)(e) of the Local Government (Miscellaneous Provisions) Act 1976 only includes that part of the whole transaction taking place in the operator's premises."

The question is, perhaps, too widely worded because it is possible to envisage activity taking place outside an operator's premises that might come within the definition provided by section 80(1). There was, however, no such activity in the circumstances of this case. I would, therefore, answer the question "Yes, in the circumstances of this case" and, accordingly, dismiss the appeal.'

[1]   [1997] RTR 257.
[2]   [1993] RTR 356; see para 12.8 above.
[3]   [1981] RTR 395; see para 12.97 below.
[4]   [1994] RTR 87; see para 12.95 below.

Advertisements for a private hire service

Windsor and Maidenhead Royal Borough Council v Khan

12.95

> Can a private hire operator advertise their business outside the district? Held: Yes. There are no restrictions on where a private hire operator can advertise their business.

Two questions were placed before the High Court for consideration in *Windsor and Maidenhead Royal Borough Council v Khan*[1]. The first was whether an offence of operating outside a controlled district was committed if an operator licensed in one district, with premises in that district, accepted a booking made by a telephone call from a person who was calling from outside that district. The second question was whether an offence was committed of operating without a licence if advertisements were placed in telephone directories which circulated not only within, but outside the area of the local authority in which the person was to operate.

[1]   [1994] RTR 87.

12.96

In relation to the first question, considerable discussion took place in the magistrates' court in relation to contract and where the contract was made. The point, however, was not pursued at the subsequent appeal to the High Court and, accordingly, only one point was considered by McCullough J when giving judgment[1] and that concerned the question of advertisements in telephone directories[2]. He observed that there was an exemption in relation to vehicle and drivers' licences when used outside the district in which they were licensed, by virtue of LG(MP)A 1976, s 75(2), but then went on (at 91B):

> 'There is no corresponding provision for operator's licences. This is not necessary because of the restrictive meaning given to the word "operate" in the Act. Section 80(1) [LG(MP)A 1976, s 80(1)] provides:
>
> > '"Operate' means in the course of business to make provision for the invitation or acceptance of bookings for a private hire vehicle ..."
>
> Thus, to take Maidenhead as an example, no operator's licence from the council is required merely because a private hire vehicle in the course of the business of its proprietor is driven through Maidenhead. An operator's licence issued by the council is only required by those who in the course of business make provision in Maidenhead for the invitation or acceptance of bookings for private hire vehicles.
>
> The defendant operates a private hire business called Top Cars. Its offices are in Slough. Slough is adjacent to or very close to the borough but outside it. It is to be presumed that either Slough does not lie within a controlled district, or, if it is within a controlled district, that the defendant held a current operator's licence issued by the district council in whose area Slough lies. He did not, as is agreed, however, hold an operator's licence issued by the council. He had advertised Top Car's services in the local Yellow Pages and Thompson's classified directories. These publications covered several areas including Slough and Maidenhead.'

He concluded (at 92L):

> 'Before this court Mr Harrison's [for the council] sole submission is that the defendant "made provision for the invitation of bookings for a private hire vehicle" in Maidenhead by placing advertisements for his private hire business in directories which circulated in Maidenhead. The fact that they also circulated in Slough is, he submits, irrelevant.
>
> I reject the submission. The considerations to which I have already referred make clear that, in its definition of the word "operate", Parliament was not referring to places which invitations might reach, but to places where provision is made for the invitation of bookings. Put an advertisement in a local newspaper in one part of England and it may be read in almost any other part of the country. The defendant made provision for the invitation of bookings at his office in Slough. What he did by advertising in the directories circulating in the area where he conducted his business, and in adjacent areas, was to inform the public that he had made such provision. His provision was nevertheless made in Slough, not in Maidenhead, nor in any of the other areas in which those directories circulate. That conclusion is not, in my judgment, affected by the fact that the directories circulated in a much wider area, or that the defendant named towns other than Slough, such as Maidenhead, in his advertisement. If Mr Harrison's submissions

were right, it would mean that the defendant was operating not just the A576 KLT [the registration number of the vehicle in question in this case], which is named in this summons, but every one of his private hire vehicles 24 hours a day, seven days a week in Maidenhead, even on days when none of his vehicles ever went anywhere near Maidenhead. That would be nonsensical.'

1   *Windsor and Maidenhead Royal Borough Council v Khan* [1994] RTR 87.

2   It is unfortunate that the first question was not pursued in the High Court and in the absence of that, a view is required. If the decision had been that an operator could only accept a booking by telephone which was actually made by a person who was telephoning from within the same district (ie the district in which the operator is licensed) it would present an extremely difficult and restrictive burden upon both operator and customer. The operator would have to enquire where the customer was located and then decide whether that was within or outside the district in which he was licensed. If it was outside, the operator would then have to inform the customer that no booking could be taken, and that they would have to call another firm in a different district. That would lead to both customer and operator dissatisfaction, as the preferred operator could not be used. Although it is impossible to foresee any decision of a court, it would seem unlikely that such an approach would find judicial favour.

Britain v ABC Cabs (Camberley) Ltd

12.97

Can a hackney carriage be used for pre-booked work outside the district in which it is licensed, and did collecting such a pre-booked customer amount to operating? Held: Hackney carriage can be used for pre-booked work outside the district in which it is licensed and such use does not amount to operating.

The question of operating a private hire vehicle had been considered much earlier in the case of *Britain v ABC Cabs (Camberley) Ltd*[1]. This case concerned the despatch of a hackney carriage from Camberley to collect a passenger from a railway station in Farnborough. The hackney carriage was licensed by Surrey Heath Borough Council, in whose area Camberley lay and Farnborough railway station was situated within the area of Rushmoor Borough Council. This raised two questions: first, whether it was an offence for a hackney carriage, licensed by a local authority which had not adopted LG(MP)A 1976, Pt II, to be used to fulfil a pre-booked journey (and thereby effectively acting as a private hire vehicle) in the area of a neighbouring local authority which had adopted LG(MP)A 1976, Pt II; and, secondly, whether the collection of a passenger within a controlled district (Rushmoor) in pursuance of a contract of hire made outside the control district (Surrey Heath) 'was operating' for the purposes of LG(MP)A 1976, Pt II. Webster J decided that (at 403J):

'The question of law on which they seek the opinion of this court is whether, on a proper construction of section 46(1)(*d*) of the Act of 1976, the collection of a passenger within a controlled district in pursuance of a contract for hire made outside the controlled district was "operating" for the purposes of that subsection of the Act.

I am satisfied that when the defendants' vehicle picked up the passenger at Farnborough Station, [which was] the only material act which the defendants did in the borough of Rushmoor controlled district, they were not "making provision for the invitation or acceptance of bookings" at all, whether for a private hire vehicle or for any other vehicle. In my judgment to conclude otherwise would be to strain the language of the definition far beyond breaking point. If they were making provision for the invitation or acceptance of bookings anywhere, they were doing that, it would seem to me, in their office at Camberley, which is not a controlled district. In my judgment therefore no offence was made out under section 46(1)(d) and the justices rightly dismissed that information.

... it follows from the conclusion which I have reached about the second case, and the views I have already expressed, in my judgment for the purposes of section 46(1)(a) the vehicle at the time and place in question was to be regarded as what in fact it was, namely, a hackney carriage in respect of which a vehicle licence is in force. In my judgment therefore no offence was made out under section 46(1)(a) ...'

¹   [1981] RTR 395.

12.98

In some parts of the country, depending upon the geography of the locality, a great many private hire vehicles are used outside their own district. Bookings are regularly made with operators who are not licensed within the district in which the person making the booking resides.

12.99

The simplest way to establish whether or not an offence has been committed is to inquire whether all three licences have been issued by the same authority? If the answer to that is 'Yes', and the 'happy family of licences' is present, then there is no restriction on the geographical area in which the journey can take place. Ultimately, this can and indeed has, led to the situation of a private hire vehicle undertaking a booking wholly within the area of one district, but the vehicle, driver and operator are licensed by and the operator is based in another, possible quite remote, district. Although this could lead to difficulties in enforcement (the practicalities of an officer wishing to inspect the records for a journey that are held some miles away), it is not, in itself, unlawful. Although extreme situations with scores of miles between locations is not particularly common, it does occur. However, the more commonly encountered scenario concerning neighbouring districts is a frequent occurrence.

Braintree District Council v Howard

12.100

> Can an unlicensed operator pass a booking to an unlicensed operator who then uses a licensed car and driver to fulfil a booking? Held: No.

The situation is different if the vehicle and driver are unlicensed. In the case of *Braintree District Council v Howard*[1], Mr Howard had not renewed his private hire vehicle and drivers' licences with Braintree District Council, so he operated from a caravan outside the district (it must be assumed that the district in which the caravan was situated was not a controlled district, that is to say, that authority had not adopted the provisions of LG(MP)A 1976). Mr Howard's wife took telephone calls at an address within Braintree district, then called Mr Howard outside the district. He arrived, as booked, at an address within Braintree district, picked up his passengers and took them to another location within the district. The whole journey took place within the district. He was prosecuted for operating a vehicle as a private hire vehicle without a licence. He was acquitted and the council appealed. The High Court upheld the appeal. As he was completely unlicensed, LG(MP)A 1976, s 56(1) did not apply, and as the journey took place wholly within a controlled district, the benefit of LG(MP)A 1976, s 75(1)(a) did not apply. Mann LJ giving judgment stated (at 199C):

'The case then seeks the opinion of this court on two questions:

"(1) whether we were right in holding, as a point of law, that the provisions of either or both of sections 56 and 75 of the Local Government (Miscellaneous Provisions) Act 1976 were relevant to the facts so as to afford a defence to the offences alleged under section 46 of that Act; and (2) whether we were right in holding as a point of law that the contract between the prosecutor's witness Mr McCloud and the defendant was made when the defendant confirmed to his wife that he was willing to undertake that work."

Mr Singh on behalf of the prosecutor submits that the justices were in error in point of law in that neither section 56 nor section 75 have any materiality as to what occurred. I am bound to agree with him. Neither section has any arguable relevance to the charges against the defendant. Section 56(1) makes the provision in regard to operators of private hire vehicles. The defendant was not charged with any offence concerning operators. However, and importantly, the section applies only to contracts "for the hire of a private hire vehicle licensed under this Part of this Act" and this vehicle was not licensed under this Part of this Act and, accordingly, that section could have no application to the case.

Section 75(1)(a), likewise, has no application to the circumstances of this case so far as the journey from the Sugar Loaves along Swan Lane [wholly within Braintree District] is concerned. Section 75(1)(a) is dealing with the problem of the vehicle which brings passengers into a controlled district. That was not the case so far as the initial journey on 17 August is concerned.

Accordingly, neither section had any materiality to the problem which was before the justices and I can surmise that the justices were attracted by those sections as offering a way of escape from convicting in regard to circumstances which they found unattractive. However, that said, the justices were in error.

In my judgment, the question which they posed must, as to the first, be answered "no" while on that conclusion on the first, the second does not arise ...'

1   [1993] RTR 193, DC.

Telephone diversion

East Staffordshire Borough Council v Rendell

12.101

> Can an operator licensed in one district divert telephone calls to be answered in a neighbouring district, or does that amount to 'operating' in the neighbouring district? Held: No they cannot, as that would amount to operating in the district in which the call was answered.

A situation concerning a telephone diversion arose in the case of *East Staffordshire Borough Council v Rendell*[1]. In this case, Mr Rendell was licensed as a private hire operator by Derbyshire Dales District Council. His base was near the border with East Staffordshire. He diverted his telephone from his base in Derbyshire Dales to a telephone situated in East Staffordshire. This meant that, when a person called the number in Derbyshire Dales to book a private hire vehicle, the telephone call was actually answered in East Staffordshire and the vehicle (licensed by Derbyshire Dales as a private hire vehicle and driven by a person holding a Derbyshire Dales private hire driver's licence) was dispatched by a person who, although he held a Derbyshire Dales operator's licence, was physically located in East Staffordshire. The matter was considered by the High Court by way of case stated, the magistrates' court having decided no offence was committed. Simon Brown LJ stated (at 6F):

> 'The ultimate question undoubtedly reduces to this: whether the respondent [Mr Rendell] by switching the telephone to Uttoxeter [in East Staffordshire] had thereby made a provision for bookings in Uttoxeter.'

He concluded his judgment (at 9F):

> 'It seems to me quite impossible on a common sense approach to the provisions here in question to regard the respondent as having done other than to make provision for the acceptance of bookings in Uttoxeter, ie, in the East Staffordshire control (sic) district where he had no licence.
>
> Certainly, on the day in question, and it appears to have been by no means an isolated day, he had made the clearest possible arrangements to ensure that those who sought to make bookings would be put through to Uttoxeter for such bookings to be accepted. In this case ... there was in my judgment, substantial provision made, a clear and effective arrangement whereby bookings could be accepted in East Staffordshire.'

Sedley J supported that view (at 11A):

> 'In my view, by publicising his Derbyshire Dales telephone number and then switching calls from there to East Staffordshire, where he had arranged for them to be answered, the respondent did two things: he made provision in Derbyshire Dales for the invitation of bookings and he also made provision in East Staffordshire for the invitation of bookings. To conclude that this was so requires no strained or expanded meaning of the statutory language, and it respects its somewhat mysterious syntax.'

1   (1995) Independent, 27 November, QBD.

12.102

This means that any diversion of a telephone call (whether a landline or a mobile phone) which is then answered by the operator outside the district in which they are licensed will amount to an offence as they will be operating without a licence in the district in which the telephone call is answered.

Even with the provisions of s 55A of the LG(MP)A 1976 in force, any diversion across borders will only be lawful if it amounts to a sub contract. This means that there must be a mechanism of accepting the booking in the district in which the initial operator is licensed, before it is subcontracted to an operator in another district.

This process could be manual, or it could be automated, but it does appear that there must be a physical presence in the district in which the operator is licensed. That may not require a human presence, but it is arguable that there should at least be (in the case of a computerised system) some form of computer that takes the booking in that district before subcontracting it out.

Where there is an automated system, a question has arisen as to whether there should be a mechanism for passengers to speak to a person acting for the operator over the telephone at all times.

R (on the application of Uber) v Transport for London

12.103

> Does a private hire operator have to make a manned telephone line available at all times? Held: This is a reasonable requirement in principle, but the legality will depend upon the actual requirement imposed.

The question of a permanently manned telephone line was considered in *R (on the application of Uber) v Transport for London*[1]. As a result of changes by Transport for London ('TfL') to the requirements for private hire licensing within Greater London, the High Court was asked to rule on the legality of three particular changes, one of which was that all private hire operators must make a permanently manned telephone line available[2].

This was considered by the judge in the following way[3]:

'32. The wording of the telephone requirement is very broad. The operator is required to:

> "Ensure that the passenger for whom the booking was made is able to speak to someone at the operating centre or other premises with a fixed address in London or elsewhere if they want to make a complaint or discuss any other matter about the carrying out of the booking."

It is not confined to a requirement to provide that facility in what the passenger believes to be an emergency, or a situation which requires immediate resolution, such as the refusal of the driver to comply with disability law in respect of the passenger, in other words, a "hotline".

33.   It requires a large appbased operator such as Uber to maintain, round the clock, a telephone service to deal with complaints and any other matter about the carrying out of the booking immediately.'

He continued[4]:

'[At present] Uber have a system which effectively sorts real emergencies from all which are only potentially critical or urgent and deals with each appropriately; the first immediately, and all others within 6 hours as to 70 per cent and within 24 hours as to 99 per cent. This is to be commended rather than criticised.'

The justification put forward by TfL was[5]:

' ... many passengers will be reassured by their ability to speak to a human being about their complaint and emergencies can be dealt with more quickly than would be the case without the intervention of a live telephone operator. A small number of real life examples are given. I accept their reasoning, but only up to a point. I can readily understand that some passengers, believing themselves to be confronted by an emergency, will find it reassuring to speak to a human telephone operator.

38.   TfL were and are entitled to identify the public interest affected as public safety and convenience, in the case of an emergency principally the former, and to conclude that a high level of protection should be given to passengers who believe that they are faced with an emergency. I also accept that in that instance there is no alternative measure which could combine reassurance and speed of response to some passengers... .

39.   Accordingly, despite the fact that Uber's current system may well provide an effective and timely response to genuine emergencies, I accept that it cannot provide the level of reassurance which some passengers may, for good reason, require. This aspect of the measure is therefore lawful. It does not follow that the regulation is lawful in its full width.'

And he concluded on this point[6]:

'TfL has not shown that less restrictive measures could not be adopted than those contained in the telephone requirement to meet the level of protection which they require for the only public interest at stake, passenger convenience... . It follows, therefore, that I must quash regulation 9(11) and leave it to [TfL] to make a fresh regulation if he considers it desirable to provide for, in colloquial terms, a "hotline" for emergencies broadly defined to include situations in which immediate action is required to remedy a breach of the law.'

Accordingly, at present such a requirement is lawful provided it is not overly onerous and disproportionate[7].

1   [2017] ACD 54, Admin Ct.
2   The other requirements considered in the judgment were:
     • the introduction of a spoken and written English test for all private hire drivers (considered in Chapter 10, para 10.60).
     • a requirement that a private hire vehicle within London has insurance for private hire work at all times (even when being used for leisure purposes); see Chapter 22, para 22.31.
3   Per Mitting J at paras 32 and 33.
4   At para 35.
5   At para 37 onwards.
6   At para 41.
7   It should be noted that at the time of writing (August 2017), both parties have indicated that they intend to seek leave to appeal to the Court of Appeal.

Location of the operator's base

12.104

It now seems clear that a private hire operator's 'base' can only be physically located within the district in which the operator is licensed. There did appear to be an argument that the provisions of LG(MP)A 1976, s 57(2)(b)(ii) allowed a base to be located outside the district, as a reference is made in the requirement for an applicant for an operator's licence to provide details of 'the address or addresses whether within the area of the council or not from which he intends to carry on business in connection with private hire vehicles licensed under this Part of this Act'. However, it now seems that the provisions of s 46(1)(d), allied to the definition of operate in s 80(1) make it clear that to operate within a district the person must have an operator's licence issued by that particular district.

Advertisements adjacent to telephones

12.105

The ruling in *Windsor and Maidenhead Royal Borough Council v Khan*[1] makes it clear that advertisements are not a provision for an invitation or acceptance of bookings. Private hire operators often advertise on or near public telephones. This occurs in pubs and clubs, as well as supermarkets and other venues. It is also the basis of the large, remote 'call-centre' operations mentioned at para 12.99 above.

Irrespective of whether the operator is licensed by the district in which these advertisements are placed, such advertisements are lawful.

1   [1994] RTR 87; see para 12.95 above.

Freephones

12.106

One of the situations which is frequently encountered is the concept of the 'freephone'. These are often located at supermarkets and shopping centres and are a dedicated phone line. The customer picks up the phone and is automatically connected to a specific private hire operator. There is no ability on the part of the customer to choose an operator; it is simply a telephone provided by that particular operator. The customer then states their location and destination and the operator despatches a vehicle to satisfy the booking.

12.107

The question becomes important if the freephone is situated outside the area in which the operator is licensed (and, again, this is a matter of geography). If that is the case, is an offence being committed? Following the approach taken in *East Staffordshire Borough Council v Rendell*[1], the answer appears to be 'No'. In the *East Staffordshire* case it was decided that the location in which the telephone was answered was the location in which the provision for the invitation of bookings was made. Accordingly, it would appear that a freephone located outside an operator's licensed district, connecting to the operator's licensed base within the licensed district, is lawful.

[1]   (1995) Independent, 27 November, QBD; see para 12.101 above.

12.108

There is no decision on this point. The matter arose in *Murtagh (t/a Rubery Rednal Cars) v Bromsgrove District Council*[1], where the freephone was located in one district, Birmingham, but was answered at the operator's licensed base in another district, Bromsgrove. Unfortunately, although the magistrates' court decided that there was no operation in Birmingham, the High Court did not find it necessary to address the point.

[1]   [2001] LLR 514, QBD; see para 12.10 above.

Mobile telephones

12.109

LG(MP)A 1976 predates even the concept of mobile telephones, but they are now an accepted and in many cases, essential, part of daily life. This leads to the question of whether a private hire operator can use a mobile telephone. This can arise in one of two situations[1].

[1]   See Chapter 9, para 9.7 for consideration of the use of mobile telephones whilst driving.

12.110

First, when the operator proposes to use a mobile telephone as his primary contact number for taking bookings. Secondly, when the operator uses a mobile telephone as a method of answering calls when the 'base' is unmanned? No Senior Court case has addressed either of these points.

12.111

In relation to the first situation, it would seem that a mobile telephone could be used as an operator's number for bookings. No requirement is laid down in LG(MP)A 1976 that a landline must be used. However, there must clearly be an identifiable premises used as the base, and those premises must be specified in the operator's licence[1]. Provided those criteria are met and all other requirements such as maintenance and storage of records are complied with, it is difficult to see the objection to a mobile telephone number. It is accepted that this will provide the operator with a degree of flexibility in his movements, and clearly he could take bookings on his mobile away from his base and it would be difficult to prove that this had been done. That begs the question of whether such an action is either a problem or an offence.

[1]   See *Kingston-upon-Hull City Council v Wilson* (1995) Times, 25 July; see para 12.43 above.

12.112

This does not seem to be a problem, provided that records are maintained and can be inspected at the operator's base. Although there may be a delay between the booking being made and the records at the base being updated, provided full records are compiled at the time the booking is made and the records at the base are updated as soon as possible, either manually or electronically, that would seem to be acceptable. There may be a delay before the records can be inspected by an authorised officer of the local authority or a constable (under the provisions of LG(MP)A 1976, s 56(2)), but such a delay can occur when using landlines if an office is not open 24 hours per day.

12.113

However, following the ruling in *East Staffordshire Borough Council v Rendell*[1], it would appear that the operator would commit an offence if he answered his mobile telephone when he was physically located outside the area in which he was licensed. If this is the case, it would be potentially very difficult to ensure compliance, and extremely difficult to enforce, as it is by no means clear which local authority area a vehicle is in at any given point[2].

[1]   (1995) Independent, 27 November, QBD; see para 12.101 above.
[2]   This can be compared with the decision in *DPP v Computer Cab Company Ltd* [1996] RTR 130 QBD; see Chapter 22, para 22.30.

12.114

The same point arises in relation to the second situation. A divert from a fixed location landline to a mobile telephone would seem to be lawful only if the mobile telephone is answered within the same district in which the operator is licensed. That would lead to a simple question of fact: was the mobile telephone answered and the booking taken, within the district. Clearly, that would be extremely difficult to prove, and also, as district boundaries are neither obvious or regular, would impose a difficult burden on an operator, who would have to decide whether it was lawful to answer a call on a mobile telephone, which may or may not lead to a booking.

12.115

Do these difficulties support a view that a condition should be imposed on an operator's licence prohibiting the use of a mobile telephone? It is difficult to see how such a prohibition could be justified, especially when the most likely operators to use such devices are persons who are both operators and drivers in a one-car firm. A prohibition would prevent an operator who is also a driver from having the safety benefits of a mobile telephone in his vehicle and that is probably unreasonable.

Again, this is an area where the law is outdated and in urgent need of revision.

Internet bookings

12.116

Advertising on the Internet and taking bookings via the Internet are not a problem. The advertising element does not differ from any other advertisement[1] and provided the booking is actually made at the operator's licensed base via a computer located there, it does not appear to infringe the ruling in *East Staffordshire Borough Council v Rendall*[2].

[1] See *Windsor v Maidenhead Royal Borough Council v Khan* [1994] RTR 87 QBD; see para 12.95 above.
[2] (1995) Independent, 27 November, QBD; see para 12.101 above.

MAKING THE BOOKING

12.117

Does the passenger have to book the vehicle personally? In many cases, the prospective passenger (or at least one of a group of passengers) will be the person who contacts the operator. However, there are a number of situations where that will not be the case.

12.118

These include hotels, businesses, pubs etc. For example, a guest at a hotel wants to travel to a meeting, or visit a local attraction. Invariably, they will ask the hotel reception to 'book a taxi'. Likewise, businesses will book vehicles to pick up customers, and other visitors attending meetings etc. Also, in some cases, a member of the staff of a pub or club will book a vehicle for customers or staff.

12.119

In the majority of cases, the call will be made to a private hire firm and a private hire vehicle and driver will be dispatched to fulfil the booking. The question raised in this scenario is whether the person who uses the car must make the call, and whether, if they do not, the person who arranges the vehicle requires an operator's licence.

12.120

There is no requirement within the LG(MP)A 1976 that the passenger must make the booking. It appears that in these scenarios outlined above, that the person making the booking is acting as the agent of the passenger and accordingly, that will be lawful.

Booking services

12.121

A further extension of this is the concept of the booking service for private hire vehicles. Can a person who is not a licensed PHV operator advertise a service of 'finding' or booking private hire vehicles?

12.122

The situation arises where a service is offered, often via the Internet, whereby a company advertises what appears to be a private hire service, but in fact is a service which simply contacts private hire companies in the area the passenger wishes to be picked up in. This is sometimes by means of a direct enquiry as to the availability of a vehicle, whilst on other occasions is effectively an open invitation to firms linked to the service to 'tender' for the booking, with the 'contract' being awarded to the lowest bidder.

12.123

Does this constitute 'in the course of business to make provision for the invitation or acceptance of bookings for a private hire vehicle'? One view is that these companies are simply acting as the agent of the hirer and therefore, no licence is required (as in the scenario above[1]). The alternative view is that as this is a service advertised as a method of securing a private hire vehicle, the answer is yes, it does, and therefore a private hire operator's licence is required.

[1]   See paras 12.118–12.120 above.

12.124

As yet there is no case on the point, so it is a matter of taking a view. It appears that the advertising of the service is a significant factor, as in the absence of such an advertisement the service would not work. This seems to make it significantly different from a non-advertised service as provided in hotels etc. Accordingly, it would seem that such a service constitutes 'in the course of business to make provision for the invitation or acceptance of bookings for a private hire vehicle', as the business consists entirely of that function. As a consequence, persons providing such a service should be licensed as private hire operators with the local authority in whose area the operators' base is located[1].

[1]   It is not possible to have a 'base' located outside the licensing councils district; see para 12.104 above.

Exempted hiring

12.125

LG(MP)A 1976, s 75[1] provides for a number of exemptions from the requirements of private hire licensing. Depending on the exemption being relied upon the effect may be that the operator (or the driver and vehicle) does not need to be licensed, but that is not always the case.

[1]   See Appendix I.

WEDDINGS AND FUNERALS

12.126

Funeral directors and others using vehicles in connection with funerals are exempted from the private hire provisions by LG(MP)A 1976, s 75(1)(c):

'(1) Nothing in this Part of this Act shall— ...
(c)   apply to a vehicle while it is being used in connection with a funeral or a vehicle used wholly or mainly, by a person carrying on the business of a funeral director, for the purpose of funerals; ...'

12.127

The effect of this is that there is no requirement for the operator, driver or vehicle to be licensed in these circumstances. It is a complete exemption from the requirements of private hire licensing. No case defines the expression 'being used in connection with a funeral', but it would appear that this is a question of fact. Likewise 'wholly or mainly' will depend upon the specific circumstances of the case. Examples of exempt use would include vehicles used to transport mourners to and from a church, cemetery, crematorium and also to the location where the funeral tea or other memorial gathering takes place, although each case would need to be considered on its own merits.

12.128

In relation to weddings, LG(MP)A 1976, s 75(1)(cc) states:

'(1) Nothing in this Part of this Act shall—
...
(cc)   apply to a vehicle while it is being used in connection with a wedding;
...'[1].

Again, this removes the need for any private hire licensing in respect of vehicles, drivers and operators used for these purposes. The position is similar to that concerning funerals and it appears that it will be a question of fact as to whether the vehicle was 'being used in connection with a wedding'. It therefore appears that the vehicles used to transport the bride, bridesmaids, groom, etc to and from the church or wedding location would not need to be licensed. That can probably be extended to the journeys from the ceremony to the reception venue. It would also seem reasonable to expect that the vehicle used to transport the bride and groom from the reception to the hotel where they are going to spend their wedding night would also be exempt as it would be the use of 'a vehicle while it is being used in connection with a wedding'. However, the journey from the hotel to the airport the following morning would seem to be too remote from the wedding ceremony to fall within the exemption.

[1]   'Wedding' is not defined in the 1976 Act, nor is it defined in the Interpretation Act 1978. Accordingly, it will carry its everyday meaning. The question is whether it extends to a Civil Partnership ceremony. The Civil Partnership Act 2004 does not address this, but it would certainly seem reasonable to apply the exemption for weddings to civil partnership ceremonies.

Other possibly exempt vehicles

12.129

Until January 2008, LG(MP)A 1976, s 75(1)(b) provided for a limited exemption from private hire licensing requirements (driver, vehicle and operator) for contracts for a vehicle and driver that lasted for seven days or longer. This was repealed as a result of the introduction of the Road Safety Act 2006, s 53.

What is the position now? On the face of it, the repeal of s 75(1)(b) should have been reasonably straightforward. Any provision of a motor vehicle and driver for hire for the purpose of carrying passengers[1] would need to be under the auspices of private hire. That would mean that the person who took the booking (the operator), the vehicle and the driver would need to be licensed in the usual way. Unfortunately, it is not that straightforward.

[1]   LG(MP)A 1976, s 80 defines a private hire vehicle as: '"private hire vehicle" means a motor vehicle constructed or adapted to seat fewer than nine passengers, other than a hackney carriage or public service vehicle or a London cab or tramcar, which is provided for hire with the services of a driver for the purpose of carrying passengers'.

12.130

There is a large range of situations where vehicles and drivers are provided to carry passengers, and the question that must be asked in each situation is: 'should this operator, driver and vehicle be licensed?'

In 2011 the Department for Transport ('DfT') issued guidance in relation to situations where in the view of the DfT private hire licences were required, and also where they were not. 'Private Hire Vehicle Licensing – A note for guidance from the Department for Transport'[1]. The note makes it clear that the DfT cannot provide a definitive legal opinion but does say[2]:

'6. However, in those 'grey areas' of the legislation where it is not clear whether a particular vehicle should be licensed or not, it is reasonable that the Department should offer a view about the extent of PHV licensing and, where possible, indicate the considerations which, in the Department's view, are relevant to an assessment of whether or not a particular vehicle should require a licence.'

1   DfT, 'Private Hire Vehicle Licensing – A note for guidance from the Department for Transport' (August 2011), available at https://www.gov.uk/government/uploads/system/uploads/attachment_data/file/3985/phv-licensing-guidance.pdf.

2   Above at paras 5 and 6.

12.131

In order to properly consider this Guidance, it is necessary to consider the case law relating to vehicles that are provided at no overt charge.

12.132

A number of commercial undertakings provide courtesy cars, including garages, hotels, pubs, nightclubs and travel agents, although there are undoubtedly other examples. In the case of garages, many provide transport from the location of their workshops to the local town centre, dropping customers who have left their car for servicing. Some also pick the customers up in the evening and take them back to the workshop. Hotels run courtesy cars for a variety of journeys. Collection from and delivery to a railway station or an airport are the most frequent examples, but sometimes hotels provide similar services to nightclubs or theatres. Pubs (especially rural pubs) provide cars to pick up and return customers, and night clubs have similar arrangements. Travel agents often provide transport to a local airport when a holiday is booked with them and collection on the client's return.

12.133

The question is whether such arrangements fall within the definition of operating and therefore require a private hire operator's licence, together with the then necessary licensing of the vehicles and drivers.

12.134

Unfortunately, there is no case specifically on the point. It is necessary to consider the matter in the light of the existing cases relating to hire, with reference to the DfT Guidance.

12.135

As can be seen above, it was decided in *St Albans District Council v Taylor*[1] that there does not have to be a payment by the passengers to the driver or operator for there to be a hiring within the provisions of LG(MP)A 1976, s 80. Indeed as Russell LJ stated:

'To constitute a hiring it is not necessary, in my judgment, that in all the circumstances there should be the payment of money. If the hirer can fairly be said to derive commercial benefit from the transaction then a hiring may take place, and in my view it did take place in the unusual circumstances of this case.'

[1]   [1991] Crim LR 852; see para 12.2 above.

12.136

To this must also be added the conclusions in the case of *Rout v Swallow Hotels Ltd*[1].

[1]   [1993] RTR 80, QBD.

Rout v Swallow Hotels Ltd

12.137

> A hotel provided a coach and a minibus which picked passengers up to bring them to the hotel and also took them to places of entertainment. There was no fixed service and it was provided at the discretion of the hotel. Did those vehicles require PSV licences and did the hotel require a PSV operators licence? Held: Yes they did.

Rout v Swallow Hotels Ltd[1] concerned a hotel which provided a 21-seater coach and an 11-seater minibus for use by guests of the hotel. The buses were provided by the hotel for a number of purposes, including collecting customers from locations to bring them to the hotel or taking them to places of entertainment. When the buses were operating and the decision as to whether or not to operate the bus at any time for any particular purpose was at the sole discretion of the hotel manager, then any resident or visitor was free to travel on the bus. No payment was made for travelling and there was no right given to any individual to make use of the service. It was entirely discretionary and if any disputes arose as to destinations, times etc, the manager exercised his discretion and made the decision.

[1]   [1993] RTR 80, QBD.

12.138

The question was raised as to whether or not they were being used to carry passengers 'for hire or reward', because if they were, then the coaches became PSVs for the purposes of the Public Passenger Vehicles Act 1981 and the hotel would have to have a PSV operator's licence and the vehicles themselves would have to comply with the fitness requirements for PSVs. Leggatt LJ set out the relevant legislative provisions[1] (at 85C):

'Section 1 of the Act of 1981 defines the term "public service vehicle". Section 1(1), so far as material, provides:

"Subject to the provisions of this section, in this Act 'public service vehicle' means a motor vehicle (other than a tramcar) which – (a) being a vehicle adapted to carry more than eight passengers, is used for carrying passengers for hire or reward…'"

[1]   *Rout v Swallow Hotels Ltd* [1993] RTR 80, QBD.

12.139

The Public Passenger Vehicles Act 1981, s 1(5), so far as material and as amended, provides:

'For the purposes of this section and Schedule 1 to this Act – (a) a vehicle is to be treated as carrying passengers for hire or reward if payment is made for, or for matters which include, the carrying of passengers, irrespective of the person to whom the payment is made … (b) a payment for the carrying of a passenger shall be treated as a fare notwithstanding that it is made in consideration of other matters in addition to the journey and irrespective of the person by or to whom it is made … (c) a payment shall be treated as made for the carrying of a passenger if made in consideration of a person's being given a right to be carried, whether for one or more journeys and whether or not the right is exercised …'

12.140

Considerable reference was made to the earlier cases of *Coward v Motor Insurers Bureau*[1] and *Albert v Motor Insurers Bureau*[2]. In addition, reference was also made to *DPP v Sikondar*[3].

[1]   [1963] 1 QB 259.
[2]   [1972] AC 301, HL.
[3]   [1993] RTR 90.

12.141

The cases referred to all considered the question of motor insurance. The House of Lords in *Albert v Motor Insurers Bureau*[1] overturned the decision in *Coward v Motor Insurers Bureau*[2] and concluded that the phrase 'a vehicle in which passengers are carried for hire or reward' meant a vehicle used for the systematic carrying of passengers for reward, not necessarily on a contractual basis, going beyond the bounds of mere social kindness and amounting to a 'business activity' as summarised from the head note in *Albert* by Leggett LJ in *Rout v Swallow Hotels*[3] at 85L. In *Sikondar*[4] the court concluded (at 96K):

'What, in our judgment, is clear is that [Public Passenger Vehicles Act 1981, s 1(5)(c)] is not to be taken as defining the only circumstances in which a vehicle is used for carrying passengers for hire or reward. In our judgment, the construction of "hire or reward" in *Albert v Motor Insurers Bureau* [1972] RTR 230 and *Motor Insurers Bureau v Meanen* [1971] 2 All ER 1372 is to be applied to that expression in section 1 of the Public

Passenger Vehicles Act 1981, so that it was not necessary in this case for the prosecution to establish a legally enforceable agreement.'

1   [1972] AC 301, HL.
2   [1963] 1 QB 259.
3   [1993] RTR 80, QBD.
4   DPP v Sikondar [1993] RTR 90.

12.142

In *Rout*[1] the court concluded, taking the previous cases into account, that these were indeed vehicles used as PSVs. Leggett LJ stated (at 88K):

'In this court in a sustained and powerful argument Mr Laprell submitted that there has to be a clear connection, if the definition of "public service vehicle" in section 1 of the Act of 1981 [Public Passenger Vehicles Act 1981, s 1] is to be satisfied, between payment and carriage, and that such a connection is absent here. He submits that the connection is made tenuous by the fact that there were some people, as is apparent from the justices findings of fact who were allowed to travel without any payment direct or indirect, such as friends of guests. But it does not seem to me that the fact that some people travelled free is relevant to the question whether guests at the hotel are indeed incidentally funding the provision of the service afforded by the coaches, however sporadic and discretionary is its operation.

Mr Laprell does not argue the absence of a payment specifically for the right to be carried means that the carrying is not for hire or reward, but he does say that it is a factor of which account should be taken in making the assessment whether the carrying of passengers was for hire or reward.

In my judgment the service is provided in connection with the hotel's business. The relevance of that is that included in the payment by a guest of the price of a room or a meal there must be taken to be an element in respect of amenities of the hotel, one of which is the provision of the vehicles. The hotel charges through the price of rooms and meals for all those amenities which it offers, whether or not individual guests avail themselves of any particular amenity or are even aware of it. The vehicles are provided by the hotel as one such amenity, and as part of the business of running the hotel, the remuneration or reward for which is included in the payments made by guests. That conclusion itself confirms the irrelevance of the fact that some passengers are carried free.

I have no hesitation in concluding that the vehicles used by the defendants were public service vehicles ...'

1   Rout v Swallow Hotels [1993] RTR 80, QBD.

12.143

Rout v Swallow Hotels[1] concerns different legislation, but it is clearly relevant to this question. The wording in the Public Passenger Vehicles Act 1981 requires passengers to be carried for hire or reward. LG(MP)A 1976, s 80 states that:

'"operate" means in the course of business to make provision for the invitation or acceptance of bookings for a private hire vehicle'

and private hire vehicle is defined as:

'a motor vehicle constructed or adapted to seat fewer than nine passengers, other than a hackney carriage or public service vehicle or a London Cab or tramcar, which is provided for hire with the services of a driver for the purpose of carrying passengers.'

It can be seen that there is no reference to reward in the private hire legislation and the emphasis is clearly on hire.

¹   [1993] RTR 80, QBD.

12.144

This is reinforced in the decision in *St Albans District Council v Taylor*¹, where it was decided that payment was not necessary for a contract of private hire to exist. The decision in *R (on the application of Arun District Council) v Spooner*² is also important as it makes it clear that operating a booking system, having a specially adapted vehicle, making a charge, and generating a profit amounts to running a business. The fact that the profits were then donated to charity was immaterial.

¹   [1991] Crim LR 852; see para 12.2 above.
²   [2007] EWHC 307 (Admin), [2007] All ER (D) 73 (Jan); see para 12.4 above.

12.145

The DfT Guidance¹ states:

'9. Of course the fundamental purpose of the PHV licensing regime is to establish a position where passengers can use these vehicles with a high degree of confidence about their safety. But, the safety concerns must be weighed up with the burdens which are placed on transport providers. This principle is at the heart of the Department's Best Practice Guidance about wider taxi and PHV licensing issues and it is also relevant in this context.

10. The key message conveyed to licensing authorities in this guidance note is to think carefully about the burden which would be placed on people and organisations who are in the "grey areas" identified by the Consultants if they were to impose a requirement for PHV licensing. We would urge licensing authorities to ask themselves – particularly in cases where the activity in question is already regulated or assessed in respect of wider duties being carried out – whether there is any real need to oblige these people or organisations to acquire licences.'

Whist it is correct that the burden on persons required to hold a licence should be considered by a local authority, that consideration cannot override a legislative requirement.

¹   DfT, *'Private Hire Vehicle Licensing – A note for guidance from the Department for Transport'* available at   https://www.gov.uk/government/uploads/system/uploads/attachment_data/file/3985/phv-licensing-guidance.pdf

12.146

The guidance lists six 'key principles' which local authorities should consider[1] and which 'should underpin the decision-making process'. It then goes on to offer guidance on nine 'sector specific' areas[2].

The key principles are detailed below, and in each case there is some further narrative contained within the guidance, key parts of which are reproduced below:

'When assessing the question of commercial benefit, licensing authorities should look fairly at all the circumstances. An assessment of whether or not the service derives a commercial benefit can be equally applied to any organisation acting as an operator of the service as well as a driver. However, in the Department's opinion, case law in this area allows licensing authorities to form a balanced and fair view of what constitutes a 'commercial benefit' rather than taking a strict and inflexible approach to remote or minor consequential benefits.'[3]:

'The Department's view is that licensing authorities are responsible for making a considered decision as to whether or not licensing should apply if the carrying of passengers is a genuinely incidental and minor part of a wider service being provided. In the Department's opinion, a distinction can be drawn between those services where carrying passengers is a genuinely incidental part of a larger service and those operations which have a separate identifiable service of carrying passengers. For example, "courtesy lifts" are a feature of many businesses which are not dedicated to transporting passengers. Many of these businesses will provide courtesy lifts on an informal basis – i.e. on the basis that a lift can be provided to customers who request such a service if a car is available at the time and someone is free to drive the customer, but no guarantee is given. This type of incidental service can be contrasted with those operations which provide dedicated transportation as part of a wider service. For example, a company organising a sporting event which agrees to organise transportation for the players or officials, is providing separate organised transportation services regardless of the fact that transportation may be a small and incidental part of the overall service.'[4]:

'The Department considers that licensing authorities should take a pragmatic approach to licensing, taking account of the underlying objective of licensing – safety. When considering services where there is an element of doubt as to whether or not PHV licensing should apply, the Department considers it relevant to investigate whether or not drivers have been assessed by an organisation in the context of their wider role (for which driving passengers is just one part). This is particularly relevant where the drivers have, for example, undergone a Criminal Records Bureau check for that wider role. One example might be in the case of care workers who use their cars to transport clients from time to time; they are likely to have been vetted for that work. The Department would question whether there is any real need to subject drivers who have been assessed in this manner to a separate licensing regime.'[5]

'This element is directed at the sorts of duties undertaken by people who are in a position of care or responsibility in respect of the passenger being carried in the vehicle. For example, in the case of genuine ambulances, the Department considers it relevant that drivers clearly have wider responsibilities for the care of their patients. Similarly, childminders have a wider responsibility and specific duties relating to the children in their care. Another example would be those who provide secure escort and custody services where drivers are under wider obligations in relation to the transport of passengers to ensure that they cannot abscond.'[6]

'PHV drivers are experts in their field and we would, of course, expect them to discharge their duties by utilising their skills to the full. However, this element of the consideration process is directed at the sorts of specialist skills which a driver must possess in order to undertake the wider work of which driving is a part. For example, the driver of an ambulance would be expected to undergo specialist training before being allowed to start work.'[7]

'This final question is included to assist licensing authorities in cases which are finely balanced where the authority is struggling to reach a decision. It relates back to the fundamental point of this guidance which is made at the outset about taking a common-sense approach to licensing. Whilst ultimately it is a matter for the courts to interpret the legislation with reference to any particular service, the Department is firmly of the opinion that in passing the relevant legislation, Parliament believed that it was establishing a regulatory mechanism for dealing with conventional private hire vehicles – albeit a range of vehicles – but whose principal purpose was to transport passengers from a to b.

Legislation by its very nature is regularly applied to situations outside of Parliament's original thinking and must constantly be interpreted to keep pace with innovation and a changing world. However, where there is an element of ambiguity in legislation and its application is unclear, Parliamentary intention can be a valid tool to aid in its interpretation. In the Department's opinion, consideration of this final question adds weight to the argument that those services which form minor or incidental parts of other services should not require licensing, for example courtesy lifts provided by garages or transport provided by child minders.'[8]

It is suggested that some of these principles do not accord with the case law in *Rout v Swallow Hotels*[9] . There is clearly a business benefit in many situations where the provision of a lift differentiates one business from a competitor, and whilst a person may have been vetted for other purposes, that does not assess their driving ability, neither does it ensure that the vehicle is safe and suitable.

---

[1]   Paragraph 12 onwards.
[2]   Paragraph 31 onwards.
[3]   At para 21.
[4]   At para 24.
[5]   At para 25.

⁶   At para 26.
⁷   At para 27.
⁸   At paras 28 and 29.
⁹   [1993] RTR 80, QBD; see para 12.137 above.

12.147

The Guidance[1] then considers 9 areas where it provides 'sector specific guidance'. The DfT's conclusions and their reasons are outlined below.

Stretched limousines

32. The Department considers that most stretched limousine operations (where the vehicle has fewer than nine passenger seats) are likely to fall within the PHV licensing regime.

35. Taking account of the principles set out in Part One of this guidance note, the Department takes the view that typical stretched limousine operations should be licensed because they involve:
- a commercial benefit on the part of the driver/organiser;
- the carrying of passengers as a main part of the service;
- drivers who are unlikely to have been vetted for wider work;
- driver duties which are restricted to driving and assisting with luggage; and
- the sort of service which Parliament would have had in mind when passing the relevant legislation.

This is clearly correct, as a stretched limousine is simply a longer and larger private hire vehicle, provided it seats up to eight passengers (any larger than that, it will be the responsibility of the Traffic Commissioners under PSV licensing).

[1]   DfT, *'Private Hire Vehicle Licensing – A note for guidance from the Department for Transport'* available at https://www.gov.uk/government/uploads/system/uploads/attachment_data/file/3985/phv-licensing-guidance.pdf

12.148

Chauffeur/Executive drivers

36. The Department considers that most chauffeur/executive operations are likely to fall within the PHV licensing regime.

39. Taking account of the principles set out in Part One of this guidance note, the Department takes the view that typical chauffeur/executive car operations should be licensed because they involve:
- a commercial benefit on the part of the driver/organiser;
- the carrying of passengers as a main part of the service;
- drivers who are unlikely to have been vetted for wider work;
- driver duties which are restricted to driving and assisting with luggage; and

- the sort of service which Parliament would have had in mind when passing the relevant legislation.

Again, this is correct as these services are simply a 'high-class' private hire service[1].

---

[1] See Chapter 13, para 13.64 for dispensation from displaying plates and other signage for 'executive' vehicles.

12.149

Event Management Companies

41. The Department considers that companies which provide a dedicated transport service for events should be subject to PHV licensing.

45. Taking account of the principles set out in Part One of this guidance note, the Department recognises that typical event management operations might involve duties beyond driving, but considers that they should be licensed because they involve:
- a commercial benefit on the part of the driver/organiser;
- the carrying of passengers as a main part of the service;
- drivers who are unlikely to have been vetted for wider work; and
- the sort of service which Parliament would have had in mind when passing the relevant legislation.

Again, as there is very little difference in the service provided between these types of operation and regular private hire services, this is correct.

12.150

Ambulances

46. The Department considers that "genuine ambulances" do not fall within the PHV licensing regime.

52. Taking account of the principles set out in Part One of this guidance note, the Department recognises that genuine ambulance services derive a commercial benefit, but consider that they should not be licensed because they involve:
- drivers who are likely to have been vetted for wider work;
- drivers who have wider duties beyond those associated with driving;
- drivers who must have specific qualifications or training which go beyond driving and general customer care; and
- the sort of service which Parliament would not have had in mind when passing the legislation.

This is a more complex area, but as most ambulance services are undertaken out of necessity rather than choice, and the commercial benefit is limited, it is probably correct.

12.151

Volunteers

53. The Department considers that genuine volunteers who receive no recompense or receive only enough to cover their actual expenses do not fall within the PHV licensing regime.

59. The Department reached its conclusion that volunteer drivers do not fall within the PHV licensing regime because of the nature of the activity in relation to the definition in the legislation. If a driver chooses to offer a substantial amount of time to this activity, this does not change the essential nature of the work; indeed, the HMRC's rules take account of the fact that some drivers will be undertaking substantial mileage and the rates reflect this.

60. Taking account of the principles set out in Part One of this guidance note, the Department considers that volunteer drivers should not be licensed because:

- the service involves no commercial benefit; and
- it is not something that Parliament would have had in mind when passing the legislation.

This is a much more difficult area. The mileage that some volunteer drivers undertake is significant, and at the mileage rates that are permitted by HMRC without counting as income[1], this can amount to a considerable sum. However, there is another tangible business benefit and that is to the NHS. The use of volunteers taking patients to and from hospital reduces the use of ambulances and must therefore amount to a benefit to the NHS.

It remains to be seen whether the courts will take the same approach as the DfT in this area.

[1] 45p per mile for the first 10,000 miles in a year, 25p thereafter.

12.152

Care and support worker services

61. The Department considers that most car journeys undertaken in the context of care and support services do not fall within the PHV licensing regime.

64. Taking account of the principles set out in Part One of this guidance note, the Department considers that people providing care and support services should not be licensed because:

- the carrying of passengers is an ancillary part of the service;
- the driver is likely to have been vetted for wider work;
- the driver will have wider duties beyond those associated with driving;
- the driver is likely to have specific qualifications or training which go beyond driving and general customer care; and
- Parliament would not have had this sort of service in mind when passing the legislation.

This seems correct, as the business benefit is harder to determine, and these journeys are probably closer to social kindness than a commercial arrangement.

12.153

Childminders

65. The Department considers that car journeys undertaken in the context of most typical childminding arrangements would not fall within the PHV licensing regime.

70. Taking account of the principles set out in Part One of this guidance note, the Department considers that typical childminders should not be licensed because:
- the carrying of passengers is an ancillary part of the service;
- the driver is likely to have been vetted for wider work;
- the driver will have wider duties beyond those associated with driving;
- the driver is likely to have specific qualifications or training which go beyond driving and general customer care; and
- Parliament would not have had this sort of service in mind when passing the legislation.

It is suggested that this part of the Guidance is wrong. Whilst the childminder will have been vetted, their driving ability and the vehicle will not. In addition, there is a clear business benefit accruing to the childminder who provides transport for children. It gives them a commercial advantage over their competitors who do not provide that additional service to their clients and the children they look after.

12.154

Rental car companies/Garages

71. The Department considers that most informal courtesy lifts offered by, for example, rental car companies or garages would not fall within the PHV licensing regime.

75. Taking account of the principles set out in Part One of this guidance note, the Department considers that rental car companies/garages should not be licensed because:
- the carrying of passengers is an ancillary part of the service; and
- Parliament would not have had this sort of service in mind when passing the legislation

Again, as with childminders, it is suggested that this part of the Guidance is also wrong, for similar reasons. In this case, the business benefit accrues to the garage or rental company that provides this service to their customers, placing them at an advantage over commercial rivals who do not provide similar lifts. In addition in this case, there is no vetting of the driver.

12.155

Secure escort and custody services

76. The Department considers that services which involve the escort and custody of people sentenced or remanded to custody, secure accommodation or alternative youth detention accommodation are not PHVs.

80. Taking account of the principles set out in Part One of this guidance note, the Department considers that secure escort and custody services should not be licensed because:
- the driver is likely to have been vetted for wider work;
- the driver will have wider duties beyond those associated with driving;
- the driver is likely to have specific qualifications or training which go beyond driving and general customer care; and
- Parliament would not have had this sort of service in mind when passing the legislation.

This seems to be correct, in part because the passengers in these vehicles are not there of their own free will.

12.156

As part of the consideration as to whether a particular service needs to be licensed as a private hire service, it is necessary to consider the question of separate fares.

12.157

One of the underpinning concepts of private hire legislation is that the vehicle is provided as a whole. In other words, the charge is for the use of the vehicle, irrespective of the number of passengers. This must be contrasted with any situation where a vehicle is provided and the passengers are charged separate fares. Such a vehicle will be caught by the Public Passenger Vehicle Act 1981, even if it seats less than nine passengers (such vehicles are referred to as 'small buses'.

CONCLUSIONS

12.158

In conclusion, it seems clear that vehicles provided with the services of a driver, for the carriage of passengers in circumstances where they are either provided in the course of a business, or the provision of the vehicle accrues some business benefit to the provider of the vehicle, the driver or both, will be licensable. The same will apply to vehicles provided with a driver where the provision goes beyond mere social kindness[1]. In many cases the DfT Guidance seems at odds with this proposition and it remains to be seen whether the courts agree with the DfT, or take the firmer line contained in *Albert v Motor Insurers Bureau*[2] and *Rout v Swallow Hotels Ltd*[3].

1   Although not defined in the cases, 'mere social kindness' would appear to include people driving
     their family members and friends around (eg children and friends to parties, parents to events).
     It would also include outings by groups and societies where some members drive others in their
     own cars.
2   [1972] AC 301, HL.
3   [1993] RTR 80, QBD; see para 12.137 above.

12.159

This then leads to the question of whether such vehicles fall within private hire
or public service vehicle licensing. That will depend on whether there is one
contract which provides the vehicle to carry a number of people (private hire)
or whether the carriage of a number of people is under separate contractual
arrangements (public service).

Small public service vehicles

12.160

In recent years, some attempts have been made to avoid the need for private hire
operator and vehicle licensing by means of a restricted passenger service vehicle
(PSV) licence under the Public Passenger Vehicles Act 1981, s 13(3). Vehicles
that carry less than nine passengers can be small PSVs[1]. Such a small PSV must
carry passengers at separate fares[2], follow a fixed route and if the commencement
and ending points of the journey are less than 15 miles apart, the route must be
registered in advance with the Traffic Commissioners. This clearly made such
attempts difficult.

1   See Public Passenger Vehicles Act 1981, s 1(1)(b). A private hire vehicle cannot carry more than
     eight passengers: see LG(MP)A 1976, s 80(1).
2   See Public Passenger Vehicles Act 1981, s 1(1)(b).

12.161

Section 79A of the Public Passenger Vehicles Act 1981 (inserted by Transport
Act 2000, s 265 was introduced to try to address this situation. It states:

'Small PSVs subject to regulation as private hire vehicles

79A–(1) If a small bus is being provided for hire with the services of a
driver for the purpose of carrying passengers otherwise than at separate
fares, it is not to be regarded as a public service vehicle for the purpose of—
(a)   Part II of the Local Government (Miscellaneous Provisions) Act 1976,
      or
(b)   any local Act applying in any area in England and Wales which
      regulates the use of private hire vehicles provided for hire with the
      services of a driver for the purpose of carrying passengers and excludes
      public service vehicles from the scope of that regulation.

(2) If a small bus is being made available with a driver to the public for hire
for the purpose of carrying passengers otherwise than at separate fares, it is

not to be regarded as a public service vehicle for the purpose of the Private Hire Vehicles (London) Act 1998.

(3) But subsection (1) or (2) does not apply where the vehicle is being so provided or made available in the course of a business of carrying passengers by motor vehicles all but a small part of which involves the operation of large buses.

(4) In this section—
"small bus" means a public service vehicle within paragraph (b) of subsection (1) of section 1 of this Act; and
"large buses" means public service vehicles within paragraph (a) of that subsection."

(5) In section 167(4) of the Criminal Justice and Public Order Act 1994 (touting for hire car services: defence in case of public service vehicles), for "passengers for public service vehicles" substitute "passengers to be carried at separate fares by public service vehicles".'

12.162

It can be seen that s 79A(1) makes it clear that, if a small PSV is carrying passengers who are not paying separate fares, then it is providing private hire services and accordingly, must be licensed as a private hire vehicle, the journey must have been booked by a private hire operator and the vehicle must be driven by a private hire driver.

12.163

Unfortunately, the vaguely worded Public Passenger Vehicle Act 1981, s 79A(3) is not as helpful. What this means is that a PSV operator whose business consists principally of using 'large buses' (which are vehicles that carry more than eight passengers) can use 'small buses' (which are vehicles that carry less than eight passengers) for carrying passengers who are not paying separate fares. In other words, that which would otherwise be a private hire service. The problem arises with the wording of s 79A(3). To enable a PSV operator to avail himself of this freedom, all but 'a small part' of his business must consist of the use of large buses. There is no indication as to how this should be assessed, and to date no cases on the point. In its letter of 9 September 2002, the Department for Transport attempted to provide some guidance (at para 13)[1]:

'What constitutes "a small part" is also not defined in legislation, and ultimately, final decisions on where the balance lies is a matter for the courts. The legislation confers the exemption on an operator whose use of small vehicles is only a small part of his business.

14. The relative size of the fleet of large and small buses is obviously very relevant and as *a rule of thumb* we believe that *if less* than 10% of the overall fleet licensed under a single PSV Operator's Licence are small vehicles the exemption will apply (eg a fleet of, say, 20 buses with 9 or more passenger

seats could run 2 additional vehicles – which could be stretched limousines that carry 8 or less passengers – for private hire work) But because the legislation refers to the size of the small and large bus business other factors (such as mileage run) should be taken into account. We would hope that in most cases it would be obvious what was and what was not, to coin a phrase, a "large bus business"' (emphasis in original).

[1]   See Appendix II.

12.164

Whether this does in fact provide any clarification remains to be seen, but it is referred to in the Guidance issued in 2016 by the Senior Traffic Commissioner[1].

[1]   Guidance of the *'Senior Traffic Commissioner, Statutory Document No. 13 – Small PSV Operations Including Limousines And Novelty Vehicles'* available from https://www.gov.uk/government/publications/traffic-commissioners-small-public-service-vehicle-operations-january-2016

Chapter 13

Private hire vehicles outside London

INTRODUCTION

13.1

Any vehicle used for private hire purposes (that is collecting a passenger for a journey which has been pre-booked) must either be licensed as a private hire vehicle under the provisions of the Local Government (Miscellaneous Provisions) Act 1976, s 48 (LG(MP)A 1976) or must be a hackney carriage[1]. LG(MP)A 1976, s 46(1)(a)[2] makes it clear that unless a vehicle is licensed under s 48 as a private hire vehicle, it is an offence to be used within a controlled district[3] as a private hire vehicle unless it is a hackney carriage This licence is either termed a 'proprietor's' licence or a 'vehicle' licence and the terms are interchangeable.

[1]   This exception will be considered at para 13.92 onwards below.
[2]   See Appendix I.
[3]   A 'controlled district' is a district where the Local Government (Miscellaneous Provisions) Act 1976 is in force. It is defined in s 80 as:
    'any area for which this Part of this Act is in force by virtue of–
    (a)   a resolution passed by a district council under section 45 of this Act; or
    (b)   section 255(4) of the Greater London Authority Act 1999;'

POWERS RELATING TO LICENSING

13.2

The powers relating to the licensing of the vehicle are contained in LG(MP)A 1976, s 48:

'48   Licensing of private hire vehicles

(1)   Subject to the provisions of this Part of this Act, a district council may on the receipt of an application from the proprietor of any vehicle for the grant in respect of such vehicle of a licence to use the vehicle as a private hire vehicle, grant in respect thereof a vehicle licence:

'Provided that a district council shall not grant such a licence unless they are satisfied—

(a) that the vehicle is—
   (i) suitable in type, size and design for use as a private hire vehicle;
   (ii) not of such design and appearance as to lead any person to believe that the vehicle is a hackney carriage;
   (iii) in a suitable mechanical condition;
   (iv) safe; and
   (v) comfortable;
(b) that there is in force in relation to the use of the vehicle a policy of insurance or such security as complies with the requirements of Part VI of the Road Traffic Act 1988,

and shall not refuse such a licence for the purpose of limiting the number of vehicles in respect of which such licences are granted by the council.

(2) A district council may attach to the grant of a licence under this section such conditions as they may consider reasonably necessary including, without prejudice to the generality of the foregoing provisions of this subsection, conditions requiring or prohibiting the display of signs on or from the vehicle to which the licence relates.'

As can be seen, this is a lengthy provision and there are a number of important points that arise from it.

13.3

It is important to recognise that the district council is not placed under a duty to issue a licence once an application has been made; it has a discretion. This can be contrasted with the requirement to issue a licence to an operator under LG(MP)A 1976, s 55(1)[1], unless, on the grounds of fitness and propriety, it has reason not to do so.

[1] See Appendix I.

13.4

LG(MP)A 1976, s 48(1) specifically includes provisos for situations where the council must not grant a licence in paras (a) and (b). Section 48(1) also expressly prohibits any refusal to grant the vehicle licence if that refusal is with a view to limiting the number of private hire vehicles licensed within the district. The consequence of this is that even if the vehicle is suitable and satisfactory, provided the refusal is not to limit numbers, the district council can exercise its discretion and refuse to grant the licence.

13.5

As with Hackney carriages, it is clear that there is no prohibition on considering the suitability of the applicant, and similar considerations apply to private hire vehicles and hackney carriages[1].

[1] See Chapter 8, para 8.98 onwards.

SUITABILITY OF THE APPLICANT/PROPRIETOR

13.6

It is important to consider what a private hire vehicle actually does. Clearly they transport people who have booked a journey via a private hire operator, from where they are to where they want to be, in a convenient, safe and comfortable manner, but the impact of a licensed private hire vehicle goes beyond that.

Private hire vehicles are seen everywhere across the United Kingdom, at all times of the day and night, in any location. As a result the presence of a private hire vehicle does not elicit any interest or curiosity. This can be contrasted with the unexpected presence of a van in the small hours of the morning.

As a consequence of this, a private hire vehicle would provide the ideal transportation system for any form of contraband, whether that is drugs, guns, illicit alcohol or tobacco, male or female prostitutes, or children who may be at risk of, or are being, abused.

In relation to private hire vehicles[1] there is no test of fitness and propriety for the proprietor. This can be contrasted with the position in relation to both hackney carriage and private hire drivers and private hire operators[2]. Section 48 of the 1976 Act gives the local authority complete discretion over granting the licence.

That discretion is usually exercised in respect of the vehicle, both its size and specification and also its mechanical and suitability, but it is equally applicable in respect of the suitability of the proprietor.

The local authority would not want to grant a private hire vehicle licence (or a fleet of private hire vehicle licences) to a proprietor if he was a drug dealer, gun-runner, person controlling prostitutes or child abuser and accordingly, local authorities must make enquiries about the character of such applicants.

[1]   Exactly the same considerations apply to hackney carriages – See Chapter 8, para 8.98 onwards.
[2]   See Chapter 10, para 10.21 for consideration of fitness and propriety for hackney carriage and private hire drivers and private hire operators.

13.7

Private hire vehicle proprietors are not excluded from the workings of the Rehabilitation of Offenders Act 1974 ('the 1974 Act')[1]. This means that convictions become 'spent' in relation to a hackney carriage proprietor. However, the ruling of the High Court in *Adamson v Waveney District Council*[2] means that local authorities can take spent convictions into account when determining the suitability of an applicant to hold a private hire vehicle proprietors licence[3].

In addition, the fact that the role of the private hire vehicle proprietor is not an exempt occupation for the 1974 Act means that it is not possible to obtain an Enhanced DBS check. However, the applicant (or licensee on renewal) can be asked to obtain a Basic Disclosure from Disclosure Scotland. This can be combined with a statutory declaration as part of the application process requiring the applicant to list all previous convictions, together with other material information in a similar fashion to hackney carriage and private hire drivers[4].

Although this is by no means a perfect system, it does give local authorities a reasonable basis for making an informed decision as to the safety and suitability of an applicant or existing private hire vehicle proprietor.

As with hackney carriage and private hire drivers, it is not only permissible but eminently sensible to have a policy in relation to previous convictions and other matters for private hire vehicle proprietors.

To enable consistent and informed decisions to be made, it is useful to have a working test of safety and suitability for private hire vehicle proprietors licence. A possible test would be:

> 'Would I be comfortable allowing this person to have control of a licensed vehicle that can travel anywhere, at any time of the day or night without arousing suspicion and be satisfied that he/she would not allow it to be used for criminal or other unacceptable purposes and be confident that he/she would maintain it to an acceptable standard throughout the period of the licence?'

It can be seen that this also encompasses a requirement on the applicant to maintain the vehicle to an acceptable standard and this will be considered below.

1   The Rehabilitation of Offenders Act 1974 (Exceptions) (Amendment) Order 2002 does not cover private hire proprietors. This can be contrasted with hackney carriage and private hire drivers.
2   [1997] 2 All ER 898, QBD – see Chapter 5, para 5.11.
3   The same is true in relation to private hire operators. However, in practice, a great many proprietors also hold operator's and driver's licences and are effectively either 'one-man-bands' or only employ a few drivers to provide cover.
4   See Chapter 10, para 10.23 onwards.

13.8

It is also useful to note that LG(MP)A 1976, s 57(1) allows the local authority to:

> 'require any applicant for a licence under the Act of 1847 or under this Part of this Act to submit to them such information as they may reasonably consider necessary to enable them to determine whether the licence should be granted and whether conditions should be attached to any such licence.'

Section 57(2)(c) allows the local authority to enquire about the character of directors and company secretaries where an application for a private hire operator's licence is made by a limited company. Although s 57(2)(c) is stated to only apply to applications for a private hire operator's licence, as that is clearly stated to be without prejudice to subsection (1), the local authority can make any enquiries that it feels are necessary in relation to an application for a private hire vehicle licence and can clearly investigate and consider the fitness and propriety of limited companies, their secretaries and directors and any convictions recorded against the company whilst an applicant was a secretary or director.

THE SAFETY OF THE VEHICLE

13.9

Section 48(1)(a)(iv) requires the Council to be satisfied that the vehicle is safe. The question arose in *Chauffeur Bikes Ltd v Leeds City Council*[1] as to whether 'safe' meant safe as a vehicle, or safe for use as a private hire vehicle.

1   [2005] EWHC 2369 (Admin), [2006] LLR 12.

Chauffeur Bikes Ltd v Leeds City Council

13.10

> Refusal of an application to licence a motorbike as a private hire vehicle as not a 'safe' vehicle. Applicant appealed. Did 'safe' mean generally safe, or safe for use as a private hire vehicle? Held: The correct interpretation was that the council had to be satisfied that the vehicle was safe for use as a private hire vehicle.

The case concerned an application to licence a motorcycle (a Honda Pan European touring motorcycle) as a private hire vehicle. The council refused the application and an appeal was lodged with the magistrates' court which was successful. The council challenged that decision on appeal to the Crown Court and the appeal was upheld. The applicant then appealed to the High Court by way of case stated. There was no dispute that a motorcycle could be licensed as a private hire vehicle; rather the dispute centred on whether it was reasonable for the local authority to refuse to licence a motorcycle as a private hire vehicle. This was outlined by Keene LJ[1]:

'[4] The issue in the present case centres on the question of safety. The Crown Court heard oral evidence from both sides, and it had a number of reports before it. As a result, it concluded that a private hire licence should be refused for the Honda motorcycle because it was unsuitable and unsafe for use as a private hire vehicle.

[5] It is clear that the court's conclusion as to unsuitability was based on safety considerations. The case stated refers to a number of factors in that connection, for example:

"Design features
(i)   People sit on the motorcycle not in it.
(ii)   The contribution to the weight of the machine by adding a passenger and the positioning of the weight of that passenger can affect the handling of the machine.
        ...
(v)   The surface area of the tyres in contact with the road is comparatively small.
(vi)   The motorcycle is susceptible to side winds because of its two wheeled configuration and its side area.

Safety issues
(vii)   Inexperienced passengers may intuitively counterbalance against the leaning over motion of a motorcycle by sitting upright in a way which may destabilise the machine.
(viii) Inexperienced passengers may react unexpectedly during the course of exposure to the ordinary incidents of motorcycle riding and thus create a dangerous situation."

There is also reference to the effect of adverse weather conditions and the reaction of inexperienced passengers to a slippery road surface and to other hazards.

[6] In addition to its conclusion on safety, as judged objectively, the case also comments at para [10] as follows:

> "The granting of such a licence would be viewed by the public as an endorsement of this form of transport as a private hire vehicle, and would encourage them to think that the dangerous potential which has been demonstrated to us on the evidence for an accident has been carefully weighed and discounted to the extent they can be assured of safe and suitable transport in such a vehicle.'"

[1]   Above, at paras 4–6.

13.11

It was argued that 'safe' was safe as a vehicle, rather than safe 'for use as a private hire vehicle'; in fact the Crown Court raised three questions for the High Court to determine[1]:

> '"(i)   Whether the Crown Court erred in finding that the requirements of section 48(i)(a)(i) and (iv) of the 1976 Act overlapped.
> (ii)   Whether the Crown Court erred in finding that the meaning of "safe" within section 48(1)(a)(iv) meant safe for use as a private hire vehicle.
> (iii) Whether the Crown Court erred in finding that the vehicle in respect of which a private hire licence was sought, namely a Honda Pan-European motorcycle, was unsuitable and unsafe for use as a private hire vehicle."'

[1]   Above, at para 10.

13.12

Keene LJ concluded as follows[1]:

> '[18] It may be that the narrow construction of the word "safe" in subpara (iv), as put forward by the appellant, is right. In other words, that subparagraph may be concerned as a criterion with whether the vehicle in question, which in terms of type, size and design is entirely suitable for private hire use, is actually safe in all respects; so that if, for example, the seatbelts in a car were too worn the vehicle would fail subpara (iv). However that does not greatly assist the appellant. I am quite satisfied that, if that construction were right, subpara (i) when it refers to suitability in terms of type, size and design for such use brings in safety as a relevant consideration. If, because of any of those factors of type, size and design, the vehicle is unsafe to be used as a private hire vehicle, then it is unsuitable for such use. Consequently a vehicle may be in a safe condition for a vehicle of its type, size and design (as this motorcycle apparently was) with the result that there was nothing wrong with its safety as motorcycles go; but

it could still for safety reasons be judged to be unsuitable in type, size or design for private hire use.

[19] As to the Crown Court's finding that this vehicle was unsuitable and unsafe for private hire use, I cannot see that its conclusion was not open to it. It did not do any comparative exercise, ie merely comparing the motorcycle with a car. Most of its specific findings related simply to the safety for such a use of this motorcycle. Certainly, given that it had both oral and written evidence before it, one cannot say that the court reached an impermissible conclusion.

[20] I recognise that motorcycles regularly carry pillion passengers in modern use and that they do so lawfully, implying that the process is not to be seen as inherently unsafe. But in such private activity the driver and the passenger would normally be known to one another and there would be the opportunity to take precautions to assess experience and to give instructions. Private hire vehicles carry ordinary members of the public who would usually be previously unknown to the driver to any significant degree. It is therefore quite a different context. In that context, there was nothing wrong in the Crown Court's comment at para [10] of the case stated (cited earlier), where in essence it suggested that the grant of a licence would indicate to the public that the private hire use of this motorcycle had been found to be safe. That would indeed be the case. The Crown Court's conclusion overall was not outside the range of conclusions which could reasonably be reached on the evidence it had.

[21] Dealing finally with the questions posed in the case, I would answer question (i) in the negative insofar as subpara (i) of s 48(1)(a) does embrace safety in the way outlined earlier. It is part of suitability for such proposed use. It then becomes unnecessary to give a definite answer to question (ii) about the meaning of 'safe' within the meaning of s 48(1)(a)(iv), although I have given an indication as to the way my mind approaches that matter earlier in this judgment. Question (iii) again should be answered in the negative.

[22] For these reasons I, for my part, would dismiss this appeal.'

[1]   Above, at paras 18–22.

13.13

That view was supported by Poole J who added an extremely important observation[1]:

'[23] I agree.

[24] This argument has been attractively presented by Mr Maddox [for the appellant]. He makes the point that there is no reason to regard the vehicle under consideration as being unsafe in itself. Does it therefore become unsafe because people are prepared to go on it? The answer, or part of it, is, I think, that the legislation, namely the 1976 Act, permits district councils

individually to consider that question. The fact that a district council, say in Kent, may come to one conclusion (as we are told was the case) does not oblige one in Yorkshire to do the same. Nor does Mr Maddox argue otherwise.'

¹   Above, at paras 23–24.

13.14

Accordingly, the conclusion was that deciding that a motorcycle was not safe for use as a private hire vehicle was not an unreasonable conclusion. This case is not authority for the proposition that motorcycles cannot be licensed as private hire vehicles, although clearly it supported the view of one local authority that such a vehicle was not safe. Each case must be considered on its merits and there is no doubt that motorcycles have been licensed as private hire vehicles in the past and no doubt will be in the future. Ultimately it is for each local authority to decide upon its policy and then consider any application that deviates on that policy on its own merits.

This decision may also have an impact on vehicles where access to particular seats is limited or restricted. A number of local authorities will not licence some 'people carriers' or multi-purpose vehicles ('MPV') to carry passengers in seats where another seat has to be moved to allow access, although it should be noted that the DfT Guidance does not take this approach[1].

¹   DfT, '*Taxi and Private Hire Vehicle Licensing: Best Practice Guidance*' (October 2006, revised March 2010), para 8, http://www.dft.gov.uk/pgr/regional/taxis/taxiandprivatehirevehiclelic1792.

'Similarly, it may be too restrictive to automatically rule out considering Multi- Purpose Vehicles, or to license them for fewer passengers than their seating capacity (provided of course that the capacity of the vehicle is not more than eight passengers)'.

Also see para 13.17 onwards.

THE TYPE OF VEHICLE

13.15

There is no such thing as a purpose-designed or purpose-built private hire vehicle, unlike a hackney carriage where 'London style' vehicles are available. Private hire vehicles come in all shapes and sizes and there is no normal or typical vehicle. LG(MP)A 1976, s 48(1)(a)[1] lays down certain criteria that have to be satisfied before the district council can license a vehicle as a private hire vehicle.

¹   See Appendix I.

Criteria as to the vehicle

13.16

The first consideration is whether it is 'suitable in type, size and design for use as a private hire vehicle'. Most local authorities have policies relating to the size and other specifications of the vehicle. These include requirements that the vehicle has four doors for driver and passenger access, together with minimum sizes for internal dimensions, such as seats and legroom, to ensure a reasonable standard of comfort for the passengers.

13.17

One area of interest concerns vehicles that are designed to carry more than four passengers in addition to the driver. In the 1970s and 1980s these used to be represented by estate cars, which had an additional row of seats fitted in the area which would normally be the boot area (traditionally, models produced by Peugeot and Citroën), but have long since been superseded by so-called 'people carriers' or multi-purpose vehicles ('MPVs'). In relation to estate cars, there was always concern about access to and egress from the rear row of seats. A great many authorities refused to license such vehicles for more than four passengers, as the only way to emerge from the rearmost row of seats was with the middle row tipped up and through the rear doors. This situation was, therefore, analogous to the use of a two-door car with passengers in the back seat, as one of the front-seat passengers would have to get out to allow the rear-seat passengers out and this was felt to be unsatisfactory. However, a number of authorities did license such vehicles as seven-seat private hire vehicles (or, in some cases, as hackney carriages).

13.18

Similar considerations can arise with the modern people carrier-type cars, depending on the configuration of seats and doors. These vary from manufacturer to manufacturer, but it is an important consideration.

13.19

The primary concern raised in relation to the problem is the method of escape from the vehicle in the case of accident or emergency. It is felt by many people that immediate access to a door is necessary for all passengers and the driver, except the passenger sitting in the middle of the rear seat, who will hopefully be able to escape once the passengers sitting to either side have done so. The problem is that, if a seat has to be tipped up to enable this escape to be facilitated, then it is possible that, for whatever reason (injury, death etc), this may not be possible if the seat is occupied. In addition, where a vehicle has access for rear passengers on one side only (as is the case for some types of MPVs), some authorities are unwilling to licence the vehicle as it means there is a risk that passengers will have to exit into passing traffic if the vehicle is parked facing oncoming traffic. The DfT has addressed this in its *Best Practice Guide*[1] where it states:

'Specification Of Vehicle Types That May Be Licensed

26. The legislation gives local authorities a wide range of discretion over the types of vehicle that they can license as taxis or PHVs. Some authorities specify conditions that in practice can only be met by purpose-built vehicles but the majority license a range of vehicles.

27. Normally, the best practice is for local licensing authorities to adopt the principle of specifying as many different types of vehicle as possible. Indeed, local authorities might usefully set down a range of general criteria, leaving it open to the taxi and PHV trades to put forward vehicles of their own choice which can be shown to meet those criteria. In that way there can be flexibility for new vehicle types to be readily taken into account.

28. It is suggested that local licensing authorities should give very careful consideration to a policy which automatically rules out particular types of vehicle or prescribes only one type or a small number of types of vehicle. For example, the Department believes authorities should be particularly cautious about specifying only purpose-built taxis, with the strict constraint on supply that that implies. But of course the purpose-built vehicles are amongst those which a local authority could be expected to license. Similarly, it may be too restrictive to automatically rule out considering Multi-Purpose Vehicles, or to license them for fewer passengers than their seating capacity (provided of course that the capacity of the vehicle is not more than eight passengers).'

¹   DfT, '*Taxi and Private Hire Vehicle Licensing: Best Practice Guidance*' (October 2006, revised March 2010), paras 26–28, available from http://www.dft.gov.uk/pgr/regional/taxis/taxiandprivatehire vehiclelic1792.

13.20

Other than that, there are no real restrictions on the type of vehicles that can be used as a private hire vehicle, other than that contained in LG(MP)A 1976, s 48(1)(a)(ii): that it is 'not of such design and appearance as to lead any person to believe that the vehicle is a hackney carriage'.

13.21

This is an interesting question and the answer as to whether a certain vehicle could appear to be a hackney carriage will to a large extent depend upon the location in which it is to be licensed. Some local authorities have adopted so called 'mandatory orders', which means that only purpose-built vehicles (currently FX4, Metro-cabs, TXI, TXII, TXIV, or Mercedes Vito Taxi vehicles) will be licensed as hackney carriages¹. This leaves the field of saloons, estate cars and people carriers open for private hire work. In other areas, hackney carriages are themselves generally saloons, estate cars and people carriers, and distinctions between private hire and hackney carriage vehicles can become blurred.

¹   See Chapter 8, paras 8.109 and 8.122.

R v Bournemouth Borough Council, ex p Thompson

13.22

Could a local authority refuse to licence a vehicle as a private hire vehicle when it had a superficial resemblance to hackney carriages in other parts of

> the country, but not that particular district? Held: No, it was a local matter and what resembled a hackney carriage elsewhere did not prevent a vehicle being licensed as a private hire vehicle.

This point was considered in *R v Bournemouth Borough Council, ex p Thompson*[1], which concerned a judicial review of a decision by Bournemouth Borough Council to grant a private hire licence to an applicant for an Austin FL2 vehicle. It was similar in appearance to the vehicle that was then being produced as a purpose-built hackney carriage, which was an Austin FX4R. That was the 'classic' London-type cab at the time and apparently the principal distinctions between a FX4R and a FL2 were the absence of a 'For Hire' raised sign on the leading edge of the roof, no division between the front and rear seats, and a front passenger seat.

[1]   (1985) 83 LGR 662.

13.23

The challenge was launched on the grounds that the decision to grant a private hire vehicle licence to such a vehicle was flawed. The application was heard by Mann J, who gave judgment[1]. He considered the facts and then said (at 667):

> 'The only way in which the decision upon his application could be flawed is by an appeal to the principle of irrationality: that is to say the principal adumbrated in *Associated Provincial Picture Houses Ltd v Wednesbury Corporation*[2], to the effect that a decision can be flawed if it is one which no reasonable local authority properly instructed could have reached. Neither the grounds on which relief is sought nor the affidavit in support of the application contain an appeal to that principle.'

He continued:

> 'It suffices for me to say that in regard to the limited function of this court, there is no material before me which would enable me to say that no committee properly instructed could reasonably have reached the conclusion which this committee did in regard to Mr Purkiss's application [the applicant]. They saw the vehicle. They knew all the local conditions. That on a later occasion – 1 November – they took a different view of the matter is, so far as I am concerned, neither here nor there.'

That dealt with the substance of the judicial review and the finding that the decision to grant the licence was not *Wednesbury* unreasonable. In relation to the question of granting an Austin FL2 a private hire vehicle licence, Mann J said (at 667):

> 'What the committee had to ask itself was this: are we satisfied that the FL2 is not of such a design and appearance as to lead to any person to believe that the vehicle is a hackney carriage? I have read the definition of "hackney carriage" incorporated from the Act of 1847 [Town Police Causes Act 1847]. Having regard to that definition, it seems to me that what the committee had to ask itself was this: is the FL2 of such design and appearance as to lead any person to believe that the vehicle is a vehicle plying for hire?

It seems to me that the question has to be asked in relation to the local circumstances. That which may give rise to a belief in London is not necessarily the same as that which might give rise to a belief in Inverness. The likelihood of the belief occurring must depend upon local conditions and upon factors such as – and I would have supposed importantly – the composition of the local hackney carriage fleet. There is, in my judgment, no such thing as a vehicle which, as a matter of law, is in all places to be regarded inexorably as a hackney carriage.'

¹   *R v Bournemouth Borough Council, ex p Thompson* (1985) 83 LGR 662.
²   [1948] KB 223.

13.24

Although the references to Inverness and London are unfortunate (as both are outside the area in which LG(MP)A 1976 can take effect), the judgment is sound. It will be a matter of local consideration for the local authority to decide upon the type of vehicles which it is prepared to licence as private hire vehicles. Obviously, if the hackney carriage fleet in the district is predominately made up of London-style cabs, then it would seem foolish to grant a private hire licence to a vehicle which bore a remarkable similarity to what would be well-known as a hackney carriage in the district. However, if the local hackney fleet is made up more of saloon- and people carrier-type vehicles plus perhaps some Eurotaxis, then the distinguishing factors may well be the question of whether or not roof signs are allowed, whether there is a hackney carriage livery, which must not be replicated on private hire vehicles, and so on. It would be for the local authority to balance these factors and come to its own conclusion in every case.

13.25

It is open to a local authority to impose a livery requirement upon private hire vehicles under LG(MP)A 1976, s 48(2), but although this is not a common option it has been imposed by some authorities.

13.26

The remaining factors contained in LG(MP)A 1976, s 48(1)(a)(iii)–(v) concern the suitability of the mechanical condition of the vehicle and the safety and comfort of the vehicle. This will involve testing the vehicle, but this is not one of the tests permitted under LG(MP)A 1976, s 50(1), and accordingly this initial test does not have to take place within the area of the local authority¹.

¹   See Chapter 8, para 8.143 onwards in relation to the testing of hackney carriages.

CONDITIONS AS TO THE VEHICLE

13.27

Once the local authority is satisfied that the provisions of LG(MP)A 1976, s 48(1) are satisfied, it can then consider whether to impose any conditions under s 48(2). There are a number of conditions which appear to be of almost universal application by local authorities under this provision, including:

- the vehicle must be safe, clean and tidy;
- the plate must be securely attached;
- provision of a first aid kit[1]; and
- provision of a fire extinguisher.

[1] This is a requirement for self-employed drivers under the Health and Safety (First-Aid) Regulations 1981 made under the Health & Safety at Work Etc. Act 1974.

13.28

As LG(MP)A 1976, s 48(2) makes specific reference to signs displayed on the vehicle (either allowing or prohibiting such signs), the question of roof signs can usefully be considered here.

Identification of a private hire vehicle

13.29

The question of how a private hire vehicle is best identified as such, whilst remaining sufficiently different in appearance from a hackney carriage, or an unlicensed private vehicle is one that causes considerable problems to local authorities.

13.30

As mentioned above, there are a number of different approaches taken by local authorities across England and Wales. These often involve some additional identification of the vehicle, over and above the basic requirement to display the identification plate issued by the local authority[1]. Methods used to assist the identification process include:

- front plates as well as rear ones;
- signs on doors and wings carrying specified information;
- roof signs;
- liveries.

[1] The duty placed upon the local authority to issue a plate is contained in LG(MP)A, s 48(5); s 48(6) requires it to be exhibited on the vehicle in accordance with conditions contained in the vehicle licence imposed under s 48(2).

PRIVATE HIRE PLATES

13.31

LG(MP)A 1976, s 48(5) requires that the council issue a plate. That plate must be 'exhibited on the vehicle' in such a way as the council requires, such requirements being specified by a condition attached to the licence. In cases where one plate is issued, the conditions usually require it to be displayed on the rear of the vehicle[1]. Across England and Wales there is a wide variation in private hire plates, with no recognisable standard in relation to size, information printed upon the plate, colour or any other aspect of design. This can be contrasted with the situation prevailing for hackney carriages[2].

1   For the situation with front plates, see para 13.37 below.
2   See Chapter 8, para 8.2.

Solihull Metropolitan Borough Council v Silverline Cars

13.32

> Can a vehicle proprietor appeal against the design of a private hire vehicle plate which a condition of the licence requires them to display? Held: No. The design of the plate (including size) is a matter for the local authority to determine.

The case of *Solihull Metropolitan Borough Council v Silverline Cars*[1] makes it clear that the design and content of the plate is entirely up to the local authority. In this case, Solihull Metropolitan Borough Council introduced a new and larger plate, by way of condition imposed upon the private hire vehicle licence granted under LG(MP)A 1976, s 48, the condition being imposed under s 48(2). The new plate measured four-and-a-half by twelve-and-three-quarter inches and replaced an earlier plate of two-and-three-quarter by three-and-three-quarter inches. The earlier plate was described in the judgment given by Mann LJ as being 'a modest mark'. Silverline Cars were aggrieved by the introduction of the new plate because their business was up-market executive hire where the appearance of the plate four-and-a-half by twelve-and-three-quarter inches would, it was alleged, adversely affect the appearance of their vehicles and, therefore, their overall business profitability. They appealed against the imposition of the condition at the magistrates' court and lost and further appealed to the Crown Court. The Crown Court decided that the new plate was 'a vulgar sign' and allowed the appeal. The local authority appealed by way of case stated. In giving the judgment of the court, Mann LJ stated (at 146L):

> 'In times past, the district council's disc was a sticker, having overall dimensions of 2¾ inches by 3¾ inches; a modest mark. However, in 1987, for reasons which I need not entertain, a larger disc came into use. Its overall dimensions were some 4½ inches by 12¾ inches.
>
> The proprietors operate a business of quality in which discretion is of the utmost importance. Whilst the proprietors were content with the smaller and earlier disc, they do not take to the larger disc which they regard as being not consonant with the nature of their undertaking. Hence the appeal to justices. Hence the appeal to the Crown Court.
>
> I have some sympathy with the proprietors in their dislike of exhibiting the larger disc. I can well understand why they regard such an exhibition as not consonant with their business. However, sympathy is not enough. As I read the statute, the design and form of the plate or disc is wholly a matter for the district council. Their decision as to a particular form of plate or

disc is no doubt subject to judicial review, in the event that the plate or disc is achieved as a result of perversity in accordance with *Associated Provincial Picture Houses Ltd v Wednesbury Corpn* [1948] KB 223. The design is not, however, a matter for the court. The court is concerned, and concerned only, with the condition as to exhibition. The matter of exhibition can be the subject of appeal, the form of the plate or disc is not the subject of appeal.'

[1]   [1989] RTR 142.

13.33

There were four questions raised in this case, concerning the type and exhibition of a private hire plate and they were dealt with comprehensively by the court. As they are useful and important points, the relevant questions and the answers given by Mann LJ[1] (at 147F) are reproduced below in full:

'Turning to the questions posed in this case, I recite them and answer them as follows:

"(a) Whether the size and design of an identification disc can be considered in an appeal against a condition prescribing the matter in which it is to be displayed," the answer is, no.

"(b) Whether on the true construction of section 48(6) of the Act [LG(MP)A 1976, s 48(6)] there is a requirement for a plate or disc to be exhibited on all licensed private hire vehicles subject to the exemptions under section 75 of the Act [LG(MP)A 1976, s 75]," the answer is, yes.

"(c) Whether the nature of the business conducted by the proprietors is relevant when considering an appeal against the condition concerning the manner of display of an identification disc," the answer is, no.

"(d) Whether it is within the court's powers to delete a condition as to display without replacing it with another condition when determining an appeal against a condition imposed under section 48(6) of the Act," the answer is, no. The court can of course vary [a condition].'

[1]   *Solihull Metropolitan Borough Council v Silverline Cars* [1989] RTR 142.

13.34

It is worth noting and does not appear to have been made clear in the *Solihull* case[1], that under LG(MP)A 1976, s 75(3)[2] it is open to the local authority to waive both the requirement to display plates on the vehicle and for the driver to wear a badge if it sees fit[3].

[1]   *Solihull Metropolitan Borough Council v Silverline Cars* [1989] RTR 142.
[2]   See para 13.64 onwards.
[3]   See para 13.64 below.

13.35

Some authorities have plates that simply state the name of the licensing authority, the licence number of the vehicle and the number of passengers it can carry.

Others also include registration number, make and colour of the vehicle and expiry date of the vehicle licence.

13.36

There is no doubt that the more information that can be contained on the plate, the more use it is to members of the public, the authority itself and the police. A number of authorities, who issue new plates on renewal, have a system of colour-coding so that at any given time there are only two colours in existence. This provides an easy visual method of establishing whether the plate has expired, but necessitates the production of a new plate each year. Other authorities are able to make their plates last for many years, as the information on them does not change. It is entirely a matter for the local authorities concerned.

13.37

Some authorities impose a condition that there should be a front as well as a rear plate, again to enable members of the public to identify private hire vehicles more readily.

13.38

The requirement to display the plate can be lifted in one of two ways. First, under LG(MP)A 1976, s 75(1)(d), if there is a contract for the hire of that specific vehicle for a period exceeding 24 hours. Secondly, under s 75(3), which allows the local authority to specify either certain occasions when the plate need not be displayed or, alternatively, that the district council can issue a notice which can be carried effectively in lieu of the plate being displayed[1].

[1]   See para 13.64 below in relation to 'Executive Hire'.

FRONT PLATES

13.39

The usual requirement is for the plate issued under s 48(5) to be required to be securely affixed to the rear of the vehicle[1]. A number of local authorities issue a second plate which is required to be fixed to the front of the vehicle. This is certainly a useful additional identification feature, making it clear that the vehicle is licensed when approached (or approaching) from the front. The DfT *Best Practice Guide*[2] commends this approach in the following terms:

> 'The licence plate is a helpful indicator of licensed status and, as such, it helps identification if licence plates are displayed on the front as well as the rear of vehicles.'

This is only part of the DfT Guidance on private hire vehicle identification. The remaining elements will be considered below in connection with the other methods outlined above.

[1]   See para 13.31 above.

² DfT, *'Taxi and Private Hire Vehicle Licensing: Best Practice Guidance'* (October 2006, revised March 2010), para 38, available from http://www.dft.gov.uk/pgr/regional/taxis/taxiandprivatehirevehicle lic1792. See Appendix II.

SIGNS ON DOORS AND WINGS CARRYING SPECIFIED INFORMATION

13.40

In recent years a number of local authorities have introduced requirements (by conditions attached to private hire vehicle licences) to display signs on the vehicle in a specified format. They often include phrases such as 'Advanced Bookings Only' or 'Pre-booked Journeys Only', and in some cases, statements that the passengers will not be covered by insurance if the vehicle was not correctly pre-booked via a private hire operator. The conditions will specify where these signs must be located, usually on the nearside and off-side doors, sometimes on the front or rear wings, and occasionally on the front or rear of the vehicle.

13.41

Again, the DfT *Best Practice Guide*[1] addresses this:

> 'a licence condition which requires a sign on the vehicle in a specified form. This will often be a sign of a specified size and shape which identifies the operator (with a telephone number for bookings) and the local licensing authority, and which also has some words such as 'pre-booked only'. This approach seems the best practice; it identifies the vehicle as private hire and helps to avoid confusion with a taxi, but also gives useful information to the public wishing to make a booking. It is good practice for vehicle identification for PHVs to include the contact details of the operator.'

¹ DfT, *'Taxi and Private Hire Vehicle Licensing: Best Practice Guidance'* (October 2006, revised March 2010), para 38, available from http://www.dft.gov.uk/pgr/regional/taxis/taxiandprivatehirevehicle lic1792. See Appendix II.

13.42

There has been debate over the way in which these signs are attached to the vehicle. They can either be adhesive and fixed permanently to the vehicle, or magnetic and be capable of being removed.

13.43

The magnetic ones are claimed to damage the paintwork of the car less than the adhesive versions, which can leave a discoloured mark on removal if they are attached for a long time. However, the ease of removal of magnetic signs leaves them vulnerable to theft, and also to use on unlicensed vehicles. As a private hire vehicle is always a private hire vehicle[1] and the plates should never be removed whilst the vehicle is licensed, the same applies to the additional signs. This certainly appears to be a compelling argument in favour of the permanently attached adhesive versions. The arguments against are the discolouration of the paintwork and consequent loss in resale value of the vehicle.

¹   See *Benson v Boyce* [1997] RTR 226, para 13.72 below.

13.44

As private hire vehicles are working vehicles, the costs associated with their use as private hire vehicles, including depreciation, must be taken into account and when balanced against the problems and risks associated with magnetic signs would seem to be sufficient reasons to require their use. To date there is no senior court decision on the point.

ROOF SIGNS

13.45

A number of authorities either allow or, in some cases, require, signs to be affixed to the doors, bonnets, boots and wings of private hire vehicles, stating the company name, telephone number etc, and this is clearly allowable as a condition under LG(MP)A 1976, s 48(2)¹. Some authorities go further and require signs stating, 'Pre-booked only' or similar words to reinforce the fact that a private hire vehicle cannot ply for hire. There has for some years been less certainty over the question of roof signs on private hire vehicles.

¹   See Appendix I.

13.46

Hackney carriages have traditionally had roof signs. Some of these illuminate only when the vehicle is for hire (as on purpose-built vehicles) and others remain illuminated all the time. Such signs can also be used on private hire vehicles but there are certain restrictions. The Transport Act 1980, s 64 states:

'64 Roof-signs on vehicles other than taxis

(1) There shall not, in any part of England and Wales outside the metropolitan police district and the City of London, be displayed on or above the roof of any vehicle which is used for carrying passengers for hire or reward but which is not a taxi—

(a)   any sign which consists of or includes the word "taxi" or "cab", whether in the singular or plural, or "hire", or any word of similar meaning or appearance to any of those words, whether alone or as part of another word; or

(b)   any sign, notice, mark, illumination or other feature which may suggest that the vehicle is a taxi.

(2) Any person who knowingly—

(a)   drives a vehicle in respect of which subsection (1) is contravened; or

(b)   causes or permits that subsection to be contravened in respect of any vehicle, shall be liable on summary conviction to a fine not exceeding £200.

(3) In this section "taxi" means a vehicle licensed under section 37 of the Town Police Clauses Act 1847, section 6 of the Metropolitan Carriage

Act 1869, section 10 of the Civic Government (Scotland) Act 1982 or any similar local enactment.'

It can be seen quite clearly from that wording that roof signs per se are not themselves illegal on private hire vehicles, but certain words are outlawed.

Yakhya v Tee

13.47

> Is a roof sign on a private hire vehicle displaying the telephone number of the operator unlawful? Held: No, only the proscribed words were illegal.

This matter was considered in *Yakhya v Tee*[1]. This case concerned a prosecution brought by Reading Borough Council against a driver of a private hire vehicle which was displaying a roof sign. On the roof sign was a telephone number. He was prosecuted under the Transport Act 1980, s 64 and convicted. He appealed by way of case stated. The appeal was heard by Robert Goff LJ and Mann J. Judgment was given by Mann J. In relation to the sign itself, he stated (at 124C):

> 'All that was stated about the sign on the roof is that it bore black numerals on a light background, the last four digits of which were 8888. However, it was agreed before the court that the whole sign was a telephone number.'

Reference was made to the case of *Breame v Anderson*[2] which concerned a similar provision of the London Cab Act 1968, s 4. In his judgment in this case, Mann J quoted (at 125A) from the judgment in *Breame*:

> 'Lord Parker CJ said, at p 39C, that the test for determining whether or not there had been a contravention of that provision [London Cab Act 1968, s 4] was:
>
> > "In my judgment one just looks at the vehicle with the sign on it, and asks as a matter of common sense: does it suggest that the vehicle is immediately for hire?"
>
> Ashworth J said, at p 39E:
>
> > "one looks at the sign on the vehicle and asks: does it suggest that which is forbidden?"'

Mann J then continued (at 125C):

> 'In our judgment, a court has to look at the vehicle of itself and in no particular context but with the sign on it and then ask, as a matter of common sense: does the sign suggest that the vehicle is a taxi?
>
> Applying that test, we ask: did the sign suggest that the vehicle was a taxi? The sign suggests a number of things. Amongst others it suggests that the vehicle was available for hire on a telephone call or it suggests a means of identifying the vehicle that a caller had ordered. Accordingly, and applying the test in *Breame v Anderson* we are of the opinion that the

conclusion reached by the justices [to convict] was such that no properly instructed and reasonable bench of justices could have reached. In fairness to the justices we record that *Breame v Anderson* was not drawn to their attention.

We now respond to the question which the justices ask. The first is:

"Whether the justices were correct in deciding that the sign displayed on the roof contravened the subsection in that it may have suggested that the vehicle was a taxi."

The answer is no. The second is:

"whether the justices were correct in inferring that any sign displayed on the roof of a private hire vehicle, and in particular a sign containing a telephone number, would be in contravention of the subsection."

The answer is no.'

1   [1984] RTR 122.
2   [1971] RTR 31.

13.48

As a consequence, a few local authorities have either allowed or insisted upon roof signs on private hire vehicles[1]. The rationale behind such requirements is to aid the identification of private hire vehicles for the public. This is a matter that is seen as especially important in large urban areas, where a major problem concerns the use of unlicensed 'pirate' vehicles (that is, unlicensed vehicles driven by unlicensed drivers and not operated by a licensed operator).

1   For example, for a number of years in the 1990s, this included Manchester, where the roof sign carried the telephone number and name of the firm, but that policy was reversed and roof signs on private hire vehicles are now prohibited by condition. In Newcastle-upon-Tyne, where the sign contains the telephone number and the words 'Advance Booking Only' they are optional, whilst Luton Borough Council make it a mandatory requirement.

13.49

The argument against roof signs is usually that they will lead to confusion in the minds of the public between private hire vehicles and hackney carriages but, in certain areas, this argument is weakened. In districts where all hackney carriages have to be purpose-built, whereas private hire vehicles will include saloon cars, estate cars and people carriers, the distinction will already be reasonably obvious. It is acknowledged that this argument about confusion would be much more apparent in an area where saloon-type vehicles were licensed as hackney carriages.

13.50

The DfT *Best Practice Guide*[1] does not regard the use of roof signs on private hire vehicles in a favourable light:

'Another approach, possibly in conjunction with the previous option, is a requirement for a roof-mounted, permanently illuminated sign with words such as 'pre-booked only'. But it can be argued that any roof-mounted sign, however unambiguous its words, is liable to create confusion with a taxi. So roof-mounted signs on PHVs are not seen as best practice.'

However, they are clearly used effectively in a number of local authority areas, and have the benefit of judicial approval.

[1] DfT, '*Taxi and Private Hire Vehicle Licensing: Best Practice Guidance*' (October 2006, revised March 2010), para 8 available from http://www.dft.gov.uk/pgr/regional/taxis/taxiandprivatehirevehicle lic1792. See Appendix II.

LIVERIES

13.51

It is open to a local authority to adopt a policy requiring a livery for private hire vehicles in just the same way as for hackney carriages[1]. To date this has not been a common approach, although some local authorities have adopted such a policy. In many other cases, the requirements for private hire colours or liveries are more simply expressed as not being the same colour as liveried hackney carriages.

[1] See Chapter 8, para 8.124 above in relation to hackney carriage liveries.

AGE POLICIES

13.52

Another consideration is the age of the vehicle in question. A number of authorities have age policies. It is arguable that these are even more important in relation to private hire vehicles than they are in relation to hackney carriages, as no private hire vehicles are purpose-built, whereas in most districts there are at least a few purpose-built hackney carriages[1].

[1] For discussion of age policies and the requirements that enable them to be adopted and used successfully in relation to hackney carriages, see Chapter 8, para 8.108 onwards.

STRETCHED LIMOUSINES

13.53

In the last few years there has been an enormous increase in the use of stretched limousines, 'a dramatically elongated saloon motorcar which is becoming familiar on our streets[1]', which have moved from their traditional use as wedding and funeral cars[2] into the mainstream private hire arena. Their use includes all the usual private hire uses, plus 'special occasions' such as outings to the races, transport to parties and balls, hen and stag nights, and children's birthday parties.

[1] Per Pitchford J in *Vehicle and Operator Services Agency v Johnson* [2003] EWHC 2104 (Admin), (2003) 167 JP 497, Admin Ct, at para 1 (see para 13.58 below).
[2] Cars used in connection with a wedding (and, it seems, a civil partnership ceremony) or funerals are exempt from private hire licensing by virtue of LG(MP)A 1976, s 75(1)(c) and (cc). See Chapter 12, para 12.126 onwards for further details.

13.54

In itself, this should not pose a problem. The services provided are those provided by private hire vehicles and there is no reason why the provisions do not apply to these vehicles. There are, however, some problems that have been encountered, including:

- some of these vehicles seat more than eight passengers;
- many of them have left-hand drive;
- many of them originate from the US;
- many of them have been converted or modified after manufacture;
- many of them have tinted windows; and
- due to their US origin, parts availability may be difficult.

13.55

For these and other reasons, a great many local authorities have been reluctant to licence these vehicles, and to insist that the operators and drivers are also correctly licensed. Unfortunately, this means that the public are being put at risk through untested and unlicensed vehicles, operators and drivers. This is addressed in the DfT *Best Practice Guide*[1] where it states:

> **'Stretched Limousines**
>
> http://www.vosa.gov.uk/vosa/vosalocations/vosaenforecementoffices.htm)
>
> 40. Local licensing authorities are sometimes asked to license stretched limousines as PHVs. It is suggested that local authorities should approach such requests on the basis that these vehicles – where they have fewer than nine passenger seats – have a legitimate role to play in the private hire trade, meeting a public demand. Indeed, the Department's view is that it is not a legitimate course of action for licensing authorities to adopt policies that exclude limousines as a matter of principle and that any authorities which do adopt such practices are leaving themselves open to legal challenge. A policy of excluding limousines creates an unacceptable risk to the travelling public, as it would inevitably lead to higher levels of unlawful operation. Public safety considerations are best supported by policies that allow respectable, safe operators to obtain licences on the same basis as other private hire vehicle operators. The Department has now issued guidance on the licensing arrangements for stretched limousines. This can be accessed on the Department's web-site at http://www.dft.gov.uk/pgr/regional/taxis/stretchlimousines.pdf.
>
> 41. The limousine guidance makes it clear that most operations are likely to fall within the PHV licensing category and not into the small bus category. VOSA will be advising limousine owners that if they intend to provide a private hire service then they should go to the local authority for PHV licences. The Department would expect licensing authorities to assess applications on their merits; and, as necessary, to be proactive in ascertaining whether any limousine operators might already be providing an unlicensed service within their district.

42. Imported stretched limousines were historically checked for compliance with regulations under the Single Vehicle Approval (SVA) inspection regime before they were registered. This is now the Individual Vehicle Approval (IVA) scheme. The IVA test verifies that the converted vehicle is built to certain safety and environmental standards. A licensing authority might wish to confirm that an imported vehicle was indeed tested by VOSA for IVA before being registered and licensed (taxed) by DVLA. This can be done either by checking the V5C (Registration Certificate) of the vehicle, which may refer to IVA under the "Special Note" section; or by writing to VOSA, Ellipse, Padley Road, Swansea, SA1 8AN, including details of the vehicle's make and model, registration number and VIN number.

43. Stretched limousines which clearly have more than 8 passenger seats should not of course be licensed as PHVs because they are outside the licensing regime for PHVs. However, under some circumstances the SVA regime accepted vehicles with space for more than 8 passengers, particularly where the precise number of passenger seats was hard to determine. In these circumstances, if the vehicle had obtained an SVA certificate, the authority should consider the case on its merits in deciding whether to license the vehicle under the strict condition that the vehicle will not be used to carry more than 8 passengers, bearing in mind that refusal may encourage illegal private hire operation.

44. Many councils are concerned that the size of limousines prevents them being tested in conventional MoT garages. If there is not a suitable MoT testing station in the area then it would be possible to test the vehicle at the local VOSA test stations. The local enforcement office may be able to advise (contact details on http://www.vosa.gov.uk).'

[1]   DfT, 'Taxi and Private Hire Vehicle Licensing: Best Practice Guidance' (October 2006, revised March 2010), paras 40–44, available at http://www.dft.gov.uk/pgr/regional/taxis/taxiandprivatehire vehiclelic1792. See Appendix II.

13.56

In August 2011 the DfT issued 'Private Hire Vehicle Licensing – A note for guidance from the Department for Transport'[1] which gave 'sector specific' Guidance. In relation to stretched limousines it states:

'Stretched limousines

32. The Department considers that most stretched limousine operations (where the vehicle has fewer than nine passenger seats) are likely to fall within the PHV licensing regime.

33. Essentially these vehicles are luxury versions of conventional "minicabs". They are in the business of transporting passengers, normally in a group, from a pick up point to a destination. They focus on providing this service in a luxurious way, but they are, nevertheless, providing a straightforward transportation service. The operator will, of course, want to be sure that the driver is highly skilled in terms of customer service.

However, aside from the size and quality of the vehicle and the possibility of in-vehicle entertainment, there is no discernible difference in the function and service provided between a conventional minicab and a stretched limousine.

34. The Department's Best Practice Guidance provides further information about the licensing of stretched limousines, for example approval certification, how to test the vehicles and how to establish the number of seats.

35. Taking account of the principles set out in Part One of this guidance note, the Department takes the view that typical stretched limousine operations should be licensed because they involve:
- a commercial benefit on the part of the driver/organiser;
- the carrying of passengers as a main part of the service;
- drivers who are unlikely to have been vetted for wider work;
- driver duties which are restricted to driving and assisting with luggage; and
- the sort of service which Parliament would have had in mind when passing the relevant legislation.'

¹   This superseded the January 2008 Department for Transport – *Guidance for operators of stretch limousines*, although that Guidance has never been formally cancelled It is contained in Appendix II.

13.57

Obviously, if a stretched limousine seats more than eight passengers, it cannot be licensed as a private hire vehicle and would need to be licensed by the Traffic Commissioners as a public service vehicle (PSV).

Number of seats

Vehicle and Operator Services Agency v Johnson

13.58

> When a vehicle has curved seating accommodation, is the capacity simply a multiple of the 400mm per person per seat, or can the design be taken into account? Held: The design, number of seat belts and the type of vehicle can all be taken into account when calculating the seating capacity.

One problem regularly encountered is establishing just how many seats a stretched limousine has. This was considered in the case of *Vehicle and Operator Services Agency v Johnson*¹. This was important as the question of whether the particular vehicle in question was a PSV or a private hire vehicle rested on the decision. The case concerned a stretched limousine and the offences were outlined at para 1 of the judgment:

'(1) using a public service vehicle without a certificate of initial fitness or a certificate under sections 55-58 Road Traffic Act 1988, contrary to section 6 Public Passenger Vehicles Act 1981; (2) using a public service vehicle when it was not operated under a public service vehicle operator's licence granted under Part 2 Public Passenger Vehicles Act 1981 contrary to section 12 of that Act; (3) permitting the driver to drive a public service vehicle carrying nine passengers for hire or reward otherwise than in accordance with the licence authorising him to drive vehicles of that class, contrary to section 87(2) Road Traffic Act 1988 and Schedule II Road Traffic Offenders Act 1988. "Vehicles of that class" were, for these purposes, a public service vehicle.'

The magistrates dismissed the case as they concluded that the vehicle was not a PSV as it was not 'a vehicle adapted to carry more than eight passengers' (Public Passenger Vehicles Act 1981, s 1(1)) and therefore no offence had been committed. The prosecutor appealed to the High Court. The case was heard by Pitchford J.

He outlined the question as follows (at para 3):

'A series of decisions of the Divisional Court, over which Lord Parker CJ presided, settled, it is common ground, that the word "adapted" used in subsection 1(1) means not "altered" but "apt", "fit" or "suitable". These decisions were *Maddox v Storer* [1962] 1 All ER 831, *Burns v Currell* [1963] 2 All ER 297 and *Wurzal v Addison* [1965] 1 All ER 20. The question for the justices was whether the vehicle as constructed was suitable for carrying nine passengers. They found it was not, and the question posed in the case stated is this:

"Were we right in finding that the stretch limousine registration MIL 2597 was not adapted to carry more than eight passengers and was therefore not a public service vehicle for the purposes of the statute and the regulations?"'

The decision revolved around the seating available. By virtue of the Public Service Vehicle (Conditions of Fitness, Equipment, Use and Certification) Regulations 1981, reg 28(1)(b), a length of 400mm measured along the front of each seat is required for each passenger. In this vehicle, the seating was not in rows, but ranged around the inside of the vehicle, some of it in an 'L' shape. Although by measuring the front edge of the seat, there was sufficient space, as a multiple of 400mm, to accommodate six people, that overlooked the effect of the corner, which reduced the available room for the passengers legs significantly. Pitchford J put it thus (at para 8):

'If the correct approach was to treat the corner seat as a straight line continuation of the bench seats, the total measurement would be 2,400 mm, which would be just enough to accommodate six people sitting in line, each occupying 400 mm each. However, the justices were not dealing with a single straight-line bench seat ... They were dealing, in effect, with an L-shaped bench whose effect was to create a corner space which could not be occupied by a passenger on one side of the corner without encroaching on the space available to a passenger on the other side of the corner. Undoubtedly six persons could squash themselves into the space available, and it is suggested that that was the case on the night [in question]. But to do so would reduce the length of the seat for use by one of those passengers below 400 mm.'

He continued (at para 9):

'Additional factors addressed to the justices were the presence of eight seat belts and the purpose of the vehicle as a luxury carrier. In this connection the justices' attention was drawn to a passage in the 20th edition of *Wilkinson's Road Traffic Offences* at page 851, in which the editors express the following opinion:

"A tantalising problem has arisen with the emergence of the 'stretch limo'. These are often designed to provide generous accommodation but for no more than eight passengers. However, the generosity of the seating space allowed is such that far more than 400 mm is given for each seat. Seat belts may be provided for only eight passengers. The question arises as to whether this is a public service vehicle. It is submitted that the nature of the use to which the vehicle is put and the requirements regarding seat belts … combine to exclude such vehicles from the definition."

10. I have no doubt that both the design of seating space provided and the number of seat belts fitted will (depending upon the circumstances) be relevant considerations. It seems to me, however, that they can seldom be determinative of the issue whether a vehicle is suitable for the carriage of more than eight passengers. Were that to be so, the operator could avoid the plain purpose of the legislation by relying on style rather than the substance of the accommodation.'

He concluded as follows (at para 11):

'It does not seem to me that the justices gave undue weight to style. While they accepted that the seating space was intended to be more generous for a passenger in a stretch limousine than in a standard car or taxi, their decision was that in normal use it was not practicable for the vehicle to carry a ninth passenger. The vehicle was not designed and laid out to carry more than eight passengers. It seems to me that the justices' observation as to the generosity of seating was apt when one considers the natural compartments into which the bench seating was divided.

12 In deciding that mere straight line measurement was not appropriate to judge the accommodation, which included a corner seat and the short arm of the L to which I have referred, I consider the justices exercised sound judgment and common sense. Their decision was, in my view, plainly open to them on the facts. Accordingly, it is my view that the question posed for the opinion of this court should be answered "yes" and the appeal should be dismissed.'

¹   [2003] EWHC 2104 (Admin), (2003) 167 JP 497, Admin Ct.

13.59

The DfT Guidance[1] and the decision in *Vehicle and Operator Services Agency v Johnson*[2] support the view that these vehicles are licensable as private hire vehicles, the only exceptions being their use either as a small PSV charging separate fares or as a small PSV where their use form a 'small part' of PSV operator's business[3]. The DfT has made it clear that it is for local authorities to decide whether to license these vehicles and to take enforcement action if they do not licence them.

[1] DfT, '*Taxi and Private Hire Vehicle Licensing: Best Practice Guidance*' (October 2006, revised March 2010), paras 40–44, available at http://www.dft.gov.uk/pgr/regional/taxis/taxiandprivatehire vehiclelic1792. See Appendix II.
[2] (30 July 2003, unreported), Admin Ct.
[3] Transport Act 2000, s 265. See Chapter 12, para 12.160 onwards and also Department for Transport letter, 9 September 2002 (see Appendix II).

13.60

In addition, by virtue of LG(MP)A 1976, s 48(1)(a) before a local authority can license a vehicle as a private hire vehicle it must be satisfied that the vehicle is:

'(i) suitable in type, size and design for use as a private hire vehicle;
(ii) not of such design and appearance as to lead any person to believe that the vehicle is a hackney carriage;
(iii) in a suitable mechanical condition;
(iv) safe; and
(v) comfortable.'

It is therefore necessary for a local authority to consider any stretched limousine in the light of these matters, plus their own vehicle policies and conditions.

13.61

It may be the case that these vehicles do not fit within a local authority's existing policies for private hire vehicles, but the authority can introduce a different set of conditions for stretched limousines and indeed, a number of local authorities have done this.

13.62

Turning to the other problems mentioned at para 13.31 above, these are not insurmountable matters for local authorities to overcome. They need to be considered in the light of LG(MP)A 1976, s 48. Many of the difficulties which these vehicles present are ultimately matters of mechanical assessment, inspection and enforcement and as such, are not in themselves any more of a problem to local authorities than existing vehicles.

13.63

As public safety is paramount, if local authorities do licence these vehicles, they must, of course, be satisfied that they can do so safely. Conversely, if they do not licence them, then the public need to be alerted to the risks that they expose themselves to by using these vehicles, and the local authority needs to take firm enforcement action, as these are unlicensed 'pirate' vehicles.

'EXECUTIVE' HIRE

13.64

There are a large number of companies who provide what they refer to as 'Executive Hire Cars'. Although clearly private hire vehicles, they are often used by companies and firms to transport visitors, senior staff members etc and are seen as being more akin to a chauffeur driven vehicle than a private hire vehicle. In many cases they will have an exemption from the requirement to display a plate, granted by the local authority under LG(MP)A 1976, s 75(3). This states:

'(3) Where a licence under section 48 of this Act is in force for a vehicle, the council which issued the licence may, by a notice in writing given to the proprietor of the vehicle, provide that paragraph (a) of subsection (6) of that section shall not apply to the vehicle on any occasion specified in the notice or shall not so apply while the notice is carried in the vehicle; and on any occasion on which by virtue of this subsection that paragraph does not apply to a vehicle section 54(2)(a) of this Act shall not apply to the driver of the vehicle.'

It can be seen that such a notice removes the need to display a plate and also dispenses with the requirement contained in s 54(2)[1] that the driver should wear his 'badge in such position and manner as to be plainly and distinctly visible'.

[1]   See Appendix I.

13.65

Notwithstanding this exemption contained in the Act, there is no definition of 'executive' car and it is for each local authority to decide which vehicles will be granted such an exemption. In the past, this tended to be decided on a case by case basis, but a number of local authorities have now adopted standards for the vehicles for which they will grant such an exemption. This usually involves not only the absence of a plate, but also removal of the common conditions requiring additional signage to be displayed on private hire vehicles. It may also allow features on the vehicle which would not normally be acceptable for a private hire vehicle including dark tinted glass to the rear windows.

There are a number of questions that the local authority need to consider when formulating and 'executive hire' policy:

* Why should the vehicle be exempt from displaying plates (and the driver exempt from the requirement to wear his badge) in the first place?
* In what circumstances would the authority allow the exemption to apply, because it should be recognised that it does not have to be whole time exemption?; and finally
* What types of vehicles would the authority wish to bring within this policy?

13.66

Such relaxation of requirements is often allied to a condition restricting the use of the vehicle to 'executive' use, although such definitions have proved difficult to determine. The aim is to enable these vehicles to be used for their more selective purpose and avoid them being used in situations where the absence of identification features might cause problems (such as late night city and town centre use), with either the licensed vehicle itself being overlooked by a passenger who had made a booking with the operator, or by allowing unlicensed vehicles to masquerade as licensed 'executive' vehicles.

13.67

Any use of the vehicle for 'normal' private hire use would then be a breach of condition, which could lead to revocation or suspension of the vehicle licence. As with so much in the areas of private hire (and hackney carriage) licensing, ultimately this will all depend on regular and effective enforcement.

There is no right of appeal against a decision by the local authority to refuse to grant an exemption under s 75(3) and the only direct means of challenge would be judicial review. However, as the requirement to display any additional signage over the plate would be imposed by means of condition attached to the vehicle licence, it is possible to appeal against those requirements. As the requirement to display the plate is a statutory requirement under s 48(6) it would only be an appeal against the additional signage.

THE PRIVATE HIRE VEHICLE LICENCE ITSELF

13.68

LG(MP)A 1976, s 48(3) and (4) outlines the requirements of the actual licence:

'(3) In every vehicle licence granted under this section there shall be specified—
(a) the name and address of—
   (i)   the applicant; and
   (ii) every other person who is a proprietor of the private hire vehicle in respect of which the licence is granted, or who is concerned, either solely or in partnership with any other person, in the keeping, employing or letting on hire of the private hire vehicle;
(b) the number of the licence which shall correspond with the number to be painted or marked on the plate or disc to be exhibited on the private hire vehicle in accordance with subsection (6) of this section;
(c) the conditions attached to the grant of the licence; and
(d) such other particulars as the district council consider reasonably necessary.
(4) Every licence granted under this section shall—
(a) be signed by an authorised officer of the council which granted it;
(b) relate to not more than one private hire vehicle; and

(c) remain in force for such period not being longer than one year as the
     district council may specify in the licence.'

13.69

The licence must include:

*   the name and address of the applicant;
*   the name and address of anyone else with an interest in the vehicle;
*   the number of the licence;
*   any conditions attached to the licence; and
*   such other particulars as the district council consider reasonably necessary.

Some authorities use this to include the make, colour and appearance of the
vehicle, together with the number of seats for passengers that it is licensed to
carry.

13.70

The licence itself can be granted for up to a year and must be signed by an
authorised officer[1] of the council.

[1]   An authorised officer is defined in s 80 as 'any officer of a district council authorised in writing
      by the council for the purposes of this Part of this Act'.

ALWAYS A PRIVATE HIRE VEHICLE

13.71

Once a vehicle has been licensed as a private hire vehicle, does that mean it is
always a private hire vehicle, in a similar manner to a hackney carriage[1]? The
answer is yes, as is clearly determined in the case of *Benson v Boyce*[2].

[1]   See *Hawkins v Edwards* [1901] 2 KB 169; see Chapter 8, para 8.4 and *Yates v Gates* [1970] 1 All
      ER 754, QBD (Chapter 8, para 8.5) which quite clearly states that a hackney carriage is always
      a hackney carriage.
[2]   [1997] RTR 226.

Benson v Boyce

13.72

> When not carrying passengers, can a private hire vehicle be driven a person
> who does not hold a private hire drivers' licence? Held: No, it is always a
> private hire vehicle and can only be driven by a licensed private hire driver,
> irrespective of whether it is carrying passengers.

In the case of *Benson v Boyce*[1] the question of whether a private hire vehicle
was always a private hire vehicle was addressed. This case concerned a vehicle
which was licensed as a private hire vehicle, but which was being driven

by a person who did not hold a private hire driver's licence. The question raised was whether a private hire vehicle is only a private hire vehicle (and, therefore, only needs to be driven by a person with a private hire driver's licence) when it is working as a private hire vehicle or is it (following the approach taken in *Yates v Gates*[2] in relation to hackney carriages) always a private hire vehicle, irrespective of whether or not it is working? Mance J delivered a lengthy judgment on behalf of the Divisional Court. In the course of this he referred to both *Yates v Gates* and *Kingston upon Hull City Council v Wilson*[3]. He observed that there was no reference to *Yates v Gates* in the *Kingston upon Hull* case. Although he did not appear to regard the *Kingston upon Hull* case as conflicting with his conclusion (or, indeed, *Yates v Gates*), he concluded (at 236G):

> 'I consider that the correct interpretation of section 46(1)(b) is that it applies to all driving in a controlled district of a vehicle characterised under section 80(1) as a private hire vehicle, whatever the specific activity in connection with which the vehicle is in fact being driven. The two questions raised by the case stated are:
> (1)   Whether it is correct that the wording "provided for hire" in section 80 of the Local Government (Miscellaneous Provisions) Act 1976 relates to the nature of the vehicle rather than to the nature of the activity?
> (2)   Whether, on the correct interpretation of Part II of the Local Government (Miscellaneous Provisions) Act 1976, the Prosecution must prove an actual hiring of the vehicle in question at the material time in order to obtain a conviction for an offence under section 46(1) (*b*) of that Act?
> In the context of this case, I would answer the first question in the affirmative and the second in the negative. I would therefore uphold the Justices' conviction of the appellant and dismiss the appeal.'

---

[1]   [1997] RTR 226.

[2]   [1970] 1 All ER 754, QBD; see Chapter 8, para 8.4.

[3]   (1995) Times, 25 July. In *Kingston upon Hull City Council v Wilson* the judge concluded that a vehicle could be licensed as a hackney carriage in one district and as a private hire vehicle in another district. At no time was any reference made to the decisions in *Hawkins v Edwards* [1901] 2 KB 169 or *Yates v Gates* [1970] 1 All ER 754, QBD, which quite clearly state that a hackney carriage is always a hackney carriage. In conflict with this, Buxton J concluded that a vehicle could indeed be a hackney carriage in one district and a private hire vehicle in a second district.

13.73

Accordingly, a vehicle cannot be a hackney carriage at some time and a private hire vehicle at another time in different districts if the characteristics of either vehicle are that they are, at all times, a hackney carriage or a private hire vehicle. Local authorities should therefore enquire whether a vehicle has been licensed in another district as a hackney carriage before they consider the grant of a private hire vehicle licence.

13.74

The consequence of this is that, at all times, a private hire vehicle must be driven by a person who holds a private hire driver's licence issued by the same authority as that which licensed the car[1].

[1]   See Chapter 14, para 14.2.

13.75

Failure to comply with this requirement will lead to an offence being committed under s 46(1)(b) of the 1976 Act. In addition, it is also possible that the driver will not be insured to drive the vehicle, which is an offence under the Road Traffic Act 1988, s 143[1].

[1]   See para 13.105 onwards, below.

METERS AND FARES

13.76

There is no power in any Act allowing a local authority to set the fares charged by private hire vehicles. It is entirely a matter for negotiation (forming a binding contract) between the hirer and the operator as to the fare that will be charged. However, that provision can be limited if a meter is fitted to the vehicle.

13.77

Again, there is no power that enables a local authority to require a meter to be fitted, but if one is fitted, LG(MP)A 1976, s 71 comes into play[1]. This states:

'**71 Taximeters**

(1) Nothing in this Act shall require any private hire vehicle to be equipped with any form of taximeter but no private hire vehicle so equipped shall be used for hire in a controlled district unless such taximeter has been tested and approved by or on behalf of the district council for the district or any other district council by which a vehicle licence in force for the vehicle was issued.

(2) Any person who—
(a)   tampers with any seal on any taximeter without lawful excuse; or
(b)   alters any taximeter with intent to mislead; or
(c)   knowingly causes or permits a vehicle of which he is the proprietor to be used in contravention of subsection (1) of this section.
shall be guilty of an offence.'

[1]   Within Greater London, it is illegal for a private hire vehicle to be fitted with a taximeter. The question of whether a smartphone (an advanced mobile telephone) which recorded distance and time was a taximeter was considered in *Transport for London v Uber London Ltd and Ors* [2015] EWHC 2918 (Admin). The High Court concluded that such a device was not a taximeter for these purposes. See Chapter 22, para 22.26 for full details.

13.78

It should be noted, however, that whilst the taximeter has to be tested and approved, there is still no power for the local authority to set a fare. The only time in which there is any form of control over the fare charged for private hire use is when a hackney carriage is used for pre-booked purposes. This only applies when the vehicle is booked other than by hailing in the street or being approached at a rank; that is, when it is pre-booked by telephone or any other means, irrespective of whether it is being dispatched by a private hire operator[1].

[1] For the use of hackney carriages for pre-booked purposes, see para 13.92.

13.79

A hackney carriage used for pre-booked purposes cannot charge more than the metered fare. In other words, the maximum that can be charged is the fare that is displayed on the meter, the meter being sealed by the licensing authority that issued the hackney carriage licence in accordance with its table of fares. However, there is nothing to prevent a hackney carriage used for either hackney carriage or pre-booked purposes charging less than the metered fare[1].

[1] See *Liverpool City Council v Curzon Ltd* (12 November 1993, unreported), QBD; see Chapter 9, para 9.29 onwards.

13.80

The authority for this proposition is s 67 of the Local Government (Miscellaneous Provisions) Act 1976 which states[1]:

'67 Hackney carriages used for private hire

(1) No hackney carriage shall be used in the district under contract or purported contract for private hire except at a rate of fares or charges not greater than that fixed by the byelaws or table mentioned in section 66 of this Act, and, when any such hackney carriage is so used, the fare or charge shall be calculated from the point in the district at which the hirer commences his journey.

(2) Any person who knowingly contravenes this section shall be guilty of an offence.

(3) In subsection (1) of this section "contract" means—

(a) a contract made otherwise than while the relevant hackney carriage is plying for hire in the district or waiting at a place in the district which, when the contract is made, is a stand for hackney carriages appointed by the district council under section 63 of this Act; and

(b) a contract made, otherwise than with or through the driver of the relevant hackney carriage, while it is so plying or waiting.'

[1] It is unfortunate that the legislation refers to the use of a hackney carriage for private hire purposes. It is clear that a hackney carriage cannot be a private hire vehicle (see LG(MP)A 1976, s 80) and a pre-booked hackney carriage is not undertaking private hire work, as that can only be undertaken by a private hire vehicle. The preferred term is 'pre-booked hackney carriage work' using the inherent right of a hackney carriage to undertake such work – see Chapter 8, para 8.155 onwards.

13.81

This section refers to the use of a hackney carriage 'in the district'. It is not clear whether this means the district in which the hackney carriage is licensed, or the district in which a hackney carriage is being used. However, in s 80 (the interpretation section) 'the district' is defined in the following terms:

'"the district", in relation to a district council in whose area the provisions of this Part of this Act are in force, means—
(a) if those provisions are in force throughout the area of the council, that area; and
(b) if those provisions are in force for part only of the area of the council, that part of that area;'

That would appear to mean that a hackney carriage used in any district in which the 1976 Act has been adopted cannot charge more than the fares set by the council that licensed that hackney carriage, as determined via that hackney carriage's meter. However, there is an alternative view that it only applies to the district in which it is licensed. In the absence of authority, it is difficult to be certain, but it is suggested that the former approach is preferable, and that the metered fare cannot be exceeded within any district where the 1976 Act has been adopted.

PROVISIONS TO ENSURE THAT A DRIVER MUST CARRY ASSISTANCE DOGS

13.82

Private hire drivers must allow assistance dogs to be carried in their vehicle. The Equality Act 2010, s 170 ('EA 2010') makes it an offence for a private hire driver to refuse to carry out a booking that was accepted by the operator:

'(a) if the booking is made by or on behalf of a disabled person or a person who wishes to be accompanied by a disabled person, and
(b) the reason for the failure or refusal is that the disabled person is accompanied by an assistance dog.'

'Assistance dog' is defined in s 173(1) as meaning:

'"assistance dog" means—
(a) a dog which has been trained to guide a blind person;
(b) a dog which has been trained to assist a deaf person;
(c) a dog which has been trained by a prescribed charity to assist a disabled person who has a disability that consists of epilepsy or otherwise affects the person's mobility, manual dexterity, physical co-ordination or ability to lift, carry or otherwise move everyday objects;
(d) a dog of a prescribed category which has been trained to assist a disabled person who has a disability (other than one falling within paragraph (c)) of a prescribed kind[1];'

Additional Assistance dogs are prescribed by reg 3 of The Disability Discrimination Act 1995 (Taxis) (Carrying of Guide Dogs etc.) (England and Wales) Regulations 2000, SI 2000/2990 as amended and include:

' "3. Prescribed charities

Each of the following is a prescribed charity for the purposes of paragraph (c) of the definition of "assistance dog" in section 173(1) of the 2010 Act (so far as that definition applies for the purposes of section 168 of that Act)—

(a) "Dogs for the Disabled" registered with the Charity Commission under registration number 1092960;

(b) "Support Dogs" registered with the Charity Commission under registration number 1017237; and

(c) "Canine Partners for Independence" registered with the Charity Commission under registration number 803680.'.

[1]   The Disability Discrimination Act 1995 (Taxis) (Carrying of Guide Dogs etc.) (England and Wales) Regulations 2000, SI 2000/2990, as amended, are now deemed to have been made under the Equality Act and were amended by the Equality Act 2010 (Commencement No. 4, Savings, Consequential, Transitional, Transitory and Incidental Provisions and Revocation) Order 2010, 2010/2317, Sch 8.

13.83

It is possible for a local authority to grant a certificate of exemption from this requirement to a private hire driver under EA 2010, s 171 and this is based on medical grounds. The licensing authority must take into account 'the physical characteristics of the private hire vehicle which the applicant drives or those of any kind of private hire vehicle in relation to which he requires the certificate' (EA 2010, s 171(2)). If such an exemption certificate is granted, it must be in the form specified in the Disability Discrimination Act 1995 (Private Hire Vehicles) (Carriage of Guide Dogs etc.) (England and Wales) Regulations 2003, reg 2 and Sch 1 (in England) or Sch 2 (in Wales)[1]. Once such a certificate has been granted, it must be displayed in accordance with reg 2(2):

'2–(2) The prescribed manner of exhibiting a notice of exemption for the purposes of section 171(4)(b) of the 2010 Act shall be by either—

(a) affixing it in a prominent position on the dashboard of the private hire vehicle, facing upwards; or

(b) affixing it to the windscreen of the private hire vehicle, facing outwards.'

[1]   SI 2003/3122. Deemed to be made under the EA 2010 by virtue of Sch 7 and art 21 of the Equality Act 2010 (Commencement No. 4, Savings, Consequential, Transitional, Transitory and Incidental Provisions and Revocation) Order 2010, SI 2010/2317 and the wording was amended by Sch 8.

13.84

Once a certificate of exemption has been granted, the original DfT *Best Practice Guide*[1] issued in 2006 suggested that a local authority considered 'providing – for use in informing passengers – Braille cards to those drivers exempted from the duty to carry prescribed assistance dogs'. Unfortunately and inexplicably, this was dropped from the 2010 revision, but there is no reason why the council cannot provide such a card and impose a condition requiring its use.

There is a right of appeal against a refusal by the licensing authority to issue an exemption certificate. This is contained in s 171 (2) which states:

> '(1) A person who is aggrieved by the refusal of a licensing authority in England and Wales to issue an exemption certificate under section 166, 169 or 171 may appeal to a magistrates' court before the end of the period of 28 days beginning with the date of the refusal.'

If the appeal is successful, the magistrates can order the licensing authority to issue the certificate (see s 172(3)).

1   DfT, '*Taxi and Private Hire Vehicle Licensing: Best Practice Guidance*' (October 2006, revised March 2010), para 17, available at http://www.dft.gov.uk/pgr/regional/taxis/taxiandprivatehirevehicle lic1792. See Appendix II.

13.85

Breach of the duty placed upon a private hire driver to undertake a journey booked by an operator because the passenger or a person accompanying the passenger has an assistance dog contrary to EA 2010, s 170 is a criminal offence under s 170(3). As the Equality Act is silent as to which body can prosecute such an offence, it is a general criminal offence and can therefore be investigated by the police and prosecuted by the Crown Prosecution Service. However it can also be investigated by, or prosecuted by the local authority under the powers contained in s 222 of the Local Government Act 1972[1]. As the local authority is the enforcing authority for all other taxi legislation, it would seem to be both reasonable and expedient for the local authority to prosecute cases such as this.

1   Section 222 states:

> '(1) Where a local authority consider it expedient for the promotion or protection of the interests of the inhabitants of their area—
> (a) they may prosecute or defend or appear in any legal proceedings and, in the case of civil proceedings, may institute them in their own name, and
> (b) they may, in their own name, make representations in the interests of the inhabitants at any public inquiry held by or on behalf of any Minister or public body under any enactment.
> (2) In this section "local authority" includes the Common Council and the London Fire and Emergency Planning Authority.'

13.86

In relation to assistance dogs, again, there have been a number of reported problems where carriage of the dog has been refused on the grounds that it may make a mess of the vehicle, either by deposit of dog hairs or worse. In addition to a breach of EA 2010, s 168, this is also a breach of the conditions of many local authorities.

PROVISION OF MOBILITY ASSISTANCE

13.87

Sections 165 and 167 of the EA 2010 came into force in April 2017. These allow a licensing authority (a local authority or TfL in London) to create a list of 'designated vehicles' which are capable of carrying passengers in wheelchairs and then require drivers of those vehicles to provide mobility assistance. These vehicles can be either hackney carriages or private hire vehicles. Section 166 is an exemption provision.

13.88

The starting point for these provisions lies with s 167:

'167 Lists of wheelchair-accessible vehicles

(1) For the purposes of section 165, a licensing authority may maintain a list of vehicles falling within subsection (2).

(2) A vehicle falls within this subsection if—
(a) it is either a taxi or a private hire vehicle, and
(b) it conforms to such accessibility requirements as the licensing authority thinks fit.

(3) A licensing authority may, if it thinks fit, decide that a vehicle may be included on a list maintained under this section only if it is being used, or is to be used, by the holder of a special licence under that licence.

(4) In subsection (3) *"special licence"* has the meaning given by section 12 of the Transport Act 1985 (use of taxis or hire cars in providing local services).

(5) "Accessibility requirements" are requirements for securing that it is possible for disabled persons in wheelchairs—
(a) to get into and out of vehicles in safety, and
(b) to travel in vehicles in safety and reasonable comfort,

either staying in their wheelchairs or not (depending on which they prefer).

(6) The Secretary of State may issue guidance to licensing authorities as to—
(a) the accessibility requirements which they should apply for the purposes of this section;
(b) any other aspect of their functions under or by virtue of this section.

(7) A licensing authority which maintains a list under subsection (1) must have regard to any guidance issued under subsection (6).'

Once a vehicle has been listed under s 167, it is then referred to as either a 'designated taxi' or a 'designated private hire vehicle' and the driver of any such vehicle who is not in possession of an exemption certificate issued under s 166 is then under a statutory duty to carry wheelchair-bound passengers and to provide 'mobility assistance' by virtue of s 165.

13.89

The duty applies when the vehicle has been hired:

'165(1) This section imposes duties on the driver of a designated taxi which has been hired—
(a) by or for a disabled person who is in a wheelchair, or
(b) by another person who wishes to be accompanied by a disabled person who is in a wheelchair.

(2) This section also imposes duties on the driver of a designated private hire vehicle, if a person within paragraph (a) or (b) of subsection (1) has indicated to the driver that the person wishes to travel in the vehicle.'

13.90

The duties imposed on the driver are detailed in sub-ss (4) and (5). Subsection (4) contains the general duties and sub-s (5) details what is meant by 'mobility assistance'.

The general duties are[1]:

'(a) to carry the passenger while in the wheelchair;
(b) not to make any additional charge for doing so;
(c) if the passenger chooses to sit in a passenger seat, to carry the wheelchair;
(d) to take such steps as are necessary to ensure that the passenger is carried in safety and reasonable comfort;
(e) to give the passenger such mobility assistance as is reasonably required.'

And mobility assistance:

'is assistance—
(a) to enable the passenger to get into or out of the vehicle;
(b) if the passenger wishes to remain in the wheelchair, to enable the passenger to get into and out of the vehicle while in the wheelchair;
(c) to load the passenger's luggage into or out of the vehicle;
(d) if the passenger does not wish to remain in the wheelchair, to load the wheelchair into or out of the vehicle.'

[1] EA 2010, s 165(4).

13.91

Failure to provide mobility assistance or to carry the passenger or discharge any of the other duties contained in s 165(4) is a criminal offence by virtue of sub-s (8), but there is a defence if the driver can show that it would not have been possible for the wheelchair to be carried safely in the vehicle (sub-s (9)(b)).

HACKNEY CARRIAGES USED FOR PRE-BOOKED PURPOSES

13.92

A question which often arises, concerns the use of hackney carriages for pre-booked purposes, which means that they are effectively being used as private hire vehicles. This can occur in one of two ways. First, the hackney carriage can be used effectively as a private hire vehicle because a booking is made with a person, either by telephone or in person and a vehicle, which is a hackney carriage, is dispatched to fulfil the booking. Secondly, a private hire operator can dispatch a hackney carriage to fulfil a private hire booking.

Such activity is clearly anticipated by the legislation, as if a hackney carriage is being used for pre-booked work, then provisions of LG(MP)A 1976, s 67 apply. This states:

'**67.—Hackney carriages used for private hire.**

(1) No hackney carriage shall be used in the district under a contract or purported contract for private hire except at a rate of fares or charges not greater than that fixed by the byelaws or tables mentioned in section 66 of this Act, and, when any such hackney carriage is so used, the fare or charge shall be calculated from the point in the district at which the hirer commences his journey.

(2) Any person who knowingly contravenes this section shall be guilty of an offence.

(3) In subsection (1) of this section "contract" means —

(a) a contract made otherwise than while the relevant hackney carriage is plying for hire in the district or waiting at a place in the district which, when the contract is made, is a stand for hackney carriages appointed by the district council under section 63 of this Act; and

(b) a contract made, otherwise than with or through the driver of the relevant hackney carriage, while it is so plying or waiting.'

13.93

In relation to the question of the requirement for a private hire operator's licence for a person who takes bookings for and dispatches hackney carriages, LG(MP)A 1976, s 46 is the relevant provision.

'46–(1)(a) No person being the proprietor of any vehicle, not being a hackney carriage or London Cab in respect of which a vehicle licence is in force, shall use or permit the same to be used in a controlled district as a private hire vehicle without having for such a vehicle a current licence under section 48 of this Act;

...

(d) No person shall in a controlled district operate any vehicle as a private hire vehicle without having a current licence under section 55 of this Act; ...'

It is an offence to contravene any of the provisions of this section by virtue of s 46(2).

13.94

As can be seen, LG(MP)A 1976, s 46(1)(a) appears to exclude a hackney carriage from the requirement to be licensed as a private hire vehicle. Does it therefore follow that a hackney carriage is excluded from the requirements of s 46(1)(d)?

13.95

In LG(MP)A 1976, s 80 the definition of private hire vehicle as:

'A motor vehicle constructed or adapted to seat fewer than nine passengers, other than a hackney carriage or public service vehicle or a London cab or tram car, which is provided for hire with the services of a driver for the purpose of carrying passengers'

excludes hackney carriages from the overall definition of private hire vehicle. This must be the correct approach as a hackney carriage is always a hackney carriage once it has been licensed (see *Hawkins v Edwards*[1]) and a private hire vehicle is always a private hire vehicle (see *Benson v Boyce*[2]) and clearly, once licensed as one type of vehicle and having that status, it would be impossible for the same vehicle to have a differing status.

[1]   [1901] 2 KB 169; see Chapter 8, para 8.4.
[2]   [1997] RTR 226; see para 13.72 above.

13.96

The definition of operate is contained in LG(MP)A 1976, s 80 as:

'means in the course of business to make provision for the invitation or acceptance of bookings for a private hire vehicle.'

13.97

Although it may appear that the effect of LG(MP)A 1976, s 46(1)(d) is to require an operator's licence for a person who operates '*any vehicle* as a private hire vehicle', the effect being to bring within the provisions of that subsection any vehicle that maybe operated for the purposes of a private hire vehicle, irrespective of whether or not the vehicle itself is actually a private hire vehicle, this view has been dismissed by the High Court in the case of *Brentwood Borough Council v Gladen*[1].

[1]   [2004] EWHC 2500 (Admin).

Brentwood Borough Council v Gladen

13.98

> Was a private hire operators licence required when booking were only taken for hackney carriages? Held: No.

This case concerned the booking and dispatch of hackney carriages. Gladen ran a business which accepted bookings for hackney carriages. A number of test purchases were undertaken by Brentwood BC, to establish that he did undertake this activity. Gladen did not hold a private hire operator's licence. He was prosecuted under LG(MP)A 1876, s 46(1)(d) and (2) for operating private hire services without having a private hire operator's licence under s 55. The situation was summarised by Collins J[1]:

'The argument was that, although they were licensed as hackney carriages and although the drivers were equally licensed as hackney carriage drivers, there was a requirement under the legislation that there should be an operator's licence under the relevant provisions of Part II of the Local Government (Miscellaneous Provisions) Act 1976 because they were, by virtue of section 46(1)(d) of the 1976 Act, to be regarded as requiring an operator's licence under that Act, to enable the particular operations to be carried out lawfully.'

There was considerable argument over whether use of a hackney carriage constituted 'operating'. This was addressed by Collins J in the following way[2]:

'15. It is important to note that Parliament, in section 80 of the Act, has defined certain terms for the purposes of Part II. It is headed, as all interpretation sections are, "In this Part of this Act, unless the subject or context otherwise requires". The relevant terms for our purposes are "operate", which is defined as meaning "in the course of business to make provision for the invitation or acceptance of bookings for a private hire vehicle"; "operator's licence", which means a licence under section 55 of the Act and "private hire vehicle", which means:

" ... a motor vehicle constructed or adapted to seat [fewer than nine passengers], other than a hackney carriage or public service vehicle [or a London cab] [or tram car], which is provided for hire with the services of a driver for the purpose of carrying passengers."

16. Now, it is, in my view, quite clear that the drafting of section 46 is with the technical meanings in mind. It is true that one could say that, in certain respects, there could have been omissions of various words if one simply went to the definition section, but that would make the wording of the section itself less than clear. It is important, therefore, to note that licensing of operators is dealt with in section 55 and that a licence under section 55 of the Act must be a licence which enables what is there set out to be done.

17. Section 55(1) provides:

"Subject to the provisions of this Part of this Act, a district council shall, on receipt of an application from any person for the grant to that person of a licence to operate private hire vehicles grant to that person an operator's licence."

So it is a licence to operate private hire vehicles.

18. Section 56 which is headed, "Operators of private hire vehicles", by subsection (2), for example, provides:

"Every person to whom a licence in force under section 55 of this Act has been granted by a district council shall keep a record in such form as the council may, by condition attached to the grant of the licence, prescribe ...

(3) Every person to whom a licence in force under section 55 of this Act has been granted by a district council shall keep such records as the council may, by condition attached to the grant of the licence [et cetera]."

19. It is clear from those provisions that it is only a person who is operating private hire vehicles who needs to be granted such a licence, and more importantly, he is the only person in respect of whom conditions under section 56 can be imposed.'

After reviewing the law and making reference to *Benson v Boyce*[3], *R v Franklyn and Carter*[4] and *R v Doncaster Metropolitan Borough Council, ex p Heath*[5] he continued[6]:

'It seems to me apparent that section 80 excludes hackney carriages from section 46(1)(d). I say that because, without going in detail over ground that I have already covered, "operate" relates to business in relation to bookings for a private hire vehicle. An "operator's licence" means a licence under section 55, and a "private hire vehicle" is defined as meaning a vehicle other than a hackney carriage. Thus, that, coupled with the provisions of section 55 and 56 which I have already read, seem to me to make it apparent that Parliament has recognised that different regimes apply to hackney carriages and to private hire vehicles, and that it is not necessary for a licensed hackney carriage, driven by a licensed hackney carriage driver, to be subject also to the requirements of an operator's licence; otherwise the limitations on the wording which Parliament has clearly set out would not be given their true meaning.

31. It is true that, if one looks at it at face value without considering the technical meaning, the words "operate any vehicle as a private hire vehicle" could lead to the belief that hackney carriages were included because a hackney carriage is obviously a vehicle. But, as it seems to me, that is quite impossible having regard to the meanings which Parliament has attached to the various words and to which I have already referred.'

1   Above, at para 3.
2   Above, at paras 15–19.
3   [1997] RTR 226.
4   (27 June 1991, unreported).
5   [2001] ACD 48, QBD (Admin Ct).
6   [2004] EWHC 2500 (Admin) at paras 30 and 31.

13.99

He then concluded[1]:

'34. I have reached the clear view that the district judge in this case was correct and that section 46(1)(d) is not breached where a licensed hackney carriage and a licensed hackney carriage driver is provided for the relevant conveyance of a passenger, albeit it is provided through an operator. In those circumstances, an operator's licence under section 55 of the Act is not appropriate, since that section does not cover hackney carriages.

35. The district judge posed this question for the opinion of the High Court:

> "Whether it is necessary to hold a licence under section 55 of the Local Government (Miscellaneous Provisions) Act 1976, in an area where that Act is in force, to operate a hackney carriage duly licensed as such under the Town Police Clauses Act 1847 as a private hire vehicle."

36. The answer to that question is: no. Accordingly, I would dismiss this appeal.'

¹   Above at paras 34–36.

13.100

Although in fact Gladen was using hackney carriages which were licensed by Brentwood BC, that is clearly not a material element of the case, as can be seen from both the judgment itself and the answer to the question posed by the magistrates. No mention is made of the fact that the vehicles were Brentwood hackney carriages, merely that they were hackney carriages, and the question posed by the magistrates and the answer given by the High Court were both unequivocal[1]:

> "'Whether it is necessary to hold a licence under section 55 of the Local Government (Miscellaneous Provisions) Act 1976, in an area where that Act is in force, to operate a hackney carriage duly licensed as such under the Town Police Clauses Act 1847 as a private hire vehicle."

The answer to that question is: no.'

It is therefore clear that hackney carriages licensed by any district council, or the PCO, can be used for private hire purposes in any district without the need for a private hire operator's licence[2].

¹   [2004] EWHC 2500 (Admin) at paras 35 and 36.
²   It is sometimes argued that the decision in *DPP v Computer Cab Company Ltd* [1996] RTR 130 QBD (see Chapter 22, para 22.30) prevents a hackney carriage driver from accepting a pre-booking if he and his hackney carriage are physically located outside the district in which they are licensed. This does not appear to be the case, as there are no equivalent provisions in the legislation applicable outside London to art 31 of the London Cab Order 1934, SI 1934/1346 – see Appendix I.

Stockton v Fidler

13.101

Does a private hire operator commit an offence if he takes bookings for, and dispatches, a hackney carriage licensed by a different authority? Held: No.

The matter was considered again by the High Court in the case of *Stockton v Fidler*[1]. Fidler was a private hire operator, licensed by Stockton-on-Tees Borough Council ('SOTBC'). As a SOTBC licensed private hire operator, he could only dispatch *private hire vehicles* licensed by SOTBC and driven by SOTBC licensed private hire drivers. However, believing that the limitation only applied to *private hire vehicles*, he dispatched hackney carriages licensed by Berwick-on-Tweed Borough Council[2], and driven by drivers who held hackney carriage drivers' licences, also issued by Berwick-on-Tweed Borough Council.

Therefore, he was charged with two offences: knowingly operating a vehicle as a private hire vehicle when the vehicle did not have a current private hire licence issued by Stockton-on-Tees Borough Council, contrary to s 46(1)(e)(i) of the 1976 Act; and knowingly operating a vehicle as a private hire vehicle when the driver did not have a current private hire driver's licence issued by Stockton-on-Tees Borough Council, contrary to s 46(1)(e)(ii) of the 1976 Act.

The case was considered by a District Judge in the magistrates' court on a preliminary point of law, and a case was stated raising the following questions:

'1 Is an offence committed under section 46(1)(e) of the Local Government (Miscellaneous Provisions) Act 1976 when a hackney carriage is operated on journeys booked and wholly contained within the area of one licensing authority when the relevant licence has been issued by a different licensing authority?

2 Is it an offence under section 45 of the Town Police clauses Act 1847 (as amended) for a hackney carriage licensed in one area to stand or ply for hire in another area where no licence has been issued to the driver or the vehicle by the licensing authority in that area?'

[1] [2010] EWHC 2430 (Admin), [2011] RTR 23, Admin Ct.
[2] At the time of the offence, Berwick-on-Tweed Borough Council was a District Council in Northumberland. Subsequent local government reorganisation resulted in Northumberland becoming a unitary authority and Berwick-on-Tweed Borough Council being abolished on 31 March 2009.

13.102

The case was heard by Munby LJ and Langstaff J. The first judgment was given by Munby LJ who opened his judgment thus[1]:

'1. What is a hackney carriage? What is the meaning of the aphorism "a hackney carriage is always a hackney carriage once it has been licensed"? Is a vehicle licensed as a hackney carriage by local authority A a hackney carriage while on the road in the area of local authority B (specifically, on the facts of the present case, is a vehicle licensed as a hackney carriage by Berwick-upon-Tweed Borough Council a hackney carriage while on the road in the area of Stockton-on-Tees Borough Council)? Does a vehicle licensed as a hackney carriage by local authority A require to be licensed as a private hire vehicle by local authority B if used for private hire in the area of local authority B (specifically, on the facts of the present case, does a vehicle licensed as a hackney carriage by Berwick-upon-Tweed Borough Council require to be licensed as a private hire vehicle by Stockton-on-Tees Borough Council if used for private hire in the area of Stockton-on-Tees Borough Council)? What is the meaning of the phrase "hackney carriage" when used in the definition of "private hire vehicle" in section 80(1) of the Local Government (Miscellaneous Provisions) Act 1976?

2. These questions are not merely of technical interest to lawyers; the answers are potentially of great significance not only to the Appellant and the Respondents in this appeal but, more generally, as some of the materials we have been referred to show, to the taxi trade, to local authorities up and down the country and, indeed, to the public at large.'

He then considered at length the legislative and judicial history of hackney carriage licensing[2]. In relation to the second question posed by the District Judge (the standing for hire issue) it was accepted that this would depend on the particular facts of the case, which had not been considered by the District Judge[3]. It was he stated, the first question concerning the taking of bookings for, and dispatch of hackney carriages licensed by another authority, which was 'the ... more difficult and important question'.

Having considered the conflicting arguments of Ms Smith for the appellant council, and Mr Roger for the respondent operator, he summarised the arguments[4]:

'55. Mr Rodger, for his part, submits that the Deputy District Judge was entirely correct in deciding the preliminary issue as she did. He relies in particular upon *Britain*, *Gladen* and *Berwick*, all of which, he submits, were correctly decided. He submits that unless what I can conveniently refer to as the 'hackney carriage exemption' – that is, the qualifying reference in the definition of a private hire vehicle in section 80(1) of the 1976 Act to "a ... vehicle ... other than a hackney carriage ... or a London cab" – is read back into the references to "a private hire vehicle" in sections 46(1)(d) and 46(1)(e) of the 1976 Act, it will not be lawful to "operate ... as a private hire vehicle" a vehicle which is licensed as a hackney carriage, even in the area in which it is so licensed, unless it is also licensed under the 1976 Act. And the latter, he says, is impossible, not least in the light of the definition of a private hire vehicle in section 80(1) of the 1976 Act and given the requirement in section 48(1)(a)(ii) of the 1976 Act that:

"a district council shall not grant ... a licence [under section 48] unless they are satisfied ... that the vehicle is ... not of such design and appearance as to lead any person to believe that the vehicle is a hackney carriage".

On the contrary, he says, the lawfulness of the use of a hackney carriage for private hire (at least in the area in which it is licensed as a hackney carriage) is assumed in section 67(1) of the 1976 Act, which provides that:

"No hackney carriage shall be used in the district under a contract or purported contract for private hire except at a rate of fares or charges not greater than that fixed by the byelaws or tables mentioned in section 66 of this Act ..."

Section 67(2) makes contravention of this provision a criminal offence.

56. Put more generally, Mr Rodger submits that a hackney carriage is always a hackney carriage, no matter what it is doing, or where, and that its use, for whatever purpose, can never make it a private hire vehicle in the statutory sense. There are, he says, entirely separate and distinct regimes for the licensing of vehicles as hackney carriages and as private hire vehicles and the regime which regulates private hire vehicles has no application to a vehicle registered as a hackney carriage. The purpose of the 1976 Act (as later, in relation to London, of the 1998 Act) was, he submits, to impose a scheme of licensing on otherwise unlicensed vehicles and their drivers; it was not to impose further regulation on already-regulated hackney carriages. To "operate" within the meaning of the 1976 Act, including for the purposes of sections 46(1)(d) and 46(1)(e), is, he says, as the definition of "operate" in section 80(1) makes clear, an activity that can be carried out only in relation to a private hire vehicle as defined by section 80(1) – and that definition explicitly excludes a hackney carriage; it is not an activity carried out, or capable of being carried out, in relation to a hackney carriage, however or wherever it is being used. The provision of a hackney carriage for hire together with the services of a driver pursuant to an advance booking is not, he submits, a licensable activity. It always has been, and continues to be, he asserts, an activity unregulated under any statute. In short, Mr Rodger prays in aid what in Button is described (page xvi) as "the inherent right of the hackney carriage proprietor to undertake pre-booked hirings anywhere in England or Wales."

57. I agree with Mr Rodger and essentially for all the reasons he has given.'

He then concluded[5]:

'58. Central to the dispute in this case, as it seems to me, are two questions of statutory construction. The first relates to the meaning of the words "hackney carriage" where they appear in the definition of "private hire vehicle" in section 80(1) of the 1976 Act. This is the issue determined by the Divisional Court in *Britain v ABC Cabs (Camberley) Ltd* [1981] RTR 395. In agreement with the decision in that case, I would hold that "hackney carriage" in section 80(1) means a hackney carriage wherever it may be licensed as such. So what I have referred to as the 'hackney carriage exemption' is not confined to hackney carriages licensed as such by the local authority which is seeking to enforce within its own area the provisions of the 1976 Act. I respectfully agree with the reasoning in *Britain* of both Webster J and, more particularly, of Ormrod LJ. Their reasoning is compelling. The decision has stood for thirty years without challenge. In my judgment it is correct and we should follow it.

59. The second question relates to whether what I have called the 'hackney carriage exemption' is to be read back into the references to a "private hire vehicle" in sections 46(1)(d) and 46(1)(e) of the 1976 Act. This is the issue determined by the Divisional Court in *Brentwood Borough Council v Gladen* [2004] EWHC 2500 (Admin), [2005] RTR 152. I agree with Collins J's decision and with his reasoning. In my judgment the words "private hire vehicle" in sections 46(1)(d) and 46(1)(e) have to be read as governed by the definition of "private hire vehicle" in section 80(1) and they are, accordingly, subject to the 'hackney carriage exemption'. This is a conclusion, moreover, which receives powerful support from the arguments which Mr Rodger has put forward (summarised in paragraph [55] above), in particular, the arguments based upon sections 48(1)(a)(ii) and 67(1).

60. I accept that in *Gladen* the court was not concerned, as we are, with a vehicle which had been licensed as a hackney carriage by another local authority. But that, in my judgment, does not take Ms Smith where she would have us go, for the 'foreign hackney carriage' point is determined against her by *Britain*.

61. Put shortly, the correct analysis, in my judgment, is this: first, and for the reasons given in *Gladen*, one has to read into the references to "private hire vehicle" in sections 46(1)(d) and 46(1)(e) the definition of "private hire vehicle" in section 80(1), including what I have called the 'hackney carriage exemption'; second, and for the reasons given in *Britain*, the words "hackney carriage" where they appear in section 80(1) are not confined to a vehicle licensed as a hackney carriage by the local authority which is seeking to enforce within its own area the provisions of the 1976 Act; they extend to any vehicle registered as a hackney carriage anywhere. And the combination of these two matters leads inexorably, as a matter of both logic and law, to the conclusion for which Mr Rodger contends.

62. For my part I would therefore answer the first question posed for our consideration by the Deputy District Judge, No. Mr Fidler was acquitted by the Deputy District Judge. His acquittal will, if my brother agrees, therefore stand.

63. I agree both with the Deputy District Judge, as also with the Deputy Judge in the *Berwick* case, that the authorities are not altogether easy to reconcile. In my judgment the decision of the District Judge in the *Wrexham* case was wrong. And if and insofar as the decision of the Divisional Court in *Wilson* conflicts with this analysis then it is, in my respectful judgment, wrong. The law, in my judgment, was and is, as Mr Rodger submitted, correctly laid down in *Britain* and *Gladen*.'

1   Above at paras 1 and 2.
2   Above at paras 3–18 and 25–47.

3   See paras 50–52 of the judgment.
4   Above at para 52 of the judgment.
5   Above at para 52 onwards of the judgment.

13.103

Lord Justice Munby reinforced that conclusion by making reference to the 'London-cab issue'[1]:

'65. The point arises in this way. It will be recalled that following the amendment of the 1976 Act by the 1985 Act, the 'hackney carriage exemption' in the definition of "private hire vehicle" in section 80(1) of the 1976 Act was extended to include a reference to "London cab". So a private hire vehicle is now defined as "a ... vehicle ... other than a hackney carriage ... or a London cab", the latter, as we have seen, being defined as a vehicle which is a hackney carriage within the meaning of the 1869 Act. Mr Rodger's point is very simple. He submits that a "London cab" is necessarily a vehicle licensed before 2000 by the Commissioner of the Metropolitan Police or since then by Transport for London; in other words a vehicle which is not and cannot be licensed by a local authority licensing vehicles under the 1976 Act. So in relation to such an authority, whether it be Berwick-upon-Tweed Borough Council or Stockton-on-Tees Borough Council or, indeed, any other local authority outside Greater London, a "London cab" is necessarily a hackney carriage licensed by another authority, now Transport for London. It follows therefore, he says, that the 'hackney carriage exemption' in the definition of a private hire vehicle in section 80(1) is not confined to a vehicle licensed as a hackney carriage by the local authority seeking to enforce within its own area the provisions of the 1976 Act. For if a vehicle licensed by Transport for London as a hackney carriage within the meaning of the 1869 Act (in other words what is called a London cab for the purposes of the 1976 Act) can be used in Stockton-on-Tees for private hire purposes without being registered by Stockton-on-Tees Borough Council as a private hire vehicle – and that is the effect of the definition of private hire vehicle in section 80(1) – then by parity of reasoning the same must apply in relation to a vehicle registered, for example by Berwick-upon-Tweed Borough Council, as a hackney carriage within the meaning of the 1847 Act.'

And he then added[2]:

'68. Mr Rodger's ... formulation of his point is, in my judgment, irrefutable. A "London cab" is necessarily and by definition a vehicle licensed as such – that is, as a hackney carriage – by Transport for London (previously the Commissioner) and not by the local authority seeking to enforce within its own area the provisions of the 1976 Act.'

1   Above at para 65.
2   Above at para 68.

13.104

That view was supported by Mr Justice Langstaff. He said[1]:

'I, too, find the answer to the first question posed by the Deputy District Judge to be of greater difficulty than that to the second. As to this first question, the authorities – in particular those of *Wilson* and *Britain* – are not easy to reconcile.'

He continued[2]:

'72. The scheme of both the Local Government (Miscellaneous Provisions) Act 1976, under which the charges here were brought, and that of the Town Police Clauses Act 1847 is to provide for local regulation of (on the one hand) private hire vehicles, and (on the other) hackney carriages. The scheme is not one of national regulation, merely administered locally. If it were, there would be no room for different councils to adopt differing requirements of applicants for the relevant licences. At first blush, therefore, and without recourse to authority or to detailed examination of the interlinking intricacies of the statutory provisions, it seems contrary to the policy adopted by the legislation to exempt a vehicle from the requirements of regulation of private hire vehicles in Stockton-on-Tees because it has been registered by another authority with different priorities and concerns to those of Stockton, as a different class of vehicle. The reasoning of Buxton J. in *Wilson* (as set out at page 13 of the Transcript, see above at paragraph 32) seems roundly dismissive of any suggestion to the contrary. It relies (page 15, transcript) on there being separate requirements (for the purposes of section 46(1)(a) of the 1976 Act) for a vehicle to be both (a) a hackney carriage and (b) to be licensed as such. It was not enough that there should simply be a licence in force in respect of the vehicle to make it a hackney carriage at the relevant time. No doubt, if the statute had wished to exempt vehicles which had been so licensed simply by virtue of that fact it would not have needed to refer to such a vehicle as actually "*being* a hackney carriage...."

73. Accordingly, as I understand his reasoning the essential question whether a vehicle is a hackney carriage is to be answered by looking to see what function the vehicle is performing at the relevant time, albeit seen in context – to determine its "characteristic use" as Mance J. described it in *Benson v Boyce*, by the use of that phrase ensuring that the forensic focus would be wider than on a short-lived use, out of character, calculated to avoid regulations otherwise applicable, such as by obscuring a licence plate or light for the course of one journey (see *Hawkins v Edwards; Yates v Gates*).

74. To determine the first question in this case, therefore, in the light of the judgments in *Wilson* it would be necessary to ask not only whether the vehicles which Mr. Fidler operated in Stockton-upon-Tees had been licensed as such in Berwick-upon-Tweed but also whether at the relevant time their characteristic use was as hackney carriages. If neither were the case, then the vehicles would not be hackney carriages, and would require

to be licensed (by Stockton-upon-Tees Borough Council) if they were to operate in other respects as private hire vehicles. Section 80(1) of the 1976 Act would not confer an exemption, because that relates to vehicles "other than hackney carriages", and the application of the statute thereby depends upon the central factual issue: is the characteristic use that of a hackney carriage? The exemption conferred by section 80(1) (on this argument) does not depend on whether the vehicle is licensed as such, but whether it is, or is not, such a vehicle.

75. I confess that both during and for some while after hearing the arguments of counsel I was attracted to this analysis, not least because it had the consequence of preserving the system of local licensing which the Acts appear to adopt. There was one principal difficulty I had in accepting it, then as now, which depends upon the wording of section 80(1) and which has led me in the event to prefer the analysis of Ormrod LJ and Webster J in *Britain v ABC Cabs*. It is what My Lord calls the "London cab" issue. The statutory definition of "London cab" is not dependent upon the characteristic use of such a vehicle as a London cab, for that use is specifically confined within geographical limits (section 4 of the 1869 Act providing, as it does, that it is a "carriage…which plies for hire within the limits of this Act…"). If the applicable legislation affords no possibility of those limits overlapping with those areas within which the 1976 Act applies then there would equally be no prospect of there being a "London cab" recognisable as such within those areas if the identity of such a cab were solely dependent on its characteristic use. Yet the definition within section 80(1) contemplates the possibility that that which is properly to be identified as a "London cab" may be a vehicle which accepts passengers for private hire in areas outside London, so that the exemption conferred from local licensing by the wording of that section has force. As my Lord holds at paragraph 68 of his judgment, I too agree that the argument to this effect made by Mr. Rodger is irrefutable, and his alternative formulation of the point equally persuasive since the geographical area within which a London cab is to be licensed as such does not (now, at any rate) overlap with those areas to which the 1976 Act applies.

76. Since the wording of the legislation has the effect, therefore, that what Mance J. described as the "characteristic use" of a vehicle is not sufficient in itself to determine what is, or is not, a hackney carriage, I too am bound to hold that "hackney carriage" in section 80(1) means a hackney carriage, wherever it may be licensed as such, and the "hackney carriage exemption" is not confined to hackney carriages licensed as such by the local authority which is seeking to enforce within its own area the provisions of the 1976 Act.

77. If and insofar as the judgments in *Britain* and those in *Wilson* are in conflict, I agree with my Lord that those in *Britain* are to be preferred. I would further add that the reasoning of Ormrod LJ in *Britain* cannot, as it seems to me, be regarded as inapplicable (despite that which appears to

have been conceded by counsel in *Wilson*) on the basis that what was under consideration was a "more composite phrase, 'being a hackney carriage in respect of which a vehicle licence is in force'.." since that phrase necessarily involves a vehicle first being identified as a hackney carriage before any consideration is given to whether or not it is licensed as such.

78. The practical result of these conclusions is not necessarily such (if one excuses the expression in the current context) as to drive a coach and horses through the control of hire vehicle licensing. No hackney carriage is exempt from local licensing as a private hire vehicle unless it is licensed as a hackney carriage somewhere, and it is an offence for it to be driven by one who is not licensed by a proper authority as its driver. No hackney carriage may ply for hire in the area of a local authority unless specifically licensed to do so within that area. (See sections 45 – 47 Town Police Clauses Act 1847). Although (as was hinted at by counsel before us) an authority such as Stockton-upon-Tees may have wished greater control over driver or vehicle in a specific case, it is not a consequence of this decision that either is without regulation, which it may be assumed will be properly and appropriately applied by whichever local authority is that which confers a licence in respect of the relevant hackney carriage, driver and employer. If it seems that there are nonetheless tensions between any policy of local licensing and regulation on the one hand, and the proper interpretation of the wording of statute as determined in this case, that must be a matter for consideration and review by Parliament rather than the courts.'

These lengthy extracts from the judgment in *Stockton v Fidler*[3] show how difficult the question was to answer, but then provide a clear judicial view, of the High Court, that a hackney carriage (whether licensed outside or within Greater London) can be used for pre-booked work anywhere without any other licence being required. It is also clear that a private hire operator can take bookings for, and dispatch hackney carriages that are licensed by any authority (including Transport for London).

[1]   Above at para 70.
[2]   Above at para 72–78.
[3]   [2010] EWHC 2430 (Admin), [2011] RTR 23, Admin Ct.

INSURANCE

13.105

The question of insurance is a source of considerable concern for all involved in private hire matters: the local authority, the drivers and the public. Private hire insurance is usually specifically for the use of the vehicle as a private hire vehicle: that is, for hire and reward providing a pre-booked service. The question that arises is whether such insurance is invalidated if the vehicle acts unlawfully and is used to ply for hire in contravention of the Town Police Clauses Act 1847, s 45 (TPCA 1847). This has been considered in a number of cases, the most recent of which has altered the position in respect of hackney carriages plying for hire outside their licensed district (or zone), but has not altered the underlying premise that the existence or otherwise of insurance cover will depend on the wording of the policy.

Telford v Wrekin Borough Council v Ahmed

13.106

> Was the offence of driving without insurance committed when a private hire vehicle was found plying or standing for hire? Held: Yes it was , but that conclusion was dependent on the wording of the insurance policy itself.

In *Telford v Wrekin Borough Council v Ahmed*[1], the facts were that a number of private hire drivers were prosecuted for unlawfully plying for hire contrary to s 45 of the TPCA 1847. Each was also prosecuted for the offence of driving without insurance contrary to the Road Traffic Act 1988, s 143. All were convicted of unlawfully plying for hire and acquitted of driving without insurance, as the district judge believed that as the insurance company would cover third-party losses, there was no offence (in fact, by the time the district judge stated his case, he had researched the authorities further and had concluded that he had erred in law). The matter came before the High Court on an appeal by way of case stated, and the judgment was handed down by McCombe J. He outlined the relevant parts of each of the defendant's insurance policies[2]:

'3 Each of the respondents was licensed by the appellant for the carrying of passengers for reward, provided that a prior booking had been made. None was licensed to ply for hire without such prior booking. Each had a motor insurance policy in respect of private hire work on prior booking. The relevant limitations to be obtained from the respondents' insurance certificates were in the following terms, which I can conveniently take from paragraph 3 of the judge's case stated:

"3 **Limitations as to use extracted from the defendants' insurance certificates**

(i) **Tanveer Ahmed (Cooperative Insurance Society)**

Persons entitled to drive: 'Any person who is driving on the order or with the permission of the policy holder.'

Limitations as to use: 'Use for any purpose excluding use for hiring (other than the carriage of passengers for hire provided that the vehicle does not stand or ply for hire) ...

and

(ii) **Christian Erkrath (Equity Red Star at Lloyd's)**

'Use for private hire, including the carriage of passengers and goods for reward. (Private hire means the letting of a vehicle supplied to the hirer direct from the policy holder's garage).'

(iii) Mirza Hussain (Equity Red Star at Lloyd's)

Identical to (ii) above.

(iv) Mohammed Khan (Equity Red Star at Lloyd's)

Identical to (ii) above but with the additional words ... 'but excluding use for public hire ...'

(v) Muslim Khan (Equity Red Star at Lloyd's)

Persons entitled to drive: 'Any person who is driving on the order or with the permission of the policy holder.'

Limitations as to use: identical to (ii) above.

(vi) David Knott (named driver on the policy) (Zenith Insurance plc)

'... use for the carriage of passengers or goods for hire and reward by prior arrangement only, provided that such use complies with the laws and regulations of the appropriate Licensing Authority.'

(vii) Zaheer Mahmood (Chaucer Insurance)

'2 Private Hire by prior booking at the policy holder's business address. Not to be used for the carriage of passengers for hire or reward except as in (ii) above ...'

(viii) Shafti Mustapha (Chaucer Insurance)

Identical to (vii) above."

The policies of insurance covered the respondents for the use of their vehicles for those uses but not for others. However in each case the insurance certificates contained a footnote in approximately the following form:

"Advice to Third Parties. Nothing in the certificate affects your right as a third party to make a claim."

A variation of that note appears on all the certificates.'

He then concluded[3]:

'9 In my judgment, the learned District Judge's second thoughts in this matter are entirely correct. Whether a policy covers a particular risk and therefore whether there is in force a valid insurance covering that risk will usually be a matter of construction of the insurance policy in question, rather than a matter of evidence. That was certainly so in the present case. In my view, it is entirely clear that the limitations to the insurance in each of these cases demonstrated that the vehicle was not covered when being used on "ply for hire" operations. The note at the foot of the certificate does not affect what was in fact covered by the policies. It merely gives notice, in layman's terms, of the consequences of arrangements made under the aegis of the Motor Insurance Bureau for the compensation of third parties for the liabilities of an uninsured driver. Equally it demonstrates that notwithstanding the absence of insurance, there is nothing to prevent such a third party making a claim against the driver. The note does not affect at all the extent of the cover afforded to the insured under the policies themselves.

10 It may be true that the policy in each of these cases remained in force notwithstanding any breach of its terms by the relevant respondent until avoided by the insurer. However the fact remained that such policy, in its unavoided form, did not cover the risk in question. In *Adams v Dunne* the risk *was* covered, notwithstanding that the policy was voidable for misrepresentation by the insured; it had not in fact been avoided at the relevant time. That is not the issue in this case.'

It can be seen therefore, that the construction of the insurance policy on a case by case basis, and the consequential effect on the passengers as to whether the driver will be indemnified by his insurers in a civil claim, or whether the claim will be one for the Motor Insurers Bureau, is vital in relation to any question of whether or not an offence under s 143 of the Road Traffic Act 1988 was committed.

[1]   (2006) EWHC 1748 (Admin), [2007] LLR 82.
[2]   Above at para 3.
[3]   Above, at paras 9 and 10.

Singh v Solihull Metropolitan Borough Council

13.107

> Was private hire insurance invalidated when the vehicle was plying for hire, and did European Directives alter that? Held: Yes it was, and European Directives did not remove criminal liability.

Telford and Wrekin[1] was followed by *Singh v Solihull Metropolitan Borough Council*[2]. In this case it was argued that the requirements of European Directives[3] which required policies of insurance to cover third-party losses amounted to defences to driving without insurance when plying for hire unlawfully. The facts were simple: a private hire vehicle was hired with immediate effect by two undercover officers of the Council. There was no defence to the prosecution for unlawful plying for hire, but in relation to driving without insurance offence, Singh appealed against conviction on the basis of the European directives and the decision of the European Court of Justice in *Ruiz Bernaldez*[4].

[1]   (2006) EWHC 1748 (Admin), [2007] LLR 82; see para 13.106 above.
[2]   [2007] EWHC 552 (Admin), [2007] 2 CMLR 47.
[3]   72/166/EEC, 84/5/EEC and 90/232/EEC.
[4]   [1996] 2 CMLR 889.

13.108

Collins J summed up in the impact of the Directives as follows[1]:

'[19] The Directives are concerned, as is apparent, with the protection of the victims of drivers. They are to ensure that there is compulsory insurance, which means that any victim is compensated, and, in the case of the Second Directive, that if the driver of the vehicle which causes the damage is either uninsured or the vehicle cannot be identified, then the victim shall have compensation and if it cannot be by the insurer, it will be by the Motor Insurers' Bureau in the case of this country or some similar body in the case of other member states. The Directive is not in terms concerned with the criminal responsibility, if any, of the driver in relation to whether he has failed to comply with the compulsory insurance laws of the country in question.'

In relation to *Ruiz Bernaldez*, he concluded that the decision was not to remove criminal liability for the domestic offence of driving without insurance.

1   (2006) EWHC 1748 (Admin), [2007] LLR 82 at para 19.

Sedgefield Borough Council v Crowe

13.109

Did hackney carriage insurance cover an unlicensed driver? Held: Yes it did, based on the wording of the policy.

In *Sedgefield Borough Council v Crowe*[1] of the question of the construction of the insurance policy as identified in *Telford and Wrekin*[2] was the determining factor. Crowe had been a hackney carriage driver, but his licence was revoked by the council. He was then observed driving a hackney carriage, for the purposes of delivering forms to the council in respect of another vehicle and also testing the vehicle for mechanical defects. At the material time, there was no suggestion that he was carrying passengers. He was prosecuted for both driving a hackney carriage without a hackney carriage driver's licence contrary to s 47 of the TPCA 1847 and driving without insurance contrary to s 143 of the Road Traffic Act 1988. He was convicted of driving without a licence, but acquitted of driving without insurance because the magistrates found that the insurance policy had covered the drivers at the material time against third-party risks.

1   [2008] All ER (D) 98 (Jul).
2   (2006) EWHC 1748 (Admin), [2007] LLR 82; see para 13.106 above.

13.110

The insurance policies stated[1]:

'Under clause 1 of the certificate – "Description of Vehicles" – it is said to apply to –

"1.….any motor car or licensed taxi the property of the policyholder or in their custody or control and for which they are legally responsible."

In [clause] 2 the policyholder is defined as –

"Mr James Crowe and Mrs Ashley Crowe T/A [trading as] Horndale Taxis"

Under clause 5 it states:

"5   Persons or classes of persons entitled to drive.

Any person who is driving on the order or with the permission of the policyholder."

In italics there is a proviso –

"Provided the person driving holds a licence to drive the vehicle or has held a licence and is not disqualified for or prohibited by law from holding or obtaining a licence.

6   Limitations as to use

Use for social domestic and pleasure purposes and for private and public hire including the carriage of passengers and goods for hire and reward.

The policy does not cover use for hiring, the letting on hire, the carriage of passengers or goods for hire or reward, racing, pacemaking, track days, use in any contest, reliability or speed trial, or use for any purpose in connection with the motor trade, except where included in 6 above.'"

[1]   Above, at para 8.

13.111

A letter from the insurance company was placed before the magistrates and in it they stated[1]: 'it is not a requirement of our policy that the driver holds a valid taxi badge'.

[1]   Above at para 12.

13.112

The local authority appealed by way of case stated, arguing that the reference in the insurance policy to 'licence' referred to a hackney carriage driver's licence, not a DVLA driver's licence.

13.113

In reference to the particular insurance policy Blake J (giving the judgment of the court) concluded as follows[1]:

'… for the reasons I have sought to give in the light of the particular terms of this insurance certificate and in the absence of any evidence to suggest that a prohibited use was being put under the terms of the insurance certificate, I would answer the questions posed by the justices as follows. In the first question –

"Can a driver of a Hackney Carriage ever be validly insured to drive the vehicle if he no longer holds a Hackney Carriage Drivers Licence ..."

I would pose the answer yes. To the second half of that first question –

"... will a driver's insurance policy to drive a Hackney Carriage fail to cover the risk if he no longer holds a Hackney Carriage Drivers Licence?"

I would answer no.'

[1]   Above, at para 21.

13.114

This clearly supports the decision in *Telford and Wrekin*[1] that the question of whether or not there is an insurance policy in place will depend, as has been stated, upon the construction of that policy in each particular case, and ultimately, it will be a matter of fact in any prosecution as to whether the vehicle was insured or not.

[1]   (2006) EWHC 1748 (Admin), [2007] LLR 82; see para 13.106 above.

Oldham BC v Sajjad

13.115

> Is hackney carriage insurance invalidated when the vehicle plies for hire in another district? Held: No, based on the wording of the policy and the prohibition on geographic restrictions on insurance contained in the Road Traffic Act 1988.

The most recent case is *Oldham BC v Sajjad*[1] which concerned a hackney carriage plying for hire outside the district in which it was licensed. A hackney carriage licensed by Rossendale BC and driven by Sajjad was hailed and responded, in Oldham, picking up two passengers. Sajjad was prosecuted for unlawful plying for hire contrary to TPCA 1847, s 45 and driving without insurance contrary to the Road Traffic Act 1988, s 143. He pleaded guilty to the plying for hire but not guilty to the no insurance charge. He was acquitted by the magistrates and the council appealed by way of case stated.

The question posed by the magistrates was[2]:

> 'Was the court right in finding from the submissions made that the certificate of insurance produced by the defendant was valid in the circumstances whereby the defendant admits that he was plying for hire in an area outside of that which the Hackney Carriage licence was granted?'

[1]   [2016] EWHC 3597 (Admin).
[2]   Above at para 17.

13.116

The appeal was heard by McCombe LJ and Kerr J, judgment being given by McCombe LJ. He recited the facts, and then detailed the terms of the insurance policy, which it must be remembered, was for a hackney carriage[1]:

> '11 The certificate of insurance stated the limitations as to use in the following terms:
> > "(a) Use for business purposes and social and domestic and pleasure purposes by any person who is entitled to drive the vehicle.
> > (b) Use for business purposes including the carriage of passengers for hire or reward under a public hire licence."'

It was argued by the council that this policy must only apply when the vehicle was being used legally, to stand or ply for hire in Rosendale and it could not cover illegal activity in Oldham, a different district. However, it was argued for Sajjad that the provisions of the Road Traffic Act itself prohibited any restriction on the geographic extent of the insurance policy. This was explained by McCombe LJ in the following way[2]:

> '19 Mr Hussain, for [Sajjad] the respondent, now submits that the restriction of the insured activity of using for business purposes including the carriage of passengers for hire or reward has been restricted by reference to an area. That restriction, accordingly offends section 148(2) of the 1988 Act. It is necessary to incorporate certain parts of the Act for the purposes of this judgment to which I will particularly refer. First to section 145 , which provides as follows:

> > "(1) In order to comply with the requirements of this Part of this Act, a policy of insurance must satisfy the following conditions...

> > (3) Subject to subsection (4) below, the policy—
> > (a) must insure such person, persons or classes of persons as may be specified in the policy in respect of any liability which may be incurred by him or them in respect of the death of or bodily injury to any person or damage to property caused by, or arising out of, the use of the vehicle on a road [or other public place] in Great Britain..."

> Section 148 of the Act then provides as follows:

> > "(1) Where a certificate of insurance ... has been delivered under section 147 of this Act to the person by whom a policy has been effected ... so much of the policy or security as purports to restrict—...
> > (a) the insurance of the persons insured by the policy, or... by reference to any of the matters mentioned in subsection (2) below shall, as respects such liabilities as are required to be covered by a policy under section 145 of this Act, be of no effect."

> Then subsection (2):

> > "Those matters are—
> > (e) the time at which or the areas within which the vehicle is used."

20 Mr Hussain's submission is that the effect of these provisions is to render the restriction on the permitted activity of use for hire or reward, is to restrict it with a restriction prohibiting the time which or the areas within which the vehicle is to be used. Moreover, what the respondent did, although a criminal offence, was nonetheless covered by the policy.'

The counter-argument put forward by the council was that the admission of a criminal offence should be sufficient to render any insurance invalid and there was no geographic restriction on the insurance policy. However, it was clear from other cases that committing a criminal offence did not necessarily invalidate insurance.

1   Above at para 11.
2   Above at para 19 onwards.

13.117

McCombe LJ distinguished this cases from the decision in *Telford and Wrekin*[1] in which he had given judgement on the basis of the wording of the insurance policy. In *Telford and Wrekin* the policy covered private hire only and therefore could not extend to cover plying for hire. He quoted paragraphs 9 and 10 of the *Telford* judgment[2] and then concluded[3]:

'26 While I said in *Telford* that the risk would usually be a matter of construction of the insurance policy in question rather than a matter of evidence, that related to the meaning of the policy as to the risk covered. I was anxious to explain in the Telford decision that the view of the witness in that case, a Mr Kemp, as to whether or not the insurer was on risk could not dictate the true meaning of the policy. The question still remains, once one has found the nature of the risk covered as a matter of language of the insurance policy, to determine whether the activity being conducted on the occasion in question is within that covered risk. Certain Mr Moss's submissions to us this morning struck me as seeking to demonstrate consequences [underlined in the original] of a particular construction of the policy rather than the questions of construction [underlined in the original] of the policy and the Act as this court has to do.

27 In the present case, the question is whether the insurance on its true construction, and with reference to the Act and on the facts as found, covered the activity being conducted by this respondent. He was covered for business use including the carriage of passengers for hire or reward under a public hire licence. The vehicle had a public hire licence but not for the type of hire and the area in question on which the respondent had been engaged by his passengers on this occasion. However, in so far as the insurance policy sought to limit the insurance to activity in a particular area, thus if the restriction is rendered ineffective by the operation of section 148 then the policy is to be read, as it seems to me, as if that restriction was treated as deleted in blue pencil from its wording. As Kerr J pointed out in the course of argument, that seems to be the effect of the opening words of

section 148(1) which say that "so much" of the policy as purports to restrict the insurance by reference to any of the matters mentioned should be of no effect. So one would therefore remove from the relevant condition the offending passage.'

After considering the decision in *Singh v Solihull Metropolitan Borough Council*[4] he concluded[5]:

'30 The question therefore, as before, is as to the construction of this policy together with the impact of the Act upon it. Does the condition here purport to restrict the insurance by reference "... the areas within which the vehicle is used."

31 In my judgment, it does purport to restrict the otherwise permitted activity of "hire or reward", which is quite general, by reference to the area restriction in the licence. Under the Act that restriction is to my mind no effect. The policy is to be read for these purposes as if the restriction were not there. Accordingly, I consider that the justices were correct in the decision that they reached, although perhaps for reasons somewhat less full than the ones that have been argued before us.

32 For these reasons therefore I would answer the question posed by the justices in the affirmative and would dismiss the appeal.'

[1]   (2006) EWHC 1748 (Admin), [2007] LLR 82; see para 13.106 above.
[2]   (2006) EWHC 1748 (Admin), [2007] LLR 82; see para 13.106 above.
[3]   Above at paras 26 and 27.
[4]   [2007] EWHC 552 (Admin), [2007] 2 CMLR 47. See para 13.107 above.
[5]   Above at para 30 onwards.

13.118

What conclusions can be drawn from these cases?

1.   That the insurance policy itself will always be the starting point;
2.   Criminal offences do not necessarily invalidate an insurance policy.

As a result, it seems that if a licensed hackney carriage is used to ply or stand for hire outside the district (or zone) in which it is licensed, provided there was a policy of insurance for hackney carriage use in force (often termed 'public hire' by insurance companies), it is likely to be insured even outside the district – see *Oldham BC v Sajjad*[1]. However, if the vehicle is a private hire vehicle and insured accordingly, it is likely that the insurance will not cover illegal plying or standing for hire – see *Telford v Wrekin Borough Council v Ahmed*[2].

Whilst acknowledging that, it does seem unfortunate that in the context of insurance indemnity, the Road Traffic Act and the insurance companies and the courts are prepared to countenance illegal activity, whether that is illegal plying or standing for hire, or driving a hackney carriage when not the holder of a hackney carriage driver's licence.

[1]   [2016] EWHC 3597 (Admin).
[2]   (2006) EWHC 1748 (Admin), [2007] LLR 82.

13.119

It is, however, quite clear that a 'policy of insurance' must be in place for the vehicle for private hire purposes before a private hire vehicle licence can be granted as a consequence of LG(MP)A 1976, s 48(1)(b).

13.120

A prosecution for driving without insurance can be brought under the Road Traffic Offenders Act 1988 and the Local Government Act 1972, s 222 allows a local authority to bring a prosecution for driving a private hire vehicle without insurance, as such a prosecution is 'expedient for the promotion or protection of the interests of the inhabitants of their area'. This was upheld in the case of *Middlesbrough Borough Council v Safeer*[1].

[1]   [2001] 4 All ER 630, QBD.

Middlesbrough Borough Council v Safeer

13.121

> Can a local authority prosecute for an offence of no insurance, notwithstanding that it is not specified as being a local authority power under the Road Traffic Offenders Act 1988, s 4? Held: Yes it can, using the powers contained in the Local Government Act 1972, s 222.

In *Middlesbrough Borough Council v Safeer*[1] there were a number of prosecutions brought by Middlesbrough Borough Council against persons for the offence of using a motor vehicle on a road without there being in force a policy of insurance relating to the use of that vehicle, contrary to the provisions of the Road Traffic Act 1988, s 143. They were convicted in the magistrates' court, and appealed to the Crown Court on the basis that the local authority had no power to bring prosecutions of this type. Accordingly, the question before the Divisional Court was whether the local authority had the power to prosecute in these circumstances.

[1]   [2001] 4 All ER 630, QBD.

13.122

Judgment was given by Mr Justice Silber[1], who outlined the arguments against the local authority having such power and also for it.

The submissions were as follows:

'The submissions

11. The respondents make three submissions to support the decision of the Crown Court. First, importance is attached to the distinction between, on the one hand, the activities which are authorised in s 222(1) of the 1972 Act [Local Government Act 1972] which refers to local authorities having the power to "prosecute or defend or appear in any legal proceedings", and

on the other hand, s 4(1) of the Road Traffic Offenders Act [Road Traffic Offenders Act 1988] which says that a council "may institute proceedings for an offence".

12. Mr Denny, on behalf of the respondents, submits that there is a substantial and relevant difference between the wording as the use of the words "may prosecute" in the 1972 Act gives a much more limited power to the local authorities than the words "may institute proceedings" in s 4(1) of the Road Traffic Offenders Act. His submission is that the use of the word "prosecute" means that it is not possible for a local authority to institute proceedings. Implicit in his submission is the fact that the word "prosecute" must only authorise procedures that occur after proceedings have been instituted.

13. I am unable to accept that submission. To my mind the use of the word "prosecute" means that the local authority is entitled to take all steps necessary to institute and pursue a prosecution. I do not accept that the word "prosecute" has any more limited meaning than that and, in particular, I do not consider that it excludes the institution of proceedings.

14. The second submission made by Mr Denny is that the Road Traffic Offenders Act is described in its preamble as being "An Act to consolidate certain enactments relating to the prosecution and punishment" of various road traffic offences. He contends that the use of the word "consolidate" means that it is a comprehensive code and sets out exclusively all the powers that might be given in relation to those matters.

15. I cannot accept this because to my mind there is nothing in the title of the Road Traffic Offenders Act, or in any provisions of it, and in particular not in s 4, which states that those contain exclusive and comprehensive powers. The powers that are set out in s 4 of that Act are just examples of rights which are given, but are specific examples, and are not limited in any way.

16. The third submission of the respondents is that the provisions of the Road Traffic Offenders Act impliedly repealed the provisions in s 222 of the 1972 [Local Government] Act. In his written submissions, counsel for the respondents relied on cases such as *Vauxhall Estates Ltd v Liverpool Corp* [1932] 1 KB 733 in which it was held that because a later Act was, in the words of Humphreys J (at 746), "totally inconsistent" with an earlier Act or in the words of Avory J (at 743–744), "so inconsistent ... that the two Acts cannot stand together" there was an implied repeal of the earlier statute.

17. The respondents contend that in this case the provisions in the later provision here and the Road Traffic Offenders Act reached that high threshold; I do not agree as there is no reason to believe that the provisions of s 4 of the Road Traffic Offenders Act should be regarded as exhaustive. There is no statement, expressed or implied, in s 4 of the Road Traffic Offenders Act which states that it sets out the only circumstances in which

the local authority can prosecute. Thus, I conclude that s 4 has no effect on any other power previously given to the local authority to prosecute.

18. I now turn to the submissions of Mr Lewis on behalf of the appellant council. He makes two basic submissions. The first submission is that as a matter of statutory construction, s 222 of the 1972 [Local Government] Act is sufficient to empower the local authority to institute criminal proceedings where they consider it expedient for the promotion of the protection of the interests of the inhabitants. As they have a regulatory power for hackney vehicles, the power to prosecute for driving without insurance is clearly apt and suitable to fall within the provisions of s 222 of the 1972 [Local Government] Act. He reinforces that point by saying that s 4 of the Road Traffic Offenders Act does not expressly prohibit or limit the powers conferred by s 222 of the 1972 [Local Government] Act. I agree with him and it is important to stress that there is nothing set out in the later Act which says that the power to prosecute is to be used solely or exclusively for the purposes set out there.

19. The second submission of the council is that there is no reason why s 4 of the Road Traffic Offenders Act should be read as being in any way an implied limitation on the powers of s 222 of the 1972 [Local Government] Act which applies where a local authority is satisfied that prosecution is in the interest of the inhabitants of an area. That is a high threshold, or certainly higher than s 4 of the Road Traffic Offenders Act which does not include this constraint. In addition s 4 of the Road Traffic Offenders Act deals primarily with offences such as the wearing of safety helmets or the use of safety equipment in cars or allowing dogs on the road. It is clearly arguable, as Mr Lewis submits, in many cases whether action to enforce such provisions falls within the scope of a power to act in the interest of local inhabitants, as opposed to acting in the interest of a particular inhabitant. Thus he says, and I agree, there is a sensible purpose in providing express powers in respect of the offences referred to in s 4 of the Road Traffic Offenders Act. To my mind there is no reason, either of language or of policy, to read s 4 as impliedly limiting or effecting any other powers of the local authority and, in particular, those in s 222 of the 1972 [Local Government] Act.'

[1]   *Middlesbrough Borough Council v Safeer* [2001] 4 All ER 630, QBD.

13.123

He concluded that local authorities could prosecute using the provisions of the Local Government Act 1972, s 222, and were not prohibited from doing so by the limited list of offences contained in the Road Traffic Offenders Act 1988, s 4[1]:

'20. In answer to the question posed I would answer that by stating that the local authority did not have the right to prosecute for an offence of having no insurance contrary to s 143 of the 1988 Act and Sch 2 to the Road

Traffic Offenders Act, the Crown Court erred in the light of s 222 of the 1972 [Local Government] Act.'

1   *Middlesbrough Borough Council v Safeer* [2001] 4 All ER 630, QBD.

TRANSFER OF PRIVATE HIRE VEHICLES

13.124

LG(MP)A 1976, s 49 applies to private hire vehicles as it does to hackney carriages. This requires the proprietor who transfers his interest in a private hire vehicle to another person to give written notice to the district council detailing the name and address of the person to whom the private hire vehicle has been transferred. This requirement is waived if that person is already registered on the licence as a person having an interest in the vehicle. Likewise, LG(MP)A 1976, s 50[1], in relation to testing, has identical implications in relation to proprietors of private hire vehicles as it does to hackney carriages[2].

1   See Appendix I.
2   See Chapter 8, para 8.133 onwards and para 8.143 onwards.

REMOVAL AND RETURN OF THE PLATE

13.125

When the vehicle licence expires or is suspended or revoked, the local authority can require the return of the plate under the provisions of LG(MP)A 1976, s 58(1). It should be noted that the return of the plate is not automatic on expiry or suspension or revocation. Such action has to be instigated by the local authority serving notice on the proprietor requiring the return of the plate within seven days of the date of service of the notice. Failure to comply, on the part of the proprietor, with such notice is an offence by virtue of s 58(2). In this case, the plate can then be removed from the private hire vehicle by an authorised officer or police constable and the proprietor can be prosecuted. The maximum fine is level 3 on the standard scale and a continuing daily fine of £10 can be levied until the plate is surrendered.

If a proprietor refuses to surrender the plate when the licence has expired, been suspended or revoked, the local authority can place a sticker on it which makes it clear the licence is suspended or revoked. These stickers cannot be removed without destroying the plate, in which case the proprietor would have to purchase a new plate when the licence is re-instated.

SUSPENSION AND REVOCATION

13.126

LG(MP)A 1976, s 60 allows the local authority to suspend, revoke or refuse to renew a vehicle licence for one of the following reasons:

'60–(1) Notwithstanding anything in the Act of 1847 [TPCA 1847] or in this Part of this Act, a district council may suspend or revoke, or (on application therefor under section 40 of the Act of 1847 or section 48 of this Act, as the case may be) refuse to renew a vehicle licence on any of the following grounds—

(a) that the hackney carriage or private hire vehicle is unfit for use as a hackney carriage or private hire vehicle;

(b) any offence under, or non-compliance with, the provisions of the Act of 1847 or of this Part of this Act by the operator or driver; or

(c) any other reasonable cause.'

13.127

The question of the unfitness of the vehicle will be a matter of fact in relation to its mechanical condition, safety and comfort. Alternatively, or if it is a vehicle which is newly presented, then it will be subject to any of the other matters contained in LG(MP)A 1976, s 48(1).

13.128

LG(MP)A 1976, s 60(1)(b)[1] allows suspension, revocation or non-renewal of a licence for any offence under either LG(MP)A 1976 or TPCA 1847 on the part of the operator or driver for any non-compliance with those provisions. Obviously, to prove an offence, a conviction will have to have been recorded, but non-compliance could be demonstrated in a way that falls short of a criminal conviction.

[1] See also Chapter 8, para 8.241.

13.129

Suspension, revocation or non-renewal can also be for 'any other reasonable cause'. Any other reasonable cause does not have be construed ejusdem generis with the preceding grounds, as demonstrated by the case of *Norwich City Council v Thurtle and Watcham*[1], which concerned the theft of car seats which were subsequently used in private hire vehicles.

[1] (21 May 1981, unreported); see Chapter 8, para 8.138.

13.130

There is some difficulty here, in relation to the suspension, revocation or refusal to renew a vehicle licence. It is obvious that, if the vehicle is unsatisfactory for use as a private hire vehicle, suspension of the licence would make sense, as the period of suspension could be used to remedy the defects in the vehicle. Likewise, if the condition of the vehicle is so severe that no amount of work will bring it up to the required standard, then the licence should be revoked or not renewed.

Leeds City Council v Hussein

13.131

> Following his arrest for violent disorder, Leeds City Council suspended the
> driver and vehicle licences. Was it lawful to suspend the vehicle licence as
> a result of actions of the proprietor, who was also the driver in question?
> Held: Yes.

It is in relation to criminal convictions that the difficulties arise. Convictions
are caused by people, not by the vehicle itself. To revoke the vehicle licence
because of someone's convictions can on occasions seem unjust. Can a local
authority justify a suspension or revocation of a vehicle licence when the driver
has not been convicted of an offence? On the one hand, provided that the vehicle
is safe and satisfactory, it can quite readily be driven by another person who
holds a private hire driver's licence and indeed, operated by another operator.
Action can be taken against the people who committed the offence or alleged
offence (assuming they hold either an operator's or driver's licence) by way of
action against those respective licences. The alternative view is that if a driver
has behaved in such a way that his driver's licence should be removed, then he
should not continue to profit from the use of his vehicle in circumstances when
he is also a vehicle proprietor. The question of whether a vehicle licence could
be suspended in the absence of a criminal conviction was considered in *Leeds
City Council v Hussein*[1]. In that case Leeds City Council suspended a private hire
driver and vehicle proprietor's licences.

> 'The reason for these suspensions was that on 2nd August 2001 the
> respondent had been charged with an offence of violent disorder arising
> out of an incident on 26th June 2001, which involved a number of private
> hire drivers and their vehicles.²'

The question arose as to whether a conviction was required before action could
be taken³ and also whether action could be taken against the vehicle licence as
well as the driver's licence. This was addressed briefly but succinctly by Silber
J in the following terms⁴:

> '17. Up until now when considering this issue I have been considering
> suspension of a driver's licence under section 61 of the 1976 Act, but a
> vehicle licence can also be suspended for the same reason, namely "any
> other unreasonable cause" as specified in section 60 of the 1976 Act. I do
> not believe that those words would have a different meaning in section 60
> from that which I have already set out in respect of the following section,
> namely section 61. So I conclude that a vehicle licence can be suspended
> even though the driver of it has not been convicted.'

It seems clear therefore that action can be taken against a vehicle licence if the
circumstances justify it.

¹   [2003] RTR 199, Admin Ct; see Chapter 10, para 10.146.

2   Per Silber J at para 2.
3   For full consideration of this part of the judgment, see para 10.146.
4   Per Silber J at para 17.

13.132

Notice of any decision to suspend, revoke or refuse to renew a vehicle licence must be given to the proprietor in writing, stating the grounds on which the licence has been suspended, together with the reasons for that decision. This must be within 14 days of the decision. If the proprietor is aggrieved by that decision, he has a right of appeal to the magistrates' court under LG(MP)A 1976, s 60(3).

IMMEDIATE SUSPENSION OR REVOCATION

13.133

The provisions of LG(MP)A 1976, s 68 apply to private hire vehicles just as they do to hackney carriages, allowing inspection of a private hire vehicle and if necessary, subsequent immediate suspension or revocation of the licence by an authorised officer of the council or a police constable:

'68 Fitness of hackney carriages and private hire vehicles

Any authorised officer of the council in question or any constable shall have power at all reasonable times to inspect and test, for the purpose of ascertaining its fitness, any hackney carriage or private hire vehicle licensed by a district council, or any taximeter affixed to such a vehicle, and if he is not satisfied as to the fitness of the hackney carriage or private hire vehicle or as to the accuracy of its taximeter he may by notice in writing require the proprietor of the hackney carriage or private hire vehicle to make it or its taximeter available for further inspection and testing at such reasonable time and place as may be specified in the notice and suspend the vehicle licence until such time as such authorised officer or constable is so satisfied:

Provided that, if the authorised officer or constable is not so satisfied before the expiration of a period of two months, the said licence shall, by virtue of this section, be deemed to have been revoked and subsections (2) and (3) of section 60 of this Act shall apply with any necessary modifications.'

If the vehicle does not satisfy the council's requirements then a notice can be issued requiring the vehicle to be submitted for a re-test and the licence can be suspended until such time as the vehicle satisfactorily passes any subsequent test. This is an extremely useful provision and is essential for keeping the private hire vehicles operating within the area of the council in a satisfactory and safe condition.

'Unfit' in this section means any non-compliance with the council's conditions, as well as mechanical unfitness. This was the decision of the Court of Appeal in *R (on the application of Wilcock) v Lancaster City Council*[1].

1   [2013] LLR 607 Admin Ct and [2014] LLR 388, CA. See Chapter 8, para 8.151 onwards for more details.

TESTING OF VEHICLES

13.134

As has been seen, LG(MP)A 1976, s 68 allows any authorised officer of the council which licenses the vehicle or any police constable to inspect and test the vehicle[1]. This is not limited to any number of tests per year and can be used for 'spot' tests where there may be concern about the safety of a particular vehicle. There is also a power to test vehicles on a regular basis. This is contained in LG(MP)A 1976, s 50 and is used by authorities to test the vehicle during the currency of the vehicle licence:

'(1) Without prejudice to the provisions of section 68 of this Act, the proprietor of any hackney carriage or of any private hire vehicle licensed by a district council shall present such hackney carriage or private hire vehicle for inspection and testing by or on behalf of the council within such period and at such place within the area of the council as they may by notice reasonably require:

Provided that a district council shall not under the provisions of this subsection require a proprietor to present the same hackney carriage or private hire vehicle for inspection and testing on more than three separate occasions during any one period of twelve months.'

[1]   See Chapter 8, para 8.150 for more details.

13.135

Many local authorities do require vehicle tests more frequently than the annual test on renewal, but the DfT casts doubt on this practice in its *Best Practice Guide*[1].

'Vehicle Testing

32. There is considerable variation between local licensing authorities on vehicle testing, including the related question of age limits. The following can be regarded as best practice:

Frequency Of Tests. The legal requirement is that all taxis should be subject to an MOT test or its equivalent once a year. For PHVs the requirement is for an annual test after the vehicle is three years old. An annual test for licensed vehicles of whatever age (that is, including vehicles that are less than three years old) seems appropriate in most cases, unless local conditions suggest that more frequent tests are necessary. However, more frequent tests may be appropriate for older vehicles (see 'age limits' below). Local licensing authorities may wish to note that a review carried out by the National Society for Cleaner Air in 2005 found that taxis were more likely than other vehicles to fail an emissions test. This finding, perhaps suggests that emissions testing should be carried out on ad hoc basis and more frequently than the full vehicle test.

Criteria For Tests. Similarly, for mechanical matters it seems appropriate to apply the same criteria as those for the MOT test to taxis and PHVs*. The MOT test on vehicles first used after 31 March 1987 includes checking of all seat belts. However, taxis and PHVs provide a service to the public, so it is also appropriate to set criteria for the internal condition of the vehicle, though these should not be unreasonably onerous.

*A manual outlining the method of testing and reasons for failure of all MOT tested items can be obtained from the Stationary Office see http:www.tsoshop.co.uk/bookstore.asp?FO=1159966&Action=Book &From=SearchResults &ProductID=0115525726

Age Limits. It is perfectly possible for an older vehicle to be in good condition. So the setting of an age limit beyond which a local authority will not license vehicles may be arbitrary and inappropriate. But a greater frequency of testing may be appropriate for older vehicles – for example, twice-yearly tests for vehicles more than five years old.

Number Of Testing Stations. There is sometimes criticism that local authorities provide only one testing centre for their area (which may be geographically extensive). So it is good practice for local authorities to consider having more than one testing station. There could be an advantage in contracting out the testing work, and to different garages. In that way the licensing authority can benefit from competition in costs. (The Vehicle Operators and Standards Agency – VOSA – may be able to assist where there are local difficulties in provision of testing stations.)

33. The Technical Officer Group of the Public Authority Transport Network has produced Best Practice Guidance which focuses on national inspection standards for taxis and PHVs. Local licensing authorities might find it helpful to refer to the testing standards set out in this guidance in carrying out their licensing responsibilities. The PATN can be accessed via the Freight Transport Association.'

This was considered in relation to hackney carriages in Chapter 8 and the comments are equally relevant to private hire vehicles[2].

---

1   DfT, '*Taxi and Private Hire Vehicle Licensing: Best Practice Guidance*' (October 2006, revised March 2010), para 17, available at http://www.dft.gov.uk/pgr/regional/taxis/taxiandprivatehirevehicle lic1792. See Appendix II.

2   See Chapter 8, para 8.143 onwards. It was stated at para 8.149: 'It is clear that the DfT view testing in a different light to some local authorities. The suggestion that an annual test is sufficient for a vehicle which may travel up to 80,000 miles per year (equivalent to 8 years average private car use) is regarded as surprising by many involved in licensing hackney carriages and private hire vehicles, and indeed by some operators. The DfT suggestion for bi-annual tests after 5 years (by which time it is entirely possible that the vehicle may have travelled 150,000 miles, and conceivably approaching 400,000 miles) seems to undervalue the importance of vehicle testing in relation to passenger carrying vehicles such as hackney carriages and private hire vehicles.'

EXEMPT VEHICLES

13.136

LG(MP)A 1976, s 75 makes it clear that certain vehicles are exempt from the requirements of LG(MP)A 1976, Pt II. These are principally vehicles to be used in connection with a funeral or used wholly or mainly for the purpose of funerals by a person who is a funeral director[1] and vehicles that are being used in connection with a wedding. There are also other situations where the DfT suggest that licensing of operators, vehicles and drivers is not required[2].

[1]   LG(MP)A 1976, s 75(1)(c).
[2]   For further consideration of this, see Chapter 12, para 12.125 onwards.

Chapter 14

Private hire drivers outside London

INTRODUCTION

14.1

The role of the private hire driver is very similar to the role of the hackney carriage driver. Each is required to hold a licence, and to drive members of the public in a licensed vehicle. Indeed, the similarities are so great that many local authorities grant combined or dual licences that serve as a licence to drive both hackney carriages and private hire vehicles.

14.2

The case of *Benson v Boyce*[1] makes it clear that a private hire vehicle is always a private hire vehicle, and this makes it imperative that anyone who drives a private hire vehicle holds a private hire driver's licence[2].

Secondly, the responsibilities placed on and the power and control available to, a private hire driver are significant. A private hire driver is responsible not only for their passengers, but also for the control of the vehicle and all other road users. Also, a private hire driver has almost complete control over the passengers, especially in the case of a lone passenger.

This chapter examines how such a licence is obtained and to whom it can be granted, but the actual considerations that apply to private hire drivers' licences are to all intents and purposes identical to those that apply to hackney carriage drivers[3]. As a consequence, many local authorities issue dual or combined licences, allowing the holder to drive both a hackney carriage and a private hire vehicle.

[1]   [1997] RTR 226; see Chapter 13, para 13.72.
[2]   As a result of this, some local authorities issue 'restricted' driver's licences for the spouses and other relatives of private hire vehicle proprietors to enable them to drive the private hire vehicle when it is not working. This is achieved by means of conditions attached to the driver's licence, limiting the use of the licence to times when the vehicle is not carrying passengers. To qualify for such a licence, the 'restricted' driver will still have to meet the requirements of LG(MP)A 1976, s 51. See para 14.27 below.
[3]   See Chapter 10.

LICENSING OF DRIVERS OF PRIVATE HIRE VEHICLES

14.3

The requirement to hold a licence is contained in the Local Government (Miscellaneous Provisions) Act 1976 (LG(MP)A 1976), s 46(1)(b):

'46 Vehicle, driver's and operators' licences

(1) Except as authorised by this Part of this Act—

(a) ...

(b) no person shall in a controlled district act as driver of any private hire vehicle without having a current licence under section 51 of this Act [LG(MP)A 1976, s 51]; ...'

14.4

The licence itself is granted under LG(MP)A 1976, s 51:

'51.— Licensing of drivers of private hire vehicles.

(1) Subject to the provisions of this Part of this Act, a district council shall, on the receipt of an application from any person for the grant to that person of a licence to drive private hire vehicles, grant to that person a driver's licence:

Provided that a district council shall not grant a licence—

(a) unless they are satisfied

    (i) that the applicant is a fit and proper person to hold a driver's licence; and

    (ii) that the applicant is not disqualified by reason of the applicant's immigration status from driving a private hire vehicle; or

(b) to any person who has not for at least twelve months been authorised to drive a motor car, or is not at the date of the application for a driver's licence so authorised.

(1ZA) In determining for the purposes of subsection (1) whether an applicant is disqualified by reason of the applicant's immigration status from driving a private hire vehicle, a district council must have regard to any guidance issued by the Secretary of State.

(1) For the purposes of subsection (1) of this section a person is authorised to drive a motor car if-

(a) he holds a licence granted under Part III of the Road Traffic Act 1988 (not being a provisional licence) authorising him to drive a motor car, or

(b) he is authorised by virtue of section 99A(1) or section 109(1)] of that Act to drive in Great Britain a motor car.

(2) A district council may attach to the grant of a licence under this section such conditions as they may consider reasonably necessary.

(3) It shall be the duty of a council by which licences are granted in pursuance of this section to enter, in a register maintained by the council for the purpose, the following particulars of each such licence, namely—
(a)   the name of the person to whom it is granted;
(b)   the date on which and the period for which it is granted; and
(c)   if the licence has a serial number, that number,
and to keep the register available at its principal offices for inspection by members of the public during office hours free of charge.'

A comparison with the provisions governing the licensing of hackney carriage drivers

14.5

The provisions of LG(MP)A 1976, s 51 are similar to those contained in LG(MP)A 1976, s 59, which govern the licensing of a hackney carriage driver.

14.6

However, because there are slight differences, it is not possible to simply treat the provisions as totally interchangeable.

14.7

Once an application has been made to the local authority for a licence to drive a private hire vehicle under LG(MP)A 1976, s 51, the local authority is under a duty to grant that licence[1], unless it is prevented from doing so under s 51(1)(a) or (b). This duty to grant a licence can be contrasted with the provisions for hackney carriage drivers' licences, where there is no requirement to grant a licence[2].

[1]   LG(MP)A 1976, s 51(1). See Appendix I.
[2]   Town Police Clauses Act 1847, s 46; see Chapter 10, para 10.2.

14.8

The criteria and qualifications for a private hire driver are the same as those for hackney carriage drivers: the person must be a fit and proper person to hold a private hire driver's licence, must have been authorised to drive a motor vehicle for a period of a least one year before the date of the application and have the right to remain and work in the UK[1].

[1]   These are considered fully in Chapter 10, para 10.9 onwards.

14.9

The methods available to assess the fitness and propriety of the applicant include an Enhanced DBS check, the requirement that the applicant complete a statutory declaration and for the local authority to undertake a DVLA check. Again, those provisions are identical to those relating to hackney carriage drivers[1].

[1]   See Chapter 10, para 10.21 onwards.

14.10

However, after that, the provisions of LG(MP)A 1976, s 51 differ from LG(MP)A 1976, s 59. Section 51(2) gives a specific power to impose conditions on a private hire driver's licence, and this can be any condition which the local authority 'consider reasonably necessary'.

'(2) A district council may attach to the grant of a licence under this section such conditions as they may consider reasonably necessary.'

Most local authorities do impose conditions on their private hire drivers' licences. As there is no specific power to make byelaws for private hire drivers, the ability to impose conditions is extremely important.

It is also possible for a local authority to have a Code of Conduct. This can apply to both hackney carriage and private hire drivers and specifies the standard of behaviour and conduct expected of a licensed driver. If the driver falls short of this standard, the council will then consider whether they remain a fit and proper person to hold the licence.

14.11

In addition, the local authority has to maintain a register of private hire drivers' licences[1], including the following details:

- the name of the person to whom it is granted;
- the date on which and the period for which it is granted; and
- if the licence has a serial number, that number.

The register must be 'available at its principal offices for inspection by members of the public during office hours free of charge'. There is no statutory requirement as to the form the register should take[2]. Accordingly, computer records can be used, provided that there is some mechanism by which the register can be inspected.

[1]   LG(MP)A 1976, s 51(3); see Appendix I.
[2]   This can be contrasted with the requirement in relation to hackney carriage proprietors' licences under the Town Police Clauses Act 1847, s 42, where the register must be maintained in a 'book'.

14.12

If a person is aggrieved by either a refusal to grant a licence under LG(MP)A 1976, s 51 or any conditions that are attached to that licence under s 51(2), he can appeal to the magistrates' court under LG(MP)A 1976, s 52:

'52 Appeals in respect of drivers' licences

Any person aggrieved by—
(1)   the refusal of the district council to grant a driver's licence under section 51 of this Act; or
(2)   any conditions attached to the grant of a driver's licence;
may appeal to a magistrates' court.'[1]

[1]   The requirements in relation to appeals are considered in Chapter 3, para 3.3 onwards.

14.13

In relation to the application and to enable the local authority fully to consider the applicant, LG(MP)A 1976, s 57 allows the local authority to seek information. This specifically refers to a medical test. Some authorities also require 'knowledge' tests of the locality and spoken English tests[1].

[1]   For full details, see Chapter 10, para 10.60 onwards.

14.14

LG(MP)A 1976, s 53(1)(a) was amended in 2015 to introduce a presumption that a private hire drivers' licence will be granted for three years.

'53.— Drivers' licences for hackney carriages and private hire vehicles.

(1) (a) Subject to section 53A, every licence granted by a district council under the provisions of this Part of this Act to any person to drive a private hire vehicle shall remain in force for three years from the date of such licence or for such lesser period, specified in the licence, as the district council think appropriate in the circumstances of the case.'

As with the identical provisions contained in s 53(1)(b) for hackney carriage drivers' licences, this is therefore not a mandatory three-year driver's licence, but rather an indication that drivers' licences should last three years. There is no further guidance as to what a district council might think to be appropriate circumstances and therefore this will remain a matter for the local authority's discretion[1].

The DfT Best Practice Guide[2] has not been reissued since the introduction of the amendment to s 51 and currently suggests that local authorities should usually grant three year licences:

'Duration of Licences

55. It is obviously important for safety reasons that drivers should be licensed. But it is not necessarily good practice to require licences to be renewed annually. That can impose an undue burden on drivers and licensing authorities alike. Three years is the legal maximum period and is in general the best approach. One argument against 3-year licences has been that a criminal offence may be committed, and not notified, during the duration of the licence. But this can of course also be the case during the duration of a shorter licence. In relation to this, authorities will wish to note that the Home Office in April 2006 issued revised guidance for police forces on the Notifiable Occupations Scheme. Paragraphs 62–65 below provide further information about this scheme.

56. However, an annual licence may be preferred by some drivers. That may be because they have plans to move to a different job or a different area, or because they cannot easily pay the fee for a three-year licence, if it is larger than the fee for an annual one. So it can be good practice to offer drivers the choice of an annual licence or a three year licence.'[3]

It does seem clear that authority cannot insist on granting a three-year licence, and if some reason an applicant wants a one-year licence, the authority should oblige.

1   For full details see Chapter 10, para 10.3 onwards.
2   DfT *'Taxi and Private Hire Vehicle Licensing: Best Practice Guidance'* (October 2006, revised March 2010), available at http://www.dft.gov.uk/pgr/regional/taxis/taxiandprivatehirevehiclelic1792.
3   That extract is obsolete, but as it is the most recent published information by the Department of Transport in relation to drivers licences it is worth noting. It is also important to recognise that the Home Office Notifiable Occupations Scheme was cancelled in March 2015.

14.15

A fee can be charged for private hire drivers' licences under LG(MP)A 1976, s 53(2):

> '(2) Notwithstanding the provisions of the Act of 1847, a district council may demand and recover for the grant to any person of a licence to drive a hackney carriage, or a private hire vehicle, as the case may be, such a fee as they consider reasonable with a view to recovering the costs of issue and administration and may remit the whole or part of the fee in respect of a private hire vehicle in any case in which they think it appropriate to do so.'

It is important to recognise that this power is limited. It only allows for the recovery of the 'costs of issue and administration' and therefore no costs in relation to the enforcement of private hire drivers' licences can be built into the licence fee[1]. It is also payable on grant, so if the application is refused, the entire fee must be refunded. It is therefore important that additional costs such as medical tests or DBS checks are not incorporated into the licence fee, but payable separately.

1   For full consideration of licence fees see Chapter 4.

14.16

LG(MP)A 1976, s 54 places a duty on the local authority to issue drivers' badges when a licence is granted under LG(MP)A 1976, s 51 to a private hire driver, and s 54(2)(a) requires the driver to wear it at all times when acting as a private hire driver. Failure on the part of a licensed private hire driver to wear the badge is an offence.

14.17

It is worth noting that, as a private hire vehicle is always a private hire vehicle, at all times, when the vehicle is being driven, the driver must wear his badge under LG(MP)A 1976, s 54(2)(a), irrespective of whether the vehicle is 'working' at the time.

14.18

A number of authorities, by condition attached to the driver's licence, require a second badge (which they issue free of charge) to be displayed in such a way within the vehicle so that the passenger can see the badge. The need for this second badge arose as it became apparent that the badge worn on the driver's chest may not easily be seen by the passenger, especially those seated behind the driver.

Drivers' hours

14.19

There are no direct controls over the hours that a private hire driver can work[1]. However, the Working Time Regulations 1998[2] as amended apply to private hire drivers. Regulation 18 was amended by the Working Time (Amendment) Regulations 2003[3] with effect from 1 August 2003 and limits a driver's working week to 48 hours, averaged over a 17-week period.

1   This can be contrasted with HGV and PSV drivers whose driving hours are regulated. There have been suggestions that private hire drivers' hours should be limited, but at present nothing has been formally proposed.
2   SI 1998/1833.
3   SI 2003/1684.

14.20

This only applies to drivers who are employed and working under a contract of employment and does not apply to self-employed drivers. It is therefore of limited application in relation to the private hire trade, where the vast majority of drivers are self-employed.

14.21

In relation to those who are employed, they can opt out of the application of the Regulations by agreeing in writing that they should not apply in accordance with reg 4(1) (this must be voluntary and the driver cannot be forced to opt out by the employer).

SUSPENSION, REVOCATION OR REFUSAL TO RENEW A PRIVATE HIRE DRIVER'S LICENCE

14.22

LG(MP)A 1976, s 61 gives the local authority powers to suspend, revoke (or on an application for renewal, refuse to renew) a private hire driver's licence. This is exactly the same as the power available for hackney carriage driver's licences under the same section[1]. This includes the ability for the local authority to suspend or revoke a private hire driver's licence with immediate effect if necessary in the interests of public safety[2]. There is the same limitation under the ruling in *R (app Singh) v Cardiff City Council*[3] on a suspension followed by a revocation, and also, suspension of a private hire drivers' licence can be used as a punishment[4].

1   See Chapter 10, para 10.133 onwards for full consideration of suspension and revocation
     powers, and the effect of such action. There is no difference between the exercise of these
     powers for private hire and hackney carriage drivers.
2   LG(MP)A 1976, s 61. See Appendix I.
3   [2012] EWHC 1852 (Admin), [2013] LLR 108.
4   For full details see Chapter 6, para 6.43 onwards and Chapter 10, para 10.154.

14.23

It is an offence under LG(MP)A 1976, s 69 for the driver of a private hire vehicle
unnecessarily to prolong, either in distance or in time, the journey without
reasonable cause[1].

1   This provision applies equally to hackney carriages and reference should be made to Chapter 9,
     para 9.43 for a detailed study of this point.

PROBLEMS ARISING FROM THE RULING IN *BENSON V BOYCE*[1]

14.24

As a private hire vehicle is always a private hire vehicle, it must be driven by a
person who is a licensed private hire driver. This has led to two areas of difficulty.

1   [1997] RTR 226.

14.25

Firstly, in relation to the testing of a vehicle, either for the MOT test or by the
local authority[1]. Generally speaking, if there is a test conducted on the public
highway, then the driver of the vehicle must be a licensed private hire driver,
but that can be overcome by the use of 'trade plates'. These are available to
motor traders and vehicle testers under the provisions of the Vehicle Excise
and Registration Act 1994, Part 1. If trade plates have been issued to be vehicle
tester, then that covers 'all vehicles which are from time to time submitted to
him for testing in the course of his business as a vehicle tester'[2]. If those vehicles
are private hire vehicles, and submitted for testing (either MOT or the council's
own tests) then they would fall within the definition. This appears to overcome
the general prohibition on anybody other than a licensed private hire driver
driving a private hire vehicle.

This can cover both commercial operations (eg, independent garages) and
in-house council testing stations[3]. The use of such plates must comply with the
requirements of both the Vehicle Excise and Registration Act 1994 and the Road
Vehicles (Registration and Licensing) Regulations[4].

An alternative solution is also possible in areas where the local authority has
its own testers. It would be possible for the local authority to license them as
private hire drivers, but, in areas where testing is undertaken by independent
garages, it would be impossible to license all possible testers of such vehicles.

1   This can be compared with the situation pertaining to hackney carriages. See para 8.153.
     A hackney carriage is always a hackney carriage and must always be driven by a licensed hackney
     carriage driver. There is, however, one exception, introduced into the Town Police Clauses
     Act 1847, s 46 by the Transport Act 1985, s 139(2) and the Transport Act 1985, Sch 7, para 3,

which allows a hackney carriage to be driven by a person not holding a hackney carriage driver's licence if the vehicle or the driver is being tested. This was introduced for hackney carriages to overcome the difficulty and a similar provision is required for private hire vehicles. However, *Hawkins v Edwards* [1901] 2 KB 169 was decided in 1901 and *Yates v Gates* [1970] 1 All ER 754, QBD dates back to 1970, and this exception was not enacted until 1985. As yet there is no indication that Parliament will act to rectify this situation for private hire vehicles and drivers.

2   Vehicle Excise and Registration Act 1994, s 11(4).

3   Vehicle Excise and Registration Act 1994, s 62(1) states: *"vehicle tester"* means a person, other than a motor trader, who regularly in the course of his business engages in the testing on roads of vehicles belonging to other persons' and '*"business"* includes the performance by a local or public authority of its functions'.

4   SI 2002/2742.

14.26

Another possibility is to consider the vehicle licence itself. It would be possible to suspend the vehicle licence under LG(MP)A 1976, s 60(1)(c) for the duration of the test, thereby allowing a non-licensed driver to drive the vehicle without contravening LG(MP)A 1976, s 46(1)(b), but this is both cumbersome and generally impractical.

14.27

The second area of difficulty concerns the spouses or partners of licensed private hire drivers. As private hire vehicles are often used as family vehicles when they are not working, it is necessary to consider the position of persons who may drive these vehicles during times that they are not working, so-called 'leisure use'[1].

Some authorities issue 'restricted' private hire driver's licences. These do not allow the holder to drive a private hire vehicle when it is working, but do permit such a vehicle to be driven at other times. This is achieved by conditions attached to the licence under LG(MP)A 1976, s 51(2).

To encourage applicants to accept these restrictions on the use of their private hire driver's licence, many local authorities do not require the applicant to sit and pass the knowledge test, or other tests that might be required for a 'full' driver's licence. These authorities then charge a lower fee for these licences. This reduced fee is justified on the basis that as fewer tests were required, the costs of issue were not as high. In these cases, such an approach seems lawful.

Where the same tests are required before grant (eg, the examination of criminal records alone, where no additional tests are undertaken for any drivers) can the authority charge a lower fee for a 'restricted' driver's licence? This does not seem possible as under LG(MP)A 1976, s 53(2), the local authority can only 'remit the whole or part of the fee in respect of a private hire vehicle licence', not a driver's licence. In fact, it is difficult to see why the local authority should wish to charge a lower fee. Before such a 'restricted' licence can be granted, the same checks must be undertaken as for a full licence, as the local authority cannot grant a licence to anyone who does not fulfil the criteria in LG(MP)A 1976, s 51(1)(a) or (b) and, therefore, where no additional tests are required, the cost to the local authority will be the same as for a full licence. It is suggested that it would be difficult to justify a complaint being made concerning the subsidy of these licences by either the other licence holders or the council itself.

[1] A proposal was contained within the Deregulation Bill in 2014 which would have allowed people who did not hold a private hire driver's licence to drive a private hire vehicle when it was not carrying passengers. This was intended to place the use of private hire vehicles outside London in a similar position to those within London (see Chapter 22, para 22.18 onwards). This proposal led to significant concern from local authorities, licensing bodies and safety campaigners, and was dropped.

14.28

The concept of a 'restricted' licence is also used by some local authorities in respect of limousines and 'executive' cars[1]. Some authorities restrict drivers to these types of vehicles alone by condition attached to the driver's licence under LG(MP)A 1976, s 51(2). As above, the incentive for accepting such restrictions are often the removal of a requirement for a knowledge test, or other associated tests.

[1] For consideration of the licensing of limousines, 'executive' and other 'specialist' vehicles, see Chapter 13, para 13.64.

Chapter 15

Enforcement within London

INTRODUCTION

15.1

Any legal requirements are meaningless and pointless unless they are enforced. If there is no sanction applied for breach of the law, the law is worthless. This is true of hackney carriage and private hire licensing, just as much as it is true of any other area of law[1].

[1]   For general commentary on enforcement, please see Chapter 6.

15.2

The duties to implement hackney carriage legislation lie with Transport for London (TfL) by virtue of the Greater London Authority Act 1999, s 253 and Sch 20, para 1. Private hire matters within London are the responsibility of TfL by virtue of the Greater London Authority Act 1999, s 254 and Sch 21. TfL is itself a body corporate created by the Greater London Authority Act 1999, s 514 and it controls hackney carriage and private hire activities via London Taxi and Private Hire (LTPH) (formerly the Public Carriage Office (PCO)).

15.3

As with local authorities outside London, from April 2014 TfL must have regard to the requirements of the Regulator's Code[1]. This is a Statutory Code of Practice made under the Legislative and Regulatory Reform Act 2006.

[1]   Available at https://www.gov.uk/government/uploads/system/uploads/attachment_data/file/300126/14-705-regulators-code.pdf

15.4

TfL should also have regard to their own enforcement and prosecutions policy (if any). This is important following the decision in *R v Glen Adaway*[1], which shows that if a local authority either fails to have regard to its own enforcement policy, or departs from it without good reason, an application for a stay in criminal proceedings can be made. The decision has been distinguished and modified in subsequent cases[2] and the current position is that an application for a prosecution to be stayed because it amounts to an abuse of process will only be likely to succeed if the decision to prosecute is *Wednesbury* unreasonable, taking into account any enforcement policy the authority may have. Although the cases specifically relate to local authorities, there is no reason why this approach will not also be applicable to TfL.

1   [2004] EWCA Crim 2831.
2   See *R (on the application of Mondelly) v Commissioner of Police for the Metropolis* (2007) 171 JP 121, [2006] EWHC 2370 (Admin) and *London Borough of Wandsworth v Rashid* [2009] EWHC 1844 (Admin), [2009] LLR 788.

CRIMINAL ENFORCEMENT

15.5

The same concepts apply to criminal enforcement within London as they do outside London. The offences may differ slightly, but a full list of criminal offences relating to hackney carriages and private hire matters is given in Table 15.1 and Table 15.2.

Table 15.1

Enforcement table – London hackney carriages

Legislation	Section or Article	Offence	Maximum Penalty
London Hackney Carriage Act 1831	35	Refusal to take a hiring	Level 1
	47	Refusal to wait after taking deposit to cover waiting time	Level 1
	50	Carrying persons other than the hirer without consent	Level 1
	51	Depriving another driver of a fare	Level 1
	56	Driver intoxicated, wanton or furious driving or wilful misconduct	Level 1
London Hackney Carriages Act 1843	10	Lending a HC driver's licence to another person	£5.00
	10	Proprietor allowing unlicensed driver to drive a HC	Level 3
	14	Making a false representation on a driver's licence application	Level 3
	17	Driver's ticket (badge) to be worn when working	Level 1
	18	Failure to return ticket (badge) on expiry or suspension etc	Level 1
	18	Using a ticket (badge) without a licence	Level 1
	18	Using a fake ticket (badge)	Level 1
	19	Using a defaced or illegible ticket (badge)	Level 1

Legislation	Section or Article	Offence	Maximum Penalty
	21	Proprietor to retain driver's licences and produce licence if summonsed	Level 1
	25	Refusal to surrender licence on suspension or revocation	Level 1
	27	Driver allowing another to drive a HC without consent of proprietor	Level 1
	27	Driving a HC without the consent of the proprietor	Level 1
	27	Failure to reveal identity of unauthorised driver	Level 1
	28	Wanton or furious driving, or careless or wilful misbehaviour causing hurt or damage	Level 1, or 2 months imprisonment
	28	Drunkenness or use of insulting or abusive language	Level 1, or 2 months imprisonment
	33	Causing an obstruction by plying other than at a stand	Level 1
	33	Causing an obstruction by loitering or wilful misbehaviour in any public street, road or place	Level 1
	33	Allowing a person other than the hirer to ride on the driving box	Level 1
London Hackney Carriage Act 1853	16	Annoying or obstructing passengers or inhabitants by any picture, placard notice or advertisement painted on or attached to an HC	Level 1 (by virtue of section 19)
	17(1)	Demanding or taking more than the correct fare	Level 3
	17(1)	Refusal to carry the number of persons permitted	Level 3
	17(1)	Refusal to carry a reasonable quantity of luggage	Level 3
	17(2)	Refusal to take a hiring up to six miles	Level 3
	17(2)	Refusal to take a hiring lasting up to one hour	Level 3
	17(2)	Refusal to drive at less than 6 mph	Level 3
	17(3)	Plying with a HC (or horse) which is unfit for use	Level 3
Metropolitan Public Carriage Act 1869	7	Use of unlicensed HC	£5.00
	7	Unlicensed HC on a stand	£5.00
	8	Unlicensed driver plying for hire in HC	Level 3

Legislation	Section or Article	Offence	Maximum Penalty
	8	Proprietor if unlicensed driver plying for hire in HC	Level 3
	8A(8)	Failure to return licence, copy licence and badge after expiry of licence limited on immigration grounds	Level 3 and continuing daily fine not exceeding £10 per day
	8A(8)	Failure to return licence, copy licence and badge after expiry of licence because right to work or remain has expired	Level 3 and continuing daily fine not exceeding £10 per day
London Cab Act 1896	1(a)	Hiring a HC without the means to pay the fare	Level 1, or 14 days imprisonment
	1(a)	Hiring a HC intending to avoid paying the fare	Level 1, or 14 days imprisonment
	1(b)	Avoiding payment of the fare	Level 1, or 14 days imprisonment
	1(c)	After failure to pay the fare, refusal to give address or providing false address	Level 1, or 14 days imprisonment
London Cab Order 1934	14(a)	Failure to produce HC licence or insurance	£2.00 (by virtue of Article 53)
	14(b)	Failure to notify change of address and send licence for alteration	£2.00 (by virtue of Article 53)
	14(c)	Failure to notify change of place HC is kept	£2.00 (by virtue of Article 53)
	14(d)	Defacing HC licence	£2.00 (by virtue of Article 53)
	14(e)	Employing unlicensed driver, or permitting unlicensed driver to drive HC	£2.00 (by virtue of Article 53)
	14(f)	Failure to produce driver's licences of all drivers of the HC	£2.00 (by virtue of Article 53)
	14(g)	Failure to allow inspection of HC	£2.00 (by virtue of Article 53)
	14(h)	Removal or concealing of HC plates or notices	£2.00 (by virtue of Article 53)
	14(h)	Alteration or obliteration of official marks on the HC	£2.00 (by virtue of Article 53)
	14(i)	Use of HC for illegal purposes	£2.00 (by virtue of Article 53)
	14(j)	Failure to keep HC in good order and repair	£2.00 (by virtue of Article 53)

Legislation	Section or Article	Offence	Maximum Penalty
	14(k)	Causing or permitting a person to appear or be carried on HC by way of advertisement	£2.00 (by virtue of Article 53)
	14(l)	Advertisements on or in HC without consent of TfL	£2.00 (by virtue of Article 53)
	14(m)	Failure to return HC licence and plates on cessation of ownership	£2.00 (by virtue of Article 53)
	15	Making false statement or withholding information to obtain HC licence	£2.00 (by virtue of Article 53)
	16	Plying for hire without plates or notices, or with defaced plates, notices or marks	£2.00 (by virtue of Article 53)
	16	Removing, concealing, obliterating or altering plates, notices or marks on HC	£2.00 (by virtue of Article 53)
	18	Use or possession of altered, irregular or counterfeit HC licence, plates, notices or marks	£2.00 (by virtue of Article 53)
	21	Failure to return HC licence and plates on expiry of licence	£2.00 (by virtue of Article 53)
	27(3)	Failure to sign driver's licence and copy	£2.00 (by virtue of Article 53)
	28	Failure to carry driver's licence or produce it	£2.00 (by virtue of Article 53)
	29(1)	Failure by cab owner to safely retain driver's licence	£2.00 (by virtue of Article 53)
	29(1)	Failure by cab owner to inform TfL of loss or damage to driver's licence	£2.00 (by virtue of Article 53)
	29(2)	Failure by cab owner to return driver's licence to driver if required to be sent to TfL	£2.00 (by virtue of Article 53)
	31(1)(i)	Plying in a HC of a type he is not permitted to drive	£2.00 (by virtue of Article 53)
	31(1)(ii)	Plying in a HC outside his permitted area	£2.00 (by virtue of Article 53)
	32	Failure to notify change of address	£2.00 (by virtue of Article 53)
	33(1)	Carrying more than the licensed number of passengers	£2.00 (by virtue of Article 53)
	33(2)	Carrying a person on the driving box or platform of a motor cab	£2.00 (by virtue of Article 53)
	33(3)	Carrying luggage on the roof unless licensed to do so	£2.00 (by virtue of Article 53)

Legislation	Section or Article	Offence	Maximum Penalty
	36	Removal or interference with taximeter, seals or marks	£2.00 (by virtue of Article 53)
	37(i)	Plying for hire without taximeter fitted	£2.00 (by virtue of Article 53)
	37(ii)	Plying for hire without taximeter having been sealed by TfL	£2.00 (by virtue of Article 53)
	37(iii)	Failure to have damaged taximeter seal replaced by TfL within 24 hours	£2.00 (by virtue of Article 53)
	38	Failure to illuminate taximeter	£2.00 (by virtue of Article 53)
	39	Failure to activate taximeter on hiring	£2.00 (by virtue of Article 53)
	39	Failure to stop taximeter at end of hiring	£2.00 (by virtue of Article 53)
	51(2)	Failure to search or look inside cab after each hiring to check for lost property	£2.00 (by virtue of Article 53)
	51(3)	Failure to take lost property to police station, or return to owner if claimed	£2.00 (by virtue of Article 53)
	4(1)	Prohibition on signs saying 'taxi', 'cab' or 'for hire' on any wedding or funeral car	Level 4
	4(2)	Prohibition on advertisements referring to 'taxi' or 'cab' except for HC services	Level 4

Table 15.2 Enforcement Table – London Private Hire (PH)

Legislation	Section or Article	Offence	Maximum Penalty
Private Hire Vehicles (London) Act 1998	2	Acting as a PH operator without an operator's licence	Level 4
	3A(7)	Failure to return licence, after expiry of licence on immigration grounds	Level 3 and continuing daily fine not exceeding £10 per day
	4(2)(b)	Operating an unlicensed driver	Level 3
	4(3)(a)	Failure to display copy of operator's licence	Level 3
	4(3)(b)	Failure to keep records at specified operator's centre	Level 3

Legislation	Section or Article	Offence	Maximum Penalty
	4(3)(c)	Failure to enter booking in records before the journey	Level 3
	4(3)(d)	Failure to keep records of vehicles and drivers used	Level 3
	4(3)(e)	Failure to produce records to constable or authorised officer	Level 3
	4(4)	Failure to preserve records after ceasing to use operating centre	Level 3
	5	Subcontracting a booking to an unlicensed PH operator	Level 3
	6	Driving an unlicensed PH vehicle	Level 4
	6	Operating an unlicensed PH vehicle	Level 4
	6	Owner permitting an unlicensed vehicle to be used as PH vehicle	Level 4
	8(2)	Failure by owner to present PH vehicle for inspection or testing	Level 3
	8(3)	Failure by owner to report accidents to TfL	Level 3
	8(4)	Failure to report change of ownership	Level 3
	10(4)	Driver using PH vehicle without disc or plate exhibited	Level 3
	10(4)	Operator using PH vehicle without disc or plate exhibited	Level 3
	10(5)	Owner permitting use of PH vehicle without disc or plate exhibited	Level 3
	11	Owner equipping PH vehicle with taximeter	Level 3
	12(2)	Driving a PH vehicle without a PH driver's licence	Level 4
	12(2)	Operating a PH vehicle when the driver is not licensed as a PH driver	Level 4
	12(3)	Owner allowing a PH vehicle to be driven by a person who is not a licensed PH driver	Level 4
	13A(7)	Failure to return licence, after expiry of licence on immigration grounds	Level 3 and continuing daily fine not exceeding £10 per day
	21(2)(a)	Failure by owner of PH vehicle to produce licence to constable or authorised officer	Level 3
	21(2)(b)	Failure by owner of PH vehicle to produce insurance certificate to constable or authorised officer	Level 3

Legislation	Section or Article	Offence	Maximum Penalty
	22(1)	Failure by PH operator to return licence after expiry or revocation	Level 3
	22(2)	Failure by owner of PH vehicle to return licence, plate or disc after expiry or revocation	Level 3
	22(3)	Failure by PH driver to return licence and badge after expiry or revocation	Level 3
	22(4)	Failure by PH operator to return licence after suspension if so directed	Level 3
	22(4) & 22(4)(a)	Failure by owner of PH vehicle to return licence, plate or disc after suspension if so directed	Level 3
	22(4) & 22(4)(b)	Failure by PH driver to return licence and badge after suspension if so directed	Level 3
	27(1)	Obstruction of constable or authorised officer	Level 3
	27(2)(a)	Failure to comply with requirement of constable or authorised officer	Level 3
	27(2)(b)	Failure to give assistance or information to constable or authorised officer	Level 3
	27(3)	Giving false information to constable or authorised officer	Level 5
	28	Making a false statement or giving false information to obtain grant, renewal or variation of any PH licence	Level 5
	30	Contravention of Regulations relating to signs or notices on vehicles	Level 4
	31	Prohibition of use of the words 'taxi', 'taxis', 'cab' or 'cabs' in advertisements for PH services	Level 4

Fixed penalty notices

15.6

Sections 17 to 22 of the Transport for London Act 2008 introduce a fixed penalty notice system for specified hackney carriage and private hire offences within London[1]. An authorised officer can issue a fixed penalty notice to any person who he has reason to believe has committed an offence[2], at a rate of penalties to be set by TfL under the provisions of s 20. At present, there is an extremely limited list of offences for which fixed penalties can apply, contained in Sch 1 to the Act. However Sch 1 itself can be amended by regulations under s 18 (see Table 15.3).

[1]   At the time of writing (August 2017) there is still no commencement date for these provisions and the power to bring the provisions into action lies with TfL under the procedure contained in s 3 of the Act.

[2]   Transport for London Act 2008, s 17(1).

Table 15.3   Fixed Penalty Notices within London

Act/Instrument	Section or Article	Description of offence
London Hackney Carriages Act 1843 (c 86)	17	Failure to wear, or to produce, badge
London Cab Order 1934 (SR&O 1934/1346)	28	Failure to produce copy of licence
	31(1)(ii)	Plying outside licensed area
	33(1)	Carrying excess passengers
Regulations for Enforcing Order at Cab Standings in the Metropolitan Police District made on 11 October 1963	(1)	Failure to attend cab at cab standing

NON-CRIMINAL ENFORCEMENT

15.7

Just as outside London, action can also be taken against a licence in cases of transgression or non-compliance with the requirements of the hackney carriage or private hire legislation.

The same rules apply, which means that it is not necessary to obtain a criminal conviction before action can be taken against a licence[1].

[1]   See *R v Maidstone Crown Court, ex p Olson* [1992] COD 496 (see Chapter 10, para 10.139); *R v Assistant Metropolitan Police Comr, ex p Foster* (18 November 1994, unreported) (see Chapter 2, para 2.37); *McCool v Rushcliffe Borough Council* [1998] 3 All ER 889, QBD (see Chapter 10, para 10.142); and *Leeds City Council v Hussain* [2002] EWHC 1145 (Admin), [2003] RTR 199 (see Chapter 10, para 10.146).

Hackney carriages

15.8

The powers in relation to hackney carriage vehicles and drivers licences are as follows.

SUSPENSION AND REVOCATION OF VEHICLE LICENCES

15.9

There are two powers to suspend a hackney carriage vehicle licence in London, but only one power to revoke such a licence. In reality it seems likely that the powers contained in the London Hackney Carriage Act 1853, s 2 are effectively obsolete, as powers to suspend or revoke the licence by reason of the condition of the cab are contained in the London Cab Order 1934, art 19(1)(b)[1]. The London Hackney Carriage Act 1853, s 2 states:

'2 If carriages not in fit condition licences may be suspended

It shall be lawful for Transport for London to cause an inspection to be made, as often as they deem it necessary, of all … hackney carriages, and of the horse or horses used in drawing the same, within the limits of this Act; and if any such carriage, or the horse or horses used in drawing the same, shall at any time be in a condition unfit for public use, Transport for London shall give notice in writing accordingly to the proprietor thereof, which notice shall be personally served on such proprietor, or delivered at his usual place of residence; and if, after notice as aforesaid, any proprietor shall use or let to hire such carriage as a … hackney carriage, or use or let to hire such horse or horses whilst in a condition unfit for public use, Transport for London shall have power to suspend, for such time as they may deem proper, the licence of the proprietor of such carriage …'

[1] SI 1934/1346.

15.10

The powers contained in the London Cab Order 1934[1] are more wide-ranging, relating to a greater range of circumstances as a result of which, action might be taken against the licence:

'19 Revocation or Suspension of Cab Licences

(1) A cab licence shall be liable to revocation or suspension by Transport for London on any of the following grounds:—

(a) if the licence has been obtained by any misrepresentation, fraud or concealment of any material circumstances; or

(b) if Transport for London, by reason of any new circumstance arising or coming to its knowledge after the grant of a licence, or by reason of the condition of the cab, is satisfied that a licence in respect of the cab in question could not in pursuance of this Order properly be granted to the licensee if he were an applicant for a new licence; or

(c) if the licensee fails to comply with any of the provisions or conditions subject to which the licence has been granted; or

(d) on any of the grounds on which a licence in respect of a hackney carriage might at the time of the commencement of the Metropolitan Public Carriage Act 1869 have been revoked or suspended;

provided that in a case where more than one licence granted to the same licensee becomes liable to revocation or suspension under this paragraph, Transport for London, if it is of opinion that it would be contrary to the public interest to revoke or suspend all of those licences, may revoke or suspend only such one or more of them as it may think fit.

(2) In the event of the revocation or suspension of a cab licence, the licensee shall, within five days after a notice to that effect has been delivered to him personally or sent to him by registered post or by the recorded delivery service at the address mentioned in or last endorsed upon the licence, send or deliver the licence to the Public Carriage Examiner at the appointed passing station for cancellation or for retention during the time of suspension, as the case may be, and if so required in the notice shall bring or send the cab to which the licence relates to that passing station in order that the plates affixed to the cab in pursuance of this Order may be removed and delivered up to the Public Carriage Examiner; and if the licensee fails to fulfil the requirements of this sub-paragraph, he shall be guilty of a breach of this Order.

(3) On the removal of a suspension of a cab licence which has not expired by the effluxion of time the Public Carriage Examiner shall return the licence to the licensee and shall cause the plates, if removed, to be re-affixed to the cab.'

[1]   SI 1934/1346.

SUSPENSION AND REVOCATION OF DRIVERS' LICENCES

15.11

In a similar fashion, there are two powers to suspend, or in this case, revoke, a hackney carriage driver's licence, although here the earlier provision contained in the London Hackney Carriages Act 1843, s 25 only allows the magistrates to take such action on conviction. The later power in the London Cab Order 1934, art 30[1] give powers to suspend or revoke to TfL/LTPH.

[1]   SI 1934/1346.

15.12

The London Hackney Carriages Act 1843, s 25 states:

'25 Licences may be revoked or suspended

... It shall be lawful for any justice of the peace before whom any driver, ... shall be convicted of any offence, whether under this Act or any other Act, if such justice in his discretion shall think fit, to revoke the licence of such driver, ... and also any other licence which he shall hold under the provisions of this Act, or to suspend the same for such time as the justice shall think proper, and for that purpose to require the proprietor, driver, ... in whose possession such licence and the ticket thereunto belonging shall then be to deliver up the same; and every proprietor, driver, ... who, being so required, shall refuse or neglect to deliver up such licence and any such ticket, or either of them, shall forfeit, so often as he shall be so required and refuse or neglect as aforesaid, the sum of level 1 on the standard scale; and the justice shall forthwith send such licence and ticket to Transport for London, who shall cancel such licence if it has been revoked by the justice, or, if it has been suspended, shall, at the end of the time for which it shall have been suspended, re-deliver such licence, with the ticket, to the person to whom it was granted.

A magistrates' court that makes an order revoking or suspending any licence under this section may, if the court thinks fit, suspend the effect of the order pending an appeal against the order.'

15.13

The London Cab Order 1934, art 30[1] provides:

'30 Revocation or Suspension of Cab-drivers' Licences

(1) A cab-driver's licence shall be liable to revocation or suspension by Transport for London if it is satisfied, by reason of any circumstances arising or coming to its knowledge after the licence was granted, that the licensee is not a fit person to hold such a licence.

(2) In the event of the revocation or suspension of a cab-driver's licence Transport for London shall cause notice thereof to be given to the licensee, and the licensee shall, within five days after such notice has been delivered to him personally or sent to him by registered post or by the recorded delivery service at the address mentioned in or last endorsed upon the licence, send or deliver the licence and his copy thereof and his badge to Transport for London for cancellation or for retention during the time of suspension, as the case may be, and if he fails so to do he shall be guilty of a breach of this Order.

(3) On the removal of a suspension of a cab-driver's licence which has not expired by the effluxion of time Transport for London shall return the licence and the copy thereof and the badge to the licensee.'

[1] SI 1934/1346.

15.14

Whilst, again, the later power is wider ranging and considerably more flexible, the fact that the powers are given to different bodies means that the earlier power is less likely to be considered obsolete, when compared with the powers to take action under the later provisions.

15.15

Rights of appeal[1] against decisions of TfL/LTPH (but not decisions of the magistrates under the London Hackney Carriages Act 1843, s 25) are contained within the Transport Act 1985, s 17. No express power of appeal seems to be granted against the decisions of the magistrates in that situation and, accordingly, it would appear that an appeal by way of case stated or judicial review are the only methods of challenging such a decision.

[1] See Chapter 3, para 3.65.

Private hire licences

15.16

In respect of private hire operators, vehicles and drivers' licences, there are powers to suspend or revoke private hire licences in the Private Hire Vehicles (London) Act 1998, ss 16 and 17.

'16 Power to suspend or revoke licences

(1) The licensing authority may suspend or revoke a licence under this Act for any reasonable cause including (without prejudice to the generality of this subsection) any ground mentioned below.

(2) A London PHV operator's licence may be suspended or revoked where—

(a) the licensing authority is no longer satisfied that the licence holder is fit to hold such a licence; or

(b) the licence holder has failed to comply with any condition of the licence or any other obligation imposed on him by or under this Act.

(3) A London PHV licence may be suspended or revoked where—

(a) the licensing authority is no longer satisfied that the vehicle to which it relates is fit for use as a private hire vehicle; or

(b) the owner has failed to comply with any condition of the licence or any other obligation imposed on him by or under this Act.

(4) A London PHV driver's licence may be suspended or revoked where—

(a) the licence holder has, since the grant of the licence, been convicted of an offence involving dishonesty, indecency or violence;

(b) the licensing authority is for any other reason no longer satisfied that the licence holder is fit to hold such a licence; or

(c) the licence holder has failed to comply with any condition of the licence or any other obligation imposed on him by or under this Act.

17 Suspension and revocation under section 16: procedure

(1) Where the licensing authority has decided to suspend or revoke a licence under section 16—

(a) the authority shall give notice of the decision and the grounds for the decision to the licence holder or, in the case of a London PHV licence, the owner of the vehicle to which the licence relates; and

(b) the suspension or revocation takes effect at the end of the period of 21 days beginning with the day on which that notice is served on the licence holder or the owner.

(2) If the licensing authority is of the opinion that the interests of public safety require the suspension or revocation of a licence to have immediate effect, and the authority includes a statement of that opinion and the reasons for it in the notice of suspension or revocation, the suspension or revocation takes effect when the notice is served on the licence holder or vehicle owner (as the case may be).

(3) A licence suspended under this section shall remain suspended until such time as the licensing authority by notice directs that the licence is again in force.

(4) The holder of a London PHV operator's or driver's licence, or the owner of a vehicle to which a PHV licence relates, may appeal to a magistrates' court against a decision under section 16 to suspend or revoke that licence.'

15.17

It can be seen that the effect of the Private Hire Vehicles (London) Act 1998, s 17(2) is to enable TfL to suspend or revoke any licence with immediate effect if that is necessary in 'the interests of public safety'. There do not appear to have been any High Court challenges to decisions made using this justification to suspend a licence with immediate effect.

15.18

The Private Hire Vehicles (London) Act 1998, s 17(4)[1] provides a right of appeal to the magistrates' court against any decision to suspend or revoke any private hire licence. Section 25(4) provides that the appeal period shall be 21 days from the day on which the notice of the decision is served on the person concerned.

[1] See Appendix I.

CONCLUSIONS

15.19

It was stated at the commencement of this chapter that it is only through enforcement that any laws have meaningful effect and this is true of hackney carriage and private hire legislation just as much as it is of other areas. Vigorous enforcement of hackney carriage and private hire provisions is essential if the ultimate aim of the licensing regime, to protect the travelling public, is to be achieved. There is no doubt that enforcement is expensive in terms of both the staff and legal costs involved, but, unless it is undertaken, the licensing of hackney carriages and private hire vehicles becomes a merely administrative exercise. That is of benefit to no one, except unscrupulous persons who do not comply with the requirements.

15.20

Licensees who pay licence fees are entitled to expect an enforcement regime which aims not only to protect the public, but also to protect them from those who do not comply with the requirements. Indeed, this is one of the justifications for levying a fee for the grant of licences.

Chapter 16

Hackney carriages within London: an introduction

LEGISLATION

16.1

Hackney carriages within London have been subjected to statutory control for longer than in the provinces, the earliest current Act dating from 1831. Hackney carriage legislation is spread over a number of Acts, Orders and Regulations, which when combined, create a similar system to that existing outside London. In addition, the Equality Act 2010 and Immigration Act 2016 apply within London as well as outside. There is one major difference between the London and provincial situations, and that is the controlling body. Within London, hackney carriages are licensed and controlled by Transport for London (TfL), a pan-London body, rather than the local authorities[1].TfL exercise their hackney carriage functions through the London Taxi and Private Hire section ('LTPH'). The London-specific legislation consists of the following.

[1] For more information on TfL/LTPH please see Chapter 2.

London Hackney Carriages Act 1831

16.2

The sections of the London Hackney Carriage Act 1831 (LHCA 1831[1]) that remain in force specify that any hackney carriage standing is plying for hire and impose an obligation on drivers to take a fare (LHCA 1831, s 35). If a driver refuses a fare then he can be brought before a magistrate to explain the situation (LHCA 1831, s 36). Anybody who damages a hackney carriage can be liable for compensation, again before a magistrate by virtue of LHCA 1831, s 41. If a driver is asked to wait with his hackney carriage for a passenger he can ask for a deposit under the provisions of LHCA 1831, s 47. It is an offence for the proprietor or driver of a hackney carriage to allow persons other than the hirer to ride in the carriage (LHCA 1831, s 50) and if one driver deprives another of a fare then that is an offence under LHCA 1831, s 51. Drivers' conduct is regulated by the LHCA 1831, s 56 and if a complaint is brought against a driver but then withdrawn, compensation can be awarded by a magistrate to the driver under LHCA 1831, s 57.

¹   See Appendix I.

London Hackney Carriages Act 1843

16.3

The London Hackney Carriages Act 1843 (LHCA 1843)[1] authorises the grant of drivers' licences together with the metal ticket of the office of hackney carriage driver (LHCA 1843, s 8), whilst LHCA 1843, s 10 makes it an offence to drive a hackney carriage without such a ticket. The remaining sections still in force (LHCA 1843, ss 14, 16, 17, 18, 19, 21 and 24) are concerned with the system of licensing of drivers. LHCA 1843, s 25 gives the power to magistrates to revoke or suspend licences. The driver of a hackney carriage needs the consent of a proprietor (LHCA 1843, s 27) and the proprietor can recover compensation from the driver in cases of bad driving or abuse of individuals under LHCA 1843, s 28. Drivers must not obstruct the highway under LHCA 1843, s 33 and any complaint must be made within seven days before justices, who can hear complaints under LHCA 1843, ss 38 and 39. LHCA 1843, s 44 makes multiple proprietors jointly and severely liable.

¹   See Appendix I.

London Hackney Carriages Act 1850

16.4

The London Hackney Carriages Act 1850[1] allows Transport for London to appoint hackney carriage stands under the London Hackney Carriages Act 1850, s 4 and to regulate their use.

¹   See Appendix I.

London Hackney Carriages Act 1853

16.5

The London Hackney Carriages Act 1853, s 3 (LHCA 1853)[1] allows Transport for London/London Taxi and Private Hire (TfL/LTPH) to suspend hackney carriage licences if a vehicle is unfit. LHCA 1853, s 7 imposes a maximum distance upon which a hackney carriage can be hired whilst LHCA 1853, s 9 determines the number of persons that a hackney carriage may carry. In addition, a reasonable amount of luggage must be carried as a consequence of LHCA 1853, s 10. LHCA 1853, s 16 prohibits certain advertisements being displayed in or on a hackney carriage. LHCA 1853, s 17 details certain offences which drivers can commit and LHCA 1853, ss 18 and 19 govern enforcement.

¹   See Appendix I.

TfL/LTPH Metropolitan Public Carriage Act 1869

16.6

The Metropolitan Public Carriage Act 1869 (MPCA 1869)[1] applies to Greater London, including the City of London, by virtue of MPCA 1869, s 2. MPCA 1869, s 4 defines hackney carriage, whilst MPCA 1869, s 6 governs the grant of a hackney carriage licence. It is an offence to use an unlicensed hackney carriage by virtue of MPCA 1869, s 7, and MPCA 1869, s 8 specifies that hackney carriages must be driven by licensed drivers. MPCA 1869, s 9 gives TfL/LTPH the power to make regulations for hackney carriages, breach of those being an offence under MPCA 1869, s 10. MPCA 1869, ss 11 and 12 are administrative sections concerning TfL/LTPH. All offences are summary under the Act (MPCA 1869, s 13). MPCA 1869, s 14 allows TfL/LTPH to attach placards or signals to lamp posts and MPCA 1869, s 15 makes it clear that previous Acts continue in force.

[1]   See Appendix I.

London Cab Act 1896

16.7

The London Cab Act 1896[1] makes it an offence to defraud hackney carriage drivers.

[1]   See Appendix I.

London Cab and Stage Carriage Act 1907

16.8

The London Cab and Stage Carriage Act 1907[1], s 1 allows TfL/LTPH to fix the fares for hackney carriages.

[1]   See Appendix I.

London Cab Order 1934

16.9

The London Cab Order 1934[1] is the legislation which regulates the day-to-day activity of hackney carriages and hackney carriage drivers within London. It has been amended a number of times, principally to update the fares which are regulated by this Order, but also to introduce mid-yearly vehicle tests and require drivers to accept payments by credit or debit card.

[1]   SI 1934/1346. See Appendix I.

16.10

Pt III of the London Cab Order 1934[1] governs applications for and grant and refusal of, hackney carriage licences, together with the conditions imposed thereon. In addition it requires hackney carriages to display their plates when plying for hire and allows for revocation, suspension, transfer and surrender of hackney carriage licences. The remaining parts cover the following areas: Pt IV governs drivers' licences; Pt V governs the carriage of persons and luggage; Pt VI concerns meters and fares; Pt VII regulates horse carriages (although there have been no licensed horse-drawn hackney carriages in London for over 60 years the provisions are still in force); Pt VIII relates to lost property and Pts IX and X are administrative.

[1]   SI 1934/1346.

London Cab Act 1968

16.11

This Act increases the power of TfL/LTPH to regulate the fares and allows hackney carriages to park (under the London Cab Act 1968, s 3)[1].

[1]   See Appendix I.

London Cab Order 1972

16.12

London Cab Order 1972[1] extends the maximum hiring to 20 miles when the cab has been hired at Heathrow Airport.

[1]   SI 1972/1047. See Appendix I.

Transport Act 1985

16.13

The Transport Act 1985, s 17[1] creates the mechanism for appeals for vehicle and driver licences.

[1]   See Appendix I.

Local Services (Operation by Taxis) (London) Regulation 1986[1], Licensed Taxis (Hiring at Separate Fares) (London) Order 1986[2] and London Taxi Sharing Scheme Order 1987[3]

16.14

When combined, these provisions create a mechanism for hackney carriages to be used as a small bus service.

[1]   SI 1986/566. See Appendix I.
[2]   SI 1986/1387. See Appendix I.
[3]   SI 1987/1535. See Appendix I.

London Taxis (Licensing Appeals) Regulations 1986

16.15

The London Taxis (Licensing Appeals) Regulations 1986[1] specify that the appeal period is 28 days from the written notice of the decision of TfL/LTPH.

[1]   SI 1986/1188. See Appendix I.

Transport for London Act 2008

16.16

This amends a number of the earlier Acts and also introduces a fixed penalty scheme to be administered by TfL in relation to a small number of specified offences[1].

[1]   Sections 17–22 and Sch 1. See Appendix I.

Chapter 17

Hackney carriage vehicles within London: definition and demand

WHAT IS A HACKNEY CARRIAGE OR LONDON CAB?

17.1

The legislation that governs the licensing of hackney carriages in Greater London uses the terms 'hackney carriage', 'cab' and 'London cab', and the use depends upon the legislation in question. However, all refer to the definition of a hackney carriage which is contained within the Metropolitan Public Carriage Act 1869, s 4 (MPCA 1869):

> '"Hackney carriage" shall mean any carriage for the conveyance of passengers which plies for hire within the limits of this Act, and is neither a stage carriage nor a tramcar.'

A stage carriage is also defined in MPCA 1869, s 4 as:

> 'In this Act "stage carriage" shall mean any carriage for the conveyance of passengers which plies for hire in any public street, road, or place within the limits of this Act, and in which the passengers or any of them are charged to pay separate and distinct or at the rate of separate and distinct fares for their respective places or seats therein.'

And the 'limits of this Act' are defined in MPCA 1869, s 2 as:

> 'The limits of this Act shall be the metropolitan police district, and the city of London.'

The 'metropolitan police district' is defined in the London Government Act 1963, s 76, as amended by the Greater London Authority Act 1999, s 323.

Subsequent legislation uses the terms 'cab' and 'London cab', but all refer to MPCA 1869 definition, eg:

- London Cab Act 1896, s 3;
- London Cab and Stage Carriage Act 1907, s 6;
- London Cab Order 1934, art 2[1].

It is odd that the London Cab Act 1968, s 1 refers to the definition in the London Cab and Stage Carriage Act 1907, when that in turn refers to MPCA 1869. Other legislation also uses the same definition, eg the Transport Act 1985, s 13(3).

1   SI 1934/1346.

17.2

Hackney carriage licences are granted by Transport for London (TfL). The actual day-to-day activities of TfL in relation to hackney carriage matters is undertaken by the London Taxi and Private Hire Directorate (LTPH))[1]. The power to grant hackney carriage licences is contained in MPCA 1869, s 6:

'(1) Transport for London shall have the function of licensing to ply for hire within the limits of this Act hackney carriages, to be distinguished in such manner as may be prescribed.

(2) A licence under this section may—
(a)   be granted on such conditions,
(b)   be in such form,
(c)   be subject to revocation or suspension in such event, and
(d)   generally be dealt with in such manner,
        as may be prescribed.'

'Prescribed' means 'prescribed by London cab order' (MPCA 1869, s 4).

1   For details of the mechanism, please see Chapter 2.

17.3

A hackney carriage licence lasts for one year unless it is revoked or suspended (MPCA 1869, s 6(4)).

17.4

The London Cab Order 1934[1] uses the expression 'cab' to mean hackney carriage. Application for a cab licence is made to TfL/LTPH on an approved form, signed by the applicant. If the applicant is a partnership or a limited company, the form is signed by the senior partner or the secretary, manager or authorised officer of the limited company and the signatory is deemed to be the applicant and the licence is issued to that person (London Cab Order 1934, art 5).

1   SI 1934/1346; see Appendix I.

17.5

Applicants must be over 21 (London Cab Order 1934, art 6[1]), and the criteria which must be met are contained in arts 7 and 8. TfL/LTPH has a discretion to refuse an application for a licence in the following cases:

- The applicant has been convicted of an indictable offence (this includes an either way offence by virtue of the Interpretation Act 1978, Sch 1 (art 7(1)).

- The applicant appears to be unfit to hold a cab licence because:
  - he or partners of his or a company he was an officer of has been convicted of an offence relating to the use of a hackney carriage, stage carriage or public service vehicle;
  - a licence relating to any such vehicle which he held either alone or as above was suspended or revoked, he failed to comply with conditions attached or was convicted of an offence under the Act under which the licence was granted; or
  - if it is for a horse drawn cab, he has been convicted of animal cruelty (art 7(2))[2].
- If the vehicle does not conform to the conditions of fitness and is not fit to be used as a hackney carriage (art 7(3)(a))[3].
- If the applicant is not of good character (art 7(3)(b)); or
  - he fails to satisfy TfL/LTPH that he (or his partnership or company) is of good business repute (art 7(3)(c)(i)); or
  - he fails to satisfy TfL/LTPH that he (or his partnership or company) has sufficient public liability insurance to fulfil his duties under the London Cab Order 1934, art 8 (art 7(3)(c)(ii)); or
  - he fails to satisfy TfL/LTPH that he (or his partnership or company), 'having regard to his general financial position, is a fit and proper person to hold a cab licence' (art 7(3)(c)(iii)).

TfL/LTPH lays down 'Conditions of Fitness' for hackney carriage vehicles. These specify the requirements of the vehicle. Until 2002/03, they had not been comprehensively reviewed since 1961. Following the comprehensive review, TfL/LTPH announced in June 2003 that the Conditions of Fitness would remain largely unchanged. This was challenged, and as a result, a further consideration of the Conditions of Fitness was undertaken. The revised version was published in 2007 and subsequent versions have been published, the most recent of which is Version 8.0 dating from October 2016[4]. TfL/LTPH approves vehicles which comply with the Conditions of Fitness.

[1]   SI 1934/1346; see Appendix I.
[2]   This remains in force, notwithstanding the fact that no horse drawn hackney carriage has been licensed in London since 1947.
[3]   The conditions of fitness.
[4]   Available   http://www.tfl.gov.uk/assets/downloads/businessandpartners/conditions-of-fitness.pdf at http://content.tfl.gov.uk/taxi-conditions-of-fitness-update.pdf

17.6

Correct insurance must be maintained for both the cab itself and third-party liabilities. This is in addition to the requirements under the Road Traffic Act 1988 by virtue of the London Cab Order 1934, art 8[1]. It is interesting to note that the London Cab Order 1934 still refers to the Road Traffic Act 1930 'as amended by any subsequent Act' rather than the Road Traffic Act 1988, Pt VI, which now governs compulsory motor insurance.

[1]   SI 1934/1346; see Appendix I.

17.7

If the application is approved, the application form is endorsed to that effect and returned to the applicant (London Cab Order 1934, art 9[1]). It is then for the applicant to present his vehicle for licensing, in accordance with the provisions of art 10. The applicant has to present the vehicle at a passing station that TfL/LTPH have nominated[2]. 'Passing station' is defined in art 2 as:

'any place appointed by TfL as a place where cabs may be examined for the purposes of this Order, and if TfL appoints any passing station for the examination of any particular cab or cabs, that passing station shall be deemed to be the appointed passing station for that cab or those cabs.'

[1] SI 1934/1346; see Appendix I.
[2] The only 'passing station' is at the LTPH offices at Penton Street.

17.8

In addition to the vehicle, the applicant must also present the approved application form, the current tax disc and certificate of motor insurance, together with other evidence (if required) of compliance with the requirement of the London Cab Order 1934, art 8[1].

[1] SI 1934/1346; see Appendix I.

17.9

This two-stage approach to licensing the vehicle is an interesting concept as it is not only the vehicle that has to be satisfactory, but also the proprietor of the vehicle. This is quite different from the approach usually taken outside London[1].

[1] See Chapter 8, para 8.98 onwards. In many cases, the hackney carriage is owned by the driver, but there are significant numbers of London cabs that are hired out to drivers by cab companies.

17.10

Similar requirements exist under the London Cab Order 1934, art 11[1] for licensing horse cabs (defined in art 2 as 'any cab drawn by animal power, and "horse" includes any animal used to draw a cab'). These are identical to the requirements for licensing motor cabs except for the requirement to produce a tax disc.

[1] SI 1934/1346; see Appendix I.

17.11

If the application is refused, refusal to grant a licence is recorded on the application form and TfL/LTPH will notify the applicant of the decision to refuse. A right of appeal then lies within the provisions of the Transport Act 1985, s 17[1].

[1] See Chapter 3, para 3.65.

17.12

Once the vehicle has been presented for licensing, the public carriage examiner must decide whether it conforms to the conditions of fitness laid down by TfL/LTPH and is fit for public use. If he finds that it is, a certificate is issued in the form specified in the London Cab Order 1934, Sch A[1]. The examiner 'shall cause the plates and notices described in Schedule B to this Order to be affixed to the cab in the positions required by that Schedule' (London Cab Order 1934, art 12(1)). It is clear that the licence plates remain the property of TfL/LTPH.

[1]   SI 1934/1346; see Appendix I.

17.13

The grant mechanism is then further complicated by the London Cab Order 1934, art 12(2)[1] as the certificate issued by the public carriage examiner together with the approved application form is then returned to TfL/LTPH who grant a cab licence in respect of that cab. TfL/LTPH have a further opportunity not to grant a licence if any new developments have come to light since the application was originally approved. Any matter that would have initially led to a refusal in accordance with art 9 would now lead to refusal.

[1]   SI 1934/1346; see Appendix I.

17.14

If the public carriage examiner is not satisfied that the submitted vehicle conforms to the conditions of fitness, or that it is not fit for public use, he must refuse to issue a certificate and report that fact to TfL/LTPH, who must then refuse to grant a cab licence. It is possible under the London Cab Order 1934, art 13[1] for the vehicle to be re-examined, in which case the licence can be granted if the examiner is then satisfied that the vehicle conforms. As outlined at para 17.11 above, if the licence is refused a right of appeal lies to the magistrates' court.

[1]   SI 1934/1346; see Appendix I.

17.15

The actual cab licence itself is issued in a form specified in London Cab Order 1934, Sch C[1]. It is granted subject to compliance by the licensee with the provisions of the Metropolitan Public Carriage Act 1869, the London Cab and Stage Carriage Act 1907, the London Cab Order 1934 and all Acts relating to Metropolitan hackney carriages that pre-date MPCA 1869. In relation to the London Cab Order 1934, art 14, paras (a) to (m) are therefore incorporated into the licence. These state:

'(a)   The licensee shall produce the licence for examination at his principal place of business when required so to do by any police constable or Public Carriage Examiner, or by any person duly authorised in that behalf by Transport for London, and shall also, if so required, produce in like manner such evidence as Transport for London may require that the owner of the cab fulfils the requirements of paragraph 8 of this Order as to liability to third parties.

(b)   The licensee, if he changes his address during the currency of the licence, shall notify such change to Transport for London within seven days from the date of such change and shall at the same time send or deliver the licence to the office of Transport for London who shall endorse upon the licence the licensee's new address and return the licence to him forthwith.

(c)   The licensee, if during the currency of the licence he changes the place at which the cab is ordinarily kept, shall notify such change to Transport for London within seven days from the date of such change.

(d)   The licensee shall not deface the licence by erasure or otherwise.

(e)   The licensee shall not employ or permit any person to act as driver of the cab when it is hired or plying for hire except a person who is licensed in pursuance of Section 8 of the Metropolitan Public Carriage Act 1869, as amended by Section 39 of the Road Traffic Act 1934, and of Part IV of this Order to drive cabs of the type to which the cab belongs.

(f)   The licensee shall produce the licences of the persons employed or permitted by him to act as drivers of the cab for examination at his principal place of business when required so to do by any police constable or Public Carriage Examiner, or by any person duly authorised in that behalf by Transport for London.

(g)   The licensee shall at all reasonable times allow to any Public Carriage Examiner facilities for the inspection of the cab and the horses (if any) used to draw the cab, and their harness, and such facilities shall include free access to his premises, whether within or outside the metropolitan area.

(h)   The licensee shall not remove or conceal any of the plates or notices affixed to the cab in pursuance of this Order, or cause or permit any person not authorised in that behalf by Transport for London to remove or conceal any such plate or notice, nor shall he alter or obliterate, or cause or permit any person not so authorised to alter or obliterate, any mark placed upon the cab in pursuance of this Order or by the authority of Transport for London.

(i)   The licensee shall not knowingly permit the cab to be used for any illegal purpose.

(j)   The licensee shall keep the cab and all its furniture and appointments in good order and repair.

(k)   The licensee shall not cause or permit any person to appear or be carried on the cab by way of advertisement.

(l)   The licensee shall not, otherwise than in accordance with the directions of Transport for London, cause or permit any object or any printed, written or other matter to appear to be displayed on the outside or inside of the cab by way of advertisement.

(m)   The licensee, if during the currency of the licence he ceases to be the owner of the cab to which the licence relates, shall forthwith notify Transport for London and return the licence to Transport for London for cancellation, and before delivering the cab to its new owner shall remove and deliver up to Transport for London or a Public Carriage Examiner the plates affixed to the cab in pursuance of this Order.'

As outside London, it appears that the maximum number of passengers that can be carried in a vehicle for it to be capable of being licensed as a hackney carriage is eight[2]. This is because any vehicle which carries more than eight will be classified as a public service vehicle (PSV) under the Public Passenger Vehicles Act 1981, s 1(1).

[1]   SI 1934/1346; see Appendix I.
[2]   At present the maximum number of passengers that can be carried in a hackney carriage in London is six, as under the Conditions of Fitness (see para 17.5 above). All the vehicles have to be approved by TfL/LTPH and all approved vehicles have six as the maximum number that can be accommodated in the passenger compartment.

STATUS OF A LONDON HACKNEY CARRIAGE

17.16

There is no case on the question of whether or not a London cab is always a hackney carriage once it has been licensed as such. Both *Hawkins v Edwards*[1] and *Yates v Gates*[2] relate to the Town Police Clauses Act 1847 for hackney carriages outside London. As the wording of the London legislation differs from TPCA 1847, it is difficult to draw direct comparisons.

[1]   [1901] 2 KB 169; see para 8.4 above.
[2]   [1970] 1 All ER 754, QBD; see para 8.5 above.

17.17

The London Cab Order 1934, art 14[1] is useful in this regard. In *Hawkins v Edwards*[2] (the case that makes it clear that outside London, a hackney carriage is always a hackney carriage) the question was raised because the prosecution was brought against a hackney carriage proprietor who had failed to display the plate. His argument was that if the vehicle was not working as a hackney carriage it was not a hackney carriage at that time. This argument was rejected[3].

Within London, art 14(h) of the London Cab Order 1934 states:

'(h)   The licensee shall not remove or conceal any of the plates or notices affixed to the cab in pursuance of this Order, or cause or permit any person not authorised in that behalf by Transport for London to remove or conceal any such plate or notice, nor shall he alter or obliterate, or cause or permit any person not so authorised to alter or obliterate, any mark placed upon the cab in pursuance of this Order or by the authority of Transport for London.'

This makes it clear that the plates cannot be removed from the vehicle at any time, which would appear to suggest, following the ruling in *Hawkins v Edwards*, that a London cab is a London cab at all times once it has been licensed, for the duration of that licence.

[1]   SI 1934/1346; see Appendix I.

2   [1901] 2 KB 169; see para 8.4 above.
3   See para 8.4 above.

17.18

Section 8(2) of MPCA 1869, s 8(2) states:

> 'No hackney carriage shall ply for hire within the limits of this Act unless under the charge of driver having a licence under this section from Transport for London.'

This suggests that it must only be driven by a licensed hackney carriage driver when it is plying for hire. This view is reinforced by the London Cab Order 1934, art 14(e)[1], which states:

> '(e) The licensee shall not employ or permit any person to act as driver of the cab when it is hired or plying for hire except a person who is licensed in pursuance of Section 8 of the Metropolitan Public Carriage Act 1869, as amended by Section 39 of the Road Traffic Act 1934, and of Part IV of this Order to drive cabs of the type to which the cab belongs.'

1   SI 1934/1346; see Appendix I.

17.19

The London Hackney Carriages Act 1843, s 10 states:

> 'every proprietor who shall knowingly suffer any person not duly licensed under the authority of this Act to act as driver of any hackney carriage, ... of which he shall be the proprietor, shall for every such offence forfeit a sum not exceeding level 3 on the standard scale: ...'

The absence of any words relating to 'plying' or 'standing' in this section also suggests that at all times a hackney carriage must be driven by a hackney carriage driver.

17.20

Finally, the London Hackney Carriage Act 1831, s 35[1] makes it clear that a hackney carriage which is standing in any street or place is deemed to be plying for hire (although the London Cab Act 1968, s 3 relaxes that to allow hackney carriage to park) and also that any driver of a hackney carriage which is not actually hired can be compelled to take a fare, subject to distance limits. This has been amended by s 10 of the Transport for London Act 2008 which allows a rank created under s 4 of the London Hackney Carriages Act 1850 to be designated by TfL as a 'rest rank'. Section 10(4) of the 2008 Act makes it clear that the driver of a hackney carriage which is standing at a rest rank is not deemed to be plying for hire and cannot be compelled to drive the hackney carriage.

1   See Appendix I.

17.21

It would therefore appear that at all times, whether working or not, a hackney carriage must be driven by a person who holds a hackney carriage driver's licence[1].

[1]   This view is not shared by TfL/LTPH who take the view that the vehicle is a hackney carriage only when it is working. In the absence of any case on the point this is an arguable question. As TfL/LTPH is the principal enforcing authority, it seems unlikely that the point will be decided.

PLYING AND STANDING FOR HIRE

17.22

Although the wording for the London legislation differs slightly from the legislation applicable outside London, overall the concept of plying and standing for hire seem to be identical. However, the distinctions between 'plying' and 'standing' that exist outside London[1] are not replicated within the London legislation. There is nothing within the London legislation that appears fundamentally to change the approach that is outlined at para 8.7 onwards above.

There is a consistent line of High Court decisions, and one significant case which has taken a similar approach but reached a slightly different conclusion. The case which appears to depart from the reasoning first established in *Sales v Lake*[2] is *Nottingham City Council v Woodings*[3]. That decision did take account of a number previous of decisions and certainly seems to represent a practical and to an extent, pragmatic view.

However, the conclusion in *Nottingham* appears at odds with the conclusions arrived at in all the previous cases. The subsequent cases of *Chorley BC v Thomas*[4], *Dudley Metropolitan Borough Council v Arif*[5] and *Gateshead Council v Henderson*[6] all refer to the *Nottingham* decision but arrive at conclusions which are clearly based on all the cases apart from *Nottingham*.

It is clear that the simple question of where the vehicle is parked is too crude an indicator as to whether or not it is plying for hire, and it is surely the case that the courts must acknowledge the existence of licensed private hire vehicles, and the requirements that they have to wait for the next booking being communicated by the operator. The *Nottingham* decision certainly does that, but stands alone, both in relation to the earlier cases and subsequent decisions. As a consequence, it should perhaps be viewed with caution. It is suggested that these cases show that there is a difference between a private hire vehicle parking in a car park, or down a side street awaiting a booking being radioed through, and a similar vehicle located outside a pub, nightclub or supermarket, knowing it may be approached by prospective passengers who have not pre-booked a journey.

[1]   See Chapter 8, para 8.8.
[2]   [1922] 1 KB 553.
[3]   *Nottingham City Council v Woodings* [1994] RTR 72.
[4]   [2001] EWHC Admin S70, [2001] LLR 62 QBD; see para 8.37 above.
[5]   [2011] EWHC 3880 (Admin), [2012] RTR 20.
[6]   [2012] LLR 610, Admin Ct.

17.23

It would appear that the decision in *Kahn v Evans*[1] whereby it was decided that a hackney carriage was plying for hire until such time as a contract for a journey came into existence would apply to London cab[2].

[1]   [1985] RTR 33.
[2]   See Chapter 8, para 8.65 above for full details relating to this matter.

17.24

There is no limitation on the area in which a London cab can work, within the area of the Metropolitan Police District and the City of London. There is, however, a limit on certain drivers' licences[1].

[1]   See Chapter 19, para 19.22.

17.25

A licensed hackney carriage which is 'found standing in any street or place' is deemed to be plying for hire under the London Hackney Carriage Act 1831, s 35. This clearly harks back to the days when hackney carriages were horse drawn, and reflected the existence of motorised cabs. It was modified by the provisions of the London Cab Act 1968, s 3 so that if a cab is parked at a designated parking place (made by an order under the Road Traffic Regulation Act 1984) it is not plying for hire.

TRANSFER OF LICENCE

17.26

There is no general concept of transfer of hackney carriage proprietors' licences within London. Obviously, as there is no limit on the number of hackney carriage licences that will be granted, the licence itself does not have a value, in contrast to the situation outside London in districts where a limited number of licences are granted by the local authority.

17.27

However, the London Cab Order 1934, art 20[1] allows a cab licence to be transferred upon the death of the licensee. TfL/LTPH can endorse the licence (which must be sent to them) and that endorsement has the effect of transferring the licence to the personal representatives of the deceased person or to the proprietor's widow or child if they are aged 21 years or over and satisfy the conditions of fitness laid down by TfL/LTPH.

[1]   SI 1934/1346; see Appendix I.

17.28

Although the wording in the London Cab Order 1934, art 20[1] makes it clear that transfer is to the licensee's widow, the use of the words 'in the event of the death of any licensee during the currency of his cab licence…', by applying the Interpretation Act 1978, s 6, it would seem that a transfer could also be made to the widower of a female cab licensee[2].

1   SI 1934/1346; see Appendix I.
2   It seems sensible to conclude that the same provisions would apply to a civil partner on the death of the other civil partner. Unfortunately, neither the Civil Partnership Act 2004 nor the Marriage (Same Sex Couples) Act 2013 make this expressly clear, and do not amend the wording of art 20.

17.29

The second paragraph of the London Cab Order 1934, art 20[1] states:

> 'In like manner and on like conditions, in the event of the marriage of a woman licensee during the currency of her licence, such licence may be transferred to her husband.'

1   SI 1934/1346; see Appendix I.

17.30

It is less clear whether it is possible for a man who holds a cab licence and marries to transfer that to his wife using these provisions and the Interpretation Act 1978, s 6. It is arguable that s 6 allows this paragraph of the London Cab Order 1934, art 20[1] to be read from a male licensee's perspective, but in absence of any case on the point this is by no means certain[2].

1   SI 1934/1346; see Appendix I.
2   Again, this should also apply to a civil partner but the Civil Partnerships Act 2004 does not make this expressly clear, and does not amend the wording of art 20.

17.31

The final possibility for a transfer is when the licence is held by an individual on behalf of a firm or company and on the death of that licensee the licence can be transferred on similar conditions to another person who would be entitled to apply for the licence on behalf of that firm or company.

Hackney carriage offences

17.32

If a person knowingly makes any false statement or knowingly withholds any material information to obtain the grant of a cab licence either for himself or anybody else then they commit an offence contrary to the London Cab Order 1934, art 15[1] and MPCA 1869, s 10[2]. Section 10 makes breach of any Order made under MPCA 1869 (and the London Cab Order 1934 is made under s 9 of the same Act), an offence punishable by a fine not exceeding level 1 on the standard scale.

1   SI 1934/1346; see Appendix I.
2   See Appendix I.

17.33

If the plates that are fixed by TfL/LTPH are not displayed, or have been defaced or any of the other required marks applied by TfL/LTPH are missing, obliterated or indistinct, then an offence is committed under the London Cab Order 1934, art 16[1].

[1]   SI 1934/1346; see Appendix I.

17.34

It is also an offence to move, conceal, obliterate or alter any plate or other mark (London Cab Order 1934, art 16(2)[1]).

[1]   SI 1934/1346; see Appendix I.

17.35

To overcome these problems, or if any plate or notice is lost then the cab owner or licensee must take the cab to the appointed passing station and a new plate or notice or mark will be issued and fixed to the vehicle by the Public Carriage examiner (London Cab Order 1934, art 16(3)[1]).

[1]   SI 1934/1346; see Appendix I.

17.36

Use of any defaced or altered plate, licence or notice or indeed counterfeit copies of any of those if they are used constitutes an offence by virtue of the London Cab Order 1934, art 18[1], and any defaced or unauthorised alteration of any details on a cab licence renders the licence itself void by virtue of art 17.

[1]   SI 1934/1346; see Appendix I.

17.37

Within three days of the expiration of the licence, the licensee or owner must return the licence and the plates to TfL/LTPH or a public carriage examiner. Although this is not a particularly long period of time, compliance has apparently never been a problem. It is clearly necessary to prevent unauthorised use of the plates after the licence has expired. Failure to comply with this requirement is an offence by virtue of the London Cab Order 1934, art 21[1].

[1]   SI 1934/1346; see Appendix I.

17.38

The London Cab Order 1934, art 22[1] makes it clear that where the licence is held by a person on behalf of a firm or company, not only the named licensee but also the firm or company is liable for any failure to comply with any of the requirements under the Order or any of the conditions or requirements attached to the licence itself.

[1]   SI 1934/1346; see Appendix I.

SUSPENSION OR REVOCATION OF LICENCES

17.39

TfL/LTPH have the power to revoke or suspend any cab licence on any of the following grounds contained in the London Cab Order 1934, art 19(1)[1]:

'(a) if the licence has been obtained by any misrepresentation, fraud or concealment of any material circumstances; or

(b) if TfL, by reason of any new circumstance arising or coming to its knowledge after the grant of a licence, or by reason of the condition of the cab, is satisfied that a licence in respect of the cab in question could not in pursuance of this Order properly be granted to the licensee if he were an applicant for a new licence; or

(c) if the licensee fails to comply with any of the provisions or conditions subject to which the licence has been granted; or

(d) on any of the grounds on which a licence in respect of a hackney carriage might at the time of the commencement of the Metropolitan Public Carriage Act 1869 have been revoked or suspended.'

[1]   SI 1934/1346; see Appendix I.

17.40

If the licensee holds more than one licence, TfL/LTPH can decide to only revoke one or more of them as it may think fit if revocation or suspension of all of the licences would be 'contrary to the public interest'.

17.41

As there is theoretically an unlimited supply of hackney carriages within London, it is difficult to see the situation in which revocation of all of a licensee's cab licences would be contrary to the public interest. It would appear that a licensee with a massive holding of licences (perhaps more than 5% of the entire hackney carriage fleet) might lead to public problems if all their licences were revoked, but unless such action is taken the sanction contained within the London Cab Order 1934, art 19[1] is considerably watered down. If a licensee knows he is only going to lose one of a number of his licences, although it will cause some hardship, it will not perhaps have the desired effect for compliance that would otherwise be required.

[1]   SI 1934/1346; see Appendix I.

17.42

Within five days of receiving the notice of suspension or revocation, which must be delivered personally or sent by registered post or recorded delivery to the address stated in the licence, the licensee must return the licence to the public carriage examiner at the passing station for cancellation and deliver the vehicle to the passing station for the removal of the plates (London Cab Order 1934, art 19(2)[1]).

[1]   SI 1934/1346; see Appendix I.

17.43

If the licence has been suspended rather than revoked, then at the end of the period of suspension the public carriage examiner must return the licence and re-attach the plates to the vehicle (London Cab Order 1934, art 19(3)[1]). Rights of appeal against suspension or revocation are contained in the Transport Act 1985, s 17 (see para 17.11 above).

[1]   SI 1934/1346; see Appendix I.

Chapter 18

The use of hackney carriages within London

INTRODUCTION

18.1

This chapter considers the practical aspects of hackney carriage use, including consideration of the use of seat belts, taximeters and fares; disabled people; stands; non-motorised hackney carriages; hiring hackney carriages at separate fares; and the use of bus lanes.

THE POWER TO SET FARES FOR HACKNEY CARRIAGES

18.2

Transport for London/London Taxi and Private Hire (TfL/LTPH) have the power to set the fares for hackney carriages within London. This is granted by the London Cab and Stage Carriage Act 1907, s 1 and is actually made by London Cab Order. The fares are governed by the provisions of the London Cab Order 1934, as amended[1] which is regularly amended by subsequent London Cab Orders to reflect the current level of fares These also apply to non-obligatory fares by virtue of the provisions of the London Cab Act 1968, s 1.

[1]   SI 1934/1346. See Appendix I.

18.3

TfL/LTPH can in fact set different fares for different classes of cabs and under different circumstances. Obviously, if horse-drawn cabs were to return to London a different scale of charges might be applicable.

18.4

The fares themselves are contained in the London Cab Order 1934, arts 40 and 41[1] and are updated regularly. It is also possible to hire cabs at fixed fares, under the provisions of art 40A[2]. Drivers must also accept payment by credit or debit card under art 31A.

1   SI 1934/1346. See Appendix I.
2   This only applies to ranks in Coventry Street and in the vicinity of Leicester Square, and
     between 10 pm and midnight on Fridays and Saturdays, and midnight and 4 am on Saturdays
     and Sundays. – See art 40A and Sch E to the London Cab Order 1934, SI 1934/1346.

Taximeters

18.5

The London Cab Order 1934, art 35[1] requires every motor cab (as opposed to a horse drawn cab) to have a taximeter fitted. It states:

'35 Approved Taximeter to be Fitted and Sealed

(1) The owner of every motor cab shall cause the cab to be fitted with a taximeter of a type approved by Transport for London.

(2) Any such meter shall be so constructed and adjusted that--

(a) after the taximeter has been started at the commencement of the hiring or at such later time as the driver thinks fit, the fare payable for the hiring as prescribed in paragraph 40 is automatically recorded and displayed by the taximeter;

(b) the total up to an amount of not less than 10p of any extra charges payable by a hirer of the cab, can be displayed by the meter.

(3) Every taximeter so fitted shall be sealed in such manner as Transport for London may from time to time direct and may be marked in such manner as Transport for London may from time to time permit, and no person shall place such seal or mark on the taximeter unless he is authorised in that behalf by Transport for London.'

1   SI 1934/1346.

18.6

It can be seen that TfL/LTPH must approve the meter. It is an offence to remove or tamper with the taximeter or to break or to deface or tamper with any seal or mark which has been placed on the meter under the direction of TfL/LTPH[1].

1   London Cab Order 1934, SI 1934/1346, art 36.

18.7

It is an offence to use a motor cab if a meter has not been fitted, if the meter has not been sealed or if the seal has been interfered with in any way. In the latter case the vehicle must be taken to a passing station[1] as soon as practical, or in any event within 24 hours so that the seal can be refixed. These offences are contained in the London Cab Order 1934, art 37[2].

1   'Passing station' is defined in the London Cab Order 1934, SI 1934/1346, art 2. The only
     'passing station' is at the LTPH offices at Penton Street.
2   SI 1934/1346. See Appendix I.

Lighting of taxi signs and taximeters

18.8

The London Cab Order 1934, art 38[1] governs the illuminating of a sign on the vehicle and the meter itself. It states:

'(1) The owner of every motor cab shall provide a lamp so placed on the cab as to render the readings on the dial of the taximeter easily legible at all times of the day and night, and shall maintain such lamp in proper working order and condition.

(2) The driver of a motor cab shall keep such lamp properly alight throughout any part of a hiring which is during the hours of darkness as defined in Section 1 of the Road Transport Lighting Act 1927, and shall light such lamp during a hiring at any other time at the request of a hirer so as to enable the hirer to read the dial of the taximeter.

(3) Where a motor cab is provided with means for illuminating either the flag of the taximeter or a sign bearing the word "Taxi" fitted with the approval of Transport for London on the top of the cab, the driver, when plying for hire with the cab during any part of the hours of darkness as aforesaid, shall cause the flag or the sign or both the flag and the sign to be illuminated.'

[1] SI 1934/1346.

18.9

In many ways, these requirements are obsolete as meters are now electronic and are automatically illuminated. However, the requirement relating to the 'Taxi' sign on the top of the cab is clearly important when the vehicle is plying for hire.

18.10

The London Cab Order 1934, art 39 makes it clear that the meter must be set in motion as soon as the cab is hired, and not before and then stopped as soon as the hiring is terminated, but art 39 allows the driver to start the meter later, or stop it earlier[1]. Section 29 of the Equality Act 2010 makes it clear that a service provider cannot discriminate against a disabled person, so it is important that the meter is not started until a wheelchair bound passenger is properly loaded and secured and is also stopped at the end of the journey, not when the unloading has been completed[2].

[1] See Chapter 19, para 19.50 in relation to accepting less than the metered fare.
[2] This is reinforced by para 1.30 of 'Access for wheelchair users to Taxis and Private Hire Vehicles – Statutory Guidance' – Department for Transport February 2017 available at https://www.gov. uk/government/publications/access-for-wheelchair-users-to-taxis-and-private-hire-vehicles

18.11

The London Cab Order 1934, art 42[1] foresees the carriage of luggage or packages without accompanying people. In those cases the scale of charges contained in the London Cab Order 1934, arts 40 and 41 also apply. There is one fundamental distinction and that is that discretion lies with the driver of the cab as to whether or not to take a hiring to carry luggage or packages, as opposed to the requirement to take a hiring for people which usually applies under the London Hackney Carriage Act 1831, s 35.

[1]   See Chapter 19, para 19.50 in relation to accepting less than the metered fare.

18.12

Outside London it is possible for the driver to offer a discount from the fare shown on the meter[1], and that appears to be the case within London. The London Cab Order 1934, art 40[2] states:

' ... the maximum fare payable for the hiring for a journey of a motor cab shall be the aggregate of the following amounts ... . '

It is clear that the fares prescribed under the London Cab Order 1934 are the maximum that can be charged, but discounts can be offered at any time.

[1]   See Chapter 9, para 9.26 onwards.
[2]   SI 1934/1346.

18.13

This prevents overcharging and any driver who charged more than the fare shown on the meter would be liable for prosecution under the Metropolitan Public Carriage Act 1869, s 10[1]. If the passenger refuses to pay the fare it is possible to seek recovery of the fare using the provisions of the London Hackney Carriages Act 1831, s 41[2], although realistically the approaches used outside London are more likely to be used from a day-to-day practice, either taking the passenger to the nearest police station and reporting them to the police for an offence under s 11 of the Fraud Act 2006, or taking them back to where the journey commenced.

[1]   See Appendix I.
[2]   See Appendix I.

DISABLED PEOPLE AND HACKNEY CARRIAGES

18.14

The provisions of Equality Act 2010 (EA 2010) apply within London in exactly the same way they apply outside London.

This means that under EA 2010, s 168 a driver must carry an assistance dog in the passenger compartment with the passenger, unless he holds an exemption certificate issued by TfL under EA 2010, s 169[1].

TfL have created and published a list of wheelchair acccesible vehicles ('designated taxis') under the provisions of EA 2010, s 167 (all hackney carriages licensed by TfL) and accordingly, all hackney carriage drivers must provide mobility assistance to wheelchair bound passengers under EA 2010, s165, unless they have been granted an exemption certificate under s 166[2].

[1]   For full details of the carriage of assistance dogs, see Chapter 9, para 9.56 onwards.
[2]   For full details of designated taxis and mobility assistance, see Chapter 9, para 9.58 onwards.

18.15

As the specification of a London cab is fixed by TfL/LTPH and currently the vehicles that satisfy that condition are all manufactured as being wheelchair-accessible, all London cabs are in fact capable of carrying disabled passengers who wish to remain in their wheelchair.

HACKNEY CARRIAGE STANDS

18.16

TfL/LTPH has the power to create stands using the powers contained in the London Hackney Carriages Act 1850, s 4.

> **'Standings for hackney carriages to be appointed and regulated by Transport for London** ... It shall be lawful for Transport for London from time to time to appoint standings for hackney carriages at such places as they shall think convenient in any street, thoroughfare, or place of public resort within the metropolitan police district, any law, statute, or custom to the contrary thereof notwithstanding, and at their discretion to alter the same, and from time to time to make regulations concerning the boundaries of the same, and the number of carriages to be allowed at any such standing, and the times at and during which they may stand and ply for hire at any such standing, and also from time to time to make such regulations as Transport for London shall deem proper for enforcing order at every such standing, and for removing any person who shall unnecessarily loiter or remain at or about any such standing; and Transport for London shall cause all the orders and regulations to be made by them as aforesaid to be advertised in the London Gazette, and a copy thereof, signed by a person authorised for the purpose by Transport for London, to be hung up for public inspection in the offices of Transport for London, and at each of the magistrates' courts acting for an area falling wholly within an inner London borough; and such copy shall be received in evidence in the said courts as if it were the original of which it purports to be a copy, and shall be taken to be a true copy of such original order or regulation, without further proof than the aforesaid signature.'

18.17

As can be seen, this is a power not only to create stands, but also to alter them, vary the number of cabs allowed to use them, maintain order on stands and remove people who abuse the stands. No consent of the Highway Authority is required and the positioning of the stand appears to be solely at the discretion of TfL/LTPH. TfL/LTPH do in practice consult all interested parties, including the taxi trade, local authorities (as highway authority), police and local residents. These 'orders and regulations' are made by a LTPH Notice, which is approved and signed by the Head of LTPH and published in the *London Gazette*. They can be inspected at the LTPH offices and all Greater London magistrates' courts (although it is not clear whether they are actually 'hung up for public inspection' in each of those places).

18.18

Section 9 of the Transport for London Act 2008 allows TfL to designate specified ranks (either permanently or for certain times and periods) as 'directional taxi ranks'. This means that a hackney carriage leaving the rank with the passenger can only do so in one specified direction. A driver can refuse to leave the rank in anything other than the designated direction, and not contravene s 35 of the London Hackney Carriage Act 1831[1]. Such directional ranks must be clearly indicated by a sign erected by TfL[2].

[1]   Transport for London Act 2008, s 9(3); see Appendix I.
[2]   Transport for London Act 2008, s 9(2); see Appendix I.

18.19

Section 10 of the Transport for London Act 2008 allows TfL to designate by means of a London Cab Order any stand or part of the stand as a 'rest rank'. This can be permanent or part-time[1], and the maximum length of time can be specified for which a hackney carriage can use the stand for resting[2].

[1]   Transport for London Act 2008, s 10(1); see Appendix I.
[2]   Transport for London Act 2008, s 10(2); see Appendix I.

18.20

Any such rest rank must clearly be identified by means of a sign (s 10(3)), and once a vehicle is parked at a rest rank, it is not deemed to be plying or standing for hire[1].

[1]   Transport for London Act 2008, s 10(4); see Appendix I.

18.21

In addition, the London Hackney Carriages Act 1850, s 4[1] also allows TfL/LTPH to control the use of the stand by regulations. There are no powers contained in the London Cab Order 1934[2] relating to the use of the stand, and these 'Licensing Authority's Regulations at Taxi Standings' are again made by PCO Notice and published in the *London Gazette*. They were last issued on 11 October 1963 and cover:

- drivers being with their cabs;
- drivers willing to be hired;
- drivers moving up;
- disabled cabs, ie broken-down vehicles; and
- drivers not causing nuisance.

[1]   See Appendix I.
[2]   SI 1934/1346; see Appendix I.

18.22

There is no need for taxi hailing points in London as, traditionally, considerable numbers of hackney carriages cruise the streets plying for hire.

BYELAWS

18.23

There are no byelaws governing the general use of hackney carriages within London, although byelaws do exist in relation to the use of hackney carriages at Heathrow Airport[1].

[1]   The relevant part of the byelaws are reproduced in Appendix I.

Non-motorised hackney carriages

HORSE-DRAWN VEHICLES

18.24

The last horse-drawn hackney carriage in London was withdrawn in 1947, when the licence was returned to the PCO. Clearly, it would be possible for horse-drawn vehicles to return, but that would need the agreement of TfL/LTPH in relation to the vehicle specification. Whether that would be forthcoming would remain to be seen. If such vehicles were licensed as hackney carriages, then clearly all the provisions of the various legislation would apply and the driver would need a hackney carriage driver's licence, for which he would have to pass 'the knowledge' test[1]. In addition, the London Cab Order 1934, Pt VII[2] specifically applies to horse-drawn vehicles.

[1]   See Chapter 19, para 19.24.
[2]   SI 1934/1346; see Appendix I.

TRISHAWS OR PEDICABS

18.25

Outside London, a trishaw is a hackney carriage[1]. In relation to this question, which was raised outside London, the Court of Appeal had no doubt that a trishaw was a hackney carriage. Within London, the definition of hackney carriage is contained in the Metropolitan Public Carriage Act 1869, s 4:

"'Hackney Carriage" shall mean any carriage for the conveyance of passengers which plies for hire within the limits of this Act, and is neither a stage carriage nor a tram car.'

[1]   See *R v Cambridge City Council, ex p Lane* [1999] EHLR 156, CA at para 9.106 above.

Oddy v Bug Bugs Ltd

18.26

> Was a trishaw a hackney carriage plying or standing for hire? Held: No, it was a stage carriage and outside legislative control.

It is difficult to see why a trishaw cannot be a hackney carriage, as it seems quite feasible for such a vehicle to ply for hire. The case of *Oddy v Bug Bugs Ltd*[1] decided otherwise. The decision in *R v Cambridge City Council, ex p Lane*[2] was distinguished on the basis that the Town Police Clauses Act 1847 (TCPA 1847) and the MPCA 1869 differed. The TCPA 1847 does not define stage carriage wheras the MPCA 1869 does in s 4:

> '"stage carriage" shall mean any carriage for the conveyance of passengers which plies for hire in any public street, road, or place within the limits of this Act, and in which the passengers or any of them are charged to pay separate and distinct or at the rate of separate and distinct fares for their respective places or seats therein.'

On the facts of the case, it was clear that the passengers were charged separate fares and accordingly the trishaw was not a hackney carriage, but a stage carriage. The consequence of this decision is that there is no regulation of trishaws in London[3].

It would also appear that trishaws could also act as private hire vehicles within London, as the requirement for a private hire vehicle to be a motor vehicle as contained in LG(MP)A 1976, s 80 is not replicated in the Private Hire Vehicles (London) Act 1998, s 1(1)(a) as the word 'motor' is omitted.

[1]   (12 November 2003, unreported), Admin Ct.
[2]   [1999] EHLR 156, CA.
[3]   TfL has been pressing for legislation to control pedicabs/trishaws, but at the time of writing (August 2017) no legislation has been forthcoming.

Hiring hackney carriages at separate fares

18.27

The provisions of the Transport Act 1985 apply in London just as they do outside London[1]. The same procedures must be followed by TfL/LTPH and by a local authority, and all other requirements are the same. This is subject to the regulations made under the Act, which are the Local Services (Operation by Taxi) (London) Regulations 1986[2] and the Licensed Taxis (Hiring at Separate Fares) (London) Order 1986[3]. A scheme exists for the whole of the Metropolitan Area under the London Taxi Sharing Scheme Order 1987[4]. All other provisions remain as for outside London.

[1]   See para 9.112 onwards above.
[2]   SI 1986/567.
[3]   SI 1986/1387.
[4]   SI 1987/1535.

Chapter 19

Hackney carriage drivers within London

INTRODUCTION

19.1

Within London, the role of the hackney carriage driver is identical in concept to that outside London. Provisions affecting hackney carriage drivers are contained in the following legislation:

- the London Hackney Carriage Act 1831 (LHCA 1831)[1];
- the London Hackney Carriages Act 1843 (LHCA 1843)[2];
- the London Hackney Carriages Act 1850;
- the London Hackney Carriage Act 1853 (LHCA 1853)[3];
- the Metropolitan Public Carriage Act 1869 (MPCA 1869)[4];
- the London Cab Act 1896 (LCA 1896)[5];
- the London Cab and Stage Carriage Act 1907 (LCSCA 1907)[6];
- the Transport for London Act 2008;
- the London Cab Order 1934, SI 1934/1346[7]; and
- the London Cab Order 1972, SI 1972/1047[8].

[1]   See Appendix I.
[2]   See Appendix I.
[3]   See Appendix I.
[4]   See Appendix I.
[5]   See Appendix I.
[6]   See Appendix I.
[7]   See Appendix I.
[8]   See Appendix I.

19.2

As outlined in Chapter 17, paras 17.16–17.21, although it seems that a London cab must only be driven by a person who holds a London cab driver's licence, this view is not supported by TfL/LTPH, who take the view that a London cab may also be driven for social, domestic and pleasure purposes by a person who is not a licensed cab driver, provided the owner has given his consent. As TfL/LTPH are the licensing authority, this matter is unlikely to be tested in court.

GRANTING THE LICENCE

19.3

The power to grant a licence is contained within LHCA 1843, s 8 and MPCA 1869, s 8. Section 8 of the 1843 Act states:

'Transport for London to grant licences to drivers of hackney carriages – At the time of granting any licence an abstract of the laws and a ticket to be given

8 … It shall be lawful for Transport for London to grant a licence to act as driver of hackney carriages, … to any person who shall produce such a certificate as shall satisfy Transport for London of his good behaviour and fitness for such situation …; and in every such licence shall be specified the number of such licence, and the proper name and surname and place of abode, and age, and a description of the person to whom such licence shall be granted …; and every such licence shall bear date on the day on which the same shall be granted, … and on every licence of a driver … Transport for London shall cause proper columns to be prepared, in which every proprietor employing the driver … named in such licence shall enter his own name and address, and the days on which such driver … shall enter and shall quit his service respectively; and in case any of the particulars entered or endorsed upon any licence in pursuance of this Act shall be erased or defaced every such licence shall be wholly void and of none effect; and Transport for London shall, at the time of granting any licence, deliver to the driver, … to whom the same shall be granted an abstract of the laws in force relating to such driver, … and of the penalties to which he is liable for any misconduct, and also a metal ticket, upon which there shall be marked or engraved his office or employment, and a number corresponding with the number which shall be inserted in such licence.'

19.4

MPCA 1869, s 8 states:

'8.— Hackney carriage to be driven by licensed drivers.

(1) Transport for London shall have the function of licensing persons to be drivers of hackney carriages.

(2) No hackney carriage shall ply for hire within the limits of this Act unless under the charge of a driver having a licence under this section from Transport for London.

(3) If any hackney carriage plies for hire in contravention of this section—
 (a) the person driving the carriage, and
 (b) the owner of the carriage, unless he proves that the driver acted without his privity or consent,
 shall each be liable to a penalty not exceeding level 3 on the standard scale.

(4) Transport for London may send to the Commissioner of Police of the Metropolis or the Commissioner of Police for the City of London—

    (a) details of a person to whom Transport for London is considering granting a licence under this section, and

    (b) a request for the Commissioner's observations;

and the Commissioner shall respond to the request.

(5) A licence under this section may—

    (a) be granted on such conditions,

    (b) be in such form,

    (c) be subject to revocation or suspension in such event, and

    (d) generally be dealt with in such manner,

as may be prescribed.

(6) Subsection (5) of this section is subject to the following provisions of this section.

(7) Subject to section 8A, a licence under this section shall, if not revoked or suspended, be in force for three years.

(8) A fee of such amount (if any) as Transport for London may determine shall be paid to Transport for London—

    (a) by any applicant for a licence under this section, on making the application for the licence;

    (b) by any applicant for the taking or re-taking of any test or examination, or any part of a test or examination, with respect to any matter of fitness, on making the application for the taking or re-taking of the test, examination or part; and

    (c) by any person granted a licence under this section, on the grant of the licence.

(9) In paragraph (b) of subsection (8) of this section *"matter of fitness"* means—

    (a) any matter as respects which Transport for London must be satisfied before granting a licence under this section; or

    (b) any matter such that, if Transport for London is not satisfied with respect to the matter, they may refuse to grant a licence under this section.

(10) Different amounts may be determined under subsection (8) of this section for different purposes or different cases.

(11) Transport for London may remit or refund the whole or part of a fee under subsection (8) of this section.'

19.5

It can be seen that before Transport for London/London Taxi and Private Hire (TfL/LTPH) can grant a licence the applicant must produce a certificate of his good behaviour and fitness to be granted such a licence. TfL/LTPH regard the DBS Enhanced Disclosure as being such a certificate. By virtue of the London Cab Order 1934, art 23[1], TfL/LTPH must issue on demand a form of requisition for a hackney carriage drivers licence. This is now the application form supplied by TfL/LTPH, which is accompanied by a declaration as to convictions, and an agreement to notify TfL/LTPH of any future convictions.

¹ SI 1934/1346; see Appendix I.

19.6

All questions required on that certificate must be answered by the applicant by virtue of LHCA 1843, s 14¹. This makes it an offence for any person to make false representations or falsely answer any questions. Interestingly, TfL/LTPH have one calendar month after the commission of the offence to issue proceedings, which is remarkably short for the issue of criminal proceedings, unless a licence is issued as a result of such false information, in which case a prosecution can be brought during the currency of the licence.

In addition, the applicant must demonstrate his right to remain and work in the UK. S8A states:

'8A Drivers' licences for persons subject to immigration control

(1) Subsection (2) applies if—

    (a) a licence under section 8 is to be granted to a person who has been granted leave to enter or remain in the United Kingdom for a limited period ("the leave period"),

    (b) the person's leave has not been extended by virtue of section 3C of the Immigration Act 1971 (continuation of leave pending variation decision), and

    (c) apart from subsection (2), the period for which the licence would have been in force would have ended after the end of the leave period.

(2) Transport for London must grant the licence for a period which ends at or before the end of the leave period.

(3) Subsection (4) applies if—

    (a) a licence under section 8 is to be granted to a person who has been granted leave to enter or remain in the United Kingdom for a limited period, and

    (b) the person's leave has been extended by virtue of section 3C of the Immigration Act 1971 (continuation of leave pending variation decision).

(4) Transport for London must grant the licence for a period that does not exceed six months.

(5) A licence under section 8 ceases to be in force if the person to whom it was granted becomes disqualified by reason of the person's immigration status from driving a hackney carriage.

(6) If a licence granted in accordance with subsection (2) or (4) expires, the person to whom it was granted must, within the period of 7 days beginning with the day after that on which it expired, return to Transport for London—

    (a) the licence,

    (b) the person's copy of the licence (if any), and

(c)   the person's driver's badge.

(7)   If subsection (5) applies to a licence, the person to whom it was granted must, within the period of 7 days beginning with the day after the day on which the person first became disqualified, return to Transport for London—

(a)   the licence,

(b)   the person's copy of the licence (if any), and

(c)   the person's driver's badge.

(8)   A person who, without reasonable excuse, contravenes subsection (6) or (7) is guilty of an offence and liable on summary conviction—

(a)   to a fine not exceeding level 3 on the standard scale, and

(b)   in the case of a continuing offence, to a fine not exceeding ten pounds for each day during which an offence continues after conviction.

(9)   The Secretary of State may by regulations made by statutory instrument amend the amount for the time being specified in subsection (8)(b).

(10) Regulations under subsection (9) may make transitional, transitory or saving provision.

(11) A statutory instrument containing regulations under subsection (9) may not be made unless a draft of the instrument has been laid before, and approved by a resolution of, each House of Parliament.

(12) For the purposes of this section a person is disqualified by reason of the person's immigration status from driving a hackney carriage if the person is subject to immigration control and—

(a)   the person has not been granted leave to enter or remain in the United Kingdom, or

(b)   the person's leave to enter or remain in the United Kingdom—

(i)   is invalid,

(ii)   has ceased to have effect (whether by reason of curtailment, revocation, cancellation, passage of time or otherwise), or

(iii) is subject to a condition preventing the person from driving a hackney carriage.

(13) Where a person is on immigration bail within the meaning of Part 1 of Schedule 10 to the Immigration Act 2016—

(a)   the person is to be treated for the purposes of this section as if the person had been granted leave to enter the United Kingdom, but

(b)   any condition as to the person's work in the United Kingdom to which the person's immigration bail is subject is to be treated for those purposes as a condition of leave.

(14) For the purposes of this section a person is subject to immigration control if under the Immigration Act 1971 the person requires leave to enter or remain in the United Kingdom.'

The Home Office issued Guidance in December 2016 to Licensing Authorities in relation to these requirements[2] and TfL must have regard to that Guidance by virtue of art 25A(3) of the London Cab Order 1934. The remainder of art 25A details how a person can be disqualified from holding a drivers' licence because of their immigration status[3].

1   See Appendix I.
2   *'Guidance for Licensing Authorities to Prevent Illegal Working in the Taxi and Private Hire Sector in England and Wales'* available at https://www.gov.uk/government/uploads/system/uploads/attachment_data/file/574059/Guidance-for-licensing-authorities-to-prevent-illegal-working-in-the-taxi-and-private-hire-sector-in-England-and-Wales.pdf See Appendix II.
3   For full details of immigration status please see Chapter 10, para 10.20 onwards.

19.7

The licence itself can be 'in such form and ... contain such particulars as Transport for London shall think fit'[1]).

1   London Cab Order 1934, art 27.

19.8

Once the licence has been issued, the particulars of it are maintained in 'books to be kept for that purpose at the Office of Transport for London' and a copy of those details are accepted by the courts provided the copy is 'certified by the person having the charge [of the book] thereof to be a true copy' by virtue of LHCA 1843, s 16[1].

1   TfL can only disclose the address of a licensee if the person making the request, in the opinion of TfL, 'has a sufficient reason for requiring that information'. See LHCA 1843, s 16(2).

19.9

Once the licence has been granted, TfL/LTPH must provide 'an abstract of the laws in force relating to such driver'[1], together with details of sanctions for non-compliance and also the driver's badge[2]. This must state that the holder is a London hackney carriage driver and carry his driver's number.

1   The 'Abstract of Laws' is available on the TfL Website http://content.tfl.gov.uk/taxi-drivers-abstract-of-laws.pdf
2   Until the amendment of s 8 of the London Hackney Carriages Act 1843 by s 11 of the Transport for London Act 2008, with effect from 22 July 2008, TfL were required to issue 'a metal ticket, upon which there shall be marked or engraved his office or employment, and a number corresponding with the number which shall be inserted in such licence'. The amendment has substituted 'badge', for 'metal ticket' and removed the requirement for engraving.

19.10

Once that badge has been issued it must be worn at all times when he is working as a hackney carriage driver and also at any time he is required to attend before a magistrate. LHCA 1843, s 17 makes it an offence for a driver to either work whilst not wearing his badge or to appear before a magistrate without wearing his badge.

19.11

It is an offence to transfer or lend the licence to any other person, or permit any other person who is not the licensee to use or wear the badge and that is punishable by a fine not exceeding level 3 on the standard scale (see LHCA 1843, s 10)[1].

[1] See Appendix I.

FEES FOR DRIVERS' LICENCES

19.12

The power to levy a fee for both application for and grant of a driver's licence is contained in MPCA 1869, s 8(8)[1].

[1] See Appendix I.

CRITERIA FOR THE GRANT OF A LICENCE

19.13

The London Cab Order 1934, art 25[1] allows TfL/LTPH to refuse to grant a cab drivers licence on two grounds:

'25 Grounds for Refusal of Cab-drivers' Licences

(1) Transport for London may in its discretion refuse to grant a cab-drivers' licence—
  (a) if the applicant fails to satisfy Transport for London that he is of good character and fit to act as a cab-driver,
  (b) if the applicant is disqualified by reason of the applicant's immigration status from driving a hackney carriage, or
  (c) if the, applicant has within the three years immediately preceding the date of his application held a cab-driver's licence and has, otherwise than by reason of illness or other unavoidable cause, failed to act as a cab-driver during any considerable part of the period for which the licence was granted or, where he has within the said three years held more than one such licence, the period for which the last of such licences was granted.'

[1] SI 1934/1346.

19.14

TfL have a statement in relation to previous convictions for hackney carriage drivers and emphasise that each application will be considered on its own merits[1]. As with hackney carriage drivers outside London, all previous convictions (except protected cautions and protected convictions) remain current by virtue of the Rehabilitation of Offenders Act 1974 (Exceptions) Order 1975[2].

[1] Available at https://tfl.gov.uk/info-for/taxis-and-private-hire/licensing/apply-for-a-taxi-driver-licence
[2] SI 1975/1023; see Appendix I and see para 10.23 onwards above.

19.15

Although the wording 'of good character and fit to act as a cab driver' is different from the concept applicable outside London of fitness and propriety, the overall effect is similar.

19.16

Ultimately, TfL/LTPH must be satisfied that the person is suitable to act as a cab driver having regard to all relevant information that it has been able to obtain about the applicant. It is suggested that the test outlined at para 10.21 above is just as applicable as a working test within London as outside. The test is 'would you (as a person with the power to grant a licence in these circumstances) allow your son or daughter, spouse or partner, mother or father, grandson or granddaughter or any person for whom you care, to get into a vehicle with this person alone?'.

19.17

If the answer to this question or whatever similar test is laid down is an unqualified 'Yes', then the test is probably satisfied. If there are any doubts in the mind of the person who makes that decision, then further consideration should be given as to whether this person is of good character and fit to act as a cab driver.

19.18

In relation to taking into account previous convictions etc, there is no difference between the position inside London and outside[1]. The immigration status of the applicant has been considered above[2], which leaves the final possibility that the applicant has held, but not used a drivers' licence for a 'considerable part' of that period. Even excluding 'illness or other unavoidable cause' it does beg the question of how TfL are going to establish this.

[1]   See Chapter 10, para 10.23 onwards.
[2]   See above Chapter 19, para 19.6 onwards and Chapter 10, para 10.20 onwards.

19.19

The other ground for refusal of a cab driver's licence is that the applicant has not obtained the age of 21 years. This is provided for in the London Cab Order 1934, art 24[1] and if a licence is granted to person under the age of 21 years, that licence is void.

[2]   SI 1934/1346; see Appendix I.

Other matters concerning drivers

19.20

If a prosecution is brought against a driver for an offence under any provision of LHCA 1831 and the driver is acquitted, LHCA 1831, s 57 allows him to claim 'such compensation for his loss of time in attending the said Justice touching or concerning such complaint or information as to the said Justice seems reasonable'. It is interesting to note that such compensation is to be paid irrespective of whether or not the driver is legally represented and it enables a person who is acquitted to claim compensation for his loss of time and not just for costs involved in instructing a solicitor. It is unclear how often this section is used and TfL/LTPH are unaware of such claims having been made.

19.21

A drivers licence will be granted for a period of three years, unless it is revoked or suspended during that time[1].

[1]   MPCA 1869, s 8(7) see Appendix I.

19.22

It is possible for TfL/LTPH to limit a driver's licence in two ways. First, it can be limited by area. This is usually as a result of an application for 'suburban' licence which does not allow the driver to drive within the centre of London. Those licences are in fact further sub-divided into nine sectors. The alternative is an application for an all-London driver's licence which is not limited within the area of Greater London. This power is contained in the London Cab Order 1934, art 27(1)(b)[1]. The second limitation is that TfL/LTPH can limit the type of cab that the driver can drive. Although this is usually a restriction on driving a manual transmission cab (99% of London cabs have automatic transmission) this would also give TfL/LTPH an opportunity to limit a driver to a horse-drawn cab should it so wish. It is an offence by virtue of art 31 of the London Cab Order 1934 for a driver to breach any condition attached to his licence relating to type of vehicle or geographic area.

[1]   SI 1934/1346; see Appendix I.

19.23

Once the licence has been granted, TfL/LTPH must issue a copy of the licence to the driver and the driver must sign both the licence and the copy. It is necessary for the driver to be issued with a copy because the proprietor of the hackney carriage which the driver is driving has to retain the cab driver's licence by virtue of LHCA 1843, s 21, but the driver must have the copy of his licence in his possession at all times when he is driving or at any time when appearing before a court. The London Cab Order 1934, art 28[1] requires this, together with the fact that he should produce it for inspection on demand by any police constable or public carriage examiner or any officer of a court. This latter point is interesting because it would appear that any solicitor could demand to see the licence of an hackney carriage driver, as solicitors are officers of the senior courts by virtue of the Solicitors Act 1974, s 50(1). It is accepted that this is unlikely to happen in reality.

The driver must also display a copy of the badge and area that he can drive in the cab with 'such notices or marks as Transport for London may from time to time direct'[2].

1   SI 1934/1346; see Appendix I.
2   London Cab Order 1934, SI 1934/1346, art 24A.

19.24

Before a licence can be granted the applicant has to satisfy TfL/LTPH as to his knowledge of London, his fitness and his driving ability. 'The knowledge' is an extremely difficult examination, administered by TfL/LTPH, which is based upon the geography of London. It is essential for any applicant to have passed this test. In addition, a medical report must be completed and the applicant is also subjected to a driving test, which is again conducted by TfL/LTPH.

SUSPENSION OR REVOCATION OF THE LICENCE

19.25

Once the licence has been granted, it can be revoked or suspended by TfL/LTPH if it is satisfied as a result of circumstances arising or coming to its knowledge 'that the licensee is not a fit person to hold' a hackney carriage drivers licence (London Cab Order 1934, art 30[1]). As the wording of art 30(1) is:

'(1) A cab-driver's licence shall be liable to revocation or suspension by Transport for London if it is satisfied, by reason of any circumstances arising or coming to [its] knowledge after the licence was granted, that the licensee is not a fit person to hold such a licence.'

It would appear that the ruling in *R (app Singh) v Cardiff City Council*[2] may also apply, thereby prohibiting TfL from first suspending a drivers licence, conducting an investigation into allegations and then revoking the licence[3].

1   SI 1934/1346; see Appendix I.
2   [2012] EWHC 1852 (Admin), [2013] LLR 108.
3   For full consideration of the decision in *R (app Singh) v Cardiff City Council* [2012] EWHC 1852 (Admin) [2013] LLR 108; see Chapter 6, para 6.33.

19.26

Once the revocation or suspension has been notified to the licensee, provided the licensee has not requested a reconsideration of the decision or appealed the decision under the provisions of the Transport Act 1985, s 17, the licensee must return the licence, copy, and badge to the TfL/LTPH within five days. Failure to comply with the requirement is an offence by virtue of the London Cab Order 1934, art 30(3)[1].

1   SI 1934/1346; see Appendix I.

19.27

If the licence has been suspended, then when that suspension has ended (provided the licence itself has not expired during the period of the suspension) TfL/LTPH must return the licence, copy and badge to the licensee. It is also possible for the court subsequent to a conviction for any offence to revoke or suspend the licence using the powers contained in LHCA 1843, s 25. This relates to any offence, whether under this or any other Act, which would suggest that it does not have to be a matter related to hackney carriage law. In such case, again, the licence must be delivered to TfL/LTPH (in this case forthwith rather than within five days) and again, if the decision was made to suspend the licence, then the licence, copy and badge must be returned to the licensee at the end of the suspension. Power is given to the magistrates' court in this situation to suspend the effect of the order pending an appeal against the order, which would appear to be by way of judicial review or case stated, as there is no right of appeal to the Crown Court.

19.28

It is an offence for a hackney carriage driver to drive either a type of vehicle for which he is not permitted to drive, or ply for hire or permit the cab to be hired in area for which it is not licensed to work (London Cab Order 1934, art 31[1]).

[1]   SI 1934/1346; see Appendix I.

19.29

Once the licence has been granted, if the licensee changes his address, he must inform TfL/LTPH within seven days by delivering his licence and the copy to it and it must endorse the new address upon the licence. Again, failure to comply is an offence (London Cab Order 1934, art 32[1]).

[1]   SI 1934/1346; see Appendix I.

A LICENSED HACKNEY CARRIAGE DRIVER

Drivers' hours

19.30

There are no direct controls over the hours that a hackney carriage driver can work[1]. However, the Working Time Regulations 1998[2] as amended, apply to hackney carriage drivers. Regulation 18 was amended by the Working Time (Amendment) Regulations 2003[3] with effect from 1 August 2003, and limits a driver's working week to 48 hours, averaged over a 17-week period.

[1]   This can be contrasted with HGV and PSV drivers whose driving hours are regulated. There have been suggestions that hackney carriage drivers' hours should be limited, but at present nothing has been formally proposed.
[2]   SI 1998/1833.
[3]   SI 2003/1684.

19.31

This only applies to drivers who are employed and working under a contract of employment and does not apply to self employed drivers. It is therefore of limited application in relation to the hackney carriage trade, where the vast majority of drivers are self employed.

19.32

In relation to those who are employed, they can opt out of the application of the Regulations by agreeing in writing that they should not apply in accordance with reg 4(1) (this must be voluntary and the driver cannot be forced to opt out by the employer)[1].

[1]   The Government's view on this is detailed at Chapter 10, para 10.78.

19.33

There are a number of provisions throughout the legislation applied to hackney carriage drivers which exist with a view to protecting the public.

The duty to take a fare

19.34

LHCA 1831, s 35 makes it clear that a hackney carriage driver must take fare. It states:

'… Every hackney carriage which shall be found standing in any street or place … shall, unless actually hired, be deemed to be plying for hire, although such hackney carriage shall not be on any standing or place usually appropriated for the purpose of hackney carriages standing or plying for hire; and the driver of every such hackney carriage which shall not be actually hired shall be obliged and compellable to go with any person desirous of hiring such hackney carriage; and upon the hearing of any complaint against the driver of any such hackney carriage for any such refusal such driver shall be obliged to adduce evidence of having been and of being actually hired at the time of such refusal, and in case such driver shall fail to produce sufficient evidence of having been and of being so hired as aforesaid he shall forfeit a sum not exceeding level 1 on the standard scale.'

19.35

Although no distance is contained within LHCA 1831, s 35, LHCA 1853, s 7[1] made it clear that the driver could not efuse a fare up to six miles in distance or which will take more than one hour from the date of hiring. This was restated in the London Cab Order 1934, art 34[2] and has since been increased to 12 miles by the London Cab (No 2) Order 2001[3]. The London Cab Order 1972[4] extends the distance from six miles to 20 miles if the hiring commences at Heathrow Airport. There is no alteration to the time-limit on hiring. There does not appear to be any minimum distance below which the driver can refuse to carry a passenger.

[1]   See Appendix I.
[2]   SI 1934/1346; see Appendix I.
[3]   See Appendix I.
[4]   SI 1972/1047; see Appendix I.

19.36

There are two defences to a refusal to drive:

The first is that the vehicle was already hired. This is contained within LHCA 1831, s 36[1]. The power lies with the person who is refused the hiring to summon the taxi driver for a failure to arry that person. The defence is that provided the driver 'in civil and explicit terms declare[d] to any person desirous to hire such hackney carriage that it [was] actually hired' then no offence is committed. There are clearly problems if it appeared that the driver used uncivil language or improperly conducted himself towards the party who wished to hire the vehicle.

[1]   See Appendix I.

19.37

If at the hearing following such a summons the magistrates decide that the complaint is not made out, the complainant must pay compensation to the driver for his loss incurred by attending the hearing. It is up to the magistrates to decide what a reasonable sum would be.

19.38

The second defence is an equivalent provision to that contained in TPCA 1847, s 53[1] whereby the driver can refuse to take a fare if he has a 'reasonable excuse' and is found in LHCA 1853, s 7[2] Section 7 states:

'The driver of every hackney carriage which shall ply for hire at any place within the limits of this Act shall (unless such driver have a reasonable excuse, to be allowed by the justice before whom the matter shall be brought in question,) drive such hackney carriage to any place to which he shall be required by the hirer thereof to drive the same, not exceeding six miles[3] from the place where the same shall have been hired, or for any time not exceeding one hour from the time when hired.'

What would constitute a 'reasonable excuse'? It would not seem to be reasonable to expect certain people to be carried in a hackney carriage, and that would seem to include drunks, vagrants, aggressive, abusive or violent persons and so on, provided any refusal does not amount to unlawful discrimination under the Equality Act 2010[4].

[1]   See Chapter 10, para 10.93 onwards and Appendix I.
[2]   See Appendix I.
[3]   Now increased to 12 miles by the London Cab (No 2) Order 2001. The London Cab Order 1972 SI 1972/1047 extends the distance from six miles to 20 miles if the hiring commences at Heathrow Airport.
[4]   There are a number of 'protected characteristics' contained within the Equality Act 2010 and it is unlawful to discriminate against a person on the basis of one of those characteristics. They are defined in s 4 and are: age; disability; gender reassignment; marriage and civil partnership; pregnancy and maternity; race; religion or belief; sex; and sexual orientation.

Hailing a cab

19.39

Does a 'cruising' hackney carriage have to respond to a prospective passenger hailing the cab? In other words, is a refusal to stop and pick a fare on the street (as opposed to a passenger approaching a hackney carriage on the rank or stand, or stationary on the street) without a reasonable excuse an offence contrary to LHCA 1853, s 7[1]?

[1]   See Appendix I.

Hunt v Morgan

19.40

> Does a cruising cab (plying for hire) have to respond to a hailing by a prospective passenger? Held: No.

This was the question raised in *Hunt v Morgan*[1]. The facts were that the hackney carriage was hailed by a prospective passenger and the driver refused to stop, having formed the 'both inaccurate and unreasonable' view that the prospective passenger was drunk. As that view was found to be both inaccurate and unreasonable by both the magistrates' court at first instance, and Quarter Sessions on appeal, it followed that there was no reasonable excuse for not taking the passenger and the question hinged on whether LHCA 1853, s 7[2] applied in these circumstances? Both the magistrates' court and Quarter Sessions found that it did, the driver was convicted and that conviction was upheld on appeal. The driver appealed by way of case stated to the High Court.

Judgment was given by Goddard LCJ, and he introduced the matter in the following terms[3]:

> 'The question raised is whether a cruising taxicab driver is bound to accept anyone who hails him. It is obviously one of general importance, not only to cab drivers, but also to the members of the public, and it seems never to have been the subject of a decision. There is, no doubt, a widely held belief that a cabman, whether on the rank or not, is bound to accept a fare unless he has a reasonable excuse for refusing, and a full examination of the statutes relating to hackney carriages in London is necessary to decide whether this belief, which, at any rate, accords with the opinion both of the learned magistrate and the appeal committee, is well-founded.'

He then reviewed the legislation, before considering s 7 and concluding[4]:

> 'One must, however, turn back to s 7, to which we have just referred, the section which imposes the duty on the driver and provides him with the defence of a reasonable excuse. The real question in this case is: What do the words in s 7, "which shall ply for hire at any place within the limits of this Act," mean? Have they got the popular meaning which would certainly include a cab driving down a street with the flag up on which the words

"For hire" appear, or must they be confined to the cabman on the rank? In our opinion, with one exception which we will mention hereafter, it is only the cabman on the rank who is obliged to accept a fare. The plying for hire referred to in s 7, which is the material section, must, we think, be so confined. It refers to the driver of every cab which shall ply for hire at any *place* within the limits of the Act and that must, in our opinion, refer to a place appointed for the standing of hackney carriages under the Act of 1843, which is to be read together with and as part of the Act of 1853. "Place" must mean a definite point, just as the same word later in the section clearly refers to a definite destination to which the driver is required to go. It cannot mean "anywhere in a street." This view is reinforced by the fact that it is actually made an offence for a cab driver to ply for hire elsewhere than at one of those places. No doubt, the cabman who has set down a fare and is proceeding to one of those places can accept a fare if he is hailed, and it could not, we think, be held, unless he was soliciting fares as he drove along the street, that he was committing an offence against s 33 of the Act of 1843.

That it is the standing cab and not the moving cab that must accept a fare seems to be shown also by s 35 of the Act of 1831. As we have already said, that Act contained no provision with regard to cab ranks or standing places, but it does provide that:

> "Every [cab] ... found standing in any street or place ... shall, unless actually hired, be deemed to be plying for hire, although such [cab] shall not be on any standing or place usually appropriated for the purpose of [cabs] standing or plying for hire ..."

The onus of proving that he was actually hired at the time of his refusal is laid on the driver. This section is unrepealed, and it would, therefore, appear that, if a cab is standing in the street, having, for instance, just set down a passenger, the driver is bound to accept as a fare any person who desires to be driven, provided that person so informs the driver while he is still stationary and not engaged. At any rate, it seems to us clear that a cab driver commits no offence under the Act of 1853 by refusing to stop when hailed, and that he can only be required to accept anyone who chooses to hire him when he is actually on a rank or is stationary in a street.'

So it is clear that a hackney carriage which is travelling, albeit one which is not hired at the time, is under no legal requirement to respond to a hailing by a prospective passenger, which allows the driver to be selective about those he decides to pick up. This conclusion may seem remarkable and it certainly appears to have come as something of a surprise to the court, as Lord Goddard CJ concluded the judgment with the following[5]:

> 'It may not be inappropriate to hope that this matter will receive the attention of the appropriate authority which, in relation to cabs, is the Home Secretary. Conditions in 1948 are very different from what they were in 1853, when taxicabs were unknown. At present, every taxicab which is not actually hired must be driven with the flag of the taximeter in the

upward position, and the words "For hire" appear on it. Modern taxicabs are now fitted with devices illuminated at night which show on the front of the roof the words "Taxi" or "For hire," and the public may well believe that in those circumstances it is open to them to demand to be driven in any cab which is not actually conveying a passenger. It is evident that in the middle of the last century when all cabs were horse-drawn, the legislature desired to discourage the crawling cab, which might easily cause obstruction in the street, for the horse would naturally be allowed to proceed at a walking pace if the cab was not actually hired. Therefore, it may well have seemed to the legislature in those days that it was desirable so far as possible to ensure that the hiring of cabs should take place at recognised ranks and not casually in the streets. Under modern conditions, the cruising taxicab is one of the commonest sights in London streets. We have, however, to deal with the law as it stands and must see that the existing statutes are not strained so as to make a man guilty of an offence unless the words of the section clearly apply to his case. A full consideration of those sections shows that the expression "Like the cabman on the rank," so often applied with regard to people bound to accept employment if offered, for instance, members of the Bar, is well-founded. It is also to be remembered that there are no fewer than six Acts on the statute book dealing with cabs in London, Acts of 1831, 1843, 1850, 1853, 1869 and 1907. Some of the sections in these numerous statutes are obsolete. Many are obscure, as may be seen from the judgment of this court in *Goodman v Serle*, and others, as this case shows, are out of date. It is, therefore, not surprising that cab drivers, the police, and magistrates, to say nothing of the general public, have difficulty in ascertaining the law on this subject and make mistakes about it. It would seem that an Act consolidating and amending, and, if possible, simplifying, the law with regard to cabs, is very desirable. The appeal is allowed with costs here and before the appeal committee.'

1   [1948] 2 All ER 1065, QBD.
2   See Appendix I.
3   [1948] 2 All ER 1065, QBD at 1066.
4   Above at 1067.
5   Above at 1068.

FARES

19.41

Fares are set by TfL/LTPH under the London Cab Order 1934, art 40[1], under the provisions contained in s 1 of the London Cab and Stage Carriage Act 1907. These are updated regularly by London Cab Order. Both arts 40 and 41 only apply to motor cabs and it is clear that some amendments to the Order would be required if horse-drawn cabs were to be licensed once again within Greater London.

Section 1 of the 1907 Act has been amended by s 15 of the Transport for London Act 2008 to regulate fares ending outside London (defined in s 6 of the 1907 Act as 'The Metropolitan Police District and the City of London' ie Greater London). A journey that commences inside London but ends outside shall be subject to the metered fare unless either an agreement was made between the hirer and the driver before the journey commenced, or if the destination is altered during the journey, at that time[2].

A driver cannot charge more than the metered fare for any journey which does not exceed 12 miles (20 miles if starting at Heathrow). However, for a journey over 12 miles within Greater London, or for a journey of any length ending outside Greater London, the driver can strike an agreement with the prospective hirer, before the hiring commences, to charge more than the metered fare. This is covered by LCSCA 1907, s 1(4) and in relation to the 12 mile limit, by the decision in *Goodman v Serle*[3].

[1] SI 1934/1346; see Appendix I.
[2] London Cab and Stage Carriage Act 1907, s 1(4); see Appendix I.
[3] [1947] 2 All ER 318, QBD.

Goodman v Serle

19.42

> If the journey under the hiring is going to be for more than 12 miles (the limit for metered fares to be mandatory) is an agreement for more than the metered fare to be paid both lawful and enforceable? Held: Yes.

This case concerned a prosecution of a hackney carriage driver under s 17(1) for charging more than the metered fare. The journey was longer than 6 miles [the limit then contained in LHCA 1857, s 7, now 12 miles] and the driver agreed a fare for the journey. The agreed fare was 12 shillings, but at the end of the journey, the metered showed the fare to be 6 shillings and 6 pence. The agreed fare was paid, and the driver prosecuted. Lord Chief Justice Goddard, giving judgment of the court, identified the question:[1]

> 'The whole question depends on whether, the distance being over six miles, the agreement to pay 12s was a lawful agreement. There appears to be no authority on the point, and it is obvious that a question of considerable importance both to cab drivers and to hirers of cabs is raised by the Case.'

There was consideration of the applicable legislation, and then the conclusion was as follows:

> 'The offence which it is said the driver has committed was an offence under s 17 of the Act of 1853, which is continued in force by s 15 of the Act of 1869, that is, demanding more than the proper fare. The proper fare is no longer that prescribed by the Act of 1853, but is the fare prescribed by the London Cab Order, 1934. As has been pointed out above, that order is made under s 9 of the Act of 1869 and for this purpose that section can be read in this way: "The Secretary of State may from time to time by order make regulations for fixing the rates or fares for distance to be paid for hackney carriages, provided that no hackney carriage shall be compelled to take any passenger a greater distance for any one drive than six miles."

In our opinion, it follows that where the cabman has agreed to convey a fare more than six miles on one drive, no fare has been prescribed and it is left to a bargain between the parties. The purpose of the Acts is to protect ordinary cab users from extortionate fares demanded by drivers who are obliged to drive them if required. Cabs which ply for hire in London streets are primarily for short distances within the area for which they are licensed, certainly for distances not exceeding six miles. There seems no reason, therefore, why one should hold that a bargain made between cab driver and hirer for a long distance journey for which a hired motor car would certainly be equally, and probably more, appropriate should be held illegal unless there are words in the statute which compel one to do so. It is true that in 1831 when the London Hackney Carriage Act was passed voiding agreements to pay more than the fare prescribed in that Act there was no distance limit laid down beyond which a driver could refuse to go, but the subsequent Acts seem clearly to contemplate that anything above six miles is to be regarded as something in the nature of an abnormal hiring. If it were laid down by this court that a driver who is hired for a long distance, which in many circumstances it might be unreasonable to oblige him to undertake, but which he might be willing to perform for a special fare, cannot make a special bargain, it might well result that no taximan would ever take a fare for a greater distance than six miles, or at the end of six miles would stop and tell his fare to alight as he was going to turn round to go home.

We do not pretend to find the construction of these Acts at all easy, and in these days of mechanical vehicles capable of far longer journeys than the old horse cabs, it might be of assistance both to the trade and the public if the Secretary of State made an order which would put the matter beyond controversy, as he has clearly power to do, but, of the two possible constructions of the Acts, we prefer the one which seems to us the more reasonable and the one productive of the least inconvenience and hardship both to the public and the drivers, and that is to regard the fares as fixed by the Secretary of State as applying only to drivers not exceeding six miles, *ie*, drivers which a taxicab driver who is hired is bound to undertake, if required. In our opinion, if a fare desires to be carried beyond that distance, the taxicab driver is at liberty to make a bargain without regard to the prescribed fares.'

At the request of a passenger, drivers must provide a receipt for the fare that has been paid[2].

[1]   *Goodman v Serle* [1947] 2 All ER 318 at 318.
[2]   London Cab Order 1934, SI 1934/1346, art 41; see Appendix I.

19.43

The London Cab Order 1934, art 42[1] allows a motor cab to be hired for the purposes of taking luggage or packages which are not accompanied by a person, but makes it clear that the driver does not have to accept any such hiring.

[1]   SI 1934/1346; see Appendix I.

19.44

In relation to luggage, LHCA 1853, s 10 requires the driver to carry a reasonable quantity of luggage for every person hiring a hackney carriage.

19.45

LHCA 1853, s 17 states:

> '... the driver of any hackney carriage, who shall ... commit any of the following offences within the limits of this Act, shall be liable to a penalty not exceeding level 3 on the standard scale for each offence, ...:
>
> 1   Every driver of a hackney carriage who shall demand or take more than the proper fare ..., or who shall refuse to admit and carry in his carriage the number of persons painted or marked on such carriage or specified in the certificate granted by Transport for London in respect of such carriage, or who shall refuse to carry by his carriage a reasonable quantity of luggage for any person hiring or intending to hire such carriage:
>
> 2   Every driver of a hackney carriage who shall refuse to drive such carriage to any place within the limits of this Act, not exceeding six miles, to which he shall be required to drive any person hiring or intending to hire such carriage, or who shall refuse to drive any such carriage for any time not exceeding one hour, if so required by any person hiring or intending to hire such carriage, or who shall not drive the same at a reasonable and proper speed, not less than six miles an hour, except in cases of unavoidable delay, or when required by the hirer thereof to drive at any slower pace:
>
> 3   Every driver of a hackney carriage who shall ply for hire with any carriage or horse which shall be at the time unfit for public use ...'

19.46

It can be seen that it is an offence to demand or take more than the proper fare (as shown on the meter calibrated in accordance with the London Cab Order 1934, art 40[1]) or to refuse to admit or carry persons or reasonable quantities of luggage.

[1]   SI 1934/1346; see Appendix I.

19.47

It is also an offence to refuse to drive within the 12 mile limit (or 20 miles if the hiring commenced at Heathrow Airport) or refuse to drive for a period up to one hour.

19.48

It is also an offence not to drive at a reasonable and proper speed of not less than six miles per hour unless the hirer requires a slower pace to be maintained or there is unavoidable delay.

19.49

Finally, under LHCA 1853, s 17[1] it is an offence for a driver to ply for hire with a hackney carriage (or a horse pulling a hackney carriage) which is at the time unfit for public use. Clearly, action would also be taken in relation to the hackney carriage itself (see para 17.39ff above), but the driver is principally liable.

[1]   See Appendix I.

Charging less than the prescribed fare

19.50

The provisions of art 35(2) of the London Cab Order 1934[1] require the meter to be set to the rates contained in art 40 and it therefore appears that all London cabs must have the meter set to the prescribed rate[2]. However it is permissible for a driver to accept less than the metered fare, as art 40 of the London Cab Order 1934[3] only refers to the maximum fare to be charged, or to stop the meter before the end of the journey under art 35(2) of the London Cab Order 1934[4].

[1]   SI 1934/1346; see Appendix I.
[2]   This contrasts with the position outside London, where the meter can be set to a lower rate under the ruling in *Liverpool City Council v Curzon Ltd* (1983, unreported); see Chapter 9, para 9.29.
[3]   SI 1934/1346; see Appendix I.
[4]   SI 1934/1346; see Appendix I.

Carrying persons other than the driver

19.51

LHCA 1831, s 50 prohibits a driver or proprietor from carrying other persons without the express consent of the hirer. If they do carry such persons, they commit an offence with a maximum penalty of level 1 on the standard scale. In *Yates v Gates*[1] it was decided that express consent means a positive consent not an acquiescence in the form of an implied consent.

This provision does not apply in certain circumstances covered by the Licensed Taxi (Hiring at Separate Fares) (London) Order 1986[2]. For such provisions to come into force, a scheme must have been laid down by TfL/LTPH under the provisions contained in the Transport Act 1985, s 10 and such a scheme exists for the whole of the Metropolitan area under the London Taxi Sharing Scheme Order 1987[3].

[1]   [1970] 1 All ER 754, QBD; see Chapter 10, para 10.115.
[2]   SI 1986/1387; see Appendix I.
[3]   SI 1987/1535; see Appendix I.

Those who are prohibited from driving a hackney carriage

19.52

It is an offence for a driver to drive a hackney carriage without the consent of the proprietor and it is also an offence for an authorised driver of a hackney carriage to allow such a person to drive a hackney carriage without the consent of the proprietor. This is governed by LHCA 1843, s 27[1], which also makes it an offence for a person who has been charged with such an offence not to reveal the name and place of abode of the unauthorised driver, and their ticket number if they are in fact licensed. Section 27 also allows a police constable to take charge of the carriage which a person was unlawfully acting as a driver of and then to deposit the same in some safe place until the proprietor can apply to have it returned.

[1]   See Appendix I.

19.53

In addition, a hackney carriage must at all times, whether working or not, be driven by a person who holds a hackney carriage driver's licence as a consequence of the LHCA 1831, s 35 and LHCA 1843, s 10[1].

[1]   See paras 17.16–17.21 and footnote and para 19.2 above. This view is not shared by TfL/LTPH who take the view that the vehicle is a hackney carriage only when it is working. In the absence of any case on the point this is an arguable question. As TfL/LTPH is the principal enforcing authority, it seems unlikely that the point will be decided.

Other matters concerning drivers

19.54

LHCA 1843, s 28, which prohibits 'wanton or furious driving' is effectively rendered obsolete by virtue of the provisions of the Road Traffic Act 1988[1]. However, s 28 is still applicable in relation to the use of insulting or abusive language or the use of any insulting gesture or misbehaviour on the part of the driver, which if proved would call in to question their retention of their drivers licence[2].

[1]   See para 10.118 above re TPCA 1847, s 61.
[2]   The issue of drivers urinating in the street had become sufficient a problem for the PCO (as LTPH was formerly known) to issue two notices about it (21/06 and 35/07) threatening miscreants with prosecution and possible action against their licence. The PCO offered the following advice in notice 35/07:

> 'It is appreciated that the number of toilets open late at night is limited but in the interest of hygiene, common decency and the reputation of the trade, drivers are asked to act in a professional manner and find alternative facilities.'

19.55

It is interesting to note that the fine is a mandatory fine, apparently level 1 on the standard scale, but there is also a power of imprisonment for a period not exceeding two months. No term of imprisonment has been imposed in respect of any of these matters in recent years.

19.56

A similar provision exists within LHCA 1831, s 56[1], whereby if by intoxication, wanton and furious driving or by any other wilful misconduct a person is injured or endangered in his life, limbs or property, then the proprietor or driver responsible commits an offence. In addition, it is an offence to use abusive or insulting language or rude behaviour towards any person or for a driver or proprietor to assault or obstruct any 'Officer of Police, Constable, or other peace officer, watchman or patrole [sic], in the execution of [their] duty'. In addition to the fine, the licence can be revoked in the case of a proprietor.

[1]   See Appendix I.

19.57

LHCA 1843, s 33[1] makes it an offence for a driver who is plying for hire other than at a stand or who is loitering and in either case causing an obstruction in any public street, road or place commits an offence. The driver also commits an offence if by wilful misbehaviour he causes a similar obstruction.

[1]   See Appendix I.

19.58

If one driver or proprietor attempts to take a fare from another proprietor or driver in a wrongful, forcible or clandestine manner he commits an offence by virtue of LHCA 1831, s 51[1].

[1]   See Appendix I.

DEPOSITS FOR WAITING

19.59

Under LHCA 1831, s 47[1], if a hirer requires a driver of a hackney carriage to wait for him, the driver can require a deposit as a guarantee that the hirer will return. It is an offence for a driver who has received a deposit not to wait and also if the driver does not account for the deposit when demanding the final fare. Waiting time itself is not covered within the London Cab Order 1934, art 40[2], but if the cab is stationary whilst hired, the meter will continue to charge in accordance with art 40(2)(b)(ii) and (3)(b)(ii).

[1]   See Appendix I.
[2]   SI 1934/1346; see Appendix I.

REFUSAL TO PAY THE FARE

19.60

It is an offence to refuse to pay the fare and in such circumstances the sum owing can be recovered in front of a magistrate, together with costs and compensation for attending and establishing the matter before the court. This provision is contained in LHCA 1831, s 41[1].

[1]   See also not having the means to pay the fare examined in para 19.70 below.

EXPIRY OF LICENCE

19.61

If the licence expires and is not renewed, or expires because the driver loses the right to work or remain in the UK, both the licence and badge (and the copy of the licence) must be returned to TfL/LTPH within three days. Failure to return it within such time constitutes an offence under LHCA 1843, s 18. It is also an offence to use, wear or detain any badge without a licence relating to the ticket or to wear a false or counterfeit badge.

19.62

In those circumstances a constable, or any person employed for those purposes by TfL/LTPH can seize and take away any such badge.

LOST BADGES

19.63

If a driver loses or mislays a badge or the badge itself becomes obliterated or defaced then, if he still has the badge he must produce it to TfL/LTPH and the driver is then entitled to have a new badge issued. The driver must pay for that. No specific fee is prescribed in LHCA 1843, s 19 (which governs this entire matter)[1].

[1] The previous fee of 15p which had existed at least since decimalisation in 1971 was altered by s 13 of the Transport for London Act 2008 allowing TfL to charge such sum as they 'shall consider reasonable'. The current fee is £15.00 – see https://tfl.gov.uk/info-for/taxis-and-private-hire/licensing/existing-licensee#on-this-page-1 .

19.64

In addition, if a lost badge is subsequently found it must be returned to TfL within three days. Failure to do so constitutes an offence.

19.65

It is also an offence to use or wear a badge when the writing is 'obliterated, defaced, or obscured, so that the same shall not be distinctly legible'.

PROPRIETOR TO RETAIN LICENCES

19.66

By virtue of LHCA 1843, s 21[1] the proprietor must hold the driver's licence whilst the driver is driving for him and the proprietor must produce that licence in any case where he is required to produce the driver before the court. As a consequence of this the driver has the copy licence, which is satisfactory for all purposes.

[1] See Appendix I.

Number of people to be carried

19.67

The maximum number of people that can be carried in a hackney carriage shall be marked on it by virtue of LHCA 1853, s 9[1], and the driver must carry any number of persons up to and including that maximum number. In addition, by virtue of LHCA 1853, s 10[2], a reasonable quantity of luggage for every person who is hiring the carriage must be also be carried. It is amplified by the London Cab Order 1934, art 33[3], which states:

'**33 Carriage of Persons and Luggage**

(1) No person other than the driver shall be carried on any cab in excess of the number of persons which it is licensed to carry, provided that, in computing such number, an infant in arms shall not count as a person and two children under 10 years of age shall count as one person.

(2) No person other than the driver shall, without the authority of Transport for London, be carried on the driving box or platform of a motor cab.

(3) No luggage shall be carried on the roof of a motor cab unless the cab is fitted for that purpose and is licensed to carry luggage on the roof.

(4) The driver of the cab, and, unless he proves that the breach occurred without his knowledge or consent, the owner thereof, shall be liable for any breach of any of the regulations in this paragraph.'

[1]   See Appendix I.
[2]   See Appendix I.
[3]   SI 1934/1346; see Appendix I.

19.68

The fact that an infant does not count as a person and that two children under the age of 10 years count as one person may be useful from the point of view of the total number of passengers that may be carried. However, it does present difficulties in relation to seat belts and child seats: see para 9.2 onwards above.

A practical approach is that no more people can be carried than the number of seats and seatbelts available, but it should be borne in mind that rear facing seats do not need to be provided with a seat belt, although in practice they often are.

19.69

The London Cab Order 1934, art 33(3)[1] is a useful provision which makes it clear that TfL/LTPH can licence hackney carriages to carry roof racks and for many hackney carriages, especially those undertaking trips to and from airports, this can be a very useful provision when the absence of luggage space in many vehicles is taken into account. No mention is made of licensing a hackney carriage to tow a trailer, which could be equally useful. Apparently there are currently no vehicles licensed by TfL/LTPH to use roof racks or tow trailers.

[1]   SI 1934/1346; see Appendix I.

Failure or no intention to pay fare

19.70

LCA 1896, s 1 makes it an offence punishable by a fine not exceeding level 1 or 14 days' imprisonment if a person:

'(a) hires a cab, knowing or having reason to believe that he cannot pay the lawful fare, or with intent to avoid payment of the lawful fare; or

(b) fraudulently endeavours to avoid payment of a fare lawfully due from him; or

(c) having failed or refused to pay a fare lawfully due from him, either refuses to give to the driver an address at which he can be found, or, with intent to deceive, gives a false address, …'

In addition, the person remains liable to pay the fare. This is also likely to be an offence under s 11 of the Fraud Act 2006.

Lost property

19.71

Anyone who finds any lost property in a cab should immediately hand it to the cab driver. This is the requirement of the London Cab Order 1934, art 51(1)[1]. This goes considerably further and places a duty upon the driver carefully to search or look inside his cab at the termination of every hiring to establish whether or not any property has been left. If he does not search immediately because it is impracticable, he must do so as soon as it is practicable thereafter, but must in the meantime look (as opposed to search) inside the cab.

[1]   SI 1934/1346; see Appendix I.

19.72

If the driver does find any property he must deposit it at a police station within 24 hours, providing details of the finding.

19.73

Liaison is required between the police and TfL/LTPH to comply with the London Cab Order 1934, art 52[1], which relates to the treatment of lost property. In practice the police now forward any such items to TfL's centralised lost property office in Baker Street.

[1]   SI 1934/1346; see Appendix I.

Chapter 20

Private hire vehicles within London: an introduction

20.1

Private hire vehicles represent a second category or type of vehicle that provide services to the public by way of private independent transportation.

20.2

The rise in the numbers of 'mini-cabs' during the 1960s and early 1970s led to the passing and introduction of the Local Government (Miscellaneous Provisions) Act 1976 (LG(MP)A 1976), which introduced a regulatory framework for the control of private hire vehicles outside Greater London. However, it did not apply within the then Metropolitan Police Area and mini-cabs remained completely unregulated in London. It was not until 1998, over two decades later, that the Private Hire Vehicles (London) Act 1998 introduced a regime similar, but by no means identical, to that which exists under LG(MP)A 1976 outside the Metropolitan area. That is administered by the London Taxi and Private Hire (LTPH), which is part of Transport for London (TfL).

20.3

A London private hire vehicle differs from a hackney carriage in a number of fundamental ways:

1. The vehicle itself cannot resemble a hackney carriage. This is to enable it to be readily identified by the public as a private hire vehicle.
2. A London private hire vehicle cannot ply for hire (that is, cruise the streets until hailed by a prospective passenger[1]) or use hackney carriage stands (there being no concept of a private hire stand).
3. A London private hire vehicle must be driven by a person who holds a London private hire driver's licence issued by TfL/LTPH (in this aspect the situation is similar to the rules governing hackney carriages).
4. However, the similarity ends at this point because a London private hire operator must control each and every London private hire vehicle. The operator is the person who takes the bookings from the customer and

arranges for the vehicle to go to wherever the customer requests. This is the only way in which private hire vehicles are able to collect their customers.

[1] See Chapter 8, para 8.7 onwards.

20.4

It can therefore be seen that there are three players involved in the private hire function: the private hire driver; the private hire operator; and the private hire vehicle. This can be contrasted with the situation that applies to hackney carriages, where all that is required is a licensed vehicle and licensed driver.

20.5

There are further variations between the London private hire and hackney carriage licensing regimes:

1. As with hackney carriages within Greater London, no limit can be placed upon the number of private hire vehicles that TfL/LTPH will license[1].
2. TfL/LTPH has no power to prescribe fares for private hire vehicles.
3. TfL/LTPH has no power to prescribe the type of vehicle, other than the requirement that the vehicle is satisfactory for its purpose, although it can lay down minimum specifications for private hire vehicles.

[1] At the time of writing (August 2017) there are suggestions that TfL may seek to have some form of limit on private hire vehicle numbers introduced.

20.6

Although the private hire regime within London can be seen therefore as rather more relaxed than the hackney carriage regime, the overriding aims of providing the public with a safe and convenient method of transport remain the same and the differences in approach in no way undermine that fundamental consideration.

20.7

Within London, the Private Hire Vehicles (London) Act 1998 and Orders made thereunder contain all the legislative provisions.

Chapter 21

Private hire operators within London

INTRODUCTION

21.1

In general terms, the provisions of the Private Hire Vehicles (London) Act 1998 (PHV(L)A 1998) are based largely upon and are similar to, the private hire provisions contained within LG(MP)A 1976 but there are some notable differences. In the absence of any senior court decisions on the legislation itself and as the wording tends to be either identical, or at least very similar to, LG(MP)A 1976, it seems likely that many of the cases decided under that legislation will apply to London.

21.2

Within PHV(L)A 1998, reference is made to the 'licensing authority', which is defined in PHV(L)A 1998, s 36[1] as Transport for London (TfL) which administers this function through the London Taxi and Private Hire Directorate (LTPH).

[1]   See Appendix I.

THE TERM 'OPERATOR'

21.3

Within London, as outside, a private hire vehicle can only be despatched to a customer by a private hire operator, by virtue of PHV(L)A 1998, s 2(1):

'No person shall in London make provision for the invitation or acceptance of, or accept, private hire bookings unless he is the holder of a private hire vehicle operator's licence for London (in this Act referred to as a "London PHV operator's licence").'

21.4

This licence allows a person to operate private hire vehicles. Contravention of this requirement is an offence punishable by a fine not exceeding level 4 on the standard scale (PHV(L)A 1998, s 2(2))[1]. A person who holds a London operator's licence is an operator, defined in PHV(L)A 1998, s 1(1)(b)and (c) as follows:

'(b) "operator" means a person who makes provision for the invitation or acceptance of, or who accepts, private hire bookings; and

(c) "operate", in relation to a private hire vehicle, means to make provision for the invitation or acceptance of, or to accept, private hire bookings in relation to the vehicle.'

[1] See Appendix I.

21.5

PHV(L)A 1998, ss 1(1)(b) and (c) and 2(2) are almost identical to the wording contained LG(MP)A 1976, s 80 as the definition of 'operate'. It would appear therefore that the decision in *St Albans District Council v Taylor*[1] (that there did not need to be any payment for there to be a 'hiring')[2], will apply within London.

[1] [1991] Crim LR 852.
[2] See para 12.2 above.

EXEMPTED HIRING

21.6

The only overt exemptions from licensing contained in PHV(L)A 1998 are to be found in PHV(L)A 1998, s 29:

'Nothing in this Act applies to any vehicle whose use as a private hire vehicle is limited to use in connection with funerals or weddings.'

21.7

It appears that it will be a question of fact as to whether the vehicle was 'being used in connection with funerals or weddings', and there is no argument of the amount of time as the words 'used wholly or mainly' that appear in LG(MP)A 1976, s 75(1)(c) in relation to funerals are absent. As is the case outside London, this would appear to apply to civil partnership ceremonies as well as weddings[1].

[1] See Chapter 12, para 12.126 onwards.

21.8

The definition of a London private hire vehicle is contained in PHV(L)A 1998, s 1(1)(a):

'(a) "private hire vehicle" means a vehicle constructed or adapted to seat fewer than nine passengers which is made available with a driver for hire for the purpose of carrying passengers, other than a licensed taxi or a public service vehicle;'

The DfT Guidance[1] *'Private Hire Vehicle Licensing – A note for guidance from the Department for Transport'* applies within London. The same reservations apply to its impact within London as apply outside[2].

[1] *'Private Hire Vehicle Licensing – A note for guidance from the Department for Transport'* available at https://www.gov.uk/government/publications/private-hire-vehicle-licensing-guidance-note

[2] See Chapter 12, para 12.129 onwards.

Courtesy cars and other 'grey' areas

21.9

As the wording of the legislation is almost identical, it would seem that the position with regard to courtesy cars, hospital cars and other 'grey' areas covered by the DfT Guidance[1] within London is the same as outside London[2].

[1] *'Private Hire Vehicle Licensing – A note for guidance from the Department for Transport'* available at https://www.gov.uk/government/publications/private-hire-vehicle-licensing-guidance-note.

[2] See para 12.129 onwards above.

THE PREMISES AND FLEET OF AN OPERATOR

21.10

The address from which an operator is licensed to accept private hire bookings is termed the 'operating centre' (PHV(L)A 1998, s 1(5))[1] and it must be within London (PHV(L)A 1998, s 3(2) and (6)(a))[2].

[1] See Appendix I.
[2] See Appendix I.

R (app Uber) v Transport for London

21.11

Was it reasonable to require a private hire operator to provide a manned telephone line for complaints etc 24 hours a day? Held: No.

Although originally there was no requirement within the Private Hire Vehicles (London) (Operators' Licences) Regulations 2000[1] that there should be any ability to deal with personal callers at the operating centre, TfL/LTPH altered the Regulations in 2016 to add the following[2]:

'At all times during the operator's hours of business and at all times during the journey, the operator shall ensure that the passenger for whom the booking was made is able to speak to someone at the operating centre if they want to make any complaint or discuss any other matter either carrying out of the booking'.

This was challenged by Uber in *R (on the application of Uber) v Transport for London*[3] and judgment was handed down by the High Court in March 2017 by Mitting J.

The requirement was addressed as follows by the judge,[4]:

'32. The wording of the telephone requirement is very broad. The operator is required to:

> "Ensure that the passenger for whom the booking was made is able to speak to someone at the operating centre or other premises with a fixed address in London or elsewhere if they want to make a complaint or discuss any other matter about the carrying out of the booking."

It is not confined to a requirement to provide that facility in what the passenger believes to be an emergency, or a situation which requires immediate resolution, such as the refusal of the driver to comply with disability law in respect of the passenger, in other words, a "hotline".

33. It requires a large appbased operator such as Uber to maintain, round the clock, a telephone service to deal with complaints and any other matter about the carrying out of the booking immediately.'

He continued[5]:

'[At present] Uber have a system which effectively sorts real emergencies from all which are only potentially critical or urgent and deals with each appropriately; the first immediately, and all others within 6 hours as to 70 per cent and within 24 hours as to 99 per cent. This is to be commended rather than criticised.'

The justification put forward by TfL was[6]:

'… many passengers will be reassured by their ability to speak to a human being about their complaint and emergencies can be dealt with more quickly than would be the case without the intervention of a live telephone operator. A small number of real life examples are given. I accept their reasoning, but only up to a point. I can readily understand that some passengers, believing themselves to be confronted by an emergency, will find it reassuring to speak to a human telephone operator.

38. TfL were and are entitled to identify the public interest affected as public safety and convenience, in the case of an emergency principally the former, and to conclude that a high level of protection should be given to passengers who believe that they are faced with an emergency. I also accept that in that instance there is no alternative measure which could combine reassurance and speed of response to some passengers… .

39. Accordingly, despite the fact that Uber's current system may well provide an effective and timely response to genuine emergencies, I accept that it cannot provide the level of reassurance which some passengers may,

for good reason, require. This aspect of the measure is therefore lawful. It does not follow that the regulation is lawful in its full width.'

And he concluded on this point[7]:

'TfL has not shown that less restrictive measures could not be adopted than those contained in the telephone requirement to meet the level of protection which they require for the only public interest at stake, passenger convenience... . It follows, therefore, that I must quash regulation 9(11) and leave it to [TfL] to make a fresh regulation if he considers it desirable to provide for, in colloquial terms, a "hotline" for emergencies broadly defined to include situations in which immediate action is required to remedy a breach of the law.'

As a consequence, this reqirement is currently suspended pending the appeal to the Court of Appeal.

Beyond that, it will a matter for each individual operator to decide how best to furnish and equip his operating centre. The centre will normally be equipped with telephone lines and other methods of communication (eg mobile telephones, fax, email and Internet), although there is a prohibition on the use of CB equipment at an operating centre or in a London private hire vehicle (Private Hire Vehicles (London) (Operators' Licences) Regulations 2000, reg 9(5)).

[1]   SI 2000/3146; see Appendix I.
[2]   They also added requirements that private hire vehicles should be insured at all times considered at Chapter 12, para 12.103 and that drivers had (and demonstrated by obtaining a qualification) a particular standard of spoken and written English considered at Chapter 10, para 10.60.
[3]   (3 March 2017, unreported), Admin Ct. At the time of writing (August 2017), an appeal to the Court of Appeal is pending.
[4]   At paras 32 and 33.
[5]   At para 35.
[6]   At para 37 onwards.
[7]   At para 41.

21.12

The fact that London private hire operators' undertakings vary enormously in range is reflected by the fact that a lower fee is charged (under the Private Hire Vehicles (London) (Operators' Licences) Regulations 2000, reg 7(2)[1]) where the operator operates no more than two private hire vehicles.

[1]   SI 2000/3146; see Appendix I.

APPLICATION FOR AN OPERATOR'S LICENCE

21.13

Any person may apply for a London private hire vehicle operator's licence. The requirements are that the applicant must state the address of the proposed operating centre (PHV(L)A 1998, s 3(2))[1] and that the application must be made on the prescribed form, including all information required by TfL/LTPH. Although it appears that TfL/LTPH can seek any information it reasonably requires (Private Hire Vehicles (London) (Operators' Licences) Regulations 2000, reg 3(1)(a)[2]) in order to enable it to determine the application, PHV(L)A 1998, s 15(3) allows for certain specific information to be demanded:

'(3) The information which an applicant for a London PHV operator's licence may be required to furnish includes in particular information about—

(a) any premises in London which he proposes to use as an operating centre;

(b) any convictions recorded against him;

(c) any business activities he has carried on before making the application;

(d) if the applicant is or has been a director or secretary of a company, that company;

(e) if the applicant is a company, information about the directors or secretary of that company;

(f) if the applicant proposes to act as an operator in partnership with any other person, information about that person.'

It is important to recognise that this is not an exhaustive list, and these are only matters 'in particular'.

[1]   See Appendix I.
[2]   SI 2000/3146; see Appendix I.

21.14

In addition, the application must be accompanied by the prescribed application fee. That fee is non-refundable if the application fails.

21.15

As a London private hire operator is not mentioned in the Rehabilitation of Offenders Act 1974 (Exceptions) Order 1975[1], applicants can only be required to obatain a basic disclosure from Disclosure Scotland to assist in verifying the information supplied in accordance with PHV(L)A 1998, s 15(3)(b), allied to a statutory declaration.

[1]   SI 1975/1023; see Appendix I.

21.16

PHV(L)A 1998, s 28 is an all-purpose prohibition on providing false or incorrect information:

'A person who knowingly or recklessly makes a statement or furnishes information which is false or misleading in any material particular for the purpose of procuring the grant or renewal of a licence under this Act, or the variation of an operator's licence under section 18 [PHV(L)A 1998, s 18], is guilty of an offence and liable on summary conviction to a fine not exceeding level 5 on the standard scale.'

21.17

This would obviously apply to any irregularities on an application form for a London private hire vehicle operator's licence.

21.18

Once the correctly completed application has been received, then TfL/LTPH must consider the application. PHV(L)A 1998, s 3(3) states:

'(3) The licensing authority shall grant a London PHV operator's licence to the applicant if the authority is satisfied that—

(a) the applicant is a fit and proper person to hold a London PHV operator's licence;

(aa) if the applicant is an individual, the applicant is not disqualified by reason of the applicant's immigration status from operating a private hire vehicle; and

(b) any further requirements that may be prescribed (which may include requirements relating to operating centres) are met.

(3A) In determining for the purposes of subsection (3) whether an applicant is disqualified by reason of the applicant's immigration status from operating a private hire vehicle, the licensing authority must have regard to any guidance issued by the Secretary of State.'

21.19

TfL/LTPH is then under a duty to grant a London private hire vehicle operator's licence to that person provided:

- they have the right to reside and work in the UK (in the case of an individual or partnership); and
- they are satisfied that the applicant is 'a fit and proper person to hold a London PHV operator's licence'.

It is also possible for TfL to decide that 'further requirements that may be prescribed (which may include requirements relating to operating centres) [must be]... met'.

These are the only grounds on which an application can be refused.

21.20

The considerations in relation both to the applicants' immigration status are identical to those outside London[1]. The same appears to be true of the concept of fitness and propriety[2].

[1]   See Chapter 12, para 12.33 onwards.
[2]   See Chapter 12, para 12.34 onwards.

21.21

The expression 'further requirements that may be prescribed (which may include requirements relating to operating centres) are met' allows the mechanism contained in the Private Hire Vehicles (London) (Operators' Licences) Regulations 2000, regs 5, 6 and 7[1] to come into play.

[1]   SI 2000/3146; see Appendix I.

21.22

Application and grant is effectively a two-stage process. TfL/LTPH considers the application and then reg 5 states:

'5–(1) If the licensing authority is satisfied that a licence may properly be—
(a)   granted for five years—
    (i)   in the terms applied for; and
    (ii)   without the need for any additional conditions other than those prescribed in regulation 9, or
(b)   varied in the terms applied for,
the authority shall approve the application and give the applicant notice of the decision.

(2) If the authority is not so satisfied and decides—
(a)   to approve the application other than in the terms applied for;
(b)   in the case of an application for the grant of a licence, to approve the application on the basis that—
    (i)   additional conditions shall be attached to the licence, or
    (ii)   the licence shall be granted for a shorter period than five years; or
(c)   to refuse the application,
the authority shall give the applicant notice of the decision and the grounds for it.[1]'

[1]   Private Hire Vehicles (London) (Operators' Licences) Regulations 2000, SI 2000/3146, reg 5.

21.23

If the application is approved under the Private Hire Vehicles (London) (Operators' Licences) Regulations 2000, reg 5(1)[1], then the applicant has to pay a further fee (with a reduction if two or less vehicles are to be operated) within 28 days of the date of the service of the notice of TfL/LTPH 's decision, and TfL/LTPH will grant the licence. The licence itself will then last for five years.

[1]   SI 2000/3146; see Appendix I.

21.24

If TfL/LTPH does not approve the application as made, alters the terms applied for or reduces the period (Private Hire Vehicles (London) (Operators' Licences) Regulations 2000, reg 5(2)[1]) or imposes additional conditions under PHV(L)A 1998, s 3(4), then the applicant can appeal against that decision or imposition of conditions using the powers contained in s 3(7)[2]. If the appeal is unsuccessful or, alternatively, if the applicant does not take up the licence within 28 days of the notice of successful application, the application fee is forfeit.

[1]   SI 2000/3146; see Appendix I.
[2]   For details on the appeals mechanism, see Chapter 3, para 3.69 onwards.

REGISTER OF LICENCES

21.25

PHV(L)A 1998, s 23 requires that all London private hire operators' licences issued must be entered on a register maintained by TfL/LTPH. This must contain:

- the number of the licence;
- the name of the person to whom the licence is granted[1];
- the date on which the licence is granted;
- the expiry date of the licence;
- the address of each operating centre specified in the licence; and
- an indication that the licence is current, suspended or revoked.

The first four categories are required by s 23(1)(a) and the last two by s 23(1)(b) and the Private Hire Vehicles (London) (Operators' Licences) Regulations 2000, reg 17(2)[2].

[1]   TfL can only disclose the address to a person 'if it appears to the authority that the person has a sufficient reason for requiring that information' (1998 Act, s 23(4)).
[2]   SI 2000/3146; see Appendix I.

21.26

The register is open to free public inspection at times and locations set by TfL/LTPH (PHV(L)A 1998, s 23(2)) which is at the main office of the PCO, plus access is available on the PCO website[1].

There is also a requirement for TfL/LTPH to maintain a supplemental register under PHV(L)A 1998, s 23(3) listing the address of each licensed operator, but that is not open to public inspection and an operator's personal address can only be disclosed if 'it appears to the authority that the person has a sufficient reason for requiring that information.' (PHV(L)A 1998, s 23(4)).

[1]   http://www.tfl.gov.uk/tfl/businessandpartners/taxisandprivatehire/ph/licensing/?mode=operators
The details on the website are not as comprehensive as those available at the offices of London Taxi and Private Hire.

21.27

Clearly, as licences will generally last for five years, it is important that TfL/LTPH is able to keep abreast of any changes in the situation of the licensee. A number of provisions address this. The Private Hire Vehicles (London) (Operators' Licences) Regulations 2000, reg 9(4)[1] requires details of any convictions to be reported to TfL/LTPH :

'(4) If, during the currency of the licence—
(a) any conviction is recorded—
   (i) where the operator is an individual, against him,
   (ii) where the operator is a firm, against any partner of that firm, or
   (iii) where the operator is another type of body or group of persons, against that body or group or any officer of that body or group;

(b)   any information provided in the application for the grant of the licence, or for any variation thereof, changes; or

(c)   any driver ceases to be available to the operator for carrying out bookings, by virtue of that driver's unsatisfactory conduct in connection with the driving of a private hire vehicle,

the operator shall, within 14 days of the date of such event, give the licensing authority notice containing details of the conviction or change, as the case may be, or, in a case falling within sub-paragraph (c), the name of the driver and the circumstances of the case.'

¹   SI 2000/3146.

21.28

Breach of this condition does not constitute a criminal offence and, accordingly, action can only be taken against the licence[1].

¹   Suspension, revocation or refusal to renew – see para 21.70 onwards.

ADDRESS FROM WHICH THE OPERATOR MAY OPERATE AND USE OF THE OPERATING CENTRE

21.29

The address or addresses which the operator intends to use as operating centres must be specified in the application (PHV(L)A 1998, s 3(2))[1] and a copy of the licence must be displayed at each of the operating centres (PHV(L)A 1998, s 4(3)(a))[2]. TfL/LTPH take the view that an operating centre must be permanent and cannot be moved even when it is not being used as an operating centre, eg a part-time operating centre. The operator can apply for a variation of the licence to remove or add new operating centres using the procedure contained in PHV(L)A 1998, s 18[3]. This requires application to be made in a particular form, at the discretion of TfL/LTPH. There is also a right of appeal if TfL/LTPH does not accede to the request.

¹   See Appendix I.
²   See Appendix I.
³   See Appendix I.

21.30

If TfL/LTPH 'is no longer satisfied that the operating centre in question meets any requirements prescribed under section 3(3)(b) [PHV(L)A 1998, s 3(3)(b)] or for any other reasonable cause' (PHV(L)A 1998, s 19(1)), then it can suspend the use of that operating centre, or vary the licence to remove that operating centre under the provisions of PHV(L)A 1998, s 19. Again, there is a right of appeal against such decisions, but it is possible for TfL/LTPH to prevent the staying of the effect of the decision pending determination of the appeal. This can be done by using the mechanism contained in s 19(3):

'(3) If the licensing authority is of the opinion that the interests of public safety require the authority's decision to have immediate effect, and the authority includes a statement of that opinion and the reasons for it in the notice, the authority's decision shall take effect when the notice is served on the licence holder.'

21.31

The operator must maintain public liability insurance for not less than £5 million for each and every operating centre to which the public have access (Private Hire Vehicles (London) (Operators' Licences) Regulations 2000, reg 9(2)[1]).

[1]   SI 2000/3146; see Appendix I.

BOOKINGS

21.32

Within London, as outside, it is the operator with whom the public has direct initial contact in order to obtain the services of a private hire vehicle. PHV(L)A 1998, ss 4 and 5 lay down the fundamental requirements that cover a provision of a private hire vehicle by an operator.

21.33

The booking must only be accepted at the operating centre (PHV(L)A 1998, s 4(1)). This outlaws the acceptance of bookings in a private hire vehicle by an operator who is also a driver[1] by mobile telephone. How this provision is enforced if a telephone divert is in operation from the booking office to a mobile telephone is not clear.

[1]   Contrast this with the situation outside London, discussed at Chapter 12, para 12.56 above.

21.34

PHV(L)A 1998, s 5 allows a booking to be sub-contracted to another operator, but only if:

'(1)
    (a) the other operator is a London PHV operator and the sub-contracted booking is accepted at an operating centre in London;
    (b) the other operator is licensed under section 55 of the Local Government (Miscellaneous Provisions) Act 1976 (in this Act referred to as "the 1976 Act") by the council of a district and the sub-contracted booking is accepted in that district; or
    (c) the other operator accepts the sub-contracted booking in Scotland.'

21.35

It is an offence for an operator to sub-contract with an unlicensed operator (PHV(L)A 1998, s 5(2)), but there is a defence of 'due diligence' in s 5(3).

21.36

PHV(L)A 1998, s 5(5) makes it clear that, irrespective of any sub-contracting, the contract for hiring the vehicle remained between the hirer and the initial operator.

Records kept by operators

21.37

PHV(L)A 1998, s 4(3) and (4) as amended by the Transport for London Act 2008, s 25 and the Private Hire Vehicles (London) (Operators' Licences) Regulations 2000, regs 10–16[1] place a duty on a private hire operator to keep various records. In relation to bookings, these can be kept in writing or 'in such other form that the information contained in it can easily be reduced to writing' (reg 10). This would clearly include a computer, which can then print out the records. In relation to the other records which are required to be kept (vehicles used – reg 12; drivers used – reg 13; complaints – reg 14; lost property – reg 15), there is no indication as to how these records should be maintained. Clearly, writing must be acceptable, but computer records must also be acceptable.

[1]   SI 2000/3146; see Appendix I.

Journeys booked

21.38

The Private Hire Vehicles (London) (Operators' Licences) Regulations 2000, reg 11[1] contains the requirements for records of bookings:

'Before the commencement of each journey booked at an operating centre specified in his licence an operator shall enter the following particulars of the booking in the record referred to in regulation 10—

(a)   the date on which the booking is made and, if different, the date of the proposed journey;

(b)   the name of the person for whom the booking is made or other identification of him, or, if more than one person, the name or other identification of one of them;

(c)   the agreed time and place of collection, or, if more than one, the agreed time and place of the first;

(d)   the main destination specified at the time of the booking;

(e)   any fare or estimated fare quoted;

(f)   the name of the driver carrying out the booking or other identification of him;

(g)   if applicable, the name of the other operator to whom the booking has been sub-contracted, and

(h)   the registered number of the vehicle to be used or such other means of identifying it as may be adopted.'

[1]   SI 2000/3146; see Appendix I.

21.39

These conditions:

1. enable the operator to identify a particular booking;
2. enable the operator to despatch a car at the right time to the right place;
3. enable TfL/LTPH to ensure that a booking was made for a particular journey; and
4. provide a comprehensive record of bookings taken by the private hire operator.

21.40

From an enforcement perspective, it is the confirmation that a booking has been made before the journey was undertaken that is important. As mentioned at Chapter 17, para 17.22 above, it is an offence for a private hire vehicle to ply for hire; that is, to respond to anything other than a pre-booking and this can frequently be evidenced by the fact that the operator has no record of the trip which was taking place when the vehicle was apprehended by enforcement officers.

21.41

Records of bookings must be preserved for six months from the date of the booking by virtue of the Private Hire Vehicles (London) (Operators' Licences) Regulations 2000, reg 16(1)(a)[1]. If the operator tape-recorded the private hire booking, the tape must be kept for six months (reg 16(2)). It is not clear how many operators do tape their bookings. If the operating centre ceases to function, the records maintained under the Private Hire Vehicles (London) (Operators' Licences) Regulations 2000, reg 10 must be preserved for six months from the date of the last entry to comply with reg 16(3). This appears somewhat odd, as reg 10 refers to the form of the record, not the content and it is suggested that the reference in reg 16(3) should be to reg 11 rather than reg 10.

[1]   SI 2000/3146; see Appendix I.

Bookings by and for disabled people accompanied by assistance dogs

21.42

Section 170 of the Equality Act 2010 (EA 2010) which forbids a private hire operator to refuse to accept a booking for a private hire vehicle for a person accompanied by an assistance dog (s 170(1)), and not to charge any more for the journey than for an equivalent journey where no assistance dog was present (s 170(2)) applies within London in the same way as outside London[1].

[1]   See Chapter 12, para 12.62 for details.

VEHICLES USED

21.43

The second category of records that the operator is required to maintain relates to vehicles used and this is required by the Private Hire Vehicles (London) (Operators' Licences) Regulations 2000, reg 12[1]:

'(1) For the purposes of section 4(3)(d) of the 1998 Act [PHV(L)A 1998, s 4(3)(d)], an operator shall keep at each operating centre specified in his licence a record, containing the particulars set out in paragraph (2), of each private hire vehicle which is available to him for carrying out bookings accepted by him at that centre.

(2) In relation to each vehicle the particulars referred to in paragraph (1) are—
(a) the make, model and colour;
(b) the registration mark;
(c) the name and address of the registered keeper;
(ca) a copy of the vehicle's London PHV licence or temporary permit granted under the Private Hire Vehicles (London) (Transitional Provisions) Regulations 2004, as appropriate;
(d) in the case of a vehicle to which paragraph 8(1) of Schedule 2 of the Private Hire Vehicles (London PHV Licences) Regulations 2004 applies, a copy of the current MOT test certificate issued in accordance with those regulations;
(e) a copy of the current certificate of insurance or certificate of security;
(f) the date on which the vehicle became available to the operator and
(g) the date on which the vehicle ceased to be so available.'

[1]   SI 2000/3146; see Appendix I.

21.44

As with operators outside London, these records can be maintained in writing, or combined with a vehicle-tracking computerised system to give the operator a continuous view of the movements of the vehicles he controls. The Private Hire Vehicles (London) (Operators' Licences) Regulations 2000, reg 12[1] states that records must be kept for 12 months from the last date on which the vehicle was available for carrying out bookings (Private Hire Vehicles (London) (Operators' Licences) Regulations 2000, reg 16(1)(b)).

[1]   SI 2000/3146; see Appendix I.

Drivers' records

21.45

Unlike the situation outside London, where any records of drivers used by an operator are left to the local decisions of the local authority, in London they are compulsory. The Private Hire Vehicles (London) (Operators' Licences) Regulations 2000, reg 13[1] places the following requirements on operators:

'(1) For the purposes of section 4(3)(d) of the 1998 Act [PHV(L)A 1998, s 4(3)(d)], an operator shall keep at each operating centre specified in his licence a record, containing the particulars set out in paragraph (2), of each driver who is available to him for carrying out bookings accepted by him at that centre.

(2) In relation to each driver the particulars referred to in paragraph (1) are—
(a)   his surname, forenames, address and date of birth;
(b)   his national insurance number;
(c)   a photocopy of his driving licence;
(ca) a copy of his London PHV driver's licence or temporary permit granted under the Private Hire Vehicles (London) (Transitional Provisions) Regulations 2003, as appropriate;
(d)   a photograph of him;
(e)   the date on which he became available to the operator, and
(f)   the date on which he ceased to be so available.'

[1]   SI 2000/3146; see Appendix I.

21.46

The Private Hire Vehicles (London) (Operators' Licences) Regulations 2000, reg 13[1] requires that records must be kept for 12 months from the last date on which the driver was available for carrying out bookings (Private Hire Vehicles (London) (Operators' Licences) Regulations 2000, reg 16(1)(b)).

[1]   SI 2000/3146; see Appendix I.

Complaints and lost property

21.47

Two other categories of mandatory records must be kept: covering complaints and lost property. In relation to complaints, the requirements are as follows (Private Hire Vehicles (London) (Operators' Licences) Regulations 2000, reg 14[1]):

'14—(1) An operator shall keep at each operating centre specified in his licence a record containing—
(a)   the particulars set out in paragraph (2) of any complaint made in respect of a private hire booking accepted by him at that centre; and
(b)   the particulars set out in paragraph (2)(d), (e), and (f) of any other complaint made in respect of his undertaking as an operator at that centre.

(2) In relation to each complaint the particulars referred to in paragraph (1) are—

(a) the date of the related booking;

(b) the name of the driver who carried out the booking;

(c) the registration mark of the vehicle used;

(d) the name of the complainant and any address, telephone number or other contact details provided by him;

(e) the nature of the complaint, and

(f) details of any investigation carried out and subsequent action taken as a result[2].'

---

[1] SI 2000/3146; see Appendix I.

[2] Private Hire Vehicles (London) (Operators' Licences) Regulations 2000, SI 2000/3146, reg 14. See Appendix I.

21.48

This appears to be aimed at enabling TfL/LTPH to assess what complaints, if any, have been received by the operator. There is no requirement placed on the operator to investigate complaints, although clearly a great many operators will not only take complaints very seriously, they will conduct an investigation. All that the regulations require is a record of what investigation was undertaken, if any, and what action resulted from the investigation.

21.49

The lost property record comprises two parts: property that has been found and property reported lost. There are requirements to record what attempts were made to trace the owner, or find the property, as appropriate (Private Hire Vehicles (London) (Operators' Licences) Regulations 2000, reg 15)[1].

'15–(1) An operator shall keep at each operating centre specified in his licence a record, containing the particulars set out in paragraph (2), of any lost property found—

(a) at that centre, or

(b) in any private hire vehicle used to carry out a booking accepted by him there.

(2) In relation to each item of lost property the particulars referred to in paragraph (1) are—

(a) the date on which it was found;

(b) the place where it was found and if it was found in a vehicle, the registration mark of that vehicle;

(c) a description of the item;

(d) evidence to show that, where practical, an attempt was made to return the item to the owner and whether or not this was successful, and

(e) in the case of any unclaimed item which has been disposed of, how it was disposed of.

(3) An operator shall keep at each operating centre specified in his licence a record, containing the particulars set out in paragraph (4), of any property reported to him at that centre as having been lost.

(4) In relation to each item of property reported as having been lost the particulars referred to in paragraph (3) are—

(a)   the date of the report;

(b)   the date on which it is alleged to have been lost;

(c)   the place where it is alleged to have been lost;

(d)   a description of the item, and

(e)   evidence to show that, where practical, an attempt was made to find the item[2].'

---

[1]   SI 2000/3146; see Appendix I.

[2]   Private Hire Vehicles (London) (Operators' Licences) Regulations 2000, SI 2000/3146, reg 15. See Appendix I.

21.50

Records of both complaints and lost property have to be kept for six months from the date the entry was made (Private Hire Vehicles (London) (Operators' Licences) Regulations 2000, reg 16(1)(c))[1].

---

[1]   SI 2000/3146; see Appendix I.

Preservation of records

21.51

The Private Hire Vehicles (London) (Operators' Licences) Regulations 2000, reg 16[1] specifies how long records must be maintained, and those requirements are:

•   bookings (including tape recordings of booking calls) – 6 months;

•   vehicle and driver records – 12 months;

•   complaints and lost property – 6 months.

If an operator ceases to use an operating centre he must preserve bookings and driver and vehicle records as above from the date of the last entry.

---

[1]   SI 2000/3146; see Appendix I.

Inspection of records

21.52

Any authorised officer of TfL/LTPH or a police constable can, on request, inspect any records maintained by an operator by virtue of PHV(L)A 1998, s 4(3)(e).

21.53

Enforcement will be undertaken by TfL/LTPH, via its authorised officers (PHV(L)A 1998, s 36) and also the police.

21.54

This is the framework within which a London private hire operator must work. It can be seen that it is broadly similar to the system that applies outside London.

OFFENCES

21.55

Breach of a number of requirements placed upon an operator constitute an offence, including the following.

Acting as an operator without a licence

21.56

It is an offence to act as a London private hire operator without holding a London private hire vehicle operator's licence. PHV(L)A 1998, s 2 lays down the requirements and specifies the offence:

'(1) No person shall in London make provision for the invitation or acceptance of, or accept, private hire bookings unless he is the holder of a private hire vehicle operator's licence for London (in this Act referred to as a "London PHV operator's licence").

(2) A person who makes provision for the invitation or acceptance of private hire bookings, or who accepts such a booking, in contravention of this section is guilty of an offence and liable on summary conviction to a fine not exceeding level 4 on the standard scale.'

21.57

This is a strict liability offence and there is no need to prove that the unlicensed operator had knowledge that he should have been licensed.

Other offences

21.58

PHV(L)A 1998, s 4[1] creates a number of offences that can be committed by an operator.

[1]   See Appendix I.

21.59

It is an offence (PHV(L)A 1998, s 4(1) and (5)) to accept a booking at anywhere other than an operating centre specified in the licence. As mentioned at Chapter 21, para 21.33 above, this will outlaw the use of mobile telephones by operators away from the operating centre. It is also an offence (s 4(4) and (5)) not to preserve records from an abandoned operating centre for less than the prescribed period (see Chapter 12, para 12.37 above).

21.60

The operator must ensure that all bookings are undertaken by either a London private hire vehicle driven by a London private hire driver, or a London cab driven by a London cab driver. This accords with the ruling in *Dittah v Birmingham City Council, Choudhry v Birmingham City Council*[1] outside London. If the operator fails in this, he commits an offence by virtue of PHV(L)A 1998, s 4(2) and (5).

[1]   [1993] RTR 356; see Chapter 12, para 12.8.

21.61

Likewise, it is also an offence to fail to comply with the following requirements laid down by PHV(L)A 1998, s 4(3):

'(3) (a)   display a copy of his licence at each operating centre specified in the licence;

(b)   keep at each specified operating centre a record in the prescribed form of the private hire bookings accepted by him there;

(c)   before the commencement of each journey booked at a specified operating centre, enter in the record kept under paragraph (b) the prescribed particulars of the booking;

(d)   keep at each specified operating centre such records as may be prescribed of particulars of the private hire vehicles and drivers which are available to him for carrying out bookings accepted by him at that centre;

(e)   at the request of a constable or authorised officer, produce for inspection any record required by this section to be kept.'

21.62

The maximum penalty for an offence under PHV(L)A 1998, s 4 is a level 3 fine, and there is a defence, if the operator can show that he exercised 'all due diligence' to avoid committing the offence.

21.63

It is also an offence for an operator to pass a booking to another operator who is not a licensed London private hire vehicle operator, or licensed as a private hire operator in the rest of England or Wales, or Scotland (PHV(L)A 1998, s 5(2))[1]. Again, a defence of 'all due diligence' is available (s 5(3)).

[1]   See Appendix I.

21.64

If requested by an authorised officer or a police constable, the operator must produce his licence for inspection under PHV(L)A 1998, s 21(1). This must be produced either forthwith or, if that is not possible, then it must be produced within six days (s 21(3)). The location for production of the licence varies depending on who made the request:

> '(3) (a)   if the request is made by a constable, at any police station within London nominated by the licence holder or vehicle owner when the request is made, or
>
> (b)   if the request is made by an authorised officer, at such place as the officer may reasonably require.'

21.65

Failure to comply without reasonable excuse is an offence under PHV(L)A 1998, s 21(4). In relation to operators' licences, this is on the face of it an odd provision. Although it is only necessary to display a copy of the licence at each operating centre, failure to display such a copy is an offence (PHV(L)A 1998, s 4(3)(a) and (5))[1]. As a result, s 21 will only appear to come into play if either no copy is displayed or, alternatively, if the police constable or authorised officer suspects that the copy is a forgery.

[1]   See Appendix I.

21.66

If the licence has expired or been revoked, it is an offence if the former licensee does not return the licence to TfL/LTPH within seven days from the date of expiry or the date on which the revocation takes effect (PHV(L)A 1998, s 22(1) and (5)) and a daily fine can be imposed for a continuing offence after conviction by virtue of s 22(6)(b)[1].

[1]   See Appendix I.

21.67

If the licence has been suspended, a notice directing the return of the licence to TfL/LTPH within seven days of the date of the suspension being effective may be issued by TfL/LTPH, a constable or an authorised officer (PHV(L)A 1998, s 22(4)). Again, non-compliance is an offence (s 22(5)) and a daily fine for non-compliance can also be imposed (s 22(6)(b)).

21.68

Wilful obstruction of an authorised officer or a constable is an offence under PHV(L)A 1998, s 27(1), as is non-compliance with any requirement (s 27(2)(a)), failure to provide assistance or information (s 27(2)(b)) or providing false information (s 27(3))[1].

[1]   See Appendix I.

21.69

As mentioned at para 21.16 above, making a false statement in support of an application for grant or renewal of a licence is an offence by virtue of PHV(L)A 1998, s 28.

SUSPENSION, REVOCATION OR REFUSAL TO RENEW AN OPERATOR'S LICENCE

21.70

Powers to suspend, or revoke an operator's licence are contained in PHV(L)A 1998, s 16. Section 16(1) is a general power given to TfL/LTPH in relation to any private hire licence, and s 16(2) specifically refers to operators' licenses.

'(1) The licensing authority may suspend or revoke a licence under this Act for any reasonable cause including (without prejudice to the generality of this subsection) any ground mentioned below.

(2) A London PHV operator's licence may be suspended or revoked where—
(a) the licensing authority is no longer satisfied that the licence holder is fit to hold such a licence;
(aa) the licence holder has, since the grant of the licence, been convicted of an immigration offence or required to pay an immigration penalty; or
(b) the licence holder has failed to comply with any condition of the licence or any other obligation imposed on him by or under this Act.

(2A) Subsection (2)(aa) does not apply if—
(a) in a case where the licence holder has been convicted of an immigration offence, the conviction is a spent conviction within the meaning of the Rehabilitation of Offenders Act 1974, or
(b) in a case where the licence holder has been required to pay an immigration penalty—
(i) more than three years have elapsed since the date on which the penalty was imposed, and
(ii) the amount of the penalty has been paid in full.'

21.71

It can be seen that there are wide-ranging grounds for suspending or revoking a licence, and that they are very similar to those contained in LG(MP)A 1976 for licences outside London.

21.72

'Any reasonable cause' in PHV(L)A 1998, s 16(1) would not appear to be constrained by the wording of s 16(2) and therefore can cover any relevant matter that the licensing authority may feel would affect the safety or security of the public[1].

1 See *Norwich City Council v Watcham and Thurtle* (21 May 1981, unreported); see Chapter 8, para 8.138.

21.73

'No longer satisfied that the licence holder is fit to hold a licence' will depend upon the criteria that TfL/LTPH applies in relation to the grant of an operator's licence, and if they have been breached, then action can clearly be taken.

Conviction for an immigration offence or required to pay an immigration penalty is slightly odd, because if the conviction is spent, it cannot be taken into account. This does not accord with the ruling in *Adamson v Waveney District Council*[1], but as it is a statutory provision, it must apply.

1 [1997] 2 All ER 898, QBD.

21.74

Failure 'to comply with any condition of the licence or any other obligation imposed on him by or under this Act' will be a matter of fact.

21.75

If TfL/LTPH decides that action should be taken against a licence, the mechanism laid down in PHV(L)A 1998, s 17 must be followed:

'(1) Where the licensing authority has decided to suspend or revoke a licence under section 16—
(a) the authority shall give notice of the decision and the grounds for the decision to the licence holder or, in the case of a London PHV licence, the owner of the vehicle to which the licence relates; and
(b) the suspension or revocation takes effect at the end of the period of 21 days beginning with the day on which that notice is served on the licence holder or the owner.

(2) If the licensing authority is of the opinion that the interests of public safety require the suspension or revocation of a licence to have immediate effect, and the authority includes a statement of that opinion and the reasons for it in the notice of suspension or revocation, the suspension or revocation takes effect when the notice is served on the licence holder or vehicle owner (as the case may be).

(3) A licence suspended under this section shall remain suspended until such time as the licensing authority by notice directs that the licence is again in force.

(4) The holder of a London PHV operator's or driver's licence, or the owner of a vehicle to which a PHV licence relates, may appeal to a magistrates' court against a decision under section 16 to suspend or revoke that licence.'

21.76

Once the decision has been taken, notice is given to the licensee and the suspension or revocation takes effect 21 days later, including the date of service (in other words, 20 clear days from the date of service or receipt of the notice). The licensee has 21 days from the date of service (arguably not including the date of service) to appeal against the decision to the magistrates' court (PHV(L)A 1998, s 25(4)[1]–in relation to appeals generally). If an appeal is lodged, then PHV(L)A 1998, s 26(1) stays the effect of the suspension or revocation until the appeal is determined. However, if TfL/LTPH 'is of the opinion that the interests of public safety' require the effect to be immediate, then provided both a statement to that effect and the reasons for it are contained within the notice of suspension or revocation, no stay is effected by virtue of any appeal lodged. It would appear, following the decisions in *R v Burton on Trent Justices, ex p Hussain*[2] and *R (app Hope and Glory Public House Ltd) v Westminster City Magistrates' Court*[3] that the reasons must be more detailed than simply stating the grounds for the decision, in this case 'the interests of public safety', and full and detailed reasons must be given to support the decision. As there is no right of appeal against a decision that the suspension should be immediate, it would appear that the only method of challenging such a decision would be by way of judicial review, as this cannot be addressed by the magistrates on appeal against the suspension or revocation itself.

[1]   See Chapter 3, para 3.69 onwards above.
[2]   (1996) 166 JP 808, (1997) 9 Admin LR 233; see Chapter 2, para 2.89.
[3]   [2011] EWCA Civ 31, [2011] 3 All ER 579, CA; see Chapter 2, para 2.92.

21.77

Complaints or prosecutions that have not resulted in a conviction could be sufficient grounds for taking action against a licensee in this situation[1].

[1]   See *R v Maidstone Crown Court, ex p Olson* [1992] COD 496 (Chapter 10, para 10.139); *McCool v Rushcliffe Borough Council* [1998] 3 All ER 889, QBD (Chapter 10, para 10.142); *Leeds City Council v Hussain* [2002] EWHC 1145 (Admin), RTR 199 (Chapter 10, para 10.146) and *R (on the application of Wrexham CBC) v Chester Crown Court* [2004] EWHC 1591 (Chapter 10, para 10.150).

PRIVATE HIRE OPERATORS: PROBLEM AREAS

21.78

There is nothing contained in PHV(L)A 1998 or the Private Hire Vehicles (London) (Operators' Licences) Regulations 2000[1] to suggest that the position outside London with regard to the following matters will not apply within London. Accordingly, it appears that a London private hire operator can take a booking for a journey:

- which commences outside London;
- which terminates outside London;
- which goes outside London on the course of its journey; or

- that never comes within London.

[1] SI 2000/3146; see Appendix I.

21.79

For more information on these areas, see para 12.94 onwards above. Although the cases to support these propositions do not specifically mention London and predate PHV(L)A 1998, it seems very unlikely that the position is different in London from the rest of the country, notwithstanding the absence of a similar provision to LG(MP)A 1976, s 75(1)[1] within the London legislation.

[1] See Appendix I.

Advertisements for a private hire service

21.80

PHV(L)A 1998, s 31[1] prohibits the use of certain words in advertisements for private hire services. The words are 'taxi', 'taxis', 'cab' or 'cabs', or 'any word so closely resembling any of those words as to be likely to be mistaken for it', but the use of the words 'minicab', 'mini-cab', 'mini cab', 'minicabs', 'mini-cabs' or 'mini cabs' does not constitute an offence (s 31(3)). Contravention is an offence by virtue of s 31(4).

[1] See Appendix I.

21.81

PHV(L)A 1998, s 31 does not prohibit advertising a non-London private hire operator within London, neither does it prevent a London private hire operator from advertising outside London. It therefore appears that the ruling in *Windsor and Maidenhead Royal Borough Council v Khan*[1] will apply and allow such advertisements.

[1] [1994] RTR 87. See para 12.95 above.

Freephones and telephone diversions

21.82

The position within London is perhaps clearer than the position outside in relation to freephones and telephone diversions as there is no provision to allow an operating centre to be located outside London, and freephone or telephone diversion must be answered not only at an address within London, but also at an address that is licensed as an operating centre.

Chapter 22

Private hire vehicles within London

INTRODUCTION

22.1

Any vehicle used as a private hire vehicle within London and operated by a London private hire operator must either be licensed as a London private hire vehicle under the provisions of the Private Hire Vehicles (London) Act 1998, s 7 (PHV(L)A 1998) or must be a London cab[1]. PHV(L)A 1998, s 6(2) and (3) makes it clear that if a vehicle is not licensed under s 7 (or a London cab) then the driver, operator and owner of the vehicle each commit an offence if it used within London as a private hire vehicle.

[1]   This exception is considered at para 22.28 below.

22.2

Private hire vehicle is defined in s 1(1)(a) as:

'(a) "private hire vehicle" means a vehicle constructed or adapted to seat fewer than nine passengers which is made available with a driver for hire for the purpose of carrying passengers, other than a licensed taxi or a public service vehicle;'.

POWERS RELATING TO LICENSING

22.3

The powers relating to the licensing of the vehicle are contained in PHV(L)A 1998, s 7:

'7 London PHV licences

(1) The owner of any vehicle constructed or adapted to seat fewer than nine passengers may apply to the licensing authority for a private hire vehicle licence for London (in this Act referred to as a "London PHV licence") for that vehicle.

(2) The licensing authority shall grant a London PHV licence for a vehicle if the authority is satisfied—

(a)   that the vehicle—

    (i)   is suitable in type, size and design for use as a private hire vehicle;

    (ii)   is safe, comfortable and in a suitable mechanical condition for that use; and

    (iii) is not of such design and appearance as would lead any person to believe that the vehicle is a London cab;

(b)   that there is in force in relation to the use of the vehicle a policy of insurance or such security as complies with the requirements of Part VI of the Road Traffic Act 1988; and

(c)   that any further requirements that may be prescribed are met.

(3) A London PHV licence may not be granted in respect of more than one vehicle.

(4) A London PHV licence shall be granted subject to such conditions as may be prescribed and such other conditions as the licensing authority may think fit.

(5) A London PHV licence shall be in such form and shall contain such particulars as the licensing authority may think fit.

(6) A London PHV licence shall be granted for one year or for such shorter period as the licensing authority may consider appropriate in the circumstances of the case.

(7) An applicant for a London PHV licence may appeal to a magistrates' court against a decision not to grant such a licence or against any condition (other than a prescribed condition) to which the licence is subject.'

As can be seen, this is a lengthy provision and there are a number of important points that arise from it.

22.4

It is important to note that the licensing authority ('licensing authority' is defined in PHV(L)A 1998, s 36 as Transport for London (TfL) which exercises these functions through London Taxi and Private Hire (LTPH)) is placed under a duty to issue a licence once an application has been made and that provided the criteria laid down in PHV(L)A 1998, s 7(2) are met, it has no discretion and must issue a licence This can be contrasted with the requirements that apply outside London under LG(MP)A 1976, s 48(1)[1].

[1]   See Chapter 13, para 13.2.

THE TYPE OF VEHICLE

22.5

Just as outside London, within London there is no such thing as a purpose-designed or purpose-built private hire vehicle. Private hire vehicles come in all shapes and sizes and there is no normal or average vehicle. PHV(L)A 1998, s 7(2) (a) lays down certain criteria that have to be satisfied before TfL/LTPH can license a vehicle as a private hire vehicle.

Criteria as to the vehicle

22.6

TfL/LTPH must be satisfied that the vehicle is 'suitable in type, size and design for use as a private hire vehicle' and 'is safe, comfortable and in a suitable mechanical condition' for use as a private hire vehicle. It is open to TfL/LTPH to prescribe further requirements under regulations (PHV(L)A 1998, s 7(2)(c) and PHV(L)A 1998, s 32(1)), and these are contained in reg 3 of and Sch 1 to the Private Hire Vehicles (London PHV Licences) Regulations 2004[1]. There are requirements in relation to the age and/or emissions of the vehicle[2]. The further requirements include:

1. the vehicle must be a light passenger vehicle;
2. it must have an MOT test not more than 14 days' old (unless the vehicle is less than 12 months old);
3. it must have an excise licence (tax disc);
4. it must be right-hand drive;
5. any wheelchair lifting equipment must have been correctly tested;
6. it must be able to carry a reasonable amount of luggage;
7. it must comply with the construction and use regulations;
8. it must be to original manufacturer specification (unless converted –see 9 below);
9. any converted vehicle must comply with the construction and use regulations;
10. there must be sufficient doors to allow safe access and egress.

[1]   See Appendix I.
[2]   Private Hire Vehicles (London PHV Licences) Regulations 2004, reg 3; Sch 1, paras 1–1E.

22.7

The next question that must be addressed by TfL/LTPH is whether the vehicle is 'of such design and appearance as to lead any person to believe that the vehicle is a London cab'[1]. For a discussion on this point in relation to the case of *R v Bournemouth Borough Council, ex p Thompson*[2]. In relation to London, all London cabs must meet the LTPH 'Conditions of Fitness' and vehicles that meet those conditions will not be licensed by TfL as a private hire vehicle.

[1]   Private Hire Vehicles (London) Act 1998, s 7(2)(a)(iii).
[2]   (1985) 83 LGR 662. A small number of Asquiths are currently licensed. Although designed to resemble a 1930s Austin, they meet all the current Conditions of Fitness. Also, since July 2008 Mercedes-Benz Vito Taxis have met the conditions of fitness. See Chapter 13, para 13.22.

22.8

TfL/LTPH has a power to test vehicles that are licensed as private hire vehicles under PHV(L)A 1998, s 8(2)[1], but as outside London, there is no overt power to conduct tests on a vehicle that is the subject of an application for a licence. However, it is clear that TfL/LTPH must conduct a test before the licence is issued to satisfy itself that the requirements laid down in PHV(L)A 1998, s 7(2)(a)(ii) are met[2].

1   See Appendix I.
2   See Appendix I.

Conditions as to the vehicle

22.9

TfL/LTPH has power under PHV(L)A 1998, s 7(4)[1] to grant the licence subject to prescribed conditions (as laid down in any regulations made under PHV(L)A 1998, s 32(1)) and 'such other conditions as the licensing authority may think fit'.

1   See Appendix I.

22.10

The prescribed conditions are contained in reg 4 of and Sch 2 to the Private Hire Vehicles (London PHV Licences) Regulations 2003. These require the owner to retain records in the use of the vehicle (paras 1–3); notify TfL/LTPH of any change of ownership (para 4); limit the number of passengers (para 5); specify the condition of the vehicle (para 6); specify requirements for vehicles exempted from displaying an identification disc (para 7); require test certificates (para 8); specify radio equipment (para 9); require compliance with the Road Vehicles (Registration and Licensing) Regulations 2002 (para 10); require the display of an additional disc (para 11); prohibit the display of out of London plates on any dual licensed vehicle (para 12); prohibit the use of any vehicle that does not meet these conditions (para 13); and prohibit the use of any vehicle that is not insured (para 14)[1].

1   See Appendix I.

ROOF SIGNS

22.11

Although there is no specific ban on roof signs being fitted to private hire vehicles within the Act, PHV(L)A 1998, s 30 allows regulations to be made prohibiting private hire vehicles from displaying 'any sign, notice or other feature of a description specified in the regulations'. The original regulations[1] were amended by the TfL board in October 2007, and new guidelines for signs on London private hire vehicles were issued in July 2008[2]. It is an offence by virtue of s 30(3) for a person to drive a vehicle with proscribed signs, notices etc or to cause or permit the signs etc to be displayed on a vehicle. The revision to reg 8 has considerably relaxed the original regulation, which amounted to an almost blanket ban on signage on private hire vehicles. The guidelines now allow:

- appropriate warning and safety signs subject to LTPH approval;
- certain roof markings, but not signs which protrude from the roof;
- limited signs and logos identifying licensed operators on the rear of the vehicle;
- other signs, for example, those allowing PHVs to pick up and drop off passengers on red routes, but only at the discretion of TfL/LTPH.

[1]   The Private Hire Vehicles (London PHV Licences) Regulations 2004 made by TfL on 16 February 2004.
[2]   PCO Notice 16/08 now contained in 'Guidelines for Advertising on licensed London Taxis and Signs on licensed London Private Hire Vehicles' revised November 2014 available at http://content.tfl.gov.uk/taxi-advertising-guidelines.pdf

THE PRIVATE HIRE VEHICLE LICENCE ITSELF

22.12

'A London PHV licence shall be in such form and shall contain such particulars as the licensing authority may think fit' (PHV(L)A 1998, s 7(5)).

Register of licences

22.13

PHV(L)A 1998, s 23 requires that all London private hire vehicle licences issued must be entered on a register maintained by TfL/LTPH. Section 23(1)(a) prescribes the information that must be contained, namely:

- the number of the licence;
- the name of the person to whom the licence is granted[1];
- the date on which the licence is granted; and
- the expiry date of the licence.

Further information is required by reg 7 of the Private Hire Vehicles (London PHV Licences) Regulations 2004:

'(a)   the registration mark of the vehicle to which the licence relates;
(b)   an indication as to whether the licence—
(i)   is a London PHV licence or a temporary permit; and
(ii)   is current, suspended or revoked.'

[1]   TfL can only disclose the address to a person 'if it appears to the authority that the person has a sufficient reason for requiring that information' (1998 Act, s 23(4)).

22.14

The register is open to free public inspection at times and locations set by TfL/LTPH (PHV(L)A 1998, s 23(2)) which is at the main office of the LTPH, plus access is available on the LTPH website[1].

[1]   http://www.tfl.gov.uk/tfl/businessandpartners/taxisandprivatehire/ph/licensing/?mode=vehicles. The details on the website are not as comprehensive as those available at the London Taxi and Private Hire Offices.

22.15

The licence itself shall be granted for 'one year or for such shorter period as the licensing authority may consider appropriate in the circumstances of the case' (PHV(L)A 1998, s 7(6)).

Private hire plates

22.16

PHV(L)A 1998, s 10 requires that TfL/LTPH issue a 'disc or plate', which must be 'exhibited on the vehicle in such as may be prescribed' whenever the vehicle is used as a private hire vehicle on a road in London (s 10(2)). The method of exhibition of the disc is prescribed in reg 5 of the Private Hire Vehicles (London PHV Licences) Regulations 2004:

> '**5.**—(1) The identification disc shall be exhibited in the manner specified in paragraph (2).
>
> (2) The disc shall be affixed to the top of the inside of the front windscreen on the passenger side of the vehicle so that—
>
> (a) on the side which faces outwards, the following particulars are clearly legible—
>
> (i) the registration mark of the vehicle;
>
> (ii) the maximum number of passengers which may be carried in the vehicle in accordance with the conditions of the licence for the vehicle;
>
> (iii) the number of the London PHV licence for the vehicle;
>
> (iv) the date of the expiry of the licence; and
>
> (v) a statement that the licence has been issued by the Public Carriage Office of Transport for London; and
>
> (b) on the side which is visible from inside the vehicle, a statement that the vehicle is licensed by the Public Carriage Office of Transport for London is clearly legible.'

22.17

The requirement to display the plate can be lifted in relation to certain specified types of use or service if TfL/LTPH 'considers it inappropriate (having regard to that service) to require the disc or plate in question to be exhibited'. This is achieved by means of a notice issued by TfL/LTPH, presumably to the holder of the vehicle licence. Interestingly, there is no requirement within PHV(L)A 1998 to carry the notice in the vehicle (contrast with LG(MP)A 1976, s 73(3)[1] outside London) and it cannot be demanded for inspection by a constable or authorised officer under PHV(L)A 1998, s 21(2).

---

[1] See Chapter 13, para 13.64 and Appendix I.

ALWAYS A PRIVATE HIRE VEHICLE?

22.18

Once a vehicle has been licensed as a London private hire vehicle, does that mean it is always a London private hire vehicle? That is clearly the case outside London[1], but is less clear within London. The possible difference in the status of a private hire vehicle within London stems from the difference in wording between the LG(MP)A 1976 and PHV(L)A 1998.

[1]   See Chapter 13, para 13.71 onwards.

22.19

Under the ruling in *Benson v Boyce*[1] Mance J held that the wording 'provided for hire' in LG(MP)A 1976, s 80 related to the nature of the vehicle rather than the nature of the activity the vehicle was being used for. The wording in PHV(L)A 1998, s 1 is different. Section 1(1)(a) states:

'"private hire vehicle" means a vehicle constructed or adapted to seat fewer than nine passengers which is made available with a driver for hire for the purpose of carrying passengers, other than a licensed taxi or a public service vehicle; ...'

[1]   [1997] RTR 226.

22.20

It can be seen that the phrase 'provided for hire with the services of a driver' (LG(MP)A 1976, s 80) has been replaced with the phrase 'made available with a driver for hire'. Although the wording is different, there seems to be little material difference between the two expressions. Without further guidance it would appear that the two expressions are so closely related that it would be unlikely that they would carry a different meaning, leading to the conclusion that a private hire vehicle in London, once licensed, is a private hire vehicle at all times. However, this conclusion is rendered considerably less certain by PHV(L)A 1998, s 1(2) and PHV(L)A 1998, s 12(1).

22.21

PHV(L)A 1998, s 12(1) states:

'No vehicle shall be used as a private hire vehicle on a road in London unless the driver holds a private hire vehicle driver's licence.'

22.22

The concept of 'use' is addressed in PHV(L)A 1998, s 1(2), which states:

'(2) Any reference in this Act to a vehicle being "used as a private hire vehicle" is a reference to a private hire vehicle which—
(a)   is in use in connection with a hiring for the purpose of carrying one or more passengers; or

(b) is immediately available to an operator to carry out a private hire booking.'

22.23

Even if the correct interpretation of PHV(L)A 1998, s 1(1)(a) is that a London private hire vehicle is a private hire vehicle at all times, the fact that an offence is only committed by an unlicensed driver when the vehicle is either being used for a hiring (s 1(2)(a)) or can be used immediately for a hiring means that, except for the purposes of insurance, the point is considerably less important. As PHV(L)A 1998, s 4(2) places duty upon an operator to ensure that a private hire vehicle which is carrying out a booking is driven by a licensed private hire driver, it would appear that a private hire vehicle driven by a person who is not the holder of a private hire driver's licence is not a private hire vehicle which is immediately available to an operator within the meaning of s 1(2)(b).

22.24

There therefore appears to be a fundamental distinction between the licensing regime outside London and within London, as it appears that a London private hire vehicle does not have to be driven by a private hire driver if it is not being used for private hire purposes.

Meters and fares

22.25

PHV(L)A 1998, s 11 contains an absolute prohibition on any licensed London private hire vehicle being fitted with a meter and the owner of a vehicle so fitted is liable on conviction in the magistrates' court to a fine not exceeding level 3. Section 11 provides:

'(1) No vehicle to which a London PHV licence relates shall be equipped with a taximeter.

(2) If such a vehicle is equipped with a taximeter, the owner of that vehicle is guilty of an offence and liable on summary conviction to a fine not exceeding level 3 on the standard scale.

(3) In this section "taximeter" means a device for calculating the fare to be charged in respect of any journey by reference to the distance travelled or time elapsed since the start of the journey (or a combination of both).'

Transport for London v Uber London Ltd

22.26

> Was a smartphone used as a journey tracker in a private hire vehicle a meter in contravention of the prohibition on meters in private hire vehicles within London? Held: No.

The question of whether a smart-phone which tracked a journey and was used to calculate the fare by accessing a remote computer was a meter was considered by the High Court in the case of *Transport for London v Uber London Ltd and others*[1].

Uber, a licensed private hire operator, calculated the fare for a journey by means of a smartphone which the driver had in the vehicle. The question for the court to answer was whether that was a meter for the purposes of PHV(L)A 1998, s 11. The case arose by means of a request by the parties for a declaration and Ousley J, giving judgment, outlined the basic position thus[2]:

'The LTDA [Licensed Taxi Drivers' Association] and LPHCA [Licensed Private Hire Car Association] contend that private hire vehicles operating within the Uber network are equipped with taximeters, in contravention of the criminal law. TfL and Uber disagree.'

It was agreed between the parties that a declaration was a sensible means of progressing the argument.

The position was outlined by the judge (and it is reproduced here in full, because it is a useful explanation of how the Uber system works)[3]:

'The facts

11. These are not in dispute. I take them largely from Ms Carss- Frisk QC's Skeleton Argument, which is supported by Uber's evidence. Uber signs up both licensed private hire vehicle drivers and licensed black cab drivers who are then able to carry out the bookings accepted and referred to them by Uber. The booking and customer billing process involves the customer using the Customer App and the Driver using the Driver App; both Apps licensed by an Uber related company. The Driver App has to be installed on the driver's Smartphone, either rented from Uber or the driver's own Smartphone. A driver using his own Smartphone can use it for the range of other purposes for which a Smartphone can be used. Smartphones rented from Uber however are disabled from making calls or sending text messages and allow only access to the Driver App and other relevant applications such as the navigation App. Those who rent the Smartphone are supplied with a phone cradle for the vehicle but are not required to use it. The driver can keep the Smartphone where they want to during the trip. The Smartphone does not have to be visible to the customer at any time. The customer obtains the Customer App by registering certain personal details with Uber and providing a valid credit or debit card number. Once registered, the customer can use the Customer App.

12. When booking, the customer can choose a particular type of vehicle. The nearest vehicle of that type available for hire will be shown on the Smartphone screen. The customer then indicates precisely where they want to be picked up, and clicks "request" to make the booking. Uber accepts the booking and Uber's servers in the United States locate the nearest available vehicle of the type requested by the customer. The servers then send the accepted booking to the Smartphone of the nearest driver, who has 15 seconds to accept the booking. If he does not accept it,

the server sends the booking to the Smartphone of the driver of the next nearest vehicle to the customer. When the driver takes on the booking, he is sent all the relevant details including the location. He can contact the customer via the Driver App but not via the customer's mobile number. The customer is sent also by the Customer App details of the driver, car and estimated time of arrival.

13. Once the driver has picked up the customer, the customer, if he has not already done so, provides the driver with details of the desired destination. The driver puts this on to his Smartphone and clicks the "begin trip" icon on his Driver App screen. If the car hired is a black cab rather than a private hire vehicle, the driver clicks on the icon and starts his taximeter simultaneously. If the Customer App is left open during the trip, the customer will see the name and photograph of the driver on the Smartphone screen as well as the intended route and estimated time of arrival. The customer cannot see the fare during the trip and no running fare is displayed on their Smartphone or that of the driver. But if they are in a black cab booked through Uber, they can see the taximeter with the fare running in the usual way.

14. At the end of the trip the driver presses the "end trip" button on the Driver App screen on his Smartphone. If the vehicle is a black cab, the driver will be prompted to enter the fare shown on the taximeter on his Smartphone through the Driver App. That is the fare. However if the vehicle is a private hire vehicle the fare is calculated by Uber's servers, to which I shall come. The fare is not calculated and displayed on a running basis, as with a black cab taximeter. The customer will be sent a fare receipt by email within seconds of the trip ending. The receipt shows the total fare charged, a map of the route, distance travelled and time taken. It provides a breakdown of the fare showing the costs of the trip, the base fare, distance and time. The fare is automatically charged to the credit or debit card of the customer. The information about the total fare charged is sent by Uber's service to the driver on the Driver App at the same time as the customer receives his receipt. There are ways in which issue can be taken by the customer with the fare charged in this way.

15. The issue in this case relates to how the fare is calculated for PHVs on the Uber network, and not to black cabs on it. The calculation is carried out by one of two servers operated by Uber in the United States. Signals are sent to the servers by the driver's Smartphone, providing GPS data from the driver's Smartphone, and time details. Server 2 calculates the fare to be paid using what Uber calls its fare calculation model, effectively a software based algorithm. Server 2 determines which fare structure applies, in this case the London fare structure. It obtains the structure from the fare structure in Server 1 which keeps the long term data for Uber. In London there is a base fare and an additional fare. The base fare depends on the type of PHV used. The additional fare is calculated by adding the total time taken to complete the trip at a particular amount per

minute depending on the vehicle plus the total distance travelled charged at a particular amount per mile also varying with the type of vehicle. There may be a further component to the additional fare depending on whether "surge pricing" is in operation, to which the customer is alerted in advance. If so, a multiplier is applied to the additional fare. Surge pricing applies and it may apply for a very short period only, a matter of minutes sometimes, so that higher prices are charged during times of high demand for drivers; the aim is to encourage more drivers to be available at particular places. Any further tolls such as airport car parking are added, promotional offers are assessed and where applicable the fare reduced accordingly. Some fares are charged at a flat rate such as trips to the London airports. It is then for the server to send its calculated final fare to the customer and private hire driver simultaneously. No fare can be calculated during a network outage.

16. A black cab fare also comprises a base fare with an additional fare calculated using distance and time but these metrics are recorded by the taximeter which is integrated and sealed into the mechanics of the black cab and the calculation is performed by the taximeter as the journey progresses.'

He went on to give his conclusion before explaining his reasoning. His conclusion was[4]:

'The issue

17 The question for decision in the light of those agreed facts is whether the Uber PHVs are equipped with a taximeter, that is, a device for calculating fares. In my judgment, these PHVs are not equipped with a taximeter as defined by section 11(3). The driver's Smartphone with the Driver's App is not a device for calculating fares by itself or in conjunction with Server 2, and even if it were, the vehicle is not equipped with it. I reach that conclusion as a matter of the ordinary meaning of the words as applied to the agreed facts.'

In relation to the first point, whether the Smartphone was a 'device for calculating fares' his explanation for finding that it was not is contained in paragraphs 18–44 of the judgment. Of these, the first three paragraphs convey the essence of the findings:

'18. The driver's Smartphone was the primary candidate device for calculating fares. Server 2 receives inputs from the driver's Smartphone, and elsewhere. The results of the calculation are transmitted to the driver and customer via their Uber APPs and to the third party which debits the customer's account. But the Smartphone carries out no calculations; that is not its purpose. The calculation is carried out in fact by Server 2 and wherever it actually does it, it is not in the vehicle.

19. LTDA and LPHCA argue that the driver's Smartphone provides inputs to the calculation in the form of time and distance for the journey, which is correct. They argue that that suffices to make the Smartphone a

device for calculating fares. Any involvement in the process of calculation was sufficient to constitute the Smartphone such a device. That is wrong.

20. A device for recording time and distance is not a device for calculating a fare based on time and distance, let alone one based on more than that, including the fare structure itself, a necessary component to the calculation. The language of the statute is quite clear. The essence of a taximeter for the purpose of section 11 is that the device must be for the calculation of the fare then to be charged, based on whatever inputs are appropriate. Such a device is not simply recording and transmitting some or all of the inputs to a calculation made elsewhere, or receiving the output, that is the calculated fare. The Smartphone is not a "thing designed or adapted for a particular functional purpose" namely calculating fares for the PHV; see the Shorter OED. It is not a taximeter. The Smartphone with its Driver's App may be essential to enabling the calculation to take place but that does not make it a device for calculating fares. Nor does that warrant treating the Smartphone as part of a single device with Server 2; it simply is not.'

There is little in the remaining 24 paragraphs that adds to this overall conclusion, but there are some very interesting judicial observations on the various arguments presented.

In relation to the second point, the judge explained this succinctly[5]:

'Are the PHVs equipped with a device for calculating fares?

45. On the second aspect of s 11, I have concluded that the Uber PHV is not equipped with the driver's Smartphone, whether the Smartphone is hired from Uber or is the driver's own. Of course the driver needs to have the Smartphone with him in the vehicle for the calculating and charging system to work but that does not mean that the vehicle is equipped with it. It is the driver who is equipped with it. The vehicle is not equipped with something that may stay in the driver's pocket, be put in multiple places over one journey, or be moved in and out of the car with the driver, and at best may rest on the cradle.

46. "Equipped" may cover many degrees of removability and attachment. Whether a vehicle is "equipped" with a device is a matter of impression, but it would stretch a broad word too far to hold that the PHV was "equipped" with a Smartphone in this context and in these circumstances. "Equipped" focuses on what the vehicle is provided with and not what the driver brings in and uses. The Act does not prohibit the driver from carrying and using a device for fare calculation nor prohibit him from providing information via a device in order for the fares to be calculated elsewhere.'

Accordingly a declaration was granted in the following terms[6]:

'A taximeter, for the purposes of Section 11 of the Private Hire Vehicles (London) Act 1998, does not include a device that receives GPS signals in the course of a journey, and forwards GPS data to a server located outside of the vehicle, which server calculates a fare that is partially or wholly determined by reference to distance travelled and time taken, and sends the fare information back to the device.'

No reference is made in PHV(L)A 1998 to fares and, accordingly, it is clear that TfL/LTPH has no power to prescribe fares for private hire vehicles.

¹ [2015] EWHC 2918 (Admin).
² At para 1.
³ Above at paras 11–14.
⁴ At para 17.
⁵ At paras 45–47.
⁶ At para 49.

Provisions to ensure that a driver must carry assistance dogs and provision of mobility assistance

22.27

The provisions of the Equality Act 2010, s 170 (EA 2010) apply within London in the same way as outside London. Accordingly, private hire drivers must carry assistance dogs in the passenger compartment, unless the driver has a certificate of medical exemption[1].

In addition, TfL/LTPH list private hire vehicles as being wheelchair accessible under EA 2010, s 167 and the driver of such a vehicle must provide mobility assistance to passengers in wheelchairs in accordance with s 165 unless they have a certificate of exemption issued under s 166. These requirements are identical to those imposed on drivers outside London[2].

¹ See Chapter 13, para 13.82 onwards, for details.
² For full details see Chapter 13, para 13.87 onwards.

HACKNEY CARRIAGES USED FOR PRE-BOOKED WORK

22.28

It is clear that PHV(L)A 1998 foresees London hackney carriages being used for pre-booked work by a private hire operator within London (effectively as a private hire vehicle, but they cannot be a private hire vehicle because the definition in PHV(L)A 1998, s 1(1) excludes a licensed taxi). PHV(L)A 1998, s 4(2)(b) allows a London private hire operator to use a London cab driven by a person who holds a London cab driver's licence to discharge a booking for a private hire vehicle. A London cab used for private hire cannot charge more than shown on the meter. Regulation 9(8) of the Private Hire Vehicles (London) (Operators' Licences) Regulations 2000[1] states:

'Where an operator provides a London cab for the purpose of carrying out a private hire booking, any fare payable in respect of the booking shall be calculated as if the vehicle was a private hire vehicle unless the fare shown on the taximeter is less.'

¹ SI 2000/3146. See Appendix I.

22.29

As outside London it appears that a person who takes bookings for hackney carriages used for private hire purposes does not need to hold a London private hire vehicle operator's licence as a consequence of PHV(L)A 1998, s 2(1) which specifically refers to the invitation or acceptance of 'private hire bookings'. PHV(L)A 1998, s 1(4) defines a private hire booking as meaning:

> 'a booking for the hire of a private hire vehicle for the purpose of carrying one or more passengers (including a booking to carry out as sub-contractor a private hire booking accepted by another operator)'

and s 1(1)(a) specifically excludes a licensed taxi from the definition of private hire vehicle ('licensed taxi' is defined in PHV(L)A 1998, s 36 as 'a Hackney carriage, a London cab or a taxi licensed under Part II of the 1982 Act[1]')[2].

[1]   Civic Government (Scotland) Act 1982, Pt II.
[2]   This view is supported by TfL/LTPH.

DPP v Computer Cab Company Ltd

22.30

> Could a London Cab, driven by a 'suburban only' driver lawfully pick up a pre-booked fare outside the 'suburban area', ie in a part of Greater London where the driver was not permitted to ply or stand for hire? Held: Yes.

It is clear that London hackney carriages can be pre-booked, which is why they are excluded from the definition of 'private hire vehicle' in s 1 of the PHV(L)A 1998. However, there are two types of London hackney carriage driver – those who are licensed for the whole of the Greater London area and those who are only licensed for a smaller part of the area[1]. In the case of *DPP v Computer Cab Company Ltd*[2] the question arose concerning a suburban hackney carriage driver accepting a booking for a pre-booked hiring, which was accepted by the driver when he was outside the restricted area in which he could ply for hire.

The facts of the case were that a booking company (Computer Cab Company Ltd) maintained a radio circuit to which hackney carriage drivers belonged. Prospective passengers contacted the booking company who then radioed the hackney carriage driver with details of the pickup point, the destination and the customer. When that booking was accepted by the driver, he would start his meter and turn off his 'For Hire' sign, although the maximum charge prior to the collection of the customer was £2.40.

Once the driver had accepted the contract from the booking company, he proceeded to where the passenger was waiting, collected him and drove him to the booked destination.

The question arose as to whether picking up a pre-booked passenger in these circumstances, from a location outside the area in which the driver was licensed to ply for hire, constituted a breach of art 31 of the London Cab Order 1934.[3] Article 31 states:

'(1)   If the holder of a cab-driver's licence
(i)   drives a cab of any type which by the terms of his licence he is not
       permitted to drive (not being a cab which is withdrawn from hire), or
(ii)   plies for hire with a cab or permits the cab to be hired in any part of
       the metropolitan area in which by a condition attached to his licence
       he is prohibited from plying for hire with a cab,
    he shall be guilty of a breach of this Order.'

In addition, art 39 states:

'The driver of a motor cab shall, as soon as the cab is hired and no sooner,
set the mechanism of the taximeter in motion, and shall, as soon as the
hiring is terminated and no sooner, stop the mechanism of the taximeter.'

which suggested that the hiring commenced when the radio booking was
accepted, when the driver started his meter and turned off his 'For Hire' sign.

The case hinged on where the contract for hire of the cab took place, with
both the booking company and the drivers arguing that it was where the call from
the booking company was accepted by the driver (which was within that part of
London where the drivers were licensed to ply for hire), whilst the Director of
Public Prosecutions (DPP) argued that it was where the customer was collected,
which was outside the drivers' area.

Judgment was given by Lord Justice Rose who stated as follows[4]:

'In my judgment, hiring is necessarily a matter of agreement. It involves
agreement between the customer on the one hand, and the driver on the
other. In the ordinary way that is an agreement which takes place in the
street. It is a process which starts with the driver plying for hire being
hailed, a discussion following as to where the customer wishes to be taken
and, apart from exceptional cases in which the driver is entitled to refuse
a particular fare (into which it is unnecessary to go), the agreement for
hiring is clearly evidenced by the customer getting in the cab and the cab
driver deleting his "For Hire" sign and starting his meter.

Whether or not, in the circumstances postulated, a hiring took place in
an area for which the drivers were not licensed, must, as it seems to me,
depend on what, if anything, remained to be agreed between the driver
and the customer within the licensed area. Mr Carter-Manning [on behalf
of the appellant, the DPP] was constrained to concede in the course of
his reply that, save possibly in relation to the precise destination, nothing
remained to be agreed between the customer and driver in the present case
once the discussions over the telephone between the customer and the first
Respondent [Computer Cab Company Limited – the booking company] and
the radio discussion between the first Respondent and the driver had taken
place. That latter conversation having taken place, the driver would know
where he had to pick up the customer; he would know, at least in general
terms, the area where the customer was to be taken; he would know that a
sum of a maximum amount of £2.40 could be charged, whatever was shown
on the meter, for the journey between his receipt of the call and picking up
the customer, and, having extinguished his "For Hire" sign so that he was no

longer plying for hire in the area where he was licensed to ply for hire and having started the meter, he would regard himself as not only contractually bound to the first Respondent, but also obliged to collect the customer.

In my judgment, once the position is reached where nothing further remains to be agreed between the driver and the customer within the unlicensed area, the conclusion is inescapable that the hiring took place in the area where these defendants were licensed. The inevitable consequence of that, as it seems to me, is that the cabs in the instant case were not permitted to be hired in the licensed area. The hiring had already taken place. It follows that the answer to the first question posed by the Stipendiary Magistrate, namely:

> "Whether, notwithstanding any prior booking arrangement or hiring agreement, the licensed cab driver for the purposes of Paragraph 31 of the London Cab Order 1934 permits his cab to be hired at the time and place at which he physically picks 'up the hirer?'"

is "No"; and, as to the second question, namely:

> "Was I correct in law, on the agreed facts, in dismissing the informations?"

the answer is "Yes".'

This case shows that hackney carriages can be pre-booked even when driven by a driver who holds a geographically limited suburban hackney carriage driver's licence, as the hiring takes place where the booking is accepted by the driver, not where the passenger is picked up.

[1] London Cab Order 1934, SI 1934/1346, reg 27(1)(b) – see Appendix I. The two categories of driver are referred to by TfL/LTPH as 'All London' or 'Suburban' drivers.
[2] [1996] RTR 130, QBD.
[3] SI 1934/1346.
[4] [1996] RTR 130 at 135E.

Insurance

22.31

There appears to be no difference in the position regarding private hire insurance within London from that which applies outside London[1]. It would therefore appear that TfL/LTPH can prosecute for no insurance in cases of unlawful plying for hire by a private hire vehicle, but not by a hackney carriage licensed outside London, or a suburban hackney carriage driver plying for hire outside his area.

In *R (on the application of Uber) v Transport for London*[2] it was accepted that it was not necessary for private hire vehicles within London to be insured for private hire use at all times, as when they were not being used for private hire purposes, the usual policy of insurance would suffice.

[1] For details, see Chapter 13, para 13.105 onwards.
[2] [2017] ACD 54, Admin Ct.

Transfer of private hire vehicles

22.32

If the ownership of a London private hire vehicle changes, PHV(L)A 1998, s 8(4) requires the previous owner to notify TfL/LTPH of the change, together with the name and address of the new owner, within 14 days.

SUSPENSION AND REVOCATION

22.33

PHV(L)A 1998, s 16(3) allows TfL/LTPH to suspend or revoke a London private hire vehicle licence for 'any reasonable cause' (sub-s (1)) including, but not limited to:

'(a) the licensing authority is no longer satisfied that the vehicle to which it relates is fit for use as a private hire vehicle; or

(b) the owner has failed to comply with any condition of the licence or any other obligation imposed on him by or under this Act.'

This is extremely similar to the wording of LG(MP)A 1976, s 60[1]; The procedure for suspension or revocation is detailed in PHV(L)A 1998, s 17, but it should be noted that the power to stay the effects of the suspension or revocation pending the determination of appeal against the decision under PHV(L)A 1998, s 26 can be blocked by TfL/LTPH in the interests of public safety by virtue of s 17(2).

[1] See Chapter 13, para 13.126 onwards.

Testing of vehicles

22.34

PHV(L)A 1998, s 9(1)[1] allows any constable or authorised officer of TfL/LTPH to inspect and test a London private hire vehicle. If, following an inspection or test, a constable or authorised officer is not satisfied as to the fitness of the vehicle, s 9(2) allows him to serve notice on the owner of the vehicle requiring the vehicle to be presented for further inspection and testing. It is also possible to suspend the vehicle licence in these circumstances.

[1] See Appendix I.

Exempt vehicles

22.35

PHV(L)A 1998, s 29[1] makes it clear that PHV(L)A 1998 does not apply to the use of vehicles whose use as private hire vehicles (ie in connection with a hiring for the purpose of carrying passengers or immediate availability to carry out a private hire booking) is limited to use in connection with funerals or weddings. As is the case outside London, this would appear to apply to civil partnership ceremonies as well as weddings[2].

[1]   See Appendix I.
[2]   See Chapter 12, para 12.126.

Chapter 23

Private hire drivers within London

PRIVATE HIRE DRIVERS

23.1

A private hire vehicle in London when working as a private hire vehicle must be driven by a person who holds a private hire driver's licence. If a private hire vehicle is driven by someone who does not hold a private hire driver's licence when it is working then an offence is committed under the Private Hire Vehicles (London) Act 1998, s 12.

'(1) No vehicle shall be used as a private hire vehicle on a road in London unless the driver holds a private hire vehicle driver's licence.'

Application for private hire driver's licence

23.2

The Private Hire Vehicles (London) Act 1998, s 13 governs the application for a driver's licence. It states:

'**13.— London PHV driver's licences.**

(1) Any person may apply to the licensing authority for a private hire vehicle driver's licence for London (in this Act referred to as a "London PHV driver's licence").

(2) The licensing authority shall grant a London PHV driver's licence to an applicant if the Authority is satisfied that—

(a) the applicant has attained the age of 21, is (and has for at least three years been) authorised to drive a motor car and is a fit and proper person to hold a London PHV driver's licence;

(aa) the applicant is not disqualified by reason of the applicant's immigration status from driving a private hire vehicle; and

(b) the requirement mentioned in subsection (3), and any further requirements prescribed by the licensing authority are met.

(2A) In determining for the purposes of subsection (2) whether an applicant is disqualified by reason of the applicant's immigration status from driving a private hire vehicle, the licensing authority must have regard to any guidance issued by the Secretary of State.

(3) The licensing authority shall require applicants to show to the authority's satisfaction (whether by taking a test or otherwise) that they possess a level—
(a) of knowledge of London or parts of London; and
(b) of general topographical skills,
which appears to the authority to be appropriate.

The licensing authority may impose different requirements in relation to different applicants.

(4) The licensing authority may send a copy of an application to the Commissioner of Police of the Metropolis or the Commissioner of Police for the City of London with a request for the Commissioner's observations; and the Commissioner shall respond to the request.

(5) A London PHV driver's licence—
(a) may be granted subject to such conditions as the licensing authority may think fit;
(b) shall be in such form and shall contain such particulars as the licensing authority may think fit; and
(c) subject to section 13A, shall be granted for three years or for such shorter period as the licensing authority may consider appropriate in the circumstances of the particular case.

(6) An applicant may appeal to a magistrates' court against a decision not to grant a London PHV driver's licence or against any condition to which such a licence is subject.

(7) For the purposes of subsection (2), a person is authorised to drive a motor car if—
(a) he holds a licence granted under Part III of the Road Traffic Act 1988 (other than a provisional licence) authorising him to drive a motor car; or
(b) he is authorised by virtue of section 99A(1) or 109(1) of that Act (Community licences and Northern Ireland licences) to drive a motor car in Great Britain.'

23.3

It can be seen that application is made to the 'licensing authority' (defined in the Private Hire Vehicles (London) Act 1998, s 36 as Transport for London (TfL) which administers this function through the London Taxi and Private Hire Directorate (LTPH) and TFL/LTPH is under a duty to grant a licence if it is satisfied that the criteria contained in the Private Hire Vehicles (London) Act 1998, s 13(2) and (3) have been met. The criteria are that the applicant is:

- at least 21 years' of age;
- has held a full drivers licence for at least three years;
- is a fit and proper person;
- Has the right to remain in, and work in the UK; and
- has passed the required knowledge test and has satisfied any additional requirements that have been prescribed by the licensing authority[1].

The additional requirements are contained in The Private Hire Vehicles (London PHV Driver's Licences) Regulations 2003, reg 3 and are that the applicant either holds a Group 2 licence[2] or satisfies TfL that he is medically fit to hold driver's licence[3].

[1]   See the Private Hire Vehicles (London PHV Driver's Licences) Regulations 2003, reg 3.
[2]   Regulation 3(3) defines a Group 2 licence as 'A "Group 2 licence" means a licence to driver a motor vehicle granted under Part III of the Road Traffic Act 1998 which is a Group 2 Licence as defined by regulation 70 of the Motor Vehicles (Driving Licences) Regulations 1999.'
[3]   Regulation 3(4) states: 'In assessing whether an applicant is medically fit to hold a London PHV driver's licence under paragraph 2(b), Transport for London shall have regard to the medical standards that would apply in relation to a Group 2 licence.'

R (on the application of Uber) v Transport for London

23.4

> Is a requirement for a private hire driver to have a qualification for spoken and written English reasonable? Held: Yes.

In 2016 TfL/LTPH altered the regulations to require an applicant for a drivers' licence to obtain a qualification in both spoken and written English. This was challenged by Uber in *R (on the application of Uber) v Transport for London*[1] and judgment was handed down by the High Court in March 2017 by Mitting J.
    The requirement was as follows[2]:

'3A (1) The English language requirement is hereby prescribed as a section 13(2)(b) requirement.

(2) The English language requirement is that the applicants must be able to communicate in English at or above level B1 on the Common European Framework of Reference for Languages ("CEFR").

(3) The ability to communicate in English for the purpose of this requirement includes speaking, listening reading and writing.

(4) The applicant may satisfy Transport for London with their ability to meet the requirement in regulation 3(A)(2), by providing:
(i)   A certificate from a test provider appointed by Transport for London confirming that the applicant's level of proficiency in the English language is at level B(1) on the CEFR or above, or;

(ii) Documentary evidence of a qualification whether or not the qualification was obtained in the United Kingdom on the basis of which Transport for London is satisfied that the applicant's level of proficiency in the English language is equivalent to level B(1) on the CEFR or above'.

The justification for this was detailed by the judge as follows[3]:

'The English language requirement.

11. A substantial proportion of Private Hire Vehicle drivers do not have English as a first language. Various estimates appear in the documents which it is unnecessary to cite because the parties are now agreed that it is approximately 75 per cent. The impact of the English language requirement as originally made was estimated by the Finance Department of TfL, after consulting with Mr Robinson, a senior official in the Taxi and Private Hire Department, who reported to Ms Chapman, the general manager of the department. It estimated the number of licensed private hire vehicle drivers at about 100,000, of whom in the three years 2017–2018, to 2019–2020, 16,300 would fail to satisfy the requirement; and a further number, an unknown fraction of those who would be deterred from reapplying for a licence by either the English language requirement, or by the rigorous application of the existing topographical test by TfL itself. It had been fraudulently administered by a number of private companies to which testing had been outsourced. Their total number was estimated at about 15,000. On any view, the number of licensed private hire vehicle drivers estimated to be likely to fail or to be deterred were substantial, not less than 20,000. In addition, it was estimated that there would be a significant impact on new applicants for licences. The model suggested that just under 20,000 would fail or be deterred from applying.

12. On a reasonably cautious view of the impact of the English language requirement, about 40,000 persons are at risk of being prevented from obtaining a private hire vehicle driver's licence in the 3 years 2017–2018 to 2019–2020. The figures are taken from TB/100/18490.

13. They have been borne out by events. Of the applicants who have taken the B(1) CEFR test administered by Trinity College London, in the 3 months, October to December 2016, 45 per cent have failed and 55 per cent have passed, TB/150/1736–7.'

The impact of such a requirement was considered:

'14. It is common ground that a measure which has had and will have such an impact on so many people must be strictly justified. European Union law is engaged in two ways: because the English language requirement affects the right of EEA nationals to "take up and pursue activities as selfemployed persons" under Article 49 of the Treaty on the Functioning of the European Union; and, because they discriminate indirectly against non UK nationals whose first language is not English, Article 2 of Council Directive 2000/431/EC of 29th June 2000 is engaged.

It provides:

"(1) For the purposes of this Directive, the principle of equal treatment shall mean that there shall be no direct or indirect discrimination based on racial or ethnic origin

(b) Indirect discrimination shall be taken to occur where an apparently neutral provision, criterion or practice would put persons of a racial or ethnic origin at a particular disadvantage compared with other persons, unless that provision, criterion or practice is objectively justified by a legitimate aim and the means of achieving that aim are appropriate and necessary."

Article 3 deals with the scope of measure:

"(1) Within the limits of the powers conferred upon the Community, the Directive shall apply to all persons as regards both the public and private sectors including public bodies in relation to:

(a) conditions for access to employment, to selfemployment and to occupation, including selection criteria and recruitment conditions whatever the branch of activity and at all levels of the professional hierarchy, including promotion."

15. Effect is given to this Directive by section 19 of the Equality Act 2010, which provides:

"(1) A person (A) discriminates against another (B) if (A) applies to (B) a provision, criterion or practice which is discriminatory in relation to a relevant protected characteristic of (B's).

(2) For the purpose of subsection (1) a provision, criterion or practice is discriminatory in relation to a relevant protected characteristic of (B's), if:

(a) (A) applies, or would apply it to persons with whom (B) does not share the characteristic.
(b) It puts or would put persons with whom (B) shares the characteristic at a particular disadvantage, when compared with persons with whom B does not share it.
(c) It puts or would put (B) at a disadvantage.
(d) (A) cannot show it to be a proportionate means of achieving a legitimate aim."

The relevant protected characteristics include race, which, by virtue of section 9(1) includes nationality and ethnic or national origins.'

The question hinged on whether this requirement was a proportionate response to the problem, and whether it could have been achieved by a less onerous method[4]. Those tests:

'18. ... requires TfL to identify the public interest in question and the level of protection which it has determined is necessary to protect that interest and to demonstrate that the required level of protection could not be attained by less restrictive means.'

It was argued by TfL that the public interest concerned the safety, welfare and convenience of passengers, and to protect that, a driver must have:

'a sufficient command of spoken English to be able to understand their requirements, including those arising unexpectedly, for example, in a medical emergency; to discuss a route or fare with them, and to explain safety requirements to them; and of written English, to understand regulatory communications to them, and traffic and other information supplied to them by TfL.'[5]

The judge was satisfied that the requirement was within the margin of appreciation (ie, the restriction allowed within Human Rights law) and the only question was whether there was a less onerous means of achieving the legitimate aim. TfL had adopted B(1) on the Common European Framework of Reference for Languages ('CEFR') as the appropriate standard. It was argued that this did not equip a driver to deal with regulatory documents issued by TfL, but the judge took the view that it would enable them to develop their language skills. In the absence of a written and spoken English test designed for taxi drivers, the judge took the view that this was a reasonable requirement. His conclusion was as follows[6]:

'27. In my judgment, TfL have demonstrated that they were and are entitled to require drivers to demonstrate that level of competence in written as well as spoken English. There is now and for the foreseeable future no practicable alternative means of achieving the protection of the legitimate public interests which TfL have identified to the level properly set by them. In reaching that conclusion, I have not found the Central Government requirement for "public facing" officials to have a sufficient command of spoken English only to deal with a comparable set of circumstances. For the reasons explained, drivers must do more than converse with passengers and understand spoken English.'

Accordingly, the requirement to obtain this qualification is a reasonable one.

[1]   (3 March 2017, unreported), Admin Ct. At the time of writing (August 2017), an appeal to the Court of Appeal is pending.
[2]   At para 9.
[3]   Paragraph 11 onwards.
[4]   See para 16.
[5]   Above at para 19.
[6]   Above at para 27

DBS Checks

23.5

Although the Private Hire Vehicles (London) Act 1998, s 13(4) refers to a request being made for the police commissioner's observations in relation to the applicant, this would appear to have been superseded by the use of the Disclosure and Barring Service (DBS)[1].

[1]   See Chapter 14, para 14.9 and Chapter 10, para 10.23 onwards.

23.6

Conditions can be imposed on the licence (Private Hire Vehicles (London) Act 1998, s 13(5)(a)) although the Private Vehicles (London PHV Driver's Licences) Regulations 2003 do not prescribe any standard conditions[1]. The licence can be in such form as TFL/LTPH think fit and can be granted for up to three years.

[1]   This can be contrasted with the position in relation to private hire vehicle licences where the Private Vehicles (London PHV Licences) Regulations 2004 prescribe standard conditions in reg 4 and Sch 2. See Appendix I.

23.7

There is a right of appeal under the Private Hire Vehicles (London) Act 1998, s 13(6) to the magistrates' court against either a refusal to grant a licence or any condition attached to the licence.

Drivers' badges

23.8

As with London hackney carriage drivers, a badge will be issued and the design can be prescribed by TFL/LTPH (see the Private Hire Vehicles (London) Act 1998, s 14(1) and (2))[1].

[1]   See The Private Hire Vehicles (London PHV Driver's Licences) Regulations 2003, reg 4. See Appendix I.

23.9

It is a requirement that when the driver is driving a private hire vehicle which is being used as a private hire vehicle he must wear the badge so that it is plainly and distinctly visible, he must produce the badge for inspection if requested by any person (Private Hire Vehicles (London) Act 1998, s 14(3) and failure to comply with that requirement is an offence by virtue of s 14(5)).

23.10

There is one exception to the requirement for a London private hire driver to wear a badge. By virtue of the Private Hire Vehicles (London) Act 1998, s 14(4) it is possible for TFL/LTPH to issue a notice which excepts a person from having to wear the badge if the vehicle concerned is being used 'to provide a service specified in the notice' and TfL/LTPH 'considers it inappropriate (having regard to that service) to require the badge to be worn'.

'(4) The licensing authority may by notice exempt a person from the requirement under subsection (3)(a), when he is the driver of a vehicle being used to provide a service specified in the notice if the authority considers it inappropriate (having regard to that service) to require the badge to be worn.'

SUSPENSION OR REVOCATION OF LICENCES

23.11

TfL/LTPH can suspend or revoke a driver's licence for one of the reasons contained in the Private Hire Vehicles (London) Act 1998, s 16(4).

'(4) A London PHV driver's licence may be suspended or revoked where—

(a)   the licence holder has, since the grant of the licence, been convicted of an offence involving dishonesty, indecency or violence;

(aa) the licence holder has, since the grant of the licence, been convicted of an immigration offence or required to pay an immigration penalty;

(b)   the licensing authority is for any other reason no longer satisfied that the licence holder is fit to hold such a licence; or

(c)   the licence holder has failed to comply with any condition of the licence or any other obligation imposed on him by or under this Act.

(5) Subsection (4)(aa) does not apply if—

(a)   in a case where the licence holder has been convicted of an immigration offence, the conviction is a spent conviction within the meaning of the Rehabilitation of Offenders Act 1974, or

(b)   in a case where the licence holder has been required to pay an immigration penalty—

(i)   more than three years have elapsed since the date on which the penalty was imposed, and

(ii)   the amount of the penalty has been paid in full.'

23.12

The procedure is detailed in the Private Hire Vehicles (London) Act 1998, s 17[1].

[1]   See Chapter 15, para 15.16 onwards.

Drivers' hours

23.13

There are no direct controls over the hours that a private hire driver can work[1]. However, the Working Time Regulations 1998[2] as amended applies to private hire drivers. Regulation 18 was amended by the Working Time (Amendment) Regulations 2003[3] with effect from 1 August 2003, and limits a driver's working week to 48 hours, averaged over a 17-week period.

[1]   This can be contrasted with HGV and PSV drivers whose driving hours are regulated. There have been suggestions that private hire drivers' hours should be limited, but at present nothing has been formally proposed.

2   SI 1998/1833.
3   SI 2003/1684.

23.14

This only applies to drivers who are employed and working under a contract of employment and does not apply to self employed drivers. It is therefore of limited application in relation to the private hire trade, where the vast majority of drivers are self employed.

23.15

In relation to those who are employed, they can opt out of the application of the Regulations by agreeing in writing that they should not apply in accordance with reg 4(1) (this must be voluntary and the driver cannot be forced to opt out by the employer).

23.16

An authorised officer or police constable can at any time require a private hire driver to produce his licence for inspection (Private Hire Vehicles (London) Act 1998, s 21(1))[1]. If the person cannot produce the licence forthwith (s 21(3)) then it can be produced at a police station if the request was made by a police constable or at a place specified by the authorised officer in other cases. In both situations it must be produced within six days. Failure to comply is an offence by virtue of s 21(4).

1   See Appendix I.

23.17

If the licence expires or has been revoked (Private Hire Vehicles (London) Act 1998, s 22(3))[1], or the driver loses the right to remain or work in the UK (Private Hire Vehicles (London) Act 1998, s 13A(6))[2], then the holder should return it to TFL/LTPH within seven days of the date of expiry or revocation. If the licence has been suspended, it must be returned within seven days of the date on which the notice of suspension was served on the individual and this can include return of the badge (s 22(4)).

1   See Appendix I.
2   See Appendix I.

23.18

The name of the licensee[1], together with the number and the date of grant and expiry and any other provisions that may be prescribed by regulation must be maintained in a register which is available for free public inspection. These provisions are contained within the Private Hire Vehicles (London) Act 1998, s 23[2].

1   TfL can only disclose the address to a person 'if it appears to the authority that the person has
     a sufficient reason for requiring that information' (Private Hire Vehicles (London) Act 1998,
     s 23(4)).
2   See Appendix I.

Legislation

Part A – Legislation applicable both outside and within London

Part B – Legislation applicable outside London

Part C – Legislation applicable within London

Byelaws

Part A – Legislation applicable both outside and within London

A1.1

Public Health Act 1925

Part VIII
Miscellaneous

76 As to public vehicles taken at railway stations In any area within which the provisions of the Town Police Clauses Act 1847 with respect to hackney carriages are in force, those provisions and any byelaws of the local authority with respect to hackney carriages shall be as fully applicable in all respects to hackney carriages standing or plying for hire at any railway station or railway premises within such area, as if such railway station or railway premises were a stand for hackney carriages or a street:

Provided that—
  (a) the provisions of this section shall not apply to any vehicle belonging to or used by any railway company for the purpose of carrying passengers and their luggage to or from any of their railway stations or railway premises, or to the driver or conductor of such vehicle;
  (b) nothing in this section shall empower the local authority to fix the site of the stand or starting place of any hackney carriage in any railway station or railway premises, or in any yard belonging to a railway company, except with the consent of that company.

Rehabilitation of Offenders Act 1974

1 Rehabilitated persons and spent convictions (1) Subject to [subsections (2), (5) and (6)] below, where an individual has been convicted, whether before or after the commencement of this Act, of any offence or offences, and the following conditions are satisfied, that is to say—

(a) he did not have imposed on him in respect of that conviction a sentence which is excluded from rehabilitation under this Act; and

(b) he has not had imposed on him in respect of a subsequent conviction during the rehabilitation period applicable to the first-mentioned conviction in accordance with section 6 below a sentence which is excluded from rehabilitation under this Act;

then, after the end of the rehabilitation period so applicable (including, where appropriate, any extension under section 6(4) below of the period originally applicable to the first-mentioned conviction) or, where that rehabilitation period ended before the commencement of this Act, after the commencement of this Act, that individual shall for the purposes of this Act be treated as a rehabilitated person in respect of the first-mentioned conviction and that conviction shall for those purposes be treated as spent.

(2) A person shall not become a rehabilitated person for the purposes of this Act in respect of a conviction unless he has served or otherwise undergone or complied with any sentence imposed on him in respect of that conviction; but the following shall not, by virtue of this subsection, prevent a person from becoming a rehabilitated person for those purposes—

(a) failure to pay a fine or other sum adjudged to be paid by or imposed on a conviction, or breach of a condition of a recognisance or of a bond of caution to keep the peace or be of good behaviour;

(b) breach of any condition or requirement applicable in relation to a sentence which renders the person to whom it applies liable to be dealt with for the offence for which the sentence was imposed, or, where the sentence was a suspended sentence of imprisonment, liable to be dealt with in respect of that sentence (whether or not, in any case, he is in fact so dealt with);

(c) failure to comply with any requirement of a suspended sentence supervision order.

[(2A) Where in respect of a conviction a person has been sentenced to imprisonment with an order under section 47(1) of the Criminal Law Act 1977, he is to be treated for the purposes of subsection (2) above as having served the sentence as soon as he completes service of so much of the sentence as was by that order required to be served in prison.]

[(2B) In subsection (2)(a) above the reference to a fine or other sum adjudged to be paid by or imposed on a conviction does not include a reference to an amount payable under a confiscation order made under Part 2 or 3 of the Proceeds of Crime Act 2002.]

(3) In this Act "sentence" includes any order made by a court in dealing with a person in respect of his conviction of any offence or offences, other than—

[(za) a surcharge imposed under section 161A of the Criminal Justice Act 2003;]

(a) an order for committal or any other order made in default of payment of any fine or other sum adjudged to be paid by or imposed on a conviction, or for want of sufficient distress to satisfy any such fine or other sum;

(b) an order dealing with a person in respect of a suspended sentence of imprisonment;

[(c) an order under section 21A of the Prosecution of Offences Act 1985 (criminal courts charge).]

[(3A) In subsection (3)(a), the reference to want of sufficient distress to satisfy a fine or other sum includes a reference to circumstances where—

(a) there is power to use the procedure in Schedule 12 to the Tribunals, Courts and Enforcement Act 2007 to recover the fine or other sum from a person, but

(b) it appears, after an attempt has been made to exercise the power, that the person's goods are insufficient to pay the amount outstanding (as defined by paragraph 50(3) of that Schedule).]

(4) In this Act, references to a conviction, however expressed, include references—

(a) to a conviction by or before a court outside [England and Wales]; and

(b) to any finding (other than a finding linked with a finding of insanity) in any criminal proceedings . . . that a person has committed an offence or done the act or made the omission charged;

and notwithstanding anything in section 9 of the Criminal Justice (Scotland) Act 1949 or [section 14 of the Powers of Criminal Courts (Sentencing) Act 2000] [or section 187 of the Armed Forces Act 2006] (conviction of a person . . . discharged to be deemed not to be a conviction) a conviction in respect of which an order is made [discharging the person concerned] absolutely or conditionally shall be treated as a conviction for the purposes of this Act and the person in question may become a rehabilitated person in respect of that conviction and the conviction a spent conviction for those purposes accordingly.

[(5) This Act does not apply to any disregarded conviction or caution within the meaning of Chapter 4 of Part 5 of the Protection of Freedoms Act 2012.

(6) Accordingly, references in this Act to a conviction or caution do not include references to any such disregarded conviction or caution.]

Amendment

Sub-s (1): words "subsections (2), (5) and (6)" in square brackets substituted by Protection of Freedoms Act 2012, s 115(1), Sch 9, para 134(1), (2).

Sub-s (2A): inserted by the Criminal Law Act 1977, s 47, Sch 9, para 11.

Sub-s (2B): inserted by the Proceeds of Crime Act 2002, s 456, Sch 11, paras 1, 7.

Sub-s (3): para (za) inserted by the Domestic Violence, Crime and Victims Act 2004, s 58(1), Sch 10, para 9.

Sub-s (3): para (c) inserted by Criminal Justice and Courts Act 2015, s 54(3), Sch 12, para 1.

Sub-s (3A): inserted by the Tribunals, Courts and Enforcement Act 2007, s 62(3), Sch 13, para 38.

Sub-s (4): in para (a) words "England and Wales" in square brackets substituted by the Legal Aid, Sentencing and Punishment of Offenders Act 2012, s 141(10), Sch 25, paras 1, 2.

Sub-s (4): in para (b) words omitted repealed by the Children Act 1989, s 108(7), Sch 15.

Sub-s (4): words "section 247 of the Criminal Procedure (Scotland) Act 1995 (c.46)" in square brackets substituted by the Criminal Justice and Licensing (Scotland) Act 2010, s 24(1).

Sub-s (4): words "section 14 of the Powers of Criminal Courts (Sentencing) Act 2000" in square brackets substituted by the Powers of Criminal Courts (Sentencing) Act 2000, ss 165(1), 167(1), Sch 9, para 47.

Sub-s (4): words "or section 187 of the Armed Forces Act 2006" in square brackets prospectively inserted by the Armed Forces Act 2006, s 378(1), Sch 16, para 63.

Sub-s (4): second words omitted repealed by the Criminal Justice Act 1991, ss 100, 101(2), Sch 11, para 20(b), Sch 13.

Sub-s (4): words "discharging the person concerned" in square brackets substituted by the Criminal Justice Act 1991, s 100, Sch 11, para 20(c).

Sub-ss (5), (6): inserted by Protection of Freedoms Act 2012, s 115(1), Sch 9, para 134(1), (3).

2 Rehabilitation of persons dealt with in service disciplinary proceedings (1) . . . , for the purposes of this Act any finding that a person is guilty of an offence in respect of any act or omission which was the subject of service disciplinary proceedings shall be treated as a conviction and any punishment awarded [or order made by virtue of Schedule 5A to the Army Act 1955 or the Air Force Act 1955 or Schedule 4A to the Naval Discipline Act 1957] in respect of any such finding shall be treated as a sentence.

(2)–(4) . . .

(5) In this Act, "service disciplinary proceedings" means any of the following—
   [(za) any proceedings (whether or not before a court) in respect of a service offence within the meaning of the Armed Forces Act 2006 (except proceedings before a civilian court within the meaning of that Act);]
   (a) any proceedings under the Army Act 1955, the Air Force Act 1955, or the Naval Discipline Act 1957 (whether before a court-martial or before any other court or person authorised thereunder to award a punishment in respect of any offence);
   (b) any proceedings under any Act previously in force corresponding to any of the Acts mentioned in paragraph (a) above;
   [(bb) any proceedings before a Standing Civilian Court established under the Armed Forces Act 1976;]

(c) any proceedings under any corresponding enactment or law applying to a force, other than a home force, to which section 4 of the Visiting Forces (British Commonwealth) Act 1933 applies or applied at the time of the proceedings, being proceedings in respect of a member of a home force who is or was at that time attached to the first-mentioned force under that section;

whether in any event those proceedings take place in [England and Wales] or elsewhere.

[(6) Section 376(1) to (3) of the Armed Forces Act 2006 ("conviction" and "sentence" in relation to summary hearings and the SAC) apply for the purposes of this Act as they apply for the purposes of that Act.]

Amendment
Sub-s (1): words omitted repealed by the Armed Forces Act 1996, s 35(2), Sch 7, Part III; words "or order made by virtue of Schedule 5A to the Army Act 1955 or the Air Force Act 1955 or Schedule 4A to the Naval Discipline Act 1957" in square brackets inserted by the Armed Forces Act 1976, s 22(5), Sch 9, para 20(1).
Sub-ss (2)–(4): repealed by the Armed Forces Act 1996, ss 13(2), (6), 35(2), Sch 7, Part III.
Sub-s (5): para (za) inserted by the Armed Forces Act 2006, s 378(1), Sch 16, para 64(a).
Sub-s (5): para (bb) inserted by the Armed Forces Act 1976, s 22(5), Sch 9, para 20(3).
Sub-s (5): words "England and Wales" in square brackets substituted by the Legal Aid, Sentencing and Punishment of Offenders Act 2012, s 141(10), Sch 25, paras 1, 3.
Sub-s (6): inserted by the Armed Forces Act 2006, s 378(1), Sch 16, para 64(b).

3 Special provision with respect to certain disposals by children's hearings under the Social Work (Scotland) Act 1968 Where a ground for the referral of a child's case to a children's hearing under the Social Work (Scotland) Act 1968 is that mentioned in section 32(2)(g) of that Act (commission by the child of an offence) and that ground has either been accepted by the child and, where necessary, by his parent or been established to the satisfaction of the sheriff under section 42 of that Act, the acceptance or establishment of that ground shall be treated for the purposes of this Act (but not otherwise) as a conviction, and any disposal of the case thereafter by a children's hearing shall be treated for those purposes as a sentence; and references in this Act to a person's being charged with or prosecuted for an offence shall be construed accordingly.

4 Effect of rehabilitation (1) Subject to sections 7 and 8 below, a person who has become a rehabilitated person for the purposes of this Act in respect of a conviction shall be treated for all purposes in law as a person who has not committed or been charged with or prosecuted for or convicted of or sentenced for the offence or offences which were the subject of that conviction; and, notwithstanding the provisions of any other enactment or rule of law to the contrary, but subject as aforesaid—
(a) no evidence shall be admissible in any proceedings before a judicial authority exercising its jurisdiction or functions in [England and Wales] to prove that any such person has committed or been charged with or

prosecuted for or convicted of or sentenced for any offence which was the subject of a spent conviction; and

(b) a person shall not, in any such proceedings, be asked, and, if asked, shall not be required to answer, any question relating to his past which cannot be answered without acknowledging or referring to a spent conviction or spent convictions or any circumstances ancillary thereto.

(2) Subject to the provisions of any order made under subsection (4) below, where a question seeking information with respect to a person's previous convictions, offences, conduct or circumstances is put to him or to any other person otherwise than in proceedings before a judicial authority—

(a) the question shall be treated as not relating to spent convictions or to any circumstances ancillary to spent convictions, and the answer thereto may be framed accordingly; and

(b) the person questioned shall not be subjected to any liability or otherwise prejudiced in law by reason of any failure to acknowledge or disclose a spent conviction or any circumstances ancillary to a spent conviction in his answer to the question.

(3) Subject to the provisions of any order made under subsection (4) below,—

(a) any obligation imposed on any person by any rule of law or by the provisions of any agreement or arrangement to disclose any matters to any other person shall not extend to requiring him to disclose a spent conviction or any circumstances ancillary to a spent conviction (whether the conviction is his own or another's); and

(b) a conviction which has become spent or any circumstances ancillary thereto, or any failure to disclose a spent conviction or any such circumstances, shall not be a proper ground for dismissing or excluding a person from any office, profession, occupation or employment, or for prejudicing him in any way in any occupation or employment.

(4) The Secretary of State may by order—

(a) make such provisions as seems to him appropriate for excluding or modifying the application of either or both of paragraphs (*a*) and (*b*) of subsection (2) above in relation to questions put in such circumstances as may be specified in the order;

(b) provide for such exceptions from the provisions of subsection (3) above as seem to him appropriate, in such cases or classes of case, and in relation to convictions of such a description, as may be specified in the order.

(5) For the purposes of this section and section 7 below any of the following are circumstances ancillary to a conviction, that is to say—

(a) the offence or offences which were the subject of that conviction;

(b) the conduct constituting that offence or those offences; and

(c) any process or proceedings preliminary to that conviction, any sentence imposed in respect of that conviction, any proceedings (whether by way of appeal or otherwise) for reviewing that conviction or any such sentence, and anything done in pursuance of or undergone in compliance with any such sentence.

(6) For the purposes of this section and section 7 below "proceedings before a judicial authority" includes, in addition to proceedings before any of the ordinary courts of law, proceedings before any tribunal, body or person having power—

(a) by virtue of any enactment, law, custom or practice;

(b) under the rules governing any association, institution, profession, occupation or employment; or

(c) under any provision of an agreement providing for arbitration with respect to questions arising thereunder;

to determine any question affecting the rights, privileges, obligations or liabilities of any person, or to receive evidence affecting the determination of any such question.

Amendment

Sub-s (1): in para (a) words "England and Wales" in square brackets substituted by the Legal Aid, Sentencing and Punishment of Offenders Act 2012, s 141(10), Sch 25, paras 1, 5.

5 Rehabilitation periods for particular sentences (1) The sentences excluded from rehabilitation under this Act are—

(a) a sentence of imprisonment for life;

(b) a sentence of imprisonment[, youth custody][, detention in a young offender institution] or corrective training for a term exceeding [forty eight months];

(c) a sentence of preventive detention; . . .

(d) a sentence of detention during Her Majesty's pleasure or for life [under section 90 or 91 of the Powers of Criminal Courts (Sentencing) Act 2000], [or under section 209 or 218 of the Armed Forces Act 2006,] [or under section 205(2) or (3) of the Criminal Procedure (Scotland) Act 1975,] [or a sentence of detention for a term exceeding [forty eight months] passed under section 91 of the said Act of 2000] [or section 209 of the said Act of 2006] [(young offenders convicted of grave crimes) or under section 206 of the said Act of 1975 (detention of children convicted on indictment)] [or a corresponding court-martial punishment];

[(da) a youth rehabilitation order under Part 1 of the Criminal Justice and Immigration Act 2008;]

[(e) a sentence of custody for life][; and]

[(f) a sentence of imprisonment for public protection under section 225 of the Criminal Justice Act 2003, a sentence of detention for public protection under section 226 of that Act or an extended sentence under section [226A, 226B,] 227 or 228 of that Act [(including any sentence within this paragraph passed as a result of any of sections 219 to 222 of the Armed Forces Act 2006)]]

and any other sentence is a sentence subject to rehabilitation under this Act.

[[(1A) In [this section]—

(a) references to section 209 of the Armed Forces Act 2006 include references to section 71A(4) of the Army Act 1955 or Air Force Act 1955 or section 43A(4) of the Naval Discipline Act 1957;

(b) the reference to section 218 of the Armed Forces Act 2006 includes a reference to section 71A(3) of the Army Act 1955 or Air Force Act 1955 or section 43A(3) of the Naval Discipline Act 1957.]]

[(2) For the purposes of this Act and subject to subsections (3) and (4), the rehabilitation period for a sentence is the period—

(a) beginning with the date of the conviction in respect of which the sentence is imposed, and

(b) ending at the time listed in the following Table in relation to that sentence:

Sentence	End of rehabilitation period for adult offenders	End of rehabilitation period for offenders under 18 at date of conviction
A custodial sentence of more than 30 months and up to, or consisting of, 48 months	The end of the period of 7 years beginning with the day on which the sentence (including any licence period) is completed	The end of the period of 42 months beginning with the day on which the sentence (including any licence period) is completed
A custodial sentence of more than 6 months and up to, or consisting of, 30 months	The end of the period of 48 months beginning with the day on which the sentence (including any licence period) is completed	The end of the period of 24 months beginning with the day on which the sentence (including any licence period) is completed
A custodial sentence of 6 months or less	The end of the period of 24 months beginning with the day on which the sentence (including any licence period) is completed	The end of the period of 18 months beginning with the day on which the sentence (including any licence period) is completed
Removal from Her Majesty's service	The end of the period of 12 months beginning with the date of the conviction in respect of which the sentence is imposed	The end of the period of 6 months beginning with the date of the conviction in respect of which the sentence is imposed
A sentence of service detention	The end of the period of 12 months beginning with the day on which the sentence is completed	The end of the period of 6 months beginning with the day on which the sentence is completed
A fine	The end of the period of 12 months beginning with the date of the conviction in respect of which the sentence is imposed	The end of the period of 6 months beginning with the date of the conviction in respect of which the sentence is imposed
A compensation order	The date on which the payment is made in full	The date on which the payment is made in full

Sentence	End of rehabilitation period for adult offenders	End of rehabilitation period for offenders under 18 at date of conviction
A community or youth rehabilitation order	The end of the period of 12 months beginning with the day provided for by or under the order as the last day on which the order is to have effect	The end of the period of 6 months beginning with the day provided for by or under the order as the last day on which the order is to have effect
A relevant order	The day provided for by or under the order as the last day on which the order is to have effect	The day provided for by or under the order as the last day on which the order is to have effect

(3) Where no provision is made by or under a community or youth rehabilitation order or a relevant order for the last day on which the order is to have effect, the rehabilitation period for the order is to be the period of 24 months beginning with the date of conviction.

(4) There is no rehabilitation period for—
    (a) an order discharging a person absolutely for an offence, or
    (b) any other sentence in respect of a conviction where the sentence is not dealt with in the Table or under subsection (3),

and, in such cases, references in this Act to any rehabilitation period are to be read as if the period of time were nil.

(5) See also—
    (a) section 8AA (protection afforded to spent alternatives to prosecution), and
    (b) Schedule 2 (protection for spent cautions).

(6) The Secretary of State may by order amend column 2 or 3 of the Table or the number of months for the time being specified in subsection (3).

(7) For the purposes of this section—
    (a) consecutive terms of imprisonment or other custodial sentences are to be treated as a single term,
    (b) terms of imprisonment or other custodial sentences which are wholly or partly concurrent (that is terms of imprisonment or other custodial sentences imposed in respect of offences of which a person was convicted in the same proceedings) are to be treated as a single term,
    (c) no account is to be taken of any subsequent variation, made by a court dealing with a person in respect of a suspended sentence of imprisonment, of the term originally imposed,
    (d) no account is to be taken of any subsequent variation of the day originally provided for by or under an order as the last day on which the order is to have effect,
    (e) no account is to be taken of any detention or supervision ordered by a court under section 104(3) of the Powers of Criminal Courts (Sentencing) Act 2000,

(f) a sentence imposed by a court outside England and Wales is to be treated as the sentence mentioned in this section to which it most closely corresponds.

(8) In this section—

"community or youth rehabilitation order" means—

(a) a community order under section 177 of the Criminal Justice Act 2003,

(b) a service community order or overseas community order under the Armed Forces Act 2006,

(c) a youth rehabilitation order under Part 1 of the Criminal Justice and Immigration Act 2008, or

(d) any order of a kind superseded (whether directly or indirectly) by an order mentioned in paragraph (a), (b) or (c),

"custodial sentence" means—

(a) a sentence of imprisonment,

(b) a sentence of detention in a young offender institution,

(c) a sentence of Borstal training,

(d) a sentence of youth custody,

(e) a sentence of corrective training,

(f) a sentence of detention under section 91 of the Powers of Criminal Courts (Sentencing) Act 2000 or section 209 of the Armed Forces Act 2006,

(g) a detention and training order under section 100 of the Powers of Criminal Courts (Sentencing) Act 2000 or an order under section 211 of the Armed Forces Act 2006,

(h) any sentence of a kind superseded (whether directly or indirectly) by a sentence mentioned in paragraph (f) or (g),

"earlier statutory order" means—

(a) an order under section 54 of the Children and Young Persons Act 1933 committing the person convicted to custody in a remand home,

(b) an approved school order under section 57 of that Act, or

(c) any order of a kind superseded (whether directly or indirectly) by an order mentioned in any of paragraphs (c) to (e) of the definition of "relevant order" or in paragraph (a) or (b) above,

"relevant order" means—

(a) an order discharging a person conditionally for an offence,

(b) an order binding a person over to keep the peace or be of good behaviour,

(c) an order under section 1(2A) of the Street Offences Act 1959,

(d) a hospital order under Part 3 of the Mental Health Act 1983 (with or without a restriction order),

(e) a referral order under section 16 of the Powers of Criminal Courts (Sentencing) Act 2000,

(f) an earlier statutory order, or

(g) any order which imposes a disqualification, disability, prohibition or other penalty and is not otherwise dealt with in the Table or under subsection (3),

but does not include a reparation order under section 73 of the Powers of Criminal Courts (Sentencing) Act 2000,

"removal from Her Majesty's service" means a sentence of dismissal with disgrace from Her Majesty's service, a sentence of dismissal from Her Majesty's service or a sentence of cashiering or discharge with ignominy,

"sentence of imprisonment" includes a sentence of penal servitude (and "term of imprisonment" is to be read accordingly),

"sentence of service detention" means—

(a) a sentence of service detention (within the meaning given by section 374 of the Armed Forces Act 2006), or a sentence of detention corresponding to such a sentence, in respect of a conviction in service disciplinary proceedings, or

(b) any sentence of a kind superseded (whether directly or indirectly) by a sentence mentioned in paragraph (a).]

Amendment

Sub-s (1): in para (b) words ", youth custody" in square brackets inserted by the Criminal Justice Act 1982, s 77, Sch 14, para 36(a).

Sub-s (1): in para (b) words "detention in a young offender institution" in square brackets inserted by the Criminal Justice Act 1988, s 123(6), Sch 8, para 9(a).

Sub-s (1): in para (b) words "forty eight months" in square brackets substituted by the Legal Aid, Sentencing and Punishment of Offenders Act 2012, s 139(1), (2).

Sub-s (1): in para (c) word omitted repealed by the Criminal Justice Act 1982, s 78, Sch 16.

Sub-s (1): in para (d) words "under section 90 or 91 of the Powers of Criminal Courts (Sentencing) Act 2000" in square brackets inserted by the Powers of Criminal Courts (Sentencing) Act 2000, s 165(1), Sch 9, para 48(1), (2)(a).

Sub-s (1): in para (d) words "or under section 209 or 218 of the Armed Forces Act 2006," in square brackets inserted by the Armed Forces Act 2006, s 378(1), Sch 16, para 65(1), (2)(a)(i).

Sub-s (1): in para (d) words "or under section 205(2) or (3) of the Criminal Procedure (Scotland) Act 1975," in square brackets inserted by the Criminal Justice (Scotland) Act 1980, s 83(2), Sch 7, para 24(a)(i).

Sub-s (1): in para (d) words from "or a sentence of detention" to "the said Act of 2000" in square brackets substituted by the Powers of Criminal Courts (Sentencing) Act 2000, s 165(1), Sch 9, para 48(1), (2)(b).

Sub-s (1): in para (d) words "forty eight months" in square brackets substituted by the Legal Aid, Sentencing and Punishment of Offenders Act 2012, s 139(1), (2).

Sub-s (1): in para (d) words "or section 209 of the said Act of 2006" in square brackets inserted by the Armed Forces Act 2006, s 378(1), Sch 16, para 65(1), (2)(a)(ii).

Sub-s (1): in para (d) words from "(young offenders convicted of grave crimes)" to "children convicted on indictment)" in square brackets substituted by the Criminal Justice (Scotland) Act 1980, s 83(2), Sch 7, para 24(a)(ii).

Sub-s (1): in para (d) words "or a corresponding court-martial punishment" in square brackets inserted by the Armed Forces Act 1976, s 22, Sch 9, para 20(4).

Sub-s (1): in para (d) words "or a corresponding court-martial punishment" in italics repealed by the Armed Forces Act 2006, s 378, Sch 16, para 65(1), (2)(a)(iii), Sch 17.

Sub-s (1): para (e) inserted by the Criminal Justice Act 1982, s 77, Sch 14, para 36(b).

Sub-s (1): in para (e) word "; and" in square brackets inserted by the Criminal Justice Act 2003, s 304, Sch 32, Pt 1, para 18(1), (2)(a).

Sub-s (1): para (f) inserted by the Criminal Justice Act 2003, s 304, Sch 32, Pt 1, para 18(1), (2)(b).

Sub-s (1): in para (f) words "226A, 226B," in square brackets inserted by the Legal Aid, Sentencing and Punishment of Offenders Act 2012, s 126, Sch 21, para 2.

Sub-s (1): in para (f) words from "(including any sentence" to "Armed Forces Act 2006)" in square brackets inserted by the Armed Forces Act 2006, s 378(1), Sch 16, para 65(1), (2)(b).

Sub-s (1A): inserted by the Armed Forces Act 1976, s 22, Sch 9, para 20(5).

Sub-s (1A): substituted by the Armed Forces Act 2006, s 378(1), Sch 16, para 65(1), (3).

Sub-s (1A): words "this section" in square brackets substituted by the Legal Aid, Sentencing and Punishment of Offenders Act 2012, s 139(1), (3).

Sub-ss (2)–(8): substituted for sub-ss (2)–(10) by the Legal Aid, Sentencing and Punishment of Offenders Act 2012, s 139(1), (4).

6 The rehabilitation period applicable to a conviction (1) Where only one sentence is imposed in respect of a conviction (not being a sentence excluded from rehabilitation under this Act) the rehabilitation period applicable to the conviction is, subject to the following provisions of this section, the period applicable to the sentence in accordance with section 5 above.

(2) Where more than one sentence is imposed in respect of a conviction (whether or not in the same proceedings) and none of the sentences imposed is excluded from rehabilitation under this Act, then, subject to the following provisions of this section, if the periods applicable to those sentences in accordance with section 5 above differ, the rehabilitation period applicable to the conviction shall be the longer or the longest (as the case may be) of those periods.

(3) Without prejudice to subsection (2) above, where in respect of a conviction a person was conditionally discharged or [a probation order was made] and after the end of the rehabilitation period applicable to the conviction in accordance with subsection (1) or (2) above he is dealt with, in consequence of a breach of conditional discharge [or a breach of the order], for the offence for which the order for conditional discharge or probation order was made, then, if the rehabilitation period applicable to the conviction in accordance with subsection (2) above (taking into account any sentence imposed when he is so dealt with) ends later than the rehabilitation period previously applicable to the conviction, he shall be treated for the purposes of this Act as not having become a rehabilitated person in respect of that conviction, and the conviction shall for those purposes be treated as not having become spent, in relation to any period falling before the end of the new rehabilitation period.

[(3A) Without prejudice to subsection (2), where—
 (a) an order is made under section 1(2A) of the Street Offences Act 1959 in respect of a conviction,
 (b) after the end of the rehabilitation period applicable to the conviction the offender is dealt with again for the offence for which that order was made, and

(c) the rehabilitation period applicable to the conviction in accordance with subsection (2) (taking into account any sentence imposed when so dealing with the offender) ends later than the rehabilitation period previously applicable to the conviction,

the offender shall be treated for the purposes of this Act as not having become a rehabilitated person in respect of that conviction, and that conviction shall for those purposes be treated as not having become spent, in relation to any period falling before the end of the new rehabilitation period.]

(4) Subject to subsection (5) below, where during the rehabilitation period applicable to a conviction—
    (a) the person convicted is convicted of a further offence; and
    (b) no sentence excluded from rehabilitation under this Act is imposed on him in respect of the later conviction;

if the rehabilitation period applicable in accordance with this section to either of the convictions would end earlier than the period so applicable in relation to the other, the rehabilitation period which would (apart from this subsection) end the earlier shall be extended so as to end at the same time as the other rehabilitation period.

(5) Where the rehabilitation period applicable to a conviction is the rehabilitation period applicable [by virtue of paragraph (g) of the definition of "relevant order" in section 5(8) above] to an order imposing on a person any disqualification, disability, prohibition or other penalty, the rehabilitation period applicable to another conviction shall not by virtue of subsection (4) above be extended by reference to that period; but if any other sentence is imposed in respect of the first-mentioned conviction for which a rehabilitation period is prescribed by any other provision of section 5 above, the rehabilitation period applicable to another conviction shall, where appropriate, be extended under subsection (4) above by reference to the rehabilitation period applicable in accordance with that section to that sentence or, where more than one such sentence is imposed, by reference to the longer or longest of the periods so applicable to those sentences, as if the period in question were the rehabilitation period applicable to the first-mentioned conviction.

(6) . . .

(7) . . .

Amendment

Sub-s (3): words "a probation order was made" in square brackets substituted by the Criminal Justice and Court Services Act 2000, s 74, Sch 7, paras 48, 50(a).

Sub-s (3): words "or a breach of the order" in square brackets substituted by the Criminal Justice and Court Services Act 2000, s 74, Sch 7, paras 48, 50(b).

Sub-s (3A): inserted by the Policing and Crime Act 2009, s 18(3).

Sub-s (5): words "by virtue of paragraph (g) of the definition of "relevant order" in section 5(8) above" in square brackets substituted by the Legal Aid, Sentencing and Punishment of Offenders Act 2012, s 139(1), (5)(a).

Sub-s (6): repealed by the Legal Aid, Sentencing and Punishment of Offenders Act 2012, s 139(1), (5)(b).

Sub-s (7): repealed by the Armed Forces Act 1996, s 35(2), Sch 7, Part III.

7 Limitations on rehabilitation under this Act, etc (1) Nothing in section 4(1) above shall affect—

(a) any right of Her Majesty, by virtue of Her Royal prerogative or otherwise, to grant a free pardon, to quash any conviction or sentence, or to commute any sentence;

(b) the enforcement by any process or proceedings of any fine or other sum adjudged to be paid by or imposed on a spent conviction;

(c) the issue of any process for the purpose of proceedings in respect of any breach of a condition or requirement applicable to a sentence imposed in respect of a spent conviction; or

(d) the operation of any enactment by virtue of which, in consequence of any conviction, a person is subject, otherwise than by way of sentence, to any disqualification, disability, prohibition or other penalty the period of which extends beyond the rehabilitation period applicable in accordance with section 6 above to the conviction.

(2) Nothing in section 4(1) above shall affect the determination of any issue, or prevent the admission or requirement of any evidence, relating to a person's previous convictions or to circumstances ancillary thereto—

(a) in any criminal proceedings before a court in [England and Wales] (including any appeal or reference in a criminal matter);

(b) in any service disciplinary proceedings or in any proceedings on appeal from any service disciplinary proceedings;

[(bb) in any proceedings under Part 2 of the Sexual Offences Act 2003, or on appeal from any such proceedings;]

[(c) in any proceedings relating to adoption, the marriage of any minor, [or the formation of a civil partnership by any minor,] the exercise of the inherent jurisdiction of the High Court with respect to minors or the provision by any person of accommodation, care or schooling for minors;

(cc) in any proceedings brought under the Children Act 1989;]

[(d) in any proceedings relating to the variation or discharge of a youth rehabilitation order under Part 1 of the Criminal Justice and Immigration Act 2008, or on appeal from any such proceedings;]

(e) . . .

(f) in any proceedings in which he is a party or a witness, provided that, on the occasion when the issue or the admission or requirement of the evidence falls to be determined, he consents to the determination of the issue or, as the case may be, the admission or requirement of the evidence notwithstanding the provisions of section 4(1); [or,

(g) . . .[; or]

[(h) in any proceedings brought under Part 7 of the Coroners and Justice Act 2009 (criminal memoirs etc).]

. . .

(3) If at any stage in any proceedings before a judicial authority in [England and Wales] (not being proceedings to which, by virtue of any of paragraphs (a) to (e) of subsection (2) above or of any order for the time being in force under subsection (4) below, section 4(1) above has no application, or proceedings to which section 8 below applies) the authority is satisfied, in the light of any considerations which appear to it to be relevant (including any evidence which has been or may thereafter be put before it), that justice cannot be done in the case except by admitting or requiring evidence relating to a person's spent convictions or to circumstances ancillary thereto, that authority may admit or, as the case may be, require the evidence in question notwithstanding the provisions of subsection (1) of section 4 above, and may determine any issue to which the evidence relates in disregard, so far as necessary, of those provisions.

(4) The Secretary of State may by order exclude the application of section 4(1) above in relation to any proceedings specified in the order (other than proceedings to which section 8 below applies) to such extent and for such purposes as may be so specified.

(5) No order made by a court with respect to any person otherwise than on a conviction shall be included in any list or statement of that person's previous convictions given or made to any court which is considering how to deal with him in respect of any offence.

Amendment
Sub-s (2): in para (a) words "England and Wales" in square brackets substituted by the Legal Aid, Sentencing and Punishment of Offenders Act 2012, s 141(10), Sch 25, paras 1, 6(1), (2).
Sub-s (2): para (bb) substituted by the Sexual Offences Act 2003, s 139, Sch 6, para 19.
Sub-s (2): paras (c), (cc) substituted for para (c) by the Children Act 1989, s 108(5), Sch 13, para 35(1), (2).
Sub-s (2): in para (c) words "or the formation of a civil partnership by any minor," in square brackets inserted by the Civil Partnership Act 2004, s 261(1), Sch 27, para 53.
Sub-s (2): para (d) substituted by the Criminal Justice and Immigration Act 2008, s 6(2), Sch 4, Pt 1, paras 20, 22.
Sub-s (2): para (e) repealed by the Children (Scotland) Act 1995, s 105(4), (5), Sch 4, para 23(4)(b), Sch 5.
Sub-s (2): para (g) repealed by the Banking Act 1987, s 108(2), Sch 7, Pt I.
Sub-s (2): word "or" in square brackets and para (h) inserted by the Coroners and Justice Act 2009, s 158(1).
Sub-s (2): final words omitted repealed by the Children (Scotland) Act 1995, s 105(4), (5), Sch 4, para 23(4)(c), Sch 5.
Sub-s (3): words "England and Wales" in square brackets substituted by the Legal Aid, Sentencing and Punishment of Offenders Act 2012, s 141(10), Sch 25, paras 1, 6(1), (2).

8 Defamation actions (1) This section applies to any action for libel or slander begun after the commencement of this Act by a rehabilitated person and founded upon the publication of any matter imputing that the plaintiff has committed or been charged with or prosecuted for or convicted of or sentenced for an offence which was the subject of a spent conviction.

(2) Nothing in section 4(1) above shall affect an action to which this section applies where the publication complained of took place before the conviction in question became spent, and the following provisions of this section shall not apply in any such case.

(3) Subject to subsections (5) and (6) below, nothing in section 4(1) above shall prevent the defendant in an action to which this section applies from relying on any defence [under section 2 or 3 of the Defamation Act 2013 which is available to him or any defence] or of absolute or qualified privilege which is available to him, or restrict the matters he may establish in support of any such defence.

(4) Without prejudice to the generality of subsection (3) above, where in any such action malice is alleged against a defendant who is relying on a defence of qualified privilege, nothing in section 4(1) above shall restrict the matters he may establish in rebuttal of the allegation.

(5) A defendant in any such action shall not by virtue of subsection (3) above be entitled to rely upon [a defence under section 2 of the Defamation Act 2013] if the publication is proved to have been made with malice.

(6) Subject to subsection (7) below a defendant in any such action shall not, by virtue of subsection (3) above, be entitled to rely on any matter or adduce or require any evidence for the purpose of establishing (whether under [section 14 of the Defamation Act 1996] or otherwise) the defence that the matter published constituted a fair and accurate report of judicial proceedings if it is proved that the publication contained a reference to evidence which was ruled to be inadmissible in the proceedings by virtue of section 4(1) above.

(7) Subsection (3) above shall apply without the qualifications imposed by subsection (6) above in relation to—

(a) any report of judicial proceedings contained in any bona fide series of law reports which does not form part of any other publication and consists solely of reports of proceedings in courts of law; and

(b) any report or account of judicial proceedings published for bona fide educational, scientific or professional purposes, or given in the course of any lecture, class or discussion given or held for any of those purposes.

(8) . . .

Amendment

Sub-s (3): words "under section 2 or 3 of the Defamation Act 2013 which is available to him or any defence" in square brackets substituted by the Defamation Act 2013, s 16(1), (2).

Sub-s (5): words "a defence under section 2 of the Defamation Act 2013" in square brackets substituted by the Defamation Act 2013, s 16(1), (3).

Sub-s (6): words "section 14 of the Defamation Act 1996" in square brackets substituted by the Defamation Act 1996, s 14(4).

Sub-s (8): repealed by the Legal Aid, Sentencing and Punishment of Offenders Act 2012, s 141(10), Sch 25, paras 1, 7.

[8A Protection afforded to spent cautions (1) Schedule 2 to this Act (protection for spent cautions) shall have effect.

(2) In this Act "caution" means—

  (a) a conditional caution, that is to say, a caution given under section 22 of the Criminal Justice Act 2003 (c 44) (conditional cautions for adults) or under section 66A of the Crime and Disorder Act 1998 (c 37) (conditional cautions for children and young persons);

  (b) any other caution given to a person in England and Wales in respect of an offence which, at the time the caution is given, that person has admitted;

  (c) . . . ,

  (d) anything corresponding to a caution . . . falling within [paragraphs (a) or (b)] (however described) which is given to a person in respect of an offence under the law of a country outside England and Wales [and which is not an alternative to prosecution (within the meaning of section 8AA)].]

Amendment

Section inserted by the Criminal Justice and Immigration Act 2008, s 49, Sch 10, paras 1, 3.

Sub-s (2): para (c) repealed by the Legal Aid, Sentencing and Punishment of Offenders Act 2012, s 135(3), Sch 24, paras 1, 2(a).

Sub-s (2): words omitted repealed by the Legal Aid, Sentencing and Punishment of Offenders Act 2012, s 135(3), Sch 24, paras 1, 2(b)(i).

Sub-s (2): words "paragraph (a) or (b)" substituted by the Legal Aid, Sentencing and Punishment of Offenders Act 2012, s 135(3), Sch 24, paras 1, 2(b)(ii).

Sub-s (2): words "and which is not an alternative to prosecution (within the meaning of section 8AA)" in square brackets inserted by the Legal Aid, Sentencing and Punishment of Offenders Act 2012, s 141(10), Sch 25, paras 1, 8.

[8AA Protection afforded to spent alternatives to prosecution (1) The following provisions of this Act apply, with the modifications specified in subsection (3), to a spent alternative to prosecution as they apply to a spent caution—

  (a) section 9A (unauthorised disclosure of spent cautions), and

  (b) paragraphs 2 to 6 of Schedule 2 (protection relating to spent cautions and ancillary circumstances).

(2) An alternative to prosecution becomes spent for the purposes of this Act when it becomes spent under the law of Scotland.

(3) The modifications mentioned in subsection (1) are—

  (a) references to cautions are to be read as references to alternatives to prosecution (and references to cautioned are to be read accordingly),

  (b) references to the offence which was the subject of the caution are to be read as references to the offence in respect of which the alternative to prosecution was given,

  (c) paragraphs (e) and (f) of paragraph 2(1) of Schedule 2 are to be read as if they were—

"(e) anything done or undergone in pursuance of the terms of the alternative to prosecution,",

(d) references to cautions for an offence are to be read as references to alternatives to prosecution in respect of an offence, and

(e) the reference in paragraph 5 of Schedule 2 to the rehabilitation period applicable to the caution is to be read as a reference to the time at which the alternative to prosecution becomes spent.

(4) In this section "alternative to prosecution" has the same meaning as in section 8B as that section has effect in the law of Scotland but disregarding subsection (1)(f) of that section.]

Amendment
Section inserted by the Legal Aid, Sentencing and Punishment of Offenders Act 2012, s 139(1), (6).

9 Unauthorised disclosure of spent convictions (1) In this section—
"official record" means a record kept for the purposes of its functions by any court, police force, Government department, local or other public authority in Great Britain, or a record kept, in Great Britain or elsewhere, for the purposes of any of Her Majesty's forces, being in either case a record containing information about persons convicted of offences; and
"specified information" means information imputing that a named or otherwise identifiable rehabilitated living person has committed or been charged with or prosecuted for or convicted of or sentenced for any offence which is the subject of a spent conviction.

(2) Subject to the provisions of any order made under subsection (5) below, any person who, in the course of his official duties, has or at any time has had custody of or access to any official record or the information contained therein, shall be guilty of an offence if, knowing or having reasonable cause to suspect that any specified information he has obtained in the course of those duties is specified information, he discloses it, otherwise than in the course of those duties, to another person.

(3) In any proceedings for an offence under subsection (2) above it shall be a defence for the defendant . . . to show that the disclosure was made—
(a) to the rehabilitated person or to another person at the express request of the rehabilitated person; or
(b) to a person whom he reasonably believed to be the rehabilitated person or to another person at the express request of a person whom he reasonably believed to be the rehabilitated person.

(4) Any person who obtains any specified information from any official record by means of any fraud, dishonesty or bribe shall be guilty of an offence.

(5) The Secretary of State may by order make such provision as appears to him to be appropriate for excepting the disclosure of specified information derived

from an official record from the provisions of subsection (2) above in such cases or classes of case as may be specified in the order.

(6) Any person guilty of an offence under subsection (2) above shall be liable on summary conviction to a fine not exceeding [level 4 on the standard scale].

(7) Any person guilty of an offence under subsection (4) above shall be liable on summary conviction to a fine not exceeding [level 5 on the standard scale] or to imprisonment for a term not exceeding six months, or to both.

(8) Proceedings for an offence under subsection (2) above shall not . . . be instituted except by or on behalf of the Director of Public Prosecutions.

Amendment
Sub-s (3): words omitted repealed by the Legal Aid, Sentencing and Punishment of Offenders Act 2012, s 141(10), Sch 25, paras 1, 9(1), (2).
Sub-ss (6), (7): maximum fines increased and converted to levels on the standard scale by the Criminal Justice Act 1982, ss 37, 38, 46.
Sub-s (8): words omitted repealed by the Legal Aid, Sentencing and Punishment of Offenders Act 2012, s 141(10), Sch 25, paras 1, 9(1), (3).

[9A Unauthorised disclosure of spent cautions (1) In this section—
  (a) "official record" means a record which—
    (i) contains information about persons given a caution for any offence or offences; and
    (ii) is kept for the purposes of its functions by any court, police force, Government department or other public authority in England and Wales;
  (b) "caution information" means information imputing that a named or otherwise identifiable living person ("the named person") has committed, been charged with or prosecuted or cautioned for any offence which is the subject of a spent caution; and
  (c) "relevant person" means any person who, in the course of his official duties (anywhere in the United Kingdom), has or at any time has had custody of or access to any official record or the information contained in it.

(2) Subject to the terms of any order made under subsection (5), a relevant person shall be guilty of an offence if, knowing or having reasonable cause to suspect that any caution information he has obtained in the course of his official duties is caution information, he discloses it, otherwise than in the course of those duties, to another person.

(3) In any proceedings for an offence under subsection (2) it shall be a defence for the defendant to show that the disclosure was made—
  (a) to the named person or to another person at the express request of the named person;
  (b) to a person whom he reasonably believed to be the named person or to another person at the express request of a person whom he reasonably believed to be the named person.

(4) Any person who obtains any caution information from any official record by means of any fraud, dishonesty or bribe shall be guilty of an offence.

(5) The Secretary of State may by order make such provision as appears to him to be appropriate for excepting the disclosure of caution information derived from an official record from the provisions of subsection (2) in such cases or classes of case as may be specified in the order.

(6) A person guilty of an offence under subsection (2) is liable on summary conviction to a fine not exceeding level 4 on the standard scale.

(7) A person guilty of an offence under subsection (4) is liable on summary conviction to a fine not exceeding level 5 on the standard scale, or to imprisonment for a term not exceeding 51 weeks, or to both.

(8) Proceedings for an offence under subsection (2) shall not be instituted except by or on behalf of the Director of Public Prosecutions.]

Amendment
Section inserted by the Criminal Justice and Immigration Act 2008, s 49, Sch 10, paras 1, 4; for transitional provisions and savings see s 148(2), Sch 27, Pt 4, para 20.

10 Orders (1) Any power of the Secretary of State to make an order under any provision of this Act shall be exercisable by statutory instrument, and an order made under any provision of this Act except section 11 below may be varied or revoked by a subsequent order made under that provision.

[(1A) Any power of the Secretary of State to make an order under any provision of this Act includes power—
  (a) to make different provision for different purposes, and
  (b) to make incidental, consequential, supplementary, transitional, transitory or saving provision.

(1B) The power of the Secretary of State to make an order under section 5(6) includes power to make consequential provision which amends or repeals any provision of this Act or any other enactment.]

(2) No order shall be made by the Secretary of State under any provision of this Act other than section 11 below unless a draft of it has been laid before, and approved by resolution of, each House of Parliament.

Amendment
Sub-ss (1A), (1B): inserted by the Legal Aid, Sentencing and Punishment of Offenders Act 2012, s 141(10), Sch 25, paras 1, 10.

11 Citation commencement and extent (1) This Act may be cited as the Rehabilitation of Offenders Act 1974.

(2) This Act shall come into force on 1st July 1975 or such earlier day as the Secretary of State may by order appoint.

(3) This Act shall not apply to Northern Ireland.

[SCHEDULE [1]
...]

[...]

Amendment

Schedule: inserted by the Armed Forces Act 1996, s 13, Sch 4.

Schedule 1: numbered as such by the Criminal Justice and Immigration Act 2008, s 49, Sch 10, paras 1, 5.

Schedule 1: repealed by the Legal Aid, Sentencing and Punishment of Offenders Act 2012, s 141(10), Sch 25, paras 1, 11.

[SCHEDULE 2
Protection for Spent Cautions]

[Preliminary

1 (1) For the purposes of this Schedule a caution shall be regarded as a spent caution—

   (a)   in the case of a conditional caution (as defined in section 8A(2)(a))[—

      (i)   at the end of the period of three months from the date on which the caution is given, or

      (ii) if earlier, when the caution ceases to have effect; and]

   (b)   in any other case, at the time the caution is given.

(2) . . .

(3) . . .

2 (1) In this Schedule "ancillary circumstances", in relation to a caution, means any circumstances of the following—

   (a)   the offence which was the subject of the caution or the conduct constituting that offence;

   (b)   any process preliminary to the caution (including consideration by any person of how to deal with that offence and the procedure for giving the caution);

   (c)   any proceedings for that offence which take place before the caution is given (including anything which happens after that time for the purpose of bringing the proceedings to an end);

   (d)   any judicial review proceedings relating to the caution;

   (e)   in the case of a [youth caution given under section 66ZA] of the Crime and Disorder Act 1998 (c 37), anything done in pursuance of or undergone in compliance with a requirement to participate in a rehabilitation programme under section [66ZB(2) or (3)] of that Act;

   (f)   in the case of a conditional caution, any conditions attached to the caution or anything done in pursuance of or undergone in compliance with those conditions.

(2) Where the caution relates to two or more offences, references in sub-paragraph (1) to the offence which was the subject of the caution include a reference to each of the offences concerned.

(3) In this Schedule "proceedings before a judicial authority" has the same meaning as in section 4.

Protection relating to spent cautions and ancillary circumstances

3 (1) A person who is given a caution for an offence shall, from the time the caution is spent, be treated for all purposes in law as a person who has not committed, been charged with or prosecuted for, or been given a caution for the offence; and notwithstanding the provisions of any other enactment or rule of law to the contrary—

(a) no evidence shall be admissible in any proceedings before a judicial authority exercising its jurisdiction or functions in England and Wales to prove that any such person has committed, been charged with or prosecuted for, or been given a caution for the offence; and

(b) a person shall not, in any such proceedings, be asked and, if asked, shall not be required to answer, any question relating to his past which cannot be answered without acknowledging or referring to a spent caution or any ancillary circumstances.

(2) Nothing in sub-paragraph (1) applies in relation to any proceedings for the offence which are not part of the ancillary circumstances relating to the caution.

(3) Where a question seeking information with respect to a person's previous cautions, offences, conduct or circumstances is put to him or to any other person otherwise than in proceedings before a judicial authority—

(a) the question shall be treated as not relating to spent cautions or to any ancillary circumstances, and the answer may be framed accordingly; and

(b) the person questioned shall not be subjected to any liability or otherwise prejudiced in law by reason of any failure to acknowledge or disclose a spent caution or any ancillary circumstances in his answer to the question.

(4) Any obligation imposed on any person by any rule of law or by the provisions of any agreement or arrangement to disclose any matters to any other person shall not extend to requiring him to disclose a spent caution or any ancillary circumstances (whether the caution is his own or another's).

(5) A caution which has become spent or any ancillary circumstances, or any failure to disclose such a caution or any such circumstances, shall not be a proper ground for dismissing or excluding a person from any office, profession, occupation or employment, or for prejudicing him in any way in any occupation or employment.

(6) This paragraph has effect subject to paragraphs 4 to 6.

4 The Secretary of State may by order—

(a) make provision for excluding or modifying the application of either or both of paragraphs (a) or (b) of paragraph 3(2) in relation to questions put in such circumstances as may be specified in the order;

(b) provide for exceptions from the provisions of sub-paragraphs (4) and (5) of paragraph 3, in such cases or classes of case, and in relation to cautions of such a description, as may be specified in the order.

5 Nothing in paragraph 3 affects—

(a) the operation of the caution in question; or

(b) the operation of any enactment by virtue of which, in consequence of any caution, a person is subject to any disqualification, disability, prohibition or other restriction or effect, the period of which extends beyond the rehabilitation period applicable to the caution.

6 (1) Section 7(2), (3) and (4) apply for the purposes of this Schedule as follows.

(2) Subsection (2) (apart from paragraphs (b) and (d)) applies to the determination of any issue, and the admission or requirement of any evidence, relating to a person's previous cautions or to ancillary circumstances as it applies to matters relating to a person's previous convictions and circumstances ancillary thereto.

(3) Subsection (3) applies to evidence of a person's previous cautions and ancillary circumstances as it applies to evidence of a person's convictions and the circumstances ancillary thereto; and for this purpose subsection (3) shall have effect as if—

(a) any reference to subsection (2) or (4) of section 7 were a reference to that subsection as applied by this paragraph; and

(b) the words "or proceedings to which section 8 below applies" were omitted.

(4) Subsection (4) applies for the purpose of excluding the application of paragraph 3(1); and for that purpose subsection (4) shall have effect as if the words " (other than proceedings to which section 8 below applies)" were omitted.

(5) References in the provisions applied by this paragraph to section 4(1) are to be read as references to paragraph 3(1).]

Amendment

Schedule 2: inserted by the Criminal Justice and Immigration Act 2008, s 49, Sch 10, paras 1, 6.

Paragraph 1: in sub-para (1)(a) words in square brackets substituted by the Legal Aid, Sentencing and Punishment of Offenders Act 2012, s 139(1), (7)(a); sub-paras (2), (3) repealed by the Legal Aid, Sentencing and Punishment of Offenders Act 2012, s 139(1), (7)(b).

Paragraph 2: words "youth caution given under section 66ZA" in square brackets substituted by the Legal Aid, Sentencing and Punishment of Offenders Act 2012, Sch 24, para 3(a); words "66ZB(2) or (3)" in square brackets substituted by the Legal Aid, Sentencing and Punishment of Offenders Act 2012, Sch 24, para 3(b).

Transport Act 1985

Part I
General provisions relating to Road Passenger Transport

Taxis and hire cars

10 Immediate hiring of taxis at separate fares (1) In the circumstances mentioned in subsection (2) below, a licensed taxi may be hired for use for the carriage of passengers for hire or reward at separate fares without thereby—

(a) becoming a public service vehicle for the purposes of the 1981 Act or any related enactment; or

(b) ceasing (otherwise than by virtue of any provision made under section 13 of this Act) to be subject to the taxi code.

(2) The circumstances are that—

(a) the taxi is hired in an area where a scheme made under this section is in operation;

(b) the taxi is licensed by the licensing authority for that area; and

(c) the hiring falls within the terms of the scheme.

(3) In this section "licensing authority" means—

(a) in relation to the London taxi area, [Transport for London] or the holder for the time being of any office designated by [Transport for London] for the purposes of this section; and

(b) in relation to any other area in England and Wales, the authority having responsibility for licensing taxis in that area.

(4) For the purposes of this section, a licensing authority may make a scheme for their area and shall make such a scheme if the holders of at least ten per cent. of the current taxi licences issued by the authority request the authority in writing to do so.

(5) Any scheme made under this section shall—

(a) designate the places in the area from which taxis may be hired under the scheme ("authorised places");

(b) specify the requirements to be met for the purposes of the scheme in relation to the hiring of taxis at separate fares; and

(c) . . .—

(i) include such provision, or provision of such description, as may be prescribed for the purposes of this sub-paragraph;

(ii) not include provision of any such description as may be prescribed for the purposes of this sub-paragraph.

(6) Subject to subsection (5) above, any scheme made under this section may, in particular, make provision with respect to—

    (a) fares;

    (b) the display of any document, plate, mark or sign for indicating an autho-
rised place or that a taxi standing at an authorised place is available for
the carriage of passengers at separate fares;

    (c) the manner in which arrangements are to be made for the carriage of
passengers on any such hiring as is mentioned in subsection (1) above;
and

    (d) the conditions to apply to the use of a taxi on any such hiring.

(7) A licensing authority may, subject to subsection (5) above, vary any scheme
made by them under this section.

(8) . . . any scheme under this section, and any variation of such a scheme, shall
be made in accordance with the prescribed procedure.

(9) For the purposes of this section—

    (a) the hiring of a taxi falls within the terms of a scheme if—

        (i) it is hired from an authorised place; and

        (ii) the hiring meets the requirements specified by the licensing author-
ity as those to be met for the purposes of the scheme; and

    (b) a taxi is hired from an authorised place if it is standing at that place when
it is hired and the persons hiring it are all present there.

(10) . . .

Amendment

Sub-s (3): in para (a) words "Transport for London" in square brackets in both places
substituted by the Greater London Authority Act 1999, s 253, Sch 20, para 8(1), (2)(a).

Sub-s (5): in para (c) words omitted repealed by the Greater London Authority Act 1999,
ss 253, 423, Sch 20, para 8(1), (2)(b), Sch 34, Pt V.

Sub-s (8): words omitted repealed by the Greater London Authority Act 1999, ss 253,
423, Sch 20, para 8(1), (2)(c), Sch 34, Pt V.

Sub-s (10): repealed by the Greater London Authority Act 1999, ss 253, 423, Sch 20,
para 8(1), (2)(d), Sch 34, Pt V.

11 Advance booking of taxis and hire cars at separate fares (1) Where the
conditions mentioned in subsection (2) below are met, a licensed taxi or licensed
hire car may be used for the carriage of passengers for hire or reward at separate
fares without thereby—

    (a) becoming a public service vehicle for the purposes of the 1981 Act or
any related enactment; or

    (b) ceasing (otherwise than by virtue of any provision made under section
13 of this Act) to be subject to the taxi code or (as the case may be) the
hire car code.

(2) The conditions are that—

    (a) all the passengers carried on the occasion in question booked their jour-
neys in advance; and

    (b) each of them consented, when booking his journey, to sharing the use of
the vehicle on that occasion with others on the basis that a separate fare

would be payable by each passenger for his own journey on that occasion.

12 Use of taxis [or hire cars] in providing local services (1) Where the holder of a taxi licence [or a private hire vehicle licence]—

(a) applies to [a] traffic commissioner for a restricted PSV operator's licence to be granted to him under Part II of the 1981 Act; and

(b) states in his application that he proposes to use one or more licensed taxis [or licensed hire cars] to provide a local service;

section 14 of the 1981 Act (conditions to be met before grant of PSV operator's licence) shall not apply and the commissioner shall grant the application.

(2) In this section "special licence" means a restricted PSV operator's licence granted by virtue of this section.

(3) . . .

(4) Without prejudice to his powers to attach other conditions under section 16 of the 1981 Act, any traffic commissioner granting a special licence shall attach to it, under that section, the conditions mentioned in subsection (5) below.

(5) The conditions are—

(a) that every vehicle used under the licence shall be one for which the holder of the licence has a taxi licence [or a private hire vehicle licence]; and

(b) that no vehicle shall be used under the licence otherwise than for the purpose of providing a local service with one or more stopping places within the area of the authority which granted [the relevant licence for that vehicle].

(6) In subsection (5)(b) above "local service" does not include an excursion or tour.

(7) The maximum number of vehicles which the holder of a special licence may at any one time use under the licence shall be the number of vehicles for which (for the time being) he holds [relevant licences]; and a condition to that effect shall be attached to every special licence under section 16(1) of the 1981 Act.

(8) Section 1(2) of the 1981 Act (vehicle used as public service vehicle to be treated as such until that use is permanently discontinued) shall not apply to any use of a licensed taxi [or a licensed hire car] for the provision of a local service under a special licence.

(9) At any time when a licensed taxi [or a licensed hire car] is being so used it shall carry such documents, plates and marks, in such manner, as may be prescribed.

(10) [At any time when a licensed taxi or a licensed hire car is being so used the prescribed provisions of the taxi code or, as the case may be, the hire car code shall apply in relation to it;] and any such provision may be so applied subject to such modifications as may be prescribed.

[(10A) In subsections (9) and (10) "prescribed" means prescribed by the appropriate authority.]

(11) For the purposes of section 12(3) of the 1981 Act (which provides that where two or more PSV operators' licences are held they must be granted . . . for different traffic areas), special licences shall be disregarded.

(12) A person may hold more than one special licence but shall not at the same time hold more than one such licence [in relation to] a particular traffic area.

(13) The following provisions shall not apply in relation to special licences or (as the case may be) the use of vehicles under such licences—

(a) sections 16(1A) and (2), 17(3)(d), 18 to 20 . . . and 26 of the 1981 Act; and

(b) section 26(5) and (6) of this Act;

and for the purposes of section 12 of that Act this section shall be treated as if it were in Part II of that Act.

Amendment

Heading: words "or hire cars" in square brackets inserted by the Local Transport Act 2008, s 53(1), (9).

Sub-s (1): words "or a private hire vehicle licence" in square brackets inserted by the Local Transport Act 2008, s 53(1), (2)(a); in para (a) word "a" in square brackets substituted by the Local Transport Act 2008 (Traffic Commissioners) (Consequential Amendments) Order 2013, SI 2013/1644, art 3, Sch 1; in para (b) words "or licensed hire cars" in square brackets inserted by the Local Transport Act 2008, s 53(1), (2)(b).

Sub-s (3): repealed by the Deregulation and Contracting Out Act 1994, ss 68, 81, Sch 14, para 8, Sch 17.

Sub-s (5): in para (a) words "or a private hire vehicle licence" in square brackets inserted by the Local Transport Act 2008, s 53(1), (3)(a); in para (b) words "the relevant license for that vehicle" in square brackets substituted by the Local Transport Act 2008, s 53(1), (3)(b).

Sub-s (7): words "relevant licences" in square brackets substituted by the Local Transport Act 2008, s 53(1), (4).

Sub-s (8): words "or a licensed hire car" in square brackets inserted by the Local Transport Act 2008, s 53(1), (5).

Sub-s (9): words "or a licensed hire car" in square brackets inserted by the Local Transport Act 2008, s 53(1), (6).

Sub-s (10): words from "At any time when" to "the hire car code shall apply in relation to it;" in square brackets substituted by the Local Transport Act 2008, s 53(1), (7).

Sub-s (10A): inserted by the Local Transport Act 2008, s 53(1), (8).

Sub-s (11): words omitted repealed by the Local Transport Act 2008 (Traffic Commissioners) (Consequential Amendments) Order 2013, SI 2013/1644, art 3, Sch 1.

Sub-s (12): words "in relation to" in square brackets substituted by the Local Transport Act 2008 (Traffic Commissioners) (Consequential Amendments) Order 2013, SI 2013/1644, art 3, Sch 1.

Sub-s (13): figure omitted repealed by the Road Traffic (Driver Licensing and Information Systems) Act 1989, s 16, Sch 6.

13 Provisions supplementary to sections 10 to 12 (1) [The appropriate authority] may by order make such modifications of the taxi code and the hire car code as [it] sees fit for the purpose of supplementing the provision of sections 10 to 12 of this Act.

(2) Any order made under subsection (1) above may, in particular, modify any provision—

(a) relating to fares payable by the hirer of a vehicle;

(b) requiring the driver of any vehicle to accept any hiring, or to drive at the direction of a hirer, or (as the case may be) of a prospective hirer, to any place within or not exceeding any specified distance or for any period of time not exceeding a specified period from the time of hiring;

(c) making the carriage of additional passengers in any vehicle which is currently subject to a hiring dependent on the consent of the hirer.

(3) In this section, and in sections 10 to 12 of this Act—

["the appropriate authority" means—

(a) in relation to—

(i) a taxi licensed under section 37 of the Town Police Clauses Act 1847 or any similar enactment which applies outside the London taxi area,

(ii) a licensed hire car licensed under section 48 of the Local Government (Miscellaneous Provisions) Act 1976, or

(iii) a taxi or private hire car licensed under section 10 of the Civic Government (Scotland) Act 1982,

the Secretary of State;

(b) in relation to—

(i) a taxi licensed under section 6 of the Metropolitan Public Carriage Act 1869, or

(ii) a licensed hire car licensed under section 7 of the Private Hire Vehicles (London) Act 1998,

Transport for London;]

"licensed taxi" means—

(a) in England and Wales, a vehicle licensed under—

(i) section 37 of the Town Police Clauses Act 1847; or

(ii) section 6 of the Metropolitan Public Carriage Act 1869;

or under any similar enactment; and

(b) in Scotland, a taxi licensed under section 10 of the Civic Government (Scotland) Act 1982;

"London taxi area" means the area to which the Metropolitan Public Carriage Act 1869 applies;

["licensed hire car" means—

(a) in England and Wales—

(i) for the purposes of section 11 of this Act, a vehicle licensed under section 48 of the Local Government (Miscellaneous Provisions) Act 1976 or section 7 of the Private Hire Vehicles (London) Act 1998,

(ii) for the purposes of section 12 of this Act, a vehicle licensed under section 48 of the Local Government (Miscellaneous Provisions) Act 1976;

    (b) in Scotland, a private hire car licensed under section 10 of the Civic Government (Scotland) Act 1982;]

"hire car code", in relation to a licensed hire car used as mentioned in section 11 [or 12] of this Act, means those provisions made by or under any enactment which would apply if it were hired by a single passenger for his exclusive use;

"related enactment", in relation to the 1981 Act, means any statutory provision (whenever passed or made) relating to public service vehicles in which "public service vehicle" is defined directly or indirectly by reference to the provisions of the 1981 Act;

"taxi code", in relation to any licensed taxi used as mentioned in section 10, 11 or 12 of this Act, means—

    (a) in England and Wales, those provisions made by or under any enactment which would apply if the vehicle were plying for hire and were hired by a single passenger for his exclusive use; and

    (b) in Scotland, the provisions of sections 10 to 23 of the Civic Government (Scotland) Act 1982, and Part I of that Act as it applies to these provisions; and

"taxi licence" means a licence under section 6 of the Metropolitan Public Carriage Act 1869, section 7 of the Town Police Clauses Act 1847 or any similar enactment, or a taxi licence under section 10 of the Civic Government (Scotland) Act 1982;

["relevant licence" means—

    (a) in relation to a licensed taxi, a taxi licence, and

    (b) in relation to a licensed hire car, a private hire vehicle licence;

"private hire vehicle licence" means—

    (a) in England and Wales, a licence under section 48 of the Local Government (Miscellaneous Provisions) Act 1976;

    (b) in Scotland, a private hire car licence under section 10 of the Civic Government (Scotland) Act 1982.]

(4) Any order made under subsection (1) above may contain such supplementary, incidental, consequential and transitional provisions (including provisions modifying any enactment contained in any Act other than this Act) as appear to the Secretary of State to be necessary or expedient in consequence of any modification of the taxi code or the private hire car code made by the order.

Amendment

Sub-s (1): words "The appropriate authority" in square brackets substituted by the Local Transport Act 2008, s 54(1), (2)(a); word "it" substituted by the Local Transport Act 2008, s 54(1), (2)(b).

Sub-s (3): definition "the appropriate authority" inserted by the Local Transport Act 2008, s 54(1), (3), (4); definition "licensed hire car" substituted by the Local Transport Act 2008, s 54(1), (3), (5); in the definition "hire car code" words "or 12" in square brackets inserted by the Local Transport Act 2008, s 54(1), (3), (7); definitions of "relevant licence" and "private hire vehicle licence" inserted by the Local Transport Act 2008, s 54(1), (3), (6).

SCHEDULE 7
Minor and Consequential Amendments

Section 139(2)

General

1 In England and Wales, the provisions made by or under any enactment which apply to motor vehicles used—

(a) to carry passengers under a contract express or implied for the use of the vehicle as a whole at or for a fixed or agreed rate or sum; and

(b) to ply for hire for such use;

shall apply to motor vehicles adapted to carry less than nine passengers as they apply to motor vehicles adapted to carry less than eight passengers.

Criminal Justice and Public Order Act 1994

Part XII
Miscellaneous and General

Taxi touts

167 Touting for hire car services (1) Subject to the following provisions, it is an offence, in a public place, to solicit persons to hire vehicles to carry them as passengers.

(2) Subsection (1) above does not imply that the soliciting must refer to any particular vehicle nor is the mere display of a sign on a vehicle that the vehicle is for hire soliciting within that subsection.

(3) No offence is committed under this section where soliciting persons to hire licensed taxis is permitted by a scheme under section 10 of the Transport Act 1985 (schemes for shared taxis) whether or not supplemented by provision made under section 13 of that Act (modifications of the taxi code).

(4) It is a defence for the accused to show that he was soliciting for [passengers to be carried at separate fares by public service vehicles] on behalf of the holder of a PSV operator's licence for those vehicles whose authority he had at the time of the alleged offence.

(5) A person guilty of an offence under this section shall be liable on summary conviction to a fine not exceeding level 4 on the standard scale.

(6) In this section—
> "public place" includes any highway and any other premises or place to which at the material time the public have or are permitted to have access (whether on payment or otherwise); and
> "public service vehicle" and "PSV operator's licence" have the same meaning as in Part II of the Public Passenger Vehicles Act 1981.

(7) . . .

Amendment
Sub-s (4): words "passengers to be carried at separate fares by public service vehicles" in square brackets substituted by the Transport Act 2000, s 265(3).
Sub-s (7): repealed by the Serious Organised Crime and Police Act 2005, s 174(2), Sch 17, Pt 2.

Equality Act 2010

Part 12
Disabled persons: transport

Chapter 1
Taxis, etc.

160 Taxi accessibility regulations (1) The Secretary of State may make regulations (in this Chapter referred to as "taxi accessibility regulations") for securing that it is possible for disabled persons—
    (a) to get into and out of taxis in safety;
    (b) to do so while in wheelchairs;
    (c) to travel in taxis in safety and reasonable comfort;
    (d) to do so while in wheelchairs.

(2) The regulations may, in particular, require a regulated taxi to conform with provision as to—
    (a) the size of a door opening for the use of passengers;
    (b) the floor area of the passenger compartment;
    (c) the amount of headroom in the passenger compartment;
    (d) the fitting of restraining devices designed to ensure the stability of a wheelchair while the taxi is moving.

(3) The regulations may also—
    (a) require the driver of a regulated taxi which is plying for hire, or which has been hired, to comply with provisions as to the carrying of ramps or other devices designed to facilitate the loading and unloading of wheelchairs;
    (b) require the driver of a regulated taxi in which a disabled person is being carried while in a wheelchair to comply with provisions as to the position in which the wheelchair is to be secured.

(4) The driver of a regulated taxi which is plying for hire or has been hired commits an offence—
    (a) by failing to comply with a requirement of the regulations, or
    (b) if the taxi fails to conform with any provision of the regulations with which it is required to conform.

(5) A person guilty of an offence under subsection (4) is liable on summary conviction to a fine not exceeding level 3 on the standard scale.

(6) In this section—
    "passenger compartment" has such meaning as is specified in taxi accessibility regulations;

"regulated taxi" means a taxi to which taxi accessibility regulations are expressed to apply.

161 Control of numbers of licensed taxis: exception (1) This section applies if—
   (a) an application for a licence in respect of a vehicle is made under section 37 of the Town Police Clauses Act 1847,
   (b) it is possible for a disabled person—
      (i) to get into and out of the vehicle in safety,
      (ii) to travel in the vehicle in safety and reasonable comfort, and
      (iii) to do the things mentioned in sub-paragraphs (i) and (ii) while in a wheelchair of a size prescribed by the Secretary of State, and
   (c) the proportion of taxis licensed in respect of the area to which the licence would (if granted) apply that conform to the requirement in paragraph (b) is less than the proportion that is prescribed by the Secretary of State.

(2) Section 16 of the Transport Act 1985 (which modifies the provisions of the Town Police Clauses Act 1847 about hackney carriages to allow a licence to ply for hire to be refused in order to limit the number of licensed carriages) does not apply in relation to the vehicle; and those provisions of the Town Police Clauses Act 1847 are to have effect subject to this section.

(3) In section 16 of the Transport Act 1985, after "shall" insert "(subject to section 161 of the Equality Act 2010)".

162 Designated transport facilities (1) The appropriate authority may by regulations provide for the application of any taxi provision (with or without modification) to—
   (a) vehicles used for the provision of services under a franchise agreement, or
   (b) drivers of such vehicles.

(2) A franchise agreement is a contract entered into by the operator of a designated transport facility for the provision, by the other party to the contract, of hire car services—
   (a) for members of the public using any part of the facility, and
   (b) which involve vehicles entering any part of the facility.

(3) In this section—
   "appropriate authority" means—
      (a) in relation to transport facilities in England and Wales, the Secretary of State;
      (b) in relation to transport facilities in Scotland, the Scottish Ministers;
   "designated" means designated by order made by the appropriate authority;
   "hire car" has such meaning as is prescribed by the appropriate authority;
   "operator", in relation to a transport facility, means a person who is concerned with the management or operation of the facility;
   "taxi provision" means a provision of—

(a) this Chapter, or

(b) regulations made in pursuance of section 20(2A) of the Civic Government (Scotland) Act 1982,

which applies in relation to taxis or drivers of taxis;

"transport facility" means premises which form part of a port, airport, railway station or bus station.

(4) For the purposes of section 2(2) of the European Communities Act 1972 (implementation of EU obligations), the Secretary of State may exercise a power conferred by this section on the Scottish Ministers.

163 Taxi licence conditional on compliance with taxi accessibility regulations (1) A licence for a taxi to ply for hire must not be granted unless the vehicle conforms with the provisions of taxi accessibility regulations with which a vehicle is required to conform if it is licensed.

(2) Subsection (1) does not apply if a licence is in force in relation to the vehicle at any time during the period of 28 days immediately before the day on which the licence is granted.

(3) The Secretary of State may by order provide for subsection (2) to cease to have effect on a specified date.

(4) The power under subsection (3) may be exercised differently for different areas or localities.

164 Exemption from taxi accessibility regulations (1) The Secretary of State may by regulations provide for a relevant licensing authority to apply for an order (an "exemption order") exempting the authority from the requirements of section 163.

(2) Regulations under subsection (1) may, in particular, make provision requiring an authority proposing to apply for an exemption order—

(a) to carry out such consultation as is specified;

(b) to publish its proposals in the specified manner;

(c) before applying for the order, to consider representations made about the proposal;

(d) to make the application in the specified form.

In this subsection "specified" means specified in the regulations.

(3) An authority may apply for an exemption order only if it is satisfied—

(a) that, having regard to the circumstances in its area, it is inappropriate for section 163 to apply, and

(b) that the application of that section would result in an unacceptable reduction in the number of taxis in its area.

(4) After consulting the Disabled Persons Transport Advisory Committee and such other persons as the Secretary of State thinks appropriate, the Secretary of State may—

(a) make an exemption order in the terms of the application for the order;

(b) make an exemption order in such other terms as the Secretary of State thinks appropriate;

(c) refuse to make an exemption order.

(5) The Secretary of State may by regulations make provision requiring a taxi plying for hire in an area in respect of which an exemption order is in force to conform with provisions of the regulations as to the fitting and use of swivel seats.

(6) Regulations under subsection (5) may make provision corresponding to section 163.

(7) In this section—

"relevant licensing authority" means an authority responsible for licensing taxis in any area of England and Wales other than the area to which the Metropolitan Public Carriage Act 1869 applies;

"swivel seats" has such meaning as is specified in regulations under subsection (5).

165 Passengers in wheelchairs (1) This section imposes duties on the driver of a designated taxi which has been hired—

(a) by or for a disabled person who is in a wheelchair, or

(b) by another person who wishes to be accompanied by a disabled person who is in a wheelchair.

(2) This section also imposes duties on the driver of a designated private hire vehicle, if a person within paragraph (a) or (b) of subsection (1) has indicated to the driver that the person wishes to travel in the vehicle.

(3) For the purposes of this section—

(a) a taxi or private hire vehicle is "designated" if it appears on a list maintained under section 167;

(b) "the passenger" means the disabled person concerned.

(4) The duties are—

(a) to carry the passenger while in the wheelchair;

(b) not to make any additional charge for doing so;

(c) if the passenger chooses to sit in a passenger seat, to carry the wheelchair;

(d) to take such steps as are necessary to ensure that the passenger is carried in safety and reasonable comfort;

(e) to give the passenger such mobility assistance as is reasonably required.

(5) Mobility assistance is assistance—

(a) to enable the passenger to get into or out of the vehicle;

(b) if the passenger wishes to remain in the wheelchair, to enable the passenger to get into and out of the vehicle while in the wheelchair;

(c) to load the passenger's luggage into or out of the vehicle;

(d) if the passenger does not wish to remain in the wheelchair, to load the wheelchair into or out of the vehicle.

(6) This section does not require the driver—

    (a) unless the vehicle is of a description prescribed by the Secretary of State, to carry more than one person in a wheelchair, or more than one wheelchair, on any one journey;

    (b) to carry a person in circumstances in which it would otherwise be lawful for the driver to refuse to carry the person.

(7) A driver of a designated taxi or designated private hire vehicle commits an offence by failing to comply with a duty imposed on the driver by this section.

(8) A person guilty of an offence under subsection (7) is liable on summary conviction to a fine not exceeding level 3 on the standard scale.

(9) It is a defence for a person charged with the offence to show that at the time of the alleged offence—

    (a) the vehicle conformed to the accessibility requirements which applied to it, but

    (b) it would not have been possible for the wheelchair to be carried safely in the vehicle.

(10) In this section and sections 166 and 167 "private hire vehicle" means—

    (a) a vehicle licensed under section 48 of the Local Government (Miscellaneous Provisions) Act 1976;

    (b) a vehicle licensed under section 7 of the Private Hire Vehicles (London) Act 1998;

    (c) a vehicle licensed under an equivalent provision of a local enactment;

    (d) a private hire car licensed under section 10 of the Civic Government (Scotland) Act 1982.

166 Passengers in wheelchairs: exemption certificates (1) A licensing authority must issue a person with a certificate exempting the person from the duties imposed by section 165 (an "exemption certificate") if satisfied that it is appropriate to do so—

    (a) on medical grounds, or

    (b) on the ground that the person's physical condition makes it impossible or unreasonably difficult for the person to comply with those duties.

(2) An exemption certificate is valid for such period as is specified in the certificate.

(3) The driver of a designated taxi is exempt from the duties imposed by section 165 if—

    (a) an exemption certificate issued to the driver is in force, and

    (b) the prescribed notice of the exemption is exhibited on the taxi in the prescribed manner.

(4) The driver of a designated private hire vehicle is exempt from the duties imposed by section 165 if—

    (a) an exemption certificate issued to the driver is in force, and

    (b) the prescribed notice of the exemption is exhibited on the vehicle in the prescribed manner.

(5) For the purposes of this section, a taxi or private hire vehicle is "designated" if it appears on a list maintained under section 167.

(6) In this section and section 167"licensing authority", in relation to any area, means the authority responsible for licensing taxis or, as the case may be, private hire vehicles in that area.

167 Lists of wheelchair-accessible vehicles (1) For the purposes of section 165, a licensing authority may maintain a list of vehicles falling within subsection (2).

(2) A vehicle falls within this subsection if—
  (a) it is either a taxi or a private hire vehicle, and
  (b) it conforms to such accessibility requirements as the licensing authority thinks fit.

(3) A licensing authority may, if it thinks fit, decide that a vehicle may be included on a list maintained under this section only if it is being used, or is to be used, by the holder of a special licence under that licence.

(4) In subsection (3) "special licence" has the meaning given by section 12 of the Transport Act 1985 (use of taxis or hire cars in providing local services).

(5) "Accessibility requirements" are requirements for securing that it is possible for disabled persons in wheelchairs—
  (a) to get into and out of vehicles in safety, and
  (b) to travel in vehicles in safety and reasonable comfort,

either staying in their wheelchairs or not (depending on which they prefer).

(6) The Secretary of State may issue guidance to licensing authorities as to—
  (a) the accessibility requirements which they should apply for the purposes of this section;
  (b) any other aspect of their functions under or by virtue of this section.

(7) A licensing authority which maintains a list under subsection (1) must have regard to any guidance issued under subsection (6).

168 Assistance dogs in taxis (1) This section imposes duties on the driver of a taxi which has been hired—
  (a) by or for a disabled person who is accompanied by an assistance dog, or
  (b) by another person who wishes to be accompanied by a disabled person with an assistance dog.

(2) The driver must—
  (a) carry the disabled person's dog and allow it to remain with that person;
  (b) not make any additional charge for doing so.

(3) The driver of a taxi commits an offence by failing to comply with a duty imposed by this section.

(4) A person guilty of an offence under this section is liable on summary conviction to a fine not exceeding level 3 on the standard scale.

169 Assistance dogs in taxis: exemption certificates (1) A licensing authority must issue a person with a certificate exempting the person from the duties imposed by section 168 (an "exemption certificate") if satisfied that it is appropriate to do so on medical grounds.

(2) In deciding whether to issue an exemption certificate the authority must have regard, in particular, to the physical characteristics of the taxi which the person drives or those of any kind of taxi in relation to which the person requires the certificate.

(3) An exemption certificate is valid—
    (a) in respect of a specified taxi or a specified kind of taxi;
    (b) for such period as is specified in the certificate.

(4) The driver of a taxi is exempt from the duties imposed by section 168 if—
    (a) an exemption certificate issued to the driver is in force with respect to the taxi, and
    (b) the prescribed notice of the exemption is exhibited on the taxi in the prescribed manner.

The power to make regulations under paragraph (b) is exercisable by the Secretary of State.

(5) In this section "licensing authority" means—
    (a) in relation to the area to which the Metropolitan Public Carriage Act 1869 applies, Transport for London;
    (b) in relation to any other area in England and Wales, the authority responsible for licensing taxis in that area.

170 Assistance dogs in private hire vehicles (1) The operator of a private hire vehicle commits an offence by failing or refusing to accept a booking for the vehicle—
    (a) if the booking is requested by or on behalf of a disabled person or a person who wishes to be accompanied by a disabled person, and
    (b) the reason for the failure or refusal is that the disabled person will be accompanied by an assistance dog.

(2) The operator commits an offence by making an additional charge for carrying an assistance dog which is accompanying a disabled person.

(3) The driver of a private hire vehicle commits an offence by failing or refusing to carry out a booking accepted by the operator—
    (a) if the booking is made by or on behalf of a disabled person or a person who wishes to be accompanied by a disabled person, and
    (b) the reason for the failure or refusal is that the disabled person is accompanied by an assistance dog.

(4) A person guilty of an offence under this section is liable on summary conviction to a fine not exceeding level 3 on the standard scale.

(5) In this section—

"driver" means a person who holds a licence under—
- (a) section 13 of the Private Hire Vehicles (London) Act 1998 ("the 1998 Act"),
- (b) section 51 of the Local Government (Miscellaneous Provisions) Act 1976 ("the 1976 Act"), or
- (c) an equivalent provision of a local enactment;

"licensing authority", in relation to any area in England and Wales, means the authority responsible for licensing private hire vehicles in that area;

"operator" means a person who holds a licence under—
- (a) section 3 of the 1998 Act,
- (b) section 55 of the 1976 Act, or
- (c) an equivalent provision of a local enactment;

"private hire vehicle" means a vehicle licensed under—
- (a) section 6 of the 1998 Act,
- (b) section 48 of the 1976 Act, or
- (c) an equivalent provision of a local enactment.

171 Assistance dogs in private hire vehicles: exemption certificates (1) A licensing authority must issue a driver with a certificate exempting the driver from the offence under section 170(3) (an "exemption certificate") if satisfied that it is appropriate to do so on medical grounds.

(2) In deciding whether to issue an exemption certificate the authority must have regard, in particular, to the physical characteristics of the private hire vehicle which the person drives or those of any kind of private hire vehicle in relation to which the person requires the certificate.

(3) An exemption certificate is valid—
- (a) in respect of a specified private hire vehicle or a specified kind of private hire vehicle;
- (b) for such period as is specified in the certificate.

(4) A driver does not commit an offence under section 170(3) if—
- (a) an exemption certificate issued to the driver is in force with respect to the private hire vehicle, and
- (b) the prescribed notice of the exemption is exhibited on the vehicle in the prescribed manner.

The power to make regulations under paragraph (b) is exercisable by the Secretary of State.

(5) In this section "driver", "licensing authority" and "private hire vehicle" have the same meaning as in section 170.

172 Appeals (1) A person who is aggrieved by the refusal of a licensing authority in England and Wales to issue an exemption certificate under section 166, 169 or 171 may appeal to a magistrates' court before the end of the period of 28 days beginning with the date of the refusal.

(2) A person who is aggrieved by the refusal of a licensing authority in Scotland to issue an exemption certificate under section 166 may appeal to the sheriff before the end of the period of 28 days beginning with the date of the refusal.

(3) On an appeal under subsection (1) or (2), the magistrates' court or sheriff may direct the licensing authority to issue the exemption certificate to have effect for such period as is specified in the direction.

(4) A person who is aggrieved by the decision of a licensing authority to include a vehicle on a list maintained under section 167 may appeal to a magistrates' court or, in Scotland, the sheriff before the end of the period of 28 days beginning with the date of the inclusion.

173 Interpretation (1) In this Chapter—
"accessibility requirements" has the meaning given in section 167(5);
"assistance dog" means—
  (a) a dog which has been trained to guide a blind person;
  (b) a dog which has been trained to assist a deaf person;
  (c) a dog which has been trained by a prescribed charity to assist a disabled person who has a disability that consists of epilepsy or otherwise affects the person's mobility, manual dexterity, physical co-ordination or ability to lift, carry or otherwise move everyday objects;
  (d) a dog of a prescribed category which has been trained to assist a disabled person who has a disability (other than one falling within paragraph (c)) of a prescribed kind;
"taxi"—
  (a) means a vehicle which is licensed under section 37 of the Town Police Clauses Act 1847 or section 6 of the Metropolitan Public Carriage Act 1869, and
  (b) in sections 162 and 165 to 167, also includes a taxi licensed under section 10 of the Civic Government (Scotland) Act 1982,
  but does not include a vehicle drawn by a horse or other animal;
"taxi accessibility regulations" has the meaning given by section 160(1).

(2) A power to make regulations under paragraph (c) or (d) of the definition of "assistance dog" in subsection (1) is exercisable by the Secretary of State.

Policing and Crime Act 2017

Part 9
Miscellaneous and general

Chapter 1
Miscellaneous

Protection of children and vulnerable adults

177 Licensing functions under taxi and PHV legislation: protection of children and vulnerable adults (1) The Secretary of State may issue guidance to public authorities as to how their licensing functions under taxi and private hire vehicle legislation may be exercised so as to protect children, and vulnerable individuals who are 18 or over, from harm.

(2) The Secretary of State may revise any guidance issued under this section.

(3) The Secretary of State must arrange for any guidance issued under this section, and any revision of it, to be published.

(4) Any public authority which has licensing functions under taxi and private hire vehicle legislation must have regard to any guidance issued under this section.

(5) Before issuing guidance under this section, the Secretary of State must consult—
- (a) the National Police Chiefs' Council,
- (b) persons who appear to the Secretary of State to represent the interests of public authorities who are required to have regard to the guidance,
- (c) persons who appear to the Secretary of State to represent the interests of those whose livelihood is affected by the exercise of the licensing functions to which the guidance relates, and
- (d) such other persons as the Secretary of State considers appropriate.

(6) In this section, "taxi and private hire vehicle legislation" means—
- (a) the London Hackney Carriages Act 1843;
- (b) sections 37 to 68 of the Town Police Clauses Act 1847;
- (c) the Metropolitan Public Carriage Act 1869;
- (d) Part 2 of the Local Government (Miscellaneous Provisions) Act 1976;
- (e) the Private Hire Vehicles (London) Act 1998;
- (f) the Plymouth City Council Act 1975 (c.xx).

1975 No 1023

Rehabilitation of Offenders Act 1974 (Exceptions) Order 1975

1 This Order may be cited as the Rehabilitation of Offenders Act 1974 (Exceptions) Order 1975 and shall come into operation on 1st July 1975.

[2 (1) In this Order, except where the context otherwise requires—
["the 2000 Act" means the Financial Services and Markets Act 2000;]
["the 2006 Act" means the Safeguarding Vulnerable Groups Act 2006;]
"the Act" means the Rehabilitation of Offenders Act 1974;
["administration of justice offence" means—
    (a) the offence of perverting the course of justice,
    (b) any offence under section 51 of the Criminal Justice and Public Order Act 1994 (intimidation etc of witnesses, jurors and others),
    (c) an offence under section 1, 2, 6 or 7 of the Perjury Act 1911 (perjury), or any offence committed under the law of any part of the United Kingdom (other than England or Wales) or of any other country where the conduct which constitutes the offence would, if it all took place in England or Wales, constitute one or more of the offences specified by paragraph (a) to (c);]
["adoption agency" has the meaning given by section 2(1) of the Adoption and Children Act 2002;
"adoption service" means the discharge by a local authority in England or Wales of relevant adoption functions within the meaning of section 43(3)(a) of the Care Standards Act 2000;
"adoption support agency" has the meaning given by section 8 of the Adoption and Children Act 2002;]
["associate", in relation to a person ("A"), means someone who is a controller, director or manager of A or, where A is a partnership, any partner of A;]
["authorised payment institution" has the meaning given by regulation 2(1) of the [Payment Services Regulations 2017];]
. . .
["childminder agency" has the meaning given in section 98(1) of the Childcare Act 2006;]
["child minding" means—
    [(a) child minding within the meaning of section 79A of the Children Act 1989; and
    (b) early years childminding within the meaning of section 96(4) of the Childcare Act 2006, or later years childminding within the meaning of section 96(8) of that Act;]]

["children's home" has the meaning given by section 1 of the Care Standards Act 2000;]

["collective investment scheme" has the meaning given by section 235 of the 2000 Act;]

[. . .]

["contracting authority" has the meaning given by regulation 2(1) of the Public Contracts Regulations 2015, regulation 4(1) of the Utilities Contracts Regulations 2016 or regulation 4 of the Concession Contracts Regulations 2016, as appropriate;]

[. . .]

["controller" has the meaning given by section 422 of the 2000 Act;]

[. . .]

["Council of Lloyd's" means the council constituted by section 3 of Lloyd's Act 1982;]

["day care" means—
   [(a) day care for which registration is required by section 79D(5) of the Children Act 1989; and
   (b) early years provision within the meaning of section 96(2) of the Childcare Act 2006 (other than early years childminding), or later years provision within the meaning of section 96(6) of that Act (other than later years childminding), for which registration is required, or permitted, under Part 3 of that Act;]]

["day care premises" means any premises on which day care is provided, but does not include any part of the premises where children are not looked after;]

["depositary", in relation to an authorised contractual scheme, has the meaning given in section 237(2) of the 2000 Act;]

[. . .]

[. . .]

["director" has the meaning given by section 417 of the 2000 Act;]

["electronic money institution" has the meaning given by regulation 2(1) of the Electronic Money Regulations 2011;]

["the FCA" means the Financial Conduct Authority;]

["fostering agency" has the meaning given by section 4(4) of the Care Standards Act 2000;

"fostering service" means the discharge by a local authority in England or Wales of relevant fostering functions within the meaning of section 43(3)(b) of the Care Standards Act 2000;]

["key worker" means—
   (a) any individual who is likely, in the course of exercising the duties of that individual's office or employment, to play a significant role in the decision making process of the FCA, the PRA or the Bank of England in relation to the exercise of its public functions (within the meaning of section 349(5) of the 2000 Act); or
   (b) any individual who is likely, in the course of exercising the duties of that individual's office or employment, to support directly an individual mentioned in paragraph (a);]

["manager" has the meaning given by section 423 of the 2000 Act;]

["open-ended investment company" has the meaning given by section 236 of the 2000 Act;]

["operator", in relation to an authorised contractual scheme, has the meaning given in section 237(2) of the 2000 Act;]

["Part 4A permission" has the meaning given by section 55A(5) of the 2000 Act;]

["payment services" has the meaning given by regulation 2(1) of the [Payment Services Regulations 2017];]

["protected caution" means a caution of the kind described in article 2A(1);]

["protected conviction" means a conviction of the kind described in article 2A(2);]

["the PRA" means the Prudential Regulation Authority;]

["recognised clearing house" means a recognised clearing house as defined in section 285 of the 2000 Act;]

["registered account information service provider" has the meaning given by regulation 2(1) of the Payment Services Regulations 2017;]

["relevant collective investment scheme" means a collective investment scheme which is recognised under section 264 (schemes constituted in other EEA States) . . . or 272 (individually recognised overseas schemes) of the 2000 Act;]

. . .

["residential family centre" has the meaning given by section 4(2) of the Care Standards Act 2000;]

["small payment institution" has the meaning given by regulation 2(1) of the [Payment Services Regulations 2017];]

["taxi driver licence" means a licence granted under—

[(i) section 46 of the Town Police Clauses Act 1847;]

(ii) section 8 of the Metropolitan Public Carriage Act 1869;

(iii) section 9 of the Plymouth City Council Act 1975;

(iv) section 51 of the Local Government (Miscellaneous Provisions) Act 1976; or

(v) section 13 of the Private Hire Vehicles (London) Act 1998;]

["trustee", in relation to a unit trust scheme, has the meaning given by section 237 of the 2000 Act;]

[. . .]

["UK recognised investment exchange" means an investment exchange in relation to which a recognition order under section 290 of the 2000 Act, otherwise than by virtue of section 292(2) of that Act (overseas investment exchanges), is in force;]

["utility" has the meaning given by regulation 5(1) of the Utilities Contracts Regulations 2016 or regulation 5 of the Concession Contracts Regulations 2016, as appropriate;]

["voluntary adoption agency" has the meaning given by section 4(7) of the Care Standards Act 2000;]

["work" includes—

(a) work of any kind, whether paid or unpaid, and whether under a contract of service or apprenticeship, under a contract for services, or otherwise than under a contract; and

(b) an office established by or by virtue of an enactment;]

["work with children" means work of the kind described in paragraph 14[, 14A, 14B or 14C] of [Part 2 of] Schedule 1 to this Order;]

. . .

(2) . . .]

[(2ZA) In this Order references to the Bank of England do not include the Bank acting in its capacity as the Prudential Regulation Authority.]

[(2A) Nothing in this Order applies in relation to a conviction for a service offence which is not a recordable service offence; and for this purpose—

(a) "service offence" means an offence which is a service offence within the meaning of the Armed Forces Act 2006 or an SDA offence within the meaning of the Armed Forces Act 2006 (Transitional Provisions etc) Order 2009;

(b) "recordable service offence" means an offence which is a recordable service offence within the meaning of the Police and Criminal Evidence Act 1984 (Armed Forces) Order 2009.]

(3) Part IV of Schedule 1 to this Order shall have effect for the interpretation of expressions used in that Schedule.

(4) In this Order a reference to any enactment shall be construed as a reference to that enactment as amended, extended or applied by or under any other enactment.

[(4A) In this Order any reference to a conviction shall where relevant include a reference to a caution, and any reference to spent convictions shall be construed accordingly.]

(5) The Interpretation Act 1889 shall apply to the interpretation of this Order as it applies to the interpretation of an Act of Parliament.

Amendment

Paras (1), (2): substituted by the Rehabilitation of Offenders Act 1974 (Exceptions) (Amendment No. 2) Order 1986, SI 1986/2268, art 2(1), Schedule, para 1.

Para (1): definition "the 2000 Act" inserted by the Rehabilitation of Offenders Act 1974 (Exceptions) (Amendment) (No. 2) Order 2001, SI 2001/3816, arts 2, 3(1).

Para (1): definition "the 2006 Act" inserted by the Rehabilitation of Offenders Act 1974 (Exceptions) (Amendment) (England and Wales) Order 2009, SI 2009/1818, arts 2, 3.

Para (1): definition "administration of justice offence" inserted by the Rehabilitation of Offenders Act 1974 (Exceptions) (Amendment) (No. 2) Order 2001, SI 2001/3816, arts 2, 3(1).

Para (1): definition "adoption agency" inserted by the Rehabilitation of Offenders Act 1974 (Exceptions) (Amendment) Order 2001, SI 2001/1192, arts 2, 3(a).

Para (1): definitions "adoption agency", "adoption service" and "adoption support agency" substituted for definition "adoption agency" by the Rehabilitation of Offenders

Act 1974 (Exceptions) Order 1975 (Amendment) (England and Wales) Order 2014, SI 2014/1707, art 3(a).

Para (1): definition "associate" inserted by the Rehabilitation of Offenders Act 1974 (Exceptions) (Amendment) (No. 2) Order 2001, SI 2001/3816, arts 2, 3(1).

Para (1): definition "authorised payment institution" inserted by the Rehabilitation of Offenders Act 1974 (Exceptions) (Amendment) (England and Wales) Order 2011, SI 2011/1800, art 2(1), (2).

Para (1): in definition "authorised payment institution" words "Payment Services Regulations 2017" in square brackets substituted by the Payment Services Regulations 2017, SI 2017/752, reg 156, Sch 8, para 6(a)(i).

Para (1): definition "the Building Societies Commission" (omitted) repealed by the Rehabilitation of Offenders Act 1974 (Exceptions) (Amendment) (No. 2) Order 2001, SI 2001/3816, arts 2, 3(3).

Para (1): definition "childminder agency" inserted by the Rehabilitation of Offenders Act 1974 (Exceptions) Order 1975 (Amendment) (England and Wales) Order 2014, SI 2014/1707, art 3(b).

Para (1): definition "child minding" inserted by the Rehabilitation of Offenders Act 1974 (Exceptions) (Amendment) Order 2001, SI 2001/1192, arts 2, 3(b).

Para (1): in definition "child minding" paras (a), (b) substituted by the Rehabilitation of Offenders Act 1974 (Exceptions) (Amendment) (England and Wales) Order 2008, SI 2008/3259, arts 2, 3(1)(a).

Para (1): definition "children's home" inserted by the Rehabilitation of Offenders Act 1974 (Exceptions) Order 1975 (Amendment) (England and Wales) Order 2014, SI 2014/1707, art 3(c).

Para (1): definition "collective investment scheme" inserted by the Rehabilitation of Offenders Act 1974 (Exceptions) (Amendment) (No. 2) Order 2001, SI 2001/3816, arts 2, 3(1).

Para (1): definition "the competent authority for listing" inserted by the Rehabilitation of Offenders Act 1974 (Exceptions) (Amendment) (No. 2) Order 2001, SI 2001/3816, arts 2, 3(1).

Para (1): definition "the competent authority for listing" (omitted) repealed by the Financial Services Act 2012 (Consequential Amendments and Transitional Provisions) Order 2013, SI 2013/472, art 3, Sch 2, para 1(1), (2)(a).

Para (1): definition "contracting authority" inserted by the Rehabilitation of Offenders Act 1974 (Exceptions) (Amendment) (England and Wales) Order 2006, SI 2006/2143, arts 2, 3(b).

Para (1): definition "contracting authority" substituted by the Public Procurement (Amendments, Repeals and Revocations) Regulations 2016, SI 2016/275, reg 3, Sch 2, paras 25, 26(1), (2).

Para (1): definition "contracting entity" inserted by the Rehabilitation of Offenders Act 1974 (Exceptions) (Amendment) (England and Wales) Order 2006, SI 2006/2143, arts 2, 3(b).

Para (1): definition "contracting entity" (omitted) repealed by the Public Procurement (Amendments, Repeals and Revocations) Regulations 2016, SI 2016/275, reg 3, Sch 2, paras 25, 26(1), (3).

Para (1): definition "controller" inserted by the Rehabilitation of Offenders Act 1974 (Exceptions) (Amendment) (No. 2) Order 2001, SI 2001/3816, arts 2, 3(1).

Para (1): definition "Council" inserted by the Rehabilitation of Offenders Act 1974 (Exceptions) (Amendment) (England and Wales) Order 2003, SI 2003/965, arts 2, 3(a).

Para (1): definition "Council" (omitted) repealed by the Rehabilitation of Offenders Act 1974 (Exceptions) (Amendment) (England and Wales) Order 2012, SI 2012/1957, arts 2, 4.

Para (1): definition "Council of Lloyd's" inserted by the Rehabilitation of Offenders Act 1974 (Exceptions) (Amendment) (No. 2) Order 2001, SI 2001/3816, arts 2, 3(1).

Para (1): definition "day care" inserted by the Rehabilitation of Offenders Act 1974 (Exceptions) (Amendment) Order 2001, SI 2001/1192, arts 2, 3(b).

Para (1): in definition "day care" paras (a), (b) substituted by the Rehabilitation of Offenders Act 1974 (Exceptions) (Amendment) (England and Wales) Order 2008, SI 2008/3259, arts 2, 3(1)(b).

Para (1): definition "day care premises" inserted by the Rehabilitation of Offenders Act 1974 (Exceptions) (Amendment) Order 2001, SI 2001/1192, arts 2, 3(b).

Para (1): definition "depositary" inserted by the Collective Investment in Transferable Securities (Contractual Scheme) Regulations 2013, SI 2013/1388, reg 7(1), (2)(a).

Para (1): definition "Directive 2004/17/EC" inserted by the Rehabilitation of Offenders Act 1974 (Exceptions) (Amendment) (England and Wales) Order 2006, SI 2006/2143, arts 2, 3(b).

Para (1): definition "Directive 2004/17/EC" (omitted) repealed by the Public Procurement (Amendments, Repeals and Revocations) Regulations 2016, SI 2016/275, reg 3, Sch 2, paras 25, 26(1), (3).

Para (1): definition "Directive 2004/18/EC" inserted by the Rehabilitation of Offenders Act 1974 (Exceptions) (Amendment) (England and Wales) Order 2006, SI 2006/2143, arts 2, 3(b).

Para (1): definition "Directive 2004/18/EC" (omitted) repealed by the Public Procurement (Amendments, Repeals and Revocations) Regulations 2016, SI 2016/275, reg 3, Sch 2, paras 25, 26(1), (3).

Para (1): definition "director" inserted by the Rehabilitation of Offenders Act 1974 (Exceptions) (Amendment) (No. 2) Order 2001, SI 2001/3816, arts 2, 3(1).

Para (1): definition "electronic money institution" inserted by the Electronic Money Regulations 2011, SI 2011/99, reg 79, Sch 4, para 7(a).

Para (1): definition "the FCA" inserted by the Financial Services Act 2012 (Consequential Amendments and Transitional Provisions) Order 2013, SI 2013/472, art 3, Sch 2, para 1(1), (2)(b).

Para (1): definitions "fostering agency" and "fostering service" substituted for definition "the FCA" by the Rehabilitation of Offenders Act 1974 (Exceptions) Order 1975 (Amendment) (England and Wales) Order 2014, SI 2014/1707, art 3(d).

Para (1): definition "key worker" inserted by the Rehabilitation of Offenders Act 1974 (Exceptions) (Amendment) (No. 2) Order 2001, SI 2001/3816, arts 2, 3(1).

Para (1): definition "key worker" substituted by the Financial Services Act 2012 (Consequential Amendments and Transitional Provisions) Order 2013, SI 2013/472, art 3, Sch 2, para 1(1), (2)(c).

Para (1): definition "manager" inserted by the Rehabilitation of Offenders Act 1974 (Exceptions) (Amendment) (No. 2) Order 2001, SI 2001/3816, arts 2, 3(1).

Para (1): definition "open-ended investment company" inserted by the Rehabilitation of Offenders Act 1974 (Exceptions) (Amendment) (No. 2) Order 2001, SI 2001/3816, arts 2, 3(1).

Para (1): definition "operator" inserted by the Collective Investment in Transferable Securities (Contractual Scheme) Regulations 2013, SI 2013/1388, reg 7(1), (2)(b).

Para (1): definition "Part IV permission" inserted by the Rehabilitation of Offenders Act 1974 (Exceptions) (Amendment) (No. 2) Order 2001, SI 2001/3816, arts 2, 3(1).

Para (1): definition "Part 4A permission" substituted for definition "Part IV permission" by the Financial Services Act 2012 (Consequential Amendments and Transitional Provisions) Order 2013, SI 2013/472, art 3, Sch 2, para 1(1), (2)(d).

Para (1): definition "payment services" inserted by the Rehabilitation of Offenders Act 1974 (Exceptions) (Amendment) (England and Wales) Order 2011, SI 2011/1800, art 2(1), (2).

Para (1): in definition "payment services" words "Payment Services Regulations 2017" in square brackets substituted by the Payment Services Regulations 2017, SI 2017/752, reg 156, Sch 8, para 6(a)(i).

Para (1): definition "protected caution" inserted by the Rehabilitation of Offenders Act 1974 (Exceptions) Order 1975 (Amendment) (England and Wales) Order 2013, SI 2013/1198, arts 2, 3(1), (2).

Para (1): definition "protected conviction" inserted by the Rehabilitation of Offenders Act 1974 (Exceptions) Order 1975 (Amendment) (England and Wales) Order 2013, SI 2013/1198, arts 2, 3(1), (2).

Para (1): definition "the PRA" inserted by the Financial Services Act 2012 (Consequential Amendments and Transitional Provisions) Order 2013, SI 2013/472, art 3, Sch 2, para 1(1), (2)(b).

Para (1): definition "recognised clearing house" inserted by the Financial Services and Markets Act 2000 (Over the Counter Derivatives, Central Counterparties and Trade Repositories) Regulations 2013, SI 2013/504, reg 28(1), (2)(b).

Para (1): definition "registered account information service provider" inserted by the Payment Services Regulations 2017, SI 2017/752, reg 156, Sch 8, para 6(a)(ii).

Para (1): definition "relevant collective investment scheme" inserted by the Rehabilitation of Offenders Act 1974 (Exceptions) (Amendment) (No. 2) Order 2001, SI 2001/3816, arts 2, 3(1).

Para (1): in definition "relevant collective investment scheme" words omitted repealed by the Alternative Investment Fund Managers Regulations 2013, SI 2013/1773, reg 81(2), Sch 2, para 2(1), (2).

Para (1): definition "relevant offence" (omitted) repealed by the Rehabilitation of Offenders Act 1974 (Exceptions) (Amendment) (England and Wales) Order 2007, SI 2007/2149, arts 2, 3(1).

Para (1): definition "residential family centre" inserted by the Rehabilitation of Offenders Act 1974 (Exceptions) Order 1975 (Amendment) (England and Wales) Order 2014, SI 2014/1707, art 3(e).

Para (1): definition "small payment institution" inserted by the Rehabilitation of Offenders Act 1974 (Exceptions) (Amendment) (England and Wales) Order 2011, SI 2011/1800, art 2(1), (2).

Para (1): in definition "small payment institution" words "Payment Services Regulations 2017" in square brackets substituted by the Payment Services Regulations 2017, SI 2017/752, reg 156, Sch 8, para 6(a)(i).

Para (1): definition "taxi driver licence" inserted by the Rehabilitation of Offenders Act 1974 (Exceptions) (Amendment) (England and Wales) Order 2003, SI 2003/965, arts 2, 3(b).

Para (1): in definition "taxi driver licence" para (i) substituted by the Rehabilitation of Offenders Act 1974 (Exceptions) (Amendment) (England and Wales) Order 2006, SI 2006/2143, arts 2, 3(a).

Para (1): definition "trustee" inserted by the Rehabilitation of Offenders Act 1974 (Exceptions) (Amendment) (No. 2) Order 2001, SI 2001/3816, arts 2, 3(1).

Para (1): definition "UK recognised clearing house" inserted by the Rehabilitation of Offenders Act 1974 (Exceptions) (Amendment) (No. 2) Order 2001, SI 2001/3816, arts 2, 3(1).

Para (1): definition "UK recognised clearing house" repealed by the Financial Services and Markets Act 2000 (Over the Counter Derivatives, Central Counterparties and Trade Repositories) Regulations 2013, SI 2013/504, reg 28(1), (2)(a).

Para (1): definition "UK recognised investment exchange" inserted by the Rehabilitation of Offenders Act 1974 (Exceptions) (Amendment) (No. 2) Order 2001, SI 2001/3816, arts 2, 3(1).

Para (1): definition "utility" inserted by the Public Procurement (Amendments, Repeals and Revocations) Regulations 2016, SI 2016/275, reg 3, Sch 2, paras 25, 26(1), (4).

Para (1): definition "voluntary adoption agency" inserted by the Rehabilitation of Offenders Act 1974 (Exceptions) Order 1975 (Amendment) (England and Wales) Order 2014, SI 2014/1707, art 3(f).

Para (1): definition "work" inserted by the Rehabilitation of Offenders Act 1974 (Exceptions) (Amendment) Order 2001, SI 2001/1192, arts 2, 3(c).

Para (1): definition "work with children" inserted by the Rehabilitation of Offenders Act 1974 (Exceptions) (Amendment) Order 2001, SI 2001/1192, arts 2, 3(c).

Para (1): in definition "work with children" words "or 14A" in square brackets inserted by the Rehabilitation of Offenders Act 1974 (Exceptions) (Amendment) (England and Wales) Order 2012, SI 2012/1957, arts 2, 7.

Para (1): in definition "work with children" words ", 14A, 14B or 14C" in square brackets substituted for "or 14A" by the Rehabilitation of Offenders Act 1974 (Exceptions) Order 1975 (Amendment) (England and Wales) Order 2014, SI 2014/1707, art 3(g).

Para (1): in definition "work with children" words "Part 2 of" in square brackets inserted by the Rehabilitation of Offenders Act 1974 (Exceptions) (Amendment) (England and Wales) Order 2008, SI 2008/3259, arts 2, 3(1)(c).

Para (1): words omitted repealed by the Rehabilitation of Offenders Act 1974 (Exceptions) (Amendment) (No. 2) Order 2001, SI 2001/3816, arts 2, 3(3).

Para (2): repealed by the Rehabilitation of Offenders Act 1974 (Exceptions) Order 1975 (Amendment) (England and Wales) Order 2013, SI 2013/1198, arts 2, 3(1), (3).

Para (2ZA): inserted by the Bank of England and Financial Services (Consequential Amendments) Regulations 2017, SI 2017/80, reg 2, Schedule, para 21.

Para (2A): inserted by the Rehabilitation of Offenders Act 1974 (Exceptions) Order 1975 (Amendment) (England and Wales) Order 2013, SI 2013/1198, arts 2, 3(1), (4).

Para (4A): inserted by the Rehabilitation of Offenders Act 1974 (Exceptions) (Amendment) (England and Wales) Order 2008, SI 2008/3259, arts 2, 3(2).

[2A (1) For the purposes of this Order, a caution is a protected caution if it was given to a person for an offence other than a listed offence and—

(a) where the person was under 18 years at the time the caution was given, two years or more have passed since the date on which the caution was given; or

(b) where the person was 18 years or over at the time the caution was given, six years or more have passed since the date on which the caution was given.

(2) For the purposes of this Order, a person's conviction is a protected conviction if the conditions in paragraph (3) are satisfied and—

(a) where the person was under 18 years at the time of the conviction, five years and six months or more have passed since the date of the conviction; or

(b) where the person was 18 years or over at the time of the conviction, 11 years or more have passed since the date of the conviction.

(3) The conditions referred to in paragraph (2) are that—

(a) the offence of which the person was convicted was not a listed offence;

(b) no sentence mentioned in paragraph (4) was imposed in respect of the conviction; and

    (c) the person has not been convicted of any other offence at any time.

(4) The sentences referred to in paragraph (3)(b) are—
    (a) a custodial sentence, and
    (b) a sentence of service detention,

within the meaning of section 5(8) of the Act, as to be substituted by section 139(1) and (4) of the Legal Aid, Sentencing and Punishment of Offenders Act 2012.

(5) In paragraphs (1) and (3)(a) "listed offence" means—
    (a) an offence under section 67(1A) of the Medicines Act 1968;
    (b) an offence under any of sections 126 to 129 of the Mental Health Act 1983;
    (c) an offence specified in the Schedule to the Disqualification from Caring for Children (England) Regulations 2002;
    (d) an offence specified in Schedule 15 to the Criminal Justice Act 2003;
    (e) an offence under section 44 of, or under paragraph 4 of Schedule 1 or paragraph 4 of Schedule 4 to, the Mental Capacity Act 2005;
    (f) an offence under section 7, 9 or 19 of the Safeguarding Vulnerable Groups Act 2006;
    (g) an offence specified in section 17(3)(a), (b) or (c) of the Health and Social Care Act 2008, apart from an offence under section 76 of that Act;
    (h) an offence specified in the Schedule to the Safeguarding Vulnerable Groups Act 2006 (Prescribed Criteria and Miscellaneous Provisions) Regulations 2009;
    (i) an offence specified in Schedule 2 or 3 of the Childcare (Disqualification) Regulations 2009;
    (j) an offence superseded (whether directly or indirectly) by any offence falling within paragraphs (a) to (i);
    (k) an offence of—
        (i) attempting or conspiring to commit any offence falling within paragraphs (a) to (j), or
        (ii) inciting or aiding, abetting, counselling or procuring the commission of any such offence,
      or an offence under Part 2 of the Serious Crime Act 2007 (encouraging or assisting crime) committed in relation to any such offence;
    (l) an offence under the law of Scotland or Northern Ireland, or any country or territory outside the United Kingdom, which corresponds to any offence under the law of England and Wales falling within paragraphs (a) to (k);
    (m) an offence under section 42 of the Armed Forces Act 2006 in relation to which the corresponding offence under the law of England and Wales (within the meaning of that section) is an offence falling within paragraphs (a) to (k); or
    (n) an offence under section 70 of the Army Act 1955, section 70 of the Air Force Act 1955 or section 42 of the Naval Discipline Act 1957 of which

the corresponding civil offence (within the meaning of that Act) is an offence falling within paragraphs (a) to (k).]

Amendment

Article inserted by the Rehabilitation of Offenders Act 1974 (Exceptions) Order 1975 (Amendment) (England and Wales) Order 2013, SI 2013/1198, arts 2, 4.

3 [(1)] [[Subject to paragraph (2), neither] section 4(2) of, nor paragraph 3(3) of Schedule 2 to,] the Act shall apply in relation to—

    (a) any question asked by or on behalf of any person, in the course of the duties of his office or employment, in order to assess the suitability—

        (i) of the person to whom the question relates for admission to any of the professions specified in Part I of Schedule 1 to this Order; or

        [(ii) of the person to whom the question relates for any office or employment specified in Part II of the said Schedule 1 [apart from one specified in paragraph [1,] 6, 16, 17, 18, 18A, 31, 32, 35 or 36] or for any other work specified in paragraph [12A, 13, [13A,] 14, 14A, [14AA,] [14B, 14C,] [14D,] [14E,] 20, 21, ... [38, 40 or 43]] of Part II of the said Schedule 1; or]

        (iii) of the person to whom the question relates or of any other person to pursue any occupation specified in Part III of the said Schedule 1 [apart from one specified in paragraph 1 or 8] or to pursue it subject to a particular condition or restriction; or

        (iv) of the person to whom the question relates or of any other person to hold a licence, certificate or permit of a kind specified in Schedule 2 to this Order [apart from one specified in paragraph 1 or 3] or to hold it subject to a particular condition or restriction,

    where the person questioned is informed at the time the question is asked that, by virtue of this Order, spent convictions are to be disclosed;

    [(aa) any question asked by or on behalf of any person, in the course of the duties of his work, in order to assess the suitability of a person to work with children, where—

        (i) the question relates to the person whose suitability is being assessed;

        (ii) the person whose suitability is being assessed lives on the premises where his work with children would normally take place and the question relates to a person living in the same household as him;

        (iii) the person whose suitability is being assessed lives on the premises where his work with children would normally take place and the question relates to a person who regularly works on those premises at a time when the work with children usually takes place; or

        (iv) the work for which the person's suitability is being assessed is child minding which would normally take place on premises other than premises where that person lives and the question relates to a person who lives on those other premises or to a person who regularly works on them at a time when the child minding takes place, and where the person to whom the question relates is informed at the time the question is asked that, by virtue of this Order, spent convictions are to be disclosed;]

[(ab) . . .]

(b) . . .

[(bb) any question asked by or on behalf of
  (i)   the Civil Aviation Authority,
  (ii) any other person authorised to provide air traffic services under section 4 or section 5 of the Transport Act 2000 (in any case where such person is a company, an "authorised company"),
  (iii) any company which is a subsidiary (within the meaning given by section 736(1) of the Companies Act 1985) of an authorised company, or
  (iv) any company of which an authorised company is a subsidiary,
  where, in the case of sub-paragraphs (iii) and (iv) of this paragraph the question is put in relation to the provision of air traffic services, and in all cases, where the question is put in order to assess, for the purpose of safeguarding national security, the suitability of the person to whom the question relates or of any other person for any office or employment where the person questioned is informed at the time the question is asked that, by virtue of this Order, spent convictions are to be disclosed for the purpose of safeguarding national security;]

[(e) any question asked by or on behalf of any person in the course of his duties as a person employed by an adoption agency for the purpose of assessing the suitability of any person to adopt children in general or a child in particular where—
  (i)   the question relates to the person whose suitability is being assessed; or
  (ii) the question relates to a person over the age of 18 living in the same household as the person whose suitability is being assessed,
  and where the person to whom the question relates is informed at the time the question is asked that, by virtue of this Order, spent convictions are to be disclosed;]

[(ea) any question asked by or on behalf of any person in the course of his duties as a person employed by a local authority in England or Wales for the purpose of preparing a report for the court under section 14A(8) of the Children Act 1989 regarding the suitability of any person to be a special guardian, where—
  (i)   the question relates to the person whose suitability is being assessed; or
  (ii) the question relates to a person over the age of 18 living in the same household as the person whose suitability is being assessed; and where the person to whom the question relates is informed at the time the question is asked that, by virtue of this Order, spent convictions are to be disclosed;]

[(f) any question asked by or on behalf of any person, in the course of the duties of his work, in order to assess the suitability of a person to provide day care where—

(i) the question relates to the person whose suitability is being assessed; or

(ii) the question relates to a person who lives on the premises which are or are proposed to be day care premises,

and where the person to whom the question relates is informed at the time the question is asked that, by virtue of this Order, spent convictions are to be disclosed];

[(fa) any question asked by or on behalf of Her Majesty's Chief Inspector of Education, Children's Services and Skills in assessing a person's suitability for registration as a childminder agency under Part 3 of the Childcare Act 2006, where the person to whom the question relates is informed at the time the question is asked that, by virtue of this Order, spent convictions are to be disclosed;]

[(g) any question asked by, or on behalf of, the person listed in the second column of any entry in the table below to the extent that it relates to a conviction . . . (or any circumstances ancillary to . . . a conviction) of any individual, but only if—

(i) the person questioned is informed at the time the question is asked that, by virtue of this Order, spent convictions . . . are to be disclosed; and

(ii) the question is asked in order to assess the suitability of the individual to whom the question relates to have the status specified in the first column of that entry

[Status	Questioner
1 A person with Part 4A permission.	The FCA, the PRA or the Bank of England.
2 (a) A person in relation to whom an approval is given under section 59 of the 2000 Act (approval for particulararrangements). (b) An associate of the person (whether or not an individual) mentioned insub-paragraph (a)).	The FCA, the PRA or the authorised person (within the meaning of section 31(2) of the 2000 Act) or the applicant for Part 4A permission who made the application for the approval of the appropriate regulator (within the meaning of section 59(4) of the 2000 Act) under section 59 of the 2000 Act in relation to the person mentioned in sub-paragraph (a) of the first column.

[Status	Questioner
3 (a) The manager or trustee of an authorised unit trust scheme (within the meaning of section 237 of the 2000 Act.)	The FCA or the unit trust scheme mentioned in the first column.
(b) An associate of the person (whether or not an individual) mentioned in sub-paragraph (a).	
[3A (a) The operator or despositary of an authorised contractual scheme (within the meaning of section 237(3) of the 2000 Act.)	The FCA.]
(b) An associate of the person (whether or not an individual) mentioned in sub-paragraph (a).	
4 (a) A director of an open-ended investment company.	The FCA, the PRA or the open-ended investment company mentioned in the first column.
(b) An associate of the person (whether or not an individual) mentioned in sub-paragraph (a).	
5 An associate of the operator or trustee of a relevant collective investment scheme.	The FCA, the PRA, the Bank of England or the collective investment scheme mentioned in the first column.
[6 An associate of a UK recognised investment exchange or recognised clearing house.	The FCA, the PRA, the Bank of England or the investment exchange or clearing house mentioned in the first column.]
7 A controller of a person with Part 4A permission.	The FCA, the PRA or the person with Part 4A permission mentioned in the first column.
8 (a) A person who carries on a regulated activity (within the meaning of section 22 of the 2000 Act) but to whom the general prohibition does not apply by virtue of section 327 of the 2000 Act (exemption from the general prohibition for members of a designated professional body).	(a) The FCA or the PRA.

[Status	Questioner
(b) An associate of the person (whether or not an individual) mentioned in sub-paragraph (a).	
9 A key worker of the FCA, the PRA or the Bank of England.	The FCA, the PRA or the Bank of England.
10 An ombudsman (within the meaning of Schedule 17 to the 2000 Act) of the Financial Ombudsman Service.	The scheme operator (within the meaning of section 225 of the 2000 Act) of the Financial Ombudsman Service.
11 An associate of the issuer of securities which have been admitted to the official list maintained by the FCA for listing under section 74 of the 2000 Act.	The FCA.
12 A sponsor (within the meaning of section 88(2) of the 2000 Act).	The FCA.
13 (a) A Primary information provider within the meaning of section 89P of the 2000 Act).	The FCA or the PRA.
(b) An associate of the person (whether or not an individual) mentioned in sub-paragraph (a).	In the case of a person mentioned in sub-paragraph (2) of the first column, the person mentioned in sub-paragraph (1) of that column.
14 An associate of a person who has Part 4A permission and who is admitted to Lloyd's as an underwriting agent (within the meaning of section 2 of Lloyd's Act 1982).	(a) The Council of Lloyd's. (b) The person with Part 4A permission specified in the first column (or a person applying for such permission).
15 An associate of the Council of Lloyd's.	The Council of Lloyd's.
[16 (a) Any member of a UK recognised investment exchange or recognised clearing house.	The UK recognised investment exchange or recognised clearing house specified in the first column.]
(b) An associate of the person (whether or not an individual) mentioned in sub-paragraph (a).	In the case of a person mentioned in sub-paragraph (b) of the first column, the person mentioned in sub-paragraph (a) of that column.
17 A director or person responsible for the management of the electronic money or payment service business of an electronic money institution.	The FCA.

[Status	Questioner
18 A controller of an electronic money institution.	The FCA.
19 A director or a person responsible for the management of an authorised payment institution or a small payment institution.	The FCA.
20 A person responsible for the management of payment services provided, or to be provided, by an authorised payment institution or a small payment institution.	The FCA.
21 A controller of an authorised payment institution or a small payment institution.	The FCA.]

[(h) any question asked by or on behalf of the [Gambling Commission] for the purpose of determining whether to grant or revoke a licence under Part I of the National Lottery etc Act 1993 where the question relates to an individual—

(i) who manages the business or any part of the business carried on under the licence (or who is likely to do so if the licence is granted), or

(ii) for whose benefit that business is carried on (or is likely to be carried on if the licence is granted),

and where the person to whom the question relates is informed at the time that the question is asked that, by virtue of this Order, spent convictions are to be disclosed];

[(i) any question asked by or on behalf of the [Care Council for Wales] for the purpose of determining whether or not to grant an application for registration under Part IV of the Care Standards Act 2000, where the person questioned is informed at the time the question is asked that, by virtue of this Order, spent convictions are to be disclosed];

[[(j) any question asked by or on behalf of a contracting authority or utility in relation to a conviction for an offence listed in regulation 57(1) of the Public Contracts Regulations 2015 or regulation 38(8) of the Concession Contracts Regulations 2016 which is a spent conviction (or any circumstances ancillary to such a conviction) for the purpose of determining whether or not a person is excluded—

(i) for the purposes of regulation 57 of the Public Contracts Regulations 2015,

(ii) from participation in a design contest for the purposes of regulation 80 of the Public Contracts Regulations 2015,

(iii) for the purposes of regulation 80 of the Utilities Contracts Regulations 2016,

(iv) from participation in a design contest for the purposes of regulation 96 of the Utilities Contracts Regulations 2016, or

(v) for the purposes of regulation 38 of the Concession Contracts Regulations 2016,

where the person questioned is informed at the time the question is asked that, by virtue of this Order, spent convictions for such offences are to be disclosed;]

(ja) . . .]

[(k) any question asked, by or on behalf of the Football Association[, Football League] or Football Association Premier League in order to assess the suitability of the person to whom the question relates or of any other person to be approved as able to undertake, in the course of acting as a steward at a sports ground at which football matches are played or as a supervisor or manager of such a person, licensable conduct within the meaning of the Private Security Industry Act 2001 without a licence issued under that Act, in accordance with . . . section 4 of that Act];

[(l) any question asked by the [Disclosure and Barring Service] for the purpose of considering the suitability of an individual to have access to information released under sections 113A and 113B of the Police Act 1997];

[(m) any question asked by or on behalf of the Master Locksmiths Association for the purposes of assessing the suitability of any person who has applied to be granted membership of that Association;

(n) any question asked by or on behalf of the Secretary of State for the purpose of assessing the suitability of any person or body to obtain or retain a licence under regulation 5 of the Misuse of Drugs Regulations 2001 or under Article 3(2) of Regulation 2004/273/EC or under article 6(1) of Regulation 2005/111/EC where—

(i) the question relates to the holder of, or an applicant for, such a licence or any person who as a result of his role in the company or other body concerned is required to be named in the application for such a licence (or would have been so required if that person had had that role at the time the application was made), and

(ii) any person to whom the question relates is informed at the time the question is asked that by virtue of this Order, spent convictions are to be disclosed;]

[(o) any question asked by or on behalf of any body which is a licensing authority within the meaning of section 73(1) of the Legal Services Act 2007 (licensing authorities and relevant licensing authorities) where—

(i) it is asked in order to assess whether, for the purposes of Schedule 13 to that Act (ownership of licensed bodies), the approval requirements are met in relation to a person's holding of a restricted interest in a licensed body; and

(ii) the person to whom the question relates is informed at the time that the question is asked that, by virtue of this Order, spent convictions are to be disclosed.]

[(2) Paragraph (1) does not apply in relation to a protected caution or a protected conviction.]

Amendment

Article renumbered as para (1) by the Rehabilitation of Offenders Act 1974 (Exceptions) Order 1975 (Amendment) (England and Wales) Order 2013, SI 2013/1198, arts 2, 5(a).

Para (1): words "Subject to paragraph (2), neither" in square brackets substituted by the Rehabilitation of Offenders Act 1974 (Exceptions) Order 1975 (Amendment) (England and Wales) Order 2013, SI 2013/1198, arts 2, 5(b).

Para (1): words "Neither section 4(2) of, nor paragraph 3(3) of Schedule 2 to," in square brackets substituted by the Rehabilitation of Offenders Act 1974 (Exceptions) (Amendment) (England and Wales) Order 2008, SI 2008/3259, art 4.

Para (1): sub-para (a)(ii) substituted by the Rehabilitation of Offenders Act 1974 (Exceptions) (Amendment) Order 2001, SI 2001/1192, arts 2, 4(1).

Para (1): in sub-para (a)(ii) words "apart from one specified in paragraph 6, 16, 17, 18, 18A, 31, 32, 35 or 36" in square brackets substituted by the Rehabilitation of Offenders Act 1974 (Exceptions) Order 1975 (Amendment) (England and Wales) Order 2013, SI 2013/1198, arts 2, 5(c)(i).

Para (1): in sub-para (a)(ii) word "1," in square brackets inserted by the Rehabilitation of Offenders Act 1974 (Exceptions) Order 1975 (Amendment) (England and Wales) Order 2016, SI 2016/824, art 2(1), (3)(a).

Para (1): in sub-para (a)(ii) words "12A, 13, 14, 14A, 20, 21, 35, 36, 37, 40, 43 or 44" in square brackets substituted by the Rehabilitation of Offenders Act 1974 (Exceptions) (Amendment) (England and Wales) Order 2009, SI 2009/1818, arts 2, 4(1).

Para (1): in sub-para (a)(ii) word "13A," in square brackets inserted by the Rehabilitation of Offenders Act 1974 (Exceptions) Order 1975 (Amendment) (England and Wales) Order 2015, SI 2015/317, art 2(1), (2).

Para (1): in sub-para (a)(ii) word "14AA," in square brackets inserted by the Rehabilitation of Offenders Act 1974 (Exceptions) Order 1975 (Amendment) (England and Wales) Order 2016, SI 2016/824, art 2(1), (2)(a).

Para (1): in sub-para (a)(ii) words "14B, 14C," in square brackets inserted by the Rehabilitation of Offenders Act 1974 (Exceptions) Order 1975 (Amendment) (England and Wales) Order 2014, SI 2014/1707, arts 2, 4(a).

Para (1): in sub-para (a)(ii) words "14D," in square brackets inserted by the Rehabilitation of Offenders Act 1974 (Exceptions) Order 1975 (Amendment) (England and Wales) Order 2014, SI 2014/1707, arts 2, 4(b).

Para (1): in sub-para (a)(ii) word "14E," in square brackets inserted by the Rehabilitation of Offenders Act 1974 (Exceptions) Order 1975 (Amendment) (England and Wales) Order 2016, SI 2016/824, art 2(1), (2)(b).

Para (1): in sub-para (a)(ii) first figures omitted repealed by the Rehabilitation of Offenders Act 1974 (Exceptions) Order 1975 (Amendment) (England and Wales) Order 2013, SI 2013/1198, arts 2, 5(c)(i).

Para (1): in sub-para (a)(ii) second figure omitted repealed by the Rehabilitation of Offenders Act 1974 (Exceptions) (Amendment) (England and Wales) Order 2012, SI 2012/1957, arts 2, 8.

Para (1): in sub-para (a)(ii) words "38, 40 or 43" in square brackets substituted by the Protection of Freedoms Act 2012 (Disclosure and Barring Service Transfer of Functions) Order 2012, SI 2012/3006, arts 18, 19.

Para (1): in sub-para (a)(iii) words "apart from one specified in paragraph 1 or 8" in square brackets inserted by the Rehabilitation of Offenders Act 1974 (Exceptions) Order 1975 (Amendment) (England and Wales) Order 2013, SI 2013/1198, arts 2, 5(c)(ii).

Para (1): in sub-para (a)(iv) words "apart from one specified in paragraph 1 or 3" in square brackets inserted by the Rehabilitation of Offenders Act 1974 (Exceptions) Order 1975 (Amendment) (England and Wales) Order 2013, SI 2013/1198, arts 2, 5(c)(ii).

Para (1): sub-para (aa) inserted by the Rehabilitation of Offenders Act 1974 (Exceptions) (Amendment) Order 1986, SI 1986/1249, art 2, Schedule, para 1.

Para (1): sub-para (aa) substituted by the Rehabilitation of Offenders Act 1974 (Exceptions) (Amendment) Order 2001, SI 2001/1192, arts 2, 4(2).

Para (1): sub-para (ab) inserted by the Rehabilitation of Offenders Act 1974 (Exceptions) (Amendment No. 2) Order 1986, SI 1986/2268, art 2(1), Schedule, para 2.

Para (1): sub-para (ab) repealed by the Rehabilitation of Offenders Act 1974 (Exceptions) (Amendment) (No. 2) Order 2001, SI 2001/3816, arts 2, 4(1), (2).

Para (1): sub-para (b) words repealed by the Rehabilitation of Offenders Act 1974 (Exceptions) Order 1975 (Amendment) (England and Wales) Order 2013, SI 2013/1198, arts 2, 5(d).

Para (1): sub-para (bb) inserted by the Rehabilitation of Offenders Act 1974 (Exceptions) (Amendment) Order 2002, SI 2002/441, arts 2, 3(3).

Para (1): sub-para (e) inserted by the Rehabilitation of Offenders Act 1974 (Exceptions) (Amendment) Order 2001, SI 2001/1192, arts 2, 4(3). (It is understood that this para has been numbered incorrectly).

Para (1): sub-para (ea) inserted by the Rehabilitation of Offenders Act 1974 (Exceptions) Order 1975 (Amendment) (England and Wales) Order 2014, SI 2014/1707, arts 2, 4(c).

Para (1): sub-para (f) inserted by the Rehabilitation of Offenders Act 1974 (Exceptions) (Amendment) Order 2001, SI 2001/1192, arts 2, 4(3). (It is understood that this para has been numbered incorrectly).

Para (1): sub-para (fa) inserted by the Rehabilitation of Offenders Act 1974 (Exceptions) Order 1975 (Amendment) (England and Wales) Order 2014, SI 2014/1707, arts 2, 4(d).

Para (1): sub-para (g) inserted by the Rehabilitation of Offenders Act 1974 (Exceptions) (Amendment) (No. 2) Order 2001, SI 2001/3816, arts 2, 4(1), (4).

Para (1): in sub-para (g) first words omitted repealed by the Rehabilitation of Offenders Act 1974 (Exceptions) (Amendment) (England and Wales) Order 2007, SI 2007/2149, arts 2, 4(2)(i).

Para (1): in sub-para (g) second word omitted repealed by the Rehabilitation of Offenders Act 1974 (Exceptions) (Amendment) (England and Wales) Order 2007, SI 2007/2149, arts 2, 4(2)(ii).

Para (1): in sub-para (g)(i) words omitted repealed by the Rehabilitation of Offenders Act 1974 (Exceptions) (Amendment) (England and Wales) Order 2007, SI 2007/2149, arts 2, 4(3).

Para (1): in sub-para (g) Table substituted by the Financial Services Act 2012 (Consequential Amendments and Transitional Provisions) Order 2013, SI 2013/472, art 3, Sch 2, para 1(1), (3)(b).

Para (1): in sub-para (g), entry 3A in the Table substituted by the Collective Investment in Transferable Securities (Contractual Scheme) Regulations 2013, SI 2013/1388, reg 7(1), (3).

Para (1): in sub-para (g), entry 6 in the Table substituted by the Financial Services and Markets Act 2000 (Over the Counter Derivatives, Central Counterparties and Trade Repositories) Regulations 2013, SI 2013/504, reg 28(1), (3)(a).

Para (1): in sub-para (g), para (a) of entry 16 in the Table substituted by the Financial Services and Markets Act 2000 (Over the Counter Derivatives, Central Counterparties and Trade Repositories) Regulations 2013, SI 2013/504, reg 28(1), (3)(b).

Para (1): sub-para (h) inserted by the Rehabilitation of Offenders Act 1974 (Exceptions) (Amendment) Order 2002, SI 2002/441, arts 2, 3(4).

Para (1): in sub-para (h) words "Gambling Commission" in square brackets substituted by the Public Bodies (Merger of the Gambling Commission and the National Lottery Commission) Order 2013, SI 2013/2329, art 4(2), Schedule, para 30.

Para (1): sub-para (i) inserted by the Rehabilitation of Offenders Act 1974 (Exceptions) (Amendment) (England and Wales) Order 2003, SI 2003/965, arts 2, 5.

Para (1): in sub-para (i) words "Care Council for Wales" in square brackets substituted by the Rehabilitation of Offenders Act 1974 (Exceptions) (Amendment) (England and Wales) Order 2012, SI 2012/1957, arts 2, 5.

Para (1): sub-para (j) inserted by the Rehabilitation of Offenders Act 1974 (Exceptions) (Amendment) (England and Wales) Order 2006, SI 2006/2143, arts 2, 4.

Para (1): sub-para (j), (ja) substituted for sub-para (j) by the Public Contracts Regulations 2015, SI 2015/102, reg 116(2), Sch 6, para 10.

Para (1): sub-para (j) substituted by the Public Procurement (Amendments, Repeals and Revocations) Regulations 2016, SI 2016/275, reg 3, Sch 2, paras 25, 27.

Para (1): sub-para (ja) repealed by the Public Procurement (Amendments, Repeals and Revocations) Regulations 2016, SI 2016/275, reg 3, Sch 2, paras 25, 28.

Para (1): sub-para (k) inserted by the Rehabilitation of Offenders Act 1974 (Exceptions) (Amendment) (England and Wales) Order 2006, SI 2006/2143, arts 2, 4.

Para (1): in sub-para (k) words ", Football League" in square brackets inserted by the Rehabilitation of Offenders Act 1974 (Exceptions) (Amendment No. 2) (England and Wales) Order 2006, SI 2006/3290, art 2(1), (2)(a).

Para (1): in sub-para (k) words omitted repealed by the Rehabilitation of Offenders Act 1974 (Exceptions) (Amendment No. 2) (England and Wales) Order 2006, SI 2006/3290, art 2(1), (2)(b).

Para (1): sub-para (l) inserted by the Rehabilitation of Offenders Act 1974 (Exceptions) (Amendment) (England and Wales) Order 2007, SI 2007/2149, arts 2, 4(4).

Para (1): in sub-para (l) words "Disclosure and Barring Service" in square brackets substituted by the Protection of Freedoms Act 2012 (Disclosure and Barring Service Transfer of Functions) Order 2012, SI 2012/3006, arts 69, 70.

Para (1): sub-paras (m), (n) inserted by the Rehabilitation of Offenders Act 1974 (Exceptions) (Amendment) (England and Wales) Order 2009, SI 2009/1818, arts 2, 4(2).

Para (1): sub-para (o) inserted by the Rehabilitation of Offenders Act 1974 (Exceptions) (Amendment) (England and Wales) (No.2) Order 2011, SI 2011/2865, art 2.

Para (2): inserted by the Rehabilitation of Offenders Act 1974 (Exceptions) Order 1975 (Amendment) (England and Wales) Order 2013, SI 2013/1198, arts 2, 5(e).

[3ZA Neither section 4(2) of, nor paragraph 3(3) of Schedule 2 to, the Act applies in relation to—

    (a) any question asked by or on behalf of any person, in the course of the duties of his office or employment, in order to assess the suitability—

        (i) of the person to whom the question relates for an office or employment specified in paragraph [1,] 6, 16, 17, 18, 18A, 31, 32, 35 or 36 of Part II of that Schedule or for any other work specified in paragraph 35 or 36 of that Part of that Schedule; or

        (ii) of the person to whom the question relates or of any other person to pursue an occupation specified in paragraph 1 or 8 of Part III of that Schedule or to pursue it subject to a particular condition or restriction; or

        (iii) of the person to whom the question relates or of any other person to hold a licence, certificate or permit of a kind specified in paragraph 1 or 3 of Schedule 2 to this Order or to hold it subject to a particular condition or restriction,

where the person questioned is informed at the time the question is asked that, by virtue of this Order, spent convictions are to be disclosed; or

(b) any question asked by or on behalf of any person, in the course of his duties as a person employed in the service of the Crown, the United Kingdom Atomic Energy Authority or the FCA or the PRA in order to assess, for the purpose of safeguarding national security, the suitability of the person to whom the question relates or of any other person for any office or employment where the person questioned is informed at the time the question is asked that, by virtue of this Order, spent convictions are to be disclosed for the purpose of safeguarding national security.]

Amendment

Article inserted by the Rehabilitation of Offenders Act 1974 (Exceptions) Order 1975 (Amendment) (England and Wales) Order 2013, SI 2013/1198, arts 2, 6.

In sub-para (a)(i) figure "1," in square brackets inserted by the Rehabilitation of Offenders Act 1974 (Exceptions) Order 1975 (Amendment) (England and Wales) Order 2016, SI 2016/824, art 2(1), (3)(b).

[**3A** (1) [Subject to paragraph (1A), neither] section 4(2) of, nor paragraph 3(3) of Schedule 2 to, the Act applies to a question to which paragraph (2) or (3) applies.

[(1A) Paragraph (1) does not apply in relation to a protected caution or a protected conviction.]

(2) This paragraph applies to any question asked by or on behalf of any person ("A"), in the course of the duties of A's office or employment, in order to assess the suitability of the person to whom the question relates ("B") for any work which is a controlled activity relating to children within the meaning of section 21 of the 2006 Act [as it had effect immediately before the coming into force of section 68 of the Protection of Freedoms Act 2012], where the person questioned is told at the time the question is asked, that by virtue of this Order, spent convictions are to be disclosed but only if that person knows that B—

(a) is a person barred from regulated activity relating to children within the meaning of section 3(2) of the 2006 Act;

(b) is included in the list kept under section 1 of the Protection of Children Act 1999; or

(c) is subject to a direction made under section 142 of the Education Act 2002.

(3) This paragraph applies to any question asked by or on behalf of any person ("A"), in the course of the duties of A's office or employment, in order to assess the suitability of the person to whom the question relates ("B") for any work which is a controlled activity relating to vulnerable adults within the meaning of

section 22 of the 2006 Act [as it had effect immediately before the coming into force of section 68 of the Protection of Freedoms Act 2012], where the person questioned is told at the time the question is asked, that by virtue of this Order, spent convictions are to be disclosed but only if that person knows that B—

(a) is a person barred from regulated activity relating to vulnerable adults within the meaning of section 3(3) of the 2006 Act; or

(b) is included in the list kept under section 81 of the Care Standards Act 2000.]

Amendment

Article inserted by the Rehabilitation of Offenders Act 1974 (Exceptions) (Amendment) (England and Wales) Order 2010, SI 2010/1153, arts 2, 3.

Para (1): words "Subject to paragraph (1A), neither" in square brackets substituted by the Rehabilitation of Offenders Act 1974 (Exceptions) Order 1975 (Amendment) (England and Wales) Order 2013, SI 2013/1198, arts 1, 7(a).

Para (1A): inserted by the Rehabilitation of Offenders Act 1974 (Exceptions) Order 1975 (Amendment) (England and Wales) Order 2013, SI 2013/1198, arts 1, 7(b).

Para (2): words "as it had effect immediately before the coming into force of section 68 of the Protection of Freedoms Act 2012" in square brackets inserted by the Rehabilitation of Offenders Act 1974 (Exceptions) (Amendment) (England and Wales) Order 2012, SI 2012/1957, arts 2, 9.

Para (3): words "as it had effect immediately before the coming into force of section 68 of the Protection of Freedoms Act 2012" in square brackets inserted by the Rehabilitation of Offenders Act 1974 (Exceptions) (Amendment) (England and Wales) Order 2012, SI 2012/1957, arts 2, 9.

4 [(1)] [[Subject to paragraph (2), neither] paragraph (b) of section 4(3) of, nor paragraph 3(5) of Schedule 2 to the Act shall apply] in relation to—

(a) the dismissal or exclusion of any person from any profession specified in Part I of Schedule 1 to this Order;

[(b) any office, employment or occupation specified in Part II [of that Schedule apart from one specified in paragraph [1,] 6, 16, 17, 18, 18A, 31, 32, 35 or 36 or in Part III of that Schedule apart from one specified in paragraph 1 or 8] or any other work specified in paragraph [12A, 13, [13A,] 14, 14A, [14AA,] [14B, 14C,] [14D,] [14E,] 20, 21, ... 40, 43 or 44] of Part II of the said Schedule 1;]

(c) . . .

[(d) [any decision by the FCA, the PRA or the Bank of England]—

(i) to refuse an application for [Part 4A permission] under the 2000 Act,

(ii) to vary or to cancel such permission (or to refuse to vary or cancel such permission) or to impose a requirement under [section 55L, 55M or 55O] of that Act or,

(iii) to make, or to refuse to vary or revoke, an order under section 56 of that Act (prohibition orders),

(iv) to refuse an application for . . . approval under section 59 of that Act or to withdraw such approval,

(v)   to refuse to make, or to revoke, an order declaring a unit trust scheme to be an authorised unit trust scheme under section 243 of the 2000 Act or to refuse to give its approval under section 251 of the 2000 Act to a proposal to replace the manager or trustee of such a scheme,

(vi) to give a direction under section 257 of the 2000 Act (authorised unit trust schemes), or to vary (or to refuse to vary or revoke) such a direction,

[(via) to refuse to make, or to revoke, an order declaring a contractual scheme to be an authorised contractual scheme under section 261D of the 2000 Act or to refuse to give its approval under section 261Q of the 2000 Act to a proposal to replace the operator or depositary of such a scheme,

(vib) to give a direction under section 261X of the 2000 Act or to vary (or to refuse to vary or revoke) such a direction,]

(vii) to refuse to make, or to revoke, an authorisation order under regulation 14 of the Open-Ended Investment Companies Regulations 2001 or to refuse to give its approval under regulation 21 of those Regulations to a proposal to replace a director or to appoint an additional director of an open-ended investment company,

(viii) to give a direction to an open-ended investment company under regulation 25 of those Regulations or to vary (or refuse to vary or revoke) such a direction,

(ix) . . . to refuse to make, or to revoke, an order declaring a collective investment scheme to be a recognised scheme under section 272 of [the 2000 Act],

(x)   to refuse to make, or to revoke, a recognition order under section 290 of the 2000 Act, otherwise than by virtue of section 292(2) of that Act, [to refuse to vary a recognition order under section 290ZA(1) of the 2000 Act, to vary a recognition order under section 290ZA(2) of the 2000 Act,] or to give a direction to a UK recognised investment exchange or [recognised clearing house] under section 296 [or 296A] of the 2000 Act,

(xi) to make, or to refuse to vary or to revoke, an order under section 329 (orders in respect of members of a designated professional body in relation to the general prohibition), . . .

(xii) to dismiss, fail to promote or exclude a person from being a key worker of [the FCA or the PRA],

[(xiii) to refuse an application for registration as an authorised electronic money institution or a small electronic money institution under the Electronic Money Regulations 2011, . . .

(xiv) to vary or cancel such registration (or to refuse to vary or cancel such registration) or to impose a requirement under regulation 7 of those Regulations,]

[(xv) to refuse an application for registration as an authorised payment institution[, a registered account information service provider] or a small payment institution under the Payment Services Regulations [2017], . . .

(xvi) to vary or cancel such registration (or to refuse to vary or cancel such registration) or to impose a requirement under regulation 7 of those Regulations,]

[(xvii) in a case requiring any decision referred to in paragraphs (i) to (xvi), where the FCA, the PRA or the Bank of England has the function of deciding whether to give consent or conditional consent in relation to the decision which is proposed in that case, to give or refuse to give consent or to give conditional consent, or

(xviii) in a case requiring any decision referred to in paragraphs (i) to (xvi), where the FCA, the PRA or the Bank of England has the power under the 2000 Act to direct another regulator as to the decision to be taken in that case, to decide whether to give a direction and, if a direction is to be given, what direction to give,]

by reason of, or partly by reason of, a spent conviction of an individual . . ., or of any circumstances ancillary to such a conviction or of a failure (whether or not by that individual) to disclose such a conviction or any such circumstances;

(e) any decision by the scheme operator (within the meaning of section 225 of the 2000 Act) of the Financial Ombudsman Service to dismiss, or not to appoint, an individual as, an ombudsman (within the meaning of Schedule 17 to the 2000 Act) of the Financial Ombudsman Service by reason of, or partly by reason of, his spent conviction . . ., or of any circumstances ancillary to such a conviction or of a failure (whether or not by that individual) to disclose such a conviction or any such circumstances;

(f) [any decision of the FCA]—

(i) to refuse an application for listing under Part VI of the 2000 Act or to discontinue or suspend the listing of any securities under section 77 of that Act,

(ii) to refuse to grant a person's application for approval as a sponsor under section 88 of the 2000 Act or to cancel such approval, . . .

(iii) to dismiss, fail to promote or exclude a person from being a key worker of [the FCA in relation to the exercise of its functions under Part 6 of the 2000 Act, or]

[(iv) to refuse to grant a person's application under information provider rules (within the meaning of section 89P(9) of the 2000 Act) for approval as a Primary information provider, to impose limitations or other restrictions on the giving of information to which such an approval relates or to cancel such an approval,]

by reason of, or partly by reason of, a spent conviction of an individual . . ., or of any circumstances ancillary to such a conviction or of a failure (whether or not by that individual) to disclose such a conviction or any such circumstances;

(g) any decision of anyone who is specified in any of sub-paragraphs 2 to 4 or 5 to 7 of the second column of the table in article 3(g), other than [the

FCA or the PRA], to dismiss an individual who has, or to fail to promote or exclude an individual who is seeking to obtain, the status specified in the corresponding entry in the first column of that table (but not, where applicable, the status of being an associate of another person), by reason of, or partly by reason of, a spent conviction of that individual or of his associate . . ., or of any circumstances ancillary to such a conviction or of a failure (whether or not by that individual) to disclose such a conviction or any such circumstances;

(h) any decision of anyone who is specified in sub-paragraph 8(a), 14(a) or 16(a) of the second column of the table in article 3(g) to dismiss an individual who has, or to fail to promote or exclude an individual who is seeking to obtain, the status specified in the corresponding entry in sub-paragraph (b) of the first column of that table (associate), by reason of, or partly by reason of, a spent conviction of that individual . . ., or of any circumstances ancillary to such a conviction or of a failure (whether or not by that individual) to disclose such a conviction or any such circumstances;

(i) any decision of the Council of Lloyd's—

(i) to refuse to admit any person as, or to exclude, an underwriting agent (within the meaning of section 2 of Lloyd's Act 1982), where that person has, or who has applied for, [Part 4A permission], or

(ii) to dismiss, or to exclude a person from being, an associate of the Council of Lloyd's,

by reason of, or partly by reason of, a spent conviction of an individual . . ., or of any circumstances ancillary to such a conviction or of a failure (whether or not by that individual) to disclose such a conviction or any such circumstances;

(j) any decision of a UK recognised investment exchange or [recognised clearing house] to refuse to admit any person as, or to exclude, a member by reason of, or partly by reason of, a spent conviction of an individual . . ., or of any circumstances ancillary to such a conviction or of a failure (whether or not by that individual) to disclose such a conviction or any such circumstances];

[(ja) any decision by the relevant registration authority, as defined by section 5 of the Care Standards Act 2000, to refuse to grant an application for registration under Part 2 of that Act or to suspend or remove or refuse to restore a person's registration under that Part of that Act;]

[(k) any decision by the [Care Council for Wales] to refuse to grant an application for registration under Part IV of the Care Standards Act 2000 or to suspend, remove or refuse to restore a person's registration under that Part;

[(ka) any decision of Her Majesty's Chief Inspector of Education, Children's Services and Skills to refuse to grant a person's application for registration as a childminder agency or to suspend, cancel or impose a condition on a person's registration as a childminder agency under Part 3 of the Childcare Act 2006;]

(l) any decision to refuse to grant a taxi driver licence, to grant such a licence subject to conditions or to suspend, revoke or refuse to renew such a licence;

(m) any decision by the Security Industry Authority to refuse to grant a licence under section 8 of the Private Security Industry Act 2001, to grant such a licence subject to conditions, to modify such a licence (including any of the conditions of that licence) or to revoke such a licence];

[(n) any decision by the Football Association[, Football League] or Football Association Premier League to refuse to approve a person as able to undertake, in the course of acting as a steward at a sports ground at which football matches are played or as a supervisor or manager of such a person, licensable conduct within the meaning of the Private Security Industry Act 2001 without a licence issued under that Act, in accordance with . . . section 4 of that Act].

[(2) Paragraph (1) does not apply in relation to a protected caution or a protected conviction.]

Amendment

Article renumbered as para (1) by the Rehabilitation of Offenders Act 1974 (Exceptions) Order 1975 (Amendment) (England and Wales) Order 2013, SI 2013/1198, arts 2, 8(a).

Para (1): words "Neither paragraph (b) of section 4(3) of, nor paragraph 3(5) of Schedule 2 to, the Act shall apply" in square brackets substituted by the Rehabilitation of Offenders Act 1974 (Exceptions) (Amendment) (England and Wales) Order 2008, SI 2008/3259, arts 2, 5.

Para (1): words "Subject to paragraph (2), neither" in square brackets substituted by the Rehabilitation of Offenders Act 1974 (Exceptions) Order 1975 (Amendment) (England and Wales) Order 2013, SI 2013/1198, arts 2, 8(b).

Para (1): sub-para (b) substituted by the Rehabilitation of Offenders Act 1974 (Exceptions) (Amendment) Order 2001, SI 2001/1192, arts 2, 5.

Para (1): in sub-para (b) words "of that Schedule apart from one specified in paragraph 6, 16, 17, 18, 18A, 31, 32, 35 or 36 or in Part III of that Schedule apart from one specified in paragraph 1 or 8" in square brackets substituted by the Rehabilitation of Offenders Act 1974 (Exceptions) Order 1975 (Amendment) (England and Wales) Order 2013, SI 2013/1198, arts 2, 8(c)(ii).

Para (1): in sub-para (b) word "1," in square brackets inserted by the Rehabilitation of Offenders Act 1974 (Exceptions) Order 1975 (Amendment) (England and Wales) Order 2016, SI 2016/824, art 2(1), (3)(c).

Para (1): in sub-para (b) words "12A, 13, 14, 14A, 20, 21, 35, 36, 37, 40, 43 or 44" in square brackets substituted by the Rehabilitation of Offenders Act 1974 (Exceptions) (Amendment) (England and Wales) Order 2009, SI 2009/1818, arts 2, 5.

Para (1): in sub-para (b) word "13A," in square brackets inserted by the Rehabilitation of Offenders Act 1974 (Exceptions) Order 1975 (Amendment) (England and Wales) Order 2015, SI 2015/317, art 2(1), (3).

Para (1): in sub-para (b) word "14AA," in square brackets inserted by the Rehabilitation of Offenders Act 1974 (Exceptions) Order 1975 (Amendment) (England and Wales) Order 2016, SI 2016/824, art 2(1), (2)(a).

Para (1): in sub-para (b) words "14B, 14C," in square brackets inserted by the Rehabilitation of Offenders Act 1974 (Exceptions) Order 1975 (Amendment) (England and Wales) Order 2014, SI 2014/1707, arts 2, 5(a).

Para (1): in sub-para (b) words "14D," in square brackets inserted by the Rehabilitation of Offenders Act 1974 (Exceptions) Order 1975 (Amendment) (England and Wales) Order 2014, SI 2014/1707, arts 2, 5(b).

Para (1): in sub-para (b) word "14E," in square brackets inserted by the Rehabilitation of Offenders Act 1974 (Exceptions) Order 1975 (Amendment) (England and Wales) Order 2016, SI 2016/824, art 2(1), (2)(b).

Para (1): in sub-para (b) first words repealed by the Rehabilitation of Offenders Act 1974 (Exceptions) Order 1975 (Amendment) (England and Wales) Order 2013, SI 2013/1198, arts 2, 8(c)(ii).

Para (1): in sub-para (b) second word omitted repealed by the Rehabilitation of Offenders Act 1974 (Exceptions) (Amendment) (England and Wales) Order 2012, SI 2012/1957, arts 2, 8.

Para (1): sub-para (c) repealed by the Rehabilitation of Offenders Act 1974 (Exceptions) Order 1975 (Amendment) (England and Wales) Order 2013, SI 2013/1198, arts 2, 8(d).

Para (1): sub-para (d) inserted by the Rehabilitation of Offenders Act 1974 (Exceptions) (Amendment No. 2) Order 1986, SI 1986/2268, art 2(1), Schedule, para 4.

Para (1): sub-paras (d)-(j) substituted, for para (d), by the Rehabilitation of Offenders Act 1974 (Exceptions) (Amendment) (No. 2) Order 2001, SI 2001/3816, arts 2, 5.

Para (1): in sub-para (d) words "any decision by the FCA, the PRA or the Bank of England" in square brackets substituted by the Financial Services Act 2012 (Consequential Amendments and Transitional Provisions) Order 2013, SI 2013/472, art 3, Sch 2, para 1(1), (4)(a)(i).

Para (1): in sub-para (d)(i) words "Part 4A permission" in square brackets substituted by the Financial Services Act 2012 (Consequential Amendments and Transitional Provisions) Order 2013, SI 2013/472, art 3, Sch 2, para 1(1), (4)(a)(ii).

Para (1): in sub-para (d)(ii) words "section 55L, 55M or 55O" in square brackets substituted by the Financial Services Act 2012 (Consequential Amendments and Transitional Provisions) Order 2013, SI 2013/472, art 3, Sch 2, para 1(1), (4)(a)(iii).

Para (1): in sub-para (d)(iv) words omitted repealed by the Financial Services Act 2012 (Consequential Amendments and Transitional Provisions) Order 2013, SI 2013/472, art 3, Sch 2, para 1(1), (4)(a)(iv).

Para (1): sub-paras (d)(via), (vib) inserted by the Collective Investment in Transferable Securities (Contractual Scheme) Regulations 2013, SI 2013/1388, reg 7(1), (4).

Para (1): in sub-para (d)(ix) words omitted repealed by the Alternative Investment Fund Managers Regulations 2013, SI 2013/1773, reg 81(2), Sch 2, para 2(1), (3)(a).

Para (1): in sub-para (d)(ix) words "the 2000 Act" in square brackets substituted by the Alternative Investment Fund Managers Regulations 2013, SI 2013/1773, reg 81(2), Sch 2, para 2(1), (3)(b).

Para (1): in sub-para (d)(x) words "to refuse to vary a recognition order under section 290ZA(1) of the 2000 Act, to vary a recognition order under section 290ZA(2) of the 2000 Act," in square brackets inserted by the Financial Services and Markets Act 2000 (Over the Counter Derivatives, Central Counterparties and Trade Repositories) Regulations 2013, SI 2013/504, reg 28(1), (4)(a)(ii).

Para (1): in sub-para (d)(x) words "recognised clearing house" in square brackets substituted by the Financial Services and Markets Act 2000 (Over the Counter Derivatives, Central Counterparties and Trade Repositories) Regulations 2013, SI 2013/504, reg 28(1), (4)(a)(ii).

Para (1): in sub-para (d)(x) words "or 296A" in square brackets inserted by the Financial Services Act 2012 (Consequential Amendments and Transitional Provisions) Order 2013, SI 2013/472, art 3, Sch 2, para 1(1), (4)(a)(v).

Para (1): in sub-para (d)(xi) word omitted repealed by the Electronic Money Regulations 2011, SI 2011/99, reg 79, Sch 4, para 7(c).

Para (1): in sub-para (d)(xii) words "the FCA or the PRA" in square brackets substituted by the Financial Services Act 2012 (Consequential Amendments and Transitional Provisions) Order 2013, SI 2013/472, art 3, Sch 2, para 1(1), (4)(a)(vi).

Para (1): in sub-paras (d)(xiii), (xiv) inserted by the Electronic Money Regulations 2011, SI 2011/99, reg 79, Sch 4, para 7(c).

Para (1): in sub-para (d)(xiii) word omitted repealed by the Rehabilitation of Offenders Act 1974 (Exceptions) (Amendment) (England and Wales) Order 2011, SI 2011/1800, art 2(1), (4)(a).

Para (1): in sub-paras (d)(xv), (xvi) inserted by the Rehabilitation of Offenders Act 1974 (Exceptions) (Amendment) (England and Wales) Order 2011, SI 2011/1800, art 2(1), (4) (b).

Para (1): in sub-para (d)(xv) words ", a registered account information service provider" in square brackets inserted by the Payment Services Regulations 2017, SI 2017/752, reg 156, Sch 8, para 6(b)(i).

Para (1): in sub-para (d)(xv) word "2017" in square brackets inserted by the Payment Services Regulations 2017, SI 2017/752, reg 156, Sch 8, para 6(b)(ii).

Para (1): in sub-para (d)(xv) word omitted repealed by the Financial Services Act 2012 (Consequential Amendments and Transitional Provisions) Order 2013, SI 2013/472, art 3, Sch 2, para 1(1), (4)(a)(vii).

Para (1): in sub-paras (d)(xvii), (xviii) inserted by the Financial Services Act 2012 (Consequential Amendments and Transitional Provisions) Order 2013, SI 2013/472, art 3, Sch 2, para 1(1), (4)(a)(viii).

Para (1): in sub-para (d) words omitted repealed by the Rehabilitation of Offenders Act 1974 (Exceptions) (Amendment) (England and Wales) Order 2007, SI 2007/2149, arts 2, 5(1).

Para (1): in sub-para (e) words omitted repealed by the Rehabilitation of Offenders Act 1974 (Exceptions) (Amendment) (England and Wales) Order 2007, SI 2007/2149, arts 2, 5(1).

Para (1): in sub-para (f) words "any decision of the FCA" in square brackets substituted by the Financial Services Act 2012 (Consequential Amendments and Transitional Provisions) Order 2013, SI 2013/472, art 3, Sch 2, para 1(1), (4)(b)(i).

Para (1): in sub-para (f)(ii) word omitted repealed by the Financial Services Act 2012 (Consequential Amendments and Transitional Provisions) Order 2013, SI 2013/472, art 3, Sch 2, para 1(1), (4)(b)(ii).

Para (1): in sub-para (f)(iii) words "the FCA in relation to the exercise of its functions under Part 6 of the 2000 Act, or" in square brackets substituted by the Financial Services Act 2012 (Consequential Amendments and Transitional Provisions) Order 2013, SI 2013/472, art 3, Sch 2, para 1(1), (4)(b)(iii).

Para (1): in sub-para (f)(iv) inserted by the Financial Services Act 2012 (Consequential Amendments and Transitional Provisions) Order 2013, SI 2013/472, art 3, Sch 2, para 1(1), (4)(b)(iv).

Para (1): in sub-para (f) words omitted repealed by the Rehabilitation of Offenders Act 1974 (Exceptions) (Amendment) (England and Wales) Order 2007, SI 2007/2149, arts 2, 5(1).

Para (1): in sub-para (g) words "the FCA or the PRA" in square brackets substituted by the Financial Services Act 2012 (Consequential Amendments and Transitional Provisions) Order 2013, SI 2013/472, art 3, Sch 2, para 1(1), (4)(c).

Para (1): in sub-para (g) words omitted repealed by the Rehabilitation of Offenders Act 1974 (Exceptions) (Amendment) (England and Wales) Order 2007, SI 2007/2149, arts 2, 5(1).

Para (1): in sub-para (h) words omitted repealed by the Rehabilitation of Offenders Act 1974 (Exceptions) (Amendment) (England and Wales) Order 2007, SI 2007/2149, arts 2, 5(1).

Para (1): in sub-para (i)(i) words "Part 4A permission" substituted by the Financial Services Act 2012 (Consequential Amendments and Transitional Provisions) Order 2013, SI 2013/472, art 3, Sch 2, para 1(1), (4)(d).

Para (1): in sub-para (i) words omitted repealed by the Rehabilitation of Offenders Act 1974 (Exceptions) (Amendment) (England and Wales) Order 2007, SI 2007/2149, arts 2, 5(1).

Para (1): in sub-para (j) words "recognised clearing house" in square brackets substituted by the Financial Services and Markets Act 2000 (Over the Counter Derivatives, Central Counterparties and Trade Repositories) Regulations 2013, SI 2013/504, reg 28(1), (4) (b).

Para (1): in sub-para (j) words omitted repealed by the Rehabilitation of Offenders Act 1974 (Exceptions) (Amendment) (England and Wales) Order 2007, SI 2007/2149, arts 2, 5(1).

Para (1): sub-para (ja) inserted by the Rehabilitation of Offenders Act 1974 (Exceptions) Order 1975 (Amendment) (England and Wales) Order 2014, SI 2014/1707, arts 2, 5(c).

Para (1): sub-para (k) inserted by the Rehabilitation of Offenders Act 1974 (Exceptions) (Amendment) (England and Wales) Order 2003, SI 2003/965, arts 2, 7.

Para (1): in sub-para (k) words "Care Council for Wales" in square brackets substituted by the Rehabilitation of Offenders Act 1974 (Exceptions) (Amendment) (England and Wales) Order 2012, SI 2012/1957, arts 2, 5.

Para (1): sub-para (ka) inserted by the Rehabilitation of Offenders Act 1974 (Exceptions) Order 1975 (Amendment) (England and Wales) Order 2014, SI 2014/1707, arts 2, 5(d).

Para (1): sub-paras (l), (m) inserted by the Rehabilitation of Offenders Act 1974 (Exceptions) (Amendment) (England and Wales) Order 2003, SI 2003/965, arts 2, 7.

Para (1): in sub-para (n) inserted by the Rehabilitation of Offenders Act 1974 (Exceptions) (Amendment) (England and Wales) Order 2006, SI 2006/2143, arts 2, 5.

Para (1): in sub-para (n) words ", Football League" in square brackets inserted by the Rehabilitation of Offenders Act 1974 (Exceptions) (Amendment No. 2) (England and Wales) Order 2006, SI 2006/3290, art 2(1), (2)(a).

Para (1): in sub-para (n) words omitted repealed by the Rehabilitation of Offenders Act 1974 (Exceptions) (Amendment No. 2) (England and Wales) Order 2006, SI 2006/3290, art 2(1), (2)(b).

Para (2): inserted by the Rehabilitation of Offenders Act 1974 (Exceptions) Order 1975 (Amendment) (England and Wales) Order 2013, SI 2013/1198, arts 2, 8(e).

[**4ZA** Neither paragraph (b) of section 4(3) of, nor paragraph 3(5) of Schedule 2 to, the Act applies in relation to—

    (a) any office, employment or occupation specified in paragraph [1,] 6, 16, 17, 18, 18A, 31, 32, 35 or 36 of Part II of that Schedule or paragraph 1 or 8 of Part III of that Schedule or any other work specified in paragraph 35 or 36 of Part II of that Schedule;

    (b) any action taken for the purpose of safeguarding national security.]

Amendment

Article inserted by the Rehabilitation of Offenders Act 1974 (Exceptions) Order 1975 (Amendment) (England and Wales) Order 2013, SI 2013/1198, arts 2, 9.

In para (a) word "1," in square brackets inserted by the Rehabilitation of Offenders Act 1974 (Exceptions) Order 1975 (Amendment) (England and Wales) Order 2016, SI 2016/824, art 2(1), (3)(d).

[4A (1) Section 4(2) of the Act shall not apply to a question asked by or on behalf of any person, in the course of the duties of the person's office or employment, in order to assess whether the person to whom the question relates is disqualified by reason of section 66(3)(c) of the 2011 Act from being elected as, or being, a police and crime commissioner.

(2) Section 4(3)(a) of the Act shall not apply in relation to any obligation to disclose any matter if the obligation is imposed in order to assess whether a person is disqualified by reason of section 66(3)(c) of the 2011 Act from being elected as, or being, a police and crime commissioner.

(3) Section 4(3)(b) of the Act shall not apply in relation to the disqualification of a person from being elected as, or being, a police and crime commissioner under section 66(3)(c) of the 2011 Act.

(4) In this article—
"the 2011 Act" means the Police Reform and Social Responsibility Act 2011; and
"police and crime commissioner" means a police and crime commissioner established under section 1 of the 2011 Act.]

Amendment

Article inserted by the Rehabilitation of Offenders Act 1974 (Exceptions) (Amendment) (England and Wales) Order 2012, SI 2012/1957, arts 2, 3.

[5 (1) [Neither section 4(1) of, nor paragraph 3(1) of Schedule 2 to, the Act shall]—
(a) apply in relation to any proceedings specified in Schedule 3 to this Order;
(b) apply in relation to any proceedings specified in paragraph (2) below to the extent that there falls to be determined therein any issue relating to a person's spent conviction . . . or to circumstances ancillary thereto;
(c) prevent, in any proceedings specified in paragraph (2) below, the admission or requirement of any evidence relating to a person's spent conviction . . . or to circumstances ancillary thereto.

[(2) The proceedings referred to in paragraph (1) above are any proceedings with respect to a decision or proposed decision of the kind specified in article [4(1)(d) to (n)].]]

Amendment

Article substituted by the Rehabilitation of Offenders Act 1974 (Exceptions) (Amendment No. 2) Order 1986, SI 1986/2268, art 2(1), Schedule, para 4.

Para (1): words "Neither section 4(1) of, nor paragraph 3(1) of Schedule 2 to, the Act shall" in square brackets substituted by the Rehabilitation of Offenders Act 1974 (Exceptions) (Amendment) (England and Wales) Order 2008, SI 2008/3259, arts 2, 6(1).

Para (1): in sub-paras (b), (c) words omitted repealed by the Rehabilitation of Offenders Act 1974 (Exceptions) (Amendment) (England and Wales) Order 2007, SI 2007/2149, arts 2, 6.

Para (2): substituted by the Rehabilitation of Offenders Act 1974 (Exceptions) (Amendment) (No. 2) Order 2001, SI 2001/3816, arts 2, 6.

Para (2): words "4(1)(d) to (n)" in square brackets substituted by the Rehabilitation of Offenders Act 1974 (Exceptions) Order 1975 (Amendment) (England and Wales) Order 2015, SI 2015/317, art 2(1), (4).

SCHEDULE 1
[Excepted Professions, Offices, Employments, Work and Occupations]

Article 2(3), 3, 4

Part I
Professions

[1   Health care professional.]

2   Barrister (in England and Wales), . . . solicitor.

3   Chartered accountant, certified accountant.

4   . . .

5   Veterinary surgeon.

6   . . .

7   . . .

[8   . . .

8A   . . .]

9   . . .

10   . . .

[11   . . .]

[12   . . .]

[13   . . .

14   Actuary.

15   Registered foreign lawyer.

[16   Chartered legal executive or other CILEx authorised person.]

17 Receiver appointed by the Court of Protection.]

[18 Home inspector.]

Amendment

Schedule heading: words in square brackets substituted by the Rehabilitation of Offenders Act 1974 (Exceptions) (Amendment) Order 2001, SI 2001/1192, arts 2, 6(1).

Para 1: substituted by the Rehabilitation of Offenders Act 1974 (Exceptions) (Amendment) (England and Wales) Order 2012, SI 2012/1957, arts 2, 6(1), (2)(a).

Para 2: words omitted repealed by the Rehabilitation of Offenders Act 1974 (Exceptions) Order 1975 (Amendment) (England and Wales) Order 2013, SI 2013/1198, arts 2, 11(1), (2)(a).

Paras 4, 6, 7: repealed by the Rehabilitation of Offenders Act 1974 (Exceptions) (Amendment) (England and Wales) Order 2012, SI 2012/1957, arts 2, 6(1), (2)(b).

Paras 8, 8A: substituted, for para 8, by the Pharmacists and Pharmacy Technicians Order 2007, SI 2007/289, art 67, Sch 1, para 12(a).

Paras 8, 8A: repealed by the Rehabilitation of Offenders Act 1974 (Exceptions) (Amendment) (England and Wales) Order 2012, SI 2012/1957, arts 2, 6(1), (2)(b).

Para 9: repealed by the Rehabilitation of Offenders Act 1974 (Exceptions) Order 1975 (Amendment) (England and Wales) Order 2013, SI 2013/1198, arts 2, 11(1), (2)(b).

Para 10: repealed by the Rehabilitation of Offenders Act 1974 (Exceptions) (Amendment) (England and Wales) Order 2012, SI 2012/1957, arts 2, 6(1), (2)(b).

Para 11: inserted by the Osteopaths Act 1993, s 39(2).

Para 11: repealed by the Rehabilitation of Offenders Act 1974 (Exceptions) (Amendment) (England and Wales) Order 2012, SI 2012/1957, arts 2, 6(1), (2)(b).

Para 12: inserted by the Chiropractors Act 1994, s 40(2).

Para 12: repealed by the Rehabilitation of Offenders Act 1974 (Exceptions) (Amendment) (England and Wales) Order 2012, SI 2012/1957, arts 2, 6(1), (2)(b).

Paras 13-17: inserted by the Rehabilitation of Offenders Act 1974 (Exceptions) (Amendment) Order 2002, SI 2002/441, arts 2, 5(1).

Para 13: repealed by the Health Care and Associated Professions (Miscellaneous Amendments and Practitioner Psychologists) Order 2009, SI 2009/1182, art 4(1), Sch 4, para 1(a).

Para 16: substituted by the Rehabilitation of Offenders Act 1974 (Exceptions) Order 1975 (Amendment) (England and Wales) Order 2014, SI 2014/1707, arts 2, 6(a).

Para 18: inserted by the Rehabilitation of Offenders Act 1974 (Exceptions) (Amendment) (England and Wales) Order 2006, SI 2006/2143, arts 2, 6.

Part II
[Offices, Employments and Work]

1 Judicial appointments.

[2 The Director of Public Prosecutions and any office or employment in the Crown Prosecution Service.]

3 . . .

[4 [Designated officers for magistrates' courts, for justices of the peace or for local justice areas], justices' clerks [and assistants to justices' clerks].]

5 ...

[6 Constables and persons appointed as police cadets to undergo training with a view to becoming constables and naval, military and air force police.

6A Persons employed for the purposes of, or to assist the constables of a police force established under any enactment.]

7 Any employment which is concerned with the administration of, or is otherwise normally carried out wholly or partly within the precincts of, a prison, remand centre, [removal centre, short-term holding facility,] [young offender institution] or young offenders institution, and members of boards of visitors appointed under section 6 of the Prison Act 1952 . . ..

8 Traffic wardens appointed under section 81 of the Road Traffic Regulation Act 1967 . . ..

[9 Officers of providers of probation services as defined in section 9 of the Offender Management Act 2007.]

10 ...

11 ...

[12 Any office or employment which is concerned with:
  (a) the provision of care services to vulnerable adults; or
  (b) the representation of, or advocacy services for, vulnerable adults by a service that has been approved by the Secretary of State or created under any enactment;

and which is of such a kind as to enable a person, in the course of his normal duties, to have access to vulnerable adults in receipt of such services.]

[12A Any work which is regulated activity relating to vulnerable adults within the meaning of Part 2 of Schedule 4 to the 2006 Act [including that Part] [as it had effect immediately before the coming into force of section 66 of the Protection of Freedoms Act 2012].]

[13 Any employment or other work which is concerned with the provision of health services and which is of such a kind as to enable the holder of that employment or the person engaged in that work to have access to persons in receipt of such services in the course of his normal duties.]

[13A Any employment or other work in England or Wales concerned with—
  (a) the investigation of fraud, corruption or other unlawful activity affecting the national health service, or
  (b) security management in the national health service,

where "the national health service" means, in respect of England, the health service continued under section 1(1) of the National Health Service Act 2006 and, in respect of Wales, that continued under section 1(1) of the National Health Service (Wales) Act 2006.]

[14   Any work which is—
(a)   work in a regulated position; or
(b)   work in a further education institution [or 16 to 19 Academy] where the normal duties of that work involve regular contact with persons aged under 18.]

[14A   Any work which is regulated activity relating to children within the meaning of Part 1 of Schedule 4 to the 2006 Act [including that Part] [as it had effect immediately before the coming into force of section 66 of the Protection of Freedoms Act 2012].]

[14AA   Any work done infrequently which, if done frequently, would be regulated activity relating to children within the meaning of Part 1 of Schedule 4 to the 2006 Act including that Part as it had effect immediately before the coming into force of section 64 of the Protection of Freedoms Act 2012.]

[14B   Any employment or other work that is carried out at a children's home or residential family centre.

[14C   Any employment or other work which is carried out for the purposes of an adoption service, an adoption support agency, a voluntary adoption agency, a fostering service or a fostering agency and which is of such a kind as to enable a person, in the course of his normal duties, to have contact with children or access to sensitive or personal information about children.]

[14D   Any employment or office which is concerned with the management of a childminder agency or any work for a childminder agency which is of such a kind as to require the person engaged in that work to enter day care premises or premises on which child minding is provided and as to enable the person, in the course of his normal duties, to have contact with children for whom child minding or day care is provided or access to sensitive or personal information about children for whom childminding or day care is provided.]

[14E   Any chairman, member or member of staff of the Independent Police Complaints Commission who in the course of his normal duties—
(a)   has contact with vulnerable adults; or
(b)   has access to sensitive or personal information about children or vulnerable adults.]

[15   Any employment in the Royal Society for the Prevention of Cruelty to Animals where the person employed or working, as part of his duties, may carry out the [humane] killing of animals.

16 Any office or employment in the Serious Fraud Office.

17 Any office or employment in [the National Crime Agency].

[**18** The Commissioners for Her Majesty's Revenue and Customs and any office or employment in their service.

18A . . .]

19 Any employment which is concerned with the monitoring, for the purposes of child protection, of communications by means of the internet.]

[**20** Any employment or other work which is normally carried out in premises approved under section 9 of the Criminal Justice and Court Services Act 2000.

21 Any employment or other work which is normally carried out in a hospital used only for the provision of high security psychiatric services.]

[**22** An individual designated under section 2 of the Traffic Management Act 2004.

23 Judges' clerks, secretaries and legal secretaries within the meaning of section 98 of the Supreme Court Act 1981.

24 Court officers and court contractors, who in the course of their work, have face to face contact with judges of the Supreme Court, or access to such judges' lodgings.

25 Persons who in the course of their work have regular access to personal information relating to an identified or identifiable member of the judiciary.

26 Court officers and court contractors, who, in the course of their work, attend either the Royal Courts of Justice or the Central Criminal Court.

27 Court security officers, and tribunal security officers.

28 Court contractors, who, in the course of their work, have unsupervised access to court-houses, offices and other accommodation used in relation to the courts.

29 Contractors, sub-contractors, and any person acting under the authority of such a contractor or sub-contractor, who, in the course of their work, have unsupervised access to tribunal buildings, offices and other accommodation used in relation to tribunals.

30 The following persons—
    (a) Court officers who execute county court warrants;

(b)   High Court enforcement officers;

(c)   sheriffs and under-sheriffs;

(d)   tipstaffs;

(e)   any other persons who execute High Court writs or warrants who act under the authority of a person listed at (a) to (d);

(f)   persons who execute writs of sequestration;

(g)   civilian enforcement officers as defined in section 125A of the Magistrates' Courts Act 1980;

(h)   persons who are authorised to execute warrants under section 125B(1) of the Magistrates' Courts Act 1980 , and any other person, (other than a constable), who is authorised to execute a warrant under section 125(2) of the 1980 Act;

(i)   persons who execute clamping orders, as defined in paragraph 38(2) of Schedule 5 to the Courts Act 2003.

31   The Official Solicitor and his deputy.

32   Persons appointed to the office of Public Trustee or deputy Public Trustee, and -officers of the Public Trustee.

33   Court officers and court contractors who exercise functions in connection with the administration and management of funds in court including the deposit, payment, delivery and transfer in, into and out of any court of funds in court and regulating the evidence of such deposit, payment, delivery or transfer and court officers and court contractors, who receive payments in pursuance of a conviction or order of a magistrates' court.]

[**34**   People working in [the [Department for Education]], the Office for Standards in Education, Children's Services and Skills . . . with access to sensitive or personal information about children . . ..

35   Any office, employment or other work which is concerned with the establishment or operation of a database under section 12 of the Children Act 2004, and which is of such a kind as to enable the holder of that office or employment, or the person engaged in that work, to have access to information included in the database.

36   Any office, employment or other work which is of such a kind that the person is or may be permitted or required to be given access to a database under section 12 of the Children Act 2004.

37   . . .

38   The chairman, other members, and members of staff (including any person seconded to serve as a member of staff) of the [Disclosure and Barring Service][, and any other work in the Disclosure and Barring Service].

39 Staff working within the Public Guardianship Office, (to be known as the Office of the Public Guardian from October 2007), with access to data relating to children and vulnerable adults.

40 The Commissioner for Older People in Wales, and his deputy, and any person appointed by the Commissioner to assist him in the discharge of his functions or authorised to discharge his functions on his behalf.

41 The Commissioners for the Gambling Commission and any office or employment in their service.

42 Individuals seeking authorisation from the Secretary of State for the Home Department to become authorised search officers.

43 Any employment or other work where the normal duties
  (a) involve caring for, training, supervising, or being solely in charge of, persons aged under 18 serving in the naval, military or air forces of the Crown; or
  (b) include supervising or managing a person employed or working in a capacity referred to in paragraph (a).]

[44 . . .]

Amendment

Part heading: words in square brackets substituted by the Rehabilitation of Offenders Act 1974 (Exceptions) (Amendment) Order 2001, SI 2001/1192, arts 2, 6(2).

Para 2: substituted by the Rehabilitation of Offenders Act 1974 (Exceptions) (Amendment) Order 2002, SI 2002/441, arts 2, 5(2)(a).

Para 3: repealed by the Rehabilitation of Offenders Act 1974 (Exceptions) (Amendment) (England and Wales) Order 2006, SI 2006/2143, arts 2, 7(a).

Para 4: substituted by the Rehabilitation of Offenders Act 1974 (Exceptions) (Amendment) Order 2001, SI 2001/1192, arts 2, 6(3).

Para 4: words "Designated officers for magistrates' courts, for justices of the peace or for local justice areas" in square brackets substituted by SI 2005/617, art 2, Schedule, para 55.

Para 4: words "and assistants to justices' clerks" in square brackets substituted by the Rehabilitation of Offenders Act 1974 (Exceptions) (Amendment) (England and Wales) Order 2006, SI 2006/2143, arts 2, 7(b)(i).

Para 5: repealed by the Rehabilitation of Offenders Act 1974 (Exceptions) Order 1975 (Amendment) (England and Wales) Order 2013, SI 2013/1198, art 11(1), (3)(a).

Paras 6, 6A: substituted for para 6 by the Rehabilitation of Offenders Act 1974 (Exceptions) Order 1975 (Amendment) (England and Wales) Order 2013, SI 2013/1198, art 11(1), (3)(b).

Para 7: words "removal centre, short-term holding facility," in square brackets inserted by the Rehabilitation of Offenders Act 1974 (Exceptions) (Amendment) (England and Wales) Order 2006, SI 2006/2143, arts 2, 7(b)(ii).

Para 7: words "young offender institution" in square brackets substituted by virtue of the Criminal Justice Act 1988, s 123(6), Sch 8, paras 1, 3(2).

Para 7: words omitted repealed by the Rehabilitation of Offenders Act 1974 (Exceptions) Order 1975 (Amendment) (England and Wales) Order 2013, SI 2013/1198, art 11(1), (3)(c).

Para 8: words omitted repealed by the Rehabilitation of Offenders Act 1974 (Exceptions) Order 1975 (Amendment) (England and Wales) Order 2013, SI 2013/1198, art 11(1), (3) (d).

Para 9: substituted by the Rehabilitation of Offenders Act 1974 (Exceptions) Order 1975 (Amendment) (England and Wales) Order 2014, SI 2014/1707, arts 2, 6(b)(i).

Paras 10, 11: repealed by the Rehabilitation of Offenders Act 1974 (Exceptions) (Amendment) Order 1986, SI 1986/1249, art 2, Schedule, para 2.

Para 12: substituted by the Rehabilitation of Offenders Act 1974 (Exceptions) (Amendment) (England and Wales) Order 2006, SI 2006/2143, arts 2, 7(c).

Para 12A: inserted by the Rehabilitation of Offenders Act 1974 (Exceptions) (Amendment) (England and Wales) Order 2009, SI 2009/1818, arts 2, 7(1)(a).

Part 12A: words "including that Part" in square brackets inserted by the Rehabilitation of Offenders Act 1974 (Exceptions) Order 1975 (Amendment) (England and Wales) Order 2015, SI 2015/317, art 2(1), (5)(a)(i).

Para 12A: words "as it had effect immediately before the coming into force of section 66 of the Protection of Freedoms Act 2012" in square brackets inserted by the Rehabilitation of Offenders Act 1974 (Exceptions) (Amendment) (England and Wales) Order 2012, SI 2012/1957 arts 2, 10(1), (2).

Para 13: substituted by the Rehabilitation of Offenders Act 1974 (Exceptions) (Amendment) Order 2001, SI 2001/1192, arts 2, 6(4).

Part 13A: inserted by the Rehabilitation of Offenders Act 1974 (Exceptions) Order 1975 (Amendment) (England and Wales) Order 2015, SI 2015/317, art 2(1), (5)(a)(ii).

Para 14: substituted by the Rehabilitation of Offenders Act 1974 (Exceptions) (Amendment) Order 2001, SI 2001/1192, arts 2, 6(5).

Para 14: in sub-para (b) words "or 16 to 19 Academy" in square brackets inserted by the Alternative Provision Academies and 16 to 19 Academies (Consequential Amendments to Subordinate Legislation) (England) Order 2012, SI 2012/979, art 2, Schedule, para 2.

Para 14A: inserted by the Rehabilitation of Offenders Act 1974 (Exceptions) (Amendment) (England and Wales) Order 2009, SI 2009/1818, arts 2, 7(1)(b).

Part 14A: words "including that Part" in square brackets inserted by the Rehabilitation of Offenders Act 1974 (Exceptions) Order 1975 (Amendment) (England and Wales) Order 2015, SI 2015/317, art 2(1), (5)(a)(iii).

Para 14A: words "as it had effect immediately before the coming into force of section 66 of the Protection of Freedoms Act 2012" in square brackets inserted by the Rehabilitation of Offenders Act 1974 (Exceptions) (Amendment) (England and Wales) Order 2012, SI 2012/1957 arts 2, 10(1), (3).

Para 14AA: inserted by the Rehabilitation of Offenders Act 1974 (Exceptions) Order 1975 (Amendment) (England and Wales) Order 2016, SI 2016/824, art 2(1), (4)(a).

Paras 14B, 14C: inserted by the Rehabilitation of Offenders Act 1974 (Exceptions) Order 1975 (Amendment) (England and Wales) Order 2014, SI 2014/1707, arts 2, 6(b)(ii).

Para 14D: inserted by the Rehabilitation of Offenders Act 1974 (Exceptions) Order 1975 (Amendment) (England and Wales) Order 2014, SI 2014/1707, arts 2, 6(b)(iii).

Para 14E: inserted by the Rehabilitation of Offenders Act 1974 (Exceptions) Order 1975 (Amendment) (England and Wales) Order 2016, SI 2016/824, art 2(1), (4)(b).

Paras 15-19: inserted by the Rehabilitation of Offenders Act 1974 (Exceptions) (Amendment) Order 2002, SI 2002/441, arts 2, 5(2)(c).

Para 15: word "humane" in square brackets inserted by the Rehabilitation of Offenders Act 1974 (Exceptions) (Amendment) (England and Wales) Order 2006, SI 2006/2143, arts 2, 7(b)(iii).

Para 17: words "the National Crime Agency" in square brackets substituted by the Crime and Courts Act 2013, s 15(1), Sch 8, para 190(1).

Paras 18, 18A: substituted, for para 18 as originally enacted, by the Rehabilitation of Offenders Act 1974 (Exceptions) (Amendment) (England and Wales) Order 2006, SI 2006/2143, arts 2, 7(d).

Para 18A: repealed by the Public Bodies (Merger of the Director of Public Prosecutions and the Director of Revenue and Customs Prosecutions) Order 2014, SI 2014/834, art 3(3)(c), Sch 3, para 1.

Paras 20, 21: inserted by the Rehabilitation of Offenders Act 1974 (Exceptions) (Amendment) (England and Wales) Order 2003, SI 2003/965, arts 2, 8.

Paras 22-33: inserted by the Rehabilitation of Offenders Act 1974 (Exceptions) (Amendment) (England and Wales) Order 2006, SI 2006/2143, arts 2, 7(e).

Paras 34-43: inserted by the Rehabilitation of Offenders Act 1974 (Exceptions) (Amendment) (England and Wales) Order 2007, SI 2007/2149, arts 2, 7.

Para 34: words "the Department for Children, Schools and Families" in square brackets substituted by the Secretaries of State for Children, Schools and Families, for Innovation, Universities and Skills and for Business, Enterprise and Regulatory Reform Order 2007, SI 2007/3224, art 15, Sch 1, para 11.

Para 34: words "Department for Education" in square brackets substituted by the Secretary of State for Education Order 2010, SI 2010/1836, art 6, Schedule, para 11(a).

Para 34: both sets of words omitted repealed by the Rehabilitation of Offenders Act 1974 (Exceptions) (Amendment) (England and Wales) Order 2012, SI 2012/1957 arts 2, 10(1), (4).

Para 37: repealed by the Rehabilitation of Offenders Act 1974 (Exceptions) (Amendment) (England and Wales) Order 2012, SI 2012/1957 arts 2, 10(1), (5).

Para 38: words "Disclosure and Barring Service" in square brackets substituted by the Protection of Freedoms Act 2012 (Disclosure and Barring Service Transfer of Functions) Order 2012, SI 2012/3006, arts 18, 20(1), (2)(a).

Para 38: words ", and any other work in the Disclosure and Barring Service" in square brackets inserted by the Protection of Freedoms Act 2012 (Disclosure and Barring Service Transfer of Functions) Order 2012, SI 2012/3006, arts 18, 20(1), (2)(b).

Para 44: inserted by the Rehabilitation of Offenders Act 1974 (Exceptions) (Amendment) (England and Wales) Order 2009, SI 2009/1818, arts 2, 7(1)(c).

Para 44: repealed by the Protection of Freedoms Act 2012 (Disclosure and Barring Service Transfer of Functions) Order 2012, SI 2012/3006, arts 18, 20(1), (3).

Part III
Regulated occupations

1 Firearms dealer.

2 Any occupation in respect of which an application to the Gaming Board for Great Britain for a licence, certificate or registration is required by or under any enactment.

3 ...

4 ...

5 ...

6 Any occupation which is concerned with—

(a) the management of a place in respect of which the approval of the Secretary of State is required by section 1 of the Abortion Act 1967; or

(b) in England and Wales, carrying on [a regulated activity in respect of which a person is required to be registered under Part 1 of the Health and Social Care Act 2008;

(c) . . ..

7 . . .

8 Any occupation in respect of which the holder, as occupier of premises on which explosives are kept, is required [pursuant to [regulations 4, 5 and 11 of the Explosives Regulations 2014] to obtain from the chief officer of police a valid explosives certificate certifying him to be a fit person to acquire or acquire and keep explosives].

[9 . . .]

[10 Approved legal services body manager.]

[11 A regulated immigration adviser.]

[12 A head of finance and administration of a licensed body.

13 A head of legal practice of a licensed body.]

[14 CILEx approved manager.]

Amendment

Para 3: repealed by the Rehabilitation of Offenders Act 1974 (Exceptions) (Amendment) (No. 2) Order 2001, SI 2001/3816, art 7(a).

Paras 4, 5: repealed by the Rehabilitation of Offenders Act 1974 (Exceptions) (Amendment No. 2) Order 1986, SI 1986/2268, art 2(1), (2)(a).

Para 6: in sub-para (b) words "a regulated activity in respect of which a person is required to be registered under Part 1 of the Health and Social Care Act 2008" in square brackets substituted by the Rehabilitation of Offenders Act 1974 (Exceptions) Order 1975 (Amendment) (England and Wales) Order 2013, SI 2013/1198, arts 2, 11(1), (4)(a)(i).

Para 6: sub-para (c) repealed by the Rehabilitation of Offenders Act 1974 (Exceptions) Order 1975 (Amendment) (England and Wales) Order 2013, SI 2013/1198, arts 2, 11(1), (4)(a)(ii).

Para 7: repealed by the Rehabilitation of Offenders Act 1974 (Exceptions) Order 1975 (Amendment) (England and Wales) Order 2013, SI 2013/1198, arts 2, 11(1), (4)(b).

Para 8: words from "pursuant to regulations 4 and 7 of the Control of Explosives Regulations 1991" to the end in square brackets substituted by the Manufacture and Storage of Explosives Regulations 2005, SI 2005/1082, reg 28(1), Sch 5, para 27(1), (2).

Para 8: words "regulations 4, 5 and 11 of the Explosives Regulations 2014" in square brackets substituted by the Explosives Regulations 2014, SI 2014/1638, reg 83(1), Sch 13, para 11(a).

Para 9: inserted, in relation to England and Wales, by the Rehabilitation of Offenders Act 1974 (Exceptions) (Amendment) Order 2002, SI 2002/441, arts 2, 5(3)(a).

Para 9: repealed by the Rehabilitation of Offenders Act 1974 (Exceptions) (Amendment) (England and Wales) Order 2003, SI 2003/965, arts 2, 9.

Para 10: inserted by the Rehabilitation of Offenders Act 1974 (Exceptions) (Amendment) (England and Wales) Order 2008, SI 2008/3259, arts 2, 7(1).

Para 11: inserted by the Rehabilitation of Offenders Act 1974 (Exceptions) (Amendment) (England and Wales) Order 2009, SI 2009/1818, arts 2, 7(2).

Paras 12, 13: inserted by the Rehabilitation of Offenders Act 1974 (Exceptions) (Amendment) (England and Wales) Order 2011, SI 2011/1800, art 2(1), (5).

Para 14: inserted by the Rehabilitation of Offenders Act 1974 (Exceptions) Order 1975 (Amendment) (England and Wales) Order 2014, SI 2014/1707, arts 2, 6(c).

Part IV

Interpretation

In this Schedule—

["actuary" means a member of the Institute of Actuaries or a member or student of [the Institute and Faculty of Actuaries];

["approved legal services body manager" means a person who must be approved by the Law Society under section 9A(2)(e) of the Administration of Justice Act 1985;]

["assistants to justices' clerks" has the meaning given by section 27(5) of the Courts Act 2003;]

["authorised search officer" means a person authorised to carry out searches in accordance with sections 40 and 41 of the Immigration, Asylum and Nationality Act 2006;]

"care services" means

(i) accommodation and nursing or personal care in a care home (where "care home" has the same meaning as in the Care Standards Act 2000);

(ii) personal care or nursing or support for a person to live independently in his own home;

(iii) social care services; or

(iv) any services provided in an establishment catering for a person with learning difficulties;]

"certified accountant" means a member of the Association of Certified Accountants;

"chartered accountant" means a member of the Institute of Chartered Accountants in England and Wales or of the Institute of Chartered Accountants of Scotland;

["chartered legal executive" means a fellow of the Chartered Institute of Legal Executives;]

[. . .]

["child" means a person under the age of eighteen (and "children" is to be construed accordingly);]

["CILEx approved manager" means a person authorised by the Chartered Institute of Legal Executives to be concerned in the management of a body which is a CILEx authorised person;

"CILEx authorised person" means a person authorised by the Chartered Institute of Legal Executives to provide a reserved legal activity in accordance with the Legal Services Act 2007;]

["court contractor" means a person who has entered into a contract with the Lord Chancellor under section 2(4) of the Courts Act 2003, such a person's sub-contractor, and persons acting under the authority of such a contractor or sub-contractor for the purpose of discharging the Lord Chancellor's general duty in relation to the courts;]

["court officer" means a person appointed by the Lord Chancellor under section 2(1) of the Courts Act 2003;]

["court security officers" has the meaning given by section 51 of the Courts Act 2003;]

. . .

"firearms dealer" has the meaning assigned to that expression by section 57(4) of the Firearms Act 1968;

["funds in court" has the meaning given by section 47 of the Administration of Justice Act 1982;]

"further education" has the meaning assigned to that expression by section 41 of the Education Act 1944 or, in Scotland, section 4 of the Education (Scotland) Act 1962;

["further education institution" has the meaning given to it by paragraph 3 of the Education (Restriction of Employment) Regulations 2000;]

["head of finance and administration of a licensed body" means an individual who is designated as head of finance and administration and whose designation is approved in accordance with licensing rules made under section 83 of, and paragraphs 13 and 14 of Schedule 11 to, the Legal Services Act 2007;

"head of legal practice of a licensed body" means an individual who is designated as head of legal practice and whose designation is approved in accordance with licensing rules made under section 83 of, and paragraphs 11 and 12 of Schedule 11 to, the Legal Services Act 2007;]

["health care professional" means a person who is a member of a profession regulated by a body mentioned in subsection (3) of section 25 of the National Health Service Reform and Health Care Professions Act 2002 (and for the purposes of this definition subsection (3A) of that section is to be ignored);]

"health services" means services provided under the National Health Service Acts 1946 to 1973 or the National Health Service (Scotland) Acts 1947 to 1973 and similar services provided otherwise than under the National Health Service;

["high security psychiatric services" has the meaning given by section 4 of the National Health Service Act 1977;]

["home inspector" means a person who is a member of a certification scheme approved by the Secretary of State in accordance with section 164(3) of the Housing Act 2004;]

. . .

["judges of the Supreme Court" means the Lord Chief Justice, the Master of the Rolls, the President of the Queen's Bench Division, the President of the Family Division, the Chancellor of the High Court, the Lords Justices of Appeal and the puisne judges of the High Court;]

"judicial appointment" means an appointment to any office by virtue of which the holder has power (whether alone or with others) under any enactment or rule of law to determine any question affecting the rights, privileges, obligations or liabilities of any person;

[. . .]

["members of the judiciary" means persons appointed to any office by virtue of which the holder has power (whether alone or with others) under any enactment or rule of law to determine any question affecting the rights, privileges, obligations or liabilities of any person;]

["personal information" means any information which is of a personal or confidential nature and is not in the public domain and it includes information in any form but excludes anything disclosed for the purposes of proceedings in a particular cause or matter;]

"proprietor" and "independent school" have the meanings assigned to those expressions by section 114(1) of the Education Act 1944 or, in Scotland, section 145 of the Education (Scotland) Act 1962;

[. . .]

[. . .]

["registered foreign lawyer" has the meaning given by section 89 of the Courts and Legal Services Act 1990;]

[. . .]

[[. . .]

[. . .]]

"registered teacher" means a teacher registered under the Teaching Council (Scotland) Act 1965 and includes a provisionally registered teacher;

["regulated immigration adviser" means any person who provides immigration advice or immigration services as defined in section 82(1) of the Immigration and Asylum Act 1999 and is—

(i)   a registered person under Part 5 of that Act, or

(ii) a person who acts on behalf of and under the supervision of such a registered person, or

(iii) a person who falls within section 84(4)(a), (b) or (c) of that Act;]

["regulated position" means a position which is a regulated position for the purposes of Part II of the Criminal Justice and Court Services Act 2000 [other than a position which would not be a regulated position if in section 36(4) of that Act "employment" included unpaid employment];]

["removal centre" and "short-term holding facility" have the meaning given by section 147 of the Immigration and Asylum Act 1999;]

"school" has the meaning assigned to that expression by section 114(1) of the Education Act 1944 or, in Scotland, section 145 of the Education (Scotland) Act 1962;

["security management" means activity carried out pursuant to the Secretary of State's security management functions within the meaning given by section 195(3) of the National Health Service Act 2006 and in respect of Wales, the corresponding functions of Welsh Ministers;]

. . .

[. . .]

"teacher" includes a warden of a community centre, leader of a youth club or similar institution, youth worker and, in Scotland, youth and community worker;

["tribunal security officers" means persons who, in the course of their work, guard tribunal buildings, offices and other accommodation used in relation to tribunals against unauthorised access or occupation, against outbreaks of disorder or against damage;]

["tribunals" means any person exercising the judicial power of the State, that is not a court listed in section 1(1) of the Courts Act 2003;]

. . .

[["vulnerable adult" has the meaning given by section 59 of the 2006 Act as it had effect immediately before the coming into force of section 65 of the Protection of Freedoms Act 2012;]].

Amendment

Definition "actuary" inserted by the Rehabilitation of Offenders Act 1974 (Exceptions) (Amendment) Order 2002, SI 2002/441, arts 2, 5(4)(a).

In definition "actuary" words "the Institute and Faculty of Actuaries" in square brackets substituted by the Rehabilitation of Offenders Act 1974 (Exceptions) (Amendment) (England and Wales) Order 2011, SI 2011/1800, art 2(1), (6)(a).

Definition "approved legal services body manager" inserted by the Rehabilitation of Offenders Act 1974 (Exceptions) (Amendment) (England and Wales) Order 2008, SI 2008/3259, arts 2, 7(2).

Definition "assistants to justices' clerks" inserted by the Rehabilitation of Offenders Act 1974 (Exceptions) (Amendment) (England and Wales) Order 2006, SI 2006/2143, arts 2, 8.

Definition "authorised search officer" inserted by the Rehabilitation of Offenders Act 1974 (Exceptions) (Amendment) (England and Wales) Order 2007, SI 2007/2149, arts 2, 8.

Definition "care services" inserted by the Rehabilitation of Offenders Act 1974 (Exceptions) (Amendment) Order 2002, SI 2002/441, arts 2, 5(4)(a).

Definition "chartered legal executive" inserted by the Rehabilitation of Offenders Act 1974 (Exceptions) Order 1975 (Amendment) (England and Wales) Order 2014, SI 2014/1707, arts 2, 6(d)(i).

Definition "chartered psychologist" (omitted) inserted by the Rehabilitation of Offenders Act 1974 (Exceptions) (Amendment) Order 2002, SI 2002/441, arts 2, 5(4)(b).

Definition "chartered psychologist" (omitted) repealed by the Health Care and Associated Professions (Miscellaneous Amendments and Practitioner Psychologists) Order 2009, SI 2009/1182, art 4(1), Sch 4, para 1(b).

Definition "child" inserted by the Rehabilitation of Offenders Act 1974 (Exceptions) (Amendment) (England and Wales) Order 2007, SI 2007/2149, arts 2, 8.

Definitions "CILEx approved manager" and "CILEx authorised person" inserted by the Rehabilitation of Offenders Act 1974 (Exceptions) Order 1975 (Amendment) (England and Wales) Order 2014, SI 2014/1707, arts 2, 6(d)(ii).

Definition "court contractor" inserted by the Rehabilitation of Offenders Act 1974 (Exceptions) (Amendment) (England and Wales) Order 2006, SI 2006/2143, arts 2, 8.

Definition "court officer" inserted by the Rehabilitation of Offenders Act 1974 (Exceptions) (Amendment) (England and Wales) Order 2006, SI 2006/2143, arts 2, 8.

Definition "court security officers" inserted by the Rehabilitation of Offenders Act 1974 (Exceptions) (Amendment) (England and Wales) Order 2006, SI 2006/2143, arts 2, 8.

Definition "dealer in securities" (omitted) repealed by the Rehabilitation of Offenders Act 1974 (Exceptions) (Amendment No. 2) Order 1986, SI 1986/2268, art 2(2)(a).

Definition "funds in court" inserted by the Rehabilitation of Offenders Act 1974 (Exceptions) (Amendment) (England and Wales) Order 2006, SI 2006/2143, arts 2, 8.

Definition "further education institution" inserted by the Rehabilitation of Offenders Act 1974 (Exceptions) (Amendment) Order 2001, SI 2001/1192, arts 2, 6(6)(a).

Definition "head of finance and administration of a licensed body" inserted by the Rehabilitation of Offenders Act 1974 (Exceptions) (Amendment) (England and Wales) Order 2011, SI 2011/1800, art 2(1), (6)(b).

Definition "head of legal practice of a licensed body" inserted by the Rehabilitation of Offenders Act 1974 (Exceptions) (Amendment) (England and Wales) Order 2011, SI 2011/1800, art 2(1), (6)(b).

Definition "health care professional" inserted by the Rehabilitation of Offenders Act 1974 (Exceptions) (Amendment) (England and Wales) Order 2012, SI 2012/1957, arts 2, 6(1), (3)(a).

Definition "high security psychiatric services" inserted by the Rehabilitation of Offenders Act 1974 (Exceptions) (Amendment) (England and Wales) Order 2003, SI 2003/965, arts 2, 10(a).

Definition "home inspector" inserted by the Rehabilitation of Offenders Act 1974 (Exceptions) (Amendment) (England and Wales) Order 2006, SI 2006/2143, arts 2, 8.

Definition "insurance company" (omitted) repealed by the Rehabilitation of Offenders Act 1974 (Exceptions) (Amendment) (No. 2) Order 2001, SI 2001/3816, arts 2, 7(b).

Definition "judges of the Supreme Court" inserted by the Rehabilitation of Offenders Act 1974 (Exceptions) (Amendment) (England and Wales) Order 2006, SI 2006/2143, arts 2, 8.

Definition "legal executive" (omitted) inserted by the Rehabilitation of Offenders Act 1974 (Exceptions) (Amendment) Order 2002, SI 2002/441, arts 2, 5(4)(c).

Definition "legal executive" (omitted) repealed by the Rehabilitation of Offenders Act 1974 (Exceptions) Order 1975 (Amendment) (England and Wales) Order 2014, SI 2014/1707, arts 2, 6(d)(iii).

Definition "members of the judiciary" inserted by the Rehabilitation of Offenders Act 1974 (Exceptions) (Amendment) (England and Wales) Order 2006, SI 2006/2143, arts 2, 8.

Definition "personal information" inserted by the Rehabilitation of Offenders Act 1974 (Exceptions) (Amendment) (England and Wales) Order 2006, SI 2006/2143, arts 2, 8.

Definition "registered chiropractor" (omitted) inserted by the Chiropractors Act 1994, s 40(4).

Definition "registered chiropractor" (omitted) repealed by the Rehabilitation of Offenders Act 1974 (Exceptions) (Amendment) (England and Wales) Order 2012, SI 2012/1957, arts 2, 6(1), (3)(b).

Definition "registered dental care professional" (omitted) inserted by the Health Care and Associated Professions (Miscellaneous Amendments and Practitioner Psychologists) Order 2009, SI 2009/1182, art 4(1), Sch 4, para 37(b).

Definition "registered dental care professional" (omitted) repealed by the Rehabilitation of Offenders Act 1974 (Exceptions) (Amendment) (England and Wales) Order 2012, SI 2012/1957, arts 2, 6(1), (3)(b).

Definition "registered foreign lawyer" inserted by the Rehabilitation of Offenders Act 1974 (Exceptions) (Amendment) Order 2002, SI 2002/441, arts 2, 5(4)(d).

Definition "registered osteopath" (omitted) inserted by the Osteopaths Act 1993, s 39(4).

Definition "registered osteopath" (omitted) repealed by the Rehabilitation of Offenders Act 1974 (Exceptions) (Amendment) (England and Wales) Order 2012, SI 2012/1957, arts 2, 6(1), (3)(b).

Definitions "registered pharmacist" and "registered pharmacy technician" (omitted) inserted by the Pharmacists and Pharmacy Technicians Order 2007, SI 2007/289, art 67, Sch 1, para 12(b).

Definitions "registered pharmacist" and "registered pharmacy technician" (omitted) substituted by the Pharmacy Order 2010, SI 2010/231, art 68, Sch 4, para 18(1).

Definitions "registered pharmacist" and "registered pharmacy technician" (omitted) repealed by the Rehabilitation of Offenders Act 1974 (Exceptions) (Amendment) (England and Wales) Order 2012, SI 2012/1957, arts 2, 6(1), (3)(b).

Definition "regulated immigration adviser" inserted by the Rehabilitation of Offenders Act 1974 (Exceptions) (Amendment) (England and Wales) Order 2009, SI 2009/1818, arts 2, 7(3).

Definition "regulated position" inserted by the Rehabilitation of Offenders Act 1974 (Exceptions) (Amendment) Order 2001, SI 2001/1192, arts 2, 6(6)(b).

In definition "regulated position" words "other than a position which would not be a regulated position if in section 36(4) of that Act "employment" included unpaid employment" in square brackets inserted by the Rehabilitation of Offenders Act 1974 (Exceptions) (Amendment) (England and Wales) Order 2012, SI 2012/1957, arts 2, 11(1), (3).

Definition "removal centre" and "short-term holding facility" inserted by the Rehabilitation of Offenders Act 1974 (Exceptions) (Amendment) (England and Wales) Order 2006, SI 2006/2143, arts 2, 8.

Definition "security management" inserted by the Rehabilitation of Offenders Act 1974 (Exceptions) Order 1975 (Amendment) (England and Wales) Order 2015, SI 2015/317, art 2(1), (5)(b).

Definition "social services" (omitted) repealed by the Rehabilitation of Offenders Act 1974 (Exceptions) (Amendment) Order 2002, SI 2002/441, arts 2, 5(4)(e).

Definition "taxi driver" (omitted) inserted by the Rehabilitation of Offenders Act 1974 (Exceptions) (Amendment) Order 2002, SI 2002/441, arts 2, 5(4)(e).

Definition "taxi driver" (omitted) repealed by the Rehabilitation of Offenders Act 1974 (Exceptions) (Amendment) (England and Wales) Order 2003, SI 2003/965, arts 2, 10(b).

Definition "tribunal security officers" inserted by the Rehabilitation of Offenders Act 1974 (Exceptions) (Amendment) (England and Wales) Order 2006, SI 2006/2143, arts 2, 8.

Definition "tribunals" inserted by the Rehabilitation of Offenders Act 1974 (Exceptions) (Amendment) (England and Wales) Order 2006, SI 2006/2143, arts 2, 8.

Definition "unit trust scheme" (omitted) repealed by the Rehabilitation of Offenders Act 1974 (Exceptions) (Amendment No. 2) Order 1986, SI 1986/2268, art 2(2)(a).

Definition "vulnerable adult" inserted by the Rehabilitation of Offenders Act 1974 (Exceptions) (Amendment) Order 2002, SI 2002/441, arts 2, 5(4)(f).

Definition "vulnerable adult" substituted by the Rehabilitation of Offenders Act 1974 (Exceptions) (Amendment) (England and Wales) Order 2012, SI 2012/1957, arts 2, 11(1), (2).

SCHEDULE 2
Excepted Licences, Certificates and Permits

Article 3

1 Firearm certificates and shot gun certificates issued under the Firearms Act 1968, and permits issued under section 7(1), 9(2) or 13(1)(c) of that Act.

2 Licences issued under section 25 of the Children and Young Persons Act 1933 (which relates to persons under the age of 18 going abroad for the purpose of performing or being exhibited for profit).

[3 Explosives certificates issued by a chief officer of police pursuant to [regulations 4, 5 and 11 of the Explosives Regulations 2014] as to the fitness of a person to acquire or acquire and keep explosives.]

[4 Taxi driver licences.

5 Licences granted under section 8 of the Private Security Industry Act 2001.]

[6 Licences granted under [section 4A of the Poisons Act 1972].]

Amendment

Para 3: substituted by the Manufacture and Storage of Explosives Regulations 2005, SI 2005/1082, reg 28(1), Sch 5, Pt 2, para 27(1), (3).

Para 3: words "regulations 4, 5 and 11 of the Explosives Regulations 2014" in square brackets substituted by the Explosives Regulations 2014, SI 2014/1638, reg 83(1), Sch 13, para 11(b).

Paras 4, 5: inserted by the Rehabilitation of Offenders Act 1974 (Exceptions) (Amendment) (England and Wales) Order 2003, SI 2003/965, arts 2, 11.

Para 6: inserted by the Control of Explosives Precursors Regulations 2014, SI 2014/1942, reg 17(1), (4).

Para 6: words "section 4A of the Poisons Act 1972" in square brackets substituted by the Deregulation Act 2015 (Poisons and Explosives Precursors) (Consequential Amendments, Revocations and Transitional Provisions) Order 2015, SI 2015/968, art 3, Schedule, para 1(1), (2).

SCHEDULE 3
Excepted Proceedings

Article 5

1 Proceedings in respect of a person's admission to, or disciplinary proceedings against a member of, any profession specified in Part I of Schedule 1 to this Order.

2 Proceedings before the Court of Appeal of the High Court in the exercise of their disciplinary jurisdiction in respect of solicitors.

3   Disciplinary proceedings against a constable.

4   Proceedings before the Gaming Board for Great Britain.

[5   Proceedings under the Mental Health Act 1983 before any tribunal.]

6   Proceedings under the Firearms Act 1968 in respect of—
   (a)   the registration of a person as a firearms dealer, the removal of person's name from a register of firearms dealers or the imposition, variation or revocation of conditions of any such registration; or
   (b)   the grant, renewal, variation or revocation of a firearm certificate; or
   (c)   the grant, renewal or revocation of a shot gun certificate; or
   (d)   the grant of a permit under section 7(1), 9(2) or 13(1)(c) of that Act.

7   Proceedings in respect of the grant, renewal or variation of a licence under section 25 of the Children and Young Persons Act 1933 (which relates to persons under the age of 18 going abroad for the purpose of performing or being exhibited for profit).

8   . . .

[9   Proceedings in respect of a direction given under section 142 of the Education Act 2002 or of any prohibition or restriction on a person's employment or work which has effect as if it were contained in such a direction.]

10   . . .

11   Proceedings in respect of an application for, or cancellation of,—
   (a)   the Secretary of State's approval of a place under section 1 of the Abortion Act 1967; or
   (b)   . . .
   (c)   . . ..

[11A   Proceedings in respect of an application for, or suspension or cancellation of, registration in respect of a regulated activity under Part 1 of the Health and Social Care Act 2008.]

12   . . .

[13   Proceedings in respect of—
   (a)   an application to the chief officer of police for an explosives certificate pursuant to regulations 4, 5 and 11 of the Explosives Regulations 2014 ("the 2014 Regulations") as to the fitness of the applicant to acquire or acquire and keep explosives, including consideration as to whether to refuse the application on any of the grounds specified in regulation 19 of the 2014 Regulations;

    (b) the revocation of such certificates pursuant to regulation 21 of the 2014 Regulations;

    (c) an appeal or application pursuant to regulation 22 of the 2014 Regulations against a decision taken under regulation 19 or 21.]

14 Proceedings by way of appeal against, or review of, any decision taken, by virtue of any of the provisions of this Order, on consideration of a spent conviction.

15 Proceedings held for the receipt of evidence affecting the determination of any question arising in any proceedings specified in this Schedule.

[**16** [Proceedings relating to a taxi driver licence.]]

[**17** Proceedings—

    (a) before the National Lottery Commission in respect of the grant or revocation of a licence under Part I of the National Lottery etc Act 1993; or

    (b) by way of appeal to the Secretary of State against the revocation of any such licence by the National Lottery Commission.]

[**17A** Proceedings relating to registration under Part II of the Care Standards Act 2000.]

[**18** Proceedings relating to registration under Part IV of the Care Standards Act 2000.

19 Proceedings under section 11 of the Private Security Industry Act 2001.]

[**19A** Proceedings relating to the grant, amendment, variation, suspension or revocation of a licence under [section 4A of the Poisons Act 1972].]

[**20** Proceedings before the Parole Board.

21 Proceedings under section 7D of the Criminal Injuries Compensation Act 1995.

22 The following proceedings under the Proceeds of Crime Act 2002—

    (a) proceedings under Chapter 2 of Part 5;

    (b) proceedings pursuant to a notice under section 317(2);

    (c) proceedings pursuant to an application under Part 8 in connection with a civil recovery investigation (within the meaning of section 341).

23 Proceedings brought before the Football Association[, Football League] or Football Association Premier League against a decision taken by the body before which the proceedings are brought to refuse to approve a person as able to undertake, in the course of acting as a steward at a sports ground at which football matches are played or as a supervisor or manager of such a person, licensable conduct within the meaning of the Private Security Industry Act 2001 without a licence issued under that Act, in accordance with . . . section 4 of that Act.]

Amendment

Para 5: substituted by the Tribunals, Courts and Enforcement Act 2007 (Transitional and Consequential Provisions) Order 2008, SI 2008/2683, art 6(1), Sch 1, para 6.

Para 8: repealed by the Rehabilitation of Offenders Act 1974 (Exceptions) (Amendment) (No. 2) Order 2001, SI 2001/3816, arts 2, 7(c).

Para 9: substituted by the Rehabilitation of Offenders Act 1974 (Exceptions) (Amendment) (England and Wales) Order 2006, SI 2006/2143, arts 2, 9(a).

Para 10: repealed by the Rehabilitation of Offenders Act 1974 (Exceptions) (Amendment No. 2) Order 1986, SI 1986/2268, art 2(2)(b).

Para 11: sub-paras (b), (c) repealed by the Rehabilitation of Offenders Act 1974 (Exceptions) Order 1975 (Amendment) (England and Wales) Order 2013, SI 2013/1198, arts 2, 12(1), (2).

Para 11A: inserted by the Rehabilitation of Offenders Act 1974 (Exceptions) Order 1975 (Amendment) (England and Wales) Order 2013, SI 2013/1198, arts 2, 12(1), (3).

Para 12: repealed by the Rehabilitation of Offenders Act 1974 (Exceptions) Order 1975 (Amendment) (England and Wales) Order 2013, SI 2013/1198, arts 2, 12(1), (4).

Para 13: substituted by the Explosives Regulations 2014, SI 2014/1638, reg 83(1), Sch 13, para 11(c).

Para 16: inserted by the Rehabilitation of Offenders Act 1974 (Exceptions) (Amendment) Order 2002, SI 2002/441, arts 2, 6(2).

Para 16: substituted by the Rehabilitation of Offenders Act 1974 (Exceptions) (Amendment) (England and Wales) Order 2003, SI 2003/965, arts 2, 12.

Para 17: inserted by the Rehabilitation of Offenders Act 1974 (Exceptions) (Amendment) Order 2002, SI 2002/441, arts 2, 6(2).

Para 17A: inserted by the Rehabilitation of Offenders Act 1974 (Exceptions) Order 1975 (Amendment) (England and Wales) Order 2014, SI 2014/1707, arts 2, 7.

Paras 18, 19: inserted by the Rehabilitation of Offenders Act 1974 (Exceptions) (Amendment) (England and Wales) Order 2003, SI 2003/965, arts 2, 13.

Para 19A: inserted by the Control of Explosives Precursors Regulations 2014, SI 2014/1942, reg 17(1), (5).

Para 19A: words "section 4A of the Poisons Act 1972" in square brackets substituted by the Deregulation Act 2015 (Poisons and Explosives Precursors) (Consequential Amendments, Revocations and Transitional Provisions) Order 2015, SI 2015/968, art 3, Schedule, para 1(1), (3).

Paras 20-23: inserted by the Rehabilitation of Offenders Act 1974 (Exceptions) (Amendment) (England and Wales) Order 2006, SI 2006/2143, arts 2, 9(b).

Para 23: in sub-para (n) words ", Football League" in square brackets inserted by the Rehabilitation of Offenders Act 1974 (Exceptions) (Amendment No. 2) (England and Wales) Order 2006, SI 2006/3290, art 2(1), (2)(a).

Para 23: in sub-para (n) words omitted repealed by the Rehabilitation of Offenders Act 1974 (Exceptions) (Amendment No. 2) (England and Wales) Order 2006, SI 2006/3290, art 2(1), (2)(b).

1979 No 1379

Taximeters (EEC Requirements) Regulations 1979

Part I
General

1 Citation and commencement These Regulations may be cited as the Taximeters (EEC Requirements) Regulations 1979 and shall come into operation on 1st December 1979.

2 Interpretation (1) In these Regulations:—

"the Directive" means Council Directive No 77/95/EEC on the approximation of the laws of the member States relating to taximeters;

"inspector" means a person authorised in writing by the Secretary of State to be an inspector for the purposes of these Regulations;

"the relevant limits of error" means the range of permissible errors laid down by item 5.1 and 5.2 of the Annex to the Directive;

"manufacturer", where more than one person is responsible for the manufacture of an instrument, means the person responsible for the final stage of manufacture;

["the principal Regulations" means the Measuring Instruments (EEC Requirements) Regulations 1988]

"taximeters" means instruments which, according to the characteristics of the vehicle in which they are installed and the tariffs for which they have been set, calculate automatically and indicate constantly when in use the fares to be paid by the users of taxi-cabs on the basis of the distance covered, and, below a certain speed, the time for which the vehicle is occupied, exclusive of various surcharges which may be authorised by local regulations in force in member States.

(2) These Regulations shall extend to Northern Ireland.

Amendment
Para (1): definition "the principal Regulations" substituted by the Measuring Instruments (EEC Requirements) (Amendment) Regulations 1988, SI 1988/1128, reg 5(a).

3 Application These Regulations apply to taximeters not containing an electronic device in the measuring sequence; and references to instruments in these Regulations are references to such taximeters.

4 Pattern approval and partial verification: the EEC signs and marks (1) The EEC signs and marks referred to in these Regulations are the following signs and marks:—

(a) The sign of EEC pattern approval described in paragraph 1 of Schedule 1 to the principal Regulations;

(b) The sign of EEC limited pattern approval described in paragraph 2 of the said Schedule 1; and

(c) The mark of EEC partial verification described in paragraph 6 of the said Schedule 1.

In these Regulations references to the United Kingdom version of a sign or mark referred to in paragraph (1) above are references to the sign or mark appropriate, in accordance with the provisions of the said Schedule, for an EEC pattern approval granted in, or an EEC partial verification carried out in, the United Kingdom.

Part II
EEC Pattern Approval and Partial Verification in the United Kingdom

5 Introductory This part of the Regulations contains provisions with respect to the grant, extension and revocation of EEC pattern approval in the United Kingdom and the carrying out of EEC partial verification in the United Kingdom and generally with respect to the application in the United Kingdom of the EEC signs and marks in relation to instruments to which these Regulations apply.

6 EEC Pattern Approval (1) [Regulations 8 to 12] (which contain amongst other things provision with respect to the grant, extension and revocation of EEC pattern approval in the United Kingdom) of the principal Regulations, and Schedule 2 to those Regulations (which regulates the conduct in the United Kingdom of EEC pattern approval), shall so far as applicable apply in relation to the pattern approval of instruments to which these Regulations apply as they apply in relation to the pattern approval of instruments to which those Regulations apply.

(2) Where an EEC pattern approval (whether granted under these Regulations or by any member State other than the United Kingdom) is in force in respect of any pattern of instrument, the manufacturer shall cause the sign of EEC pattern approval, or where the pattern approval is a limited pattern approval, the sign of EEC limited pattern approval, to be affixed to instruments conforming to the approved pattern on the dial or on a sealed plate, and the sign must be easily visible and legible under normal conditions of installation.

Amendment

Para (1): words "Regulations 8 to 12" in square brackets substituted by the Measuring Instruments (EEC Requirements) (Amendment) Regulations 1988, SI 1988/1128, reg 5(b).

7 EEC partial verification (1) An application for consideration of any instrument for EEC partial verification shall be made to the Secretary of State in such manner as he may direct.

(2) The Secretary of State shall determine whether an EEC pattern approval is in force in respect of the instrument and, if so, whether it conforms to the approved pattern.

(3) Where the Secretary of State is satisfied
(a) that the instrument conforms to the requirements of the Directive; and
(b) that an EEC pattern approval is in force in respect of the instrument and that the instrument conforms to the approved pattern, and bears the sign required by Regulation 6 (2) above;

he shall cause to be affixed to the instrument the United Kingdom mark of EEC partial verification.

(4) If the Secretary of State refuses to cause any mark of EEC partial verification to be affixed to an instrument he shall give to the applicant a statement in writing of his reasons for the refusal.

(5) Where an EEC pattern approval is subject to a condition limiting the number of instruments which may be submitted for partial verification by reference to the pattern in question, a person who makes an application, or causes or permits the making of an application, which if granted would contravene the condition shall be guilty of an offence unless it is shown that he did not know, and had no reason to believe, that it would or might contravene the condition.

Part III
Whole Measuring Systems

8 (1) Whole measuring systems for use in the United Kingdom shall be adjusted in such a way that the relevant limits of error are asymmetric in relation to the zero error and that all errors are in favour of the hirer.

(2) In this Regulation "whole measuring system" means the vehicle and the taxi-meter bearing an EEC mark which is installed in it.

Part IV
Supplementary Provisions

9 Enforcement of conditions applicable to EEC limited pattern approval Where an EEC limited pattern approval is subject to a condition limiting the use of instruments of the pattern in question a person who, knowing that any such condition applies to any instrument, disposes of the instrument to any other person in a state in which it could be used without informing that other person of the condition, shall be guilty of an offence, and the instrument shall be liable to be forfeited.

10 Effect of revocation of EEC pattern approval (1) Where an EEC pattern approval is revoked, whether under these Regulations or by any member State other than the United Kingdom, any person who, knowing that the pattern approval has been revoked, disposes of an instrument of the pattern in question bearing any EEC sign or mark related to that pattern approval to any other person in a condition in which it could be used without informing that other person of the revocation, shall be guilty of an offence and the instrument shall be liable to be forfeited.

(2) Paragraph (1) above does not apply if any such sign or mark on the instrument has been obliterated under Regulation 13 below.

(3) For the purposes of this Regulation and Regulations 11 and 13 below, an EEC sign or mark shall be regarded as related to a pattern approval if it is a sign framed by reference to that pattern approval or a mark of EEC partial verification which was affixed by reference to conformity to the pattern which was the subject of that pattern approval.

(4) A certificate by the Secretary of State stating that an EEC pattern approval granted by any member State other than the United Kingdom has been revoked and thereby ceased to have effect on a date specified shall be conclusive as to the matters certified in any proceedings for an offence under this Regulation.

11 Effect of non-extension of EEC pattern approval Where an EEC pattern approval, whether granted under these Regulations or by any member State other than the United Kingdom, is not extended—

    (a) these Regulations shall, in relation to any instrument of the pattern in question which was used before the pattern approval ceased to have effect, apply as if the pattern approval had continued in force;

    (b) the manufacturer of any instrument of the pattern in question, bearing any EEC sign or mark related to that pattern approval, which has not been so used shall be guilty of an offence, if, after the pattern approval has ceased to have effect, he disposes of the instrument to any other person, and the instrument shall be liable to be forfeited.

12 Temporary prohibition of sale (1) Where the Secretary of State is satisfied that instruments constructed according to a pattern in respect of which an EEC pattern approval granted by a member State other than the United Kingdom is in force reveal in service a defect of a general nature which makes them unsuitable for their intended use, he may issue a prohibition notice under this Regulation with respect to instruments of that pattern.

(2) Regulation 10 above shall apply, with the necessary modifications, so long as a prohibition notice issued under this Regulation is in force with respect to instruments of any pattern, as it applies in a case where pattern approval is revoked by the Secretary of State.

(3) A prohibition notice under this Regulation shall give particulars of the pattern to which it relates.

(4) The Secretary of State may withdraw a prohibition notice at any time.

(5) If the Secretary of State issues a prohibition notice under this Regulation he shall give a statement in writing of his grounds for doing so to any person appearing to him to be concerned.

(6) The Secretary of State shall cause to be published—
- (a) any prohibition notice issued under this Regulation; and
- (b) notice of withdrawal of any such prohibition notice.

13 Obliteration of EEC signs and marks (1) An inspector may obliterate any EEC sign or mark affixed to an instrument not incorporated in a vehicle if he is satisfied—
- (a) that the instrument bearing the sign or mark falls outside the relevant limits of error, or
- (b) that the instrument does not comply in any other respect with the requirements of the Directive.

(2) Without prejudice to paragraph (1) above, an inspector may, at the request of any person appearing to him to be the owner of an instrument, obliterate any EEC sign or mark on the instrument which is related to an EEC pattern approval (whether granted under these Regulations or by any member State other than the United Kingdom) which the inspector is satisfied has ceased to have effect.

(3) Subject to paragraph (4) below, obliteration under this Regulation shall be carried out by an inspector by means of punches or pincers of a six-pointed star design as shown in the following illustration:

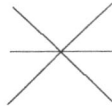

(4) Paragraph (3) above shall not apply where in the opinion of the inspector it would be impossible to obliterate any EEC sign or mark by the method there specified; and in any such case obliteration shall be carried out in such other manner as the Secretary of State may direct, whether generally or in relation to signs or marks of any particular description.

14 Unauthorised application of EEC signs and marks, etc (1) Subject to paragraph (2) below, any person who, in the case of any instrument—
- (a) not being an inspector or a person acting under the authority of an inspector, marks in any manner any plug, seal or plate used or designed for use for the reception of any EEC mark; or
- (b) not being a manufacturer authorised or required to do so under any provision of these Regulations, or the duly authorised agent of any such manufacturer, marks any such instrument with any EEC sign; or
- (c) forges, counterfeits or, except in accordance with Regulation 13 above, in any way alters or defaces any EEC sign or mark; or
- (d) removes any EEC sign or mark and inserts it into any instrument; or
- (e) makes any alteration in the instrument after any EEC sign or mark has been applied to it in accordance with these Regulations, so that it no longer complies with the requirements of the Directive;

shall be guilty of an offence.

(2) A person shall not be guilty of an offence under paragraph (1) above by reason solely of the destruction or obliteration of any sign, mark, plug, seal or plate in the course of the adjustment or repair of any instrument by, or by the duly authorised agent of, a person who is the manufacturer of, or regularly engaged in the business of repairing, instruments.

(3) Any person who sells or exposes or offers for sale any instrument which to his knowledge—

(a) bears any EEC sign or mark which is a forgery or counterfeit, or which has been transferred from another instrument, or which has been altered or defaced otherwise than under Regulation 13 above, or as permitted by virtue of paragraph (2) above, or

(b) does not comply with the requirement of the Directive by reason of any alteration made in the instrument after any EEC sign or mark was applied to it in accordance with these Regulations;

shall be guilty of an offence.

(4) Any instrument in respect of which an offence under this Regulation was committed, and any implement used in the commission of the offence, shall be liable to be forfeited.

15 Powers of inspection and entry (1) Subject to the production if so requested of his authority, an inspector may, at all reasonable times—

(a) inspect and test any instrument not incorporated in a vehicle;

(b) enter any premises at which he has reasonable cause to believe any such instruments are manufactured or stored, not being premises used only as a private dwelling house.

(2) Subject to the production if so requested of his authority, an inspector may at any time seize and detain any article which he has reasonable cause to believe is liable to be forfeited under these Regulations.

(3) If a justice of the peace, by information on oath—

(a) is satisfied that there is reasonable ground to believe that any such instrument or article as is mentioned in paragraph (1) or (2) above is manufactured or stored on any premises, or that any offence under these Regulations has been, is being or is about to be committed on any premises; and

(b) is also satisfied either—

(i) that admission to the premises has been refused, or a refusal is apprehended, and that notice of the intention to apply for a warrant has been given to the occupier, or

(ii) that an application for admission, or the giving of such a notice, would defeat the object of the entry, or that the case is one of urgency, or that the premises are unoccupied or the occupier is temporarily absent;

the justice may by warrant under his hand, which shall continue in force for a period of one month, authorise an inspector to enter the premises, if need be by force. In the application of this paragraph to Scotland, the expression "a justice of the peace" shall be construed as including the sheriff. In the application of this paragraph to Northern Ireland, for the word "information" there shall be substituted the word "complaint".

(4) An inspector entering any premises by virtue of this Regulation may take with him such other persons and such equipment as may appear to him necessary; and on leaving any premises which he has entered by virtue of a warrant under paragraph (3) above, being premises which are unoccupied or the occupier of which is temporarily absent, he shall leave them as effectively secured against trespassers as he found them.

(5) If any inspector or other person who enters any work-place by virtue of this Regulation discloses to any person any information obtained by him in the work-place with regard to any secret manufacturing process or trade secret, he shall, unless the disclosure was made in the performance of his duty, be guilty of an offence.

16 Obstruction of inspectors (1) Any person who—
- (a) wilfully obstructs an inspector acting in the execution of any provision of these Regulations; or
- (b) without reasonable cause fails to give any inspector acting as aforesaid any assistance or information which the inspector may reasonably require of him for the purposes of the performance by the inspector of his functions under these Regulations;

shall be guilty of an offence.

(2) If any person, in giving an inspector any such information as is mentioned in paragraph (1) above, gives any information which he knows to be false, he shall be guilty of an offence.

(3) Nothing in this Regulation shall be construed as requiring any person to answer any question or give any information if to do so might incriminate him.

17 Offences by corporations Regulation 24 of the principal Regulations (offences by corporations) shall apply in relation to offences under these Regulations as it applies in relation to offences under those Regulations.

18 Prosecution and punishment of offences Proceedings for any offence under these Regulations shall not—
- (a) in England and Wales, be instituted except by or on behalf of the Secretary of State or the chief officer of police for a police area; or
- (b) in Northern Ireland, be instituted except by or on behalf of the Department of Commerce for Northern Ireland or the Director of Public Prosecutions for Northern Ireland.

19 Any person guilty of an offence under Regulation 14, 15 or [16] above shall be liable on summary conviction to a fine not exceeding [£2000], and any person guilty of an offence under any other provision of these Regulations shall be liable on summary conviction to a fine not exceeding [£400].

Amendment

Words in square brackets substituted by the EEC Requirements (Amendment) Regulations 1985, SI 1985/306, reg 5.

2000 No 412

Greater London Authority Act 1999 (Hackney Carriages and Private Hire Vehicles) (Transitional and Consequential Provisions) Order 2000

1 Citation and commencement This Order may be cited as the Greater London Authority Act 1999 (Hackney Carriages and Private Hire Vehicles) (Transitional and Consequential Provisions) Order 2000 and shall come into force on 13th March 2000.

2 Interpretation In this Order—
"the 1847 Act" means the Town Police Clauses Act 1847;
"the 1869 Act" means the Metropolitan Public Carriage Act 1869;
"the 1976 Act" means the Local Government (Miscellaneous Provisions) Act 1976;
"the 1999 Act" means the Greater London Authority Act 1999;
"the appointed day" means 1st April 2000 being the day on which section 323 of the 1999 Act comes into force;
"excluded district" means a wholly excluded district or a partially excluded district;
"partially excluded district" means a district part of which ceases to be within the metropolitan police district on the appointed day;
"excluded part" in relation to a partially excluded district means the part of the district which ceases to be within the metropolitan police district on the appointed day;
"wholly excluded district" means a district the whole of which ceases to be within the metropolitan police district on the appointed day.

3 Hackney carriage byelaws having effect in a partially excluded district Any byelaws made or having effect as if made by the council of a partially excluded district under section 68 of the 1847 Act and in force in part of the district shall, from the appointed day, have effect as if made in relation to the whole of that district.

4 Anticipatory powers of excluded district councils (1) The powers conferred by this article shall be exercisable by the council of an excluded district for the purpose of securing that—
(a) hackney carriages and their drivers; and
(b) private hire vehicles, their drivers and operators,

may be licensed and able to operate lawfully in relation to the whole of that district from the appointed day.

(2) The council of a wholly excluded district may at any time before the appointed day—

(a) license hackney carriages under section 37 of the 1847 Act to ply for hire in its district;

(b) license persons under section 46 of the 1847 Act to drive hackney carriages licensed to ply for hire in its district.

(3) Section 48 of the 1976 Act shall apply in relation to applications for vehicle licences made at any time before the appointed day to the council of a wholly excluded district or the council of a partially excluded district to which Part II of the 1976 Act did not apply before the coming into force of this order.

(4) Section 55 of the 1976 Act shall apply in relation to applications made at any time before the appointed day to the council of an excluded district for licences to operate private hire vehicles in any part of its district to which the 1976 Act will not apply until the appointed day.

(5) Section 51 of the 1976 Act shall apply in relation to applications for licences to drive private hire vehicles made at any time before the appointed day to the council of a wholly excluded district or the council of a partially excluded district to which Part II of the 1976 Act did not apply on the coming into force of this Order.

(6) A licence granted pursuant to paragraph (2), (3), (4) or (5) shall not come into force before the appointed day.

(7) Subject to the foregoing provisions of this article, the council of an excluded district, may at any time before the appointed day—

(a) issue any disc, plate or badge in relation to any licence issued pursuant to this article on such terms as to its use and display before that day as it may think fit;

(b) do anything appearing to it to be appropriate or expedient for the purpose of establishing and operating a licensing system; or

(c) do anything else which it considers appropriate to fulfil the purpose specified in paragraph (1).

5 Hackney carriage or hackney carriage driver licences in force in the metropolitan police district before the appointed day Notwithstanding the provisions of section 415 of the 1999 Act a licence in force immediately before the appointed day and granted—

(a) under section 6 of the 1869 Act (hackney carriage licences); or

(b) under section 8 of that Act (hackney carriage driver licences),

shall, on the appointed day, cease to have effect in relation to any excluded district.

6 Hackney carriage standings in partially excluded districts (1) Any standings for hackney carriages appointed by the Commissioner of Police of the Metropolis under section 4 of the London Hackney Carriages Act 1850 ("the 1850 Act") in any highway in the excluded part of a partially excluded district shall from the appointed day be deemed to have been appointed by the council of that district under section 63 of the 1976 Act.

(2) So far as any provisions of regulations made under section 4 of the 1850 Act by the Commissioner of Police of the Metropolis relating to any such standings fix—

    (a) the boundaries of the standings;

    (b) the number of carriages that may wait there; or

    (c) the times of day at which they may wait,

those provisions of the regulations shall have effect as if they had been determined by the council of the district in appointing the standings under section 63 of the 1976 Act, but the regulations shall otherwise cease to have effect in relation to the standings.

(3) In this article "standings" include stands.

7 Consequential modification of the 1976 Act (1) The 1976 Act shall be amended as follows.

(2) In section 74—

    (a) for "a day fixed by resolution under section 45 of this Act" there shall be substituted "the relevant day"; and

    (b) at the end there shall be inserted the following paragraph—

"In this section "the relevant day" means—

    (a) in relation to a district the whole or part of which ceased to be within the metropolitan police district by virtue of the coming into force of section 323 of the Greater London Authority Act 1999 (alteration of the metropolitan police district), 1st April 2000;

    (b) in any other case, a day fixed by resolution under section 45 of this Act."

(3) In section 80(1) of the 1976 Act for the definition of "controlled district" there shall be substituted—

    ""controlled district" means any area for which this Part of this Act is in force by virtue of—

        (a) a resolution passed by a district council under section 45 of this Act; or

        (b) section 255(4) of the Greater London Authority Act 1999;".

2000 No 2990

Disability Discrimination Act 1995 (Taxis) (Carrying of Guide Dogs etc) (England and Wales) Regulations 2000

1 Citation, commencement, interpretation and extent (1) These Regulations may be cited as the Disability Discrimination Act 1995 (Taxis) (Carrying of Guide Dogs etc) (England and Wales) Regulations 2000 and shall come into force—
  (a) for the purposes of regulation 2(1) on 1st December 2000; and
  (b) for all other purposes on 31st March 2001.

[(2) In these Regulations "the 2010 Act" means the Equality Act 2010.]

(3) These Regulations extend to England and Wales.

Amendment

Para (2): substituted by the Equality Act 2010 (Commencement No. 4, Savings, Consequential, Transitional, Transitory and Incidental Provisions and Revocation) Order 2010, SI 2010/2317, art 24, Sch 8, para 2(1), (2).

2 Notices of exemption (1) The prescribed notice of exemption for the purposes of [section 169(4)(b) of the 2010 Act] shall be—
  (a) in the case of a driver of a taxi to whom the [exemption certificate] has been issued by a licensing authority in England, the notice set out in Schedule 1 to these Regulations; and
  (b) in the case of a driver of a taxi to whom the [exemption certificate] has been issued by a licensing authority in Wales, the notice set out in Schedule 2 to these Regulations.

[(2) The prescribed manner of exhibiting a notice of exemption for the purposes of [section 169(4)(b) of the 2010 Act] shall be—
  (a) by displaying it—
    (i) on the nearside of and immediately behind the windscreen of the taxi facing outwards; and
    (ii) in a manner that readily permits its removal;
  (b) so that—
    (i) its front is clearly visible from the outside of the taxi; and
    (ii) its back is clearly visible from the driver's seat of the taxi.]

Amendment

Para (1): words "section 169(4)(b) of the 2010 Act" in square brackets substituted by the Equality Act 2010 (Commencement No. 4, Savings, Consequential, Transitional,

Transitory and Incidental Provisions and Revocation) Order 2010, SI 2010/2317, art 24, Sch 8, para 2(1), (3).

Para (1): in sub-para (a) words "exemption certificate" in square brackets substituted by the Equality Act 2010 (Commencement No. 4, Savings, Consequential, Transitional, Transitory and Incidental Provisions and Revocation) Order 2010, SI 2010/2317, art 24, Sch 8, para 2(1), (4).

Para (1): in sub-para (b) words "exemption certificate" in square brackets substituted by the Equality Act 2010 (Commencement No. 4, Savings, Consequential, Transitional, Transitory and Incidental Provisions and Revocation) Order 2010, SI 2010/2317, art 24, Sch 8, para 2(1), (5).

Para (2): substituted by the Disability Discrimination Act 1995 (Taxis) (Carrying of Guide Dogs etc.) (England and Wales) (Amendment) Regulations 2006, SI 2006/1616, reg 2(1), (2).

Para (2): words "section 169(4)(b) of the 2010 Act" in square brackets substituted by the Equality Act 2010 (Commencement No. 4, Savings, Consequential, Transitional, Transitory and Incidental Provisions and Revocation) Order 2010, SI 2010/2317, art 24, Sch 8, para 2(1), (6).

[3 Prescribed charities Each of the following is a prescribed charity for the purposes of paragraph (c) of the definition of "assistance dog" in section 173(1) of the 2010 Act (so far as that definition applies for the purposes of section 168 of that Act)—

    (a) "Dogs for the Disabled" registered with the Charity Commission under registration number 1092960;

    (b) "Support Dogs" registered with the Charity Commission under registration number 1017237; or

    (c) "Canine Partners for Independence" registered with the Charity Commission under registration number 803680.]

Amendment

Regulation substituted by the Equality Act 2010 (Commencement No. 4, Savings, Consequential, Transitional, Transitory and Incidental Provisions and Revocation) Order 2010, SI 2010/2317, art 24, Sch 8, para 2(1), (7).

SCHEDULE 1

Regulation 2(1)(a)

1 Form of front of notice of exemption in England

[SECTION 169 EQUALITY ACT 2010]

NOTICE OF EXEMPTION

(Name of taxi licensing authority)

Driver's name

Licence No

The person named above is exempt from carrying guide dogs, hearing dogs, or assistance dogs in the taxi specified at "A" below or in a kind of taxi specified at "B" below.

A   Registration number of specified taxi*

B   Kind of taxi*

(a) Taxis with fixed partition segregating the
    driver from the passenger compartment*
(b) Taxis without fixed partition segregating the
    driver from the passenger compartment*

This notice expires _____ 20 __

*Delete as appropriate

ED

Amendment

Words "Section 169 Equality Act 2010" in square brackets substituted by the Equality Act 2010 (Commencement No. 4, Savings, Consequential, Transitional, Transitory and Incidental Provisions and Revocation) Order 2010, SI 2010/2317, art 24, Sch 8, para 2(1), (8).

[2 Form of back of notice of exemption in England

WARNING

Only the driver named overleaf may display this notice when driving the vehicle. The notice may also remain on display when the vehicle is parked provided it has been driven by, and is to be driven by, the named driver. Otherwise the named driver must remove the notice."

Amendment

Form substituted by the Disability Discrimination Act 1995 (Taxis) (Carrying of Guide Dogs etc.) (England and Wales) (Amendment) Regulations 2006, SI 2006/1616, reg 2(1), (3), Sch 1.

SCHEDULE 2

Regulation 2(1)(b)

1 Form of front of notice of exemption in Wales

[ADRAN 169 DEDDF CYDRADDOLDEB]

HYSBYSIAD EITHRIO

[SECTION 169 EQUALITY ACT 2010]
NOTICE OF EXEMPTION

(Enw'r awdurdod trwyddedu tacsis)
[(Name of taxi licensing authority)] _____

Enw'r gyrrwr
[Driver's name] _____

Rhif y Drwydded _____
[Licence No]

Mae'r sawl a enwir uchod wedi'i eithrio rhag cludo cŵn tywys, cŵn i'r byddar, neu gŵn cymorth yn y tacsi a nodir yn "A" isod neu mewn math o dacsi a nodir yn "B" isod.
[The person named above is exempt from carrying guide dogs, hearing dogs, or assistance dogs in the taxi specified at "A" below or in a kind of taxi specified at "B" below.]

A   Rhif cofrestru'r tacsi penodedig* _____ B Math o dacsi* _____
[A   Registration number of specified taxi*]   [B   Kind of taxi*]

(a) Tacsis â rhaniad sefydlog sy'n gwahanu'r gyrrwr wrth adran y teithiwr*
[(a) Taxis with fixed partition segregating the driver from the passenger compartment*]

(b) Tacsis nad oes ganddynt raniad sefydlog sy'n gwahanu'r
gyrrwr wrth adran y teithiwr*
[(b) Taxis without fixed partition segregating the
driver from the passenger compartment*]

Mae'r hysbysiad hwn yn dirwyn i ben yn _____ 20___

[This notice expires _____ 20__]

*Dileer fel y bo'n briodol
[*Delete as appropriate]

Amendment

Words "Adran 169 Deddf Cydraddoldeb 2010" in square brackets substituted by the Equality Act 2010 (Commencement No. 4, Savings, Consequential, Transitional, Transitory and Incidental Provisions and Revocation) Order 2010, SI 2010/2317, art 24, Sch 8, para 2(1), (9)(a).

Words "Section 169 Equality Act 2010" in square brackets substituted by the Equality Act 2010 (Commencement No. 4, Savings, Consequential, Transitional, Transitory and Incidental Provisions and Revocation) Order 2010, SI 2010/2317, art 24, Sch 8, para 2(1), (9)(b).

[2 Form of back of notice of exemption in Wales

RHYBUDD WARNING

Dim ond y sawl a enwir drossodd a all arddangos
yr hysbysiad hwy wrth yrru'r cerbyd. Gellir
arddangos yr Hysbysiad hwn pan fydd y cerbyd
wedi'i barcio cyhyd ag y bydd yn cael ei yrru gan,
ac i'w yrru gan, y gyrrwr a enwyd.
Fel arall rhaid I'r gyrrwr dynnu'r hysbysiad.

[Only the driver named overleaf may display this
Notice when driving the vehicle. The notice may also
remain on display when the vehicle is parked
provided it has been driven by, and is to be driven by,
the named driver. Otherwise the named driver must remove the notice.]"

Amendment
Form substituted by the Disability Discrimination Act 1995 (Taxis) (Carrying of Guide
Dogs etc.) (England and Wales) (Amendment) Regulations 2006, SI 2006/1616, reg 2(1),
(4), Sch 2.

2016 No 1153

Measuring Instruments Regulations 2016

Part 1
Introductory

1 Citation, commencement and extent (1) These Regulations may be cited as the Measuring Instruments Regulations 2016.

(2) These Regulations come into force on 28th December 2016.

(3) These Regulations extend to Northern Ireland except Part 6.

2 Interpretation (1) In these Regulations—
"the 1985 Act" means the Weights and Measures Act 1985;
"accreditation" bears the same meaning as in point 10 of Article 2 of RAMS;
"accreditation certificate" means a certificate, issued by the United Kingdom Accreditation Service or a national accreditation body in another EEA state, attesting that a conformity assessment body meets the notified body requirements;
"active electrical energy meter" means a device which measures the active electrical energy consumed in a circuit which is intended for residential, commercial or light industrial use;
"authorised representative" means any person established within the European Economic Area who has received a written mandate from a manufacturer to act on the manufacturer's behalf in relation to specified tasks;
"automatic weighing instrument" means an instrument that—
 (a) determines the mass of a product without the intervention of an operator; and
 (b) follows a predetermined programme of automatic processes characteristic of the instrument intended to determine the mass of a body by using the action of gravity on that body;
"automatic gravimetric filing instrument" means an automatic weighing instrument that fills containers with a predetermined and virtually constant mass of product from bulk;
"automatic catchweigher" means an automatic weighing instrument that determines the mass of pre-assembled discrete loads (for example prepackages) or single loads of loose material;
"automatic checkweigher" means an automatic catchweigher which subdivides articles of different mass into two or more sub-groups according to the value of the difference between their mass and the nominal set point;

"automatic discontinuous totaliser" means an automatic weighing instrument that—

(a) determines the mass of a bulk product by dividing the product into discrete loads;

(b) determines in sequence and sums the mass of each discrete load; and

(c) delivers each discrete load to bulk;

"automatic rail-weighbridge" means an automatic weighing instrument having a load receptor inclusive of rails for conveying railway vehicles;

"automatic weight grading instrument" means an instrument which sub-divides articles of different mass into several sub-groups, each characterised by a given mass range;

"beltweigher" means an automatic weighing instrument that continuously determines the mass of a bulk product on a conveyor belt without systematic subdivision of the product without interrupting the movement of the conveyor belt;

"capacity serving measure" means a capacity serving measure (such as a drinking glass, jug or thimble measure) designed to determine a specified volume of a liquid (other than a pharmaceutical product) which is sold for immediate consumption;

"CE marking" means a marking which takes the form set out in Annex II of RAMS;

"commencement date" means the date referred to in regulation 1(2);

"Commission" means the Commission of the European Union;

"competent authority" means any person who is pursuant to regulation 67 (enforcement of the Regulations), authorised to enforce these Regulations;

"compliance notice" means a notice served in accordance with regulation 68(2);

"conformity assessment" means the process demonstrating whether the essential requirements relating to a measuring instrument have been met;

"conformity assessment body" means a body that performs conformity assessment activities including calibration, testing, certification and inspection;

"dimensional measuring instrument" means—

(a) a length measuring instrument that serves for the determination of the length of rope type materials (for example textiles, bands, cables) during feed motion of the product to be measured;

(b) an area measuring instrument which serves for the determination of the area of irregular shaped objects, for example for leather; or

(c) a multi-dimensional measuring instrument which serves for the determination of the edge length (length, height, width) of the smallest enclosing rectangular parallelepiped of a product;

"the Directive" means Directive 2014/32/EU of the European Parliament and of the Council of 26 February 2014 on the harmonisation of the laws of the Member States relating to the making available on the market of measuring instruments and references to the Directive (or a specific provision of it) are references to the Directive (or that provision) as from time to time amended;

"disqualification mark" means a mark or sticker the design of which is published by the Secretary of State and which may be affixed to a regulated measuring instrument in accordance with regulation 72 (disqualification);

"distributor" means any person in the supply chain, other than a manufacturer or an importer, who makes a measuring instrument available on the market;

"economic operator" means a manufacturer, authorised representative, importer or distributor;

"enforcement notice" means a notice served in accordance with regulation 69(2);

"enforcement officer" means—

(a) an inspector; or

(b) a person appointed by the Secretary of State to act on the Secretary of State's behalf to enforce these Regulations;

"essential requirements" means, in relation to a measuring instrument (or a class of that measuring instrument), the requirements specified as being applicable in relation to that measuring instrument (or that class) in Schedule 1;

"EU declaration of conformity" means a declaration of conformity required to be drawn up in accordance with chapter 3 of Part 4;

"EU-design examination certificate" means an EU-design certificate issued by a notified body in accordance with Module H1 of Annex II to the Directive;

"EU-type examination certificate" means an EU-type examination certificate issued by a notified body in accordance with Module B of Annex II to the Directive;

"exhaust gas analyser" means a measuring instrument that serves, in relation to a motor vehicle engine with spark ignition, to determine at the moisture level of the sample analysed the volume fractions of the following exhaust gas components—

(a) carbon monoxide;

(b) carbon dioxide;

(c) oxygen; and

(d) hydrocarbons;

"gas meter" means an instrument designed to measure, memorise and display the quantity of fuel gas (volume or mass) that has passed it which is intended for residential, commercial or light industrial use;

"harmonised standard" has the meaning set out in point 1(c) of Article 2 of Regulation (EU) 1025/2012 of the European Parliament and of the Council on European standardisation (as amended from time to time);

"importer" means any person who—

(a) is established within the European Economic Area; and

(b) places a measuring instrument from a third country on the European Economic Area market;

"in writing" includes text that is—

(a) transmitted by electronic means;

(b) received in legible form; and

(c) capable of being used for subsequent reference;

"M marking" means a marking applied to a measuring instrument which consists of the capital letter 'M' and the last two digits of the year of its affixing surrounded by a rectangle, the height of which is equal to that of the CE marking applied to that instrument;

"measuring instrument" has the meaning in regulation 3(1);

"make available on the market" means any supply of a measuring instrument for distribution, or use on the European Economic Area market in the course of a commercial activity, whether in return for payment or free of charge, and related expressions are to be construed accordingly;

"manufacturer" means a person who—

(a) manufactures a measuring instrument, or has a measuring instrument designed or manufactured, and markets that measuring instrument under their name or trade mark; or

(b) is to be treated as a manufacturer by virtue of regulation 6(2);

"market surveillance authority" means the Secretary of State acting in the capacity of the market surveillance authority pursuant to the designation made by regulation 62 (the market surveillance authority) and where the context requires includes a market surveillance authority in another EEA state;

"material measure" means—

(a) a material measure of length; or

(b) a capacity serving measure;

"material measure of length" means an instrument comprising scale marks whose distances are given in legal units of length;

"national accreditation body" means the national accreditation body as defined in point 11 of Article 2 of RAMS;

"non-prescribed measuring instrument" means a measuring instrument of a kind referred to in regulation 3(3);

"non-water liquid measuring system" means a measuring system for the continuous and dynamic measurement of quantities of liquids other than water where—

(a) the system comprises a meter and all devices required to ensure correct measurement or intended to facilitate the measuring operations; and

(b) the expression "meter" means an instrument designed to measure continuously, memorise and display the quantity at metering conditions of liquid flowing through the measurement transducer in a closed, fully charged conduit;

"normative document" means a document containing technical specifications adopted by the International Organisation of Legal Metrology;

"notified body" means a conformity assessment body that has been notified to the Commission in accordance with Part 5 and includes, where the context so requires, a notified body designated as such in another EEA state in accordance with the Directive;

"notified body requirements" means the requirements set out in Schedule 5 (notified body requirements);

"notifying authority" means the notifying authority within the meaning of regulation 54 (the notifying authority)

"place on the market" means the first making available of a measuring instrument on the market, in the European Economic Area and related expressions are to be construed accordingly;

"putting into use" means the first use of a measuring instrument intended for the end-user for the purposes for which it was intended and related expressions are to be construed accordingly;

"RAMS" means Regulation (EC) 765/2008 of the European Parliament and of the Council setting out the requirements for accreditation and market surveillance relating to the marketing of products and repealing Regulation (EEC) No 339/93 (as from time to time amended);

"recall" means any measure aimed at achieving the return of a regulated measuring instrument that has already been made available to the end-user and related expressions are to be construed accordingly;

"regulated measuring instrument" means an instrument of the kind referred to in regulation 3(2);

"relevant conformity assessment procedure" means, in relation to a particular measuring instrument, a conformity assessment procedure specified in Schedule 1 as being applicable to that instrument;

"relevant economic operator" means, in relation to a measuring instrument, an economic operator with obligations in respect of that measuring instrument under Part 2;

"re-qualification mark" means a mark or sticker, the design of which is published by the Secretary of State and which is affixed to a regulated measuring instrument in accordance with regulation 73 (re-qualification);

"sub-assembly" means a hardware device mentioned as such in the instrument-specific annexes to the Directive that functions independently and makes up a measuring instrument together with other sub-assemblies with which it is compatible, or with a measuring instrument with which it is compatible;

"taximeter" means a device that works together with a signal generator to make a measuring instrument with the device measuring duration, calculating distance on the basis of a signal delivered by the distance signal generator and calculating and displaying the fare to be paid for a trip on the basis of the calculated distance or the measured duration of the trip, or both;

"technical documentation" means documentation prepared in accordance with Chapter 2 of Part 4;

"technical specification" means a document that prescribes technical requirements to be fulfilled by a measuring instrument;

"thermal energy meter" means an instrument designed to measure the thermal energy which, in a thermal energy exchange circuit, is given up by a liquid called the thermal energy-conveying liquid which is intended for residential, commercial or light industrial use and includes the following sub-assemblies, flow sensors, temperature sensor pairs and calculators where these are manufactured separately;

"Union harmonisation legislation" means any European Union legislation harmonising the conditions for the marketing of products;

"United Kingdom Accreditation Service" means the company limited by guarantee incorporated in England and Wales under number 3076190;

"volume conversion device" means a device fitted to a gas meter that automatically converts the quantity measured at metering conditions into a quantity at the specified conditions to which the measured quantity of fluid is converted;

"water meter" means an instrument designed to measure, memorise and display, the volume at metering conditions of water passing through the measurement transducer for the measurement of volumes of clean, cold or heated water intended for residential, commercial or light industrial use

"weights and measures authority" means a local weights and measures authority within the meaning set out in section 69 of the Weights and Measures Act 1985; and

"withdraw", when used in relation to a measuring instrument, means taking any measure aimed at preventing a measuring instrument in the supply chain from being made available on the market and related expressions are to be construed accordingly.

(2) A regulated measuring instrument that meets the requirements of the Directive by virtue of the laws of another EEA state is to be treated as meeting the requirements of these Regulations (except any requirement of these Regulations for anything to be written in English) and references to a regulated measuring instrument being in conformity with these Regulations are to be construed accordingly.

(3) Other expressions used in these Regulations have in relation to the application of these Regulations to—

(a) Great Britain, the same meanings as in the Weights and Measures Act 1985; and

(b) Northern Ireland, the same meanings as it the Weights and Measures (Northern Ireland) Order 1981.

3 Meaning of "measuring instrument" and related expressions and application of these Regulations (1) In these Regulations the expression "measuring instruments" comprises the following—

(a) water meters;

(b) gas meters and sub-assemblies for inclusion in, or attachment to, gas meters in the form of volume conversion devices;

(c) active electrical energy meters;

(d) thermal energy meters and any of the following sub-assemblies—
   (i) flow sensors;
   (ii) temperature sensor pairs; and
   (iii) calculators;

(e) non-water liquid measuring systems;

(f) automatic weighing instruments of the following kinds—
   (i) automatic catchweighers;
   (ii) automatic gravimetric filling instruments;
   (iii) discontinuous totalisers;
   (iv) beltweighers; and
   (v) automatic rail weighbridges;

(g) taximeters;

(h) material measures;

(i) dimensional measuring instruments; and

(j) exhaust gas analysers.

(2) In these Regulations a reference to a regulated measuring instrument means a measuring instrument of any of the following descriptions —

(a) water meters used for trade for the supply of potable water in the temperature range from 0.1°C to and including 30°C;

(b) gas meters for use for trade except a gas meter which is used under an agreement providing for the supply of a quantity of gas at a rate of flow which, if measured at a temperature of 15°C and a pressure of 1013.25 millibars, would exceed 1600 cubic meters an hour (or the equivalent quantity in kilograms);

(c) active electrical energy meters for use for trade other than an instrument which is used under an agreement providing for the supply of active electrical energy where—
   (i) the maximum quantity supplied exceeds 100 kilowatts per hour; and
   (ii) the instrument provides measurement on a half-hourly basis;

(d) non-water liquid measuring systems for use for trade of the following descriptions—
   (i) a measuring system which is used for the continuous and dynamic measurement in a quantity not exceeding 100 litres or 100 kilograms of a liquid fuel, lubricant or a mixture of fuel and lubricant other than—
      (aa) liquefied petroleum gas; or
      (bb) liquefied natural gas;
   (ii) a measuring system (other than one used in connection with the refuelling of aircraft, ships or hovercraft) which is used for the continuous and dynamic measurement in a quantity exceeding 100 litres or 100 kilograms of liquid fuel delivered from a road tanker other than—
      (aa) liquefied gases;

         (bb) lubricating oils;

         (cc) liquid fuels of a temperature below -153°C; or

         (dd) liquid fuels of a dynamic viscosity exceeding 100 millipascal seconds at 15°C;

(e) automatic weighing instruments of the following kinds which are for use for trade—

    (i) automatic gravimetric filling instruments;

    (ii) automatic catchweighers (other than automatic checkweighers and automatic weight grading instruments);

    (iii) automatic rail-weighbridges;

    (iv) beltweighers; and

    (v) discontinuous totalisers;

(f) taximeters intended for use for the protection of consumers;

(g) material measures which are for use for trade of the following kinds—

    (i) material measures of length (excluding dipping and strapping tapes);

    (ii) capacity serving measures for the measurement of draft beer or cider of the following capacities: ⅓ pint, ½ pint, ⅔ pint, 1 pint, 2 pints, 4 pints, 8 pints and 16 pints;

    (iii) capacity serving measures for the measurement of liquids other than draft beer or cider of the following capacities in millilitres (ml) and litres (l): 5 ml, 10 ml, 20 ml, 25 ml, 35 ml, 50 ml, 70 ml, 100 ml, 125 ml, 150 ml, 175 ml, 200 ml, 250 ml, 500 ml, 1 l, 2 l, 2.5 l, 5 l, 10 l and 20 l;

(h) exhaust gas analysers intended for use for the protection of the environment and public health except where the exhaust gas analyser includes or is connected to a device which is not used for the protection of the environment and public health;

(3) In these Regulations "non-prescribed measuring instruments" are measuring instruments that are neither regulated measuring instruments nor measuring instruments referred to in paragraph (4) and Schedule 2.

(4) These Regulations do not apply to the putting into use of the instruments listed in Schedule 2.

4 Revocations and transitional and consequential provisions Schedule 3 (revocations, and transitional and consequential provisions) has effect.

5 Exception for trade fairs, exhibitions and demonstration Nothing in these Regulations prevents the showing and use of a regulated measuring instrument which is not in conformity with the requirements of these Regulations at a trade fair, exhibition or demonstration for the marketing of regulated measuring instruments, provided that a visible sign clearly indicates—

(a) the name and date of the trade fair or exhibition;

(b) that the instrument is not in conformity with these Regulations; and

(c) that the instrument is not available for sale until brought into conformity with these Regulations.

Part 2
Regulated measuring instruments – obligations of economic operators

Chapter 1
Obligations of manufacturers and persons to be treated as manufacturers

6 Introductory (1) This Chapter applies in relation to the placing on the market or the putting into use of a regulated measuring instrument by a manufacturer.

(2) The obligations in this Chapter also apply to an importer or distributor who—

(a) places a regulated measuring instrument on the market under the name or trade mark of that importer or distributor; or

(b) modifies a regulated measuring instrument already placed on the market in such a way that compliance with these Regulations may be affected,

and the expression "manufacturer" is to be construed accordingly.

7 Manufacturers' responsibilities – design, conformity assessment and marking of regulated measuring instruments A manufacturer must not place on the market or put into use a regulated measuring instrument unless the manufacturer has—

(a) designed and manufactured the instrument in accordance with the essential requirements;

(b) drawn up technical documentation in relation to the instrument;

(c) carried out (or procured the carrying out of) the relevant conformity assessment procedure which has demonstrated compliance of the instrument with the applicable requirements;

(d) drawn up an EU declaration of conformity; and

(e) affixed to the instrument—

(i) the CE marking; and

(ii) the M marking.

8 Manufacturers – obligations in respect of records A manufacturer must keep the technical documentation and the EU declaration of conformity for a period of 10 years beginning with the day after the day on which the regulated measuring instrument to which it relates has been placed on the market.

9 Manufacturers' obligations to ensure continuing conformity with essential requirements (1) Manufacturers must have procedures in place for series production of regulated measuring instruments by them to ensure that instruments so manufactured continue to meet the essential requirements.

(2) The procedures mentioned in paragraph (1) must adequately take into account changes in—

(a) measuring instrument design or characteristics; and

(b) changes in the harmonised standards, normative documents or in other technical specifications by reference to which the conformity of the regulated measuring instrument is declared.

(3) When deemed appropriate with regard to the performance of a regulated measuring instrument, manufacturers must—
- (a) carry out sample testing of regulated measuring instruments manufactured by them made available on the market;
- (b) investigate complaints about regulated measuring instruments manufactured by them;
- (c) if necessary, keep a register of—
  - (i) such complaints;
  - (ii) non-conforming measuring instruments; and
  - (iii) measuring instrument recalls; and
- (d) keep distributors informed of any monitoring undertaken by them.

10 Manufacturers' obligations in relation to the marking of regulated measuring instruments with serial numbers etc. (1) A manufacturer must ensure that a regulated measuring instrument, which that manufacturer has placed on the market, bears a type, batch or serial number or other element allowing identification of that instrument.

(2) Paragraph (1) does not apply where the dimensions of the regulated measuring instrument are too small or it is of too sensitive a composition to allow it to bear the information required by that paragraph and in such a case the information must be marked on the instrument's packaging (if any) and the accompanying documents required by these Regulations.

11 Manufacturers to mark contact details on regulated measuring instruments where possible (1) A manufacturer must indicate on every regulated measuring instrument manufactured by that manufacturer, the manufacturer's name, registered trade name or registered trade mark and the postal address at which the manufacturer can be contacted.

(2) Paragraph (1) does not apply where the dimensions of the regulated measuring instrument are too small or it is of too sensitive a composition to allow it to bear the information required by that paragraph and in such a case the information must be marked on the instrument's packaging (if any) and the accompanying documents required by these Regulations.

(3) The address required by this regulation must indicate a single point at which the manufacturer can be contacted.

(4) The contact details required by this regulation must be in a language easily understood by end-users and market surveillance authorities and, in the case of regulated measuring instruments made available in the United Kingdom, they must be in English.

12 Documentation to accompany regulated measuring instruments (1) A manufacturer must ensure that regulated measuring instruments that the manufacturer has placed on the market are accompanied by—

(a) a copy of the EU declaration of conformity relating to the instruments;

(b) information on the operation of the instruments including, where relevant, the following—

    (i) rated operating conditions;

    (ii) mechanical and electromagnetic environment classes;

    (iii) the upper and lower temperature limit, whether condensation is possible or not, open or closed location;

    (iv) instructions for installation, maintenance, repairs, permissible adjustments;

    (v) instructions for correct operation and any special conditions of use; and

    (vi) conditions for compatibility with interfaces, sub-assemblies or measuring instruments.

(2) Paragraph (1)(b) does not apply where the simplicity of the regulated measuring instrument makes the supply of the information referred to in that paragraph unnecessary.

(3) Information supplied in accordance with this regulation must be in a language that can easily be understood by end-users and where the end users are in the United Kingdom, the information must be in English.

(4) Such instructions and information (and any labelling) relating to a regulated measuring instrument must be clear, understandable and intelligible.

13 Action to be taken where regulated measuring instruments placed on the market are not in conformity with the essential requirements (1) This regulation applies where a manufacturer considers or has reason to believe that a regulated measuring instrument placed on the market by that manufacturer is not in conformity with the requirements of these Regulations.

(2) The manufacturer must immediately take the corrective measures necessary to bring the regulated measuring instrument into conformity or withdraw or recall it, if appropriate.

(3) Where the regulated measuring instrument presents a risk, the manufacturer must immediately inform the competent national authorities of the EEA states in which the instrument has been made available on the market to that effect giving details, in particular, of the non-compliance and of any corrective measures taken.

14 Provision of information to the competent authority (1) A manufacturer must, further to a reasoned request from a competent authority, provide the competent authority with all the information and documentation in paper or electronic form necessary to demonstrate the conformity of a regulated measuring instrument manufactured by it with the requirements of these Regulations.

(2) Information and documentation supplied to a competent authority pursuant to this regulation must be supplied in English.

(3) A manufacturer must co-operate with a competent authority, at the request of that authority, on any action to eliminate the risks posed by regulated measuring instruments that the manufacturer has placed on the market.

15 Use of authorised representatives by manufacturers (1) A manufacturer may, by a written mandate, appoint an authorised representative to discharge the responsibilities under these Regulations in relation to the placing on the market of a regulated measuring instrument.

(2) A representative appointed under paragraph (1) may not discharge the manufacturer's obligations under regulation 7(a) and 7(b).

(3) An authorised representative shall be treated as being authorised to—
    (a) keep the EU declaration of conformity and the technical documentation at the disposal of the market surveillance authority for 10 years beginning with the day after the day the regulated measuring instrument has been placed on the market;
    (b) provide a competent authority, further to a reasoned request from that authority, with all the information and documentation necessary to demonstrate the conformity of a regulated measuring instrument; and
    (c) cooperate with a competent authority, at its request on any action taken to eliminate the risks posed by regulated measuring instruments covered by its mandate.

Chapter 2
Obligations of importers

16 Introductory This Chapter applies to the placing on the market or the putting into use of a regulated measuring instrument from a country outside the European Economic Area that is imported into the United Kingdom.

17 Ensuring compliance of regulated measuring instruments (1) An importer must only place compliant regulated measuring instruments on the market.

(2) An importer must ensure that—
    (a) the appropriate conformity assessment procedure has been carried out by the manufacturer of the regulated measuring instrument (or by the importer where the importer is to be regarded as the manufacturer by virtue of regulation 6(2));
    (b) the manufacturer has drawn up the technical documentation (or that the importer has done so where the importer is treated as the manufacturer by virtue of regulation 6(2));
    (c) the regulated measuring instrument bears the CE marking and the M marking;

(d) the regulated measuring instrument is accompanied by a copy of the EU declaration of conformity and the documents referred to in regulation 12 (documentation to accompany regulated measuring instruments); and

(e) the manufacturer (or the importer where he is treated as the manufacturer) has complied with the requirements of regulations 10 (manufacturers' obligations in relation to the marking of regulated measuring instruments with serial numbers etc.) and 11 (manufacturers to mark contact details on regulated measuring instruments where possible).

18 Importers duty to notify manufacturer and market surveillance authorities of non-compliant regulated measuring instruments that present a risk Where an importer considers or has reason to believe that the regulated measuring instrument is not in conformity with the essential requirements and presents a risk, the importer must inform the manufacturer and the market surveillance authority.

19 Requirements to mark importers' details on regulated measuring instruments (1) An importer must indicate on regulated measuring instruments imported by that importer, the importer's name, registered trade name or trademark and the postal address at which the importer can be contacted.

(2) Where a regulated measuring instrument is too small or of too sensitive a composition to allow it to bear the information required by paragraph (1), such information must be marked on any packaging in which the instrument is supplied and on any accompanying documents.

(3) Any contact details required by this regulation must be in a language easily understood by end-users and market surveillance authorities and, in the case of regulated measuring instruments made available in the United Kingdom, they must be in English.

20 Importers' duty to ensure that regulated measuring instruments are accompanied by relevant documentation (1) An importer must ensure that regulated measuring instruments imported by that importer are, where relevant, accompanied by the following instructions and information in a language easily understood by end-users—

(a) rated operating conditions;

(b) mechanical and electromagnetic environment classes;

(c) the upper and lower temperature limit, whether condensation is possible or not, open or closed location;

(d) instructions for installation maintenance, repairs, permissible adjustments;

(e) instructions for correct operation and any special conditions of use; and

(f) conditions for compatibility with interfaces, sub-assemblies or measuring instruments.

(2) Where the end users are in the United Kingdom, the instructions and information referred to in paragraph (1) must be in English.

21 Duty of importers to ensure proper conditions of storage and transport An importer must, in respect of regulated measuring instruments under the importer's responsibility ensure that the conditions of their storage or transport are not such as to jeopardise their continuing compliance with the essential requirements.

22 Duties of importers with regard to monitoring etc. (1) When deemed appropriate with regard to the performance of a regulated measuring instrument imported by an importer, the importer must—
  (a) carry out a sample testing of regulated measuring instruments made available on the market by the importer;
  (b) investigate complaints about regulated measuring instruments imported by the importer ; and
  (c) if necessary, keep a register of—
      (i)   such complaints;
      (ii) non-conforming regulated measuring instruments; and
      (iii) regulated measuring instrument recalls; and
  (d) where the importer is not also the distributor of the regulated measuring instrument, keep distributors to whom the importer has supplied regulated measuring instruments informed of any monitoring undertaken by that importer.

23 Action to be taken by importers where regulated measuring instruments placed on the market by them are not in conformity with essential requirements (1) This regulation applies where an importer considers, or has reason to believe, that a regulated measuring instrument placed on the market by the importer is not in conformity with the requirements of these Regulations.

(2) The importer must immediately take the corrective measures necessary to bring the regulated measuring instrument into conformity or withdraw or recall it, if appropriate.

(3) Where the regulated measuring instrument presents a risk, the importer must immediately inform the competent authority to that effect, giving details, in particular, of the non-compliance of the instrument and of the corrective measures taken by that importer.

24 Requirement for importer to keep copy of EU declaration of conformity An importer must, for a period of 10 years beginning with the day after the day on which the regulated measuring instrument is placed on the market, keep a copy of the EU declaration of conformity at the disposal of the market surveillance authorities and ensure that the technical documentation can be made available to those authorities upon request.

25 Provision of information to the competent authority (1) The importer must, further to a reasoned request from a competent authority, provide the competent authority with all the information and documentation in paper or electronic form necessary to demonstrate the conformity of the regulated measuring instrument with the requirements of these Regulations.

(2) Information and documentation supplied to a competent authority pursuant to this regulation must be supplied in English.

(3) An importer must co-operate with a competent authority, at its request, as regards any action to eliminate the risks posed by any regulated measuring instrument that the importer has placed on the market.

Chapter 3
Obligations of distributors

26 Introductory This Chapter applies in relation to the making available on the market or the putting into use of a regulated measuring instrument by a distributor.

27 Distributors – duty to act with due care Before making the regulated measuring instrument available on the market or putting it into use, the distributor must act with due care in relation to the requirements of these Regulations.

28 Distributors – verification obligations (1) The distributor must verify that the regulated measuring instrument bears the CE marking and the M marking.

(2) The distributor must verify that the regulated measuring instrument is accompanied by—
  (a) a copy of the EU declaration of conformity relating to it; and
  (b) information on the operation of the instrument including where relevant the following—
      (i)   rated operating conditions;
      (ii) mechanical and electromagnetic environment classes;
      (iii) the upper and lower temperature limit, whether condensation is possible or not, open and closed location
      (iv) instructions for installation, maintenance, repairs, permissible adjustments;
      (v)   instructions for correct operation and any special conditions of use; and
      (vi) conditions for compatibility with interfaces, sub-assemblies or measuring instruments.

(3) Paragraph (2)(b) does not apply where the simplicity of the regulated measuring instrument makes the supply of the information referred to in that paragraph unnecessary.

(4) Instructions and information supplied in accordance with this regulation must be in a language that can be easily understood by end-users and where those end users are in the United Kingdom must be in English.

(5) The distributor must verify that the manufacturer and the importer have complied with the requirements set out in regulation 10 (manufacturers' obligations in relation to the marking of regulated measuring instruments with serial numbers etc.), regulation 11 (manufacturers to mark contact details on regulated measuring instruments where possible) and regulation 19 (requirements to mark importers' details on regulated measuring instruments).

29 Distributors not to make non-conforming regulated measuring instruments available on the market etc. (1) This regulation applies where a distributor considers, or has reason to believe, that a regulated measuring instrument is not in conformity with the essential requirements.

(2) Where this regulation applies, the distributor must not make the regulated measuring instrument available on the market or put it into use until it has been brought into conformity.

(3) Where the regulated measuring instrument presents a risk, the distributor must immediately inform—
  (a) the manufacturer;
  (b) the importer (where the distributor is not also the manufacturer or importer); and
  (c) the market surveillance authorities,

to that effect, giving details, in particular, of the non-compliance of the instrument and of the corrective measures taken by that distributor.

30 Duty of distributors to ensure proper conditions of storage and transport A distributor must, in respect of regulated measuring instruments under that distributor's responsibility, ensure that the conditions of their storage or transport are not such as to jeopardise their continuing compliance with the essential requirements.

31 Action to be taken by distributors where regulated measuring instruments placed on the market by them are not in conformity with essential requirements (1) This regulation applies where a distributor considers, or has reason to believe, that a regulated measuring instrument placed on the market or put into use by that distributor is not in conformity with the requirements of these Regulations.

(2) The distributor must immediately take the corrective measures necessary to bring the regulated measuring instrument into conformity, or withdraw or recall it, if appropriate.

(3) Where the regulated measuring instrument presents a risk, the distributor must immediately inform the competent authority to that effect, giving details, in particular, of the non-compliance of the instrument and of the corrective measures taken by that distributor.

32 Provision of information to the competent authority (1) The distributor must, further to a reasoned request from a competent authority, provide that authority with all the information and documentation in paper or electronic form necessary to demonstrate the conformity of the regulated measuring instrument with the requirements of these Regulations.

(2) Information and documentation supplied to a competent authority pursuant to this regulation must be supplied in English.

(3) A distributor must co-operate with a competent authority, at its request, as regards any action to eliminate the risks posed by any regulated measuring instrument that the distributor has placed on the market.

Chapter 4
Identification of economic operators

33 (1) Economic operators must, on request, identify to the market surveillance authorities—
   (a) any economic operator who has supplied them with a regulated measuring instrument; and
   (b) any economic operator to whom they have supplied a regulated measuring instrument.

(2) Economic operators must be able to present the information referred to in paragraph (1) for 10 years beginning with the day after the day on which they have been supplied with the regulated measuring instrument and for 10 years day beginning with the day after the day they have supplied the instrument.

(3) The Secretary of State may impose a monetary penalty on an economic operator who fails to comply with an obligation imposed on it under this regulation.

(4) Schedule 7 has effect in relation to a monetary penalty imposed under paragraph (3).

Part 3
Non-prescribed measuring instruments

34 Introductory This Part applies where a manufacturer wishes to place on the market or put into use a non-prescribed measuring instrument in another EEA state where that measuring instrument must comply with the essential requirements under the law relating to legal metrological control of that EEA state.

35 Establishing compliance with the essential requirements – non-prescribed measuring instruments A manufacturer may demonstrate compliance with the essential requirements in respect of a non-prescribed measuring instrument in the same manner as a regulated measuring instrument and the requirements of Part 4 accordingly apply.

Part 4
Conformity of measuring instruments

Chapter 1
Establishing compliance with the essential requirements

36 Introductory This chapter applies for the purposes of establishing whether a measuring instrument (whether it is a regulated measuring instrument or a non-prescribed measuring instrument) complies with the essential requirements.

37 Methods of establishing conformity with the essential require-ments Conformity with the essential requirements may be established in relation to a measuring instrument—
  (a) through conformity with harmonised standards (or parts of those standards) covering the essential requirements where the harmonised standards have been published in the Official Journal of the European Union;
  (b) through conformity with parts of normative documents which cover the essential requirements where the parts of the normative documents have been included in a list published in the Official Journal of the European Union; or
  (c) through the use by the manufacturer of any other technical solution that complies with the essential requirements.

38 Presumptions of conformity of measuring instruments (1) Measuring instruments which are in conformity with harmonised standards (or parts of those standards) of a kind mentioned in regulation 37(a), are to be presumed to be in conformity with the essential requirements covered by those standards (or parts of those standards).

(2) Measuring instruments which are in conformity with parts of normative documents of a kind mentioned in regulation 37(b), are to be presumed to be in conformity with the essential requirements covered by those parts of normative documents.

(3) To benefit from a presumption of conformity under paragraphs (1) or (2), the manufacturer must correctly apply solutions mentioned in the relevant harmonised standards or in the normative documents.

(4) Compliance with the appropriate tests mentioned in regulation 45(1)(i) is to be presumed if the corresponding test programme has been performed in accordance with the documents mentioned in paragraphs (1) and (2) and if the test results ensure compliance with the essential requirements.

39 Conformity assessment procedures (1) Conformity assessment of a measuring instrument with the essential requirements must be established by the application at the choice of the manufacturer, of one of the conformity assessment procedures listed as applicable in relation to the measuring instrument in Schedule 1.

(2) A notified body must carry out the conformity assessment procedure selected by the manufacturer in accordance with the requirements of Schedule 4.

(3) The documents and correspondence relating to the conformity assessment procedures referred to in this regulation which are carried out in the United Kingdom must be drawn up in English.

40 Capacity serving measures – accredited in house bodies (1) This regulation applies to the conformity assessment of capacity serving measures.

(2) An accredited in-house body may be used to carry out conformity assessment activities for the undertaking of which it forms part for the purposes of implementing the procedures set out in Module A2 of Annex II to the Directive.

(3) The body must constitute a separate and distinct part of the undertaking and must not participate in the design, production, supply, installation, use or maintenance of the measuring instrument it assesses.

(4) An accredited in-house body must meet the following requirements—
    (a) it must be accredited in accordance with RAMS;
    (b) the body and its personnel must be organisationally identifiable and have reporting methods within the undertaking of which they form a part which ensure their impartiality and demonstrate it to the relevant national accreditation body;
    (c) neither the body, nor its personnel shall be responsible for the design, manufacture, supply, installation, operation or maintenance of the measuring instruments they assess nor shall they engage in any activity that might conflict with their independence of judgment or integrity in relation to their assessment activities; and
    (d) it must supply its services exclusively to the undertaking of which it forms a part.

(5) An accredited in-house body need not be notified to the notifying authority or the Commission, but information concerning its accreditation must be given by the undertaking of which it forms part to the notifying authority at the request of that authority.

41 Subsidiaries and contractors (1) Where a notified body subcontracts specific conformity assessment activities, or has such activities carried out by a subsidiary, the activities are only to be treated as having been carried out by a notified body for the purposes of regulation 39 (conformity assessment procedures) where the conditions in paragraphs (2) and (3) are met.

(2) The notified body must—
    (a) ensure that the subcontractor or subsidiary meets the notified body requirements; and
    (b) inform the Secretary of State accordingly.

(3) The notified body must have obtained the agreement of the client to the use of a subcontractor or subsidiary.

(4) Where a notified body subcontracts specific conformity assessment activities, or has such activities carried out by a subsidiary, the notified body must for a period of at least 10 years beginning on the day on which the activities are carried out, keep at the disposal of the Secretary of State the documentation concerning—

(a) the assessment of the qualifications of the subcontractor or the subsidiary; and

(b) the conformity assessment activities carried out by the subcontractor or subsidiary.

(5) When monitoring a notified body in accordance with regulation 58 (monitoring), the Secretary of State must treat the notified body as responsible for the tasks performed by a subcontractor or subsidiary, wherever the subcontractor or subsidiary is established.

42 Fees (1) A United Kingdom notified body may charge fees in connection with, or incidental to, the carrying out of conformity assessment procedures or specific tasks as it may determine.

(2) The fees referred to in paragraph (1) must not exceed the following—

(a) the costs incurred or to be incurred by the United Kingdom notified body in performing the relevant function; and

(b) an amount on account of profit which is reasonable in the circumstances having regard to—

(i) the character and extent of the work done or to be done by that notified body on behalf of the applicant; and

(ii) the commercial rate normally charged on account of profit for that work or similar work.

(3) The power in paragraph (1) includes the power to require payment of fees or a reasonable estimate of such fees in advance of carrying out the work requested by the applicant.

(4) Where any fees payable to a United Kingdom notified body pursuant to this regulation remain unpaid 28 days after either the work has been requested or payment of the fees has been requested in writing, whichever is the later, the notified body may by 14 days' notice in writing provide that, unless the fees are paid before the expiry of the notice, the certificate or notification appropriate to the relevant conformity assessment procedure may be suspended until payment of the fees has been received.

(5) This regulation does not apply to the Secretary of State.

Chapter 2
Requirements as to the technical documentation required for the purposes of conformity assessment

43 Application of this Chapter The technical documentation required for the purposes of conformity assessment under these Regulations must satisfy the requirements of this Chapter.

44 General requirements to be met by technical documentation (1) The technical documentation must—

   (a) render the design, manufacture and operation of the measuring instrument intelligible; and

   (b) permit an assessment of its conformity with the applicable requirements of the Directive.

(2) The technical documentation must be sufficiently detailed to ensure compliance with the following requirements—

   (a) the definition of the metrological characteristics;

   (b) the reproducibility of the metrological performances of produced measuring instruments when properly adjusted using appropriate intended means; and

   (c) the integrity of the measuring instrument.

45 Specific information to be included in technical documentation (1) The technical documentation must, insofar as relevant for assessment and identification of either the measuring instrument or its type (or both), include the following information—

   (a) a general description of the measuring instrument;

   (b) the conceptual design and manufacturing drawings and plans of components, sub-assemblies, circuits etc.;

   (c) manufacturing procedures to ensure consistent production;

   (d) if applicable, a description of the electronic devices with drawings, diagrams, flow diagrams of the logic and general software information explaining their characteristics and operation;

   (e) descriptions and explanations necessary for the understanding of the information referred to in sub-paragraphs (b) to (d);

   (f) a list of any harmonised standards and normative documents which have been applied in full or in part, the references of which have been published in the Official Journal of the European Union;

   (g) descriptions of the solutions adopted to meet the essential requirements where harmonised standards or normative documents have not been applied, including a list of other relevant technical specifications applied;

   (h) results of design calculations, examinations etc.;

   (i) the appropriate test results, where necessary to demonstrate that the type or measuring instruments or both comply with the following—

      (i) the requirements of the Directive under declared rated operating conditions and under specified environmental disturbances; and

      (ii) the durability specifications for gas, water and thermal-energy meters as well as for liquids other than water; and

   (j) the EU-type examination certificates or EU design examinations certificates in respect of measuring instruments containing parts identical to those in the design.

(2) The manufacturer must specify where seals and markings have been applied.

(3) The manufacturer must indicate the conditions for compatibility with interfaces and sub-assemblies where relevant.

Chapter 3
Requirement relating to EU declarations of conformity

46 Application of Chapter This Chapter applies in relation to EU declarations of conformity made in relation to a measuring instrument for the purposes of these Regulations.

47 Form and contents of EU declaration of conformity etc. (1) The EU declaration of conformity must—
    (a) state that the fulfilment of the essential requirements has been demonstrated in relation to the measuring instrument;
    (b) contain the elements specified in the relevant conformity assessment modules set out in Annex II to the Directive and be updated when appropriate;
    (c) have the model structure set out in Annex XIII to the Directive.

(2) Where a regulated measuring instrument is placed or made available on the market in the United Kingdom, the EU declaration of conformity in relation to the instrument must be in English.

48 Measuring instruments that require more than one declaration of conformity (1) This regulation applies where a measuring instrument is subject to a requirement of European Union legislation for an EU declaration of conformity otherwise than by virtue of these Regulations.

(2) Where this regulation applies, a single EU declaration of conformity must be drawn up covering all applicable requirements which identifies the Union acts concerned including their publication references.

49 Responsibility of manufacturer that draws up declaration of conformity A manufacturer, who draws up an EU declaration of conformity in relation to a measuring instrument, is responsible for compliance of the measuring instrument with the requirements of these Regulations.

Chapter 4
Conformity marking

50 Conformity with Directive requirements to be indicated by the CE marking The conformity of a measuring instrument with the requirements of these Regulations must be indicated by the presence on it of the CE marking and the M marking.

51 General principles relating to the M marking The general principles set out in article 30 of RAMS apply to the M marking with such modifications as are necessary in the circumstances.

52 Rules and conditions for affixing the CE marking and the M marking (1) The CE marking and the M marking ("the markings") must be affixed to a measuring instrument in accordance with the provisions of this regulation.

(2) The markings must be affixed visibly, legibly and indelibly to the measuring instrument or its data plate.

(3) Paragraph (2) does not apply where it is not possible or not warranted on account of the nature of the measuring instrument, in which case the markings must be affixed to the documents which accompany the measuring instrument and any packaging.

(4) When a measuring instrument consists of a series of devices, not being sub-assemblies, operating together, the markings must be affixed on the instrument's main device.

(5) The markings must be affixed before the measuring instrument is placed on the market.

(6) The markings may be affixed to the measuring instrument during the fabrication process, if justified.

(7) The M marking must immediately follow the CE marking.

(8) The markings must immediately be followed by the identification number of the notified body where that body is involved in the production control phase as set out in Annex II to the Directive.

(9) The identification number of the notified body referred to in paragraph (8) must—

    (a) be affixed by the body itself, or under its instructions by the manufacturer or his authorised representative; and

    (b) be indelible or self-destructive upon removal.

(10) The markings and (where applicable) the identification number of the notified body may be followed by any other mark indicating a special risk or use.

Part 5
Notification of conformity assessment bodies

53 Introductory (1) This Part applies to the notification to the Commission and other EEA states of the bodies authorised to carry out conformity assessment procedures in the United Kingdom in relation to measuring instruments.

(2) For the purposes of this Part, a notified body is a conformity assessment body—

    (a) which has been notified to the Commission and to other EEA states under regulation 55 (notification); and

    (b) in respect of which no objections are raised by the Commission or other EEA states—

        (i) within 2 weeks of a notification, where an accreditation certificate is used; or

(ii) within 2 months of a notification, where accreditation is not used.

(3) Paragraph (2) has effect subject to regulation 60 (changes to notifications).

54 The notifying authority (1) The notifying authority for the purposes of these Regulations is the Secretary of State.

(2) The functions of the notifying authority are—
- (a) to assess whether applicants for recognition as conformity assessment bodies meet the requirements for recognition as such;
- (b) where an assessment that a body is qualified to act as a conformity assessment body is made, to notify the Commission of that fact; and
- (c) to carry out such monitoring of bodies notified to the Commission to ensure continuing compliance with the requirements of these Regulations.

(3) The notifying authority may delegate the performance of its functions to a body that meets the requirements of Articles 24(3) and 25 of the Directive but in the event of such a delegation the notifying authority remains fully responsible for the performance of those functions.

(4) The notifying authority must supply such information as the Commission may request in relation to a body notified by it.

55 Notification (1) The Secretary of State may notify to the Commission and the other EEA states only those conformity assessment bodies that qualify for notification.

(2) A conformity assessment body qualifies for notification if the first and the second conditions below are met.

(3) The first condition is that the conformity assessment body makes an application to the Secretary of State for notification and that application is accompanied by—
- (a) a description of—
  - (i) the conformity assessment activities that the conformity assessment body intends to carry out;
  - (ii) the conformity assessment module for which the conformity assessment body claims to be competent; and
  - (iii) the measuring instrument for which the conformity assessment body claims to be competent; and either
- (b) an accreditation certificate; or
- (c) the documentary evidence necessary for the Secretary of State to verify, recognise and regularly monitor the conformity assessment body's compliance with the notified body requirements.

(4) The second condition is that the Secretary of State is satisfied that the conformity assessment body meets the requirements of Schedule 5 ("the notified body requirements").

(5) For the purposes of paragraph (4), the Secretary of State may accept an accreditation certificate, provided in accordance with paragraph (3) (b), as sufficient evidence that the conformity assessment body meets the notified body requirements.

(6) When deciding whether to notify a conformity assessment body that qualifies for notification to the Commission and the other EEA states, the Secretary of State may—

    (a) have regard to any other matter which appears to the Secretary of State to be relevant; and

    (b) set conditions that the conformity assessment body must meet.

(7) The Secretary of State must inform the Commission of the United Kingdom's procedures for the assessment and notification of conformity assessment bodies, and any changes to those procedures.

56 Presumption of conformity of notified bodies (1) Where a conformity assessment body demonstrates its conformity with the criteria laid down in a harmonised standard (or part of such a standard), the reference of which has been published in the Official Journal of the European Union, the Secretary of State is to presume that the conformity assessment body meets the notified body requirements covered by that standard (or part of that standard).

(2) The presumption in paragraph (1) is rebuttable.

57 Contents of notification A notification under regulation 55 (notification) must include—

    (a) details of—

        (i) the conformity assessment activities in respect of which the conformity assessment body has made its application for notification;

        (ii) the conformity assessment module in respect of which the conformity assessment body has made its application for notification;

        (iii) the measuring instrument in respect of which the conformity assessment body has made its application for notification; and either

    (b) an accreditation certificate; or

    (c) documentary evidence which attests to—

        (i) the conformity assessment body's competence; and

        (ii) the arrangements in place to ensure that the conformity assessment body will be monitored regularly and will continue to meet the notified body requirements.

58 Monitoring (1) The Secretary of State must monitor each notified body with a view to verifying that the notified body—

    (a) continues to meet the notified body requirements;

    (b) meets any conditions set in accordance with regulation 55(6)(b); and

    (c) carries out its functions in accordance with these Regulations.

(2) The Secretary of State must inform the Commission of the United Kingdom's procedures for the monitoring of notified bodies, and any changes to those procedures.

59 Delegation to the United Kingdom Accreditation Service The Secretary of State may authorise the United Kingdom Accreditation Service to carry out the following activities on behalf of the Secretary of State—

(a) assessing whether a conformity assessment body meets the notified body requirements; and

(b) monitoring notified bodies.

(2) Where the Secretary of State authorises the United Kingdom Accreditation Service pursuant to paragraph (1), the Secretary of State remains fully responsible for anything done pursuant to that authorisation.

60 Changes to notifications (1) Where the Secretary of State determines that a notified body no longer meets a notified body requirement, or that it is failing to fulfil any of its obligations under these Regulations other than conditions set in accordance with regulation 55(6)(b), the Secretary of State must restrict, suspend or withdraw the body's status as a notified body under regulation 55 (notification).

(2) With the consent of a notified body, or where the Secretary of State determines that a notified body no longer meets a condition set in accordance with regulation 55(6)(b), the Secretary of State may restrict, suspend or withdraw the body's status as a notified body under regulation 55.

(3) In deciding what action is required under paragraph (1) or (2), the Secretary of State must have regard to the seriousness of the failure.

(4) Before taking action under paragraph (1) or (2), the Secretary of State must—

(a) give notice in writing that the Secretary of State intends to take such action and the reasons for taking such action; and

(b) give the notified body an opportunity to make representations within a reasonable period from the date of that notice and consider any such representations.

(5) Where the Secretary of State takes action under paragraph (1) or (2), the Secretary of State must immediately inform the Commission and the other EEA states.

(6) Where the Secretary of State has taken action in respect of a notified body under paragraph (1) or (2), or where a notified body has ceased its activity, the body must—

(a) on the request of the Secretary of State, transfer its files to another notified body or to the Secretary of State; or

(b) in the absence of a request under sub-paragraph (a), ensure that its files are kept available for the Secretary of State and each enforcing authority for such period as the Secretary of State may specify.

(7) The Secretary of State may impose a monetary penalty on a United Kingdom notified body that fails to comply with any requirement imposed by or under paragraph (6).

(8) Schedule 7 has effect in relation to a monetary penalty imposed under paragraph (7)

Part 6
Use for trade of certain regulated measuring instruments

61 The use for trade of the following equipment must comply with the requirements of Schedule 6—

(a) water meters for the supply of potable water in the temperature range from 0.1°C to and including 30°C;

(b) measuring systems which are used for the continuous and dynamic measurement in a quantity not exceeding 100 litres or 100 kilograms of a liquid fuel, lubricant or a mixture of fuel and lubricant other than—
  (i) liquefied petroleum gas; or
  (ii) liquefied natural gas;

(c) measuring systems (other than one used in connection with the refuelling of aircraft, ships or hovercraft) which are used for the continuous and dynamic measurement in a quantity exceeding 100 litres or 100 kilograms of liquid fuel delivered from a road tanker other than—
  (i) liquefied gases;
  (ii) lubricating oils;
  (iii) liquid fuels of a temperature below -153°C; or
  (iv) liquid fuels of a dynamic viscosity exceeding 100 millipascal seconds at 15°C;

(d) automatic catchweighers;

(e) automatic gravimetric filling instruments;;

(f) automatic discontinuous totalisers;

(g) automatic rail weighbridges;

(h) beltweighers;

(i) material measures of length; and

(j) capacity serving measures.

Part 7
Market surveillance and enforcement

Chapter 1
Market surveillance

62 The market surveillance authority The Secretary of State is the market surveillance authority for the purposes of these Regulations and RAMS.

63 Regulated measuring instruments presenting a risk (1) This regulation applies where the market surveillance authority has sufficient reason to believe that a regulated measuring instrument presents a risk on grounds of public interest, public health, public safety, public order, protection of the environment, protection of consumers, the levying of taxes and duties or fair trading.

(2) Where this regulation applies the market surveillance authority must carry out an evaluation of the regulated measuring instrument covering all relevant requirements of these Regulations which apply to that instrument.

(3) The relevant economic operators in relation to the regulated measuring instrument must co-operate as necessary with the market surveillance authority for that purpose.

(4) Where in the course of the evaluation referred to in paragraph (2), the market surveillance authority finds that the regulated measuring instrument does not comply with the essential requirements applicable to it, it must without delay issue a direction which requires the relevant economic operator to—
    (a) take all appropriate corrective actions;
    (b) withdraw the instrument from the market; or
    (c) recall it within a reasonable period commensurate with the nature of the risk.

(5) Where the market surveillance authority acts under paragraph (4), it must without delay inform the notified body that carried out the conformity assessment procedure in respect of the regulated measuring instrument of—
    (a) the respect in which the instrument is not in conformity with the requirements of these Regulations; and
    (b) the actions that the authority is requiring the relevant economic operator to take.

(6) Where the market surveillance authority considers that non-compliance is not restricted to the United Kingdom, it must inform the Commission and the other EEA states of the results of the evaluation and of the actions which they have required the economic operator to take.

(7) The economic operator must ensure that all appropriate corrective action is taken in respect of all the regulated measuring instruments concerned that it has made available on the market throughout the European Economic Area.

(8) Where the relevant economic operator does not take adequate corrective action within a reasonable period, the market surveillance authority must take all provisional measures to prohibit or restrict the regulated measuring instrument being made available on the market, to withdraw the instrument from the market or to recall it.

(9) Where the market surveillance authority takes measures under paragraph (8), the market surveillance authority must notify the Commission and the other EEA States of those measures without delay.

(10) A notification under paragraph (9) must include all available details, in particular—
    (a) the data necessary for the identification of the non-compliant regulated measuring instrument;
    (b) the origin of the instrument;
    (c) the nature of the non-compliance alleged and the risk involved;
    (d) the nature and duration of the measures taken;

(e) the arguments put forward by the relevant economic operator; and

(f) whether the non-compliance is due to either of the following—

  (i) failure of the regulated measuring instrument to meet the requirements relating to a risk;

  (ii) shortcomings in the harmonised standards referred to in regulation 37(a).

64 EU safeguard procedure (1) Where another EEA State has initiated the procedure under Article 42 of the Directive, the Market surveillance authority must without delay, inform the Commission and the other EEA States of—

(a) any measures taken by a competent authority in respect of the regulated measuring instrument;

(b) any additional information which the market surveillance authority has at its disposal relating to the lack of conformity of the regulated measuring instrument; and

(c) any objections that the market surveillance authority may have to the measure taken by the EEA State initiating the procedure.

(2) Where a measure taken by another EEA state in respect of a regulated measuring instrument is considered justified under Article 42 of the Directive, the market surveillance authority must ensure that appropriate measures to withdraw the instrument are taken in respect of the regulated measuring instrument without delay.

(3) If, pursuant to Article 43 of the Directive, the Commission considers a direction given pursuant to regulation 63(4) is unjustified, the market surveillance authority must forthwith withdraw it and notify other enforcement authorities and economic operators affected accordingly.

65 Compliant regulated measuring instruments which present a risk (1) This regulation applies where, having carried out an evaluation under regulation 63, the market surveillance authority finds that although a regulated measuring instrument is in compliance with the requirements of these Regulations, it presents a risk on grounds of public interest, public health, public safety, public order, protection of the environment, protection of consumers, the levying of taxes and duties or fair trading.

(2) Where this regulation applies, the market surveillance authority must issue a direction requiring the economic operator to—

(a) take all appropriate measures to ensure that the regulated measuring instrument concerned, when placed on the market, no longer presents that risk;

(b) withdraw the regulated measuring instrument from the market; or

(c) recall it within a reasonable period, commensurate with the nature of the risk as it may prescribe.

(3) Where this regulation applies, the market surveillance authority must immediately inform the Commission and the other EEA states of all available details including—

(a) the data necessary for the identification of the regulated measuring instrument concerned;

(b) the origin and supply chain of the regulated measuring instrument;

(c) the nature of the risk involved; and

(d) the nature and duration of the national measures taken.

66 Provisions as to directions under regulations 63 and 65 (1) This regulation applies in relation to directions given under regulations 63 and 65.

(2) A direction must—

(a) be in writing;

(b) describe the regulated measuring instrument to which it relates in a manner sufficient to identify that instrument;

(c) specify the risk identified by the market surveillance authority;

(d) specify the steps that the economic operator must take (including the time period within which they must be taken).

(3) The Secretary of State may impose a monetary penalty on an economic operator who fails to comply with a direction given under regulation 63 or 65.

(4) Schedule 7 has effect in relation to a monetary penalty imposed under paragraph (3).

Chapter 2
Enforcement authorities and procedures

67 Enforcement of the Regulations (1) The Secretary of State—

(a) must enforce these regulations where required to do so in the capacity of the market surveillance authority; and

(b) may otherwise than in the capacity of market surveillance authority, enforce these Regulations in Great Britain,

and for the purposes of this paragraph may appoint a person to act on his behalf.

(2) In Great Britain it is the duty of every local weights and measures authority to enforce these Regulations within its area in relation to regulated measuring instruments other than—

(a) gas meters;

(b) active electrical energy meters;

(c) taximeters; and

(d) exhaust gas analysers.

(3) In Northern Ireland—

(a) the Department for Infrastructure must enforce these Regulations in relation to regulated measuring instruments of the following kinds—

(i) taximeters; and

(ii) exhaust gas analysers.

(b) the Utility Regulator (or the Secretary of State pursuant to arrangements made under paragraph (7)) must enforce the Regulations) in relation to regulated measuring instruments of the following kinds—

(i) gas meters; and

(ii) active electrical energy meters.

(c) the Department for the Economy must enforce these Regulations (other than Part 6) insofar as they relate to regulated measuring instruments of the following kinds—

(i) cold water meters;

(ii) automatic weighing instruments;

(iii) material measures; and

(iv) non-water liquid measuring systems.

(4) No proceedings for an offence under these Regulations may be instituted in England and Wales except by or on behalf of a competent authority.

(5) Nothing in these Regulations shall authorise a competent authority to bring proceedings in Scotland for an offence.

(6) No proceedings shall be instituted in Northern Ireland for an offence under these Regulations in respect of a regulated measuring instrument except—

(a) by or on behalf of a competent authority which has responsibility for enforcing these Regulations in respect of that regulated measuring instrument; or

(b) the Director of Public Prosecutions for Northern Ireland.

(7) The Secretary of State and the Utility Regulator may, in relation to the enforcement of these Regulations in Northern Ireland, enter into arrangements for the Secretary of State to act on behalf of the Utility Regulator for, or in connection with, the carrying out of some or all of the functions conferred on the Utility Regulator by these Regulations.

68 Compliance notice procedure (1) This regulation applies where a competent authority has reasonable grounds for considering that one or more of the following breaches applies in relation to a regulated measuring instrument that has been placed on the market or put into use—

(a) the CE marking or the M marking has been affixed in violation of Article 30 of the RAMS regulation or the requirements of these Regulations;

(b) the CE marking or the M marking has not been affixed;

(c) the identification number of the notified body, where the notified body is involved in the production control phase has—

(i) been affixed otherwise than in accordance with the requirements of these Regulations; or

(ii) not been affixed;

(d) the EU declaration of conformity has not been drawn up correctly;

(e) the technical documentation is either not available or is not complete;

(f) the information referred to in regulation 11 or regulation 20 is false or incomplete; or

(g) any other failure—

(i) by a manufacturer to comply with the requirements of Chapter 1 of Part 2; or

(ii) by an importer to comply with the requirements of Chapter 2 of Part 2.

(2) The competent authority may serve a notice in writing ("a compliance notice") on the economic operator it considers is the responsible for the breach which must—

(a) describe the regulated measuring instrument to which it relates in a manner sufficient to identify that instrument;

(b) specify which of the circumstances in paragraph (1) applies in relation to the regulated measuring instrument;

(c) require the economic operator on whom the notice is served to take steps to remedy the matters referred to in paragraph (b);

(d) specify the date, being not less than 21 days from the date of the notice, by which the steps specified in it must be taken; and

(e) warn the economic operator that, where the non-conformity continues beyond the date specified in sub-paragraph (d), the competent authority may take further action under regulation 69 (enforcement notices) in respect of that regulated measuring instrument.

(3) Where a compliance notice is served by a competent authority other than the Secretary of State, it must at the same time as it serves that notice, send a copy to the Secretary of State.

69 Enforcement notices (1) This regulation applies where a competent authority has reasonable grounds for considering that an economic operator on whom a compliance notice has been served by the competent authority has failed to comply with that notice.

(2) The competent authority may serve a notice ("an enforcement notice") on the economic operator which must—

(a) be in writing;

(b) describe the regulated measuring instrument to which it relates in a manner sufficient to identify that instrument;

(c) specify, with reasons, the respects in which, in the opinion of the competent authority, the compliance notice has not been complied with; and

(d) specify the steps that the economic operator must take to comply with the compliance notice; and

(e) specify the date, being not less than 21 days from the date of the notice, by which the economic operator to whom the notice is given is required to comply with it.

(3) An enforcement notice may impose either or both of the following requirements—

(a) that the regulated measuring instrument is to be withdrawn from the market unless the steps referred to in paragraph (2)(d) are taken; or

(b) that the placing on the market or putting into use of the regulated measuring instrument is to be prohibited or restricted unless the steps referred to in paragraph (2)(d) are taken.

(4) Where an enforcement notice is served by a competent authority other than the Secretary of State, it must at the same time as it serves that notice send a copy of the notice to the Secretary of State.

(5) If the Secretary of State is of the opinion that consideration ought to be given as to whether a certificate or notification which is granted by a United Kingdom notified body should be withdrawn, the Secretary of State must inform that notified body of that fact.

(6) If the Secretary of State is of the opinion that consideration ought to be given as to whether a certificate or notification which is granted by a notified body in another EEA state should be withdrawn, the Secretary of State must inform the market surveillance authority in that state of that fact.

70 Review of enforcement decisions of a competent authority (1) Where a notice is served under regulation 68 (compliance notice procedure) or 69 (enforcement notices) is by a competent authority other than the Secretary of State, an economic operator who is aggrieved by the decision to serve the notice may, in accordance with paragraphs (2) and (3) apply to the Secretary of State to review the decision; and on such application the Secretary of State may—

    (a) hold an inquiry in connection with the decision; and

    (b) appoint an assessor for the purposes of assisting him with his review or any such inquiry.

(2) An application under paragraph (1) must be made by notice in writing to the Secretary of State, and must be sent to the Secretary of State not later than 21 days after the date of the notice of the decision in respect of which the application for review is sent to the economic operator.

(3) A notice of application for review under this regulation must state the grounds on which the application is made.

(4) The Secretary of State must, within a reasonable time, inform the economic operator and the authority referred to in paragraph (1) in writing of the Secretary of State's decision whether to uphold the decision of that authority and—

    (a) in a case where the Secretary of State upholds that decision, must also state the grounds for the Secretary of State's decision; and

    (b) in a case where the Secretary of State does not uphold that decision, may—

        (i) where the review relates to regulation 68 give instructions for the withdrawal of the notice given under paragraph (2) of that regulation; or

        (ii) where the review relates to regulation 69, give instructions for the withdrawal of the notice given under paragraph (1) of that regulation.

71 Offence of failure to comply with an enforcement notice (1) This paragraph applies where an enforcement notice has, pursuant regulation 69 (enforcement notices), been served on an economic operator by a competent authority other than the Secretary of State and either—

    (a) the time for making an application by the economic operator for a
        review pursuant to regulation 70 (review of enforcement decisions of a
        competent authority) has expired without such application having been
        made; or
    (b) an application for review has been made by the economic operator and
        determined without an instruction for the withdrawal of the notice
        being given and a period of 21 days has elapsed beginning with the day
        after notice of the outcome of the review has been served on the eco-
        nomic operator.

(2) Where paragraph (1) applies, if the economic operator on whom the compliance notice has been served fails to comply with the requirements of that notice,
that economic operator is guilty of an offence.

(3) An economic operator that fails to comply with an enforcement notice
served on the economic operator by the Secretary of State is guilty of an offence.

72 Disqualification (1) This regulation and regulation 73 (re-qualification)
apply only in relation to a regulated measuring instruments of the following
kinds—
    (a) cold water meters;
    (b) automatic weighing instruments;
    (c) material measures; and
    (d) non-water liquid measuring systems.

(2) Where the circumstances in paragraph (3) apply, an inspector may affix a
disqualification mark to a regulated measuring instrument which bears the—
    (a) CE marking;
    (b) M marking; and
    (c) identification number of the notified body which carried out the confor-
        mity assessment procedure in respect of the instrument.

(3) The circumstances referred to in paragraph (2) are that the instrument is
used for trade in circumstances where—
    (a) the instrument does not conform to the essential requirements (other
        than the requirements relating to maximum permissible errors);
    (b) the instrument is not in conformity with any EU-type examination cer-
        tificate or EU-design examination certificate which applies to it;
    (c) by reason of any adjustment, alteration, addition, repair or replacement,
        it is likely that the instrument has ceased to conform with the essential
        requirements (other than the requirements relating to maximum per-
        missible errors); or
    (d) any requirements applicable to the instrument by virtue of Part 6 are
        not met.

(4) Where one or more of the markings and identification requirements referred
to in paragraph (2) is not affixed to a regulated measuring instrument, the inspector may affix a disqualification mark to the instrument.

(5) Where it appears to the inspector that the nature or degree of non-compliance of the regulated measuring instrument under paragraph (2) is not such that a disqualification mark should be immediately affixed to it or to any sealing device on it, the inspector may give to any person in possession of the instrument a notice requiring the person to ensure that the instrument is made to comply with the essential requirements before the expiry of 21 days from the date of the notice or such longer period as may be specified in the notice.

(6) If a notice given under paragraph (5) is not complied with, the inspector must affix a disqualification mark to the regulated measuring instrument or to any sealing device on it.

(7) Any disqualification mark which is affixed to a regulated measuring instrument under this regulation must be affixed in such a position that it is clearly visible when the instrument is in its regular operating position or where it is affixed to any sealing device on the instrument, it must be affixed in such a position that it obliterates as far as possible any inscription on that sealing device.

(8) A person is guilty of an offence if that person uses for trade a regulated measuring instrument to which there is affixed a disqualification mark, unless a re-qualification mark has been affixed to it in accordance with regulation 73 (requalification).

73 Re-qualification (1) This regulation applies where—
  (a) a disqualification mark has been affixed to a regulated measuring instrument in accordance with regulation 72 (disqualification);
  (b) a notice has been served under regulation 72(5); or
  (c) a regulated measuring instrument is intended to be used for trade in the circumstances referred to in regulation 72(3)(a) to (iv) or (3) but a disqualification mark has not been affixed to the instrument or to any sealing device on it.

(2) A person requiring a re-qualification mark to be affixed to a regulated measuring instrument must submit it, in such manner as may be directed, to an inspector or approved verifier and provide such assistance as the inspector or approved verifier may reasonably require.

(3) An inspector or approved verifier may affix a re-qualification mark to that regulated measuring instrument or to any sealing device if satisfied that the instrument is compliant with
  (a) the essential requirements;
  (b) any EU-type examination certificate or EU-design examination certificate which applies to it; and
  (c) any requirements applicable to that instrument by virtue of Schedule 6 other than the provisions relating to maximum permissible errors are met.

(4) For the purposes of being satisfied that a re-qualification mark may be affixed to a regulated measuring instrument or any sealing device on it under this regulation, an inspector or approved verifier may take such steps as the inspector

or approved verifier considers appropriate, including testing the instrument by means of such test equipment as the inspector or approved verifier considers appropriate and suitable for the purpose.

(5) There may be charged in respect of any steps taken under paragraph (4) such fees as are reasonable in the circumstances.

(6) The inspector or approved verifier must keep a record of any test carried out under paragraph (4).

(7) Where a re-qualification mark is affixed to a regulated measuring instrument pursuant to paragraph (3), it must be affixed in such a position that it obliterates as far as possible any disqualification mark.

74 Testing of regulated measuring instruments (1) Where an inspector considers that a test of a regulated measuring instrument is necessary, otherwise than for the purposes of regulation 73, the inspector may require the controller of the instrument to provide to the inspector such equipment, test liquid, materials, qualified personnel or other assistance as the inspector may reasonably require.

(2) Every regulated measuring instrument submitted for testing by its controller must be in a clean condition.

(3) Paragraphs (4) to (9) of this regulation only apply to regulated measuring instruments that are non-water liquid measuring systems.

(4) No regulated measuring instrument shall be tested until it is installed ready for use and complete with all its parts.

(5) A regulated measuring instrument must be tested by an inspector under practical working conditions with a test liquid which must be—
    (a) the liquid fuel that the instrument is intended to deliver; or
    (b) a liquid having properties which replicate in all respects relevant to testing those of the liquid fuel that the instrument is intended to deliver.

(6) An inspector may open a locked or sealed tank or container for the purpose of testing a regulated measuring instrument or returning any liquid withdrawn during testing.

(7) Any liquid withdrawn during testing must be—
    (a) returned to the tank or container from which it was withdrawn if the inspector is of the opinion that it is reasonable and practicable to do so and the controller agrees; or
    (b) placed in another suitable receptacle reasonably convenient for the purpose that is provided by the controller.

(8) An inspector, if requested to do so by the controller, must give to the controller a signed and dated statement of the quantity of liquid withdrawn during testing.

(9) An inspector must—

(a) securely re-fasten any tank or container opened under paragraph (6) immediately after the conclusion of any test or after returning any liquid withdrawn during testing; and

(b) replace any sealing device broken by the inspector.

(10) In this regulation references to the "controller" of a regulated measuring instrument are to the person who has control of the instrument or whom the inspector has reasonable cause to believe has control of the instrument.

Part 8
Offences

75 Unauthorised application of authorised marks (1) Subject to paragraph (2), a person is guilty of an offence, if that person—

(a) affixes an authorised mark to a regulated measuring instrument otherwise than in accordance with these Regulations;

(b) alters or defaces an authorised mark affixed to a regulated measuring instrument;

(c) removes an authorised mark affixed to a regulated measuring instrument; or

(d) affixes any other form of marking to a regulated measuring instrument which is likely to deceive any person as to the meaning or form, or both, of an authorised mark.

(2) Where the alteration, defacement or removal of an authorised mark is occasioned solely—

(a) in the course of the adjustment or repair of a regulated measuring instrument by a person engaged in the business of repair of such instruments or by that person's duly authorised agent; or

(b) by an enforcement officer or approved verifier in the carrying out of any of their functions under these Regulations,

that person (or that person's authorised agent), enforcement officer or approved verifier is not guilty of an offence under paragraph (1)(b) or (1)(c).

(3) A person is guilty of an offence if that person places on the market or puts into use or uses for trade a regulated measuring instrument—

(a) from which, to that person's knowledge, an authorised mark has been removed; or

(b) which to that person's knowledge bears—

(i) an authorised mark affixed otherwise than in accordance with these Regulations;

(ii) an authorised mark that has been altered or defaced otherwise than in the circumstances referred to in paragraph (2); or

(iii) any mark which is likely to deceive any person as to the meaning or form, or both, of an authorised mark.

(4) A regulated measuring instrument in respect of which an offence under this regulation has been committed and any implement used in the commissioning of the offence is liable to be forfeited.

(5) In this regulation "authorised mark" means—
   (a) the CE marking;
   (b) the M marking;
   (c) the identification number of the notified body which carried out the conformity assessment procedure in respect of the relevant regulated measuring instrument;
   (d) a disqualification mark; or
   (e) a re-qualification mark.

76 Offences by economic operators etc. (1) In this regulation "event of default" means—
   (a) the placing on the market or putting into use of a regulated measuring instrument which—
      (i)   does not meet the essential requirements applicable to it;
      (ii) has not been the subject of an applicable conformity assessment procedure;
      (iii) does not bear the markings or inscriptions required by these Regulations; or
      (iv) is not accompanied by the documents and information required by these Regulations; or
   (b) any failure to—
      (i)   create or maintain any records required to be created or maintained under these Regulations; or
      (ii) provide to a competent authority documents or information pursuant to a requirement imposed by or under these Regulations; or
   (c) any failure to comply with an obligation under regulation 74(1) or 74(2)

(2) Where an event of default mentioned in paragraph (1)(a) or 1(b) occurs as a result of the failure of an economic operator to comply with an obligation imposed on the economic operator by any provision of these Regulations, the economic operator is guilty of an offence.

(3) Where there is an event of default of a kind referred to in paragraph (1)(c), the person on whom the obligation is imposed under section 74(1) or 74(2) is guilty of an offence.

77 Penalties for offences A person guilty of an offence under any provision of these Regulations is liable, on summary conviction—
   (a) in England and Wales to a fine; and
   (b) in Scotland or Northern Ireland to a fine not exceeding level 5 on the standard scale.

78 Defence of due diligence (1) In proceedings against a person for an offence under these Regulations (other than regulation 75(3)), it is a defence for that person to show that that person took all reasonable steps and exercised all due diligence to avoid committing the offence.

(2) Where, in proceedings against a person for such an offence the defence provided by paragraph (1) involves an allegation that the commission of the offence was due to—

    (a) the act or default of another; or

    (b) reliance on information given by another,

that person shall not, without the leave of the court, be entitled to rely on the defence, unless, not less than seven clear days before the hearing of the proceedings (or, in Scotland, the trial diet), that person has served a notice under paragraph (3) on the person bringing the proceedings.

(3) A notice under this paragraph must give such information identifying or assisting in the identification of the person who committed the act or default or gave the information as is in the possession of the person serving the notice at the time that person serves it.

(4) A person shall not be entitled to rely on the defence provided by paragraph (1) by reason of reliance on information supplied by another, unless that person shows it was reasonable in all the circumstances for that person to have relied on the information, having regard in particular to—

    (a) the steps which that person took, and those which might reasonably have been taken, for the purpose of verifying the information; and

    (b) whether that person had any reason to disbelieve the information.

79 Liability of persons other than the principal offender (1) Where the commission by a person ("A") of an offence under these Regulations is due to the act or default of another person ("B") in the course of any business of A, B is guilty of the offence and may be proceeded against and punished, whether or not proceedings are taken against A.

(2) Where a body corporate commits an offence under these Regulations and it is proved that the offence was committed—

    (a) with the consent or connivance of an officer of the body corporate,

    (b) as a result of the negligence of an officer of the body corporate

the officer as well as the body corporate is guilty of the offence.

(3) In paragraph (2), a reference to an officer of a body corporate includes a reference to—

    (a) a director, manager, secretary or other similar officer of the body corporate;

    (b) a person purporting to act as a director, manager, secretary or other similar officer; and

    (c) if the affairs of the body corporate are managed by its members, a member

(4) In this regulation, references to a "body corporate" include references to a partnership in Scotland, and in relation to such partnership, any reference to a director, manager, secretary or other similar officer of a body corporate is a reference to a partner.

Part 9
Miscellaneous and supplemental

80 Service of documents etc. (1) Any document required or authorised by these Regulations to be served on a person may be so served—
 (a) by delivering it to that person or by leaving it at that person's proper address or by sending it by post to that person at that address;
 (b) if the person is a body corporate, by serving it in accordance with sub-paragraph (a) on the secretary or clerk of that body; or
 (c) if the person is a partnership, by serving it in accordance with that sub-paragraph on a partner or on a person having control or management of the partnership business.

(2) For the purposes of paragraph (1), and for the purposes of section 7 of the Interpretation Act 1978 (which relates to the service of documents by post) in its application to that paragraph, the proper address of any person on whom a document is to be served in accordance with these Regulations is that person's last known address except that—
 (a) in the case of service on a body corporate or its secretary or clerk, it is the address of the registered or principal office of the body corporate; and
 (b) in the case of service on a partnership or a partner or a person having the control or management of a partnership business, it is the principal office of the partnership,

and for the purposes of this paragraph the principal office of a company registered outside the United Kingdom or of a partnership carrying on business outside the United Kingdom is its principal office within the United Kingdom.

81 Review (1) The Secretary of State must from time to time—
 (a) carry out a review of these Regulations;
 (b) set out the conclusions of the review in a report; and
 (c) publish the report.

(2) In carrying out the review the Secretary of State must, so far as is reasonable, have regard to how the Directive is implemented in other EEA states.

(3) The report must, in particular—
 (a) set out the objectives intended to be achieved by the regulatory system established by these Regulations;
 (b) assess the extent to which those objectives are achieved; and
 (c) assess whether those objectives remain appropriate and, if so, the extent to which they could be achieved by a system that imposes less regulation.

(4) The first report under this regulation must be published no later than 5 years after the date of the coming into force of these Regulations.

(5) Reports under this regulation are afterwards to be published at intervals not exceeding 5 years.

Schedule 1
Essential requirements and applicable conformity assessment procedures

1 Introductory The essential requirements and conformity assessment procedure applicable to measuring instruments are as set out in this Schedule.

9 Taximeters (1) The essential requirements in relation to taximeters are—
    (a) the requirements of Annex 1 of the Directive; and
    (b) the specific requirements in Annex IX.

(2) The conformity assessment procedures specified in the modules in Annex II to the Directive applicable to taximeters are—
    (a) B and F;
    (b) B and D; or
    (c) H1.

Schedule 2
Measuring instrument which may continue to be put into use

Taximeters

13 A Taximeter—
    (a) in respect of which a certificate of approval was granted before 30th October 2006; and
    (b) which was passed as fit for use before 30th October 2016 for the protection of consumers and marked under the Metropolitan Conditions of Fitness.

2017 No 342

Equality Act 2010 (Taxis and Private Hire Vehicles) (Passengers in Wheelchairs – Notices of Exemption) Regulations 2017

1 Citation, commencement and interpretation (1) These Regulations may be cited as the Equality Act 2010 (Taxis and Private Hire Vehicles) (Passengers in Wheelchairs – Notices of Exemption) Regulations 2017 and come into force on 6th April 2017.

(2) In these Regulations "the Act" means the Equality Act 2010.

2 Notices of exemption (1) The prescribed notice of exemption for the purposes of section 166(3)(b) and (4)(b) of the Act is—

(a) in the case of a driver of a designated taxi or a designated private hire vehicle to whom an exemption certificate has been issued by a licensing authority in England or Scotland, the notice set out in Schedule 1; and

(b) in the case of a driver of a designated taxi or a designated private hire vehicle to whom an exemption certificate has been issued by a licensing authority in Wales, the notice set out in Schedule 2.

(2) Each notice of exemption must have the exterior dimensions of 10cm x 10cm.

(3) The prescribed manner of exhibiting a notice of exemption for the purposes of section 166(3)(b) and (4)(b) of the Act is—

(a) by displaying it—

(i) on the nearside of and immediately behind the windscreen of the vehicle; and

(ii) in a manner that readily permits its removal;

(b) so that—

(i) its front is clearly visible from the outside of the vehicle; and

(ii) its back is clearly visible from the driver's seat of the vehicle.

Schedule 1

1. Form of front of notice of exemption in England and Scotland

Section 166 Equality Act 2010

Notice Of Exemption

Name of licensing authority

_____

Driver's name

_____

Licence No.

_____

The person named above is exempt from the duties required by section 165 of the Equality Act 2010.

Ew

This notice expires _____ **20** _____

2. Form of back of notice of exemption in England and Scotland

Attention

Only the driver named overleaf may display this notice when driving the vehicle. The notice may also remain on display when the vehicle is parked provided it has been driven by, and is to be driven by, the named driver. Otherwise the named driver must remove the notice.

Schedule 2

1. Form of front of notice of exemption in Wales

Adran 166 O Ddeddf Cydraddoldeb 2010
Section 166 Equality Act 2010

Hysbysiad Am Esemptiad
Notice Of Exemption

Enw'r awdurdod trwyddedu *Name of licensing authority*

Enw'r gyrrwr *Driver's name*

Rhif y Drwydded *Licence No.*

Mae'r person a enwir uchod yn esempt rhag y dyletswyddau gofynnol yn adran 165 o Ddeddf Cydraddoleb 2010.
The person named above is exempt from the duties required by section 165 of the Equality Act 2010.

Daw'r hysbysiad hwn i ben ar _____ **20** _____

This notice expires _____ *20* _____

Ew

2. Form of back of notice of exemption in Wales

Rhybudd Attention

Dim ond y gyrrwr a enwir dros y ddalen all arddangos yr Hysbysiad hwn wrth yrru'r cerbyd. Gellir hefyd barhau i arddangos yr hysbysiad pan fydd y cerbyd wedi'i barcio cyhyd ag y bydd yn cael ei yrru gan, ac i'w yrru gan, y gyrrwr a enwyd. Fel arall rhaid i'r gyrrwr a enwyd dynnu'r hysbysiad oddi yno.

Only the driver named overleaf may display this Notice when driving the vehicle. The notice may also remain on display when the vehicle is parked provided it has been driven by, and is to be driven by, the named driver. Otherwise the named driver must remove the notice.

Town Police Clauses Act 1847

3. Interpretations in this and the special Act:

The following words and expressions, in both this and the special Act, and any Act incorporated therewith, shall have the meanings hereby assigned to them, unless there be something in the subject or context repugnant to such construction; (that is to say,)

Words importing the singular number shall include the plural number, and words importing the plural number shall include the singular number:

Words importing the masculine gender shall include females:

The word "person" shall include a corporation, whether aggregate or sole:

The word "lands" shall include messuages, lands, tenements, and hereditaments of any tenure:

The word "street" shall extend to and include any road, square, court, alley, and thoroughfare or public passage within the limits of the special Act:

The word "month" shall mean calendar month:

[. . .] [1]

[. . .] [2]

[. . .] [3]

The word "cattle" shall include horses, asses, mules, sheep, goats, and swine.

Amendment

1. Words repealed by Statute Law (Repeals) Act 1993, Sch 1(XIV), para.1.

2. Words repealed by Courts Act 2003, Sch.10 para 1 (as SI 2005/910).

3. Definition of “quarter sessions” repealed by Courts Act 1971, Sch. 11, Pt IV.

Hackney carriages

37 Hackney carriages to be licensed. The commissioners may from time to time licence to ply for hire within the prescribed distance, or if no distance is prescribed, within five miles from the General Post Office of the city, town, or place to which the special Act refers, (which in that case shall be deemed the prescribed distance,) such number of hackney coaches or carriages of any kind or description adapted to the carriage of persons as they think fit.

38 What to be deemed hackney carriages Every wheeled carriage, whatever may be its form or construction, used in standing or plying for hire in any street within the prescribed distance, and every carriage standing upon any street within the prescribed distance, having thereon any numbered plate required by this or the special Act to be fixed upon a hackney carriage, or having thereon any plate resembling or intended to resemble any such plate as aforesaid, shall be deemed to be a hackney carriage within the meaning of this Act; and in all proceedings at law or otherwise the term "hackney carriage" shall be sufficient to describe any such carriage: Provided always, that no stage coach used for the purpose of standing or plying for passengers to be carried for hire at separate fares, and duly licensed for that purpose, and having thereon the proper numbered plates required by law to be placed on such stage coaches, shall be deemed to be a hackney carriage within the meaning of this Act.

39 . . .

Amendment
Section repealed by the Transport Act 1981, s 40(1), Sch 12, Pt III.

40 Persons applying for licence to sign a requisition Before any such licence is granted a requisition for the same, in such form as the commissioners from time to time provide for that purpose, shall be made and signed by the proprietor or one of the proprietors of the hackney carriage in respect of which such licence is applied for; and in every such requisition shall be truly stated the name and surname and place of abode of the person applying for such licence, and of every proprietor or part proprietor of such carriage, or person concerned, either solely or in partnership with any other person, in the keeping, employing, or letting to hire of such carriage; and any person who, on applying for such licence, states in such requisition the name of any person who is not a proprietor or part proprietor of such carriage, or who is not concerned as aforesaid in the keeping, employing, or letting to hire of such carriage, and also any person who wilfully omits to specify truly in such requisition as aforesaid the name of any person who is a proprietor or part proprietor of such carriage, or who is concerned as aforesaid in the keeping, employing, or letting to hire of such carriage, shall be liable to a penalty not exceeding [level 1 on the standard scale].

Amendment
Maximum penalty increased by the Criminal Justice Act 1967, s 92(1), Sch 3, Part I, and converted to a level on the standard scale by the Criminal Justice Act 1982, ss 37, 38, 46.

41 What shall be specified in the licences In every such licence shall be specified the name and surname and place of abode of every person who is a proprietor or part proprietor of the hackney carriage in respect of which such licence is granted, or who is concerned, either solely or in partnership with any other person, in the keeping, employing, or letting to hire of any such carriage, and also the number of such licence which shall correspond with the number to be painted or marked on the plates to be fixed on such carriage, together with such other particulars as the commissioners think fit.

42 Licences to be registered Every licence shall be made out by the clerk of the commissioners, and duly entered in a book to be provided by him for that purpose; and in such book shall be contained columns or places for entries to be made of every offence committed by any proprietor or driver or person attending such carriage; and any person may at any reasonable time inspect such book, without fee or reward.

43 Licence to be in force for one year only Every licence so to be granted shall be under the common seal of the commissioners, if incorporated, or, if not incorporated, shall be signed by two or more of the commissioners, and shall not include more than one carriage so licensed, and shall be in force for one year only from the day of the date of such licence or until the next general licensing meeting, in case any general licensing day be appointed by the commissioners.

44 Notice to be given by proprietors of hackney carriages of any change of abode So often as any person named in any such licence as the proprietor or one of the proprietors, or as being concerned, either solely or in partnership with any person, in the keeping, employing, or letting to hire of any such carriage, changes his place of abode, he shall, within seven days next after such change, give notice thereof in writing, signed by him, to the commissioners, specifying in such notice his new place of abode; and he shall at the same time produce such licence at the office of the commissioners, who shall by their clerk, or some other officer, endorse thereon and sign a memorandum specifying the particulars of such change; and any person named in any such licence as aforesaid as the proprietor, or one of the proprietors, of any hackney carriage, or as being concerned as aforesaid, who changes his place of abode and neglects or wilfully omits to give notice of such change, or to produce such licence in order that such memorandum as aforesaid may be endorsed thereon, within the time and in the manner limited and directed by this or the special Act, shall be liable to a penalty not exceeding [level 1 on the standard scale].

Amendment
Maximum penalty increased by the Criminal Justice Act 1967, s 92(1), Sch 3, Part I, and converted to a level on the standard scale by the Criminal Justice Act 1982, ss 37, 38, 46.

45 Penalty for plying for hire without a licence If the proprietor or part proprietor of any carriage, or any person so concerned as aforesaid, permits the same to be used as a hackney carriage plying for hire within the prescribed distance without having obtained a licence as aforesaid for such carriage, or during the time that such licence is suspended as hereinafter provided, or if any person be found driving, standing, or plying for hire with any carriage within the prescribed distance for which such licence as aforesaid has not been previously obtained, or without having the number of such carriage corresponding with the number of the licence openly displayed on such carriage, every such person so offending shall for every such offence be liable to a penalty not exceeding [level 4 on the standard scale].

Amendment
Maximum penalty on any conviction increased and converted to a level on the standard scale by the Criminal Justice Act 1982, ss 37, 39, 46, Sch 3.

46 Drivers not to act without first obtaining a licence No person shall act as driver of any hackney carriage licensed in pursuance of this or the special Act to ply for hire within the prescribed distance without first obtaining a licence from the commissioners, which licence shall be registered by the clerk to the commissioners, [and such fee as the commissioners may determine shall be paid] for the same; and every such licence shall be in force until the same is revoked except during the time that the same may be suspended as after mentioned.

Amendment
Words in square brackets substituted by the Local Government, Planning and Land Act 1980, s 1(6), Sch 6.

47 Penalty on drivers acting without licence, or proprietors employing unlicensed drivers If any person acts as such driver as aforesaid without having obtained such licence, or during the time that his licence is suspended, or if he lend or part with his licence, except to the proprietor of the hackney carriage, or if the proprietor of any such hackney carriage employ any person as the driver thereof who has not obtained such licence, or during the time that his licence is suspended, as herein-after provided, every such driver and every such proprietor shall for every such offence respectively be liable to a penalty not exceeding [level 3 on the standard scale].

Amendment
Enhanced penalty on a subsequent conviction abolished, maximum penalty on any conviction increased and converted to a level on the standard scale by the Criminal Justice Act 1982, ss 35, 37, 38, 46.

48 Proprietor to retain licences of drivers, and to produce the same before justices on complaint In every case in which the proprietor of any such hackney carriage permits or employs any licensed person to act as the driver thereof, such proprietor shall cause to be delivered to him, and shall retain in his possession, the licence of such driver, while such driver remains in his employ; and in all cases of complaint, where the proprietor of a hackney carriage is summoned to attend before a justice, or to produce the driver, the proprietor so summoned shall also produce the licence of such driver, if he be then in his employ; and if any driver complained of be adjudged guilty of the offence alleged against him, such justice shall make an endorsement upon the licence of such driver, stating the nature of the offence and amount of the penalty inflicted; and if any such proprietor neglect to have delivered to him and to retain in his possession the licence of any driver while such driver remains in his employ, or if he refuse or neglect to produce such licence as aforesaid, such proprietor shall for every such offence be liable to a penalty not exceeding [level 1 on the standard scale].

Amendment
Maximum penalty increased by the Criminal Law Act 1977, s 31(6), and converted to a level on the standard scale by the Criminal Justice Act 1982, ss 37, 46.

49 Proprietor to return licence to drivers except in case of misconduct When any driver leaves the service of the proprietor by whom he is employed without having been guilty of any misconduct, such proprietor shall forthwith return to such driver the licence belonging to him; but if such driver have been guilty of any misconduct, the proprietor shall not return his licence, but shall give him notice of the complaint which he intends to prefer against him, and shall forthwith summon such driver to appear before any justice to answer the said complaint; and such justice, having the necessary parties before him, shall inquire into and determine the matter of complaint, and if upon inquiry it appear that the licence of such driver has been improperly withheld, such justice shall direct the immediate re-delivery of such licence, and award such sum of money as he thinks proper to be paid by such proprietor to such driver by way of compensation.

50 Revocation of licences of proprietors or drivers The commissioners may, upon the conviction for the second time of the proprietor or driver of any such hackney carriage for any offence under the provisions of this or the special Act with respect to hackney carriages, or any byelaw made in pursuance thereof, suspend or revoke, as they deem right, the licence of any such proprietor or driver.

51 Number of persons to be carried in a hackney carriage to be painted thereon *No hackney carriage shall be used or employed or let to hire, or shall stand or ply for hire, within the prescribed distance, unless the number of persons to be carried by such hackney carriage, in words at length, and in form following, (that is to say,) "To carry .... persons," be painted on a plate placed on some conspicuous place on the outside of such carriage, and in legible letters, so as to be clearly distinguishable from the colour of the ground whereon the same are painted, one inch in length, and of a proportionate breadth; and the driver of any such hackney carriage shall not be required to carry in or by such hackney carriage a greater number of persons than the number painted thereon.*

Amendment
Repealed, in relation to tramcars and trolley vehicles, by the Transport Charges &c (Miscellaneous Provisions) Act 1954, ss 14(1), 15(2), Sch 2, Part IV.

52 Penalty for neglect to exhibit the number, or for refusal to carry the prescribed number *If the proprietor of any hackney carriage permit the same to be used, employed, or let to hire, or if any person stand or ply for hire with such carriage, without having the number of persons to be carried thereby painted and exhibited in manner aforesaid, or if the driver of any such hackney carriage refuse, when required by the hirer thereof, to carry in or by such hackney carriage the number of persons painted thereon, or any less number, every proprietor or driver so offending shall be liable to a penalty not exceeding [level 1 on the standard scale].*

Amendment

Repealed, in relation to tramcars and trolley vehicles, by the Transport Charges &c (Miscellaneous Provisions) Act 1954, ss 14(1), 15(2), Sch 2, Part IV.

Maximum penalty increased by the Criminal Law Act 1977, s 31(6), and converted to a level on the standard scale by the Criminal Justice Act 1982, ss 37, 46.

53 Penalty on driver for refusing to drive A driver of a hackney carriage standing at any of the stands for hackney carriages appointed by the commissioners, or in any street, who refuses or neglects, without reasonable excuse, to drive such carriage to any place within the prescribed distance, or the distance to be appointed by any byelaw of the commissioners, not exceeding the prescribed distance, to which he is directed to drive by the person hiring or wishing to hire such carriage, shall for every such offence be liable to a penalty not exceeding [level 2 on the standard scale].

Amendment

Maximum penalty increased and converted to a level on the standard scale by the Criminal Justice Act 1982, ss 37, 39, 46, Sch 3.

54 Penalty for demanding more than the sum agreed for If the proprietor or driver of any such hackney carriage, or if any other person on his behalf, agree beforehand with any person hiring such hackney carriage to take for any job a sum less than the fare allowed by this or the special Act, or any byelaw made thereunder, such proprietor or driver shall be liable to a penalty not exceeding [level 1 on the standard scale] if he exact or demand for such job more than the fare so agreed upon.

Amendment

Maximum penalty increased by the Criminal Law Act 1977, s 31(6), and converted to a level on the standard scale by the Criminal Justice Act 1982, ss 37, 46.

55 Agreement to pay more than the legal fare No agreement whatever made with the driver, or with any person having or pretending to have the care of any such hackney carriage, for the payment of more than the fare allowed by any byelaw made under this or the special Act, shall be binding on the person making the same; and any such person may, notwithstanding such agreement, refuse, on discharging such hackney carriage, to pay any sum beyond the fare allowed as aforesaid; and if any person actually pay to the driver of any such hackney carriage, whether in pursuance of any such agreement or otherwise, any sum exceeding the fare to which such driver was entitled, the person paying the same shall be entitled, on complaint made against such driver before any justice of the peace, to recover back the sum paid beyond the proper fare, and moreover such driver shall be liable to a penalty for such exaction not exceeding [level 3 on the standard scale]; and in default of the repayment by such driver of such excess of fare, or of payment of the said penalty, such justice shall forthwith commit such driver to prison, there to remain for any time not exceeding one month, unless the said excess of fare and the said penalty be sooner paid.

Amendment

Maximum penalty increased and converted to a level on the standard scale by the Criminal Justice Act 1982, ss 37, 39, 46, Sch 3.

56 Agreements to carry passengers a discretionary distance for a fixed sum If the proprietor or driver of any such hackney carriage, or if any other person on his behalf, agree with any person to carry in or by such hackney carriage persons not exceeding in number the number so painted on such carriage as aforesaid, for a distance to be in the discretion of such proprietor or driver, and for a sum agreed upon, such proprietor or driver shall be liable to a penalty not exceeding [level 1 on the standard scale] if the distance which he carries such persons be under that to which they were entitled to be carried for the sum so agreed upon, according to the fare allowed by this or the special Act, or any byelaw made in pursuance thereof.

Amendment

Maximum penalty increased by the Criminal Law Act 1977, s 31(6), and converted to a level on the standard scale by the Criminal Justice Act 1982, ss 37, 46.

57 Deposit to be made for carriages required to wait When any hackney carriage is hired and taken to any place, and the driver thereof is required by the hirer there to wait with such hackney carriage, such driver may demand and receive from such hirer his fare for driving to such place, and also a sum equal to the fare of such carriage for the period, as a deposit over and above such fare, during which he is required to wait as aforesaid, or if no fare for time be fixed by the byelaws, then the sum of [7p] for every half hour during which he is so required to wait, which deposit shall be accounted for by such driver when such hackney carriage is finally discharged by such hirer; and if any such driver who has received any such deposit as aforesaid refuses to wait as aforesaid, or goes away or permits such hackney carriage to be driven or taken away without the consent of such hirer, before the expiration of the time for which such deposit was made, or if such driver on the final discharge of such hackney carriage refuse duly to account for such deposit, every such driver so offending shall be liable to a penalty not exceeding [level 1 on the standard scale].

Amendment

First sum in square brackets substituted by the Decimal Currency Act 1969, s 10,; the maximum penalty increased by the Criminal Law Act 1977, s 31(6), and converted to a level on the standard scale by the Criminal Justice Act 1982, ss 37, 46.

58 Penalty on proprietors, etc convicted of overcharging Every proprietor or driver of any such hackney carriage who is convicted of taking as a fare a greater sum than is authorized by any byelaw made under this or the special Act shall be liable to a penalty not exceeding [level 3 on the standard scale], and such penalty may be recovered before one justice; and in the conviction of such proprietor or driver an order may be included for payment of the sum so overcharged, over and above the penalty and costs; and such overcharge shall be returned to the party aggrieved . . .

Amendment
Maximum penalty increased and converted to a level on the standard scale by the Criminal Justice Act 1982, ss 37, 39, 46, Sch 3; words omitted repealed by the Statute Law Revision Act 1894.

59 Penalty for permitting persons to ride without consent of hirer Any proprietor or driver of any such hackney carriage which is hired who permits or suffers any person to be carried in or upon or about such hackney carriage during such hire, without the express consent of the person hiring the same, shall be liable to a penalty not exceeding [level 1 on the standard scale].

Amendment
Maximum penalty increased by the Criminal Law Act 1977, s 31(6), and converted to a level on the standard scale by the Criminal Justice Act 1982, ss 37, 46.

60 No unauthorized person to act as driver No person authorized by the proprietor of any hackney carriage to act as driver of such carriage shall suffer any other person to act as driver of such carriage without the consent of the proprietor thereof; and no person, whether licensed or not, shall act as driver of any such carriage without the consent of the proprietor; and any person so suffering another person to act as driver, and any person so acting as driver without such consent as aforesaid, shall be liable to a penalty not exceeding [level 1 on the standard scale] for every such offence.

Amendment
Maximum penalty increased by the Criminal Law Act 1977, s 31(6), and converted to a level on the standard scale by the Criminal Justice Act 1982, ss 37, 46.

61 Penalty on drivers for drunkenness, furious driving, etc If the driver or any other person having or pretending to have the care of any such hackney carriage be intoxicated while driving, or if any such driver or other person by wanton and furious driving, or by any other wilfil misconduct, injure or endanger any person in his life, limbs, or property, he shall be liable to a penalty not exceeding [level 1 on the standard scale]; . . .

Amendment
Maximum penalty increased by the Criminal Law Act 1977, s 31(6), and converted to a level on the standard scale by the Criminal Justice Act 1982, ss 37, 46; words omitted repealed by the Statute Law (Repeals) Act 1989.

62 Penalties in case of carriages being unattended at places of public resort If the driver of any such hackney carriage leave it in any street or at any place of public resort or entertainment, whether it be hired or not, without someone proper to take care of it, any constable may drive away such hackney carriage and deposit it, and the horse or horses harnessed thereto, at some neighbouring livery stable or other place of safe custody; and such driver shall be liable to a penalty not exceeding [level 1 on the standard scale] for such offence; and in default of payment of the said penalty upon conviction, and of the expences of taking and keeping the said hackney carriage and horse or horses, the same, together with the harness belonging thereto, or any of them, shall be sold by order of the justice before whom such conviction is made, and after deducting from the produce of such sale the amount of the said penalty, and of all costs and expences, as well of the proceedings before such justice as of the taking, keeping, and sale of the said hackney carriage, and of the said horse or horses and harness, the surplus (if any) of the said produce shall be paid to the proprietor of such hackney carriage.

Amendment
Maximum penalty increased by the Criminal Law Act 1977, s 31(6), and converted to a level on the standard scale by the Criminal Justice Act 1982, ss 37, 46.

63 Compensation for damage done by driver In every case in which any hurt or damage has been caused to any person or property as aforesaid by the driver of any carriage let to hire, the justice before whom such driver has been convicted may direct that the proprietor of such carriage shall pay such a sum, not exceeding five pounds, as appears to the justice a reasonable compensation for such hurt or damage; and every proprietor who pays any such compensation as aforesaid may recover the same from the driver, and such compensation shall be recoverable from such proprietor, and by him from such driver, as damages.

64 Penalty on drivers obstructing other drivers Any driver of any hackney carriage who suffers the same to stand for hire across any street or alongside of any other hackney carriage, or who refuses to give way, if he conveniently can, to any other carriage, or who obstructs or hinders the driver of any other carriage in taking up or setting down any person into or from such other carriage, or who wrongfully in a forcible manner prevents or endeavours to prevent the driver of any other hackney carriage from being hired, shall be liable to a penalty not exceeding [level 1 on the standard scale].

Amendment
Maximum penalty increased by the Criminal Law Act 1977, s 31(6), and converted to a level on the standard scale by the Criminal Justice Act 1982, ss 37, 46.

65 Compensation to drivers attending to answer complaints not substantiated If the driver of any such hackney carriage be summoned or brought before any justice to answer any complaint or information touching or concerning any offence alleged to have been committed by such driver against the provisions of this or the special Act, or any byelaw made thereunder, and such complaint or information be afterwards withdrawn or quashed or dismissed, or if such driver be acquitted of the offence charged against him, the said justice, if he think fit, may order the complainant or informant to pay to the said driver such compensation for his loss of time in attending the said justice touching or concerning such complaint or information as to the said justice seems reasonable; . . .

Amendment
Words omitted repealed by the Statute Law (Repeals) Act 1989.

66 Fare unpaid may be recovered as a penalty If any person refuse to pay on demand to any proprietor or driver of any hackney carriage the fare allowed by this or the special Act, or any byelaw made thereunder, such fare may, together with costs, be recovered before one justice as a penalty.

67 . . .

Amendment
Section repealed by the Criminal Damage Act 1971, s 11(8), Schedule, Pt I, and SI 1977/426, art 13(6), Sch 2.

68 Byelaws for regulating hackney carriages The commissioners may from time to time (subject to the restrictions of this and the special Act) make byelaws for all or any of the purposes following; (that is to say,)

For regulating the conduct of the proprietors and drivers of hackney carriages plying within the prescribed distance in their several employments, and determining whether such drivers shall wear any and what badges, and for regulating the hours within which they may exercise their calling:

For regulating the manner in which the number of each carriage, corresponding with the number of its licence, shall be displayed:

For regulating *the number of persons to be carried by such hackney carriages, and in what manner such number is to be shown on such carriage, and* what number of horses or other animals is to draw the same, and the placing of check strings to the carriages, and the holding of the same by the driver, and how such hackney carriages are to be furnished or provided:

For fixing the stands of such hackney carriages, and the distance to which they may be compelled to take passengers, not exceeding the prescribed distance:

For fixing the rates or fares, as well for time as distance, to be paid for such hackney carriages within the prescribed distance, and for securing the due publication of such fares:

For securing the safe custody and re-delivery of any property accidentally left in hackney carriages, and fixing the charges to be made in respect thereof.

Amendment
Words from "the number" to "such carriage, and" repealed, in relation to tramcars or trolley vehicles, by the Transport Charges &c (Miscellaneous Provisions) Act 1954, ss 14(1), 15(2), Sch 2, Part IV.

Public Health Act 1875

Part IV
Local Government Provisions

Police Regulations

171 Incorporation of certain provisions of 10 & 11 Vict c 89 The provisions of the Town Police Clauses Act 1847, with respect to the following matters, (namely,)

(1) With respect to obstructions and nuisances in the streets; and
(2) With respect to fires; and
(3) With respect to places of public resort; and
(4) With respect to hackney carriages; . . .

shall, for the purpose of regulating such matters in urban districts, be incorporated with this Act,

The expression in the provisions so incorporated "the superintendent constable," and the expression "any constable or other officer appointed by virtue of this or the special Act", shall, for the purposes of this Act, respectively include any superintendent of police, and any constable or officer of police acting for or in the district of any urban authority; and the expression "within the prescribed distance" shall for the purposes of this Act mean within any urban district.

Notwithstanding anything in the provisions so incorporated, a license granted to the driver of any hackney carriage in pursuance thereof shall be in force for one year only from the date of the license, or until the next general licensing meeting where a day for such meeting is appointed.

Amendment
Words omitted repealed by the Public Health Act 1936, s 346, Sch 3, Part I.

Town Police Clauses Act 1889

3 Defining "omnibus" The term "omnibus," where used in this Act, shall include—

> Every omnibus, char-à-banc, wagonette, brake, stage coach, and other carriage plying or standing for hire by or used to carry passengers at separate fares, to, from, or in any part of the prescribed distance;

but shall not include—

> Any tramcar or tram carriage . . .:

> Any carriage starting from and previously hired for the particular passengers thereby carried at any livery stable yard (within the prescribed distance) whereat horses are stabled and carriages let for hire, the said carriage starting from the said stable yard and being bonâ fide the property of the occupier thereof, and not standing or plying for hire within the prescribed distance:

> Any omnibus belonging to or hired or used by any railway company for conveying passengers and their luggage to or from any railway station of that company, and not standing or plying for hire within the prescribed distance:

> Any omnibus starting from outside the prescribed distance, and bringing passengers within the prescribed distance, and not standing or plying for hire within the prescribed distance.

Amendment
Words omitted repealed by the Transport and Works Act 1992, s 68(1), Sch 4, Pt I.

4 Extending certain provisions of principal Act to omnibuses (1) The several terms "hackney carriages", "hackney coach", "carriages", and "carriage", whenever used in sections thirty-seven, forty to fifty-two (both inclusive), fifty-four, fifty-eight, and sixty to sixty-seven (both inclusive) of the principal Act shall, notwithstanding anything contained in section thirty-eight of that Act, be deemed to include every omnibus.

(2) The word "driver" or "drivers" when used in any of the said sections of the principal Act shall be deemed to include every conductor of any omnibus.

(3) For the purposes of sections fifty-four, fifty-eight, and sixty-six of the principal Act, the fare, according to the statement of fares exhibited on any omnibus, shall be deemed to be the fare allowed by the principal Act or authorised by any byelaw under that Act.

5 Licences may be granted for short periods Any licence may be granted under the principal Act to continue in force for such less period than one year as the Commissioners may think fit, and shall specify in the licence.

6 Byelaws The Commissioners may from time to time make byelaws for all or any of the following purposes, that is to say:—

> For regulating the conduct of the proprietors, drivers, and conductors of omnibuses plying within the prescribed distance in their several employments, and determining whether such drivers and conductors shall wear any and what badges:

> For regulating the manner in which the number of each omnibus corresponding with the number of its licence shall be displayed:

> . . .

> For regulating the number and securing the fitness of the animals to be allowed to draw an omnibus, and for the removal therefrom of unfit animals:

> For securing the fitness of the omnibus and the harness of the animals drawing the same:

> For fixing the stands for omnibuses and the points at which they may stop a longer time than is necessary for the taking up and setting down of passengers desirous of entering or leaving the same:

> For securing the safe custody and re-delivery of any property accidentally left in any omnibus, and fixing the charge to be made in respect thereof;

> To provide for the carrying and the lighting of proper lamps for denoting the direction in which the omnibus is proceeding, and promoting the safety and convenience of the passengers carried thereby:

> To provide for the exhibition on some conspicuous part of every omnibus of a statement in legible letters and figures of the fares to be demanded and received from the persons using or carried for hire in such omnibus:

> To prevent within the prescribed distance—

>> (a) the owner, driver, or conductor of any omnibus, or any other person on their or his behalf, by touting, calling out, or otherwise, from importuning any person to use or to be carried for hire in such omnibus, to the annoyance of such person or of any other person;

>> (b) the blowing of or playing upon horns or other musical instruments, or the ringing of bells, by the driver or conductor of any omnibus, or by any person travelling on or using any such omnibus.

Provided that nothing in this Act contained shall empower the Commissioners to fix the site of the stand of any omnibus in any railway station, or in any yard adjoining or connecting therewith, except with the consent of the railway company owning such site.

Amendment
Words omitted repealed by the Transport Charges, etc (Miscellaneous Provisions) Act 1954, s 14(1), Sch 2, Part IV.

Public Health Act 1936

Part XII
General

Appeals and other applications to courts of summary jurisdiction, and appeals to the
[Crown Court]

300 Appeals and applications to courts of summary jurisdiction (1) Where any enactment in this Act provides—

(a) for an appeal to a court of summary jurisdiction against a requirement, refusal or other decision of a council; or

(b) for any matter to be determined by, or an application in respect of any matter to be made to, a court of summary jurisdiction,

the procedure shall be by way of complaint for an order, and the Summary Jurisdiction Acts shall apply to the proceedings.

(2) The time within which any such appeal may be brought shall be twenty-one days from the date on which notice of the council's requirement, refusal or other decision was served upon the person desiring to appeal, and for the purposes of this subsection the making of the complaint shall be deemed to be the bringing of the appeal.

(3) In any case where such an appeal lies, the document notifying to the person concerned the decision of the council in the matter shall state the right of appeal to a court of summary jurisdiction and the time within which such an appeal may be brought.

NOTES

Amendment
Cross-heading: words in square brackets substituted by virtue of the Courts Act 1971, s 56(2), Sch 9, Pt I.

301 Appeals to [Crown Court] against decisions of justices Subject as hereinafter provided, where a person aggrieved by any order, determination or other decision of a court of summary jurisdiction under this Act is not by any other enactment authorised to appeal to [the Crown Court], he may appeal to such a court:

Provided that nothing in this section shall be construed as conferring a right of appeal from the decision of a court of summary jurisdiction in any case if each of the parties concerned might under this Act have required that the dispute should be determined by arbitration instead of by such a court.

Amendment
Words in square brackets substituted by the Courts Act 1971, s 56(2), Sch 9, Pt I.

302 Effect of decision of court upon an appeal Where upon an appeal under this Act a court varies or reverses any decision of a council, it shall be the duty of the council to give effect to the order of the court and, in particular, to grant or issue any necessary consent, certificate or other document, and to make any necessary entry in any register.

Local Government Act 1972

SCHEDULE 14
Amendment and Modification of Public Health Acts, Etc

Section 180

Part I
The Public Health Act 1936

1 . . .

2 Any reference to an urban authority or rural authority shall be construed as a reference to a local authority.

3 . . .

4 Without prejudice to paragraph 2 above, the following provisions, that is to say, sections . . . *79, 80,* . . . 263 and 264 shall apply throughout the district of every local authority.

5–17 . . .

18 The powers conferred by Part VIII on local authorities within the meaning of the Public Health Act 1936 shall be exercisable not only by such authorities but also by all local authorities within the meaning of this Act, whether or not they are local authorities within the meaning of that Act, and references in that Part to a local authority shall be construed accordingly.

19 . . .

20 Any reference in section 278 to a local authority shall include a reference to a county council . . .

21, 22 . . .

Amendment

Paras 1, 9, 22: amend the Public Health Act 1936.

Para 3: repealed by the Statute Law (Repeals) Act 2004, s 1(1), Sch 1, Pt 13.

Para 4: first words omitted repealed by the Building Act 1984, s 133(2), Sch 7; words in italics prospectively repealed by the Control of Pollution Act 1974, s 108, Sch 4, as from a day to be appointed; second words omitted repealed by the Environmental Protection Act 1990, s 162, Sch 16, Part III.

Paras 5-8: repealed by the Control of Pollution Act 1974, s 108, Sch 4.

Para 10: repealed by the Building Act 1984, s 133(2), Sch 7.

Paras 11, 12: repealed by the Environmental Protection Act 1990, s 162, Sch 16, Part III.

Paras 13-16: repealed by the Public Health (Control of Disease) Act 1984, s 78, Sch 3.

Para 17: repealed by the National Health Service Reorganisation Act 1973, s 57, Sch 5.

Para 19: repealed by the Statute Law (Repeals) Act 2004, s 1(1), Sch 1, Pt 13.

Para 20: words omitted repealed by the Local Government Act 1985, s 102, Sch 17.

Para 21: repealed by the Statute Law (Repeals) Act 2004, s 1(1), Sch 1, Pt 13.

Part II
Other Enactments

Public Health Acts 1875 to 1925

23 Subject to the following provisions of this Schedule and the provisions of Schedule 26 to this Act, all the provisions of the Public Health Acts 1875 to 1925 shall extend throughout England and Wales, whether or not they so extended immediately before 1st April 1974.

24 Paragraph 23 above shall not apply to the following enactments, that is to say—
(a) so much of section 160 of the Public Health Act 1875 as incorporates the provisions of the Towns Improvement Clauses Act 1847 with respect to the naming of streets (hereafter in this Schedule referred to as "the original street-naming enactment");
(b) section 171(4) of the said Act of 1875;
(c) . . .
(d) sections 21, 82, 83. . . of the Public Health Acts Amendment Act 1907; and
(e) sections 17 to 19 and 76 of the Public Health Act 1925;

and those enactments shall, subject to paragraph 25 below, apply to those areas, and only those, to which they applied immediately before 1st April 1974.

25 (1) Subject to [sub-paragraph (2)] below, a local authority may after giving the requisite notice resolve that any of the enactments mentioned in paragraph 24 above shall apply throughout their area or shall cease to apply throughout their area (whether or not, in either case, the enactment applies only to part of their area).

(2) A resolution under this paragraph disapplying—
(a) section 171(4) of the Public Health Act 1875;
(b) . . .
(c) section 82, 83 . . . of the Public Health Acts Amendment Act 1907; or
(d) section 76 of the Public Health Act 1925;

must be passed before 1st April 1975, but any other resolution under this paragraph may be passed at any time.

(3) A resolution under this paragraph applying either of the following provisions, that is to say, section 21 of the said Act of 1907 or section 18 of the said Act of 1925, throughout an area shall have effect as a resolution disapplying the other provision throughout that area and a resolution under this paragraph applying either of the following provisions, that is to say, the original street-naming enactment or section 19 of the said Act of 1925, throughout an area shall have effect as a resolution disapplying the other provision throughout that area.

(4) ...

(5) The notice which is requisite for a resolution given under sub-paragraph (1) above is a notice—

    (a) given by the local authority in question of their intention to pass the resolution given by advertisement in two consecutive weeks in a local newspaper circulating in their area; and

    (b) served, not later than the date on which the advertisement is first published, on the council of every parish or community whose area, or part of whose area, is affected by the resolution or, in the case of a parish so affected but not having a parish council (whether separate or common), on the chairman of the parish meeting.

(6) The date on which a resolution under this paragraph is to take effect shall—

    (a) ... be a date specified therein, being not earlier than one month after the date of the resolution; ...

    (b) ...

(7) A copy of a resolution of a local authority under this paragraph, certified in writing to be a true copy by the proper officer of the authority, shall in all legal proceedings be received as evidence of the resolution having been passed by the authority.

26 The following enactments shall not extend to Greater London, that is to say—

    (a) sections 160 and 171 of the Public Health Act 1875;

    (b) ...

    (c) sections 21 and 80 of the Public Health Acts Amendment Act 1907 and so much of section 81 of that Act as relates to the Town Police Clauses Act 1847;

    (d) sections 17 to 19, 75 and 76 of the Public Health Act 1925.

27 (1) The powers conferred on certain authorities by the enactments to which this paragraph applies shall be exercisable not only by those authorities, but also by all local authorities within the meaning of this Act, whether or not they are local authorities for the purposes of the Public Health Acts 1875 to 1925, and references in those enactments to an urban authority or a local authority shall be construed accordingly.

(2) This paragraph applies to the following enactments, that is to say—

    (a) section 164 of the Public Health Act 1875;

(b) section 44 of the Public Health Acts Amendment Act 1890;

(c) Part VI of the Public Health Acts Amendment Act 1907, as amended by Part VI of the Public Health Act 1925.

28 A district council [or, where they are not the highway authority, the council of a Welsh principal area] shall not without the consent of the highway authority—

(a) provide a clock under section 165 of the Public Health Act 1875 in a case where it overhangs a highway; or

(b) exercise any power under section 40 or 42 of the Public Health Acts Amendment Act 1890 or section 14 or 75 of the Public Health Act 1925 in relation to a highway.

29 A highway authority who are not a local authority within the meaning of the Public Health Acts 1875 to 1925 may exercise concurrently with the local authority powers conferred on the latter by section 153 of the Public Health Act 1875.

30 Any reference in section 161 of the said Act of 1875 to an urban authority shall, in relation to a metropolitan road within the meaning of the London Government Act 1963, be construed as a reference to the Greater London Council alone.

31 A local authority within the meaning of the Public Health Acts 1875 to 1925 may exercise the powers conferred by section 31 of the Public Health Acts Amendment Act 1907 without being empowered by an order made by the Secretary of State.

32 So much of section 76 of the said Act of 1907 as enables the Secretary of State to make rules governing the exercise by local authorities of their powers under that section shall cease to have effect.

33, 34 . . .

35, 36 . . .

37 The powers conferred on a local authority by section 34 of that Act shall as respects England be exercisable also by a county council and references in that section to a local authority shall be construed accordingly.

38, 39 . . .

40 The powers conferred on a local authority by sections 44 and 46 of that Act shall, in the case of a street outside Greater London which is a highway, be exercisable by the highway authority as well as by the local authority.

41 . . .

42 The powers conferred by sections 52 to 54 of that Act on local authorities shall be exercisable not only by such authorities, but also by all local authorities within the meaning of this Act, whether or not they are local authorities within the meaning of that Act, and references in those sections to a local authority shall be construed accordingly.

43–49 . . .

Amendment

Para 24: sub-para (c) repealed by the Local Government (Miscellaneous Provisions) Act 1982, s 47, Sch 7, Pt I.

Para 24: in sub-para (d) words omitted repealed by the Statute Law (Repeals) Act 2004, s 1(1), Sch 1, Pt 13.

Para 25: in para (1) words "sub-paragraph (2)" in square brackets substituted by the Legislative Reform (Local Authority Consent Requirements) (England and Wales) Order 2008, SI 2008/2840, art 3(1)(a).

Para 25: sub-para (2)(b) repealed by the Local Government (Miscellaneous Provisions) Act 1982, s 47, Sch 7, Pt I.

Para 25: in sub-para (2)(c) words omitted repealed by the Statute Law (Repeals) Act 2004, s 1(1), Sch 1, Pt 13.

Para 25: para (4) repealed by the Legislative Reform (Local Authority Consent Requirements) (England and Wales) Order 2008, SI 2008/2840, art 3(1)(b).

Para 25: in sub-para (6)(a) words omitted repealed by the Legislative Reform (Local Authority Consent Requirements) (England and Wales) Order 2008, SI 2008/2840, art 3(1)(c)(i).

Para 25: sub-para (6)(b) repealed by the Legislative Reform (Local Authority Consent Requirements) (England and Wales) Order 2008, SI 2008/2840, art 3(1)(c)(ii).

Para 26: sub-para (b) repealed by the Local Government (Miscellaneous Provisions) Act 1982, s 47, Sch 7, Pt I.

Para 28: words in square brackets inserted by the Local Government (Wales) Act 1994, s 66(5), Sch 15, para 63.

Para 33: repealed by the Statute Law (Repeals) Act 2004, s 1(1), Sch 1, Pt 13.

Para 34: amends the Parish Councils Act 1957, s 3(1).

Paras 35, 36: repealed by the Statute Law (Repeals) Act 2004, s 1(1), Sch 1, Pt 13.

Paras 38, 39: repealed by the Public Health (Control of Disease) Act 1984, s 78, Sch 3.

Para 41: repealed by the Litter Act 1983, s 12(3), Sch 2.

Para 43: repealed by the Local Government Act 1985, s 102, Sch 17.

Para 44: repealed by the Statute Law (Repeals) Act 2004, s 1(1), Sch 1, Pt 13.

Para 45: repealed by the Refuse Disposal (Amenity) Act 1978, s 12(2), Sch 2.

Paras 46, 47: repealed by the Public Health (Control of Disease) Act 1984, s 78, Sch 3.

Para 48: repealed by the National Health Service Reorganisation Act 1973, s 57, Sch 5.

Para 49: amends the Deposit of Poisonous Waste Act 1972, s 5; prospectively repealed by the Control of Pollution Act 1974, s 108, Sch 4.

Local Government (Miscellaneous Provisions) Act 1976

Part II
Hackney Carriages and Private Hire Vehicles

45 Application of Part II (1) The provisions of this Part of this Act, except this section, shall come into force in accordance with the following provisions of this section.

(2) If the Act of 1847 is in force in the area of a district council, the council may resolve that the provisions of this Part of this Act, other than this section, are to apply to the relevant area; and if the council do so resolve those provisions shall come into force in the relevant area on the day specified in that behalf in the resolution (which must not be before the expiration of the period of one month beginning with the day on which the resolution is passed).

In this subsection "the relevant area", in relation to a council, means—
   (a) if the Act of 1847 is in force throughout the area of the council, that area; and
   (b) if the Act of 1847 is in force for part only of the area of the council, that part of that area.

(3) A council shall not pass a resolution in pursuance of the foregoing subsection unless they have—
   (a) published in two consecutive weeks, in a local newspaper circulating in their area, notice of their intention to pass the resolution; and
   (b) served a copy of the notice, not later than the date on which it is first published in pursuance of the foregoing paragraph, on the council of each parish or community which would be affected by the resolution or, in the case of such a parish which has no parish council, on the chairman of the parish meeting.

(4) If after a council has passed a resolution in pursuance of subsection (2) of this section the Act of 1847 comes into force for any part of the area of the council for which it was not in force when the council passed the resolution, the council may pass a resolution in accordance with the foregoing provisions of this section in respect of that part as if that part were included in the relevant area for the purposes of subsection (2) of this section.

46 Vehicle, drivers' and operators' licences (1) Except as authorised by this Part of this Act—
   (a) no person being the proprietor of any vehicle, not being a hackney carriage [or London Cab] in respect of which a vehicle licence is in force, shall use or permit the same to be used in a controlled district as a pri-

vate hire vehicle without having for such a vehicle a current licence under section 48 of this Act;

(b) no person shall in a controlled district act as driver of any private hire vehicle without having a current licence under section 51 of this Act;

(c) no person being the proprietor of a private hire vehicle licensed under this Part of this Act shall employ as the driver thereof for the purpose of any hiring any person who does not have a current licence under the said section 51;

(d) no person shall in a controlled district operate any vehicle as a private hire vehicle without having a current licence under section 55 of this Act;

(e) no person licensed under the said section 55 shall in a controlled district operate any vehicle as a private hire vehicle—

   (i) if for the vehicle a current licence under the said section 48 is not in force; or

   (ii) if the driver does not have a current licence under the said section 51.

(2) If any person knowingly contravenes the provisions of this section, he shall be guilty of an offence.

Amendment
Sub-s (1): words in square brackets inserted by the Transport Act 1985, s 139(2), Sch 7, para 17.

47 Licensing of hackney carriages (1) A district council may attach to the grant of a licence of a hackney carriage under the Act of 1847 such conditions as the district council may consider reasonably necessary.

(2) Without prejudice to the generality of the foregoing subsection, a district council may require any hackney carriage licensed by them under the Act of 1847 to be of such design or appearance or bear such distinguishing marks as shall clearly identify it as a hackney carriage.

(3) Any person aggrieved by any conditions attached to such a licence may appeal to a magistrates' court.

48 Licensing of private hire vehicles (1) Subject to the provisions of this Part of this Act, a district council may on the receipt of an application from the proprietor of any vehicle for the grant in respect of such vehicle of a licence to use the vehicle as a private hire vehicle, grant in respect thereof a vehicle licence:

Provided that a district council shall not grant such a licence unless they are satisfied—

(a) that the vehicle is—

   (i) suitable in type, size and design for use as a private hire vehicle;

   (ii) not of such design and appearance as to lead any person to believe that the vehicle is a hackney carriage;

      (iii) in a suitable mechanical condition;

      (iv) safe; and

      (v) comfortable;

  (b) that there is in force in relation to the use of the vehicle a policy of insurance or such security as complies with the requirements of [Part VI of the Road Traffic Act 1988],

and shall not refuse such a licence for the purpose of limiting the number of vehicles in respect of which such licences are granted by the council.

(2) A district council may attach to the grant of a licence under this section such conditions as they may consider reasonably necessary including, without prejudice to the generality of the foregoing provisions of this subsection, conditions requiring or prohibiting the display of signs on or from the vehicle to which the licence relates.

(3) In every vehicle licence granted under this section there shall be specified—

  (a) the name and address of—

      (i) the applicant; and

      (ii) every other person who is a proprietor of the private hire vehicle in respect of which the licence is granted, or who is concerned, either solely or in partnership with any other person, in the keeping, employing or letting on hire of the private hire vehicle;

  (b) the number of the licence which shall correspond with the number to be painted or marked on the plate or disc to be exhibited on the private hire vehicle in accordance with subsection (6) of this section;

  (c) the conditions attached to the grant of the licence; and

  (d) such other particulars as the district council consider reasonably necessary.

(4) Every licence granted under this section shall—

  (a) be signed by an authorised officer of the council which granted it;

  (b) relate to not more than one private hire vehicle; and

  (c) remain in force for such period not being longer than one year as the district council may specify in the licence.

(5) Where a district council grant under this section a vehicle licence in respect of a private hire vehicle they shall issue a plate or disc identifying that vehicle as a private hire vehicle in respect of which a vehicle licence has been granted.

(6)

  (a) Subject to the provisions of this Part of this Act, no person shall use or permit to be used in a controlled district as a private hire vehicle a vehicle in respect of which a licence has been granted under this section unless the plate or disc issued in accordance with subsection (5) of this section is exhibited on the vehicle in such manner as the district council shall prescribe by condition attached to the grant of the licence.

  (b) If any person without reasonable excuse contravenes the provisions of this subsection he shall be guilty of an offence.

(7) Any person aggrieved by the refusal of a district council to grant a vehicle licence under this section or by any conditions specified in such a licence, may appeal to a magistrates' court.

Amendment
Sub-s (1)(b): words in square brackets substituted by the Road Traffic (Consequential Provisions) Act 1988, s 4, Sch 3, para 16.

49 Transfer of hackney carriages and private hire vehicles (1) If the proprietor of a hackney carriage or a private hire vehicle in respect of which a vehicle licence has been granted by a district council transfers his interest in the hackney carriage or private hire vehicle to a person other than the proprietor whose name is specified in the licence, he shall within fourteen days after such transfer give notice in writing thereof to the district council specifying the name and address of the person to whom the hackney carriage or private hire vehicle has been transferred.

(2) If a proprietor without reasonable excuse fails to give notice to a district council as provided by subsection (1) of this section he shall be guilty of an offence.

50 Provisions as to proprietors (1) Without prejudice to the provisions of section 68 of this Act, the proprietor of any hackney carriage or of any private hire vehicle licensed by a district council shall present such hackney carriage or private hire vehicle for inspection and testing by or on behalf of the council within such period and at such place within the area of the council as they may by notice reasonably require:

Provided that a district council shall not under the provisions of this subsection require a proprietor to present the same hackney carriage or private hire vehicle for inspection and testing on more than three separate occasions during any one period of twelve months.

(2) The proprietor of any hackney carriage or private hire vehicle—
   (a) licensed by a district council under the Act of 1847 or under this Part of this Act; or
   (b) in respect of which an application for a licence has been made to a district council under the Act of 1847 or under this Part of this Act;

shall, within such period as the district council may by notice reasonably require, state in writing the address of every place where such hackney carriage or private hire vehicle is kept when not in use, and shall if the district council so require afford to them such facilities as may be reasonably necessary to enable them to cause such hackney carriage or private hire vehicle to be inspected and tested there.

(3) Without prejudice to the provisions of [section 170 of the Road Traffic Act 1988], the proprietor of a hackney carriage or of a private hire vehicle licensed by a district council shall report to them as soon as reasonably practicable, and

in any case within seventy-two hours of the occurrence thereof, any accident to such hackney carriage or private hire vehicle causing damage materially affecting the safety, performance or appearance of the hackney carriage or private hire vehicle or the comfort or convenience of persons carried therein.

(4) The proprietor of any hackney carriage or of any private hire vehicle licensed by a district council shall at the request of any authorised officer of the council produce for inspection the vehicle licence for such hackney carriage or private hire vehicle and the certificate of the policy of insurance or security required by [Part VI of the Road Traffic Act 1988] in respect of such hackney carriage or private hire vehicle.

(5) If any person without reasonable excuse contravenes the provisions of this section, he shall be guilty of an offence.

Amendment
Sub-ss (3), (4): words in square brackets substituted by the Road Traffic (Consequential Provisions) Act 1988, s 4, Sch 3, para 16.

51 Licensing of drivers of private hire vehicles (1) Subject to the provisions of this Part of this Act, a district council shall, on the receipt of an application from any person for the grant to that person of a licence to drive private hire vehicles, grant to that person a driver's licence:

Provided that a district council shall not grant a licence—
    (a) unless they are satisfied[—
        (i)] that the applicant is a fit and proper person to hold a driver's licence;
        [and
        (ii) that the applicant is not disqualified by reason of the applicant's immigration status from driving a private hire vehicle; or]
    [(b) to any person who has not for at least twelve months been authorised to drive a motor car, or is not at the date of the application for a driver's licence so authorised].

[(1ZA) In determining for the purposes of subsection (1) whether an applicant is disqualified by reason of the applicant's immigration status from driving a private hire vehicle, a district council must have regard to any guidance issued by the Secretary of State.]

[(1A) . . .]

[(1B) For the purposes of subsection (1) of this section a person is authorised to drive a motor car if—
    (a) he holds a licence granted under Part III of the Road Traffic Act 1988 (not being a provisional licence) authorising him to drive a motor car, or
    (b) he is authorised by virtue of section 99A(1) [or section 109(1)] of that Act to drive in Great Britain a motor car.]

(2) A district council may attach to the grant of a licence under this section such conditions as they may consider reasonably necessary.

(3) It shall be the duty of a council by which licences are granted in pursuance of this section to enter, in a register maintained by the council for the purpose, the following particulars of each such licence, namely—

    (a) the name of the person to whom it is granted;

    (b) the date on which and the period for which it is granted; and

    (c) if the licence has a serial number, that number,

and to keep the register available at its principal offices for inspection by members of the public during office hours free of charge.

Amendment

Sub-s (1): in para (a) "— (i)" in square brackets inserted by the Immigration Act 2016, s 37, Sch 5, paras 17, 18(1), (2)(a).

Sub-s (1): in para (a) word "and" and sub-para (a)(ii) in square brackets substituted by the Immigration Act 2016, s 37, Sch 5, paras 17, 18(1), (2)(b).

Sub-s (1): para (b) substituted by the Driving Licences (Community Driving Licence) Regulations 1996, SI 1996/1974, reg 5, Sch 4, para 2(2).

Sub-s (1ZA): inserted by the Immigration Act 2016, s 37, Sch 5, paras 17, 18(1), (3).

Sub-s (1A): inserted by the Road Traffic Act 1991, s 47(1).

Sub-s (1A): repealed by the Police Act 1997, s 134, Sch 9, para 34, Sch 10.

Sub-s (1B): inserted by the Driving Licences (Community Driving Licence) Regulations 1996, SI 1996/1974, reg 5, Sch 4, para 2(3).

Sub-s (1B): in para (b) words in square brackets inserted by the Deregulation (Taxis and Private Hire Vehicles) Order 1998, SI 1998/1946, art 2.

52 Appeals in respect of drivers' licences Any person aggrieved by—

    (1) the refusal of the district council to grant a driver's licence under section 51 of this Act; or

    (2) any conditions attached to the grant of a driver's licence;

may appeal to a magistrates' court.

53 Drivers' licences for hackney carriages and private hire vehicles

(1)

    (a) [Subject to section 53A, every] licence granted by a district council under the provisions of this Part of this Act to any person to drive a private hire vehicle shall remain in force for three years from the date of such licence or [for such lesser period, specified in the licence, as the district council think appropriate in the circumstances of the case].

    (b) Notwithstanding the provisions of the Public Health Act 1875 and the Town Police Clauses Act 1889, [but subject to section 53A,] every licence granted by a district council under the provisions of the Act of 1847 to any person to drive a hackney carriage shall remain in force for three years from the date of such licence or [for such lesser period, specified in the licence, as the district council think appropriate in the circumstances of the case].

(2) Notwithstanding the provisions of the Act of 1847, a district council may demand and recover for the grant to any person of a licence to drive a hackney carriage, or a private hire vehicle, as the case may be, such a fee as they consider reasonable with a view to recovering the costs of issue and administration and may remit the whole or part of the fee in respect of a private hire vehicle in any case in which they think it appropriate to do so.

(3) The driver of any hackney carriage or of any private hire vehicle licensed by a district council shall at the request of any authorised officer of the council or of any constable produce for inspection his driver's licence either forthwith or—

(a) in the case of a request by an authorised officer, at the principal offices of the council before the expiration of the period of five days beginning with the day following that on which the request is made;

(b) in the case of a request by a constable, before the expiration of the period aforesaid at any police station which is within the area of the council and is nominated by the driver when the request is made.

(4) If any person without reasonable excuse contravenes the provisions of this section, he shall be guilty of an offence.

Amendment

Sub-s (1): in para (a) words "Subject to section 53A, every" in square brackets substituted by the Immigration Act 2016, s 37, Sch 5, paras 17, 19(a).

Sub-s (1): in para (a) words "for such lesser period, specified in the licence, as the district council think appropriate in the circumstances of the case" in square brackets substituted by the Deregulation Act 2015, s 10(1), (2)(a).

Sub-s (1): in para (b) words "but subject to section 53A," in square brackets inserted by the Immigration Act 2016, s 37, Sch 5, paras 17, 19(b).

Sub-s (1): in para (b) words "for such lesser period, specified in the licence, as the district council think appropriate in the circumstances of the case" in square brackets substituted by the Deregulation Act 2015, s 10(1), (2)(b).

[53A Drivers' licences for persons subject to immigration control (1) Subsection (2) applies if—

(a) a licence within section 53(1)(a) or (b) is to be granted to a person who has been granted leave to enter or remain in the United Kingdom for a limited period ("the leave period");

(b) the person's leave has not been extended by virtue of section 3C of the Immigration Act 1971 (continuation of leave pending variation decision); and

(c) apart from subsection (2), the period for which the licence would have been in force would have ended after the end of the leave period.

(2) The district council which grants the licence must specify a period in the licence as the period for which it remains in force; and that period must end at or before the end of the leave period.

(3) Subsection (4) applies if—

(a) a licence within section 53(1)(a) or (b) is to be granted to a person who has been granted leave to enter or remain in the United Kingdom for a limited period; and

(b) the person's leave has been extended by virtue of section 3C of the Immigration Act 1971 (continuation of leave pending variation decision).

(4) The district council which grants the licence must specify a period in the licence as the period for which it remains in force; and that period must not exceed six months.

(5) A licence within section 53(1)(a) ceases to be in force if the person to whom it was granted becomes disqualified by reason of the person's immigration status from driving a private hire vehicle.

(6) A licence within section 53(1)(b) ceases to be in force if the person to whom it was granted becomes disqualified by reason of the person's immigration status from driving a hackney carriage.

(7) If a licence granted in accordance with subsection (2) or (4) expires, the person to whom it was granted must, within the period of 7 days beginning with the day after that on which it expired, return the licence and the person's driver's badge to the district council which granted the licence.

(8) If subsection (5) or (6) applies to a licence, the person to whom it was granted must, within the period of 7 days beginning with the day after the day on which the person first became disqualified, return the licence and the person's driver's badge to the district council which granted the licence.

(9) A person who, without reasonable excuse, contravenes subsection (7) or (8) is guilty of an offence and liable on summary conviction—
(a) to a fine not exceeding level 3 on the standard scale; and
(b) in the case of a continuing offence, to a fine not exceeding ten pounds for each day during which an offence continues after conviction.

(10) The Secretary of State may by regulations made by statutory instrument amend the amount for the time being specified in subsection (9)(b).

(11) Regulations under subsection (10) may make transitional, transitory or saving provision.

(12) A statutory instrument containing regulations under subsection (10) may not be made unless a draft of the instrument has been laid before, and approved by a resolution of, each House of Parliament.]

Amendment
Section inserted by the Immigration Act 2016, s 37, Sch 5, paras 17, 20.

54 Issue of drivers' badges (1) When granting a driver's licence under section 51 of this Act a district council shall issue a driver's badge in such a form as may from time to time be prescribed by them.

(2)
  (a) A driver shall at all times when acting in accordance with the driver's licence granted to him wear such badge in such position and manner as to be plainly and distinctly visible.
  (b) If any person without reasonable excuse contravenes the provisions of this subsection, he shall be guilty of an offence.

55 Licensing of operators of private hire vehicles (1) Subject to the provisions of this Part of this Act, a district council shall, on receipt of an application from any person for the grant to that person of a licence to operate private hire vehicles grant to that person an operator's licence:

Provided that a district council shall not grant a licence unless they are satisfied[—
  (a)] that the applicant is a fit and proper person to hold an operator's licence[; and
  (b) if the applicant is an individual, that the applicant is not disqualified by reason of the applicant's immigration status from operating a private hire vehicle.]

[(1A) In determining for the purposes of subsection (1) whether an applicant is disqualified by reason of the applicant's immigration status from operating a private hire vehicle, a district council must have regard to any guidance issued by the Secretary of State.]

[(2) [Subject to section 55ZA, every] licence granted under this section shall remain in force for five years or for such lesser period, specified in the licence, as the district council think appropriate in the circumstances of the case.]

(3) A district council may attach to the grant of a licence under this section such conditions as they may consider reasonably necessary.

(4) Any applicant aggrieved by the refusal of a district council to grant an operator's licence under this section, or by any conditions attached to the grant of such a licence, may appeal to a magistrates' court.

Amendment
Sub-s (1): "— (a)" in square brackets inserted by the Immigration Act 2016, s 37, Sch 5, paras 17, 21(1), (2)(a).
Sub-s (1): word "and" and para (b) in square brackets inserted by the Immigration Act 2016, s 37, Sch 5, paras 17, 21(1), (2)(b).
Sub-s (1A): inserted by the Immigration Act 2016, s 37, Sch 5, paras 17, 21(1), (3).
Sub-s (2): substituted by the Deregulation Act 2015, s 10(1), (3).
Sub-s (2): words "Subject to section 55ZA, every" in square brackets substituted by the Immigration Act 2016, s 37, Sch 5, paras 17, 21(1), (4).

[55ZA Operators' licences for persons subject to immigration control (1) Subsection (2) applies if—
  (a) a licence under section 55 is to be granted to a person who has been granted leave to enter or remain in the United Kingdom for a limited period ("the leave period");

(b) the person's leave has not been extended by virtue of section 3C of the Immigration Act 1971 (continuation of leave pending variation decision); and

(c) apart from subsection (2), the period for which the licence would have been in force would have ended after the end of the leave period.

(2) The district council which grants the licence must specify a period in the licence as the period for which it remains in force; and that period must end at or before the end of the leave period.

(3) Subsection (4) applies if—
   (a) a licence under section 55 is to be granted to a person who has been granted leave to enter or remain in the United Kingdom for a limited period; and
   (b) the person's leave has been extended by virtue of section 3C of the Immigration Act 1971 (continuation of leave pending variation decision).

(4) The district council which grants the licence must specify a period in the licence as the period for which it remains in force; and that period must not exceed six months.

(5) A licence under section 55 ceases to be in force if the person to whom it was granted becomes disqualified by reason of the person's immigration status from operating a private hire vehicle.

(6) If a licence granted in accordance with subsection (2) or (4) expires, the person to whom it was granted must, within the period of 7 days beginning with the day after that on which it expired, return the licence to the district council which granted the licence.

(7) If subsection (5) applies to a licence, the person to whom it was granted must, within the period of 7 days beginning with the day after the day on which the person first became disqualified, return it to the district council which granted the licence.

(8) A person who, without reasonable excuse, contravenes subsection (6) or (7) is guilty of an offence and liable on summary conviction—
   (a) to a fine not exceeding level 3 on the standard scale; and
   (b) in the case of a continuing offence, to a fine not exceeding ten pounds for each day during which an offence continues after conviction.

(9) The Secretary of State may by regulations made by statutory instrument amend the amount for the time being specified in subsection (8)(b).

(10) Regulations under subsection (9) may make transitional, transitory or saving provision.

(11) A statutory instrument containing regulations under subsection (9) may not be made unless a draft of the instrument has been laid before, and approved by a resolution of, each House of Parliament.]

Amendment

Section inserted by the Immigration Act 2016, s 37, Sch 5, paras 17, 22.

[55A Sub-contracting by operators (1) A person licensed under section 55 who has in a controlled district accepted a booking for a private hire vehicle may arrange for another person to provide a vehicle to carry out the booking if—

    (a) the other person is licensed under section 55 in respect of the same controlled district and the sub-contracted booking is accepted in that district;

    (b) the other person is licensed under section 55 in respect of another controlled district and the sub-contracted booking is accepted in that district;

    (c) the other person is a London PHV operator and the subcontracted booking is accepted at an operating centre in London; or

    (d) the other person accepts the sub-contracted booking in Scotland.

(2) It is immaterial for the purposes of subsection (1) whether or not subcontracting is permitted by the contract between the person licensed under section 55 who accepted the booking and the person who made the booking.

(3) Where a person licensed under section 55 in respect of a controlled district is also licensed under that section in respect of another controlled district, subsection (1) (so far as relating to paragraph (b) of that subsection) and section 55B(1) and (2) apply as if each licence were held by a separate person.

(4) Where a person licensed under section 55 in respect of a controlled district is also a London PHV operator, subsection (1) (so far as relating to paragraph (c) of that subsection) and section 55B(1) and (2) apply as if the person holding the licence under section 55 and the London PHV operator were separate persons.

(5) Where a person licensed under section 55 in respect of a controlled district also makes provision in the course of a business for the invitation or acceptance of bookings for a private hire car or taxi in Scotland, subsection (1) (so far as relating to paragraph (d) of that subsection) and section 55B(1) and (2) apply as if the person holding the licence under section 55 and the person making the provision in Scotland were separate persons. In this subsection, "private hire car" and "taxi" have the same meaning as in sections 10 to 22 of the Civic Government (Scotland) Act 1982.

(6) In this section, "London PHV operator" and "operating centre" have the same meaning as in the Private Hire Vehicles (London) Act 1998.]

Amendment

Section inserted by the Deregulation Act 2015, s 11.

[55B Sub-contracting by operators: criminal liability (1) In this section—

    "the first operator" means a person licensed under section 55 who has in a controlled district accepted a booking for a private hire vehicle and then made arrangements for another person to provide a vehicle to carry out the booking in accordance with section 55A(1);

"the second operator" means the person with whom the first operator made the arrangements (and, accordingly, the person who accepted the sub-contracted booking).

(2) The first operator is not to be treated for the purposes of section 46(1)(e) as operating a private hire vehicle by virtue of having invited or accepted the booking.

(3) The first operator is guilty of an offence if—

(a) the second operator is a person mentioned in section 55A(1)(a) or (b),

(b) the second operator contravenes section 46(1)(e) in respect of the sub-contracted booking, and

(c) the first operator knew that the second operator would contravene section 46(1)(e) in respect of the booking.]

Amendment
Section inserted by the Deregulation Act 2015, s 11.

56 Operators of private hire vehicles (1) For the purposes of this Part of this Act every contract for the hire of a private hire vehicle licensed under this Part of this Act shall be deemed to be made with the operator who accepted the booking for that vehicle whether or not he himself provided the vehicle.

(2) Every person to whom a licence in force under section 55 of this Act has been granted by a district council shall keep a record in such form as the council may, by condition attached to the grant of the licence, prescribe and shall enter therein, before the commencement of each journey, such particulars of every booking of a private hire vehicle invited or accepted by him, whether by accepting the same from the hirer or by undertaking it at the request of another operator, as the district council may by condition prescribe and shall produce such record on request to any authorised officer of the council or to any constable for inspection.

(3) Every person to whom a licence in force under section 55 of this Act has been granted by a district council shall keep such records as the council may, by condition attached to the grant of the licence, prescribe of the particulars of any private hire vehicle operated by him and shall produce the same on request to any authorised officer of the council or to any constable for inspection.

(4) A person to whom a licence in force under section 55 of this Act has been granted by a district council shall produce the licence on request to any authorised officer of the council or any constable for inspection.

(5) If any person without reasonable excuse contravenes the provisions of this section, he shall be guilty of an offence.

57 Power to require applicants to submit information (1) A district council may require any applicant for a licence under the Act of 1847 or under this Part of this Act to submit to them such information as they may reasonably consider necessary to enable them to determine whether the licence should be granted and whether conditions should be attached to any such licence.

(2) Without prejudice to the generality of the foregoing subsection—

    (a) a district may require an applicant for a driver's licence in respect of a hackney carriage or a private hire vehicle—

        (i) to produce a certificate signed by a registered medical practitioner to the effect that he is physically fit to be the driver of a hackney carriage or a private hire vehicle; and

        (ii) whether or not such a certificate has been produced, to submit to examination by a registered medical practitioner selected by the district council as to his physical fitness to be the driver of a hackney carriage or a private hire vehicle;

    (b) a district council may require an applicant for an operator's licence to submit to them such information as to—

        (i) the name and address of the applicant;

        (ii) the addresses or address whether within the area of the council or not from which he intends to carry on business in connection with private hire vehicles licensed under this Part of this Act;

        (iii) any trade or business activities he has carried on before making the application;

        (iv) any previous application he has made for an operator's licence;

        (v) the revocation or suspension of any operator's licence previously held by him;

        (vi) any convictions recorded against the applicant;

    as they may reasonably consider necessary to enable them to determine whether to grant such licence;

    (c) in addition to the information specified in paragraph (b) of this subsection, a district council may require an applicant for an operator's licence to submit to them—

        (i) if the applicant is or has been a director or secretary of a company, information as to any convictions recorded against that company at any relevant time; any trade or business activities carried on by that company; any previous application made by that company for an operator's licence; and any revocation or suspension of an operator's licence previously held by that company;

        (ii) if the applicant is a company, information as to any convictions recorded against a director or secretary of that company; any trade or business activities carried on by any such director or secretary; any previous application made by any such director or secretary for an operator's licence; and any revocation or suspension of an operator's licence previously held by such director or secretary;

        (iii) if the applicant proposes to operate the vehicle in partnership with any other person, information as to any convictions recorded against that person; any trade or business activities carried on by that person; any previous application made by that person for an operator's licence; and any revocation or suspension of an operator's licence previously held by him.

(3) If any person knowingly or recklessly makes a false statement or omits any material particular in giving information under this section, he shall be guilty of an offence.

58 Return of identification plate or disc on revocation or expiry of licence etc (1) On—

(a) the revocation or expiry of a vehicle licence in relation to a hackney carriage or private hire vehicle; or
(b) the suspension of a licence under section 68 of this Act;

a district council may by notice require the proprietor of that hackney carriage or private hire vehicle licensed by them to return to them within seven days after the service on him of that notice the plate or disc which—

(a) in the case of a hackney carriage, is required to be affixed to the carriage as mentioned in section 38 of the Act of 1847; and
(b) in the case of a private hire vehicle, was issued for the vehicle under section 48(5) of this Act.

(2) If any proprietor fails without reasonable excuse to comply with the terms of a notice under subsection (1) of this section—

(a) he shall be guilty of an offence and liable on summary conviction to a fine not exceeding [level 3 on the standard scale] and to a daily fine not exceeding ten pounds; and
(b) any authorised officer of the council or constable shall be entitled to remove and retain the said plate or disc from the said hackney carriage or private hire vehicle.

Amendment
Sub-s (2): first-mentioned maximum fine increased and converted to a level on the standard scale by virtue of the Criminal Justice Act 1982, ss 37, 38, 46.

59 Qualifications for drivers of hackney carriages (1) Notwithstanding anything in the Act of 1847, a district council shall not grant a licence to drive a hackney carriage—

(a) unless they are satisfied[—
(i)] that the applicant is a fit and proper person to hold a driver's licence; [and
(ii) that the applicant is not disqualified by reason of the applicant's immigration status from driving a hackney carriage; or]
[(b) to any person who has not for at least twelve months been authorised to drive a motor car, or is not at the date of the application for a driver's licence so authorised].

[(1ZA) In determining for the purposes of subsection (1) whether an applicant is disqualified by reason of the applicant's immigration status from driving a hackney carriage, a district council must have regard to any guidance issued by the Secretary of State.]

[(1A) . . .]

[(1A) For the purposes of subsection (1) of this section a person is authorised to drive a motor car if—
  (a) he holds a licence granted under Part III of the Road Traffic Act 1988 (not being a provisional licence) authorising him to drive a motor car, or
  (b) he is authorised by virtue of section 99A(1) [or section 109(1)] of that Act to drive in Great Britain a motor car.]

(2) Any applicant aggrieved by the refusal of a district council to grant a driver's licence on the ground that he is not a fit and proper person to hold such licence may appeal to a magistrates' court.

Amendment
Sub-s (1): in para (a) "— (i)" in square brackets inserted by the Immigration Act 2016, s 37, Sch 5, paras 17, 23(1), (2)(a).
Sub-s (1): word "and" and sub-para (ii) in square brackets substituted by the Immigration Act 2016, s 37, Sch 5, paras 17, 23(1), (2)(b).
Sub-s (1): para (b) substituted by the Driving Licences (Community Driving Licence) Regulations 1996, SI 1996/1974, reg 5, Sch 4, para 2(4).
Sub-s (1ZA): inserted by the Immigration Act 2016, s 37, Sch 5, paras 17, 23(1), (3).
First sub-s (1A): (as inserted by the Road Traffic Act 1991, s 47(1)) repealed by the Police Act 1997, s 134, Sch 9, para 34, Sch 10.
Second sub-s (1A): inserted by the Driving Licences (Community Driving Licence) Regulations 1996, SI 1996/1974, reg 5, Sch 4, para 2(5).
Second sub-s (1A): in para (b) words in square brackets inserted by the Deregulation (Taxis and Private Hire Vehicles) Order 1998, SI 1998/1946, art 3.

60 Suspension and revocation of vehicle licences (1) Notwithstanding anything in the Act of 1847 or in this Part of this Act, a district council may suspend or revoke, or (on application therefor under section 40 of the Act of 1847 or section 48 of this Act, as the case may be) refuse to renew a vehicle licence on any of the following grounds—
  (a) that the hackney carriage or private hire vehicle is unfit for use as a hackney carriage or private hire vehicle;
  (b) any offence under, or non-compliance with, the provisions of the Act of 1847 or of this Part of this Act by the operator or driver; or
  (c) any other reasonable cause.

(2) Where a district council suspend, revoke or refuse to renew any licence under this section they shall give to the proprietor of the vehicle notice of the grounds on which the licence has been suspended or revoked or on which they have refused to renew the licence within fourteen days of such suspension, revocation or refusal.

(3) Any proprietor aggrieved by a decision of a district council under this section may appeal to a magistrates' court.

61 Suspension and revocation of drivers' licences (1) Notwithstanding anything in the Act of 1847 or in this Part of this Act, a district council may suspend or revoke or (on application therefor under section 46 of the Act of 1847 or section 51 of this Act, as the case may be) refuse to renew the licence of a driver of a hackney carriage or a private hire vehicle on any of the following grounds—
    (a) that he has since the grant of the licence—
        (i) been convicted of an offence involving dishonesty, indecency or violence; or
        (ii) been convicted of an offence under or has failed to comply with the provisions of the Act of 1847 or of this Part of this Act;
    [(aa)   that he has since the grant of the licence been convicted of an immigration offence or required to pay an immigration penalty;] or
    (b) any other reasonable cause.

[(1A) Subsection (1)(aa) does not apply if—
    (a) in a case where the driver has been convicted of an immigration offence, the conviction is a spent conviction within the meaning of the Rehabilitation of Offenders Act 1974, or
    (b) in a case where the driver has been required to pay an immigration penalty—
        (i) more than three years have elapsed since the date on which the penalty was imposed, and
        (ii) the amount of the penalty has been paid in full.]

(2)
    (a) Where a district council suspend, revoke or refuse to renew any licence under this section they shall give to the driver notice of the grounds on which the licence has been suspended or revoked or on which they have refused to renew such licence within fourteen days of such suspension, revocation or refusal and the driver shall on demand return to the district council the driver's badge issued to him in accordance with section 54 of this Act.
    (b) If any person without reasonable excuse contravenes the provisions of this section he shall be guilty of an offence and liable on summary conviction to a fine not exceeding [level 1 on the standard scale].

[(2ZA) The requirement in subsection (2)(a) to return a driver's badge does not apply in a case where section 62A applies (but see subsection (2) of that section).]

[(2A) Subject to subsection (2B) of this section, a suspension or revocation of the licence of a driver under this section takes effect at the end of the period of 21 days beginning with the day on which notice is given to the driver under subsection (2)(a) of this section.

(2B) If it appears that the interests of public safety require the suspension or revocation of the licence to have immediate effect, and the notice given to the driver under subsection (2)(a) of this section includes a statement that that is so and an explanation why, the suspension or revocation takes effect when the notice is given to the driver.]

(3) Any driver aggrieved by a decision of a district council under [subsection (1) of] this section may appeal to a magistrates' court.

Amendment

Sub-s (1): para (aa) inserted by the Immigration Act 2016, s 37, Sch 5, paras 17, 24(1), (2).

Sub-s (1A): inserted by the Immigration Act 2016, s 37, Sch 5, paras 17, 24(1), (3).

Sub-s (2): maximum fine increased and converted to a level on the standard scale by virtue of the Criminal Justice Act 1982, ss 37, 38, 46.

Sub-s (2ZA): inserted by the Immigration Act 2016, s 37, Sch 5, paras 17, 24(1), (4).

Sub-ss (2A), (2B): inserted by the Road Safety Act 2006, s 52(1), (2).

Sub-s (3): words in square brackets inserted by the Road Safety Act 2006, s 52(1), (3).

62 Suspension and revocation of operators' licences (1) Notwithstanding anything in this Part of this Act a district council may suspend or revoke, or (on application therefor under section 55 of this Act) refuse to renew an operator's licence on any of the following grounds—

(a) any offence under, or non-compliance with, the provisions of this Part of this Act;

(b) any conduct on the part of the operator which appears to the district council to render him unfit to hold an operator's licence;

(c) any material change since the licence was granted in any of the circumstances of the operator on the basis of which the licence was granted;

[(ca)   that the operator has since the grant of the licence been convicted of an immigration offence or required to pay an immigration penalty;] or

(d) any other reasonable cause.

[(1A) Subsection (1)(ca) does not apply if—

(a) in a case where the operator has been convicted of an immigration offence, the conviction is a spent conviction within the meaning of the Rehabilitation of Offenders Act 1974, or

(b) in a case where the operator has been required to pay an immigration penalty—

(i) more than three years have elapsed since the date on which the penalty was imposed, and

(ii) the amount of the penalty has been paid in full.]

(2) Where a district council suspend, revoke or refuse to renew any licence under this section they shall give to the operator notice of the grounds on which the licence has been suspended or revoked or on which they have refused to renew such licence within fourteen days of such suspension, revocation or refusal.

(3) Any operator aggrieved by a decision of a district council under this section may appeal to a magistrates' court.

Amendment

Sub-s (1): para (ca) inserted by the Immigration Act 2016, s 37, Sch 5, paras 17, 25(1), (2).

Sub-s (1A): inserted by the Immigration Act 2016, s 37, Sch 5, paras 17, 25(1), (3).

[62A Return of licences suspended or revoked on immigration grounds (1) Subsection (2) applies if—

    (a) under section 61 a district council suspend, revoke or refuse to renew the licence of a driver of a hackney carriage or a private hire vehicle on the ground mentioned in subsection (1)(aa) of that section, or

    (b) under section 62 a district council suspend, revoke or refuse to renew an operator's licence on the ground mentioned in subsection (1)(ca) of that section.

(2) The person to whom the licence was granted must, within the period of 7 days beginning with the relevant day, return to the district council—

    (a) the licence, and

    (b) in the case of a licence of a driver of a hackney carriage or a private hire vehicle, the person's driver's badge.

(3) In subsection (2) "the relevant day" means—

    (a) where the licence is suspended or revoked, the day on which the suspension or revocation takes effect;

    (b) where the district council refuse to renew the licence, the day on which the licence expires as a result of the failure to renew it.

(4) A person who, without reasonable excuse, contravenes subsection (2) is guilty of an offence and liable on summary conviction—

    (a) to a fine not exceeding level 3 on the standard scale, and

    (b) in the case of a continuing offence, to a fine not exceeding ten pounds for each day during which an offence continues after conviction.

(5) The Secretary of State may by regulations made by statutory instrument amend the amount for the time being specified in subsection (4)(b).

(6) Regulations under subsection (5) may make transitional, transitory or saving provision.

(7) A statutory instrument containing regulations under subsection (5) may not be made unless a draft of the instrument has been laid before, and approved by a resolution of, each House of Parliament.]

Amendment

Section inserted by the Immigration Act 2016, s 37, Sch 5, paras 17, 26.

63 Stands for hackney carriages (1) For the purposes of their functions under the Act of 1847, a district council may from time to time appoint stands for hackney carriages for the whole or any part of a day in any highway in the district which is maintainable at the public expense and, with the consent of the owner, on any land in the district which does not form part of a highway so maintainable and may from time to time vary the number of hackney carriages permitted to be at each stand.

(2) Before appointing any stand for hackney carriages or varying the number of hackney carriages to be at each stand in exercise of the powers of this section, a

district council shall give notice to the chief officer of police for the police area in which the stand is situated and shall also give public notice of the proposal by advertisement in at least one local newspaper circulating in the district and shall take into consideration any objections or representations in respect of such proposal which may be made to them in writing within twenty-eight days of the first publication of such notice.

(3) Nothing in this section shall empower a district council to appoint any such stand—

(a) so as unreasonably to prevent access to any premises;

(b) so as to impede the use of any points authorised to be used in connection with a [local service within the meaning of the Transport Act 1985] [or PSV operator's licence granted under [the Public Passenger Vehicles Act 1981]], as points for the taking up or setting down of passengers, or in such a position as to interfere unreasonably with access to any station or depot of any passenger road transport operators, except with the consent of those operators;

(c) on any highway except with the consent of the highway authority,

and in deciding the position of stands a district council shall have regard to the position of any bus stops for the time being in use.

(4) Any hackney carriage byelaws for fixing stands for hackney carriages which were made by a district council before the date when this section comes into force in the area of the council and are in force immediately before that date shall cease to have effect, but any stands fixed by such byelaws shall be deemed to have been appointed under this section.

(5) The power to appoint stands for hackney carriages under subsection (1) of this section shall include power to revoke such appointment and to alter any stand so appointed and the expressions "appointing" and "appoint" in subsections (2) and (3) of this section shall be construed accordingly.

Amendment

Sub-s (3): first words in square brackets substituted by the Transport Act 1985, s 1, Sch 1, para 2.

Sub-s (3): second words in square brackets substituted by the Transport Act 1980, s 43, Sch 5, Part II, words in square brackets therein substituted by the Public Passenger Vehicles Act 1981, s 88, Sch 7, para 19.

64 Prohibition of other vehicles on hackney carriage stands (1) No person shall cause or permit any vehicle other than a hackney carriage to wait on any stand for hackney carriages during any period for which that stand has been appointed, or is deemed to have been appointed, by a district council under the provisions of section 63 of this Act.

(2) Notice of the prohibition in this section shall be indicated by such traffic signs as may be prescribed or authorised for the purpose by the Secretary of State in pursuance of his powers under [section 64 of the Road Traffic Regulation Act 1984].

(3) If any person without reasonable excuse contravenes the provisions of this section, he shall be guilty of an offence.

(4) In any proceedings under this section against the driver of a public service vehicle it shall be a defence to show that, by reason of obstruction to traffic or for other compelling reason, he caused his vehicle to wait on a stand or part thereof and that he caused or permitted his vehicle so to wait only for so long as was reasonably necessary for the taking up or setting down of passengers.

Amendment
Sub-s (2): words in square brackets substituted by the Road Traffic Regulation Act 1984, s 146, Sch 13, para 36.

65 Fixing of fares for hackney carriages (1) A district council may fix the rates or fares within the district as well for a time as distance, and all other charges in connection with the hire of a vehicle or with the arrangements for the hire of a vehicle, to be paid in respect of the hire of hackney carriages by means of a table (hereafter in this section referred to as a "table of fares") made or varied in accordance with the provisions of this section.

(2)

(a) When a district council make or vary a table of fares they shall publish in at least one local newspaper circulating in the district a notice setting out the table of fares or the variation thereof and specifying the period, which shall not be less than fourteen days from the date of the first publication of the notice, within which and the manner in which objections to the table of fares or variation can be made.

(b) A copy of the notice referred to in paragraph (a) of this subsection shall for the period of fourteen days from the date of the first publication thereof be deposited at the offices of the council which published the notice, and shall at all reasonable hours be open to public inspection without payment.

(3) If no objection to a table of fares or variation is duly made within the period specified in the notice referred to in subsection (2) of this section, or if all objections so made are withdrawn, the table of fares or variations shall come into operation on the date of the expiration of the period specified in the notice or the date of withdrawal of the objection or, if more than one, of the last objection, whichever date is the later.

(4) If objection is duly made as aforesaid and is not withdrawn, the district council shall set a further date, not later than two months after the first specified date, on which the table of fares shall come into force with or without modifications as decided by them after consideration of the objections.

(5) A table of fares made or varied under this section shall have effect for the purposes of the Act of 1847 as if it were included in hackney carriage byelaws made thereunder.

(6) On the coming into operation of a table of fares made by a council under this section for the district, any hackney carriage byelaws fixing the rates and fares or any table of fares previously made under this section for the district, as the case may be, shall cease to have effect.

(7) Section 236(8) (except the words "when confirmed") and section 238 of the Local Government Act 1972 (except paragraphs (c) and (d) of that section) shall extend and apply to a table of fares made or varied under this section as they apply to byelaws made by a district council.

66 Fares for long journeys (1) No person, being the driver of a hackney carriage licensed by a district council, and undertaking for any hirer a journey ending outside the district and in respect of which no fare and no rate of fare was agreed before the hiring was effected, shall require for such journey a fare greater than that indicated on the taximeter with which the hackney carriage is equipped or, if it is not equipped with a taximeter, greater than that which, if the current byelaws fixing rates or fares and in force in the district in pursuance of section 68 of the Act of 1847 or, as the case may be, the current table of fares in force within the district in pursuance of section 65 of this Act had applied to the journey, would have been authorised for the journey by the byelaws or table.

(2) If any person knowingly contravenes the provisions of this section, he shall be guilty of an offence.

67 Hackney carriages used for private hire (1) No hackney carriage shall be used in the district under contract or purported contract for private hire except at a rate of fares or charges not greater than that fixed by the byelaws or table mentioned in section 66 of this Act, and, when any such hackney carriage is so used, the fare or charge shall be calculated from the point in the district at which the hirer commences his journey.

(2) Any person who knowingly contravenes this section shall be guilty of an offence.

(3) In subsection (1) of this section "contract" means—
    (a) a contract made otherwise than while the relevant hackney carriage is plying for hire in the district or waiting at a place in the district which, when the contract is made, is a stand for hackney carriages appointed by the district council under section 63 of this Act; and
    (b) a contract made, otherwise than with or through the driver of the relevant hackney carriage, while it is so plying or waiting.

68 Fitness of hackney carriages and private hire vehicles Any authorised officer of the council in question or any constable shall have power at all reasonable times to inspect and test, for the purpose of ascertaining its fitness, any hackney carriage or private hire vehicle licensed by a district council, or any taximeter affixed to such a vehicle, and if he is not satisfied as to the fitness of the hackney carriage or private hire vehicle or as to the accuracy of its taximeter he may by notice in writing require the proprietor of the hackney carriage or private hire vehicle to make it or its taximeter available for further inspection and testing at such reasonable time and place as may be specified in the notice and suspend the vehicle licence until such time as such authorised officer or constable is so satisfied:

Provided that, if the authorised officer or constable is not so satisfied before the expiration of a period of two months, the said licence shall, by virtue of this section, be deemed to have been revoked and subsections (2) and (3) of section 60 of this Act shall apply with any necessary modifications.

69 Prolongation of journeys (1) No person being the driver of a hackney carriage or of a private hire vehicle licensed by a district council shall without reasonable cause unnecessarily prolong, in distance or in time, the journey for which the hackney carriage or private hire vehicle has been hired.

(2) If any person contravenes the provisions of this section, he shall be guilty of an offence.

70 Fees for vehicle and operators' licences (1) Subject to the provisions of subsection (2) of this section, a district council may charge such fees for the grant of vehicle and operators' licences as may be resolved by them from time to time and as may be sufficient in the aggregate to cover in whole or in part—
  (a) the reasonable cost of the carrying out by or on behalf of the district council of inspections of hackney carriages and private hire vehicles for the purpose of determining whether any such licence should be granted or renewed;
  (b) the reasonable cost of providing hackney carriage stands; and
  (c) any reasonable administrative or other costs in connection with the foregoing and with the control and supervision of hackney carriages and private hire vehicles.

(2) The fees chargeable under this section shall not exceed—
  (a) for the grant of a vehicle licence in respect of a hackney carriage, twenty-five pounds;
  (b) for the grant of a vehicle licence in respect of a private hire vehicle, twenty-five pounds; and
  (c) for the grant of an operator's licence, twenty-five pounds per annum;

or, in any such case, such other sums as a district council may, subject to the following provisions of this section, from time to time determine.

(3)
  (a) If a district council determine that the maximum fees specified in subsection (2) of this section should be varied they shall publish in at least one local newspaper circulating in the district a notice setting out the variation proposed, drawing attention to the provisions of paragraph (b) of this subsection and specifying the period, which shall not be less than twenty-eight days from the date of the first publication of the notice,

within which and the manner in which objections to the variation can be made.

(b) A copy of the notice referred to in paragraph (a) of this subsection shall for the period of twenty-eight days from the date of the first publication thereof be deposited at the offices of the council which published the notice and shall at all reasonable hours be open to public inspection without payment.

(4) If no objection to a variation is duly made within the period specified in the notice referred to in subsection (3) of this section, or if all objections so made are withdrawn, the variation shall come into operation on the date of the expiration of the period specified in the notice or the date of withdrawal of the objection or, if more than one, of the last objection, whichever date is the later.

(5) If objection is duly made as aforesaid and is not withdrawn, the district council shall set a further date, not later than two months after the first specified date, on which the variation shall come into force with or without modification as decided by the district council after consideration of the objections.

(6) A district council may remit the whole or part of any fee chargeable in pursuance of this section for the grant of a licence under section 48 or 55 of this Act in any case in which they think it appropriate to do so.

71 Taximeters (1) Nothing in this Act shall require any private hire vehicle to be equipped with any form of taximeter but no private hire vehicle so equipped shall be used for hire in a controlled district unless such taximeter has been tested and approved by or on behalf of the district council for the district or any other district council by which a vehicle licence in force for the vehicle was issued.

(2) Any person who—
  (a) tampers with any seal on any taximeter without lawful excuse; or
  (b) alters any taximeter with intent to mislead; or
  (c) knowingly causes or permits a vehicle of which he is the proprietor to be used in contravention of subsection (1) of this section.

shall be guilty of an offence.

72 Offences due to fault of other person (1) Where an offence by any person under this Part of this Act is due to the act or default of another person, then, whether proceedings are taken against the first-mentioned person or not, that other person may be charged with and convicted of that offence, and shall be liable on conviction to the same punishment as might have been imposed on the first-mentioned person if he had been convicted of the offence.

(2) Section 44(3) of this Act shall apply to an offence under this Part of this Act as it applies to an offence under Part I of this Act.

73 Obstruction of authorised officers (1) Any person who—
  (a) wilfully obstructs an authorised officer or constable acting in pursuance of this Part of this Act or the Act of 1847; or

(b) without reasonable excuse fails to comply with any requirement properly made to him by such officer or constable under this Part of this Act; or

(c) without reasonable cause fails to give such an officer or constable so acting any other assistance or information which he may reasonably require of such person for the purpose of the performance of his functions under this Part of this Act or the Act of 1847;

shall be guilty of an offence.

(2) If any person, in giving any such information as is mentioned in the preceding subsection, makes any statement which he knows to be false, he shall be guilty of an offence.

74 Saving for certain businesses Where any provision of this Part of this Act coming into operation on [the relevant day] requires the licensing of a person carrying on any business, or of any vehicle used by a person in connection with any business, it shall be lawful for any person who—

(a) immediately before that day was carrying on that business; and

(b) had before that day duly applied for the licence required by that provision;

to continue to carry on that business until he is informed of the decision with regard to his application and, if the decision is adverse, during such further time as is provided under section 77 of this Act.

[In this section "the relevant day" means—

(a) in relation to a district the whole or part of which ceased to be within the metropolitan police district by virtue of the coming into force of section 323 of the Greater London Authority Act 1999 (alteration of the metropolitan police district), 1st April 2000;

(b) in any other case, a day fixed by resolution under section 45 of this Act.]

Amendment

Words "the relevant day" in square brackets substituted by the Greater London Authority Act 1999 (Hackney Carriages and Private Hire Vehicles) (Transitional and Consequential Provisions) Order 2000, SI 2000/412, art 7(1), (2)(a).

Words from "In this section" to "section 45 of this Act" in square brackets inserted by the Greater London Authority Act 1999 (Hackney Carriages and Private Hire Vehicles) (Transitional and Consequential Provisions) Order 2000, SI 2000/412, art 7(1), (2)(b).

75 Saving for certain vehicles etc (1) Nothing in this Part of this Act shall—

(a) apply to a vehicle used for bringing passengers or goods within a controlled district in pursuance of a contract for the hire of the vehicle made outside the district if the vehicle is not made available for hire within the district;

(b) ...

(c) apply to a vehicle while it is being used in connection with a funeral or a vehicle used wholly or mainly, by a person carrying on the business of a funeral director, for the purpose of funerals;

[(cc) apply to a vehicle while it is being used in connection with a wedding;]

(d) require the display of any plate, disc or notice in or on any private hire vehicle licensed by a council under this Part of this Act during such period that such vehicle is used for carrying passengers for hire or reward—

(i) . . .

(ii) under a contract for the hire of the vehicle for a period of not less than 24 hours.

(2) Paragraphs (a), (b) and (c) of section 46(1) of this Act shall not apply to the use or driving of a vehicle or to the employment of a driver of a vehicle while the vehicle is used as a private hire vehicle in a controlled district if a licence issued under section 48 of this Act by the council whose area consists of or includes another controlled district is then in force for the vehicle and a driver's licence issued by such a council is then in force for the driver of the vehicle.

[(2A) Where a vehicle is being used as a taxi or private hire car, paragraphs (a), (b) and (c) of section 46(1) of this Act shall not apply to the use or driving of the vehicle or the employment of a person to drive it if—

(a) a licence issued under section 10 of the Civic Government (Scotland) Act 1982 for its use as a taxi or, as the case may be, private hire car is then in force, and

(b) the driver holds a licence issued under section 13 of that Act for the driving of taxis or, as the case may be, private hire cars.

In this subsection, "private hire car" and "taxi" have the same meaning as in sections 10 to 22 of the Civic Government (Scotland) Act 1982.]

[(2B) Paragraphs (a), (b) and (c) of section 46(1) of this Act shall not apply to the use or driving of a vehicle, or to the employment of a driver of a vehicle, if—

(a) a London PHV licence issued under section 7 of the Private Hire Vehicles (London) Act 1998 is in force in relation to that vehicle; and

(b) the driver of the vehicle holds a London PHV driver's licence issued under section 13 of that Act.]

(3) Where a licence under section 48 of this Act is in force for a vehicle, the council which issued the licence may, by a notice in writing given to the proprietor of the vehicle, provide that paragraph (a) of subsection (6) of that section shall not apply to the vehicle on any occasion specified in the notice or shall not so apply while the notice is carried in the vehicle; and on any occasion on which by virtue of this subsection that paragraph does not apply to a vehicle section 54(2)(a) of this Act shall not apply to the driver of the vehicle.

Amendment

Sub-s (1): para (b) repealed by the Road Safety Act 2006, ss 53, 59, Sch 7.

Sub-s (1): para (cc) inserted and para (d)(i) repealed by the Transport Act 1985, s 139(2), Sch 7.

Sub-s (2A): inserted by the Civic Government (Scotland) Act 1982, s 16.

Sub-s (2B): inserted by the Private Hire Vehicles (London) Act 1998, s 39(1), Sch 1, para 1.

76 Penalties Any person who commits an offence against any of the provisions of this Part of this Act in respect of which no penalty is expressly provided shall be liable on summary conviction to a fine not exceeding [level 3 on the standard scale].

Amendment
Maximum fine increased and converted to a level on the standard scale by virtue of the Criminal Justice Act 1982, ss 37, 38, 46.

77 Appeals (1) Sections 300 to 302 of the Act of 1936, which relate to appeals, shall have effect as if this Part of this Act were part of that Act.

(2) If any requirement, refusal or other decision of a district council against which a right of appeal is conferred by this Act—
    (a) involves the execution of any work or the taking of any action; or
    (b) makes it unlawful for any person to carry on a business which he was lawfully carrying on up to the time of the requirement, refusal or decision;

then, until the time for appealing has expired, or, when an appeal is lodged, until the appeal is disposed of or withdrawn or fails for want of prosecution—
    (i) no proceedings shall be taken in respect of any failure to execute the work, or take the action; and
    (ii) that person may carry on that business.

[(3) Subsection (2) of this section does not apply in relation to a decision under subsection (1) of section 61 of this Act which has immediate effect in accordance with subsection (2B) of that section.]

[(4) On an appeal under this Part of this Act or an appeal under section 302 of the Act of 1936 as applied by this section, the court is not entitled to entertain any question as to whether—
    (a) a person should be, or should have been, granted leave to enter or remain in the United Kingdom; or
    (b) a person has, after the date of the decision being appealed against, been granted leave to enter or remain in the United Kingdom.]

Amendment
Sub-s (3): inserted by the Road Safety Act 2006, s 52(1), (4).
Sub-s (4): inserted by the Immigration Act 2016, s 37, Sch 5, paras 17, 27.

78 Application of provisions of Act of 1936 Subsection (1) of section 283 and section 304 of the Act of 1936 shall have effect as if references therein to that Act included a reference to this Part of this Act.

79 Authentication of licences Notwithstanding anything in section 43 of the Act of 1847, any vehicle or driver's licence granted by a district council under that Act, or any licence granted by a district council under this Part of this Act, shall not be required to be under the common seal of the district council, but if not so sealed shall be signed by an authorised officer of the council.

[79A Persons disqualified by reason of immigration status (1) For the purposes of this Part of this Act a person is disqualified by reason of the person's immigration status from carrying on a licensable activity if the person is subject to immigration control and—

    (a) the person has not been granted leave to enter or remain in the United Kingdom; or

    (b) the person's leave to enter or remain in the United Kingdom—

        (i) is invalid;

        (ii) has ceased to have effect (whether by reason of curtailment, revocation, cancellation, passage of time or otherwise); or

        (iii) is subject to a condition preventing the person from carrying on the licensable activity.

(2) Where a person is on immigration bail within the meaning of Part 1 of Schedule 10 to the Immigration Act 2016—

    (a) the person is to be treated for the purposes of this Part of this Act as if the person had been granted leave to enter the United Kingdom; but

    (b) any condition as to the person's work in the United Kingdom to which the person's immigration bail is subject is to be treated for those purposes as a condition of leave.

(3) For the purposes of this section a person is subject to immigration control if under the Immigration Act 1971 the person requires leave to enter or remain in the United Kingdom.

(4) For the purposes of this section a person carries on a licensable activity if the person—

    (a) drives a private hire vehicle;

    (b) operates a private hire vehicle; or

    (c) drives a hackney carriage.]

Amendment
Section inserted by the Immigration Act 2016, s 37, Sch 5, paras 17, 28.

[79B Immigration offences and immigration penalties (1) In this Part of this Act "immigration offence" means—

    (a) an offence under any of the Immigration Acts;

    (b) an offence under section 1 of the Criminal Attempts Act 1981 of attempting to commit an offence within paragraph (a); or

    (c) an offence under section 1 of the Criminal Law Act 1977 of conspiracy to commit an offence within paragraph (a).

(2) In this Part of this Act "immigration penalty" means a penalty under—

(a) section 15 of the Immigration, Asylum and Nationality Act 2006 ("the 2006 Act"); or

(b) section 23 of the Immigration Act 2014 ("the 2014 Act").

(3) For the purposes of this Part of this Act a person to whom a penalty notice under section 15 of the 2006 Act has been given is not to be treated as having been required to pay an immigration penalty if—

(a) the person is excused payment by virtue of section 15(3) of that Act; or

(b) the penalty is cancelled by virtue of section 16 or 17 of that Act.

(4) For the purposes of this Part of this Act a person to whom a penalty notice under section 15 of the 2006 Act has been given is not to be treated as having been required to pay an immigration penalty until such time as—

(a) the period for giving a notice of objection under section 16 of that Act has expired and the Secretary of State has considered any notice given within that period; and

(b) if a notice of objection was given within that period, the period for appealing under section 17 of that Act has expired and any appeal brought within that period has been finally determined, abandoned or withdrawn.

(5) For the purposes of this Part of this Act a person to whom a penalty notice under section 23 of the 2014 Act has been given is not to be treated as having been required to pay an immigration penalty if—

(a) the person is excused payment by virtue of section 24 of that Act; or

(b) the penalty is cancelled by virtue of section 29 or 30 of that Act.

(6) For the purposes of this Part of this Act a person to whom a penalty notice under section 23 of the 2014 Act has been given is not to be treated as having been required to pay an immigration penalty until such time as—

(a) the period for giving a notice of objection under section 29 of that Act has expired and the Secretary of State has considered any notice given within that period; and

(b) if a notice of objection was given within that period, the period for appealing under section 30 of that Act has expired and any appeal brought within that period has been finally determined, abandoned or withdrawn.]

Amendment
Section inserted by the Immigration Act 2016, s 37, Sch 5, paras 17, 28.

80 Interpretation of Part II (1) In this Part of this Act, unless the subject or context otherwise requires—

"the Act of 1847" means the provisions of the Town Police Clauses Act 1847 with respect to hackney carriages;

"the Act of 1936" means the Public Health Act 1936;

. . .

"authorised officer" means any officer of a district council authorised in writing by the council for the purposes of this Part of this Act;

"contravene" includes fail to comply;

["controlled district" means any area for which this Part of this Act is in force by virtue of—

(a) a resolution passed by a district council under section 45 of this Act; or

(b) section 255(4) of the Greater London Authority Act 1999;]

"daily fine" means a fine for each day during which an offence continues after conviction thereof;

"the district", in relation to a district council in whose area the provisions of this Part of this Act are in force, means—

(a) if those provisions are in force throughout the area of the council, that area; and

(b) if those provisions are in force for part only of the area of the council, that part of that area;

"driver's badge" means, in relation to the driver of a hackney carriage, any badge issued by a district council under byelaws made under section 68 of the Act of 1847 and, in relation to the driver of a private hire vehicle, any badge issued by a district council under section 54 of this Act;

"driver's licence" means, in relation to the driver of a hackney carriage, a licence under section 46 of the Act of 1847 and, in relation to the driver of a private hire vehicle, a licence under section 51 of this Act;

"hackney carriage" has the same meaning as in the Act of 1847;

"hackney carriage byelaws" means the byelaws for the time being in force in the controlled district in question relating to hackney carriages;

["London cab" means a vehicle which is a hackney carriage within the meaning of the Metropolitan Public Carriage Act 1869;]

"operate" means in the course of business to make provision for the invitation or acceptance of bookings for a private hire vehicle;

"operator's licence" means a licence under section 55 of this Act;

"private hire vehicle" means a motor vehicle constructed or adapted to seat [fewer than nine passengers], other than a hackney carriage or public service vehicle [or a London cab] [or tramcar], which is provided for hire with the services of a driver for the purpose of carrying passengers;

"proprietor" includes a part-proprietor and, in relation to a vehicle which is the subject of a hiring agreement or hire-purchase agreement, means the person in possession of the vehicle under that agreement;

"public service vehicle" has the same meaning as in [the Public Passenger Vehicles Act 1981];

"taximeter" means any device for calculating the fare to be charged in respect of any journey in a hackney carriage or private hire vehicle by reference to the distance travelled or time elapsed since the start of the journey, or a combination of both; and

"vehicle licence" means in relation to a hackney carriage a licence under sections 37 to 45 of the Act of 1847 [in relation to a London cab a licence under section 6 of the Metropolitan Public Carriage Act 1869] and in relation to a private hire vehicle means a licence under section 48 of this Act.

(2) In this Part of this Act references to a licence, in connection with a controlled district, are references to a licence issued by the council whose area consists of or includes that district, and "licensed" shall be construed accordingly.

(3) Except where the context otherwise requires, any reference in this Part of this Act to any enactment shall be construed as a reference to that enactment as applied, extended, amended or varied by, or by virtue of, any subsequent enactment including this Act.

[(4) In this Part of this Act, except where the context otherwise requires, references to a district council shall, in relation to Wales, be construed as references to a county council or county borough council.]

Amendment

Sub-s (1): definition "the Act of 1972", omitted, repealed by the Road Traffic (Consequential Provisions) Act 1988, s 3(1), Sch 1, Pt I.

Sub-s (1): definition "controlled district" substituted by the Greater London Authority Act 1999 (Hackney Carriages and Private Hire Vehicles) (Transitional and Consequential Provisions) Order 2000, SI 2000/412, art 7(1), (3).

Sub-s (1): definition "London cab" inserted by the Transport Act 1985, s 139(2), Sch 7, para 17(3)(a).

Sub-s (1): in definition "private hire vehicle" words "fewer than nine passengers" in square brackets substituted by the Transport Act 1980, s 43, Sch 5, Pt II.

Sub-s (1): in definition "private hire vehicle" words "or a London cab" in square brackets inserted by the Transport Act 1985, s 139(2), Sch 7, para 17(3)(b).

Sub-s (1): in definition "private hire vehicle" words "or tramcar" in square brackets inserted by the Transport and Works Act 1992, s 62(3).

Sub-s (1): in definition "public service vehicle" words "the Public Passenger Vehicles Act 1981" in square brackets substituted by the Public Passenger Service Vehicles Act 1981, s 88, Sch 7, para 20.

Sub-s (1): in definition "vehicle licence" words from "in relation to" to "Metropolitan Public Carriage Act 1869" in square brackets inserted by the Transport Act 1985, s 139(2), Sch 7, para 17(3)(c).

Sub-s (4): inserted by the Local Government Reorganisation (Wales) (Consequential Amendments No. 3) Order 1996, SI 1996/3071, art 2, Schedule, para 1(8).

Transport Act 1980

Part IV
Miscellaneous and General

64 Roof-signs on vehicles other than taxis (1) There shall not, in any part of England and Wales outside the metropolitan police district and the City of London, be displayed on or above the roof of any vehicle which is used for carrying passengers for hire or reward but which is not a taxi—

(a) any sign which consists of or includes the word "taxi" or "cab", whether in the singular or plural, or "hire", or any word of similar meaning or appearance to any of those words, whether alone or as part of another word; or

(b) any sign, notice, mark, illumination or other feature which may suggest that the vehicle is a taxi.

(2) Any person who knowingly—

(a) drives a vehicle in respect of which subsection (1) is contravened; or

(b) causes or permits that subsection to be contravened in respect of any vehicle,

shall be liable on summary conviction to a fine not exceeding [level 3 on the standard scale].

(3) In this section "taxi" means a vehicle licensed under section 37 of the Town Police Clauses Act 1847, section 6 of the Metropolitan Carriage Act 1869, [section 10 of the Civic Government (Scotland) Act 1982] or any similar local enactment.

Amendment

Sub-s (2): maximum penalty increased and converted to a level on the standard scale by the Criminal Justice Act 1982, ss 37, 38, 46.

Sub-s (3): words inserted by the Transport Act 1985, s 139(2), Sch 7, para 20.

Public Passenger Vehicles Act 1981

Part I
Preliminary

Definition and classification of public service vehicles

1 Definition of "public service vehicle" (1) Subject to the provisions of this section, in this Act "public service vehicle" means a motor vehicle (other than a tramcar) which—
  (a) being a vehicle adapted to carry more than eight passengers, is used for carrying passengers for hire or reward; or
  (b) being a vehicle not so adapted, is used for carrying passengers for hire or reward at separate fares in the course of a business of carrying passengers.

(2) For the purposes of subsection (1) above a vehicle "is used" as mentioned in paragraph (a) or (b) of that subsection if it is being so used or if it has been used as mentioned in that paragraph and that use has not been permanently discontinued.

(3) A vehicle carrying passengers at separate fares in the course of a business of carrying passengers, but doing so in circumstances in which the conditions set out in Part I, or III of Schedule 1 to this Act are fulfilled, shall be treated as not being a public service vehicle unless it is adapted to carry more than eight passengers.

(4) For the purposes of this section a journey made by a vehicle in the course of which one or more passengers are carried at separate fares shall not be treated as made in the course of a business of carrying passengers if—
  (a) the fare or aggregate of the fares paid in respect of the journey does not exceed the amount of the running costs of the vehicle for the journey; and
  (b) the arrangements for the payment of fares by the passenger or passengers so carried were made before the journey began;

and for the purposes of paragraph (a) above the running costs of a vehicle for a journey shall be taken to include an appropriate amount in respect of depreciation and general wear.

(5) For the purposes of this section, . . . and Schedule 1 to this Act—
  (a) a vehicle is to be treated as carrying passengers for hire or reward if payment is made for, or for matters which include, the carrying of passengers, irrespective of the person to whom the payment is made and, in the case of a transaction effected by or on behalf of a member of any association of persons (whether incorporated or not) on the one hand

and the association or another member thereof on the other hand, notwithstanding any rule of law as to such transactions;

(b) a payment for the carrying of a passenger shall be treated as a fare notwithstanding that it is made in consideration of other matters in addition to the journey and irrespective of the person by or to whom it is made;

(c) a payment shall be treated as made for the carrying of a passenger if made in consideration of a person's being given a right to be carried, whether for one or more journeys and whether or not the right is exercised.

(6) Where a fare is paid for the carriage of a passenger on a journey by air, no part of that fare shall be treated for the purposes of subsection (5) above as paid in consideration of the carriage of the passenger by road by reason of the fact that, in case of mechanical failure, bad weather or other circumstances outside the operator's control, part of that journey may be made by road.

Amendment
Sub-ss (3), (5): words omitted repealed by the Transport Act 1985, s 139(3), Sch 8.

2 . . .

Amendment
Section repealed by the Transport Act 1985, s 139(3), Sch 8.

SCHEDULE 1
Public Service Vehicles: Conditions Affecting Status or Classification

Sections 1, 2

Part I
Sharing of Taxis and Hire-Cars

1 The making of the agreement for the payment of separate fares must not have been initiated by the driver or by the owner of the vehicle, by any person who has made the vehicle available under any arrangement, or by any person who receives any remuneration in respect of the arrangements for the journey.

2 (1) The journey must be made without previous advertisement to the public of facilities for its being made by passengers to be carried at separate fares, except where the local authorities concerned have approved the arrangements under which the journey is made as designed to meet the social and welfare needs of one or more communities, and their approvals remain in force.

(2) In relation to a journey the local authorities concerned for the purposes of this paragraph are those in whose area any part of the journey is to be made; and in this sub-paragraph "local authority" means—

(a) in relation to England and Wales, [the council of a county, metropolitan district or London borough and the Common Council of the City of London];

(b) in relation to Scotland, a [council constituted under section 2 of the Local Government etc (Scotland) Act 1994].

3 . . .

Amendment

Para 2: in sub-para (2), in para (a) words in square brackets substituted by the Local Government Act 1985, s 8, Sch 5, para 3, in para (b) words in square brackets substituted by the Local Government etc (Scotland) Act 1994, s 180(1), Sch 13, para 121(5).

Para 3: repealed by the Transport Act 1985, s 139(3), Sch 8.

Part II

. . .

. . .

Amendment

Part repealed by the Transport Act 1985, s 139(2), (3), Sch 7, para 21(2), Sch 8.

Part III
Alternative Conditions Affecting Status or Classification

5 Arrangements for the bringing together of all the passengers for the purpose of making the journey must have been made otherwise than by, or by a person acting on behalf of—

(a) the holder of the PSV operator's licence under which the vehicle is to be used, if such a licence is in force.

(b) the driver or the owner of the vehicle or any person who has made the vehicle available under any arrangement, if no such licence is in force,

and otherwise than by any person who receives any remuneration in respect of the arrangements.

6 The journey must be made without previous advertisement to the public of the arrangements therefor.

7 All passengers must, in the case of a journey to a particular destination, be carried to, or to the vicinity of, that destination, or, in the case of a tour, be carried for the greater part of the journey.

8 No differentiation of fares for the journey on the basis of distance or of time must be made.

Part IV
Supplementary

9 For the purposes of paragraphs 2 and 6 above no account shall be taken of any such advertisement as follows, that is to say—

 (a) a notice displayed or announcement made—

 (i) at or in any place of worship for the information of persons attending that place of worship;

 (ii) at or in any place of work for the information of persons who work there; or

 (iii) by any club or other voluntary association at or in any premises occupied or used by the club or association;

 (b) a notice contained in any periodical published for the information of, and circulating wholly or mainly among—

 (i) persons who attend or might reasonably be expected to attend a particular place of worship or a place of worship in a particular place; or

 (ii) persons who work at a particular place of work or at any of two or more particular places of work; or

 (iii) the members of a club or other voluntary association.

Transport Act 1981

Part V
Miscellaneous and General

35 Charges for licensing of cabs and cab drivers (1), (2) . . .

(3) Where section 70 of the Local Government (Miscellaneous Provisions) Act 1976 (fees for vehicle and operator's licences) is not in force in the area of a district council, the sums to be paid for a licence granted by the council under section 37 of the Town Police Clauses Act 1847 (licensing of cabs outside London) shall be such as the council may determine, and different sums may be so determined with respect to different descriptions of vehicle; and the sums so determined shall be such as appear to the council to be sufficient in the aggregate to cover in whole or in part—

   (a) the reasonable cost of the carrying out by or on behalf of the district council of inspections of hackney carriages for the purpose of determining whether any such licence should be granted or renewed;
   (b) the reasonable cost of providing hackney carriage stands; and
   (c) any reasonable administrative or other costs in connection with the foregoing and with the control and supervision of hackney carriages.

[(3A) In subsection (3) above, references to a district council shall be read, in relation to Wales, as references to a county council or a county borough council.]

(4) This section does not extend to Scotland.

(5) This section comes into force on such day as the Secretary of State may by order made by statutory instrument, appoint, and different days may be so appointed for different purposes.

Amendment
Sub-ss (1), (2): repealed by the Greater London Authority Act 1999, s 423, Sch 34, Pt V.
Sub-s (3A): inserted by the Local Government (Wales) Act 1994, s 22(1), Sch 7, para 37.

Transport Act 1985

Part I
General provisions relating to Road Passenger Transport

Taxis and hire cars

15 Extension of taxi licensing in England and Wales (1) Where, immediately before the commencement of this section, the provisions of the Town Police Clauses Act 1847 with respect to hackney carriages and of the Town Police Clauses Act 1889 (as incorporated in each case in the Public Health Act 1875) were not in force throughout the whole of the area of a district council in England and Wales whose area lies outside the area to which the Metropolitan Public Carriage Act 1869 applies, those provisions (as so incorporated) shall—

(a) if not then in force in any part of the council's area, apply throughout that area; and

(b) if in force in part only of its area, apply also in the remainder of that area.

(2) Where part only of a district council's area lies outside the area to which the Act of 1869 applies, that part shall, for the purposes of subsection (1) above, be treated as being the area of the council.

(3) So much of any local Act as enables a district council to bring to an end the application of the provisions mentioned in subsection (1) above to the whole or any part of their area shall cease to have effect.

16 Taxi licensing: control of numbers The provisions of the Town Police Clauses Act 1847 with respect to hackney carriages, as incorporated in any enactment (whenever passed), shall [(subject to section 161 of the Equality Act 2010)] have effect—

(a) as if in section 37, the words "such number of" and "as they think fit" were omitted; and

(b) as if they provided that the grant of a licence may be refused, for the purpose of limiting the number of hackney carriages in respect of which licences are granted, if, but only if, the person authorised to grant licences is satisfied that there is no significant demand for the services of hackney carriages (within the area to which the licence would apply) which is unmet.

Amendment
Words "(subject to section 161 of the Equality Act 2010)" in square brackets inserted by the Equality Act 2010, s 161(3).

SCHEDULE 7
Minor and Consequential Amendments

Section 139(2)

The Town Police Clauses Act 1847

3 Section 46 of the Town Police Clauses Act 1847 (drivers not to act without first obtaining a licence) shall not apply to a person driving a hackney carriage licensed under that Act for the purpose of or in connection with—

   (a) any test of the mechanical condition or fitness of the hackney carriage or its equipment carried out for the purposes of [section 45 of the Road Traffic Act 1988] (tests of satisfactory condition of vehicles other than goods vehicles) or for the purposes of any requirements with respect to such condition or fitness imposed by or under any other enactment; or

   (b) any test of that person's competence to drive a hackney carriage carried out for the purposes of any application made by him for a licence to drive a hackney carriage.

Amendment

Para 3(a): words "section 45 of the Road Traffic Act 1988" in square brackets substituted by the Road Traffic (Consequential Provisions) Act 1988, s 4, Sch 3, para 31.

1986 No 567

Local Services (Operation by Taxis) Regulations 1986

1 Citation and commencement These Regulations may be cited as the Local Services (Operation by Taxis) Regulations 1986 and shall come into operation on 16th April 1986.

2 Interpretation (1) In these Regulations—
"the 1847 Act" means the Town Police Clauses Act 1847;
"the 1976 Act" means the Local Government (Miscellaneous Provisions) Act 1976;
"the 1985 Act" means the Transport Act 1985;
"local service" has the meaning given by section 2 of the 1985 Act;
"local taxi area" means the area in which a vehicle is licensed to ply for hire under section 37 of the 1847 Act;
"special licence" means a restricted PSV operator's licence granted by virtue of section 12 of the 1985 Act;
"licensed taxi" and "taxi code" have the meanings given by section 13(3) of the 1985 Act; and
"taximeter" has the meaning given by section 80(1) of the 1976 Act.

(2) Any reference in these Regulations to the 1847 Act is a reference to that Act as it applies in relation to a vehicle as a part of the taxi code (and accordingly as it so applies as incorporated, extended or applied by or under any enactment).

3 Application These Regulations apply to a licensed taxi which is licensed under section 37 of the 1847 Act, at any time when that vehicle is being used to provide a local service under a special licence.

4 Prescribed Provisions (1) The provisions specified in the first column of the Table to the extent that they are part of the taxi code, subject to the exceptions and modifications specified in the second column thereof, are hereby prescribed as applying in relation to a vehicle to which these Regulations apply.

(2) Where any part of the taxi code is contained in provisions made by or under any local Act, then any such provisions which have substantially similar purpose and effect to those provisions prescribed by paragraph (1) of this regulation are hereby prescribed as applying in relation to a vehicle to which these Regulations apply.

(3) The provisions so prescribed shall apply—
(a) whether or not the use of the vehicle to provide a local service is within the local taxi area for that vehicle, and accordingly any limitation in

those provisions to that area shall have no effect when the vehicle is being so used; and

(b) subject to the modification that any reference to a hackney carriage includes a reference to a vehicle to which these Regulations apply.

TABLE

Column 1	Column 2
Provisions Prescribed	**Modifications**
The 1847 Act, sections 37–65	Section 52 is modified by the omission of the words from "or if the driver" to "or any less number"; and sections 53–59, 62 and 64 are excepted.
Public Health Act 1875, section 251	None
The 1976 Act, Part II	Sections 63, 65–7, 69, and 75 are excepted Section 64(1) is modified by the omission of the words "other than a hackney carriage".
Any byelaws made under section 68 of the 1847 Act or conditions attached to a licence under section 47 of the 1976 Act with the purpose in either case of regulating—	None

a. the display of the licence number on the vehicle;

b. the number of persons that may be carried in the vehicle;

c. the wearing of a badge by the driver;

d. the safe custody and redelivery of any property accidentally left in the vehicle;

e. the reporting of accidents

f. the tampering with any taximeter with which the vehicle is provided;

g. the civil and orderly behaviour of the driver and the precautions to be taken by him in regard to the safety of passengers; and

h. the equipment and fittings of the vehicle;

and any byelaws prescribing penalties for breach of the above-mentioned byelaws

5 The holder of a special licence shall during such time as the vehicle is being used to provide a local service cause—

(a) to be displayed on the vehicle a notice clearly legible from the front which includes the word "BUS" in letters at least 60 millimetres high and indicates either the destination of the vehicle, or its route, or the nature of the service being provided;

(b) any notice which the vehicle is required to display to indicate that it is available for exclusive hire (including any such notice which bears any of the words "hire", "taxi" or "cab") not to be illuminated by any light forming part of the equipment of the vehicle;

(c) a fare table to be displayed in the vehicle in a manner clearly legible by passengers, and containing sufficient information for any passenger to ascertain the fare for his journey or the manner in which that fare is computed.

1986 No 1386

Licensed Taxis (Hiring at Separate Fares) Order 1986

1 Citation and Commencement This Order may be cited as the Licensed Taxis (Hiring at Separate Fares) Order 1986 and shall come into operation on 3rd September 1986.

2 Interpretation (1) In this Order:
    "the 1847 Act" means the Town Police Clauses Act 1847;
    "authorised place" has the meaning given by section 10(5) of the 1985 Act;
    "the 1976 Act" means the Local Government (Miscellaneous Provisions) Act 1976;
    "the 1985 Act" means the Transport Act 1985; and
    "taxi" means a vehicle licensed under section 37 of the 1847 Act.

(2) Any reference in this Order to the 1847 Act is a reference to that Act as it applies in relation to a vehicle as a part of the taxi code (and accordingly as it so applies as incorporated, extended or applied by or under any enactment).

3 Application (1) This Order applies in relation to a taxi:
    (1) standing at an authorised place and available for hire under the terms of a scheme for the immediate hiring of taxis at separate fares;
    (2) hired under the terms of such a scheme; or
    (3) being used for the carriage of passengers at separate fares where the conditions in section 11(2) of the 1985 Act are met.
    (2) Article 4(2) of this Order applies in addition to a taxi proceeding to an authorised place.

4 Modifications of the taxi code In its application as specified in article 3 of this Order, the taxi code shall be modified as follows:
    (1) in section 52 of the 1847 Act, the words from "or if the driver" to "every proprietor" shall be omitted;
    (2) any requirement in a byelaw made under section 68 of the 1847 Act or in a condition attached to a licence under section 47 of the 1976 Act that an unhired taxi shall proceed to a stand shall be satisfied if the taxi proceeds to an authorised place; and
    (3) the following provisions shall not apply:
        (a) any provision in so far as it prohibits the driver from touting orally at an authorised place for passengers to share the taxi with a passenger who has already requested a service at separate fares;
        (b) any byelaws made under section 68 of the 1847 Act or conditions attached to licences under section 47 of the 1976 Act with the purpose in either case of regulating:

   (i) the rates or fares to be paid;

   (ii) the use of any taxi meter with which the vehicle is equipped;

   (iii) the journey which a driver is required to undertake; or

   (iv) the luggage required to be carried;

(c) any table of fares having effect pursuant to section 65(5) of the 1976 Act as if included in byelaws made under section 68 of the 1847 Act;

(d) sections 53 to 59 of the 1847 Act;

(e) sections 66 and 67 of the 1976 Act; and

(f) any provisions which have substantially similar purpose and effect to the provisions described in sub-paragraphs (*b*), (*d*) or (*e*) of this paragraph made by or under any local Act.

1998 No 1946

Deregulation (Taxis and Private Hire Vehicles) Order 1998

Whereas:
  (a) the Secretary of State is of the opinion that certain provisions of the Local Government (Miscellaneous Provisions) Act 1976 impose burdens affecting persons in the carrying on of a trade, business or profession or otherwise and that by amending or repealing the provisions concerned it is possible to remove or reduce the burdens concerned without removing any necessary protection;
  (b) he has consulted such organisations as appear to him to be representative of interests substantially affected by his proposals and such other persons as he considers appropriate;
  (c) it appears to the Secretary of State that it is appropriate, following that consultation, to proceed with the making of this Order;
  (d) a document setting out the Secretary of State's proposals has been laid before Parliament as required by section 3 of the Deregulation and Contracting Out Act 1994 and the period for Parliamentary consideration under section 4 has expired;
  (e) the Secretary of State has had regard to the representations made during that period;
  (f) a draft of this Order has been laid before Parliament with a statement giving details of such representations and the changes to the Secretary of State's proposals in the light of those representations; and
  (g) a draft of this Order has been approved by resolution of each House of Parliament:

Now, therefore, the Secretary of State, in exercise of the powers conferred by section 1 of the Deregulation and Contracting Out Act 1994, hereby makes the following Order:—

NOTES

Notwithstanding the repeal for certain purposes of the Deregulation and Contracting Out Act 1994, s 1 this Order was continued in force by virtue of the Regulatory Reform Act 2001, s 12(4); following the repeal of that section this Order is continued in force by virtue of the Legislative and Regulatory Reform Act 2006, s 30(5).

1 Citation and commencement This Order may be cited as the Deregulation (Taxis and Private Hire Vehicles) Order 1998 and shall come into force 28 days after the day on which it is made.

2 Qualifications for drivers of private hire vehicles In section 51 of the Local Government (Miscellaneous Provisions) Act 1976 (licensing of drivers of private hire vehicles), in subsection (1) as inserted by the Driving Licences (Community Driving Licence) Regulations 1996, in paragraph (b) after "section 99A(1)" there shall be inserted "or section 109(1)".

3 Qualifications for drivers of taxis In section 59 of the Local Government (Miscellaneous Provisions) Act 1976 (qualifications for drivers of hackney carriages), in subsection (1A) as inserted by the Driving Licences (Community Driving Licence) Regulations 1996, in paragraph (b) after "section 99A(1)" there shall be inserted "or section 109(1)".

2008 No 2840

Legislative Reform (Local Authority Consent Requirements) (England and Wales) Order 2008

1 Citation, commencement and extent (1) This Order may be cited as the Legislative Reform (Local Authority Consent Requirements) (England and Wales) Order 2008 and shall come into force on the day after the day on which it is made.

(2) This Order extends to England and Wales only.

...

3 Hackney carriage licence zones (1) Subject to paragraph (2), in paragraph 25 of Schedule 14 to the Local Government Act 1972 (amendment and modification of Public Health Acts 1875 to 1925) ("paragraph 25")—
- (a) in sub-paragraph (1), for "sub-paragraphs (2) and (4)" there shall be substituted "sub-paragraph (2)";
- (b) sub-paragraph (4) shall be repealed; and
- (c) in sub-paragraph (6)—
    - (i) in paragraph (a), the words from "except" to "any area," shall be omitted; and
    - (ii) paragraph (b) and the preceding "and" shall be repealed.

(2) Where, before the date on which this Order comes into force—
- (a) a local authority, after giving the requisite notice, passes a resolution under paragraph 25 that section 171(4) of the Public Health Act 1875 (incorporation of certain provisions of the Town Police Clauses Act 1847(6))(7) shall apply throughout its area; and
- (b) that resolution is neither approved nor disapproved by the Secretary of State or, in relation to a local authority in Wales, the Welsh Ministers,

the date on which that resolution is to take effect shall be the date which is 35 days after the date on which this Order comes into force.

London Hackney Carriage Act 1831

1 . . .

Amendment

Section repealed by the Statute Law Revision Act 1874.

2, 3 . . .

Amendment

Sections repealed by the Revenue Act 1869, s 39, Sch (E).

4 . . .

Amendment

Section repealed by the Statute Law (Repeals) Act 1989, s 1(1), Schedule, Pt X.

5–17 . . .

Amendment

Sections repealed by the Revenue Act 1869, s 39, Sch (E).

18 . . .

Amendment

Section repealed by the Statute Law (Repeals) Act 1976, s 1(1), Sch 1, Pt XVII.

19–25 . . .

Amendment

Sections repealed by the Revenue Act 1869, s 39, Sch (E).

26 . . .

Amendment

Section repealed by the Statute Law Revision Act 1874.

27, 28 . . .

Amendment

Sections repealed by the Statute Law (Repeals) Act 1993, s 1(1), Sch 1, Pt XV, Group 2.

29 ...

Amendment
Section repealed by the Statute Law Revision Act 1874.

30–33 ...

Amendment
Section repealed by the Revenue Act 1869, s 39, Sch (E).

34 ...

Amendment
Section repealed by the Statute Law Revision Act 1874.

35 Hackney carriages standing in any street shall be deemed to be plying for hire; and the drivers thereof refusing to go with any person shall forfeit forty shillings ... Every hackney carriage which shall be found standing in any street or place ... shall, unless actually hired, be deemed to be plying for hire, although such hackney carriage shall not be on any standing or place usually appropriated for the purpose of hackney carriages standing or plying for hire; and the driver of every such hackney carriage which shall not be actually hired shall be obliged and compellable to go with any person desirous of hiring such hackney carriage; and upon the hearing of any complaint against the driver of any such hackney carriage for any such refusal such driver shall be obliged to adduce evidence of having been and of being actually hired at the time of such refusal, and in case such driver shall fail to produce sufficient evidence of having been and of being so hired as aforesaid he shall forfeit [a sum not exceeding level 1 on the standard scale].

Amendment
First words omitted repealed by the Statute Law Revision (No 2) Act 1888.
Second words omitted repealed by the Statute Law (Repeals) Act 1976, s 1(1), Sch 1, Pt XVII.
Maximum fine increased by the Criminal Justice Act 1967, s 92(1), Sch 3, Pt I, and converted to a level on the standard scale by the Criminal Justice Act 1982, ss 37, 38, 46.

36 Compensation to be made to drivers improperly summoned for refusing to carry any person Provided always, ... that if the driver of any hackney carriage shall in civil and explicit terms declare to any person, desirous to hire such hackney carriage that it is actually hired and shall afterwards, notwithstanding such reply, be summoned to answer for his refusal to carry such person in his said hackney carriage, and shall upon the hearing of the complaint produce sufficient evidence to prove that such hackney carriage was at the time actually and bona fide hired, and it shall not appear that he used uncivil language, or that he improperly conducted himself towards the party by whom he shall be so summoned, the justice before whom such complaint shall be heard shall order the person who shall have summoned such driver to make to him such compensation for his loss of time in attending to make his defence to such complaint as such justice shall deem reasonable . . .

Amendment

First words omitted repealed by the Statute Law Revision (No 2) Act 1888; second words omitted repealed by the Statute Law (Repeals) Act 1976, s 1(1), Sch 1, Pt XVII.

37 . . .

Amendment

Section repealed by the Statute Law (Repeals) Act 1973, s 1(1), Sch 1, Pt VI.

38–40 . . .

Amendment

Sections repealed by the Statute Law Revision Act 1874.

41 Persons refusing to pay the driver his fare, or in injuring his carriage, to be liable to make compensation . . . If any person shall refuse or omit to pay the driver of any hackney carriage the sum justly due to him for the hire of such hackney carriage, or if any person shall deface or in any manner injure any such hackney carriage, it shall be lawful for any justice of the peace, upon complaint thereof made to him, to grant a summons, or, if it shall appear to him necessary, a warrant, for bringing before him or any other justice such defaulter or defender, and, upon proof of the facts made upon oath before any such justice, to award reasonable satisfaction to the party so complaining for his fare or for his damages and costs, and also a reasonable compensation for his loss of time in attending to make and establish such complaint . . .

Amendment

First words omitted repealed by the Statute Law Revision (No 2) Act 1888; second words omitted repealed by the Statute Law (Repeals) Act 1976, s 1(1), Sch 1, Pt XVII.

42 . . .

Amendment

Section repealed by the Statute Law Revision Act 1874.

43–45 . . .

Amendment

Sections repealed by the Statute Law (Repeals) Act 1973, s 1(1), Sch 1, Pt VI.

46 . . .

Amendment

Section repealed by the Statute Law Revision Act 1874.

47 Driver may demand deposit when required to wait with carriage—Penalty on such driver refusing to wait, or to account for the deposit, etc, forty shillings . . . Where any hackney carriage shall be hired and taken to any place of public resort, or elsewhere, and the driver thereof shall be required there to wait with such hackney carriage, it shall be lawful for such driver to demand and receive from the person so hiring and requiring him to wait as aforesaid a reasonable sum as a deposit, over and above the fare to which such driver shall be entitled for driving thither, which sum so demanded and received shall be accounted for by such driver when such hackney carriage shall be finally discharged; and if any such driver who shall have received any such deposit as aforesaid shall refuse to wait with such hackney carriage at the place where he shall be so required to wait, or if such driver shall go away, or shall permit such hackney carriage to be driven or taken away, without the consent of the person making such deposit, before the expiration of the time for which the sum so deposited shall be a sufficient compensation, . . . or if such driver on the final discharge of such hackney carriage shall refuse duly to account for such deposit, every such driver so offending shall forfeit [level 1 on the standard scale].

Amendment
First words omitted repealed by the Statute Law Revision (No 2) Act 1888.
Second words omitted repealed by the Statute Law Revision Act 1874.
Maximum fine increased by the Criminal Law Act 1977, s 31(6), and converted to a level on the standard scale by the Criminal Justice Act 1982, ss 37, 46.

48 . . .

Amendment
Section repealed by the Statute Law Revision Act 1959.

49 . . .

Amendment
Section repealed by the Revenue Act 1869, s 39, Sch (E).

50 Penalty for permitting persons to ride without consent of the hirer, twenty shillings . . . If the proprietor or driver of any hackney carriage which shall be hired shall permit or suffer any person to ride or be carried in, upon, or about such hackney carriage, without the express consent of the person hiring the same, such proprietor or driver shall forfeit [level 1 on the standard scale].

Amendment
Words omitted repealed by the Statute Law Revision (No 2) Act 1888.
Maximum fine increased by the Criminal Law Act 1977, s 36(1), and converted to a level on the standard scale by the Criminal Justice Act 1982, ss 37, 46.

51 Penalty for depriving drivers of other hackney carriages of their fares; twenty shillings . . . If any proprietor or driver of any hackney carriage . . .

shall wrongfully, in a forcible or clandestine manner, take away the fare from any other such proprietor or driver who, in the judgement of any justice of the peace before whom any complaint of such offence shall be heard, shall appear to be fairly entitled to such fare; every such proprietor, driver, . . . so offending shall forfeit [level 1 on the standard scale].

Amendment

First words omitted repealed by the Statute Law Revision (No 2) Act 1888.

Second and third words omitted repealed by the Statute Law Revision (No 2) Act 1888, and the Statute Law (Repeals) Act 1976.

Maximum fine increased by the Criminal Law Act 1977, s 36(1), and converted to a level on the standard scale by the Criminal Justice Act 1982, ss 37, 46.

52–54 . . .

Amendment

Sections repealed by the Statute Law Revision (No 2) Act 1888.

55 . . .

Amendment

Section repealed by the London Cab Act 1968, s 3(1).

56 Penalty on proprietors or drivers misbehaving, £5—Licences may be revoked . . . If the proprietor or driver of any hackney carriage, or any other person having the care thereof, shall, by intoxication, or by wanton and furious driving, or by any other wilful misconduct, injure or endanger any person in his life, limbs, or property, or if any such proprietor or driver . . . shall make use of any abusive or insulting language, or be guilty of other rude behaviour, to or towards any person whatever, or shall assault or obstruct . . . any officer of police, constable, . . . watchman, or patrole, in the execution of his duty, every such proprietor, driver, . . . or other person so offending in any of the several cases aforesaid, shall forfeit [a sum not exceeding level 1 on the standard scale] . . . ; . . ..

Amendment

First, second, third, fifth and sixth words omitted repealed by the Summary Jurisdiction Act 1884, s 4, Schedule, the Statute Law Revision (No 2) Act 1888, the Statute Law (Repeals) Act 1976 and the Statute Law (Repeals) Act 1989.

Fourth words omitted repealed by the Statute Law (Repeals) Act 2004, s 1(1), Sch 1, Pt 14.

Penalty increased to £25 by the Criminal Law Act 1977, s 31(6), and converted to level 1 on the standard scale by the Criminal Justice Act 1982, ss 37, 46.

Final words omitted repealed by the Statute Law (Repeals) Act 2004, s 1(1), Sch 1, Pt 14.

57 Where complaints against drivers are withdrawn, etc, justice may award compensation to them for their loss of time in attending to answer

the same . . . If any driver of a hackney carriage . . . shall be summoned or brought before any justice of the peace to answer any complaint or information touching or concerning any offence committed or alleged to have been committed by such driver . . . against the provisions of this Act, and such complaint or information shall afterwards be withdrawn or quashed or dismissed, or if the defendant shall be acquitted of the offence charged against him, it shall be lawful for the said justice, if he shall think fit, to order and award that the complainant or informant shall pay to the said driver . . . such compensation for his loss of time in attending the said justice touching or concerning such complaint or information as to the said justice shall seem reasonable . . .

Amendment

Final words omitted repealed by the Statute Law (Repeals) Act 1976, s 1(1), Sch 1, Pt XVII; other words omitted repealed by the Statute Law Revision (No 2) Act 1888.

58 . . .

Amendment

Section repealed by the Revenue Act 1869, s 39, Sch (E).

59, 60 . . .

Amendment

Section repealed by the Statute Law (Repeals) Act 1973, s 1(1), Sch 1, Pt VI.

61 . . .

Amendment

Section repealed by the Revenue Act 1869, s 39, Sch (E).

62, 63 . . .

Amendment

Sections repealed by the Statute Law (Repeals) Act 1976, s 1(1), Sch 1, Pt XVII.

64 . . .

Amendment

Section repealed by the Statute Law Revision Act 1874.

65 . . .

Amendment

Section repealed by the Summary Jurisdiction Act 1884, s 4, Schedule.

66, 67 . . .

Amendment
Sections repealed by the Statute Law Revision Act 1874.

68 . . .

Amendment
Section repealed by the Statute Law (Repeals) Act 1976, s 1(1), Sch 1, Pt XVII.

69 . . .

Amendment
Section repealed by the Summary Jurisdiction Act 1884, s 4, Schedule.

70, 71 . . .

Amendment
Sections repealed by the Statute Law (Repeals) Act 1976, s 1(1), Sch 1, Pt XVII.

72 . . .

Amendment
Section repealed by the Statute Law Revision Act 1874.

73 . . .

Amendment
Section repealed by the Public Authorities Protection Act 1893, s 2, Schedule.

74 Construction of the terms used in this Act Whenever in this Act, with reference to any person, . . . matter, or thing, any word or words is or are used importing the singular number or the masculine gender only, yet such word or words shall be understood to include several persons . . . as well as one person . . ., females as well as males, bodies politic or corporate as well as individuals, and several matters or things as well as one matter or thing unless it be otherwise specially provided, or there be something in the subject or context repugnant to such construction.

Amendment
Words omitted repealed by the Statute Law (Repeals) Act 2004, s 1(1), Sch 1, Pt 14.

75–78 . . .

Amendment
Sections repealed by the Statute Law Revision Act 1874.

SCHEDULE (A)

. . .

Amendment
Schedule repealed by the Revenue Act 1869, s 39, Sch (E).

SCHEDULE (B)

. . .

Amendment
Schedule repealed by the Revenue Act 1869, s 39, Sch (E).

SCHEDULE (C)

. . .

Amendment
Schedule repealed by the Revenue Act 1869, s 39, Sch (E).

SCHEDULE (D)

. . .

Amendment
Schedule repealed by the Summary Jurisdiction Act 1884, s 4, Schedule.

London Hackney Carriages Act 1843

1 ...

Amendment

Section repealed by the Statute Law Revision Act 1874 (No 2).

2 Interpretation of terms . . . the word "proprietor" shall include every person who, either alone or in partnership with any other person, shall keep any hackney carriage . . . , or who shall be concerned otherwise than as a driver or attendant in employing for hire any hackney carriage or any metropolitan stage carriage . . .

Amendment

Words omitted repealed by the Statute Law Revision (No 2) Act 1888, the Statute Law (Repeals) Act 1976 and the Statute Law (Repeals) Act 1989.

3 Provisions of 1 & 2 Will 4, c 22, extended to this Act . . . So much of the London Hackney Carriage Act 1831 as relates to hackney carriages . . . and not hereby repealed, . . . shall extend and apply to hackney carriages . . . within the meaning of this Act . . .

Amendment

Words omitted repealed by the Statute Law Revision Act 1874 (No 2), and the Statute Law Revision Act 1891.

4 . . . .

Amendment

Section repealed by the Statute Law (Repeals) Act 1973, s 1(1), Sch 1, Pt VI.

5, 6 . . .

Amendment

Section repealed by the Statute Law Revision Act 1874 (No 2).

7 . . .

Amendment

Section repealed by the Statute Law (Repeals) Act 1976, s 1(1), Sch 1, Pt XVII.

8 [Transport for London] to grant licences to drivers of hackney carriages—At the time of granting any licence an abstract of the laws and a [badge] to be given . . . It shall be lawful for [Transport for London] to grant a licence to act as driver of hackney carriages, . . . to any person who shall produce such a certificate as shall satisfy [Transport for London] of his good behaviour and fitness for such situation . . . ; and in every such licence shall be specified the number of such licence, and the proper name and surname and place of abode, and age, and a description of the person to whom such licence shall be granted . . . ; and every such licence shall bear date on the day on which the same shall be granted, . . . and on every licence of a driver . . . [Transport for London] shall cause proper columns to be prepared, in which every proprietor employing the driver . . . named in such licence shall enter his own name and address, and the days on which such driver . . . shall enter and shall quit his service respectively; and in case any of the particulars entered or endorsed upon any licence in pursuance of this Act shall be erased or defaced every such licence shall be wholly void and of none effect; and [Transport for London] shall, at the time of granting any licence, deliver to the driver, . . . to whom the same shall be granted an abstract of the laws in force relating to such driver, . . . and of the penalties to which he is liable for any misconduct, and also a [badge], upon which there shall be marked . . . his office or employment, and a number corresponding with the number which shall be inserted in such licence.

Amendment

Section heading: words "Transport for London" in square brackets substituted by virtue of the Greater London Authority Act 1999, s 253, Sch 20, paras 1(2), (3), 10.

Section heading: word "badges" in square brackets substituted by virtue of the Transport for London Act 2008, s 11(2).

Words omitted repealed by the Statute Law Revision Act 1874 (No 2), the Statute Law Revision Act 1891, and the Statute Law (Repeals) Act 1976.

Words "Transport for London" in square brackets in each place they occur substituted by the Greater London Authority Act 1999, s 253, Sch 20, paras 1(2), (3), 10.

Words "badge" in square brackets substituted by the Transport for London Act 2008, s 11(1)(a).

Final words omitted repealed by the Transport for London Act 2008, s 11(1)(b).

9 . . .

Amendment

Section repealed by the Statute Law Revision Act 1874 (No 2).

10 Penalty on persons acting as drivers, etc, without licences and [badges], [level 3 on the standard scale]; on proprietors suffering drivers to do, [level 3 on the standard scale]—Employment of unlicensed drivers, etc, in case of necessity . . . every person to whom a licence and [badge] shall have been granted who shall, except in compliance with the provisions of this Act, transfer or lend such licence, or permit any other person to use or wear such [badge], shall for every such offence forfeit the sum of five pounds; and every proprietor who shall knowingly suffer any person not duly licensed under the authority of this Act to act as driver of any hackney carriage, . . . of which he shall be the proprietor, shall for every such offence forfeit a sum not exceeding level 3 on the standard scale: . . .

Amendment

Section heading: maximum penalty on summary conviction in any instance now level 3 on the standard scale by virtue of the Criminal Justice Act 1967, s 92(1), Sch 3, Pt I, and the Criminal Justice Act 1982, ss 35, 37, 38, 46.

Section heading: word "badges" in square brackets substituted by virtue of the Transport for London Act 2008, s 11(2).

Words omitted repealed by the Statute Law Revision Act 1874 (No 2), the Statute Law Revision Act 1891, the Statute Law (Repeals) Act 1976 and the Statute Law (Repeals) Act 1993.

Word "badge" in square brackets in both places it occurs substituted by the Transport for London Act 2008, s 11(2).

Maximum penalty on summary conviction in any instance now level 3 on the standard scale by virtue of the Criminal Justice Act 1967, s 92(1), Sch 3, Pt I, and the Criminal Justice Act 1982, ss 35, 37, 38, 46.

11–13 . . .

Amendment

Sections repealed by the Statute Law Revision Act 1874 (No 2).

14 Persons applying for licences to sign a requisition for the same, etc— Penalty on applicants or referees making false representations . . . Before any such licence as aforesaid shall be granted a requisition for the same, in such form as [Transport for London] shall from time to time appoint for that purpose, and accompanied with such certificate as herein-before is required, shall be made and signed by the person by whom such licence shall be required; and in every such requisition all such particulars as [Transport for London] shall require shall be truly set forth; and every person applying for or attempting to procure any such licence who shall make or cause to be made any false representation in regard to any of the said particulars, . . . or who shall not truly answer all questions which shall be demanded of him in relation to such application for a licence, and also every person to whom reference shall be made who shall, in regard to such application, wilfully and knowingly make any misrepresentation, shall forfeit for every such offence a sum not exceeding level 3 on the standard scale; and it shall be lawful for [Transport for London] to proceed for recovering of such penalty before any magistrate at any time within one calendar month after the commission of the offence, or during the currency of the licence so improperly obtained.

Amendment

First words omitted repealed by the Statute Law Revision Act 1891.

Words "Transport for London" in square brackets in each place they occur substituted by the Greater London Authority Act 1999, s 253, Sch 20, para 1(2), (3).

Second words omitted repealed by the Forgery and Counterfeiting Act 1981, s 30, Schedule, Pt I.

Maximum penalty now level 3 on the standard scale by virtue of the Criminal Justice Act 1967, s 92(1), Sch 3, Pt I, and the Criminal Justice Act 1982, ss 37, 38, 46.

15 ...

Amendment
Section repealed by the Statute Law (Repeals) Act 1976, s 1(1), Sch 1, Pt XVII.

16 Particulars of licences to be entered in a book at [Transport for London's] office—Copies of entries to be evidence—Copies of particulars to be given on application, without fee [(1)] ... The particulars of every licence which shall be granted as aforesaid shall be entered in books to be kept for that purpose at the office of [Transport for London]; and in all courts, and before any justice of the peace, and upon all occasions whatsoever, a copy of an entry made in any such book, and certified by the person having the charge thereof to be a true copy, shall be received as evidence, and be deemed sufficient proof of all things therein registered, without requiring the production of the said book, or of any licence, or of any requisition or other document upon which any such entry may be founded; and[, subject to subsection (2),] every person applying at all reasonable times shall be furnished with a certified copy of the particulars respecting any licensed person, without payment of any fee.

[(2) Transport for London may disclose the address of a licensed person to any person only if it appears to Transport for London that the person has a sufficient reason for requiring that information.]

Amendment
Section heading: words "Transport for London's" in square brackets substituted by virtue of the Greater London Authority Act 1999, s 253, Sch 20, Pt I, para 1(2), (3).
Sub-s (1): numbered as such by the Transport for London Act 2008, s 12(1), (2).
Sub-s (1): words omitted repealed by the Statute Law Revision Act 1891.
Sub-s (1) words "Transport for London" in square brackets substituted by the Greater London Authority Act 1999, s 253, Sch 20, para 1(2), (3).
Sub-s (1): words ", subject to subsection (2)," in square brackets inserted by the Transport for London Act 2008, s 12(1), (3).
Sub-s (2): inserted by the Transport for London Act 2008, s 12(1), (4).

17 [Badges] to be worn by drivers, etc ... Every licensed driver ... shall at all times during his employment, and when he shall be required to attend before any justice of the peace, wear his [badge] conspicuously upon his breast, in such manner that the whole of the writing thereon shall be distinctly legible; and every driver ... who shall act as such, or who shall attend when required before any justice of the peace, without wearing such [badge] in manner aforesaid, or who, when thereunto required, shall refuse to produce such [badge] for inspection, or to permit any person to note the writing thereon, shall for every such offence forfeit [a sum not exceeding level 1 on the standard scale].

Amendment
Section heading: word "Badges" square brackets substituted by virtue of the Transport for London Act 2008, s 11(2).

Words omitted repealed by the Statute Law Revision Act 1874 (No 2), the Statute Law Revision Act 1891, and the Statute Law (Repeals) Act 1976.

Word "badge" in square brackets in each place it occurs substituted by the Transport for London Act 2008, s 11(2).

Maximum fine increased by the Criminal Law Act 1977, s 92(1), Sch 3, Pt I, and converted to a level on the standard scale by the Criminal Justice Act 1982, ss 37, 38, 46.

18 Licences and [badges] to be delivered up on the discontinuance of licences [(1)] . . . Upon the expiration of any licence granted under this Act the person to whom such licence shall have been granted shall deliver such licence and the [badge] relating thereto to [Transport for London]; and every such person who, after the expiration of such licence, shall wilfully neglect for three days to deliver the same to [Transport for London], and also every person who shall use or wear or detain any [badge] without having a licence in force relating to such [badge], or who shall for the purpose of deception use or wear or have any [badge] resembling or intended to resemble any [badge] granted under the authority of this Act, shall for every such offence forfeit the sum of [level 1 on the standard scale]; and it shall be lawful for [Transport for London], or for any person employed by [Transport for London] for that purpose, to prosecute any person so neglecting to deliver up his licence or [badge], at any period within twelve calendar months after the expiration of the licence; and it shall be lawful for any constable . . . or any person employed for that purpose by [Transport for London], to seize and take away any such [badge], wheresoever the same may be found, in order to deliver the same to [Transport for London].

[(2) Subsection (1) does not require the delivery of a licence and badge on the expiry of the licence if the licence was granted in accordance with section 8A(2) or (4) of the Metropolitan Public Carriage Act 1869 (but see section 8A(6) of that Act).]

Amendment

Section heading: word "badges" in square brackets substituted by virtue of the Transport for London Act 2008, s 11(2).

Section renumbered as para (1) by the Immigration Act 2016, s 37, Sch 5, para 1(1), (2).

Sub-s (1): first words omitted repealed by the Statute Law Revision Act 1891.

Sub-s (1): word "badge" in square brackets in each place it occurs substituted by the Transport for London Act 2008, s 11(2).

Sub-s (1): words "Transport for London" in square brackets in each place they occur substituted by the Greater London Authority Act 1999, s 253, Sch 20, para 1(2)-(4).

Sub-s (1): penalty increased to £25 by the Criminal Law Act 1977, s 31(6), and converted to level 1 on the standard scale by the Criminal Justice Act 1982, ss 37, 46.

Sub-s (1): final words omitted repealed by the Statute Law (Repeals) Act 2004, s 1(1), Sch 1, Pt 14.

Sub-s (2): inserted by the Immigration Act 2016, s 37, Sch 5, para 1(1), (3).

19 New [badges] to be delivered instead of defaced or lost [badges] . . . Whenever the writing on any [badge] shall become obliterated or defaced, so that the same shall not be distinctly legible, and also whenever any [badge] shall be proved to the satisfaction of [Transport for London] to have been lost or mislaid, the person to whom the licence relating to any such [badge] shall have been granted shall deliver such [badge] (if he shall have the same in his possession) and shall produce such licence to [Transport for London], and such person shall then be entitled to have a new [badge] delivered to him, upon payment, [to Transport for London], of such sum of money [as Transport for London shall consider reasonable]: Provided always, that if any [badge] which shall have been proved as aforesaid or represented to have been lost or mislaid shall afterwards be found the same shall forthwith be delivered to [Transport for London]; and every person into whose possession any such [badge] as last aforesaid shall be or come who shall refuse or neglect for three days to deliver the same to [Transport for London], and also every person licensed under the authority of this Act who shall use or wear the [badge] granted to him after the writing thereon shall be obliterated, defaced, or obscured, so that the same shall not be distinctly legible, shall for every such offence forfeit the sum of [level 1 on the standard scale].

Amendment

Section heading: word "badges" in square brackets in both places it occurs substituted by virtue the Transport for London Act 2008, s 11(2).

Words omitted repealed by the Statute Law Revision Act 1891.

Word "badge" in square brackets in each place it occurs substituted by the Transport for London Act 2008, s 11(2).

Words "Transport for London" in square brackets in each place they occur substituted by the Greater London Authority Act 1999, s 253, Sch 20, para 1(2), (3).

Words "to Transport for London" in square brackets substituted by the Greater London Authority Act 1999, s 253, Sch 20, para 1(2), (5).

Words "as Transport for London shall consider reasonable" in square brackets substituted by the Transport for London Act 2008, s 13.

Maximum fine increased by the Criminal Law Act 1977, s 31(6), and converted to a level on the standard scale by the Criminal Justice Act 1982, ss 37, 46.

20 . . .

Amendment

Section repealed by the Forgery and Counterfeiting Act 1981, s 30, Schedule, Pt I.

21 Proprietor to retain the licence of drivers or conductors employed by him, and produce them in case of complaint—Particulars of convictions to be endorsed on licences . . . Every proprietor of a hackney carriage . . . who shall permit or employ any licensed person to act as the driver . . . thereof shall require to be delivered to him, and shall retain in his possession, the licence of such driver . . . while such driver . . . shall remain in his service; and in all cases of complaint where the proprietor of a hackney carriage . . . shall be summoned to produce the driver . . . of such carriage before a justice of the peace he shall also produce the licence of such driver . . . , if at the time of receiving the summons such driver or conductor shall be in his service; and if any driver . . . complained of shall be adjudged guilty of the offence alleged against him the justice of the peace before whom he shall be convicted shall in every case endorse upon the licence of such driver . . . the nature of the offence, and the amount of the penalty inflicted; and every proprietor who shall neglect to require to be delivered to him, and to retain in his possession, the licence of any driver . . . during such period as such driver . . . shall remain in his service, or who shall refuse or neglect to produce such licence as aforesaid, shall for every such offence forfeit [a sum not exceeding level 1 on the standard scale].

Amendment
First words omitted repealed by the Statute Law Revision Act 1891; other words omitted repealed by the Statute Law (Repeals) Act 1976, s 1(1), Sch 1, Pt XVII; penalty increased to £25 by the Criminal Law Act 1977, s 31(6), and converted to level 1 on the standard scale by the Criminal Justice Act 1982, ss 37, 46.

22, 23 . . .

Amendment
Sections repealed by the Statute Law (Repeals) Act 1993, s 1(1), Sch 1, Pt XV, Group 2.

24 Proceedings with respect to licences on quitting service [(1)] . . . When any licensed driver . . . shall leave the service of any proprietor such proprietor shall, upon demand thereof, return to him his licence: Provided always, that if the said proprietor shall have any complaint against the said driver . . . it shall be lawful for such proprietor to retain the licence for [a time which, excluding any day mentioned in subsection (2), does not exceed] twenty-four hours after the demand thereof, and within that time to apply to [a magistrates' court] . . . for a summons against him; and the said proprietor, [when applying] for the summons, shall deposit the licence with the [designated officer for the] [magistrates' court] . . .; and in case any proprietor who upon demand thereof shall have refused or neglected to deliver to any driver . . . his licence shall not within [that time] apply for such summons, and deposit the licence as aforesaid, or shall not appear to prosecute his complaint at the time mentioned in the summons, it shall be lawful for such driver . . . to apply [to a magistrates' court] . . . for a summons against such proprietor; and upon hearing and deciding the case the justice, if he shall think there was no just cause for detaining the licence, or that there has been needless delay on the part of the proprietor in bringing the matter to a hearing, shall have power to order the said proprietor to pay such compensation to the said driver . . . as the said justice shall think reasonable; . . . and the justice shall cause the licence to be delivered to the said driver . . . , unless any misconduct shall be proved against him, by reason whereof the justice shall think that such licence should be revoked or suspended; and so long as any proprietor shall neglect to apply for such summons and deposit the licence, after demand thereof, any justice of the peace may in like manner from time to time order compensation to be paid by him to the same driver . . . ; and no proprietor shall, under any pretext or by virtue of any claim whatever, retain beyond the time aforesaid the licence of his driver . . . .

[(2) The days are—
- (a) Saturday or Sunday;
- (b) Christmas Day or Good Friday;
- (c) a day which is a bank holiday in England and Wales under the Banking and Financial Dealings Act 1971.]

Amendment

Sub-s (1): numbered as such by the Courts Act 2003, s 109(1), Sch 8, para 14(1), (2).

Sub-s (1): first words omitted repealed by the Statute Law Revision Act 1891.

Sub-s (1): second and third words omitted repealed by the Statute Law (Repeals) Act 1976, s 1(1), Sch 1, Pt XVII.

Sub-s (1): words "a time which, excluding any day mentioned in subsection (2), does not exceed" in square brackets substituted by the Courts Act 2003, s 109(1), Sch 8, para 14(1), (3)(a).

Sub-s (1): words "a magistrates' court" in square brackets substituted by the Courts Act 2003, s 109(1), Sch 8, para 14(1), (3)(b).

Sub-s (1): fourth words omitted repealed by the Access to Justice Act 1999, s 106, Sch 15, Pt V, Table (1).

Sub-s (1): words "when applying" in square brackets substituted by the Courts Act 2003, s 109(1), Sch 8, para 14(1), (3)(c).

Sub-s (1): words "designated officer for the" in square brackets substituted by the Courts Act 2003, s 109(1), Sch 8, para 14(1), (3)(d).

Sub-s (1): words "magistrates' court" in square brackets in each place they occur substituted by the Access to Justice Act 1999, s 78(2), Sch 11, para 6(b).

Sub-s (1): fifth words omitted repealed by the Access to Justice Act 1999, s 106, Sch 15, Pt V, Table (1).

Sub-s (1): sixth and seventh words omitted repealed by the Statute Law (Repeals) Act 1976, s 1(1), Sch 1, Pt XVII.

Sub-s (1): words "that time" in square brackets substituted by the Courts Act 2003, s 109(1), Sch 8, para 14(1), (3)(e).

Sub-s (1): words "to a magistrates' court" in square brackets substituted by the Courts Act 2003, s 109(1), Sch 8, para 14(1), (3)(f).

Sub-s (1): eighth words omitted repealed by the Access to Justice Act 1999, s 106, Sch 15, Pt V, Table (1).

Sub-s (1): ninth, tenth, eleventh, twelfth and final words omitted repealed by the Statute Law (Repeals) Act 1976, s 1(1), Sch 1, Pt XVII.

Sub-s (2): inserted by the Courts Act 2003, s 109(1), Sch 8, para 14(1), (4).

25 Licences may be revoked or suspended . . . It shall be lawful for any justice of the peace before whom any driver, . . . shall be convicted of any offence, whether under this Act or any other Act, if such justice in his discretion shall think fit, to revoke the licence of such driver, . . . and also any other licence which he shall hold under the provisions of this Act, or to suspend the same for such time as the justice shall think proper, and for that purpose to require the proprietor, driver, . . . in whose possession such licence and the [badge] thereunto belonging shall then be to deliver up the same; and every proprietor, driver, . . . who, being so required, shall refuse or neglect to deliver up such licence and any such [badge], or either of them, shall forfeit, so often as he shall be so required and refuse or neglect as aforesaid, the sum of [level 1 on the standard scale];

and the justice shall forthwith send such licence and [badge] to [Transport for London], who shall cancel such licence if it has been revoked by the justice, or, if it has been suspended, shall, at the end of the time for which it shall have been suspended, re-deliver such licence, with the [badge], to the person to whom it was granted.

[A magistrates' court that makes an order revoking or suspending any licence under this section may, if the court thinks fit, suspend the effect of the order pending an appeal against the order.]

Amendment
Words omitted repealed by the Statute Law Revision Act 1874 (No 2), the Statute Law Revision Act 1891, and the Statute Law (Repeals) Act 1976.
Word "badge" in square brackets in each place it occurs substituted by the Transport for London Act 2008, s 11(2).
Penalty increased to £25 by the Criminal Law Act 1977, s 31(6), and converted to level 1 on the standard scale by the Criminal Justice Act 1982, ss 37, 46.
Words "Transport for London" in square brackets substituted by the Greater London Authority Act 1999, s 253, Sch 20, para 1(2), (3).
Words from "A magistrates' court" to "against the order." in square brackets inserted by the Transport Act 1985, s 139(2), Sch 7, para 2.

26 . . .

Amendment
Section repealed by the Revenue Act 1869, s 39, Sch (E).

27 No person to act as driver, etc of any carriage without the consent of the proprietor . . . Every driver . . . authorized by any proprietor to act as driver of any hackney carriage, . . . who shall suffer any other person to act as driver of such hackney carriage without the consent of the proprietor thereof, and also every person, whether duly licensed or not, who shall act as driver . . . of any such carriage without the consent of the proprietor thereof, shall forfeit the sum of [level 1 on the standard scale]; and every driver . . . charged with such offence who, when required by a justice of the peace so to do, shall not truly make known the name and place of abode of the person so suffered by him to act as driver . . . without consent of the proprietor, and also the number of the [badge] of such person (if licensed), shall be liable to a further penalty of [level 1 on the standard scale]; and it shall be lawful for any police constable, [if necessary, to take charge of the carriage and every horse in charge of any person unlawfully acting as driver and to deposit the same in some place of safe custody until the same can be applied for by the proprietor].

Amendment
First words omitted repealed by the Statute Law Revision Act 1874 (No 2), and the Statute Law Revision Act 1891.
Other words omitted repealed by the Statute Law (Repeals) Act 1976, s 1(1), Sch 1, Pt XVII.

Maximum fine increased by the Criminal Law Act 1977, s 31(6), and converted to a level on the standard scale by the Criminal Justice Act 1982, ss 37, 46.

Word "badge" in square brackets substituted by the Transport for London Act 2008, s 11(2).

Words from "if necessary, to take charge" to "by the proprietor" in square brackets substituted by the Police and Criminal Evidence Act 1984, s 119, Sch 6, para 4.

28 Punishment for furious driving, and wilful misbehaviour—Compensation for injury, etc—Proprietor paying compensation may recover from driver, etc . . . Every driver of a hackney carriage . . . who shall be guilty of wanton or furious driving, or who by carelessness or wilful misbehaviour shall cause any hurt or damage to any person or property being in any street or highway, and also every driver, . . . who during his employment shall be drunk, or shall make use of any insulting or abusive language, or shall be guilty of any insulting gesture or any misbehaviour, shall for every such offence [of which he is convicted before the justice] forfeit the sum of [level 1 on the standard scale]; *or it shall be lawful for the justice before whom such complaint shall be brought, if in his discretion he shall think proper, instead of inflicting such penalty, forthwith to commit the offender to prison for any period not exceeding two calendar months* . . .

Amendment

First, second, third and final words omitted repealed by the Statute Law Revision Act 1874 (No 2), the Statute Law Revision Act 1891, the Statute Law (Repeals) Act 1976 and the Statute Law (Repeals) Act 1993.

Words "of which he is convicted before the justice" in square brackets prospectively inserted by the Criminal Justice Act 2003, s 304, Sch 32, Pt 2, para 147.

£3 penalty increased to £25 by the Criminal Law Act 1977, s 31(6), and converted to level 1 on the standard scale by the Criminal Justice Act 1982, ss 37, 46.

Words from "; or it shall" to "two calendar months" in italics prospectively repealed by the Criminal Justice Act 2003, s 332, Sch 37, Pt 9.

29 . . .

Amendment

Section repealed by the London Government Act 1963, ss 83(1), 93(1), Sch 17, para 29, Sch 18, Pt II.

30 . . .

Amendment

Section repealed by the Statute Law (Repeals) Act 1976, s 1(1), Sch 1, Pt XVII.

31 . . .

Amendment

Section repealed by the Statute Law Revision Act 1966.

32 ...

Amendment

Section repealed by the Statute Law (Repeals) Act 1973, s 1(1), Sch 1, Pt VI.

33 Penalty on drivers for loitering or causing any obstruction, etc ...
Every driver of a hackney carriage who shall ply for hire elsewhere than at some standing or place appointed for that purpose, or who by loitering or by any wilful misbehaviour shall cause any obstruction in or upon any public street, road, or place, . . . and every driver of a hackney carriage, whether hired or unhired, allowing any person beside himself, not being the hirer or a person employed by such hirer, to ride on the driving box, . . . shall for every such offence forfeit [a sum not exceeding level 1 on the standard scale].

Amendment

First words omitted repealed by the Statute Law Revision Act 1891.

Second and third words omitted repealed by the Statute Law (Repeals) Act 1976, s 1(1), Sch 1, Pt XVII.

Maximum fine increased by the Criminal Law Act 1967, s 92(1), Sch 3, Pt I, and converted to a level on the standard scale by the Criminal Justice Act 1982, ss 37, 38, 46.

34 ...

Amendment

Section repealed by the Statute Law Revision Act 1874 (No 2).

35 ...

Amendment

Section repealed by the Statute Law (Repeals) Act 1993, s 1(1), Sch 1, Pt XV, Group 2.

36, 37 ...

Amendment

Sections repealed by the Statute Law (Repeals) Act 1976, s 1(1), Sch 1, Pt XVII.

38 Complaints to be made within [twenty eight] . . . All complaints under the provisions of the London Hackney Carriage Act 1831, or of this Act, or of the orders and regulations made in pursuance of either of them, . . . shall be made within seven days next after the day on which the cause of complaint shall have arisen.

Amendment

Section heading: words "twenty eight" in square brackets substituted by the Transport for London Act 2008, s 14.

First words omitted repealed by the Statute Law Revision Act 1891; second words omitted repealed by the Statute Law (Repeals) Act 1976, s 1(1), Sch 1, Pt XVII.

39 Justices may hear complaints and award penalties . . . It shall be lawful for any justice of the peace to hear and determine all complaints under the provisions of this Act or of the London Hackney Carriage Act 1831, and to adjudge the payment of any penalty or of any sum of money under either of the said Acts, or of the orders and regulations made pursuant to either of them, and to order payment of the same, with or without costs, either immediately, or at such time and place, and by such instalments, as he shall think fit; . . .

Amendment
First words omitted repealed by the Statute Law Revision Act 1891; second words omitted repealed by the Statute Law (Repeals) Act 1976, s 1(1), Sch 1, Pt XVII.

40–43 . . .

Amendment
Section repealed by the Statute Law (Repeals) Act 1976, s 1(1), Sch 1, Pt XVII.

44 Where there are more proprietors than one alone may be proceeded against . . . In every case where there shall be more than one proprietor of any hackney carriage . . . it shall be sufficient, in any information, summons, order, conviction, warrant, or any other proceeding under the provisions of this Act, or of the London Hackney Carriage Act 1831, to name one of such proprietors without reference to any other or others of them, and to describe and proceed against him as if he were sole proprietor.

Amendment
First words omitted repealed by the Statute Law Revision Act 1891; second words omitted repealed by the Statute Law (Repeals) Act 1976, s 1(1), Sch 1, Pt XVII.

45, 46 . . .

Amendment
Section repealed by the Statute Law (Repeals) Act 1976, s 1(1), Sch 1, Pt XVII.

47 . . .

Amendment
Section repealed by the Public Authorities Protection Act 1893, s 2, Schedule.

48 . . .

Amendment
Section repealed by the Statute Law Revision Act 1959.

SCHEDULE

. . .

Amendment
Schedule repealed by the Statute Law (Repeals) Act 1976, s 1(1), Sch 1, Pt XVII.

London Hackney Carriages Act 1850

1 . . .

Amendment
Section repealed by the Statute Law Revision Act 1875.

2 . . .

Amendment
Section repealed by the Statute Law (Repeals) Act 2004, s 1(1), Sch 1, Pt 14.

3 . . .

Amendment
Section repealed by the Statute Law Revision Act 1891.

4 Standings for hackney carriages to be appointed and regulated by [Transport for London] . . . It shall be lawful for [Transport for London] from time to time to appoint standings for hackney carriages at such places as they shall think convenient in any street, thoroughfare, or place of public resort within the metropolitan police district, any law, statute, or custom to the contrary thereof notwithstanding, and at their discretion to alter the same, and from time to time to make regulations concerning the boundaries of the same, and the number of carriages to be allowed at any such standing, and the times at and during which they may stand and ply for hire at any such standing, and also from time to time to make such regulations as [Transport for London] shall deem proper for enforcing order at every such standing, and for removing any person who shall unnecessarily loiter or remain at or about any such standing; and [Transport for London] shall cause all the orders and regulations to be made by them as aforesaid to be advertised in the London Gazette, and a copy thereof, [signed by a person authorised for the purpose by Transport for London], to be hung up for public inspection in [the offices of Transport for London], and at each of the [magistrates' courts acting for an area falling wholly within an inner London borough]; and such copy shall be received in evidence in the said courts as if it were the original of which it purports to be a copy, and shall be taken to be a true copy of such original order or regulation, without further proof than [the aforesaid signature].

Amendment
Words "Transport for London" in square brackets in section heading substituted by virtue of the Greater London Authority Act 1999, s 253, Sch 20, paras 2(1), (2)(a), 11.
Words omitted repealed by the Statute Law Revision Act 1891.

Words "Transport for London" in square brackets in each place they occur substituted by the Greater London Authority Act 1999, s 253, Sch 20, paras 2(1), (2)(a), 11.

Words "signed by a person authorised for the purpose by Transport for London" in square brackets substituted by the Greater London Authority Act 1999, s 253, Sch 20, paras 2(1), (2)(b), 11.

Words "the offices of Transport for London" in square brackets substituted by the Greater London Authority Act 1999, s 253, Sch 20, paras 2(1), (2)(c), 11.

Words from "magistrates' courts acting" to "an inner London borough" in square brackets substituted by the Access to Justice Act 1999, s 78(2), Sch 11, para 7.

Words "the aforesaid signature" in square brackets substituted by the Greater London Authority Act 1999, s 253, Sch 20, paras 2(1), (2)(d), 11.

5 . . .

Amendment

Section repealed by the Statute Law Revision Act 1892.

6 . . .

Amendment

Section repealed by the Statute Law (Repeals) Act 1981.

7 . . .

Amendment

Section repealed by the Statute Law Revision Act 1892.

8 This Act to be construed with 6 & 7 Vict c 86 . . . This Act shall be construed as one Act with the London Hackney Carriages Act 1843, and . . . all the provisions of the said Act, except so far as is herein otherwise provided, shall extend to this Act, and to all things done in execution of this Act.

Amendment

Words omitted repealed by the Statute Law Revision Act 1891.

9, 10 . . .

Amendment

Sections repealed by the Statute Law Revision Act 1875.

London Hackney Carriage Act 1853

1 . . .

Amendment
Section repealed by the Statute Law Revision Act 1892.

2 If carriages not in fit condition licences may be suspended [(1)] It shall be lawful for [Transport for London] to cause an inspection to be made, as often as they deem it necessary, of all . . . hackney carriages, and of the horse or horses used in drawing the same, within the limits of this Act; and if any such carriage, or the horse or horses used in drawing the same, shall at any time be in a condition unfit for public use, [Transport for London] shall give notice in writing accordingly to the proprietor thereof, [which notice—
    (a) shall be personally served on the proprietor or delivered at his usual place of residence, and
    (b) may be personally served on the driver of the carriage;

and if, after notice has been served on the proprietor or driver as mentioned in paragraph (a) or (b), the carriage is used or let to hire as a hackney carriage, or the horse is, or the horses are, used or let, whilst in a condition unfit for public use], [Transport for London] shall have power to suspend, for such time as they may deem proper, the licence of the proprietor of such carriage . . ..

[(2) A proprietor of a hackney carriage whose licence is suspended under subsection (1) shall not be guilty of an offence under section 7 of the Metropolitan Public Carriage Act 1869 (c 115) in respect of the carriage unless he has been given written notice in accordance with subsection (1).]

Amendment
Sub-s (1): numbered as such by the Transport for London Act 2008, s 16(1), (2).

Sub-s (1): first words omitted repealed by the Statute Law (Repeals) Act 1976, s 1(1), Sch 1, Pt XVII; second words omitted repealed by the Statute Law Revision Act 1892.

Sub-s (1): words "Transport for London" in square brackets in each place they occur substituted by the Greater London Authority Act 1999, s 253, Sch 20, paras 3(1), (2), 12.

Sub-s (1): words from "which notice—" to "for public use" in square brackets substituted by the Transport for London Act 2008, s 16(1), (3).

Sub-s (2): inserted by the Transport for London Act 2008, s 16(1), (4).

3 . . .

Amendment
Section repealed by the Statute Law Revision Act 1892.

4-6 ...

Amendment
Sections repealed by the Statute Law (Repeals) Act 1973, s 1(1), Sch 1, Pt VI.

7 Distances, etc which drivers of hackney carriages shall be required to drive The driver of every hackney carriage which shall ply for hire at any place within the limits of this Act shall (unless such driver have a reasonable excuse, to be allowed by the justice before whom the matter shall be brought in question,) drive such hackney carriage to any place to which he shall be required by the hirer thereof to drive the same, not exceeding six miles from the place where the same shall have been hired, or for any time not exceeding one hour from the time when hired: ...

Amendment
Words omitted repealed by the Statute Law (Repeals) Act 1973, s 1(1), Sch 1, Pt VI.

8 ...

Amendment
Section repealed by the Statute Law Revision Act 1892.

9 Number of persons to be carried ... *The driver of any such hackney carriage shall, if required by the hirer thereof, carry in and by such carriage the number of persons painted or marked thereon, or any less number of persons.*

Amendment
Repealed, in relation to tramcars and trolley vehicles, by the Transport Charges &c (Miscellaneous Provisions) Act 1954, s 14(1), Sch 2, Pt IV.
Words omitted repealed by the Statute Law Revision Act 1892.

10 A reasonable quantity of luggage to be carried The driver of every hackney carriage within the limits of this Act shall carry in or upon such carriage a reasonable quantity of luggage for every person hiring such carriage ...

Amendment
Words omitted repealed by the Statute Law (Repeals) Act 1973, s 1(1), Sch 1, Pt VI.

11 ...

Amendment
Section repealed by the Statute Law (Repeals) Act 1976, s 1(1), Sch 1, Pt XVII.

12, 13 ...

Amendment
Sections repealed by the Statute Law (Repeals) Act 1993, s 1(1), Sch 1, Pt XV, Group 2.

14, 15 . . .

Amendment
Sections repealed by the Statute Law (Repeals) Act 1976, s 1(1), Sch 1, Pt XVII.

16 Pictures, advertisements, etc, not to be carried in thoroughfares It shall not be lawful for any person to carry about on any carriage or on horseback or on foot, in any thoroughfare or public place within the limits of this Act, to the obstruction or annoyance of the inhabitants or passengers, any picture, placard, notice, or advertisement, whether written, printed, or painted upon or posted or attached to any part of such carriage, or on any board, or otherwise.

17 Drivers liable to penalties for certain offences . . . the driver of any hackney carriage, who shall . . . commit any of the following offences within the limits of this Act, shall be liable to a penalty not exceeding [level 3 on the standard scale] for each offence, . . . :

1   Every driver of a hackney carriage who shall demand or take more than the proper fare . . . , or who shall refuse to admit and carry in his carriage the number of persons painted or marked on such carriage or specified in the certificate granted by [Transport for London] in respect of such carriage, or who shall refuse to carry by his carriage a reasonable quantity of luggage for any person hiring or intending to hire such carriage:

2   Every driver of a hackney carriage who shall refuse to drive such carriage to any place within the limits of this Act, not exceeding six miles, to which he shall be required to drive any person hiring or intending to hire such carriage, or who shall refuse to drive any such carriage for any time not exceeding one hour, if so required by any person hiring or intending to hire such carriage, or who shall not drive the same at a reasonable and proper speed, not less than six miles an hour, except in cases of unavoidable delay, or when required by the hirer thereof to drive at any slower pace:

3   Every driver of a hackney carriage who shall ply for hire with any carriage or horse which shall be at the time unfit for public use . . .

Amendment
First and second words omitted repealed by the Statute Law (Repeals) Act 1976, s 1(1), Sch 1, Pt XVII.
Maximum penalty increased and converted to a level on the standard scale by the Criminal Justice Act 1982, ss 37, 39, 46, Sch 3.
Third words omitted repealed by the Statute Law (Repeals) Act 1976, s 1(1), Sch 1, Pt XVII, and the Summary Jurisdiction Act 1884, s 4.
In para 1 words omitted repealed by the Statute Law (Repeals) 1973.
In para 1 words "Transport for London" in square brackets substituted by the Greater London Authority Act 1999, s 253, Sch 20, para 3(1), (3).
In para 3 words omitted repealed by the Summary Jurisdiction Act 1884, s 4.

18 Jurisdiction of police magistrates It shall be lawful for [two justices of the peace] to hear and determine all offences against the provisions of this Act,

and also all disputes or causes of complaint that may arise out of the same;
... ...

Amendment

Words "two justices of the peace" in square brackets substituted by the Access to Justice Act 1999, s 78(2), Sch 11, para 8(a).

First words omitted repealed by the Access to Justice Act 1999, ss 78(2), 106, Sch 11, para 8(b), Sch 15, Pt V, Table (3).

Second words omitted repealed by the Access to Justice Act 1999, s 106, Sch 15, Pt V, Table (1).

Final words omitted repealed by the London Cab Act 1896, s 2.

19 Penalty for offences against Act For every offence against the provisions of this Act, for which no special penalty is herein-before appointed, the offender shall be liable to a penalty not exceeding [level 1 on the standard scale], ...

Amendment

Words omitted repealed by the Summary Jurisdiction Act 1884, s 4, Schedule, and the Statute Law (Repeals) Act 1976; maximum penalty increased and converted to a level on the standard scale by the Criminal Justice Act 1982, ss 37, 38, 46.

20 Powers of Commissioners of Police Limits of Act [In this Act] the words "the limits of this Act" shall include every part of the Metropolitan Police District and City of London.

Amendment

Words in square brackets substituted by the Greater London Authority Act 1999, s 253, Sch 20, para 3(1), (4).

21 Construction This Act shall be construed as one Act with the London Hackney Carriages Act 1843 and the Act passed in the thirteenth year of the reign of her Majesty, chapter seven; and all the provisions of the said Acts, except so far as is herein otherwise provided, shall extend to this Act, and to all things done in execution of this Act.

22 ...

Amendment

Section repealed by the Statute Law Revision Act 1892.

SCHEDULE (A)

...

Amendment

Schedule repealed by the Statute Law (Repeals) Act 1973, s 1(1), Sch 1, Pt VI.

SCHEDULE (B)

. . .

___

Amendment
Schedule repealed by the Statute Law Revision Act 1892.

SCHEDULE (C)

. . .

___

Amendment
Schedule repealed by the Statute Law Revision Act 1892.

Metropolitan Public Carriage Act 1869

1 Short title This Act may be cited for all purposes as "The Metropolitan Public Carriage Act 1869".

2 Limits of Act The limits of this Act shall be the metropolitan police district, and the city of London . . .

Amendment

Words omitted repealed by the Statute Law (Repeals) Act 1989.

3 . . .

Amendment

Repealed by the Statute Law Revision (No 2) Act 1893.

4 Interpretation In this Act "stage carriage" shall mean any carriage for the conveyance of passengers which plies for hire in any public street, road, or place within the limits of this Act, and in which the passengers or any of them are charged to pay separate and distinct or at the rate of separate and distinct fares for their respective places or seats therein.

"Hackney carriage" shall mean any carriage for the conveyance of passengers which plies for hire within the limits of this Act, and is [neither a stage carriage nor a tramcar].

["London cab order" shall mean an order made by Transport for London.

"Prescribed" shall mean prescribed by London cab order.]

[Any power to make a London cab order under this Act includes power to vary or revoke a previous such order.]

Amendment

In definition "Hackney carriage" words "neither a stage carriage nor a tramcar" in square brackets substituted by the Transport and Works Act 1992, s 62(1).

Definitions "London cab order" and "Prescribed" substituted for definition "Prescribed" as originally enacted by the Greater London Authority Act 1999, s 253, Sch 20, paras 5(1), (2)(a), 14.

Words from "Any power to" to "previous such order." in square brackets inserted by the Greater London Authority Act 1999, s 253, Sch 20, paras 5(1), (2)(b), 14.

5 . . .

Amendment

Section repealed by the Statute Law (Repeals) Act 1976, s 1(1), Sch 1, Pt XVII.

Licensing Hackney and Stage Carriages

[6 Grant of hackney carriage licences (1) Transport for London shall have
the function of licensing to ply for hire within the limits of this Act hackney carriages, to be distinguished in such manner as may be prescribed.

(2) A licence under this section may—
    (a) be granted on such conditions,
    (b) be in such form,
    (c) be subject to revocation or suspension in such event, and
    (d) generally be dealt with in such manner,

as may be prescribed.

(3) Subsection (2) of this section is subject to the following provisions of this
section.

(4) A licence under this section shall, if not revoked or suspended, be in force
for one year.

(5) A fee of such amount (if any) as Transport for London may determine shall
be paid to Transport for London—
    (a) by any applicant for a licence under this section, on making the applica-
         tion for the licence;
    (b) by any applicant for the taking or re-taking of any test or examination,
         or any part of a test or examination, with respect to any matter of fit-
         ness, on making the application for the taking or re-taking of the test,
         examination or part; and
    (c) by any person granted a licence under this section, on the grant of the
         licence.

(6) In paragraph (b) of subsection (5) of this section "matter of fitness" means—
    (a) any matter as respects which Transport for London must be satisfied
         before granting a licence under this section; or
    (b) any matter such that, if Transport for London is not satisfied with
         respect to the matter, they may refuse to grant a licence under this sec-
         tion.

(7) Different amounts may be determined under subsection (5) of this section
for different purposes or different cases.

(8) Transport for London may remit or refund the whole or part of a fee under
subsection (5) of this section.

(9) Provision shall be made by London cab order—
    (a) for the transfer of a licence under this section to the [surviving spouse or
         surviving civil partner] or to any child of full age of any person to whom
         such a licence has been granted who may die during the continuance of
         the licence leaving a [surviving spouse or surviving civil partner] or child
         of full age; . . .
    (b) . . ..]

Amendment

Section substituted by the Greater London Authority Act 1999, s 253, Sch 20, paras 5(1), (3), 14.

Sub-s (9): in para (a) words "surviving spouse or surviving civil partner" in square brackets substituted by the Marriage (Same Sex Couples) Act 2013 (Consequential and Contrary Provisions and Scotland) Order 2014, SI 2014/560, art 2, Sch 1, para 1(a)(i).

Sub-s (9): in para (a) word omitted repealed by the Marriage (Same Sex Couples) Act 2013 (Consequential and Contrary Provisions and Scotland) Order 2014, SI 2014/560, art 2, Sch 1, para 1(a)(ii).

Sub-s (9): para (b) repealed by the Marriage (Same Sex Couples) Act 2013 (Consequential and Contrary Provisions and Scotland) Order 2014, SI 2014/560, art 2, Sch 1, para 1(b).

7 Penalty on use of unlicensed carriage If any unlicensed hackney . . . carriage plies for hire, the owner of such carriage shall be liable to a penalty not exceeding five pounds for every day during which such unlicensed carriage plies. And if any unlicensed hackney carriage is found on any stand within the limits of this Act, the owner of such carriage shall be liable to a penalty not exceeding five pounds for each time it is so found. The driver also shall in every such case be liable to a like penalty unless he proves that he was ignorant of the fact of the carriage being an unlicensed carriage.

Any hackney . . . carriage plying for hire, and any hackney carriage found on any stand without having such distinguishing mark, or being otherwise distinguished in such manner as may for the time being be prescribed . . ., shall be deemed to be an unlicensed carriage.

Amendment

First and second words omitted repealed by the Statute Law (Repeals) Act 1976, s 1(1), Sch 1, Pt XVII.

Maximum penalty on any conviction now level 4 on the standard scale by virtue of the Criminal Justice Act 1967, s 92(1), Sch 3, Part I, and the Criminal Justice Act 1982, ss 37, 39, 46, Sch 3.

Final words omitted repealed by the Greater London Authority Act 1999, ss 253, 423, Sch 20, paras 5(1), (4), 14, Sch 34, Pt V.

Licensing Drivers of Hackney and Stage Carriages

[8 Hackney carriage to be driven by licensed drivers (1) Transport for London shall have the function of licensing persons to be drivers of hackney carriages.

(2) No hackney carriage shall ply for hire within the limits of this Act unless under the charge of a driver having a licence under this section from Transport for London.

(3) If any hackney carriage plies for hire in contravention of this section—
    (a) the person driving the carriage, and
    (b) the owner of the carriage, unless he proves that the driver acted without his privity or consent,

shall each be liable to a penalty not exceeding level 3 on the standard scale.

(4) Transport for London may send to the Commissioner of Police of the Metropolis or the Commissioner of Police for the City of London—

  (a) details of a person to whom Transport for London is considering granting a licence under this section, and

  (b) a request for the Commissioner's observations;

and the Commissioner shall respond to the request.

(5) A licence under this section may—

  (a) be granted on such conditions,

  (b) be in such form,

  (c) be subject to revocation or suspension in such event, and

  (d) generally be dealt with in such manner,

as may be prescribed.

(6) Subsection (5) of this section is subject to the following provisions of this section.

(7) [Subject to section 8A, a] licence under this section shall, if not revoked or suspended, be in force for three years.

(8) A fee of such amount (if any) as Transport for London may determine shall be paid to Transport for London—

  (a) by any applicant for a licence under this section, on making the application for the licence;

  (b) by any applicant for the taking or re-taking of any test or examination, or any part of a test or examination, with respect to any matter of fitness, on making the application for the taking or re-taking of the test, examination or part; and

  (c) by any person granted a licence under this section, on the grant of the licence.

(9) In paragraph (b) of subsection (8) of this section "matter of fitness" means—

  (a) any matter as respects which Transport for London must be satisfied before granting a licence under this section; or

  (b) any matter such that, if Transport for London is not satisfied with respect to the matter, they may refuse to grant a licence under this section.]

(10) Different amounts may be determined under subsection (8) of this section for different purposes or different cases.

(11) Transport for London may remit or refund the whole or part of a fee under subsection (8) of this section.]

Amendment

Section substituted by the Greater London Authority Act 1999, s 253, Sch 20, paras 5(1), (5), 14.

Sub-s (7): words "Subject to section 8A, a" in square brackets substituted by the Immigration Act 2016, s 37, Sch 5, paras 2, 3.

[8A Drivers' licences for persons subject to immigration control (1) Subsection (2) applies if—

    (a) a licence under section 8 is to be granted to a person who has been granted leave to enter or remain in the United Kingdom for a limited period ("the leave period"),

    (b) the person's leave has not been extended by virtue of section 3C of the Immigration Act 1971 (continuation of leave pending variation decision), and

    (c) apart from subsection (2), the period for which the licence would have been in force would have ended after the end of the leave period.

(2) Transport for London must grant the licence for a period which ends at or before the end of the leave period.

(3) Subsection (4) applies if—

    (a) a licence under section 8 is to be granted to a person who has been granted leave to enter or remain in the United Kingdom for a limited period, and

    (b) the person's leave has been extended by virtue of section 3C of the Immigration Act 1971 (continuation of leave pending variation decision).

(4) Transport for London must grant the licence for a period that does not exceed six months.

(5) A licence under section 8 ceases to be in force if the person to whom it was granted becomes disqualified by reason of the person's immigration status from driving a hackney carriage.

(6) If a licence granted in accordance with subsection (2) or (4) expires, the person to whom it was granted must, within the period of 7 days beginning with the day after that on which it expired, return to Transport for London—

    (a) the licence,

    (b) the person's copy of the licence (if any), and

    (c) the person's driver's badge.

(7) If subsection (5) applies to a licence, the person to whom it was granted must, within the period of 7 days beginning with the day after the day on which the person first became disqualified, return to Transport for London—

    (a) the licence,

    (b) the person's copy of the licence (if any), and

    (c) the person's driver's badge.

(8) A person who, without reasonable excuse, contravenes subsection (6) or (7) is guilty of an offence and liable on summary conviction—

    (a) to a fine not exceeding level 3 on the standard scale, and

    (b) in the case of a continuing offence, to a fine not exceeding ten pounds for each day during which an offence continues after conviction.

(9) The Secretary of State may by regulations made by statutory instrument amend the amount for the time being specified in subsection (8)(b).

(10) Regulations under subsection (9) may make transitional, transitory or saving provision.

(11) A statutory instrument containing regulations under subsection (9) may not be made unless a draft of the instrument has been laid before, and approved by a resolution of, each House of Parliament.

(12) For the purposes of this section a person is disqualified by reason of the person's immigration status from driving a hackney carriage if the person is subject to immigration control and—

    (a) the person has not been granted leave to enter or remain in the United Kingdom, or

    (b) the person's leave to enter or remain in the United Kingdom—

        (i) is invalid,

        (ii) has ceased to have effect (whether by reason of curtailment, revocation, cancellation, passage of time or otherwise), or

        (iii) is subject to a condition preventing the person from driving a hackney carriage.

(13) Where a person is on immigration bail within the meaning of Part 1 of Schedule 10 to the Immigration Act 2016—

    (a) the person is to be treated for the purposes of this section as if the person had been granted leave to enter the United Kingdom, but

    (b) any condition as to the person's work in the United Kingdom to which the person's immigration bail is subject is to be treated for those purposes as a condition of leave.

(14) For the purposes of this section a person is subject to immigration control if under the Immigration Act 1971 the person requires leave to enter or remain in the United Kingdom.]

Amendment
Section inserted by the Immigration Act 2016, s 37, Sch 5, paras 2, 4.

Regulations relating to Hackney and Stage Carriages

9 Regulations as to hackney and stage carriages [Transport for London may from time to time by London cab order] make regulations for all or any of the following purposes; that is to say,

(1) For regulating *the number of persons to be carried in any hackney . . . carriage*, and in what manner such number is to be shown on such carriage, and how such hackney carriages are to be furnished or fitted:

(2) For fixing the stands of hackney carriages, . . . and the persons to attend at such stands:

(3) For fixing the rates or fares, as well for time as distance, to be paid for hackney carriages, and for securing the due publication of such fares; . . .

(4) For forming, in the case of hackney carriages, a table of distances, as evidence for the purpose of any fare to be charged by distance, by the preparation of a book, map, or plan, or any combination of a book, map, or plan:

(5) For securing the safe custody and re-delivery of any property accidentally left in hackney . . . carriages and fixing the charges to be paid in respect thereof, with power to cause such property to be sold or to be given to the finder in the event of its not being claimed within a certain time:

Subject to the following restrictions:—

(1) In fixing the stands for hackney carriages within the city of London . . . the consent of the Court of the Lord Mayor and Aldermen shall be required to any stand appointed by [Transport for London]:

(2), (3) . . .

[(4) Any power of Transport for London to fix by regulations made by London cab order under this section any rates or fares to be paid for hackney carriages is exercisable subject to and in accordance with any directions given to Transport for London by the Mayor of London as to the basis on which those rates or fares are to be calculated.]

Amendment

Words "Transport for London may from time to time by London cab order" in square brackets substituted by the Greater London Authority Act 1999, s 253, Sch 20, paras 5(1), (6)(a), 14.

Words from "the number of persons" to "carriage, and" repealed, in relation to tramcars or trolley vehicles by the Transport Charges etc (Miscellaneous Provisions) Act 1954, s 14(1), Sch 2, Pt IV.

Words omitted repealed by the Road Transport Lighting Act 1927, s 11(1), Schedule, the Statute Law Revision Act 1966, the London Cab Act 1968, s 5(2), the Statute Law (Repeals) Act 1973, the Statute Law (Repeals) Act 1976 and the Statute Law (Repeals) Act 1989.

In para (1) of the restrictions words "Transport for London" in square brackets substituted by the Greater London Authority Act 1999, s 253, Sch 20, paras 5(1), (6)(b), 14.

Para (4) of the restrictions inserted by the Greater London Authority Act 1999, s 253, Sch 20, paras 5(1), (6)(c), 14.

---

10 Penalties of breach of regulations [Where Transport for London is authorised to make a London cab order under this Act, Transport for London] may annex a penalty not exceeding [level 1 on the standard scale or not exceeding a lesser amount] for the breach of such order or of any part or parts thereof, or of any regulation or regulations thereby made; and any penalties under this section shall be deemed to be penalties under this Act, and may be enforced accordingly.

Amendment

Words from "Where Transport for" to "Transport for London" in square brackets substituted by the Greater London Authority Act 1999, s 253, Sch 20, paras 5(1), (7), 14.

Maximum penalty increased and converted to a reference to the standard scale by the Criminal Justice Act 1982, ss 37, 40, 46.

[11 Grant of licences by other persons at direction of TFL [Any licence which may be granted by Transport for London under this Act may, if Transport for London so directs, be granted by such person as may be appointed for the purpose in the direction.]

Amendment

Section substituted by the Greater London Authority Act 1999, s 253, Sch 20, paras 5(1), (8), 14.

12 Powers to carry Act into execution [Transport for London] may appoint such officers and constables of the metropolitan police force, and for the city of London of the city police, as [Transport for London] thinks fit to perform any duties required to be performed for the purposes of carrying this Act into execution, and may award such sums by way of compensation for their services out of the monies raised under this Act as [Transport for London] may think just.

Amendment

Words "Transport for London" in square brackets in each place they occur substituted by the Greater London Authority Act 1999, s 253, Sch 20, paras 5(1), (9), 14.

Legal Proceedings and Miscellaneous

13 Recovery of penalties All penalties under this Act may be recovered -summarily . . .

Amendment

Words omitted repealed by the Statute Law (Repeals) Act 1989.

14 Placard, etc may be affixed to lamp post [Transport for London] may cause to be attached to any lamp post any placard or signal for the purpose of -carrying into effect the provisions of this Act.

Amendment

Words "Transport for London" in square brackets substituted by the Greater London Authority Act 1999, s 253, Sch 20, paras 5(1), (10), 14.

15 Existing Acts to continue in force All the provisions of the Acts relating to hackney carriages . . . in force at the time of the commencement of this Act shall, subject to any alteration made therein by this Act or [by any London cab order] made in pursuance of this Act, continue in force, and all such provisions of the said Acts as relate to licences granted under those Acts, or any of them, shall, subject to any alteration as aforesaid, apply to licences granted under this Act.

Amendment

Words omitted repealed by the Statute Law (Repeals) Act 1976, s 1(1), Sch 1, Pt XVII.

Words "by any London cab order" in square brackets substituted by the Greater London Authority Act 1999, s 253, Sch 20, paras 5(1), (11), 14.

London Cab Act 1896

1 Penalties for defrauding cabmen If any person commits any of the following offences with respect to a cab, namely:—

    (a) hires a cab, knowing or having reason to believe that he cannot pay the lawful fare, or with intent to avoid payment of the lawful fare; or

    (b) fraudulently endeavours to avoid payment of a fare lawfully due from him; or

    (c) having failed or refused to pay a fare lawfully due from him, either refuses to give to the driver an address at which he can be found, or, with intent to deceive, gives a false address,

he shall be liable on summary conviction to pay, in addition to the lawful fare, a fine not exceeding [level 1 on the standard scale], or, in the discretion of the court, to be imprisoned for a term not exceeding fourteen days; and the whole or any part of any fine imposed may be applied in compensation to the driver.

Amendment

Maximum fine increased and converted to a level on the standard scale by the Criminal Justice Act 1982, ss 37, 38, 46.

2 . . .

Amendment

Section repealed by the Statute Law Revision Act 1950, s 1(1), First Schedule.

3 Meaning of cab In this Act the expression "cab" shall mean any hackney carriage within the meaning of the Metropolitan Public Carriage Act 1869.

4 Short title This Act may be cited as the London Cab Act 1896.

London Cab and Stage Carriage Act 1907

1 Fares for taximeter cabs (1) [Transport for London] shall have power by regulations made [by London cab order] under section nine of the Metropolitan Public Carriage Act 1869 to fix the fares to be paid for the hire in London of cabs fitted with taximeters, either on the basis of time or distance or both, and so as to differ for different classes of cabs and under different circumstances. . . .

(2) . . .

[(3) The power conferred by subsection (1) of this section is subject to paragraph (4) of the restrictions specified in section nine of the said Act of 1869.]

[(4) The fare for a cab journey starting within London but ending outside London shall be—
  (a) such fare as may be agreed between the driver and the passenger—
      (i) before the commencement of the journey, or
      (ii) where, after the commencement of the journey, the driver and the passenger agree to change the destination of the journey, at the time when the destination of the journey is changed, or
  (b) if no fare is so agreed, the fare shown on the taximeter.

(5) A driver of a cab who demands or takes more than the proper fare for a journey undertaken as mentioned in subsection (4) of this section is guilty of an offence and liable on summary conviction to a fine not exceeding level 3 on the standard scale.]

Amendment
Sub-s (1): words "Transport for London" in square brackets substituted by the Greater London Authority Act 1999, s 253, Sch 20, paras 6(1), (2)(a), 15(1).
Sub-s (1): words "by London cab order" in square brackets inserted by the Greater London Authority Act 1999, s 253, Sch 20, paras 6(1), (2)(b), 15(1).
Sub-s (1): words omitted repealed by the Statute Law (Repeals) Act 1973, s 1(1), Sch 1, Pt VI.
Sub-s (2): repealed by the Statute Law (Repeals) Act 1976, s 1(1), Sch 1, Pt XVII.
Sub-s (3): inserted by the Greater London Authority Act 1999, s 253, Sch 20, paras 6(1), (3), 15(1).
Sub-ss (4), (5): inserted by the Transport for London Act 2008, s 15.

2 Abolition of privileged cab system (1) In the admission of cabs to a railway station, or in the treatment of cabs while in a railway station, the company having the control of the station shall not show any preference to any cab, or give any cab a privilege, which is not given to other cabs; and where any charge is made in respect of the admission of any cab to a railway station for the purpose of plying for hire therein, the charge made shall not exceed such sum as may be allowed by [Transport for London].

(2) If it is proved to the satisfaction of [Transport for London] that it will not be possible to obtain a sufficient supply of cabs at a railway station for the proper accommodation of the public, unless the operation of this section is suspended or modified as respects that section, [Transport for London] may [by London cab order] so modify or suspend the operation of this section with respect to that station, subject to such conditions as may be specified in the order.

(3) In this section the expression "railway station" includes the precincts thereof and the approaches thereto.

(4) Nothing in this section shall affect the liability of cabs or the drivers thereof to comply with any regulations or conditions which may be made by the company having control of a railway station for the purpose of maintaining order or dealing with the traffic at such station, including regulations as to—

    (i)   The number of cabs to be admitted at any one time;

    (ii) The rejection of cabs and drivers unfit for admission; and

    (iii) The expulsion of any cabman who has been guilty of misconduct, or of a breach of the company's byelaws or regulations.

(5) . . .

Amendment

Sub-s (1): words "Transport for London" in square brackets substituted by the Greater London Authority Act 1999, s 253, Sch 20, paras 6(1), (4)(a), 15(2).

Sub-s (2): words "Transport for London" in square brackets in both places they occur substituted by the Greater London Authority Act 1999, s 253, Sch 20, paras 6(1), (4)(b)(i), 15(3).

Sub-s (2): words "by London cab order" in square brackets substituted by the Greater London Authority Act 1999, s 253, Sch 20, paras 6(1), (4)(b)(ii), 15(3).

Sub-s (5): repealed by the Statute Law Revision Act 1927.

3 . . .

Amendment

Section repealed by the Statute Law (Repeals) Act 1976, s 1(1), Sch 1, Pt XVII.

4 . . .

Amendment

Section repealed by the London Government Act 1963, ss 83(1), 93(1), Sch 17, para 29, Sch 18, Pt II.

5 . . .

Amendment

Section repealed by the Statute Law (Repeals) Act 1976, s 1(1), Sch 1, Pt XVII.

6 Definitions (1) In this Act the expression "stage carriage" has the same meaning as in the Metropolitan Public Carriage Act 1869 as amended by this

Act, the expression "cab" has the same meaning as the expression "hackney carriage" has in that Act, the expression "fare" includes any payment to be made for the carriage of luggage on a cab, and any other payment to be made in respect of the hire of a cab, [the expression "London cab order" has the same meaning as in the Metropolitan Public Carriage Act 1869] and the expression "taximeter" means any appliance for measuring the time or distance for which a cab is used, or for measuring both time and distance, which is for the time being approved for the purpose by or on behalf of [Transport for London].

(2) It is hereby declared that for the purposes of any Act relating to hackney carriages . . . or cabs, in London, the expressions "hackney carriage" . . . or "cab" include any such vehicle, whether drawn or propelled by animal or mechanical power . . . .

(3) In this Act the expression "London" means the Metropolitan Police District and the City of London.

[(4) Any power to make a London cab order under or by virtue of this Act includes power to vary or revoke a previous such order.]

Amendment

Sub-s (1): words "the expression "London cab order" has the same meaning as in the Metropolitan Public Carriage Act 1869" in square brackets inserted by the Greater London Authority Act 1999, s 253, Sch 20, para 6(1), (5)(a).

Sub-s (1): words "Transport for London" in square brackets substituted by the Greater London Authority Act 1999, s 253, Sch 20, paras 6(1), (5)(b), 15(4).

Sub-s (2): first and second words omitted repealed by the Statute Law (Repeals) Act 1976; final words omitted repealed by the Statute Law Revision Act 1927.

Sub-s (4): inserted by the Greater London Authority Act 1999, s 253, Sch 20, para 6(1), (6).

7 Short title and extent of Act (1) This Act may be cited as the London Cab and Stage Carriage Act 1907.

(2) This Act shall only apply to London as defined by this Act.

London Cab Act 1968

1 Power to regulate fares for non-obligatory journeys (1) The power of [Transport for London] under paragraph (3) of section 9 of the Metropolitan Public Carriage Act 1869 and section 1 of the London Cab and Stage Carriage Act 1907 (regulations governing cab fares in London) shall include power to pre-scribe fares for the hire of cabs in respect of all journeys in London whether or not the journey is one which the driver of the cab is obliged by law to undertake.

[(1A) The power conferred by subsection (1) of this section is subject to para-graph (4) of the restrictions specified in section 9 of the said Act of 1869.]

(2) In this section "cab", "fare" and "London" have the same meaning as in the said Act of 1977, and for the purposes of this section a journey shall be treated as a journey in London if it begins and ends there.

Amendment
Sub-s (1): words "Transport for London" in square brackets substituted by the Greater London Authority Act 1999, s 253, Sch 20, para 7(1), (2).
Sub-s (1A): inserted by the Greater London Authority Act 1999, s 253, Sch 20, para 7(1), (3).

2 Power to increase length of obligatory journeys (1) [Transport for London] may [by London cab order] direct that for the reference to the distance of six miles in section 7 and paragraph (2) of section 17 of the London Hackney Carriage Act 1853 (being the length of a journey which the driver of a cab is by law obliged to undertake) there shall be substituted a reference to such greater distance as appears to [Transport for London] to be appropriate.

(2) [A London cab order] under this section may be limited so as to apply only in relation to hirings in respect of journeys which begin, or which end, at such places as may be specified in the order, and may substitute different distances in relation to such hirings or any of them and in relation to other hirings.

(3) The power to make [London cab orders] under this section includes power to vary or revoke a previous [such] order . . ..

(4) Before making [any London cab order] under this section [Transport for London] shall consult with such bodies appearing to [Transport for London] to represent the owners and drivers of cabs as [Transport for London] considers appropriate.

Amendment
Sub-s (1): words "Transport for London" in square brackets in both places they occur substituted by the Greater London Authority Act 1999, s 253, Sch 20, paras 7(1), (4)(a) (i), (iii), 16(1).

Sub-s (1): words "by London cab order" in square brackets substituted by the Greater London Authority Act 1999, s 253, Sch 20, paras 7(1), (4)(a)(ii), 16(1).

Sub-s (2): words "A London cab order" in square brackets substituted by the Greater London Authority Act 1999, s 253, Sch 20, para 7(1), (4)(b).

Sub-s (3): words "London cab orders" in square brackets substituted by the Greater London Authority Act 1999, s 253, Sch 20, para 7(1), (4)(c)(i).

Sub-s (3): word "such" in square brackets inserted by the Greater London Authority Act 1999, s 253, Sch 20, para 7(1), (4)(c)(ii).

Sub-s (3): words omitted repealed by the Greater London Authority Act 1999, ss 253, 423, Sch 20, para 7(1), (4)(c)(iii), Sch 34, Pt V.

Sub-s (4): words "any London cab order" in square brackets substituted by the Greater London Authority Act 1999, s 253, Sch 20, para 7(1), (4)(d)(i).

Sub-s (4): words "Transport for London" in square brackets in each place they occur substituted by the Greater London Authority Act 1999, s 253, Sch 20, para 7(1), (4)(d) (ii), (iii).

3 Relaxation of restrictions on the parking of cabs (1) . . .

(2) In section 35 of the said Act of 1831 (under which a cab found standing in any street or place is, in certain circumstances, deemed to be plying for hire) the reference to a street or place shall not include a reference to any parking place for the time being designated by an order in force under the Road Traffic Regulation Act [1984] or to any part of a road the use of which as a parking place is for the time being authorised by an order in force under that Act.

(3) Notwithstanding anything in any enactment whereby the said section 35 has effect in relation to premises of the British Railways Board [or Transport for London or any of its subsidiaries (within the meaning of the Greater London Authority Act 1999) the reference] in that section to a street or place shall not include a reference to any part of those premises which is set aside by [the body concerned] as a parking place for vehicles.

Amendment

Sub-s (1): repealed by the Statute Law (Repeals) Act 2004, s 1(1), Sch 1, Pt 14.

Sub-s (2): date in square brackets substituted by the Road Traffic Regulation Act 1984, s 146, Sch 13, para 4.

Sub-s (3): words "or Transport for London or any of its subsidiaries (within the meaning of the Greater London Authority Act 1999) the reference" in square brackets substituted by the Transport for London (Consequential Provisions) Order 2003, SI 2003/1615, art 2, Sch 1, para 3(1), (2).

Sub-s (3): words "the body concerned" in square brackets substituted by the Transport for London (Consequential Provisions) Order 2003, SI 2003/1615, art 2, Sch 1, para 3(1), (3).

4 . . .

Amendment

Section repealed, except in relation to any vehicle whose use as a private hire vehicle is limited to use in connection with funerals or weddings, by the Private Hire Vehicles (London) Act 1998, ss 29, 39(2), Sch 2.

[4A . . .]

Amendment

Section inserted by the London Cab Act 1973, s 2.

Section repealed, except in relation to any vehicle whose use as a private hire vehicle is limited to use in connection with funerals or weddings, by the Private Hire Vehicles (London) Act 1998, ss 29, 39(2), Sch 2.

[4B London cab orders (1) In this Act, "London cab order" means an order made by Transport for London.

(2) Any power to make a London cab order under or by virtue of this Act includes power to vary or revoke a previous such order.]

Amendment

Section inserted by the Greater London Authority Act 1999, s 253, Sch 20, para 7(1), (6).

5 Short title and repeals (1) This Act may be cited as the London Cab Act 1968.

(2) . . .

Amendment

Sub-s (2): repealed by the Statute Law (Repeals) Act 2004, s 1(1), Sch 1, Pt 14.

Transport Act 1985

Part I
General provisions relating to Road Passenger Transport

Taxis and hire cars

17 London taxi and taxi driver licensing: appeals (1) In this section—
"licence" means a licence under section 6 of the Metropolitan Public Carriage Act 1869 (taxi licences) or under section 8 of that Act (taxi driver
licences); and
"licensing authority" means the person empowered to grant a licence.

(2) Where the licensing authority has refused to grant, or has suspended or
revoked, a licence the applicant for, or (as the case may be) holder of, the licence
may, before the expiry of the [designated period]—
(a) require the authority to reconsider his decision; or
(b) appeal to [a magistrates'] court.

(3) Any call for a reconsideration under subsection (2) above must be made to
the licensing authority in writing.

(4) On any reconsideration under this section the person calling for the decision to be reconsidered shall be entitled to be heard either in person or by his
representative.

(5) If the person calling for a decision to be reconsidered under this section is
dissatisfied with the decision of the licensing authority on reconsideration, he
may, before the expiry of the [designated period], appeal to [a magistrates'] court.

(6) On any appeal to it under this section, the court may make such order as it
thinks fit; and any order which it makes shall be binding on the licensing authority.

(7) Where a person holds a licence which is in force when he applies for a new
licence in substitution for it, the existing licence shall continue in force until
the application for the new licence, or any appeal under this section in relation
to that application, is disposed of, but without prejudice to the exercise in the
meantime of any power of the licensing authority to revoke the existing licence.

(8) For the purposes of subsection (7) above, where the licensing authority
refuses to grant the new licence the application shall not be treated as disposed
of—
(a) where no call for a reconsideration of the authority's decision is made
under subsection (2) above, until the expiry of the [designated period];
(b) where such a reconsideration is called for, until the expiry of the [desig-
nated period] which begins by reference to the decision of the authority
on reconsideration.

(9) Where the licensing authority suspends or revokes a licence, or confirms a decision to do so, he may, if the holder of the licence so requests, direct that his decision shall not have effect until the expiry of the [designated period].

(10) In this section . . .
    ["designated period" means such period as may be specified for the purpose
        by London cab order;
    "London cab order" means an order made by Transport for London].

[(11) Any power to make a London cab order under this section includes power to vary or revoke a previous such order.]

Amendment

Sub-s (2): words "designated period" in square brackets substituted by the Greater London Authority Act 1999, s 253, Sch 20, para 8(1), (3)(a); in para (b) words "a magistrates'" in square brackets substituted by the Courts Act 2003, s 109(1), Sch 8, para 293(1), (2).

Sub-s (5): words "designated period" in square brackets substituted by the Greater London Authority Act 1999, s 253, Sch 20, para 8(1), (3)(a); words "a magistrates'" in square brackets substituted by the Courts Act 2003, s 109(1), Sch 8, para 293(1), (2).

Sub-s (8): in paras (a), (b) words "designated period" in square brackets substituted by the Greater London Authority Act 1999, s 253, Sch 20, para 8(1), (3)(a).

Sub-s (9): words "designated period" in square brackets substituted by the Greater London Authority Act 1999, s 253, Sch 20, para 8(1), (3)(a).

Sub-s (10): definition "the appropriate court" (omitted) repealed by the Courts Act 2003, s 109(1), (3), Sch 8, para 293(1), (3), Sch 10; definitions "designated period" and "London cab order" inserted by the Greater London Authority Act 1999, s 253, Sch 20, para 8(1), (3)(b).

Sub-s (11): inserted by the Greater London Authority Act 1999, s 253, Sch 20, para 8(1), (3)(c).

Private Hire Vehicles (London) Act 1998

Introductory

1 Meaning of "private hire vehicle", "operator" and related expressions (1) In this Act—

    (a) "private hire vehicle" means a vehicle constructed or adapted to seat fewer than nine passengers which is made available with a driver . . . for hire for the purpose of carrying passengers, other than a licensed taxi or a public service vehicle; . . .

    (b) "operator" means a person who makes provision for the invitation or acceptance of, or who accepts, private hire bookings[; and

    (c) "operate", in relation to a private hire vehicle, means to make provision for the invitation or acceptance of, or to accept, private hire bookings in relation to the vehicle.]

(2) Any reference in this Act to a vehicle being "used as a private hire vehicle" is a reference to a private hire vehicle which—

    (a) is in use in connection with a hiring for the purpose of carrying one or more passengers; or

    (b) is immediately available to an operator to carry out a private hire booking.

(3) Any reference in this Act to the operator of a vehicle which is being used as a private hire vehicle is a reference to the operator who accepted the booking for the hiring or to whom the vehicle is immediately available, as the case may be.

(4) In this Act "private hire booking" means a booking for the hire of a private hire vehicle for the purpose of carrying one or more passengers (including a booking to carry out as sub-contractor a private hire booking accepted by another operator).

(5) In this Act "operating centre" means premises at which private hire bookings are accepted by an operator.

Amendment

Sub-s (1): in para (a) words omitted repealed by the Road Safety Act 2006, ss 54, 59, Sch 7.

Sub-s (1): in para (a) word omitted repealed by the Immigration Act 2016, s 37, Sch 5, paras 34, 35(a).

Sub-s (1): para (c) and word in square brackets preceding it inserted by the Immigration Act 2016, s 37, Sch 5, paras 34, 35(b).

Regulation of private hire vehicle operators in London

2 Requirement for London operator's licence (1) No person shall in London make provision for the invitation or acceptance of, or accept, private hire bookings unless he is the holder of a private hire vehicle operator's licence for London (in this Act referred to as a "London PHV operator's licence").

(2) A person who makes provision for the invitation or acceptance of private hire bookings, or who accepts such a booking, in contravention of this section is guilty of an offence and liable on summary conviction to a fine not exceeding level 4 on the standard scale.

3 London operator's licences (1) Any person may apply to the [licensing authority] for a London PHV operator's licence.

(2) An application under this section shall state the address of any premises in London which the applicant proposes to use as an operating centre.

(3) The [licensing authority] shall grant a London PHV operator's licence to the applicant if [the authority] is satisfied that—
- (a) the applicant is a fit and proper person to hold a London PHV operator's licence;
- [(aa)   if the applicant is an individual, the applicant is not disqualified by reason of the applicant's immigration status from operating a private hire vehicle; and]
- (b) any further requirements that may be prescribed (which may include requirements relating to operating centres) are met.

[(3A) In determining for the purposes of subsection (3) whether an applicant is disqualified by reason of the applicant's immigration status from operating a private hire vehicle, the licensing authority must have regard to any guidance issued by the Secretary of State.]

(4) A London PHV operator's licence shall be granted subject to such conditions as may be prescribed and such other conditions as the [licensing authority] may think fit.

(5) [Subject to section 3A, a] London PHV operator's licence shall be granted for five years or such shorter period as the [licensing authority] may consider appropriate in the circumstances of the case.

(6) A London PHV operator's licence shall—
- (a) specify the address of any premises in London which the holder of the licence may use as an operating centre;
- (b) be in such form and contain such particulars as the [licensing authority] may think fit.

(7) An applicant for a London PHV operator's licence may appeal to a magistrates' court against—
- (a) a decision not to grant such a licence;
- (b) a decision not to specify an address proposed in the application as an operating centre; or
- (c) any condition (other than a prescribed condition) to which the licence is subject.

Amendment

Sub-s (1): words "licensing authority" in square brackets substituted by the Greater London Authority Act 1999, s 254, Sch 21, paras 1, 2.

Sub-s (3): words "licensing authority" in square brackets substituted by the Greater London Authority Act 1999, s 254, Sch 21, paras 1, 2.

Sub-s (3): words "the authority" in square brackets substituted by the Greater London Authority Act 1999, s 254, Sch 21, paras 1, 3.

Sub-s (3): para (aa) substituted for "and" by the Immigration Act 2016, s 37, Sch 5, paras 34, 36(1), (2).

Sub-s (3A): inserted by the Immigration Act 2016, s 37, Sch 5, paras 34, 36(1), (3).

Sub-s (4): words "licensing authority" in square brackets substituted by the Greater London Authority Act 1999, s 254, Sch 21, paras 1, 2.

Sub-s (5): words "Subject to section 3A, a" in square brackets substituted by the Immigration Act 2016, s 37, Sch 5, paras 34, 36(1), (4).

Sub-s (5): words "licensing authority" in square brackets substituted by the Greater London Authority Act 1999, s 254, Sch 21, paras 1, 2.

Sub-s (6): in para (b) words "licensing authority" in square brackets substituted by the Greater London Authority Act 1999, s 254, Sch 21, paras 1, 2.

[3A London PHV operator's licences for persons subject to immigration control (1) Subsection (2) applies if—

    (a) a London PHV operator's licence is to be granted to a person who has been granted leave to enter or remain in the United Kingdom for a limited period ("the leave period");

    (b) the person's leave has not been extended by virtue of section 3C of the Immigration Act 1971 (continuation of leave pending variation decision); and

    (c) apart from subsection (2), the period for which the licence would have been granted would have ended after the end of the leave period.

(2) The licence must be granted for a period which ends at or before the end of the leave period.

(3) Subsection (4) applies if—

    (a) a London PHV operator's licence is to be granted to a person who has been granted leave to enter or remain in the United Kingdom for a limited period; and

    (b) the person's leave has been extended by virtue of section 3C of the Immigration Act 1971 (continuation of leave pending variation decision).

(4) The licence must be granted for a period which does not exceed six months.

(5) A London PHV operator's licence ceases to be in force if the person to whom it was granted becomes disqualified by reason of the person's immigration status from operating a private hire vehicle.

(6) If subsection (5) applies to a licence, the person to whom it was granted must, within the period of 7 days beginning with the day after the day on which the person first became disqualified, return it to the licensing authority.

(7) A person who, without reasonable excuse, contravenes subsection (6) is guilty of an offence and liable on summary conviction—

(a) to a fine not exceeding level 3 on the standard scale; and

(b) in the case of a continuing offence, to a fine not exceeding ten pounds for each day during which an offence continues after conviction.

(8) The Secretary of State may by regulations amend the amount for the time being specified in subsection (7)(b).]

Amendment
Section inserted by the Immigration Act 2016, s 37, Sch 5, paras 34, 37.

4 Obligations of London operators (1) The holder of a London PHV operator's licence (in this Act referred to as a "London PHV operator") shall not in London accept a private hire booking other than at an operating centre specified in his licence.

(2) A London PHV operator shall secure that any vehicle which is provided by him for carrying out a private hire booking accepted by him in London is—

(a) a vehicle for which a London PHV licence is in force driven by a person holding a London PHV driver's licence; or

(b) a London cab driven by a person holding a London cab driver's licence.

(3) A London PHV operator shall—

(a) display a copy of his licence at each operating centre specified in the licence;

(b) keep at each specified operating centre a record in the prescribed form of the private hire bookings accepted by him there;

(c) before the commencement of each journey booked at a specified operating centre, enter in the record kept under paragraph (b) the prescribed particulars of the booking;

(d) *keep at each specified operating centre such records as may be prescribed of particulars of the private hire vehicles and drivers which are available to him for carrying out bookings accepted by him at that centre;*

[(d) keep at the specified operating centre or, where more than one operating centre is specified, at one of the operating centres such records as may be prescribed of particulars of the private hire vehicles and drivers which are available to him for carrying out bookings accepted by him at that or, as the case may be, each centre;

(da) where more than one operating centre is specified—

(i) give notice to the licensing authority, and

(ii) display at each specified operating centre a notice,

stating the address of the operating centre at which the records are kept under paragraph (d);]

(e) at the request of a constable or authorised officer, produce for inspection any record required by this section to be kept.

(4) If a London PHV operator ceases to use an operating centre specified in his licence he shall preserve any record he was required by this section to keep there for such period as may be prescribed.

(5) A London PHV operator who contravenes any provision of this section is guilty of an offence and liable on summary conviction to a fine not exceeding level 3 on the standard scale.

(6) It is a defence in proceedings for an offence under this section for an operator to show that he exercised all due diligence to avoid committing such an offence.

Amendment
Sub-s (3): para (d) prospectively substituted, by subsequent paras (d), (da), by the Transport for London Act 2008, s 25.

5 Hirings accepted on behalf of another operator (1) A London PHV operator ("the first operator") who has in London accepted a private hire booking may not arrange for another operator to provide a vehicle to carry out that booking as sub-contractor unless—
   (a) the other operator is a London PHV operator and the sub-contracted booking is accepted at an operating centre in London;
   (b) the other operator is licensed under section 55 of the Local Government (Miscellaneous Provisions) Act 1976 (in this Act referred to as "the 1976 Act") by the council of a district and the sub-contracted booking is accepted in that district; or
   (c) the other operator accepts the sub-contracted booking in Scotland.

(2) A London PHV operator who contravenes subsection (1) is guilty of an offence and liable on summary conviction to a fine not exceeding level 3 on the standard scale.

(3) It is a defence in proceedings for an offence under this section for an operator to show that he exercised all due diligence to avoid committing such an offence.

(4) It is immaterial for the purposes of subsection (1) whether or not sub--contracting is permitted by the contract between the first operator and the person who made the booking.

(5) For the avoidance of doubt (and subject to any relevant contract terms), a contract of hire between a person who made a private hire booking at an operating centre in London and the London PHV operator who accepted the booking remains in force despite the making of arrangements by that operator for another contractor to provide a vehicle to carry out that booking as sub-contractor.

Regulation of private hire vehicles in London

6 Requirement for private hire vehicle licence (1) A vehicle shall not be used as a private hire vehicle on a road in London unless a private hire vehicle licence is in force for that vehicle.

(2) The driver and operator of a vehicle used in contravention of this section are each guilty of an offence.

(3) The owner of a vehicle who permits it to be used in contravention of this section is guilty of an offence.

(4) It is a defence in proceedings for an offence under subsection (2) for the driver or operator to show that he exercised all due diligence to prevent the vehicle being used in contravention of this section.

(5) A person guilty of an offence under this section is liable on summary conviction to a fine not exceeding level 4 on the standard scale.

(6) In this section "private hire vehicle licence" means—
    (a) except where paragraph (b) or (c) applies, a London PHV licence;
    (b) if the vehicle is in use for the purposes of a hiring the booking for which was accepted outside London in a controlled district, a licence under section 48 of the 1976 Act issued by the council for that district; and
    (c) if the vehicle is in use for the purposes of a hiring the booking for which was accepted in Scotland, a licence under section 10 of the Civic Government (Scotland) Act 1982 (in this Act referred to as "the 1982 Act"),

and for the purposes of paragraph (b) or (c) it is immaterial that the booking in question is a sub-contracted booking.

(7) This section does not apply to a vehicle used for the purposes of a hiring for a journey beginning outside London in an area of England and Wales which is not a controlled district.

7 London PHV licences (1) The owner of any vehicle constructed or adapted to seat fewer than nine passengers may apply to the [licensing authority] for a private hire vehicle licence for London (in this Act referred to as a "London PHV licence") for that vehicle.

(2) The [licensing authority] shall grant a London PHV licence for a vehicle if [the authority] is satisfied—
    (a) that the vehicle—
        (i) is suitable in type, size and design for use as a private hire vehicle;
        (ii) is safe, comfortable and in a suitable mechanical condition for that use; and
        (iii) is not of such design and appearance as would lead any person to believe that the vehicle is a London cab;
    (b) that there is in force in relation to the use of the vehicle a policy of insurance or such security as complies with the requirements of Part VI of the Road Traffic Act 1988; and
    (c) that any further requirements that may be prescribed are met.

(3) A London PHV licence may not be granted in respect of more than one vehicle.

(4) A London PHV licence shall be granted subject to such conditions as may be prescribed and such other conditions as the [licensing authority] may think fit.

(5) A London PHV licence shall be in such form and shall contain such particulars as the [licensing authority] may think fit.

(6) A London PHV licence shall be granted for one year or for such shorter period as the [licensing authority] may consider appropriate in the circumstances of the case.

(7) An applicant for a London PHV licence may appeal to a magistrates' court against a decision not to grant such a licence or against any condition (other than a prescribed condition) to which the licence is subject.

Amendment

Sub-s (1): words "licensing authority" in square brackets substituted by the Greater London Authority Act 1999, s 254, Sch 21, paras 1, 2.

Sub-s (2): words "licensing authority" in square brackets substituted by the Greater London Authority Act 1999, s 254, Sch 21, paras 1, 2.

Sub-s (2): words "the authority" in square brackets substituted by the Greater London Authority Act 1999, s 254, Sch 21, paras 1, 4.

Sub-s (4): words "licensing authority" in square brackets substituted by the Greater London Authority Act 1999, s 254, Sch 21, paras 1, 2.

Sub-s (5): words "licensing authority" in square brackets substituted by the Greater London Authority Act 1999, s 254, Sch 21, paras 1, 2.

Sub-s (6): words "licensing authority" in square brackets substituted by the Greater London Authority Act 1999, s 254, Sch 21, paras 1, 2.

8 Obligations of owners of licensed vehicles (1) This section applies to the owner of any vehicle to which a London PHV licence relates.

(2) The owner shall present the vehicle for inspection and testing by or on behalf of the [licensing authority] within such period and at such place as [the authority] may by notice reasonably require.

The vehicle shall not be required to be presented under this subsection on more than three separate occasions during any one period of 12 months.

(3) The owner shall (without prejudice to section 170 of the Road Traffic Act 1988) report any accident to the vehicle materially affecting—
    (a) the safety, performance or appearance of the vehicle, or
    (b) the comfort or convenience of persons carried in the vehicle,

to the [licensing authority] as soon as reasonably practical and in any case within 72 hours of the accident occurring.

(4) If the ownership of the vehicle changes, the person who was previously the owner shall within 14 days of the change give notice to the [licensing authority] of that fact and the name and address of the new owner.

(5) A person who, without reasonable excuse, contravenes any provision of this section is guilty of an offence and liable on summary conviction to a fine not exceeding level 3 on the standard scale.

Amendment

Sub-s (2): words "licensing authority" in square brackets substituted by the Greater London Authority Act 1999, s 254, Sch 21, paras 1, 2.

Sub-s (2): words "the authority" in square brackets substituted by the Greater London Authority Act 1999, s 254, Sch 21, paras 1, 5.

Sub-s (3): words "licensing authority" in square brackets substituted by the Greater London Authority Act 1999, s 254, Sch 21, paras 1, 2.

Sub-s (4): words "licensing authority" in square brackets substituted by the Greater London Authority Act 1999, s 254, Sch 21, paras 1, 2.

9 Fitness of licensed vehicles (1) A constable or authorised officer has power at all reasonable times to inspect and test, for the purpose of ascertaining its fitness, any vehicle to which a London PHV licence relates.

(2) If a constable or authorised officer is not satisfied as to the fitness of such a vehicle he may by notice to the owner of the vehicle—

    (a) require the owner to make the vehicle available for further inspection and testing at such reasonable time and place as may be specified in the notice; and

    (b) if he thinks fit, suspend the London PHV licence relating to that vehicle until such time as a constable or authorised officer is satisfied as to the fitness of the vehicle.

(3) A notice under subsection (2)(b) shall state the grounds on which the licence is being suspended and the suspension shall take effect on the day on which it is served on the owner.

(4) A licence suspended under subsection (2)(b) shall remain suspended until such time as a constable or authorised officer by notice to the owner directs that the licence is again in force.

(5) If a licence remains suspended at the end of the period of two months beginning with the day on which a notice under subsection (2)(b) was served on the owner of the vehicle—

    (a) a constable or authorised officer may by notice to the owner direct that the licence is revoked; and

    (b) the revocation shall take effect at the end of the period of 21 days beginning with the day on which the owner is served with that notice.

(6) An owner may appeal against a notice under subsection (2)(b) or (5) to a magistrates' court.

10 Identification of licensed vehicles (1) The [licensing authority] shall issue a disc or plate for each vehicle to which a London PHV licence relates which identifies that vehicle as a vehicle for which such a licence is in force.

(2) No vehicle to which a London PHV licence relates shall be used as a private hire vehicle on a road in London unless the disc or plate issued under this section is exhibited on the vehicle in such manner as may be prescribed.

(3) The [licensing authority] may by notice exempt a vehicle from the requirement under subsection (2) when it is being used to provide a service specified in the notice if [the authority] considers it inappropriate (having regard to that service) to require the disc or plate in question to be exhibited.

(4) The driver and operator of a vehicle used in contravention of subsection (2) are each guilty of an offence.

(5) The owner of a vehicle who permits it to be used in contravention of subsection (2) is guilty of an offence.

(6) It is a defence in proceedings for an offence under subsection (4) for the driver or operator to show that he exercised all due diligence to prevent the vehicle being used in contravention of subsection (2).

(7) A person guilty of an offence under this section is liable on summary conviction to a fine not exceeding level 3 on the standard scale.

Amendment
Sub-s (1): words "licensing authority" in square brackets substituted by the Greater London Authority Act 1999, s 254, Sch 21, paras 1, 2.
Sub-s (3): words "licensing authority" in square brackets substituted by the Greater London Authority Act 1999, s 254, Sch 21, paras 1, 2.
Sub-s (3): words "the authority" in square brackets substituted by the Greater London Authority Act 1999, s 254, Sch 21, paras 1, 6.

11 Prohibition of taximeters (1) No vehicle to which a London PHV licence relates shall be equipped with a taximeter.

(2) If such a vehicle is equipped with a taximeter, the owner of that vehicle is guilty of an offence and liable on summary conviction to a fine not exceeding level 3 on the standard scale.

(3) In this section "taximeter" means a device for calculating the fare to be charged in respect of any journey by reference to the distance travelled or time elapsed since the start of the journey (or a combination of both).

Regulation of drivers of private hire vehicles in London

12 Requirement for private hire vehicle driver's licence (1) No vehicle shall be used as a private hire vehicle on a road in London unless the driver holds a private hire vehicle driver's licence.

(2) The driver and operator of a vehicle used in contravention of this section are each guilty of an offence.

(3) The owner of a vehicle who permits it to be used in contravention of this section is guilty of an offence.

(4) It is a defence in proceedings against the operator of a vehicle for an offence under subsection (2) for the operator to show that he exercised all due diligence to prevent the vehicle being used in contravention of this section.

(5) A person guilty of an offence under this section is liable on summary conviction to a fine not exceeding level 4 on the standard scale.

(6) In this section "private hire vehicle driver's licence" means—
- (a) except where paragraph (b) or (c) applies, a London PHV driver's licence;
- (b) if the vehicle is in use for the purposes of a hiring the booking for which was accepted outside London in a controlled district in England and Wales, a licence under section 51 of the 1976 Act issued by the council for that district; and
- (c) if the vehicle is in use for a hiring the booking for which was accepted in Scotland, a licence under section 13 of the 1982 Act,

and for the purposes of paragraph (b) or (c) it is immaterial that the booking in question is a sub-contracted booking.

(7) This section does not apply to the use of a vehicle for the purposes of a hiring for a journey beginning outside London in an area of England and Wales which is not a controlled district.

13 London PHV driver's licences (1) Any person may apply to the [licensing authority] for a private hire vehicle driver's licence for London (in this Act referred to as a "London PHV driver's licence").

(2) The [licensing authority] shall grant a London PHV driver's licence to an applicant if [the authority] is satisfied that—
- (a) the applicant has attained the age of 21, is (and has for at least three years been) authorised to drive a motor car and is a fit and proper person to hold a London PHV driver's licence;
- [(aa) the applicant is not disqualified by reason of the applicant's immigration status from driving a private hire vehicle; and]
- (b) the requirement mentioned in subsection (3), and any further requirements prescribed by the [licensing authority], are met.

[(2A) In determining for the purposes of subsection (2) whether an applicant is disqualified by reason of the applicant's immigration status from driving a private hire vehicle, the licensing authority must have regard to any guidance issued by the Secretary of State.]

(3) The [licensing authority] shall require applicants to show to [the authority's] satisfaction (whether by taking a test or otherwise) that they possess a level—
- (a) of knowledge of London or parts of London; and
- (b) of general topographical skills,

which appears to [the authority] to be appropriate.

The [licensing authority] may impose different requirements in relation to different applicants.

(4) The [licensing authority] may send a copy of an application to the Commissioner of Police of the Metropolis or the Commissioner of Police for the City of

London with a request for the Commissioner's observations; and the Commissioner shall respond to the request.

(5) A London PHV driver's licence—

(a) may be granted subject to such conditions as the [licensing authority] may think fit;

(b) shall be in such form and shall contain such particulars as the [licensing authority] may think fit; and

(c) [subject to section 13A,] shall be granted for three years or for such shorter period as the [licensing authority] may consider appropriate in the circumstances of the particular case.

(6) An applicant may appeal to a magistrates' court against a decision not to grant a London PHV driver's licence or against any condition to which such a licence is subject.

(7) For the purposes of subsection (2), a person is authorised to drive a motor car if—

(a) he holds a licence granted under Part III of the Road Traffic Act 1988 (other than a provisional licence) authorising him to drive a motor car; or

(b) he is authorised by virtue of section 99A(1) or 109(1) of that Act (Community licences and Northern Ireland licences) to drive a motor car in Great Britain.

Amendment

Sub-s (1): words "licensing authority" in square brackets substituted by the Greater London Authority Act 1999, s 254, Sch 21, paras 1, 2.

Sub-s (2): words "licensing authority" in square brackets in both places they occur substituted by the Greater London Authority Act 1999, s 254, Sch 21, paras 1, 2.

Sub-s (2): words "the authority" in square brackets substituted by the Greater London Authority Act 1999, s 254, Sch 21, paras 1, 7(1), (2).

Sub-s (2): para (aa) substituted for "and" by the Immigration Act 2016, s 37, Sch 5, paras 34, 38(1), (2).

Sub-s (2A): inserted by the Immigration Act 2016, s 37, Sch 5, paras 34, 38(1), (3).

Sub-s (3): words "licensing authority" in square brackets in both places they occur substituted by the Greater London Authority Act 1999, s 254, Sch 21, paras 1, 2.

Sub-s (3): words "the authority's" in square brackets substituted by the Greater London Authority Act 1999, s 254, Sch 21, paras 1, 7(1), (3)(a).

Sub-s (3): words "the authority" in square brackets substituted by the Greater London Authority Act 1999, s 254, Sch 21, paras 1, 7(1), (3)(b).

Sub-s (4): words "licensing authority" in square brackets substituted by the Greater London Authority Act 1999, s 254, Sch 21, paras 1, 2.

Sub-s (5): words "licensing authority" in square brackets in each place they occur substituted by the Greater London Authority Act 1999, s 254, Sch 21, paras 1, 2.

Sub-s (5): in para (c) words "subject to section 13A," in square brackets inserted by the Immigration Act 2016, s 37, Sch 5, paras 34, 38(1), (4).

[13A London PHV driver's licences for persons subject to immigration control (1) Subsection (2) applies if—

(a) a London PHV driver's licence is to be granted to a person who has been granted leave to enter or remain in the United Kingdom for a limited period ("the leave period");

(b) the person's leave has not been extended by virtue of section 3C of the Immigration Act 1971 (continuation of leave pending variation decision); and

(c) apart from subsection (2), the period for which the licence would have been granted would have ended after the end of the leave period.

(2) The licence must be granted for a period which ends at or before the end of the leave period.

(3) Subsection (4) applies if—

(a) a London PHV driver's licence is to be granted to a person who has been granted leave to enter or remain in the United Kingdom for a limited period; and

(b) the person's leave has been extended by virtue of section 3C of the Immigration Act 1971 (continuation of leave pending variation decision).

(4) The licence must be granted for a period which does not exceed six months.

(5) A London PHV driver's licence ceases to be in force if the person to whom it was granted becomes disqualified by reason of the person's immigration status from driving a private hire vehicle.

(6) If subsection (5) applies to a licence, the person to whom it was granted must, within the period of 7 days beginning with the day after the day on which the person first became disqualified, return the licence and the person's driver's badge to the licensing authority.

(7) A person who, without reasonable excuse, contravenes subsection (6) is guilty of an offence and liable on summary conviction—

(a) to a fine not exceeding level 3 on the standard scale; and

(b) in the case of a continuing offence, to a fine not exceeding ten pounds for each day during which an offence continues after conviction.

(8) The Secretary of State may by regulations amend the amount for the time being specified in subsection (7)(b).]

Amendment
Section inserted by the Immigration Act 2016, s 37, Sch 5, paras 34, 39.

14 Issue of driver's badges (1) The [licensing authority] shall issue a badge to each person to whom [the authority] has granted a London PHV driver's licence.

(2) The [licensing authority] may prescribe the form of badges issued under this section.

(3) A person issued with such a badge shall, when he is the driver of a vehicle being used as a private hire vehicle,

[(a)] wear the badge in such position and manner as to be plainly and distinctly visible [and—

(b) at the request of any person, produce the badge for inspection].

(4) The [licensing authority] may by notice exempt a person from the requirement under *subsection (3)* [subsection (3)(a)], when he is the driver of a vehicle being used to provide a service specified in the notice if [the authority] considers it inappropriate (having regard to that service) to require the badge to be worn.

(5) Any person who without reasonable excuse contravenes subsection (3) is guilty of an offence and liable on summary conviction to a fine not exceeding level 3 on the standard scale.

Amendment

Sub-s (1): words "licensing authority" in square brackets substituted by the Greater London Authority Act 1999, s 254, Sch 21, paras 1, 2.

Sub-s (1): words "the authority" in square brackets substituted by the Greater London Authority Act 1999, s 254, Sch 21, paras 1, 8(1), (2).

Sub-s (2): words "licensing authority" in square brackets substituted by the Greater London Authority Act 1999, s 254, Sch 21, paras 1, 2.

Sub-s (3): para (a) prospectively numbered as such by the Transport for London Act 2008, s 23(1).

Sub-s (3): para (b) and word "and" immediately preceding it prospectively inserted by the Transport for London Act 2008, s 23(1).

Sub-s (4): words "licensing authority" in square brackets substituted by the Greater London Authority Act 1999, s 254, Sch 21, paras 1, 2.

Sub-s (4): words "subsection (3)" in italics prospectively repealed and subsequent words in square brackets prospectively substituted by the Transport for London Act 2008, s 23(2).

Sub-s (4): words "the authority" in square brackets substituted by the Greater London Authority Act 1999, s 254, Sch 21, paras 1, 8(1), (3).

Licences: general provisions

15 Applications for licences (1) An application for the grant of a licence under this Act shall be made in such form, and include such declarations and information, as the [licensing authority] may require.

(2) The [licensing authority] may require an applicant to furnish such further information as [the authority] may consider necessary for dealing with the application.

(3) The information which an applicant for a London PHV operator's licence may be required to furnish includes in particular information about—

(a) any premises in London which he proposes to use as an operating centre;

(b) any convictions recorded against him;

(c) any business activities he has carried on before making the application;

(d) if the applicant is or has been a director or secretary of a company, that company;

(e) if the applicant is a company, information about the directors or secretary of that company;

(f) if the applicant proposes to act as an operator in partnership with any other person, information about that person.

(4) An applicant for a London PHV driver's licence may be required by the [licensing authority]—

(a) to produce a certificate signed by a registered medical practitioner to the effect that—

(i) he is physically fit to be the driver of a private hire vehicle; and

(ii) if any specific requirements of physical fitness have been prescribed for persons holding London PHV licences, that he meets those requirements; and

(b) whether or not such a certificate has been produced, to submit to examination by a registered medical practitioner selected by the [licensing authority] as to his physical fitness to be the driver of such a vehicle.

(5) The provisions of this Act apply to the renewal of a licence as they apply to the grant of a licence.

Amendment

Sub-s (1): words "licensing authority" in square brackets substituted by the Greater London Authority Act 1999, s 254, Sch 21, paras 1, 2.

Sub-s (2): words "licensing authority" in square brackets substituted by the Greater London Authority Act 1999, s 254, Sch 21, paras 1, 2.

Sub-s (2): words "the authority" in square brackets substituted by the Greater London Authority Act 1999, s 254, Sch 21, paras 1, 9.

Sub-s (4): words "licensing authority" in square brackets in both places they occur substituted by the Greater London Authority Act 1999, s 254, Sch 21, paras 1, 2.

16 Power to suspend or revoke licences (1) The [licensing authority] may suspend or revoke a licence under this Act for any reasonable cause including (without prejudice to the generality of this subsection) any ground mentioned below.

(2) A London PHV operator's licence may be suspended or revoked where—

(a) the [licensing authority] is no longer satisfied that the licence holder is fit to hold such a licence;

[(aa) the licence holder has, since the grant of the licence, been convicted of an immigration offence or required to pay an immigration penalty;] or

(b) the licence holder has failed to comply with any condition of the licence or any other obligation imposed on him by or under this Act.

[(2A) Subsection (2)(aa) does not apply if—

(a) in a case where the licence holder has been convicted of an immigration offence, the conviction is a spent conviction within the meaning of the Rehabilitation of Offenders Act 1974, or

(b) in a case where the licence holder has been required to pay an immigration penalty—

(i)   more than three years have elapsed since the date on which the penalty was imposed, and

(ii) the amount of the penalty has been paid in full.]

(3) A London PHV licence may be suspended or revoked where—

(a) the [licensing authority] is no longer satisfied that the vehicle to which it relates is fit for use as a private hire vehicle; or

(b) the owner has failed to comply with any condition of the licence or any other obligation imposed on him by or under this Act.

(4) A London PHV driver's licence may be suspended or revoked where—

(a) the licence holder has, since the grant of the licence, been convicted of an offence involving dishonesty, indecency or violence;

[(aa) the licence holder has, since the grant of the licence, been convicted of an immigration offence or required to pay an immigration penalty;]

(b) the [licensing authority] is for any other reason no longer satisfied that the licence holder is fit to hold such a licence; or

(c) the licence holder has failed to comply with any condition of the licence or any other obligation imposed on him by or under this Act.

[(5)   Subsection (4)(aa) does not apply if—

(a) in a case where the licence holder has been convicted of an immigration offence, the conviction is a spent conviction within the meaning of the Rehabilitation of Offenders Act 1974, or

(b) in a case where the licence holder has been required to pay an immigration penalty—

(i)   more than three years have elapsed since the date on which the penalty was imposed, and

(ii) the amount of the penalty has been paid in full.]

Amendment

Sub-s (1): words "licensing authority" in square brackets substituted by the Greater London Authority Act 1999, s 254, Sch 21, paras 1, 2.

Sub-s (2): in para (a) words "licensing authority" in square brackets substituted by the Greater London Authority Act 1999, s 254, Sch 21, paras 1, 2.

Sub-s (2): para (aa) inserted by the Immigration Act 2016, s 37, Sch 5, paras 34, 40(1), (2).

Sub-s (2A): inserted by the Immigration Act 2016, s 37, Sch 5, paras 34, 40(1), (3).

Sub-s (3): in para (a) words "licensing authority" in square brackets substituted by the Greater London Authority Act 1999, s 254, Sch 21, paras 1, 2.

Sub-s (4): para (aa) inserted by the Immigration Act 2016, s 37, Sch 5, paras 34, 40(1), (4).

Sub-s (4): in para (b) words "licensing authority" in square brackets substituted by the Greater London Authority Act 1999, s 254, Sch 21, paras 1, 2.

Sub-s (5): inserted by the Immigration Act 2016, s 37, Sch 5, paras 34, 40(1), (5).

17 Suspension and revocation under section 16: procedure (1) Where the [licensing authority] has decided to suspend or revoke a licence under section 16—

(a) [the authority] shall give notice of the decision and the grounds for the decision to the licence holder or, in the case of a London PHV licence, the owner of the vehicle to which the licence relates; and

(b) the suspension or revocation takes effect at the end of the period of 21 days beginning with the day on which that notice is served on the licence holder or the owner.

(2) If the [licensing authority] is of the opinion that the interests of public safety require the suspension or revocation of a licence to have immediate effect, and [the authority] includes a statement of that opinion and the reasons for it in the notice of suspension or revocation, the suspension or revocation takes effect when the notice is served on the licence holder or vehicle owner (as the case may be).

(3) A licence suspended under this section shall remain suspended until such time as the [licensing authority] by notice directs that the licence is again in force.

(4) The holder of a London PHV operator's or driver's licence, or the owner of a vehicle to which a PHV licence relates, may appeal to a magistrates' court against a decision under section 16 to suspend or revoke that licence.

Amendment

Sub-s (1): words "licensing authority" in square brackets substituted by the Greater London Authority Act 1999, s 254, Sch 21, paras 1, 2.

Sub-s (1): in para (a) words "the authority" in square brackets substituted by the Greater London Authority Act 1999, s 254, Sch 21, paras 1, 10(1), (2).

Sub-s (2): words "licensing authority" in square brackets substituted by the Greater London Authority Act 1999, s 254, Sch 21, paras 1, 2.

Sub-s (2): words "the authority" in square brackets substituted by the Greater London Authority Act 1999, s 254, Sch 21, paras 1, 10(1), (3).

Sub-s (3): words "licensing authority" in square brackets substituted by the Greater London Authority Act 1999, s 254, Sch 21, paras 1, 2.

18 Variation of operator's licence at the request of the operator (1) The [licensing authority] may, on the application of a London PHV operator, vary his licence by adding a reference to a new operating centre or removing an existing reference to an operating centre.

(2) An application for the variation of a licence under this section shall be made in such form, and include such declarations and information, as the [licensing authority] may require.

(3) The [licensing authority] may require an applicant to furnish such further information as he may consider necessary for dealing with the application.

(4) The [licensing authority] shall not add a reference to a new operating centre unless [the authority] is satisfied that the premises in question meet any requirements prescribed under section 3(3)(b).

(5) An applicant for the variation of a London PHV operator's licence under this section may appeal to a magistrates' court against a decision not to add a new operating centre to the licence.

Amendment

Sub-s (1): words "licensing authority" in square brackets substituted by the Greater London Authority Act 1999, s 254, Sch 21, paras 1, 2.

Sub-s (2): words "licensing authority" in square brackets substituted by the Greater London Authority Act 1999, s 254, Sch 21, paras 1, 2.

Sub-s (3): words "licensing authority" in square brackets substituted by the Greater London Authority Act 1999, s 254, Sch 21, paras 1, 2.

Sub-s (4): words "licensing authority" in square brackets substituted by the Greater London Authority Act 1999, s 254, Sch 21, paras 1, 2.

Sub-s (4): words "the authority" in square brackets substituted by the Greater London Authority Act 1999, s 254, Sch 21, paras 1, 11.

19 [Variation of operator's licence by the licensing authority] (1) The [licensing authority] may—
- (a) suspend the operation of a London PHV operator's licence so far as relating to any operating centre specified in the licence; or
- (b) vary such a licence by removing a reference to an operating centre previously specified in the licence,

if [the authority] is no longer satisfied that the operating centre in question meets any requirements prescribed under section 3(3)(b) or for any other reasonable cause.

(2) Where the [licensing authority] has decided to suspend the operation of a licence as mentioned in subsection (1)(a) or vary a licence as mentioned in subsection (1)(b)—
- (a) [the authority] shall give notice of the decision and the grounds for it to the licence holder; and
- (b) the decision shall take effect at the end of the period of 21 days beginning with the day on which the licence holder is served with that notice.

(3) If the [licensing authority] is of the opinion that the interests of public safety require [the authority's] decision to have immediate effect, and [the authority] includes a statement of that opinion and the reasons for it in the notice, [the authority's] decision shall take effect when the notice is served on the licence holder.

(4) If a licence is suspended in relation to an operating centre, the premises in question shall not be regarded for the purposes of this Act as premises at which the licence holder is authorised to accept private hire bookings, until such time as the [licensing authority] by notice states that the licence is no longer suspended in relation to those premises.

(5) The holder of a London PHV operator's licence may appeal to a magistrates' court against a decision under subsection (1).

Amendment

Provision heading: substituted by the Greater London Authority Act 1999, s 254, Sch 21, paras 1, 12(1), (5).

Sub-s (1): words "licensing authority" in square brackets substituted by the Greater London Authority Act 1999, s 254, Sch 21, paras 1, 2.

Sub-s (1): words "the authority" in square brackets substituted by the Greater London Authority Act 1999, s 254, Sch 21, paras 1, 12(1), (2).

Sub-s (2): words "licensing authority" in square brackets substituted by the Greater London Authority Act 1999, s 254, Sch 21, paras 1, 2.

Sub-s (2): in para (a) words "the authority" in square brackets substituted by the Greater London Authority Act 1999, s 254, Sch 21, paras 1, 12(1), (3).

Sub-s (3): words "licensing authority" in square brackets substituted by the Greater London Authority Act 1999, s 254, Sch 21, paras 1, 2.

Sub-s (3): words "the authority's" in square brackets in both places they occur substituted by the Greater London Authority Act 1999, s 254, Sch 21, paras 1, 12(1), (4)(a).

Sub-s (3): words "the authority" in square brackets substituted by the Greater London Authority Act 1999, s 254, Sch 21, paras 1, 12(1), (4)(b).

Sub-s (4): words "licensing authority" in square brackets substituted by the Greater London Authority Act 1999, s 254, Sch 21, paras 1, 2.

20 Fees for grant of licences, etc (1) The [licensing authority] may by regulations provide for prescribed fees to be payable—

    (a) by an applicant for a licence under this Act, or for the variation of a London operator's licence under section 18, on making the application;

    (b) by a person granted a licence or variation, on the grant or variation of the licence and (if the regulations so provide) at such times while the licence is in force as may be prescribed.

(2) Regulations under this section may provide for fees to be payable by instalments, or for fees to be remitted or refunded (in whole or part), in prescribed cases.

(3) The [licensing authority] may decline to proceed with—

    (a) an application for, or for the variation of, a licence; or

    (b) the grant or variation of a licence,

until any prescribed fee (or instalment) due in respect of the application or grant is paid.

Amendment

Sub-s (1): words "licensing authority" in square brackets substituted by the Greater London Authority Act 1999, s 254, Sch 21, paras 1, 2.

Sub-s (3): words "licensing authority" in square brackets substituted by the Greater London Authority Act 1999, s 254, Sch 21, paras 1, 2.

21 Production of documents (1) The holder of a London PHV operator's licence or a London PHV driver's licence shall at the request of a constable or authorised officer produce his licence for inspection.

(2) The owner of a vehicle to which a London PHV licence relates shall at the request of a constable or authorised officer produce for inspection—

(a) the London PHV licence for that vehicle;

(b) the certificate of the policy of insurance or security required in respect of the vehicle by Part VI of the Road Traffic Act 1988.

(3) A document required to be produced under this section shall be produced either forthwith or—

(a) if the request is made by a constable, at any police station within London nominated by the licence holder or vehicle owner when the request is made, or

(b) if the request is made by an authorised officer, at such place as the officer may reasonably require,

before the end of the period of 6 days beginning with the day on which the request is made.

(4) A person who without reasonable excuse contravenes this section is guilty of an offence and liable on summary conviction to a fine not exceeding level 3 on the standard scale.

22 Return of licences, etc (1) [Without prejudice to subsection (1A),] the holder of a London PHV operator's licence shall return the licence to the [licensing authority] after the expiry or revocation of that licence, within the period of 7 days after the day on which the licence expires or the revocation takes effect.

[(1A) Where the suspension or revocation of a London PHV operator's licence has immediate effect by virtue of section 17(2), the holder of the licence shall, at the request of a constable or authorised officer, forthwith return the licence to the constable or officer.]

(2) [Without prejudice to subsection (2A),] the owner of a vehicle to which a London PHV licence relates shall return the licence and *the plate or disc* [every plate or disc] which was issued for the vehicle under section 10 [or any regulations made under this Act] to the [licensing authority] after the expiry or revocation of that licence within the period of 7 days after the day on which the licence expires or the revocation takes effect.

[(2A) Where the suspension or revocation of a London PHV licence has immediate effect by virtue of section 9(3) or 17(2), the owner of the vehicle to which the licence relates shall, at the request of a constable or authorised officer, forthwith return to the constable or officer the licence and every plate or disc which was issued for the vehicle under section 10 or any regulations made under this Act.]

(3) [Without prejudice to subsection (3A),] the holder of a London PHV driver's licence shall return the licence and his driver's badge to the [licensing authority] after the expiry or revocation of that licence, within the period of 7 days after the day on which the licence expires or the revocation takes effect.

[(3A) Where the suspension or revocation of a London PHV driver's licence has immediate effect by virtue of section 17(2), the holder of the licence shall, at the request of a constable or authorised officer, forthwith return his driver's badge to the constable or officer.]

(4) [Without prejudice to subsections (1A), (2A) and (3A),] on the suspension of a licence under this Act, the [licensing authority], a constable or an authorised officer may by notice direct the holder of the licence, or the owner of the vehicle, to return the licence to [the authority, constable or officer (as the case may be)] within the period of 7 days after the day on which the notice is served on that person.

A direction under this subsection may also direct—
  (a) the return by the vehicle owner of *the disc or plate* [every disc or plate] which was issued for the vehicle under section 10 [or any regulations made under this Act] (in the case of a London PHV licence); or
  (b) the return by the licence holder of the driver's badge (in the case of a London PHV driver's licence).

(5) A person who without reasonable excuse fails to comply with any requirement or direction under this section to return a licence, disc, plate or badge is guilty of an offence.

(6) A person guilty of an offence under this section is liable on summary conviction—
  (a) to a fine not exceeding level 3 on the standard scale; and
  (b) in the case of a continuing offence, to a fine not exceeding ten pounds for each day during which an offence continues after conviction.

(7) A constable or authorised officer is entitled to remove and retain *the plate or disc* [every disc or plate] from a vehicle to which an expired, suspended or revoked London PHV licence relates following—
  (a) a failure to comply with subsection (2) or a direction under subsection (4);
  (b) a suspension or revocation of the licence which has immediate effect by virtue of section 9(3) or 17(2).

Amendment

Sub-s (1): words "Without prejudice to subsection (1A)," in square brackets prospectively inserted by the Transport for London Act 2008, s 24(1), (2).

Sub-s (1): words "licensing authority" in square brackets substituted by the Greater London Authority Act 1999, s 254, Sch 21, paras 1, 2.

Sub-s (1A): prospectively inserted by the Transport for London Act 2008, s 24(1), (3).

Sub-s (2): words "Without prejudice to subsection (2A)," in square brackets prospectively inserted by the Transport for London Act 2008, s 24(1), (4)(a).

Sub-s (2): words "the plate or disc" in italics prospectively repealed and subsequent words in square brackets prospectively substituted by the Transport for London Act 2008, s 24(1), (4)(b).

Sub-s (2): words "or any regulations made under this Act" in square brackets prospectively inserted by the Transport for London Act 2008, s 24(1), (4)(c).

Sub-s (2): words "licensing authority" in square brackets substituted by the Greater London Authority Act 1999, s 254, Sch 21, paras 1, 2.

Sub-s (2A): prospectively inserted by the Transport for London Act 2008, s 24(1), (5).

Sub-s (3): words "Without prejudice to subsection (3A)," in square brackets prospectively inserted by the Transport for London Act 2008, s 24(1), (6).

Sub-s (3): words "licensing authority" in square brackets substituted by the Greater London Authority Act 1999, s 254, Sch 21, paras 1, 2.

Sub-s (3A): prospectively inserted by the Transport for London Act 2008, s 24(1), (7).

Sub-s (4): words "Without prejudice to subsections (1A), (2A) and (3A)," in square brackets prospectively inserted by the Transport for London Act 2008, s 24(1), (8)(a).

Sub-s (4): words "licensing authority" in square brackets substituted by the Greater London Authority Act 1999, s 254, Sch 21, paras 1, 2.

Sub-s (4): words "the authority, constable or officer (as the case may be)" in square brackets substituted by the Greater London Authority Act 1999, s 254, Sch 21, paras 1, 13.

Sub-s (4): in para (a) words "the disc or plate" in italics prospectively repealed and subsequent words in square prospectively substituted by the Transport for London Act 2008, s 24(1), (8)(b).

Sub-s (4): words "or any regulations made under this Act" in square brackets prospectively inserted by the Transport for London Act 2008, s 24(1), (8)(b).

Sub-s (7): words "the plate of disc" in italics prospectively repealed and subsequent words in square brackets prospectively substituted by the Transport for London Act 2008, s 24(1), (9).

23 Register of licences (1) The [licensing authority] shall maintain a register containing the following particulars for each licence issued under this Act, namely—

    (a) the number of the licence, the name . . . of the person to whom it is granted, the date on which it is granted and the expiry date; and

    (b) such other particulars as may be prescribed.

(2) The register [kept under subsection (1)] shall be available for inspection free of charge by members of the public at such place or places, and during such hours, as are determined by the [licensing authority].

[(3) The licensing authority shall maintain a supplementary register containing, for each licence issued under this Act, the address of the person to whom it is granted.

(4) The licensing authority may disclose the address of a licence holder to any person only if it appears to the authority that the person has a sufficient reason for requiring that information.]

Amendment

Sub-s (1): words "licensing authority" in square brackets substituted by the Greater London Authority Act 1999, s 254, Sch 21, paras 1, 2.

Sub-s (1): in para (a) words omitted repealed by the Transport for London Act 2008, s 26(1), (2).

Sub-s (2): words "kept under subsection (1)" in square brackets inserted by the Transport for London Act 2008, s 26(1), (3).

Sub-s (2): words "licensing authority" in square brackets substituted by the Greater London Authority Act 1999, s 254, Sch 21, paras 1, 2.

Sub-ss (3), (4): inserted by the Transport for London Act 2008, s 26(1), (4).

24 [Delegation of functions by the licensing authority] (1) The functions of the [licensing authority] under this Act (apart from any power to make subordinate legislation) may be exercised by any person appointed by the [licensing authority] for the purpose to such extent and subject to such conditions as may be specified in the appointment.

(2) An appointment under this section may authorise the person appointed to retain any fees received by him.

(3) It is the duty of a person appointed under this section to comply with any directions given to him by the [licensing authority] in relation to the exercise of functions under this Act.

Amendment
Provision heading: substituted by the Greater London Authority Act 1999, s 254, Sch 21, paras 1, 14.
Sub-s (1): words "licensing authority" in square brackets in both places they occur substituted by the Greater London Authority Act 1999, s 254, Sch 21, paras 1, 2.
Sub-s (3): words "licensing authority" in square brackets substituted by the Greater London Authority Act 1999, s 254, Sch 21, paras 1, 2.

25 Appeals (1) This section applies to any appeal which lies under this Act to a magistrates' court against a decision of the [licensing authority], a constable or an authorised officer in relation to, or to an application for, a licence under this Act.

(2) If the [licensing authority] has exercised the power to delegate functions under section 24, such an appeal shall be heard by [a magistrates' court].

(3) Any such appeal shall be by way of complaint for an order and the Magistrates' Courts Act 1980 shall apply to the proceedings.

(4) The time within which a person may bring such an appeal is 21 days from the date on which notice of the decision appealed against is served on him.

(5) In the case of a decision where an appeal lies, the notice of the decision shall state the right of appeal to a magistrates' court and the time within which an appeal may be brought.

(6) An appeal against any decision of a magistrates' court in pursuance of an appeal to which this section applies shall lie to the Crown Court at the instance of any party to the proceedings in the magistrates' court.

(7) Where on appeal a court varies or reverses any decision of the [licensing authority], a constable or an authorised officer, the order of the court shall be given effect to by the [licensing authority] or, as the case may be, a constable or authorised officer.

[(8) On an appeal under this Act to the magistrates' court or the Crown Court, the court is not entitled to entertain any question as to whether—
    (a) a person should be, or should have been, granted leave to enter or remain in the United Kingdom; or

(b)   a person has, after the date of the decision being appealed against, been granted leave to enter or remain in the United Kingdom.]

Amendment

Sub-s (1): words "licensing authority" in square brackets substituted by the Greater London Authority Act 1999, s 254, Sch 21, paras 1, 2.

Sub-s (2): words "licensing authority" in square brackets substituted by the Greater London Authority Act 1999, s 254, Sch 21, paras 1, 2.

Sub-s (2): words "a magistrates' court" in square brackets substituted by the Courts Act 2003 (Consequential Provisions) Order 2005, SI 2005/886, art 2, Schedule, para 54.

Sub-s (7): words "licensing authority" in square brackets in both places they occur substituted by the Greater London Authority Act 1999, s 254, Sch 21, paras 1, 2.

Sub-s (8): inserted by the Immigration Act 2016, s 37, Sch 5, paras 34, 41.

26 Effect of appeal on decision appealed against (1) If any decision of the [licensing authority] against which a right of appeal is conferred by this Act—
   (a)   involves the execution of any work or the taking of any action;
   (b)   makes it unlawful for any person to carry on a business which he was lawfully carrying on at the time of the decision,

the decision shall not take effect until the time for appealing has expired or (where an appeal is brought) until the appeal is disposed of or withdrawn.

(2) This section does not apply in relation to a decision to suspend, vary or revoke a licence if the notice of suspension, variation or revocation directs that, in the interests of public safety, the decision is to have immediate effect.

Amendment

Sub-s (1): words "licensing authority" in square brackets substituted by the Greater London Authority Act 1999, s 254, Sch 21, paras 1, 2.

27 Obstruction of authorised officers etc (1) A person who wilfully obstructs a constable or authorised officer acting in pursuance of this Act is guilty of an offence and liable on summary conviction to a fine not exceeding level 3 on the standard scale.

(2) A person who, without reasonable excuse—
   (a)   fails to comply with any requirement properly made to such person by a constable or authorised officer acting in pursuance of this Act; or
   (b)   fails to give a constable or authorised officer acting in pursuance of this Act any other assistance or information which he may reasonably require of such person for the purpose of performing his functions under this Act,

is guilty of an offence and liable on summary conviction to a fine not exceeding level 3 on the standard scale.

(3) A person who makes any statement which he knows to be false in giving any information to an authorised officer or constable acting in pursuance of this Act

is guilty of an offence and liable on summary conviction to a fine not exceeding level 5 on the standard scale.

28 Penalty for false statements A person who knowingly or recklessly makes a statement or furnishes information which is false or misleading in any material particular for the purpose of procuring the grant or renewal of a licence under this Act, or the variation of an operator's licence under section 18, is guilty of an offence and liable on summary conviction to a fine not exceeding level 5 on the standard scale.

29 Saving for vehicles used for funerals and weddings Nothing in this Act applies to any vehicle whose use as a private hire vehicle is limited to use in connection with funerals or weddings.

Further controls

30 Prohibition of certain signs, notices etc (1) The [licensing authority] may make regulations prohibiting the display in London on or from vehicles (other than licensed taxis and public service vehicles) of any sign, notice or other feature of a description specified in the regulations.

(2) Before making the regulations the [licensing authority] shall consult such bodies appearing to [the authority] to represent the London cab trade and the private hire vehicle trade in London as [the authority] considers appropriate.

(3) Any person who—
    (a) drives a vehicle in respect of which a prohibition imposed by regulations under this section is contravened; or
    (b) causes or permits such a prohibition to be contravened in respect of any vehicle,

is guilty of an offence and liable on summary conviction to a fine not exceeding level 4 on the standard scale.

Amendment
Sub-s (1): words "licensing authority" in square brackets substituted by the Greater London Authority Act 1999, s 254, Sch 21, paras 1, 2.
Sub-s (2): words "licensing authority" in square brackets substituted by the Greater London Authority Act 1999, s 254, Sch 21, paras 1, 2.
Sub-s (2): words "the authority" in square brackets in both places they occur substituted by the Greater London Authority Act 1999, s 254, Sch 21, paras 1, 15.

31 Prohibition of certain advertisements (1) This section applies to any advertisement—
    (a) indicating that vehicles can be hired on application to a specified address in London;
    (b) indicating that vehicles can be hired by telephone on a telephone number being the number of premises in London; or

(c)   on or near any premises in London, indicating that vehicles can be hired at those premises.

(2)   No such advertisement shall include—
(a)   any of the following words, namely "taxi", "taxis", "cab" or "cabs", or
(b)   any word so closely resembling any of those words as to be likely to be mistaken for it,

(whether alone or as part of another word), unless the vehicles offered for hire are London cabs.

(3)   An advertisement which includes the word "minicab", "mini-cab" or "mini cab" (whether in the singular or plural) does not by reason only of that fact contravene this section.

(4)   Any person who issues, or causes to be issued, an advertisement which contravenes this section is guilty of an offence and liable on summary conviction to a fine not exceeding level 4 on the standard scale.

(5)   It is a defence for a person charged with an offence under this section to prove that—
(a)   he is a person whose business it is to publish or arrange for the publication of advertisements;
(b)   he received the advertisement in question for publication in the ordinary course of business; and
(c)   he did not know and had no reason to suspect that its publication would amount to an offence under this section.

(6)   In this section—
"advertisement" includes every form of advertising (whatever the medium) and references to the issue of an advertisement shall be construed accordingly;
"telephone number" includes any number used for the purposes of communicating with another by electronic means; and "telephone" shall be construed accordingly.

Miscellaneous and supplementary

32 Regulations (1) The [licensing authority] may make regulations for any purpose for which regulations may be made under this Act [(other than section [3A(8), 13A(8) or] 37)] or for prescribing anything which falls to be prescribed under any provision of this Act [(other than section 37)].

(2)   Regulations under this Act may—
(a)   make different provision for different cases;
(b)   provide for exemptions from any provision of the regulations; and
(c)   contain incidental, consequential, transitional and supplemental provision.

[(2A) The power to make regulations conferred on the Secretary of State by section 3A(8) or 13A(8) is exercisable by statutory instrument.

(2B) A statutory instrument containing regulations under either of those sections may not be made unless a draft of the instrument has been laid before, and approved by a resolution of, each House of Parliament.]

(3) Any power to make regulations [conferred on the Secretary of State by section 37] is exercisable by statutory instrument which shall be subject to annulment in pursuance of a resolution of either House of Parliament.

[(4) Any power of the licensing authority to make regulations under this Act includes power to vary or revoke previous regulations made under this Act (other than regulations made under section [3A(8), 13A(8) or] 37).

(5) Subsection (4) applies notwithstanding that the previous regulations in question were made by the Secretary of State by statutory instrument.

(6) The licensing authority shall secure that any regulations made under this Act by the authority are printed and published.

(7) A fee may be charged for the sale of regulations printed and published under subsection (6).]

Amendment
Sub-s (1): words "licensing authority" in square brackets substituted by the Greater London Authority Act 1999, s 254, Sch 21, paras 1, 2.
Sub-s (1): words "(other than section 37)" in square brackets in both places they occur inserted by the Greater London Authority Act 1999, s 254, Sch 21, paras 1, 16(1), (2).
Sub-s (1): words "3A(8), 13A(8) or" in square brackets inserted by the Immigration Act 2016, s 37, Sch 5, paras 34, 42(1), (2).
Sub-ss (2A), (2B): inserted by the Immigration Act 2016, s 37, Sch 5, paras 34, 42(1), (3).
Sub-s (3): words "conferred on the Secretary of State by section 37" in square brackets substituted by the Greater London Authority Act 1999, s 254, Sch 21, paras 1, 16(1), (3).
Sub-ss (4)-(7): inserted by the Greater London Authority Act 1999, s 254, Sch 21, paras 1, 16(1), (4).
Sub-s (4): words "3A(8), 13A(8) or" in square brackets inserted by the Immigration Act 2016, s 37, Sch 5, paras 34, 42(1), (2).

33 Offences due to fault of other person (1) Where an offence by any person under this Act is due to the act or default of another person, then (whether proceedings are taken against the first mentioned person or not) that other person is guilty of the offence and is liable to be proceeded against and punished accordingly.

(2) Where an offence under this Act committed by a body corporate is proved to have been committed with the consent or connivance of, or attributable to any neglect on the part of, any director, manager, secretary or other similar officer of the body corporate (or any person purporting to act in that capacity), he as well as the body corporate is guilty of the offence is liable to be proceeded against and punished accordingly.

34 Service of notices (1) Any notice authorised or required under this Act to be given to any person may be served by post.

(2) For the purposes of section 7 of the Interpretation Act 1978 any such notice is properly addressed to a London PHV operator if it is addressed to him at any operating centre of his in London.

(3) Any notice authorised or required under this Act to be given to the owner of a vehicle shall be deemed to have been effectively given if it is given to the person who is for the time being notified to the [licensing authority] for the purposes of this Act as the owner of the vehicle (or, if more than one person is currently notified as the owner, if it is given to any of them).

Amendment

Sub-s (3): words "licensing authority" in square brackets substituted by the Greater London Authority Act 1999, s 254, Sch 21, paras 1, 2.

35 References to the owner of a vehicle (1) For the purposes of this Act the owner of a vehicle shall be taken to be the person by whom it is kept.

(2) In determining, in the course of any proceedings for an offence under this Act, who was the owner of a vehicle at any time it shall be presumed that the owner was the person who was the registered keeper of the vehicle at that time.

(3) Notwithstanding that presumption—
  (a) it is open to the defence to show that the person who was the registered keeper of a vehicle at any particular time was not the person by whom the vehicle was kept at that time; and
  (b) it is open to the prosecution to prove that the vehicle was kept at that time by some person other than the registered keeper.

(4) In this section "registered keeper", in relation to a vehicle, means the person in whose name the vehicle was registered under the Vehicle Excise and Registration Act 1994.

[35A Persons disqualified by reason of immigration status (1) For the purposes of this Act a person is disqualified by reason of the person's immigration status from carrying on a licensable activity if the person is subject to immigration control and—
  (a) the person has not been granted leave to enter or remain in the United Kingdom; or
  (b) the person's leave to enter or remain in the United Kingdom—
    (i) is invalid;
    (ii) has ceased to have effect (whether by reason of curtailment, revocation, cancellation, passage of time or otherwise); or
    (iii) is subject to a condition preventing the person from carrying on the licensable activity.

(2) Where a person is on immigration bail within the meaning of Part 1 of Schedule 10 to the Immigration Act 2016—
  (a) the person is to be treated for the purposes of this Act as if the person had been granted leave to enter the United Kingdom; but

    (b) any condition as to the person's work in the United Kingdom to which the person's immigration bail is subject is to be treated for those purposes as a condition of leave.

(3) For the purposes of this section a person is subject to immigration control if under the Immigration Act 1971 the person requires leave to enter or remain in the United Kingdom.

(4) For the purposes of this section a person carries on a licensable activity if the person—
    (a) operates a private hire vehicle; or
    (b) drives a private hire vehicle.]

Amendment
Section inserted by the Immigration Act 2016, s 37, Sch 5, paras 34, 43.

[35B Immigration offences and immigration penalties (1) In this Act "immigration offence" means—
    (a) an offence under any of the Immigration Acts;
    (b) an offence under section 1 of the Criminal Attempts Act 1981 of attempting to commit an offence within paragraph (a); or
    (c) an offence under section 1 of the Criminal Law Act 1977 of conspiracy to commit an offence within paragraph (a).

(2) In this Act "immigration penalty" means a penalty under—
    (a) section 15 of the Immigration, Asylum and Nationality Act 2006 ("the 2006 Act"), or
    (b) section 23 of the Immigration Act 2014 ("the 2014 Act").

(3) For the purposes of this Act a person to whom a penalty notice under section 15 of the 2006 Act has been given is not to be treated as having been required to pay an immigration penalty if—
    (a) the person is excused payment by virtue of section 15(3) of that Act; or
    (b) the penalty is cancelled by virtue of section 16 or 17 of that Act.

(4) For the purposes of this Act a person to whom a penalty notice under section 15 of the 2006 Act has been given is not to be treated as having been required to pay an immigration penalty until such time as—
    (a) the period for giving a notice of objection under section 16 of that Act has expired and the Secretary of State has considered any notice given within that period; and
    (b) if a notice of objection was given within that period, the period for appealing under section 17 of that Act has expired and any appeal brought within that period has been finally determined, abandoned or withdrawn.

(5) For the purposes of this Act a person to whom a penalty notice under section 23 of the 2014 Act has been given is not to be treated as having been required to pay an immigration penalty if—

(a)   the person is excused payment by virtue of section 24 of that Act; or

(b)   the penalty is cancelled by virtue of section 29 or 30 of that Act.

(6) For the purposes of this Act a person to whom a penalty notice under section 23 of the 2014 Act has been given is not to be treated as having been required to pay an immigration penalty until such time as—

(a)   the period for giving a notice of objection under section 29 of that Act has expired and the Secretary of State has considered any notice given within that period; and

(b)   if a notice of objection was given within that period, the period for appealing under section 30 of that Act has expired and any appeal brought within that period has been finally determined, abandoned or withdrawn.]

Amendment
Section inserted by the Immigration Act 2016, s 37, Sch 5, paras 34, 43.

36 Interpretation In this Act, unless the context otherwise requires—

"authorised officer" means an officer authorised in writing by the [licensing authority] for the purposes of this Act;

["controlled district" means any area for which Part II of the 1976 Act is in force by virtue of—

(a)   a resolution by a district council under section 45 of that Act; or

(b)   section 255(4) of the Greater London Authority Act 1999;]

"driver's badge" means the badge issued to the holder of a London PHV driver's licence;

"hackney carriage" means a vehicle licensed under section 37 of the Town Police Clauses Act 1847 or any similar enactment;

"licensed taxi" means a hackney carriage, a London cab or a taxi licensed under Part II of the 1982 Act;

["the licensing authority" means Transport for London;]

"London" means the area consisting of the metropolitan police district and the City of London (including the Temples);

"London cab" means a vehicle licensed under section 6 of the Metropolitan Public Carriage Act 1869;

"London PHV driver's licence" means a licence under section 13;

"London PHV licence" means a licence under section 7;

"London PHV operator" has the meaning given in section 4(1);

"London PHV operator's licence" means a licence under section 2;

"notice" means notice in writing;

["operate" has the meaning given in section 1(1);]

"operating centre" has the meaning given in section 1(5);

"operator" has the meaning given in section 1(1);

"prescribed" means prescribed in regulations under section 32(1);

"private hire vehicle" has the meaning given in section 1(1);

"public service vehicle" has the same meaning as in the Public Passenger Vehicles Act 1981, "road" means any length of highway or of any other road to which the public has access (including bridges over which a road passes);

"the 1976 Act" means the Local Government (Miscellaneous Provisions) Act 1976;

"the 1982 Act" means the Civic Government (Scotland) Act 1982; and

"vehicle" means a mechanically propelled vehicle (other than a tramcar) intended or adapted for use on roads.

Amendment

In definition "authorised officer" words "licensing authority" in square brackets substituted by the Greater London Authority Act 1999, s 254, Sch 21, paras 1, 2.

Definition "controlled district" substituted by the Greater London Authority Act 1999 (Commencement No. 8 and Consequential Provisions) Order 2000, SI 2000/3145, art 3.

Definition "the licensing authority" inserted by the Greater London Authority Act 1999, s 254, Sch 21, paras 1, 17.

Definition "operate" inserted by the Immigration Act 2016, s 37, Sch 5, paras 34, 44.

37 Power to make transitional etc provisions (1) The Secretary of State may by regulations make such transitional provisions and such savings as he considers necessary or expedient in preparation for, in connection with, or in consequence of—

(a) the coming into force of any provision of this Act; or

(b) the operation of any enactment repealed or amended by a provision of this Act during any period when the repeal or amendment is not wholly in force.

(2) Regulations under this section may modify any enactment contained in this or in any other Act.

[(3) Before making regulations under this section the Secretary of State shall consult the licensing authority.]

Amendment

Sub-s (3): inserted by the Greater London Authority Act 1999, s 254, Sch 21, paras 1, 18.

38 . . .

Amendment

Section repealed by the Greater London Authority Act 1999, ss 254, 423, Sch 21, paras 1, 19, Sch 34, Pt V.

39 Consequential amendments and repeals (1) Schedule 1 (minor and consequential amendments) shall have effect.

(2) The enactments mentioned in Schedule 2 are repealed to the extent specified.

40 Short title, commencement and extent (1) This Act may be cited as the Private Hire Vehicles (London) Act 1998.

(2) This Act (apart from this section) shall come into force on such date as the Secretary of State may by order made by statutory instrument appoint; but different dates may be appointed for different purposes.

An order under this subsection may contain any provision which could be made under section 37 in connection with any provision brought into force by the order.

(3) Any provision of this Act which amends or repeals any other Act has the same extent as the provision being amended or repealed.

(4) Subject to subsection (3), this Act extends only to England and Wales.

SCHEDULE 1
Minor and Consequential Amendments

Section 39(1)

Local Government (Miscellaneous Provisions) Act 1976 (c 57)

1 In section 75 of the Local Government (Miscellaneous Provisions) Act 1976 (exemptions), after subsection (2A) there shall be inserted the following subsection—

"(2B) Paragraphs (a), (b) and (c) of section 46(1) of this Act shall not apply to the use or driving of a vehicle, or to the employment of a driver of a vehicle, if—
    (a) a London PHV licence issued under section 7 of the Private Hire Vehicles (London) Act 1998 is in force in relation to that vehicle; and
    (b) the driver of the vehicle holds a London PHV driver's licence issued under section 13 of that Act."

Public Passenger Vehicles Act 1981 (c 14)

2 In section 79 of the Public Passenger Vehicles Act 1981 (vehicles excluded from regulation as private hire vehicles), after the word "1982" there shall be inserted the words ", in the Private Hire Vehicles (London) Act 1998".

Civic Government (Scotland) Act 1982 (c 45)

3 In section 21 of the Civic Government (Scotland) Act 1982 (offences), after subsection (3) there shall be inserted the following subsection—

"(3A) Subsection (1)(b) above does not apply to the operation of a vehicle within an area in respect of which its operation or its driver is not licensed if there are in force—
    (a) in respect of the vehicle, a licence under section 7 of the Private Hire Vehicles (London) Act 1998; and
    (b) in respect of its driver, a licence under section 13 of that Act."

Transport Act 1985 (c 67)

4 In section 13(3) of the Transport Act 1985 (defined terms for sections 10 to 13 of that Act), in the definition of "licensed hire car", at the end there shall be inserted the words "or section 7 of the Private Hire Vehicles (London) Act 1998".

SCHEDULE 2
Repeals

Section 39(2)

Chapter	Short title	Extent of repeal
1968 c 7	London Cab Act 1968.	Sections 4 and 4A.
1973 c 20	London Cab Act 1973.	The whole Act.
1990 c 42	Broadcasting Act 1990.	In Schedule 20, paragraph 10.
1992 c 42	Transport and Works Act 1992.	Section 62(2).

Greater London Authority Act 1999

Part IV
Transport

Chapter XI
Hackney Carriages and Private Hire Vehicles

253 Hackney carriages Schedule 20 to this Act (which makes provision about hackney carriages) shall have effect.

254 The Private Hire Vehicles (London) Act 1998 (1) Except as provided by the following provisions of this section, the functions of the Secretary of State under the Private Hire Vehicles (London) Act 1998 are transferred by this subsection to Transport for London.

(2) Subsection (1) above does not apply to any functions of the Secretary of State under section 37, 38 or 40 of that Act (transitional provisions, financial provisions and commencement etc).

(3) Schedule 21 to this Act (which makes amendments to the Private Hire Vehicles (London) Act 1998 in consequence of subsections (1) and (2) above) shall have effect.

(4) Any regulations made, licence issued, authorisation granted, or other thing done under the Private Hire Vehicles (London) Act 1998, other than section 37, 38 or 40, by or in relation to the Secretary of State before the coming into force of this section shall have effect as from the coming into force of this section as made, issued, granted or done by or in relation to Transport for London.

255 Provisions consequent on alteration of metropolitan police district (1) Where, by virtue of the coming into force of section 323 below, the whole or any part of the area of a district council ceases to be within the metropolitan police district, the following provisions of this section shall have effect.

(2) The provisions of the Town Police Clauses Act 1847 with respect to hackney carriages, as incorporated in the Public Health Act 1875, shall apply throughout the council's area.

(3) The council's area shall constitute a single licensing area for the purposes of those provisions, without the passing of any resolution under Part II of Schedule 14 to the Local Government Act 1972 (extension resolutions).

(4) The provisions of Part II of the Local Government (Miscellaneous Provisions) Act 1976 (hackney carriages and private hire vehicles) shall also apply

throughout the council's area, without the passing of any resolution under section 45 of that Act (application of Part II).

(5) Where an order is made under section 425 below bringing section 323 below into force, the provision that may be made by virtue of section 420 or 425 below includes provision enabling or facilitating—

(a) the making of byelaws,

(b) the issuing of licences, discs or plates, and

(c) the establishment and operation of a licensing system,

in relation to hackney carriages or private hire vehicles by a district council falling within subsection (1) above in preparation for the coming into force of this section.

(6) The provision that may be made by virtue of subsection (5) above includes provision for the application of any enactment with or without modification.

(7) Subsections (5) and (6) above are without prejudice to the provision that may be made by virtue of sections 420 and 425 below.

SCHEDULE 20
Hackney Carriages

Section 253

Part I
Transfers of Functions and Amendments

The London Hackney Carriages Act 1843

1 (1) All the jurisdiction, powers, authorities, privileges, interests and duties which, immediately before the coming into force of this paragraph, were vested in or exercisable by the Commissioners of Police of the Metropolis by virtue of section 2 of the London Hackney Carriages Act 1850 (transfer of functions of registrar of metropolitan public carriages to Commissioners of Police of the Metropolis) are transferred to and vested in Transport for London by this subparagraph.

(2) The London Hackney Carriages Act 1843 shall accordingly be amended as follows.

(3) For "the registrar" and "the said registrar", wherever occurring, there shall be substituted "Transport for London".

(4) In section 18 (licences and tickets to be delivered up on discontinuance of licence) for "him" there shall be substituted "Transport for London".

(5) In section 19 (new tickets to be delivered instead of defaced or lost tickets) for "for the use of Her Majesty" there shall be substituted "to Transport for London".

The London Hackney Carriages Act 1850

2 (1) The London Hackney Carriages Act 1850 shall be amended as follows.

(2) In section 4 (standings for hackney carriages to be appointed and regulated by the Commissioners of Police of the Metropolis)—
  (a) for "the said Commissioners of Police" and, where first and second occurring, "the said commissioners" there shall be substituted "Transport for London";
  (b) for "signed by one of the said commissioners" there shall be substituted "signed by a person authorised for the purpose by Transport for London";
  (c) for "the office of the Commissioners of Police in the City of Westminster" there shall be substituted "the offices of Transport for London";
  (d) for "the signature of the said commissioner" there shall be substituted "the aforesaid signature".

The London Hackney Carriage Act 1853

3 (1) The London Hackney Carriage Act 1853 shall be amended as follows.

(2) In section 2 (powers of inspection of carriages etc) for—
  (a) "the said Commissioners of Police", and
  (b) "the said commissioners", in both places where those words occur,

there shall be substituted "Transport for London".

(3) In section 17 (penalties for offences) in paragraph 1 (excessive fares and refusal to carry authorised number of passengers or reasonable quantity of luggage) for "the said Commissioners of Police" there shall be substituted "Transport for London".

(4) In section 20 (powers of Commissioners of Police etc) for the words from the beginning to "appoint; and" there shall be substituted "In this Act".

. . .

4 . . .

The Metropolitan Public Carriage Act 1869

5 (1) The Metropolitan Public Carriage Act 1869 shall be amended as follows.

(2) In section 4 (interpretation)—
  (a) for the definition of "Prescribed" there shall be substituted the following definitions—
    ""London cab order" shall mean an order made by Transport for London.
    "Prescribed" shall mean prescribed by London cab order."; and
  (b) at the end of the section there shall be added the following paragraph—

"Any power to make a London cab order under this Act includes power to vary or revoke a previous such order."

(3) For section 6 (grant of hackney carriage licences) there shall be substituted—

"6 Grant of hackney carriage licences (1) Transport for London shall have the function of licensing to ply for hire within the limits of this Act hackney carriages, to be distinguished in such manner as may be prescribed.

(2) A licence under this section may—
    (a) be granted on such conditions,
    (b) be in such form,
    (c) be subject to revocation or suspension in such event, and
    (d) generally be dealt with in such manner,

as may be prescribed.

(3) Subsection (2) of this section is subject to the following provisions of this section.

(4) A licence under this section shall, if not revoked or suspended, be in force for one year.

(5) A fee of such amount (if any) as Transport for London may determine shall be paid to Transport for London—
    (a) by any applicant for a licence under this section, on making the application for the licence;
    (b) by any applicant for the taking or re-taking of any test or examination, or any part of a test or examination, with respect to any matter of fitness, on making the application for the taking or re-taking of the test, examination or part; and
    (c) by any person granted a licence under this section, on the grant of the licence.

(6) In paragraph (b) of subsection (5) of this section "matter of fitness" means—
    (a) any matter as respects which Transport for London must be satisfied before granting a licence under this section; or
    (b) any matter such that, if Transport for London is not satisfied with respect to the matter, they may refuse to grant a licence under this section.

(7) Different amounts may be determined under subsection (5) of this section for different purposes or different cases.

(8) Transport for London may remit or refund the whole or part of a fee under subsection (5) of this section.

(9) Provision shall be made by London cab order—
    (a) for the transfer of a licence under this section to the widow or to any child of full age of any person to whom such a licence has been granted who may die during the continuance of the licence leaving a widow or child of full age; and

(b) for the transfer of a licence under this section to the husband of any woman to whom such a licence has been granted and who marries during the continuance of the licence."

(4) In section 7 (penalty on use of unlicensed carriage) the words "by the said Secretary of State" shall cease to have effect.

(5) For section 8 (hackney carriage to be driven by licensed drivers) there shall be substituted—

"8 Hackney carriage to be driven by licensed drivers (1) Transport for London shall have the function of licensing persons to be drivers of hackney carriages.

(2) No hackney carriage shall ply for hire within the limits of this Act unless under the charge of a driver having a licence under this section from Transport for London.

(3) If any hackney carriage plies for hire in contravention of this section—
    (a) the person driving the carriage, and
    (b) the owner of the carriage, unless he proves that the driver acted without his privity or consent,

shall each be liable to a penalty not exceeding level 3 on the standard scale.

(4) Transport for London may send to the Commissioner of Police of the Metropolis or the Commissioner of Police for the City of London—
    (a) details of a person to whom Transport for London is considering granting a licence under this section, and
    (b) a request for the Commissioner's observations;

and the Commissioner shall respond to the request.

(5) A licence under this section may—
    (a) be granted on such conditions,
    (b) be in such form,
    (c) be subject to revocation or suspension in such event, and
    (d) generally be dealt with in such manner,

as may be prescribed.

(6) Subsection (5) of this section is subject to the following provisions of this section.

(7) A licence under this section shall, if not revoked or suspended, be in force for three years.

(8) A fee of such amount (if any) as Transport for London may determine shall be paid to Transport for London—
    (a) by any applicant for a licence under this section, on making the application for the licence;
    (b) by any applicant for the taking or re-taking of any test or examination, or any part of a test or examination, with respect to any matter of fitness, on making the application for the taking or re-taking of the test, examination or part; and

(c) by any person granted a licence under this section, on the grant of the licence.

(9) In paragraph (b) of subsection (8) of this section "matter of fitness" means—
    (a) any matter as respects which Transport for London must be satisfied before granting a licence under this section; or
    (b) any matter such that, if Transport for London is not satisfied with respect to the matter, they may refuse to grant a licence under this section.

(10) Different amounts may be determined under subsection (8) of this section for different purposes or different cases.

(11) Transport for London may remit or refund the whole or part of a fee under subsection (8) of this section."

(6) In section 9 (regulations as to hackney and stage carriages)—
    (a) for "The said Secretary of State may from time to time by order" there shall be substituted "Transport for London may from time to time by London cab order";
    (b) in paragraph (1) of the restrictions (consents required for stands in the City appointed by the Secretary of State) for "the Secretary of State" there shall be substituted "Transport for London"; and
    (c) at the end of the restrictions there shall be added—

"(4) Any power of Transport for London to fix by regulations made by London cab order under this section any rates or fares to be paid for hackney carriages is exercisable subject to and in accordance with any directions given to Transport for London by the Mayor of London as to the basis on which those rates or fares are to be calculated."

(7) In section 10 (power of Secretary of State to annex penalty for breach of order) for "Where the Secretary of State is authorised to make any order under this Act, he" there shall be substituted "Where Transport for London is authorised to make a London cab order under this Act, Transport for London".

(8) For section 11 (other persons by whom licences may be granted) there shall be substituted—

"11 Grant of licences by other persons at direction of TfL Any licence which may be granted by Transport for London under this Act may, if Transport for London so directs, be granted by such person as may be appointed for the purpose in the direction."

(9) In section 12 (powers to carry Act into execution)—
    (a) for "The said Secretary of State" there shall be substituted "Transport for London"; and
    (b) for "he", in both places where it occurs, there shall be substituted "Transport for London".

(10) In section 14 (power to affix placards etc to lamp posts) for "The Commissioner of the Metropolitan Police" there shall be substituted "Transport for London".

(11) In section 15 (existing Acts to continue in force) for "by any order or regulation of the said Secretary of State" there shall be substituted "by any London cab order".

The London Cab and Stage Carriage Act 1907

6 (1) The London Cab and Stage Carriage Act 1907 shall be amended as follows.

(2) In section 1(1) (power of Secretary of State to fix, by order under section 9 of the 1869 Act, fares for cabs fitted with taximeters)—
   (a) for "The Secretary of State" there shall be substituted "Transport for London";
   (b) after "regulations made" there shall be inserted "by London cab order".

(3) At the end of section 1 there shall be inserted—

"(3) The power conferred by subsection (1) of this section is subject to paragraph (4) of the restrictions specified in section nine of the said Act of 1869."

(4) In section 2 (abolition of privileged cab system)—
   (a) in subsection (1) (charges for admission to railway station not to exceed sum allowed by Secretary of State) for "the Secretary of State" there shall be substituted "Transport for London"; and
   (b) in subsection (2) (power of Secretary of State by order to suspend or modify the section in relation to a station if satisfied of insufficient supply of cabs at the station)—
      (i) for "the Secretary of State", in both places, there shall be substituted "Transport for London"; and
      (ii) for "by order" there shall be substituted "by London cab order".

(5) In section 6 (definitions) in subsection (1)—
   (a) after the definition of the expression "fare" there shall be inserted "the expression "London cab order" has the same meaning as in the Metropolitan Public Carriage Act 1869"; and
   (b) in the definition of "taximeter" (which requires the device to be approved by or on behalf of the Secretary of State) for "the Secretary of State" there shall be substituted "Transport for London".

(6) At the end of that section there shall be added—

"(4) Any power to make a London cab order under or by virtue of this Act includes power to vary or revoke a previous such order."

The London Cab Act 1968

7 (1) The London Cab Act 1968 shall be amended as follows.

(2) In section 1(1) (which extends the power of the Secretary of State to set fares under the Acts of 1869 and 1907) for "the Secretary of State" there shall be substituted "Transport for London".

(3) After subsection (1) of section 1 there shall be inserted—

"(1A) The power conferred by subsection (1) of this section is subject to paragraph (4) of the restrictions specified in section 9 of the said Act of 1869."

(4) In section 2 (power to increase length of obligatory journeys)—
    (a) in subsection (1) (the power)—
        (i) for "The Secretary of State" there shall be substituted "Transport for London";
        (ii) for "by order" there shall be substituted "by London cab order"; and
        (ii) for "him" there shall be substituted "Transport for London";
    (b) in subsection (2) (power to limit application of order) for "An order" there shall be substituted "A London cab order";
    (c) in subsection (3) (power includes power to vary or revoke previous orders and is exercisable by statutory instrument subject to negative parliamentary procedure)—
        (i) for "orders" there shall be substituted "London cab orders";
        (ii) after "previous" there shall be inserted "such"; and
        (iii) the words from "and shall be exercisable" to the end of the subsection shall cease to have effect; and
    (d) in subsection (4) (duty to consult before making order)—
        (i) for "any order" there shall be substituted "any London cab order";
        (ii) for "the Secretary of State" there shall be substituted "Transport for London"; and
        (iii) for "him" and "he" there shall be substituted "Transport for London".

(5) In section 4A (power of Secretary of State by order to prohibit signs etc on private hire cars)—
    (a) in subsection (1)—
        (i) for "The Secretary of State" there shall be substituted "Transport for London"; and
        (ii) for "by order" there shall be substituted "by London cab order";
    (b) in subsection (2), for "by an order" there shall be substituted "by a London cab order";
    (c) in subsection (3) (power includes power to vary or revoke previous orders and is exercisable by statutory instrument subject to negative parliamentary procedure)—
        (i) for "orders" there shall be substituted "London cab orders";
        (ii) after "previous" there shall be inserted "such"; and
        (iii) the words from "and shall be exercisable" to the end of the subsection shall cease to have effect;
    (d) in subsection (4) (duty to consult before making order)—
        (i) for "order" there shall be substituted "London cab order";
        (ii) for "the Secretary of State" there shall be substituted "Transport for London"; and

(iii) for "him" and "he" there shall be substituted "Transport for London"; and

(e) in subsection (5) (relationship to section 4) for "an order" there shall be substituted "a London cab order".

(6) After section 4A there shall be inserted—

"4B London cab orders (1) In this Act, "London cab order" means an order made by Transport for London.

(2) Any power to make a London cab order under or by virtue of this Act includes power to vary or revoke a previous such order."

The Transport Act 1985

8 (1) The Transport Act 1985 shall be amended as follows.

(2) In section 10 (immediate hiring of taxis at separate fares)—
   (a) in subsection (3)(a) (meaning of "licensing authority" in relation to the London taxi area) for "the Secretary of State", in both places, there shall be substituted "Transport for London";
   (b) in subsection (5)(c), the words "if made otherwise than by the Secretary of State" shall cease to have effect;
   (c) in subsection (8), the words "Except in the case of a scheme made by the Secretary of State," shall cease to have effect; and
   (d) subsection (10) (power of Secretary of State to make scheme exercisable by order) shall cease to have effect.

(3) In section 17 (London taxi and taxi driver licensing: appeals)—
   (a) in subsections (2), (5), (8)(a) and (b) and (9) (which relate to reconsideration or appeal within the prescribed period) for "prescribed period", in each place, there shall be substituted "designated period";
   (b) in subsection (10), after the definition of "the appropriate court" there shall be inserted the following definitions—
   ""designated period" means such period as may be specified for the purpose by London cab order;
   "London cab order" means an order made by Transport for London"; and
   (c) after subsection (10) there shall be added—

"(11) Any power to make a London cab order under this section includes power to vary or revoke a previous such order."

Amendment

Para 4: repealed by the Statute Law (Repeals) Act 2004, s 1(1), Sch 1, Pt 14.

Part II
Transitional Provisions

Saving

9 This Part of this Schedule is without prejudice to the provision that may be made under any power conferred on a Minister of the Crown by this Act to make subordinate legislation, within the meaning of the Interpretation Act 1978.

The London Hackney Carriages Act 1843

10 (1) Any licence to act as driver of hackney carriages—
   (a) which was issued under section 8 of the London Hackney Carriages Act 1843 by or on behalf of the Commissioner of Police of the Metropolis, and
   (b) which is in force immediately before the coming into force of paragraph 1 above,

shall have effect as from the coming into force of that paragraph as if it had been issued by Transport for London.

(2) Any metal ticket—
   (a) which was issued under that section by or on behalf of the Commissioner of Police of the Metropolis, and
   (b) which is in force immediately before the coming into force of paragraph 1 above,

shall have effect as from the coming into force of that paragraph as if it had been issued by Transport for London.

The London Hackney Carriages Act 1850

11 Any regulations made or other thing done under section 4 of the London Hackney Carriages Act 1850 by or on behalf of a Commissioner of Police of the Metropolis and in force or otherwise having effect immediately before the coming into force of paragraph 2 above shall have effect as from the coming into force of that paragraph as if made or done by or, in the case of a signature, by a person authorised for the purpose by, Transport for London.

The London Hackney Carriage Act 1853

12 Any notice given under section 2 of the London Hackney Carriage Act 1853 and having effect immediately before the coming into force of sub-paragraph (2) of paragraph 3 above shall have effect as from the coming into force of that sub-paragraph as a notice given by Transport for London.

. . .

13 . . .

The Metropolitan Public Carriage Act 1869

14 (1) Any order—
   (a) made by or on behalf of the Secretary of State under or by virtue of any enactment contained in the Metropolitan Public Carriage Act 1869, and
   (b) in force immediately before the coming into force of any provision of [paragraph 5] above in relation to that enactment,

shall, to the extent that the provision made by the order could be made by Transport for London, have effect as from the coming into force of that provision in relation to that enactment as a London cab order, but with the substitution for references to the Secretary of State of references to Transport for London.

(2) Any licence granted under section 6 or 8 of that Act and in force immediately before the coming into force of sub-paragraph (3) or (5) of paragraph 5 above in relation to that section shall have effect as from the coming into force of that sub-paragraph in relation to that section as a licence granted under that section by Transport for London.

(3) Any suspension or revocation of a licence under section 6 or 8 of that Act having effect immediately before the coming into force of sub-paragraph (3) or (5) of paragraph 5 above shall have effect as from the coming into force of that sub-paragraph in relation to that section as the suspension or revocation of the licence by Transport for London.

(4) Any appointment made under section 12 of that Act by the Secretary of State and in force immediately before the coming into force of sub-paragraph (9) of paragraph 5 above shall have effect as from the coming into force of that sub-paragraph as an appointment made by Transport for London.

The London Cab and Stage Carriage Act 1907

15 (1) Any regulations made by the Secretary of State by order by virtue of section 1 of the London Cab and Stage Carriage Act 1907 and in force immediately before the coming into force of sub-paragraph (2) of paragraph 6 above shall have effect as from the coming into force of that paragraph as regulations made by London cab order by virtue of that section.

(2) Any sum for the time being allowed by the Secretary of State under subsection (1) of section 2 of that Act immediately before the coming into force of paragraph (a) of sub-paragraph (4) of paragraph 6 above shall have effect as from the coming into force of that paragraph as the sum for the time being allowed under that subsection by Transport for London until such time as Transport for London allow a different sum.

(3) Any order made by the Secretary of State under section 2 of that Act and in force immediately before the coming into force of paragraph (b) of sub--paragraph (4) of paragraph 6 above shall have effect as from the coming into force of that paragraph as a London cab order.

(4) Any approval given by or on behalf of the Secretary of State for the purposes of the definition of "taximeter" in section 6(1) of that Act and in force immediately before the coming into force of the amendment made by paragraph (b) of sub-paragraph (5) of paragraph 6 above shall have effect as from the coming into force of that amendment as an approval given by Transport for London.

The London Cab Act 1968

16 (1) Any order made by the Secretary of State under section 2 of the London Cab Act 1968 and in force immediately before the coming into force of paragraph (a) of sub-paragraph (4) of paragraph 7 above shall have effect as from the coming into force of that paragraph as a London cab order.

(2) Any order made by the Secretary of State under section 4A of that Act and in force immediately before the coming into force of paragraph (a) of sub-paragraph (5) of paragraph 7 above shall have effect as a London cab order as from the coming into force of that paragraph.

The Transport Act 1985

17 (1) Any scheme made under section 10 of the Transport Act 1985 by the Secretary of State and in force immediately before the coming into force of paragraph (a) of sub-paragraph (2) of paragraph 8 above shall have effect as from the coming into force of that paragraph as a scheme made by Transport for London.

(2) Any regulations prescribing a period for the purposes of a provision of that Act specified in paragraph (a) of sub-paragraph (3) of paragraph 8 above and in force immediately before the coming into force of that paragraph shall, until such time as a period is specified by London cab order for the purposes of that provision, continue in force and have effect as if the period so prescribed were the period specified for the purposes of that provision by London cab order.

Amendment
Para 13: repealed by the Statute Law (Repeals) Act 2004, s 1(1), Sch 1, Pt 14.
Para 14: in sub-para (1)(b) words "paragraph 5" in square brackets substituted by the Transport for London Act 2016, s 7.

SCHEDULE 21
The Private Hire Vehicles (London) Act 1998

Section 254

1 The Private Hire Vehicles (London) Act 1998 shall be amended as follows.

2 Except in sections 37, 38 and 40, for "Secretary of State", wherever occurring, there shall be substituted "licensing authority".

3 In section 3(3) (grant of London operator's licences) for "he" there shall be substituted "the authority".

4 In section 7(2) (grant of London PHV licences) for "he" there shall be substituted "the authority".

5 In section 8(2) (presentation of vehicle for inspection and testing) for "he" there shall be substituted "the authority".

6 In section 10(3) (exemption from exhibiting disc or plate) for "he" there shall be substituted "the authority".

7 (1) Section 13 (London PHV driver's licences) shall be amended as follows.

(2) In subsection (2) (grant of London PHV driver's licence) for "he" there shall be substituted "the authority".

(3) In subsection (3) (requirements as to knowledge of London and topographical skill)—
    (a) for "his" there shall be substituted "the authority's"; and
    (b) for "him" there shall be substituted "the authority".

8 (1) Section 14 (issue of driver's badges) shall be amended as follows.

(2) In subsection (1) (duty to issue badge) for "he" there shall be substituted "the authority".

(3) In subsection (4) (exemption from wearing badge) for "he" in the second place where it occurs there shall be substituted "the authority".

9 In section 15(2) (further information to be furnished with application for licence) for "he" there shall be substituted "the authority".

10 (1) Section 17 (suspension and revocation under section 16: procedure) shall be amended as follows.

(2) In subsection (1)(a) (duty to give notice of decision and grounds for it) for "he" there shall be substituted "the authority".

(3) In subsection (2) (immediate commencement of suspension or revocation in interests of public safety) for "he" there shall be substituted "the authority".

11 In section 18(4) (reference to new operating centre not to be added unless satisfied that premises meet prescribed requirements) for "he" there shall be substituted "the authority".

12 (1) Section 19 (variation of operator's licence) shall be amended as follows.

(2) In subsection (1) (suspension or variation as to operating centre) for "he" there shall be substituted "the authority".

(3) In subsection (2)(a) (duty to give notice of decision and grounds for it) for "he" there shall be substituted "the authority".

(4) In subsection (3) (immediate commencement of suspension or revocation in interests of public safety)—
(a) for "his" in both places where it occurs there shall be substituted "the authority's"; and
(b) for "he" there shall be substituted "the authority".

(5) The sidenote to the section accordingly becomes "Variation of operator's licence by the licensing authority."

13 In section 22(4) (notice directing return of licence) for "him" there shall be substituted "the authority, constable or officer (as the case may be)".

14 The sidenote to section 24 becomes "Delegation of functions by the licensing authority."

15 In section 30(2) (consultation with cab and private hire trade before making regulations prohibiting certain signs, notices etc) for "him" and "he" there shall be substituted "the authority".

16 (1) Section 32 (regulations) shall be amended as follows.

(2) In subsection (1) (purpose for which regulations may be made) after "this Act", in both places, there shall be inserted "(other than section 37)".

(3) In subsection (3) (power to make regulations to be exercisable by statutory instrument subject to negative parliamentary procedure) for "conferred by this Act" there shall be substituted "conferred on the Secretary of State by section 37".

(4) At the end of the section there shall be added—

"(4) Any power of the licensing authority to make regulations under this Act includes power to vary or revoke previous regulations made under this Act (other than regulations made under section 37).

(5) Subsection (4) applies notwithstanding that the previous regulations in question were made by the Secretary of State by statutory instrument.

(6) The licensing authority shall secure that any regulations made under this Act by the authority are printed and published.

(7) A fee may be charged for the sale of regulations printed and published under subsection (6)."

17 In section 36 (interpretation) after the definition of "licensed taxi" there shall be inserted—
""the licensing authority" means Transport for London;".

18 In section 37 (power of Secretary of State to make transitional provisions etc) at the end there shall be added—

"(3) Before making regulations under this section the Secretary of State shall consult the licensing authority."

19 Section 38 (financial provisions relating to the Secretary of State) shall cease to have effect.

Transport for London Act 2008

Part 3
London cabs and private hire vehicles

London cabs: general provisions

9 Power to designate directional taxi ranks (1) TfL may by London cab order designate any standing for hackney carriages appointed under section 4 of the London Hackney Carriages Act 1850 (c. 7) to be a directional taxi rank—
    (a) at all times; or
    (b) for such times of the day, days or other periods as may be specified in the order.

(2) Where TfL designates a directional taxi rank, TfL shall cause a sign to be displayed at the rank clearly indicating—
    (a) the direction or directions in which the drivers of vehicles plying for hire at that rank are required to travel if so requested by any person wishing to hire the vehicle in question; and
    (b) the times, days or other periods for which the rank is designated to be a directional taxi rank.

(3) Notwithstanding section 35 of the London Hackney Carriage Act 1831 (c. 22) and section 17 of the London Hackney Carriage Act 1853 (c. 33), the driver of a hackney carriage plying for hire at a directional taxi rank may refuse to drive his vehicle in a direction which is not the specified direction or, where more than one direction is specified, which is not one of the specified directions.

(4) Where it appears to TfL to be desirable or expedient TfL may suspend the operation of a designation under this section for such period or periods as TfL thinks fit.

(5) In this section—
    "directional taxi rank" means a standing for hackney carriages whose drivers are plying for hire only for journeys in a specified direction or in one of several specified directions;
    "London cab order" means an order made under section 9 of the Metropolitan Public Carriage Act 1869 (c. 115); and
    "specified direction", in relation to a directional taxi rank, means the direction (or any of the directions) specified in the designation relating to that rank.

10 Power to designate rest ranks (1) TfL may by London cab order designate any standing (or part of a standing) for hackney carriages appointed under section 4 of the London Hackney Carriages Act 1850 (c. 7) to be a rest rank—

(a)   at all times; or

(b)   for such times of the day, days or other periods as may be specified in the order.

(2) TfL may by London cab order prescribe the maximum length of time during which a hackney carriage may stand at a rest rank; and different maximum lengths of time may be prescribed—

(a)   for different rest ranks; or

(b)   for different times of the day, days or other periods.

(3) Where TfL designates a rest rank, TfL shall cause a sign to be displayed at the rank clearly indicating that the rank (or the relevant part of it) is a rest rank.

(4) Notwithstanding section 35 of the London Hackney Carriage Act 1831 (c. 22) and section 17 of the London Hackney Carriage Act 1853 (c. 33), the driver of a hackney carriage which is standing at a rest rank shall not be deemed to be plying for hire and, accordingly, may not be compelled to drive his vehicle to any place by any person wishing to hire it.

(5) Where it appears to TfL to be desirable or expedient TfL may suspend the operation of a designation under this section for such period or periods as TfL thinks fit.

(6) In this section "London cab order" means an order made under section 9 of the Metropolitan Public Carriage Act 1869 (c. 115).

11 Taxi drivers' badges (1) In section 8 of the London Hackney Carriages Act 1843 (c. 86) (metal ticket to be issued to licensed driver of hackney carriage)

(a)   for "metal ticket" substitute "badge", and

(b)   omit "or engraved".

(2) In sections 10, 17, 18, 19, 25 and 27, for "ticket", in each case where that word occurs, substitute "badge".

12 Public register of cab licences not to include holders' addresses (1) Section 16 of the London Hackney Carriages Act 1843 shall be amended as follows.

(2) Re-number the existing provision subsection (1).

(3) In that subsection, after "may be founded; and" insert ", subject to subsection (2),".

(4) After that subsection, insert—

"(2) Transport for London may disclose the address of a licensed person to any person only if it appears to Transport for London that the person has a sufficient reason for requiring that information.".

13 Cost of replacement badges In section 19 of the London Hackney Carriages Act 1843 (cost of replacement badge to be such sum, not exceeding 15p, as TfL shall from time to time appoint) for ", not exceeding 15p, as Transport for

London shall from time to time appoint" substitute "as Transport for London shall consider reasonable".

14 Time limit for making complaints In section 38 of the London Hackney Carriages Act 1843 (complaints to be made within 7 days) and in the heading to that section for "seven" substitute "twenty eight".

15 Fares for journeys ending outside London (1) After subsection (3) of section 1 of the London Cab and Stage Carriage Act 1907 (c. 55) (fares for taximeter cabs) insert—

"(4) The fare for a cab journey starting within London but ending outside London shall be—
    (a) such fare as may be agreed between the driver and the passenger—
        (i) before the commencement of the journey, or
        (ii) where, after the commencement of the journey, the driver and the passenger agree to change the destination of the journey, at the time when the destination of the journey is changed, or
    (b) if no fare is so agreed, the fare shown on the taximeter.

(5) A driver of a cab who demands or takes more than the proper fare for a journey undertaken as mentioned in subsection (4) of this section is guilty of an offence and liable on summary conviction to a fine not exceeding level 3 on the standard scale.".

(2) Nothing in this section shall affect the operation of section 35 of the London Hackney Carriage Act 1831 (c. 22), sections 7 and 17 of the London Hackney Carriage Act 1853 (c. 33) or any other enactment which makes provision as regards the obligation of drivers of hackney carriages to drive their vehicles on certain journeys if so requested by persons wishing to hire them.

16 Unfit cabs (1) Section 2 of the London Hackney Carriage Act 1853 (service of notice on proprietor of unfit cab and suspension of licence) shall be amended as follows.

(2) Re-number the existing provision subsection (1).

(3) In that subsection, for the words from "which notice shall be personally served" to "horses whilst in a condition unfit for public use" substitute

"which notice—
    (a) shall be personally served on the proprietor or delivered at his usual place of residence, and
    (b) may be personally served on the driver of the carriage;

and if, after notice has been served on the proprietor or driver as mentioned in paragraph (a) or (b), the carriage is used or let to hire as a hackney carriage, or the horse is, or the horses are, used or let, whilst in a condition unfit for public use,".

(4) After that subsection, insert—

"(2) A proprietor of a hackney carriage whose licence is suspended under sub-section (1) shall not be guilty of an offence under section 7 of the Metropolitan Public Carriage Act 1869 (c. 115) in respect of the carriage unless he has been given written notice in accordance with subsection (1).".

London cabs and private hire vehicles: fixed penalties

17 Fixed penalty cab and private hire vehicle offences (1) Where on any occasion an authorised officer finds a person who he has reason to believe has on that occasion committed an offence under any of the enactments—

(a) specified in columns (1) and (2) of the table set out in Schedule 1 to this Act; and

(b) described in column (3) of that table;

the authorised officer may give that person a notice offering him the opportunity of discharging any liability to conviction for that offence by payment of a fixed penalty.

(2) Sections 18 to 21 (fixed penalties) shall apply in respect of fixed penalty notices under this section.

(3) Schedule 2 to this Act shall have effect with respect to financial provisions relating to the administration and enforcement of this section and sections 18 to 21 (fixed penalties).

(4) In subsection (1) "authorised officer" means a person authorised in writing by TfL for the purposes of sections 17 to 21 of this Act.

18 Power to amend Schedule 1 (1) The Secretary of State may, after consulting—

(a) the Mayor,

(b) the Greater London Assembly,

(c) TfL,

(d) every London borough council,

(e) the Common Council of the City of London, and

(f) such bodies or persons as appear to him to be representative of persons who would be affected by the proposed regulations,

by regulations, amend Schedule 1 to this Act by adding a relevant offence to, or removing a relevant offence from, the offences for the time being mentioned in the table set out in that Schedule.

(2) In subsection (1) "relevant offence" means an offence under an enactment regulating hackney carriages or private hire vehicles in London or the drivers, proprietors or operators of such carriages or vehicles.

19 Fixed penalty notices (1) The provisions of this section shall have effect in relation to notices ("fixed penalty notices") which may be given under section 17 (fixed penalty cab and private hire vehicle offences).

(2) Where a person is given a fixed penalty notice in respect of an offence—

    (a) no proceedings shall be instituted for that offence before the expiration of 28 days following the date of the notice;

    (b) he shall not be convicted of that offence if he pays the fixed penalty before the expiration of that period; and

    (c) in the case of an offence in respect of which (but for this paragraph) section 38 of the London Hackney Carriages Act 1843 (c. 86) (which as amended by section 14 (time limit for making complaints) requires complaints for certain offences to be made within 28 days) applies, proceedings may (notwithstanding that section) be instituted for that offence until the expiration of 42 days following the date of the notice.

(3) A fixed penalty notice under this section shall give such particulars of the circumstances alleged to constitute the offence as are necessary for giving reasonable information of the offence and shall state—

    (a) the period during which, by virtue of subsection (2), proceedings will not be taken for the offence;

    (b) the amount of the fixed penalty;

    (c) the name of the person to whom and the address at which the fixed penalty may be paid; and

    (d) the consequences of not making any payment within the period for payment;

and, without prejudice to payment by any other method, payment of the fixed penalty may be made by pre-paying and posting to that person at that address a letter containing the amount of the penalty (in cash or otherwise).

(4) Where a letter is sent in accordance with subsection (3) payment shall be regarded as having been made at the time at which that letter would be delivered in the ordinary course of post.

(5) The form of notices under this section shall be such as the Secretary of State may by regulations prescribe.

(6) The fixed penalty payable in pursuance of a fixed penalty notice under this section shall be paid to TfL.

(7) In any proceedings a certificate which—

    (a) purports to be signed by or on behalf of the chief finance officer of TfL; and

    (b) states that payment of a fixed penalty was or was not received by a date specified in the certificate,

shall be evidence of the facts stated.

20 Levels of fixed penalties (1) It shall be the duty of TfL to set the levels of fixed penalties payable to TfL.

(2) Different levels may be set for different cases or classes of case.

(3) In setting the level of fixed penalty under subsection (1) TfL shall take into account the maximum fine for the particular fixed penalty offence in question and may take account of—

    (a) any reasonable costs or expected costs incurred or to be incurred in connection with the administration of the provisions of the enactment under which the particular fixed penalty offence is created; and

    (b) the cost or expected cost of enforcing the provisions of the relevant enactment.

(4) Levels of fixed penalties set by TfL in accordance with this section may only come into force in accordance with section 21 (fixed penalties: reserve powers of Secretary of State).

(5) TfL shall publish, in such manner as the Mayor may determine, the levels of fixed penalties which have been set by TfL in accordance with this section.

21 Fixed penalties: reserve powers of Secretary of State (1) Where TfL sets any levels of fixed penalties under subsection (1) of section 20 (levels of fixed penalties), TfL shall notify the Secretary of State of the levels of fixed penalties so set.

(2) Where notification of any levels of fixed penalties is required to be given under subsection (1), the levels of fixed penalties shall not come into force until after the expiration of—

    (a) the period of one month beginning with the day on which the notification is given; or

    (b) such shorter period as the Secretary of State may allow.

(3) If, before the expiration of that period, the Secretary of State gives notice to TfL that he objects to the levels of fixed penalties on the grounds that some or all of them are or may be excessive, those levels of fixed penalties shall not come into force unless and until the objection has been withdrawn.

(4) If, at any time before the levels of fixed penalties required to be notified under subsection (1) to the Secretary of State have come into force, the Secretary of State considers that some or all of them are excessive, he may make regulations setting the levels of fixed penalties.

(5) Levels of fixed penalties set under subsection (4) must be no higher than those notified under subsection (1).

(6) Where the Secretary of State makes any such regulations TfL must not set any further fixed penalties under subsection (1) until after the expiration of the period of 12 months beginning with the day on which the regulations are made.

22 Regulations Any power to make regulations under section 18, 19 or 21—

    (a) includes power to make provision in respect of such cases only as may be specified in the regulations and to make different provision for different circumstances, and

    (b) shall be exercised by statutory instrument subject to annulment in pursuance of a resolution of either House of Parliament.

Private hire vehicles

23 Production of London PHV driver's badge (1) In section 14(3) of the 1998 Act (obligation of driver of London private hire vehicle to wear badge) before "wear the badge in such position and manner as to be plainly and distinctly visible" insert "(a)" and after those words insert
      "and—
    (b) at the request of any person, produce the badge for inspection.".

(2) In section 14(4) of the 1998 Act (power of TfL to exempt a driver from a requirement to wear his badge) for "subsection (3)" insert "subsection (3)(a)".

24 Return of licences etc. on suspension or revocation (1) Section 22 of the 1998 Act (return of licences etc.) shall be amended as follows.

(2) In subsection (1), at the beginning insert "Without prejudice to subsection (1A),".

(3) After subsection (1) insert—

"(1A) Where the suspension or revocation of a London PHV operator's licence has immediate effect by virtue of section 17(2), the holder of the licence shall, at the request of a constable or authorised officer, forthwith return the licence to the constable or officer.".

(4) In subsection (2)—
    (a) at the beginning insert "Without prejudice to subsection (2A),";
    (b) for "the plate or disc" substitute "every plate or disc"; and
    (c) after "section 10" insert "or any regulations made under this Act".

(5) After subsection (2) insert—

"(2A) Where the suspension or revocation of a London PHV licence has immediate effect by virtue of section 9(3) or 17(2), the owner of the vehicle to which the licence relates shall, at the request of a constable or authorised officer, forthwith return to the constable or officer the licence and every plate or disc which was issued for the vehicle under section 10 or any regulations made under this Act.".

(6) In subsection (3), at the beginning insert "Without prejudice to subsection (3A),".

(7) After subsection (3) insert—

"(3A) Where the suspension or revocation of a London PHV driver's licence has immediate effect by virtue of section 17(2), the holder of the licence shall, at the request of a constable or authorised officer, forthwith return his driver's badge to the constable or officer.".

(8) In subsection (4)—
- (a) at the beginning insert "Without prejudice to subsections (1A), (2A) and (3A),"; and
- (b) in paragraph (a), for "the disc or plate" substitute "every disc or plate" and after "section 10" insert "or any regulations made under this Act".

(9) In subsection (7), for "the plate or disc" substitute "every disc or plate".

25 Obligation of London operators to keep records In section 4(3) of the 1998 Act (records to be kept by London operators), for paragraph (d) substitute—
> "(d) keep at the specified operating centre or, where more than one operating centre is specified, at one of the operating centres such records as may be prescribed of particulars of the private hire vehicles and drivers which are available to him for carrying out bookings accepted by him at that or, as the case may be, each centre;
> (da) where more than one operating centre is specified—
>> (i) give notice to the licensing authority, and
>> (ii) display at each specified operating centre a notice,
> stating the address of the operating centre at which the records are kept under paragraph (d);".

26 Public register of licences not to include holders' addresses (1) Section 23 of the 1998 Act (particulars to be kept in public register of licences) shall be amended as follows.

(2) In subsection (1)(a), leave out "and address".

(3) In subsection (2), after "the register" insert "kept under subsection (1)".

(4) After subsection (2) insert—

"(3) The licensing authority shall maintain a supplementary register containing, for each licence issued under this Act, the address of the person to whom it is granted.

(4) The licensing authority may disclose the address of a licence holder to any person only if it appears to the authority that the person has a sufficient reason for requiring that information.".

1934 No 1346

London Cab Order 1934

Part I
Short Title and Interpretation

1 Short title This Order may be cited as the "London Cab Order 1934".

2 Definition and Interpretation (1) In this Order, unless the context otherwise requires, the following expressions have the meanings hereby respectively assigned to them:—

. . .

"Receiver" means the Receiver for the Metropolitan Police District and includes any person authorised by him to receive payments or give receipts on his behalf;

"Metropolitan area" means the area consisting of the City of London and the Metropolitan Police District;

"Passing station" means any place appointed by [Transport for London] as a place where cabs may be examined for the purposes of this Order, and if [Transport for London] appoints any passing station for the examination of any particular cab or cabs, that passing station shall be deemed to be the appointed passing station for that cab or those cabs;

"Public Carriage Examiner" means any person appointed by [Transport for London] to examine and inspect public carriages for the purposes of the Metropolitan Public Carriage Act 1869;

"Cab" has the same meaning as the expression "hackney carriage" has in the Metropolitan Public Carriage Act 1869;

"Motor Cab" means any mechanically-propelled cab;

"Horse cab" means any cab drawn by animal power, and "horse" includes any animal used to draw a cab;

"Cab licence" means a licence in pursuance of Section 6 of the Metropolitan Public Carriage Act 1869 and of Part III of this Order in respect of a cab;

"Cab-driver's licence" means a licence in pursuance of Section 8 of the Metropolitan Public Carriage Act 1869, as amended by Section 39 of the Road Traffic Act 1934, and of Part IV of this Order to drive cabs;

"Owner" or "Cab-owner" in relation to a cab which is the subject of a hiring agreement or hire purchase agreement means the person in possession of the cab under that agreement; and

"Licensee" means any person to whom a licence is granted.

(2) The Interpretation Act 1889 applies for the purpose of the interpretation of this Order as it applies for the purpose of the interpretation of an Act of Parliament.

Amendment

Para (1): definition "the Assistant Commissioner" (omitted) repealed by the London Cab Order 1934 (Modification) Order 2000, SI 2000/1666, art 3(1).

Para (1): in definition "Passing station" words "Transport for London" in square brackets in both places they occur substituted by virtue of the London Cab Order 1934 (Modification) Order 2000, SI 2000/1666, art 3(2).

Para (1): in definition "Public Carriage Examiner" words "Transport for London" in square brackets substituted by virtue of the London Cab Order 1934 (Modification) Order 2000, SI 2000/1666, art 3(2).

Part II
Licensing Authority

4 Power of [Transport for London] to vary directions, etc Any appointment made or approval or direction given by [Transport for London] under this Order may at any time be revoked or varied by [it].

Amendment

Words "Transport for London" in square brackets and word "it" in square brackets substituted by virtue of the London Cab Order 1934 (Modification) Order 2000, SI 2000/1666, art 3(2).

Part III
Cab Licences

[5 Applications for Cab Licences (1) Every application for a cab licence shall be made in such form, and include such declarations and information as Transport for London may require.

(2) Where the cab is jointly owned or owned by a partnership firm or a limited liability company, the application shall be made in the name of one of the joint owners or by the senior partner of the firm, or the Secretary, Manager or other duly authorised officer of the company, as the case may be, and that person shall for the purposes of this Part of this Order be deemed to be the applicant for the licence, and the licence if granted shall be issued to him

(3) Transport for London may in its discretion require applicants to provide different information depending on whether or not the applicant has previously held or currently holds a cab licence or cab drivers licence.]

Amendment

Substituted by the London Cab Order 2007, arts 2, 3.

6 Disqualification of persons under 21 A cab licence shall not be granted to a person under the age of 21 years, and if granted to any such person shall be void.

[7 Grant of Cab Licences Transport for London shall grant a cab licence if it is satisfied that:--

(a) the applicant is a fit and proper person to hold a cab licence;

(b) the vehicle in respect of which the application is made conforms to the conditions of fitness from time to time laid down by Transport for London; and

(c) the requirements of paragraph 8 of this Order as to liability to third parties are met.]

Amendment
Substituted by the London Cab Order 2007, arts 2, 4.

8 Cab-owner's Liability to Third Parties (1) The liability to third parties to which this paragraph relates is any liability (other than a contractual liability) incurred by the owner or driver of a cab, as a consequence of the user of the cab, in respect of

(a) the death of or bodily injury to any person, other than a person employed by the owner of the cab whose death or injury arises out of and in the course of his employment, and

(b) damage to animals or to property not belonging to the cab-owner or cab-driver nor held in trust by him nor under his charge or control not being conveyed in the cab, and not being damage to any bridge, weigh-bridge, viaduct, or road, or any property thereunder.

(2) Subject as hereinafter provided there shall be in force in relation to every cab a policy of insurance issued by an insurer approved by [Transport for London] which insures the owner of the cab and any other person who drives the cab with his permission in respect of any liability to third parties to which this paragraph relates: provided that

(a) a policy of insurance or a security complying with Part II of the Road Traffic Act 1930, as amended by any subsequent Act, shall be a sufficient fulfilment of the requirements of this paragraph in respect of so much of the liability as it covers, and

(b) any other liability to which this paragraph relates shall not be required to be covered for an amount in excess of £10,000 (or, in the case of a horse cab, £1,000) in respect of any claim or series of claims arising out of any one accident or occurrence.

(3) [Transport for London] may, in any case where [it] is satisfied that the financial position of the owner of a cab is such as to enable him and the cab-driver to meet without insurance any liability to third parties to which this paragraph relates, or any part of that liability, direct that the requirements of this paragraph (not being requirements of Part II of the Road Traffic Act 1930 as amended by any subsequent Act) either shall not apply in relation to that cab or shall apply with such modifications as [it] may direct, and in any such case those requirements shall either have no effect or have effect as so modified, as the case may be.

(4) If the owner of any cab in respect of which a cab licence is in force fails to fulfil the requirements of this paragraph as to liability to third parties, he shall be guilty of a breach of this Order: provided that the cab-owner shall not be guilty

of a breach of this Order by reason only of failure to fulfil the requirements of this paragraph during any period during which the cab is withdrawn from hire.

Amendment

Para (2): words "Transport for London" in square brackets substituted by virtue of the London Cab Order 1934 (Modification) Order 2000, SI 2000/1666, art 3(2).

Para (3): words "Transport for London" in square brackets and word "it" in square brackets in both places it occurs substituted by virtue of the London Cab Order 1934 (Modification) Order 2000, SI 2000/1666, art 3(2).

9 . . .

Amendment

Repealed by the London Cab Order 2007, arts 2, 5.

[10 Presentation of Motor Cabs for Licensing The applicant for licence for a motor cab shall present the vehicle for inspection and testing by Transport for London within such period and at such place Transport for London may by notice require.]

Amendment

Substituted by the London Cab Order 2007, arts 2, 6.

[11 Presentation of Horse Cab for Licensing The applicant for licence for a horse cab shall present the vehicle for inspection and testing by Transport for London within such period and at such place Transport for London may by notice require.]

Amendment

Substituted by the London Cab Order 2007, arts 2, 7.

[12 Affixing of plates, etc (1) On granting a cab licence Transport for London shall cause to be affixed to the cab

(a) the plates and notices described in Schedule B to this Order in the positions required by that Schedule; and

(b) such notices or marks as Transport for London may from time to time direct.

(2) The said plates shall remain the property of Transport for London.]

Amendment

Substituted by the London Cab Order 2007, arts 2, 8.

13 . . .

Amendment

Repealed by the London Cab Order 2007, arts 2, 9.

14 Form of Cab Licence and Conditions to be complied with Every cab licence shall be in the form contained in Schedule C to this Order, and shall be in force for a period of one year unless sooner revoked or suspended, and shall be granted subject to the provisions specified therein and subject also to the following conditions:—

(a) The licensee shall produce the licence for examination at his principal place of business when required so to do by any police constable or Public Carriage Examiner, or by any person duly authorised in that behalf by [Transport for London], and shall also, if so required, produce in like manner such evidence as [Transport for London] may require that the owner of the cab fulfils the requirements of paragraph 8 of this Order as to liability to third parties.

(b) The licensee, if he changes his address during the currency of the licence, shall notify such change to [Transport for London] within seven days from the date of such change and shall at the same time send or deliver the licence to the office of [Transport for London] who shall endorse upon the licence the licensee's new address and return the licence to him forthwith.

(c) The licensee, if during the currency of the licence he changes the place at which the cab is ordinarily kept, shall notify such change to [Transport for London] within seven days from the date of such change.

(d) The licensee shall not deface the licence by erasure or otherwise.

(e) The licensee shall not employ or permit any person to act as driver of the cab when it is hired or plying for hire except a person who is licensed in pursuance of Section 8 of the Metropolitan Public Carriage Act 1869, as amended by Section 39 of the Road Traffic Act 1934, and of Part IV of this Order to drive cabs of the type to which the cab belongs.

(f) The licensee shall produce the licences of the persons employed or permitted by him to act as drivers of the cab for examination at his principal place of business when required so to do by any police constable or Public Carriage Examiner, or by any person duly authorised in that behalf by [Transport for London].

(g) The licensee shall at all reasonable times allow to any Public Carriage Examiner facilities for the inspection of the cab and the horses (if any) used to draw the cab, and their harness, and such facilities shall include free access to his premises, whether within or outside the metropolitan area.

(h) The licensee shall not remove or conceal any of the plates or notices affixed to the cab in pursuance of this Order, or cause or permit any person not authorised in that behalf by [Transport for London] to remove or conceal any such plate or notice, nor shall he alter or obliterate, or cause or permit any person not so authorised to alter or obliterate, any mark placed upon the cab in pursuance of this Order or by the authority of [Transport for London].

(i) The licensee shall not knowingly permit the cab to be used for any illegal purpose.

(j) The licensee shall keep the cab and all its furniture and appointments in good order and repair.

(k) The licensee shall not cause or permit any person to appear or be carried on the cab by way of advertisement.

[(l) The licensee shall not, otherwise than in accordance with the directions of Transport for London, cause or permit any object or any printed, written or other matter to appear to be displayed on the outside or inside of the cab or presented to any passenger by way of advertisement.]

[(m) The licensee, if during the currency of the licence he ceases to be the owner of the cab to which the licence relates, shall within 14 days of the change of ownership:–

(i) notify Transport for London and return the licence to Transport for London for cancellation, and before delivering the cab to its new owner remove and deliver up to Transport for London or a Public Carriage Examiner the plates affixed to the cab in pursuance of this Order; or

(ii) apply jointly with the new owner to Transport for London, in accordance with paragraph 14A, to have the licence transferred to the new owner.]

[(n) Throughout the currency of the licence two test certificates issued in accordance with section 45(2)(c) of the Road Traffic Act 1988 ("MOT certificates") must be in force in relation to the vehicle as follows:

(i) the first MOT certificate must relate to an examination of the vehicle which took place not more than 14 days before the end of the day on which the vehicle was presented for licensing (the day of presentation being regarded as "Day 1" for those purposes); and

(ii) the second MOT certificate must relate to an examination of the vehicle which took place not more than 14 days before the end of the sixth month anniversary of the date of grant of the licence (the day of the six month anniversary being regarded as "Day 1" for the purposes of that requirement).]

(o) . . .

Amendment

In paras (a)-(c), (f), (h) words "Transport for London" in square brackets in each place they occur substituted by virtue of the London Cab Order 1934 (Modification) Order 2000, SI 2000/1666, art 3(2).

Para (l): substituted by the London Cab Order 2010, art 3.

Para (m): substituted by the London Cab Order 2007, arts 2, 10(1)(a).

Para (n): inserted by the London Cab (MOT Test Requirements) (No. 3) Order 2012, arts 2, 3.

Para (o): repealed by the London Cab Order (No. 2) 2008, arts 2, 3.

[**14A Transfer of Cab Licence** Transport for London shall transfer a licence from a previous vehicle owner to a new owner upon an application being made in accordance with paragraph 14(m)(ii) if:--

(a) the application is made in such form, and include such declarations and information as Transport for London may require; and

(b) the new owner satisfies Transport for London that he is a fit and proper person to hold a cab licence.]

Amendment

Article inserted by the London Cab Order 2007, arts 2, 11.

15 Obtaining Licence by False Statements or by Withholding Information If any person for the purpose of obtaining the grant of a cab licence to himself or to any other person knowingly makes any false statement or withholds any material information, he shall be guilty of a breach of this Order.

16 Plying for hire without plates, etc, or with plates, etc, defaced (1) If the owner of a cab, or, where the owner is a firm or company, the person holding the licence in respect of the cab on its behalf, causes or permits the cab to ply for hire.

(a) without any of the plates or notices affixed thereto in pursuance of this Order, or with any such plate or notice so defaced that any figure thereon is illegible, or

(b) without any of the marks placed thereupon in pursuance of this Order or by the authority of [Transport for London], or with any such mark so obliterated, or indistinct that any material particular thereon is illegible,

he shall be guilty of a breach of this Order.

(2) If any person without lawful authority removes, conceals, obliterates or alters any such plate notice or mark, he shall be guilty of a breach of this Order.

(3) If any such plate or notice is lost, or has become defaced, or if any such mark has become obliterated or indistinct, the cab-owner or the licensee, as the case may be, shall bring or send the cab to the appointed passing station and the Public Carriage Examiner shall affix a new plate or notice or place a new mark on the cab, as may be required.

[(4) If a licensed cab is granted a new licence that is to take effect following the expiration of the current licence it may ply for hire whilst displaying plates and notices related to that new licence rather than the current licence.]

Amendment

Para (1): in sub-para (b) words "Transport for London" in square brackets substituted by virtue of the London Cab Order 1934 (Modification) Order 2000, SI 2000/1666, art 3(2).
Para (4): inserted by the London Cab Order 2007, arts 2, 12.

17 Defaced or Altered Cab Licences to be Void A cab licence which is defaced or on which there is an unauthorised erasure or alteration of any material particular shall be void.

18 Possession of Defaced, etc, Cab Licence or Plates, etc If any person uses or has in his possession without lawful authority any altered or irregular cab licence, or any altered or irregular plate notice or mark required for the purposes of this Order, or any counterfeit of any such licence plate notice or mark, he shall be guilty of a breach of this Order.

19 Revocation or Suspension of Cab Licences (1) A cab licence shall be liable to revocation or suspension by [Transport for London] on any of the following grounds:—
  (a) if the licence has been obtained by any misrepresentation, fraud or concealment of any material circumstances; or
  (b) if [Transport for London], by reason of any new circumstance arising or coming to [its] knowledge after the grant of a licence, or by reason of the condition of the cab, is satisfied that a licence in respect of the cab in question could not in pursuance of this Order properly be granted to the licensee if he were an applicant for a new licence; or
  (c) if the licensee fails to comply with any of the provisions or conditions subject to which the licence has been granted; or
  (d) on any of the grounds on which a licence in respect of a hackney carriage might at the time of the commencement of the Metropolitan Public Carriage Act 1869 have been revoked or suspended;

provided that in a case where more than one licence granted to the same licensee becomes liable to revocation or suspension under this paragraph, [Transport for London], if [it] is of opinion that it would be contrary to the public interest to revoke or suspend all of those licences, may revoke or suspend only such one or more of them as [it] may think fit.

(2) In the event of the revocation or suspension of a cab licence, the licensee shall, within five days after a notice to that effect has been delivered to him personally or sent to him by registered post [or by the recorded delivery service] at the address mentioned in or last endorsed upon the licence, send or deliver the licence to the Public Carriage Examiner at the appointed passing station for cancellation or for retention during the time of suspension, as the case may be, and if so required in the notice shall bring or send the cab to which the licence relates to that passing station in order that the plates affixed to the cab in pursuance of this Order may be removed and delivered up to the Public Carriage Examiner; and if the licensee fails to fulfil the requirements of this sub-paragraph, he shall be guilty of a breach of this Order.

(3) On the removal of a suspension of a cab licence which has not expired by the effluxion of time the Public Carriage Examiner shall return the licence to the licensee and shall cause the plates, if removed, to be re-affixed to the cab.

Amendment
Para (1): words "Transport for London" in square brackets in both places they occur substituted by virtue of the London Cab Order 1934 (Modification) Order 2000, SI 2000/1666, art 3(2).

Para (1): in sub-para (b) word "its" in square brackets substituted by virtue of the London Cab Order 1934 (Modification) Order 2000, SI 2000/1666, art 3(2).

Para (1): word "it" in square brackets in both places it occurs substituted by virtue of the London Cab Order 1934 (Modification) Order 2000, SI 2000/1666, art 3(2).

Para (2): words in square brackets inserted by the London Cab Order 1962, SI 1962/289, art 1.

20 Transfer of Cab Licences on Death, etc In the event of the death of any licensee during the currency of his cab licence, the licence shall be sent or delivered to the office of [Transport for London], who may by endorsement thereon transfer the licence to the personal representative of the deceased person, or to [the licensee's] [surviving spouse, surviving civil partner] or child, if such representative or [surviving spouse, surviving civil partner] or child is of full age and, in accordance with the provisions of this Part of this Order, satisfies [Transport for London] of his or her fitness to hold such licence.

. . .

In the case of a licence held on behalf of a firm or company, the licence may, in like manner and on like conditions, be transferred from the licensee to any other person who would be entitled under this Part of this Order to apply for a licence on behalf of the firm or company.

Amendment

Words "Transport for London" in square brackets in both places they occur substituted by virtue of the London Cab Order 1934 (Modification) Order 2000, SI 2000/1666, art 3(2).

Word " the licensee's" in square brackets substituted by the Marriage (Same Sex Couples) Act 2013 (Consequential Provisions) Order, SI 2014/107, art 2, Sch 1, para 1(a).

Words "surviving spouse, surviving civil partner" in square brackets in both places they occur substituted by the Marriage (Same Sex Couples) Act 2013 (Consequential Provisions) Order, SI 2014/107, art 2, Sch 1, para 1(b).

Para omitted repealed by the Marriage (Same Sex Couples) Act 2013 (Consequential Provisions) Order, SI 2014/107, art 2, Sch 1, para 1(c).

21 Cab Licences to be Surrendered on Expiry and Plates Removed The owner of a cab, or, where the owner is a firm or company, the person holding the licence in respect of the cab on its behalf, shall, not later than three days after the expiration of the period for which the licence in respect of the cab was granted, deliver up the licence and the plates affixed to the cab in pursuance of this Order to [Transport for London] or a Public Carriage Examiner, and if he fails so to do he shall be guilty of a breach of this Order.

Amendment

Words "Transport for London" in square brackets substituted by virtue of the London Cab Order 1934 (Modification) Order 2000, SI 2000/1666, art 3(2).

22 Responsibility of Firm or Company Where a cab licence is held by any person on behalf of a firm or company, both that person and the firm or company, as the case may be, shall be deemed to be the licensee in respect of that licence, and shall as such be liable for any breach of this Order or any failure to comply with any of the provisions or conditions subject to which the licence is granted.

Part IV
Cab-Drivers' Licences

23 Requisitions for Cab-drivers' Licences [Transport for London] shall furnish on demand to any person applying for a cab-driver's licence the form of requisition appointed for that purpose in pursuance of Section 14 of the London Hackney Carriages Act 1843.

Amendment
Words "Transport for London" in square brackets substituted by virtue of the London Cab Order 1934 (Modification) Order 2000, SI 2000/1666, art 3(2).

24 Disqualification of Persons under 21 A cab-driver's licence shall not be granted to a person under the age of 21 years, and if granted to any such person shall be void.

25 Grounds for Refusal of Cab-drivers' Licences (1) Transport for London may in its discretion refuse to grant a cab-drivers' licence–
  (a) if the applicant fails to satisfy Transport for London that he is of good character and fit to act as a cab-driver,
  (b) if the applicant is disqualified by reason of the applicant's immigration status from driving a hackney carriage, or
  (c) if the applicant has within the three years immediately preceding the date of his application held a cab-driver's licence and has, otherwise than by reason of illness or other unavoidable cause, failed to act as a cab-driver during any considerable part of the period for which the licence was granted or, where he has within the said three years held more than one such licence, the period for which the last of such licences was granted.]

Amendment
Article substituted by the London Cab (No. 2) Order 2016, arts 2, 3.

[25A Immigration matters (1) For the purposes of paragraph 25, a person is disqualified by reason of the person's immigration status from driving a hackney carriage if the person is subject to immigration control and—
  (a) the person has not been granted leave to enter or remain in the United Kingdom, or
  (b) the person's leave to enter or remain in the United Kingdom—
    (i) is invalid,
    (ii) has ceased to have effect (whether by reason of curtailment, revocation, cancellation, passage of time or otherwise), or

(iii) is subject to a condition preventing the person from driving a hackney carriage.

(2) For the purposes of this paragraph and paragraph 25, a person is subject to immigration control if under the Immigration Act 1971 the person requires leave to enter or remain in the United Kingdom.

(3) In determining for the purposes of paragraph 25 whether an applicant is disqualified by reason of the applicant's immigration status from driving a hackney carriage, Transport for London must have regard to any guidance issued by the Secretary of State.

(4) Where a person is at large in the United Kingdom by virtue of paragraph 21(1) of Schedule 2 to the Immigration Act 1971 (temporary admission or release from detention)–
    (a) the person is to be treated for the purposes of this Order as if the person has been granted leave to enter the United Kingdom, but
    (b) any restriction as to employment imposed under paragraph 21(2) of Schedule 2 to the 1971 Act is to be treated as a condition of leave.

(5) Where a person is on immigration bail within the meaning of Part 1 of Schedule 10 to the Immigration Act 2016 –
    (a) the person is to be treated for the purposes of paragraph 25 as if the person had been granted leave to enter the United Kingdom, but
    (b) any condition as to the person's work in the United Kingdom to which the person's immigration bail is subject is to be treated for those purposes as a condition of leave.]

Amendment
Article inserted by the London Cab (No. 2) Order 2016, arts 2, 4(1).

26 Fees for Cab-drivers' Licences and for driving tests (1), (2) . . .

(3) If an applicant for a cab-driver's licence has failed on two occasions to pass the driving test on any type of cab, or if the holder of a cab-driver's licence who has applied to have his licence made available for an additional type of cab has failed on two occasions to pass the driving test on that type, he shall, if allowed by [Transport for London] to undergo any further driving test on that type, pay to the Receiver [12(1/2) p] in respect of the third and each subsequent driving test.

Amendment
Paras (1), (2): repealed by the London Cab Order 1982, SI 1982/311, art 2.
Para (3): words "Transport for London" in square brackets substituted by virtue of the London Cab Order 1934 (Modification) Order 2000, SI 2000/1666, art 3(2).
Para (3): sum "12(1/2)p" in square brackets substituted by the Decimal Currency Act 1969, s 10.

27 Form of Cab-driver's Licence and Issue of Copy of Licence (1) Every cab-driver's licence shall be [in such form and subject to (a) and (b) contain such

particulars as Transport for London shall think fit] . . . provided that in any such licence [Transport for London] may

    (a) limit in such manner as [it] thinks fit the types of cabs which the licensee may be permitted to drive, and

    (b) in any case where the licensee has not satisfied [Transport for London] that he has an adequate knowledge of the metropolitan area, attach a condition prohibiting the licensee from plying for hire with a cab in the said area except in such part or parts thereof as may be specified, being a part or parts in respect of which he has satisfied [Transport for London] that he has an adequate knowledge.

(2) When a cab-driver's licence is issued, a copy of the licence shall also be issued to the licensee.

(3) Immediately after the licensee shall have received his licence and his copy thereof, he shall sign both the licence and the copy with his usual signature in the space provided, and if he fails so to do he shall be guilty of a breach of this Order.

Amendment

Para (1): words "in such form and subject to (a) and (b) contain such particulars as Transport for London shall think fit" in square brackets substituted by the London Cab Order 2012, arts 2, 3(1).

Para (1): words omitted revoked by the London Cab (No. 2) Order 2016, arts 2, 5.

Para (1): words "Transport for London" in square brackets in each place they occur substituted by virtue of the London Cab Order 1934 (Modification) Order 2000, SI 2000/1666, art 3(2).

Para (1): in sub-para (a) word "it" in square brackets substituted by virtue of the London Cab Order 1934 (Modification) Order 2000, SI 2000/1666, art 3(2).

28 Production of Copy of Licence A cab-driver shall have his copy of his cab-driver's licence in his possession at all times during his employment as a cab-driver or when appearing before a court and shall produce it for inspection on demand by any police constable or Public Carriage Examiner or any officer of a court, and if he fails so to do he shall be guilty of a breach of this Order.

[28A Cab-drivers to display driver's badge details and licensed area A cab-driver shall affix to the cab operated when plying for hire the following:

    (a) the display of the driver's badge number and licensed area in the form that Transport for London shall think fit; and

    (b) such notices or marks as Transport for London may from time to time direct with regard to (a)]

Amendment

Inserted by the London Cab Order 2012, arts 2, 4.

29 Responsibility of Cab-owners for Safe Custody and Return of Cab-drivers' Licences (1) While a cab-driver's licence is retained by a cab-owner in pursuance of section 21 of the London Hackney Carriages Act 1843, the cab-owner shall preserve it undamaged and undefaced, and shall make no mark upon it otherwise than as provided in Section 8 of that Act, and, if the licence becomes defaced or is lost, shall forthwith furnish to [Transport for London] as full a statement as may be of the circumstances in which it was defaced or lost, and, in the case of a defaced licence, shall at the same time send or deliver it to [Transport for London].

(2) If at any time the licensee is required to send or deliver his licence to [Transport for London] the cab-owner shall thereupon return the licence to the licensee for that purpose.

(3) If any cab-owner acts in contravention of or fails to comply with any of the provisions of this paragraph, he shall be guilty of a breach of this Order.

Amendment
Paras (1), (2): words "Transport for London" in square brackets in each place they occur substituted by virtue of the London Cab Order 1934 (Modification) Order 2000, SI 2000/1666, art 3(2).

30 Revocation or Suspension of Cab-drivers' Licences (1) A cab-driver's licence shall be liable to revocation or suspension by [Transport for London] if [it] is satisfied, by reason of any circumstances arising or coming to [its] knowledge after the licence was granted, that the licensee is not a fit person to hold such a licence.

[(2) A relevant circumstance for the purposes of sub-paragraph (1) includes, but is not limited to, whether the licensee has been convicted of an immigration offence or required to pay an immigration penalty unless:
    (a) in a case where the driver has been convicted of an immigration offence, the conviction is a spent conviction within the meaning of the Rehabilitation of Offenders Act 1974, or
    (b) in a case where the driver has been required to pay an immigration penalty –
        (i) more than three years have elapsed since the date on which the penalty was imposed, and
        (ii) the amount of the penalty has been paid in full.

(3) In the event of the revocation or suspension of a cab-driver's licence Transport for London shall cause notice thereof to be given to the licensee, and the licensee shall, within five days after such notice has been delivered to him personally or sent to him by registered post or by the recorded delivery service at the address mentioned in or last endorsed upon the licence, send or deliver the licence and his copy thereof and his badge to Transport for London for cancellation or for retention during the time of suspension, as the case may be, and if he fails so to do he shall be guilty of a breach of this Order.

(4) On the removal of a suspension of a cab-driver's licence which has not expired by the effluxion of time Transport for London shall return the licence and the copy thereof and the badge to the licensee.]

Amendment

Para (1): words "Transport for London" in square brackets in each place they occur substituted by virtue of the London Cab Order 1934 (Modification) Order 2000, SI 2000/1666, art 3(2).

Para (1): words "it", "its" in square brackets substituted by virtue of the London Cab Order 1934 (Modification) Order 2000, SI 2000/1666, art 3(2).

Paras (2)-(4): substituted for paras (2), (3) as originally enacted by the London Cab (No. 2) Order 2016, arts 2, 6.

[30A Immigration offences and immigration penalties (1) In this Cab Order "immigration offence" means—

- (a) an offence under any of the Immigration Acts,
- (b) an offence under section 1 of the Criminal Attempts Act 1981 of attempting to commit an offence within paragraph (a), or
- (c) an offence under section 1 of the Criminal Law Act 1977 of conspiracy to commit an offence within paragraph (a).

(2) In this Cab Order "immigration penalty" means a penalty under—

- (a) section 15 of the Immigration, Asylum and Nationality Act 2006 ("the 2006 Act"), or
- (b) section 23 of the Immigration Act 2014 ("the 2014 Act").

(3) For the purposes of this Cab Order a person to whom a penalty notice under section 15 of the 2006 Act has been given is not to be treated as having been required to pay an immigration penalty if—

- (a) the person is excused payment by virtue of section 15(3) of that Act, or
- (b) the penalty is cancelled by virtue of section 16 or 17 of that Act.

(4) For the purposes of this Cab Order a person to whom a penalty notice under section 15 of the 2006 Act has been given is not to be treated as having been required to pay an immigration penalty until such time as—

- (a) the period for giving a notice of objection under section 16 of that Act has expired and the Secretary of State has considered any notice given within that period, and
- (b) if a notice of objection was given within that period, the period for appealing under section 17 of that Act has expired and any appeal brought within that period has been finally determined, abandoned or withdrawn.

(5) For the purposes of this Cab Order a person to whom a penalty notice under section 23 of the 2014 Act has been given is not to be treated as having been required to pay an immigration penalty if—

- (a) the person is excused payment by virtue of section 24 of that Act, or
- (b) the penalty is cancelled by virtue of section 29 or 30 of that Act.

(6) For the purposes of this Cab Order a person to whom a penalty notice under section 23 of the 2014 Act has been given is not to be treated as having been required to pay an . immigration penalty until such time as—

(a) the period for giving a notice of objection under section 29 of that Act has expired and the Secretary of State has considered any notice given within that period, and

(b) if a notice of objection was given within that period, the period for appealing under section 30 of that Act has expired and any appeal brought within that period has been finally determined, abandoned or withdrawn.]

Amendment
Article inserted by the London Cab (No. 2) Order 2016, arts 2, 7.

31 Breach of Terms or Conditions of Cab-driver's Licence (1) If the holder of a cab-driver's licence

(i) drives a cab of any type which by the terms of his licence he is not permitted to drive (not being a cab which is withdrawn from hire), or

(ii) plies for hire with a cab or permits the cab to be hired in any part of the metropolitan area in which by a condition attached to his licence he is prohibited from plying for hire with a cab,

he shall be guilty of a breach of this Order.

(2) Section 35 of the London Hackney Carriage Act 1831 and paragraph (2) of Section 17 of the London Hackney Carriage Act 1853 shall not apply in the case of a cab-driver who is in any part of the metropolitan area in which by a condition attached to his licence he is prohibited from plying for hire with a cab.

[**31A Debit and Credit Card Acceptance** (1) Every cab-driver's licence shall be granted subject to a condition that, if so requested by a passenger, the licensee shall accept payment by credit or debit card using a payment device approved by Transport for London.]

Amendment
Article inserted by the London Cab Order 2016, arts 2, 4(1).

32 Change of Cab-driver's Address to be Notified (1) If during the currency of his licence the holder of a cab-driver's licence changes his address, he shall, within seven days of such change of address, notify the change and send or deliver his licence and his copy thereof to [Transport for London], who shall endorse the new address upon the licence and the copy and return them to the licensee.

(2) If a licensee fails to comply with the requirements of this paragraph, he shall be guilty of a breach of this Order.

(3) This paragraph shall have effect in substitution for the provisions of Section 15 of the London Hackney Carriages Act 1843.

Amendment
Para (1): words "Transport for London" in square brackets substituted by virtue of the London Cab Order 1934 (Modification) Order 2000, SI 2000/1666, art 3(2).

Part V
Regulations as to Number of Persons to be Carried in Cabs as to Cab Fittings and as to the Distances to which Cabs may be Compelled to Take Passengers

33 Carriage of Persons and Luggage (1) No person other than the driver shall be carried on any cab in excess of the number of persons which it is licensed to carry, provided that, in computing such number, an infant in arms shall not count as a person and two children under 10 years of age shall count as one person.

(2) No person other than the driver shall, without the authority of [Transport for London], be carried on the driving box or platform of a motor cab.

(3) No luggage shall be carried on the roof of a motor cab unless the cab is fitted for that purpose and is licensed to carry luggage on the roof.

(4) The driver of the cab, and, unless he proves that the breach occurred without his knowledge or consent, the owner thereof, shall be liable for any breach of any of the regulations in this paragraph.

Amendment
Para (2): words "Transport for London" in square brackets substituted by virtue of the London Cab Order 1934 (Modification) Order 2000, SI 2000/1666, art 3(2).

[34 Distance for which cab drivers may be compelled to drive (1) In the London Hackney Carriage Act 1853, for the references to six miles in section 7 and in paragraph (2) of section 17 of there shall be in each case be substituted a reference to twelve miles.

(2) Nothing in this paragraph affects the London Cab Order 1972.]

Amendment
Article substituted by the London Cab (No 2) Order 2001, arts 2, 3.

Part VI
Regulations as to Taximeters and Fares for Motor Cabs

35 Approved Taximeter to be Fitted and Sealed [(1) The owner of every motor cab shall cause the cab to be fitted with a taximeter of a type approved by [Transport for London].

(2) . . . Any such meter shall be so construed and adjusted that—
   [(a) after the taximeter has been started at the commencement of the hiring or at such later time as the driver thinks fit, the fare payable for the hiring, as prescribed in paragraph 40 is automatically recorded and displayed by the taximeter;] and
   (b) the total up to an amount of not less than 10p of any extra charges payable by a hirer of the cab, can be displayed by the meter.

[(2A) . . .]

(3) Every taximeter so fitted shall be sealed in such manner as [Transport for London] may from time to time direct and may be marked in such manner as [Transport for London] may from time to time permit, and no person shall place such seal or mark on the taximeter unless he is authorised in that behalf by [Transport for London].

(4) . . .]

Amendment

Article substituted by the London Cab Order 1985, SI 1985/933, art 3.

Paras (1), (3): words "Transport for London" in square brackets in each place they occur substituted by virtue of the London Cab Order 1934 (Modification) Order 2000, SI 2000/1666, art 3(2).

Para (2): words omitted repealed by the London Cab (No. 2) Order 1990, SI 1990/2003, reg 3(a).

Para (2): sub-para (a) substituted by the London Cab Order 2010, arts 2, 4.

Para (2A): inserted by the London Cab (No 2) Order 2001, arts 2, 4(1), (3).

Para (2A): repealed by the London Cab Order 2002, arts 2, 3(1), (3).

Para (4): repealed by the London Cab (No. 2) Order 1990, SI 1990/2003, reg 3(b).

---

36 Removal of or tampering with Taximeters No person shall, without the authority of [Transport for London], remove or tamper with the taximeter fitted to a motor cab in respect of which a cab licence is in force, or the mechanism by which the taximeter is operated, or break, alter, deface, or otherwise tamper with any seal or mark placed on the taximeter by direction of [Transport for London].

Amendment

Words "Transport for London" in square brackets in both places they occur substituted by virtue of the London Cab Order 1934 (Modification) Order 2000, SI 2000/1666, art 3(2).

---

37 Plying for Hire without Taximeters or with Taximeters not Sealed, etc The owner or driver of a motor cab shall not cause or permit the cab to ply for hire

   (i)   if a taximeter is not fitted thereto as provided in this Part of this Order, or

   (ii) if such taximeter has not been sealed and marked in accordance with the directions (if any) of [Transport for London], or

   (iii) if the seal or any mark placed on such taximeter by direction of [Transport for London] is broken, altered, defaced, or otherwise tampered with and if as soon as practicable and in any event within 24 hours thereafter the cab is not brought or sent to the appointed passing station in order that a new seal or mark may be placed on the taximeter.

Amendment

In paras (ii), (iii) words "Transport for London" in square brackets substituted by virtue of the London Cab Order 1934 (Modification) Order 2000, SI 2000/1666, art 3(2).

38 Lighting of Taximeters and "Taxi" signs (1) The owner of every motor cab shall provide a lamp so placed on the cab as to render the readings on the dial of the taximeter easily legible at all times of the day and night, and shall maintain such lamp in proper working order and condition.

(2) The driver of a motor cab shall keep such lamp properly alight throughout any part of a hiring which is during the hours of darkness as defined in Section 1 of the Road Transport Lighting Act 1927, and shall light such lamp during a hiring at any other time at the request of a hirer so as to enable the hirer to read the dial of the taximeter.

(3) Where a motor cab is provided with means for illuminating either the flag of the taximeter or a sign bearing the word "Taxi" fitted with the approval of [Transport for London] on the top of the cab, the driver, when plying for hire with the cab during any part of the hours of darkness as aforesaid, shall cause the flag or the sign or both the flag and the sign to be illuminated.

Amendment
Para (3): words "Transport for London" in square brackets substituted by virtue of the London Cab Order 1934 (Modification) Order 2000, SI 2000/1666, art 3(2).

[39 Starting and stopping the taximeter (1) The driver of a motor cab shall start the taximeter no sooner than when the cab is hired or at such later time as the driver thinks fit.

(2) The driver of a motor cab shall stop the taximeter no later than when the hiring is terminated or at such earlier time as the driver thinks fit.]

Amendment
Article substituted by the London Cab Order 2010, arts 2, 5.

[40 Fares for motor cabs (1) Subject to sub-paragraphs (3) and (4), the maximum fare payable for the hiring for a journey of a motor cab shall be the aggregate of the following amounts—
   (a) a hiring charge of £1.80; and
   (b) a sum arrived at by reference to the length and duration of the journey in accordance with such of the rates specified in sub-paragraph (2) as are applicable in the circumstances of the journey.

[(2) Exclusive of sums payable by virtue of sub-paragraph (4), the rates are—
   (a) for any part of the journey which takes place between the hours of 5 am and 8 pm, on any day except a Saturday, Sunday or public holiday,
      (i) during which the cab travels at a speed exceeding 4.65 metres per second, the rate of 20p for [117.4] metres or the rate of 20p for 86.9 metres for distance travelled in excess of [9626.8] metres;
      (ii) during which the cab is stationary or travels at a speed not exceeding 4.65 metres per second, the rate of 20p for [25.2] seconds or the rate of 20p for 18.7 seconds for distance travelled in excess of [9626.8] metres;

(b) for any part of the journey that takes place on a Saturday or Sunday (other than a public holiday) between the hours of 5 am and 8 pm, or on any day (other than a public holiday) between the hours of 8 pm and 10 pm,

    (i) during which the cab travels at a speed exceeding 4.65 metres per second, the rate of 20p for [95.5] metres or the rate of 20p for 86.9 metres for distance travelled in excess of [9645.5] metres;

    (ii) during which the cab is stationary or travels at a speed not exceeding 4.65 metres per second, the rate of 20p for [20.5] seconds or the rate of 20p for 18.7 seconds for distance travelled in excess of [9645.5] metres;

(c) for any part of the journey that takes place between 10 pm on any day and 5 am on the following day or at any time on a public holiday--

    (i) during which the cab travels at a speed exceeding 4.65 metres per second, the rate of 20p for 81.2 metres or the rate of 20p for 86.9 metres for distance travelled in excess of 9656.1 metres;

    (ii) during which the cab is stationary or travels at a speed not exceeding 4.65 metres per second, the rate of 20p for 17.5 seconds or the rate of 20p for 18.7 seconds for distance travelled in excess of 9656.1metres.]

(3) Where the sum arrived at in accordance with sub-paragraphs (1) and (2)--

    (a) is less than [£2.60] the fare shall be [£2.60];

    (b) exceeds [£2.60] but is not a multiple of 20p, the fare shall be the sum so arrived at rounded up to the next highest multiple of 20p.

(4) In addition to the fare for hiring a motor cab provided for in sub-paragraphs (1) to (3), the following maximum amounts shall, subject to sub-paragraph (5), be payable by the hirer for the whole of the journey to which the hiring relates-

    (a) £4.00 for a hiring beginning or ending between the hours of 8 pm on 24 December and 6 am on 27 December or the hours of 8 pm on 31 December and 6 am on 2 January;

    (b) [£2 for a hiring arranged by telephone, mobile phone, smart phone, mobile application, any application software and by use of the internet];

    (c) [£2.80] for a hiring beginning at a rank at Heathrow Airport;

    (d) £40.00 if, during the hiring, the cab is soiled in such a way that it has to be taken out of service for cleaning;

    (e) . . .

(5) The amounts provided for in sub-paragraph (4) shall only be payable--

    (a) in the case of that prescribed by sub-paragraph (4)(d) and (4)(e), if and to the extent that the amount is displayed on a notice prominently displayed in the cab so as to be clearly legible by the hirer and the driver chooses to levy an amount;

    [(aa) in the case of that prescribed by sub-paragraph 4(b) above, if and to the extent that the amount is shown on the taximeter and the applicable terms and conditions of the person arranging the hiring make provision for a driver to levy such an amount for the arrangement of a hiring by mobile application, any application software and by the use of the internet;]

(b) in any other case, if and to the extent that the amount is shown on the taximeter.

(6) In sub-paragraph (2) "public holiday" means Christmas Day, Boxing Day, New Year's Day, Good Friday, Easter Sunday and any other day which is a bank holiday in England and Wales under the Banking and Financial Dealings Act 1971 or by Royal Proclamation.]

Amendment
Article substituted by the London Cab Order 2010, arts 2, 6.
Para (2): substituted by the London Cab Order 2016, arts 2, 3(1), (2).
Para (2): in sub-paras (a)(i) figures "117.4" and "9626.8" in square brackets substituted by the London Cab Order 2017, arts 2, 3(1), (2).
Para (2): in sub-paras (a)(ii) figures "25.2" and "9626.8" in square brackets substituted by the London Cab Order 2017, arts 2, 3(1), (2).
Para (2): in sub-paras (a)(i) figures "95.5" and "9645.5" in square brackets substituted by the London Cab Order 2017, arts 2, 3(1), (3).
Para (2): in sub-paras (a)(i) figures "20.5" and "9645.5" in square brackets substituted by the London Cab Order 2017, arts 2, 3(1), (3).
Para (3): in sub-paras (a) and (b) figure "£2.60" in square brackets in all places it occurs substituted by the London Cab Order 2016, arts 2, 3(1), (3).
Para (4): sub-para (b) substituted by the London Cab Order 2014, arts 2, 3.
Para (4): in sub-para (c) figure "2.80" in square brackets in all places it occurs substituted by the London Cab Order 2014, arts 2, 3.
Para (4): sub-para (e) repealed by the London Cab Order 2016, arts 2, 3(1), (4).
Para (5): sub-para (aa) inserted by the London Cab Order 2014, arts 2, 3.

[40A Fixed Fare Arrangements (1) Schedule E to this Order, which specifies the circumstances under which the driver of a motor cab must charge a fixed fare for carrying one or more passengers to a single destination, shall have effect.

(2) Paragraphs 39 and 40 shall not apply when the driver of a motor cab opts to carry passengers in accordance with the fixed fare arrangements set out in Schedule E to this Order.]

Amendment
Article inserted by the London Cab (No 2) Order 2001, arts 2, 6.
Article repealed by the London Cab Order 2002, arts 2, 5.
Article inserted by the London (Fixed Fares) Cab Order 2010, arts 2, 3.

[41 Provision of receipt on request The driver of a motor cab shall, if so requested by a passenger during or immediately after a journey, provide the passenger with a receipt for the fare paid by him for that journey.]

Amendment
Article repealed by the London Cab Order 2004, arts 2, 3.
Article inserted by virtue of the London Cab Order 2007, arts 2, 14.

42 Motor Cabs Hired for Luggage Unaccompanied by Passengers The scales prescribed in this Part of this Order for the hiring of a motor cab and for extra charges for luggage . . . shall apply in any case where the driver of a motor cab accepts a hiring for the carriage of articles of luggage or packages . . . unaccompanied by any person in like manner as if one person were carried in the cab with the said articles or packages . . . : provided that the cab-driver shall not be compelled to accept such a hiring.

Amendment

Words omitted repealed by the London Cab Order 1980, SI 1980/588, arts 2, 4.

Part VII
Regulations as to fares for horse cabs

43 'Four-mile circle' In this Part of this Order the expression 'the four-mile circle' means the circumference of a circle the radius of which is four miles from Charing Cross.

44 Hiring to be by distance unless stipulated by time The hiring of a horse cab shall be by distance unless at the commencement of the hiring the hirer shall stipulate that the hiring shall be by time.

45 Hiring charge may be made Whether the hiring is by distance or by time, the driver of a horse cab shall, if a notice to that effect in a form approved by the Commissioner of Police is kept conspicuously displayed inside the cab, in such position as the Commissioner of Police may from time to time direct, be entitled to charge for each separate hiring a hiring charge of 6d. in addition to the fare for distance or time and the extra charges prescribed in this Part of this Order.

46(1) Scale of fares for horse cabs hired by distance If a horse cab is hired by distance the fare payable for distance shall be in accordance with whichever of the following scales is appropriate:

	*s.	d.
(a) if the cab is hired and discharged within the four-mile circle,	1	0
for two miles or any less distance		
for more than two miles		
for each mile and for any part of a mile in excess of the last completed mile	0	6
or		
(b) if the cab is hired within but is discharged outside the four-mile circle,		
for one mile or any less distance	1	0
for more than one mile		
for each mile ended within the circle	0	6
for each mile ended outside the circle and for any part of a mile in excess of the last completed mile	1	0

	*s.	d.

or
(c) if the cab is hired outside the four-mile circle, wherever
discharged,

	s.	d.
for one mile or any less distance	1	0
for more than one mile		
for each mile or any part of a mile in excess of the last completed mile	1	0

provided that in any case the driver may, if he so desires, notify in some manner approved by the Commissioner of Police that he is willing to accept a fare of 6d. for a distance not exceeding one mile.

* [While Part VII remains in force, the extent of amendment of the fees and the provisions is not generally certain.]

(2) The fare payable for distance under one of the scales prescribed in this para-graph shall not include any extra charges which may become payable by the hirer as provided in this Part of this Order.

47 Extra charge for waiting by horse cabs hired by distance If a horse cab which is hired by distance waits at the request of the hirer for one or more peri-ods which together amount to or exceed fifteen minutes, an extra charge shall become payable by the hirer in accordance with the following scale:

	s.	d.
in respect of each completed 15 minutes during which the cab waits (whether in one or more stoppages) in the case of a four-wheel cab hired within the four-mile circle	0	6
in the case of a four-wheel cab hired outside the four-mile circle, or a hansom wherever hired	0	8

provided that no extra charge shall be payable if the total period of such waiting in the course of the hiring is less than 15 minutes.

48 Scale of fares for horse cabs hired by time (1) If a horse cab is hired by time the fare payable for time shall be in accordance with whichever of the fol-lowing scales is appropriate:

	s.	d.
(a) in the case of a four-wheel cab hired and discharged within the four-mile circle for one hour or any less period	2	0
for more than one hour for each fifteen minutes and for any shorter period in excess of the last completed fifteen minutes	0	6

or

	s.	d.

(b) in the case of a four-wheel cab either hired or discharged
   outside the four-mile circle, or of a hansom wherever
   hired or discharged

	s.	d.
for one hour or any less period	2	6

for more than one hour
for each fifteen minutes and for any shorter period

in excess of the last completed fifteen minutes	0	8

(2) The fare payable for time under one of the scales prescribed in this paragraph shall not include any extra charges which may become payable by the hirer as provided in this Part of this Order.

49 Extra charges for additional passengers and for luggage in horse cabs In addition to the fare payable for the hiring of a horse can, whether by distance or by time, as provided in this Part of this Order, extra charges in accordance with the following scales shall be payable by the hirer for the carriage of additional passengers and of luggage, such extra charges to be for the whole of the journey for which the additional passengers or the luggage are carried, that is to say:

	s.	d.

(i) for luggage carried on the box or roof of the cab, or on the
   footboard of a hansom if the doors do not close over it—
   for each bicycle, perambulator or child's mail-cart (not

being a folded mail-cart)	0	6
for each article or package of any other description	0	2

(ii) for additional passengers, in any case where the cab is
    licensed to carry more than two persons—

for each additional passenger beyond two	0	6]

provided that for the purpose of computing the extra charge for additional passengers an infant in arms shall not count as a passenger, and two children under 10 years of age shall count as one passenger.

50 Horse cabs hired for luggage unaccompanied by passengers The scales prescribed in this Part of the Order for the hiring of a horse cab by distance (including the hiring charge), and for extra charges for waiting at the request of the hirer, and for luggage, shall apply in any case where the driver of a horse cab accepts a hiring for the carriage of articles of luggage or packages unaccompanied by any person in like manner as if one person were carried in the cab with the said articles or packages: provided that the cab-driver shall not be compelled to accept such a hiring.

Part VIII
Regulations as to Property Accidentally Left in Cabs

51 Care and Disposal of Property left in Cabs (1) Any person who finds any property accidentally left in a cab shall immediately hand the same to the cab-driver.

(2) Immediately after the termination of every hiring of a cab, the cab-driver shall carefully search the cab, or, if careful search is then impracticable, shall look inside the cab, to ascertain whether any property has been accidentally left therein, and if he does not carefully search the cab at the termination of the hiring he shall do so as soon as practicable thereafter.

(3) Any cab-driver who finds any property left in the cab or to whom any such property is handed shall, within 24 hours, deposit such property at a police station in the metropolitan area, in the state in which it was found by, or handed to, him, and shall truly state the particulars of such finding: provided that if such property is sooner claimed by the owner thereof and satisfactory proof of ownership is given, it shall be restored to the owner forthwith instead of being deposited at a police station.

52 Disposal by Assistant Commissioner of deposited property (1) If any property found in a cab and deposited at a police station by the cab-driver be not claimed within three months from the last day of the month in which the property reaches [the police station] and proved to the satisfaction of [Transport for London] to belong to the claimant, [Transport for London] may at [its] discretion either deliver the property to the cab-driver, or sell or otherwise dispose of the property and pay to the cab-driver such reasonable award as [it] shall give, but so that the award shall not in any case be less than [5p] or exceed,

> for property consisting of or comprising coin, paper money, any gold or silver article, jewellery, watch or clock, and not being of greater value than £10, [15p] in the £ on the value of the property.

or,

> for property of any other kind and not being of greater value than £10, [12½p] in the £ on the value of the property,

or,

> for property above the value of £10, such a sum as [Transport for London] shall deem reasonable:

Provided that a cab-driver who has failed to satisfy [Transport for London] that he has complied fully with the Regulations in this Part of this Order shall not be entitled to receive any award in accordance with the foregoing scale, but [Transport for London] may, at [its] discretion, in any such case award such sum as [it] may consider reasonable in all the circumstances.

(2) If any property found in a cab and deposited at a police station by the cab-driver be claimed within three months from the last day of the month in which the property is received at [the police station], and the claimant proves to the satisfaction of [Transport for London] that he is entitled thereto, the property shall be delivered to him on payment to [Transport for London] of—

> (a) a fee in respect of the cost of collecting, keeping in safe custody, and restoring lost property;
> (b) an award to the cab-driver by whom the property was deposited; and
> (c) such additional sum (if any) as may be payable as hereinafter provided.

(3) The fee payable under sub-paragraph (2) of this paragraph shall be determined in accordance with the following scale, but so that the fee payable in any one case shall not be less than [2½p] or exceed £10:

    for property of the value of £10 or under, a sum equal to [2½p] in the £ on the value of the property;

    for property above the value of £10, a sum equal to [2½p] in the £ on the first £10 of the value of the property and [5p] in the £ on any amount by which the value of the property exceeds £10:

Provided that if, in the opinion of [Transport for London], the payment of such fee would for any reason be inequitable, [it] may at [its] discretion waive payment thereof or accept such sum as [it] may consider reasonable in all the circumstances.

(4) The award to be paid to the cab-driver under sub-paragraph (2) of this paragraph shall be such reasonable sum as may be awarded by [Transport for London], having regard to all the circumstances, including the value of the property: provided that the award shall not be less than [5p] or exceed a sum calculated in accordance with the scale laid down in sub-paragraph (1) of this paragraph.

(5) The value of any property for the purposes of this paragraph shall, in the case of property sold by [Transport for London], be the sum for which it is sold, and in any other case shall be its value as estimated by [Transport for London], having due regard to the value placed upon it by the claimant: provided that a claimant may, if he so desires, cause the property to be submitted for valuation to a valuer to be chosen by [Transport for London] and in any such case the fee payable by the claimant shall be determined upon the basis of the value put upon the property by such valuer, and the cost of such valuation shall be paid to [Transport for London] by the claimant.

(6) If the property is forwarded to the claimant by post or other means, the cost of postage or other means of conveyance and any other expenses so incurred shall be paid to [Transport for London] by the claimant.

(7) In the case of any unclaimed property contained in any package, bag or other receptacle, [Transport for London] may cause the property to be opened and the contents examined if [it] deems it necessary to do so for the purpose either

    (a) of identifying and tracing the owner of the property, or

    (b) of ascertaining the nature of its contents with a view to securing its safe custody or ascertaining whether the property is of a perishable nature.

In the case of any property which is claimed by any person [Transport for London] may, if the claim of that person to be entitled to the property cannot otherwise be established to the satisfaction of [Transport for London], require the claimant to open the property and to submit the contents to examination for the purpose of establishing his claim to ownership.

Amendment
Paras (1), (2): words "the police station" in square brackets substituted by the London Cab Order 1971, SI 1971/333, art 4.

Paras (1)-(7): words "Transport for London" in square brackets in each place they occur substituted by virtue of the London Cab Order 1934 (Modification) Order 2000, SI 2000/1666, art 3(2).

Paras (1), (3): word "its" in italics in each place it occurs substituted by virtue of the London Cab Order 1934 (Modification) Order 2000, SI 2000/1666, art 3(2).

Paras (1), (3), (7): word "it" in square brackets in each place it occurs substituted by virtue of the London Cab Order 1934 (Modification) Order 2000, SI 2000/1666, art 3(2).

Para (1): sums "5p", "15p" in square brackets substituted by the Decimal Currency Act 1969, s 10.

Para (1): sum "12(½)p" in square brackets substituted by the Decimal Currency Act 1969, s 10.

Para (3): sum "2(½)p" in square brackets in each place it occurs substituted by the Decimal Currency Act 1969, s 10.

Paras (3), (4): sum "5p" in square brackets substituted by the Decimal Currency Act 1969, s 10.

Part IX
General

53 Penalty I annex a penalty not exceeding £2.00 for any breach of this Order or of any Regulations in Parts V, VI, VII or VIII thereof.

55 Reprinting of Order (1) Where by any subsequent Order of [Transport for London] for the time being in force any paragraphs words or figures are ordered to be added to or omitted from this Order, or to be substituted for any other paragraphs words or figures in this Order, then copies of this Order printed under the authority of His Majesty's Stationery Office after the amending Order takes effect may be printed with the paragraphs words or figures added or omitted or substituted, and with the paragraphs thereof so numbered, as may be ordered in the amending Order, and this Order shall be construed as if it had at the time when the amending Order takes effect been made with such addition omission or substitution.

(2) A reference in any document to this Order or to any provisions thereof shall, unless the context otherwise requires, be construed as referring to this Order as amended by any subsequent Order for the time being in force.

Amendment
Para (1): words "Transport for London" in square brackets substituted by virtue of the London Cab Order 1934 (Modification) Order 2000, SI 2000/1666, art 3(2).

Part X
Transitory Provisions and Commencement

57 Commencement This Order shall come into force on the 1st day of January, 1935.

SCHEDULE A

. . .

. . .

Amendment
Schedule repealed by the London Cab Order 2007, arts 2, 15.

SCHEDULE B
Description of Plates, etc to be affixed to Cabs

Article 12

The plates and notices to be affixed to a cab in pursuance of paragraph 12 of this Order shall be in accordance with the following descriptions, and, subject as provided in the description in each case, shall bear such devices or marks and generally be of such form, and shall be affixed in such conspicuous and convenient positions, as [Transport for London] may from time to time direct. The expression "the number of the cab" means the number allotted to the cab by [Transport for London] as the number by which it is to be distinguished.

(1) a plate, to be affixed on the outside of the back of the cab, bearing the following particulars:—
Cab No......
Licensed to carry.....persons.

(2) a plate, to be affixed inside the cab, bearing the number of the cab.

(3) a plate to be affixed inside the cab, bearing a notice in which is set forth particulars of the fares and charges which the cab-driver shall be entitled to demand from a hirer of the cab, and bearing also the following notice:—

If the hirer of this cab wishes to make any complaint about the cab or the cab-driver, he may communicate with [Transport for London] at .... , quoting the number of the cab and (if necessary) the number of the driver's badge.

Applications for property accidentally left in this cab should be made to [the police station] at ....

Amendment
Words "Transport for London" in square brackets in each place they occur substituted by virtue of the London Cab Order 1934 (Modification) Order 2000, SI 2000/1666, art 3(2).
Words "the police station" in square brackets substituted by the London Cab Order 1971, SI 1971/333, art 4.

[SCHEDULE C
Form of Cab Licence

Article 14

*Motor/Horse Cab Licence

Cab Licence No: .... Start Date: ....

*Vehicle Registration Mark: .... Expiry Date: ....

Having been appointed by Transport for London to grant Cab Licences under the Metropolitan Public Carriage Act 1869, hereby grant to** .... a Cab Licence in respect of the *motor/horse cab identified above to ply for hire within the Metropolitan Police District and the City of London.

The number of persons that this cab is licensed to carry is ....

***This cab is licensed to carry luggage on the roof.

This licence is granted subject to compliance by the licensee with the provisions of all Acts, Regulations and Orders relating to the use of *motor/horse cabs and the licence conditions specified therein.

This licence shall be in force for one year from the Start Date specified above unless sooner revoked or suspended. Where the period between Date of Issue and Expiry Date is more than 12 months, this licence has been issued on the basis that there is a pre-existing valid licence which covers the intervening period.

Signed on behalf of Transport for London .... Date of issue: ....

Notes on completing the licence (not to be printed in licence)

*The licence shall specify, either motor cab or horse cab, as the case may be. Delete the word "motor" or "horse" as appropriate. Omit reference to vehicle registration mark for horse cabs.

**Where a licensee is himself the owner or part owner of the cab, his name and address are to be inserted here, with the words "on behalf of ....", as necessary. Where the owner is a firm or company, the name of the licensee shall be inserted and the name and address of the firm or company, with the licensee's position therein, eg, "A B, Senior Partner of the firm of B and C (or Secretary of X Y & Co Ltd), on behalf of that firm (or company), of (insert address of firm or company)."

***This sentence relating to the carriage of luggage is only to be included on the licence if the vehicle is to be licensed to carry luggage on the roof in other cases it must be omitted.]

Amendment
Schedule substituted by the London Cab Order 2007, arts 2, 16.

SCHEDULE D

· · ·

· · ·

Amendment
Schedule repealed by the London Cab Order 2012, arts 2, 3(2).

[Schedule E
Fixed fare arrangements

1 Preliminary and interpretation (1) In the circumstances specified in this Schedule, the driver of a motor cab must charge a fixed fare for carrying one or more passengers to a single destination.

(2) In this Schedule—

"Applicable Fare Zone" means, in respect of any proposed journey by motor cab under the fixed fare arrangements specified in this Schedule, the Fare Zone within which the passenger's specified destination lies;

"Applicable Fixed Fare" means the fare payable in respect of any proposed journey by motor cab under the fixed fare arrangements specified in this Schedule, being the fare specified in column 3 of the table in Annex 2 to this Schedule that corresponds with the Applicable Fare Zone for that journey;

"Designated Rank" means a taxi rank referred to in the first column of the table in Annex 1 to this Schedule;

"Fare Zone" means any one of the fare zones referred to in the first column of the table in Annex 2 to this Schedule;

"Fare Zone Map" means a plan of Greater London showing the Fare Zones as may from time to time be publicised by TfL as being the Fare Zone Map for the purposes of this Schedule;

"Operative Date" means a date publicised by TfL as being a date on which fixed fare arrangements shall commence at a Designated Rank for the purposes of this Schedule;

"Operative Period" means a period which starts on an Operative Date and ends on such later date as may be publicised by TfL; and

"TfL" means Transport for London.

(3) The distances referred to in the second column of the table in Annex 2 to this Schedule are approximate.

2 Application (1) During an Operative Period, the provisions of this Schedule shall apply to motor cabs standing for hire or hired at a Designated Rank.

(2) During the hours of operation identified in the second column of the table in Annex 1 to this Schedule, any motor cab standing for hire at a Designated Rank must be hired for the carriage of passengers in accordance with the fixed fare arrangements specified in this Schedule.

3 Fixed fare arrangements Where the driver of a motor cab has opted to carry a passenger in accordance with the fixed fare arrangements specified in this Schedule, the fare payable shall be the Applicable Fixed Fare for the proposed journey.

4 Seeking to hire a motor cab under fixed fare arrangements (1) A person may only seek to hire a motor cab under a fixed fare arrangement in circumstances where:

  (a) that person's journey will commence at a Designated Rank during the hours of operation identified in the second column of the table in Annex 1 to this Schedule;

  (b) that person is travelling to a single destination without any intermediate stops; and

  (c) that destination is readily identifiable and lies within a Fare Zone.

5 Determination and payment of the Applicable Fixed Fare (1) The Applicable Fixed Fare in respect of any journey must be determined, in accordance with the provisions of this paragraph, before the commencement of the journey from the Designated Rank.

(2) The Applicable Fixed Fare will be determined, having regard to a person's stated destination and, where necessary, after consulting the Fare Zone Map in order to determine the Applicable Fare Zone.

(3) If, after being informed of the Applicable Fixed Fare, a person decides to proceed to be carried as a passenger, the Applicable Fixed Fare must be paid in full before the commencement of the journey and once the journey has commenced, no refund of the Applicable Fixed Fare, in full or in part, will be payable under any circumstances.

(4) If, after being informed of the Applicable Fixed Fare, a person decides not to be carried as a passenger under the fixed fare arrangements specified in this Schedule, no fare or other charge shall be payable by that person.

6 Operation of the Taximeter (1) When a motor cab is hired under the fixed fare arrangements specified in this Schedule, the driver of the motor cab shall not start the taximeter during the course of the passenger's journey except under the circumstances specified in paragraph 6 (2) below.

(2) In the event that a passenger requests the driver of a motor cab, after the passenger's journey has commenced, to carry the passenger or, in the case of more than one passenger, at least one of them, to a different destination to that specified before the commencement of the journey, then the driver of the motor cab may agree to carry a passenger to the different destination and in doing so, may start the taximeter as soon as,

  (a) in the case of an additional destination, the original destination has been reached; or

  (b) in the case of an alternative destination, the driver of the motor cab and the passenger agree that the taximeter should be started and, in each case, no sooner and the driver of the motor cab shall stop the taximeter no later than when the hiring is terminated or at such earlier time as the driver thinks fit.

(3) Nothing in paragraph 6(2) above shall oblige the driver of a motor cab to carry the passenger or passengers beyond the original destination specified before the commencement of the journey.

(4) Notwithstanding the provisions of paragraph 40A(2) of the Order, in any case where the driver of a motor cab starts the taximeter during the course of a journey which commenced on a fixed fare basis in accordance with paragraph 6(2) above, the fare payable for the remainder of the passenger's journey will be determined in accordance with the provisions of paragraph 40 of the Order and any fare payable shall be paid by the passenger to the driver of the motor cab at the termination of the passenger's journey and such fare shall be payable in addition to the Applicable Fixed Fare paid before the journey commenced.

7 **Multiple Passengers** Nothing in this Schedule shall prohibit the driver of a motor cab from carrying more than one passenger to a single destination in accordance with the fixed fare arrangements specified in this Schedule but the driver of a motor cab may not charge more than once for the same journey, and any reference within this Schedule to a passenger shall be construed as a reference to 'passengers' where the circumstances so require.

Annex 1 to the Schedule

Paragraphs 1(2), 2(2) and 4(1)(a)

Designated Rank and Hours of Operation

Designated Rank	Hours of Operation
Taxi rank at Coventry Street for four cabs on the north side of the carriageway, commencing 5.4 metres east of the north-eastern kerb line of Rupert Street, and continuing eastwards by the kerb for 24.1 metres together with any feeder ranks as may serve it from time to time or such other rank within the vicinity of Leicester Square, London, WC2 as may from time to time be publicised by TfL as being a Designated Rank for the purposes of this Schedule.	Between 22.00 hours and 24.00 hours on Fridays and Saturdays; and Between 0.00 hours and 04.00 hours on Saturdays and Sundays or such other hours of operation as may from time to time be publicised by TfL as being the Hours of Operation for the purposes of this Schedule.

Annex 2 to the Schedule

Paragraph 1(1) and 1(3)

Applicable Fixed Fares

Fare Zone	Distance measured in a straight line from Designated Rank	Applicable Fixed Fare
1	Not farther than three miles	£20.00
2	In excess of three miles but not farther than seven miles	£30.00
3	In excess of seven miles but not farther than ten miles	£40.00
4	In excess of ten miles but not farther than twelve miles or the boundary of Greater London if reached first	£50.00]

Amendment
Schedule inserted by the London (Fixed Fares) Cab Order 2010, arts 2, 4.

Regulations for Enforcing Order at Cab Standings in the Metropolitan Police District

By virtue of the provisions of section 4 of the London Hackney Carriages Act, 1850, I, the undersigned, Commissioner of Police of the Metropolis, hereby make the following regulations to be observed by drivers of cabs at all cab standings within the Metropolitan Police District:-

(1) The drivers of the first two cabs on the standing or any separate portion of the standing shall at all times be with their cabs and shall be available for hiring immediately they are required.

(2) No driver shall allow his cab to remain on the standing or any portion of the standing unless he is willing to accept any lawful hiring that may be offered.

(3)
    (i)   All drivers must move their cabs up as vacancies occur, and vacancies must not be filled, in any other manner.
    (ii)   When the standing is divided into several portions, the driver of the leading cab on each portion shall move his cab up to fill any vacancy in the next portion (or in such other portion as may be set out in the Regulations appointing the standing) immediately such vacancy occurs.

(4) No disabled cab shall remain on the standing longer than is reasonably necessary to effect its removal, unless such disablement is temporary and is remedied without delay.

(5) Drivers must not congregate unnecessarily on, or obstruct, the carriageway or footway, and their behaviour must be such that no annoyance or disturbance is caused or is likely to be caused to residents or other persons in the vicinity.

(6) The provisions of these Regulations are in addition to not in derogation of the provisions of any regulations applying to particular standings.

The Regulations made by the Commissioner of Police of the Metropolis on the 8th July, 1960, are hereby revoked.

Commissioner of Police of the Metropolis
Metropolitan Police Office,
New Scotland Yard,
London, SW1.

11th October, 1963

Any person offending against the Regulations is liable to a penalty not exceeding forty shillings.

1972 No 1047

London Cab Order 1972

1   This Order may be cited as the London Cab Order 1972 and shall come into operation on 7th August 1972.

2   The Interpretation Act 1889 shall apply to the interpretation of this Order as it applies to the interpretation of an Act of Parliament.

3   In relation to hirings in respect of journeys which begin at Heathrow Airport, London, for the reference to the distance of six miles in section 7 and paragraph (2) of section 17 of the London Hackney Carriage Act 1853 (being the length of a journey which the driver of a cab is by law obliged to undertake) there shall be substituted a reference to the distance of twenty miles.

1986 No 566

Local Services (Operation by Taxis) (London) Regulations 1986

1 Citation and commencement These Regulations may be cited as the Local Services (Operation by Taxis) (London) Regulations 1986 and shall come into operation on 16th April 1986.

2 Interpretation In these Regulations—
"the 1985 Act" means the Transport Act 1985;
"special licence" means a restricted PSV operator's licence granted by virtue of section 12 of the 1985 Act; and
"licensed taxi", "London taxi area" and "taxi code" have the meanings given by section 13(3) of the 1985 Act.

3 Application These Regulations apply to a licensed taxi which is licensed under section 6 of the Metropolitan Public Carriage Act 1869, at any time when that vehicle is being used to provide a local service under a special licence.

4 Prescribed Provisions (1) The provisions specified in the first column of the Table to the extent that they are part of the taxi code, except those provisions specified in the second column thereof, are hereby prescribed as applying in relation to a vehicle to which these Regulations apply.

(2) The provisions so prescribed shall apply:
(a) whether or not the use of the vehicle to provide a local service is within the London taxi area, and accordingly any limitation in those provisions to that area shall have no effect when the vehicle is being so used; and
(b) subject to the modification that any reference to a hackney carriage includes a reference to a vehicle to which these Regulations apply.

TABLE

Column 1	Column 2
Provisions Prescribed	**Provisions Excepted**
London Hackney Carriage Act 1843	Sections 3 and 33
London Hackney Carriage Act 1853	Sections 7, 9, 10, 12, 13, 16, 17, 18 and 19
Metropolitan Public Carriage Act 1869	Sections 2, 9 and 10
The London Cab Order 1934	Articles 31(1)(ii) and (2), 34, 35(2) and (4), 38–50 and Schedule E

5 Notice and Fare Table The holder of a special licence shall during such time as the vehicle is being used to provide a local service cause—

(a) to be displayed on the vehicle a notice clearly legible from the front which includes the word "BUS" in letters at least 60 millimetres high and indicates either the destination of the vehicle, or its route, or the nature of the service being provided;

(b) any notice which the vehicle is required to display to indicate that it is available for exclusive hire (including any such notice which bears the words "hire", "taxi" or "cab") not to be illuminated by any light forming part of the equipment of the vehicle;

(c) a fare table to be displayed in the vehicle in a manner clearly legible by passengers, and containing sufficient information for any passenger to ascertain the fare for his journey or the manner in which that fare is computed.

1986 No 1188

London Taxis (Licensing Appeals) Regulations 1986

1 Citation and commencement These Regulations may be cited as the London Taxis (Licensing Appeals) Regulations 1986 and shall come into operation on 1st August 1986.

2 Prescribed period The period prescribing for the purposes of both subsections (2) and (5) of section 17 of the Transport Act 1985 shall be 28 days from the date of the written notice of the decision of the licensing authority.

1986 No 1387

Licensed Taxis (Hiring at Separate Fares) (London) Order 1986

1 Citation and Commencement This Order may be cited as the Licensed Taxis (Hiring at Separate Fares) (London) Order 1986 and shall come into operation on 3rd September 1986.

2 Interpretation In this Order:—
"the 1985 Act" means the Transport Act 1985;
"authorised place" has the meaning given by section 10(5)(*a*) of the 1985 Act; and
"taxi" means a vehicle licensed under section 6 of the Metropolitan Public Carriage Act 1869.

3 Application This Order applies in relation to a taxi:—
(1) standing at an authorised place and available for hire under a scheme for the immediate hiring of taxis at separate fares;
(2) hired under such a scheme at separate fares; or
(3) being used for the carriage of passengers at separate fares where the conditions in section 11(2) of the 1985 Act are met.

4 Modifications of the taxi code (1) Neither the provisions of the taxi code specified in the Table, nor any provisions of that code in so far as it prohibits the driver from touting orally at an authorised place for passengers to share the taxi with a passenger who has already requested a service at separate fares, shall apply.

(2) For the purposes of section 33 of the London Hackney Carriage Act 1843, an authorised place shall be treated as a place appointed for the purpose of plying for hire.

TABLE

Provisions	Subject matter of provisions
London Hackney Carriage Act 1831	
Section 35	Obligatory hirings
Section 50	Hirer's consent to other passengers
London Hackney Carriage Act 1853	
Section 7	Obligatory journeys
Section 9	Number of persons to be carried at the instance of the hirer
Section 10	Carriage of luggage
Section 17(1) and (2)	Penalties
London Cab Order 1934	
Article 34	Obligatory journeys
Articles 38–50	Fares

1987 No 1535

London Taxi Sharing Scheme Order 1987

1   This Order may be cited as the London Taxi Sharing Scheme Order 1987 and shall come into force on 28th September 1987.

2   The Secretary of State hereby makes the London Taxi Sharing Scheme as set out in the Annex to this Order.

3   The Heathrow Taxi Sharing Scheme Order 1987 and the London (British Rail) Taxi Sharing Scheme Order 1987 are hereby revoked.

ANNEX
The London Taxi Sharing Scheme 1987

1 Designation of authorised places and interpretation (1) There is hereby designated as an authorised place every place at which a taxi may lawfully ply for hire.

(2) In this Scheme—
"authorised place" means any place designated in paragraph 1(1) from which taxis may be hired under the terms of the Scheme;
"exclusive service" means a service other than at separate fares;
"shared service" means a service at separate fares;
"taxi" means a vehicle licensed under section 6 of the Metropolitan Public Carriage Act 1869; and, except where otherwise stated, any reference to a numbered paragraph or Schedule is a reference to the paragraph or Schedule bearing that number in this Scheme.

2 Application (1) The requirements of this Scheme shall apply to taxis standing for hire or hired at separate fares under this Scheme for a journey from an authorised place.

(2) Any taxi may at the option of the holder of the licence for that vehicle be used for the carriage of passengers at separate fares under the terms of this Scheme.

(3) When a taxi is hired in accordance with this Scheme, the provisions of this Scheme applying to the journey for which it is hired shall apply to any part of that journey outside the London taxi area as they apply to any part within that area.

3 Availability A taxi shall be available for hire under this Scheme when it is standing at an authorised place and displaying a notice containing the words specified in paragraph 4.

4 Signs on vehicles There shall be displayed on any taxi standing for hire under this Scheme (in addition to any other sign, mark or notice which is required to be displayed on the taxi) a notice containing the words "Shared Taxi".

5 Fares (1) The taxi meter shall be set in motion only when the taxi leaves the authorised place and shall display the fare for an exclusive service payable under paragraphs 40 and 41(2) of the London Cab Order 1934.

(2) The maximum amount payable by a passenger sharing a service shall be the aggregate of:—
  (a) the amount calculated in accordance with the conversion table set out in Schedule 1 as the time when the passenger is set down and according to the number of passengers who arranged the shared service; and
  (b) any charge for luggage payable under paragraph 41(1) of the London Cab Order 1934.

(3) No fare shall be charged for any child under the age of two years, and no such child shall be counted when calculating the number of people sharing the vehicle.

(4) For the purpose of computing fares, each child over the age of two years but under the age of ten years shall be charged at half fare and when calculating the number of people sharing the vehicle—
  (a) if an even number of children are being carried, one half of that number shall be counted; and
  (b) if an odd number of such children are being carried, one half of the even number immediately following that odd number shall be counted.

6 Fare Tables (1) The driver of a taxi to which this Scheme applies shall at all times carry in his taxi—
  (a) a copy of the conversion table set out in Schedule 1; and
  (b) a copy of the fare table set out in Schedule 2.

(2) The driver shall produce the tables specified in paragraph 6(1) to any passenger who asks to see them or either of them.

7 Obligatory hirings The driver of a taxi available for hire under this Scheme who—
  (a) is not waiting with a person seeking a shared service for another person to offer to share the taxi; and
  (b) would, apart from the Licensed Taxis (Hiring at Separate Fares) (London) Order 1986, be required to accept the hiring,

shall not without reasonable excuse refuse a hiring to two or more persons seeking a shared service to the same destination; but he may, with the agreement of those persons, wait for a reasonable period for further passengers to share the hiring.

8 Arrangements for a shared service (1) If a person seeks to hire for a shared service a taxi available for hire under this Scheme and the driver is unable to find at least one other person to share the hiring within a reasonable time, then no fare or other charge shall be payable and the driver shall be free to seek an alternative hiring provided that the driver and the first mentioned person may continue to wait for another person to offer to share the taxi for so long as they both agree to do so.

(2) The driver of a taxi available for hire under this Scheme may refuse to accept as a passenger for a shared service any person on the grounds that his intended destination could not be reached without an excessive or unreasonable addition to the length or duration of the journey of any passenger previously accepted for a journey, but shall not refuse to carry a person already accepted by him as a passenger because his destination is not on such grounds compatible with that of a person who subsequently seeks a shared service.

(3) Before the commencement of any journey from the authorised place by a taxi for the purpose of a shared service, any person may (notwithstanding any earlier agreement) decide not to be carried as a passenger and no fare or other charge shall be payable by that person.

9 Cessation of availability If—
    (a) a person at any time seeks to hire for an exclusive service a taxi available for hire under this Scheme;
    (b) the driver is not waiting with a person seeking a shared service for another person to offer to share the taxi; and
    (c) the driver either—
        (i) would, apart from the Licensed Taxis (Hiring at Separate Fares) (London) Order 1986, be required to accept the hiring; or
        (ii) accepts the hiring although not required to do so,

then that taxi shall thereupon cease to be available for hire under this Scheme until the expiry of that hiring.

10 Luggage The driver shall not refuse to carry in his taxi the luggage of a passenger if the luggage can be accommodated safely within the luggage compartment of the taxi with the luggage of other passengers already accepted by him.

11 Route to be followed The route taken by the taxi and the order in which passengers are set down shall be determined by the driver, but he shall not unreasonably prolong the journey of any passenger.

SCHEDULE 1
CONVERSION TABLE FOR USE IN CALCULATING SHARED FARES

Paragraph 5

Maximum amount payable by each passenger

Fare displayed on meter	NUMBER SHARING			
	2	3	4	5
80p	50p	40p	40p	30p
£1.00	70p	60p	50p	40p
£1.20	80p	70p	50p	50p
£1.40	90p	80p	60p	60p
£1.60	£1.00	90p	70p	60p
£1.80	£1.20	£1.00	80p	70p
£2.00	£1.30	£1.10	90p	80p
£2.20	£1.40	£1.20	£1.00	90p
£2.40	£1.60	£1.30	£1.10	£1.00
£2.60	£1.70	£1.40	£1.20	£1.00
£2.80	£1.80	£1.50	£1.30	£1.10
£3.00	£2.00	£1.70	£1.40	£1.20
£3.20	£2.10	£1.80	£1.40	£1.30
£3.40	£2.20	£1.90	£1.50	£1.40
£3.60	£2.30	£2.00	£1.60	£1.40
£3.80	£2.50	£2.10	£1.70	£1.50
£4.00	£2.60	£2.20	£1.80	£1.60
£4.20	£2.70	£2.30	£1.90	£1.70
£4.40	£2.90	£2.40	£2.00	£1.80
£4.60	£3.00	£2.50	£2.10	£1.80
£4.80	£3.10	£2.60	£2.20	£1.90
£5.00	£3.30	£2.80	£2.30	£2.00
£5.20	£3.40	£2.90	£2.30	£2.10

£5.40	£3.50	£3.00	£2.40	£2.20
£5.60	£3.60	£3.10	£2.50	£2.20
£5.80	£3.80	£3.20	£2.60	£2.30
£6.00	£3.90	£3.30	£2.70	£2.40
£6.20	£4.00	£3.40	£2.80	£2.50
£6.40	£4.20	£3.50	£2.90	£2.60
£6.60	£4.30	£3.60	£3.00	£2.60
£6.80	£4.40	£3.70	£3.10	£2.70
£7.00	£4.60	£3.90	£3.20	£2.80
£7.20	£4.70	£4.00	£3.20	£2.90
£7.40	£4.80	£4.10	£3.30	£3.00
£7.60	£4.90	£4.20	£3.40	£3.00
£7.80	£5.10	£4.30	£3.50	£3.10
£8.00	£5.20	£4.40	£3.70	£3.20
£8.20	£5.30	£4.40	£3.70	£3.30
£8.40	£5.50	£4.60	£3.80	£3.40
£8.60	£5.60	£4.70	£3.90	£3.40
£8.80	£5.70	£4.80	£4.00	£3.50
£9.00	£5.90	£5.00	£4.10	£3.60
£9.20	£6.00	£5.10	£4.20	£3.70
£9.40	£6.10	£5.20	£4.20	£3.80
£9.60	£6.20	£5.30	£4.30	£3.80
£9.80	£6.40	£5.40	£4.40	£3.90
£10.00	£6.50	£5.50	£4.50	£4.00

Where the fare displayed on the meter exceeds £10, the shared fare shall be calculated by repeated use of the conversion table for each multiple of £10 and for any sum by which the fare displayed exceeds the highest multiple of £10.

SCHEDULE 2
FARE TABLE FOR SHARED SERVICE

Paragraph 6

1 Total fare At any time when the taxi is shared the fare payable by each passenger shall be the sum of the basic fare specified in paragraph 2 of this Table and the permitted luggage charge.

2 Basic fare The basic fare shall be calculated by applying the conversion table carried by the driver to the sum displayed on the meter when the passenger leaves the taxi.

3 Sum displayed on the meter The meter will be started when the taxi leaves the authorised place and will operate at the normal rate for an exclusive service. It may include any additional charges that would apply to an exclusive service, with the exception of the charges for additional passengers and for luggage.

4 Number sharing The basic fare is calculated from the sum displayed on the meter according to the number of passengers sharing the taxi when it leaves the authorised place.

5 Child fares Children under the age of 2 years are carried free, and those aged between 2 and 10 years will be charged half fare. For the purpose of calculating the number of people sharing the taxi, children under the age of 2 years are not counted and, for children aged between 2 and 10 years—
   (a)   1 or 2 children count as 1 person;
   (b)   3 or 4 children count as 2 persons; and
   (c)   5 or 6 children count as 3 persons.

2000 No 1666

London Cab Order 1934 (Modification) Order 2000

1 Citation and commencement This Order may be cited as the London Cab Order 1934 (Modification) Order 2000 and shall come into force on 3rd July 2000.

2 Modification of the London Cab Order 1934 The London Cab Order 1934 shall have effect in accordance with the following provisions of this Order.

3 References to the Assistant Commissioner, the Commissioner and the Secretary of State (1) In paragraph 2(1) the definition of "the Assistant Commissioner" shall be omitted.

(2) Any reference to the Assistant Commissioner, the Commissioner of Police or the Secretary of State shall be treated as a reference to Transport for London.

4 Modification of forms in Schedules A document which is required to be in the form contained in Schedule—
- (a) A (form of certificate to be given by public carriage examiner in relation to an application for a cab licence);
- (b) B (description of plates etc to be affixed to cabs);
- (c) C (form of cab licence); or
- (d) D (form of cab-driver's licence),

may be modified so far as may be necessary in consequence of any provision of Schedule 20 (hackney carriages) to the Greater London Authority Act 1999 or of this Order.

2000 No 3146

Private Hire Vehicles (London) (Operators' Licences) Regulations 2000

Part I
General

1 Citation and commencement These Regulations may be cited as the Private Hire Vehicles (London) (Operators' Licences) Regulations 2000 and shall come into force on 22nd January 2001.

2 Interpretation In these Regulations, unless the context otherwise requires—

"the 1998 Act" means the Private Hire Vehicles (London) Act 1998;

"application" means an application for the grant or variation of a licence;

["business name" means a name which if used by a person for the purpose of carrying on business would make him subject to the Companies Act 2006;]

"CB apparatus" means wireless telegraphy apparatus known as "Citizens' Band" which is designed or adapted, or has facilities permitting its adaptation, for the purpose of transmitting spoken messages on the frequency band 26.1 MHz to 28 MHz;

"certificate of insurance" and "certificate of security" shall be construed in accordance with section 147 of the Road Traffic Act 1988;

"Community licence" and "Northern Ireland licence" have the same meanings as in section 108(1) of the Road Traffic Act 1988;

"driving licence" means a licence to drive a motor car granted under Part III of the Road Traffic Act 1988 (other than a provisional licence), or a licence authorising the driving of a motor car by virtue of section 99A(1) or 109(1) of that Act (Community licences and Northern Ireland licences);

"firm" has the same meaning as in section 4 of the Partnership Act 1890;

"licence" means a London PHV operator's licence;

"licensing authority" means the person appointed under section 24(1) of the 1998 Act for the purpose of exercising the functions of the Secretary of State under that Act or, where no such appointment has been made, the Secretary of State;

"MOT test certificate" means, in relation to a vehicle to which section 47 of the Road Traffic Act 1998 applies, a test certificate issued in respect of the vehicle as mentioned in subsection (1) of that section;

"national insurance number" has the same meaning as in regulation 1(2) of the Social Security (Contributions) Regulations 1979;

"officer", in relation to a body corporate, shall be construed in accordance with section 744 of the Companies Act 1985;

"operator" means a London PHV operator and in relation to a licence means the operator to whom the licence was granted;

"registered keeper" means, in relation to a vehicle, the person in whose name the vehicle is registered under the Vehicle Excise and Registration Act 1994;

"registration mark" means, in relation to a vehicle, the mark assigned to the vehicle in accordance with section 23 of the Vehicle Excise and Registration Act 1994;

"variation" means a variation of a licence at the operator's request under section 18 of the 1998 Act; and

"wireless telegraphy apparatus" shall be construed in accordance with section 19(1) of the Wireless Telegraphy Act 1949.

Amendment

Definition "business name" substituted by the Private Hire Vehicles (London) (Operators' Licences) (Amendment) Regulations 2016, regs 2, 3.

Part II
Applications

3 Manner of making applications Every application shall—
  (a) be made on a form supplied by the licensing authority and include the information and declarations required by that form;
  (b) be signed—
     (i) if made by an individual, by that person,
     (ii) if made by a firm, by one of the partners of that firm with the authority of the others, or
     (iii) if made by any other body or group of persons, by one or more individual persons authorised for that purpose by the body or group; and
  (c) be accompanied by the appropriate fee prescribed by regulation 4.

4 Fees The appropriate fee for the purpose of regulation 3 is—
  (a) [£703] in the case of an application for the grant of a licence; and
  [(b) £50 in the case of an application for variation of a licence to remove an existing reference to one or more operating centres.]
  [(c) £200 in the case of an application for variation of a licence to add a reference to one or more operating centres.]

Amendment

In para (a) figure "£703" in square brackets substituted by the Private Hire Vehicles (London) (Operators' Licences) (Amendment) Regulations 2006, regs 2, 3(1).

Para (b) substituted by the Private Hire Vehicles (London) (Operators' Licences) (Amendment) Regulations 2010, regs 2, 3(1).

Para (c) inserted by the Private Hire Vehicles (London) (Operators' Licences) (Amendment) Regulations 2010, regs 2, 3(2).

5 Determination of applications (1) If the licensing authority is satisfied that a licence may properly be—

    (a) granted for five years—

        (i) in the terms applied for; and

        (ii) without the need for any additional conditions other than those prescribed in regulation 9, or

    (b) varied in the terms applied for,

the authority shall approve the application and give the applicant notice of the decision.

(2) If the authority is not so satisfied and decides—

    (a) to approve the application other than in the terms applied for;

    (b) in the case of an application for the grant of a licence, to approve the application on the basis that—

        (i) additional conditions shall be attached to the licence, or

        (ii) the licence shall be granted for a shorter period than five years; or

    (c) to refuse the application,

the authority shall give the applicant notice of the decision and the grounds for it.

Part III
Licences

6 Grant and variation (1) Where the decision has been made to approve an application in accordance with regulation 5(1) or 5(2)(a) or (b) the licensing authority shall, provided that any appropriate fee prescribed by regulation 7 is received within the period of 28 days commencing on the date specified in paragraph (2), grant or vary the licence, as the case may be, and send the licence or any replacement licence to the applicant.

(2) The date referred to in paragraph (1) is—

    (a) the date of service of the notice given in accordance with regulation 5; or

    (b) where an appeal is brought against that decision, the date of disposal or withdrawal of that appeal.

(3) If any appropriate fee prescribed by regulation 7 is not received by the licensing authority in accordance with paragraph (1) the approval will lapse, the application will be deemed to have been withdrawn and the licensing authority shall be entitled to retain the fee accompanying it.

7 Fees (1) Subject to paragraph (2), for the purpose of regulation 6 the fee for the grant of a licence for a period of five years is [£1707].

(2) Where an applicant for the grant of a licence meets the requirement set out in paragraph (3), he may elect that the amount of [£550] shall be substituted for the amount of [£1707] referred to in paragraph (1).

(3) The requirement referred to in paragraph (2) is that no more than two private hire vehicles will be available to the applicant for carrying out bookings accepted by him at all the operating centres which will be specified in his licence.

(4) Subject to paragraphs (5) and (6), for the purpose of regulation 6 the fee for the grant of a licence for a period of less than five years is an amount equal to that proportion of the amount of [£1707] which the proposed period of the licence bears in relation to the period of five years.

(5) Where an applicant for the grant of a licence meets the requirement set out in paragraph (3), he may elect that the amount of [£550] shall be substituted for the amount of [£1707] referred to in paragraph (4).

(6) Where the calculation of any fee in accordance with paragraph (4) would have the result that the amount payable would include a fraction of a pound then the amount payable shall be adjusted downwards to the nearest pound.

Amendment
Para (1): sum "£1707" in square brackets substituted by the Private Hire Vehicles (London) (Operators' Licences) (Amendment) Regulations 2006, regs 2, 3(2).
Para (2): sums "£550" and "£1707" in square brackets substituted by the Private Hire Vehicles (London) (Operators' Licences) (Amendment) Regulations 2006, regs 2, 3(2), (3).
Para (4): sum "£1707" in square brackets substituted by the Private Hire Vehicles (London) (Operators' Licences) (Amendment) Regulations 2006, regs 2, 3(2).
Para (5): sums "£550" and "£1707" in square brackets substituted by the Private Hire Vehicles (London) (Operators' Licences) (Amendment) Regulations 2006, regs 2, 3(2), (3).

8 Refund of fees (1) Subject to paragraph (5), where the licensing authority is satisfied that—
    (a) an operator has ceased to operate from every operating centre specified in his licence, other than by reason of the suspension or revocation of that licence;
    (b) that operator has transferred some or all of his undertaking as an operator to another person, and
    (c) before the date of the transfer the transferee has been granted a new licence in relation to any operating centre specified in the transferor's licence,

the licensing authority shall, upon receipt of a written request for a refund accompanied by the transferor's licence, refund a proportion of the fee paid for the grant of that licence being an amount calculated in accordance with paragraph (3).

(2) Subject to paragraph (5), where a licence has been granted following an election made under regulation 7(2) or (5) and before its expiry the operator has been granted a new licence in circumstances where he did not meet the requirement set out in regulation 7(3) in relation to all of the operating centres to be

specified in that licence, the licensing authority shall, upon receipt of a written request for a refund accompanied by the first mentioned licence, refund a proportion of the fee paid for the grant of that licence being an amount calculated in accordance with paragraph (3).

(3) Subject to paragraph (4), the amount referred to in paragraphs (1) and (2) shall be that proportion of the fee which the number of full years remaining on the licence bears to the period for which the licence was granted, the number of full years being calculated from the date of receipt by the licensing authority of both the request for a refund and the licence.

(4) Where the calculation in accordance with paragraph (3) would have the result that the amount refundable would include a fraction of a pound then the amount refundable shall be adjusted downwards to the nearest pound.

(5) Where a proportion of the fee paid for the grant of a licence is refunded in accordance with paragraph (1) or (2), that licence shall cease to have effect.

9 Conditions (1) Every licence shall be granted subject to the conditions set out in the following provisions of this regulation.

(2) In respect of any operating centre specified in the licence which is accessible to members of the public, the operator shall maintain in force a policy of insurance against public liability risks which provides a minimum indemnity of £5,000,000 in respect of any one event.

[(3) Before the commencement of each journey, the operator shall—
    (a) agree the fare with the person making the private hire booking, or
    (b) provide an accurate estimate of that fare to the person maing the private hire booking.

What constitutes an accurate estimate for the purposes of this condition may be specified by the licensing authority from time to time.]

(4) If, during the currency of the licence—
    (a) any conviction is recorded—
        (i) where the operator is an individual, against him,
        (ii) where the operator is a firm, against any partner of that firm, or
        (iii) where the operator is another type of body or group of persons, against that body or group or any officer of that body or group;
    (b) any information provided in the application for the grant of the licence, or for any variation thereof, changes; or
    (c) any driver ceases to be available to the operator for carrying out bookings, by virtue of that drivers's unsatisfactory conduct in connection with the driving of a private hire vehicle,

the operator shall, within 14 days of the date of such event, give the licensing authority notice containing details of the conviction or change, as the case may be, or, in a case falling within sub-paragraph (c), the name of the driver and the circumstances of the case.

(5) No CB apparatus shall be used in connection with a private hire booking at any operating centre specified in the licence or in any private hire vehicle available for carrying out bookings accepted at any such operating centre.

(6) The operator shall preserve records in accordance with regulation 16(1)(a) and (b).

(7) The operator shall establish and maintain a procedure for dealing with—
    (a) complaints, and
    (b) lost property,

arising in connection with any private hire booking accepted by him and shall keep and preserve records in accordance with regulations 14, 15 and 16(1)(c).

(8) Where an operator provides a London cab for the purpose of carrying out a private hire booking, any fare payable in respect of the booking shall be calculated as if the vehicle was a private hire vehicle unless the fare shown on the taximeter is less.

(9) In the case of a licence granted following an election made under regulation 7(2) or (5), the operator must, during the currency of the licence, continue to meet the requirement that no more than two private hire vehicles are available to him for carrying out bookings accepted by him at all the operating centres specified in his licence.

[(10) Before the commencement of each journey, the operator shall provide to the passenger for whom the booking was made particulars of the driver and the private hire vehicle carrying out that booking. The licensing authority shall specify from time to time the particulars which are to be provided and how they are to be provided.

(11) [At all times during the operator's hours of business and at all times during a journey, the operator shall ensure that the passenger for whom the booking was made is able to speak to a person at the operating centre or other premises with a fixed address in London or elsewhere (whether inside or outside the United Kingdom) which has been notified to the licensing authority in writing if the passenger wants to make a complaint or discuss any other matter about the carrying out of the booking with the operator.]

(12) The operator shall provide to the licensing authority such particulars of drivers and private hire vehicles as may be specified by the licensing authority from time to time.]

[(13) The operator shall notify the licensing authority of any material changes to its operating model that may affect the operator's compliance with the 1998 Act, these Regulations or any conditions of that operator's licence, before those changes are made.]

Amendment
Para (3): substituted by the Private Hire Vehicles (London) (Operators' Licences) (Amendment) Regulations 2016, regs 2, 4(1).

Paras (10)-(12): inserted by the Private Hire Vehicles (London) (Operators' Licences) (Amendment) Regulations 2016, regs 2, 4(2).

Paras (11): substituted by the Private Hire Vehicles (London) (Operators' Licences) (Amendment) Regulations 2017, regs 2, 3.

Para (13): inserted by the Private Hire Vehicles (London) (Operators' Licences) (Amendment) (No. 2) Regulations 2016, regs 2, 3.

Part IV
Records

10 Form of record of private hire bookings The record which an operator is required to keep by virtue of section 4(3)(b) of the 1998 Act at each operating centre specified in his licence of the private hire bookings accepted by him there shall be kept—

(a) in writing, or

(b) in such other form that the information contained in it can easily be reduced to writing.

11 Particulars of private hire bookings Before the commencement of each journey booked at an operating centre specified in his licence an operator shall enter the following particulars of the booking in the record referred to in regulation 10—

(a) the date on which the booking is made and, if different, the date of the proposed journey;

(b) the name of the person for whom the booking is made or other identification of him, or, if more than one person, the name or other identification of one of them;

(c) the agreed time and place of collection, or, if more than one, the agreed time and place of the first;

(d) the main destination . . .;

[(e) the agreed fare or estimated fare;]

(f) the name of the driver carrying out the booking or other identification of him;

(g) if applicable, the name of the other operator to whom the booking has been sub-contracted, and

(h) the registered number of the vehicle to be used or such other means of identifying it as may be adopted.

Amendment

In sub-para (d): words omitted repealed by the Private Hire Vehicles (London) (Operators' Licences) (Amendment) Regulations 2016, regs 2, 5(1).

Sub-para (e): substituted by the Private Hire Vehicles (London) (Operators' Licences) (Amendment) Regulations 2016, regs 2, 5(2).

12 Particulars of private hire vehicles (1) For the purposes of section 4(3)(d) of the 1998 Act, an operator shall keep at each operating centre specified in his licence a record, containing the particulars set out in paragraph (2), of each private hire vehicle which is available to him for carrying out bookings accepted by him at that centre.

(2) In relation to each vehicle the particulars referred to in paragraph (1) are—
    (a) the make, model and colour;
    (b) the registration mark;
    (c) the name and address of the registered keeper;
    [(ca) a copy of the vehicle's London PHV licence or temporary permit granted under the Private Hire Vehicles (London) (Transitional Provisions) Regulations 2004, as appropriate;]
    (d) in the case of a vehicle to which [paragraph 8(1) of Schedule 2 of the Private Hire Vehicles (London PHV Licences) Regulations 2004] applies, a copy of the current MOT test certificate [issued in accordance with those regulations];
    (e) a copy of the current certificate of insurance or certificate of security;
    (f) the date on which the vehicle became available to the operator and
    (g) the date on which the vehicle ceased to be so available.

Amendment

Para (2): sub-para (ca) inserted by the Private Hire Vehicles (London) (Operators' Licences) (Amendment) Regulations 2004, regs 2, 3.

Para (2): sub-para (d) words "paragraph 8(1) of Schedule 2 of the Private Hire Vehicles (London PHV Licences) Regulations 2004" in square brackets substituted by Private Hire Vehicles (London) (Operators' Licences) (Amendment) Regulations 2011, regs 2, 3(1).

Para (2): sub-para (d) words "issued in accordance with those regulations" in square brackets inserted by Private Hire Vehicles (London) (Operators' Licences) (Amendment) Regulations 2011, regs 2, 3(2).

13 Particulars of drivers (1) For the purposes of section 4(3)(d) of the 1998 Act, an operator shall keep at each operating centre specified in his licence a record, containing the particulars set out in paragraph (2), of each driver who is available to him for carrying out bookings accepted by him at that centre.

(2) In relation to each driver the particulars referred to in paragraph (1) are—
    (a) his surname, forenames, address and date of birth;
    (b) his national insurance number;
    (c) a photocopy of his driving licence;
    [(ca) a copy of his London PHV driver's licence or temporary permit granted under the Private Hire Vehicles (London) (Transitional Provisions) Regulations 2003, as appropriate;]
    (d) a photograph of him;
    (e) the date on which he became available to the operator, and
    (f) the date on which he ceased to be so available.

Amendment

Para (2): sub-para (ca) inserted by the Private Hire Vehicles (London) (Operators' Licences) (Amendment) Regulations 2003, regs 2, 3.

14 Record of complaints (1) An operator shall keep at each operating centre specified in his licence a record containing—

- (a) the particulars set out in paragraph (2) of any complaint made in respect of a private hire booking accepted by him at that centre; and
- (b) the particulars set out in paragraph (2)(d), (e), and (f) of any other complaint made in respect of his undertaking as an operator at that centre.

(2) In relation to each complaint the particulars referred to in paragraph (1) are—

- (a) the date of the related booking;
- (b) the name of the driver who carried out the booking;
- (c) the registration mark of the vehicle used;
- (d) the name of the complainant and any address, telephone number or other contact details provided by him;
- (e) the nature of the complaint, and
- (f) details of any investigation carried out and subsequent action taken as a result.

15 Record of lost property (1) An operator shall keep at each operating centre specified in his licence a record, containing the particulars set out in paragraph (2), of any lost property found—

- (a) at that centre, or
- (b) in any private hire vehicle used to carry out a booking accepted by him there.

(2) In relation to each item of lost property the particulars referred to in paragraph (1) are—

- (a) the date on which it was found;
- (b) the place where it was found and if it was found in a vehicle, the registration mark of that vehicle;
- (c) a description of the item;
- (d) evidence to show that, where practical, an attempt was made to return the item to the owner and whether or not this was successful, and
- (e) in the case of any unclaimed item which has been disposed of, how it was disposed of.

(3) An operator shall keep at each operating centre specified in his licence a record, containing the particulars set out in paragraph (4), of any property reported to him at that centre as having been lost.

(4) In relation to each item of property reported as having been lost the particulars referred to in paragraph (3) are—

- (a) the date of the report;
- (b) the date on which it is alleged to have been lost;
- (c) the place where it is alleged to have been lost;
- (d) a description of the item, and
- (e) evidence to show that, where practical, an attempt was made to find the item.

16 Preservation of records (1) Subject to paragraph (3), an operator shall preserve the particulars of—

(a) each private hire booking recorded in accordance with regulation 11 for [twelve months] from the date on which the booking was accepted;

(b) each private hire vehicle and driver recorded in accordance with regulations 12 and 13 for twelve months from the date on which the vehicle or, as the case may be, the driver ceased to be available for carrying out bookings;

(c) each complaint and item of lost property recorded in accordance with regulations 14 and 15 for [twelve months] from the date on which they were entered in the respective record.

(2) Where an operator tape-records a private hire booking he shall preserve the tape-recording of that conversation for a period of [twelve months].

(3) For the purpose of section 4(4) of the 1998 Act, if an operator ceases to use an operating centre specified in his licence, he shall, in relation to that operating centre, preserve—

(a) the record referred to in regulation 10 for [twelve months]; and

(b) the records kept in accordance with regulations 12 and 13 for twelve months,

from the date of the last entry.

Amendment

Para (1): in sub-para (a) words "twelve months" in square brackets substituted by the Private Hire Vehicles (London) (Operators' Licences) (Amendment) Regulations 2016, regs 2, 6.

Para (1): in sub-para (c) words "twelve months" in square brackets substituted by the Private Hire Vehicles (London) (Operators' Licences) (Amendment) Regulations 2016, regs 2, 6.

Para (2): words "twelve months" in square brackets substituted by the Private Hire Vehicles (London) (Operators' Licences) (Amendment) Regulations 2016, regs 2, 6.

Para (3): in sub-para (a) words "twelve months" in square brackets substituted by the Private Hire Vehicles (London) (Operators' Licences) (Amendment) Regulations 2016, regs 2, 6.

Part V
Other Matters

17 Register of licences (1) The register maintained by the licensing authority in relation to each licence issued under the 1998 Act shall contain, in addition to the matters set out in section 23(1)(a) of that Act, the further particulars set out in paragraph (2).

(2) In relation to each licence the further particulars referred to in paragraph (1) are—

(a) the address of each operating centre specified in the licence; and

(b) an indication that it is current, suspended or revoked.

18 Issue of replacement licences (1) Subject to paragraph (2), where an operator notifies the licensing authority that—

(a) he has adopted, altered or dispensed with a business name;

(b) he has changed his name; or

(c) his licence has been lost, destroyed or defaced,

[the licensing authority may issue a replacement licence].

(2) Except where a licence has been lost or destroyed, no replacement shall be issued until the original licence has been returned to the licensing authority.

Amendment

Para (1): words "the licensing authority may issue a replacement licence" in square brackets substituted by the Private Hire Vehicles (London) (Operators' Licences) (Amendment) Regulations 2016, regs 2, 7.

19 Continuance of licence on death, bankruptcy etc (1) This regulation applies in relation to a licence granted in the sole name of an individual in the event of—

(a) the death of that individual;

(b) the bankruptcy of that individual; or

(c) that individual becoming a [person who lacks capacity (within the meaning of the Mental Capacity Act 2005) to carry on the activities covered by the licence].

(2) After the happening of the event mentioned in paragraph (1)(a) the licensing authority may direct that the licence shall not be treated as terminated when the individual died but suspended until the date when a direction under paragraph (3) comes into force.

(3) After the happening of any of the events mentioned in paragraph (1) the licensing authority may direct that a person carrying on the business of the operator is to be treated for the purposes of the 1998 Act as if he were the operator for such purpose and to such extent as is specified in the direction for a period not exceeding—

(a) six months from the date of the coming into force of that direction; or

(b) if less, the remainder of the period of the licence.

Amendment

Para (1): in sub-para (c) words from "person who lacks capacity" to the end of the paragraph in square brackets substituted by the Private Hire Vehicles (London) (Operators' Licences) (Amendment) Regulations 2009, regs 2, 3.

20 Transitional provisions (1) Subject to paragraph (2), where an application is received by the licensing authority before 22nd August 2001 but no determination under regulation 5 has been made in relation to that application before 22nd October 2001, the licensing authority shall—

(a) issue the applicant with a temporary permit, in the terms applied for, to make provision for the invitation or acceptance of, or accept, private hire bookings, or

(b) make a temporary variation of the applicant's licence in the terms applied for,

which shall have effect from the latter date as if it were a licence granted or, as the case may be, variation made under the 1998 Act.

(2) Any temporary permit issued or variation made under paragraph (1) shall, unless the permit or, as the case may be, the licence to which the variation applies, has already been suspended or revoked under the 1998 Act, cease to have effect for the purposes of that Act—

(a) on the grant or variation of a licence pursuant to the outstanding application; or

(b) where no such licence is granted or varied, on the expiry of the period of 28 days commencing on the date specified in paragraph (3).

(3) The date referred to in paragraph (2)(b) is—

(a) the date of service of the notice given in accordance with regulation 5 of a decision in relation to the outstanding application; or

(b) where an appeal is brought against that decision, the date of disposal or withdrawal of that appeal.

2003 No 655

Private Hire Vehicles (London) (Transitional and Saving Provisions) Regulations 2003

1 Citation and commencement These Regulations may be cited as the Private Hire Vehicles (London) (Transitional and Saving Provisions) Regulations 2003 and shall come into force on 1st April 2003.

2 Interpretation In these Regulations—
"the 1998 Act" means the Private Hire Vehicles (London) Act 1998;
"application deadline" in relation to an existing driver means the date specified under regulation 4(1) as the application deadline for that driver;
"existing driver" means an individual who is registered with Transport for London as an existing driver in accordance with article 3(1);
"the first appointed day" means 1st April 2003;
"the second appointed day" means 1st June 2003; and
"temporary permit" means a temporary permit issued under regulation 5(1).

3 Registration of existing drivers (1) Subject to the provisions of this regulation, an individual who has been the driver of a vehicle used as a private hire vehicle on roads in London under a booking which was—
(a) made through a London PHV operator ("the relevant operator"); and
(b) accepted at an operating centre specified in the relevant operator's London PHV operator's licence,

may apply to be registered with Transport for London as an existing driver by delivering to Transport for London the form provided by it for the purpose completed to show such particulars as Transport for London may reasonably require.

(2) The form shall be signed by the applicant and countersigned by the relevant operator.

(3) The form shall be treated as validly delivered to Transport for London if, and only if, it is received by Transport for London on the second appointed day or at any time before that day, whether before or after the making of these Regulations.

4 Application deadlines (1) Transport for London shall by notice given to each existing driver specify an application deadline by which that driver is invited to submit an application for a London PHV driver's licence.

(2) Transport for London shall not be required to consider any application for a London PHV driver's licence from an existing driver until after the application deadline.

5 Issue of temporary permits [(1) Transport for London may issue a temporary permit to—

    (a) any existing driver; or

    (b) an applicant for a London PHV driver's licence who, at any time before [1st January 2007], has submitted an application which—

        (i) meets all requirements of Transport for London made pursuant to section 15(1), (2) and (4) of the 1998 Act; and

       (ii) for which any prescribed fee (or instalment) due in accordance with regulations made by Transport for London under section 20 has been paid.]

(2) Subject to regulation 6 and, except for the purposes of section 14(1) (driver's badges) of the 1998 Act, a temporary permit shall have effect as if it were London PHV driver's licence and may in particular be suspended or revoked under section 16 of that Act accordingly.

Amendment

Para (1): substituted by the Private Hire Vehicles (London) (Transitional and Saving Provisions) (Amendment) Regulations 2003, SI 2003/3028, regs 2, 3.

Para (1): in sub-para (b) words "1st January 2007" in square brackets substituted by the Private Hire Vehicles (London) (Transitional and Saving Provisions) (Amendment) Regulations 2006, SI 2006/584, reg 2.

6 Duration of temporary permits (1) A temporary permit shall cease to have effect on whichever of the following dates falls first—

    (a) if a London PHV driver's licence is granted to the holder of the temporary permit, the date on which the licence was granted;

    (b) if an application for a London PHV driver's licence by the holder of the temporary permit is refused, the date on which the time for appealing against the refusal of the application expires or (where an appeal is brought) the date on which the appeal is disposed of or withdrawn;

  [(bb) in the case of a temporary permit issued pursuant to regulation 5(1) (b), on the last day of the period of 3 months beginning with the day on which the temporary permit is issued or such later date (if any) as Transport for London may from time to time notify to the holder;]

    (c) if the temporary permit is revoked, the date on which the revocation takes effect in accordance with section 17(1) or (2) of the 1998 Act; or

    (d) if the temporary permit ceases to have effect in accordance with paragraph (3), the date specified or agreed as mentioned in paragraph (2).

(2) If an application for a London PHV driver's licence is not received from the holder of a temporary permit by the application deadline, Transport for London may give notice to the holder that, if an application is not received by Transport for London from him by the date specified in the notice or such later date as Transport for London may agree, the temporary permit is to cease to have effect.

(3) If no such application is received by the date so specified or agreed, the temporary permit shall thereupon cease to have effect.

Amendment
Para (1): sub-para (bb) inserted by the Private Hire Vehicles (London) (Transitional and Saving Provisions) (Amendment) Regulations 2003, SI 2003/3028, regs 2, 4.

7 Modification of section 13 of the 1998 Act (1) In relation to an application for a London PHV driver's licence who is an existing driver and the holder of a temporary permit or London PHV driver's licence, section 13 of the 1998 Act shall have effect subject to the following modifications.

(2) In subsection (2) for the words "the requirement mentioned in subsection (3), and any further" there shall be substituted "any".

(3) Subsection (3) shall be omitted.

8 Saving for private hire vehicles licensed in Plymouth In relation to private hire vehicles licensed under the Plymouth City Council Act 1975, the 1998 Act shall have effect as if—
    (a) in section 5(1), at end of paragraph (c), there were inserted—
"or;
    (d) the other operator is licensed under the 1975 Act.";
    (b) in section 6(6)—
        (i) the word "and" at the end of paragraph (b) were omitted;
        (ii) at the end of paragraph (c) there were inserted—
"and
    (d) if the vehicle is in use for the purposes of a hiring the booking for which was accepted in the City of Plymouth, a licence issued under the 1975 Act,";
    (c) for "paragraph (b) or (c)" (in both places) there were substituted "paragraph (b), (c) or (d)";
    (d) in section 12(6)—
        (i) in paragraph (b) the word "and" were omitted; and
        (ii) after paragraph (c) there were inserted—
"and
    (d) if the vehicle is in use for the purposes of a hiring the booking for which was accepted in the City of Plymouth, a licence under the 1975 Act.";
and
    (e) in section 36, after the definition of "road" there were inserted the following definition—
""the 1975 Act" means the Plymouth City Council Act 1975;".

Private Hire Vehicles (London PHV Driver's Licences) Regulations 2003

Transport for London, in exercise of the powers conferred on it by sections 13(2), 14(2), 15(4)(a)(ii), 20(1) and (2), 23(1)(b) and 32(1) and (2) of the Private Hire Vehicles (London) Act 1998 and of all other powers enabling it in that behalf, hereby makes the following Regulations:—

1 Citation and commencement These Regulations may be cited as the Private Hire Vehicles (London PHV Driver's Licences) Regulations 2003 and shall come into force on 1st April 2003.

2 Interpretation In these Regulations—
"the 1998 Act" means the Private Hire Vehicles (London) Act 1998;
"licence" except in regulations 3 and 5 mean a London PHV driver's licence or a driver's temporary permit;
"the register" means the register of licences which the licensing authority is required to maintain under section 23(1) of the 1998 Act;
"section 13(2)(b) requirement" means a requirement which, in accordance with section 13(2)(b)of the 1998 Act, the licensing authority must be satisfied has been met, before granting a London PHV driver's licence to an applicant; and
"driver's temporary permit" means a temporary permit issued under regulation 5 of the Private Hire Vehicles (London) (Transitional and Saving Provisions) Regulations 2003.

3 The physical fitness requirement (1) The physical fitness requirement is hereby prescribed as a section 13(2)(b) requirement.

(2) The physical fitness requirement is that the applicant—
(a) is the holder of a Group 2 licence; or
(b) satisfies Transport for London that he [is medically fit to hold a London PHV driver's licence.]

(3) A "Group 2 licence" means a licence to drive a motor vehicle granted under Part III of the Road Traffic Act 1988 which is a Group 2 licence as defined by regulation 70 of the Motor Vehicles (Driving Licences) Regulations 1999.

(4) [In assessing whether an applicant is medically fit to hold a London PHV driver's licence under paragraph 2(b), Transport for London shall have regard to the medical standards that would apply in relation to a Group 2 licence.]

Amendment

Para (2): in sub-para (b) words "is medically fit to hold a London PHV driver's licence." in square brackets substituted by the Private Hire Vehicles (London PHV Driver's Licences) (Amendment) Regulations 2009, regs 2, 3(1).

Para (4): substituted by the Private Hire Vehicles (London PHV Driver's Licences) (Amendment) Regulations 2009, regs 2, 3(2).

[3A The English language requirement (1) The English language requirement is hereby prescribed as a section 13(2)(b) requirement.

(2) The English language requirement is that the applicant must be able to communicate in English at or above level B1 on the Common European Framework of Reference for Languages ("CEFR").

(3) The ability to communicate in English for the purposes of this requirement includes speaking, listening, reading and writing.

(4) Applicants may satisfy Transport for London of their ability to meet the requirement in regulation 3A(2) by providing:
  (i) a certificate from a test provider appointed by Transport for London confirming that the applicant's level of proficiency in the English language is at level B1 on the CEFR or above; or
  (ii) documentary evidence of a qualification (whether or not the qualification was obtained in the United Kingdom) on the basis of which Transport for London is satisfied that the applicant's level of proficiency in the English language is equivalent to level B1 on the CEFR or above.]

Amendment
Regulation inserted by the Private Hire Vehicles (London PHV Driver's Licences) (Amendment) Regulations 2016, regs 2, 3.
Regulation substituted for reg 3A (as inserted) by the Private Hire Vehicles (London PHV Driver's Licences) (Amendment) (No. 2) Regulations 2016, regs 2, 3.

[3B Transitional provisions The English language requirement will apply to all applications received by Transport for London on or after 14 October 2016, but in respect of applications received on or before 30 September 2017, the applicant must satisfy Transport for London that they have met the requirement in regulation 3A(2) on any date on or before 30 September 2017.]

Amendment
Regulation substituted for reg 3A (as inserted) by the Private Hire Vehicles (London PHV Driver's Licences) (Amendment) (No. 2) Regulations 2016, regs 2, 3.
Regulation substituted by the Private Hire Vehicles (London PHV Driver's Licences) (Amendment) Regulations 2017, regs 2, 3.

4 Form of driver's badge (1) The driver's badge shall be in a form which meets the requirements specified in paragraph (2).

(2) The requirements are that the badge—
  (a) states the name of the licence holder ("the holder") to whom it has been issued;
  (b) states the number and expiry date of the holder's licence;
  (c) includes a photographic image of the holder; and

(d) states on the reverse that it is the property of Transport for London and is to be returned to a specified address in the event of its being found.

5 Fees (1) The fee payable, on the making of an application, by an applicant for a London PHV driver's licence shall be [£157].

(2) The fee payable by a person granted a London PHV driver's licence ("the licence fee")—
(a) shall unless already paid, be payable on the grant of the licence; and
(b) shall be [£105].

(3) Paragraphs (1) and (2) apply to the renewal of a licence as they apply to the grant of a licence.

(4) Where a London PHV driver's licence ceases to have effect (whether by revocation or otherwise) on the ground that—
(a) the holder of the licence is no longer physically fit to hold such a licence;
(b) the licence is surrendered by the holder; or
(c) the holder dies,

a refund of a proportion of the licence fee shall be payable, in accordance with the following provisions of this regulation, to the holder, or in a case falling within sub-paragraph (c) the holder's personal representatives.

(5) A refund shall be payable upon receipt of a written request by the holder of the licence accompanied by the licence and the driver's badge issued to the holder.

(6) The amount refundable shall be equal to that proportion of the licence fee which the number of whole months remaining unexpired of the period for which the licence was granted bears to the whole of that period, rounded up to the nearest whole pound.

Amendment
Para (1): figure "£157" in square brackets substituted by the Private Hire Vehicles (London PHV Driver's Licences) (Amendment) Regulations 2004, regs 2, 3(1).
Para (2): in sub-para (b) figure "£105" in square brackets substituted by the Private Hire Vehicles (London PHV Driver's Licences) (Amendment) Regulations 2004, regs 2, 3(2).

6 Register of licences The register shall contain, in addition to the particulars specified in section 23(1)(a) of the 1998 Act, an indication in relation to each licence as to whether—
(a) it is a London PHV driver's licence or a driver's temporary permit; and
(b) it is current, suspended or revoked.

Private Hire Vehicles (London PHV Licences) Regulations 2004

Transport for London, in exercise of the powers conferred upon it by sections 7(2)(c) and (4), 10(2), 20(1), 23(1)(b) and 32(1) and (2) of the Private Hire Vehicles (London) Act 1998 and, after consultation with bodies appearing to it to represent the London cab trade and the private hire vehicle trade in London, by section 30 of that Act, and of all other powers enabling it in that behalf, hereby makes the following Regulations:—

1 Citation and commencement These Regulations may be cited as the Private Hire Vehicles (London PHV Licences) Regulations 2004 and shall come into force on 8th March 2004.

2 Interpretation (1) In these Regulations—
"the 1988 Act" means the Road Traffic Act 1988;
"the 1998 Act" means the Private Hire Vehicles (London) Act 1998;
"construction and use requirements" has the meaning given by section 41(7) of the 1988 Act;
"EEA State" means a State which was a party to the Agreement on the European Economic Area signed at Oporto on 2nd May 1992 as adjusted by the Protocol signed at Brussels on 17th March 1993 or which, by virtue of a subsequent agreement, falls to be treated as if it were a party to that agreement;
"the identification disc" means the disc or plate issued for a vehicle in accordance with section 10(1) of the 1998 Act;
"the register" means the register of licences which the licensing authority is required to maintain under section 23(1) of the 1998 Act;
"temporary permit" means a temporary permit issued under regulation 5 of the Private Hire Vehicles (London) (Transitional Provisions) Regulations 2004; and
"test certificate" has the meaning given by section 45(2)(b) of the 1988 Act.

(2) A reference in these Regulations to the number of passengers that a vehicle is licensed to carry is a reference to the maximum number of passengers that may be carried in the vehicle in accordance with the conditions of the licence.

3 Further requirements that must be met (1) In addition to the requirements specified in section 7(2)(a) and (b) of the 1998 Act the requirements specified in Schedule 1 are hereby prescribed under section 7(2)(c) as requirements that Transport for London must be satisfied are met before granting a London PHV licence in respect of a vehicle.

(2) Transport for London may exempt a vehicle from any of the requirements of this regulation and Schedule 1 if Transport for London—

(a) is so requested by the applicant for a London PHV licence for the vehicle; and

(b) is satisfied that, having regard to exceptional circumstances, it is reasonable to do so.

4 Prescribed licence conditions The conditions specified in Schedule 2 are hereby prescribed as conditions subject to which a London PHV licence is to be granted in respect of a vehicle.

5 Exhibition of identification disc (1) The identification disc shall be exhibited in the manner specified in paragraph (2).

(2) The disc shall be affixed to the top of the inside of the front windscreen on the passenger side of the vehicle so that—

(a) on the side which faces outwards, the following particulars are clearly legible—

    (i) the registration mark of the vehicle;

    (ii) the maximum number of passengers which may be carried in the vehicle in accordance with the conditions of the licence for the vehicle;

    (iii) the number of the London PHV licence for the vehicle;

    (iv) the date of the expiry of the licence; and

    (v) a statement that the licence has been issued by the Public Carriage Office of Transport for London; and

(b) on the side which is visible from inside the vehicle, a statement that the vehicle is licensed by the Public Carriage Office of Transport for London is clearly legible.

6 Fees (1) The fee payable, on the making of an application, by an applicant for a London PHV licence shall be [£87].

(2) The fee payable by a person granted a London PHV licence—

(a) shall unless already paid, be payable on the grant of the licence; and

(b) shall be [£27].

(3) Paragraphs (1) and (2) apply to the renewal of a licence as they apply to the grant of a licence.

Amendment

Para (1): figure "£87" in square brackets substituted by the Private Hire Vehicles (London PHV Licences) (Amendment) Regulations 2009, regs 2, 3.

Para (2): in sub-para (b) figure "£27" in square brackets substituted by the Private Hire Vehicles (London PHV Licences) (Amendment) Regulations 2006, regs 2, 3(2).

7 Register of licences In addition to the particulars specified in section 23(1) (a) of the 1998 Act, the register shall contain the following particulars for each London PHV licence issued or having effect under that Act—

(a) the registration mark of the vehicle to which the licence relates;

(b) an indication as to whether the licence—
  (i) is a London PHV licence or a temporary permit; and
  (ii) is current, suspended or revoked.

8 Prohibition of certain signs, notices etc. [No signs or advertising material shall be displayed on or from a private hire vehicle], except:
  (a) badges or emblems on the radiator or windscreen which are issued by an organisation—
    (i) providing vehicle repair or recovery services; or
    (ii) concerned with driving skills and qualifications; . . .
  (b) a sign displayed temporarily on a stationary vehicle which contains, and contains only:
    (i) the name and address of a person operating the private hire vehicle, or the name under which he carries on that business and its address; and
    (ii) the name of a passenger for whom a private hire booking has been [made; or]
  [(c) other signs or advertising material in such locations and for such purposes as the licensing authority may approve from time to time for either:
    (i) specified private hire vehicles; or
    (ii) all private hire vehicles.]

Amendment

Words "No signs or advertising material shall be displayed on or from a private hire vehicle" in square brackets substituted by the Private Hire Vehicles (London PHV Licences) (Amendment) Regulations 2016, regs 2, 3.

Para (a): in sub-para (ii) word omitted repealed by the Private Hire Vehicles (London PHV Licences) (Amendment) Regulations 2007, regs 2, 3(1).

Para (b): words "made; or" in square brackets substituted by the Private Hire Vehicles (London PHV Licences) (Amendment) Regulations 2007, regs 2, 3(3).

Para (c): inserted by the Private Hire Vehicles (London PHV Licences) (Amendment) Regulations 2007, regs 2, 3(4).

SCHEDULE 1
REQUIREMENTS PRESCRIBED UNDER SECTION 7(2)(c)
OF THE 1998 ACT

Regulation 3

1 Vehicle type The vehicle must be a light passenger vehicle as defined by section 85 of the Road Traffic Act 1988.

[1A Vehicle age limits before 1 January 2018 Where on or before 31 December 2017 a London PHV licence is granted:
    (1) On renewal, the vehicle shall not be over 10 years of age as calculated from the date on which the vehicle was first registered under the Vehicle and Excise Registration Act 1994; and
    (2) Otherwise than on renewal, then the vehicle shall not be over 5 years of age as so calculated.

1B Vehicle emission standards before 1 January 2018 Where on or before 31 December 2017 a London PHV licence is granted otherwise than on renewal the vehicle shall comply with the Euro 4 standard as set out in Directive 70/220/EEC.

1C Vehicle age limits and emission standards after 1 January 2018 Where a London PHV licence is granted (including on renewal) on or after 1 January 2018 the vehicle shall not be over 10 years of age as calculated from the date on which the vehicle was first registered under the Vehicle and Excise Registration Act 1994.

1D
    (1) Where on or after 1 January 2018 a London PHV licence is granted otherwise than on renewal between any of the dates stated in Column 2 of the Table below, and the vehicle is of the age indicated in Column 1, then it shall comply with the corresponding requirements set out in—
        (a) Column 3 as to the applicable minimum emission standard (Euro standard) of the vehicle as determined under (as appropriate and as amended) Directive 70/220/EEC (for Euro 4) or Regulation 715/2007/EC (for Euro 6); and
        (b) Column 4 as to whether or not the vehicle must be a zero-emission capable ("ZEC") vehicle as defined in sub-paragraph (2) below.

Table

	1	2	3	4
	Vehicle's age as calculated by reference to date of its first registration under the Vehicle and Excise Registration Act 1994	Date of grant of London PHV licence	Requirement to meet the stated Euro standard as a minimum	Requirement for the vehicle to be a ZEC vehicle as defined in paragraph 1D (2) below.
A	All vehicles of any age	Between 1 January 2018 until 31 December 2019 (incl.)	Euro 6 or (if a petrol-hybrid vehicle) Euro 4	No
B	Over 18 months old	Between 1 January 2020 until 31 December 2022 (incl.)	Euro 6	No
C	Under 18 months old	On or after 1 January 2020	Euro 6	Must be a ZEC vehicle
D	All vehicles of any age.	On or after 1 January 2023	Euro 6	Must be a ZEC vehicle

(2) A vehicle is a ZEC vehicle if it meets either of the following requirements:

    (a) It must emit no more than 50g/km CO_2 exhaust emissions (at tail-pipe) as determined in accordance with Regulation 715/2007/EC and UN ECE Regulation 101 (as amended) and be capable of being operated with no (zero) such exhaust emissions for a minimum range of 16.093 km (10 miles); or

    (b) It must emit no more than 75g/km CO_2 exhaust emissions (at tail-pipe) as determined in accordance with Regulation 715/2007/EC and UN ECE Regulation 101 (as amended) and be capable of being operated with no (zero) such emissions for a minimum range of 32.187 km (20 miles).

(3) Nothing in sub-paragraph (1) above shall prevent a London PHV licence being granted to a vehicle before 1 January 2020 if it meets—

    (a) the requirements of a ZEC vehicle under sub-paragraph (2) above; and

(b) (as a minimum) the Euro 6 emission standard as determined under Regulation 715/2007/EC (as amended).

1E For the purposes of paragraphs 1C and 1D above the references to Directive 70/220/EEC and Regulation 715/2007/EC are to be construed as a reference to those instruments as amended from time to time in accordance with or pursuant to paragraph 1A of Schedule 2 to the European Communities Act 1972 (as amended).]

2 Test certificates Unless the date on which the vehicle was first registered under the Vehicle Excise and Registration Act 1994 fell within the period of 12 months ending with the date on which the vehicle is produced for inspection by Transport for London, a test certificate must have been issued for the vehicle within the period of 14 days ending with the date of that inspection.

3 Licences A vehicle licence taken out under the Vehicle Excise and Registration Act 1994 must be in force for the vehicle.

4 Vehicle to have right hand drive The steering wheel of the vehicle must be on the right hand or off-side of the vehicle.

5 Wheelchair lifting equipment Any equipment fitted to the vehicle for the purpose of lifting a wheelchair into the vehicle must have been tested in accordance with the requirements of the Lifting Operations and Lifting Equipment Regulations 1998.

6 Luggage space The vehicle must have a boot or luggage compartment which provides sufficient space to carry a reasonable amount of luggage for as many passengers as it is licensed to carry.

7 Construction and type approval requirements (1) The vehicle must comply with—
(a) all construction and use requirements applicable to it; and
(b) all type approval requirements so applicable.

(2) For the purposes of paragraph (1) "type approval requirements" has the meaning given by section 54(1) of the 1988 Act and a vehicle shall be taken to comply with those requirements if—
(a) an EC certificate of conformity (as defined by section 85 of that Act);
(b) a Minister's approval certificate issued under section 58(1) of that Act; or
(c) a Department's approval certificate issued under Article 31A(4) of the Road Traffic (Northern Ireland) Order 1981 has effect with respect to it.

8 Compliance with the manufacturer's specification Unless it has been modified or converted as mentioned in paragraph 9, the vehicle must comply with the original manufacturer's specification with respect to the braking system, steering, engine, transmission, fuel system, suspension and lighting.

9 Modified or converted vehicle (1) Where a vehicle has been modified or converted since a certificate of the kind referred to in paragraph 7(2)(a), (b) or (c) was issued in respect of it, evidence must be produced to satisfy Transport for London that the vehicle as converted or modified complies with construction and use requirements.

(2) Where a vehicle has been converted or modified so as to be capable of propulsion otherwise than by petrol or diesel fuel, evidence must be produced to satisfy Transport for London that the conversion has been carried out, and subsequently tested at the recommended frequency, by a converter of vehicles who is listed as an approved supplier in relation to vehicles of the type in question—
  (a) in the PowerShift Register or the CleanUp Register maintained by the Energy Saving Trust; or
  (b) in a register maintained in an EEA State by a body equivalent to the Energy Saving Trust for purposes similar to those for which the PowerShift and CleanUp Registers are maintained.

10 Doors and windows (1) The number of doors must be sufficient to allow safe access and egress for the number of passengers which the vehicle is licensed to carry.

(2) If the vehicle is fitted with a single door for the passenger compartment, that door must be fitted to the left hand or near side of the vehicle.

(3) Any devices fitted to the vehicle for operating doors and windows must be—
  (a) fitted to each door;
  (b) in full working order; and
  (c) accessible to passengers.

(4) Any child locks fitted to the vehicle must be in full working order.

[**11 Insurance** The vehicle must be insured to carry passengers for hire or reward.]

Amendment
Paras 1A-1E: inserted by the Private Hire Vehicles (London PHV Licences) (Amendment) Regulations 2015, regs 2, 3.
Para 11: inserted by the Private Hire Vehicles (London PHV Licences) (Amendment) Regulations 2016, regs 2, 4.

SCHEDULE 2
PRESCRIBED CONDITIONS OF LONDON PHV LICENCES

Regulation 4

1 Use by persons other than the owner 1. The owner of the vehicle shall keep a record, containing the information specified in condition 2, of each occasion on which the owner—

 (a) allocates the vehicle to a London PHV operator for use as a private hire vehicle; or

 (b) not being London PHV operator, permits any person to use the vehicle as a private hire vehicle.

2 Contents of record kept under condition 1 The record kept under condition 1 shall include—

 (a) the registration mark of the vehicle;

 (b) the name and address of the London PHV operator to whom the vehicle is allocated or of the driver permitted to use the vehicle;

 (c) the number of the operator's London PHV operator's licence or of the driver's London PHV driver's licence;

 (d) the date from which the vehicle was allocated to the operator or the driver was permitted to use it; and

 (e) the date on which the vehicle ceased to be so allocated or used.

3 Retention and production of record The record kept under condition 1—

 (a) shall be retained by the owner for a period of at least 12 months beginning with the date specified in condition 2(e); and

 (b) shall be produced by the owner for inspection at the request of an authorised officer.

4 Change of ownership Where the ownership of the vehicle changes and the new owner intends to use the vehicle, or permit the vehicle to be used as a private hire vehicle, the new owner shall—

 (a) notify the change to Transport for London in writing;

 (b) return the existing licence to Transport for London for alteration of the owner's name;

 (c) provide a declaration in writing to Transport for London—

  (i) that the Secretary of State for Transport has been notified of the change in accordance with the Road Vehicles (Registration and Licensing) Regulations 2002;

  [(ii) that the vehicle is insured to carry passengers for hire or reward]; and

  (iii) unless the vehicle was first registered under the Vehicle Excise and Registration Act 1994 within the period of 12 months ending with the date of the declaration, a test certificate was issued within the period of 6 months ending with the date of the declaration.

5 Number of passengers The number of passengers carried in the vehicle must not at any time exceed—

(a) the number of passengers that it is licensed to carry; or

(b) the number of passenger seats fitted with seat belts.

6 Condition of the vehicle The vehicle shall be maintained in good and efficient mechanical condition and be properly adjusted.

7 Vehicles exempted from requirement to display an identification disc If the vehicle has been exempted by Transport for London pursuant to section 10(3) of the 1998 Act from the requirement under section 10(2) (display of identification disc), the London PHV licence in force for the vehicle, or a copy thereof, shall be carried in the vehicle while it is being used as a private hire vehicle.

8 Test certificates (1) Subject to paragraph (2), on any day during the currency of the licence a test certificate must have been issued for the vehicle within the period of 6 months ending with the day in question.

(2) Paragraph (1) does not apply where a test certificate was not required to be produced in accordance with paragraph 2 of Schedule 1 when the current licence for the vehicle was issued.

9 Communication devices (1) All radio equipment fitted to the vehicle must be fitted securely and safely and in accordance with guidelines for the time being published by the Radio Communications Agency.

(2) All two-way radio equipment must be of a type for the time being approved by the Radio Communications Agency.

10 Compliance with the Road Vehicles (Registration and Licensing) Regulations 2002 The owner shall comply with all relevant requirements of the Road Vehicles (Registration and Licensing) Regulations 2002 in relation to the vehicle.

11 Display of additional disc (1) Without prejudice to regulation 5 and section 10 of the 1998 Act, an additional disc issued by Transport for London shall be displayed on the rear windscreen of the vehicle while it is being used as a private hire vehicle, so that—

(a) on the side which faces outwards, the particulars specified in regulation 5(2)(a) are clearly legible; and

(b) on the side which faces inwards, particulars of how any passenger may make a complaint about the service provided by means of the vehicle and the address to which any complaint may be sent are clearly legible.

(2) This condition does not apply while a vehicle is being used in circumstances when it is, by virtue of a notice under section 10(3) of the 1998 Act, exempted from the requirement to comply with section 10(2).

12 Vehicle licensed outside London If a licence granted under section 48 of the Local Government (Miscellaneous Provisions) Act 1976 (licensing of private hire vehicles in England and Wales outside Greater London) or an equivalent provision of a local Act is in force for the vehicle, the plate or disc issued in respect of the vehicle under section 48(5) of that Act (or its equivalent) shall not be displayed on the vehicle whilst it is being used as a private hire vehicle under its London PHV licence.

13 Compliance with licensing requirements The owner shall not use the vehicle, or permit it to be used, as a private hire vehicle at any time when the vehicle is in such a condition that it would not meet the requirements of paragraphs 2 to 11 of Schedule 1.

[14 Insurance (1) The vehicle must be insured to carry passengers for hire or reward at all times for the duration of the licence.

(2) Details of the insurance must be displayed in the vehicle at all times for the duration of the licence. Transport for London shall specify from time to time the details which are to be displayed and how they are to be displayed.]

[15 Advertising No advertising material shall be displayed in the vehicle other than in accordance with such requirements as Transport for London may specify from time to time.]

Amendment

Para 4: sub-para (c)(ii) substituted by the Private Hire Vehicles (London PHV Licences) (Amendment) Regulations 2016, regs 2, 5(i).

Para 14: substituted by the Private Hire Vehicles (London PHV Licences) (Amendment) Regulations 2016, regs 2, 5(ii).

Para 15: inserted by the Private Hire Vehicles (London PHV Licences) (Amendment) Regulations 2016, regs 2, 5(iii).

Heathrow Byelaws 2014

3. Prohibited acts

3.28 Private hire vehicles No person shall cause or permit a Private Hire Vehicle to enter the Airport for the purpose of loading passengers unless that Private Hire Vehicle has been pre-booked or is to be parked in an official car park in anticipation of such a booking.

3.29 Loading of private hire vehicles No person shall cause or permit a Private Hire Vehicle to load passengers at the Airport other than in an official car park.

4. Acts for which permission is required

4.14 Taxi touting No person shall in the Terminal Building or other public building, car park or any other public place on the Airport offer his or any other Vehicle (unless that Vehicle is a Taxi or Public Service Vehicle) for hire.

9. Taxis

9.1 Ply for hire No person shall cause or permit a Taxi to ply for hire or load passengers unless:
   (a) He is authorised to do so by the Airport Company; and
   (b) He does so from an Authorised Stranding provided that it shall not be an offence to load passengers in a public car park or at a distance of more than half a mile from the nearest of such Authorised Standings or, with the consent of the a Constable or an Airport Official at any distance from such Authorised Standings.

9.2 Authorised standing No person shall cause or permit any Vehicle other than a Taxi to stand on an Authorised Standing.

9.3 Permitted number standing No person shall cause or permit a Taxi to stand on an Authorised Standing in excess of the maximum permitted number of Taxis as indicated by a Sign at the head of the Authorised Standing.

9.4 Taxi drivers Taxi drivers on an Authorised Standing shall be with their Taxis and be available and willing to be hired immediately.

9.5 Disabled taxis Disabled Taxis shall not be left by their drivers on an Authorised Standing or Taxi Feeder Park longer than is reasonably necessary to effect removal unless such disablement is temporary and is remedied without delay.

9.6 Obstruction Taxi drivers shall not obstruct the carriageway, footpath or buildings or cause annoyance or disturbance to persons in the vicinity.

9.7 Washing down No person shall wash down or clean out a Taxi on an Authorised Standing.

9.8 Wearing of badge Taxi and Private Hire Vehicle drivers shall display their Badge at all times whilst on the Airport.

9.9 Taxi Feeder Park No person shall drive a Taxi on to an Authorised Standing without having first driven through a Taxi Feeder Park unless at the direction or with the consent of a Constable, an Airport Official or the Airport Company.

9.10 Entering taxi feeder park No person shall bring a Taxi into the Taxi Feeder Park unless he has been permitted to do so by the Airport Company and displays a Ticket issued for that purpose in the windscreen of the Taxi.

9.11 No more than one taxi No person who has driven a Taxi onto the Airport shall, while that Taxi remains on the Airport, drive another Taxi onto the Airport.

9.12 Taxi feeder park parking No person shall without the permission of the Airport Company leave a Taxi on a Taxi Feeder Park unless willing to be despatched immediately to an Authorised Standing.

9.13 Filling vacancies Drivers shall move up their Taxis on an authorised standing or Taxi Feeder Park by filling vacancies as they occur.

9.14 Taxi feeder park good order Taxi drivers who are for the time being in a Taxi Feeder Park shall comply with such directions for ensuring good order and an orderly movement of traffic within that Taxi Feeder Park as may be given by a Constable, an Airport Official or the Airport Company.

9.15 Leaving taxi feeder park Taxi drivers who are for the time being in a Taxi Feeder Park shall:
    (a) Leave the Taxi Feeder Park by an exit for the time being designated for that purpose and in the order in which they entered immediately they are required to do so by a Constable, or an Airport Official; and
    (b) Proceed directly and without delay to the Authorised Standing provided that nothing in this byelaw shall apply to anything to the contrary done at the direction of, or with the consent of a Constable, the Airport Company or an Airport Official.

9.16 Defacing tickets No person shall deface, alter or amend any Ticket issued for the purpose referred to in byelaw 9.11.

Circulars

Part C – Circulars/Guidance applicable within London

A2.1

Equality Act Guidance Note A –
Taxi and Private Hire Vehicles (DfT 2010)

Provisions coming into effect in October 2010

INTRODUCTION

The Equality Act 2010 brings together in one Act a number of different pieces of legislation about discrimination, – including disability discrimination. The new Act includes many of the taxi and private hire vehicle (PHV) provisions which were in the Disability Discrimination Act 1995, but it also includes some important changes.

Sections 160 to 173 of the Equality Act 2010 relate specifically to taxis and private hire vehicles (PHVs).

The Equality Act 2010 can be viewed at http://www.opsi.gov.uk/acts/acts2010/ukpga_20100015_en_1

Some of the taxi/PHV provisions are being brought into force on 1st October 2010.

This guidance note explains which taxi/PHV sections are being brought into force on that date and is designed for licensing authorities.

A separate guidance note has been prepared specifically for the taxi and PHV trades.

DUTIES TO ASSIST PASSENGERS IN WHEELCHAIRS.

Sections 165, 166 and 167 of the Equality Act 2010 deal with the imposition of duties on the drivers of wheelchair accessible taxis and PHVs to assist passengers who use wheelchairs.

The duties which had been contained in the Disability Discrimination Act 1995 had never been brought into force so when the duties are actually brought into force – at a later date, but not before April 2011 – it will constitute a substantive change in the law.

The duties – Section 165 places duties on drivers of designated wheelchair accessible taxis and PHVs. Designated vehicles are those listed by the licensing authority under section 167 (see 'Lists of wheelchair accessible vehicles', below).

The duties are:

- to carry the passenger while in the wheelchair;

- not to make any additional charge for doing so;
- if the passenger chooses to sit in a passenger seat to carry the wheelchair;
- to take such steps as are necessary to ensure that the passenger is carried in safety and reasonable comfort; and
- to give the passenger such mobility assistance as is reasonably required.

This section will be commenced at a later date, but not before April 2011.

Exemptions from the duties – Section 166 allows licensing authorities to exempt drivers from the duties to assist passengers in wheelchairs if they are satisfied that it is appropriate to do so on medical grounds or because the driver's physical condition makes it impossible or unreasonably difficult for him or her to comply with the duties.

This section will be commenced on 1 October 2010.

Consequently, from October, taxi and PHV drivers who drive designated wheelchair accessible taxis or PHVs will be able to apply for exemptions. Licensing authorities that intend to maintain a list of wheelchair accessible taxis and PHVs licensed in their area should therefore be putting in place a system for assessing drivers and a system for granting exemption certificates for those drivers who they consider should be exempt.

The Department will be making regulations early in 2011 specifying the exact format for the Exemption Notices that licensing authorities will issue and exempt drivers will be required to display in their vehicles. The Department will also arrange for the printing and distribution of the Exemption Notices (which will be similar to the Notices for drivers who are exempt from carrying guide dogs). These will be ready shortly after the regulations come into force early in 2011.

Lists of wheelchair accessible vehicles – Section 167 allows licensing authorities to maintain a list of "designated vehicles", that is, a list of wheelchair accessible taxis and PHVs licensed in their area. The consequence of being on this list is that the driver must undertake the duties in section 165.

This section will be commenced at a later date (not before April 2011).

So, although the list of designated vehicles will have no actual effect in law until the duties are commenced, we would urge licensing authorities to start maintaining a list as soon as possible for the purpose of liaising with the trade and issuing exemption certificates.

Also, from October, it will be possible for drivers to appeal against a decision by the licensing authority not to grant an exemption; the appeal will go to the magistrates' court.

When section 167 comes into force, and the lists of designated vehicles have a statutory effect, it will be possible for the owner of a vehicle to appeal against a licensing authority's decision to include his or her vehicle on the list. This appeal will also go to the magistrates' court.

Separate, and more detailed, guidance will be issued about the accessibility requirements which licensing authorities should apply in relation to this provision and other aspects of their functions under this new approach. This guidance will be issued in the autumn.

GUIDE DOGS AND ASSISTANCE DOGS

Sections 168 to 171 of the Equality Act 2010 deal with the carriage of guide dogs and other assistance dogs and England and Wales.

These sections have simply been lifted from the Disability Discrimination Act 1995 which imposed duties on taxi and PHV drivers (and PHV operators) to accept guide dogs.

When these sections come into force on 1 October, the existing sections in the Disability Discrimination Act 1995 will be repealed.

So, the change is largely a technical one rather than one with any practical implications.

There is nothing new and nothing additional that drivers (and PHV operators) need to do in relation to assistance dogs. The existing obligations will carry on after 1 October but simply under different legislation.

However, there is one important point to note. The legislation bringing these sections of the Equality Act into force on 1 October is designed to ensure a smooth transition from the assistance dogs provisions in the Disability Discrimination Act 1995 to those contained in the Equality Act 2010.

The legislation will ensure that:

- The Exemption Notice Regulations[1] made under sections 37 and 37A of the Disability Discrimination Act 1995 will continue to have effect – as though they had been made under the Equality Act 2010;
- Taxi and PHV drivers who are already exempt from the duty to carry guide dogs can continue to rely on their certificate of exemption issued by a licensing authority even though the certificate refers to the Disability Discrimination Act 1995;
- Licensing authorities will continue to be able to issue certificates to drivers who are exempt from the duty to carry guide dogs even though the certificates say "issued under section 37 or 37A of the Disability Discrimination Act 1995" on them. The certificates are now deemed to have been issued under the Equality Act 2010;
- Licensing authorities will continue to be able to issue the yellow Exemption Notices provided by the Department which exempt drivers must display on their vehicles (and exempt drivers will continue to be able to display them), even though the Notices refer to the Disability Discrimination Act 1995.

The comprehensive guidance issued by the Department in 2007 about the duties to carry assistance dogs and the procedure for granting medical exemptions etc still stands. This is because there has been no substantive change in the actual duties or the assessment of applicants for medical exemptions. The Guidance can be viewed at:

http://www.dft.gov.uk/adobepdf/259428/323526/19560LicensingAuthoriti es321.pdf

The position in relation to the carriage of assistance dogs in Scotland also remains the same, but the means of achieving this is different. Essentially although the relevant sections of the Disability Discrimination Act 1995 will be repealed, the legislation which brings the Equality Act into force will ensure that the provisions inserted into section 20 of the Civic Government (Scotland) Act 1982 remain.

[1]   The Disability Discrimination Act 1995 (Taxis) (Carrying of Guide Dogs etc.) (England and Wales) Regulations 2000 (SI 2000/2990) (as amended) and The Disability Discrimination Act 2003 (Private Hire Vehicles) (Carriage of Guide Dogs etc) (England and Wales) Regulations 2003 (SI 2003/3122) (as amended).

THE CONTROL OF TAXI NUMBERS

Since the Transport Act 1985 it has been possible for licensing authorities in England and Wales (outside of London) to refuse a taxi licence application if they are satisfied that there is no significant unmet demand for taxis in their licensing area.

Section 161 of the Equality Act 2010 qualifies the law in this area, to ensure licensing authorities that have relatively few wheelchair accessible taxis operating in their area, do not refuse licences to such vehicles for the purposes of controlling taxi numbers.

For section 161 to have effect, the Secretary of State must make regulations specifying:

- the proportion of wheelchair accessible taxis that must operate in an area before the respective licensing authority is lawfully able to refuse to license such a vehicle on the grounds of controlling taxi numbers; and
- the dimensions of a wheelchair that a wheelchair accessible vehicle must be capable of carrying in order for it to fall within this provision.

The DfT plans to consult on the content of regulations before section 161 comes in to force; the actual date will be announced in due course, but it will not be before April 2011.

Equality Act Guidance Note B – Taxi and Private Hire Drivers (DfT 2010)

ARE YOU A TAXI OR PRIVATE HIRE VEHICLE DRIVER?

There are some changes in the law which will come into effect in October 2010 which might affect you.

The Equality Act, which was passed earlier this year, includes some provisions relating specifically to taxis and private hire vehicles (PHVs) and disability.

Certain parts of the Act do not become law until the Government makes commencement orders to bring each part of it into force. The Government intends to bring into force several parts of the Act in October 2010, including some, but not all, of the provisions that are specific to taxis and PHVs. Other provisions will come into force later – but not before April 2011.

This note describes what will happen in October in relation to those parts of the Act that are specific to taxis and PHVs, and what the implications will be for taxi and PHV drivers.

This note focuses on the implications for the taxi and PHV trades of the October provisions. A separate note has been prepared for licensing authorities.

DUTIES ON DRIVERS TO ASSIST PASSENGERS IN WHEELCHAIRS.

The Equality Act is due to place duties on the drivers of designated wheelchair accessible taxis and PHVs to provide physical assistance to passengers in wheelchairs. A further announcement will be made on when the duties will come into force, but it will not be before April 2011.

The duties will apply to the driver of any wheelchair accessible taxi or PHV which is on the licensing authority's list of "designated vehicles".

If you are the driver of a wheelchair accessible taxi or PHV, it is advised that you find out whether your licensing authority intends to maintain a list of designated vehicles, and therefore whether the duties are likely to apply to you.

Before the duties are brought into force, any drivers who suffer from a disability or a condition which would make it difficult for them to provide physical assistance can apply for an exemption from the duties to offer assistance.

The opportunity to apply for exemptions starts on 1 October.

What do I need to do?

If you are the driver of a wheelchair accessible taxi or PHV, the first thing you need to do is establish whether your licensing authority intends to keep a list of designated vehicles. We are encouraging licensing authorities to make their decision known to drivers and perhaps establish a "shadow" list as soon as possible.

If your licensing authority does intend to maintain a list of designated vehicles, and your wheelchair accessible vehicle is to be included on the list, you will be required to carry out the duties to assist wheelchair users.

What are the duties?

The duties being placed on the drivers of designated wheelchair accessible taxis and PHVs are:

- to carry the passenger while in a wheelchair
- not to make any additional charge for doing so
- if the passenger chooses to sit in a passenger seat, to carry the wheelchair
- to take such steps as are necessary to ensure that the passenger is carried in safety and reasonable comfort; and
- to give the passenger such mobility assistance as is reasonably required.

What does mobility assistance mean?

Mobility assistance essentially means helping passengers who use wheelchairs by providing physical assistance.

If the passenger wishes to remain in the wheelchair, the driver must help the passenger to get into and out of the vehicle.

If the passenger wants to transfer to a seat, the driver must help him or her to get out of the wheelchair and into a seat and back into the wheelchair; the driver must also load the wheelchair into the vehicle.

The driver must also offer to load the passenger's luggage into and out of the vehicle.

What if my licensing authority does not intend to keep a list of designated vehicles?

If a licensing authority does not intend to maintain a list of designated vehicles then the duties will not apply; the duties only apply to drivers of vehicles which are on the licensing authority's list of designated vehicles.

What if I have a back condition which makes it impossible for me to help a passenger in a wheelchair get into a cab?

The new Act allows for exemptions from the duties on medical grounds or if the driver's physical condition makes it impossible or unreasonably difficult for him or her to comply with those duties.

It is the responsibility of drivers who require an exemption to apply for one from their licensing authority before the duties come into force; they will have at least six months to go through this process.

Who decides if a driver is exempt?

The local licensing authority decides if a driver should be exempt from the duties.

What if the licensing authority says that I am ok to carry out the duties and I disagree?

The legislation allows a driver to appeal to the magistrates' court within 28 days if the licensing authority decides not to issue an exemption certificate.

How will passengers know that I am exempt from the duties to assist passengers?

The Department will be printing and issuing to licensing authorities special Exemption Notices which exempted drivers must display on their vehicles in order that passengers will know that the driver is exempt from duties.

When will the duties come into force?

A further announcement will be made about when the actual duties to assist will come into force, but it will not be before April 2011.

Drivers with a medical condition that prevents them from carrying out the duties will be able to apply to their licensing authority for an exemption from October 2010, before the duties come into force.

GUIDE DOGS

The other thing that will happen on the 1st of October is that the duties placed on taxi and PHV drivers and on PHV operators to carry guide dogs and other assistance dogs will transfer from the Disability Discrimination Act 1995 to the Equality Act 2010.

In practice, the duties will remain exactly the same as they are now.

Any person who is currently exempt from the duty to carry an assistance dog on medical grounds will continue to be exempt.

That is because we have made a change in the law so that all existing exemption certificates and all existing exemption notices remain in force as though they had been made under the Equality Act 2010.

Will I have to take a different approach to the carriage of guide dogs from 1 October?

No. The change is a purely technical one; the duties to carry guide dogs and other assistance dogs will not change at all.

I have an exemption certificate which says that it was issued under the Disability Discrimination Act 1995 – do I have to get a new one?

No, you do not have to get a new certificate, the certificate which you have been granted remains valid until its expiry date.

I have a special notice in my taxi/PHV which says that I am exempt from carrying guide dogs and mentions the Disability Discrimination Act 1995 – do I need to get a new one?

No, you do not have to get a new exemption notice; the notice which was provided by the licensing authority remains valid until its expiry date.

Code of Practice for Horse Drawn Vehicles (DfT 2011)

This Code of Practice contains guidance jointly reviewed and agreed by the following organisations:

The Department of the Environment, Transport and the Regions

The British Driving Society The British Horse Society

The Heavy Horse Driving Committee

The Joint National Horse Education & Training Council

International League for the Protection of Horses

INTRODUCTION

Due to the increasing popularity of horse drawn vehicles on the road, a working group was set up which includes organisations experienced in the use of such vehicles. The main aim of the group was to produce a Code of Practice which could be used by drivers and operators of horse drawn vehicles, and especially those who use such vehicles to carry paying passengers.

The Code provides a simple but authoritative guide to the recommended minimum levels of competence (the 'road driving assessment') for drivers of horse drawn vehicles. The Code also includes full details of vehicle safety checks (the 'carriage check list').

NOTE

This Code of Practice should not be treated as a legal document. The emphasis is on the safety of the driver and passengers, carriage and horse(s) and other road users. Every effort has been made to provide true, helpful and accurate information.

SCOPE OF THE CODE

The Code applies to all types of horse drawn vehicles used on the road but it is primarily aimed at those vehicles carrying paying passengers (i.e. vehicles used for 'hire and reward'). The type of vehicles referred to in the Code are: two or four wheeled modern carriages, two or four wheeled traditional carriages and horse drawn passenger carrying vehicles. The Code applies to these carriages whether driven to a single horse or pairs or teams of horses.

OBJECTIVES

The Code's objectives are:

- To provide guidance for new and existing drivers of horse drawn vehicles carrying paying passengers

- To summarise the road driving assessment for single, pair and teams of horses
- To provide details of a recognised carriage safety check list

THE ROAD DRIVING ASSESSMENT

This test is the recommended minimum competence for driving horses/ponies and vehicles carrying paying passengers on the public highway. The assessment is not a compulsory requirement for those wishing to drive horses but may be required if an operator wants to receive a local authority licence to operate a passenger carrying service. Applications for an assessment may be made either to the British Driving Society or the Heavy Horse Training Committee who appoint a panel of assessors. There is a small fee for the assessment and on satisfactory completion a certificate of competence (Road Driving Certificate) will be granted.

The practical driving section of the assessment, which can be carried out at the driver or operator's premises, may be taken with a single, pair or team and will carry the relevant certification. The harnessing and underpinning of knowledge must include a single and a pair.

Grandfather rights for this assessment can be retained by attaining a certificate of Approved Prior Learning. This certificate can only be issued by a group of approved and qualified assessors, namely the Harness Horse Training Board, the British Driving Society or the Heavy Horse Training Committee.

Method of Inspection

The competence will be assessed by direct observation of practical performance and oral questioning of underpinning knowledge. The assessment will be in line with safe yard practice and will take approximately 2 hours.

The British Driving Society Proficiency Test and the Heavy Horse Training Committee Road Driving Assessment test are directly accreditable.

THE CARRIAGE CHECK LIST

This is a comprehensive list of safety checks that should be carried out to ensure that the carriage and its fittings are safe and in good working condition. The checks can be carried out either by the driver/operator or by a panel appointed by the British Driving Society or the Heavy Horse Training Committee.

THE ROAD DRIVING ASSESSMENT

Section A: Prepare horse and vehicle for road use

Performance Criteria

1. Control of the horse is maintained at all times

2.   Harness is selected and fitted to the horse for road use
3.   Horse is safely hitched to the vehicle following laid down procedures
4.   The controlling position adopted is appropriate to the vehicle in use
5.   The health, safety and security of the horse, self and others is maintained throughout

Range Statement

Harness: Show; exercise

Vehicle: Two wheeled; four wheeled

Knowledge and Understanding

1.   Correct fitting of harness
2.   Dangers of inappropriate procedures and adjustments to harness
3.   Safety precautions to be taken when handling horses
4.   State of feet and the effect on pulling power
5.   Implications of the Road Traffic Act when preparing vehicle
6.   Importance of safety checks
7.   Mounting and dismounting procedures
8.   Why is it important to adopt the correct driving position?

Section B: Carry out road driving manoeuvres

Performance Criteria

1.   Horse and vehicle are driven smoothly at a speed appropriate to road conditions
2.   Obstacles encountered during driving are safely negotiated
3.   The vehicle is correctly positioned on the road for safe and effective driving
4.   Road safety procedures are adhered to at all times
5.   Agreed cooling down procedures are followed on completion of work
6.   The health, safety and security of horse, self and others is maintained throughout

Range Statement

Conditions: Traffic; road surface; weather; noise level; gradients; pedestrians

Obstacles: Road junctions; stationary vehicles; traffic lights; roundabouts

Knowledge and Understanding

1.   Horses' reactions when working alone and in company
2.   Importance of returning a horse 'cool' from work
3.   Effects of weather on road surfaces
4.   Operating limits on vehicles

5. Application of the Highway Code and Road Traffic Acts
6. Use of the whip
7. Procedures in the event of a road traffic accident
8. Types of hand signals

Section C: Attend to horse and vehicle after driving

Performance Criteria

1. Vehicle is parked and secured at designated location
2. Horse is unhitched from the vehicle, harness removed and returned to relevant location
3. Approved cooling down procedures are implemented before horse is returned to stables
4. Control of the horse is maintained at all times
5. The health, safety and security of the horse, self and others is maintained throughout

Range Statement

Vehicles: Two wheeled; four wheeled

Knowledge and Understanding

1. Safety procedure when unhitching
2. Recommended cooling down procedures
3. Methods of braking and securing vehicles
4. Circumstances when assistance is required
5. Correct storage and security of vehicle

CARRIAGE CHECK LIST

Section A – 2 Wheel Carriages (Traditional)

Area of inspection	Check	Reason for rejection
WHEELS	1. End play on axle	End play of 12mm or more
	2. Tight joints into hub	Any looseness found in these areas, by using manual force
	Spokes into felloes	Any looseness found in these areas, by using manual force
	Steel rim or clincher on felloes	Any looseness found in these areas, by using manual force
	3. Rubbers for protrusion	Rubbers protruding from the channel
	4. General soundness of wood	Evidence of woodworm, rot or cracks

Area of inspection	Check	Reason for rejection
AXLES	1. Collinge axle – nuts and split pin in place	Signs of corrosion, looseness or missing components
	2. Mail axle – check hub bolts and nuts on inside of moon plate	Signs of corrosion, looseness or missing components
	3. Lubrication (both axle types)	Lack of lubrication
	4. Washers and seals	Signs of corrosion, looseness or missing components
SHAFTS	1. Thickness and strength	Inadequate thickness and strength in keeping with carriage size
	2. Wood and laminations	Evidence of woodworm, rot or cracks and delaminations
	3. Slack and movement where shaft joins vehicle at drawbar	Excessive slackness and movement
	4. Shaft fixings, bolt and bolt attachments	Signs of corrosion, looseness or missing components
	5. Tug stops and breeching staples	Incorrectly positioned, signs of corrosion, looseness or missing components and excessive wear
SPRINGS	1. Leaves and fixings, especially ends of full elliptic springs	Broken, excessive wear or collapsed
	2. U-bolts supporting Springs and their fixings to the axle	Signs of corrosion, looseness or missing components
	3. Threads of nuts	Stripped or worn threads
	4. Leatherwork and tension brackets on C springs	Deterioration of leatherwork and tension brackets
BODY	1. Woodwork	Evidence of woodworm, rot or cracks
	2. Panels	Cracks and safety related damage
	3. Spring mountings and shaft fixings	Signs of corrosion, looseness or missing components
	4. All bolts and screws	Insecure or general looseness

Area of inspection	Check	Reason for rejection
	5. Seat securing mechanism	Insecure or general looseness
	6. Cushion straps	Missing or damaged, insecure or general looseness
	7. Straps and mounting irons	Missing or damaged, insecure or general looseness and deterioration
SWINGLETREE	1. Swingletree (wood or metal) including trace hooks and fixing bolts, chains (if fitted)	Insecure, hook screws not in place, signs of corrosion, worn or missing components, evidence of woodworm, rot, cracks and safety related damage

Section B – 2 Wheel Carriages (Modern)

Area of inspection	Check	Reason for rejection
	If not steel: check as for traditional; otherwise	
WHEELS/AXLES	1. Welds	Evidence of fatigue or cracks
	2. Bearings Adjustment	Excessive play, roughness or tightness
	If not steel: check as for traditional; otherwise:	
SHAFTS	1. Material and construction (especially where shaft joins carriage)	Evidence of fatigue (often indicated by cracks in paintwork), excessive wear around bolt mountings, incorrect components
	2. Tug stops and breeching staples	Incorrectly positioned, signs of corrosion, looseness or missing components and excessive wear
	As for traditional vehicle, and:	
SPRINGS	1. Coil spring	Incomplete, cracked or fractured, worn or corroded so that its cross-sectional area is seriously weakened
	2. Damper Unit (if fitted)	Damage, corrosion, insecurity of attachment and fluid leakage

Area of inspection	Check	Reason for rejection
	3. Rubber suspension unit	Looseness, cracks or fractures, damage or corrosion, separation between flexible element and metal
	As for traditional vehicle, and:	
BODY AND SWINGLETREE	1. Sliding body balance system (if used)	Insecure, hook screws not in place, signs of corrosion, missing or loose components, evidence of woodworm, rot, cracks and safety related damage

Section C – 4 Wheel Carriages (Traditional)

Area of inspection	Check	Reason for rejection
ADDITIONAL CHECKS	As for 2 wheel carriages,	and:
	1. Forecarriage turntable and centre pin	Excessive play, worn centre pin, woodworm, rot or cracks
	2. Support plates	Insufficient lubrication
	3. Polehousing, polepin polehead and bearing (if fitted)	Stress cracking, excessive wear and excessive play in bearing
	4. Shaft bolts (if fitted)	Signs of corrosion, looseness or missing components
	5. Mounting steps, rails etc. and seats	Sharp edges, insecure, worn or inappropriate components
	6. Hoods and folding moveable safety features	Sharp edges, insecure, worn or inappropriate components
	7. Brakes: (a) Traditional	Worn, damaged or insecure blocks, excessive play or wear to linkage
	(b) Modern (hydraulic)	Low fluid level or leakage, worn pads, excessive play or wear to linkage, damage to hydraulic line

Section D – 4 Wheel Carriages (Modern)

Area of inspection	Check	Reason for rejection
ADDITIONAL CHECKS	As for 2 wheel carriages and 4 wheel traditional, and:	
	1. Ball bearing turntable (if fitted)	Excessive play and insufficient lubrication
	2. Pole springing system	Signs of corrosion, missing or loose components

Horse

It is recommended that any horse which is to be used for the carriage of passengers should be at least six years old. It is not the aim of this Code to set out guidance or information on veterinary checks for horses and it is recommended that operators seek the advice of a veterinary surgeon on the suitability of any animal for the purpose of drawing a carriage.

Harness

Drivers should ensure that all harnesses are properly fitted and appropriate for their particular use. Harnesses should also be regularly checked for soundness and safety.

FURTHER READING

The British Driving Society Introduction to Driving
(The British Driving Society) published by the BDS, Warwick

Breaking a Horse to Harness
(Sallie Walrond) published by J A Allen, London

Driving a Harness Horse
(Sallie Walrond) published by J A Allen, London

The Art of Driving
(Max Pape) published by J A Allen, London

Licensing Motorcycles as Private Hire Vehicles – A guidance note from the Department for Transport (DfT 2012)

1. The Department for Transport recognises that questions about whether and how to license motorcycles as private hire vehicles (PHVs) have implications nationally. We are therefore publishing guidance to assist licensing authorities who are considering this issue.

2. In drawing up the guidance, we recognise that there is a balance to be struck between the flexibility provided by motorcycle PHVs and the safety risks associated with these vehicles.

3. The Department is also mindful of the important judgment in the case of Leeds City Council v Chauffeur Bikes Ltd – mentioned below.

4. Leaving aside the Leeds judgment for the moment, the Department's starting point is to take account of the main thrust of the taxi/PHV Best Practice Guidance which urges licensing authorities to accept for licensing as wide a range of vehicles as possible and to ensure that any constraints or restrictions are in place for a very good reason.

5. The Department would want to be convinced that there was strong evidence and compelling reasons if we were to provide guidance which advised licensing authorities not to accept motorcycles as PHVs. After all, such guidance, if accepted by licensing authorities, would mean putting a number of established operators out of business.

6. We do not consider that there is a compelling case for ruling out motorcycles as PHVs on safety grounds.

7. It is in the nature of this sort of niche market that passengers will weigh up the risks involved and act accordingly. Many people would never choose to use motorcycle PHVs because of the risks they perceive whereas others regard riding pillion as a convenient and practical form of transport.

8. The Department's key point is that the risks associated with riding as a pillion passenger on a motorcycle are not sufficiently high as to provide guidance which rules them out of the licensing system altogether.

9. However, there is an important High Court judgment on this issue – *Leeds City Council v Chauffeur Bikes Ltd*[1] – which we must mention in this regard and which local licensing authorities should consider before determining a local policy on whether or not to license motorcycles as PHVs.

10. The High Court held that a motorcycle could be in a safe condition for a motorcycle but it could still, for safety reasons, be judged to be unsuitable in type, size or design for use as a private hire vehicle. On that basis, the Court

decided that the motorcycle in question could rightly be held to be unsuitable and unsafe for private hire use.

11. The Department forms the opinion that this case does not automatically rule out the licensing of motorcycles as PHVs. Whilst licensing authorities clearly must follow the principles established by the High Court in this judgment, we would urge them to consider applications in the light of their available powers to ensure adequate standards are met and the sorts of risks identified by the Court are mitigated.

12. The following sections outline the standards and conditions which the Department considers to represent Best Practice when licensing motorcycles as PHVs.

¹ *Chauffeur Bikes Ltd v Leeds City Council* [2006] R.T.R. 7

APPLICATIONS – PRE-REQUISITES BEFORE GRANTING A LICENCE

A1 – Vehicles

(i)   When assessing applications for a vehicle licence in respect of a motorcycle, licensing authorities should bear in mind that motorcycles must be approved for road use and comply with the Road Vehicles (Construction and Use) Regulations 1986 S.I. 1986 No 1078, as amended, and the Road Vehicles Lighting Regulations 1989 S.I. 1989 No 1796 as amended.

(ii)   Licensing authorities should ensure that the vehicle is suitable for the role of carrying passengers. As with conventional cars presented for PHV licensing, the Department envisages that a range of motorcycles would be suitable for licensing. Larger more powerful motor-vehicles (e.g. over 750cc or equivalent) are more stable which is particularly useful when carrying pillion passengers. However, there may be occasions when the licensing authority judges that a lighter vehicle is appropriate. Licensing authorities should satisfy themselves that any vehicle presented to them would be capable of carrying a pillion passenger in reasonable safety and comfort.

(iii)   Handrails and a seat back are features which might contribute to a more comfortable riding experience, but the Department recommends that these elements are best left to the discretion of vehicle owners who will want to decide on a commercial basis whether to incorporate them.

(iv)   It is likely that passengers using motorcycle PHVs will have some luggage with them and the vehicle must be capable of storing this luggage. The passenger should never be expected to hold any luggage whilst riding pillion. Generally, motorcycles will have guidelines from the manufacturer about the amount of luggage which can be stored on the vehicle and licensing authorities will want to ensure that this is sufficiently reasonable for the likely demand.

(v)   The motorcycle should have footrests suitable for pillion passengers. Standard footrests are likely to be suitable for the majority of passengers.

(vi) The vehicle must have hire and reward insurance. Additional fittings or modifications to the vehicle for its use as a PHV such as backrests, luggage racks, containers or driver information systems must be declared and must comply with motorcycle and components' manufacturers' recommendations for such additional equipment. The owner must declare that any modifications comply with the Construction and Use Regulations referred to in A1(i) above.

(vii) Anti-lock brakes (ABS) can reduce the stopping distance and improve stability during braking in wet weather. The Department recommends that ABS should be fitted to any motorcycles which are licensed as PHVs.

A2 – Riders

(i) When assessing applications for a driver licence from an individual who declares an intention to ride motorcycle PHVs, a licensing authority must, of course, ensure that they comply with the requirements in section 51 of the Local Government (Miscellaneous Provisions) Act 1976 or section 13 of the Private Hire Vehicles (London) Act 1998.

(ii) And, in order to be granted a licence, the applicant must hold a current valid full motorcycle driving licence issued by the DVLA, for the type of vehicle being used.

(iii) Motorcycle accident rates decrease steeply as riders become more experienced so, in addition to these requirements, it is crucial that a licensing authority satisfies itself that the applicant is suitably competent at, and experienced in, riding a motorcycle to an appropriate standard, including taking passengers and carrying luggage.

(iv) As regards competence, the Department recommends that applicants for a motorcycle PHV driver's licence should, as a minimum, have successfully completed the Institute of Advanced Motorist or The Royal Society for the Prevention of Accidents (RoSPA) advanced rider schemes or another course which is demonstrably equivalent or superior. Successful completion of one of these courses is a good indicator of an individual's ability to ride safely and competently in terms of awareness, anticipation, vehicle handling and general roadcraft.

(v) The question of experience is a more subjective one and a licensing authority will want to enquire about an applicant's practical experience of riding motorcycles and taking pillion passengers. The Department recommends that applicants should have at least five years' experience of riding motorcycles. In addition to any self-declaration, the Department recommends that any operator considering taking a motorcycle rider onto his or her circuit should undertake their own practical assessment of the rider, including taking pillion passengers. Of course, there may well be occasions when the owner/rider is also the operator. The Department does not want to discourage this practice, but it is crucial that the licensing authority can satisfy itself as comprehensively as possible about the applicant's actual riding experience, particularly as regards taking pillion passengers.

(vi)   The Department does not consider that an age limit should be imposed for riders, but it is likely that experience requirements combined with potential insurance limitations would effectively rule out young riders.

(vii)   The Department's Best Practice Guidance in respect of wider taxi and PHV licensing suggests that licensing authorities should satisfy themselves about an applicant's ability to communicate with passengers in English. This requirement is all the more important with motorcycle PHV riders where a rider might have to communicate safety instructions to passengers.

C1 – Vehicle licences

(i)   The vehicle should be operated in accordance with the manufacturer's specifications in all respects.

(ii)   The Department recommends that licensing authorities should test motorcycle PHVs twice per year, as permitted in the legislation.

(iii)   The display of the disc, and any permitted signage, must not interfere with the safety or operation of the vehicle.

(iv)   The vehicle should not be loaded beyond the manufacturer's recommendations.

(v)   If luggage is carried, it must be made secure so as not to affect the stability of the vehicle or the visibility of the driver. Purpose-built containers (panniers) are likely to be the most suitable means of carrying luggage.

(vi)   Luggage must not be carried by a passenger (passengers need their hands free to secure themselves to the motorcycle).

(vii)   The vehicle should be able to accelerate and maintain a road speed appropriate to the traffic conditions in which it operates.

C2 – Driver licences

(i)   The driver and the passenger must comply with the requirement to wear a safety helmet. The helmet must properly fit the individual user and be securely fastened, or it will be less effective and possibly dangerous. Operators should have a selection of helmets and determine at the time of booking which size helmet the rider should bring with them.

(ii)   Whilst there is no legislation on protective clothing, it is strongly recommended that appropriate protective clothing is worn. The driver should wear protective clothing to guard them in the event of an accident. They should also offer protective clothing to passengers. The Department recommends that riders should, as a minimum, offer passengers gloves, a jacket and trousers. The clothing offered to passengers should ideally be CE marked to indicate compliance with recognised safety standards. Guidance about protective clothing can be found at http://think.direct.gov.uk/motorcycles.html

(iii)   Communication between the rider and the passenger is an essential component of a safe journey. Accordingly, the Department recommends that the driver and passenger should be linked through the safety helmets via a driver/pillion intercom system. The rider should instruct the passenger on how to use the system.

(iv)   It should be borne in mind that some passengers might never have ridden on a motorcycle. The driver should, at the point of pick-up, determine whether a passenger is experienced on a motorcycle. If not, the driver should deliver a short and basic briefing to passengers before commencing a journey, instructing them how to react to driving conditions such as cornering etc, and reminding them that they are choosing to accept that there are some risks involved in travelling by motorcycle that do not arise when travelling in cars. The driver should also remind passengers that they need to co-operate with the driver to assist in keeping the vehicle stable, for example, on corners.

(v)   The driver should refuse to carry any passenger who cannot be carried safely e.g. because they cannot be properly equipped with appropriate helmet and safety clothing, appear to be under the influence of alcohol or drugs, cannot reach the foot pegs or are not able to understand the safety instructions.

(vi)   The driver should ride safely at all times giving due regard to the safety of his/her passenger environmental factors, traffic conditions and other road users.

C3 – Operator licences

(i)   The operator's website (if any) should display an image of the PHV operator licence, and operators should provide a copy of the licence to passengers on request.

(ii)   Operators should indicate how they propose to meet the requirement for drivers on their circuit to ensure that passengers have properly fitting and secured helmets and adequate protective clothing, including gloves, jackets and trousers.

(iii)   Operators should advise passengers, at the time of booking, that they should wear sturdy boots which cover their ankles and they should alert the hirer to maximum luggage dimensions and weights.

(iv)   Operators should provide a written statement to the licensing authority setting out how they intend to assess any riders who want to join their operation.

(v)   If helmets are to be shared between drivers or passengers, operators should indicate how they will ensure adequate hygiene and fitment between users. The Department recommends that operators should offer disposable helmet inserts/balaclavas for passengers to wear.

(vi)   Operators must implement and ensure compliance with a health and safety policy.

(vii)   Operators should ensure that suitable maintenance plans are in place for the motorcycles on their circuits and they should hold the service records for these vehicles.

(viii) If the pillion passenger cannot reach the footrests, travel should not be allowed to occur.

(ix) The Department considers that, due to the risks involved, and the fact that the rider is dependent on the passenger being sufficiently cooperative, operators should not accept bookings which involve carrying a passenger who is under 16 years of age.

Regulators' Code (BIS 2014)

FOREWORD

In the Autumn Statement 2012 Government announced that it would introduce a package of measures to improve the way regulation is delivered at the frontline such as the Focus on Enforcement review of appeals, the proposed Growth Duty for non-economic regulators and the Accountability for Regulator Impact measure.

This Government is committed to reducing regulatory burdens and supporting compliant business growth through the development of an open and constructive relationship between regulators and those they regulate. The Regulators' Code provides a flexible, principles based framework for regulatory delivery that supports and enables regulators to design their service and enforcement policies in a manner that best suits the needs of businesses and other regulated entities.

Our expectation is that by clarifying the provisions contained in the previous Regulators' Compliance Code, in a shorter and accessible format, regulators and those they regulate will have a clear understanding of the services that can be expected and will feel able to challenge if these are not being fulfilled.

Regulators within scope of the Regulators' Code are diverse but they share a common primary purpose – to regulate for the protection of the vulnerable, the environment, social or other objective. This Code does not detract from these core purposes but seeks to promote proportionate, consistent and targeted regulatory activity through the development of transparent and effective dialogue and understanding between regulators and those they regulate.

I believe the Regulators' Code will support a positive shift in how regulation is delivered by setting clear expectations and promising open dialogue. Ultimately this will give businesses greater confidence to invest and grow.

Michael Fallon

Minister of State for Business and Enterprise

Department for Business, Innovation and Skills

REGULATORS' CODE

This Code was laid before Parliament in accordance with section 23 of the Legislative and Regulatory Reform Act 2006 ("the Act"). Regulators whose functions are specified by order under section 24(2) of the Act must have regard to the Code when developing policies and operational procedures that guide their regulatory activities. Regulators must equally have regard to the Code when setting standards or giving guidance which will guide the regulatory activities of other regulators. If a regulator concludes, on the basis of material evidence, that a specific provision of the Code is either not applicable or is outweighed by another relevant consideration, the regulator is not bound to follow that provision, but should record that decision and the reasons for it.

1. Regulators should carry out their activities in a way that supports those they regulate to comply and grow

1.1   Regulators should avoid imposing unnecessary regulatory burdens through their regulatory activities[1] and should assess whether similar social, environmental and economic outcomes could be achieved by less burdensome means. Regulators should choose proportionate approaches to those they regulate, based on relevant factors including, for example, business size and capacity.

1.2   When designing and reviewing policies, operational procedures and practices, regulators should consider how they might support or enable economic growth for compliant businesses and other regulated entities[2], for example, by considering how they can best:
- understand and minimise negative economic impacts of their regulatory activities;
- minimising the costs of compliance for those they regulate;
- improve confidence in compliance for those they regulate, by providing greater certainty; and
- encourage and promote compliance.

1.3   Regulators should ensure that their officers have the necessary knowledge and skills to support those they regulate, including having an understanding of those they regulate that enables them to choose proportionate and effective approaches.

1.4   Regulators should ensure that their officers understand the statutory principles of good regulation[3] and of this Code, and how the regulator delivers its activities in accordance with them.

[1]   The term 'regulatory activities' refers to the whole range of regulatory options and interventions available to regulators.

[2]   The terms 'business or businesses' is used throughout this document to refer to businesses and other regulated entities.

[3]   The statutory principles of good regulation can be viewed in Part 2 (21) on page 12: http://www.legislation.gov.uk/ukpga/2006/51/pdfs/ukpga_20060051_en.pdf.

2. Regulators should provide simple and straightforward ways to engage with those they regulate and hear their views

2.1   Regulators should have mechanisms in place to engage those they regulate, citizens and others to offer views and contribute to the development of their policies and service standards. Before changing policies, practices or service standards, regulators should consider the impact on business and engage with business representatives.

2.2   In responding to non-compliance that they identify, regulators should clearly explain what the non-compliant item or activity is, the advice being given, actions required or decisions taken, and the reasons for these. Regulators should provide an opportunity for dialogue in relation to the advice, requirements or decisions, with a view to ensuring that they are acting in a way that is proportionate and consistent.

This paragraph does not apply where the regulator can demonstrate that immediate enforcement action is required to prevent or respond to a serious breach or where providing such an opportunity would be likely to defeat the purpose of the proposed enforcement action.

2.3   Regulators should provide an impartial and clearly explained route to appeal against a regulatory decision or a failure to act in accordance with this Code. Individual officers of the regulator who took the decision or action against which the appeal is being made should not be involved in considering the appeal. This route to appeal should be publicised to those who are regulated.

2.4   Regulators should provide a timely explanation in writing of any right to representation or right to appeal. This explanation should be in plain language and include practical information on the process involved.

2.5   Regulators should make available to those they regulate, clearly explained complaints procedures, allowing them to easily make a complaint about the conduct of the regulator.

2.6   Regulators should have a range of mechanisms to enable and regularly invite, receive and take on board customer feedback, including, for example, through customer satisfaction surveys of those they regulate[4].

---

[4]   The Government will discuss with national regulators a common approach to surveys to support benchmarking of their performance.

3. Regulators should base their regulatory activities on risk

3.1   Regulators should take an evidence based approach to determining the priority risks in their area of responsibility, and should allocate resources where they would be most effective in addressing those priority risks.

3.2   Regulators should consider risk at every stage of their decision-making processes, including choosing the most appropriate type of intervention or way of working with those regulated; targeting checks on compliance; and when taking enforcement action.

3.3   Regulators designing a risk assessment framework[5], for their own use or for use by others, should have mechanisms in place to consult on the design with those affected, and to review it regularly.

3.4   Regulators, in making their assessment of risk, should recognise the compliance record of those they regulate, including using earned recognition approaches and should consider all available and relevant data on compliance, including evidence of relevant external verification.

3.5   Regulators should review the effectiveness of their chosen regulatory activities in delivering the desired outcomes and make any necessary adjustments accordingly.

5 The term 'risk assessment framework' encompasses any model, scheme, methodology or risk rating approach that is used to inform risk-based targeting of regulatory activities in relation to individual businesses or other regulated entities.

4. Regulators should share information about compliance and risk

4.1 Regulators should collectively follow the principle of "collect once, use many times" when requesting information from those they regulate.

4.2 When the law allows, regulators should agree secure mechanisms to share information with each other about businesses and other bodies they regulate, to help target resources and activities and minimise duplication.

5. Regulators should ensure clear information, guidance and advice is available to help those they regulate meet their responsibilities to comply

5.1 Regulators should provide advice and guidance that is focused on assisting those they regulate to understand and meet their responsibilities. When providing advice and guidance, legal requirements should be distinguished from suggested good practice and the impact of the advice or guidance should be considered so that it does not impose unnecessary burdens in itself.

5.2 Regulators should publish guidance, and information in a clear, accessible, concise format, using media appropriate to the target audience and written in plain language for the audience.

5.3 Regulators should have mechanisms in place to consult those they regulate in relation to the guidance they produce to ensure that it meets their needs.

5.4 Regulators should seek to create an environment in which those they regulate have confidence in the advice they receive and feel able to seek advice without fear of triggering enforcement action.

5.5 In responding to requests for advice, a regulator's primary concerns should be to provide the advice necessary to support compliance, and to ensure that the advice can be relied on.

5.6 Regulators should have mechanisms to work collaboratively to assist those regulated by more than one regulator. Regulators should consider advice provided by other regulators and, where there is disagreement about the advice provided, this should be discussed with the other regulator to reach agreement.

6. Regulators should ensure that their approach to their regulatory activities is transparent

6.1 Regulators should publish a set of clear service standards, setting out what those they regulate should expect from them.

6.2 Regulators' published service standards should include clear information on:

a) how they communicate with those they regulate and how they can be contacted;

b) their approach to providing information, guidance and advice;

c) their approach to checks on compliance[6], including details of the risk assessment framework used to target those checks as well as protocols for their conduct, clearly setting out what those they regulate should expect;

d) their enforcement policy, explaining how they respond to non-compliance;

e) their fees and charges, if any. This information should clearly explain the basis on which these are calculated, and should include an explanation of whether compliance will affect fees and charges; and

f) how to comment or complain about the service provided and routes to appeal.

6.3 Information published to meet the provisions of this Code should be easily accessible, including being available at a single point[7] on the regulator's website that is clearly signposted, and it should be kept up to date.

6.4 Regulators should have mechanisms in place to ensure that their officers act in accordance with their published service standards, including their enforcement policy.

6.5 Regulators should publish, on a regular basis, details of their performance against their service standards, including feedback received from those they regulate, such as customer satisfaction surveys, and data relating to complaints about them and appeals against their decisions.

[6] Including inspections, audit, monitoring and sampling visits, and test purchases.

[7] This requirement may be satisfied by providing a single web page that includes links to information published elsewhere.

MONITORING THE EFFECTIVENESS OF THE REGULATORS' CODE

The Government is committed to making sure the Regulators' Code is effective. To make sure that the Code is being used effectively, we want businesses, regulated bodies and citizens to challenge regulators who they believe are not acting in accordance with their published policies and standards. It is in the wider public interest that regulators are transparent and proportionate in their approaches to regulation.

The Government will monitor published policies and standards of regulators subject to the Regulators' Code, and will challenge regulators where there is evidence that policies and standards are not in line with the Code or are not followed.

Guidance for Licensing Authorities to Prevent Illegal Working in the Taxi and Private Hire Sector in England and Wales (Home Office 2016)

1. INTRODUCTION

The Immigration Act 2016 (the 2016 Act) amended existing licensing regimes in the UK to seek to prevent illegal working in the private hire vehicle (PHV) and taxi sector[1]. With effect from 1 December 2016, the provisions in the 2016 Act prohibit all licensing authorities[2] across the UK from issuing to anyone who is disqualified by reason of their immigration status and they discharge this duty by conducting immigration checks. The 2016 Act also embeds other immigration safeguards into the existing licensing regimes across the UK.

[1] Outside London, these provisions also apply to pedi-cabs by virtue of being 'hackney carriages'.

[2] The exceptions are London taxis, for which Transport for London will make equivalent provision by amending the London Cab Order 1934 and booking offices in Scotland, where the Civic Government (Scotland) Act 1982 (Licensing of Booking Offices) Order 2009 will be amended by a consequential amendment.

1.1   What does this measure do?

The provisions in the 2016 Act amend existing licensing regimes to prevent people without lawful immigration status and the right to work from holding an operator or a PHV or taxi driver licence[3]. This has been achieved by adapting the following existing licensing legislation across the UK: London Hackney Carriages Act 1843; the London Cab Order 1934; Private Hire Vehicles (London) Act 1998; Metropolitan Public Carriage Act 1869; Local Government (Miscellaneous Provisions) Act 1976; Plymouth City Council Act 1975; Road Traffic Offenders (Northern Ireland) Order 1996 and the Taxi Act (Northern Ireland) 2008. The Civic Government (Scotland) Act 1982 (Licensing of Booking Offices) Order 2009 will also be amended in due course in respect of booking offices in Scotland.

The new provisions mean that driver and operator licences must not be issued to people who are illegally present in the UK, who are not permitted to work, or who are permitted to work but are subject to a condition that prohibits them from holding such a licence.

Licensing authorities must discharge this duty by requiring the applicant to submit one of a number of prescribed documents which show that the applicant has permission to be in the UK and undertake work as an operator or a private hire or taxi driver. The check must be performed when the applicant first applies for a licence or first applies to renew or extend their licence whether for the full statutory term or a lesser period on or after 1 December 2016. For those who have limited permission to be in the UK, the licensing authority must repeat the check at each subsequent application to renew or extend the licence until such time as the applicant demonstrates that they are entitled to remain indefinitely in the UK.

Where a person's immigration permission to be in the UK is time-limited to less than the statutory length for a driver or operator licence, the licence must be issued for a duration which does not exceed the applicant's period of permission to be in the UK and work. In the event that the Home Office cuts short or ends a person's immigration permission (referred to as curtailment or revocation), any licence issued as a consequence of an application which was made on or after 1 December 2016, that the person holds will automatically lapse.

The provisions also add immigration offences and penalties to the list of grounds on which operator and private hire and taxi driver licences may be suspended or revoked by licensing authorities. In circumstances where the operator or driver licence expires, is revoked or suspended on immigration grounds, it must be returned to the issuing licence authority. Failure to return the licence will be a criminal offence, punishable on conviction in a Magistrates' Court by a fine (see chapter 5).

3   The provisions do not prevent people without lawful immigration status who already hold a licence from continuing to doing so.

1.2   Purpose of this guidance

This guidance is issued for use by licensing authorities in England and Wales. Equivalent guidance will be issued for the relevant licence issuing bodies in Scotland and Northern Ireland.

Licensing authorities are under a duty not to issue licences to people who are disqualified by their immigration status from holding them. In determining whether someone is disqualified, licensing authorities are under a statutory duty to have regard to this guidance.

The requirement to check the immigration status of licence applicants does not amend or replace the existing 'fit and proper' person test that licensing authorities must perform; this includes the obtaining of a Certificate of Good Conduct for applicants who have resided abroad for a period of time.

1.3   Who is disqualified from holding a licence?

A person is disqualified from holding an operator or a PHV or taxi driver licence by reason of their immigration status if:

- the person requires leave to enter or remain in the UK and has not been granted it; or
- the person's leave to enter or remain in the UK
  - is invalid, has ceased to have effect (whether by reason of curtailment, revocation, cancellation, passage of time, or otherwise), or
  - is subject to a condition preventing the person from doing work of that kind.

A person is also disqualified from holding a licence if they are subject to a condition on their permission to be in the UK preventing them from holding licence, for example, they are subject to an immigration restriction that does not permit them to work.

1.4 For whom is this guidance relevant?

This guidance applies to applications and requests to renew or extend a current licence sent to licensing authorities on or after 1 December 2016.

It should be used by licensing authority staff responsible for the issue, renewal, suspension and revocation of operator or PHV or taxi driver licences.

These provisions only apply to the applicant and do not apply to the MOT or other vehicle check. They also do not apply to a DVLA or DVA driver's licence, although the Immigration Act 2014 and the 2016 Act introduced provisions regarding the issue and revocation of such licences in respect of illegal migrants and, upon commencement, will provide, through section 44 of the 2016 Act, a new criminal offence of driving illegally in the UK.

1.5 When will this guidance be relevant?

The checking requirements are not retrospective. Licensing authorities do not have to check the immigration status of those people who already hold a licence which was issued before 1 December 2016, or who sent their licence application to the licensing authority before this date. The check must be performed when the applicant first applies i.e. sends the application for a licence to the licensing authority or first applies to renew their licence or extend their licence on or after 1 December 2016. A postmark may be acceptable evidence of date of application.

For those who have time-limited permission to be in the UK, the check must be repeated at each subsequent application to renew or extend the licence until such time as the applicant demonstrates that they are entitled to remain indefinitely in the UK, and as a result, there are no restrictions on their ability to work. The documents referred to in the list of acceptable documents in Annex A will indicate whether the individual has temporary permission to be in the UK or is entitled to remain indefinitely and work in the UK. The list of acceptable documents is explained further in section 3.

1.5 How should this guidance be used?

This guidance sets out what licensing authorities need to know about their legal duty not to issue a licence to a person who is disqualified from holding one because of that person's immigration status. It sets out how licensing authorities should discharge this duty by conducting document checks. It explains on whom a licensing authority needs to make checks, when, and how to do the checks correctly.

1.6   References in this guidance

References to 'we' or us' in this guide are to the Home Office. References to 'you' and 'your' are to the licensing authority.

'Days' means calendar days, i.e. including Saturdays, Sundays and bank holidays.

'A current document' means a document that has not expired.

2. RIGHT TO A LICENCE CHECK

2.1   What does 'right to a licence' mean?

For the purposes of this guidance, 'a right to a licence' means that someone is not disqualified by their immigration status from holding an operator or a PHV or taxi driver licence. There may be other reasons why you may be prohibited from issuing a licence, which still stand. This guidance does not relate to these other reasons, for example, the fit and proper person test.

For all operator and PHV and taxi driver licence applications made (sent) on or after 1 December 2016, you must comply with the legal requirement not to issue a licence to someone who is disqualified from holding the licence by reason of their immigration status. You must discharge this duty by requiring the applicant to submit one of a number of prescribed documents which show that the applicant has permission to be in the UK and undertake work as an operator or PHV or taxi driver. The check must be performed when the applicant first applies for a licence or first applies to renew or extend their licence, whether for the full statutory term or for a lesser period, on or after 1 December 2016. For those who have time-limited permission to be in the UK, you must repeat the check at each subsequent application to renew or extend the licence until such time as the applicant demonstrates that they are entitled to remain indefinitely in the UK. The documents referred to in the list of acceptable documents in Annex A will indicate whether the individual has temporary permission to be in the UK or is entitled to remain indefinitely in the UK. The list of acceptable documents is explained in section 3.

You must be satisfied that the person is not disqualified from holding a licence before you issue a licence to that person.

Checking a person's documents to determine if they can hold the licence comprises three key steps:

1.   Obtain the person's original document(s);
2.   Check the document(s) in the presence of the applicant; and
3.   Make and retain a clear copy of the document(s).

You can find detailed information on how to correctly conduct right to a licence checks and a list of acceptable documents later in this guidance. You are responsible for conducting the visual inspection of the document(s) presented to you.

2.2 Why do you need to do checks?

Licensing authorities have a legal duty not to issue operator or PHV or taxi driver licences to people disqualified by their immigration status from holding them, in order to prevent illegal working in the private hire vehicle and taxi sector. In order to discharge this duty, this guidance requires you to conduct document checks as part of the licence application process.

The checks should establish whether or not an applicant has a lawful immigration status in the UK, or is prohibited from working because they are in the UK illegally, or is subject to a condition that prevents them from holding a licence.

2.3 Who do you conduct checks on?

You should conduct 'right to a licence' checks in accordance with section 3 of this guidance on all applicants for operator or PHV or taxi driver licences. This means you should ask all applicants for such licences to provide you with one of the original documents/combination of documents set out at Annex A to this guidance.

To ensure that you do not discriminate against anyone, you should treat all licence applicants in the same way when they first apply on or after 1 December 2016 during the licence application process. This will also demonstrate a fair, transparent and consistent application process. You should not make assumptions about a person's right to work in the UK or their immigration status on the basis of their nationality, ethnic or national origin, accent, the colour of their skin, or the length of time they have been resident in the UK.

2.4 When do you conduct checks?

The immigration checks have been developed to fit within the existing licensing regimes and to keep the additional requirements and burdens to a minimum. Accordingly, you should incorporate the right to a licence check into your existing application process at any point before a decision is made on the application. The check could be carried out, for example, when the applicant first lodges their application, or at a subsequent interview. Your guidance to applicants should make clear when the check will be performed in order that the applicant may submit the necessary documents at the appropriate time.

You may need to amend your application forms to include a declaration stating that the applicant has to have the correct immigration status to apply for the licence, that they must provide to you immigration status documents in line with Annex A in order for their application to be considered valid and that they understand that the licence will lapse if they are no longer entitled to work in the UK. The application form or supporting guidance should state which document or documents must be submitted by the applicant (as set out in Annex A) and when and indicate that you may check their immigration status with us. The right to work check will be conducted by you during a face to face meeting with the applicant.

The declaration itself can be a succinct statement, such as:-

'Your right to work in the UK will be checked as part of your licence application, this could include the licensing authority checking your immigration status with the Home Office. We may otherwise share information with the Home Office. You must therefore provide a document or document combination that is stipulated as being suitable for this check. The list of documents is set out at [guidance link]. You must provide the original document(s), such as your passport or biometric residence permit, as indicated in the published guidance, so that the check can take place. The document(s) will be copied and the copy retained by the licensing authority. The original document will be returned to you. Your application will not be considered valid until all the necessary information and original document(s) have been produced and the relevant paid has been paid.

If there are restrictions on the length of time you may work in the UK, your licence will not be issued for any longer than this period. In such circumstances the check will be repeated each time you apply to renew or extend your licence, If, during this period, you are disqualified from holding a licence because you have not complied with the UK's immigration laws, your licence will lapse and you must return it to the licensing authority. Failure to do so is a criminal offence.'

If the applicant fails to provide document(s) specified in Annex A that demonstrate a right to a licence in accordance with your published application process, you should consider whether to offer a further opportunity to provide the documents before rejecting the application, if your usual process allows this.

2.5   When does a migrant's status come to an end?

Migrants who are subject to UK immigration control may be granted permission to enter or remain in the UK, with a condition permitting employment, on a time-limited basis or on an indefinite basis. When the person's stay is time limited, this will be shown in their immigration documentation. It is possible for a migrant to apply to extend their stay, and if they do so before their previous status expires, they continue to have any right to work that they previously had while their application and any associated administrative review or appeal are outstanding. In such cases, a person's status may be confirmed by you contacting the Home Office's Evidence and Enquiry Unit.

3. HOW DO YOU CONDUCT CHECKS?

3.1   Three-step check

There are three basic steps to conducting a right to work check. Remember three keywords:

1. Obtain
2. Check
3. Copy

Illustration 1: Summary of a right to a licence check

Obtain

Obtain original versions of one or more acceptable documents.

Check

Check the document's validity in the presence of the holder

Copy

make and retain a clear copy.

Illustration 2 explains in more detail what you need to do in each of the three steps to correctly conduct a check.

Illustration 2: The Three-Step Check

Step 1 Obtain

You must obtain original document(s) from either List A or List B of acceptable documents at Annex A.

Step 2 Check

You must check that the document(s) are genuine and that the person presenting them is the licence applicant, the rightful holder of the document(s), and not disqualified from obtaining a licence. You must check:

- photographs and dates of birth are consistent across documents and with the person's appearance in order to detect impersonation;
- expiry dates for permission to be in the UK have not passed;
- any work restrictions to determine if the applicant is prohibited from holding a licence;
- the documents are genuine, have not been tampered with and belong to the holder; and
- the reasons for any difference in names across documents (e.g. original marriage certificate, divorce decree absolute, deed poll). These supporting documents should also be photocopied and a copy retained.

Guidance on examining and identifying fraudulent identity documents may be found here. A checklist which may assist you is at Annex B of this guidance.

Step 3 Copy

You must make a clear copy of each document checked and retain these copies securely, with other licence application documents. If you do not retain the copy, you will have to repeat the check if someone permitted to remain indefinitely in the UK applies to renew or extend their licence. You should copy:

- Passports: any page with the document expiry date, the holder's nationality, date of birth, signature, immigration permission expiry date, biometric details, photograph and any page containing information indicating the holder has an entitlement to enter or remain in the UK and is not prohibited by their conditions of work from holding the licence.
- All other documents: the document in full, including both sides of a Biometric Residence Permit and a Residence Card (biometric format).

Step 1: Obtain acceptable documents
Lists of acceptable documents for checks

You must undertake a document check in respect of every application for a new licence or to renew, or extend an existing licence, which is made on or after 1 December 2016. Once you have done this, you will only be required to undertake a further document check when the applicant subsequently applies to renew or extend their licence if they have time-limited immigration permission to be in the UK and work, unless you did not retain a copy of the document or documents which indicated that they have no restrictions on their right to stay and work in the UK.

The full range of the documents you may accept for checks is set out in two lists – List A and List B. These lists are contained in Annex A to this guidance. You will note that the lists contain more secure documents such as national passports, biometric residence permits and residence cards (biometric format) – these documents are preferred because they are more secure. Applicants may not hold these documents, so the list also contains other acceptable evidence of immigration status. Please note that a UK driver's licence is not evidence of lawful status and a right to work.

You must obtain an original document, or document combination, specified in one of these lists in order to comply with step 1 of the 3-step check. This is because scanned and photocopied documents make forgeries less easy to identify.

List A contains the range of documents which you may accept for a person who has a permanent right to remain in the UK. This includes UK passports (which may have expired). Following the correct checks, you may grant a licence for a period of up to the maximum statutory period for that type of licence. This is because there are no limitations on the type of work the applicant can undertake, or for how long. When the applicant provides document(s) from List A and you have retained the copy, a further check will not be necessary when they subsequently apply to renew or extend their licence. If you do not retain the copy, you will have to repeat the check when they next apply to renew or extend their licence.

List B contains the range of documents which may be accepted for a person who has a temporary right to be in the UK. If you conduct the check correctly you may issue the licence for a period up to the expiry date of the person's leave indicated by the document, although this must not exceed the maximum statutory period for which such a licence may be issued. You will need to request the original document and check these on each occasion that the applicant subsequently applies to renew or extend their licence until such time as the applicant provides document(s) from List A that demonstrates that they have a permanent right to remain in the UK.

A number of the documents in the list will only demonstrate a right to a licence if the document is current when the check takes place, including passports issued outside the European Economic Area which are endorsed to say that the holder has indefinite leave to remain (ILR) in the UK. Provided the passport endorsed with ILR is current when the check takes place, a licence may be granted up to the statutory maximum even though the passport might time-expire before the licence time-expires. If the passport which is endorsed with ILR is not current when the check takes place, you may invite the applicant to apply to the Home Office for a biometric residence permit. Further information on this application is contained here. Once the application has been made, you may verify this check through the Evidence and Enquiry Unit and, once successfully verified, grant the licence for a maximum period of six months from the date of the verification.

Some documents, such as British passports, do not have to be current in order to demonstrate a right to a licence. However, you still need to check carefully that the document relates to the applicant and, if necessary, request further evidence before issuing the licence. Annex A clearly indicates which documents must be current to demonstrate the right to a licence.

Biometric Residence Permits

For most non-European Economic Area (non-EEA) migrants granted permission to be in the UK, the document you are likely to see to demonstrate a right to work is a Biometric Residence Permit (BRP). The Home Office began issuing BRPs in November 2008. Since July 2015, BRPs have been the only evidence of lawful residence currently issued by the Home Office to most non-EEA nationals and their dependants granted permission to remain in the UK for more than six months.

BRPs are credit-card sized immigration documents that contain a secure embedded chip and incorporate sophisticated security safeguards to combat fraud and tampering. They provide evidence of the holder's immigration status in the UK including the date on which the person's entitlement to work in the UK is due to expire. In most cases, this will be the expiry date of the BRP. However, where the BRP indicates that a person has indefinite leave to enter or remain (ILE or ILR) in the UK, this means that there is no time limit on the holder's ability to live and work in the UK (although the BRP itself is valid for 10 years) after which the holder needs to apply for a replacement). BRPs contain the holder's unique biometric identifiers (fingerprints and digital photo) within the chip, are highly resistant to forgery and counterfeiting, display a photo and biographical information on the face of the document and details of entitlements, such as access to work and/or public funds. BRPs therefore provide you with a secure and simple means to conduct a right to a licence check.

Migrants overseas granted permission to enter the UK for more than six months are issued with a vignette (sticker) in their passport, which will be valid for 30 days, to enable them to travel to the UK. Following their arrival, they will have 10 days or before their vignette expires (whichever is the later) to collect their BRP from the Post Office branch detailed in their decision letter. You should not issue the licence on the basis of the 30 day vignette, but wait until you have seen and checked the related BRP.

Residence cards (biometric format)

From 6 April 2015, we started issuing Residence Cards (including Permanent Residence Cards and Derivative Residence Cards) for non-EEA family members of EEA and Swiss nationals in a biometric format. From this date, we stopped issuing a vignette in the passport or standalone document, though these will continue to be acceptable documents for the purpose of right to work checks, as long as they are valid. The new Residence Cards (biometric format) closely resemble Biometric Residence Permits as indicated above.

Step 2: Check the validity of document(s)

You should check the validity of the original document(s), in the presence of the holder. This may be the physical presence of the applicant or by live video conference. In the event that it is not possible for the applicant to attend in person, you must have the original document(s) at the time you conduct the check against the person by video. Therefore, the document will need to be sent by secure mail or delivered by hand to you beforehand so that it can be checked against the holder. This is to safeguard against a document being presented by someone to whom it does not belong.

Where a person presents a document and it is reasonably apparent that the person presenting the document is not the person referred to in that document, even if the document itself is genuine, you should not accept it as evidence of lawful immigration status and, therefore, the applicant's right to hold a licence.

Some documents, such as UK birth certificates, do not include a photograph. You may consider requesting and checking additional documentary evidence of the person's identity, for example their DVA or DVLA licence. You may accept a UK birth certificate issued by the General Register Office even though it has been endorsed as being "certified to be a true copy of an entry in a register in my custody" or contain words to the same effect.

Guidance on checking documents has been made available to employers, including local authorities as employers, who have a duty to undertake right to work checks on their employees. You may find this helpful and it is available here. Guidance on examining and identifying fraudulent identity documents may be found here. This contains a helpful checklist which has been reproduced in Annex B.

You must perform the check carefully. You must make a visual inspection of the original document, and then check the details and any photograph of the holder against the holder to identify reasonably apparent forgeries and imposters.

You are not required to use artificial aids, such as an ultra violet lamp or a magnifying glass, although you will find such aids useful when performing the check. You may also wish to consider using a commercially available document scanner to help check the authenticity of biometric documents presented to you, notably passports and biometric residence permits (BRPs). Guidance about using such technology is available at this link.

If someone gives you a false document or a genuine document that does not belong to them, you may use this link to report the individual to the Home Office. You may also contact Crimestoppers.

You may obtain further assistance on document types from your Local Partnership Manager (LPM) or email I&SDLPMSsupportTeam@homeoffice. gsi.gov.uk. In most cases, your LPM or your local Immigration, Compliance and Enforcement (ICE) team will also be your first point of contact if you suspect that you have encountered a forged or counterfeit document (though they are unable to respond to requests for immigration status checks. Please see section 3.2 below).

Step 3: Retain a copy of document(s)

You should keep a copy of every document you have checked. This could be a hard or an electronic copy. You should keep the copy securely in accordance with data protection principles. Provided the specified document or documents are in List A, if you retained the copy, you will not have to repeat the check when the licence holder subsequently applies to you to renew or extend their licence.

3.2   Home Office verification checks

In most cases, you should be able to make an assessment that the person is not disqualified from holding a licence by making a visual check of the document(s) against the person presenting them. This will include all cases where the applicant is a British citizen.

If you require an immigration status check, you may contact the Home Office's Evidence and Enquiry Unit. Your Local Partnership Manager will have their contact details. The Evidence and Enquiry Unit will aim to respond to your request within 10 working days.

It is only necessary to contact the Home Office's Evidence and Enquiry Unit in the following circumstances to verify that someone has the right to hold a licence:

1.   You are presented with a Certificate of Application which is less than six months old and indicates that work is permitted; or
2.   You are satisfied that you have not been provided with any acceptable documents because the person has an outstanding application for permission to remain in the UK with the Home Office which was made before their previous immigration leave expired or has an appeal or administrative review pending against a Home Office decision that grants them a right to work and, therefore, cannot provide to you evidence of their right to a licence.

In these two circumstances, the Evidence and Enquiry Unit will confirm the individual's immigration status. You will still have to determine whether the applicant should be granted a licence. A licence issued as a consequence of this check must be limited, as indicated below, to a maximum period of six months. Upon any subsequent application to renew the licence, you must carry out a further document check before issuing the licence. You are prohibited by statute from issuing a licence if a person is disqualified by their immigration status.

If you are making a check because the licence applicant has an outstanding immigration application with the Home Office, or a pending appeal or administrative review against a Home Office decision, we suggest that you wait at least 14 days after the application, appeal or administrative review was made before requesting the Evidence and Enquiry Unit to confirm the status. This is to allow time for that application, appeal or administrative review to be registered with the Home Office.

3.4 Duration of licences

If a person provides you with acceptable documents from List A at Annex A, there is no restriction on their right to work in the UK so their immigration status does not prevent you from issuing them a licence for up to the statutory maximum period. Provided you retained a copy of the document or documents that were originally checked, you will not be required to repeat the check when the applicant applies to renew or extend their licence with you.

If a person provides you with acceptable document(s) from List B, this means that there are restrictions on their right to live and work in the UK. Their licence must not be issued for a period that exceeds their permission to be in the UK (up to the statutory maximum period for that type of licence).

When the licence has been issued on the basis of a Certificate of Application which states that work is permitted and which has been verified by our Evidence and Enquiry Unit, the licence may only be issued for a maximum period of six months from the date of the Certificate of Application.

When the licence has been issued on the basis that the applicant has an outstanding in-time[4] Home Office application, appeal or administrative review which has been verified by our Evidence and Enquiry Unit, the licence may be issued for a maximum period of six months from the date of the licence decision.

[4] An in-time application is one that was submitted before the applicant's earlier immigration permission to be in the UK expired, and so, by operation of statute, extends their permission until a decision has been made on the application.

3.5 When will a licence lapse?

A licence issued in respect of an application made on or after 1 December 2016, will lapse when the holder's permission to be in the UK comes to an end. This could be because their permission to be in the UK has time-expired or because we have brought it to an end (for example, we have curtailed their permission to be in the UK). You are under no duty to carry out on-going immigration checks to see whether a licence holder's permission to be in the

UK has been brought to an end. The migrant will be aware when their time limited permission has come to an end and we will inform them if we curtail their permission to be in the UK.

4. ELIGIBILITY OF CERTAIN CATEGORIES OF MIGRANT TO HOLD LICENCES

It is important to determine that an applicant for a licence is not only in the UK lawfully and has permission to work, but that they are not prevented from undertaking work as a taxi operator or driver.

The following section provides clarification on several specific immigration categories. If you require further advice in relation to these or other immigration categories, you may contact your Local Partnership Manager.

4.1 Tier 1: Entrepreneur

A person granted leave to enter or remain in the UK as a Tier 1 (Entrepreneur) migrant, is prohibited from engaging in employment except where they are working for the business which they have established, joined or taken over. They will comply with this restriction if, for example, they are employed as the director of the business in which they have invested, or if they are working in a genuinely self-employed capacity. They may not, however, be considered to be working for their own business if the work they undertake amounts to no more than employment by another business (for example, where their work is no more than the filling of a position or vacancy with, or the hire of their labour to that business, including where it is undertaken through engagement with a recruitment or employment agency). In this capacity, they would have a contract of service. This applies even if it is claimed that such work is undertaken on a self-employed basis.

You must therefore be satisfied that the applicant is genuinely engaged in running their own business as a taxi operator or driver. You should consider requesting evidence of an applicant's appropriate registration of their business or for self employment with HM Revenue and Customs as part of the consideration of any application. If an applicant is deemed to be effectively an employee and the business is not their own, their application should be rejected.

For more information, please see the policy guidance for Tier 1 (Entrepreneur) on GOV.UK.

4.2 Tier 2: Skilled workers

A person granted immigration leave under Tier 2 as a Skilled Worker is granted permission to work for a specified employer (a sponsor) in a specified capacity. It is unlikely they would qualify for a licence in this sector. A dependant of a Tier 2 migrant may qualify for a licence, as the same restrictions do not apply.

4.3 Tier 4: Students

A Tier 4 student may have permission to work for a limited number of hours during term time whilst studying in the UK, and full time during holidays. There are restrictions in place as to who is eligible to work and this will be indicated in their BRP or passport vignette. This right to work will be dependent on them continuing to follow their course of study. They cannot be self-employed, but they may, however, qualify for a licence if directly employed. Where a Tier 4 student has completed their course, they are only able to work if they were initially given permission to work as part of their conditions as a student, until that permission expires or otherwise comes to an end.

4.4 Asylum seekers

Asylum seekers do not usually have permission to work and when they do, this is only in a shortage occupation which will not involve the PHV and taxi sector and therefore they must not be granted a licence if their application is made on or after 1 December 2016.

An Application Registration Card (ARC) is provided to a person who has claimed asylum in the UK, pending consideration of their case. An ARC may exceptionally state that the holder has a right to work, but this will only be in a shortage occupation. You must not grant a PHV or taxi operator or driver licence on the basis of the ARC. However, you should check whether the asylum seeker has alternative evidence of a right to hold a licence.

A person who has been recognised by the UK as a refugee is issued with a BRP and has no restrictions on their right to work in the UK whilst their BRP remains valid.

4.5 Nationals from the European Economic Area (EEA)

EEA and Swiss nationals have the right to work in the UK. However, you should not issue a licence to any individual simply on the basis that they claim to be an EEA national. You should also be aware that not all EEA nationals are permitted to work in the UK without restrictions (please see separate guidance in respect of Croatian nationals). You should require any person who claims to be an EEA national to produce a valid EEA passport or EEA national identity card that confirms that they are a national of an EEA country or Switzerland.

4.6 Non-EEA Family Members of EEA nationals

Non-EEA nationals who are the direct family members of an EEA (or Swiss) national who is exercising European Union Treaty rights or has permanent residence, are also entitled to live and work in the UK. You should not grant a licence to any individual simply on the basis that they claim to be the family member of an EEA national. You should also be aware that not all family members of EEA nationals are permitted to work in the UK.

There is no mandatory requirement for non-EEA nationals who are resident in the UK as a family member of an EEA national to register with the Home Office or to obtain documentation issued by the Home Office.

Consequently, it is open to any non-EEA national who has an enforceable EU law right to work in the UK – as a direct family member of an EEA national or by virtue of a derivative right of residence – to demonstrate the existence of that right through means other than those documents in Annex A.

In such cases, you may choose to accept such alternative evidence. You should ask to see the following:

- evidence of the applicant's own identity – such as a passport,
- evidence of their relationship with the EEA family member – e.g. a marriage certificate, civil partnership certificate or birth certificate, and
- evidence that the EEA national has a right of permanent residence in the UK or is one of the following if they have been in the UK for more than 3 months:
  (i)   working e.g. employment contract, wage slips, letter from the employer,
  (ii) self-employed e.g. contracts, invoices, or audited accounts with a bank,
  (iii) studying e.g. letter from the school, college or university and evidence of sufficient funds, or
  (iv) self-sufficient e.g. bank statements.

For family members of EEA nationals who are studying or financially independent you must also see evidence that the EEA national and any family members hold comprehensive sickness insurance in the UK. This can include a private medical insurance policy, an EHIC card or an S1, S2 or S3 form.

You must only accept original documents as evidence.

In the event that a non-EEA national is found not to qualify to work in the UK you will have issued a licence which is invalid.

4.7   Croatian nationals

Croatian nationals' access to the UK labour market are subject to transitional arrangements set out in the Accession of Croatia (Immigration and Worker Authorisation) Regulations 2013. Under these Regulations, a Croatian national who wishes to work in the UK and who is subject to the worker authorisation requirement will need to obtain an accession worker authorisation document (permission to work) before starting any employment.

This means that since 1 July 2013, a Croatian national will only be able to work in the UK if they hold a valid accession worker authorisation document (such as a purple registration certificate) or if they are exempt from work authorisation. The list of exempt categories is contained in our guidance.

Croatian students who have been issued with a yellow registration certificate are only permitted to work for 20 hours a week during term time and full time during the holidays.

5. REVOCATION OF LICENCES

We may provide you with information, or you may obtain information from other sources, which will cause you to wish to suspend or revoke a licence on the basis that the licence holder's immigration status has changed on or after 1 December 2016, for example their permission to be in the UK has been curtailed, they have been served with a deportation order or they have been convicted of an immigration offence (generally, but not limited to, convictions under the Immigration Act 1971) or subjected to an immigration penalty which has not been cancelled following an objection or appeal. An immigration penalty will have been issued, for example, because they employed an illegal worker or let premises to someone who does not have a right to rent. Please note that civil penalties may be issued to UK citizens as well as migrants who breach the relevant regulations.

On any appeal relating to an operator or driver licence decision whether it is to grant, revoke or suspend the licence, the court is not entitled to consider whether the licence holder should have been convicted of an immigration offence or received an immigration penalty or should have been granted by the Home Office permission to be in the UK. This is because separate rights of immigration appeal, or to have an immigration decision administratively reviewed, exist.

Upon receiving such information, you may also wish to consider whether the licence holder continues to meet the 'fit and proper' test.

5.1   Return of the licence

The licence holder is required to return the licence to you, once that licence has expired, or been suspended or revoked on immigration grounds. This is underpinned by criminal offences of failing to comply with the return requirement under existing taxi licensing legislation.

If the licence holder, without a reasonable excuse, fails within 7 days to return the licence, badge and any other evidence of identification issued by you to you, they commit an offence. The maximum fine is level 3 on the standard scale.

6. PROVIDING INFORMATION TO THE HOME OFFICE

These new provisions to prevent illegal working in relation to PHV and taxi operator and driver licences, do not specifically mandate licensing authorities to report to the Home Office cases in which you have refused an application for an operator or driver licence or subsequently suspended or revoked a licence on immigration grounds.

However, you are requested to provide the Home Office with this information, in order that other appropriate enforcement action may be taken against a person, including revoking their UK driving licence. This information exchange is supported by section 55 of the Immigration Act 2016 which expands the existing information sharing gateway at section 20 of the Immigration and Asylum Act 1999 (the 1999 Act) and gives public authorities a clear statutory authority to supply information or documents to the Home Office which may be used for immigration purposes. See: Factsheet. Any information should be sent using the template at Annex C to tphlicensing@homoffice.gsi.gov.uk.

In addition, section 20A of the 1999 Act, as amended by section 55 of the 2016 Act, places a duty on local authorities to provide Home Office immigration officials with nationality documents which are in their possession, but only when specifically requested to do so. See: Factsheet. So you may be asked for copies of nationality documents which you have retained as part of the licensing application if they belong to someone who is liable for removal from the UK.

7. DO YOU HAVE ANY QUESTIONS?

In the first instance, please refer to this guidance. You may also wish to look at the further useful information provided in the existing illegal working guidance. Employers already have a duty to do checks. However, as most PHV and taxi licence holders are self employed, their right to work and immigration status is not checked, so through these new provisions and this guidance we aim to prevent illegal working in this sector. When dealing with a licence application, you must check the immigration status of all applicants, including those who are not self employed.

The illegal working guidance is available at:

https://www.gov.uk/government/publications/right-to-work-checks-employers-guide and includes:

- An employer's guide to the administration of the civil penalty scheme;
- An employer's guide to acceptable right to work documents;
- Frequently asked questions;
- Code of practice on preventing illegal working: Civil penalty scheme for employers;
- Code of practice for employers: Avoiding unlawful discrimination while preventing illegal working;
- An employer's 'Right to Work Checklist';
- The online interactive tool 'Employer Checking Service Enquiries; and
- The online interactive tool 'Check if someone can work in the UK'.

Guidance on examining and identifying fraudulent identity documents may be found here

If you have questions about a person's immigration status, you may contact the Home Office's Evidence and Enquiry Unit.

Your Local Partnership Manager will be able to assist you if you with question about document types or if you suspect you have been provided with a forged document. They cannot confirm a person's immigration status.

8. ANNEX A
LISTS OF ACCEPTABLE DOCUMENTS FOR RIGHT TO A LICENCE CHECKS

The lists of documents are based on those prescribed to show evidence of a right to work.

List A: No immigration restrictions on right to a licence in the UK. Once you have undertaken the necessary check once in respect of an application made on or after 1 December 2016, if you retained the copy, you will not have to repeat the check when they subsequently apply to renew or extend their licence.

1.   A passport showing the holder, or a person named in the passport as the child of the holder, is a British citizen or a citizen of the UK and Colonies having the right of abode in the UK.

2.   A passport or national identity card showing the holder, or a person named in the passport as the child of the holder, is a national of a European Economic Area country or Switzerland.

3.   A Registration Certificate or Document Certifying Permanent Residence issued by the Home Office to a national of a European Economic Area country or Switzerland.

4.   A Permanent Residence Card issued by the Home Office to the family member of a national a European Economic Area country or Switzerland.

5.   A current Biometric Immigration Document (Biometric Residence Permit) issued by the Home Office to the holder indicating that the person named is allowed to stay indefinitely in the UK, or has no time limit on their stay in the UK.

6.   A current passport endorsed to show that the holder is exempt from immigration control, is allowed to stay indefinitely in the UK, has the right of abode in the UK, or has no time limit on their stay in the UK.

7.   A current Immigration Status Document issued by the Home Office to the holder with an endorsement indicating that the named person is allowed to stay indefinitely in the UK or has no time limit on their stay in the UK, together with an official document giving the person's permanent National Insurance number and their name issued by a Government agency or a previous employer. An example of an Immigration Status Document may be found here.

8.   A full birth or adoption certificate issued in the UK which includes the name(s) of at least one of the holder's parents or adoptive parents, together with an official document giving the person's permanent National Insurance number and their name issued by a Government agency or a previous employer.

9. A birth or adoption certificate issued in the Channel Islands, the Isle of Man or Ireland, together with an official document giving the person's permanent National Insurance number and their name issued by a Government agency or a previous employer.

10. A certificate of registration or naturalisation as a British citizen, together with an official document giving the person's permanent National Insurance number and their name issued by a Government agency or a previous employer.

List B: Immigration restrictions on the right to a licence in the UK. You may issue the licence (subject to statutory limitations) up to the expiry date of the permission to work in the UK. You will need to check immigration status each time they make an application to renew or extend their licence.

1. A current passport endorsed to show that the holder is allowed to stay in the UK and is currently allowed to do the type of work in question.

2. A current Biometric Immigration Document (Biometric Residence Permit) issued by the Home Office to the holder which indicates that the named person can currently stay in the UK and is allowed to do the work in question.

3. A current Residence Card (including an Accession Residence Card or a Derivative Residence Card) issued by the Home Office to a non-European Economic Area national who is a family member of a national of a European Economic Area country or Switzerland or who has a derivative right of residence.

   This guidance [link to page 16] provides further information on checking a non-European Economic Area national family member's right to a licence.

4. A current Immigration Status Document containing a photograph issued by the Home Office to the holder with a valid endorsement indicating that the named person may stay in the UK, and is allowed to do the type of work in question, together with an official document giving the person's permanent National Insurance number and their name issued by a Government agency or a previous employer.

1. A Certificate of Application issued by the Home Office under regulation 17(3) or 18A (2) of the Immigration (European Economic Area) Regulations 2006, to a family member of a national of a European Economic Area country or Switzerland stating that the holder is permitted to take employment which is less than 6 months old together with Verification from the Home Office Evidence and Enquiry Unit. The licence may be granted for six months from the date of the Certificate of Application.

2. A Verification issued by the Home Office Evidence and Enquiry Unit to you, which indicates that the named person may stay in the UK because they have an in time application, appeal or administrative review and which is outstanding. The licence may be issued for six months from the date of the licence decision.

9. ANNEX B
CHECKLIST ON EXAMINING AND IDENTIFYING FRAUDULENT IDENTITY DOCUMENTS

	Cause for concern?	
	Yes	No
Does the document allow the person to live and work in the UK?		
Is the person presenting the document the same as the image or photograph?		
Is the document genuine or counterfeit? Check for:		
General quality/cover – Is it manufactured to a high standard?		
Watermarks – view the page with a light source, e.g. a torch or lamp		
UV reaction – If a UV light is available, check if the document reacts dull		
Random fibres – Are there random fibres on each of the document's pages?		
Print quality – Is the quality of the print of a high standard (no dots)?		
Intaglio ink on inside cover of passports – Is there raised ink on the document?		
Optically variable ink – Move the document under a light source		
Machine readable zone (font) – If available, use an online MRZ checker		

	Cause for concern?	
	Yes	No
Holographic devices – Move the document under a light source		
Have any pages been substituted? Check for:		
Construction / page alignment / page numbers / page design		
Counterfeit pages (see above)		
Has the photograph / image been substituted? Check for:		
Damage around the photograph / image		
Any safeguards over photograph / image e.g. ink stamp, emboss, laminate		
Correct image type		
Evidence of a second laminate – move the document under a light source		
Have any details been altered? Check for:		
Damage to paper around details e.g. date of birth		
Is the document a fantasy / pseudo document? – Can you find in on the PRADO or EDISON websites?		

Glossary of terms used in Annex B.

Background print – Areas on secure documents which are printed to a high standard. Using magnification, solid lines and detailed designs should be visible.

Intaglio Ink – A printing process which results in the ink having a raised and rough feel and which is found on the inside of most (not all) passports. It often involves a hidden pattern, revealed when the page is viewed at an oblique angle.

MRZ – A machine readable zone which allows for optical character recognition of characters which match a specific font.

Optically Variable Ink – A clear colour change from one colour to another which should be seen when the document is tilted.

Random Fibres – Security fibres which appear randomly across the paper. They can be visible to the naked eye or react when exposed to UV light.

Watermark – Created during the paper manufacturing process by varying the thickness of paper. It should consist of subtle changes in tone and both lighter and darker areas.

Further guidance on examining identity documents and examples of these techniques may be found here.

10. ANNEX C
PHV AND TAXI LICENCE REFERRAL FORM

PHV and taxi driver/operator licence referral form

Please complete the below details and press submit to return to Immigration Enforcement

Licensing Authority Details
Name
Email
Licensing Authority
Date Referred

Individual's details
Home Office Reference (if known)
Surname
Forename(s)
Gender
Nationality
Date of birth
Other known names
Last known address
Postcode
Contact number
Driving licence number
NI Number
Document type presented
Document number

Action taken
Driver or operator licence
First application or renewal
Licence denied or revoked
Date
If revoked, has the licence been returned?

If email doesn't open after clicking button – check whether you see "Security Warning, Macros have been disabled." message above. If yes click options and enable this content.

Email form to the Home Office

Access for wheelchair users to Taxis and Private Hire Vehicles (DfT 2017)

MINISTERIAL FOREWORD

This Government is committed to ensuring that transport works for everyone, including disabled people. Since joining the Department for Transport in 2015, and taking on Ministerial responsibility for transport accessibility, I have made it my mission to challenge the status quo and encourage innovative thinking to improve access to transport across the modes.

I know however, that despite the real improvements which have taken place in recent years, some disabled passengers still face discrimination when attempting to travel. I am clear that this is unacceptable.

Owners of assistance dogs are already protected by provisions in the Equality Act 2010 which make it unlawful to refuse or charge them extra. I want similar protections to apply to wheelchair users, which is why I am delighted that we have commenced the remaining parts of sections 165 and 167 of the Equality Act 2010, making it a criminal offence for drivers of designated taxi and private hire vehicles to refuse to carry passengers in wheelchairs, to fail to provide them with appropriate assistance, or to charge them extra. I hope that in so doing we will send a clear signal to the minority of drivers who think it acceptable to discriminate on grounds of disability that such behaviour will not be tolerated – and, more importantly, to enable wheelchair users to travel with confidence.

Andrew Jones MP,
Parliamentary Under Secretary of State, Department for Transport

1. INTRODUCTION

Status of guidance

1.1 This guidance document has been issued in order to assist local licensing authorities (LAs) in the implementation of legal provisions intended to assist passengers in wheelchairs in their use of designated taxi and private hire vehicle (PHV) services. It provides advice on designating vehicles as being wheelchair accessible so that the new protections can apply, communicating with drivers regarding their new responsibilities and handling requests from drivers for exemptions from the requirements.

1.2 This is a statutory guidance document, issued under section 167(6) of the Equality Act 2010 and constitutes the Secretary of State's formal guidance to LAs in England, Wales and Scotland on the application of sections 165 to 167 of the Equality Act 2010. LAs must have regard to this guidance document.

2. PUTTING THE LAW INTO PRACTICE

Background

2.1   We have commenced sections 165 and 167 of the Equality Act 2010 ("the Act"), in so far as they were not already in force. Section 167 of the Act provides LAs with the powers to make lists of wheelchair accessible vehicles (i.e. "designated vehicles"), and section 165 of the Act then requires the drivers of those vehicles to carry passengers in wheelchairs, provide assistance to those passengers and prohibits them from charging extra.

2.2   The requirements of section 165 do not apply to drivers who have a valid exemption certificate and are displaying a valid exemption notice in the prescribed manner. An exemption certificate can be issued under section 166 of the Act, which is already in force. This allows LAs to exempt drivers from the duties under section 165 where it is appropriate to do so, on medical grounds or because the driver's physical condition makes it impossible or unreasonably difficult for them to comply with those duties.

2.3   On 15th September 2010, the Department for Transport issued guidance on the Act which stated, in relation to section 167, "although the list of designated vehicles will have no actual effect in law until the duties are commenced, we would urge licensing authorities to start maintaining a list as soon as possible for the purpose of liaising with the trade and issuing exemption certificates".

2.4   We therefore recognise that may LAs have already implemented some of these provisions, including publishing lists of wheelchair accessible vehicles and exempting drivers. Therefore, there are likely to be a range of approaches being used in practice by LAs across England, Wales and Scotland.

Transitionary arrangements

2.5   We want to ensure that the commencement of sections 165 and 167 of the Act has a positive impact for passengers in wheelchairs, ensures they are better informed about the accessibility of designated taxis and PHVs in their area, and confident of receiving the assistance they need to travel safely.

2.6   But we recognise that LAs will need time to put in place the necessary procedures to exempt drivers with certain medical conditions from providing assistance where there is good reason to do so, and to make drivers aware of these new requirements. In addition, LAs will need to ensure that their new procedures comply with this guidance, and that exemption notices are issued in accordance with Government regulations. This will ensure that we get a consistent approach and the best outcomes for passengers in wheelchairs.

2.7   As such, we would encourage LAs to put in place sensible and manageable transition procedures to ensure smooth and effective implementation of this new law. LAs should only publish lists of wheelchair accessible vehicles for the purposes of section 165 of the Act when they are confident that those procedures have been put in place, drivers and owners notified of the new requirements and given time to apply for exemptions where appropriate. We would expect these arrangements to take no more than a maximum of six months to put in place, following the commencement of these provisions, but this will of course be dependent on individual circumstances.

2.8   A flowchart setting out the sorts of processes that a LA could follow is set out below. This is an indicative illustration, and it will be down to each LA to determine the actions they need to take to ensure this new law is implemented effectively in their area.

Licensing Authorities review this guidance document and compare against any existing policies

⬇

Licensing Authorities prepare draft lists of designated wheelchair accessible vehicles

⬇

Licensing Authorities set out policies for exempting drivers on medical and physical condition grounds

⬇

Licensing Authorities inform owners that their vehicles will be placed on the list and alert drivers to their upcoming duties

⬇

Drivers apply for exemptions where necessary

⬇

Licensing authority issues exemptions

⬇

Licensing authority publishes list of designated wheelchair accessible vehicles and duties on drivers take effect

3. VEHICLES

Overview

3.1   Section 167 of the Act permits, but does not require, LAs to maintain a designated list of wheelchair accessible taxis and PHVs.

3.2 Whilst LAs are under no specific legal obligation to maintain a list under section 167, the Government recommends strongly that they do so. Without such a list the requirements of section 165 of the Act do not apply, and drivers may continue to refuse the carriage of wheelchair users, fail to provide them with assistance, or to charge them extra.

Vehicles that can be designated

3.3 We want to ensure that passengers in wheelchairs are better informed about the accessibility of the taxi and PHV fleet in their area, confident of receiving the assistance they need to travel safely, and not charged more than a non-wheelchair user for the same journey.

3.4 The Act states that a vehicle can be included on a licensing authority's list of designated vehicles if it conforms to such accessibility requirements as the licensing authority thinks fit. However, it also goes on to explain that vehicles placed on the designated list should be able to carry passengers in their wheelchairs should they prefer.

3.5 This means that to be placed on a licensing authority's list a vehicle must be capable of carrying some – but not necessarily all – types of occupied wheelchairs. The Government therefore recommends that a vehicle should only be included in the authority's list if it would be possible for the user of a "reference wheelchair"[1] to enter, leave and travel in the passenger compartment in safety and reasonable comfort whilst seated in their wheelchair.

3.6 Taking this approach allows the provisions of section 165 of the Act apply to a wider range of vehicles and more drivers than if LAs only included on the list vehicles capable of taking a larger type of wheelchair.

3.7 The Government recognises that this approach will mean that some types of wheelchair, particularly some powered wheelchairs, may be unable to access some of the vehicles included in the LA's list. The Act recognises this possibility, and section 165(9) provides a defence for the driver if it would not have been possible for the wheelchair to be carried safely in the vehicle. Paragraph 3.10 of this guidance below aims to ensure that users of larger wheelchairs have sufficient information about the vehicles that will be available to them to make informed choices about their journeys.

[1] As defined in Schedule 1 of the Public Service Vehicle Accessibility Regulations 2000

Preparing and publishing lists of designated vehicles

3.8 We want to ensure that passengers in wheelchairs have the information they need to make informed travel choices, and also that drivers and vehicle owners are clear about the duties and responsibilities placed on them.

3.9 Before drivers can be subject to the duties under section 165 of the Act, the LA must first publish their list of designated vehicles, and clearly mark it as 'designated for the purposes of section 165 of the Act'.

3.10   LAs should ensure that their designated lists are made easily available to passengers, and that vehicle owners and drivers are made aware. Lists should set out the details of the make and model of the vehicle, together with specifying whether the vehicle is a taxi or private hire vehicle, and stating the name of operator. Where possible it would also be helpful to include information about the size and weight of wheelchair that can be accommodated, and whether wheelchairs that are larger than a "reference wheelchair" can be accommodated.

3.11   However, we recognise that some passengers in wheelchairs may prefer to transfer from their wheelchair into the vehicle and stow their wheelchair in the boot. Although the legal requirement for drivers to provide assistance does not extend to the drivers of vehicles that cannot accommodate a passenger seated in their wheelchair, we want to ensure that these passengers are provided with as much information as possible about the accessibility of the taxi and PHV fleet in their area.

3.12   We would therefore recommend that LAs also publish a list of vehicles that are accessible to passengers in wheelchairs who are able to transfer from their wheelchair into a seat within the vehicle. It should be made clear however that this list of vehicles has not been published for the purposes of section 165 of the Act and drivers of those vehicles are therefore not subject to the legal duties to provide assistance. Authorities may however wish to use existing licensing powers to require such drivers to provide assistance, and impose licensing sanctions where this does not occur.

Appeals

3.13   Section 172 of the Act enables vehicle owners to appeal against the decision of a LA to include their vehicles on the designated list. That appeal should be made to the Magistrate's Court, or in Scotland the sheriff, and must be made within 28 days of the vehicle in question being included on the LA's published list.

4. DRIVERS

Driver responsibilities

4.1   Section 165 of the Act sets out the duties placed on drivers of designated wheelchair accessible taxis and PHVs.

4.2   The duties are:
- to carry the passenger while in the wheelchair;
- not to make any additional charge for doing so;
- if the passenger chooses to sit in a passenger seat to carry the wheelchair;
- to take such steps as are necessary to ensure that the passenger is carried in safety and reasonable comfort; and
- to give the passenger such mobility assistance as is reasonably required.

4.3   The Act then goes on to define mobility assistance as assistance:
- To enable the passenger to get into or out of the vehicle;
- If the passenger wishes to remain in the wheelchair, to enable the passenger to get into and out of the vehicle while in the wheelchair;
- To load the passenger's luggage into or out of the vehicle;
- If the passenger does not wish to remain in the wheelchair, to load the wheelchair into or out of the vehicle.

4.4   Once the duties are commenced, it will be an offence for the driver (unless exempt) of a taxi or PHV which is on the licensing authority's designated list to fail to comply with them. We encourage LAs to provide drivers of taxis and PHVs who are not exempt from the duties with clear guidance on their duties with respect to the carriage of passengers in wheelchairs, either as part of existing driver-facing guidance, or as supplementary communication. The Disabled Persons Transport Advisory Committee's Disability Equality and Awareness Training Framework for Transport Staff[2] may provide a useful resource.

4.5   Although each situation will be different, we take the view that reasonable mobility assistance will be subject to other applicable law, including health and safety legislation. However, we would always expect drivers to provide assistance such as folding manual wheelchairs and placing them in the luggage compartment, installing the boarding ramp, or securing a wheelchair within the passenger compartment.

4.6   Depending on the weight of the wheelchair and the capability of the driver, reasonable mobility assistance could also include pushing a manual wheelchair or light electric wheelchair up a ramp, or stowing a light electric wheelchair in the luggage compartment.

4.7   It is our view that the requirement not to charge a wheelchair user extra means that, in practice, a meter should not be left running whilst the driver performs duties required by the Act, or the passenger enters, leaves or secures their wheelchair within the passenger compartment. We recommend that licensing authority rules for drivers are updated to make clear when a meter can and cannot be left running.

[2]   http://webarchive.nationalarchives.gov.uk/20080804135759/http:/www.dptac.gov.uk/education/stafftraining/pdf/trainingframework-nontabular.pdf

Applying for and issuing exemptions

4.8   Some drivers may have a medical condition or a disability or physical condition which makes it impossible or unreasonably difficult for them to provide the sort of physical assistance which these duties require. That is why the Act allows LAs to grant exemptions from the duties to individual drivers. These provisions are contained in section 166, and were commenced on 1st October 2010.

4.9   Section 166 allows LAs to exempt drivers from the duties to assist passengers in wheelchairs if they are satisfied that it is appropriate to do so on medical or physical grounds. The exemption can be valid for as short or long a time period as the LA thinks appropriate, bearing in mind the nature of the medical issue. If exempt, the driver will not be required to perform any of the duties. Since October 2010, taxi and PHV drivers who drive wheelchair accessible taxis or PHVs have therefore been able to apply for exemptions. If they do not do so already, LAs should put in place a system for assessing drivers and a system for granting exemption certificates for those drivers who they consider should be exempt.

4.10 We suggest that authorities produce application forms which can be submitted by applicants along with evidence supporting their claim. We understand that some licensing authorities have already put in place procedures for accessing and exempting drivers, and as an absolute minimum, we think that the evidence provided should be in the form of a letter or report from a general practitioner.

4.11 However, the Government's view is that decisions on exemptions will be fairer and more objective if medical assessments are undertaken by professionals who have been specifically trained and who are independent of the applicant. We would recommend that independent medical assessors are used where a long-term exemption is to be issued, and that LAs use assessors who hold appropriate professional qualifications and who are not open to bias because of a personal or commercial connection to the applicant. LAs may already have arrangements with such assessors, for example in relation to the Blue Badge Scheme.

4.12 If the exemption application is successful then the LA should issue an exemption certificate and provide an exemption notice for the driver to display in their vehicle. As section 166 has been in force since 2010, many LAs will already have processes in place for issuing exemption certificates, and as such we do not intend to prescribe the form that those certificates should take. We are however keen to ensure that passengers in wheelchairs are able to clearly discern whether or not a driver has been exempted from the duties to provide assistance, and as such will prescribe the form of and manner of exhibiting a notice of exemption.

4.13 If the exemption application is unsuccessful we recommend that the applicant is informed in writing within a reasonable timescale and with a clear explanation of the reasons for the decision.

Demonstrating exemptions

4.14 In addition to the exemption certificate, exempt drivers need to be issued with a notice of exemption for display in their vehicle.

4.15 The Department will soon make regulations which will prescribe the form of and manner of exhibiting a notice of exemption. Where a driver has been exempted from the duties under section 165 of the Act, they must display an exemption notice in the vehicle they are driving in the form and manner prescribed by the regulations. If the notice is not displayed then the driver could be prosecuted if they do not comply with the duties under section 165 of the Act.

4.16 The Department aims to distribute copies of the notice of exemption to LAs, but they are of course free to produce their own in accordance with the regulations.

4.17 Only one exemption notice should be displayed in a vehicle at any one time.

Appeals

4.18 Section 172 of the Act enables drivers to appeal against the decision of a LA not to issue an exemption certificate. That appeal should be made to the Magistrate's Court, or a sheriff in Scotland, and must be made within 28 days beginning with the date of the refusal.

4.19 LAs may choose to establish their own appeal process in addition to the statutory process but this would need to be undertaken rapidly in order to allow any formal appeal to the Magistrate's Court to be made within the 28 day period.

5. ENFORCEMENT

Licensing measures and prosecution

5.1 It is important to note that a driver will be subject to the duties set out in section 165 of the Equality Act 2010 if the vehicle they are driving appears on the designated list of the LA that licensed them, and the LA has not provided them with an exemption certificate, regardless of where the journey starts or ends.

5.2 The Government expects LAs to take tough action where drivers breach their duties under section 165 of the Act.

5.3 LAs have wide-ranging powers to determine the rules by which taxis and private hire vehicles within their respective areas may operate. We recommend that they use these powers to ensure that drivers who discriminate against disabled passengers are held accountable.

5.4 If a driver receives a conviction for breaching their duties under section 165 of the Act, it would be appropriate for the authority to review whether or not they remained a fit and proper person to hold a taxi or PHV drivers' licence. The Government's presumption is that a driver who wilfully failed to comply with section 165 would be unlikely to remain a "fit and proper person".

5.5 Authorities might also apply conditions which enable them to investigate cases of alleged discrimination and take appropriate action, even where prosecution did not proceed.

A2.8

Regulation of taxis and private hire vehicles: understanding the impact on competition (Competition and Markets Authority April 2017)

Regulation of taxis and private hire vehicles: understanding the impact on competition

April 2017

About the Competition and Markets Authority

CMA
Competition & Markets Authority

- On 1 April 2014, the Competition and Markets Authority (CMA) became the UK's lead competition and consumer body. The CMA brought together the competition and consumer protection functions of the Office of Fair Trading and the Competition Commission

- The CMA has a statutory duty to seek to promote competition for the benefit of consumers. The CMA has an advocacy function, which involves giving information or advice to public authorities on the impact on competition of public policy.

- As part of this work, HM Treasury has asked the CMA to consider how local authorities can support competition, and to challenge them when they do not.

www.gov.uk/government/organisations/competition-and-markets-authority

The purpose of this guidance note

CMA
Competition & Markets Authority

- As part of our work on local authorities' impact on competition, the CMA has undertaken a review of taxi and PHV licensing conditions.

- The CMA recognises that taxi and PHV licensing conditions play a crucial role in ensuring the safety of passengers. Regulations on vehicle safety and driver suitability are clearly necessary to ensure safety.

- This guide is designed to help local authorities understand the impact some licensing conditions can have on consumers and hence help to reach the right balance between ensuring passenger safety and avoiding consumers having to face higher prices or lower service quality.

- The CMA has found that some licensing conditions are likely to restrict or distort competition in ways that may result in higher prices and/or worse service for consumers.

- The CMA recognises that licensing authorities face competing pressures and tough decisions over how to strike the right balance.

- The CMA's short report on the impact that licensing conditions can have on consumer welfare is available on request.

Competition and regulation

CMA
Competition & Markets Authority

- Competition is a process of rivalry between firms that benefits consumers. Competition can exert downward pressure on prices and upward pressure on quality, because greater competition means that firms must fight harder to attract and retain customers.

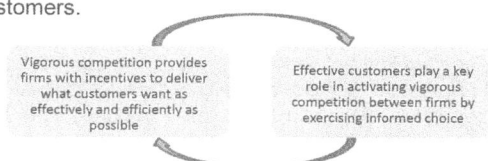

> Vigorous competition provides firms with incentives to deliver what customers want as effectively and efficiently as possible

> Effective customers play a key role in activating vigorous competition between firms by exercising informed choice

- Effective and fair competition is underpinned by competition and consumer protection laws which govern how businesses can compete.

- Government may impose additional regulations in a market where, for example, there are concerns around consumer safety.

- The CMA's view is that competition should only be restricted by regulatory rules to the extent that is necessary to protect consumers.

- This guide illustrates how some licensing conditions can affect consumers' interests, in order to help ensure conditions are targeted and proportionate.

Background

CMA
Competition & Markets Authority

- The CMA's understanding of the hackney carriage and PHV markets is informed by the OFT's 2003 market study and the subsequent impact evaluation in 2007, the examination of a merger between private hire operators in Sheffield and our recent evidence review and analysis of licensing conditions. We also considered the 2014 Law Commission report on Taxi and Private Hire services.

- The OFT's 2003 market study found, among other things, that:
  - Passengers are in a relatively weak position to compare offers and negotiate prices in the hail and rank (taxi) trade. There is therefore a need for fare regulation of taxis. This also provides a justification for greater regulation of service standards of taxis compared to PHVs.
  - Quantity regulations on taxis are not necessary to ensure either the safety or quality of taxis, or that passengers are charged reasonable fares. However, quantity regulations may damage consumer welfare by reducing the availability and increasing waiting times for taxis.

- As part of our review of licensing conditions, the CMA has written to several licensing authorities, including Transport for London[1] and Sheffield City Council[2], to highlight where conditions may restrict competition and harm consumer welfare.

[1] CMA response to TfL consultation
[2] CMA letter to Sheffield City Council

CMA view of taxi and private hire trades (1 of 2)

CMA — Competition & Markets Authority

The two tier system

- Taxis' right to ply for hire necessitates different regulation for taxis and PHVs. Passengers are in a weak position to judge the quality or to compare prices of taxis; it is therefore necessary to regulate taxi fares (and service standards).
- The scope for competition between taxis and PHVs, increasing with the emergence of app-based models, can deliver benefits for passengers. To facilitate this, regulatory distinctions between taxis and PHVs should not go beyond what is required by legislation or necessary to protect passengers.

Private Hire

- Passengers are in a better position to assess the quality and compare the prices of private hire operators than they are with taxis. Competition can generally work well between private hire operators.
- There is a need to ensure passenger safety, but licensing conditions that go beyond this may reduce passenger choice, and increase cost and prices.
- Some conditions may also create barriers to entry, reducing the number of operators, and hence reducing competitive pressure on operators to reduce prices or improve service quality.

CMA view of taxi and private hire trades (2 of 2)

CMA — Competition & Markets Authority

Hackney carriages

- As noted above, there is a need to regulate the prices and service standards of taxis, owing to their unique right to ply for hire. There is also a need, as with the private hire trade, to ensure the safety of passengers.
- Quantity restrictions are not necessary to ensure the safety of passengers, or to ensure that fares are reasonable. However, they can harm passengers by reducing availability, increasing waiting times, and reducing the scope for downward competitive pressure on fares.
- The CMA takes the view that concerns around congestion, air pollution and enforcement costs can generally be addressed through measures less harmful to passengers' interests than quantity restrictions.
- If the removal of quantity restrictions leads to increased waiting times for taxi drivers between journeys, this indicates that price competition which would benefit passengers is not occurring. Licensing authorities should monitor waiting times and consider adjusting the regulated fare cap to address mismatches between supply and demand. Addressing such mismatches is likely to benefit passengers.

Licensing conditions that can have negative impacts on consumers

CMA
Competition & Markets Authority

- The CMA's competition impact assessment guidelines can help those designing policy or regulations to assess their impact on competition and the interests of consumers.
- These guidelines contain four tests which help policy makers assess whether their proposals will limit competition:
  1. Will the measures directly or indirectly limit the number or range of suppliers?
  2. Will the measure limit the ability of suppliers to compete?
  3. Will the measure limit suppliers' incentives to compete?
  4. Will the measure limit the choices and information available to consumers?
- Considering these questions will help ensure local authorities are aware of the restrictions they may be introducing on competition and may encourage them to consider alternative courses of action where possible.

www.gov.uk/government/publications/competition-impact-assessment-guidelines-for-policymakers

Examples of conditions that may harm the interests of passengers (1 of 2)

CMA
Competition & Markets Authority

Competition Impact Assessment test	Examples	Nature of harm
1. Limiting the number or range of suppliers	Quantity restrictions on taxis	Quantity restrictions may cause harm to passengers through reduced availability, increased waiting times, reduced scope for downward competitive pressure on fares and reduced choice. They also may increase the risk to passenger safety if they encourage the use of illegal, unlicensed drivers and vehicles.
1. Limiting the number or range of suppliers	Restricting market development by: - Banning drivers from working for more than one operator - Conditions on vehicle signage that make it difficult for drivers to work for more than one operator	Such conditions make it difficult for firms to enter the market or expand by recruiting existing drivers on a part time basis. They may also encourage drivers to move to the largest operator. This may reduce the number of firms, thereby reducing competitive pressure to reduce prices or improve service quality.
2 & 3. Limiting the ability and incentives of suppliers to compete	Service provision is over-regulated beyond passenger needs/wants: - Compulsory landline helpline, sometimes having to be based within the authority - Minimum number of days advance booking function - Extensive navigational skills assessments for PHV drivers	Private hire is a market where passengers are likely to be in a good position to trade off price and quality levels that best suit their needs. If sufficient numbers of passengers desire a high service standard, then it is likely that some operators will offer it. Over-regulation of service standards is likely to mean higher costs and therefore higher fares for passengers, especially those who would most value a low cost service. It may also create barriers to entry, thereby reducing the number of operators, and hence competitive pressure between them.

Examples of conditions that may harm the interests of passengers (2 of 2)

CMA
Competition & Markets Authority

Competition Impact Assessment test	Example	Nature of harm
2 & 3. Limiting the ability and incentives of suppliers to compete	Introducing restrictions on business models or unnecessary distinction between conditions imposed on PHVs and taxis: - Prescribing the method in which pre-booked fares should be recorded (eg written records) - Restrictions on advertising products on vehicles - Restrictions on where PHVs can park - Requirement to specify *exact* fare in advance - Approval required for any changes to operating model	Restrictions on how PHV operators must operate are likely to reduce innovation that could reduce costs or improve the quality of service for passengers. Conditions that apply to PHV operators and not to taxis may increase, relatively, PHV operating costs. Such conditions may therefore make it harder for PHV operators to attract passengers who might otherwise use taxis, potentially resulting in passengers paying higher fares or receiving lower service quality.
4. Limiting choices and information available to consumers	Banning aspects of service valued by passengers: - Displays of vehicle availability in-app - Compulsory minimum waiting times between booking and journey start	Banning aspects of service that passengers might find valuable is likely to directly harm their welfare.

What to do if you are considering reviewing your licensing regime

CMA
Competition & Markets Authority

- Ensure your proposed measures are necessary to achieve your objective(s)
- Consider the questions set out in the CMA's competition impact assessment guidelines
- Where measures are likely to restrict competition and harm consumer welfare, consider whether alternative, less-restrictive measures could be employed to achieve your objective(s) and if not, whether the objectives really do necessitate the restriction
- The CMA's short report which contains further detail and information on our view on taxi and PHV licensing conditions is available on request.
- If you would like to discuss these issues, including issues not addressed in this review, you can contact advocacy@cma.gsi.gov.uk for further advice.

Joint Circular from the DOT
Circular 3/85, 4 December 1985
Scottish Development Department
Circular 32/85
WO Circular 64/85

TRANSPORT ACT 1985

INTRODUCTION

1. This circular describes the provisions of the Transport Act 1985 as they affect local authorities in Great Britain though it does not purport to provide an interpretation of the law. It also explains the steps by which it is intended to bring in the new arrangements. Separate circulars, DTp 4/85 (WO 63/85) for England and Wales and SDD 30/85 for Scotland, describe the provisions about local authority and Passenger Transport Executive ('PTE') bus undertakings and their transfer to public transport companies and contain the statutory advice of the Secretary of State under sections 59, 68 and 69. The Departments will also be issuing shortly a Code of Practice on Tendering, and further guidance on concessionary fare schemes. A list of these and other proposed Departmental publications about the Act is at Annex 1.

Interpretation

2. References throughout this circular to county councils should be read as meaning non-metropolitan councils in Scotland. 'The Act' means the Transport Act 1985 and references to sections are to sections of that Act 1985 and references to sections are to sections of that Act unless otherwise stated. 'London' means the present administrative area of Greater London. 'The 1968 Act' means the Transport Act 1968 and 'the 1981 Act' means the Public Passenger Vehicles Act 1981.

Main provisions of the Act

3. The purpose of the Act is to establish the disciplines of a competitive market in the provision of local bus services. To achieve this the Act –

(1) in Parts I and II abolishes road service licensing everywhere in Great Britain outside London and replaces it with a system of registration; and reduces the barriers between bus and taxi operations;

(2) in Part III provides for the reorganisation and privatisation of the National Bus Company and its subsidiaries;

(3) in Part IV revises the public transport powers and responsibilities of local authorities and PTEs to suit competitive conditions; and

provides for the transfer of existing local authority and PTE bus undertakings to public transport companies at arms length from their parent authorities;

(4) in Part V sets out new requirements for co–operation between social services, education and public transport authorities, and for tendering for subsidised local services; and contains provisions about travel concession schemes, and about certain grants;

(5) in Part VI applies to the bus industry various provisions of existing competition law and covers various miscellaneous matters;

(6) in schedule 6 sets out the arrangements for the transition from the old system to the new. The transitional period will run from 6 January to 25 October 1986.

This Act does not weaken the existing requirements for PSV operator licences and driver licences for vehicles and maintenance standards; these essential quality controls remain intact. Indeed, the Act contains some additional powers to control the behaviour of operators of local services.

Implementation

4. Authorities with public transport responsibilities have a heavy programme of work throughout 1986 to implement the Act. Many are already well advanced in their planning. Authorities' attention is particularly drawn to two matters on which very prompt action will need to be taken. The first is the preparation of new public transport policies and consultation on those policies, including specific consideration of the scope for co–ordination with education and social services transport. The requirements are set our in paragraphs 43 – 50, 65 – 70 and 81 – 86; these affect PTAs and county councils. Only when those policies are settled, can these authorities proceed to secure the particular services, which require subsidy through a process of open tendering. The tendering is to be completed by 26 October 1986. Authorities will no doubt wish to complete the policy formulation stage by Easter 1986 at the latest. The second area needing quick action is the publication by 8 April 1986 of proposed concessionary fare schemes, for those authorities who wish to have power to compel operators to participate in them. This is set out in paragraphs 114 and 115.

PART I: GENERAL PROVISIONS RELATING TO ROAD PASSENGER TRANSPORT

Note. Paragraphs 5–18 are not relevant to hackney carriage and private hire licensing.

Taxis and hire cars

19. Sections 10 to 17 deal with (taxis and hire cars. Apart from section 12, this circular is concerned only with those provisions as they affect taxi and hire car operation in England and Wales. The Scottish Development Department will be issuing a separate circular for Scotland in due course.

Sharing of taxis & hire cars in England and Wales

20. Sections 10 and 11 provide for the sharing of taxis and hire cars in England and Wales by passengers paying separate fares. Section 10 provides for taxi sharing schemes and section 11 allows pre-booked passengers to be carried at separate fares in licensed taxis and licensed hire cars. These sections will be brought into force in early Summer 1986 with the necessary regulations and orders. Discussions are already taking place with the Association of District Councils and Association of Metropolitan Authorities about the future advice to be given to taxi licensing authorities about taxi sharing schemes made under section 10.

Taxis providing local services: special licences

21. Section 12 lays down conditions under which taxis may be used to provide local services throughout Great Britain. In line with the other provisions relating to local services, this section will be brought into force on January 6. Vehicles operated under section 12 will be subject to hybrid controls. Vehicle quality and safety standards will continue to be the responsibility of the district council, as the taxi licensing authority. The service will, like any other local service, be subject to regulation by the traffic commissioner. Since such control may be exercised by means of conditions attached to the operator's licence, this section makes provision for a taxi proprietor to obtain a 'special licence' under conditions, which recognise that he has already satisfied his district council of his suitability to operate passenger carrying services. The object of this section is, therefore, to put a taxi proprietor wishing to operate local services on the same footing as a bus operator – making him subject to equivalent but not identical controls.

22. The holder of a taxi licence will from 6 January be able to apply to the traffic commissioner for a special PSV operator's licence which will enable him to register local services (whether those provided without subsidy or ones to be provided under a contract for service subsidies with a local authority or PTE). A local authority can consider a tender from a taxi proprietor who has not yet obtained his special licence but will not be able to award a contract until he has done so. During the transitional period a holder of a special PSV operator's licence will be able to apply for a road service licence just like any other PSV operator's licence holder. Regulations governing the operation of vehicles under section 12 will be in place by 1 March 1986 to permit service to be provided under road service licences from that date.

Taxis providing local services in London

23. Similar arrangements will apply in London, where the Assistant Commissioner of the Metropolitan Police, as the taxi licensing authority, will be responsible for ensuring quality control of taxis used to provide local services. Holding a special PSV operator's licence will enable the holder of a London taxi licence to operate local services from 1 March 1986 under agreement with London Regional Transport or under a London local service licence granted under Part II of the Act.

Section 13

24. Section 13 will be brought into force on 6 January in order to provide the definitions required by section 12. Regulations made under section 13 will modify the taxi and hire car codes as they apply to vehicles operated under sections 10 and 11. These regulations will be brought into force with those sections.

Extension of taxi licensing In England and Wales

25. Section 15 extends taxi licensing to all districts and parts of districts in England DOT Circular 3/85, SDD Circular 32/85, WO Circular 64/85 and Wales where there is no such licensing at present. The section will be brought into force later. District councils which license taxis in part or parts only of their area may wish to reconsider their policy on this matter with a view to rationalising their arrangements for taxi licensing before this section is brought into force. This would be achieved by resolution made under paragraph 25 of schedule 14 to the Local Government Act 1972 and, if appropriate, section 45 of the Local Government (Miscellaneous Provisions) Act 1976. The Department is willing to advise any district council on the procedure necessary and on the way in which they might implement taxi licensing.

Grant of taxi licences: vehicles with 8 passenger seats

26. Section 16 will also be brought into effect on 6 January. This section Qualifies the power which district councils now have under the Town Police Clauses Act 1847 to refuse to grant taxi licences in support of a policy of limiting the number of taxis in their area. Under the section a district may refuse an application for a licence in order to limit the number of taxis if, but only if, they are satisfied that there is no significant unmet demand for taxi services within the area to which the licence would apply. An applicant whose licence is refused by a district council has a right of appeal to the Crown Court. The section does not require district councils to limit the number of taxis licences they issue for this reason; it forbids them to restrict numbers for any other reason. The powers of district councils to refuse licences or put conditions on them, relating to the fitness of the applicant or his vehicle are undiminished. In view of the fact that these vehicles may now be authorised to carry passengers at separate fares, district councils may wish to review the conditions of fitness laid down for these vehicles and the enforcement of maintenance standards. The attention of district councils is drawn to the provisions of paragraph 1 of schedule 7, which establishes that taxis may be licensed with up to eight passenger seats.

Advice on the grant of taxi licences

27. District councils may wish to review their policy on the control of taxi numbers in the light of the section. Limitation of taxi numbers can have many undesirable effects – an insufficiency of taxis, either generally or at particular times or in particular places; insufficient competition between the providers of

taxi services, to the detriment of their customers; and prices for the transfer of taxi licences from one person to another which imply an artificial restriction of supply. Under the section a district council may refuse a licence to restrict numbers only if satisfied that there is not significant unmet demand for taxis in the relevant area. If there is an appeal, it will be for the council to convince the court that they had reasonable grounds for being so satisfied. It will not, in general, be sufficient for a district council to rely on the assertion of existing taxi licence holders that the demand is already catered for. They have evidence only of the demand, which they satisfy, and it will be for the council themselves to seek for and examine the evidence of unmet demand. There may be those who have given up trying to use taxis because of the inadequacy of the service and there may be latent demand in parts of a district that have not been adequately served – where those who wish to use taxis may not have demonstrated their demand since there had been no opportunity of having it satisfied. Moreover, if the applicant for a new taxi licence proposed to use it to provide a new service – for instance under section 12 – and had reasonable grounds to believe that there would be demand for his service if he provided it, a council which wished to refuse a licence would have to satisfy themselves that that demand would not be forthcoming. Overcrowding at taxis ranks is not of itself evidence that there is no unmet demand. It may be that the provision of ranks has hitherto been too limited and the council should look actively for sites for further ranks.

28. There are a number of district councils which already exercise no control on the number of taxis in their areas without causing problems of over–supply. However, the Department accepts that in some areas the total abandonment of quantity control could lead to an initial over–supply of taxis before market forces could bring about an equilibrium between supply and demand. In order to avoid possible disruption, a district council faced with a large number of new applicants could, in the Department's view, reasonably grant a proportion of the applications, deferring consideration of the remainder until the effects of granting the first tranche could be assessed.

A2.10

DOT Circular 7/86, 18 December 1986

TRANSPORT ACT 1985: THE SHARING OF TAXIS AND HIRE CARS

Contents   **Paragraph**

INTRODUCTION

1. This Circular contains guidance for local authorities in England (outside London) and Wales on the provisions contained in the Transport Act 1985 'the 1985 Act' under which licensed taxis or hire cars may he used to carry passengers at separate fares. It has no legal force. Whilst every care has been taken in composing the descriptions of the various legislative provisions, those descriptions should not be taken as authoritative interpretations of the provisions. Authorities should seek their own advice on the precise interpretation of the legislation. The arrangement applying in Scotland is the subject of a separate circular (No 25/1986) issued by the Scottish Development Department.

2. Prior to the 1985 Act, the sharing of taxis and hire cars was permitted under the conditions laid down in Part I of Schedule I to the Public Passenger Vehicles Act 1981 ('the 1981 Act'). These permitted a group of people travelling together to agree among themselves to contribute to a single fare for the hire of the vehicle but, in particular, prohibited the driver from initiating the arrangement. Sharing was also permitted under an arrangement approved by a County Council (or Metropolitan District Council) for the provision of services designed to meet the social and welfare needs of one or more communities. The relevant paragraphs of Schedule 1 to the 1981 Act have nor been repealed and taxis and hire cars may continue to be shared in accordance with those conditions. These are set out at Annex A.

3. Taxi and hire car sharing could also be authorised by county councils under the provisions of Sections 47 to 49 of the 1981 Act. These provided for the authorisation of individual services in specially designated 'Experimental Areas'. In view of the more general provisions of the 1985 Act, Sections 47 to 49 of the 1981 Act were repealed with effect from 26 October 1986.

4. The effect of the 1985 Act was to extend greatly the circumstances under which taxis and hire cars may be used to provide shared services. For England and Wales, three new forms of service were permitted – (a) under section 12, a licensed taxi may be used to provide local 'bus' services; (b) under section 11, a licensed taxi or licensed hire car may be used to carry pre-booked passengers at separate fares; (c) under Section 10, taxi licensing authorities are empowered to set up schemes under which licensed taxis may be used to stand for shared hire only or for either shared or exclusive hire (at the discretion of the first hirer).

5. The legal provisions which apply to each of these forms of sharing are described in Parts I to III of this Circular. A feature that is common to them all is that they apply only to licensed vehicles. This requirement was imposed in order that the vehicles should be subject to the quality control of a licensing authority. For this purpose, the vehicle and driver remain subject to the same regime as would apply to them if they were used for exclusive hire.

6. The vehicle-operating regime differs according to the type of service involved. Pre-booked hiring of taxis and hire cars under the provisions of Section 11 is the simplest form of shared operation and no special provision is made to regulate the manner or circumstances under which this service may be offered. Local services operated under the provisions of Section 12 are subject to the same control by the Traffic Commissioner as any other local service. The use of taxis to stand for shared hire under the provisions of Section 10 is regulated according to a local taxi sharing scheme set up by the taxi licensing authority, (the district council). District councils are given wide discretion to control the extent of taxi sharing in their area and the manner in which the service is to be provided The Department's advice on the making of taxi sharing schemes is given in Part IV and model provisions are set out in Annex C of this Circular.

7. This Circular is concerned with the implementation of the 1985 Act. The financial and manpower effects for local authorities of the Act as a whole are described in paragraphs 188 to 191 of Department of Transport Circular 3/85 (Welsh Office Circular 64/85).

PART 1. SECTION 12 – THE USE OF TAXIS IN PROVIDING LOCAL SERVICES

8. Section 12 of the 1985 Act was brought into force on 6 January 1986. It lays down the conditions under which taxis may be used to provide local services throughout Great Britain. Taken together with the regulations made under Sections 12(9) and (10)[1] the provisions of the section define the legislative framework within which such vehicles operate. The principle underlying these provisions is that the service has to be registered with the Traffic Commissioner in the same way as any other local bus service, but that vehicle quality and safety standards continue to be the responsibility of the authority that licensed the taxi. This is achieved by making the vehicle subject to the selective application of public service vehicle and taxi legislation.

[1]   The Local Services (Operation by Taxis) Regulations 1986 SI 1986/567. The Local Services (Operation by Taxis) (London) Regulations 1986 SI 1986/566.

Public service vehicle controls

9. When used to provide a local service, a taxi becomes a public service vehicle, subject to most of the provisions of the 1981 Act. The most significant modification of these provisions is made in Section 12(1) of the 1985 Act which provides that the holder of a taxi licence has a right to be granted a restricted public service vehicle operator's licence under Part II of the 1981 Act (a 'special licence') for use in providing a local service with his licensed taxi. Since operating standards will remain the responsibility of the taxi licensing authority he is not required to meet the conditions laid down in Section 14 of the 1981 Act.

10. Section 12(4) of the 1985 Act requires the Traffic Commissioner on granting a special licence, to attach the conditions mentioned in Section 12(5). These conditions provide that only licensed taxis may be used under a special licence and limit such use to the provision of a local service that is not an excursion or tour. (This second condition does not prevent the vehicle from being used, for example, to provide a normal, exclusive taxi service since the vehicle would not then be being used under the special licence) The third condition that must be attached to a special licence requires that every local service operated under the licence must have at least one stopping place (defined in Section 137 of the 1985 Act as a point where passengers are taken up or set down) in the taxi licensing area in which the vehicle is licensed. This condition does not prevent such a service from also having stopping places in other taxi licensing areas.

11. Section 1(2) of the 1981 Act is disapplied by Section 12(8) of the 1985 Act, with the result that the vehicle ceases to be a public service vehicle at any time when it is not being used to provide a local service. The disapplication of this section permits a licensed taxi to alternate between providing local services and operating as an exclusive taxi or a taxi shared under the provisions of Section 10 or 11 of the 1985 Act. Furthermore, number of other provisions of the 1981 Act are disapplied by Section 12(13) of the 1985 Act. These are as follows—

(a) *Sections 16(1A) and (2) of the 1981 Act*, which limit to two the number of vehicles which may be operated under a restricted operator's licence and empower the Traffic Commissioner to attach conditions to an operator's licence specifying different maximum numbers for different descriptions of vehicles. These provisions are replaced by those of Section 12(7) of the 1985 Act, there being only one description of vehicle which may be operated under a special licence: namely one for which the holder of the licence has a taxi licence. As many vehicles may be operated under a special licence as the holder holds taxi licences.

(b) *Section 17(3)(d) of the 1981 Act*, which empowers the Traffic Commissioner to revoke or suspend a restricted public service vehicle operator's licence if it appears to him that the holder no longer satisfies the requirements of good repute or financial standing. These requirements do not apply to a special licence (see paragraph 9 above).

(c) *Section 18 of the 1981 Act*, which requires all vehicles operated under a public service vehicle operator's licence to exhibit an operator's disc showing particulars of the operator of the vehicle and of the public service vehicle operator's licence under which it is being used. Instead, the vehicle remains subject to any requirements of the taxi code[1] regarding the display of information concerning its taxi licence.

(d)   *Sections 19 and 20 of the 1981 Act*, which impose duties on the holder of a public service vehicle operator's licence to give to the Traffic Commissioner certain information including information about conditions relevant to good repute and about the vehicles operated under that licence. This is not required since quality control of special licence holders and their vehicles remains the responsibility of the taxi licensing authority.

(e)   *Section 22 of the 1981 Act*, which requires that the driver of a public service vehicle shall be licensed for the purpose under that section. These vehicles remain licensed taxis and, under the taxi code, may be driven only by the holder of a taxi driver's licence. It was therefore not necessary to retain duplicate driver licensing requirements under the 1981 Act.

(f)   *Section 26 of the 1981 Act*, which makes provision for regulations to be made with respect to the number of persons who may be carried in a public service vehicle and the mark to be carried on the vehicle showing that number. These matters are regulated under the taxi code.

(g)   *Subsections (5) and (6) of Section 26 of the 1985 Act*, which make provision for the Traffic Commissioner to attach to an operator's licence a condition restricting to specified vehicles the vehicles which may be used under that licence. The vehicles used under a special licence are restricted to those for which the holder has a taxi licence and their fitness is regulated under the taxi code. The further provisions of Section 26(4) and (5) are not therefore required. It should be noted however, that the Traffic Commissioner retains the power to attach conditions to a special licence under Section 26(1) of the 1985 Act (for failing to operate a local service in a satisfactory manner) or under Section 8 of that Act (for the purpose of enforcing traffic regulation conditions).

[1]   'Taxi code' is defined in Section 13 of the 1985 Act as 'those provisions made by or under any enactment which would apply (to a licensed taxi) if the vehicle were plying for hire and were hired by a single passenger for his exclusive use'.

Controls under the taxi code

12. Section 12(10) of the 1985 Act provides a power for the Secretary of State to make regulations prescribing those provisions of the taxi code that are to apply to a licensed taxi when it is being used to provide a local service under a special PSV operator's licence. Since there are in Great Britain three different licensing regimes for taxis, three sets of Regulations have been made. The Local Services (Operation by Taxis) Regulations 1986, SI 1986/567, apply to vehicles licensed under Section 37 of the Town Police Clauses Act 1847 (that is, to taxis licensed in England (outside London) and Wales). The Local Services (Operation by Taxis) (London) Regulations 1986, 31 1986/566, apply to vehicles licensed in London

under Section 6 of the Metropolitan Public Carriage Act 1869, and the Local Services (Operation by Taxis) (Scotland) Regulations 1986, SI 1986/1239/S.106, apply to vehicles licensed in Scotland under section 10 of the Civic Government (Scotland) Act 1982. These regulations have the common purpose of providing that the quality, safety and enforcement aspects of vehicle operation continue to be regulated by the authority that licensed the taxi.

13. For England (outside London) and Wales, the regulations apply to these vehicles the greater part of the taxi code that is contained in the 1847 Act and in the Local Government (Miscellaneous Provisions) Act 1976 (the 1976 Act) where Part II of that Act has been adopted. In particular –

(a) Section 46 of the 1847 Act provides that these vehicles may be driven only by a licensed taxi driver;

(b) Section 50 of the 1847 Act and Section 60 of the 1976 Act provide a power to suspend or revoke the vehicle licence; and

(c) Section 68 of the 1976 Act provides a power for vehicles to be inspected and tested by authorised officers and for the licences of defective vehicles to be suspended.

14. The provisions of the taxi code which are not applied to these vehicles are those, which conflict with their use to carry passengers at separate fares. In particular –

(a) *Section 46 of the 1847* Act under which the driver of a taxi may be compelled to accept a hiring;

(b) Sections 54 to 58 the 1847 Act and byelaws made under Section 68 of that Act which serve to control the fares, which may be charged. As with any other local service, the operator of a taxi used to provide a local service is free to determine what fares to charge.

(c) Section 52 (Part) and 59 of the 1847 Act and Section 69 of the 1976 Act which specify certain rights of the exclusive hirer of a taxi providing a conventional service.

15. These Regulations also contain provisions made under Section 12(9) of the 1985 Act requiring that when a taxi is being used to provide a local service –

(a) it must carry a sign which includes the word 'BUS' and which indicates the service being provided;

(b) any 'taxi' or 'for hire' sign must not be illuminated; and

(c) a fare table must be displayed in the vehicle.

PART II. SECTION 11 ADVANCE BOOKING OF TAXIS AND HIRECARS AT SEPARATE FARES

16. Section 11 of the 1985 Act which applies only to England and Wales, was brought into force on 1 July 1 1986. It makes provision for the carriage at separate fares in licensed taxis and hire cars of passengers who have booked their journeys in advance. This form of shared operation does not involve standing or plying for hire on the street and is therefore open to hire cars as will as taxis. The

primary purpose is to permit taxi radio circuits and hire car operators to offer a prospective passenger the choice of either an exclusive service, as at present, or a shared service at a lower fare. They are not required to offer a shared service but, where the travel needs of a prospective passenger can be accommodated on a vehicle which has been previously booked they may, subject to the consent of the first passenger, combine what would otherwise be two or more separate journeys. Such a service may be offered only if all passengers have booked their journey in advance and consented to the sharing of the vehicle on the basis of separate fares.

17. Such services may be provided only by licensed taxis or licensed hire cars. When providing such a service the vehicle does not become a public service vehicle for the purpose of the 1981 Act, but continues to be subject to regulation as a taxi or hire car. There is nothing in the hire car code[1] which conflicts with the provision of these services and, for them, no further regulations are required. There are, however, provisions of the taxi code that are incompatible with the provision of shared services. These are disapplied in two Orders[2] made under Section 13 of the 1985 Act. These Orders apply also to taxis available for immediate hiring at separate fares under the provisions of Section 10 of the 1985 Act and are discussed at greater length in Part III of this Circular, However, one aspect of the Orders which is particularly relevant to services provided under Section 11 is the disapplication of taxi fares control. There is no power under Section 11 for the taxi licensing authority to exercise this control over pre-booked services and consequently the Orders have the effect of putting prebooked shared taxis on the same footing as shared hire cars providing a similar service.

[1]   'hire car code' is defined in section 13 of the 1985 Act as 'those provisions made by or under any enactment which would apply (to a licensed hire car) if it were hired by a single passenger for his exclusive use'.

[2]   Licensed Taxis (Hiring at Separate Fares) Order 1986, Act 1986/1386. The licensed Taxi (Hiring at Separate fares (London) Order 1986 SI 1986/1387.

PART III. SECTION 10 – IMMEDIATE HIRING OF TAXIS AT SEPARATE FARES

18. Section 10 of the 1985 Act applies only to England and Wales and lays down the conditions under which a taxi may be hired at separate fares for a journey commencing there and then. The principal conditions are that –

(a)   all passengers board the vehicle at the same place;

(b)   the boarding place has been authorised by the authority responsible for licensing taxis in the area in which that place is situated;

(c)   the hiring is in accordance with any other requirement laid down by that authority; and

(d)   the vehicle is licensed as a taxi by the same authority.

19. Provided the conditions are met, the vehicle is exempt from being a public service vehicle for the purposes of the 1981 Act or related enactments. When offering or providing such a service the vehicle does not cease to be subject to

the taxi code (except as provided for by Order made under Section 13 of the 1985 Act).

20. That the vehicle must be a licensed taxi and remains subject to the taxi code ensures that both the vehicle and driver are subject to the quality control of the taxi licensing system. That it must be licensed by the same authority that designates the place at which shared services may be offered restricts this form of service to the same vehicles as may offer exclusive taxi services in that area. That all passengers must board the vehicle at the same place prevents the vehicle from picking up passengers in the course of the journey. (This restriction does not, of course, apply to a local service operated under the provisions of Section 12 of the 1985 Act or to a vehicle booked in advance to pick up passengers at several places under the provisions of Section 11).

Application of the taxi code

21. The taxi code applies to vehicles used to provide these shared services as modified by two Orders[1] made under Section 13 of the 1985 Act. These Orders display parts of the taxi code, which are incompatible with the provision of shared services. These include –

    (a)   the right of the hirer to demand to be carried to any place within the compellable distance;

    (b)   the right of the hirer to determine which or how many people should be carried, or to require luggage to be carried;

    (c)   conditions which require the driver of an unhired taxi to drive to the nearest taxi stand – he may instead go to a place authorised by the licensing authority for the provision of shared services –

    (d)   regulations which prohibit the driver from seeking further passengers to share the vehicle and

    (e)   regulations governing exclusive fares

[1]   The Licensed Taxi (Hiring at Separate Fares) Order 1986, SI 1986/1386. The Licensed Taxi (Hiring at Separate Fares) London) Order 1986, SI 1986/1387.

Taxi sharing schemes

22. Central to the legal framework for the operation of these shared services is the making of a scheme by the taxi licensing authority. The authority has discretion over whether or not to make a scheme except that it is required under Section 10(4) to do so if requested by the holders of at least 10% of current taxi licences, (not 10% of licence holders). Irrespective of whether the scheme is made as a result of such a request it is for the licensing authority to decide the form and nature of the scheme.

23. Every scheme must –

    (a)   designate the places in the area from which shared taxis may be hired (the 'authorised places');

(b)   specify the requirements to be met in relation to the hiring of taxis at separate fares;

(c)   include any provision that the Secretary of State requires by regulations to be included;

(d)   not include any provision that the Secretary of State by regulations prohibits from being included; and

(e)   be made in accordance with the prescribed procedure.

Procedure for making a Scheme

24. The procedures to be followed by a district council in making a taxi sharing scheme are laid down in the Taxis (Schemes for Hire at Separate Fares) Regulations 1986, SI 1986/1779. These require the authority to obtain the consent of the highway authority in respect of any authorised place and of the landowner in respect of any such place that is not on the highway. The authority is required to consult the chief constable, the county council (or in the case of a metropolitan district, the Passenger Transport Authority) and the local taxi owners and drivers (or their representatives). It is then required to publish the proposed scheme and invite representations. After considering such representations, the scheme may be made with or without modification but, if significant modification is made, the council is required to consult again on the modified aspects of the scheme. A similar procedure must be followed in varying a scheme.

Obligatory provisions

25. The description of the provisions required by the Secretary of State to be included in all schemes are prescribed in the Taxis (Schemes for Hire at Separate fares) Regulations 1986. These are as follows –

(a)   any vehicle licensed by the licensing authority to ply for hire in an area where a scheme is in operation may at the option of the holder of the licence be used for the carriage of passengers at separate fares under the terms of the scheme;

(b)   the provisions of the scheme shall apply to any part of a shared journey outside the area in which the scheme is in operation as well as to the part within that area; and

(c)   any vehicle standing for hire under the terms of the scheme at an authorised place shall display (in addition to any sign, mark or notice which it is required to display by the taxi code) a notice indicating that the vehicle is available for shared hire.

26. The first of these provisions is intended to ensure that the scheme is open to all taxis in the area but that no proprietor may be compelled to participate. The second provides that a vehicle leaving its licensing area in the course of a shared hiring remains subject to its own local scheme (it cannot of course be used to ply for hire – whether shared or exclusive – outside its own area). The third condition is designed to ensure that vehicles used under a scheme carry a clear indication of the service available, for the benefit of travellers and enforcement officials.

27. The Secretary of State has not at present used his powers under Section 10(5) of the 1985 Act to prescribe provisions, which may not be included in a local authority scheme. He will, however, treat this as a reserve power to be used if, for instance, there is evidence that licensing authorities are imposing conditions against the interests of the travelling public.

Authorised places

28. Subject to the consultations and consents provided for by the Taxis (Scheme for Hire at Separate Fares) Regulations 1986 – any place may be designated as a place from which taxis may be hired at separate fares. Such places may form part of an existing taxi rank, or may be separate from the facilities for exclusive taxis.

Signing of authorised places

29. For authorised places on the highway the local authority should place a road marking in the form of diagram 1028.1 in Schedule 2 to the Traffic Signs Regulations and General Directions 1981, SI 1981/859 to indicate the extent of the authorised place to both taxi drivers and other road users. The legend 'TAXIS' should be used where the place is for both exclusive and shared taxis. Where the place is to be used only by shared taxis the legend should be varied to 'SHARED TAXIS' (See drawing WM1028. 1 at Annex B).

30. An informatory sign WBM (R) 857.1 is available to indicate how many taxis may use the stand and also to provide prospective passengers with information on the operation of a shared taxi scheme such as fare tables, times of operation or other relevant details. This information may be changed as necessary from time to time. Three variants of the sign are available headed 'TAXIS', 'SHARED TAXIS' and 'TAXIS AND SHARED TAXIS'. Details of the designs are given in Annex B.

31. Designation of a taxi rank under Section 64 of the Local Government (Miscellaneous Provisions) Act 1976 automatically prohibits the stopping of all other vehicles on the rank and this should be indicated by signs in the form of diagrams 642 and 642.1 in the Traffic Signs Regulations or in the form of WBM(R) 650.1 (see drawing at Annex B). Where problems are likely to be experienced with other vehicles waiting or loading on a place authorised for use by shared taxis only, a parking place order should be made under Section 32 of the Road Traffic Regulation Act 1984 to restrict the use of the place to shared taxis. The order may either just prohibit waiting by other vehicles (which will still allow them to load or unload goods or passengers) or prohibit the stopping of all other vehicles for any purpose including loading or unloading. The restriction should be signed by the appropriate variant of the regulatory sign WBM (R) 650.1. In all cases where this sign is used the diagram 1028.1 roads marking should be coloured yellow, notwithstanding the provisions of Regulation 24(4) of the Traffic Signs Regulations.

32. In all cases the highway authority (when different from the taxi licensing authority) should be consulted before any road markings or signs are installed.

Furthermore all the signs and road markings referred to above, except the diagram 1028.1 road marking with the legend 'TAXIS', coloured in accordance with the provisions of Regulation 24(4), and the signs in diagrams 642 and 642.1, require authorisation by the appropriate Department of Transport Regional Office or by the Welsh Office before they are installed. Any further advice on signing should also be sought from the Regional Office or the Welsh Office.

Other requirements of the scheme

33. Section 12(6) of the 1985 Act contains a list, which is not exhaustive, of matters for which a scheme may make provision. These are –

    (*a*)   fares;
    (*b*)   the signs to be carried on vehicles used under the scheme and those used to mark authorised places;
    (*c*)   the manner in which arrangements are to be made for the carriage of passengers at separate fares; and
    (*d*)   the conditions to apply to the use of a taxi on a shared hiring.

34. The effect of the Licensed Taxis (Hiring at Separate Fares) Order 1986 is to disapply any provision of the taxi code which, in its existing form, is incompatible with taxi sharing. It is open to the licensing authority to replace or reinstate in a suitable form any such provision as part of its scheme, (provided these do not conflict with the obligatory provisions described in paragraph 25). The Department's guidance on the additional requirements of the scheme is contained in Part IV of this Circular.

PART IV. GUIDANCE ON THE MAKING OF TAXI SHARING SCHEMES

35. Guidance is given in Part III on the statutory requirements governing the form and content of taxi sharing schemes and the procedure by which they are to be made. This part of the Circular sets out the Department's guidance on the options open to a licensing authority in formulating its scheme. A model taxi sharing schemes is given in Annex C. This is not intended to provide a blueprint for local schemes. Rather, having decided what provisions are required, a district council may find certain of the model provisions helpful in drafting its scheme.

General

36. In preparing their local schemes district councils should bear in mind the general principles that lay behind the Government's promotion of the idea of taxi sharing and its approval by Parliament. Taxi sharing was seen as providing district councils with the opportunity to improve the public transport facilities available in their areas and to permit the taxi trade to widen its market and share in the new opportunities opened up by the 1985 Act. A shared taxi journey should give the taxi proprietor a greater return while being significantly less expensive for each passenger. This will bring travel by taxi within the reach of many more people.

37. It was decided not to set up a new class of vehicle authorised to offer only a shared service. In order to make the most efficient use of the vehicles available, the driver should be free to switch between exclusive and shared operations according to demand. In practice, although the making of the scheme is entirely the responsibility of the licensing authority, vehicles will be made available for shared hire only to the extent that the provisions of the scheme are acceptable to the taxi trade and, equally, there will be enough customers to make a scheme a success only if the provisions of the scheme are attractive to a significant proportion of the travelling public.

38. Taxi drivers and proprietors will need to be reassured that taxi sharing will not reduce the earnings or size of the taxi trade by combining existing passengers into fewer journeys. Shared taxis, with their lower fares, offer the prospect of attracting more passengers, so increasing total taxi revenue as well as benefiting the travellers. The trade will wish to put this to the test and licensing authorities may adopt an incremental approach, starting with a relatively limited scheme that can be extended once experience has been gained.

39. A second benefit of this approach is that it would be possible initially to provide for sharing where it is likely to cause few problems. The level of control which will need to be exercised on the operation of shared taxi services will depend very much on the type of scheme being set up. A service from an out-of-town shopping centre to residential estates is unlikely to raise the same problems as one operating from a city centre late at night. Licensing authorities will find no shortage of possible problems which could be dealt with only by extensive regulation. Rather than seeking to provide for these at the outset, the initial scheme might be restricted to locations or times of day when difficulties would not be expected to occur and the operation of the scheme could be subject to minimal regulations. As experience is gained, the scheme could be extended and regulations added to deal with any particular problems as they arise.

Authorised places

40. The designation of authorised places will generally involve two types of decision: where in the licensing area the authorised places should be located and whether they should be combined with exclusive taxi ranks or segregated from them. It is suggested that the licensing authorities should first determine where shared facilities would provide maximum benefit to travellers in the area. They may wish to look first to the provision of services at out-of-town shopping centres, hospitals, railway stations, airports or other facilities that attract relatively large numbers of passengers. The scheme could later be varied to include, for example, night services from a city centre.

41. In rural areas and small towns there may be few places where there is a particularly high demand for taxis. Equally taxi sharing is likely to cause few problems and the authorities for such areas are advised to consider designating all taxi ranks as authorised places.

42. In larger conurbations authorities may initially wish to specify the destinations to be served by shared taxis from each of the authorised places. For instance, shared taxis from a shopping centre might initially be limited to serving one or two residential estates. Shared taxis from the railway station might be authorised to operate only to the city centre. Such an arrangement would avoid, at the outset, any problems associated with assembling groups of passengers to share, and it is amenable to a simple flat rate or zonal fare tariff. Again, once experience has been gained, the scheme might be extended to additional destinations.

43. Whether authorised places should be combined with exclusive taxi ranks must to some extent depend on the space available. Where space is limited, as in many city and town centres, the best use of available space is likely to be achieved by combining shared and exclusive ranks. Except at the busiest ranks in the larger cities it should be enough simply to designate the entire rank as being available for both shared and exclusive services. However, where there may be confusion at, for example, an airport or busy railway terminus it may be preferable to divide the rank, reserving some spaces for the use of shared taxis only, so that both the drivers and prospective passengers choose in advance whether to go to the shared or exclusive part of the rank.

Exclusive and shared compellability

44. 'Exclusive compellability' is the existing right of the hirer of a taxi to demand an exclusive service and to be carried to any place in the licensing area. 'Shared compellability' would be the right of the first passenger who wished to share the vehicle to require the driver to take him to his chosen destination if at least one further passenger could be found.

45. The disapplication of Section 53 of the 1847 Act provided for in the Licensed Taxis (Hiring at Separate Fares) Order has the effect of disapplying exclusive compellability. Unless this is reinstated or replaced by shared compellability as part of the scheme, it will be open to the driver of a taxi operating under the scheme to refuse to accept a hiring, either exclusive or shared.

46. Whether exclusive compellability should be reinstated will depend on the way in which the scheme is to operate. There can be no case for allowing a taxi driver to refuse a hiring if his vehicle is standing at a place from which exclusive taxis may be hired. Thus, at a combined shared/exclusive rank, irrespective of whether a driver is offering a shared service, he should be deemed also to be available for exclusive hire by providing in the scheme for exclusive compellability. Where shared and exclusive taxis are segregated (even if only at different parts of the same taxi rank) or where there is an exclusive service available nearby, a passenger should probably not be given the right to demand such a service from a taxi standing for shared hire.

47. A special case might be where an authorised place has been designated for the provision of a shared service to a particular destination – for example into a city centre in the morning peak hours. The driver of a taxi offering such a service

may be doing so only because he wishes to travel in that particular direction and he would offer no service at all rather than risk being compelled to accept a hiring in the wrong direction. In this case it would be reasonable not to reinstate exclusive compellability but instead to give the passenger the right to be carried to the specified destination at a discounted fare, even if no other passenger can be found to share the vehicle.

48. As a general feature of schemes, licensing authorities may wish to provide for shared compellability in support of passengers wanting to share the vehicle to a destination which is unpopular with taxi drivers (perhaps because there is difficulty in obtaining a return fare). There should then be no circumstance in which a passenger is unable to make his journey, although he cannot always be guaranteed a shared service at a discounted fare.

Signs on vehicles and at authorised places

49. As described in paragraph 25 every scheme must contain provision for a sign to be carried on a vehicle standing for hire under the scheme. The form and wording of this sign and the manner in which it is to be displayed are left to the discretion of the licensing authority. It is advised to avoid complex and expensive requirements that might act as a barrier to taxi proprietors wishing to participate in the scheme. In many cases a simple but uniform sign displayed in the windscreen of the vehicle will be adequate. If the desired operational flexibility is to be achieved, the sign should be capable of being easily removed and replaced.

50. The wording of the sign will depend on the type of service permitted under the scheme and authorities are advised to use a form of words that conveys as precisely as possible what is on offer. For example if the scheme provides generally for exclusive compellability a sign such as that used in Queensland Australia may be appropriate; this reads, 'This vehicle may be shared at the free choice of the first hirer'. A similar message is conveyed more briefly but less precisely by signs reading 'Shared or exclusive hire', 'Available for shared hire' or 'Shared hirings accepted'. Where the scheme does not provide for exclusive compellability, this might be made clear by a sign reading 'Shared hire only'. Although some of these signs might be rather large it should be noted that they are required to be displayed only when the vehicle is stationary.

51. Details of the signing arrangements at authorised places are given in paragraphs 29 to 32.

Operation

52. As suggested earlier, it may not be necessary at the outset to regulate every aspect of the arrangements for sharing and the conditions under which a taxi may be so hired. Much can be left to the goodwill and commonsense of those involved, with the power to introduce additional regulations kept in reserve. Moreover, the way in which sharing will operate will depend on other aspects of

the scheme, such as whether combined or separate ranks have been designated and whether exclusive or shared compellability has been instated.

53. All schemes will need to make clear the respective roles of the passengers and the driver in the arrangements for sharing. It is suggested that the driver should be made responsible for deciding whether the destination of subsequent passengers can reasonably be accommodated on a journey serving that of the first passenger. Under this arrangement, the first passenger, having elected to share the vehicle, would not have the right to choose or reject fellow passengers but any passenger should be allowed to decide not to travel without incurring a financial penalty.

54. The driver should also be made responsible for determining the route of the vehicle and the order in which passengers are set down, subject to the condition that he should not unreasonably prolong the journey of any passenger.

55. Licensing authorities may also wish to specify in the scheme the manner in which the arrangements to share the vehicle are to be made. This would include regulating such aspects as the period for which the driver must wait for further passengers to the same or similar destination and determining what may happen if no further passengers come forward.

Fares

56. Any scheme for shared fares should offer an incentive both to the taxi proprietor and to the intending passengers. The driver should receive more in fares than for an exclusive hire and each passenger should pay less. However, care has to be taken to strike a balance between these incentives. If shared fares are set too high, passengers will not make use of the service; if the margin for the driver is set too low, there will be no incentive for him to participate in the scheme. How these margins should be set will be a matter for the judgement of the licensing authority; but if they are not balanced both the taxi trade and their passengers will be denied the benefits of a properly operating system for shared fares.

57. However the fare is to be calculated it should be made apparent to the passengers that the specified shared fare is to be paid by each person and is not the fare for the hire of the vehicle. It should also be made clear that sharing is an additional facility. Thus a group of people travelling together may continue to hire as a whole a taxi available for exclusive hire, paying the exclusive fare plus the permitted extra charge for additional passengers. If however, they chose to hire the vehicle on a shared basis they will each pay the shared fare.

58. There are four basic ways in which shared fares might be charged by taxi drivers, though there are many possible variations. The four methods are –

    (*a*)   a flat fare system;
    (*b*)   a zonal system;
    (*c*)   modified use of existing meters; or
    (*d*)   use of special (or specially adapted) meters.

Flat fare systems

59. These systems have two major advantages: they are easily understood and passengers know in advance how much their journey will cost. They will be particularly applicable where all passengers travel much the same distance. An obvious example would be airport taxis: all passengers would be coming from (or going to) the airport and the other end of their journey will usually be close to the town centre. So a large part of the journey will be common for all passengers. Other examples where a flat fare system might be appropriate would be where a common taxi journey is from a close group of small towns and villages into a neighbouring city centre (and back) or even for all journeys made entirely within a small town. But licensing authorities will be best placed to identify for their own areas trips for which a flat charge would be appropriate.

60. A flat fare system does not necessarily mean that the fare should be like a bus fare, ie not dependent on the number of passengers travelling. It could readily be provided that the more passengers who are sharing the taxi the less each would pay. Such an arrangement might be necessary to maintain the correct balance between the interests of the passengers and the driver, without introducing too complicated a fare system.

Zonal systems

61. The simplest extension of a flat fare system would be to introduce destination zones by, for example, treating different residential estates as separate fare zones for journeys from a shopping centre. At its most comprehensive, a zonal system involves dividing the licensing area into zones and laying down the fare per passenger for journeys between each pair of zones. This may be done in a fare table (to be displayed in the vehicle together with the zonal map) or by specifying the fare according to the number of different zones through which the passenger is carried. Such a system might be appropriate for larger towns.

62. The major disadvantage of a zonal system is that, unless there are very few zones, it is too complex for the fare to vary according to the number of passengers carried and so the last passenger left in the vehicle receives an exclusive service at the shared rate. In consequence, zonal fares tend to be pitched at a relatively high level.

63. It is worth noting that a zonal system may be used to compute both shared and exclusive fares (as is done in Washington DC). Consequently, where a full zonal system is introduced for the purpose of calculating shared fares; it might also be applied to exclusive fares, so dispensing with the need for taxi meters.

Metered systems

64. Although they do not permit passengers to know their fare in advance, taxi meters are familiar and give the public confidence that they are not being overcharged. Meters are available which are capable of computing shared fares where passengers board and alight at different points on the route. However,

the form of sharing permitted under Section 10 of the 1985 Act requires that all passengers must board the vehicle at the same place. It follows that full shared metering is not essential for the schemes to be set up under the 1985 Act. Moreover, time has to be allowed for the public to become used to shared taxis, for the trade to test whether such a service is worthwhile commercially and for more meter manufacturers to be persuaded that there is a large enough potential market for a shared taxi meter.

65. Because all passengers must board the vehicle at the same authorised place it is possible to use an unmodified taxi meter to compute shared fares. The fare shown on a normal taxi meter when each passenger alights is directly related to the distance that he has been carried. And it would be possible to provide that each passenger should pay a stipulated proportion of the fare shown on the meter when he leaves the taxi. However, no matter how that proportion is defined, such schemes have a number of drawbacks. First, there may be arguments over the arithmetic, even if the percentages are kept simple; and as the scheme becomes more complex so does the scope for argument. Secondly, where each passenger pays the same proportion of the metered fare, the return to the driver shows enormous variation. He stands to lose money where the last passenger left in the taxi gets off long after the others, and so enjoys a long exclusive ride at the discounted rate. The use of an unmodified taxi meter is therefore best suited to the case where all passengers travel to the same destination.

Metered systems – modified existing meters

66. The problem outlined above would be overcome if the meter could be adapted to run at a rate that was dependent on the number of people using the vehicle at that particular time. It is understood that most modern meters are capable of holding 4 separate tariffs. So they can be programmed to run at a rate appropriate to the number of people of sharing –

Tariff 1 – Exclusive rate
Tariff 2 – Two people sharing
Tariff 3 – Three people sharing
Tariff 4 – Four or more people sharing.

67. Tariff I would therefore be 100% of the exclusive rate, and Tariff 2, 3 and 4 would represent progressively smaller percentages (in that order) of the exclusive rate. If, for example, four people boarded a shared taxi the meter would be set at Tariff 4. When the first passenger left it would be stopped (not set to zero) and he would pay the amount shown on the meter, which would then be set to run at Tariff 3. This sequence would be repeated until the last passenger remained, when the meter would be set to run at the exclusive rate. In this way, most existing meters could be used to operate as a full shared meter for the type of sharing provided for in the Act.

68. The main limitation on using existing meters in this way is that they are generally capable of holding only 4 tariffs. If taxi sharing proves popular it may well be more efficient to use larger vehicles (a taxi may be licensed with up to

8 -passenger seats) and the Government would not wish to see the method of regulating fares inhibit what might otherwise be a beneficial change. This, however, is unlikely to be a problem at the outset when few vehicles are licensed to carry more than 5 passengers. More seriously, many licensing authorities require the use of two or more metered tariffs for the metering of exclusive fares. For example, different tariffs may be laid down for immediate and pre-booked hirings or, as in London, a second tariff may be brought in automatically on long journeys. In some cases these problems may be overcome by the simple expedient of employing Tariff 3 for three or more people sharing; in others it may preclude the use of adapted taxi meters.

Metered systems – special meters

69. It is understood that most meter manufacturers intend developing fully shared meters capable of storing in separate memories the fare so far for each passenger (and incrementing them in accordance with the fare scheme in operation), and perhaps of displaying them simultaneously or in rotation. Such meters will be capable of handling up to 8 tariffs and, if sharing proves popular, they will almost certainly become the standard for the next generation of taxi meters. Licensing authorities are, however, cautioned against prematurely requiring their taxi trades to invest in new meters.

Tariff structure

70. In fixing the shared tariff it will be necessary for licensing authorities to decide

(*a*) whether there should be any initial hiring charge and if so how it should be treated;

(*b*) whether the shared tariff should include waiting time;

(*c*) how 'extras' should be handled; and

(*d*) the level of discount.

Although each of these matters may be decided separately, they will, in combination, determine the balance that is struck between the interests of the passengers and the drivers.

71. The initial hiring charge could be retained, with every passenger paying the charge at the exclusive rate. Alternatively, it could be discounted at the same rate as the distance tariff or abandoned altogether.

72. So far as waiting time is concerned, it is suggested that this should be metered in exactly the same way as for the existing exclusive tariff. It would not be possible to share a luggage charge since it would not apply to all passengers and it is suggested that this charge should be dropped. It would also be simpler to drop 'extras' that depend on the time of day or day of operation but these could be treated in the same way as the initial hiring charge. Charges for additional passengers should be dropped.

73. It is recommended that licensing authorities adopt the simplest arrangements for the above elements of the tariff and, in discussion with their taxi trade, use the discount rates to set fares which apportion the benefits of sharing fairly between them and their passengers.

Publicity

74. Licensing authorities will wish to ensure that potential users of shared service are aware of the scheme and have some understanding of how to use it. Publication of the scheme, as well as fulfilling a statutory requirement, will provide an opportunity of explaining how the scheme will operate. This is likely to create considerable interest and generate publicity in the local press and radio. Newspaper articles might be made available and a press release issued at little cost. In some circumstances the printing and distribution of an explanatory leaflet might be appropriate, possibly as a joint venture with the taxi trade.

PUBLIC PASSENGER VEHICLES ACT 1981, ANNEX A
SCHEDULE 1, PART 1

(As amended by the Transport Act 1985)

SHARING OF TAXIS AND HIRE-CARS

1. The making of the agreement for the payment of separate fares must not have been initiated by the driver or by the owner of the vehicle, by any person who has made the vehicle available under any agreement, or by any person who receives any remuneration in respect of the arrangements for the journey.

2. (1) The journey must be made without previous advertisement to the public of facilities for its being made by passengers to be carried at separate fares, except where the local authorities concerned have approved the arrangements under which the journey is made as designed to meet the social and welfare needs of one or more communities, and their approvals remain in force.

(2) In relation to a journey the local authorities concerned for the purposes of this paragraph are those in whose area part of the journey is to be made; and in this subparagraph 'local authority' means –

  (a) in relation to England and Wales, the council of a county, metropolitan district or London borough and the Common Council of the City of London;
  (b) in relation to Scotland, a regional or islands council.

Note See Annex B overleaf.

MODEL TAXI SHARING SCHEME ANNEX C

The District Council of.....................[1] in exercise of the powers conferred by Section 10(4) of the Transport Act 1985 and having obtained the consents and

TRAFFIC SIGNS AT TAXI RANKS   ANNEX B

WM 642

WBM 650.1

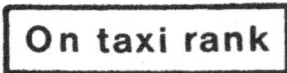

WM 642.1

WBM (R) 857.1
Variants

WM 1028.1
Variant

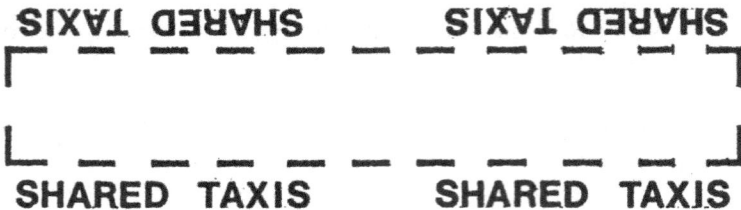

carried out the consultations required by the Taxis (Schemes for Hire at Separate Fares) Regulations 1986[2] hereby resolve to make the following scheme.

[1] Add name of Council.
[2] SI 1986/1779.

Citation and Commencement

1. This scheme may be cited as the.................[1] (Taxi Hire at Separate Fares) Scheme 19 – and shall come into operation on.................19 .

[1] Add name of Council.

Interpretation

2. In this scheme, unless the context otherwise requires

'the Act' means the Transport Act 1985;
'the Council' means the district council of...............[1]
'taxi' means a vehicle licensed by the Council under Section 37 of the Town Police Clauses Act 1847;
'authorised place' has the meaning given by Section 10(5) of the Act;
'designated area' means[2]
'exclusive service' means a service other than at separate fares; and 'shared service' means a service at separate fares.

[1] Add name of Council.
[2] Describe here the licensing area for taxis under Section 37 of the Town Police Clauses Act 1847. If the Council licenses taxis in part only of the district the designated area will comprise only that part of the district. If the Council licenses taxis in two or more parts of the district, the designated area will comprise one only of those parts and separate schemes will be necessary for each licensing area.

Application

3. (1) Any taxi licensed by the Council to ply for hire in the designated area may at the option of the holder of the licence be used for the carriage of passengers at separate fares under the terms of this scheme.

(2) When a taxi is hired in accordance with this scheme, the provisions of the scheme applying to the journey for which it is hired shall apply to any part of that journey outside the designated area as they apply to any part within that area.

Authorised places

4. The places listed in Schedule 1 to this scheme, are authorised places [at the times and for the journeys indicated in that Schedule].

Signs on vehicles

5. There should be displayed on any taxi available for hire under the terms of this scheme at an authorised place (in addition to any other sign, mark or

notice which is required to be displayed on the taxi) a notice containing the sign described [illustrated] in Schedule 2 to this scheme[1].

[1]   This is the minimum requirement for the display on the notice. The Council may, if it considers necessary, impose additional requirements relating to the manner in which the notice is constructed and displayed.

Fares

6. The fare payable by each passenger for a journey made under this scheme shall be calculated in accordance with Schedule 3 to this scheme.

7. The fare table specified in Schedule 4 to this scheme shall be displayed in a manner that is clearly legible to passengers, in any vehicle standing for hire or hired under this scheme.

Taxi meters

81. (1) Any taxi standing for hire or hired under this Scheme shall be fitted with a taxi meter capable of displaying a fare calculated in accordance with Schedule 3 to this Scheme.

(2) The meter shall be set in motion only when the taxi leaves the authorised place and shall display the fare calculated in accordance with Schedule 3 to this scheme and appropriate to the number of passengers in the taxi at that time.

(3) When any passenger leaves the taxi, the meter shall be stopped (but not returned to zero) and shall be restarted at the tariff appropriate to the number of passengers remaining in it when the taxi continues the journey for which it is hired under this scheme.

[1]   Paragraph 8 would apply only if metered fares are specified in Schedule 3.

Operation

9. A taxi shall be available for hire under this scheme when it is standing at an authorised place and displaying the sign specified in paragraph 5 thereof.

10[1]. If –

    (*a*)   a person at any time seeks to hire for an exclusive service a taxi available for hire under this scheme; and –

    (*b*)   the driver and a person seeking a shared service are not waiting for another person to offer to share the taxi; and

    (*c*)   the driver either

        i.   would, apart from the Licensed Taxis (Hiring at Separate Fares) Order 1986, be required to accept the hiring; or

        ii.   accepts the hiring although not required to do so,

    then that taxi shall thereupon cease to be available for hire under this scheme until the expiry of that hiring.

10^2. If –

(a)   a person at any time seeks to hire for an exclusive service a taxi available for hire under this scheme; and

(b)   the driver and a person seeking a shared service are not waiting for another person to offer to share the taxi; and

(c)   the driver accepts the hiring although not required to do so,

then that taxi shall thereupon cease to be available for hire under this scheme until the expiry of that hiring.

11.   If a person seeks to hire for a shared service a taxi available for hire under this scheme and the driver is unable to find at least one other person to share the hiring within [. . . minutes] [a reasonable time] then, no fare shall be payable and, subject to paragraph 10 of this scheme, the driver shall be free to seek an alternative hiring, provided that the driver and that person may continue to wait for another person to offer to share the taxi for so long as they both agree to do so.

12^3.   The driver of a taxi available for hire under this scheme shall not unreasonably refuse a hiring to two or more persons seeking a shared service to any destination within the designated area [indicated in Schedule 1].

13.   Before a taxi has left an authorised place for the purpose of a shared service, any person may decide not to be carried as a passenger (notwithstanding any earlier agreement) and no fare shall be payable by him.

14.   The driver may decline to accept as a passenger any person on the grounds that his intended destination could not be reached without an excessive or unreasonable addition to the journey distance of any passenger previously accepted for a journey, or that his luggage could not be accommodated safely within the luggage compartment of the taxi, but shall not refuse to carry a person already accepted by him as a passenger because his destination or luggage are not on such grounds compatible with those of a person who subsequently seeks a service.

15.   The driver shall not refuse to carry luggage in his taxi provided that the luggage can be accepted safely within the luggage compartment of the taxi having regard to the luggage of other passengers.

16.   The route taken by the taxi and the order in which passengers are set down shall be determined by the driver, but he shall not unreasonably prolong the journey of any passenger.

[1]   The two versions of paragraph 10 are alternatives; the first provides for 'exclusive compellability', the second does not.

[2]   The two versions of paragraph 10 are alternatives; the first provides for 'exclusive compellability', the second does not.

[3]   Paragraph 12 provides for 'shared compellability' and should be omitted if that is not required.

SCHEDULE 1 – AUTHORISED PLACES

The places listed in column 1 are designated as places from which taxis may be hired under the scheme.

[For each authorised place, passengers may be carried at separate fares to the corresponding places shown in column 2. Where there are no places listed in column 2 against a particular authorised place, passengers may be carried to any destination, without limitation.]

[The times at which the scheme shall operate at each authorised place are listed in column 3. Where no times are listed against an authorised place, the scheme shall operate at all times from that place.]

Column 1	Column 2	Column 3
Market Place (Hackney Carriage Stand)		
[Named] Shopping Centre	[Named] residential estates	
Railway Station Forecourt		Monday to Friday 5pm to 8pm

SCHEDULE 2 – SIGNS ON VEHICLES

1. This appendix should contain a description or drawing of the sign prescribed for the purpose of paragraph 5 of the scheme.

SCHEDULE 3 – FARES

The fare to be charged to each person for services provided under the scheme shall be based on the distance and time elements of the fare for an exclusive service as contained in [byelaw no] [the table of fares made by the Council under Section 65 of the Local Government (Miscellaneous Provisions) Act 1976] as amended or replaced and in force from time to time.

The following tariffs shall apply –

> 4 people sharing: for each person X% of the exclusive tariff
> 3 people sharing: for each person Y% of the exclusive tariff
> 2 people sharing: for each person Z% of the exclusive tariff

No additional charge shall be made for the carriage of luggage.

No fare shall be charged for children under the age of 5 unless they occupy a separate seat which would otherwise have been taken by a fare paying passenger.

SCHEDULE 4 – FARE TABLE

In every vehicle used under the scheme there shall be displayed in a manner that is clearly legible to passengers the following sign –

'FARE TABLE FOR SHARED SERVICES'

1. The taxi meter on this vehicle is capable of metering shared fares.

2. During any time that the vehicle is shared the meter will record the separate fare payable by each of the passengers.

3. The rate at which the fare increases depends on the number of passengers sharing in accordance with the following table –

    4 people sharing: X% of normal tariff
    3 people sharing: Y% of normal tariff
    2 people sharing: Z% of normal tariff

4. The normal tariff is shown on the second fare table displayed in this vehicle.

5. No additional charge shall be made for the carriage of luggage.

6. No fare shall be charged for children under the age of 5 years unless they occupy a separate seat, which would otherwise have been taken by a farepaying passenger.

Note: The above provisions would apply to metered fares. For zonal fares a fare table and map would be required. For flat fares between authorised places and specified destinations a fare table would be required together with a definition of the destinations to be served.

DOT Circular 8/86, 17 November 1986

TRANSPORT ACT 1985: SECTION 15:
EXTENSION OF TAXI LICENSING THROUGHOUT
ENGLAND AND WALES

INTRODUCTION

1. This Circular applies to England (outside London) and Wales. It provides guidance to local authorities on the effect of Section 15 of the Transport Act 1985 ('the 1985 Act'), though it does not purport to provide an interpretation of the law. Section 15 has the effect of extending taxi licensing throughout England and Wales. Provision is made in the Transport Act 1985 (Commencement Number 6) Order 1986, SI 1986/1794 (c. 63) to bring this section into force with effect from 1 January 1987.

THE PURPOSE OF SECTION 15

2. The 1985 Act contains provisions under which taxis may be used to carry passengers at separate fares. (These are described in Departmental Circular 7/86). These vehicles are not subject to all of the controls exercised under public service vehicle legislation. In order to safeguard quality and safety standards these provisions extend only to vehicles, which are subject to controls under a taxi licensing system.

3. Shared taxi services are thought likely to be of particular benefit in rural areas where conventional bus services may be uneconomic and smaller vehicles can cope with the demand. However, in many such areas there is at present no taxi licensing, with the result that taxi proprietors are prevented from offering this wider range of services in areas where they might be of great benefit.

4. Section 15 extends to previously uncontrolled areas the consumer protection afforded by the licensing of taxis and taxi drivers. Moreover, with the extension of taxi licensing throughout England and Wales all taxi proprietors will be able to benefit from the opportunity to provide shared services and no area will be deprived of such services by the absence of a licensing system.

THE PRESENT ARRANGEMENTS

5. In England (outside London) and Wales, taxis may be licensed by district councils under the hackney carriage provisions of the Town Police Clauses Act 1847 ('the 1847 Act'). By virtue of Section 171(4) of the Public Health Act 1875 ('the 1875 Act') these provisions were applied to the urban districts which were formed under the 1875 Act. Part II of Schedule 14 to the Local Government Act 1972 ('the 1972 Act') provided that Section 171(4) of the 1875 Act should

apply to those areas, and only those, to which it applied immediately before 1 April 1974. However, under paragraph 25 of that Schedule, district councils were empowered to resolve that section 171(4) of the 1875 Act should apply throughout their area or should cease to apply throughout their area (whether or not it previously applied only to part of their area). A resolution disapplying this provision had to be passed before 1 April 1975 but no time limit was placed on the extension of taxi licensing throughout a local authority area.

6. The cumulative effect is that there are areas of England and Wales where taxis are licensed under the provisions of the 1847 Act either because they were urban districts in 1875 or because an extension resolution has been passed by the district council under the provisions of the 1972 Act. Conversely, there are areas where there is no taxi licensing under the 1847 Act either because they were not urban districts in 1875 or because licensing has been disapplied by a resolution passed before 1 April 1975.

7. Such areas may be combined in a single district with the result that there may be districts with the following licensing arrangements –

- (a) taxis licensed throughout the district as a single taxi licensing area (this would arise where the district was formed from a single 1875 urban district or where an extension resolution has been passed under the 1972 Act);
- (b) taxis licensed throughout the district, but in two or more distinct taxi licensing areas (this would arise where the district was formed from two or more 1875 urban districts);
- (c) taxis licensed in part or parts only of the district (this would arise where the district was formed from one or more 1875 urban districts but also contained some area that was not such a district); or
- (d) taxis licensed in no part of the district (this would arise where the district contained no 1875 urban districts or where licensing had been disapplied by a resolution passed under the 1972 Act).

8. There are some 260 districts in categories (a) and (b) which license taxis throughout their areas. These will not be affected by Section 15 of the 1985 Act. There are about 50 districts in each of categories (c) and (d) with partial licensing or none at all, and it is these, which will be affected by Section 15.

THE EFFECT OF SECTION 15

9. Section 15 of the 1985 Act applies the taxi licensing provisions of the 1847 Act to all districts and parts of districts in England (outside the Metropolitan Police District) and Wales. By virtue of Section 15(1)(a), where there is at present no area of a district in which taxis are licensed (category (d) of paragraph 7 above), the 1847 Act will apply throughout the district. Where taxis are already licensed in part or parts of the district (category (c) of paragraph 7 above), Section 15(1)(b) creates an additional licensing area comprising so much of the district as is not already subject to the provisions of the 1847 Act (or of the Metropolitan Public Carriage Act 1869).

10. Except as described below, from 1 January 1987 it will be an offence for a vehicle to be used to stand or ply for hire in a street or public place in England or Wales unless it is licensed for that purpose in accordance with the provisions of the 1847 Act.

11. The exceptions to paragraph 10 are –

(*a*) a public service vehicle operated under the provisions of the Public Passenger Vehicles Act 1981; or

(*b*) a vehicle standing or plying for hire in the Metropolitan Police District (which must be licensed in accordance with the provisions of the Metropolitan Public Carriage Act 1869); or

(*c*) a vehicle to which the saving provision of the Commencement Order applies (see paragraph 13 below).

12. It follows that the councils for those districts affected by Section 15 should be prepared from 1 January 1987 to consider applications for taxi licences. An applicant who is refused such a licence or whose application is not considered within a reasonable time would have a right of appeal to a Crown Court by virtue of the Public Health Act 1875 and the Public Health Acts Amendment Act 1890.

TRANSITIONAL PROVISIONS

13. The Order commencing Section 15 of the 1985 Act makes two transitional provisions. The first is a saving provision permitting existing taxi proprietors and drivers to continue until 1 April 1987 to provide a service without holding the necessary licences. This will apply to taxi proprietors and drivers who before 1 January 1987 were operating without a licence in an area affected by Section 15. It will also apply to proprietors and drivers who were licensed in an adjacent area but were similarly providing a service in the new licensing area.

14. The second transitional provision empowers a district council to resolve before 1 January 1987 to adopt Part II of the Local Government (Miscellaneous Provisions) Act 1976 (see paragraphs 19 and 20). This modifies taxi licensing under the 1847 Act and also provides for the licensing of hire cars. It cannot normally be adopted unless the 1847 Act is already in place. This transitional provision permits those councils that wish to adopt these provisions to bring them into force at the same time as the 1847 Act.

ZONING

15. Where a district contains two or more 1875 urban districts (and an extension resolution has not been made under the 1972 Act) each of those areas will be separate zones for the purpose of taxi licensing. That is, a taxi licence granted for one such area does not permit the vehicle to be used to stand or ply for hire in another. A council may resolve to amalgamate such zones and so licence taxis throughout its district as a single taxi licensing area but there is no statutory power under which a council may choose to divide its district into zones for the purpose of taxi licensing.

16. Where a district council has no taxi licensing controls, the effect of Section 15 will be to make the entire district a single licensing area. Where there are already taxi controls in part or parts of a district, Section 15 will create an additional licensing area. Existing licensing zones will be unaffected unless and until the council passes an extension resolution.

17. The benefits or otherwise of retaining licensing zones are closely related to the question of taxi quantity control, in that zoning serves to support limitation of taxi numbers in urban areas. The Government's guidance on quantity control is contained in paragraphs 26 to 28 of Departmental Circular 3/85 (Welsh Office Circular 64/85) in relation to Section 16 of the 1985 Act. In considering whether to support quantity control by the retention of licensing zones councils will wish to take account of the reduced efficiency resulting from requiring a taxi arriving in one zone from another to return empty. Furthermore, since zones are totally independent licensing areas, the council will be required to exercise separate control for each area. This could involve increased administrative costs in preparing licensing conditions and making byelaws, regulations and taxi sharing schemes for each area.

18. It will remain open to councils with more than one licensing zone to pass an extension resolution to combine these into a single licensing area. For the reasons given in the previous paragraph, the Government recommends this.

THE LOCAL GOVERNMENT (MISCELLANEOUS PROVISIONS) ACT 1976

19. Part II of this Act provides for the licensing of hire cars and modifies the licensing of taxis under the 1847 Act. This legislation is adoptive and may be brought into force by council resolution only for those areas in which the 1847 Act is in force. Section 15 has no effect on the application of these provisions. However, a transitional provision is made in the commencement of Section 15 to enable a district council to resolve in advance of the coming into force of the 1847 Act, to adopt Part II of the 1976 Act (see paragraph 14).

20. The 1976 Act provides additional powers for ensuring that vehicles are suitable for use as taxis and that they are maintained in a satisfactory condition. In particular, sections 50 and 68 contain specific powers to inspect and test taxis and section 60 provides the power to suspend, revoke or refuse to renew a licence. In addition, the 1976 Act permits taxi fares to be set by council resolution rather than byelaw. However, in considering whether to adopt these provisions, councils will wish to be aware that Part II of the 1976 Act must be adopted in its entirety, including the provision for licensing hire cars.

THE METROPOLITAN POLICE DISTRICT

21. Section 15 of the 1985 Act does not apply to the Metropolitan Police District where the licensing of taxis and taxi drivers is done under the Metropolitan Public Carriage Act 1869. As the Metropolitan Police District is not precisely the same as the administrative area of Greater London there are a few districts,

which have the 1869 Act in force in part of their area. Section 15 'extends the application of the 1847 Act to those parts of such districts which are not covered by the 1869 Act.

CONTROLS

22. The 1847 Act requires a district council that licenses taxis to accept and consider applications for taxi and taxi drivers' licences and to maintain a register of licences granted. In addition it empowers such an authority to make bylaws for the purposes of –

(a)   specifiying how licence plates are to be carried on the vehicle;
(b)   laying down requirements for vehicle construction and fitting;
(c)   regulating the fares to be charged and the use of an approved taxi meter,
(d)   regulating the behaviour of taxi proprietors and drivers;
(e)   fixing taxi stands; and
(f)   securing the safe custody and re-delivery of lost property.

specifying how licence plates are to be carried on the vehicle; laying down requirements for vehicle construction and fitting; regulating the fares to be charged and the use of an approved taxi meter, regulating the behaviour of taxi proprietors and drivers; fixing taxi stands; and securing the safe custody and re-delivery of lost property.

The Home Office issued a set of model byelaws in 1974 and these are annexed. [The model byelaws have subsequently been updated, and the current model is reproduced at Appendix 2.10]

23. It will be for each council to decide on the level of control appropriate to local circumstances. It has been open to councils since 1972 to resolve to extend taxi licensing throughout their district. Consequently, none of the areas affected by Section 15 are those for which the responsible council has seen a compelling need to apply taxi licensing. In view of this the Government does not recommend the setting up of an extensive or burdensome licensing system. The application of taxi licensing to previously uncontrolled areas was provided for in the 1985 Act in order to protect the safety of passengers. While regulating vehicle and driver standards the Council may not consider it necessary to control the way in which the taxi service is operated. In particular, the Government can see no reason why a council should seek to limit the number of taxis licensed to operate in these areas. There may be no need to control taxi fares; in the past these have been set by the operators, and councils may wish to allow this to continue. On the same basis, the imposition of exacting constructional requirements for vehicles is unlikely to be justified: such regulatory requirements impose a cost on the taxi trade, which must ultimately be borne by taxi passengers.

VEHICLE STANDARDS

24. The only vehicle requirement imposed by national legislation (other than those governing the fitness of any road vehicle) is in respect of seating capacity.

A vehicle adapted to carry more than eight passengers that is used for hire or reward is a public service vehicle. Consequently, a taxi may have no more than eight passenger seats. Historically, taxis have been saloon cars licensed to carry four or five passengers and the attention of licensing authorities is drawn to the higher legal seating limit. Vehicles adapted to carry seven or eight passengers may be particularly suitable for the provision of shared taxi or 'bus' services and their use should not be precluded by vehicle licensing pre-conditions. Such preconditions may be laid down in order to ensure that a vehicle is suitable in type and design for use as a taxi. In deciding whether there is a need to prescribe such conditions councils will wish to consider whether their absence has resulted in this operation of unsuitable vehicles or is likely to do so.

25. A council will wish to ensure that the vehicles that it licences are mechanically sound, roadworthy and safe. This is normally achieved by granting licences for one year subject to the vehicle passing an annual test. Testing may be delegated to suitable garage companies in the area or other local agents or, where the council has its own testing facilities; they may undertake this work themselves. The cost of vehicle testing may be recovered as part of the licence fee (see paragraph 29) and should not be charged separately.

26. Some councils set advisory age limits on the vehicles they are prepared to licence. These cannot be rigidly enforced and if a vehicle proves to be in a satisfactory condition it should be licensed regardless of its age. It has recently come to the notice of the Department that some councils are proposing to insist that any vehicle submitted for initial licensing must be new. This is seen as an unwarranted restriction on entry to the trade for would-be taxi proprietors.

DRIVERS' STANDARDS

27. A district council will wish to satisfy itself that an applicant for a taxi driver's licence is a fit and proper person. The Medical Commission on Accident Prevention has drawn up guidelines on medical fitness of applicants for the holders of vocational driving licences (Medical Aspects of Fitness to Drive, £3 inc p & p from 35–43 Lincolns Inn Fields, London WC2A 3PN).

28. Many councils set a special driving test for taxi drivers and some test their geographical knowledge of the taxi licensing area. Neither of these tests are likely to be appropriate for the licensing of taxi drivers in an area to which Section 15 applies.

FINANCIAL AND MANPOWER EFFECTS

29. This Circular is concerned with the implementation of the 1985 Act. The financial and manpower effects for local authorities of the Act as a whole are described in paragraphs 188 to 191 of Department Circular 3/85 (Welsh Office Circular 64/85). Under Section 35 of the Transport Act 1981, a district council may recover in the form of licensing fees the reasonable administrative or other costs incurred in connection with the licensing, control and supervision of taxis.

MODEL BYELAWS FOR HACKNEY CARRIAGES   ANNEX

(revised 1974)

[Note: When submitting draft byelaws for provisional approval it is Important that the required assurances should be given about the siting of stands [No 15, footnote (1)] the operation of taximeters [No 15, footnote (2) and No 4, footnote (1)(a)] and, where appropriate, about the custody of lost property [No 17, footnote (1).]

BYELAWS

Made under section 68 of the Town Police Clauses Act 1847, and section 171 of thePublic Health Act 1875, by the[1] with respect to hackney carriages in[2]

Interpretation

1. Throughout these byelaws 'the Council' means the[1]   and 'the district' means[2]   .

Notes.

1   Insert 'District Council of

2   Insert name of district.

Provisions regulating the manner in which the number of each hackney carriage corresponding with the number of its licence, shall be displayed

2.

    (*a*)   The proprietor of a hackney carriage shall cause the number of the licence granted to him in respect of the carriage to be legibly painted or marked on the outside and inside of the carriage, or on plates affixed thereto,

    (*b*)   A proprietor or driver of a hackney carriage shall –

        i.   not wilfully or negligently cause or suffer any such number to be concealed from public view while the carriage is standing or plying for hire;

        ii.   not cause or permit the carriage to stand or ply for hire with any such painting, marking or plate so defaced that any figure or material particular is illegible.

Provisions regulating how hackney carriages are to be furnished or provided

3. The proprietor of a hackney carriage shall –

    (*a*)   provide sufficient means by which any person in the carriage may communicate with the driver,

    (*b*)   cause the roof or covering to be kept water-tight;

    (*c*)   provide any necessary windows and a means of opening and closing not less than one window on each side;

    (*d*)   cause the seats to be properly cushioned or covered;

(e)   cause the floor to be provided with a proper carpet, mat, or other suitable covering;

(f)   cause the fittings and furniture generally to be kept in a clean condition, well maintained and in every way fit for public service;

(g)   provide means for securing luggage if the carriage is so constructed as to carry luggage;

(h)   provide an efficient fire extinguisher which shall be carried in such a position as to be readily available or use; and

(i)   provide at least two doors for the use of persons conveyed in such carriage and a separate means of ingress and egress for the driver.

4.[1] The proprietor of a hackney carriage shall cause any taximeter with which the carriage is provided to be so constructed, attached, and maintained as to comply with the following requirements, that is to say –

(a)   the taximeter shall be fitted with a key, flag, or other device the turning of which will bring the machinery of the taximeter into action and cause the word 'HIRED' to appear on the face of the taximeter,

(b)   such key, flag, or other device shall be capable of being locked in such a position that the machinery of the taximeter is not in action and that no fare is recorded on the face of the taximeter;

(c)   when the machinery of the taximeter is in action there shall be recorded on the face of the taximeter in clearly legible figures a fare not exceeding the rate or fare which the proprietor or driver is entitled to demand and take for the hire of the carriage by [time as well as for] distance in pursuance of the byelaw[2] in that behalf;

(d)   the word 'FARE' shall be printed on the face of the taximeter in plain letters so as clearly to apply to the fare recorded thereon;

(e)   the taximeter shall be so placed that all letters and figures on the face thereof are at all times plainly visible to any person being conveyed in the carriage, and for that purpose the letters and figures shall be capable of being suitably illuminated during any period of hiring; and

(f)   the taximeter and all the fittings thereof shall be so affixed to the carriage with seals or other appliances that it shall not be practicable for any person to tamper with them except by breaking, damaging or permanently displacing the seals or other appliances.

Notes.

1   (a)   An assurance should be given that proprietors of cabs already fitted with taximeters will have no difficulty in complying with the byelaws relating to taximeters, and, where the byelaws will require all cabs to be fitted with meters, that the other proprietors will be able to obtain and fit suitable meters and 'FOR HIRE' signs by the time the byelaws may be expected to come into operation.

      (b)   Where the Council wishes to require all cabs to be fitted with a taximeter, the following form of words may be used;

           'The proprietor of a hackney carriage shall cause the same to be provided with a taximeter so constructed, attached and maintained as to comply with the following requirements, that is to say,'

      (c)   Where taximeters are not in use and their use cannot be foreseen, model byelaws 4, 5 and 6 may be omitted. If they are omitted, the heading preceding model byelaw 5 should remain.

2   On adoption of Local Government (Miscellaneous Provisions) Act 1976 'byelaw' should be deleted and 'tariff fixed by the Council' should be inserted.

Provisions regulating the conduct of the proprietors and drivers of hackney carriages plying within the district in their several employments, and determining whether such drivers shall wear any and what badges

5. The driver of a hackney carriage provided with a taximeter shall –

   (*a*)   when standing or plying for hire, keep the key, flag or other device fitted in pursuance of the byelaw in that behalf locked in the position in which no fare is recorded on the face of the taximeter,

   (*b*)   Before beginning a journey for which a fare is charged for distance [and time], bring the machinery of the taximeter into action by moving the said key, flag or other device, so that the word 'HIRED' is legible on the face of the taximeter and keep the machinery of the taximeter in action until the termination of the hiring; and

   (*c*)   cause the dial of the taximeter to be kept properly illuminated throughout any part of a hiring which is during the hours of darkness as defined for the purposes of the Road Traffic Act 1972, and also at any other time at the request of the hirer.

6. A proprietor or driver of a hackney carriage shall not tamper with or permit any person to tamper with any taximeter with which the carriage is provided, with the fittings thereof, or with the seals affixed thereto.

7. The driver of a hackney carriage shall, when plying for hire in any street and not actually hired –

   (*a*)   proceed with reasonable speed to one of the stands fixed by the byelaw in that behalf;

   (*b*)   if a stand, at the time of his arrival, is occupied by the full number of carriages authorized to occupy it, proceed to another stand;

   (*c*)   on arriving at a stand not already occupied by the full number of carriages authorized to occupy it, station the carriage immediately behind the carriage or carriages on the stand and so as to face in the same direction; and

   (*d*)   from time to time when any other carriage immediately in front is driven off or moved forward cause his carriage to be moved forward so as to fill the place previously occupied by the carriage driven off or moved forward.

8. A proprietor or driver of a hackney carriage, when standing or plying for hire, shall not, by calling out or otherwise, importune any person to hire such carriage and shall not make use of the services of any other person for the purpose.

9. The driver of a hackney carriage shall behave in a civil and orderly manner and shall take all reasonable precautions to ensure the safety of persons conveyed in or entering or alighting from the vehicle.

10. The proprietor or driver of a hackney carriage who has agreed or has been hired to be in attendance with the carriage at an appointed time and place shall,

unless delayed or prevented by some sufficient cause, punctually attend with such carriage at such appointed time and place.

11. The driver of a hackney carriage when hired to drive to any particular destination shall, subject to any directions given by the hirer, proceed to that destination by the shortest available route[1].

Note.

1   Where the Local Government (Miscellaneous Provisions) Act 1976 has been adopted, this byelaw will be replaced by the provisions of Section 69 of that Act.

12. A proprietor or driver of a hackney carriage shall not convey or permit to be conveyed in such carriage any greater number of persons than the number of persons specified on the plate affixed to the outside of the carriage.

13. If a badge has been provided by the Council and delivered to the driver of a hackney carriage he shall, when standing or plying for hire, and when hired, wear that badge in such position and manner as to be plainly visible.

14. The driver of a hackney carriage so constructed as to carry luggage shall, when requested by any person hiring or seeking to hire the carriage –

(*a*)   convey a reasonable quantity of luggage;

(*b*)   afford reasonable assistance in loading and unloading; and

(*c*)   afford reasonable assistance in removing it to or from the entrance of any building, station, or place at which he may take up or set down such person.

Provisions fixing the stands of hackney carriages[1]

15. 'Each of the several places specified in the following list shall be a stand for such number of hackney carriages as is specified in the list[2,3].

Notes.

1   Assurances are required that –

(a)   the proposed stands are not situated on parking places provided by the Council under section 32 of the Road Traffic Regulation Act 1984, or an earlier similar provision;

(b)   the police are in agreement with the siting of the stands, so far as traffic considerations are concerned; and

(c)   i.   the proposed stands are situated on roads for the maintenance of which the Council is responsible; or

ii.   where any other person or authority is responsible for the maintenance of the road, the consent of that authority or person has been obtained. (In the case of a stand on railway property such consent should, if possible, be in terms, which relieve proprietors and drivers of the necessity to obtain permission individually to use the stand.)

2   Descriptions of the stands should be sufficient to enable them to be identified (eg against the kerb opposite nos 93 to 97 King Street.)

3   This byelaw will cease to have effect on adoption of Local Government (Miscellaneous Provisions) Act 1976 by virtue of Section 63(4) of that Act.

Provisions fixing the rates or fares to be paid for hackney carriages within the district, and securing the due publication of such fares[1]

16. The proprietor or driver of a hackney carriage shall be entitled to demand and take for the hire of the carriage the rate or fare prescribed by the attached

table[2,5] the rate or fare being calculated by distance unless the hirer express at the commencement of the hiring his desire to engage by time[3].

Provided always that where a hackney carriage furnished with a taximeter shall be hired by distance the proprietor or driver thereof shall not be entitled to demand and take a fare greater than that recorded on the face of the taximeter, save for any extra charges authorised by the attached table[5] which it may not be possible to record on the face of the taximeter[4].

Notes.
1   The desirability of consultations with the local cab trade, whilst at the same time bearing in mind the interests of the cab using public, should not be overlooked when fares are being considered, in view of the possibility of objections being made at a later stage.
2   In compiling the table, care should be taken to ensure that no difficulties will arise as to the recording of the fares by taximeters. An assurance should be given that the fares will be capable of being recorded in the prescribed units by all taximeters likely to be employed on cabs in the district, or, alternatively, that no taximeters are in use in the district and that their use in the future is not foreseen.
3   When no fares for time are prescribed, hirings by time will be uncontrolled and the fare will be subject to individual contract in each case. In view of the difficulty of fixing fares for time, which are reasonable to both parties, this is generally regarded as preferable.
4   This proviso should be included whether or not taximeters are introduced in case they are introduced on a voluntary basis before further byelaws are made.
5   On adoption of the Local Government (Miscellaneous Provisions) Act 1976 'attached table' should be deleted and 'Council' inserted.

17.

    (*a*)   The proprietor of a hackney carriage shall cause a statement of the fares fixed by byelaw[1] to be exhibited inside the carriage, in clearly distinguishable letters and figures.

    (*b*)   The proprietor or driver of a hackney carriage bearing a statement of fares in accordance with this byelaw shall not wilfully or negligently cause or suffer the letters of figures in the statement to be concealed or rendered illegible at any time while the carriage is plying or being used for hire.

Note.
1   On adoption of the Local Government (Miscellaneous Provisions) Act 1976 'byelaw' should be deleted and 'council resolution' inserted.

Provisions securing the safe custody and re-delivery of any property accidentally left in hackney carriages, and fixing the charges to be made in respect thereof

18. The proprietor or driver of a hackney carriage shall immediately after the termination of any hiring or as soon as practicable thereafter carefully search the carriage for any property which may have been accidentally left therein.

19. The proprietor or driver of a hackney carriage shall, if any property accidentally left therein by any person who may have been conveyed in the carriage be found by or handed to him –

    (*a*)   carry it as soon as possible and in any event within 48 hours, if not sooner claimed by or on behalf of its owner, to[1] the office of the

Council, and leave it in the custody of the officer in charge of the office on his giving a receipt for it; and

(*b*)   be entitled to receive from any person to whom the property shall be redelivered an amount equal to five pence in the pound of its estimated value (or the fare for the distance from the place of finding to the office of the Council, whichever be the greater) but not more than five pounds.

Note.
1   It may be desired to substitute 'a police station in the district'. In this case an assurance will be required that the consent of the police has been obtained.

Penalties

20. Every person who shall offend against any of these byelaws shall be liable on summary conviction to a fine not exceeding one hundred pounds and in the case of a continuing offence to a further fine not exceeding five pounds for each day during which the offence continues after conviction therefor.

Repeal of byelaws[1]

21. The byelaws relating to hackney carriages which were made by the Council[2] on the day of and which were confirmed by[3] on the day of are hereby repealed.

Notes.
1   If there are no byelaws in force upon the subject, this should be stated and the clause struck out.
2   State names in full of all local authorities whose byelaws are to be repealed.
3   State the confirming authority, e.g. The Local Government Board; the Minister of Health; One of the Principal Secretaries of State of His Late Majesty King George VI; One of Her Majesty's Principal Secretaries of State.

Table of fares in relation to byelaw 16[1]

		New pence
(i)	Mileage	
If the distance does not exceed one mile		V
	for the whole distance	
If the distance exceeds one mile		
	for the first mile	V
	For each subsequent yards or uncompleted part thereof	W
(ii)	Waiting time[2]	
For each period of minutes or uncompleted part thereof		W
(iii)	Extra charges[3]	
a.	For hirings begun between p.m./Midnight and a.m.	X% of the above rate or fare

b.   For each article of luggage conveyed outside
     the passenger compartment of the carriage   Yp

c.   For each person in excess of   Xp

Notes.

1   On adoption of the Local Government (Miscellaneous Provisions) Act 1976 this table will be
    replaced by the 'Table of Fares' provided for by Section 65 of that Act.

2   Where taximeters are in use, or are likely to be brought into use, it will be necessary to permit all
    waiting time to be charged in order to prevent contravention of byelaw 4(c). Taximeters record
    all waiting, whether at the hirer's request or due to traffic congestion.

3   The 'extra charges' table is included only for the guidance of local authorities who wish to
    prescribe extra charges; it should not be taken as indicating that all or any of the extra charges
    should necessarily be prescribed.

DOT Circular 4/87, 16 November 1987

TRANSPORT ACT 1985:
QUANTITY CONTROL OF TAXIS

1. A number of District Councils have approached the Department for further advice on the application of Section 16 of the Transport Act 1985.

2. Previous advice on the effect of this Section on the grant of taxi licences was contained in paragraphs 27 and 28 of Department of Transport Circular 3/85 (Welsh Office Circular 64/85).

3. Of the Court cases that have been brought since this legislation came into force on 6 January 1986, three have been heard in the High Court. Two of these (*R v Gravesham Borough Council ex parte Gravesham Association of Licensed Hackney Carriage Owners and R v Transport Committee of Great Yarmouth ex parte Sawyer* (C0/572/86 and C0/601/86 unreported) took the form of judicial reviews of resolutions made by the licensing authorities to de-restrict the number of licences issued. In his judgement on both cases, Mr Justice Hodgson said:

> "It follows that, in my judgement, an authority which was exercising a restriction policy prior to 1986 could rescind that policy and adopt in its place a policy with no numerical ceiling to the number of licences issued. A policy, in other words, of allowing market forces to take their course. It could also adopt such a policy whether or not there was unmet demand, so that there was no obligation on an authority to consider the question of demand at all. It follows that the adopting of a policy of de-restriction could not of itself be attacked in any circumstances as irrational. I have therefore to consider the two cases on the basis that the decisions are unimpeachable, unless it can be shown that there was some procedural impropriety or that, in arriving at its decision, either authority took into account irrelevant matter or failed to take into account relevant matters."

4. The Judge dismissed both Applications. Mr Sawyer appealed the Judge's decision and the appeal was heard on 16 June 1987 by Lord Justice Dillon, Lord Justice Woolf and Lord Justice Bingham (reported in the Times Law Report for 18 June 1987). The appellant argued that Mr Justice Hodgson was in error in saying that the policy of derestriction could not of itself be attacked in any circumstancs as irrational. Lord Justice Woolf commented that "the passage of which complaint is made is to be construed not as indicating that [it is] impossible for the Court to intervene, but as being a reference to the practical difficulties involved in doing SO". The Court of Appeal upheld the judgement at first instance.

5. In the third case (*R v Reading Borough Council ex parte Egan and Same v Same ex parte Sullman* (C0/318/86 and C0/612/86, as reported in the Times Law Report for 12 June 1987) applications were bought for an order of certiorari to quash a decision made by the Transport Committee of the Reading Borough Council

"that in accordance with the suggestion of the Department of Transport in paragraph 28 of Circular 3/85, the Chief Executive and Town Clerk be authorised to issue up to 30 new Hackney Carriage licences (to be issued by ballot, on the basis of 1 licence per applicant) and that other applications be deferred until the effects of granting these additional licences have been assessed".

6. The question before the Court, therefore, was (to quote from the judgement):

"Whether a Council which is unsure of the presence or absence of unmet demand, but which fears that immediate and total de-restriction may cause over-provision, is entitled to issue a limited number of further licences as a temporary measure, and as a means of obtaining the evidence by which the presence or absence of unmet demand can finally be established."

7. In answering this question, Mr Justice Nolan said that such a Council was "obliged to grant applications for licences in respect of suitably qualified vehicles without limit of number" and that "Paragraph 28 of the Circular appears to me to incorporate an erroneous view of the law".

8. It follows from these judgements that:

a.   a Council may adopt a policy of de-restricting the number of taxi licences that it issues, without considering the question of demand;

b.   it is not open to a Council which is unsure of the presence or absence of significant unmet demand to refuse to grant any application for a taxi licence for the purpose of limiting the number of taxi licences; and

c.   a Council which believes that there is significant unmet demand and is able to quantify the extent of that demand must grant at least such number of taxi licences as it considers necessary to ensure that no significant unmet demand remains.

9. It is, of course, open to a Council which is satisfied that there is no significant unmet demand to refuse to grant additional taxi licences.

10. The advice contained in Paragraph 28 of Circular 3/85 is now withdrawn.

A2.13

DOT Circular 2/92; HO Circular 13/92

DISCLOSURE OF CRIMINAL RECORDS: APPLICANTS FOR HACKNEY CARRIAGE & PRIVATE HIRE VEHICLE DRIVERS' LICENCES

SUMMARY

1. This circular advises local authorities on the procedures to adopt for checking with the police the criminal convictions of applicants for hackney carriage and private hire vehicle drivers' licences. They apply where –

- local authorities have responsibilities under the Local Government (Miscellaneous Provisions) Act 1976; or
- any local Act contains a provision requiring a local authority to be satisfied as to the fimess of an applicant to hold a licence to drive a hackney carriage or a private hire vehicle.

2. This facility does not apply to local authorities who have not adopted the Local Government (Miscellaneous Provisions) Act 1976 and therefore license hackney carriage drivers by virtue of the Town Police Clauses Act 1847 only.

Annex A – explains the procedure.
Annex B – sets out a model local policy statement.
Annex C – is a model request for a police check.
Annex D – contains example guidelines relating to the relevance of convictions.

ACTION

3. The procedure described in Annex A comes into effect on 1 April 1992. Local authorities responsible for the licensing of drivers of hackney carriages or private hire vehicles are asked to adopt it for gaining access to the police records described, and to nominate an officer to liaise with the police. The name of the nominated officer should be given to the police as soon as possible.

BACKGROUND

4. These arrangements stem from Section 47 of the Road Traffic Act 1991 which provides that a council may send to the chief officer of police for the police area in which the council is situated a copy of an application for a hackney carriage or private hire vehicle driver's licence and may request the chief officer's observations on it. The chief officer is required to respond to the request. The arrangements are intended to assist local authorities in satisfying themselves that applicants are fit and proper persons to hold driver licences. The arrangements do not apply to London.

5. This Circular has been drawn up in consultation with representatives of the local authority associations, the Association of Chief Police Officers and taxi trade associations.

ENQUIRIES

6. Contact points for enquiries are:

From local authorities	From the Police:
Mrs. K Turnbull	Mr F E Whittaker
Department of Transport	F2 Division
Room S15/20	Home Office
2 Marsham Street	50 Queen Anne's Gate
LONDON SW1P 3EB	LONDON SW 1H 9AT

ANNEX A

DISCLOSURE OF CRIMINAL RECORDS

APPLICANTS FOR HACKNEY CARRIAGE AND PRIVATE HIRE VEHICLE DRIVERS' LICENCES

Scope

1. The legislation provides that local authorities with responsibilities under the Local Government (Miscellaneous Provisions Act 1976 (the Act)) or equivalent local legislation may ask the chief officer of police for their area for his observations on –

- any application for a licence to drive a hackney carriage;
- any application for renewal of a licence to drive a hackney carriage;
- any application for a licence to drive a private hire vehicle under Section 51 of the Act;
- any application for renewal of a licence to drive a private hire vehicle

where the application was received on or after 1 April 1992 or was under consideration at that date.

The police check

2. In all cases the police check will be made against the index to the national collection of criminal records maintained on the Police National Computer (PNC). These records include details of persons convicted of all offences, broadly speaking, for which a term of imprisonment may be given.

3. Hackney carriage and private hire vehicle (PHV) driver licences may run for up to three years, although many authorities re-grant them annually. Because

of constraints on resources authorities should note that, in commenting on an application, the police will normally only conduct a criminal record check if the licence is being granted or re-granted for the first time under these arrangements, or if a period of three years has elapsed since the applicant was last subject to a criminal record check (but see also paragraphs 17 and 25).

Nominated officer

4. An officer in each local authority to whom these arrangements apply should take responsibility for requesting checks from the police. Authorities should give their police force details of their nominated officer as soon as possible. He or she should be responsible for –

- overseeing the operation of the checking procedure within the authority;
- ensuring that requests fall within the terms of the legislation and this circular;
- ensuring that requests are made at the right time;
- ensuring that the provisions of the Rehabilitation of Offenders Act 1974 are observed;
- ensuring that information received from the police is released only to those who need to see it, and
- ensuring that records are kept securely and for no longer than is -necessary.

Procedure

5. Police checks should not take the place of normal licensing procedures. Other checks to establish a person's integrity and fitness to hold a licence to drive a hackney carriage or PHV should be carried out, and attempts made to account satisfactorily for any unexplained gaps in employment.

6. A police check should not be requested if an applicant is unsuitable for other reasons.

7. In considering applications from potential licence holders authorities should be aware that applicants do not have to reveal, and licensing authorities must not take into account, offences which are spent under the Rehabilitation of Offenders Act 1974, although these may be included in any record provided by the police. The nominated officer should take responsibility for identifying spent convictions and ensuring that those considering the application are not influenced by them.

8. An applicant should be informed in writing that a police check will be carried out.

9. Authorities should make every effort to confirm the identity of the applicant before the police are asked to process a check. Verification of identity, date of birth and any change of name should be obtained. Apart from checking any available documentation such as birth certificate, passport, driving licence etc,

it is recommended that independent verification of the applicant's identity is sought, perhaps from a previous employer. Incomplete or incorrect identification details may invalidate the police check and lead to a failure to discover relevant convictions.

10. Authorities may wish to consider making a policy statement available to people who will be subject to a criminal records check under these arrangements. A model statement is offered at Annex B.

11. When a police check is desired, the request should be sent to the Chief Constable of the police force for the area in which the applicant has applied for a licence. Requests should be made in a form consistent with the model layout shown at Annex C.

12. The police will reply to the nominated officer either indicating that there is no trace on national police records of a record which matches the details provided, or that those details appear identical with the person whose record will be attached. The record will contain details of all convictions recorded nationally against that person.

13. It should be noted that the police record will not include details of motoring convictions. Such information may be obtained from the Driver and Vehicle Licensing Agency. This will be provided on receipt of a written request, which must include the subject's driver number, or failing that, their full name and date of birth. A fee of £3.50 (for each individual enquiry) is payable at the time the request is made. The information given will include endorsement/ disqualification details. Requests should be sent to –

> DEU (Data Subject Enquiries)
> Room C 1/16
> DVLA
> Longview Road
> Swansea 5A6 7JL.

14. Where

- the information provided by the police differs from that provided by the applicant, and is of significance, the nominated officer should discuss the discrepancy with the applicant before reaching any final decision in which the nature of the information received is a factor;
- there is disagreement, the person should have the opportunity to see the information provided by the police.

15. It should be noted that applicants themselves may reveal certain minor convictions or cautions which are not recorded in the national collection of criminal records and, therefore, not included in the convictions provided by the police. In general, corroboration of such convictions or cautions should not be sought from the police.

16. A person who believes the information provided by the police is incorrect and who wishes to make representations to the police should do so in the first

place through the nominated officer. Authorities will want to ensure that cases of this kind are dealt with at an appropriate level.

Checks on persons already in possession of hackney carriage/phv drivers' licences

17. Checks should not normally be made on persons other than in connection with an application for grant or renewal of a licence. If, however, serious allegations are made against a driver, or previously unrevealed information comes to light and the nominated officer is satisfied that the information cannot be verified in any other way, a police check may be requested. This should not be done without the knowledge of the individual concerned who must be given an opportunity to discuss the outcome of the check.

Use of information

18. The fact that a person has a criminal record or is known to the police does not necessarily mean that he or she is unfit to hold a driver's licence. The authority concerned should make a balanced judgement about a person's suitability taking into account only those offences which are considered relevant to the person's suitability to hold a licence. A person's suitability should be looked at as a whole in the light of all the information available.

19. In deciding the relevance of convictions, authorities will want to bear in mind that offences which took place many years in the past may often have less relevance than recent offences. Similarly, a series of offences over a period of time is more likely to give cause for concern than an isolated minor conviction. In any event the importance of rehabilitation must be weighed against the need to protect the public.

20. In order to ensure consistent and fair treatment when determining whether or not criminal convictions render an applicant unsuitable to hold a licence, local authorities may find it very helpful to draw up detailed policy guidelines containing general criteria against which applications may be considered. The guidelines at Annex D are based on those used by the Metropolitan Police and are offered to local authorities as an example which they may wish to use or adapt.

21. Where it is discovered that a driver, licensed prior to implementation of section 47, had failed to disclose past convictions, local authorities will need to consider carefully whether they should now refuse to re-grant the driver licence. In most cases, if those convictions are such that they would now lead to the refusal of a licence, refusal should be considered. If, however, previously unrevealed convictions are discovered which would not now disqualify the individual from holding a licence, consideration should normally be given to granting it. It is possible that a significant proportion of drivers will be shown to have concealed previous convictions and it is recommended that local authorities develop a consistent and fair policy when dealing with them.

Appeals

22. Any person who is aggrieved by the licensing authority's decision to refuse a driver's licence may appeal to a Magistrates' Court.

Storage and destruction of records

23. Any information the police supply will be of a sensitive and personal nature. It must be used only in connection with the application which gave rise to the request for a check to be made. The nominated officer must ensure it is kept securely while the licensing process takes its course and that the information is not kept for longer than is necessary. An indication on the Authority's own record that a check with the police has been carried out may be made but should not refer to specific offences.

Checks on applicants from overseas

24. Other than in exceptional circumstances, the police cannot –

- make enquiries about the antecedents of people from overseas; or
- establish details of convictions acquired outside the United Kingdom.

Applicants from certain EC countries may, however, be able to produce certificates of good conduct.

Police reporting of convictions as they occur

25. If a police force is able to identify that the holder of a driver licence has acquired a relevant conviction, it will give details to the local nominated officer. This will occur only where the police are aware that a person is licensed under the Act and so will not mean that the nominated officer will automatically get information about all relevant convictions.

Police monitoring

26. Where possible forces are asked to collate the following information in respect of each authority with which they deal:

- number of PNC checks requested,
- time taken to process checks,
- number of positive traces, and
- any apparent difficulties with these arrangements, including the resource implications.

27. The results of this monitoring will be kept under review by the Home Office in conjunction with the Association of Chief Police Officers and the local authority associations.

[Annex A is no longer relevant due to the availability of Criminal Records Bureau Disclosures]

ANNEX B

STATEMENT OF POLICY ABOUT RELEVANT CONVICTIONS

(See Annex A, paragraph 10)

When formulating their own policy, local authorities may wish to consider using the following statement, suitably adapted:

> 'When submitting an application for a licence to drive a hackney carriage or private hire vehicle you are requested to declare any convictions or cautions you may have, unless they are regarded as "spent:" under the Rehabilitation of Offenders Act 1974. The information you give will be treated in confidence and will only be taken into account in relation to your application.
>
> You should be aware that the licensing authority is empowered in law to check with the police for the existence and content of any criminal record held in the name of an applicant. Information received from the police will be kept in strict confidence while the licensing process takes its course and will be retained for no longer than is necessary.
>
> The disclosure of a criminal record or other information will not debar you from gaining a licence unless the authority considers that the conviction renders you unsuitable. In making this decision the authority will consider the nature of the offence, how long ago and what age you were when it was committed and any other factors which may be relevant. [Authorities may wish to refer to any guidelines to which they adhere.] Any applicant refused a driver's licence on the ground that he/she is not a fit and proper person to hold such a licence has a right of appeal to a Magistrates' Court.
>
> If you would like to discuss what effect a conviction might have on your application you may telephone [A N Other on 012 – 345 – 6789] in confidence, for advice.'

[Annex C is no longer relevant due to the availability of Criminal Records Bureau Disclosures]

ANNEX D

It is recommended that local authorities adopt their own guidelines relating to the relevance of convictions for use in determining applications for hackney carriage and private hire vehicle (PHV) drivers, licences. The following is an example only and is based on criteria used by the Metropolitan Police.

GUIDELINES RELATING TO THE RELEVANCE OF CONVICTIONS

General policy

1. Each case will be decided on its own merits.

2. A person with a current conviction for serious crime need not be permanently barred from obtaining a licence but should be expected to remain free of conviction for 3 to 5 years, according to the circumstances, before an application is entertained. Some discretion may be appropriate if the offence is isolated and there are mitigating circumstances. However, the overriding consideration should be the protection of the public.

3. The following examples afford a general guide on the action to be taken where convictions are admitted.

(a) Minor traffic offences

Convictions for minor traffic offences, eg obstruction, waiting in a restricted street, speeding etc, should not prevent a person from proceeding with an application. If sufficient points have been accrued to require a period of disqualification of the applicant's driving licence then a hackney carriage or PHV licence may be granted after its restoration but a warning should be issued as to future conduct.

(b) Major traffic offences

An isolated conviction for reckless driving or driving without due care and attention etc, should normally merit a warning as to future driving and advice on the standard expected of hackney carriage and PHV drivers. More than one conviction for this type of offence within the last two years should merit refusal and no further application should be considered until a period of 1 to 3 years free from convictions has elapsed.

(c) Drunkenness

(i) With motor vehicle

A serious view should be taken of convictions of driving or being in charge of a vehicle while under the influence of drink. An isolated incident should not necessarily debar an applicant but strict warnings should be given as to future behaviour. More than one conviction for these offences should raise grave doubts as to the applicant's fitness to hold a licence. At least 3 years should elapse (after the restoration of the driving licence) before an applicant is considered for a licence. If there is any suggestion that the applicant is an alcoholic, a special medical examination should be arranged before the application is entertained. If the applicant is found to be an alcoholic a period of years should elapse after treatment is complete before a further licence application is considered.

(ii) Not in motor vehicle

An isolated conviction for drunkenness need not debar an applicant from gaining a licence. However, a number of convictions for drunkenness could indicate a medical problem necessitating critical examination (see (i) above). In some cases, a warning may be sufficient.

(d) Drugs

An applicant with a conviction for a drug related offence should be required to show a period of at least 3 years free of convictions before an application is entertained, or 5 years after detoxification treatment if he/she was an addict.

(e) Indecency offences

As hackney carriage and PHV drivers often carry unaccompanied passengers, applicants with convictions for indecent exposure, indecent assault, importuning, or any of the more serious sexual offences, should be refused until they can show a substantial period (at least 3 to 5 years) free of such offences. More than one conviction of this kind should preclude consideration for at least 5 years. In either case if a licence is granted a strict warning as to future conduct should be issued.

(f) Violence

As hackney carriage and PHV drivers maintain close contact with the public, a firm line should be taken with applicants who have convictions for grievous bodily harm, wounding or assault. At least 3 years free of such convictions should be shown before an application is entertained and even then a strict warning should be administered.

(g) Dishonesty

Hackney carriage and PHV drivers are expected to be persons of trust. The widespread practice of delivering unaccompanied property is indicative of the trust that business people place in drivers. Moreover, it is comparatively easy for a dishonest driver to defraud the public by demanding more than the legal fare etc. Overseas visitors can be confused by the change in currency and became 'fair game' for an unscrupulous driver. For these reasons a serious view should be taken of any conviction involving dishonesty. In general, a period of 3 to 5 years free of conviction should be required before entertaining an application.

Hackney Carriage Byelaws:
Local Government Reorganisation (England)

1. This note explains the Department of Transport's position in respect of hackney carriage byelaws submitted by those local licensing authorities affected by changes arising from the Local Government Act 1992. This advice concerns only England. Different considerations apply to Wales by virtue of the Local Government (Wales) Act 1994.

THE LOCAL GOVERNMENT ACT 1992

2. Essentially, the 1992 Act allowed for three types of changes to be implemented –

- a structural change involving the replacement, in a non-metropolitan area, of the two principal tiers of local government with a single tier;
- a boundary change which may be made for the purposes of facilitating a structural change or independently of such a change. It may involve the alteration of a local government area, the constitution of a local government area by the amalgamation of more such areas or the abolition of an area and its distribution amongst other areas;
- electoral changes which are changes in the electoral arrangements for a local government area, whether made in consequence of any structural or boundary change or independently of any such change.

3. So far as taxi licensing is concerned, structural changes are not in themselves a problem; where one tier of local government ceases to exist, without boundary changes, all the functions of local government in the area are exercisable by a single authority. Neither is there a problem in respect of electoral changes. The problems affecting taxi licensing are generated by the boundary changes that accompany structural changes.

DEVELOPMENT OF TAXI ZONES

4. In considering the effect of boundary changes on taxi licensing, it is first appropriate to trace the history of the zoning concept up to the coming into force on 1st January 1987 of section 15 of the Transport Act 1985.

i 1847–1974

5. The Town Police Clauses Act 1847 refers to 'the prescribed distance' and defines the word 'prescribed' as referring to such matter as may be prescribed or provided for in the special Act. The prescribed distance is particularly relevant as the distance within which a hackney carriage may be licensed to ply for hire (section 37) and the distance within which the driver of the hackney carriage can be compelled to go (section 53). There are numerous other references to it.

6. Section 5 (repealed) of the Public Health Act 1875 provided that England (except the metropolis) should consist of districts to be called urban sanitary districts and rural sanitary districts which were to be subject to the jurisdiction of local authorities, respectively called urban sanitary authorities and rural sanitary authorities, which were invested with various powers mentioned in the Act. Section 171 (which is still in force) dealt with the Town Police Clauses Act 1847. That Act was originally a clauses Act, that is to say it had no independent existence of its own and only applied to an area if there was a special Act so applying it. Section 171 of the 1875 Act applied the provisions of the 1847 Act with respect to hackney carriages and provided that, for the purposes of regulating hackney carriages in urban districts, those provisions should be incorporated with the 1875 Act; the expression 'within the prescribed distance' was defined for the purposes of that Act as meaning within any urban district.

7. At this point there was no concept of 'zoning'; a single urban authority licensed hackney carriages to ply for hire within the whole of the urban district.

8. Under the Local Government Act 1894, urban sanitary authorities became urban districts and urban sanitary authorities urban district councils, except where the area consisted of a borough. Under the Local Government Act 1933 the relevant areas for taxi licensing were county districts, which could be either urban district councils or non-county boroughs, and county boroughs. In a few cases taxi licensing was extended to rural districts by virtue of orders under section 276 of the Public Health Act 1875.

ii Local Government Act 1974

9. In 1974 effect was given to the reorganisation set out in the Local Government Act 1972. All local authorities inside England and Wales were abolished and a new two-tier system of county councils and district councils was constituted. They key provision of the 1972 Act is section 180. This provides that for the purposes of (inter alia) the Public Health Act 1875, the local authority and sanitary authority (whether urban or not) for a district is the district council. Section 180 introduced Schedule 14, Part II of which provided that section 171(4) of the Public Health Act 1875 should apply to those areas, and only those, to which it applied immediately before 1st April 1974. In the Department's view, it is this provision, which established the concept of zoning.

10. What it meant in practice was that the taxi licensing situation within new district councils effectively became 'frozen'; a prescribed distance before the change remained a prescribed distance after the change. Consequently, a new district council which, for example, incorporated two former urban districts (i.e. two district prescribed distances) would administer taxi licensing for those two districts or 'zones'. The new district council might also have inherited an area which was not a former urban district and where taxis had not been licensed; in the absence of any action on the part of the new district council, the effect of the 1972 Act was to leave that remaining area unlicensed.

11. Paragraph 25 of Schedule 14, however, enabled a local authority after giving the requisite notice to resolve that section 171(4) should apply throughout their area or cease to apply throughout their area (whether or not, in either case the enactment applied only to part of their area). A resolution disapplying section 171(4) had to be passed before 1st April 1975, but a resolution that section 171(4) should apply throughout their area could be passed at any time. Such a resolution does not have effect unless approved by the Secretary of State.

12. Consequently, a new district council, on coming into being under the 1972 Act, had three options in respect of taxi licensing –

(i)   it could do nothing, in which case taxis would be licensable in those of the areas included in the new district in which taxis were previously licensable. These would comprise separate taxi licensing zones. The remainder of the district would not be subject to taxi licensing.

(ii)   it could pass a resolution disapplying section 171(4) of the Public Health Act 1875 which meant that taxi licensing would cease in those urban districts where taxis had previously been licensed and there would be no taxi licensing at all within the new district council's area. Such a resolution had to be passed before 1 April 1975.

(iii) it could pass a resolution applying section 171(4) throughout the area, which meant that the former urban districts [and boroughs] where taxis had previously been licensed would merge with the remainder of the new district to create a single taxi licensing area comprising the whole of the new district council's area.

13. At this point the legislation cuts adrift from the phrase 'within the prescribed distance', but that continues to be a key expression in the 1847 Act. In the Department's view it is clear that, so long as the hackney carriage provisions in the 1847 Act continue to apply after 1st April 1974 to an area where they applied immediately before that date the words 'within the prescribed distance' continue to refer to that area but, when a resolution that section 171(4) of the 1875 Act should apply throughout the district becomes effective, those words refer to the whole district.

iii Transport Act 1985

14. The next significant legislative change affecting taxi licensing areas was the enactment of section 15 of the Transport Act 1985. This provides that where, immediately before the commencement of section 15, the provisions of the 1847 Act with respect to hackney carriages were not in force throughout the whole area of a district council in England and Wales those provisions (as incorporated by the 1875 Act) shall

• if not then in force in part of the council's area, apply throughout that area; and

• if in force in part only of its area, apply also in the remainder of that area.

15. Again the Act does not make specific reference to the prescribed distance. However, in the Department's opinion, the construction of section 15 certainly recognises that a district might have distinct prescribed distances or taxi licensing zones as a result of the changes generated by the Local Government Act 1972.

16. The effect of the 1985 Act was explained in Circular 8/86 (copies available from Miss P Brown on 0171 271 5056). If taxi licensing had not previously applied at all in a district then section 15(1) (a) meant that it applied throughout that district and the whole of the district was 'within the prescribed distance' for the purposes of the 1847 Act. If, however, the 1847 Act only applied in part of the district (ignoring by virtue of section 15(2) any part of the district in the Metropolitan Police district) then the effect of section 15(1) (*b*) was that the 1847 Act 'applied also' in the remainder of the district; that remaining area constituted a separate zone, so that the words 'within the prescribed distance' referred to each of the zones and not to the district as a whole.

17. Relating section 15 to the three options which a district council could have taken in 1974 (paragraph 12 above) –

- in case (i) (where taxis were licensed in one or more distinct zones within the district), the effect of section 15 would have been to create an additional taxi licensing zone comprising that part of the district which was not already subject to taxi licensing;
- in case (ii) (where taxis were not licensed at all in the district), the effect of section 15 would have been to create a single taxi licensing comprising the whole of the district; and
- in case (iii) (where the whole of the district comprised a single taxi licensing area by virtue of having passed an extension resolution) the effect of section 15 would have been nil; the intention of section 15 was to extend taxi licensing to those areas where taxis had not previously been licensed.

18. If a council falling into the case (i) category wanted to turn the whole of its district into a single licensing zone, it could do so by passing a resolution under Schedule 14 of the Local Government Act 1972 ('an extension resolution') providing that the 1847 Act as to apply throughout the district.

19. Two circumstances support the Department's position. One is the subtle difference of wording between paragraphs (a) and (*b*) of section 15(1) ('apply throughout' as against 'apply also'). The other is the fact that the references to section 171(4) of the 1875 Act in Part II of Schedule 14 to the 1972 Act were not repealed. Accordingly, after section 15 was enacted, Parliament left in force provisions of the 1972 Act enabling a district council to apply section 171(4) 'throughout their area'. There is little substance to the argument that Schedule 14 of the 1972 Act became redundant after the coming into force of section 15 of the 1985 Act. The 1985 Act neither repealed nor amended Schedule 14 of the 1972 Act.

The effect of the Local Government Act 1992

20. Any new area constituted by an order made under the 1992 Act will be an area within all of which taxi licensing applies. However, the new area may include the whole or parts of single zone districts and/or of multiple zone districts. The possible combinations of circumstances are numerous which is why it is important to be clear as to the underlying principles.

21. The relevant provisions which impinge on taxi licensing areas are regulations 4 and 5 of the Local Government Changes for England Regulations 1994 (as amended by SI 1995/1748).

22. The Department takes the view that the general effect of these provisions in regard to taxi licensing may be summarised as follows –

- As with the 1972 reorganisation, the taxi licensing situation is effectively 'frozen' until further action is taken. Licences granted by a transferor authority continue in force in the areas in relation to which they were granted. Thus a licence granted in respect of an area which is split between two district councils is treated as granted by each of those councils in relation to so much as that area as lies within each new local government area. When that licence comes to an end, the licensee will have to apply for a new licence to one or other or both of the successor authorities.
- Nothing in the reorganisation effects any byelaws. Thus, if a new area to which taxi byelaws apply, becomes split between two districts, the byelaws will continue in force in the areas in respect of which they were made and will be treated as made by the successor council in relation to the part of the original area falling within their local government area.
- The reorganisation will not affect taxi zones. Thus, if a new area comprises the whole or parts of existing taxi licensing areas, those areas will continue to be separate licensing areas unless and until the local authority passes a resolution under Schedule 14 to the 1972 Act to apply the 1847 Act throughout its area (referred to in Circular 8/86 as 'an extension resolution').

EXAMPLES

23. A first example is a new unitary authority comprising the whole of two former districts, A and B, each of which was a single taxi licensing zone. Licences granted by the transferor councils will continue in force as respects the areas for which they were granted. Likewise byelaws will continue in force for the two areas. It follows that new taxi licences can only be granted for one or other area. There would be nothing, however, to prevent the council of the new unitary authority from granting an applicant a licence to ply for hire in zone A and a licence to ply for hire in zone B. If the Council wished to combine the two zones, it could do so by passing an extension resolution and making byelaws to apply throughout the district. Both would have to be approved by the Secretary of State.

24. A second example is a unitary authority where the new area comprises the whole of one former district and parts of three districts contiguous with it. On the day when the unitary authority is formed, taxi licences granted by all four of the former councils will continue in force with respect to the areas for which they were granted. Thus, the unitary authority will, by default, comprise four separate taxi licensing zones – A being the whole of the former district which remains intact and B, C and D being parts of former neighbouring districts which have been surrendered to the new unitary authority. Four separate sets of byelaws would continue to apply. The licence for B would be valid not only in the relevant part of the new district but also in that part of the existing prescribed distance which lies outside the new unitary authority. The same applies to C and D.

25. One the expiration of a licence relating to B, C and D, the holder will have to decide which council to apply to for a new licence. One option would be to apply to the new unitary authority, which would mean that a driver could ply for hire within the relevant zone of the unitary authority, but not in the area of the council, which had issued his expired licence. Another option would be for the licence holder to apply to the council, which had issued his expired licence in which case his new licence would not permit him to ply for hire within the area of the new unitary authority.

26. Again, however, there would be nothing to prevent the unitary authority from granting to the same applicant separate licences to ply for hire within two or more of those zones.

27. Here too, as in the first example, the unitary authority concerned could combine its zones by passing an extension resolution and making a uniform set of byelaws, subject to the approval of the Secretary of State.

28. The second example would also apply mutatis mutandis, to cases of boundary changes involving two or more district councils, where a unitary authority was not involved.

CONCLUSION

29. A key consideration underpinning the local government reorganisation was the importance of maintaining continuity as far as practicable. This advice note suggests that continuity in terms of the area in which a taxi driver can ply for hire is the natural course when unitary authorities are created. A change in the area in which a driver could ply for hire would only come if the licensing authority chooses to amalgamate the prescribed distances which it inherits, or if a licence to ply for hire within a prescribed distance which has been split by the reorganisation expires and a decision has to be made about where to operate in future.

30. The Department takes the view that if a unitary authority wishes to amalgamate its taxi licensing zones and apply taxi licensing uniformly to its area, then it must pass a resolution under Schedule 14 of the Local Government Act

1972, and secure the approval of the Secretary of State. If it does not do so the Department will decline to confirm byelaws for the new district as a whole.

Department of Transport
Buses and Taxis Division
May 1997

Applications for the Secretary of State's approval to extension resolutions; and hackney carriage byelaws in *draft form* should be sent to –

Miss P A Brown
Buses and Taxis Division
3/12 Great Minster House
76 Marsham Street
LONDON
SW1P 4DR

Local Government Reorganisation (Wales) Hackney Carriage Byelaws

1. This note explains the position of the Department of the Environment, Transport and the Regions (DETR) in respect of hackney carriage byelaws submitted by those local licensing authorities affected by changes arising from the Local Government (Wales) Act 1994. This advice concerns only Wales. A separate advice note has been prepared in respect of local government reorganisation in England.

THE LOCAL GOVERNMENT (WALES) ACT 1994

2. In Wales, local government has been completely restructured by the 1994 Act. This Act replaced the county councils and district councils by new unitary principal areas known as counties and county boroughs. The existing communities are continued in being, as are their councils. The 1994 Act allows for the making of changes to the boundaries and electoral arrangements of local government areas. A boundary change may involve the alteration of a local government area; the constitution of a new local government area by the amalgamation of more such areas or communities or by the aggregation of parts of such areas or by the separation of part of such an area; the abolition of an area or community and its distribution among other principal areas or communities and the constitution of a new community. The 1994 Act also allows a change in electoral arrangements for any local government area which is either consequential on any change in local government areas resulting from any boundary changes or is independent of a change in the boundaries of a particular area.

3. So far as taxi licensing is concerned, structural changes are not in themselves a problem; the 1994 Act provides for the transfer of functions to the new unitary authorities. Electoral changes do not present any problems either. However, the problems affecting taxi licensing are generated by the boundary changes that accompany structural changes.

DEVELOPMENT OF TAXI ZONES

4. In considering the effect of boundary changes on taxi licensing, it is first appropriate to trace the history of the zoning concept up to the coming in to force on 1 January 1987 of section 15 of the Transport Act 1985.

i 1847–74

5. The Town Police Clauses Act 1847 refers to 'the prescribed distance' and defines the word 'prescribed' as referring to such matter as may be prescribed or provided for in the special Act. The prescribed distance is particularly relevant

as the distance within which a hackney carriage may be licensed to ply for hire (section 37) and the distance within which the driver of the hackney carriage can be compelled to go (section 53). There are numerous other references to it.

6. Section 5 (repealed) of the Public Health Act 1875 provided that England and Wales (except the metropolis) should consist of districts to be called urban sanitary districts and rural sanitary districts which were to be subject to the jurisdiction of local authorities, respectively called urban sanitary authorities and rural sanitary authorities, which were invested with various powers mentioned in the Act. Section 171 (which is still in force) dealt with the Town Police Clauses Act 1847. That Act was originally a clauses Act, that is to say it had no independent existence of its own and only applied to an area if there was a special Act so applying it. Section 171 of the 1875 Act applied the provisions of the 1847 Act with respect to hackney carriages and provided that, for the purposes of regulating hackney carriages in urban districts, those provisions should be incorporated with the 1875 Act; the expression 'within the prescribed distance' was defined for the purposes of that Act as meaning within any urban district.

7. At this point there was no concept of 'zoning'; a single urban authority licensed hackney carriages to ply for hire within the whole of the urban sanitary district.

8. Under the Local Government Act 1894, urban sanitary districts became urban districts and urban sanitary authorities urban district councils, except where the area consisted of a borough. Under the Local Government Act 1933, the relevant areas for taxi licensing were county districts, which could be either urban district councils or non-county boroughs, and county boroughs. In a few cases taxi licensing was extended to rural districts by virtue of orders under section 276 of the Public Health Act 1875.

ii Local Government Act 1972

9. In 1974, effect was given to the reorganisation set out in the Local Government Act 1972. All local authorities inside England and Wales were abolished and a new two-tier system of county councils and district councils was constituted. So far as taxi licensing is concerned, the key provision of the 1972 Act is section 180. This provides that for the purposes of (inter alia) the Public Health Act 1875, the local authority and sanitary authority (whether urban or not) for a district is the district council. Section 180 introduced Schedule 14, Part II of which provided that section 171(4) of the Public Health Act 1875 should apply to those areas, and only those, to which it applied immediately before 1 April 1974. In the view of DETR, it is this provision, which established the concept of zoning.

10. What it meant in practice was that the taxi licensing situation within new district councils effectively became 'frozen' until the taking of action as mentioned in paragraph 11 below; a prescribed distance before the change remained a prescribed distance after the change. Consequently, a new district council which, for example, incorporated two former urban districts (i.e. two distinct prescribed

distances) would administer taxi licensing for those two districts or 'zones'. The new district council might also have inherited an area which was not a former urban district and where taxis had not been licensed; in the absence of any action on the part of the new district council the effect of the 1972 Act was to leave that remaining area unlicensed.

11. Paragraph 25 of Schedule 14, however, enabled a local authority after giving the requisite notice to resolve that section 171(4) should apply throughout their area or cease to apply throughout their area (whether or not, in either case, the enactment applied only to part of their area). A resolution disapplying section 171(4) had to be passed before 1 April 1975, but a resolution that section 171(4) should apply throughout their area could be passed at any time. Such a resolution does not have effect unless approved by the Secretary of State.

12. Consequently, a new district council, on coming into being under the 1972 Act, had three options in respect of taxi licensing –

(i) It could do nothing, in which case taxis would continue to be licensable in those of the areas included in the new district in which taxis were previously licensable. These would comprise separate taxi licensing zones. The remainder of the district would not be subject to taxi licensing; or

(ii) it could pass a resolution disapplying section 171(4) of the Public Health Act 1875 which meant that taxi licensing would cease in those urban districts where taxis had previously been licensed and there would be no taxi licensing at all within the new district council's area. Such a resolution had to be passed before 1 April 1975; or

(iii) subject to the approval of the Secretary of State, it could pass a resolution applying section 171(4) throughout the area, which meant that the former urban districts (and boroughs) where taxis had previously been licensed would merge with the remainder of the new district to create a single taxi licensing area comprising the whole of the new district council's area.

13. At this point the legislation cuts adrift from the phrase 'within the prescribed distance', but that continues to be a key expression in the 1847 Act. In the view of DETR, it is clear that, so long as the hackney carriage provisions in the 1847 Act continue to apply after 1 April 1974 to an area where they applied immediately before that date, the words 'within the prescribed distance' continue to refer to that area but, when a resolution that section 171(4) of the 1875 Act should apply throughout the district becomes effective, those words refer to the whole district.

iii Transport Act 1985

14. The next significant legislative change affecting taxi licensing areas was the enactment of section 15 of the Transport Act 1985. This provides that where, immediately before the commencement of section 15, the provisions of the 1847 Act with respect to hackney carriages were not in force throughout the

whole of the area of a district council in England and Wales, those provisions (as incorporated by the 1875 Act) shall –

- if not then in force in part of the council's area, apply throughout that area; and
- if in force in part only of its area, apply also in the remainder of that area.

15. Again, the Act does not make specific reference to the prescribed distance. However, in the opinion of DETR, the construction of section 15 certainly recognises that a district might have distinct prescribed distances or taxi licensing zones as a result of the changes generated by the Local Government Act 1972.

16. The effect of the 1985 Act was explained in Circular 8/86 (copies available from Miss P Brown on 0171 271 5056). If taxi licensing had not previously applied at all in a district then section 15(1) (a) meant that it applied throughout that district and the whole of the district was 'within the prescribed distance' for the purposes of the 1847 Act. If, however, the 1847 Act only applied in part of the district (ignoring by virtue of section 15(2) any part of the district in the Metropolitan Police district) then the effect of section 15(1) (b) was that the 1847 Act 'applied also' in the remainder of the district; that remaining area constituted a separate zone, so that the words 'within the prescribed distance' referred to each of the zones and not to the district as a whole.

17. Relating section 16 to the three options which a district council could have taken in 1974 (paragraph 12 above) –

- in case (i) (where taxis were licensed in one or more distinct zones within the district), the effect of section 15 would have been to create an additional taxi licensing zone comprising that part of the district which was not already subject to taxi licensing;
- in case (ii) (where taxis were not licensed at all in the district), the effect of section 15 would have been to create a single taxi licensing comprising the whole of the district; and
- in case (iii) (where the whole of the district comprised a single taxi licensing area by virtue of having passed an extension resolution) the effect of section 15 would have been nil; the intention of section 15 was to extend taxi licensing to those areas where taxis had not previously been licensed.

18. If a council falling into the case (i) category wanted to turn the whole of its district into a single licensing zone, it could do so by passing a resolution under Schedule 14 of the Local Government Act 1972 ('an extension resolution') providing that the 1847 Act as to apply throughout the district.

19. Two circumstances support the position of DETR. One is the subtle difference of wording between paragraphs (a) and (b) of section 15(1) ('apply throughout' as against 'apply also'). The other is the fact that the references to section 171(4) of the 1875 Act in Part II of Schedule 14 to the 1972 Act were

not repealed. Accordingly, after section 15 was enacted, Parliament left in force provisions of the 1972 Act enabling a district council to apply section 171(4) 'throughout their area'. There is little substance to the argument that Schedule 14 of the 1972 Act became redundant after the coming into force of section 15 of the 1985 Act. The 1985 Act neither repealed nor amended Schedule 14 of the 1972 Act.

THE LOCAL GOVERNMENT (WALES) ACT 1994

20. Any new principal area under the 1994 Act will be an area within all of which taxi licensing applies. However, the new area may include the whole or parts of single zone districts or of multiple zone districts. The possible combinations of circumstances are numerous which is why it is important to be clear as to the underlying principles.

21. DETR takes the view that –

- as with the 1972 reorganisation, the taxi licensing situation is effectively 'frozen' until further action is taken. Licences granted by a transferor authority continue in force in the areas in relation to which they were granted. Thus a licence granted in respect of an area which is split between two unitary authorities is treated as granted by each of those authorities in relation to so much as that area as lies within each new authority area. When that licence comes to an end, the licensee will have to apply for a new licence to one or other or both of the successor authorities;

- nothing in the reorganisation affects any byelaws. Thus, if an area to which taxi byelaws apply, becomes split between two unitary authorities, the byelaws will continue in force in the areas in respect of which they were made and will be treated as made by the successor authority in relation to the part of the original area falling within their local government area; and

- the reorganisation will not affect taxi zones. Thus, if a new area comprises the whole or parts of existing taxi licensing areas, those areas will continue to be separate licensing areas unless and until with the approval of the Secretary of State for the Environment, Transport and the Regions, the unitary authority passes a resolution under Schedule 14 to the 1972 Act to apply the 1847 Act throughout its area (referred to in Circular 8/86 as 'an extension resolution').

EXAMPLES

22. A first example is a new unitary authority comprising the whole of two former districts, A and B, each of which was a single taxi licensing zone. Licences granted by the transferor authorities will continue in force as respects the areas for which they were granted. Likewise byelaws will continue in force for the two areas. It follows that new taxi licences can only be granted for one or other area. There would be nothing, however, to prevent the council of the new unitary

authority from granting an applicant a licence to ply for hire in zone A and a licence to ply for hire in zone B. If the authority wished to combine the two zones, it could do so by passing an extension resolution and making byelaws to apply throughout the district. Both would have to be approved by the Secretary of State.

23. A second example is a unitary authority where the new area comprises the whole of one former district and parts of three districts contiguous with it. On the day when the unitary authority is formed, taxi licences granted by all four of the former authorities will continue in force with respect to the areas for which they were granted. Thus, the unitary authority will, by default, comprise four separate taxi licensing zones – A being the whole of the former district which remains intact and B, C and D being parts of former neighbouring districts which have been surrendered to the new unitary authority. Four separate sets of byelaws would continue to apply. The licence for B would be valid not only in the relevant part of the new district but also in that part of the existing prescribed distance which lies outside the new unitary authority. The same applies to C and D.

24. One the expiration of a licence relating to B, C or D, the holder will have to decide which authority to apply to for a new licence. One option would be to apply to the new unitary authority, which would mean that a driver could ply for hire within the relevant zone of the unitary authority, but not in the area of the council which had issued his expired licence. Another option would be for the licence holder to apply to the authority which had issued his expired licence in which case his new licence would not permit him to ply for hire within the area of the new unitary authority.

25. Again, however, there would be nothing to prevent the unitary authority from granting to the same applicant separate licences to ply for hire within two or more of those zones.

26. Here too, as in the first example, the unitary authority concerned could combine its zones by passing an extension resolution and making a uniform set of byelaws, subject to the approval of the Secretary of State.

CONCLUSION

27. A key consideration underpinning the reorganisation of local government in both England and Wales was the importance of maintaining continuity as far as practicable. This advice note suggests that continuity in terms of the area in which a taxi driver can ply for hire is the natural course when unitary authorities are created. A change in the area in which a driver could ply for hire would only come if the licensing authority chooses to amalgamate the prescribed distances which it inherits, or if a licence to ply for hire within a prescribed distance which has been split by the reorganisation expires and a decision has to be made about where to operate in future.

28. DETR takes the view that if a unitary authority wishes to amalgamate its taxi licensing zones and apply taxi licensing uniformly to its area, then it must

pass a resolution under Schedule 14 of the Local Government Act 1972, and secure the approval of the Secretary of State. If it does not do so, the Department of the Environment, Transport and the Regions will decline to confirm byelaws for the new district as a whole.

Applications for the approval of the Secretary of State for the Environment, Transport and the Regions to extension resolutions; and hackney carriage byelaws in draft form should be sent to –

Miss P A Brown
Buses and Taxis Division
Zone 3/12
Department of the Environment, Transport and the Regions
Great Minster House
76 Marsham Street
LONDON
SW1P 4DR

Department of the Environment, Transport and the Regions
Buses and Taxis Division
February 1998

Transport Circular 4/94
November 1994

THE DEPARTMENT OF TRANSPORT

TAXI TOUTING

To:
The Chief Executive
   Metropolitan District Councils
   District Councils in England and Wales
   London Borough Councils
The Commissioner of Police for the Metropolis
The Commissioner of Police for the City of London
Chief Officers of Police including the British Transport Police
Clerks to Police Authorities
Clerks to the Justices
Chairmen of Benches
Crown Prosecution Service
British Tourist Authority
London Taxi Board
National Association of Taxi & Private Hire Licensing & Enforcement Officers

TAXI TOUTING

This Circular is to draw Section 167 of the Criminal Justice and Public Order Act 1994 to your attention. This section of the Act came into force on 3 November 1994.

The provisions of this section are designed to make it easier for the police, in particular, to take effective action against touts who offer to the public the services of cars acting as unlicensed taxis. This is known to be particularly a problem in London, but the Act applies to the whole of England and Wales.

Please note that the provision only deals with the problem of touting. The law on the associated problem of illegal plying for hire has not been changed.

Subsection (1) makes it an offence in a public place for a person to solicit others to hire vehicles to carry them as passengers. "Soliciting" is normally a proactive process. So people who legitimately offer the services of hire vehicles where they are approached by the public and react to that approach will not be affected by this provision. Examples are taxis at ranks, the taxi booking desks at Heathrow, private hire vehicle offices and the car booking kiosks at airports.

Subsection (2) provides that the soliciting offence in (1) does not have to refer to any particular vehicle. This means that a police officer taking action against the tout in a street does not have to prove in court that the tout was acting in concert with the driver of a particular vehicle.

The expression "public place" is defined in subsection (6) and is deliberately drawn very widely. It will include places such as railway stations and airports, to which the public is permitted access. It therefore extends beyond the streets and roads and would cover for instance touting from a shop doorway.

Subsection (2) provides that a taxi driver merely sitting in a taxi with a "For Hire" or "Taxi" sign displayed will not be committing an offence; nor will the driver of a taxi or private hire vehicle with a sign indicating that it can be hired by telephone. Equally under subsection (3) no offence will be committed where a person is soliciting others to hire licensed taxis under a scheme for shared taxis provided for by section 10 of the Transport Act 1985. Lastly, subsection (4) provides a specific defence for persons who solicit customers for Public Service Vehicles on behalf and with the permission of the holder of the relevant PSV Operator's licence.

Subsection (5) provides a penalty of level four for persons found guilty of an offence under subsection (1). This is the same as for some other taxi offences, in particular illegally plying for hire.

Subsection (6) contains definitions.

Subsection (7) provides that offences under this section shall be added to the list of arrestable offences at s 24 (2) of the Police and Criminal Evidence Act 1984.

I would be grateful if Clerks to the Justices could pass a copy of this Circular to the Chairman of Bench in their area. Likewise Chief Executives of District Councils should draw it to the attention of the Hackney Carriage Licensing/Enforcement Officer.

ENQUIRIES

Mrs K Turnbull
Department of Transport,
Room 515110,
2 Marsharn Street,
LONDON SW1 P 3EB

Tel: 071-276 4896

P E PICKERING

Assistant Secretary

A2.17

Department for Transport

Rupert Cope
Head of Taxi/PHV Branch
Buses and Taxis Division
Integrated and Local Transport
Directorate 3/12
Great Minster House
76 Marsham Street
LONDON
SW1 P 4DR

Direct line: 020 7944 2291
Divisional Enquiries: 020 7944 2293

Fax: 020 7944 2279

GTN: 3533 2291

rupert.cope@dft.gsi.gov.uk

Web site: www.dft.gov.uk

Our Ref: PT2 1012182

9 September 2002

- Chief Executives
- Taxi/PHV Licensing Officers
- District & Borough Councils
- Unitary Authorities in England and Wales
- Head of Public Carriage Office,
- Transport for London (items 1 &2)
- Scottish Executive (items 1&2)
- Department of Environment, Northern Ireland (items 1 &2)
- DPTAC (item 1)
- Traffic Area Offices (item 2)
- Vehicle Inspectorate (item 2)
- The Home Office/ACP0 (item 2)
- National Assembly for Wales (item 3)

Dear Sir/Madam

Taxi and Private Hire Vehicle Licensing Issues

1. I am writing to inform you about three matters relating to hackney carriage (taxi) and private hire vehicle (PHV) legislation, one of which – stretched limousines – also relates to public service vehicle (PSV – bus) legislation, namely:

(1) Local accessibility policies for taxis prior to taxi regulations being made under the Disability Discrimination Act 1995;
(2) Stretched Limousines; and
(3) Taxi Byelaws

(1) Local accessibility policies for taxis prior to taxi regulations being made under the Disability Discrimination Act 1995

2. As you know, we planned to make taxi accessibility regulations under the Disability Discrimination Act 1995 (DDA) effective between 2002 and 2012. When we realised that this could not be achieved in a way that would be acceptable to both disabled people and the taxi trade, the Minister announced in 2000 that regulations would not be introduced in 2002. Since that time we have been exploring a range of options to help to increase the number of accessible taxis available to disabled people throughout the country. We hope to issue further information on our future plans shortly.

3. In the meantime, local licensing authorities may of course make their own policy with regard to accessible taxis for their area, and many do so.

4. As we suggested in our letter to Chief Executives of 31 January 2000, local licensing authorities wishing to set local accessibility standards are advised to look at the various accessible vehicles on offer and judge their suitability against local circumstances and operating conditions. One effective way of making comparisons is to invite several manufacturers to present vehicles on the same day and to invite local disability organisations to try out the options and to offer comments. There are a number of vehicles currently available, which offer good accessibility, and from discussions with industry the Department expects that several vehicles are likely to be suitable.

5. We would stress that the adoption of a policy for accessible taxis is entirely a matter for local consideration and decision. There are several options for such policies which could result in the taxi fleet being wholly or partly accessible. Some authorities require the whole taxi fleet to be accessible whilst others require all new taxi licences issued to be for accessible vehicles only. Moreover, some authorities in areas where the number of taxi licences is controlled have issued additional licences specifically for accessible vehicles in order to improve the number of accessible taxis in their area.

6. In assessing the accessibility of particular vehicles, licensing authorities will want to ensure that they meet the needs of the widest range of disabled people, not only those who are wheelchair users. They will also wish to assure themselves that the equipment provided for wheelchair access and securing is appropriate. For example, the design should allow for wheelchair users to travel facing forward or rearward – never sideways.

7. The choice of vehicle is clearly important. However, unless the drivers know how to use the equipment which is provided for disabled people, for example, the ramps for wheelchair access, and have an understanding of the needs of disabled people, then many of the benefits of accessible transport will be lost. Licensing authorities will therefore want to consider what training is necessary for drivers, both would-be and existing, to help them better meet the needs of their disabled passengers.

8. We know that some authorities have been holding back on any local initiative in this area in anticipation of national regulations. We would urge them not

to do so. As and when any national requirements are introduced there will be a sufficient lead-time for any necessary changes to be made. In the meantime licensing authorities may be able to make significant improvements in the availability of taxis to disabled people in their area.

9. Some points to consider and questions which we consider might be useful for licensing authorities when making an accessibility policy for their area are attached as an annex to this letter. Please note that neither list is meant to be exhaustive.

(2) Stretched Limousines

10. The number of stretched limousines being imported from abroad, particularly the United States, seems to be increasing. It is quite legal to import these vehicles. However, their use has led to licensing problems both for those licensing PSVs in traffic area offices and for those licensing PHVs in local government. In turn, this has led further to problems for enforcement authorities.

11. For licensing and enforcement purposes, stretched limousines can come within the licensing regimes for either PSVs or PHVs. However, it is the Department's view that such vehicles do not meet the requirements for minibuses (ie vehicles with more than 8 passenger seats) in the UK PSV Construction and Use Regulations. **So these vehicles cannot lawfully carry more than 8 passengers**. If they do so, it is matter for the appropriate enforcement authorities – the Vehicle Inspectorate or the police – to take the necessary action for the law being broken.

Licensing stretched limousines as small PSVs

12. If a stretched limousine is licensed as a small PSV, (carrying 8 or less passengers), **separate fares** must be charged. The term 'separate fares' is not defined in legislation. However, we believe it represents a charge made directly or indirectly to each passenger for carriage which is unaffected by the number of fare payers. This is the way fares are often structured, for example, on a local bus service. Subject to any concessions that the operator may give, each passenger pays the same fare for the same journey, regardless of how many other passengers on the bus wish to make that journey.

13. There is one exception to the requirement for separate fares to be charged. 'Big bus' operators (ie those operating vehicles with 9 or more passenger seats) can run small PSVs for some private hire work, provided the operation of these vehicles represents a small part of their overall business. What constitutes 'a small part' is also not defined in legislation, and ultimately, final decisions on where the balance lies is a matter for the courts. The legislation confers the exemption on an operator whose use of small vehicles is only a small part of his business.

14. The relative size of the fleet of large and small buses is obviously very relevant and as a rule of thumb we believe that if less than 10% of the overall fleet

licensed under a single PSV Operator's Licence are small vehicles the exemption will apply (e.g. a fleet of, say, 20 buses with 9 or more passenger seats could run 2 additional vehicles – which could be stretched limousines that carry 8 or less passengers – for private hire work). But because the legislation refers to the size of the small and large bus business other factors (such as mileage run) should be taken into account. We would hope that in most cases it would be obvious what was and what was not, to coin a phrase, a 'large bus business'.

15. If a particular journey carried out at separate fares has start and finish points or stopping places that are more than 15 miles apart (as the crow flies), there is no requirement to register it as a local service. However, if stopping places (or start and finish points) on individual journeys (even one-off trips) are less than 15 miles apart, then that journey falls into the category of a 'local service' and must be registered in advance as a local bus service with the appropriate Traffic Commissioner. Generally, registered bus services must operate to a fixed route and timetable, but the Traffic Commissioner may accept other particulars, so long as a complete description of the service is provided to his satisfaction. Operating a local service without first registering it may result in disciplinary action by the Traffic Commissioner.

16. In practical terms, because of the separate fares and route registration requirements outlined above, stretched limousines are more likely to fall within the licensing regime for PHVs. However, because vehicles with up to 8 passenger seats *may* be licensed as PSVs or PHVs, PSV licensing staff in traffic area offices and local government PHV licensing officers need to liaise closely where there is any doubt on licensing matters concerning stretched limousines. Similarly, the relevant enforcement authorities for PSVs (Vehicle Inspectorate or the police) need to work closely with local PHV licensing enforcement officers in this respect (see paragraph 23 below).

Licensing stretched limousines as PHVs

17. As stated in the previous paragraph, stretched limousines are in our view more likely to fall within the licensing regime for PHVs.

18. Each local licensing authority in England and Wales (district/borough councils, unitary authorities or Transport *for* London) may decide which vehicles are suitable for licensing as PHVs in their area. Accordingly, it is for each licensing authority to decide for its area whether they wish to license stretched limousines as PHVs, taking into account local circumstances.

19. Clearly, it is not for central Government to pre-empt any local decision in this regard but each licensing authority will want to consider all aspects of the suitability of such vehicles, especially any safety considerations, taking into account local needs and circumstances.

20. However, if a licensing authority decides that stretched limousines are not suitable to be licensed as PHVs in accordance with its licensing policies to meet local needs and circumstances, we consider that such vehicles can only be used lawfully for hire or reward in that licensing area if they are licensed as small

PSVs; are operating under a full set of PHV licences issued by another licensing authority; or are being used in accordance with paragraph 22 below.

21. The licensing process allows for would-be licence holders, who are refused a licence on the grounds that a vehicle is unsuitable to be licensed as a PHV, to appeal against the decision in the local magistrates' court.

22. If vehicles with up to 8 passenger seats, including stretched limousines, are used solely for weddings and/or funerals, they are exempt from PHV licensing requirements. Additionally, in England and Wales outside London vehicles with up to 8 passenger seats, including stretched limousines, may carry passengers for hire or reward under a contract for a period of not less than seven days.

23. As mentioned in paragraph 16 above, because vehicles with up to 8 passenger seats may be licensed as PHVs or PSVs, local government PHV licensing officers and PSV licensing staff in traffic area offices need to liaise closely where there is any doubt on licensing matters concerning stretched limousines. Similarly, the relevant enforcement authorities for PHVs (local PHV licensing officers or the police) need to work closely with the Vehicle Inspectorate in this respect.

(3) Taxi Byelaws: section 68 of the Town Police Clauses Act 1847

24. We thought it might be helpful to use the opportunity presented by this letter to remind licensing authorities of their obligations and our expectations in undertaking the byelaw-making process.

25. To assist licensing authorities, a set of model byelaws was included as an annex to Circular 8/86. As originally drafted, the model byelaws provided options depending on whether or not the council making the byelaws had adopted Part II of the Local Government (Miscellaneous Provisions) Act 1976 (the 1976 Act). However, since all but one provincial area of England and Wales is now subject to the licensing provisions contained in the 1976 Act, the model byelaws have been revised to take account of this development. The actual policy has not been revised – just the presumption that the 1976 Act has been adopted meaning, for example, that the fixing of fares and the appointing of stands are dealt with under that Act rather than by means of byelaws.

26. For the purposes of consistency, we would expect draft byelaws to be based on the model. That is not to say that we would automatically dismiss any deviation from the wording of the model; it is fully realised that licensing authorities often want to tailor their licensing policies to their own circumstances. However, when a deviation is proposed, we do need to be satisfied that there is a genuine reason for it and that it is not simply change for the sake of change.

27. When submitting draft byelaws for provisional approval, it would help to avoid correspondence and would help the byelaws to be made sooner if:

    (i)   any proposed deviation from the model was accompanied by both a detailed explanation of the licensing authority's policy and the reasons for the model's inadequacy;

(ii) the text had been checked to ensure that not only did it make sense but also that it made a coherent whole with no repetition or contradiction;

(iii) the entire document had been scrutinised by the licensing authority's lawyers to ensure that the question of validity had been properly addressed; and

(iv) in respect of Wales, if the authority intends submitting a Welsh language version of the byelaws they do so as early as possible.

All this would be with the aim of helping us to help licensing authorities.

28. When making hackney carriage byelaws, it is important to bear in mind that hackney carriage proprietors and drivers can be prosecuted and fined for contravening the byelaws. From a practical point of view, the provisions need to be clearly and unambiguously set out both so that taxi proprietors and drivers understand what their obligations are and so that the courts have the minimum of difficulty in enforcement.

29. Additionally, the licensing authority must be satisfied that the byelaws are certain, reasonable, intra vires and are not contrary to, or inconsistent with, the general law. These are all factors which the confirming authorities – in England, the Secretary of State or, in respect of Wales, the Minister for Environment – will have regard to when considering drafts.

30. Licensing authorities in England can obtain copies of the model byelaws by contacting Pippa Brown on 020 7944 2278; an electronic version can also be obtained using the e-mail address: pippaa.brown@dft.gsi.gov.uk. If you have any queries about hackney carriage byelaws please contact Miss Brown, preferably in writing at the above address or by e-mail.

31. Licensing authorities in Wales can obtain copies of the model byelaws by contacting Mike Spearing at the National Assembly for Wales on 02920 826518; an electronic version can also be obtained using the e-mail address: michael. spearing@wales.gov.uk. If you have any queries about hackney carriage byelaws please contact Mr Spearing, preferably in writing at the above address or by e-mail.

Yours faithfully

R F Cope

ANNEX

LOCAL ACCESSIBILITY POLICIES FOR TAXIS

Points to consider when assessing vehicles

- Other authorities may already have experience of introducing accessible vehicles, or are in the process of doing so. Sharing experience and resources may be useful.

- The vehicles should be available for viewing, but it might also be useful to invite the companies involved to provide data on the basic specification of their vehicles, and information on any optional extras. This information can then be made available to those attending the viewing or to others with an interest who are unable to attend in person. The companies should also make clear what specification of their vehicle is on display.
- It will be important to involve local disabled people and their organisations in the assessment process. In doing so authorities will want to consider the accommodation provided – which should preferably be somewhere with weather protection and access to facilities such as toilets and refreshments. They will also need to ensure disabled people can get to the venue and may wish to provide transport support.
- Authorities will want to ensure that the vehicles meet the needs of the widest range of disabled people, not only those who are wheelchair users.
- The wheelchair users who participate should ideally represent a cross-section of wheelchair users, eg users of both manual and powered wheelchairs. They should be invited to look at wheelchair entry, exit and the restraint equipment provided for wheelchairs and occupants.
- This exercise should help authorities to establish their minimum standard for accessible taxis which ideally should provide for a range of vehicles, catering for the needs of the widest range of disabled people. A list of the vehicles, including the specifications, which are accepted for licensing should be publicly available.
- It is important, however, that new designs of vehicle are not excluded because they do not feature on the published list. The minimum standard set by the authority could, therefore, be used as the benchmark against which to assess any new vehicle presented to the authority for licensing as a taxi.

DfT

September 2002

LOCAL ACCESSIBILITY POLICIES FOR TAXIS

Useful questions when assessing vehicles

Entry for Ambulant and Semi-ambulant Passengers

How easy do people find it to enter and exit the vehicle?

How easy is it to open and close the door from both inside and outside the vehicle?

Are grab handles provided in appropriate places; are they highly visible and are they helpful?

Would the doors be sufficiently illuminated at night?

Assisted Entry

On vehicles with a high floor height, is a step provided and how easy is it to use?

Is a swivel seat provided and how helpful is it?

Entry for wheelchair users

How easy is it for wheelchair occupants to enter, exit and manoeuvre within the vehicle?

Are the wheelchair and occupant restraint systems suitable for a range of wheelchairs?

Internal Features

How easy is it for people with different disabilities to locate and operate passenger controls within the passenger area?

Safety Considerations

Is there a slip-resistant surface to the ramp, step (where fitted) and vehicle floor?

What is the Safe Working Load of the ramp?

Do the wheelchair and occupant restraint systems secure the wheelchair and occupant safely? Have they been tested in the vehicle?

Are the wheelchair and occupant restraint systems easy to use?

To which one of the following has the vehicle been tested in the converted state:

- –   European Community Whole Vehicle Type Approval
- –   UK Low Volume National Type Approval
- –   Single Vehicle Approval?

DfT

September 2002

Department for Transport
Guidance notes and model byelaws

INTRODUCTION

1. The purpose of this guidance note is to assist local licensing authorities in England who are considering making hackney carriage byelaws under section 68 of the Town Police Clauses Act 1847.

BYELAWS OR CONDITIONS OF LICENCE?

2. As a first step, licensing authorities will want to consider whether their regulatory objectives – in terms of exerting controls over taxi owners and drivers – can best be achieved by attaching conditions to licences or by making byelaws. Conditions can be attached to hackney carriage vehicle licences by virtue of section 47 of the Local Government (Miscellaneous Provisions) Act 1976.

3. It appears to have been accepted amongst local licensing authorities that the judgment in the case of *Wathan v Neath and Port Talbot CBC* [2002] EWHC 16341 established a principle that there was no power available in law to attach conditions to a hackney carriage driver's licence.

4. The Department's view is that the decision in *Wathan* is being misinterpreted; and that the power to grant a licence to a hackney carriage driver under s.46 of the Town Police Clauses Act 1847 implies a power to attach conditionls to that licence.

5. *Hewison v Skegness Urban District Council* [1963] 1 QB 5841 held that whether or not an authority could impose conditions to a licence depended on what the statutory power to grant the licence said or implied. In deciding whether conditions can be imposed on a hackney carriage driver's licence, certain considerations must be taken into account, including (i) whether or not the statutory regime contains preconditions for the grant of a licence – an absence of statutory criteria makes it easier to imply a power to impose conditions; and (ii) enforcement. There is a mechanism to enforce any breach of a condition under section 50 of the 1847 Act and section 61 of the 1976 Act.

6. These considerations have informed our view that the power to grant a licence to a hackney carriage driver under section 46 of the 1847 Act implies a power to attach conditions to that licence.

7. By contrast, in the case of *Wathan v Neath and Port Talbot CBC*, the court was asked if section 57 of the Local Government (Miscellaneous Provisions) Act 1976 empowers authorities to attach conditions to a hackney carriage driver's licence. The court held that it did not, because section 57 concerns licence applications and whether conditions should be attached to a licence. We accept the conclusion of the court in relation to the question put to it; section 57 does

not, as the judgment makes clear, confer a power to impose conditions. However this was, in our view, because section.57 impliedly assumes that there was already such a power, presumably deriving from section 46 of the 1847 Act.

8. We recognise that there are arguments against this view, and it will be a matter for each licensing authority, in conjunction with its own legal advisers, to determine whether it is proper to attach conditions to a licence. Ultimately, of course, whether section 46 provides such a power will be a matter for the courts to decide.

9. While, in the Department's opinion, there is no need – at least on legal grounds – for licensing authorities to abandon their conditions of licence and re-enact the relevant obligations or prohibitions in byelaws, some local licensing authorities might decide that hackney carriage byelaws suit their purposes better than conditions of licence (eg the varying approaches to penalties for offences or consequences for breaches might be a relevant consideration).

CONSIDERATIONS WHEN MAKING HACKNEY CARRIAGE BYELAWS

(i) Extent of vires

10. Having considered the matter carefully, we take the view that the byelaw-making power in the 1847 Act should be considered in the context of local authorities' wider responsibilities in relation to hackney carriage licensing ie. that the purpose of the power is to enable local licensing authorities to regulate hackney carriage drivers and proprietors in such a way as to ensure that they are fit and proper persons and in order to ensure the safety of the travelling public. In reaching this conclusion, it is relevant to note that the 1847 Act refers to the conduct of both drivers and proprietors "plying . . . in their several employments", suggesting that plying is not restricted just to drivers seeking hirings, but is a way of defining the running of a taxi business. Moreover, section 68 also refers to regulating things such as the maintenance of the carriage. We therefore take the view that section 68 allows byelaws to cover all areas associated with the business of running hackney carriages in which the licensing authority has a genuine and legitimate interest.

(ii) Model byelaws

11. The Department has produced a set of model byelaws as a basis for local licensing authorities. This is attached at Annex **A**. The model byelaws cover the range of standard controls which most local authorities would want to impose and we would expect local authorities to base their byelaws on the model.

(iii) Deviations from the model

12. Where a local authority wishes to introduce a byelaw which deviates from the model, we shall expect local authorities to take a rigorous approach in

-drafting to ensure that the tests of legal validity are met. These are set out in Kruse v Johnson [1898] 2 QB 911 as comprising 4 elements essential to validity:

- byelaws must be within the powers of the local authority which makes them;
- byelaws must not be repugnant to the general law;
- byelaws must be certain and positive in their terms; and
- byelaws must be reasonable.

13. If a local authority identifies *a* policy objective which it wishes to reflect in byelaws, the onus will be on the local authority to draft a suitable byelaw to put to the Department for provisional approval.

14. The onus will also be on the local authority to satisfy itself as to the validity of any proposed byelaw which it submits to the Department for approval. We would expect local authorities to have sought their own legal advice and to provide an explanation as to why they consider that any proposed byelaw is valid. We would stress that confirmation by the Secretary of State does not endow the byelaws with legal validity – only the courts can determine whether a byelaw is valid. To this extent, it is crucial that any draft byelaws are seen and approved by the Council's legal advisers. Any request for provisional approval of byelaws which deviate from the model should be accompanied by an explanation of the policy objective, a justification of their validity and confirmation that the byelaws have been approved by legal advisers.

(iv) Secretary of State's role

15. Section 236(7) of the Local Government Act 1972 gives the Secretary of State power to confirm or refuse byelaws which are submitted to him. Confirmation depends on validity. In confirming a byelaw, the Secretary of State is not purporting to give legal effect to something which would not otherwise be lawful.

16. The principal element of the approval and confirmation process will involve consideration of the policy issues, mainly whether the objective is reasonable and the byelaw appropriate to achieve it. We shall reach a view at the provisional approval stage and we shall also continue to consider any objections put to the Secretary of State when the byelaws have been advertised.

THE BYELAW MAKING PROCEDURE

17. A description of the procedure for making byelaws is attached at Annex B.

Buses and Taxis Division

July 2005

02079445980

ANNEX A
MODEL BYELAWS FOR HACKNEY CARRIAGES

BYELAWS

Made under section 68 of the Town Police Clauses Act 1847, and section 171 of the Public Health Act 1875, by the council of *[name of council]* with respect to hackney carriages in *[name of district]*.

INTERPRETATION

1. Throughout these byelaws "the Council" means *[name of council]* and "the district" means *[name of district]*.

PROVISIONS REGULATING THE MANNER IN WHICH THE NUMBER OF EACH HACKNEY CARRIAGE CORRESPONDING WITH THE NUMBER OF ITS LICENCE, SHALL BE DISPLAYED

2. (a) The proprietor of a hackney carriage shall cause the number of the licence granted to him in respect of the carriage to be legibly painted or marked on the outside and inside of the carriage, or on plates affixed thereto.

(b) A proprietor or driver of a hackney carriage shall:

(i)   not wilfully or negligently cause or suffer any such number to be concealed from public view while the carriage is standing or plying for hire; and

(ii)   not cause or permit the carriage to stand or ply for hire with any such painting marking or plate so defaced that any figure or material particular is illegible.

PROVISIONS REGULATING HOW HACKNEY CARRIAGES ARE TO BE FURNISHED OR PROVIDED

3. The proprietor of a hackney carriage shall:

(a)   provide sufficient means by which any person in the carriage may communicate with the driver;

(b)   cause the roof or covering to be kept water-tight;

(c)   provide any necessary windows and a means of opening and closing not less than one window on each side;

(d)   cause the seats to be properly cushioned or covered;

(e)   cause the floor to be provided with a proper carpet, mat or other suitable covering;

(f)   cause the fittings and furniture generally to be kept in a clean condition, well maintained and in every way fit for public service;

(g)   provide means for securing luggage if the carriage is so constructed as to carry luggage;

(h)   provide an efficient fire extinguisher which shall be carried in such a position as to be readily available for use; and

(i)   provide at least two doors for the use of persons conveyed in such carriage and a separate means of ingress and egress for the driver.

4.[1] The proprietor of a hackney carriage shall cause any taximeter with which the carriage is provided to be so constructed, attached and maintained as to comply with the following requirements, that is to say:

(a)   the taximeter shall be fitted with a key, flag or other device the turning of which will bring the machinery of the taximeter into action and cause the word "HIRED" to appear on the face of the taximeter;

(b)   such key, flag or other device shall be capable of being locked in such a position that the machinery of the taximeter is not in action and that no fare is recorded on the face of the taximeter;

(c)   when the machinery of the taximeter is in action there shall be recorded on the face of the taximeter in clearly legible figures, a fare not exceeding the rate or fare which the proprietor or driver is entitled to demand and take for the hire of the carriage by time as well as for distance in pursuance of the tariff fixed by the Council;

(d)   the word "FARE" shall be printed or1 the face of the taximeter in plain letters so as clearly to apply to the fare recorded thereon;

(e)   the taximeter shall be so placed that all letters and figures on the face thereof are at all times plainly visible to any person being conveyed in the carriage, and for that purpose the letters and figures shall be capable of being suitably illuminated during any period of hiring; and

(f)   the taximeter and all the fittings thereof shall be so affixed to the carriage wi,th seals or other appliances that it shall not be practicable for any person to tamper with them except by breaking, damaging or permanently displacing the seals or other appliances.

[1]   (a) An assurance should be given that proprietors of cabs already fitted with taximeters will have no difficulty in complying with the byelaws relating to taximeters an4 where the byelaws will require all cabs to be fitted with meters, that the other proprietors will be able to obtain and fit suitable meters and "FOR HIRE" signs by the time the byelaws may be expected to come into operation.
(b) Where the Council wishes to require all cabs to be fitted with a taximeter, the following form of words may be used: "The proprietor of a hackney carriage shall cause the same to be provided with a taximeter so constructed, attached and maintained as to comply with the following requirements, that is to say:–
(c) Where taximeters are not in use and their use cannot be foreseen, model byelaws 4, 5 and 6 may be omitted. If they are omitted, the heading preceding model byelaw 5 should remain.

PROVISIONS REGULATING THE CONDUCT OF THE PROPRIETORS AND DRIVERS OF HACKNEY CARRIAGES PLYING WITHIN THE DISTRICT IN THEIR SEVERAL EMPLOYMENTS, AND DETERMINING WHETHER SUCH DRIVERS SHALL WEAR ANY AND WHAT BADGES

5. The driver of a hackney carriage provided with a taximeter shall:

(a)   when standing or plying for hire, keep the key, flag or other device fitted in pursuance of the byelaw in that behalf locked in the position in which no fare is recorded on the face of the taximeter;

(b)   before beginning a journey for which a fare is charged for distance and time, bring the machinery of the taximeter into action by moving the said key, flag or other device so that the word "HIRED" is legible on the face of the taximeter and keep the machinery of the taximeter in action until the termination of the hiring; and

(c)   cause the dial of the taximeter to be kept properly illuminated throughout any part of a hiring which is between half-an-hour after sunset and half-an-hour before sunrise, and also at any other time at the request of the hirer.

6. A proprietor or driver of a hackney carriage shall not tamper with or permit any person to tamper with any taximeter with which the carriage is provided, with the fittings thereof, or with the seals affixed thereto.

7. The driver of a hackney carriage shall, when plying for hire in any street and not actually hired:

(a)   proceed with reasonable speed to one of the stands appointed by the Council;

(b)   if a stand, at the time of his arrival, is occupied by the full number of carriages authorised to occupy it, proceed to another stand;

(c)   on arriving at a stand not already occupied by the full number of carriages authorised to occupy it, station the carriage immediately behind the carriage or carriages on the stand and so as to face in the sarrle direction; and

(d)   from time to time, when any other carriage immediately in front is driven off or moved forward cause his carriage to be moved forward so as to fill the place previously occupied by the carriage driven off or moved forward.

8. A proprietor or driver of a hackney carriage, when standing or plying for hire, shall not make use of the services of any other person for the purpose of importuning any person to hire such carriage.

9. The driver of a hackney carriage shall behave in a civil and orderly manner and shall take all reasonable precautions to ensure the safety of persons conveyed in or entering or alighting from the vehicle.

10. The proprietor or driver of a hackney carriage who has agreed or has been hired to be in attendance with the carriage at an appointed time and place shall, unless delayed or prevented by some sufficient cause, punctually attend with such carriage at such appointed time and place.

11. A proprietor or driver of a hackney carriage shall not convey or permit to be conveyed in such carriage any greater number of persons than the number of persons specified on the plate affixed to the outside of the carriage.

12. If a badge has been provided by the Council and delivered to the driver of a hackney carriage he shall, when standing or plying for hire, and when hired, wear that badge in such position and manner as to be plainly visible.

13. The driver of a hackney carriage so constructed as to carry luggage shall, when requested by any person hiring or seeking to hire the carriage:

    (a)   convey a reasonable quantity of luggage;

    (b)   afford reasonable assistance in loading and unloading; and

    (c)   afford reasonable assistance in removing it to or from the entrance of any building, station or place at which he may take up or set down such person.

PROVISIONS FIXING THE RATES OR FARES TO BE PAID FOR HACKNEY CARRIAGES WITHIN THE DISTRICT AND SECURING THE DUE PUBLICATION OF SUCH FARES

14. (i) The proprietor or driver of a hackney carriage shall be entitled to demand and take for the hire of the carriage the rate or fare prescribed by the Council, the rate or fare being calculated by a combination of distance and time unless the hirer express at the commencement of the hiring his desire to engage by time.

(ii)[1] Where a hackney carriage furnished with a taximeter is hired by distance and time the proprietor or driver thereof shall not be entitled to demand and take a fare greater than that recorded on the taxirneter, save for any extra charges authorised by the Council which it may not be possible to record on the face of the taxirneter.

15. (i) The proprietor of a hackney carnage shall cause a statement of the fares fixed by council resolution to be exhibited inside the carriage, in clearly distinguishable letters and figures.

(ii) The proprietor or driver of a hackney carriage bearing a statement of fares in accordance with this byelaw shall not wilfully or negligently cause or suffer the letters or figures in the statement to be concealed or rendered illegible at any tirne while the carriage is plying or being used for hire.

[1]   This provision should be included whether or not taximeters are introduced in case they are introduced on a voluntary basis before further byelaws are made.

PROVISIONS SECURING THE SAFE CUSTODY AND RE-DELIVERY OF ANY PROPERTY ACCIDENTALLY LEFT IN HACKNEY CARRIAGES, AND FIXING THE CHARGES TO BE MADE IN RESPECT THEREOF

16. The proprietor or driver of a hackney carriage shall immediately after the termination of any hiring, or as soon as practicable thereafter, carefully search the carriage for any property which may have been accidentally left therein.

17. The proprietor or driver of a hackney carriage shall, if any property accidentally left therein by any person who may have been conveyed in the carriage be found by or handed to him:

(a) carry it as soon as possible and in any event within 48 hours if not sooner claimed by or on behalf of its owner, to the office of the council[1] and leave it in the custody of the officer in charge of the office on his giving a receipt for it; and

(b) be entitled to receive from any person to whom the property shall be re-delivered an amount equal to five pence in the pound of its estimated value (or the fare for the distance from the place of finding to the office of the Council, whichever be the greater) but not more than five pounds.

[1] It may be desired to substitute "a police station in the district". In this case, an assurance will be required that the consent of the police has been obtained.

PENALTIES

18. Every person who shall offend against any of these byelaws shall be liable on summary conviction to a fine not exceeding Level 2 on the Standard Scale and in the case of a continuing offence to a further fine not exceeding two pounds for each day during which the offence continues after conviction therefor.

REPEAL OF BYE LAWS[1]

19. The byelaws relating to hackney carriages which were made by ....
Council[2] on the .... day of .... and which were confirmed by ....[3]
on the ..... day of .... are hereby repealed.

[1] If there are no byelaws in force upon the subject, this should be stated and the clause struck out.
[2] State the names in full of all local authorities whose byelaws are to be repealed
[3] State the confirming authority.

ANNEX B
HACKNEY CARRIAGE BYELAWS: – THE BYELAW-MAKING PROCESS

Prior to seeking provisional approval

- Consider the model set of byelaws (see Annex A). Electronic version from Darwin Gunewardena – Darwin.Gunewardena@dft.gsi.gov.uk
- Identify any policy objectives which you wish to include which are not incorporated in the model.
- Consider with legal advisers whether the policy objectives could be incorporated in the byelaws.
- Draft appropriate byelaws with accompanying justification of policy objective and statement regarding their legal validity.

Submitting to the Department for provisional approval

- Submit the proposed draft byelaws for provisional approval. It is preferable to submit a full set of byelaws so that all the provisions can be considered together rather than by seeking provisional approval in a piecemeal manner. The byelaws should be sent to Darwin Gunewardena – either using the e-mail address above or at 311 3 Great Minster House, 76 Marsham Street, London, SW1 P 4DR.
- Identify in the covering letter those byelaws which deviate from the model.
- Set out in the covering letter the policy objective to be achieved in respect of each byelaw which deviates from the model (including why the model is not suitable in the case of a minor deviation).
- Confirm in the covering letter that the byelaws have been approved by the Council's legal advisers and that they are satisfied that each proposed byelaw is valid in legal terms.
- You will receive an acknowledgement from the Department on receipt of draft byelaws. However, please bear in mind that if we have a substantial number of requests for approval and confirmation, there might well be a delay in processing requests.

Submitting to the Department for confirmation.

- Having followed the making, sealing and advertising procedure in s.236 of the Local Government Act 1972, please submit the byelaws to Darwin Gunewardena for confirmation.
- We shall require two sealed copies of the byelaws for confirmation – one for our retention and one which will be returned to the council.
- Please submit evidence that the statutory procedure in respect of advertising the byelaws has been followed (a copy of the page(s) of the relevant local papers is sufficient for this purpose).

Coming into operation

- The Department will agree a coming into operation date with the local authority. The standard period is four weeks from confirmation, but this can be adapted if the local authority has specific reasons. We would, however, expect sufficient time between confirmation and coming into operation as to enable the byelaws to be printed and distributed to owners and drivers.

Department for Transport

Buses and Taxis Division

July 2005

Road Safety Act 2006: Private Hire Vehicles – Guidance Note

TABLE OF CONTENTS

ROAD SAFETY ACT 2006: SECTIONS 53 AND 54

REPEAL OF THE PHV CONTRACT EXEMPTION

A note from the Department for Transport

INTRODUCTION

1. This note relates to private hire vehicles – PHVs. in England and Wales only, as PHV licensing is devolved in Scotland and Northern Ireland.

2. It responds to the main questions that have been raised with the Department by local licensing authorities, and others, concerning two forthcoming changes

to PHV licensing legislation provided for in the Road Safety Act 2006 ("the 2006 Act"):–

–   Section 53 of the 2006 Act repeals section 75(1)(b) of the Local Government (Miscellaneous Provisions) Act 1976 which is commonly known as "the contract exemption", and currently exempts from PHV licensing requirements vehicles engaged on contracts lasting not less than seven days. The provision affects England and Wales outside London; our letter of 28 February 2007 (copy attached), stated that the intention was to bring the provision into force in January 2008 and Ministers have now decided that the precise coming into force date will be 28 January 2008.

–   Section 54 of the 2006 Act amends the definition of "private hire vehicle" in the Private Hire Vehicles London. Act 1998 – which has much the same end result in terms of requiring vehicles in London engaged on contracts – to provide services to specific groups rather than the public at large to be licensed. As also foreseen in our February letter, Ministers have decided that this change will come into force on 31 March 2008.

3. Whilst this note is written largely in terms of the impact that the repeal of the contract exemption will have outside London, the points it makes are also generally relevant to what will be the position within London when section 54 of the 2006 Act comes into force.

4. We sought the views of stakeholders on a draft of this guidance and are grateful for the comments which we received.

THE DEPARTMENT'S VIEW, NOT LEGAL ADVICE

5. It is not the role of the Department to interpret the law or to provide legal advice. Nothing in this note should be regarded as a definitive statement of what the law means and it should not be relied upon as legal advice. It is clear from the views we received that many stakeholders would find it helpful if the guidance could give stronger advice on the impact of the repeal of the contract exemption, but we would stress that it is a matter for local licensing authorities to make decisions on what the law requires in particular cases, seeking their own legal advice when necessary. Organisations that may be affected by the changes described in paragraph 2 should also consider seeking their own independent legal advice. Ultimately it is for the Courts to provide a definitive interpretation of the law.

6. However the Department is able to offer a view on the questions that have been raised and what follows covers each of these in turn.

WHAT IS A PRIVATE HIRE VEHICLE?

7. A PHV is defined in legislation as "a motor vehicle constructed or adapted to seat fewer than nine passengers, other than a hackney carriage or public

service vehicle or a London cab or tramcar, which is provided for hire with the services of a driver for the purpose of carrying passengers". The repeal of the contract exemption will not change this definition. All that will happen when the contract exemption is repealed is that vehicles outside London which fall within the definition of a PHV in the Local Government (Miscellaneous Provisions) Act 1976 ("the 1976 Act") and which have not been licensed because of relying on the contract exemption will be brought within the PHV licensing regime.

8. PHVs are often referred to as "minicabs" but the definition brings into the PHV licensing regime a wider range of vehicles than just the conventional minicab. For example, in considering whether a particular vehicle falls within the definition of "private hire vehicle" it is not relevant that all hirings are charged through a business account without any cash changing hands between the driver and passenger; what is relevant is whether the vehicle has fewer than nine passenger seats and is made available for hire with the services of a driver for the purpose of carrying passengers. Nor does the definition say that the vehicle has to be hired frequently or for a number of different purposes for it be a PHV. It is not relevant, for example, whether the vehicle only carries out one trip per day on the same route; what is relevant is whether the vehicle is provided for hire with the services of a driver for the purpose of carrying passengers. This is explained in more detail in the sections which follow below.

9. A further general point to note is that PHV licensing is designed to cover exclusive hirings, where the vehicle is hired as a whole. It is therefore necessary to consider the manner in which the vehicle is provided. If passengers pay individual fares as part of the contractual arrangements PHV licensing is unlikely to apply. Where a vehicle is not being exclusively hired it may be that the vehicle is being used to carry passengers for hire or reward at separate fares, which would make the Public Service Vehicle (PSV ie bus) licensing regime relevant. It would then also be relevant whether the vehicle is being used "in the course of a business of carrying passengers" – for the purposes of the definition of a PSV in the Public Passenger Vehicles Act 1981. The various categories into which the -vehicles could fall are described in greater detail below.

WHAT DID THE CONTRACT EXEMPTION COVER?

10. At present that is before section 53 of the 2006 Act comes into force., by virtue of section 75(1)(b) of the 1976 Act a vehicle in England and Wales outside London which would otherwise need to be licensed as a PHV is exempt from PHV licensing requirements if it is used for contracts lasting not less than seven days. Similarly, the operator and driver of that vehicle are exempt from PHV licensing requirements.

11. It is important, in the Department's view, to note that the contract exemption is quite narrow. This is because case law has established that for section 75-1.-b. of the1976 Act to apply the following conditions must all be satisfied:

(i)　the vehicle must be hired under a contract for use of a specific, identified vehicle, not merely a contract for the provision of a service;

(ii)　the contract must be for a period of at least seven days;

(iii)　a notice period for termination of the contract must be specified in the contract.

12. Licensing authorities, and transport providers considering whether they will be affected by the repeal of the exemption, will need to consider whether the vehicles in question are in fact currently within the scope of the exemption. Any vehicle which satisfies the definition of a PHV and has been relying on the contract exemption in error should have been licensed as a PHV already and the need to be licensed does not arise from repeal of the exemption.

WHAT ARE THE ALTERNATIVES TO PHV LICENSING?

13. The definition of "private hire vehicle" set out above encompasses a range of vehicles and a range of services, but it does not follow that every vehicle with fewer than nine passenger seats which is used to carry passengers for some sort of recompense must necessarily be licensed in the PHV category.

14. As mentioned above, a PHV is licensed first and foremost to provide exclusive hirings, in other words hirings in which the vehicle is hired as a whole by a single person or group. The hirings must be made through a licensed PHV operator for a specified charge. (As an adjunct to the main purpose of providing exclusive hirings, a licensed PHV operator can, in certain circumstances, "marry-up" hirings to a similar destination and charge passengers separate fares – but the primary purpose of a PHV is to provide exclusive hirings and any vehicles with fewer than nine passenger seats which provide exclusive hirings should be considered in the context of the definition of "private hire vehicle".)

Small PSVs

15. It is possible for vehicles with fewer than nine passenger seats which carry passengers at a commercial rate to fall within the Public Service Vehicle – PSV. Operator licensing regime – they are known as "small PSVs". The main characteristic of a small PSV – which distinguishes it from a PHV – is that the small PSV provides a service at separate fares that is, where each passenger pays his or her own fare for a particular journey. Small PSVs are not normally allowed to provide exclusive hirings – the exception to this rule being where the vehicles are a small part of a big bus operator's business.. The operator of any small PSV would need to hold a PSV Operator's licence, granted by the relevant Traffic Commissioner.

16. Of course, as mentioned above, where a vehicle is already licensed as a PHV, it can offer a service at separate fares in specific circumstances, but the small PSV category applies where a vehicle provides a service at separate fares and is not licensed as a PHV.

Car sharing schemes

17. It is also possible for vehicles with fewer than nine passenger seats to provide a service involving the carriage of passengers which is neither a PHV nor a small PSV – the vehicle could fall within the rules governing car sharing schemes. The main characteristic of a vehicle which is being used legitimately under the car sharing rules is that the total of any charges should be agreed in advance and must not exceed the running costs – including wear and tear and depreciation. of the vehicle for the journey. In other words, it is a form of transport which is provided by volunteers who do not make a profit from the service.

18. The rules governing car sharing are contained in section 1–4. of the Public Passenger Vehicles Act 1981 ("the 1981 Act"). A useful leaflet about how these schemes work has been prepared by the Community Transport Association and can be accessed on their website: http://www.communitytransport.com/index.aspx?id=104 (the relevant document is "Using MPVs and Smaller Vehicles").

19. Car sharing schemes have a valuable role to play and repeal of the contract exemption is not intended to bring them within the PHV licensing regime where they are legitimately operating under the 1981 Act.

Hackney carriages (taxis)

20. For the sake of completeness, it is worth mentioning that vehicles with fewer than nine passenger seats which provide exclusive hirings can be licensed as hackney carriages – or taxis. As well as carrying out pre-booked hirings, a hackney carriage is permitted to stand at ranks or be hailed in the street so the passenger arranges the hiring directly with the driver – unlike PHVs where the hiring must be made through a licensed operator. It is unlikely that vehicles which have been exempt from PHV licensing by virtue of the contract exemption would want to enter the hackney carriage licensing regime, but it would, at least in theory, be an option for the vehicle owners to consider.

21. This brief outline of the various categories into which a vehicle with fewer than nine passenger seats could potentially fall demonstrates the complexity of the legislation. That is why the Department stresses the importance of independent legal advice. The views which follow below focus on the position in relation to PHV licensing; they are offered in general terms noting that individual cases should, of course, be considered according to their particular circumstances.

WILL I HAVE TO BE LICENSED IN EVERY AREA IN WHICH I WISH TO UNDERTAKE A HIRING?

22. This is a question that has been asked by some transport providers who will be affected by the repeal of the contract exemption. The law on "cross border" hirings is complex and it may be appropriate for those involved to seek their own advice in particular cases.

23. The legislation governing PHVs in England and Wales is couched in terms of PHVs being regulated according to the "controlled district" in which they are operated. A controlled district comprises the area of a local district or borough council or unitary authority.

24. The Department takes the view that a licensed PHV can undertake a hiring which goes beyond the boundary of, or is wholly outside, its controlled district. However this is subject to a requirement that the vehicle and the driver are both licensed by the same local authority that granted a licence to the operator who arranged the hiring, and also that the operator has a licence for the area in which he intends to operate.

25. We would emphasise again that our view should not be regarded as a substitute for independent legal advice, and that much may depend upon the facts of a particular case.

BEST PRACTICE GUIDANCE

26. It is worth mentioning in this note the relevance of the Department's Best Practice Guidance which was published in October 2006 – it can be accessed on the Department's website (www.dft.gov.uk). Licensing authorities will be faced with a number of applications for PHV licences from drivers, operators and vehicle owners whose circumstances might be different from the more conventional applications which they routinely receive.

27. There are likely, for example, to be drivers who currently drive for a commercial rate but are dedicated to just a single contract, for example, a school run involving the same journey twice a day during term time. Licensing authorities must, of course, satisfy themselves that an applicant for a PHV driver's licence is a fit and proper person to hold such a licence, but they would want to take account of the nature of the work carried out by the applicant in doing so. In relation to topographical knowledge, the Guidance suggests that licensing authorities might adopt a lighter touch in relation to PHV drivers than taxi drivers.

HOW DOES THE REPEAL OF THE CONTRACT EXEMPTION
AFFECT "AMBULANCES"?

28. A number of providers of "ambulance" services have asked if the services they provide will come within the PHV licensing regime following the repeal of the contract exemption. Bearing in what is said above (paragraph 11) on the narrowness of the contract exemption, the Department is doubtful that many providers of an ambulance service currently rely on the contract exemption in order to be able to provide their service outside the PHV licensing regime. In particular, we understand that many private ambulance vehicles are provided under contracts for the provision of ambulance services, rather than for use of a specific vehicle, and therefore cannot rely on the exemption.

29. That of course still leaves the basic question of whether a particular vehicle comes within the definition of a PHV quoted above. A wide range of vehicles and operations appear to come under the broad "ambulance" heading, and it seems to the Department that the vehicles can be divided into three categories:

- emergency/specialist ambulance vehicles – likely to accommodate a stretcher and specialist equipment, and to require the presence of health professionals. Licensing authorities may wish to make use in this connection of the fact these vehicles are exempt from road tax by virtue of the Vehicle Excise and Registration Act 1994 and cannot be used for "social" hirings. The Annex to this note sets out the definition in the 1994 Act.

- vehicles which operate as part of a formal Patient Transport Service[1] – usually non-emergency, planned transport of patients, where the booking will only be made if the person to be carried has been assessed by a health professional as having a medical need for transport; these vehicles will be contracted to a health care provider and cannot be used for "social" hirings; licensing authorities can verify with the owner of a vehicle that it is being used in connection with such a contract. An exemption from road tax as mentioned under the first bullet point – and described in the annex – might also be relevant. Patient Transport Services encompass a wide range of vehicles, ranging from specialist to less specialist types, to allow for transport consistent with a patient's needs.

- other vehicles used to transport passengers to and from hospitals and other medical facilities on an ad-hoc basis without falling within either of the above two categories. These vehicles might perhaps be driven by volunteers or perhaps the operator has made a commercial decision to dedicate the operation to medical-related journeys, but the key point is that they are not operated as part of a formal Patient Transport Service scheme and are not within the definitions in the Annex.

[Note: in practice there is some overlap between the first two ambulance categories, (eg: during a crisis a non-emergency ambulance may become an emergency ambulance).]

30. In considering which of these categories falls within the definition of PHV, there are a number of factors that we recommend licensing authorities take into account. The Department believes that there is a significant difference between vehicles arranged by a health provider and used because a person is assessed as having a medical need for transport, and other vehicles used to provide transport to health facilities. It is significant that details of the former, being provided as part of a wider healthcare package, would be subject to the laws on patient confidentiality (so the providers could not comply with PHV licensing requirements to allow licensing officers to check records). The Department also considers it significant whether the vehicles in question are permitted to carry out health-related work only, taking account of the descriptions in the first two bullet points. The signs displayed by the vehicle are a factor too, (but will not be

determinative, eg: if the vehicle is also used for social events). The Department considers it irrelevant whether the vehicles are provided by the NHS or private sector.

31. There is no specific exemption in the PHV licensing legislation for an ambulance and the Government has no plans to introduce such an exemption. It appears to the Department that a court would be unlikely to consider that Parliament intended vehicles in the first two categories – ie: emergency/specialist ambulances and vehicles used under Patient Transport Services schemes. to be within the PHV definition. Therefore an exemption would not be necessary or appropriate. In reaching this conclusion the Department took account of the specific characteristics of the vehicles in the first two categories, most particularly the fact that they form part of a wider healthcare package and can only carry patients who have been assessed as having a medical need for transport. Moreover, they cannot be used for non-medical/health-related work, the drivers should have training and background checks in connection with the service they provide, and the records of any transport provided are subject to the laws on patient confidentiality. In short, if checks are in place for these services, they could legitimately be regarded as distinct from the PHV licensing regime.

32. In the Department's view, vehicles in the third category which are provided for hire but which, though choice (commercial or otherwise), are dedicated to hospital-related journeys may well fall within the PHV definition. There will, inevitably, be cases where a licensing authority decides that a vehicle which presents itself as an ambulance actually falls within the PHV category on account of the nature of the work which it provides. For example, the Department has been made aware of vehicles which describe themselves as ambulances but actually carry out a variety of bookings ranging from patient transfer to evening social events.

HOW WILL SERVICES PROVIDED BY VOLUNTEERS BE AFFECTED (INCLUDING VOLUNTARY CAR SCHEMES)?

33. Government Ministers welcome the valuable service provided by the many volunteers who offer their time freely to transport less fortunate members of society to and from health appointments and various social events and engagements. Their efforts and kindness benefit society as a whole by contributing towards social inclusion. The Department is aware of concerns about the actual dividing line between volunteers who provide a service using small vehicles and licensed PHV drivers who provide a service on a commercial basis. Each sector has a valuable role to play and this note endeavours to assist those who want to understand what constitutes volunteering and when a service becomes commercial.

34. The Department's view is that the phrase "for hire" in the definition of a PHV implies that there must be an element of commercial benefit to an arrangement for PHV licensing requirements to apply. As a consequence of this we consider that services provided by genuine volunteers who receive no recompense or

receive only enough to cover their actual expenses are unlikely to satisfy the definition of a PHV. Therefore in our view such services would not have needed to rely on the contract exemption to avoid PHV licensing requirements and as such its repeal will not affect them in any way.

35. There is case law which indicates that a service becomes commercial if there is any form of profit or gain by the transport provider (ie: if the service is not simply an act of social kindness). Drivers will want to satisfy themselves that they are not making a profit from the service they provide if they want to avoid falling within the definition of "private hire vehicle". It is worth reiterating at this point the importance of drivers seeking independent legal advice if they are in any doubt about their own particular case.

36. In determining whether a particular volunteer service is operating legitimately outside the PHV licensing regime, one useful method of calculating the profitability or otherwise of the service might be to consider the rates charged in the context of the rules set out by HM Revenue and Customs (HMRC) for taxation purposes. The rules are explained in a fact sheet which can be accessed on the HMRC's website. Essentially, volunteer drivers' tax free allowance is 40 pence on the first 10,000 miles in the tax year; and 25 pence on each mile over 10,000 in the tax year. The HMRC fact sheet explains how to calculate income from volunteer driving.

37. The particular point has been raised whether voluntary car schemes will be affected by the repeal of the contract exemption. It is our understanding that many such schemes involve the payment of separate fares and as such fall outside the PHV licensing regime and outside the PSV licensing regime – the rules governing car sharing are covered in paragraphs 17–19. The repeal of the contract exemption will not change this.

HOW WILL THE CHANGE AFFECT "STRETCHED LIMOUSINES"?

38. Some stretched limousines may fall within the definition of PHV and may have been relying on the contract exemption. However, the points made in paragraph 11 are of course relevant. In particular, it should be noted that the contract exemption cannot be correctly relied on by services which involve a series of one-off hirings lasting a day or perhaps just an evening – as seems to be the case for many services provided by stretched limousines.

CHILDMINDERS

39. There are a considerable variety of childminding arrangements. In considering whether the repeal of the contract exemption is relevant, much will depend on the particular facts of each case.

40. The Department's view is that it is possible that a childminder who uses his or her own car to drive a child to and from school or for any outings as part of his/her childminding business might fall within the PHV definition. However

we consider it unlikely that a court would consider that Parliament intended that the majority of the many thousands of childminders across England and Wales should have to obtain PHV licences in order to be able to transport children in their care. As such, we would expect the courts to seek to interpret the definition of a PHV in such a way that most typical childminder arrangements do not fall within its scope.

41. In our view the following further considerations are also likely to be relevant:–

–   Whether the childminder actually has the transport of the child in his or her care in the motor vehicle as a requirement of the contract, (ie whether the child has a right to be carried in the childminder's vehicle in return for the payment provided, or whether other modes of transport are an option).

–   Whether the vehicle is hired as a whole – the concept of exclusive hirings is covered in paragraph 14. Childminders may be caring for different children under different contracts at the same time. These children may be simultaneously carried in the vehicle for the same journeys (e.g. where the children attend the same school) or for overlapping journeys (e.g. if children are dropped off or collected in turn from different schools). Where this is the situation, the vehicle as a whole has not been exclusively hired by any particular parent.

–   Whether separate fares are being charged; if they are, the vehicle is not a PHV.

42. If a vehicle only provides a service which would place it in the PHV category only for part of the year (eg during term time) and not during other times, it would still require a PHV licence in order to provide a lawful PHV service at the times when it is operating as such.

DISTRIBUTION OF THIS NOTE

43. This note is being sent to taxi/PHV licensing authorities and other relevant organisations. It has also been placed on the Department's website.

Buses and Taxis Division

Department for Transport

ANNEX

IS THE VEHICLE EXEMPT FROM ROAD TAX BY VIRTUE OF THE VEHICLE EXCISE AND REGISTRATION ACT 1994?

Schedule 2 to the Vehicle Excise and Registration Act 1994 identifies an ambulance as a vehicle which is exempt from road tax; it defines an ambulance as:

- A vehicle which:
  - (a) is constructed or adapted for, and used for no other purpose than, the carriage of sick, injured or disabled people to or from welfare centres or places where medical or dental treatment is given, and
  - (b) is readily identifiable as a vehicle used for the carriage of such people by being marked "Ambulance" on both sides.

A2.20

Guidance for operators of stretch limousines

INTRODUCTION

This Guidance tries to answer basic questions to assist owners and operators of stretched limousines.

It is only intended for general help; it is not a legal document. For details of the law you will need to refer to the relevant legislation.

Operations for hire, or any sort of payment will require some form of licence, for use either as a public service vehicle or as a private hire vehicle, depending on the type of vehicle and the way it is used. Public service vehicle operators' licences apply across Great Britain and are issued by the Traffic Commissioners. Licences for private hire vehicles are issued by local authorities in England and Wales, but this does not apply in Scotland as the legal framework is different. Section 4 explains which type of licence is needed and where to obtain more information about the licensing requirements.

Further information on specific aspects of the law can be found in the documents listed in this Guidance. If after considering the additional documents you are still unsure about any aspect of the law you may wish to consider seeking independent legal advice.

1. HOW DO I REGISTER MY LIMOUSINE FOR USE ON THE ROAD IN GREAT BRITAIN?

If you buy a brand new vehicle in Great Britain (GB) the dealer will usually arrange for it to be registered for you. Further information can be obtained from the Direct.Gov website, Motoring section:

http://www.direct.gov.uk/Motoring/BuyingAndSellingAVehicle/RegisteringAVehicle/fs/en

A vehicle imported into GB for use on the public road must be licensed and registered immediately after arrival. Information on the procedures for importing, licensing and registering vehicles purchased outside Great Britain can be found on the website above under "Registering an Imported vehicle".

The vast majority of Limousines imported in to GB are exported from the USA. Legislation governing the construction and use of vehicles is significantly different in America and therefore the vehicles will need modifications (significant modifications in the case of larger vehicles) before being compliant with GB requirements.

Limousines with up to 8 passenger seats

Smaller limousines, those with up to 8 passenger seats, will in almost all cases, not be type approved to British or European standards and thus will need to undergo the Single Vehicle Approval (SVA) scheme. The SVA scheme is a pre-registration inspection for cars and light goods vehicles that have not been type-approved to British or European standards. The main purpose of the scheme is to ensure that these vehicles have been designed and constructed to modern safety and environmental standards before they can be used on public roads.

Limousines where the number of passenger seats is around 8–10 but is hard to determine.

The SVA scheme can only be used to approve passenger cars seating up to 8 passengers plus the driver. In some cases it was difficult to determine the exact number of seats because, for example, the vehicle has long bench seats. In those cases, the Vehicle and Operator Services Agency (VOSA) was prepared to accept a declaration from the applicant for SVA that the seating capacity does not exceed 8 passengers, and that the applicant will undertake to inform any other person that may use the vehicle of that limitation. These vehicles were then registered with a passenger seating capacity of 8. From summer 2008 this will no longer be possible.

Limousines with more than 8 passenger seats.

Larger limousines are not suitable for the SVA scheme. Currently the system for registering large limousines is essentially based on self-declaration that the vehicle is compliant with British laws. The Driver and Vehicle Licensing Agency (DVLA) will accept a COIF (Certificate of Initial Fitness) as confirming that the vehicle complies with GB construction standards, or if a COIF is not available they may request that the vehicle is checked to ensure that it meets GB construction standards. From summer 2008, it is expected that all limousines submitted for registration without a COIF will have to be inspected by VOSA for compliance with GB construction standards before they can be registered with DVLA.

There are very few limousine types that are currently compliant with COIF, which is an inspection carried out by VOSA to check that a vehicle with more than 8 passenger seats complies with GB construction requirements, and is a requirement for a limousine used for carrying paying passengers.

The Department is aware that vehicles not complying with GB construction regulations have been registered and is taking steps to prevent this. For most of these vehicles it will be expensive to convert them so that they comply.

2. CAN I CONVERT A CAR THAT IS ALREADY REGISTERED INTO A LIMOUSINE, BY STRETCHING IT?

It is possible to take a car which is already registered with DVLA and convert it into a Limousine, using reputable coachbuilders here or in the USA. Once the vehicle has been converted you are legally required to notify DVLA of the changes, since the identity of the vehicle may be brought into question. It is possible that the passenger capacity or the taxation class of the vehicle would have changed, so the V5 registration document would no longer be valid. A future buyer of the vehicle will be suspicious if the vehicle in front of him/her is not as described on the V5.

If a vehicle or its chassis has been cut in half and extended, the vehicle would need to be inspected by DVLA and would be assessed as being in one of two categories, either as radically altered from its original specification, or, if a kit of new parts has been used in the build, as a kit conversion. The registration number will change because this is not the same vehicle as that described on the vehicle records and it would be misleading to retain the original registration number when the vehicle has undergone such major modifications.

DVLA issues a guide to the registration of rebuilt, radically altered and kit converted vehicles, in the form of an information leaflet INF 26, which is available from DVLA Local Offices. Information is also available on www.direct. gov.uk . You will be required to show receipts, build plans and photographs of the build if you are applying for kit conversion status.

DVLA advises that before modifying a vehicle which has a cherished registration mark, the vehicle keeper may wish to consider securing the mark, which may be lost if the vehicleâs identity is changed.

If, following modification, the identity of the vehicle is changed then evidence of type approval will be required in order to register the vehicle. This will normally be SVA. However, if the number of passenger seats now exceeds 8 then the vehicle is not normally subject to SVA, but should be submitted to VOSA for "COIF" (Certificate of Initial Fitness) certification if it is to be used for hire and reward, as most limousines are.

Evidence required before undergoing SVA.

Before a converter submits his vehicle to VOSA for SVA inspection, he will have to provide evidence to demonstrate the modified vehicle's capability to operate at weights higher than the original vehicle's maximum gross weight, if this will be exceeded when the vehicle is full of passengers. Key components such as the axles, suspension and brakes may have to be upgraded to take the extra weight of the converted vehicle, compared to the original base vehicle.

More information

For further information on registering a rebuilt, radically altered or kit converted vehicle, see the following link on the Direct.gov website:

http://www.direct.gov.uk/Motoring/BuyingAndSellingAVehicle/ RegisteringAVehicle/RegisteringAVehicleArticles/fs/en?CONTENT_ ID=10014246&chk=VsQ/Fs

3. CAN I USE MY LIMOUSINE TO CARRY FARE-PAYING PASSENGERS?

Theoretically yes, but you will need some form of operator' s licence.

Virtually any motor vehicle used in Great Britain to carry passengers for hire/ hire or reward on a commercial basis needs a licence of some kind. The type of licence required depends upon on the capacity of the vehicle and the type of operation undertaken.

Operating hire or reward services without the requisite operator's licence is a criminal offence.

Hire or reward is any sort of payment which gives a person a right to be carried on a vehicle regardless of whether a profit is made or not. The payment may be made by the person himself, or on his behalf. It may be a direct payment (such as a fare, hire charge or other payment made directly in respect of the journey) or an indirect payment (such as a membership subscription to a club, payment for a bed in a hotel or payment for concert tickets).

4. WHAT TYPE OF OPERATORS LICENCE DO I NEED?

For vehicles constructed or adapted to carry more than 8 passengers, the licence required is a public service vehicle (PSV) operatorâs licence issued by the Traffic Commissioner.

For vehicles adapted to carry 8 passengers or fewer, it is either:

(a)   a private hire vehicle (PHV) licence if the vehicle is hired out, with a driver, as a whole (ie: an exclusive hiring). In England and Wales these licences are administered by the relevant local authority or Transport for London (TfL) who have discretion as to what vehicles they will license. The situation is similar in Scotland with the Scottish Executive having legislative responsibility.

(b)   a PSV operator's licence if the vehicle is used for carrying passengers at separate fares "in the course of a business of carrying passengers", once again issued by the Traffic Commissioner. This type of operation is known as a small PSV.

Information on the PSV operator licensing regime is contained in the guidance booklet PSV437 which can be obtained from any of VOSAâs traffic area offices (for address and contact details see appendix 1) or can be accessed on the VOSA website (www.vosa.gov.uk).

In England and Wales, information on the local private hire vehicle requirements can be obtained from your local licensing authority (district/borough councils, unitary authorities or TfL). Given that most operations are likely to be exclusive hirings the vast majority of Limousine operations will fall within the requirements of the PHV operator regime.

If you need further information about the operation in Scotland of small passenger-carrying vehicles (with 8 or fewer passenger seats) ask the Scottish Traffic Area for a copy of the note "Licensing of Small Passenger Carrying Vehicles".

You will also need to ensure that you have the appropriate vehicle and operator insurance for your operation. Operating without valid vehicle insurance could result in your vehicle being impounded.

5. WHAT CAN I DO IF MY LOCAL AUTHORITY WILL NOT LICENSE MY VEHICLE AS A PHV?

Each local licensing authority in England and Wales may decide which vehicles are suitable for licensing as PHVs in their area. Accordingly, it is for each licensing authority to decide for its area whether they wish to license stretched limousines as PHVs, taking into account local circumstances. It is important to note that vehicles can only be licensed as PHVs if they have fewer than 9 passenger seats.

The Department for Transport has issued best practice guidance to local licensing authorities in England and Wales on the licensing of taxis and PHVs. That guidance encourages local authorities to consider the licensing of limousines on a case by case basis and not to impose a blanket ban on the type of vehicle.

The licensing process allows for would-be licence holders, who are refused a licence on the grounds that a vehicle is unsuitable to be licensed as a PHV, to appeal against the authority's decision in the local magistrates' court.

6. ARE THERE ANY EXCEPTIONS TO THE REQUIREMENT TO LICENSE AS A PHV OPERATOR?

If vehicles with up to 8 passenger seats, including stretched limousines, are used solely for weddings and/or funerals, they are exempt from PHV licensing requirements.

7. ARE THERE ANY CONDITIONS PLACED ON THE OPERATORS OF SMALL PSVS?

When granting an application for a Small PSV licence to the operator of a stretch limousine the Traffic Commissioner may attach a standard set of conditions to the licence. The conditions generally imposed for limousine operators are:

- When using a stretch limousine under a PSV licence the vehicle will not carry more than 8 passengers.
- Passengers must be carried at separate fares (see below).
- If any journey is less than 15 miles measured in a straight line, then it must be registered as a local service with the Traffic Commissioner prior to its operation.
- The registration numbers of all vehicles which are used under the PSV operator's licence are to be logged with the Traffic Commissioner within seven days of their acquisition. If a vehicle is no longer used under the PSV licence that fact must also be notified to the Traffic Commissioner within seven days of it cessation.
- Before being used under a PSV licence stretch limousines must pass a Single Vehicle Approval test and hold a relevant annual test certificate.

8. WHAT IS A SEPARATE FARE?

If a limousine is licensed as a small PSV, (carrying 8 or less passengers), separate fares must be charged. The term "separate fares" is not defined in legislation. However, we believe it represents a charge made directly or indirectly to each passenger for carriage which is unaffected by the number of fare payers. This is the way fares are often structured, for example, on a local bus service. Subject to any concessions that the operator may give, each passenger pays the same fare for the same journey, regardless of how many other passengers on the bus wish to make that journey.

9. MUST I ALWAYS CHARGE SEPARATE FARES IF I OPERATE AS A SMALL PSV?

In most cases the answer is yes, otherwise you will be operating as a PHV and will need to be licensed accordingly.

There is one exception to the requirement for separate fares to be charged. "Big bus" operators (ie those operating vehicles with 9 or more passenger seats) can run small PSVs for some private hire work, provided the operation of these -vehicles represents a small part of their overall business. What constitutes "a small part" is also not defined in legislation, and ultimately, final decisions on where the balance lies is a matter for the courts. The legislation confers the exemption on an operator whose use of small vehicles is only a small part of his business.

The *relative size* of the fleet of large and small buses is obviously very relevant and as a *rule of thumb* we believe that if less than 10% of the overall fleet licensed under a single PSV Operator's Licence are small vehicles the exemption will apply (e.g. a fleet of, say, 20 buses with 9 or more passenger seats could run 2 additional vehicles – which could be stretched limousines that carry 8 or less passengers – for private hire work). But because the legislation refers to the size of the small and large bus business other factors (such as mileage run) should be taken into account. We would hope that in most cases it would be obvious what was and what was not, to coin a phrase, a "large bus business".

You will need to make the Traffic Commissioner aware if you are a big bus operator wishing to run stretch limousines, so that the standard conditions attached to the PSV licence can be reconsidered.

10. CAN I USE THE LIMOUSINE TO CARRY MORE THAN 8 PASSENGERS?

Only if you have a PSV operator licence that allows for that. In order to obtain such a licence you will need to prove that your vehicle complies with legally required safety standards. In order to prove this, your vehicle will need to have a Certificate of Initial Fitness (COIF) issued by VOSA.

However, most limousines imported from the USA cannot obtain such a certificate because they do not comply with GB construction and use regulations. In particular, the regulations require any passenger vehicle carrying more than eight people to have exits big enough to get passengers out quickly in the event of an emergency. Many limousines do not comply with this requirement. In addition, the regulations require European-approved lamps, mirrors, tyres, seat belts and glass, which are not present on American vehicles, and the regulations on turning circle are not met by most stretched American vehicles.

If your vehicle is able to comply with the safety standards, guidance on obtaining a PSV licence is available in the booklet PSV 437. The guidance provides details of the type of services that you may provide using such a licence but you will also need to consider the impact of the drivers' hours and driver licensing requirements for PSV vehicles. Guidance on drivers hours is available in the document PSV 375 (also available from VOSA) and driver licence information is available from DVLA (www.dvla.gov.uk or tel: 0870 240 0009).

11. WHAT TYPE OF SERVICE CAN I OPERATE WITH A SMALL PSV?

You can operate either a local service (standard or flexibly routed) or operate excursions and tours.

Note: you cannot do any work which needs a PHV licence without the required licence.

Also, there are restrictions on the carriage of alcohol on vehicles used to take passengers to certain sporting events.

Further information on the operation of PSV vehicles can be found in the guidance document PSV 437 and information on local services can be found in PSV353A (local service registrations) and PSV358A (flexible local bus service registrations) from either the Traffic Area Offices or via the VOSA website.

12. WHAT IS A LOCAL SERVICE?

It is a bus service using Public Service Vehicles (PSVs) to carry passengers at separate fares over short distances. The route can be of any overall length, as long as throughout its length passengers can get off within 24.15 kms (15 miles) (measured in a straight line) of the place where they were picked up. Local services must be registered with the Traffic Commissioner.

The legislation specifying what service particulars must be registered with the Traffic Commissioner for a local service imposes different requirements according to whether the service in question is a "standard service" (ie a conventional registered local service) or a âflexible serviceâ. Further information on the description and operation of local services are contained in the guidance notes mentioned in the previous section.

13. ARE EXCURSIONS AND TOURS LOCAL BUS SERVICES?

On an excursion or tour all the passengers must travel together to the same place or places and then return together to the place where they got on. (They need not get on at exactly the same place.)

Excursions and tours only need to be registered with the traffic commissioner as a local service if all three of the following points are met:

- separate fares are paid;
- the whole journey is within a 15 mile radius of the starting point;
- they run one or more times a week for at least 6 weeks in a row.

It is accepted that most limousine operators running a small PSV taking ad hoc bookings will not need to register all of their likely journeys as local services because of the final point above. However, if you are not sure how long or how often the service will run you should register it to be on the safe side.

Any excursion or tour which is a local bus service and has a stop in London must also have a London service permit. Again you should contact Transport for London for details.

APPENDIX 1: VOSA TRAFFIC AREA OFFICES

All correspondence should be addressed to the Clerk to the Traffic Commissioner

North Eastern
Hillcrest House
386 Harehills Lane
Leeds
LS9 6NF

Telephone: 0870 606 0440

Fax: 0113 249 8142

North Western
Hillcrest House
386 Harehills Lane
Leeds
LS9 6NF

Telephone: 0870 606 0440

Fax: 0113 249 8142

West Midland
38 George Road, Edgbaston,
Birmingham B15 1PL

Telephone: 0870 606 0440

Fax:

0121 456 4250 (Lic)

0121 456 3513 (Comp)

Eastern
City House
126–130 Hills Road
Cambridge
CB2 1NP

Telephone: 0870 606 0440

Fax:

01223 309 684 (Lic)

01223 309 681 (Comp)

Western
2 Rivergate
Temple Quay
Bristol
BS1 6EH

Telephone: 0870 606 0440

Fax: 0117 929 8352

South Eastern and Metropolitan
Ivy House
3 Ivy Terrace
Eastbourne
BN21 4QT

Telephone: 0870 606 0440

Fax: 01323 726 679

Scottish
J Floor
Argyle House
3 Lady Lawson Street
Edinburgh
EH3 9SE

Telephone: 0870 606 0440

Fax: 0131 229 0682

Welsh
38 George Road, Edgbaston,
Birmingham B15 1PL

Telephone: 0870 606 0440

Fax:

0121 456 4250 (Lic)

0121 456 3513 (Comp)

A2.21

Nigel Dotchkin
Head of Disability and Equalities
Accessibility & Equalities Unit
Zone 2/23
Great Minster House
76 Marsham Street
London SW1P 4DR

Tel: 020 7944 4912

Fax: 020 7944 6102

E-Mail: nigel.dotchkin@dft.gov.uk

Web site: www.dft.gov.uk

Chief Executives

Local licensing authorities

TAXI ACCESSIBILITY

I have received a number of enquiries about whether there is currently a Government target that all taxis in local authority areas should become wheelchair accessible over a 10 year period from 2010. This letter clarifies the position.

In 2003, the Government stated that it intended to set standards for wheelchair accessible taxis and to introduce regulations that would apply to mainly urban local authority areas (so-called 'Phase 1' authorities). As you may know, the regulation making powers relating to accessible vehicles are contained in the Disability Discrimination Act 1995 and do not apply to private hire vehicles.

Since then, however, the Department has received a number of representations making the case for a broader range of disabled people's needs to be met in any regulations, rather than restricting the requirements only to wheelchair users. We have been looking at how this could be achieved but it is a complex matter. As a result, regulations have not been made.

Ministers remain keen to make progress on taxi accessibility and therefore intend to develop a consultation package for summer 2008 to seek views on the way forward.

I hope that your authority will engage in this forthcoming consultation and I would welcome your comments at that time on the way that taxi accessibility might best be achieved. To help us develop the consultation package, we intend to set up a small informal stakeholder group, including representatives from the Institute of Licensing and the National Association of Licensing and Enforcement Officers, as well as from the taxi trade and disability groups.

I have also enclosed a copy of the report by the ECMT (European Conference of Ministers of Transport) Taxi Group, which contains information that you may find of interest. You will note that it advocates a mixed fleet of accessible taxis. This will certainly be one of the options on which we will be seeking your views during the consultation process.

In the meantime, accessible taxi policies remain a matter for individual local licensing authorities with previous guidance that has been issued by the Department.

I should be grateful if you would pass the second copy of this letter to the Council's Taxi Licensing Officer.

NIGEL DOTCHKIN

Taxi and Private Hire Vehicle Licensing: Best Practice Guidance (DfT, March 2010)

INTRODUCTION

1. The Department first issued Best Practice Guidance in October 2006 to assist those local authorities in England and Wales that have responsibility for the regulation of the taxi and private hire vehicle (PHV) trades.

2. It is clear that many licensing authorities considered their licensing policies in the context of the Guidance. That is most encouraging.

3. However, in order to keep our Guidance relevant and up to date, we embarked on a revision. We took account of feedback from the initial version and we consulted stakeholders in producing this revised version.

4. The key premise remains the same – it is for individual licensing authorities to reach their own decisions both on overall policies and on individual licensing matters, in the light of their own views of the relevant considerations. This Guidance is intended to assist licensing authorities but it is only guidance and decisions on any matters remain a matter for the authority concerned.

5. We have not introduced changes simply for the sake of it. Accordingly, the bulk of the Guidance is unchanged. What we have done is focus on issues involving a new policy (for example trailing the introduction of the Safeguarding Vulnerable Groups legislation); or where we consider that the advice could be elaborated (eg enforcement); or where progress has been made since October 2006 (eg the stretched limousine guidance note has now been published).

THE ROLE OF TAXIS AND PHVS

6. Taxis (more formally known as hackney carriages) and PHVs (or minicabs as some of them are known) play an important part in local transport. In 2008, the average person made 11 trips in taxis or private hire vehicles. Taxis and PHVs are used by all social groups; low-income young women (amongst whom car ownership is low) are one of the largest groups of users.

7. Taxis and PHVs are also increasingly used in innovative ways – for example as taxi-buses – to provide innovative local transport services (see paras 92-95)

THE ROLE OF LICENSING: POLICY JUSTIFICATION

8. The aim of local authority licensing of the taxi and PHV trades is to protect the public. Local licensing authorities will also be aware that the public should have reasonable access to taxi and PHV services, because of the part they play in local transport provision. Licensing requirements which are unduly stringent will

tend unreasonably to restrict the supply of taxi and PHV services, by putting up the cost of operation or otherwise restricting entry to the trade. Local licensing authorities should recognise that too restrictive an approach can work against the public interest – and can, indeed, have safety implications.

9. For example, it is clearly important that somebody using a taxi or PHV to go home alone late at night should be confident that the driver does not have a criminal record for assault and that the vehicle is safe. But on the other hand, if the supply of taxis or PHVs has been unduly constrained by onerous licensing conditions, then that person's safety might be put at risk by having to wait on late-night streets for a taxi or PHV to arrive; he or she might even be tempted to enter an unlicensed vehicle with an unlicensed driver illegally plying for hire.

10. Local licensing authorities will, therefore, want to be sure that each of their various licensing requirements is in proportion to the risk it aims to address; or, to put it another way, whether the cost of a requirement in terms of its effect on the availability of transport to the public is at least matched by the benefit to the public, for example through increased safety. This is not to propose that a detailed, quantitative, cost-benefit assessment should be made in each case; but it is to urge local licensing authorities to look carefully at the costs – financial or otherwise – imposed by each of their licensing policies. It is suggested they should ask themselves whether those costs are really commensurate with the benefits a policy is meant to achieve.

SCOPE OF THE GUIDANCE

11. This guidance deliberately does not seek to cover the whole range of possible licensing requirements. Instead it seeks to concentrate only on those issues that have caused difficulty in the past or that seem of particular significance. Nor for the most part does the guidance seek to set out the law on taxi and PHV licensing, which for England and Wales contains many complexities. Local licensing authorities will appreciate that it is for them to seek their own legal advice.

CONSULTATION AT THE LOCAL LEVEL

12. It is good practice for local authorities to consult about any significant proposed changes in licensing rules. Such consultation should include not only the taxi and PHV trades but also groups likely to be the trades' customers. Examples are groups representing disabled people, or Chambers of Commerce, organisations with a wider transport interest (eg the Campaign for Better Transport and other transport providers), womens' groups or local traders.

ACCESSIBILITY

13. The Minister of State for Transport has now announced the way forward on accessibility for taxis and PHVs. His statement can be viewed on the

Department's web-site at: http://www.dft.gov.uk/press/speechesstatements/ statements/accesstotaxis. The Department will be taking forward demonstration schemes in three local authority areas to research the needs of people with disabilities in order to produce guidance about the most appropriate provision. In the meantime, the Department recognises that some local licensing authorities will want to make progress on enhancing accessible taxi provision and the guidance outlined below constitutes the Department's advice on how this might be achieved in advance of the comprehensive and dedicated guidance which will arise from the demonstration schemes.

14. Different accessibility considerations apply between taxis and PHVs. Taxis can be hired on the spot, in the street or at a rank, by the customer dealing directly with a driver. PHVs can only be booked through an operator. It is important that a disabled person should be able to hire a taxi on the spot with the minimum delay or inconvenience, and having accessible taxis available helps to make that possible. For PHVs, it may be more appropriate for a local authority to license any type of saloon car, noting that some PHV operators offer accessible vehicles in their fleet. The Department has produced a leaflet on the ergonomic requirements for accessible taxis that is available from: http://www.dft.gov.uk/ transportforyou/access/taxis/pubs/research

15. The Department is aware that, in some cases, taxi drivers are reluctant to pick up disabled people. This may be because drivers are unsure about how to deal with disabled people, they believe it will take longer for disabled people to get in and out of the taxi and so they may lose other fares, or they are unsure about insurance arrangements if anything goes wrong. It should be remembered that this is no excuse for refusing to pick up disabled people and that the taxi industry has a duty to provide a service to disabled people in the same way as it provides a service to any other passenger. Licensing authorities should do what they can to work with operators, drivers and trade bodies in their area to improve drivers' awareness of the needs of disabled people, encourage them to overcome any reluctance or bad practice, and to improve their abilities and confidence. Local licensing authorities should also encourage their drivers to undertake disability awareness training, perhaps as part of the course mentioned in the training section of this guidance that is available through Go-Skills.

16. In relation to enforcement, licensing authorities will know that section 36 of the Disability Discrimination Act 1995 (DDA) was partially commenced by enactment of the Local Transport Act 2008. The duties contained in this section of the DDA apply only to those vehicles deemed accessible by the local authority being used on "taxibus" services. This applies to both hackney carriages and private hire vehicles.

17. Section 36 imposes certain duties on drivers of "taxibuses" to provide assistance to people in wheelchairs, to carry them in safety and not to charge extra for doing so. Failure to abide by these duties could lead to prosecution through a Magistrates' court and a maximum fine of £1,000.

18. Local authorities can take action against non-taxibus drivers who do not abide by their duties under section 36 of the DDA (see below). This could involve for example using licence conditions to implement training requirements or, ultimately, powers to suspend or revoke licences. Some local authorities use points systems and will take certain enforcement actions should drivers accumulate a certain number of points

19. There are plans to modify section 36 of the DDA. The Local Transport Act 2008 applied the duties to assist disabled passengers to drivers of taxis and PHVs whilst being used to provide local services. The Equality Bill which is currently on its passage through Parliament would extend the duties to drivers of taxis and PHVs whilst operating conventional services using wheelchair accessible vehicles. Licensing authorities will be informed if the change is enacted and Regulations will have to be made to deal with exemptions from the duties for drivers who are unable, on medical grounds to fulfil the duties.

Duties to carry assistance dogs

20. Since 31 March 2001, licensed taxi drivers in England and Wales have been under a duty (under section 37 of the DDA) to carry guide, hearing and other prescribed assistance dogs in their taxis without additional charge. Drivers who have a medical condition that is aggravated by exposure to dogs may apply to their licensing authority for an exemption from the duty on medical grounds. Any other driver who fails to comply with the duty could be prosecuted through a Magistrates' court and is liable to a fine of up to £1,000. Similar duties covering PHV operators and drivers have been in force since 31 March 2004.

21. Enforcement of this duty is the responsibility of local licensing authorities. It is therefore for authorities to decide whether breaches should be pursued through the courts or considered as part of the licensing enforcement regime, having regard to guidance issued by the Department. http://www.dft.gov.uk/transportforyou/access/taxis/pubs/taxis/carriageofassistancedogsinta6154?page=2

Duties under the Part 3 of the DDA

22. The Disability Discrimination Act 2005 amended the DDA 1995 and lifted the exemption in Part 3 of that Act for operators of transport vehicles. Regulations applying Part 3 to vehicles used to provide public transport services, including taxis and PHVs, hire services and breakdown services came into force on 4 December 2006. Taxi drivers now have a duty to ensure disabled people are not discriminated against or treated less favourably. In order to meet these new duties, licensing authorities are required to review any practices, policies and procedures that make it impossible or unreasonably difficult for a disabled person to use their services.

23. The Disability Rights Commission, before it was incorporated into the Equality and Human Rights Commission, produced a Code of Practice to explain the Part 3 duties for the transport industry; this is available at http://www.

equalityhumanrights.com/uploaded_files/code_of_practice_provision_and_use
_of_transport_vehicles_dda.pdf. There is an expectation that Part 3 duties also
now demand new skills and training; this is available through GoSkills, the sector
skills council for road passenger transport. Go-Skills has also produced a DVD
about assisting disabled passengers. Further details are provided in the training
section of this guidance.

24. Local Authorities may wish to consider how to use available courses to
reinforce the duties drivers are required to discharge under section 3 of DDA,
and also to promote customer service standards for example through GoSkills.

25. In addition recognition has been made of a requirement of basic skills prior
to undertaking any formal training. On-line tools are available to assess this
requirement prior to undertaking formal training.

VEHICLES

Specification of vehicle types that may be licensed

26. The legislation gives local authorities a wide range of discretion over the
types of vehicle that they can license as taxis or PHVs. Some authorities specify
conditions that in practice can only be met by purpose-built vehicles but the
majority license a range of vehicles.

27. Normally, the best practice is for local licensing authorities to adopt the
principle of specifying as many different types of vehicle as possible. Indeed,
local authorities might usefully set down a range of general criteria, leaving it
open to the taxi and PHV trades to put forward vehicles of their own choice
which can be shown to meet those criteria. In that way there can be flexibility for
new vehicle types to be readily taken into account.

28. It is suggested that local licensing authorities should give very careful
consideration to a policy which automatically rules out particular types of
vehicle or prescribes only one type or a small number of types of vehicle. For
example, the Department believes authorities should be particularly cautious
about specifying only purpose-built taxis, with the strict constraint on supply
that that implies. But of course the purpose-built vehicles are amongst those
which a local authority could be expected to license. Similarly, it may be too
restrictive to automatically rule out considering Multi-Purpose Vehicles, or to
license them for fewer passengers than their seating capacity (provided of course
that the capacity of the vehicle is not more than eight passengers).

29. The owners and drivers of vehicles may want to make appropriate adaptations
to their vehicles to help improve the personal security of the drivers. Licensing
authorities should look favourably on such adaptations, but, as mentioned in
paragraph 35 below, they may wish to ensure that modifications are present
when the vehicle is tested and not made after the testing stage.

Tinted windows

30. The minimum light transmission for glass in front of, and to the side of, the driver is 70%. Vehicles may be manufactured with glass that is darker than this fitted to windows rearward of the driver, especially in estate and people carrier style vehicles. When licensing vehicles, authorities should be mindful of this as well as the large costs and inconvenience associated with changing glass that conforms to both Type Approval and Construction and Use Regulations.

Imported vehicles: type approval (see also "stretched limousines", paras 40-44 below)

31. It may be that from time to time a local authority will be asked to license as a taxi or PHV a vehicle that has been imported independently (that is, by somebody other than the manufacturer). Such a vehicle might meet the local authority's criteria for licensing, but the local authority may nonetheless be uncertain about the wider rules for foreign vehicles being used in the UK. Such vehicles will be subject to the 'type approval' rules. For passenger cars up to 10 years old at the time of first GB registration, this means meeting the technical standards of either:

-    a European Whole Vehicle Type approval;
-    a British National Type approval; or
-    a Individual Vehicle Approval.

Most registration certificates issued since late 1998 should indicate the approval status of the vehicle. The technical standards applied (and the safety and environmental risks covered) under each of the above are proportionate to the number of vehicles entering service. Further information about these requirements and the procedures for licensing and registering imported vehicles can be seen at www.businesslink.gov.uk/vehicleapprovalschemes

Vehicle testing

32. There is considerable variation between local licensing authorities on vehicle testing, including the related question of age limits. The following can be regarded as best practice:

- • **Frequency Of Tests.** The legal requirement is that all taxis should be subject to an MOT test or its equivalent once a year. For PHVs the requirement is for an annual test after the vehicle is three years old. An annual test for licensed vehicles of whatever age (that is, including vehicles that are less than three years old) seems appropriate in most cases, unless local conditions suggest that more frequent tests are necessary. However, more frequent tests may be appropriate for older vehicles (see 'age limits' below). Local licensing authorities may wish to note that a review carried out by the National Society for Cleaner Air in 2005 found that taxis were more likely than other vehicles to fail an emissions test. This finding, perhaps suggests that emissions testing should be carried out on ad hoc basis and more frequently than the full vehicle test.

- **Criteria For Tests**. Similarly, for mechanical matters it seems appropriate to apply the same criteria as those for the MOT test to taxis and PHVs*. The MOT test on vehicles first used after 31 March 1987 includes checking of all seat belts. However, taxis and PHVs provide a service to the public, so it is also appropriate to set criteria for the internal condition of the vehicle, though these should not be unreasonably onerous.
- **Age Limits**. It is perfectly possible for an older vehicle to be in good condition. So the setting of an age limit beyond which a local authority will not license vehicles may be arbitrary and inappropriate. But a greater frequency of testing may be appropriate for older vehicles – for example, twice-yearly tests for vehicles more than five years old.
- **Number Of Testing Stations**. There is sometimes criticism that local authorities provide only one testing centre for their area (which may be geographically extensive). So it is good practice for local authorities to consider having more than one testing station. There could be an advantage in contracting out the testing work, and to different garages. In that way the licensing authority can benefit from competition in costs. (The Vehicle Operators and Standards Agency – VOSA – may be able to assist where there are local difficulties in provision of testing stations.)

33. The Technical Officer Group of the Public Authority Transport Network has produced Best Practice Guidance which focuses on national inspection standards for taxis and PHVs. Local licensing authorities might find it helpful to refer to the testing standards set out in this guidance in carrying out their licensing responsibilities. The PATN can be accessed via the Freight Transport Association.

* A manual outlining the method of testing and reasons for failure of all MOT tested items can be obtained from the Stationary Office see http:www.tsoshop.co.uk/bookstore.asp?FO=1159966& Action=Book&From=SearchResults&ProductID=0115525726

Personal security

34. The personal security of taxi and PHV drivers and staff needs to be considered. The Crime and Disorder Act 1998 requires local authorities and others to consider crime and disorder reduction while exercising all of their duties. Crime and Disorder Reduction Partnerships are also required to invite public transport providers and operators to participate in the partnerships. Research has shown that anti-social behaviour and crime affects taxi and PHV drivers and control centre staff. It is therefore important that the personal security of these people is considered.

35. The owners and drivers of vehicles will often want to install security measures to protect the driver. Local licensing authorities may not want to insist on such measures, on the grounds that they are best left to the judgement of the owners

and drivers themselves. But it is good practice for licensing authorities to look sympathetically on – or actively to encourage – their installation. They could include a screen between driver and passengers, or CCTV. Care however should be taken that security measures within the vehicle do not impede a disabled passenger's ability to communicate with the driver. In addition, licensing authorities may wish to ensure that such modifications are present when the vehicle is tested and not made after the testing stage.

36. There is extensive information on the use of CCTV, including as part of measures to reduce crime, on the Home Office website (e.g. http://scienceandresearch.homeoffice.gov.uk/hosdb/cctv-imaging-technology/CCTV-and-imaging-publications) and on the Information Commission's Office website (www.ico.gov.uk). CCTV can be both a deterrent to would-be trouble makers and be a source of evidence in the case of disputes between drivers and passengers and other incidents. There is a variety of funding sources being used for the implementation of security measures for example, from community safety partnerships, local authorities and drivers themselves.

37. Other security measures include guidance, talks by the local police and conflict avoidance training. The Department has recently issued guidance for taxi and PHV drivers to help them improve their personal security. These can be accessed on the Department's website at: http://www.dft.gov.uk/pgr/crime/taxiphv/. In order to emphasise the reciprocal aspect of the taxi/PHV service, licensing authorities might consider drawing up signs or notices which set out not only what passengers can expect from drivers, but also what drivers can expect from passengers who use their service. Annex B contains two samples which are included for illustrative purposes but local authorities are encouraged to formulate their own, in the light of local conditions and circumstances. Licensing authorities may want to encourage the taxi and PHV trades to build good links with the local police force, including participation in any Crime and Disorder Reduction Partnerships.

Vehicle identification

38. Members of the public can often confuse PHVs with taxis, failing to realise that PHVs are not available for immediate hire and that a PHV driver cannot be hailed. So it is important to distinguish between the two types of vehicle. Possible approaches might be:

- **a licence condition that prohibits PHVs from displaying any identification at all apart from the local authority licence plate or disc.** The licence plate is a helpful indicator of licensed status and, as such, it helps identification if licence plates are displayed on the front as well as the rear of vehicles. However, requiring some additional clearer form of identification can be seen as best practice. This is for two reasons: firstly, to ensure a more positive statement that the vehicle **cannot** be hired immediately through the driver; and secondly because it is quite reasonable, and in the interests of the travelling public, for a

PHV operator to be able to state on the vehicle the contact details for hiring;

- **a licence condition which requires a sign on the vehicle in a specified form**. This will often be a sign of a specified size and shape which identifies the operator (with a telephone number for bookings) and the local licensing authority, and which also has some words such as 'pre-booked only'. This approach seems the best practice; it identifies the vehicle as private hire and helps to avoid confusion with a taxi, but also gives useful information to the public wishing to make a booking. It is good practice for vehicle identification for PHVs to include the contact details of the operator.

- Another approach, possibly in conjunction with the previous option, is **a requirement for a roof-mounted, permanently illuminated sign with words such as 'pre-booked only'**. But it can be argued that any roof-mounted sign, however unambiguous its words, is liable to create confusion with a taxi. So roof-mounted signs on PHVs are not seen as best practice.

Environmental considerations

39. Local licensing authorities, in discussion with those responsible for environmental health issues, will wish to consider how far their vehicle licensing policies can and should support any local environmental policies that the local authority may have adopted. This will be of particular importance in designated Air Quality Management Areas (AQMAs), Local authorities may, for example, wish to consider setting vehicle emissions standards for taxis and PHVs. However, local authorities would need to carefully and thoroughly assess the impact of introducing such a policy; for example, the effect on the supply of taxis and PHVs in the area would be an important consideration in deciding the standards, if any, to be set. They should also bear in mind the need to ensure that the benefits of any policies outweigh the costs (in whatever form).

Stretched limousines

40. Local licensing authorities are sometimes asked to license stretched limousines as PHVs. It is suggested that local authorities should approach such requests on the basis that these vehicles – where they have fewer than nine passenger seats – have a legitimate role to play in the private hire trade, meeting a public demand. Indeed, the Department's view is that it is not a legitimate course of action for licensing authorities to adopt policies that exclude limousines as a matter of principle and that any authorities which do adopt such practices are leaving themselves open to legal challenge. A policy of excluding limousines creates an unacceptable risk to the travelling public, as it would inevitably lead to higher levels of unlawful operation. Public safety considerations are best supported by policies that allow respectable, safe operators to obtain licences on the same basis as other private hire vehicle operators. The Department has now issued

guidance on the licensing arrangements for stretched limousines. This can be accessed on the Department's web-site at http://www.dft.gov.uk/pgr/regional/taxis/stretchlimousines.pdf.

41. The limousine guidance makes it clear that most operations are likely to fall within the PHV licensing category and not into the small bus category. VOSA will be advising limousine owners that if they intend to provide a private hire service then they should go to the local authority for PHV licences. The Department would expect licensing authorities to assess applications on their merits; and, as necessary, to be proactive in ascertaining whether any limousine operators might already be providing an unlicensed service within their district.

42. Imported stretched limousines were historically checked for compliance with regulations under the Single Vehicle Approval (SVA) inspection regime before they were registered. This is now the Individual Vehicle Approval (IVA) scheme. The IVA test verifies that the converted vehicle is built to certain safety and environmental standards. A licensing authority might wish to confirm that an imported vehicle was indeed tested by VOSA for IVA before being registered and licensed (taxed) by DVLA. This can be done either by checking the V5C (Registration Certificate) of the vehicle, which may refer to IVA under the "Special Note" section; or by writing to VOSA, Ellipse, Padley Road, Swansea, SA1 8AN, including details of the vehicle's make and model, registration number and VIN number.

43. Stretched limousines which clearly have more than 8 passenger seats should not of course be licensed as PHVs because they are outside the licensing regime for PHVs. However, under some circumstances the SVA regime accepted vehicles with space for more than 8 passengers, particularly where the precise number of passenger seats was hard to determine. In these circumstances, if the vehicle had obtained an SVA certificate, the authority should consider the case on its merits in deciding whether to license the vehicle under the strict condition that the vehicle will not be used to carry more than 8 passengers, bearing in mind that refusal may encourage illegal private hire operation.

44. Many councils are concerned that the size of limousines prevents them being tested in conventional MoT garages. If there is not a suitable MoT testing station in the area then it would be possible to test the vehicle at the local VOSA test stations. The local enforcement office may be able to advise (contact details on http://www.vosa.gov.uk).

QUANTITY RESTRICTIONS OF TAXI LICENCES OUTSIDE LONDON

45. The present legal provision on quantity restrictions for taxis outside London is set out in section 16 of the Transport Act 1985. This provides that the grant of a taxi licence may be refused, for the purpose of limiting the number of licensed taxis 'if, but only if, the [local licensing authority] is satisfied that there is no significant demand for the services of hackney carriages (within the area to which the licence would apply) which is unmet'.

46. Local licensing authorities will be aware that, in the event of a challenge to a decision to refuse a licence, the local authority concerned would have to establish that it had, reasonably, been satisfied that there was no significant unmet demand.

47. Most local licensing authorities do not impose quantity restrictions; the Department regards that as best practice. Where restrictions are imposed, the Department would urge that the matter should be regularly reconsidered. The Department further urges that the issue to be addressed first in each reconsideration is whether the restrictions should continue at all. It is suggested that the matter should be approached in terms of the interests of the travelling public – that is to say, the people who use taxi services. What benefits or disadvantages arise for them as a result of the continuation of controls; and what benefits or disadvantages would result for the public if the controls were removed? Is there evidence that removal of the controls would result in a deterioration in the amount or quality of taxi service provision?

48. In most cases where quantity restrictions are imposed, vehicle licence plates command a premium, often of tens of thousands of pounds. This indicates that there are people who want to enter the taxi market and provide a service to the public, but who are being prevented from doing so by the quantity restrictions. This seems very hard to justify.

49. If a local authority does nonetheless take the view that a quantity restriction can be justified in principle, there remains the question of the level at which it should be set, bearing in mind the need to demonstrate that there is no significant unmet demand. This issue is usually addressed by means of a survey; it will be necessary for the local licensing authority to carry out a survey sufficiently frequently to be able to respond to any challenge to the satisfaction of a court. An interval of three years is commonly regarded as the maximum reasonable period between surveys.

50. As to the conduct of the survey, the Department's letter of 16 June 2004 set out a range of considerations. But key points are:

- the length of time that would-be customers have to wait at ranks. However, this alone is an inadequate indicator of demand; also taken into account should be...
- waiting times for street hailings and for telephone bookings. But waiting times at ranks or elsewhere do not in themselves satisfactorily resolve the question of unmet demand. It is also desirable to address...
- latent demand, for example people who have responded to long waiting times by not even trying to travel by taxi. This can be assessed by surveys of people who do not use taxis, perhaps using stated preference survey techniques.
- peaked demand. It is sometimes argued that delays associated only with peaks in demand (such as morning and evening rush hours, or pub closing times) are not 'significant' for the purpose of the Transport Act 1985. The Department does not share that view. Since the peaks

in demand are by definition the most popular times for consumers to use taxis, it can be strongly argued that unmet demand at these times should not be ignored. Local authorities might wish to consider when the peaks occur and who is being disadvantaged through restrictions on provision of taxi services.

- consultation. As well as statistical surveys, assessment of quantity restrictions should include consultation with all those concerned, including user groups (which should include groups representing people with disabilities, and people such as students or women), the police, hoteliers, operators of pubs and clubs and visitor attractions, and providers of other transport modes (such as train operators, who want taxis available to take passengers to and from stations);

- publication. All the evidence gathered in a survey should be published, together with an explanation of what conclusions have been drawn from it and why. If quantity restrictions are to be continued, their benefits to consumers and the reason for the particular level at which the number is set should be set out.

- financing of surveys. It is not good practice for surveys to be paid for by the local taxi trade (except through general revenues from licence fees). To do so can call in question the impartiality and objectivity of the survey process.

51. Quite apart from the requirement of the 1985 Act, the Department's letter of 16 June 2004 asked all local licensing authorities that operate quantity restrictions to review their policy and justify it publicly by 31 March 2005 and at least every three years thereafter. The Department also expects the justification for any policy of quantity restrictions to be included in the Local Transport Plan process. A recommended list of questions for local authorities to address when considering quantity controls was attached to the Department's letter. (The questions are listed in Annex A to this Guidance.)

TAXI FARES

52. Local licensing authorities have the power to set taxi fares for journeys within their area, and most do so. (There is no power to set PHV fares.) Fare scales should be designed with a view to practicality. The Department sees it as good practice to review the fare scales at regular intervals, including any graduation of the fare scale by time of day or day of the week. Authorities may wish to consider adopting a simple formula for deciding on fare revisions as this will increase understanding and improve the transparency of the process. The Department also suggests that in reviewing fares authorities should pay particular regard to the needs of the travelling public, with reference both to what it is reasonable to expect people to pay but also to the need to give taxi drivers sufficient incentive to provide a service when it is needed. There may well be a case for higher fares at times of higher demand.

53. Taxi fares are a maximum, and in principle are open to downward negotiation between passenger and driver. It is not good practice to encourage such

negotiations at ranks, or for on-street hailings; there would be risks of confusion and security problems. But local licensing authorities can usefully make it clear that published fares are a maximum, especially in the context of telephone bookings, where the customer benefits from competition. There is more likely to be a choice of taxi operators for telephone bookings, and there is scope for differentiation of services to the customer's advantage (for example, lower fares off-peak or for pensioners).

54. There is a case for allowing any taxi operators who wish to do so to make it clear – perhaps by advertising on the vehicle – that they charge less than the maximum fare; publicity such as '5% below the metered fare' might be an example.

DRIVERS

Duration of licences

55. It is obviously important for safety reasons that drivers should be licensed. But it is not necessarily good practice to require licences to be renewed annually. That can impose an undue burden on drivers and licensing authorities alike. Three years is the legal maximum period and is in general the best approach. One argument against 3-year licences has been that a criminal offence may be committed, and not notified, during the duration of the licence. But this can of course also be the case during the duration of a shorter licence. In relation to this, authorities will wish to note that the Home Office in April 2006 issued revised guidance for police forces on the Notifiable Occupations Scheme. Paragraphs 62-65 below provide further information about this scheme.

56. However, an annual licence may be preferred by some drivers. That may be because they have plans to move to a different job or a different area, or because they cannot easily pay the fee for a three-year licence, if it is larger than the fee for an annual one. So it can be good practice to offer drivers the choice of an annual licence or a three-year licence.

Acceptance of driving licences from other EU member states

57. Sections 51 and 59 of the Local Government (Miscellaneous Provisions) Act 1976 as enacted stated that an applicant for a taxi or private hire vehicle (PHV) driver's licence must have held a full ordinary GB driving licence for at least 12 months in order to be granted a taxi or PHV driver's licence. This requirement has subsequently been amended since the 1976 Act was passed. The Driving Licences (Community Driving Licence) Regulations 1996 (SI 1996 No 1974) amended sections 51 and 59 of the 1976 Act to allow full driving licences issued by EEA states to count towards the qualification requirements for the grant of taxi and PHV driver's licences. Since that time, a number of central and eastern European states have joined the EU and the EEA and the Department takes the view that drivers from the Accession States are eligible to acquire a taxi or PHV

driver's licence under the 1976 Act if they have held an ordinary driving licence for 12 months which was issued by an acceding State (see section 99A(i) of the Road Traffic Act 1988). To complete the picture, the Deregulation (Taxis and Private Hire Vehicles) Order 1998 (SI 1998 No 1946) gave equal recognition to Northern Ireland driving licences for the purposes of taxi and PHV driver licensing under the 1976 Act (see section 109(i) of the Road Traffic Act 1988, as amended).

Criminal record checks

58. A criminal record check is an important safety measure particularly for those working closely with children and the vulnerable. Taxi and PHV drivers can be subject to a Standard Disclosure (and for those working in "Regulated Activity" to an Enhanced Disclosure[1]) through the Criminal Records Bureau. Both levels of Disclosure include details of spent and unspent convictions, cautions reprimands and final warnings. An Enhanced Disclosure may also include any other information held in police records that is considered relevant by the police, for example, details of minor offences, non-conviction information on the Police National Computer such as Fixed Penalty Notices and, in some cases, allegations. An Enhanced Disclosure is for those working in Regulated Activity and the Government has produced guidance in relation to this and the new "Vetting and Barring Scheme" which is available at www.isagov.org.uk/ default.aspx?page=402. [The Department will issue further advice as the new SVG scheme develops.]

59. In considering an individual's criminal record, local licensing authorities will want to consider each case on its merits, but they should take a particularly cautious view of any offences involving violence, and especially sexual attack. In order to achieve consistency, and thus avoid the risk of successful legal challenge, local authorities will doubtless want to have a clear policy for the consideration of criminal records, for example the number of years they will require to have elapsed since the commission of particular kinds of offences before they will grant a licence.

60. Local licensing authorities will also want to have a policy on background checks for applicants from elsewhere in the EU and other overseas countries. One approach is to require a certificate of good conduct authenticated by the relevant embassy. The Criminal Records Bureau website (www.crb.gov.uk) gives information about obtaining certificates of good conduct, or similar documents, from a number of countries.

61. It would seem best practice for Criminal Records Bureau disclosures to be sought when a licence is first applied for and then every three years, even if a licence is renewed annually, provided drivers are obliged to report all new convictions and cautions to the licensing authority.

[1]   "Regulated Activity" is defined in The Safeguarding Vulnerable Groups Act 2006 (Miscellaneous Provisions) Regulations 2009

Notifiable occupations scheme

62. Under this Scheme, when an individual comes to the notice of the police and identifies their occupation as a taxi or PHV driver, the police are requested to notify the appropriate local licensing authority of convictions and any other relevant information that indicates that a person poses a risk to public safety. Most notifications will be made once an individual is convicted however, if there is a sufficient risk, the police will notify the authority immediately.

63. In the absence of a national licensing body for taxi and PHV drivers, notifications are made to the local licensing authority identified on the licence or following interview. However, it is expected that all licensing authorities work together should they ascertain that an individual is operating under a different authority or with a fraudulent licence.

64. The police may occasionally notify licensing authorities of offences committed abroad by an individual however it may not be possible to provide full information.

65. The Notifiable Occupations Scheme is described in Home Office Circular 6/2006 which is available at http://www.basingstoke.gov.uk/CommitteeDocs/Committees/Licensing/20070710/3%20yr%20licences-update%20on%20hants%20constab%20procedures%20re%20Home%20office%20circ%20 6;2006-%20Appendix%202.pdf. Further information can also be obtained from the Criminal Records Team, Joint Public Protection Information Unit, Fifth Floor, Fry Building, 2 Marsham Street, London SW1P 4DF; e-mail Samuel. Wray@homeoffice.gsi.gov.uk.

Immigration checks

66. The Department considers it appropriate for licensing authorities to check on an applicant's right to work before granting a taxi or PHV driver's licence. It is important to note that a Criminal Records Bureau check is not a Right to Work check and any enquires about the immigration status of an individual should be addressed to the Border and Immigration Agency. Further information can be found at www.bia.homeoffice.gov.uk/employingmigrants. More generally, the Border and Immigration Agency's Employers' Helpline (0845 010 6677) can be used by licensing staff to obtain general guidance on immigration documentation, although this Helpline is not able to advise on individual cases. The authority can obtain case specific immigration status information, including whether a licensing applicant is permitted to work or details of work restrictions, from the Evidence and Enquiry Unit, Floor 12, Lunar House, Wellesley Road, Croydon CR9 2BY . Further details on the procedures involved can be obtained by contacting the Unit (020 8196 3011).

Medical fitness

67. It is clearly good practice for medical checks to be made on each driver before the initial grant of a licence and thereafter for each renewal. There is

general recognition that it is appropriate for taxi/PHV drivers to have more stringent medical standards than those applicable to normal car drivers because:

- they carry members of the general public who have expectations of a safe journey;
- they are on the road for longer hours than most car drivers; and
- they may have to assist disabled passengers and handle luggage.

68. It is common for licensing authorities to apply the "Group 2" medical standards – applied by DVLA to the licensing of lorry and bus drivers – to taxi and PHV drivers. This seems best practice. The Group 2 standards preclude the licensing of drivers with insulin treated diabetes. However, exceptional arrangements do exist for drivers with insulin treated diabetes, who can meet a series of medical criteria, to obtain a licence to drive category C1 vehicles (ie 3500-7500 kgs lorries); the position is summarised at Annex C to the Guidance. It is suggested that the best practice is to apply the C1 standards to taxi and PHV drivers with insulin treated diabetes.

Age limits

69. It does not seem necessary to set a maximum age limit for drivers provided that regular medical checks are made. Nor do minimum age limits, beyond the statutory periods for holding a full driver licence, seem appropriate. Applicants should be assessed on their merits.

Driving proficiency

70. Many local authorities rely on the standard car driving licence as evidence of driving proficiency. Others require some further driving test to be taken. Local authorities will want to consider carefully whether this produces benefits which are commensurate with the costs involved for would-be drivers, the costs being in terms of both money and broader obstacles to entry to the trade. However, they will note that the Driving Standards Agency provides a driving assessment specifically designed for taxis.

Language proficiency

71. Authorities may also wish to consider whether an applicant would have any problems in communicating with customers because of language difficulties.

Other training

72. Whilst the Department has no plans to make training courses or qualifications mandatory, there may well be advantage in encouraging drivers to obtain one of the nationally-recognised vocational qualifications for the taxi and PHV trades. These will cover customer care, including how best to meet the needs of people

with disabilities. More information about these qualifications can be obtained from GoSkills, the Sector Skills Council for Passenger Transport. GoSkills is working on a project funded by the Department to raise standards in the industry and GoSkills whilst not a direct training provider, can guide and support licensing authorities through its regional network of Regional Managers.

73. Some licensing authorities have already established training initiatives and others are being developed; it is seen as important to do this in consultation with the local taxi and PHV trades. Training can cover customer care, including how best to meet the needs of people with disabilities and other sections of the community, and also topics such as the relevant legislation, road safety, the use of maps and GPS, the handling of emergencies, and how to defuse difficult situations and manage conflict. Training may also be considered for applicants to enable them to reach an appropriate standard of comprehension, literacy and numeracy. Authorities may wish to note that nationally recognised qualifications and training programmes sometimes have advantages over purely local arrangements (for example, in that the qualification will be more widely recognised).

Contact details are:

GoSkills, Concorde House, Trinity Park, Solihull, Birmingham, B37 7UQ.
Tel: 0121-635-5520
Fax: 0121-635-5521
Website: www.goskills.org
e-mail: info@goskills.org

74. It is also relevant to consider driver training in the context of the 2012 Olympic and Paralympic Games which will take place at a number of venues across the country. One of the key aims of the Games is to "change the experience disabled people have when using public transport during the Games and to leave a legacy of more accessible transport". The Games provide a unique opportunity for taxi/PHV drivers to demonstrate their disability awareness training, and to ensure all passengers experience the highest quality of service.

Topographical knowledge

75. Taxi drivers need a good working knowledge of the area for which they are licensed, because taxis can be hired immediately, directly with the driver, at ranks or on the street. So most licensing authorities require would-be taxi-drivers to pass a test of local topographical knowledge as a pre-requisite to the first grant of a licence (though the stringency of the test should reflect the complexity or otherwise of the local geography, in accordance with the principle of ensuring that barriers to entry are not unnecessarily high).

76. However, PHVs are not legally available for immediate hiring in the same way as taxis. To hire a PHV the would-be passenger has to go through an operator, so the driver will have an opportunity to check the details of a route before starting a journey. So it may be unnecessarily burdensome to require a would-be

PHV driver to pass the same 'knowledge' test as a taxi driver, though it may be thought appropriate to test candidates' ability to read a map and their knowledge of key places such as main roads and railway stations. The Department is aware of circumstances where, as a result of the repeal of the PHV contract exemption, some people who drive children on school contracts are being deterred from continuing to do so on account of overly burdensome topographical tests. Local authorities should bear this in mind when assessing applicants' suitability for PHV licences.

PHV OPERATORS

77. The objective in licensing PHV operators is, again, the safety of the public, who will be using operators' premises and vehicles and drivers arranged through them.

Criminal record checks

78. PHV operators (as opposed to PHV drivers) are not exceptions to the Rehabilitation of Offenders Act 1974, so Standard or Enhanced disclosures cannot be required as a condition of grant of an operator's licence. But a Basic Disclosure, which will provide details of unspent convictions only, could be seen as appropriate, after such a system has been introduced by the Criminal Records Bureau. No firm date for introduction has yet been set; however, a feasibility study has been completed; the Criminal Records Bureau is undertaking further work in this regard. Overseas applicants may be required to provide a certificate of good conduct from the relevant embassy if they have not been long in this country. Local licensing authorities may want to require a reference, covering for example the applicant's financial record, as well as the checks outlined above.

Record keeping

79. It is good practice to require operators to keep records of each booking, including the name of the passenger, the destination, the name of the driver, the number of the vehicle and any fare quoted at the time of booking. This information will enable the passenger to be traced if this becomes necessary and should improve driver security and facilitate enforcement. It is suggested that 6 months is generally appropriate as the length of time that records should be kept.

Insurance

80. It is appropriate for a licensing authority to check that appropriate public liability insurance has been taken out for premises that are open to the public.

Licence duration

81. A requirement for annual licence renewal does not seem necessary or appropriate for PHV operators, whose involvement with the public is less direct

than a driver (who will be alone with passengers). Indeed, a licence period of five years may well be appropriate in the average case. Although the authority may wish to offer operators the option of a licence for a shorter period if requested.

Repeal of the PHV contract exemption

82. Section 53 of the Road Safety Act 2006 repealed the exemption from PHV licensing for vehicles which were used on contracts lasting not less than seven days. The change came into effect in January 2008. A similar change was introduced in respect of London in March 2008. As a result of this change, local licensing authorities are considering a range of vehicles and services in the context of PHV licensing which they had not previously licensed because of the contract exemption.

83. The Department produced a guidance note in November 2007 to assist local licensing authorities, and other stakeholders, in deciding which vehicles should be licensed in the PHV regime and which vehicles fell outside the PHV definition. The note stressed that it was a matter for local licensing authorities to make decisions in the first instance and that, ultimately, the courts were responsible for interpreting the law. However, the guidance was published as a way of assisting people who needed to consider these issues. A copy of the guidance note can be found on the Department's web-site at: http://www.dft.gov. uk/pgr/regional/taxis/rsa06privatehirevehicles As a result of a recent report on the impact of the repeal of the PHV contract exemption, the Department will be revising its guidance note to offer a more definite view about which vehicles should be licensed as PHVs. The report is also on the Department's web-site at: http://www.dft.gov.uk/pgr/regional/taxis/phvcontractexemption/.

ENFORCEMENT

84. Well-directed enforcement activity by the local licensing authority benefits not only the public but also the responsible people in the taxi and PHV trades. Indeed, it could be argued that the safety of the public depends upon licensing authorities having an effective enforcement mechanism in place. This includes actively seeking out those operators who are evading the licensing system, not just licensing those who come forward seeking the appropriate licences. The resources devoted by licensing authorities to enforcement will vary according to local circumstances, including for example any difficulties with touting by unlicensed drivers and vehicles (a problem in some urban areas). Local authorities will also wish to liaise closely with the police. Multi-agency enforcement exercises (involving, for example, the Benefits Agency) have proved beneficial in some areas.

85. Local licensing authorities often use enforcement staff to check a range of licensed activities (such as market traders) as well as the taxi and PHV trades, to make the best use of staff time. But it is desirable to ensure that taxi and PHV enforcement effort is at least partly directed to the late-night period, when

problems such as touting tend most often to arise. In formulating policies to deal with taxi touts, local licensing authorities might wish to be aware that the Sentencing Guidelines Council have, for the first time, included guidance about taxi touting in their latest Guidelines for Magistrates. The Guidelines, which came into effect in August 2008, can be accessed through the SGC's web-site – www.sentencing-guidelines.gov.uk.

86. Some local licensing authorities employ taxi marshals in busy city centres where there are lots of hirings, again perhaps late at night, to help taxi drivers picking up, and would-be passengers queuing for taxis.

87. As part of enforcement, local licensing authorities will often make spot checks, which can lead to their suspending or revoking licences. They will wish to consider carefully which power should best be used for this purpose. They will note, among other things, that section 60 of the Local Government (Miscellaneous Provisions) Act 1976 provides a right of appeal for the licence-holder, whereas section 68, which is also sometimes used, does not; this can complicate any challenge by the licence-holder.

88. Section 52 of the Road Safety Act 2006 amended the Local Government (Miscellaneous Provisions) Act 1976 such that local authorities can now suspend or revoke a taxi or PHV driver's licence with immediate effect on safety grounds. It should be stressed that this power can only be used where safety is the principal reason for suspending or revoking and where the risk justifies such an approach. It is expected that in the majority of cases drivers will continue to work pending appeal and that this power will be used in one-off cases. But the key point is that the law says that the power must be used in cases which can be justified in terms of safety. The Department is not proposing to issue any specific guidance on this issue, preferring to leave it to the discretion of licensing authorities as to when the power should be used.

TAXI ZONES

89. The areas of some local licensing authorities are divided into two or more zones for taxi licensing purposes. Drivers may be licensed to ply for hire in one zone only. Zones may exist for historical reasons, perhaps because of local authority boundary changes.

90. The Department recommends the abolition of zones. That is chiefly for the benefit of the travelling public. Zoning tends to diminish the supply of taxis and the scope for customer choice – for example, if fifty taxis were licensed overall by a local authority, but with only twenty five of them entitled to ply for hire in each of two zones. It can be confusing and frustrating for people wishing to hire a taxi to find that a vehicle licensed by the relevant local authority is nonetheless unable to pick them up (unless pre-booked) because they are in the wrong part of the local authority area. Abolition of zones can also reduce costs for the local authority, for example through simpler administration and enforcement. It can also promote fuel efficiency, because taxis can pick up a passenger anywhere in

the local authority area, rather than having to return empty to their licensed zone after dropping a passenger in another zone.

91. It should be noted that the Government has now made a Legislative Reform Order which removed the need for the Secretary of State to approve amalgamation resolutions made by local licensing authorities The Legislative Reform (Local Authority Consent Requirements)(England and Wales) Order 2008 came into force in October 2008. Although these resolutions no longer require the approval of the Secretary of State, the statutory procedure for making them – in paragraph 25 of schedule 14 to the Local Government Act 1972- remains the same.

FLEXIBLE TRANSPORT SERVICES

92. It is possible for taxis and PHVs to provide flexible transport services in a number of different ways. Such services can play a valuable role in meeting a range of transport needs, especially in rural areas – though potentially in many other places as well. In recent years there has been a significant increase in the provision of flexible services, due partly to the availability of Rural Bus Subsidy Grant and Rural Bus Challenge Support from the Department.

93. The Department encourages local licensing authorities, as a matter of best practice, to play their part in promoting flexible services, so as to increase the availability of transport to the travelling public. This can be done partly by drawing the possibilities to the attention of taxi and PHV trade. It also should be borne in mind that vehicles with a higher seating capacity than the vehicles typically licensed as taxis (for example those with 6, 7 or 8 passenger seats) may be used for flexible services and should be considered for licensing in this context.

94. The main legal provisions under which flexible services can be operated are:

- **Shared taxis and PHVs – advance bookings (section 11, Transport Act 1985):** licensed taxis and PHVs can provide a service at separate fares for up to eight passengers sharing the vehicle. The operator takes the initiative to match up passengers who book in advance and agree to share the vehicle at separate fares (lower than for a single hiring). An example could be passengers being picked up at home to go to a shopping centre, or returning from the shops to their homes. The operator benefits through increased passenger loadings and total revenues.

- **Shared taxis – immediate hirings (section 10, Transport Act 1985):** such a scheme is at the initiative of the local licensing authority, which can set up schemes whereby licensed taxis (not PHVs) can be hired at separate fares by up to eight people from ranks or other places that have been designated by the authority. (The authority is required to set up such a scheme if holders of 10% or more of the taxi licences in the area ask for one.) The passengers pay only part of the metered fare, for example in going home after a trip to the local town, and without pre-booking, but the driver receives more than the metered fare.

- **Taxibuses (section 12, Transport Act 1985):** owners of licensed taxis can apply to the Traffic Commissioner for a 'restricted public service vehicle (PSV) operator licence'. The taxi owner can then use the vehicle to run a bus service for up to eight passengers. The route must be registered with the Traffic Commissioner and must have at least one stopping place in the area of the local authority that licensed the taxi, though it can go beyond it. The bus service will be eligible for Bus Service Operators Grant (subject to certain conditions) and taxibuses can be used for local authority subsidised bus services. The travelling public have another transport opportunity opened for them, and taxi owners have another business opportunity. The Local Transport Act 2008 contains a provision which allows the owners of PHVs to acquire a special PSV operator licence and register a route with the traffic commissioner. A dedicated leaflet has been sent to licensing authorities to distribute to PHV owners in their area alerting them to this new provision.

95. The Department is very keen to encourage the use of these types of services. More details can be found in the Department's publication 'Flexible Transport Services' which can be accessed at:. http://www.dft.gov.uk/pgr/regional/buses/bol/flexibletransportservices

LOCAL TRANSPORT PLANS

96. The Transport Act 2000 as amended by the Transport Act 2008, requires local transport authorities in England outside London to produce and maintain a Local Transport Plan (LTP), having regard to any guidance issued by the Secretary of State. The latest guidance published in July 2009 will cover the next round of LTPs from 2011. LTPs set out the authority's local transport strategies and policies for transport in their area, and an implementation programme. 82 LTPs covering all of England outside London have been produced and cover the period up to 2011. From 2011 local authorities will have greater freedom to prepare their LTPs to align with wider local objectives.

97. All modes of transport including taxi and PHV services have a valuable part to play in overall transport provision, and so local licensing authorities have an input to delivering the LTPs. The key policy themes for such services could be availability and accessibility. LTPs can cover:

- quantity controls, if any, and plans for their review;
- licensing conditions, with a view to safety but also to good supply of taxi and PHV
- services;
- fares;
- on-street availability, especially through provision of taxi ranks;
- vehicle accessibility for people with disabilities;
- encouragement of flexible services.

ANNEX A
TAXI AND PRIVATE HIRE VEHICLE LICENSING: BEST PRACTICE
GUIDANCE

Useful questions when assessing quantity controls of taxi licences

- Have you considered the Government's view that quantity controls should be removed unless a specific case that such controls benefit the consumer can be made?

Questions relating to the policy of controlling numbers

- Have you recently reviewed the need for your policy of quantity controls?
- What form did the review of your policy of quantity controls take?
- Who was involved in the review?
- What decision was reached about retaining or removing quantity controls?
- Are you satisfied that your policy justifies restricting entry to the trade?
- Are you satisfied that quantity controls do not:
  - reduce the availability of taxis;
  - increase waiting times for consumers;
  - reduce choice and safety for consumers?
- What special circumstances justify retention of quantity controls?
- How does your policy benefit consumers, particularly in remote rural areas?
- How does your policy benefit the trade?
- If you have a local accessibility policy, how does this fit with restricting taxi licences?

Questions relating to setting the number of taxi licences

- When last did you assess unmet demand?
- How is your taxi limit assessed?
- Have you considered latent demand, ie potential consumers who would use taxis if more were available, but currently do not?
- Are you satisfied that your limit is set at the correct level?
- How does the need for adequate taxi ranks affect your policy of quantity controls?

Questions relating to consultation and other public transport service provision

- When consulting, have you included etc
  - all those working in the market;
  - consumer and passenger (including disabled) groups;
  - groups which represent those passengers with special needs;
  - local interest groups, eg hospitals or visitor attractions;
  - the police;
  - a wide range of transport stakeholders eg rail/bus/coach providers and traffic managers?

- Do you receive representations about taxi availability?
- What is the level of service currently available to consumers (including other public transport modes)?

ANNEX B
TAXI AND PRIVATE HIRE VEHICLE LICENSING: BEST PRACTICE GUIDANCE

Notice for taxi passengers – what you can expect from the taxi trade and what the taxi trade can expect from you

The driver will:

- Drive with due care and courtesy towards the passenger and other road users.
- Use the meter within the licensed area, unless the passenger has agreed to hire by time.
- If using the meter, not start the meter until the passenger is seated in the vehicle.
- If travelling outside the licensed area, agree the fare in advance. If no fare has been negotiated in advance for a journey going beyond the licensing area then the driver must adhere to the meter.
- Take the most time-efficient route, bearing in mind likely traffic problems and known diversions, and explain any diversion from the most direct route.

The passenger will:

- Treat the vehicle and driver with respect and obey any notices (e.g. in relation to eating in the vehicle).
- Ensure they have enough money to pay the fare before travelling. If wishing to pay by credit card or to stop on route to use a cash machine, check with the driver before setting off.
- Be aware of the fare on the meter and make the driver aware if it is approaching the limit of their financial resources.
- Be aware that the driver is likely to be restricted by traffic regulations in relation to where s/he can stop the vehicle.

Notice for PHV passengers – what you can expect from the PHV trade and what the PHV trade can expect from you

The driver will:

- Ensure that the passenger has pre-booked and agrees the fare before setting off.
- Drive with due care and courtesy towards the passenger and other road users.
- Take the most time-efficient route, bearing in mind likely traffic problems and known diversions, and explain any diversion from the most direct route.

The passenger will:

- Treat the vehicle and driver with respect and obey any notices (eg. in relation to eating in the vehicle).
- Ensure they have enough money to pay the fare before travelling. If wishing to pay by credit card or to stop on route to use a cash machine, check with the driver before setting off.
- Be aware that the driver is likely to be restricted by traffic regulations in relation to where s/he can stop the vehicle.

ANNEX C
TAXI AND PRIVATE HIRE VEHICLE LICENSING: BEST PRACTICE GUIDANCE

Assessing applicants for a taxi or PHV driver licence in accordance with C1 standard

Exceptional circumstances under which DVLA will consider granting licences for vehicles over 3.5 tonnes or with more than 8 passenger seats.

Insulin treated diabetes is a legal bar to driving these vehicles. The exceptional arrangements that were introduced in September 1998 were only in respect of drivers who were employed to drive small lorries between 3.5 tonnes and 7.5 tonnes (category C1). The arrangements mean that those with good diabetic control and who have no significant complications can be treated as "exceptional cases" and may have their application for a licence for category C1 considered. The criteria are

- To have been taking insulin for at least 4 weeks;
- Not to have suffered an episode of hypoglycaemia requiring the assistance of another person whilst driving in the last 12 months;
- To attend an examination by a hospital consultant specialising in the treatment of diabetes at intervals of not more than 12 months and to provide a report from such a consultant in support of the application which confirms a history of responsible diabetic control with a minimal risk of incapacity due to hypoglycaemia;
- To provide evidence of at least twice daily blood glucose monitoring at times when C1 vehicles are being driven (those that have not held C1 entitlement in the preceding 12 months may provide evidence of blood glucose monitoring while driving other vehicles);
- To have no other condition which would render the driver a danger when driving C1 vehicles; and
- To sign an undertaking to comply with the directions of the doctor(s) treating the diabetes and to report immediately to DVLA any significant change in condition.

Private Hire Vehicle Licensing – A note for guidance from the Department for Transport (DfT 2011)

INTRODUCTION

1. This note relates to private hire vehicles (PHVs) in England and Wales only, as responsibility for PHV licensing policy is devolved to Scotland and Northern Ireland.

2. It was clear that the repeal of the PHV contract exemption[1] and the change to the definition of "private hire vehicle" in the London PHV legislation[2] brought into focus a variety of activities which were not regarded as 'conventional' PHV services but which involved the carriage of passengers in a vehicle with fewer than nine passenger seats. A number of such activities were identified by the In House Policy Consultants (IHPC) commissioned by the Department to evaluate the impact of the repeal of the contract exemption – in particular, activities that were specifically identified by some local authorities as requiring licensing under the PHV licensing regime.

3. It was particularly disappointing to note from the IHPC report[3] that only 50% of respondents thought that the objective of the repeal – improving public safety – had been achieved. The principal reason given was that the legislation was not being consistently and rigorously enforced. Respondents felt there were too many grey areas where licensing authorities were not sure whether vehicles used for certain types of activities should be licensed. A view which emerged from the stakeholders was that the Department's guidance note of November 2007 which accompanied the repeal of the PHV contract exemption was couched in a non-committal way leaving licensing authorities and operators unsure about the status of many activities.

4. It was also clear that those involved with the operation of vehicles used for these activities (i.e. activities where there was an element of doubt about whether PHV licensing applied) were looking to the Department to provide a definitive statement about whether they should in fact be licensed.

5. The Department is not in a position to provide the sort of definitive statement that stakeholders are seeking; to do so would be to give the impression that the Department was responsible for interpreting the law. The Department is not responsible for interpreting the law – that is a matter for the courts.

6. However, in those 'grey areas' of the legislation where it is not clear whether a particular vehicle should be licensed or not, it is reasonable that the Department should offer a view about the extent of PHV licensing and, where possible, indicate the considerations which, in the Department's view, are relevant to an assessment of whether or not a particular vehicle should require a licence.

7. This note therefore moves away from the repeal of the PHV contract exemption, back to first principles. It sets out the key principles and characteristics which the Department considers define a private hire vehicle and, against that background, offers a straightforward view about whether the various services identified by the Consultants as falling within a grey area should actually require licences.

8. We would expect that this guidance note would have a degree of persuasive value in terms of assisting with local authority decision-making. But, any transport providers reading this note should be aware that it does not carry the force of law and the Department would urge people who are in any doubt about their legal position to seek independent legal advice.

9. Of course the fundamental purpose of the PHV licensing regime is to establish a position where passengers can use these vehicles with a high degree of confidence about their safety. But, the safety concerns must be weighed up with the burdens which are placed on transport providers. This principle is at the heart of the Department's Best Practice Guidance about wider taxi and PHV licensing issues and it is also relevant in this context.

10. The key message conveyed to licensing authorities in this guidance note is to think carefully about the burden which would be placed on people and organisations who are in the "grey areas" identified by the Consultants if they were to impose a requirement for PHV licensing. We would urge licensing authorities to ask themselves – particularly in cases where the activity in question is already regulated or assessed in respect of wider duties being carried out – whether there is any real need to oblige these people or organisations to acquire licences.

11. It should be stressed that the key principles set out in Part One of this guidance note are designed to assist with licensing authorities' consideration of any given case where the decision is not clear-cut. It is not designed to be a "tick-box" exercise which leads automatically to a "yes" or "no" answer. It is the responsibility of licensing authorities to reach informed decisions based on an assessment of each case and this note is designed to help them do so.

[1]   The Road Safety Act 2006 repealed section 75(1)(b) of the Local Government (Miscellaneous Provisions) Act 1976 which contained an exemption from PHV licensing for vehicles used on contracts lasting not less than seven days (commonly known as the 'contract exemption'); the repeal came into force in January 2008.

[2]   The Road Safety Act 2006 amended the definition of "private hire vehicle" in section 1 of the Private Hire Vehicles (London) Act 1998 by removing the words "to the public".

[3]   http://www.dft.gov.uk/pgr/regional/taxis/phvcontractexemption/

PART ONE – KEY PRINCIPLES

Definition of private hire vehicle

12. Section 80 of the Local Government (Miscellaneous Provisions) Act 1976[4] defines a private hire vehicle as:

"A motor vehicle constructed or adapted to seat fewer than nine passengers, other than a hackney carriage or public service vehicle or a London cab or tramcar, which is provided for hire with the services of a driver for the purpose of carrying passengers"

13. It is clear that a range of vehicles could potentially fall within this definition – certainly more vehicles than those which are solely used to provide a conventional "minicab" service. Licensing authorities will be aware of existing case law in this area and this guidance note is not intended to conflict with any of the binding principles already established by the courts. However, in the Department's opinion, there remains an element of flexibility for licensing authorities to take a balanced view of the specific facts of any one case. This guidance note attempts to assist licensing authorities with their decision making by setting out what the Department considers are relevant considerations and example parameters as to which services should have their vehicles treated as PHVs and which should not.

14. It should be stressed that this is the Department's view of what the law means; it represents our best effort to clarify issues which have not been clarified by the courts. We recognise that in due course the courts might interpret the law differently from the view set out in this guidance note. In those circumstances, we would look again at this guidance note.

15. The Department sought the views of stakeholders on a draft of this guidance and is grateful for the comments received. Some revisions to the initial draft version have been made on the basis of the feedback we received.

---

[4]   The definition in the Private Hire Vehicles (London) Act 1998, is similar though not identical.

Deciding what is, and what is not, a private hire vehicle?

16. In the Department's view, whether PHV licensing is required in a particular case will depend on a careful assessment of all the facts. The Department would discourage licensing authorities from adopting blanket policies on particular types of services, for example a policy which requires all childminders who drive a child to school to be licensed, as often consideration of the specific facts of how a particular vehicle is used will be necessary to reach a decision.

17. In offering advice about what is and what is not a PHV, the Department considers that there are some key principles which should underpin the decision-making process.

18. We would recommend that licensing authorities when deliberating over a particular service where it is not clear whether or not licensing should apply, ask themselves the following questions – and consider the points which the Department offers as a guide.

Question 1 Is there a commercial benefit?	
If the driver or the operating organisation / person derives a commercial benefit, it should be subject to further scrutiny.	If the carrying of passengers yields no commercial benefit, it is unlikely to require private hire licensing.

19. A key characteristic of a typical private hire vehicle operator and driver is that they charge a fare at a commercial rate that will generate a profit.

20. Accordingly, if the driver of a vehicle used for carrying passengers is doing no more than collecting expenses, then the vehicle should not, in the Department's view, be subject to PHV licensing.

21. The definition of private hire vehicle in legislation refers to a vehicle being "provided for hire". Case law has established that there does not need to be the payment of money for a hiring to take place. However, there will need to be some element of commercial benefit to the person providing the vehicle. When assessing the question of commercial benefit, licensing authorities should look fairly at all the circumstances. An assessment of whether or not the service derives a commercial benefit can be equally applied to any organisation acting as an operator of the service as well as a driver. However, in the Department's opinion, case law in this area allows licensing authorities to form a balanced and fair view of what constitutes a 'commercial benefit' rather than taking a strict and inflexible approach to remote or minor consequential benefits.

Question 2 Is carrying passengers in a vehicle with fewer than nine passenger seats an ancillary part, or a main part, of the overall service?	
If carrying passengers is a main part, or an obviously separate and identifiable part, the service is more likely to require further scrutiny.	If carrying passengers is an ancillary part, the service is less likely to be private hire.

22. A characteristic of a typical private hire vehicle operation is that the operator wants to transport passengers from a start point to a destination; that is the main purpose of the business.

23. It is clear that there are a number of services provided by various people and organisations which involve carrying passengers as a purely incidental and minor part of the wider service. When looking at services where there is an element of doubt as to whether or not PHV licensing should apply, the Department considers it relevant to look at the overall services being provided and the characteristic use of any vehicles in question.

24. The Department's view is that licensing authorities are responsible for making a considered decision as to whether or not licensing should apply if the carrying of passengers is a genuinely incidental and minor part of a wider

service being provided. In the Department's opinion, a distinction can be drawn between those services where carrying passengers is a genuinely incidental part of a larger service and those operations which have a separate identifiable service of carrying passengers. For example, "courtesy lifts" are a feature of many businesses which are not dedicated to transporting passengers. Many of these businesses will provide courtesy lifts on an informal basis – i.e. on the basis that a lift can be provided to customers who request such a service if a car is available at the time and someone is free to drive the customer, but no guarantee is given. This type of incidental service can be contrasted with those operations which provide dedicated transportation as part of a wider service. For example, a company organising a sporting event which agrees to organise transportation for the players or officials, is providing separate organised transportation services regardless of the fact that transportation may be a small and incidental part of the overall service.

Question 3
Has the driver been vetted to provide the wider service of which driving is a part?

If the driver has not been vetted for wider work, the Department considers that the service is likely to require further scrutiny.	If the driver has been vetted for wider work, the Department considers that the service is less likely to require private hire licensing.

25. The Department considers that licensing authorities should take a pragmatic approach to licensing, taking account of the underlying objective of licensing – safety. When considering services where there is an element of doubt as to whether or not PHV licensing should apply, the Department considers it relevant to investigate whether or not drivers have been assessed by an organisation in the context of their wider role (for which driving passengers is just one part). This is particularly relevant where the drivers have, for example, undergone a Criminal Records Bureau check for that wider role. One example might be in the case of care workers who use their cars to transport clients from time to time; they are likely to have been vetted for that work. The Department would question whether there is any real need to subject drivers who have been assessed in this manner to a separate licensing regime.

Question 4
Is the driver under any explicit or implicit obligation to undertake any duties or tasks beyond driving (and assisting with entry/exit and assisting with luggage)?

If the driver's duties are restricted to driving and assisting with luggage, the Department considers that the service is more likely to be private hire.	If the driver has wider duties beyond those associated with driving, the Department considers that the service is less likely to be private hire.

26. This element is directed at the sorts of duties undertaken by people who are in a position of care or responsibility in respect of the passenger being carried in the vehicle. For example, in the case of genuine ambulances, the Department considers it relevant that drivers clearly have wider responsibilities for the care of their patients. Similarly, childminders have a wider responsibility and specific duties relating to the children in their care. Another example would be those who provide secure escort and custody services where drivers are under wider obligations in relation to the transport of passengers to ensure that they cannot abscond.

Question 5 Does the service require a specific qualification or level of training on the part of the driver which goes beyond the driving and courtesy skills associated with conventional private hire?	
If the driver does not require any specific qualifications or training which go beyond driving and general customer care, the Department considers that the service is more likely to be private hire.	If the driver must have specific qualifications or training which go beyond driving and general customer care, the Department considers that the service is less likely to be private hire.

27. PHV drivers are experts in their field and we would, of course, expect them to discharge their duties by utilising their skills to the full. However, this element of the consideration process is directed at the sorts of specialist skills which a driver must possess in order to undertake the wider work of which driving is a part. For example, the driver of an ambulance would be expected to undergo specialist training before being allowed to start work.

Question 6 Would Parliament have had this service in mind in passing the legislation governing private hire vehicles?	
If Parliament would have had this sort of service in mind when passing the relevant legislation, the Department considers that the service is more likely to be private hire.	If Parliament would not have had this sort of service in mind when passing the legislation, the Department considers that the service is less likely to be private hire.

28. This final question is included to assist licensing authorities in cases which are finely balanced where the authority is struggling to reach a decision. It relates back to the fundamental point of this guidance which is made at the outset about taking a common-sense approach to licensing. Whilst ultimately it is a matter for the courts to interpret the legislation with reference to any particular service, the Department is firmly of the opinion that in passing the relevant legislation, Parliament believed that it was establishing a regulatory mechanism for dealing

with conventional private hire vehicles – albeit a range of vehicles – but whose principal purpose was to transport passengers from a to b.

29. Legislation by its very nature is regularly applied to situations outside of Parliament's original thinking and must constantly be interpreted to keep pace with innovation and a changing world. However, where there is an element of ambiguity in legislation and its application is unclear, Parliamentary intention can be a valid tool to aid in its interpretation. In the Department's opinion, consideration of this final question adds weight to the argument that those services which form minor or incidental parts of other services should not require licensing, for example courtesy lifts provided by garages or transport provided by child minders.

Insurance

30. The issue of insurance does not feature in this guidance note as relevant to the question of whether or not a particular service falls within the PHV licensing regime. However, the Department views correct insurance cover as an extremely important issue which may, of course, be affected by an assessment of whether or not a particular service is operating within the PHV regime. Licensing authorities may wish to make enquiries about the insurance cover held by transport providers as part of their investigations and decision making process. We would urge licensing authorities to communicate to transport providers the importance of checking with their insurance provider that the services they are providing are adequately covered by the relevant policy of insurance and stress that any conclusions reached in the licensing process will not necessarily be relevant to an assessment of whether or not the insurance policy is adequate. It should be noted that this guidance note has been shown to the Association of British Insurers at the draft stage and they were satisfied with the guidance contained in it.

PART TWO – SECTOR-SPECIFIC GUIDANCE

31. This section of the guidance note deals with those sectors mentioned in the IHPC report as being "grey areas" in the context of PHV licensing. It takes each sector in turn and, using the key principles outlined in Part One, offers a general opinion on whether they should be licensed as private hire. As mentioned above, licensing authorities are encouraged to look at the specific facts of any one case and reach a conclusion based on those individual facts rather than automatically placing particular types of services into the licensed or non-licensed category.

Stretched limousines

32. The Department considers that most stretched limousine operations (where the vehicle has fewer than nine passenger seats) are likely to fall within the PHV licensing regime.

33. Essentially these vehicles are luxury versions of conventional "minicabs". They are in the business of transporting passengers, normally in a group, from a pick up point to a destination. They focus on providing this service in a luxurious way, but they are, nevertheless, providing a straightforward transportation service. The operator will, of course, want to be sure that the driver is highly skilled in terms of customer service. However, aside from the size and quality of the vehicle and the possibility of in-vehicle entertainment, there is no discernable difference in the function and service provided between a conventional minicab and a stretched limousine.

34. The Department's Best Practice Guidance provides further information about the licensing of stretched limousines, for example approval certification, how to test the vehicles and how to establish the number of seats.

35. Taking account of the principles set out in Part One of this guidance note, the Department takes the view that typical stretched limousine operations should be licensed because they involve:

- a commercial benefit on the part of the driver/organiser;
- the carrying of passengers as a main part of the service;
- drivers who are unlikely to have been vetted for wider work;
- driver duties which are restricted to driving and assisting with luggage; and
- the sort of service which Parliament would have had in mind when passing the relevant legislation.

Chauffeur/Executive drivers

36. The Department considers that most chauffeur/executive operations are likely to fall within the PHV licensing regime.

37. It seems to the Department that the primary function of a chauffeur/executive driver and vehicle is to transport passengers from a to b, albeit in a higher quality vehicle than a conventional minicab. As with stretched limousines, the Department, whilst recognising that the drivers might have a more dedicated focus on higher quality customer care, considers that chauffeur vehicles would fall within the PHV category.

38. The Department would take this opportunity, though, to highlight for licensing authorities section 75(3) of the 1976 Act which allows them to modify requirements for the display of plates on vehicles and the wearing of badges by drivers.

39. Taking account of the principles set out in Part One of this guidance note, the Department takes the view that typical chauffeur/executive car operations should be licensed because they involve:

- a commercial benefit on the part of the driver/organiser;
- the carrying of passengers as a main part of the service;
- drivers who are unlikely to have been vetted for wider work;

- driver duties which are restricted to driving and assisting with luggage; and
- the sort of service which Parliament would have had in mind when passing the relevant legislation.

40. Licensing authorities might want to remind chauffeur/executive car drivers and owners of the importance of making all bookings through a licensed operator. This is particularly important in "one-man-band" cases where the owner of the vehicle is also the driver and takes the bookings himself; he would need a separate PHV operator's licence.

Event management companies

41. The Department considers that companies which provide a dedicated transport service for events should be subject to PHV licensing.

42. The Department is aware of the existence of companies who specialise in providing transport services for events or those who specialise in the organisation or management of events, of which, a part includes the provision of transport services. Due to the numbers of people involved in, or attending, the event in question, organisers often want to call in a specialist company to provide transport. Nevertheless, these vehicles are providing a dedicated transport service and the company itself is acting as an operator in terms of arranging the hirings.

43. Of course, each operation must be assessed individually, but in general terms, the Department considers that these companies are acting as PHV operators and the vehicles and drivers used by them should be licensed.

44. It may well be the case that the drivers' customer care obligations go slightly beyond the requirements associated with a conventional private hire driver, but the essential nature of the work is to provide transport from a to b.

45. Taking account of the principles set out in Part One of this guidance note, the Department recognises that typical event management operations might involve duties beyond driving, but considers that they should be licensed because they involve:

- a commercial benefit on the part of the driver/organiser;
- the carrying of passengers as a main part of the service;
- drivers who are unlikely to have been vetted for wider work; and
- the sort of service which Parliament would have had in mind when passing the relevant legislation.

Ambulances

46. The Department considers that "genuine ambulances" do not fall within the PHV licensing regime.

47. We recognise that there is a great deal of debate about what constitutes a genuine ambulance and a wide range of vehicles and operations appear to come under the broad "ambulance" heading.

48. It seems to the Department that "genuine ambulances" fall into two categories:

- emergency/specialist ambulance vehicles – likely to accommodate a stretcher and specialist equipment, and to require the presence of health professionals. Licensing authorities may wish to make use in this connection of the fact these vehicles are exempt from road tax by virtue of the Vehicle Excise and Registration Act 1994[5] and cannot be used for "social" hirings.

- vehicles which operate as part of a formal Patient Transport Service[6] – usually non-emergency, planned transport of patients, where the booking will only be made if the person to be carried has been assessed by a health professional as having a medical need for transport; these vehicles will be contracted to a health care provider and cannot be used for "social" hirings; licensing authorities can verify with the owner of a vehicle that it is being used in connection with such a contract. An exemption from road tax as mentioned under the first bullet point might also be relevant. Patient Transport Services encompass a wide range of vehicles, ranging from specialist to less specialist types, to allow for transport consistent with a patient's needs.

49. It is these categories of vehicle/service which the Department has in mind in reaching the conclusion that "genuine ambulances" do not need to be licensed. And, it should be stressed that the vehicles referred to in the second category above are vehicles solely dedicated to patient transport service work; if the vehicles, at other times, carry out social hirings then they would not fall into this category.

50. There is a category of vehicle/service which the operator might describe as an ambulance because it carries out predominantly transport work involving medical-related journeys, but which the Department does not recognise as a genuine ambulance. These vehicles transport passengers to and from hospitals and other medical facilities on an ad-hoc basis but do not fall within either of the above two categories. They might, for example, be under the control of an operator who has made a commercial decision to provide a dedicated service involving medical-related journeys, but the key point is that if they do not (i) meet the definition of "ambulance" in the Vehicle Excise and Registration Act 1994; or (ii) operate under the auspices of a formal Patient Transport Service, then the Department would advise that they are likely to be private hire. It may well be the case that other considerations apply (taking account of the six questions in Part One of this Guidance Note) but they are unlikely to be ruled out of PHV licensing because they are ambulances.

51. The Department is aware of plans to bring private ambulances under the control of the Care Quality Commission in 2011; the vehicles will be registered and the drivers will undergo training and CRB checks. This move will go a

long way towards helping licensing authorities to determine whether a particular service is a genuine ambulance and whether or not it should be licensed as PHV. This note has been shown to the Care Quality Commission who considered that the guidance was in line with their own view of what constitutes an ambulance.

52. Taking account of the principles set out in Part One of this guidance note, the Department recognises that genuine ambulance services derive a commercial benefit, but consider that they should not be licensed because they involve:

- drivers who are likely to have been vetted for wider work;
- drivers who have wider duties beyond those associated with driving;
- drivers who must have specific qualifications or training which go beyond driving and general customer care; and
- the sort of service which Parliament would not have had in mind when passing the legislation.

5   Schedule 2 to the Vehicle Excise and Registration Act 1994 identifies an ambulance as a vehicle which is exempt from road tax; it defines an ambulance as:
- A vehicle which -
  (a) is constructed or adapted for, and used for no other purpose than, the carriage of sick, injured or disabled people to or from welfare centres or places where medical or dental treatment is given, and
  (b) is readily identifiable as a vehicle used for the carriage of such people by being marked "Ambulance" on both sides.

6   In the Department's view, "a formal Patient Transport Service" can be taken here to include services contracted to private healthcare providers, subject to the other requirements identified in this paragraph being met.

Volunteers

53. The Department considers that genuine volunteers who receive no recompense or receive only enough to cover their actual expenses do not fall within the PHV licensing regime.

54. The definition of "private hire vehicle" states that the vehicle must be "provided for hire". It is clear that in order to satisfy this requirement there must be some form of commercial benefit to the person providing the vehicle.

55. The Government recognises the importance of volunteers who willingly give their own time to assist others and are not paid a wage for doing so. It is important that they should continue to be able to do so in order to contribute towards social inclusion objectives.

56. It should be noted that car sharing is a quite lawful and legitimate form of transport provision. The rules governing car sharing are contained in section 1(4) of the Public Passenger Vehicles Act 1981 ("the 1981 Act"). A useful leaflet about how these schemes work has been prepared by the Community Transport Association and can be accessed on their web-site: http://www.ctauk.org/ (the relevant document is "Using MPVs and Smaller Vehicles").

57. In determining whether a particular volunteer service is operating legitimately outside the PHV licensing regime, one useful method of calculating

the profitability or otherwise of the service might be to consider the rates charged in the context of the rules set out by HM Revenue and Customs (HMRC) for taxation purposes. The rules are explained in a fact sheet which can be accessed on the HMRC's web-site http://www.hmrc.gov.uk/mileage/volunteer-drivers.htm. The updated rates are in this fact sheet: http://www.hmrc.gov.uk/budget2011/individuals-mainannouncements.pdf. Essentially, volunteer drivers' tax free allowance is 45 pence on the first 10,000 miles in the tax year; and 25 pence on each mile over 10,000 in the tax year. The HMRC fact sheet explains how to calculate income from volunteer driving.

58. The Department recognises that the licensed trade has concerns about the total mileage undertaken by some volunteer drivers which they consider amounts to being in the business of providing transport in such a way as to make a profit. Furthermore, in addition to drivers, licensing authorities will be aware that the fundamental question of whether or not a commercial benefit is derived from the service can equally be applied to any organisation acting as an operator of the service in question. As mentioned in Part One of this guidance note, the Department would urge licensing authorities to make a balanced and fair assessment of whether or not a 'commercial benefit' is derived in any particular case, rather than taking a strict and inflexible approach to this question.

59. The Department reached its conclusion that volunteer drivers do not fall within the PHV licensing regime because of the nature of the activity in relation to the definition in the legislation. If a driver chooses to offer a substantial amount of time to this activity, this does not change the essential nature of the work; indeed, the HMRC's rules take account of the fact that some drivers will be undertaking substantial mileage and the rates reflect this.

60. Taking account of the principles set out in Part One of this guidance note, the Department considers that volunteer drivers should not be licensed because:

- the service involves no commercial benefit; and
- it is not something that Parliament would have had in mind when passing the legislation.

Care and support worker services

61. The Department considers that most car journeys undertaken in the context of care and support services do not fall within the PHV licensing regime.

62. This section refers to people who provide regulated or unregulated care and support to adults in their own homes, in community settings, in residential or nursing care homes or as part of Shared Lives schemes.

63. The provision of a transport service in this context can be either where a member of staff within a care home drives one of the residents to, for example, the shops or a health appointment; or where a care worker visits a person in their own home for the purpose of providing a general care package, of which driving them to the shops, to an appointment or to any other activity is one part. This includes cases where care is funded by a personal budget, Direct Payment or the individual's own money.

64. Taking account of the principles set out in Part One of this guidance note, the Department considers that people providing care and support services should not be licensed because:

- the carrying of passengers is an ancillary part of the service;
- the driver is likely to have been vetted for wider work;
- the driver will have wider duties beyond those associated with driving;
- the driver is likely to have specific qualifications or training which go beyond driving and general customer care; and
- Parliament would not have had this sort of service in mind when passing the legislation.

Childminders

65. The Department considers that car journeys undertaken in the context of most typical childminding arrangements would not fall within the PHV licensing regime.

66. We recognise that there is a variety of childminding arrangements and, on examining the facts of particular cases, there may well be circumstances where this principle does not apply. However, the Department's guidance in the above statement reflects a typical childminding arrangement where a childminder uses his or her own car to transport one or more children to and from, for example, school.

67. This conclusion reflects the principles underlying most of the questions in Part One of the guidance note. A childminder will have undergone a whole raft of suitability checks and the service he or she provides goes well beyond driving. It seems to the Department to be unnecessarily burdensome for childminders to be drawn into the PHV licensing regime.

68. Childminders are already vetted; they are carrying out work where the driving element is incidental rather than central, they require specialist skills and they have responsibilities to the passengers which go beyond driving.

69. The Department considers it most unlikely that a court would conclude that Parliament intended that the majority of the many thousands of childminders across England and Wales should have to obtain PHV licences in order to be able to transport children in their care.

70. Taking account of the principles set out in Part One of this guidance note, the Department considers that typical childminders should not be licensed because:

- the carrying of passengers is an ancillary part of the service;
- the driver is likely to have been vetted for wider work;
- the driver will have wider duties beyond those associated with driving;
- the driver is likely to have specific qualifications or training which go beyond driving and general customer care; and
- Parliament would not have had this sort of service in mind when passing the legislation.

Rental car companies / Garages

71. The Department considers that most informal courtesy lifts offered by, for example, rental car companies or garages would not fall within the PHV licensing regime.

72. It is quite common for rental car companies and garages to provide a 'courtesy lift' service for customers – perhaps because they have dropped off the rental car at the company's office and need to get back into town, or, in the case of garages, because the car needs to stay at the garage for repair and the owner needs to get home. Such lifts are provided as an ancillary service to the main purpose of the business.

73. The Department recognises that an assessment of the individual facts of each case will be necessary. In reaching the conclusion that most services of this nature would fall outside of the licensing regime, the Department has taken the view that most services will be of an 'informal' nature. By this the Department means that the service will not usually be a contractual arrangement or form part of the contract for wider services and will not be advertised as such. A service of this nature will usually be provided on the basis that a lift may be available if a vehicle is available and a member of staff is free at the time, but no guarantee is given. Furthermore, vehicles are usually used on an ad hoc basis rather than specific vehicles being allocated for this purpose – the vehicles are simply part of the hire fleet or garage test cars which are predominantly used for other purposes. However, a more formal arrangement or the allocation of specific cars purely for the purpose of courtesy lifts and no other, or limited other, functions would suggest that the service is more likely to fall within the licensing regime.

74. These types of companies do not dedicate themselves to the transportation of passengers; they simply offer lifts as a convenience to their customers as an informal and ancillary service to their main business. The Department does not consider that Parliament had this sort of service in mind when it passed the national PHV licensing legislation in 1976. Whilst it is clear that an assessment of the individual facts of any one case will be necessary, the Department would encourage licensing authorities to take a pragmatic approach to these types of grey area services. In the Department's opinion, a distinction can be drawn between those companies who offer an informal and ad hoc courtesy lift service making use of any available cars and staff and those companies who provide a separate dedicated transport service for customers. As discussed in Part One, in assessing the fundamental question of whether the service derives a commercial benefit, the Department would once again urge licensing authorities to make a balanced and fair assessment on the individual facts of any one case.

75. Taking account of the principles set out in Part One of this guidance note, the Department considers that rental car companies/garages should not be licensed because:

- the carrying of passengers is an ancillary part of the service; and
- Parliament would not have had this sort of service in mind when passing the legislation

Secure escort and custody services

76. The Department considers that services which involve the escort and custody of people sentenced or remanded to custody, secure accommodation or alternative youth detention accommodation are not PHVs.

77. There is a whole category of service provision involving the transportation of people who are sentenced to be remanded to custody and must be carried from, for example, a prison or young offenders institution, to a court. An important consideration is that these services require the involvement of specialists who are in a particular position of authority and responsibility. In order to carry out their duties, the drivers have undertaken training in physical control methods and have had criminal record checks.

78. The Department takes the view that the special characteristics of this work take them outside the realm of PHV licensing; what is most crucial is the element of control which the drivers have, and, going back to the first principles outlined in Part One, the drivers will already have been assessed for their wider responsibilities.

79. There is a further category of transport closely allied to this but which is more in the nature of social care than secure care, for example journeys involving contact visits for children in care and transporting children who have absconded from care homes. The Department's advice is to take account of the general principles outlined in Part One of this note in reaching a decision, most particularly is determining whether the drivers have already been assessed for the purposes of carrying out this work and whether they have had specialist training relating to their wider care responsibilities. In general terms the Department considers that these services should not fall within the PHV licensing regime, but we recognise that there might be services where these characteristics do not feature and they are simply a PHV operator which has decided to serve a niche market.

80. Taking account of the principles set out in Part One of this guidance note, the Department considers that secure escort and custody services should not be licensed because:

- the driver is likely to have been vetted for wider work;
- the driver will have wider duties beyond those associated with driving;
- the driver is likely to have specific qualifications or training which go beyond driving and general customer care; and
- Parliament would not have had this sort of service in mind when passing the legislation.

Taxi and PHV licensing – Councillors' handbook (England and Wales) (Local Government Association revised August 2017)

FOREWORD

Taxis and Private Hire Vehicles (PHVs) are vital to our communities; whether it's the iconic black cab in our cities or the flexible minicab in a rural district. As elected members, we are responsible for ensuring the public travel safely and receive a good level of service, and that our systems attract good, reputable drivers.

Our critical responsibilities in licensing these drivers and vehicles have been highlighted by recent examples of licensed vehicle drivers and/or operators being involved in the sexual exploitation of children. Taxis are regularly used to transport children during the school run. Elderly and disabled users also rely heavily on the door-to-door service taxis and PHVs provide, as it is often the only way for many residents to access local services. Clearly, drivers must therefore command the highest level of confidence before they can be entrusted with this responsibility. It is essential that we take seriously our responsibility to determine whether someone is a lit and proper' person to hold a licence.

There are economic benefits too in enabling visitors to move quickly and safely through your area. Taxis and PHVs have a particularly important role in the night-time economy, ensuring the public return home safely, and can be helpful in ensuring that people disperse quickly and peacefully after events.

Unfortunately, the existing licensing system is outdated and needs urgent reform. One of the main pieces of legislation dates from 1847, which means it predates even the earliest motor vehicles, let alone online and mobile booking apps. The Local Government Association (LGA) is lobbying for a Taxi and PHV Licensing Reform Bill to modernise the governance system for taxis and PHVs and better protect passengers from the many and varied risks which now exist. Until then, it is incumbent on us to do the best we can with the tools at our disposal.

We have developed this handbook to help you use these tools and understand some of the key issues concerning taxi and PHV licensing. It is intended to be used as a starting point to explain some of the difficulties that can arise in this complex area of business regulation, but of course is not a replacement for the training provided by your own authority.

We hope you find it useful.

Councillor Simon Blackburn

The regulatory framework for taxis and PHVs an overview

TERMINOLOGY

Taxis are referred to in legislation, regulation and common language as 'hackney carriages', 'black cabs' and 'cabs'. The term 'taxi' is used throughout this handbook and refers to all such vehicles.

Private hire vehicles (PHVs) include a range of vehicles such as minicabs, executive cars, limousines and chauffeur services. The term 'PHV' is used throughout this handbook to refer to all such vehicles.

Councils are only responsible for the licensing of vehicles which carry up to a maximum of eight passengers. Vehicles with a seating capacity of more than eight passenger seats, which can include some stretch limousines, are licensed by the Traffic Commissioners, who are appointed by the Transport Secretary.

LEGISLATION

Taxi and Private Hire Vehicle (PHV) legislation is primarily concentrated in the Town Police Clauses Act 1847 (the 1847 Act) and the Local Government (Miscellaneous Provisions) Act 1976 (the 1976 Act). The legislation provides a broad framework for the licensing of drivers, vehicles and operators but the detail of how this is done, including standards and conditions, is the responsibility of individual district and unitary councils (licensing authorities'). There are a number of other Acts which also have an impact; for example the Equalities Act 2010, which places a duty on councils to take steps to meet the needs of disabled people where these are different from the needs of other people, and enables regulations to improve disabled access to taxis.

This mix of legislation is widely regarded as outdated and in 2014 the Law Commission published the results of a three year study into consolidating and updating the laws governing both taxis and PHVs into a single piece of legislation[1]. The Government has yet to respond to the report, although two clauses were brought forward early in the Deregulation Act 2015. A third clause, permitting anyone to drive a licensed vehicle when it was 'off-duty' was removed after lobbying from the LGA and other stakeholders.

The LGA, in consultation with our member councils, does not fully agree with all the Law Commission's proposals, but feels that it does provide a sound basis for the reform that is very urgently needed. The LGA will therefore be lobbying for a Taxi and PHV Licensing Reform Bill to be brought forward in the next Parliament.

[1]   The full report can be found on the Law Commission's website:

http://lawcommissionjustice.gov.uk/areas/taxi-and-private-hire-services.htm

Facts and figures:

- In England and Wales, there were around 76,000 taxis and 166,000 PHVs as at the end of March 2015.

- There are an estimated 297,000 licensed taxi and PHV drivers in England and Wales.
- Taxis and PHVs together account for just over one per cent of all trip stages per person per year in Great Britain. This is about 600 million trip stages or around 3 million miles a year.
- An estimated 58 per cent of all taxis are wheelchair accessible in England and Wales.

DIFFERENCES BETWEEN TAXIS AND PHVS

One of the key differences between the vehicles is that a PHV, unlike a taxi, cannot ply for hire, which means that all journeys must be pre-booked in advance through a licensed operator. It is an offence for PHVs to pick up passengers from any location unless pre-booked. Local councils can, if they wish, also regulate the fares charged by taxis, whereas there is no power to do so with PHVs.

	Taxi	**Private Hire**
Ply for hire	✓	x
Pre booked	✓	✓
Operating from a rank	✓	x
Fare meter required	✓	x
Fare tariff set by council	✓	x
Number of vehicles may be restricted by councils	✓	x
Taxis require two types of licence:		Hackney carriage proprietors (vehicle) licence Hackney carriage drivers licence
The provision of a private hire service requires three types of licence:		Private hire operators licence Private vehicle licence Private hire drivers licence

COUNCIL ROLE IN TAXI AND PHV LICENSING IN ENGLAND AND WALES

Taxi and PHV licensing in England and Wales is undertaken by licensing authorities (district and unitary councils), which have the responsibility for ensuring the public travel in safe, well maintained vehicles driven by competent drivers; as well as providing a fair and reasonable service for the taxi and PHV trade.

In London, taxi and PHV licensing is the responsibility of Transport for London and delivered by London Taxi and Private Hire, which is accountable to the

Mayor of London and responsible for delivering the Mayor's Transport Strategy. Local councils in London have no direct role in licensing taxis and PHVs.

To deliver their responsibilities, councils' core functions in taxi and PHV licensing can be summarised as:

- setting the local framework, which can include safeguarding standards, fares, vehicles standards or limits on vehicle numbers
- considering applications and safeguarding the public by issuing, reviewing or revoking licences
- undertaking inspection and enforcement activities to ensure the required standards are being maintained.

Taxi and private hire licensing may be undertaken within a single department but usually sits within one of the council's regulatory services such as environmental health or legal services. It is often also combined with other licensing functions. The committee overseeing decisions is often referred to as the 'Regulatory Committee' to distinguish it from the committee overseeing decisions under the Licensing Act 2003 (Alcohol and regulated entertainment).

In providing the licensing function, the council, under the provisions of the 1976 Act, is entitled to levy fees to recover the reasonable cost associated with:

- recovering the costs of the issue and administration of drivers' licences
- the inspection of vehicles for the purposes of determining whether any such licence should be granted or renewed
- the provision of hackney carriage stands
- any administrative or other costs in connection with the control and supervision of hackney carriage and private hire vehicles.

With the exception of drivers' licences, the council is required to consult upon the fees it intends to levy through a public notice procedure. In determining the fees to be charged, it would be reasonable to do so with a view to achieving full cost recovery.

Licensing income from these schemes must therefore be 'ring-fenced' in that licensing fees and charges cannot be spent on other areas of council activity — even other areas of licensing business. It is important to ensure that applicants and licensees receive value for money. As a councillor you should ensure that your authority's budgets can stand up to scrutiny by the District Auditor and under the Freedom of Information Act, which has been increasingly used in recent years by licensees and trade associations.

There are no statutory timescales or performance measures for taxi/PHV licensing, unlike some other licensing regimes. However many councils use internal targets to measure the service being provided to applicants and licensees. A periodic review of the licensing service's processes and procedures can help to improve this. One council, for instance, subjected its licensing procedures to a business review and succeeded in reducing the time taken to process vehicle licences from 45 days to just one day. However, whilst it is important to be as efficient as possible, the council's primary function is to protect the public.

Refocusing a service on its public protection role typically leads to improvements in efficiency while strengthening the service's delivery of its primary function, and there are tried and tested systems thinking approaches to achieve this.

Department for Transport's (DfT) role

The DfT's role is that of regulatory ownership and maintenance of the regulatory framework for taxis and private hire vehicles. The Department collects and publishes statistics on a regular basis and produces guidance to assist local councils in carrying out their taxi and PHV licensing functions. The guidance is considered to be 'best practice' and addresses a number of issues where inconsistency of approach exists in taxi and private hire licensing in England and Wales. The Policing and Crime Bill, once enacted, will introduce the power for government to produce statutory guidance on using licensing to prevent harm to children and vulnerable adults, and councils will have to have regard to this guidance. This handbook will be updated to reflect the statutory guidance once it is produced.

Strengths and weaknesses of the current system

Councils have a wide range of powers that can be used to regulate taxis and PHVs, protecting the public and supporting local economies; but there are also some anomalies within the existing system.

Local councils have the power to attach conditions to the licences of operators, taxis (vehicles), PHVs, and PHV drivers, but not the licences of taxi drivers. They can also influence the local context in which vehicles operate, and a range of licensing policies have been developed to do this by councils, but they vary from relatively relaxed to very strict regimes. Many councils have also adopted local bylaws under the Town Police Clauses Act 1889 that regulate driver conduct, which can helpfully provide some of the otherwise missing influence over the conduct of taxi drivers.

However, over time this has created differing standards with little coordination within regions or nationally. The result is varying standards of service for passengers, particularly disabled users; confusion for taxi and PHV businesses; some types of vehicles operating unregulated; and taxis working in areas in which they are not licensed to do so. This is far from ideal.

Nonetheless, taken together these policies and bylaws offer a reasonable standard of influence when it comes to assessing applications to the licensing committee. The situation for enforcement activities is much less positive.

- First and foremost, councils have no ability to stop vehicles, which leaves them only able to intervene when a vehicle is stationary, and unable to prevent it being driven off — only the police may stop a vehicle.
- Secondly, a council may only take action against a vehicle or driver that it has licensed, meaning that there is absolutely nothing that a council can do if a vehicle or driver licensed elsewhere is operating in their area, other than complain to the 'home' authority.

This is why the issue of cross-border hiring is the most acute taxi/PHV licensing problem facing many councils today. For example if a driver applies to a council for a licence only to be refused by the licensing committee due to police concerns, it is still possible that a neighbouring council could still choose to licence the driver based on the same information. Once a driver is granted a licence, they will be able to operate across council areas including the one which initially refused the licence.

This situation could pose a risk to communities, as well as the reputation of local government as a whole and every council should use all opportunities to protect other communities outside of its immediate responsibility.

Councils following best practice will meet or communicate regularly with licensing committees and officers in neighbouring councils to ensure critical information is shared and that there is a consistency and robustness in decision-making. By working together, local government can make sure that this vital service is safe, respected, and delivering for local communities.

The following sections of this handbook set out guidance on how councils can deliver the best possible licensing regulation.

ROLE OF COUNCILLORS

Councillors and the council's regulatory/licensing committee

Councils will usually operate with a regulatory/licensing committee which may be made up of non-executive/cabinet councillors, and sometimes with sub-committees made up of councillors of the parent committee. Where this is the case, the role of the parent committee is to consider and propose policy, including setting the overall approach of the council, conditions and standards for vehicles and drivers.

Apart from setting taxi fares and ranks, taxi/PHV licensing is a 'council' and not an 'executive' function.

Developing a policy

There is no requirement to create a single licensing statement or policy for taxi and PHV licensing in the way that there is for the Licensing Act 2003 and Gambling Act 2005. However, the LGA strongly encourages licensing authorities to create a unified policy that brings together all their procedures in one place; this could include policies on convictions, determining the 'fit and proper' person test, licence conditions, and vehicle standards.

Creating a single, unified policy that is reviewed on a regular basis will provide clarity for drivers and operators, as well as strengthening the council's position if there is a challenge against a decision in court.

For the purposes of simplicity, the rest of this document will refer to a single licensing statement, even though a licensing authority may choose to retain separate policy documents.

It is important to take account of the views of the trade, customers and other stakeholders when establishing the policy, in the same way the council would do when developing any other licensing policy.

Decision making

Decision-making in respect of individual cases, whether applications for licences or where matters are brought to the attention of the council following the grant of a licence (for example breach of conditions, convictions, driving endorsements, etc), are often made by a regulatory/licensing subcommittee. This sits as a quasi-judicial body and therefore must follow the rules of natural justice — anyone affected by a decision has a right to be heard and no one should be a judge in his own cause. All decisions should be made without 'fear or favour', however difficult they may be.

Sub-committees have a range of options available to them including:

- in the case of licence applications, to grant a licence, with or without conditions (but not for taxi drivers)
- in the case of licence applications, to refuse a licence
- in the case of existing licences where matters are brought to the council's attention, to
  - do nothing (but members should set out reasons for this to protect the council in the future)
  - suspend a licence
  - introduce conditions on a PHV driver's or operator's licence
  - revoke a licence.

Suspension can be particularly helpful in improving standards or addressing complaints. For instance, a licence can be suspended until such time as the driver can undergo additional driver training or receive other improvement support. However, you cannot suspend a licence as an interim measure pending a final decision being made at a later date — it must always be used as a final decision[2]. In other words, the suspension is lifted once the required action has been completed, with no threat of further penalty. In this context, suspension is not a punishment but a tool to protect the public from risk until corrective action has been completed by the driver.

Although the suspension must in itself be a final decision, if new evidence comes to light at a later date, as can happen in a court case, the committee may take a new decision based on the new evidence. This would not fall foul of the Singh v Cardiff court case and decision, which considered the issue of suspension, because the decision to suspend would be made on the facts known at that time, and the decision to revoke would be made on the facts known at the later date.

However, the same case law has also determined that there are instances where a suspension can be used as a lesser sanction than revocation.

"The relevant disciplinary body may conclude that even if the misconduct has been established, that the appropriate sanction should be something less than complete revocation of the [licence]. It may be, for example, a suspension for a period of one year, will constitute sufficient sanction in the interests of the public[3]"

Councils may attach conditions to taxi and PHV licences (except taxi driver licences) — either standard ones that apply to every licence or specific ones bespoke for individual applicants. In either case the conditions must not:

- exceed the council's powers set out in the controlling legislation ('ultra vires')
- be unreasonable or disproportionate
- be beyond the applicant's powers to comply with
- be for an ulterior motive.

They must:

- be clearly stated in order that they can be properly understood to be complied with and enforced.

[2]   This was established in R (application of Singh) v Cardiff City Council [2012] EWCH 1852 (Admin)

[3]   Singh vs Cardiff

Decision-making may also be delegated to officers, and is an important tool where a serious offence is committed and immediate revocation is needed. All councils should consider having a delegation system in place for this contingency; the chief executive or deputy is often nominated for this role.

Both applicants seeking new licences and the holders of existing licences will have the right of appeal to the local magistrates' court if they are aggrieved by the decision of the council. In all cases where a licence is suspended or revoked, reasons must be given for that decision. Drivers must reach the standard of a lit and proper' person with each case being dealt with on its own merits, normally with reference to an objective policy published by the council.

In doing so, councillors must remember established case law which says "[Consideration of a licence] does not require any consideration of the personal circumstances, which are irrelevant, except perhaps in very rare cases to explain or excuse some conduct of the driver".[4] The overriding consideration is the safety of the public which may, in some cases, outweigh the right of the applicant to hold or continue to hold a licence.

Training of councillors

No councillor should be permitted to sit on a committee or sub-committee without having been formally trained. As a minimum, training should cover licensing procedures, natural justice, understanding the risks of child sexual exploitation, and disability equality, as well as any additional issues deemed locally appropriate.

It is important that training does NOT simply relate to procedures, but also covers the making of difficult and potentially controversial decisions, and the use of case study material can be helpful to illustrate this.

All training should be formally recorded by the council and require a signature from the councillor.

In addition to in-house training, there are a number of independent training providers, including the professional bodies — the National Association of Enforcement and Licensing Officers (NALEO) and the Institute of Licensing (104 The LGA has also made available a free online module on regulatory services for all councillors to use: https://lms.learningnexus.co.uk/LGA/

Appearance of bias

While third party lobbying of elected members is legitimate and certain councillors may make representations to the licensing committee on behalf of 'interested parties', it is crucial for the licensing authority and its committee to ensure that there is neither actual nor an appearance of bias in its decision-making. It should also be remembered that concerns about political lobbying were the basis of the concerns which lead to the first Nolan Committee on Standards in Public Life.[5]

Section 25 of the Localism Act 2011 does not prevent members from publicly expressing a view about an issue or giving the appearance of having a closed mind towards an issue on which they are to adjudicate.

[4] Leeds City Council v Hussain [2002] EWHC 1145 Admin, Siber J

[5] https://www.gov.uk/government/uploads/system/uploads/attachment_data/file/336919/1stInquiry Report.pdf

However it is recommended that to avoid an appearance of bias the following advice should be observed:

- No member sitting on the licensing sub-committee can represent one of the interested parties or the applicant. If s/he wishes to do so s/he must excuse him/herself from membership of the sub-committee which is considering the application. Case law has also established they should not be in the room for the hearing once an interest has been declared.
- If a member who sits on the licensing sub-committee is approached by persons wishing to lobby him/her as regards the licence application then that member must politely explain that they cannot discuss the matter and refer the lobbyist to his/her ward member or the licensing officer who can explain the process of decision making. If the member who sits on the licensing sub-committee wishes to represent them then s/he will need to excuse him/herself from the licensing sub-committee.

- Members who are part of the licensing sub-committee must avoid expressing personal opinions prior to licensing sub-committee decision. To do so will indicate that the member has made up his/her mind before hearing all the evidence and that their decision may not be based upon the licensing objectives nor the statement of licensing policy.

- Members must not pressurise licensing officers to make any particular decisions or recommendations as regards applications.

- Political group meetings should never be used to decide how any members on the licensing sub-committee should vote. The view of the Ombudsman is that using political whips in this manner may well amount to findings of maladministration. It may be advisable that the chair of the licensing sub-committee should state, during proceedings, that no member of the sub-committee is bound by any party whip.

- Councillors must not be members of the licensing sub-committee if they are involved in campaigning about the particular application.

- Other members (ie those who do not sit on the licensing sub-committee) need to be careful when discussing issues relating to matters which may come before the licensing sub-committee members as this can easily be viewed as bias / pressure and may well open that sub-committee member to accusations of such. While a full prohibition upon discussing such issues with committee members by other members may be impractical and undemocratic, local authorities are advised to produce local guidance for members on how such matters can be dealt with.[6] Such guidance could include a definition of what is viewed as excessive eg attempting to obtain a commitment as to how the member might vote.

- Members must also be aware of the need to declare any pecuniary or non-pecuniary interests in matters that may come before them, whether these relate to policy issues or to specific applications.

- Member behaviour is also governed by the member's code of conduct which you should have regard to, and most authorities also have a member/officer protocol which governs how members and officers should interact and the differences in their roles and responsibilities.

- Members should consult their monitoring officers for further advice where necessary.

A well-defined policy and comprehensive scheme of delegations to officers can go a long way to avoiding many of these pitfalls, although, of course, members must retain full oversight of how the scheme is working.

6   "It is undemocratic and impractical to try to prevent councillors from discussing applications with whomever they want; local democracy depends on councillors being available to people who want to speak to them. The likely outcome of a prohibition would be that lobbying would continue but in an underhand and covert way." (Nolan Committee Report into Standards in Public Life, p. 72)

THE 'FIT AND PROPER' PERSON TEST[7]

Passengers should be at the centre of a licensing authority's taxi licensing policies and processes. As the Casey Review into Rotherham[8] noted 'The safety of the public should be the uppermost concern of any licensing and enforcement regime: when determining policy, setting standards and deciding how they will be enforced.' There is no area where this is more important than in the application of the 'fit and proper person' test.

Licensing authority responsibilities

A licensing authority **must not grant a taxi or PHV driver's licence unless it is satisfied that the applicant is a fit and proper person** to hold such a licence. This is very different to the Licensing Act 2003 or Gambling Act 2005, where the presumption is to permit a licence application.

A licensing authority is also entitled to suspend or revoke a taxi or PHV driver's licence if there is evidence to suggest that the individual is not a fit and proper person, and specifically[9]:

- if s/he has been convicted since the grant of the licence of an offence involving dishonesty, violence or indecency
- for non-compliance with the licensing requirements of [the 1847 Act or the 1976 Act] and related legislation, or
- for any other reasonable cause.

Properly applying the 'fit and proper' person test is essential for ensuring a robust licensing scheme that protects safety and commands the confidence of the general public.

On receiving an application, councils should first check the applicant's right to work. This ensures that applications are not heard where the applicant has no legal right to work in the UK, and is a requirement of the Immigration Act 2016. In addition to checks of standard documents, council may wish to use the Home Office's free checking service for new or existing drivers[10].

Once this is established, an inquiry into an applicant's fitness to be licensed is likely to include enquiries into his health, local knowledge and understanding of the responsibilities of a licensed driver. However, character is usually investigated first.

Most councils have adopted a formal statement of policy about the relevance of convictions and how this assists in determining whether an applicant is fit and proper. While each application must be determined on its individual merits, the convictions policy should set out a recommended minimum period free of conviction for offences falling into broad categories as a guideline for licensing committees.

[7] The text in this section draws heavily on an article by Ian de Prez, Solicitor Advocate for Suffolk Coastal District Council, in Local Government Lawyer magazine. We are grateful to Mr de Prez and Local Government Lawyer for their permission to reproduce the points from the article.

8   Casey, L. 'Report of Inspection of Rotherham Metropolitan Borough Council', 2015

9   S60(1)(a)(b)(c), Local Government (Miscellaneous Provisions) Act 1976

10   The service can be contacted at: evidenceandenquiry@homeoffice.gsi.gov.uk

The reason a person's past criminal conduct is taken into consideration is that it can indicate **what is likely to happen in the future if a licence is granted**.

However, councils should not focus solely on an applicant's convictions as an indication of their character. For instance, failure to comply with regulatory requirements may not itself be criminal, but may demonstrate a concerning tendency to disregard licence conditions. Factors such as anti-social behaviour, solvency and sobriety may also be relevant.

Convictions policy

It is important to set out how your sub-committee will view convictions, spent or otherwise, and ideally include it as part of your consolidated taxi licensing policy. Decisions on licensing drivers are exempt from the provisions of the Rehabilitation of Offenders Act and so historic convictions that might otherwise be considered as spent or expired can be taken into consideration.

As set out above, licensing authorities should set out their approach in their convictions policy, which should be regularly reviewed and updated as appropriate. The LGA has developed a sample convictions policy which sits alongside this handbook. This should be used to assist licensing authorities in developing their own policies, rather than directly replicated.

In particular, **the LGA encourages councils to take a strong stance on indecency offences, such as those relating to sexual assault or rape**. While each case must be considered on its own merits, the default position should be that if an applicant has a previous conviction for a sexual offence, a licence will not be issued. Members should be aware of the wide range of criminal offences identified in the Sexual Offences Act 2003 that are very strong indicators of risk if an offender were enabled to be alone in a licensed vehicle with a young person or vulnerable adult.

In addition to indecency offences, Parliament also singled out offences of violence and dishonesty as being of particular concern and relevance when issuing licences, and your policy should weight these offences accordingly. Again, while each case must be considered on its own merits, the LGA policy sets out a default position whereby an applicant with a conviction for a violent offence or driving offence involving a loss of life will be refused a licence.

The convictions policy should set out expectations for how the licensing authority will remain updated about relevant convictions after the point at which a licence has been granted. The Disclosure and Barring Service (DBS) update service, which costs an applicant £13 a year as of November 2016, can help to ensure that licensing authorities receive relevant information as quickly as possible. **The LGA suggests that all licensing authorities consider making it mandatory for drivers to register for the update service and**

nominate the licensing authority to receive updates. Licensees should be able to provide evidence of continuous registration and nomination throughout the duration of their licence.

If licensees are obliged under their licence to inform the local authority of their arrest or conviction and they fail to do so (or where they fail to notify the police that they hold a licence), this should be viewed particularly seriously as it prevents the local authority from taking that information into account when protecting public safety. This is also a breach of condition and can be actioned by the authority on that basis. Whilst the law does not allow conditions to be added to a Hackney Carriage Driver licence, many councils only issue 'dual' Private Hire / Hackney Carriage Driver licences in order to address this point. Alternatively, licensing authorities may wish to attach a condition to hackney carriage vehicle licences for the proprietor to notify the licensing authority as soon as they become aware that a driver of the vehicle is arrested, charged, cautioned or convicted of an offence.

Use of soft intelligence

It is important to remember that your decisions need not, and should not, be based solely on convictions. Licensing committees are able to take into account soft intelligence provided by the police and other partners, as well as of the applicant's responses in the committee hearing. Crucially, the evidential threshold for licensing committees is **not** the 'beyond reasonable doubt' standard which is the criminal standard of proof for criminal trials.

Anecdotal evidence suggests that some authorities have been reluctant to attach much weight to non-conviction information, and in some instances have even doubted the propriety of reporting it to members. However, there is no doubt that this information can and should be taken into account and may sometimes be the sole basis for a refusal, a suspension or revocation.

When dealing with allegations rather than convictions and cautions, a decision maker must not start with any assumptions about them. Allegations will have been disclosed because they reasonably might be true, not because they definitely are true. It is good practice for the decision makers, with the help of their legal adviser, to go through the contents of an enhanced disclosure certificate with an applicant/ driver and see what they say about it. If, as sometimes happens in practice, admissions are made about the facts, that provides a firm basis for a decision.

It will not be possible to give a comprehensive list of points that will be considered as part of the fit and proper person test, but each council should set out in writing, preferably as part of its licensing statement, an outline of how the council intends to approach these decisions and what factors will carry the most weight.

Decision making

A reasonable rule of thumb is to ask yourself 'Would I be happy letting my wife/ husband/ daughter/son be driven by this driver?'. If you are not confident that the answer is 'yes', then you should refuse the licence. In short, if you are 51 per cent certain that the applicant may not be a fit and proper person then you are able to, and should, refuse the licence. You should not give a driver the benefit of the doubt at this stage in the process.

A licensing authority can take into account any spent conviction but of course must do so in a fair and proportionate way, following the authority's policy. It is still appropriate to note the distinction between spent and unspent convictions when considering an application, and there will be many cases in which a particular spent conviction is no longer relevant because sufficient time has passed to demonstrate a change of character. Sometimes an applicant/driver will assert that he was wrongly convicted, or only pleaded guilty to get it over with, to shield a family member or to avoid the risk of a more severe sentence. However the licensing authority should not go behind the existence of the conviction in an attempt to 're-try' the case." Sub-committee members should also be mindful that if a person claims to have perverted the course of justice by lying to protect as relative or friend, that in itself may demonstrate a dishonest character.

When making decisions at both the application stage, or in a disciplinary situation with an existing driver, the sole deciding factor should be the safety of the travelling public. Exceptional mitigation may be relevant to assessing the risk to the travelling public if it shows that the driver/ applicant acted out of character, so that the misdemeanour is unlikely to be repeated — but **personal circumstances, and specifically the potential economic hardship of an applicant or driver, are not a factor to weigh in the balance against the safety of passengers**[11].

In the case of McCool v Rushcliffe Borough Council[12], Lord Bingham said this:

> "One must it seems to me approach this case bearing in mind the objectives of this licensing regime which is plainly intended among other things to ensure so far as possible that those licensed to drive private hire vehicles are suitable persons to do so, namely that they are safe drivers with good driving records and adequate experience; sober, mentally and physically fit, honest and not persons who would take advantage of their employment to abuse or assault passengers."

Lord Bingham's view has since been confirmed in two further court cases — Anwar v Cherwell District Council and Leeds Council v Hussain.

Councils have a broad discretion when refusing to grant a licence, providing the decision is reasonable, proportionate and — ideally — in line with a published policy. If the decision departs from the policy, then the council should state the reasons for this in writing to the applicant.

Where you have refused a licence, or granted a licence subject to strict conditions or criteria, or for a shorter period than three years, then you must set out these reasons in writing. Applicants have a right of appeal to the magistrates' court against those decisions and it aids both applicants and the court to understand the nature of the decision being appealed against.

A decision to revoke, suspend or refuse to renew a licence will engage the licensee's rights under the Human Rights Act 1998 (the 1998 Act) by providing a right to a fair hearing and a right to an independent and impartial appeal tribunal (in this case the magistrates' court). It may also engage the licensee's rights not to be deprived of their underlying economic interests in the licence unless that can be justified in the public interest and is proportionate.

There have been a number of challenges to decisions to suspend or revoke licences on the basis that a licence is a personal piece of property, and therefore revocation infringes the driver's human rights. However, case law has established that a decision maker dealing with a currently licensed driver should not regard the licence as a piece of property under the 1998 Act.[13]

11   Nottingham City Council v Farooq [1998] EWHC Admin 991
12   [1998] 3 All ER 889
13   Cherwell District Council v Anwar [2011] EWHC 2943 (Admin)

PHV operator responsibilities

Taxi and PHV licensing is not an area where there is much scope for self-regulation, but PHV operators do have a key role in ensuring that their drivers are fit and proper persons, that the vehicles they use are adequate and insured, that their staff handle customer information correctly, and that everyone is properly trained in their roles including awareness of child sexual exploitation (CSE) and disability equality.

Your policy should therefore cover the responsibility of PHV operators for ensuring that their drivers are fit and proper persons; as part of the process of granting and monitoring an operator licence, you may wish to require operators to demonstrate what steps they are taking to ensure that their drivers are fit and proper persons, as well as appropriately trained.

This responsibility is even more important now that the Deregulation Act has enabled operators to sub-contract bookings to other providers. There are existing obligations on operators who seek to pass on a booking and the first operator will always retain overall responsibility for its fulfilment. However, there is scope for councils to enhance this responsibility by placing conditions on an operator's licence to require them to set out how they will handle subcontracting and ensure consumer protection.

It is also appropriate to remind operators that they have responsibilities towards their drivers and should ensure that they are not working excessive hours. A recent case in Mansfield of a driver falling asleep at the wheel and causing a fatality was investigated by the Coroner, who recommended greater attention was given to ensuring drivers were not unduly fatigued. This is most effectively done by the operator, who will have more regular contact with the driver and should be reminding them of the serious consequences that can result if they drive for excessive hours.

These are areas that have not yet been tested through the courts and offers a fertile ground for those innovative councils who wish to make full use of their powers to protect their communities. We encourage councils to explore this, and to share their new practice with the LGA and other licensing authorities.

Changes in technology mean that there are newly emerging operator models, which can require scrutiny to ensure that they comply with the law as it stands. Functions and processes that are well established among non-digital operators may need to be questioned and traced when considering a proposal to operate online. A checklist of questions to ask is included at the end of this handbook, although the list is not exhaustive.

Monitoring complaints

All councils should have a robust system for recording complaints, including analysing trends across the whole system as well as complaints against individual drivers. Complaints about drivers should be taken seriously and drivers with a number of complaints made against them should be contacted by the council and concerns raised with the driver and operator (if appropriate). Further action must be determined by the council, which could include no further action, the offer of training, a formal review of the licence, or formal enforcement action.

The licensing committee should review the complaints procedure and records regularly, and always before a review of the licensing policy. It is expected that councils will carry out 'mystery shopping' and test purchasing checks on licensed vehicles; and the committee should have oversight of this to ensure that the council is properly carrying out its enforcement responsibilities.

Penalty points enforcement system: Rother District Council

When taxi and PHV drivers contravene conditions of their licence the only sanctions available to members of taxi licensing committees is that of revocation or suspension. For minor infringements, such as not displaying a name badge at all times, revocation or suspension can be too harsh a punishment. Drivers who make an error in judgement on any given day, with a previous unblemished career, may face all or nothing decisions by councillors if they are reported to committee following a complaint from a member of the public.

Also once drivers are licensed there is limited information available to continually assess whether they are fit and proper persons, and as such for members to have a clear view of their past conduct when drivers are called to committee for hearings.

In light of this Rother District Council decided to develop a 'penalty points enforcement scheme', where drivers can carry a fixed number of points for minor matters of misconduct that would allow the driver to continue driving until such time as they either reached the level set by members, at which point there would be a hearing, or if officers decided that the nature of the complaint against a driver was too serious to deal with under the scheme.

Rother found that on the whole the trade agreed that the process led to improvements in behaviour, especially by those drivers who tend not to take their role as licensed drivers too seriously. The trade appreciated that the scheme is transparent and clear, and removes any ambiguity about whether officers or members felt that a matter was serious, or when the driver thought it was very minor.

The penalty points enforcement scheme gives councillors a more influential role in the licensing process, and it allows drivers to understand that members make the decisions on fitness and propriety and not officers. However, it is worth noting that the accumulation of points cannot automatically lead to a sanction and that the 'fitness' or otherwise of a licensee has to be dealt with separately and in its own way.

Many other councils have introduced similar schemes and there has been a noticeable improvement in both standards of behaviour and standards of compliance. Councils should have regard to case law that has established parameters for these schemes, including a judgement in Singh v Cardiff that the scheme must not fetter the discretion of the decision maker.

Scrutiny

Public scrutiny is an essential part of ensuring that government remains effective and accountable, and this is especially true of quasi-judicial systems like taxi and PHV licensing. Scrutiny ensures that executives and committees are held accountable for their decisions, that their decision-making process is clear and accessible to the public and that there are opportunities for the public and their representatives to influence and improve public policy.

There are a number of aspects of taxi and PHV licensing that are suitable for a scrutiny investigation, ranging from a review of the policy and framework, including how it contributes to a wider transport policy, its success in delivering accessible transport for disabled users, or the handling of complaints; to more specialist subjects such as the setting of fees, provision of taxi ranks, or the age and maintenance of the fleet.

The Centre for Public Scrutiny[14] provides guidance on how to hold effective scrutiny, and also has a number of case studies from councils that have already held scrutiny enquiries into their taxi and PHV licensing systems.

[14] www.cfps.org.uk

PUBLIC PROTECTION AND ENFORCEMENT

Partnership working and information sharing

Effective partnership working between local licensing authorities, the Driver and Vehicle Standards Agency (DVSA), police, other council services such as trading standards and environmental health, as well as the local trade, is vital to ensuring effective taxi and PHV regulation.

It is particularly important to join-up enforcement operations with the police as taxi licensing officers do not have powers to stop and search vehicles. Similarly, licensing officers may only take action against drivers and vehicles that they have licensed, which is why the issue of cross-border usage is so problematic (see below). You should ensure your council taxi licensing officers meet regularly with their local police force and develop good relationships.

As a councillor, you are well placed to shape and influence how this crucial partnership relationship between your council and other bodies works and develops. There are many areas across England and Wales where these partnerships are working well.

It is particularly important to have effective intelligence sharing protocols in place with the local police force. The police have powers to disclose information under common law, which enables them to share information about relevant investigations with licensing teams even before an arrest or conviction is made.

The Home Office's abolition of the Notifiable Occupations Scheme has led to significant inconsistencies between councils and police forces when it comes to sharing soft intelligence. A replacement scheme has been developed, called the Common Law Disclosure Policy, but reports from the ground raise significant concerns about the way it has been implemented, and the LGA is raising this with the Home Office.

In the meantime all licensing authorities should use their local relationships to continue the flow of information. Councillors should seek the support of their local police and crime commissioner if necessary.

Sharing intelligence: Norfolk councils and Norfolk Constabulary

Safeguarding information sharing process

What is the issue?

Licences are issued by the local authority for a wide variety of purposes. For example, a licence is required to drive either a licensed hackney or a private hire vehicle (a dual licence allows a driver to drive a hackney carriage vehicle or private hire vehicle) and all PHV drivers must work for a licensed private hire operator. When a licence is refused, suspended or revoked by the licensing authority or there are any other concerns raised which may be considered a safeguarding issue it has been agreed that the licensing authority will notify the police for intelligence purposes.

Why is this necessary?

Licence holders can operate in positions of trust and it is vital that any relevant information about safeguarding issues is shared so that individuals are blocked from becoming taxi operators or holding any other kind of licence in different council areas across the county/ country. Without effective information sharing, there is a real risk of unsuitable people being granted licences to operate which puts people at risk.

How will this work?

When a licence is refused/suspended/revoked due to a 'safeguarding' issue then licensing authorities are to complete a template and submit it the police electronically via secure email. The referral template should also be used to report any safeguarding concerns about any licence holder. The police will create an intelligence report which becomes disclosable as part of any subsequent DBS check undertaken anywhere in the country, thereby reducing the risk of unsuitable persons being granted a licence.

What is a 'safeguarding issue'?

Physical — Including hitting, slapping, pushing, kicking, restraint or inappropriate sanctions.

Sexual — Including rape and sexual assault or sexual acts to which the vulnerable person (including any young person) has not consented, could not consent or was pressured into consenting.

Psychological — Including emotional abuse, threats of harm or abandonment, deprivation of contact, humiliation, blaming, controlling, intimidation, coercion, harassment, verbal abuse, isolation or withdrawal from services or supportive networks.

Financial — Including theft, fraud, exploitation, pressure in connection with wills, property or inheritance or financial transactions, the misuse or misappropriation of property, possessions or benefits.

Neglect/failure to act — Including ignoring medical or physical care needs, failure to provide access to appropriate health care, social care, education services or misuse of medication, adequate nutrition or heating.

Discriminatory — Including racist, sexist behaviour and harassment based on a person's ethnicity, race, culture, sexual orientation, age or disability, and other forms of harassment, slurs or similar treatment.

Institutional abuse — This can sometimes happen in residential homes, nursing homes or hospitals when people are mistreated because of poor or inadequate care, neglect and poor practice that affects the whole of that service.

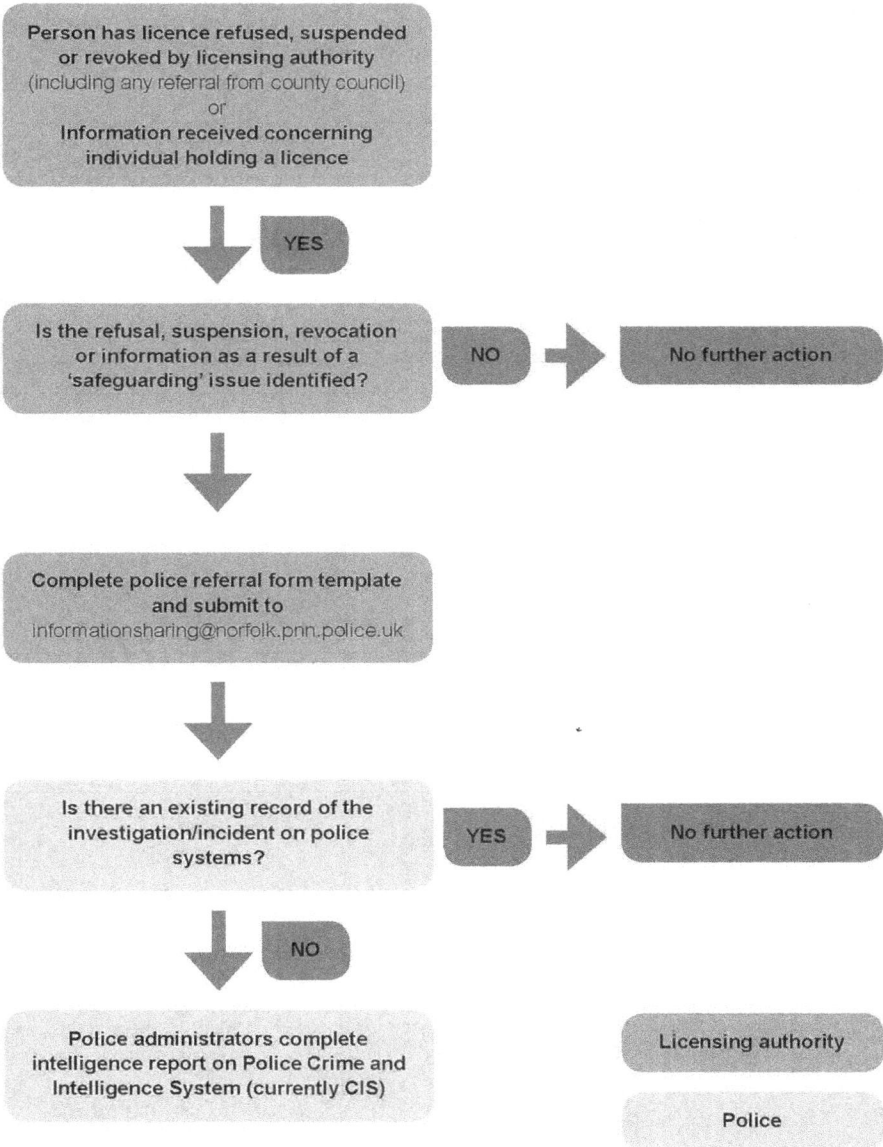

Person has licence refused, suspended or revoked by licensing authority (including any referral from county council) or Information received concerning individual holding a licence

YES

Is the refusal, suspension, revocation or information as a result of a 'safeguarding' issue identified?

NO → No further action

Complete police referral form template and submit to informationsharing@norfolk.pnn.police.uk

Is there an existing record of the investigation/incident on police systems?

YES → No further action

NO

Police administrators complete intelligence report on Police Crime and Intelligence System (currently CIS)

Licensing authority

Police

Police Referral Form Template

(submit to informationsharing@norfolk.pnn.police.uk)

Local Authority	
Disclosing Officer	
Role	
Driver/Applicant/Subject	
Surname	
Forename(s)	
Date of Birth	
Home Address	
Telephone	
Type of Licence Application (if applicable)	
Vehicle Details (if known/ applicable) *include registrtaion / make / model	
Information/Intelligence	

Refusal	Yes/No	Suspension	Yes/No	Revocation	Yes/No	Information	Yes/No
Date of refusal / suspension / revocation / information							
Circumstances * (must include any relevant time / date / location information)							
Additional Information							

*   Circumstances should provide sufficient summary information to identify threats and risks associated with the applicant / driver. Full records of any investigation need not be disclosed on the IR as these will be retained locally by relevant authority

Joint operations: Blaenau Gwent Council

Blaenau Gwent Council's Licensing Team coordinated roadside checks on taxis and private hire vehicles to make sure Blaenau Gwent pupils travelled to school safely.

On the morning of the school run the council's licensing team, officers from the council's school transport division and technical experts from DVSA checked 16 buses and eight taxis.

The school run checks were followed up with detailed safety inspections that resulted in one notice and a number of warnings.

- One deferred prohibition notice was issued for a defect. The company was told to carry out the repairs within a time period.
- Four drivers were given advice regarding minor defects.
- Six warnings were given for not wearing seatbelts.
- Four enquiries were made by Blaenau Gwent Council's education division about school contracts operating logistics.

During the day, Gwent Police traffic officers gave out 16 fixed penalties for no seatbelts, two fixed penalties for using mobile telephones while driving and ordered repairs for a cracked windscreen.

Chair of Blaenau Gwent Council's Licensing Committee, Councillor Jim Watkins said:

"We are committed to maintaining and improving the standards of the home-to-school transport service provided by independent operators and those contracted to us. Our regular check-ups are important. We have to thank our partners in Gwent Police and the DVSA, and the operators as well, for their cooperation."

Managing cross border hiring

Cross border hiring is a term to describe when a taxi is lawfully used for PHV purposes in a district outside which it has been licensed to operate. This is a problem in many areas because there are disparities in conditions on licences; a prospective driver in one council district may apply to be licensed as a driver in another district because there are lower standards in driver testing, cheaper licence fees or less rigorous/fewer pre-licence checks. The term 'cross border' is also used when a PHV in one district picks up a passenger from another district. This is legal, provided either that the driver, vehicle and operator are all licensed by the first district; or that the operator sub-contracts the booking to an operator licensed in another council area.

This is also problematic, because when a taxi is being driven for PHV purposes in another district, the local council has no powers to intervene if the driver contravenes any condition of the licence or provides a poor service to the passenger; all that can be done is to write to the authority that issued the licence, where this is known. This practice is also unfair on the trade in the local area, as they may face competition from drivers who may have paid cheaper licence fees or undergone less rigorous checks elsewhere. These safeguards are rarely visible to consumers, who therefore cannot make an informed decision to use the more heavily checked and therefore safer, albeit more expensive, option.

As a councillor you can take some simple steps to ensure that your local authority is not having a detrimental impact on other authorities and their communities. Ask your taxi and PHV licensing service whether they have a high enough standard of conditions (see councillor checklist) and consider where an applicant intends to work when issuing licences.

You do have the legal right to refuse to issue a licence if the applicant does not intend to work mainly in your area and should recognise that the reputational impact to your council of knowingly licensing taxis to operate elsewhere could severely limit your ability to develop partnership working with neighbouring authorities.

If you seek to include a section on this in your licensing policy, then it is important to remember that a 'hackney carriage' cannot 'work' or 'operate' as a PHV. The law simply allows them to be used for 'private hire purposes'. This may sound like semantics, but has been tested in the courts and means that you cannot use your greater power to condition PHV driver licences to regulate the driver of a hackney carriage, even though they may at times be working in the same manner as a PHV driver (ie making pre-booked journeys, rather than plying for hire).

The most notable piece of case law on cross-border hiring was between Newcastle City Council and Berwick Borough Council. Between 2006 and 2008, Berwick's licensed fleet had grown from 46 taxis to 672. Many of the fleet were not operating in Berwick but had applied there as a result of a less stringent application process and were operating in neighbouring or nearby areas.

In his judgment, the judge rejected Berwick's arguments that it is obliged by law to issue a hackney carriage licence to any applicant, so long as they and their vehicles are fit.

Commenting on the potentially 'undesirable consequences' of Berwick's stance, he said the council is having to carry out its enforcement powers from a distance and faces difficulty in keeping its licensed cabs under observation.

He said: "It seems to me that it must be desirable for an authority issuing licences to hackney carriages to be able to restrict the issuing of those licences to proprietors and drivers which are intending to ply for hire in that authority's area."

He said the intention of the licensing system is that "it should operate in such a way that the authority licensing hackney carriages is the authority for the area in which those vehicles are generally used".

The judge added: "If the hackney carriages are used in areas remote from Berwick-upon-Tweed, enforcement will be very difficult and impracticable.

"It seems to me it is very difficult to exercise proper control over hackney carriages which are never, or rarely, used in the prescribed area.

"It is also undesirable for authorities to be faced with a proliferation of hackney carriages licensed outside the area in which they are being used and therefore not subject to the same conditions and bylaws as apply to those vehicles licensed in the area."

Judge Symons said he would leave it to the judgment and common sense of the borough council to decide how to react to his ruling, that it does have a 'discretion' to refuse to licence taxis if there is no 'unmet demand' for cabs in Berwick itself.

"While I cannot at the moment conceive of it being rational to grant a licence to those who intend to operate their hackney carriages remotely from Berwick-upon-Tweed, I am not prepared to say that it is bound to be unlawful" he concluded.

Until the Law Commission's proposals extending an authorised officer's powers are enacted, the protocol[15] below could be used by authorities to ensure rogue drivers and vehicles are prevented from hiding 'over the border' or routinely operating outside the reach of enforcement by their licensing authority.

It allows councils to authorise officers from other councils to use enforcement powers on their behalf. This enables those councils to then take action against vehicles which are licensed by the other authority when they cross over council boundaries.

This practice was recently highly commended by the then Transport Minister Baroness Kramer, citing some of Merseyside councils' practices since 1995. Transport is also often one of the issues identified as a priority by combined authorities. These new structures will make sharing enforcement powers increasingly attractive and could pave the way to extending your regulatory reach beyond your borders. In time, a shared framework similar to Transport for London could evolve.

The protocol is suggested as an easy way forward for those authorities wishing to consider such joint authorisations of officers.

Protocol
1. All authorities agree what level of expertise/qualification/skills is the minimum for approval of authorisation of each individual.
2. All authorities establish, via their own schemes of delegation, what procedural steps need to be taken to validly authorise (ie chief officer's report, sub-committee or full committee decision).
3. All authorities agree the form and wording of the 'letter of authorisation' and 'photo warrant card' to be issued.
4. Each 'requesting council' formally requests authorisation of named individual officers.
5. Each 'receiving council' obtains authorisation and provides a 'letter of authorisation' in respect of the other authority's officers.
6. Each employing authority provides its own officers with a photo warrant card specifying that for the purposes of [specify Acts of Parliament] that officer [name] is a duly authorised officer of [list all authorising councils].
7. Each authority provides all officers with copies of appropriate bylaws, conditions and agreed methodologies/reporting mechanisms for dealing with defective vehicles and other issues from other areas.

8. Each authority seeks political and financial approval for pre-planned joint operations both with each other and also police/HMRC Customs & Excise.
9. Data sharing protocols, as required, be established between authorities, including standard incident reporting templates/operation logs to be used by all for consistency and scheme recording.

[15] The relevant enabling legislation is Section 32 Part I of the Local Government (Miscellaneous Provisions) Act 1976: 32 Power of local authorities to execute works outside their areas. 'Any power to execute works which is conferred on a local authority by any enactment may, unless the contrary intention appears in that or any other enactment, be exercised outside as well as inside the area of the authority.'

Child sexual exploitation

As set out in the fit and proper person section above, protecting all passengers lies at the heart of taxi and PHV licensing systems. However, recent cases have shown that licensing authorities must ensure that their licensing regimes effectively protect some of their most vulnerable residents, including children at risk of sexual exploitation. A detailed exploration of tackling child sexual exploitation (CSE) is outside the remit of this guide, but all councillors and officers, across all services, should familiarise themselves with the LGAs guides on CSE.[16]

Sadly, both licensed premises and licensed vehicles have been used as opportunities to sexually exploit children, as recent high profile cases have underlined. The Government commissioned Dame Louise Casey CB to investigate reports into the governance of Rotherham Council following widespread allegations of child sexual exploitation. Her subsequent review contained two chapters on the role that licensing could and should have played in preventing some of this exploitation, and the report is essential reading for any councillor joining a licensing committee. The full report and documents relating to the Rotherham investigation can be found at: www.gov.uk/government/collections/inspection-into-the-governance-of-rotherham-council

It is important to recognise that this is a subject that needs to be sensitively handled to avoid drivers feeling that they are being treated as potential criminals. However, the sensitivity around the subject must not mean that the issue is not discussed or that training is not provided. There are two particular points licensing authorities should be aware of:

The first is that we know that many victims of exploitation are too traumatised for investigations to proceed to court, meaning that issues do not always show up through disclosure. This makes additional soft intelligence from all other sources critical to licensing deliberations — as outlined in the 'use of soft intelligence' section above.

The second is that taxi and PHV drivers can be a valuable source of intelligence about exploitation if they know what to look for. For this reason, many councils now make CSE training a mandatory part of the licensing application process, which the LGA supports.

Your local safeguarding boards also have an important role to play in licensing and you should ensure that safeguarding boards understand the role that licensing can play in their discussions. Your licensing officers should also be fully engaged with relevant safeguarding discussions.

This is particularly important in two-tier areas, with licensing located in the districts and child protection in the county council. A number of serious case reviews have highlighted a failure of communication between the two-tiers of local government as a contributing factor to child exploitation going undetected.

If allegations of CSE or other serious offences are made, then your council should have in place procedures to allow a rapid response from the council. In the most serious cases, it will not be appropriate to wait until a licensing committee or sub-committee can be held. Councils should consider how they can structure their scheme of delegations to enable the effective use of immediate powers of suspension and revocation in appropriate cases.

[16]   http://www.local.gov.uk/web/guest/children-and-young-peopleNjournal_
content/56/10180/3790391/ARTICLE

Operation Sanctuary

Operation Sanctuary investigated allegations of a series of sexual offences predominantly within Newcastle, but also in other local authority areas, involving a number of men from a range of communities and vulnerable female victims, including teenagers and young adults.

Operation Sanctuary was about targeting men exploiting vulnerable teenagers and women and stopping their behaviour. Commenting at the time, Northumbria Police stated:

'These crimes are happening behind closed doors, in local streets and it is likely that people living nearby recognise the behaviour we describe. It may be groups of men going into properties with teenage girls or one or two women. They might see women under the influence of drink or drugs who might appear distressed in some way. We need them to report this to us. If it is innocent then nothing will happen to them. But this allows us to check and may avoid someone else becoming a victim.

We also know some of these girls and women may frequent certain businesses which brings them into contact with these men so we will be visiting the premises and speaking to those who work there and those who hang around.

We also believe that the victims are transported in taxis to the different addresses — again we will be speaking to all taxi firms to ask for their help if they spot anything that appears suspicious or fits the description of what we are looking at.

To date 30 people have been arrested for conspiracy to rape women (28 men and two women).Those arrested come from a range of communities and backgrounds.'

As part of Operation Sanctuary, officers delivered leaflets in Newcastle city centre to taxi drivers, hotels, and other businesses.

The leaflets advised them of the ongoing operation, how it affected them and what to look out for to identify any potential vulnerable girls or young women.

This helped to keep people informed and updated about the operation, as well as aware of how everyone has a part to play in ensuring information is reported to police.

Installing CCTV in cabs

A number of councils require CCTV to be installed in taxis and PHVs, as a way of reducing crimes and providing evidence to support prosecution. This approach can benefit both passengers and drivers, who can equally be the subjects of assaults, abuse or fraud. However, it is important recognise that the cost of installing such equipment, can be an issue for drivers.

Consultation with your driver community will help determine a suitable approach; including the period of time allowed for installation if you decide to introduce this approach.

It is important to be aware of surveillance and data protection issues when considering the use of CCTV, particularly with regard to the recording of conversations.

The Information Commissioner's Office (ICO) has said it is not normally justified to use CCTV to record conversations between members of the public as 'it is highly intrusive', but have also stated that council applications to install cameras in cabs are likely to be acceptable because of the number of crimes being committed in taxis[17].

As well as assessing the impact on privacy, we have accepted they [councils] can take into account factors such as the likelihood of crimes being committed against drivers and passengers; the vulnerable one-to-one situation; the fact that taxis are travelling all over the area at different times of day; and CCTV can protect both the driver and passengers."'

It is therefore essential that licensing authorities take account of people's right to privacy when deciding whether to impose CCTV as a licence condition for taxis. Whether the installation of CCTV is mandatory or voluntary it is essential that the local authority has a strict specification for permissible systems to ensure that there are adequate safeguards, such as who can access the footage.

It is also important to note that the use of CCTV inside and outside the vehicle are treated differently, and that once a passenger is inside a vehicle that they have hired they have a right to privacy. This means that they must be notified that the vehicle has a CCTV system in operation.

Some councils have chosen to specify that audio recording should only be activated when there is a specific threat, in the same way that a panic button could be used.

Transport for London, acting on advice from the ICO, recommend:

- Where recording is triggered due to a specific threat, eg a 'panic button' is utilised. Where this audio recording facility is utilised a reset function must be installed which automatically disables audio recording and returns the system to normal default operation after a specified time period has elapsed.
- The time period that audio recording may be active should be the minimum possible and should be declared at the time of submission for approval of the equipment.

Any specified company, organisation or individual vehicle owner who has a CCTV system installed in a licensed vehicle must register with the ICO ('notification') and obtain documented evidence of that registration. This documentary evidence may be required to be presented to an official of the taxis and private hire team (TPH) at any time during the term of the TPH vehicle licence. The notification requires renewal on an annual basis and payment of the appropriate fee.

Due to the complexity of surveillance and privacy legislation and case law, this information is provided only as a summary. The Information Commissioner's Code of Practice provides a helpful starting point, and references case law on when audio is and is not appropriate.[18] The LGA is however working with councils that have introduced a requirement for mandatory CCTV to produce a short guide on the issues to consider.

[17] The Information Commissioner's Office: https://ico.org.uk/about-the-ico/news-and-events/
news-and-blogs/2014/10/ico-warns-
cctv-operators-that-use-of-surveillance-cameras-must-be-necessary-and-proportionate/
https://ico.org. Aimed ia/about-the-ico/documents/1042192/ico-annual-report-201213. pdf
(page 39)

[18] https://ico.org.uk/media/for-organisations/documents/1542/cctv-code-of-practice.pdf

DISABILITY AND EQUALITY ISSUES

The Equality Act 2010 sets out obligations for public bodies to advance equality of opportunity among people and eliminate discrimination. Councils should think about how they can fulfil this obligation in relation to taxi and PHV licensing. Although there are few specific requirements that councils must implement in relation to disability issues, the LGA encourages councils to go beyond what is strictly required by introducing wheelchair accessible vehicle lists and mandatory disability training for all drivers.

Accessibility requirements – wheelchairs

In April 2017, various parts of the Equality Act 2010 relating to taxis and PHVs were enacted, meaning new duties were placed on both drivers and councils around accessibility for passengers in wheelchairs. The Department for Transport's (DfT) updated statutory guidance[19] on access for wheelchair users to taxis and PHVs sets out these new requirements and is a useful tool to support councils with these changes.

The new provisions give councils the power, although not a duty, to maintain a statutory list of designated wheelchair accessible vehicles they license that meet "such accessibility requirements as the licensing authority thinks fit".[20] Where councils opt to do so, drivers of taxis and PHVs designated as being wheelchair accessible must comply with the requirements of Section 165 of the Equality Act 2010, unless they have been issued with an exemption certificate. Prior to April 2017, while some councils had designated vehicles as wheelchair accessible, the obligations on drivers under section 165 were not in force.

Under section 165 of the Equality Act taxi/ PHV drivers are obligated to carry passengers while in a wheelchair without additional charge. Drivers are also required to give the passenger any mobility assistance that is reasonably required, for example help getting in or out of the taxi and with loading luggage. Drivers who believe that for medical or physical reasons they should be exempt from these duties are required to apply to the council for exemption. Whilst there is no prescribed format for the exemption certificates that councils issue to drivers, there is a prescribed format for the exemption notices[21], which are separate to certificates and will need to be issued by the council and displayed in the vehicle by drivers. Prescribed exemption notices should be issued to new and existing exemption holders and a consistent process for handling exemption applications implemented to support this. Any appeal against a refusal to grant exemption will need to be heard by a Magistrate's court.

As these new powers requiring taxis and PHVs to carry wheelchair users only apply if the council has published a statutory list of wheelchair accessible vehicles, the LGA strongly recommends that councils do so, to increase access for wheelchair users and ensure that enforcement action can be taken against drivers where necessary. Publishing a statutory list also sends a strong signal to the trade locally that they are expected to follow access requirements. Following the implementation of the Equalities Act provisions, campaign groups have submitted Freedom of Information requests to identify which councils are and are not intending to develop a statutory list, and it is likely that this level of engagement with the issue will be maintained in the coming years.

The statutory guidance sets out in more detail what the statutory lists should include, for example the details of the make and model of the vehicle and the name of the driver and/or PHV operator. The guidance also recommends that a separate, non-statutory list should be developed of vehicles that are accessible to passengers in wheelchairs if they transfer from their wheelchair.

For councils not currently publishing a statutory list but planning to do so, it is important that transition plans are in place and communicated to licence holders. Consideration should be given to whether operator and driver licence conditions could be reviewed to aid enforcement.

[19]   www.gov.uk/government/uploads/system/uploads/attachment_data/file/593350/access-for-wheelchair-users-taxis-and-private-hire-vehicles.pdf

[20]   'Accessibility requirements' are "requirements for securing that it is possible for disabled persons in wheelchairs: (i) to get into and out of vehicles in safety, and (ii) to travel in vehicles in

safety and reasonable comfort, either staying in their wheelchairs or not (depending on which they prefer).

[21]   www.legislation.gov.uk/uksi/2017/342/pdfs/uksi_20170342_en.pdf

Accessibility requirements – guide dogs

Media stories and research by the charity Guide Dogs show there is a widespread problem of assistance dog owners being refused access to taxis and PHVs[22] despite the legal requirement for taxis and PHVs to carry guide dogs unless the driver has a valid medical exemption certificate. Similarly, there are many stories of extra or over-charging for users of wheelchairs. Councils should make clear to drivers that they cannot charge a disabled passenger more than any other passenger.

Working with disabled people locally to carry out mystery shopping of taxis and PHVs can provide valuable insight into whether drivers are complying with their legal duties. However, figures suggest that only 20 per cent of councils assess the quality of services provided to assistance dog owners in their areas. Only 18 local authorities conduct mystery shopping or surveys to ensure that taxi and PHV drivers are meeting their obligations.[23]

In relation to assistance dogs, Guide Dogs have developed some standard wording which they encourage councils to include in their taxi licensing policies, as well as a guidance note[24] on access to taxis and minicabs for guide dog owners.

[22]   www.guidedogs.org.uldmedia/7868390/access-all-areas-main-reportimal.pdf
[23]   Data gathered by Guide Dogs following a Freedom of Information request in November 2015.
[24]   www.guidedogs.org.uldmedia/824002²/ₐccess-guide-taxis.pdf

Disability equality training

Disability equality training can support taxi and PHV drivers to understand and meet requirements under the Equality Act. The LGA supports the call for disability equality training to be mandatory for taxi and PHV drivers; currently, less than a third of councils make this a mandatory component of a licence. At a time when council enforcement and discretionary travel resources are heavily under pressure, engaging with your driver community to ensure they are aware of their responsibilities should not be underestimated and can repay the small investment needed.

Although many councils have chosen to provide their own training support on disability issues, there are also a number of other providers who offer this training. It is important to remember that stories and information given by people who have a disability is much more powerful and resonant than just numbers or tables on a spreadsheet, or lists of things not to do. You may therefore want to work with your local disability and victim groups to co-design this element of training.

Guide Dogs suggestions for taxi licensing policy

Taxi and PHV Policy — assistance dogs
The law

Under the Equality Act 2010, licensed drivers of taxis and private hire vehicles are under a duty to carry passengers with guide, hearing and other assistance dogs without additional charge.

When carrying such passengers, drivers have a duty to:

a) convey the disabled passenger's dog and allow it to remain under the physical control of the owner; and
b) not to make any additional charge for doing so.

We would ask Licensing Authorities to use their best endeavours to ensure that licensed drivers of taxis and private hire vehicles ask the passenger where they prefer to sit with their dog in the vehicle.

Enforcement

Under the Equality Act 2010, it is an offence for any operator or driver to refuse to carry assistance dogs or to charge more for the fare or booking. On conviction for such an offence, drivers can be fined up to £1,000 and have their licence removed.

To ensure best practice in achieving effective enforcement the Licensing Authority will use its best endeavours to:

• investigate all reported violations of the Act with a view to pursuing a conviction
• work together in conjunction with assistance dog owners by various means such as, but not limited to, test purchases to ensure that licensing requirements are being complied with
• ensure that all taxi and private hire vehicle drivers undertake disability equality training, which includes information regarding the carriage of assistance dogs.

Medical Exemption Certificates

Drivers who have a certifiable medical condition which is aggravated by exposure to dogs may apply to the council for exemption from the duty on medical grounds. All other taxi and private hire vehicle drivers are required to carry assistance dogs. Drivers must place the notice of exemption in an easily accessible place, for example on the windscreen or in a prominent position on the dashboard.

The Licencing Authority will:

• where an exemption certificate is issued, provide an additional tactile and/or large print resource to taxi and private hire vehicle drivers (as a reasonable adjustment within the Equality Act) so that assistance dog owners who are blind can identify that the driver has been issued with a certificate

- only issue an exemption certificate when it is authorised by a medical practitioner and is accompanied by medical evidence, for example a blood test, a skin prick test or clinical history.

Promoting equality awareness: Stockport Metropolitan Borough Council

Stockport Council's licensing team has worked in partnership with Disability Stockport to produce a brochure that includes:

- the contact details of licensed drivers who have successfully completed disability awareness training provided by Disability Stockport and Solutions SK, funded by Stockport Council
- information to enable disabled passengers to book transport with providers who best suit their needs
- guidance to passengers on the types of licensed vehicles available for hire in Stockport
- guidance to disabled passengers on how to hire a licensed vehicle in Stockport and what service they should expect
- advice to licensed drivers on how to assist disabled passengers
- guidance to licensed drivers on what is expected of them further to their disability awareness training
- information on how to improve the service and awareness of it.

The guide has been recognised as good practice by the Government's Accessible Britain Challenge. The guide can be found at: www.stockport.gov. uk/general-information-and-applications-taxi-licensing/stockport-disability- aware-transport-providers-guide

Mystery Shopping Case Study: Kirklees Council

Kirklees Council's licensing team has been involved in a mystery shopping exercise with local guide dog owners. The activity saw guide dog owners making mystery shopping telephone calls to local taxi and PHV firms requesting a driver and informing them that they had an assistance dog. The guide dog owners then informed the council about which companies refused them access, or provided them with a substandard service.

Kirklees Council's licensing team then wrote to all the firms contacted in the mystery shopping stating the law. A second round of mystery shopping calls then took place, and for any taxi or PHV operators that guide dog owners still had concerns about, the licencing team visited them to speak about their legal obligations.

This was followed up by mystery shopping in person in partnership with West Yorkshire Police and Kirklees Council. As a result of the mystery shop, Kirklees Council have taken action against three drivers. Kirklees Licensing team have continued

OTHER ISSUES

Quantity restrictions

Quantity restriction is a term used to describe a local council imposing limits on the number of taxi licences within its area. This is often seen as a controversial issue because in those areas that continue to impose quantity restrictions, the taxi trade is often a strong advocate of keeping a 'restricted fleet'. Currently only 88 councils in England and Wales continue to restrict numbers. The decision to restrict taxis is left to the local council, but the LGA suggests that councils consider the DfT's view and state your reasons for departing from it when setting out your licensing policy.

'Most local licensing authorities do not impose quantity restrictions; the Department regards that as best practice. Where restrictions are imposed, the Department would urge that the matter should be regularly reconsidered. The Department further urges that the issue to be addressed first in each reconsideration is whether the restrictions should continue at all. It is suggested that the matter should be approached in terms of the interests of the travelling public.' **DfT Taxi and PHV Licensing Best Practice Guidance on quantity restrictions**.

Restricting the number of taxis: Stockport Metropolitan Borough Council

Local councils which limit the number of taxis within their fleets should regularly produce an unmet demand survey. The survey reviews the consumer demand for taxis and considers factors such as the length of time customers wait at ranks and waiting times for street hailings and telephone bookings.

In 2008 Stockport Metropolitan Borough Council carried out an unmet demand and public opinion survey, which indicated that there was no significant unmet demand. Stockport licensing committee agreed to maintain a limit on the number of taxis currently licensed by the authority. To ensure this was a balanced decision Stockport considered the guidance issued by the DfT in relation to maintaining limits and various consumer reports which indicate that a general increase in the number of taxis is beneficial for consumers. While maintaining a limit the committee also agreed to increase that limit by five licences per year over the next three years.

They further committed to reviewing current rank facilities including creating new ranks, particularly night-time ranks in busy areas. The policy is kept under continuous review, with the most recent survey in late 2014 determining that there was no unmet demand and that restrictions should be maintained, although there is scope for providing additional ranking facilities.

Lifting quantity restrictions: Salford City Council

Salford City Council previously had a policy of limiting taxi licence numbers. An unmet demand survey had been carried out in 2004 which recommended an increase in the issue of one licence which brought the total number of taxis in Salford to 79. If the council wished to retain this limit, an additional unmet demand survey would have been required in 2007 costing the council additional resources. It was recognised that a complete review of taxi and private hire licensing functions was required.

The decision to delimit was based on a number of factors:

- the Office of Fair Trading (OFT), now the Competition and Markets Authority (CMA), market study into 'The Regulation of Licensed Taxi and Private Hire Services in the UK' and the Department for Transport's 'Taxi and Private Hire Best Practice Guidance' which called for the removal of quantity restrictions
- the National Consumer Council's campaign calling for the removal of quantity restrictions
- representations from certain members of the taxi and private hire trades that wheelchair users were unable to hire taxis at certain times of the day or in certain areas of the city
- feedback following consultation with the public, business community, wheelchair users, elected members and the taxi trade as to taxi availability.

Following adoption of the policy to delimit taxi numbers an interim injunction was served on the council, on behalf of two taxi proprietors who operated a total of 18 vehicles, preventing implementation of the policy pending a judicial review.

The case was heard in the High Court where the judge ruled that none of the grounds put forward by the claimants were properly arguable for the purpose of judicial review, and the council were awarded their costs in full.

Stretched limousines and larger vehicles

Many of these vehicles were built in America and do not comply with British requirements for a vehicle of this passenger capacity. This is also true of many other novelty vehicles, which should always be considered on a case-by-case basis. The recent Law Commission report proposed bringing all such vehicles within a standard licensing scheme and the LGA supports this proposal.

Limousines with up to eight passenger seats

These vehicles should be licensed by your council. To become 'road legal' vehicles must meet certain standards before they can be licensed. Vehicles that meet these standards and operate unlicensed pose a risk to public safety.

Limousines with over eight passenger seats

The DVSA licenses vehicles over eight seats such as buses and HGVs, and as such any stretched limousine which has a seating capacity of over eight passenger seats cannot be licensed by councils as a PHV. The LGA has highlighted concerns that drivers of vehicles with more than eight seats are not subject to the same checks as taxi and PHV drivers, and is arguing that anyone driving a vehicle used for these purposes should be subject to the same checks.

Stretched limousine enforcement: Basingstoke District Council

In 2006 following concerns from the trade and parents, Basingstoke District Council developed a strategy to stop unlicensed stretched limousines plying their trade. Unlicensed vehicles are often in a dangerous state of disrepair and extremely unsafe for the public to travel in, and drivers who are not checked may have a prior serious criminal record.

Enforcement activity was targeted by writing to all secondary schools within the borough to ask where and when their summer proms were to be held. They provided the schools with an advisory letter, which gave advice to parents about ensuring that the limousines they booked were properly licensed and what evidence to look for.

Basingstoke carried out over 16 joint enforcement operations at the summer balls over the next three years with local traffic police and DVSA checking over 100 vehicles and drivers.

The checks were carried out to ensure the safety of the pupils, and Basingstoke arranged private hire companies to be on standby if necessary and take any affected pupils home as a priority.

The majority of limousines checked were unlicensed by local councils or DVSA, and some drivers had serious criminal records, no DVLA licence and no insurance.

Where there had been serious issues such as unlicensed vehicles or drivers arrested the parents who booked the vehicles were advised in case they wished to claim back costs from the company and so they could also avoid using them again in the future.

CHECKLIST FOR COUNCILLORS IN ENGLAND AND WALES

This list is intended to help you gauge your council's effectiveness in providing a competent taxi and PHV licensing service. The answers should help you determine the quality of the service your council delivers, and whether changes should be made.

- Are the needs and safety of passengers placed at the centre of your licensing system?
- Are drivers assessed against agreed and appropriate standards to ensure they are lit and proper' and entitled to hold a licence? Many councils

require applicants to undertake Group 2 medical checks, enhanced Disclosure and Barring Service (DBS) checks, and local knowledge tests before they are licensed to carry the public.

- Are your drivers provided with training on disability equality, spotting child sexual exploitation and other locally relevant issues?
- Does your council have a taxi and PHV licensing policy document, which has been subject to regular review and has regard to the Department for Transport's Best Practice Guidance (last issued March 2010) and has been consulted on with the trade and user groups?
- Do your taxi licensing officers have a regular dialogue with neighbouring councils, with a view to adopting consistent standards, developing a common approach and to share relevant information?
- Do you have sufficient information and understanding to challenge or defend your council's taxi and PHV licensing activity in the context of an overview and scrutiny committee?
- Does your council have a multi-agency enforcement programme with the police, DVSA and neighbouring councils? Such operations help ensure the public remain safe.
- Does your council have adequate numbers of accessible taxis — to ensure people who are vulnerable in society such as disabled users can utilise the service?
- Does your council have effective consultation methods with taxi and PHV representatives and taxi users? Many councils have taxi liaison forums which meet on a regular basis.
- Are vehicles subject to agreed and routine stringent testing to ensure they are mechanically safe and suitable to transport the public?
- Are your licensing fees and charges sufficient to provide the resources for an efficient licensing service but which does not create a surplus? If there is a surplus, is this returned through a reduction in future fees?
- Does your council license stretched limousines under eight passenger seats? Many vehicles are operating unlicensed and unchecked as some councils refuse to license such vehicles.

OPERATOR LICENSING: CHECKLIST FOR COUNCILLORS

New and emergent technologies are enabling vehicles to be booked through non-traditional methods that can require additional scrutiny to ensure that they comply with the law as it stands. These are some of the issues you may want to consider when deciding whether to license such operators:

- PHV operator licences are required for anyone who makes provision in the course of business for the invitation or acceptance of bookings for PHVs, so you need to consider:
- Who will invite the booking? If passengers are invited to make bookings through an app, does the app belong to the applicant? If not, it may be that the applicant is not the right person to be licensed.

- Who will accept the booking? If it is the driver who accepts (for instance, by pressing 'accept' on a smartphone app), the driver may need to be licensed as a PHV operator too. This may depend on who the passenger has a contract with — is it the app provider or the driver?
- What does the applicant intend to do in your district? Some models can mean that all the activities of inviting or accepting bookings happen remotely outside your authority's jurisdiction and control.
- Can vehicles be booked in advance, or can customers only 'book' a vehicle at the time they want it?
- If there is no facility to pre-book, you should satisfy yourself that the vehicles are not unlawfully plying for hire, and you should be clear in your reasons why you have come to this conclusion.
- Can passengers specify a vehicle to suit their needs, for instance a wheelchair accessible vehicle, saloon, number of seats, etc? If not, how will the applicant ensure that an appropriate vehicle is sent to the customer?
- How will complaints be dealt with?
- Is the fare structure transparent and well publicised? Remember that passengers who have had too much to drink can be vulnerable and may not realise they are being charged two or three times the normal fare. How will the applicant ensure that vulnerable passengers are not taken advantage of?
- Does the applicant intend to use Hackney Carriages and/or minibuses to fulfil bookings? Operator licences only govern PHV bookings, so bookings that are fulfilled by Hackney Carriages and/or minibuses are not subject to the safeguards in the operator licence. How can you ensure that passengers receive the protection they expect when they make a booking through a PHV operator?
- Some app-based booking platforms require passengers to enter into a separate contract for hire with the driver. If this is the case, you should consider whether the driver also needs to be licensed as an operator.[25] What safeguards will be in place to ensure that passengers can seek redress against the operator rather than the driver when things go wrong?

[25] See Blueline v Newcastle City Council: http://www.licensingresource.co.uk/sites/default/files/2599.pdf

GLOSSARY

1847 Act — Town Police Clauses Act 1847

1976 Act — Local Government (Miscellaneous Provisions) Act 1976

1998 Act — Human Rights Act 1998. This Act transposed the European Convention on Human Rights into UK law.

App — Application. A tool that can be downloaded to a phone or smart device and used to engage a licensed vehicle. These may use taxis, PHVs, or both.

CSE — Child sexual exploitation. Sexual exploitation of children and young people under 18 involves exploitative situations, contexts and relationships where young people (or a third person or persons) receive 'something' (eg food, accommodation, drugs, alcohol, cigarettes, affection, gifts, money) as a result of them performing, and/or another or others performing on them, sexual activities.

DVSA — The Driver and Vehicle Standards Agency is an executive agency of the Department for Transport and is responsible for setting and improving standards for driving, including the roadworthiness of vehicles.

DVLA — The Driver and Vehicle Licensing Agency is an executive agency of the Department for Transport and maintains registers of drivers and vehicles in Great Britain.

Hackney carriage — See Taxi

IoL — The Institute of Licensing is a membership body for licensing officers, licensing lawyers and the licensed trade

NALEO — The National Association of Licensing and Enforcement Officers is a professional body for licensing officers.

PHV — See 'Private hire vehicle'

Ply for hire — To be hailed in the street to pick up a passenger. This can only be done by taxis.

Private hire vehicle — Private hire vehicles (PHVs) include a range of vehicles including minicabs, executive cars, limousines and chauffeur services. They must be pre-booked and cannot be hailed by people on the street.

Taxi — Taxis are referred to in legislation, regulation and common language as 'hackney carriages', 'black cabs' and 'cabs'. They can be hailed in the street, but can also be pre-booked.

LTPH Conditions of Fitness

2016 (Version 8.0 10th October 2016). Originally published 2007; updated: Version 3.0 25th February 2009; Version 4.0 27th April 2009; Version 5.0 22nd October 2009; Version 6.0 (undated); Version 7.0 30th September 2011; Version 8.0 10th October 2016.

Notes

i   In this document the "Licensing Authority" means Transport for London which will exercise, through the Head of Policy and Service Development at the London Taxi and Private Hire office (LTPH) , the duties imposed by the London Cab Order 1934 as amended by the Greater London Authority Act 1999.

ii   Any reference to a taxi in this document refers to a motorised taxi.

iii   In this document the term "approved" or "approved by LTPH" means approval by the LTPH Head of Policy and Service Development who is the technical representative of the Licensing Authority. A "licence" and "licensed" (and cognate expressions) refer to the granting by the Licensing Authority of a taxi licence under section 11 of the Metropolitan Public Carriage Act 1869.

iv   The address for all communications to LTPH is:
Transport for London – Taxi and Private Hire
4th Floor – Yellow Zone
Palestra
197 Blackfriars Road
Southwark
London
SE1 8NJ
e-mail: enquires@tfl.gov.uk

v   The Conditions of Fitness ("CoF") in Part 2 and Directions in Part 3 are laid down or made in accordance with the terms of paragraphs 7 and 14 respectively of the London Cab Order 1934, as amended.

vi   Following the reviews of the CoF carried out in 2003–5 this document sets out the Conditions of Fitness for London taxis in force from 1 January 2007. LTPH intends as far as possible to maintain a stable platform for vehicle manufacturers and will not therefore expect to review the CoF fully for about 10 years. However, LTPH reserves the right to amend the CoF should there be situations which require it, such as amendments to national or international laws with respect to road vehicles or air quality. These may include, for example, changes arising from disability legislation or the implementation of European emissions and air quality laws. The publication of the Mayor's Air Quality Strategy in December 2010 to accommodate European emissions and air quality laws has resulted in the introduction into the CoF of age based limits for taxis (see below).

Construction and licensing of taxis in London

In accordance with the provisions of paragraph 7 of the London Cab Order 1934, in pursuance of the Metropolitan Public Carriage Act 1869, no vehicle shall be licensed as a taxi unless it is fit for public service and conforms to the requirements in this document unless the Licensing Authority exempts a vehicle from those requirements after a request to do so by the applicant and where, having regard to exceptional circumstances, the Authority is satisfied it is reasonable to do so.

NB Please refer to TPH Notice 09/11 which sets out the exemptions and applicable conditions from the requirements as to the maximum age limit (see section 5.A below) and relevant and applicable exhaust emissions standards see section 13 below). The Licensing Authority retains the general discretion to grant exemptions in other circumstances where it considers it reasonable to do so.

PART 1
PROCEDURE TO BE FOLLOWED BY MANUFACTURERS AND OWNERS OF TAXIS FOR USE IN LONDON

1   Approval of new types of taxi

1.1   An application for the approval of a new type of taxi must be made in writing to LTPH and must be accompanied by dimensioned drawings or blueprints, together with detailed specifications and any particulars required by the Vehicle Policy Manager.

1.2   Before constructing any new type of taxi, manufacturers are advised to study the Conditions of Fitness set out in Part 2 of this document and to send to the Vehicle Policy Manager at LTPH, dimensioned drawings or blueprints, together with detailed specifications of the proposed vehicle, or vehicle conversion, for advice as to its general suitability for public service in London. It is also advisable to arrange for a preliminary inspection of the vehicle.

1.3   Manufacturers should address any current guidance issued by the DfT for the design of taxis and indicate to LTPH the extent to which those guidelines have been accommodated. In particular, manufacturers should demonstrate that they have taken account of current DfT guidance as regards ergonomic requirements for accessible taxis.

1.4   Arrangements must then be made to present the completed vehicle for inspection by LTPH. When presented, every facility must be given for the inspection and testing of the vehicle. A declaration must be provided by the manufacturer or authorised person that the vehicle conforms to the law and is safe for use as a public carriage, together with a certificate of registration and summarised documentary evidence that the vehicle meets the regulations specified in paragraph 5.1.

1.5   Any proposed alterations to the original specification must be submitted to LTPH for approval.

2   Existing approved types of taxi

2.1   New taxis of an existing approved type which are offered for licensing for the first time must be presented, by appointment, for inspection by LTPH or its approved agent. If the vehicle conforms to the approved type, a Certificate of Approval will be issued by or on behalf of the Licensing Authority.

3 Presentation for renewal of licence

3.1   To renew the licence of an existing taxi, the vehicle must be presented for inspection with the current licence. If any approved alterations have been carried out since the last inspection, these must be notified when the licence is renewed and appropriate documentation must be submitted.

3.2   Every taxi in service must be fully equipped to approved standards in order that wheelchair passengers may be carried.

3.3   From 1st January 2017 every taxi in service must be equipped with a TfL approved card payment system. The card payment device must be installed within the passenger compartment.

4 General

4.1   It must be understood that, although the conditions set out in this document have been complied with, approval will be withheld if the Licensing Authority is of the opinion that a vehicle is unsuitable for public use.

4.2   Although LTPH may extend approval of any particular type of taxi to all other taxis conforming to the design of that type, it must be understood that LTPH may withdraw such general approval if, in it's opinion, any unsuitable features arise.

PART 2
CONDITIONS OF FITNESS

The Conditions of Fitness in Part 2 are operative from 1 January 2007. Vehicles type approved before this date remain subject to the conditions in force at the time of approval except that the conditions in paragraphs 15.1 and 15.2 apply to all licensed vehicles.

5 General construction

5.1   Every new type of taxi must comply in all respects with the requirements of the Motor Vehicle (Type Approval) Regulations 1980, the Motor Vehicle (Type Approval) Regulations (Great Britain) 1984, the Motor Vehicles (EC Type Approval) Regulations 1998 and with any further national or international legislation as may be applicable. They must also comply in use with the Road Vehicles (Construction and Use) Regulations 1986 (C & U). Every new type of taxi offered for approval must comply in all respects with British and European vehicle regulations and be "type approved" to the requirements of the M1 category of European Whole Type Approval Directive 2007/46/EC as amended. Those taxis which have not been "type approved" to the M1 category (e.g. conversions) must be presented with approved certification that the specific vehicle meets the requirements of that category.

5.2   Taxis offered for type approval must be so constructed as to facilitate the carriage of disabled persons and must be capable as a minimum of accommodating a disabled person in a DfT reference wheelchair in the passenger compartment.

5A   Maximum age of vehicles

5A.1   From 1st January 2012, no licence will be issued to a vehicle over 15 years of age as calculated from the date on which the vehicle was first registered under the Vehicle and Excise Registration Act 1994.
NB: TPH Notice 09/11 sets out the circumstances in which the Licensing Authority will grant exemptions to vehicles from the 15 year maximum age limit for taxis.

Modifications/Additional Equipment

5.3   No equipment and/or fittings, other than those approved, may be attached to, or carried on the inside or outside of, the vehicle.
5.4   No modification may be carried out to a taxi without prior approval from LTPH. Before considering any unapproved modification to a taxi, approval must be sought from LTPH.
5.5   Guidance for in-cab modifications such as surveillance systems, etc. may be obtained from LTPH.

6   Steering

6.1   The steering wheel must be on the offside of the vehicle.

7   Manoeuvrability requirement

7.1   The vehicle must be capable of being turned on either lock so as to proceed in the opposite direction without reversing between two vertical parallel planes not more than 8.535 metres apart.
7.2   The wheel turning circle kerb to kerb on either lock must be not less than 7.62 metres in diameter.
N.B. These requirements were fully reviewed in 2005 (See PCO Notice 43/05).

8   Tyres

8.1   All tyres must comply with the relevant legislation. Specifically, retread tyres must comply with BS AU 144E as amended and be marked accordingly.
8.2   Tyres must be of the designated size, speed and weight rating for that make and model of vehicle as prescribed by the vehicle manufacturer.

9   Brakes

9.1   An anti-lock braking system is to be fitted.

10 Interior lighting

10.1 Adequate lighting must be provided for the driver and passengers.

10.2 Separate lighting controls for both passenger and driver must be provided. In the case of the passenger compartment, an illuminated control switch must be fitted in an approved position. This must be within reach of wheelchair passengers. Lighting must also be provided at floor level to each passenger door and be activated by the opening of the doors.

11 Electrical equipment

11.1 Any additional electrical installation and/or after-market components to be used within the taxi must meet the requirements of the relevant Automotive Electro Magnetic Compatibility (EMC) Directive, as amended, and be marked accordingly.

12 Fuel systems

12.1 A device must be provided whereby the supply of fuel to the engine may be immediately cut off. A manually operated device must have its location together with the means of operation and "off" position clearly marked on the outside of the vehicle. In the case of a vehicle fitted with an automatic inertia fuel cut off switch, no markings are required. Any engine powered by liquid petroleum gas (LPG), compressed natural gas (CNG), liquid natural gas (LNG), petrol or any combination of these fuels must be fitted with an automatic inertia fuel cut off device. They must also have a manually operated fuel cut off device externally mounted which is easily visible and readily accessible at all times from the outside of the vehicle with its location and means of operation clearly marked.

13 Exhaust emissions standards

13.1 New taxi models must meet the current and relevant EC Directive for exhaust emissions, i.e. the respective Euro standard. Current, approved, taxi models must meet prescribed emissions standards.
NB: TPH Notice 09/11 sets out the relevant and applicable standards, and exemptions to them.

14 Body

14.1 The body must be of the fixed head type with a partially glazed partition separating the passenger from the driver.

14.2 The overall length must not exceed 5 metres. This is essential for determining the size of taxi ranks, other pick-up points and for the free access and flow of other vehicles in London's congested streets.

15 Facilities for the disabled

15.1 Every taxi must be equipped to approved standards in order that wheelchair passengers may be carried.

15.2   Approved anchorages must be provided for wheelchair tiedowns and the wheelchair passenger restraint. These anchorages must be either chassis or floor linked and capable of withstanding approved dynamic or static tests. Restraints for wheelchair and occupant must be independent of each other. Anchorages must also be provided for the safe stowage of a wheelchair when not in use, whether folded or otherwise, if carried within the passenger compartment. All anchorages and restraints must be so designed that they do not cause any danger to other passengers.

15.3   The door and doorway must be so constructed as to permit an unrestricted opening across the doorway of at least 75cm. The minimum angle of a hinged door when opened must be 90 degrees

15.4   The clear height of the doorway must be not less than 1.2 metres.

15.5   Grab handles must be placed at door entrances to assist the elderly and disabled. All grab handles must be in a contrasting colour.

15.6   The top of the tread for any entrance should normally be at floor level of the passenger compartment and comply with the following requirements:
   a)   be not more than 380 mm from the ground, (measured at the centre of the tread width);
   b)   the surface shall be covered in a slip-resistant material;
   c)   have a band of colour across the entire width of the edge which shall contrast with the remainder of the tread and floor covering.

Should any entrance be more than 380 mm from the ground, an external interim step must be made available when the associated passenger door is opened and comply with the following requirements
   a)   not be more than 380 mm in height from the ground, (measured at the centre of the step width;
   b)   not be less than 250 mm deep;
   c)   the surface shall be covered in a slip-resistant material;
   d)   have a band of colour across its leading edge which shall contrast with the remainder of the step and floor covering;
   e)   not be capable of operation whilst the vehicle is in motion;
   f)   if automatic or powered, be fitted with a safety device which stops the motion of the step if the step is subject to a reactive force not exceeding 150N in any direction and if that motion could cause injury to the passenger;
   g)   can fold or retract so that it does not project beyond the side face of the vehicle and the vehicle is not capable of being driven away unless the step is so folded or retracted.

15.7   The vertical distance between the highest part of the floor and the roof in the passenger compartment must not be less than 1.3 metres.

15.8   Where seats are placed facing each other, there must be a minimum space of 42.5cm between any part of the front of a seat and any part of any other seat which faces it, provided adequate foot room is maintained at floor level.

15.9   Where all seats are placed facing to the front of the vehicle, there must be clear space of at least 66cm in front of every part of each seat squab, measured along a horizontal plane at the centre of the cushion.

15.10 A ramp for the loading of a wheelchair and occupant must be available at all times for use, as a minimum, at the nearside passenger door on all new vehicles presented for licensing. The ramp must have a safety lip, be 70cm wide, as a minimum, and comprise a single non-slip surface. It is desirable for this facility to be available at the offside passenger door also. An adequate locking device must be fitted to ensure that the ramp does not slip or tilt when in use. Provision must be made for the ramp to be stowed safely when not in use.

16 Passenger compartment

16.1 When fitted, occasional seats must be at least 40cm in width and the distance from the back of the upholstery to the front edge of the seat must be not less than 35.5cm.

16.2 Occasional seats must be so arranged as to rise automatically when not in use. They must be placed at least 4cm apart. When not in use, they must not obstruct doorways.

16.3 The rear seat dimensions must be adequate to carry the appropriate number of adult passengers comfortably.

16.4 Suitable means must be provided to assist persons to rise from the rear seat with particular attention to the needs of the elderly and disabled.

16.5 Lap and diagonal seatbelts must be fitted on all seats (including rear facing seats).

16.6 Colour contrasting sight patches are required on all passenger seats.

16.7 Head restraints must be fitted for all (forward and rear facing) seats. The design of headrests should maximise rear sightlines for the driver when any of the passenger seats are not occupied.

16.8 An induction loop system (or equivalent) must be fitted.

16.9 A TfL approved card payment device must be installed.

17 Driver's compartment

17.1 The driver's compartment must be so designed that the driver has adequate room, can easily reach, and quickly operate, the controls.

17.2 The controls must be so placed as to allow reasonable access to the driver's seat and, when centrally placed, controls must be properly protected from contact with luggage.

17.3 Every vehicle must be provided with an approved means of communication between the passenger and the driver. If a sliding window is fitted on the glazed partition, the maximum width of the opening must not exceed 11.5cm.

17.4 Where a single-piece glazed partition is fitted, a facility must be provided for making payment to the driver.

18 Visibility

18.1 Driver Visibility

A single-piece, full width rear window must be fitted. The design of headrests should maximise rear sightlines for the driver when any of the passenger seats are not occupied.

18.2 Passenger Visibility

The windows should maximise passenger visibility into and out of the vehicle.

The top of the window line for front and side windows, when measured vertically to the top of the visible portion of the glass, must not be less than 780mm on any glass panel forward of or beside the seated passenger. The vertical distance is to be measured through the E point as defined in Directive 77/649/EEC, from the top of the uncompressed rear forward-facing passenger seat cushion to the first point of totally obscured glass. Manufacturers are to declare conformity to this condition in drawing format.

The bottom of the window line for front and side windows must be low enough to afford passengers adequate visibility out of the vehicle.

A proportion of the window area in the passenger compartment must be available for opening by the seated passenger.

18.3 Windows must permit maximum visibility into, and out of, the vehicle. They must have no more than 25% tint value.

18.4 Passenger windows must be capable of being opened easily by passengers, including those in wheelchairs, when seated. The control for opening a window must be clearly identified to prevent it being mistaken for any other control.

19 Heating and ventilation

19.1 An adequate heating and ventilation system must be provided for the driver and passengers and means provided for independent control by the driver and the passengers. All switches must be within easy reach of seated passengers, including those in wheelchairs.

20 Door fittings

20.1 An approved type of automatic door securing device must be fitted to passenger doors to prevent them being opened when the vehicle is in motion. When the vehicle is stationary, the passenger doors must be capable of being readily opened from the inside and outside of the vehicle by one operation of the latch mechanism. The door must not open from the inside if the driver has the foot brake depressed. The interior door handle must be clearly identified to prevent it being mistaken for any other control.

21 Fare table and number plate

21.1 A frame must be provided for the fare table and fixed in an approved place. A position for an interior number plate is to be provided with the words "The number of this taxi is…." shown immediately above the position of the plate.

22 Floor covering

22.1 The flooring of the passenger compartment must be covered with a slip resistant material, which can be easily cleaned.

22.2 The floor covering must not impede the movement of wheelchairs. The colour of the floor covering must contrast with any upstand areas around it and with the colour of the seats.

23 Luggage

23.1 Suitable dedicated provision for the secure carriage of luggage must be made, separated from the passenger compartment and proportionate in size to the number of passengers carried.

24 Taximeter

24.1 Taximeters must comply with the regulations set out in the PCO document 'Approved Taximeters – Specification for use in London 2006'.

24.2 A taximeter of an approved type must be fitted in an approved position. A designated pulse output point must be provided that has a pulse output compatible with the taximeter fitted and, subject to the vehicle and/ or taximeter manufacturer's declaration, operates the taximeter within prescribed tolerances.

24.2 Taximeters must be capable of issuing a receipt that contains prescribed details. If this is achieved by the addition of a printer, it must meet with relevant Automotive EMC Directives, be marked accordingly and fitted in an approved position. The receipt must contain, as a minimum, the date and time of issue, the metered fare, extras and total fare. All of this information must be obtained from the taximeter in a 'read only' format. Manually input information is not permitted. Additional information, such as the start time and time taken for journey, distance travelled etc, may be permitted by application to LTPH.

25 "Taxi" sign

25 A "Taxi" sign approved by LTPH, clearly visible both by day and night when the taxi is available for hire, must be fitted.

26 Radio apparatus

26.1 Where apparatus for the operation of a two-way radio system is fitted to a taxi, no part of the apparatus may be fixed in the passenger compartment or in the rear boot compartment if LPG tanks or equipment are situated therein. Any additional electrical installation and/or after-market components to be used within the taxi must meet the requirements of the relevant Automotive Electro Magnetic Compatibility (EMC) Directive, as amended, and be marked accordingly.

26.2   Any other radio equipment, either in the passenger or driver compartment, must be approved by LTPH.

27   Maintenance

27.1   Vehicles, including all fittings, advertisements, etc., must be maintained to approved standards. The vehicles should always be kept clean and in good working order. Vehicles will at all times be subject to test and inspection and should it be found that a vehicle is not being properly maintained or kept in good working order, a notice will be served on the owner prohibiting him/her using the vehicle until the defect has been rectified.

27.2   Safety-critical parts used for the repair and maintenance of taxis, such as brake, steering and suspension parts, should be approved in advance by LTPH as meeting the requirements of the relevant block exemption regulations.

28   Certificate of insurance and form of holder

28.1   A current certificate of insurance as required by any Acts or Regulations relating to motor vehicles must be carried in a holder securely affixed to the taxi in an approved position. Key information on this certificate, including the registration number (if applicable), the owner's name and the expiry date of the insurance, must be not less than 12 point font size. The certificate must also state that the policy complies with the requirements of the London Cab Order 1934.

PART 3
DIRECTIONS

The Directions in Part 3 apply to all licensed vehicles.

29   Advertisements

29.1   Suitable advertisements may be allowed on the exterior or interior of the taxi subject to the approval of the Licensing Authority.

29.2   Advertisements will not be approved for use unless they comply with the current directions as contained in the 'Guidelines for Advertising on Licensed London Taxis'.

29.3   No material may be placed on the glazed areas other than notices which may be approved from time to time, however, suitable advertisements may be allowed on the rear windscreen as directed in the 'Guidelines for Advertising on Licensed London Taxis'.

29.4   Applications for approval of advertisements must be made in writing to Cab Advertising Approvals at LTPH or by email to: tph.enquiries@tfl.gov.uk

29.5   Further information and guidance on advertising matters can be obtained from Cab Advertising Approvals at LTPH or by email to: tph.enquiries@tfl.gov.uk

30   Badges/Emblems

30.1   In addition to advertisements displayed in accordance with paragraph 29 above, vehicles may display the official badge or emblem of organisations:

(a)   which provide emergency vehicle repair and/or recovery services; and/or,

(b)   membership of which indicates that the driver possesses professional skills/qualifications, which enhance the taxi service provided to the public.

30.2   Badges may be affixed to the front of the vehicle only in such a manner as not to be detrimental to the operation of the vehicle, likely to cause injury to any person, or to detract from any authorised sign which the vehicle may be required to display.

30.3   No advertisement, badge or emblem, including the stick-on type is to be exhibited other than is provided for in the directions contained in this paragraph or paragraph 29.

Index

[All references are to paragraph number]